Dictionary of World Philosophy

CONSULTANT EDITORS

Dictionary of
World Philosophy

A. Pablo Iannone

ROUTLEDGE
ROUTLEDGE
Taylor & Francis Group

London and New York

First published 2001
by Routledge
11 New Fetter Lane, London EC4P 4EE

Simultaneously published in the USA and Canada
by Routledge
29 West 35th Street, New York, NY 10001

Routledge is an imprint of the Taylor & Francis Group

© 2001 Routledge

Typeset in Sabon by Taylor & Francis Books Ltd
Printed and bound in Great Britain by TJ International, Padstow, Cornwall

British Library Cataloguing in Publication Data
A catalogue record for this book is available from the British Library

Library of Congress Cataloging in Publication Data
Iannone, A. Pablo.
Dictionary of world philosophy / A. Pablo Iannone.
Includes bibliographical references.
1. Philosophy–Dictionaries. I. Title.
B41 .I26
2001
103–dc21
00-142471

ISBN 0–415–17995–5

To my wife, Mary Kay Garrow, for her unfaltering support and encouragement, and to our daughters, Alejandra Emilia and Catalina Patricia, whose support, encouragement, and expectation kept me at work on a frequently tedious – however interesting – project, and whose joy of life, love of learning, ever-expanding search for their place in the universe, and desire for a good world give concrete meaning to this book's aspirations.

To abandon the subjectivity of a Johnson or a Webster is feasible, even desirable. To abandon all humanity, to achieve some Platonic perfection of an entirely disinterested dictionary is impossible....The intrusion may be limited, but to ask otherwise is not merely to chase the sun, but to suppose one can catch it too.

(Jonathon Green, *Chasing the Sun: Dictionary Makers and the Dictionaries They Make*)

A book is the dialogue it establishes with its reader and the intonation it imposes upon his voice and the changing and durable images it leaves in his memory.

(Jorge Luis Borges, "A Note on (toward) Bernard Shaw")

All writing depends on the generosity of the reader.

(Alberto Manguel, *A History of Reading*)

Contents

Preface

In Jorge Luis Borges's "The Library of Babel," the universe is envisioned as a library composed of an indefinite number of incessantly and insufficiently lighted hexagonal galleries, each wall containing five shelves, each shelf containing thirty-five books of uniform format, and each book – however minutely – different in content from all others, but the entire (formless and chaotic) set of books containing all the possible combinations of twenty-five symbols.[1] The narrator acknowledges that, as a youth, he wandered, like many others, through the library's galleries in search of a catalog of catalogs, a compendium of all the rest, which would help organize and understand the chaotic library-universe and its contents. The task of writing the present dictionary has at times felt disquietly analogous to that of "The Library of Babel"'s wanderers.

This is no reason for wonder. After all, a dictionary, especially a dictionary of philosophy – a characteristically comprehensive branch of inquiry that yields characteristically comprehensive worldviews – is not unlike the compendium sought by the wanderers in "The Library of Babel." Further, the purposes and nature of dictionaries have grown in complexity throughout history in a manner that, at times, prompted confusion, when not dictionary wars. The earliest recorded dictionaries, those of 2500 BCE Sumerian-Akkadian scribes, had the buttressing of conquest as an aim. By providing translations of Akkadian terms, they were meant to help the Sumerian conquerors rule over the vanquished Akkadian population.[2] By contrast, beginning with the fourth century BCE, the Greek compilers of words, though like the Sumerians concerned with earlier works, aimed at making accessible words – say, four centuries' old Homeric words – which had become hard to understand over time because linguistic and related practices had changed substantially.[3]

Dictionaries of this type soon became the norm in scholarly circles and so remained until the late Middle Ages. They were written for their peers by compilers of words in modern times called lexicographers – from the Greek *lexicon* ("dictionary") and *graphos* ("writing" or "writer"), i.e. writers of dictionaries. In the Western world, the language of scholarship eventually became Latin. The main purpose of dictionaries, however, remained the same for centuries: that of reporting the meaning of difficult scholarly words.

This situation changed in the Renaissance, when, in addition to the previous purpose, dictionaries began to recommend and promote attitudes, and express unusual ideas. Initially these were the ideas of the rediscovered Greco-Roman world. Eventually, they included still other – new – ideas, and dictionaries accordingly began to coin new terms, sometimes even in the vernacular rather than in Latin.[4]

Such a development could not but politicize the role of lexicographers. From being guardians of the classic past, they became promoters of new attitudes and, eventually, gatekeepers in the flow of information. To be sure, they had always decided what entries to compile. However, once the promotion of new attitudes became a purpose of lexicographers and their dictionaries, the issue arose whether their decisions were bound to be hopelessly arbitrary and biased or whether, though subjective and not neutral because made by actual human beings who have their preferences and ideals, they none the less could be balanced and open to reason.

This issue has been enhanced in our times. Like all times, they are not easy times in which to live. Yet, they are especially complicated because of the unprecedented fragmentation they involve between the myriad of cultures which are coming into increasing – sometimes conflictive – contact during the turn of the century; between one philosophical – or intellectual, or artistic – tradition and another; between the business, technology, and policy-making sectors; and between a number of the societal sectors just indicated and the general public. This dictionary partly grew from the realization that such fragmentation constitutes a significant obstacle to a range of human activities that are crucial to any human flourishing. For, at the very least, it is a significant obstacle to mutual understanding and any reasonably harmonious interactions between groups, these and their members, and individuals with each other. Especially in cross-cultural interactions, it undermines the flourishing of ethnic groups and their members when they are – but sometimes also when they are not – disadvantaged.

The dictionary builds on work I carried out in a range of philosophical and related areas, which led to my *Contemporary Moral Controversies in Technology* (Oxford, 1987); *Contemporary Moral Controversies in Business* (Oxford, 1989), *Through Time and Culture* (Prentice Hall, 1994), and, perhaps most notably, *Philosophy as Diplomacy* (Humanities Press, 1994) and *Philosophical Ecologies* (Humanity Books, 1999). These provided evidence for the said lack of integration, and began to formulate ways of addressing the problems it poses.

The dictionary also benefited from many outstanding works of reference, among them such encyclopedias and dictionaries as Edward Craig and Dr Luciano Floridi, eds, *Routledge Encyclopedia of Philosophy* (Routledge, 1998); William L. Reese, *Dictionary of Philosophy and Religion* (Humanities Press, 1996); Stuart Brown, Diané Collinson, and Robert Wilkinson, eds, *Biographical Dictionary of Twentieth-Century Philosophers* (Routledge, 1996); Ellis Cashmore *et al.*, *Dictionary of Race and Ethnic Relations* (Routledge, 1996); Robert Audi, ed., *The Cambridge Dictionary of Philosophy* (Cambridge, 1995); Stephen Schuhmacher and Gert Woerner, eds, *The Encyclopedia of Eastern Philosophy and Religion* (Shambhala, 1994); John Grimes, *A Concise Dictionary of Indian Philosophy* (SUNY, 1989); A.R. Lacey, *A Dictionary of Philosophy* (Scribner's, 1976); Paul Edwards, *Encyclopedia of Philosophy* (Macmillan, 1967); and José Ferrater Mora, *Diccionario de Filosofía* (Sudamericana, 1965).

In attempting to help further address contemporary fragmentation problems, this dictionary departs from the predominant trend of using one or more editors to combine the contributions of hundreds, if not thousands, of philosophers. To be sure, this approach has produced outstanding works, as evidenced by the multi-authored dictionaries and encyclopedias included among those just listed. Yet, arguably in part as a result of sheer lack of communication – when not of conflicting personalities or methodological inflexibilities – between contributors, such works sometimes display a lack of cohesiveness, even of consistency, which can only contribute to further contemporary fragmentation. This is not to say that the present dictionary simply reverts to the good old single-author days when, as the lexicographer Henri Béjoint said, "dictionaries were much worse, and also much better."[5] Instead, it seeks a balance between these extremes by relying on the advice of a manageable number of editorial consultants who review lists of entries and drafts of the entries' content, while a single author writes the drafts as well as the final version of the manuscript.

In moving the said integrative project further, this dictionary presents and discusses a great variety of philosophical traditions in a manner that tries to be sensitive to the different concerns that motivate them. Some of these traditions developed in Asia and Europe, while others flourished in the Americas, Africa, or Oceania. The criterion used in this dictionary to include specific philosophical traditions is that they have been the subject of substantial studies from a philosophical standpoint, e.g. traditional studies in the history of philosophy or more recent studies in ethnophilosophy. This approach makes room for traditions such as those in Asia, Europe, and India, which have been long recognized in scholarly philosophical studies. It also makes room for other traditions such as those that flourished in the pre-Hispanic Americas, sub-Saharan Africa, and among the Māori, which have been the subject of more recent or recently more numerous philosophical studies.

Whenever it is likely to be illuminating (and without succumbing to the temptations of simplistic equal-space rules), this dictionary points out the contributions of different philosophical traditions on a specific topic, as well as the differences and similarities between these traditions' predominant motives in addressing the topics. That is, this dictionary makes a concerted effort to be truly a dictionary of *world* philosophy, a conception under which all philosophical traditions, be they Chinese, European, or Indian, are treated on a par with each other. The reader should accordingly expect the entries to include more cultural and widely historical commentary than that found in other dictionaries of philosophy.

Also, some distinctions (e.g. between philosophy and religion or between metaphysics and epistemology) are quite sharply drawn in what has come to be called Western philosophy, i.e. philosophy significantly tracing back to the Greco-Roman world and predominantly practiced in France, Germany, Great Britain, the United States, and their geographical areas of influence on the planet, e.g. Australia and New Zealand, and Latin America. By contrast, the said distinctions are not so sharply, if at all, drawn in other philosophical traditions, say, those in India, China, and even in areas where Western philosophy is the majority tradition, as made plain, for example, by Navajo thought in the United States, and Māori thought in New Zealand. Accordingly, readers should expect the entries to include more discussion of religious, social, or other topics, as well as more combined discussions of more than one area of Western philosophy, than that found in primarily or exclusively Western-influenced dictionaries of philosophy.

These differences in philosophical approaches and, generally, ways of thinking are understandably correlated with the – often sharply different – histories and social-life structures of the traditions in question. It is crucial to keep them in mind when comparing philosophical traditions from different cultures. One such cultural difference, for example, is described by the Japanese historian H. Paul Varley in discussing the Japanese director

Ozu Yasuhirō's focus on the conflict between the traditional and the modern in the Japanese family:

> Social pressures today...are much less severe...; but the domestic dilemma remains, with *giri* often taken to mean the demands of the traditional Japanese family and *ninjō* the pull of modern ways.
>
> To understand why this should represent a specially Japanese, rather than universal problem, we must note that there are few analogues to the Japanese family and the enormous importance it continues to hold in Japanese society. It is simply a fact...that the Japanese are overwhelmingly group-oriented: they work in groups, they play in groups, they seem happiest in groups. Such extraordinary feeling for collective behavior has its origin in the family, and any rejection of, or failure to conform to, the family raises for the Japanese the most serious questions about his role in society as a whole.[6]

The differences between East Asian and Western cultures are not simply a matter of social preferences. A wide range of current studies indicate that, for example, reasoning in Chinese, Japanese, and Korean cultures focuses more on relations among objects and the context in which they interact, while reasoning in Western cultures focuses more on general, context-independent categories and predominantly uses formal logic.[7] Recent memory studies indicate that East Asians attend to background and global aspects of an image, while Westerners focus on a few discrete objects.[8] Also, in thinking about opposing views, East Asians seek to retain elements of each in a middle way, while members of Western cultures try to establish which view is correct and discard the others.[9]

Equally significant – though by no means the same – points of difference can be made between social features of predominant European or English-speaking North American cultures on the one hand, and social features of African, Chinese, Indian, Latin American, Māori, Native American, and other cultures, on the other hand. Indeed, though perhaps not always so sharp, differences can be found within any of the groups just listed, and these are reflected in their various philosophical traditions.

For example, three groups have recently been studied in Guatemala's rainforest: native Itzag Maya, Q'eqchi' Maya who moved to the area about twenty years ago, and Spanish-speaking Ladinos who moved to the area at about the same time. The Itzag Maya clear less land yearly and cultivate more plant species on average than the other two groups. In addition, they possess detailed knowledge of their environment, and seem to act out of a concern for their environment, not fear of social consequences (they do not punish members of their groups who cut down too many trees or otherwise act selfishly). By contrast, the Q'eqchi' Maya do not show any ecological concerns despite concerted community efforts to foster ecological awareness among them. The Ladinos appear to be adopting some sounder ecological practices, though it is not clear how they learn them.[10]

As for Western cultures, significant differences are found between them. In fact, recent studies indicate that different Western spelling systems, and possibly other culture-specific ways of organizing knowledge, significantly influence readers' strategies for decoding texts and even the brain functions they use in doing so. For example, in Italian, written letters almost always correspond to consistent sounds; while in English they do not: think of learning to read such similarly spelled, yet very differently pronounced, words as *cough*, *dough*, and *tough*. A team of Italian and British neuroscientists has recently found that, in decoding Italian text, English readers take much longer to begin reading than Italian readers. This is associated with the reading strategies used by each group. Italian readers simply match written letters to corresponding sounds, while English readers use additional strategies. These differences are reflected in the brain functions used. The Italians' matching of written letters to corresponding sounds is an activity carried out in one area of the brain network, i.e. the area concerning reading comprehension. By contrast, in decoding English text, English readers primarily use two areas of that network, both different from that used by Italians.[11]

One should accordingly keep in mind these cultural and related – some quite unexpected – differences when dealing, as this dictionary does, with the concepts and philosophical traditions found in world philosophy.

The comprehensive aims of the present work, together with the aim of producing a manageable dictionary, led to some difficult decisions. One concerned the manner in which information about philosophers should be presented. The decision was that the present work should be a *dictionary of terms*, and information about philosophers should be introduced to the extent it is relevant to the terms used as entries. Thus, the biographical information to be found here is no substitute for that to be found in a full-fledged encyclopedia of philosophy or in a biographical dictionary of philosophers. Though often substantial, biographical information provided in the present dictionary is not the primary concern. The dictionary focuses on terms and the conceptual, theoretical, factual, and related matters they involve.

When needed and feasible, etymological information was included, both at the beginning of most entries and in the text following them. In providing such information about words derived from the Greek, sometimes the infinitive is given, while other times the first-person present indicative is given. This was largely dictated by the practices of the sources used and by the way in which the readers' needs seemed best served in each case.

As regards transliteration, all terms from non-roman alphabets have been romanized in the present dictionary. Diacritical marks have been used according to current predominant conventions. When conventions conflict, those have been followed – typically simple ones – that appear likely to help a wider readership.

The same concern with meeting the widely ranging needs of a varied readership – from scholars to students pursuing their inquiries in different places or languages on earth – has been used to select the works cited at the end of the entries. That is, without disregarding the need to cite standard works, as needed, the dictionary cites recent publications, or works published in places or languages of direct interest to the entries.

This concern with meeting the needs of the dictionary's readership is also the ground for the dictionary's extensive cross-referencing. Dummy entries are listed accompanied with one or more entries where they are discussed. In the actual entries, cross-references appear typically in SMALL CAPS. Additionally, *italic* type has been used in many instances: as emphasis for terms being introduced, or which have etymological or theoretical significance, or because they are works being cited, or because the use of italics is likely to help readers.

As always, I accept responsibility for my mistakes, but there would have been many more had I not benefited from the many learned and wise corrections and suggestions provided by the dictionary's excellent and patient consultant editors: Professors David Braybrooke, Charles Butterworth, Lorraine Code, Antonio S. Cua, Kwame Gyekye, Steven Heine, Asa Kasher, Yong Choon Kim, Florencia Luna, Enrique E. Marí, Jitendra N.

Mohanty, Amy Oliver, John Patterson, and Suzanne Stern-Gillet. I am extremely grateful to all of them for their careful, informed help.

I am also grateful to those of my colleagues at Central Connecticut State University who commented on the project or offered suggestions at various points or, simply, with whom I recently had philosophical discussions which helped improve this dictionary. They include Felton Best, David Blitz, Brian O'Connell, John Seddon, Bill Sokolowski, David Vance, and, especially, those who, in effect, acted as additional consultant editors, reviewing entries, and giving me detailed – in some cases, extensive – written comments: Don Adams, Margaret Ayotte-Levvis, Parker English, Eleanor Godway, Gary Levvis, and Joe McKeon. My special thanks also to Bertrand Stern-Gillet for his comments on markets and his help with globalization sources.

For their extremely effective library support services, I also thank the staff at the Central Connecticut State University Elihu Burritt Library, especially Steve Cauffman, John Cayer, Emily S. Chasse, Rick Churchill, Norma Chute, Cheryl Dreher, Marie A. Kascus, Barbara Sullivan Meagher, Faith A. Merriman, Joan G. Packer, Nicholas G. Tomaiuolo, June Sapia Welwood, and Tzou Min Hsiung. I should also mention and thank the Connecticut State University for providing funds for research in support of the work that led to this book, and the Central Connecticut State University College of Arts and Sciences, for granting reassigned time to pursue the project. And I very much thank Fiona Cairns, Senior Editor at Routledge (who put the idea of writing this dictionary in my head), for her editorial sense and encouragement, and all the Routledge editorial staff members with whom I had the pleasure of working during the book's planning and production process: Lauren Dallinger, Tony Nixon, Dominic Shryane, and Andrew Varney.

What I owe my wife, Mary Kay Garrow, for her unwavering help and encouragement, I cannot possibly repay. As for our daughters, Alejandra Emilia and Catalina Patricia, they have played an essential part in all this by being with us, which has filled my life with happiness; by their support and trust, which inspired me to persevere through the periods of tedium that any project of this type must entail; and by their love of life and learning, which gives meaning to the aspirations of this book.

Cheshire, Connecticut API
May 2000

Notes

1 Jorge Luis Borges, "The Library of Babel," *Labyrinths* (New York: New Directions, 1964), pp. 51–8, esp. 51–4. See also the fascinating CD by Pablo Pereyra entitled "La Biblioteca Total: Viaje por el Universo de J.L. Borges" (Buenos Aires: La Nación, 1996).
2 Jonathon Green, *Chasing the Sun* (New York: Henry Holt, 1996), pp. 1–2.
3 Green, *Chasing the Sun*, p. 2.
4 Green, *Chasing the Sun*, p. 3.
5 Quoted in Green, *Chasing the Sun*, p. 10.
6 H. Paul Varley, *Japanese Culture*, 3rd edn (Honolulu: University of Hawaii Press, 1984).
7 Bruce Bower, "Cultures of Reason," *Science News*, Vol. 157 (January 22, 2000), p. 57.
8 Bower, "Cultures of Reason," p. 57.
9 Bower, "Cultures of Reason," p. 57.
10 Bower, "Cultures of Reason," p. 58.
11 Bruce Brower, "Readers' Brains Go Native," p. 58.

Entries A–Z

A
a
a fortiori
a priori–a posteriori
abazimu
Abdera, School of
abduction
ābhāsa-vāda
abhāva
abhidharma
Abhidarmakosha
abhihitānvaya-vāda
abhinava-anyathā-khyāti
abhinivesha
abortion
absolute
abstract
Academy
accident
accidentalism
acosmism
act
action
actionism
activism
actual
actualism
ad
adequate
adhyāsa
ādhyātmā
Advaita
aesthetics
affectio
affirmative
African philosophy

Afrocentricity
āgama
age of the world
agent
Agikuyu
agnosticism
Agriculture School
ahamkāra
ahimsā
ākāsa
Akhbārīs
akrasia
ālaya-vijñāna Vijñāna
alchemy
alethiology
Alexandrian School
Allāh
ambiguity
analogy
analysis
analytic–synthetic distinction
anattā
animism
anthropocentrism
anthropology
anthropomorphism
antinomy
anumāna
applied
Arabic philosophy
archetype
argument
Arianism
Aristotelianism
Arminianism
Arrow's theorem

A A letter used in philosophy as a symbol for the following. First, the predicate of a proposition in formulas of the form *AB*, which are to be read as "*A* is a predicate of *B*" – in the *Prior Analytics* and some other works by the Greek philosopher Aristotle (384–322 BCE).

Second, any universal affirmative proposition; that is, any proposition having the standard form "All *S* are *P*," such as "All triangles are figures" and "All humans are mammals" – in the work of the Scholastics and most logic writers after them.

Third, a formulation of the identity principle, *A=A*, meaning any item is identical to itself – in many classical texts.

Fourth, a formulation of the law of identity expressed in the logic of classes, an area of modern logic, by means of the same formula used in classical logic to express the principle of identity: *A=A*. By contrast, the principle of identity is expressed in another modern logic area, sentential logic, by means of the formulas $p \supset p$ and $p \equiv p$, and the law of reflexivity is expressed in the logic of identity by means of the formula $(x)(x=x)$.

Fifth, relations between subject and object in discussions by German idealists, especially Johann Gottlieb Fichte (CE 1762–1814) and Friedrich Wilhelm Joseph Schelling (CE 1775–1854). Fichte uses the formula *A=A* as a conditional to mean: if *A* exists, then *A* exists. Schelling uses *A* together with the symbols "−," which represents being in itself; "+," which represents being outside itself; and "±", which represents the subject–object totality.

Sixth, the so-called simple abstracts in modern logic. This way, the letter *A* and other capitals such as "*B*" and "*C*" are predicate letters. Sometimes the lower-case versions of these letters are used for the same purpose.

Seventh, the inclusive disjunction, as in *Apq*, in Polish logic notation (e.g. Lukasiewicz's). In the notation formulated by the English philosopher Bertrand Russell (CE 1872–1970), this is formulated as *pvq*. The Polish logician Jan Lukasiewicz (CE 1878–1956) sometimes also uses the letter *A* to indicate (together with "*E*", "*I*", and "*O*") one of the constants of quantificational logic, as in *Aab*, which can be read as "every *a* is a *b*."

Eighth, one of the categories of modal propositions in scholastic discussions of modal logic (see LOGIC).

See also: categorical; identity; logic; syllogism

Further reading
Kneale, William and Kneale, Martha (1962) *The Development of Logic*, Oxford: Oxford University Press.
Scholz, Heinrich (1961) *Concise History of Logic*, New York: Philosophical Library.

a A Latin preposition used in many philosophical locutions. Among them are the following. First, *a dicto secundum quid ad dictum simpliciter*. This refers to an invalid inference of the form: a subject has a certain feature in some respect; hence, it has it in all respects, e.g. "Fido is a big dog. Hence, Fido is a big being." To state that the argument is not valid, the following formula is used: *a dicto secundum* *quid ad dictum simpliciter non valet consequentia.*

Second, *a fortiori*. See A FORTIORI below.

Third, *a parte ante, a parte post.* Scholastic philosophers used these expressions to describe the temporal relations between the existence of the soul and that of the body. The soul was said to have existed *a parte ante* if its existence preceded that of the body (or *a parte ante perpetua* if it had preceded it for ever). In contrast, the soul was said to have existed *a parte post* if its existence had not preceded that of the body, but, instead, had began with that of the body. These authors however agreed that the soul remained after the body's dissolution. See also A PRIORI–A POSTERIORI below.

Fourth, *a parte rei.* Scholastic philosophers used this expression to mean that something, say, Mount Everest, was what it was independently of the operations of the understanding, that is, *a parte rei*, and not as a result from the operations of the understanding (*secundum intellectum*). Sometimes, the *secundum intellectum* sense contrasted with *a parte rei* is designated with the expression *quad nos*, i.e. evident to us.

Fifth, *a posteriori*. See A PRIORI–A POSTERIORI below.

Sixth, *a se.* Scholastic philosophers used this expression to contrast what is *a se*, that is, from itself or, in other words, completely independent and self-sufficient, with what is *ab alio* or, in other words, proceeds from something else. For example, they said God was *a se*, because He depended on nothing for its existence; while human beings were *ab alio*, because they proceeded from other beings, their parents.

Seventh, *a simultaneo*. See A PRIORI–A POSTERIORI below.

a fortiori A Latin expression applied to arguments in two ways. First, from the premise that any items which have a certain feature also have an additional feature, and that given items have the first feature to an eminent degree, the argument concludes that *a fortiori* – i.e. even more so – the latter items must have the additional feature. An example is: typical motor-vehicle driving involves a moderate amount of risk, which calls for careful driving. Some motor-vehicle driving conditions involve high risk. Hence, even more so, they call for careful driving. This sort of argument has found a variety of applications in statistical and other studies involving non-deductive forms of reasoning, for example in the social sciences.

Second, from premises that involve comparative terms such as "greater than" and "lesser than," a conclusion is drawn on the basis of transitivity. An example is: Peter is older than Kevin and Kevin is older than Tom. Hence, *a fortiori*, Peter is older than Tom.

See also: probability; relation

Further reading

Grabenhorst, Thomas Kyrill (1990) *Das argumentum a fortiori: eine Pilot-Studie anhand der Praxis von Entscheidungsbegrundungen,* Frankfurt am Main and New York: P. Lang.

Lavin, Milton L. (1970) *A Fortiori Bayesian Inference in Psychological Research,* Cambridge, MA: MIT.

Prior, Arthur N. (1948–9) "Arguments a fortiori," *Analysis* 9: 49–50.

a priori–a posteriori This distinction has been widely used in modern philosophy and, less, in scholastic philosophy. A priori is frequently applied to beliefs or claims, meaning that they are justified in a manner prior to or independent of sensory, introspective, and any other types of experience. It is contrasted with a posteriori, or empirical; that is, applied to beliefs or claims whose justification is at least partly based on such experience. For example, it may justifiably be claimed that we know a priori whether it is, or is not, raining here and now – we do not need to check to know this. However, we can only know *a posteriori* whether, in fact, it is raining here and now, because we need to use our senses to find out.

The *a priori–a posteriori* distinction concerns the justification of the belief or claim, not how it or any concepts it involves are acquired. Hence, if a belief or claim is said to be known a priori, it is irrelevant to make the objection that experience is necessary to acquire it or some concepts it involves.

Also, the a priori–a posteriori distinction involves a conception of experience that is narrower than that of any conscious process whatsoever. For the latter would presumably be involved even in a priori justifications.

Instead, the distinction involves a conception of experience as any input received from the world around us.

A priori is sometimes also applied to proofs or arguments. In this regard, some medieval philosophers applied the expression *a simultaneo* to syllogisms where neither the middle term is ontologically prior with regard to the conclusion, nor the conclusion is ontologically prior with regard to the middle term. For example, in the ontological proof – also called ontological argument – for the existence of God, this existence is derived from the essence or concept of God, which cannot be said to be the cause or the effect of God's existence. The said medieval philosophers contrasted this type of proof with a priori proofs, where the middle term is supposed to have ontological or physical priority with regard to the conclusion. For example, the spirituality of the soul (in the middle term) is supposed to be ontologically prior to, and used as a basis to conclude the soul's immortality. They also contrasted *a simultaneo* proofs with *a posteriori* proofs, where the middle term has neither priority nor posteriority with regard to the conclusion, for example, when the soul's operations are used in the middle term to prove the nature of the soul.

See also: knowledge; philosophy of religion

Further reading
BonJour, Laurence (1997) *In Defense of Pure Reason: A Rationalist Account of A Priori Justification*, Cambridge, UK and New York: Cambridge University Press.
Hick, John (1964) *The Existence of God*, New York and London: Macmillan & Collier Macmillan.
Moser, Paul K. (1987) *A Priori Knowledge*, Oxford and New York: Oxford University Press.
Pap, A. (1944) "The different kinds of a priori," *The Philosophical Review* LIII: 464–84.

a simultaneo *see* a priori–a posteriori

abazimu Some African philosophers use this term (or its singular, *umuzimu*) to denote *spirits of the dead* in dealing with the problem of human immortality. For example, the contemporary African philosopher Alexis Kagame uses *abazimu* to mean non-living beings with intelligence. Though these beings are understood to be immortal, they are supposed to have a beginning: they began to exist when humans began to exist.

There is some controversy in African ethnophilosophy, however, concerning the acceptability of the terms *abazimu* and *umuzimu*. Kagame thinks the origin of *abazimu* as an opposite of *umuzima*, which means "the living," results from a reconstruction of the Kinyarwanda language by missionaries, and thus considers *abazimu* strictly a non-African import. By contrast, the contemporary African philosopher D.S. Masolo argues that this is a peculiarity of Kinyarwanda and that things are otherwise, for example, in the Kiswahili language. This, however, does not settle the question, given that Kiswahili is a mixture of Arabic and Bantu.

See also: identity; metaphysics

Further reading
Kagame, Alexis (1956) *La Philosophie Bantu-Rwandaise de l'etre*, Brussels: Academie Royale des Sciences Coloniales; reprinted as *Bantu-Rwandan Philosophy of Being*, New York: Johnson Reprint Corporation, 1984.
Masolo, D.A. (1994) *African Philosophy in Search of Identity*, Bloomington, IN and Edinburgh: Indiana University Press and Edinburgh University Press.

Abdera, School of An early atomism school that developed in the city of Abdera, in the Northern Greek region of Thrace. It includes the philosophers Leucippus (*fl. c.* 440 BCE) and his disciple Democritus (460–370 BCE). The philosopher Protagoras (490–*c.* 410 BCE), who also lived in Abdera, is not part of this school, which is also distinguished from the later version of atomism in Epicureanism, the philosophy formulated by the philosopher Epicurus of Athens (341–270 BCE).

Leucippus, in *The Great World System*, and Democritus in *The Little World System* and other writings, hypothesized the existence of tiny, invisible, internally solid, homogeneous things – atoms (literally meaning the uncuttable) – and the void or empty space. Those adopting this corpuscular model tried to meet Eleatic objections against change by explaining macroscopic, qualitative, changes as arrangements and rearrangements of groups of atoms, which they supposed to be constantly in motion and to differ among themselves only quantitatively: in size, shape, and speed. Given the right conditions – which the *Abderites* (the members or followers of the School of Abdera) understood in causal terms – a concentration of colliding atoms could start a vortex that would draw other atoms, eventually generating an entire world. Living things in such a world develop from slime through the activity of soul atoms, which are finer and more spherical than other atoms, and are diffused through our bodies. A slight loss of these atoms causes us to sleep. A greater loss occurs when we faint; a total loss, in death.

However, internal change to the atoms was, according to the Abderites, impossible. For change would involve some cutting, which could occur only through the penetration of an instrument, say, a blade, into empty spaces or void, and there was no void in the atoms.

Since the atoms are invisible and all properties are properties of atoms, the senses cannot give us reliable knowledge, but reason can. Also, given that, on this philosophy, death is the loss of soul atoms, personal immortality is impossible. Given this, Democritus argued that the aim of life is a state of balance achieved through moderation in satisfying pleasures. Envy and ambition were incompatible with such balance, while democracy was the social ordering that best suited it.

See also: atomism; Greek philosophy

Further reading
Copleston, Frederick, S.J. (1962) *A History of Philosophy, Vol. I, Greece & Rome, Part I*, revised edn, Garden City, NY, Doubleday. Chapter Ten, "The Atomists."
Kaufmann, Walter, and Baird, Forrest E. (1994) *Ancient Philosophy*, Englewood Cliffs, NJ: Prentice Hall. "Democritus (and Leucippus)," pp. 37–45.

abduction A type of reasoning contrasted with deductive reasoning and, in some cases, with inductive reasoning. Various accounts have been influential. First, for the Greek philosopher Aristotle (384–322 BCE), abduction (in Greek, *apagoge*) was a type of syllogistic inference that conveyed no certainty on the

conclusion because of a weak connection between either the major and the middle terms, or the middle and the minor terms.

Second, for the United States philosopher Charles Sanders Peirce (CE 1839–1914), abduction (or the abductive method or retroduction, or method of hypothesis) was one of the three basic forms of inference, by contrast with deduction and induction. For him, deduction was typified by the following form of argument (often called *modus ponendo ponens*): if a certain event, H, occurs, then a result R is to be observed; but H occurs; hence, R is to be observed. Induction, meanwhile, was typified by the form of argument often called induction by enumeration: a number of observations of the event H are accompanied by a number of observations of the result R. Hence, if a certain event, H, occurs, then a result R is to be observed. By contrast with these forms of argument, abduction was an argument that inferred a hypothesis or explanation: if the event H occurred, then the result R would be observed. However, the event R is observed; hence, the event H must have occurred. Later versions of this type of argument have been called arguments to the best explanation, i.e. arguments that involve the view that event H must have occurred because H is the best available (or simply the best) explanation of the observed data.

Third, after the first half of the twentieth century, the term abduction also began to be widely used to refer to rules of reasoning for the discovery, not the JUSTIFICATION, of scientific hypotheses or theories. A distinction between the context of discovery and the context of justification was drawn by the German philosopher Hans Reichenbach (CE 1891–1953), but he thought reasoning was relevant to justification, while discovery was merely a matter of psychology.

The philosopher Norwood Russell Hanson (CE 1924–67) later tried to distinguish reasons for accepting a particular hypothesis (which he thought characteristic in justifications) from reasons suggesting that the true hypothesis will be of a specified kind (which he thought were reasons typically based on analogies and characteristic of discoveries). However, his attempts at developing logics of abductive or retroductive reasoning for these latter reasons were thought by many to amount to logics of justification.

The contemporary Austrian-American philosopher Herbert Feigl distinguished between two classes of justification. One was validation or *justificatio cognitionis*, which is involved in the application of inductive, deductive, or other principles to infer consequences from them. The other, vindication or *justificatio actionis*, applies to the principles themselves and takes, and should take, pragmatic considerations into account.

Of late, rather than focusing, as these previous attempts, on the formulation of a logic of discovery, the search has focused on such things as procedures or strategies for discovery, and conditions under which research programs or traditions can lead to discoveries or become sterile. These and the preceding studies, however, deal with concerns that are heuristic (from the Greek *heuristikos* and the Latin *heuristicus*: to find out or discover): that of intelligence as ability to search and reason in finding solutions to problems. In artificial intelligence studies, heuristics is the area of inquiry that studies this ability and describes its rules; though, in general, it studies any rules of discovery.

See also: deduction; induction; positivism

Further reading
Buchler, Justus (1955) *Philosophical Writings of Peirce*, New York: Dover. Chapter 11: "Abduction and Induction."
Lakatos, Imre and Musgrave, Alan (1970) *Criticism and the Growth of Knowledge*, London and New York: Cambridge University Press.
McKeon, Richard (1966) *The Basic Works of Aristotle*, New York: Random House. Prior Analytics, II, 25, 69 at 20–3.

ābhāsa-vāda This term means "theory of appearance." It has two main philosophical uses. First, in Advaita-Vedānta, it refers to the theory that the individual soul is merely an illusory appearance – a projection – of Brahman-intelligence. This view is a variation of *pratibimba-vāda*, the theory that the individual (*jīva*) is an appearance of Brahman as reflected in ignorance. To provide an understanding of

this more general theory, the analogy of a reflection in a mirror is sometimes used.

Second, the term also refers to the creation theory of the Shaiva School, or Shaivinism, which sees Shiva as the supreme being who creates, maintains, and destroys the universe, and of the Shākta School, or Shaktism, which reveres Shakti as the force that maintains the universe and makes life possible. According to this creation theory, the universe is made up of appearances that are all real as aspects of the ultimate reality.

See also: Brahman; Hinduism; philosophy of mind

Further reading
Chatterjee, Satishchandra (1950) *The Fundamentals of Hinduism*, Calcutta: Das Gupta.
Chaudhuri, Anil Kumar Ray (1955) *Self and Falsity in Advaita Vedanta: with an Appendix on Theories of Reality in Indian Philosophy*, Calcutta: Progressive Publishers.
Renou, Louis (1962) *Hinduism*, New York: Braziller. Chapter 5: "Religious Sects."

abhāva This controversial term means non-existence in the sense of the absence of objects. According to the Buddhist Prbāhkara Mīmāmsā and Vishishtādvaita Schools, negation does not exist at all; hence, talk of non-existence makes no sense. By contrast, the Nyāya-Vaiśeṣika, Bhatta Mīmāmsā and Dvaita Schools hold that non-existence is a distinct category.

Under the general view that non-existence is a distinct category, two main kinds of non-existence have been distinguished. The first is not comparative. It includes three subdivisions: prior non-existence, as when one says "I did not exist before being born"; annihilative non-existence, as when one says "I will not exist after dying"; and absolute non-existence, as when one says "A square circle cannot possibly exist." The second main kind of non-existence is comparative and concerns the type of situation in which one object, e.g. a turtle, is not another, e.g. a hare (which can be exemplified by the sentence "A turtle being a hare does not exist"). This kind of non-existence is also called reciprocal non-existence.

See also: Hinduism

Further reading
Datta, Srilekha (1991) *The Ontology of Negation*, Calcutta: Jadavpur University, Calcutta, K.P. Bagchi & Co.
Ingalls, D.H. (1951) *Materials for the Study of Navya-Nyāya Logic*, Cambridge, MA: Harvard University Press.

abhidharma This term literally means primary teaching. As a proper name, *abhidharma* refers both to the earliest texts presenting, in a reflective and systematic manner, the main philosophical and psychological categories in Buddhism, and to the content of these texts. The earlier of these texts were produced up to about the second century CE, and provided schematic definitions of terms in the question and answer form characteristic of catechisms. Later works tended to include more extensive discussions of metaphysical topics – for example, the existence of past objects – and of logical topics – for example, the nature of reference. These texts received their final codification around the middle of the fifth century CE. As a corpus, they constitute the dogmatic basis of the Hīnayāna – Small Vehicle – School, which relies on the early Buddhist texts, and the Mahāyāna – Great Vehicle – School, which relies both on early and later texts.

The Abhidharma of the Hīnayāna School is written in Pali and includes seven books: the *Book of the Elements of Existence* lists and organizes mental and material elements; the *Book of Classifications* characterizes aggregates, fields, and faculties; the *Book of Points of Controversy* discusses matters of controversy significant for the history of Buddhism; the *Book of Individuals* describes types of individuals among the clergy and lay people; the *Book of Elements* discusses the elements; the *Book of Pairs* is about the positive and the negative aspects of each topic it addresses; and the *Book of Causality* describes the causal connections between individual *dharmas*.

The Abhidharma of the Mahāyāna School, written in Sanskrit, is also composed of seven books: the *Book of the Recitations of the Teaching* presents the elements of the doctrine divided into monads, diads, triads, etc.; the *Book of the Things* is in part exactly like the previously mentioned *Book of Classifications*; the *Book of Descriptions* offers reasons to believe many myths; the *Book of Understandings* overlaps with various Hīnayāna School books; the *Book of Elements* is practically identical to the Hīnayāna *Book of Elements*; the *Book of Literary Treatises* discusses characterizations of the elements of the Buddhist doctrine and their subdivisions; and the *Book of the Starting Point of Knowledge* discusses such things as propensities and knowledge.

See also: Buddhism

Further reading
Kasyapa, Jagadisa, Bhikkhu (1954) *The Abhidhamma Philosophy: or, The Psycho-Ethical Philosophy of Early Buddhism*, Kadamkuan, Patna: Swatantra Nava Bharat Press.
van Gorkom, Nina (1997) *Abhidhamma in Daily Life*, London: Triple Gem Press.

Abhidarmakosha This text, whose title literally means *Treasure Chamber of the Abhidharma*, is the most important compilation of the Sarvāstivāda School of Mahāyāna Buddhism. Composed by the Indian philosopher Vasubandu (fourth or fifth century CE) in Kashmir, it is a collection of 600 verses accompanied by a prose commentary. Today, only the Chinese and Tibetan versions remain. This book represents the transition from the Hīnayāna to the Mahāyāna School and, as the basic text of Chinese Buddhism, it significantly contributed to the spread of Buddhism in China. It is divided into nine parts, each devoted primarily to one of the following topics: elements, faculties, worlds, modes of existence, propensities, the path of liberation, knowledge, concentration, and theories of the individual. This last part is a critique of the Vātsīputrīya view that postulates an independently existing entity.

See also: Buddhism

Further reading
Desmarais, Michele Marie (1992) *Concepts of Mental Health and Mental Illness: A Comparison of Definitions and Checklists in the Abhidharmakosabhasya and the Diagnostic and Statistical Manual of Mental Disorders*, Vancouver, BC: University of British Columbia.
Steenburg, David John Frederick (1988) *The Role of Intention in Perception According to Vasubandhu's Abhidharmakosabhasya: The*

Background to Buddhist Soteriology, Ottawa: National Library of Canada.

abhihitānvaya-vāda This term, meaning "the relatedness of the designated entities," refers to a theory of meaning of sentences. According to this Bhatta Mīmānsa theory, words have their own separate meanings independently of any sentences. These isolated meanings combine in sentences to produce the meaning of these sentences. Hence, what a sentence means results from a construction based on the isolated meanings of the words, which are combined to produce a collective meaning. This also applies to past uses of language. One first remembers the isolated meanings of the words in a remembered sentence and, then, a collective memory gives the sentence a collective meaning.

See also: Hinduism

abhinava-anyathā-khyāti The name of a relatively late theory of error found in the Dvaita Vedānta School, it is a combination of two theories. The first is *asat-khyāti* ("apprehension of the non-existent"), the theory of error held by the Mādhyamika Buddhist School, in which the object of erroneous belief is thought to be unreal. The second is *anyathā-khyāti* ("apprehension-otherwise"), the Nyāya-Vaiśeṣika School theory of error, in which the object of erroneous belief is real, but appears to be other than it is or, in other words, is placed in the wrong category. The *abhinava-anyathā-khyāti* theory of error holds that the object of erroneous belief is unreal, but its substratum is real. For example, the belief that a stick seen in a glass of water is bent has an unreal object, a bent stick, but a real substratum: that of the representations that constitute the visual illusion.

See also: epistemology; knowledge

Further reading
Nagaraja Rao, P. (1976) *The Epistemology of Dvaita Vedanta*, Adyar, Madras, and Wheaton, IL: Adyar Library and Research Centre; Agents, Theosophical Pub. House.
Sharma, B.N. Krishnamurti (1981) *History of the Dvaita School of Vedanta and Its Literature: From the Earliest Beginnings to Our Own Time*, 2nd rev. edn, Delhi: Motila Banarsidass.

Shiv Kumar (1984) *Samkhya-Yoga Epistemology*, Delhi: Eastern Book Linkers.

abhinivesha This term, which ordinarily means "will-to-live," "strong desire," or "self-love," is used in Indian philosophy in general, and in Sāmkhya-Yoga philosophy in particular, to indicate an affliction (*klesha*) regarded as an aspect of a more comprehensive affliction, ignorance (*AVIDYĀ*): an instinctive clinging to one's own life and dreading one's own death. Other specific afflictions that are also aspects of ignorance are egoism (*asmitā*), attachment (*rāga*), and aversion (*dvesa*). Despite the derogatory connotations of this characterization, *abhinivesha* is not always a bad thing. Indeed, it is sometimes commendable to display self-love and a will-to-live, and to prosper materially, so long as this is done in a balanced, not blinkered or one-sided, manner.

See also: avidyā; Hinduism

Further reading
Catalina, Francis V. (1968) *A Study of the Self Concept of Sankhya Yoga Philosophy*, Delhi: Munshiram Manoharlal.
Das, Kalicharan (1975) *Concept of Personality in Samkhya-Yoga and the Gita*, Gauhati: Gauhati University.
Shiv Kumar (1984) *Samkhya-Yoga Epistemology*, Delhi: Eastern Book Linkers.

Further reading
Bhatt, Govardhan P. (1989) *The Basic Ways of Knowing: An In-Depth Study of Kumarila's Contribution to Indian Epistemology*, 2nd rev. edn, Delhi, India: Motilal Banarsidass.
Shastri, Biswanarayan (1995) *Mimamsa Philosophy and Kumarila Bhatta*, New Delhi: Rashtriya Sanskrit Sansthan.

abjection *see* feminist philosophy

ableism *see* ethics; justice

Aborigines *see* culture

abortion A term that, in philosophy, theology, and social debates, often means the deliberate termination of pregnancy before the fetus is able to survive outside the uterus. However, participants in these debates sometimes use the term abortion simply to mean the termination of pregnancy before birth, regardless of whether the fetus is viable or not. The morality of abortion has long been debated in the West.

The Greek philosopher Aristotle (384–322 BCE) held that the soul attached itself to the fetus about 120 days after conception; hence, only then did the fetus become human and, since it is not wrong to kill non-humans, abortion was acceptable before the first 120 days of pregnancy. The Bible never explicitly forbids abortions, and Islam has largely inherited Aristotle's view. By contrast, early fathers of the Christian Church – for example, the philosopher Augustine (CE 354–430), who was born in the African city of Thagaste, the Latin author Tertullian (CE c. 155–c. 240), who was born in the African city of Carthage, the Dalmatian theologian Jerome (c. CE 347–420), and the Patriarch of Constantinople, Chrysostom (CE ?347–407) – argued that abortion was a sin, an unnatural interference with the process of natural generation, and the wrongful killing of a human being. Following the philosopher Aquinas (CE 1225–74, born near the city of Naples, in what is now Italy), the Bavarian philosopher Albertus Magnus (CE 1206–80), held the view that abortion was acceptable before the first forty days of pregnancy for males, but for a longer period, i.e. before the first ninety days of pregnancy, for females. The Catholic Church used to hold this view as well, which, among other reasons, led to charges that the Church was sexist.

Today, philosophical and social arguments against abortion, and on behalf of the *right to life* of the fetus, primarily argue that abortion is the wrongful killing of a human being because the embryo is a human being from the time of conception (or, at least, from some later point in the pregnancy), and that the killing of an innocent human being such as the embryo is murder.

Arguments for the moral permissibility of at least some abortions are often based on the view that each woman has an overriding *right to her own body* and abortion is a way of exercising this right. In this connection, the contemporary United States philosopher Judith Jarvis Thomson, for example, has argued that even if the fetus is a person, the woman carrying it is not always obligated to carry it to term. In support of her position, she asks us to imagine that we wake up connected to a violinist who needs to remain thus connected

for nine months. Thomson holds that the reader has no obligation to remain thus connected and considers this case to be analogous to that of a pregnant woman.

Along different lines, some contemporary philosophers and Catholic theologians hold that a modified version of the *principle of double effect* is the only justification of deadly acts, including abortion. Traditionally, this principle says that one may act in ways that foreseeably lead to deadly results, so long as: first, one's action has a good result; second, one did not intend the deadly result to occur as an end or as a means; third, one did not bring about the good result by means of the deadly one; and fourth, the good result was sufficiently significant to outweigh the deadly one. The modern modification occurs in the third and fourth conditions. In the case of abortion, this means that the aim of saving the mother's life can be achieved so long as one does not intend to kill the fetus, even if it has been foreseen that this will happen. Also, weighing the life of a mother against that of the fetus is no longer required (on the grounds that weighing incommensurable goods is impossible).

Other grounds are *consequentialist*: abortions are necessary to curb overpopulation; to prevent the birth of children who, because unwanted, are likely to become social misfits; or to prevent the birth of children who, because unwanted, are likely to undergo much suffering.

Grounds such as the right to life, the right to one's own body, and the consequentialist grounds just mentioned are often used in attempts to establish, not simply the moral permissibility of *acts* of abortion, but what policies – whether *pro-choice* or *pro-life* – are justified concerning abortion. The relative strength of such grounds for this purpose, however, depends on whether, how, and to what extent policies should enforce right conduct, and this is a matter of debate between authoritarian and liberal conceptions of policy.

See also: ethics

Further reading
Baird, Robert M. and Rosenbaum, Stuart E. (1989) *The Ethics of Abortion: Pro-Life! vs. Pro-Choice!*, Buffalo, NY: Prometheus Books.

Cohen, Marshall, Nagel, Thomas, and Scanlon, Thomas (1974) *The Rights and Wrongs of Abortion*, Princeton, NJ: Princeton University Press.

Kamm, F.M. (1992) *Creation and Abortion: A Study in Moral and Legal Philosophy*, New York: Oxford University Press.

Warren, Mary Anne (1973) "On the Moral and Legal Status of Abortion," *The Monist* 57(1), January: 43–61

absence *see* logic

absolute This term derives from the Latin *absolutus*, which means *completed* or *perfect*. It has a variety of uses involving such connotations as fixed, independent, unqualified, unconditional, and completed. It has accordingly been opposed to whatever is changing, dependent, qualified, conditional, incomplete, or relative – the term most often contraposed to absolute. It found its main philosophical use in Western metaphysics, where idealists have used it as a noun to describe an independent reality, the absolute, expressed in all things. In Eastern thought, it has been used in the twentieth century by the Indian philosopher Sri Aurobindo (CE 1872–1950) as a term synonymous with BRAHMAN. Philosophers have attempted to investigate the absolute's nature and kinds. They accordingly talk of the absolute pure and simple, or *absolutum simpliciter*, that some, following the philosopher Nicholas of Cusa (CE 1401–1464) – born in the city of Kues, whose name was rendered as *Cusa* in Italian and other Romance languages, in what is now Germany – consider identical with God; others with Being; and still others with the One, the Principle of all things, or the Ultimate Cause of everything. Philosophers contrast the absolute *simpliciter* with the absolute with regard to a kind or *absolutum secundum quid*.

There are also additional, less traditional, interpretations of the absolute. The German philosopher Johann Gottlieb Fichte (CE 1762–1814) used it to refer to the ego as the power leading to knowledge and reality. The German philosopher Friedrich Wilhelm Joseph Schelling (CE 1775–1854) used it to refer to the unconditional ground, indeed identity, of subject and object. The German philosopher Georg Wilhelm Friedrich Hegel (CE 1770–1831), in criticizing Schelling, defined the absolute as spirit:

the necessity embodied and developed in the world through history. This view influenced the thought of such nineteenth-century philosophers as the British philosophers Bernard Bosanquet (CE 1848–1923) and Francis Herbert Bradley (CE 1846–1924), and the United States philosopher Josiah Royce (1855–1916 CE).

As an adjective, the term absolute has been applied to a variety of concepts in such expressions as:

1　Absolute right: see ETHICS.
2　Absolute principle: see ETHICS.
3　Absolute space: see METAPHYSICS; PHILOSOPHY OF SCIENCE.
4　Absolute time: see METAPHYSICS; PHILOSOPHY OF SCIENCE.
5　Absolute threshold: see PHILOSOPHY OF MIND.
6　Absolute truth: see TRUTH.

See also: ethics; idealism; metaphysics; philosophy of science; truth

Further reading
Findlay, J.N. (1970) *Ascent to the Absolute: Metaphysical Papers and Lectures*, London and New York: Allen & Unwin and Humanities Press.

Klemm, David E. and Zoller, Gunter (1997) *Figuring the Self: Subject, Absolute, and Others in Classical German Philosophy*, Albany: State University of New York Press.

Simha, Kaliprasada (1991) *The Absolute in Indian Philosophy*, Varanasi, Delhi: Chaukhambha Orientalia.

abstinence *see* Jewish philosophy

abstract Term derived from the Latin verb *abstrahere*, which means to draw from, or to put aside. To say that something is abstract is to say that it has been drawn from something else, or put aside. *Abstract items* or *abstract entities* are called *abstractions* or *abstracta*, and are typically contrasted with those that are concrete, i.e. complete and actual. Abstractions can be of many kinds; but philosophers have concentrated on cases where the entities abstracted are general or universals (also called *universalia*), and generic notions (such as numbers, sets, geometrical figures, propositions, properties, and relations). These abstractions – e.g. the square – are said to be ab-stracted from particulars – e.g. from particular squares

– but include no feature peculiar to any of these particulars.

Abstractions have been associated with ontological realism. Early examples are the Ideas or Forms characterized by the Greek philosopher Plato (428–348 BCE). For him, these abstractions, from the form of a square to that of a chariot, were the only real entities instantiated in particular objects of the world of appearances surrounding us, such as particular squares and particular chariots. The Forms had no spatiotemporal location and were simply in a relation of instantiation or exemplification to the particulars that were their examples or instances. That is, the Forms were TRANSCENDENT to the particulars; in other words, neither in them nor in our minds. This type of position is called realism.

On Plato's account, there was no form for simply being a particular, hence particulars had no reality. The Greek philosopher Aristotle (384–322 BCE) is often interpreted to have held, in contrast with Plato, that only particulars, or primary substances, were genuinely real, and abstract entities or universals had no existence apart from particulars but existed in them, i.e. they were immanent; in other words, in the particulars. While this distinction between primary and secondary substances is correctly ascribed to Aristotle concerning his earlier *Categories*, he later considerably modified – or even abandoned – the distinction in *Metaphysics*, especially in book Z. In any case, the distinction belongs in a version of substantialism that became most influential in the history of philosophy. In this connection, Aristotle used the term *ousia*, i.e. substance, to denote the individual existing thing. He divided substances into *ousia prote* or first substance, i.e. the primary subject of predication, and *ousia deutera*, or secondary substance, i.e. a genus, which he thought to be less substantial than a species belonging to it and even less substantial than individuals belonging to the species.

In the West during the Middle Ages, philosophers such as Augustine (CE 354–430) – born in Thagaste, North Africa – and Aquinas (CE 1225–74) – born near the city of Naples, in what is now Italy – upheld realism, i.e. they accepted the existence of abstract entities.

Others, for example the English philosopher William Ockham (*c.* CE 1285–1347), held that similar objects could be denoted by the same name without there being any need for an abstract entity they all shared. Because Ockham considered the primary names to be mental in nature, his position is sometimes interpreted as exemplifying CONCEPTUALISM, the view that there are no universals and that the classificatory function which universals are supposed to have is actually a function of mental entities – e.g. representations, or classificatory abilities – called concepts. An alternative to both realism and conceptualism is NOMINALISM, the view that there are no universals and that the classificatory function which universals are supposed to have is actually a function of words such as nouns, adjectives, and verbs, or of uses of such words. The French philosopher and theologian Peter Abelard (CE 1079–1142) had already sought a middle way between realism and nominalism, by arguing that what we predicate of many things is not a mere *flatus vocis* or word, but a *sermo*, i.e. the content of a word. This content, he argued, is derived from the particulars by abstraction, but is not in the particulars. It is simply a common though confused image of many things. This would seem to indicate Abelard leaned towards the nominalist or, at least, the conceptualist camp. Yet, at the same time, he argues that the exemplars – from the Latin *exemplum*, i.e. *model* or *example* – are in God's mind, which makes his position lean towards realism.

The neo-Scholastics of the seventeenth century adhered to a realist version of abstract entities in their conception of COMPLEXUM SIGNIFICABILE, what is signified only by a *complexum* (i.e. by a statement or declarative sentence), which was what today is taken to be a proposition. In modern philosophy, rationalists such as the French philosopher René Descartes (CE 1596–1650) and his followers upheld the existence of abstract entities, which could be known, like mathematical truths, through the sheer use of reason. Alternatively, empiricists like the Scottish philosopher David Hume (CE 1711–76) and the Irish philosopher George Berkeley (CE 1685–1753) rejected abstract entities on the grounds that they could not be known through the senses.

In the twentieth century, the English philosopher Gilbert Ryle (CE 1900–76), for example, conceived of categories – which are paradigms of abstraction – as word-types. He applied this conception to a characterization of a category mistake: the placing of an item in the wrong category, because of some misunderstanding concerning the nature of this entity. For example, upon seeing a university's campus buildings, one may ask, "Which one is the university?", mistakenly implying that the university is one of the buildings that, at best, can be its embodiment or part of its concrete existence.

Controversies about abstract entities have not remained entirely restricted to epistemology and metaphysics. Instead, they have been recurrent in other philosophical areas such as aesthetics and ethics. In ethics, for example, some philosophers, from Plato to the British philosophers G.E. Moore (CE 1873–1958) and W.D. Ross (CE 1877–1971), have argued for the existence and usefulness of abstract entities such as moral principles, rules, or values discoverable through reason or intellectual intuition alone. While others, from the Greek philosopher Protagoras (c. 490–c. 420 BCE), through Hume, to the United States philosopher Charles L. Stevenson (CE 1908–79), the contemporary British philosopher R.M. Hare, and the French philosopher Jean-Paul Sartre (CE 1905–80), have argued that such abstract entities do not exist or, if they exist, have little use in dealing with ethical problems. In contemporary ethics, the term abstract has been used in discussing conceptions of ethics that focus on ideals far removed from reality, treating social – from economic to political – circumstances as moral externalities. In feminism, the term has been used in discussing conceptions of masculinity.

See also: complexum significabile; definition; metaphysics; quality

Further Reading

Broad, C.D. (1971) *Five Types of Ethical Theory*, London: Humanities Press and Routledge & Kegan Paul.

Hartsock, Nancy C.M. (1985 [1983]) *Money, Sex, and Power: Toward a Feminist Histor-ical Materialism*, Boston: Northeastern University Press.

Iannone, A. Pablo (1994) *Philosophy as Diplomacy*, Atlantic Highlands, NJ: Humanities Press.

Rogers, A.K. (1971) *Morals in Review*, New York: AMS Press.

Weinberg, Julius Rudolph (1965) *Abstraction, Relation, and Induction: Three Essays in the History of Thought*, Madison: University of Wisconsin Press.

abstraction *see* abstract

absurd *see* existentialism

Academy The school established by the Greek philosopher Plato (428–348 BCE) in Athens around 385 BCE, named after and located near a public park and gymnasium dedicated to the Greek hero Academus. The school specialized in mathematics, music, astronomy, and dialectics, and survived until CE 529, when it was dissolved, together with other pagan schools, by the Roman Emperor Justinian I (CE 483–565). The Academy's history is divided into a variety of periods. Some prefer to talk of the *Old Academy* – including Plato, Speusippus (c. 407–339 BCE), Xenocrates (396–314 BCE), and their followers – and the *New Academy* – the Skeptical Academy of the third and second centuries BCE. Others talk of five periods: Old (as above), Middle (Arcesilaus, c. 315–241 BCE), New (Carneades, c. 213–129 BCE), Fourth (Philo of Larissa, second–first century BCE), and Fifth (Antiochus of Ascalon, c. 130–c. 68 BCE). Still others prefer a tripartite division – the Old, Middle or Second, and New or Third. There are also those who prefer to talk of these three divisions plus the Very New or Fourth, also sometimes called the *School of Athens*, which was part of Neoplatonism.

For most of its history, the Academy was devoted to elucidating doctrines that were not quite explicit in Plato's dialogues. We know them largely through Aristotle's works. There are two opposed first principles, the One and the Indefinite Dyad; these generate Forms or Ideas, which may be identified with numbers, and from these derive intermediate mathematical objects and perceptible things.

The Old or First Academy was highly influenced by late Pythagoreans, often identifying ideas with numbers. Given Plato's indebtedness to Socrates (470–400 BCE), it was also one of the Socratic Schools. The Second emphasized probability and shifted its position towards SCEPTICISM. Indeed, its founder, Arcesilaus, held the doctrine of *eulogon*: that the guide to life was to be probability. The Third emphasized skepticism even more. The Fourth was an early example of eclecticism, seeking to select what was valid from all philosophies, and towards the end – which, as stated, some call the School of Athens – was Neoplatonic. A term sometimes used in this context is synchretism (from the Greek *synkretizein*, i.e. *to combine*), which denotes the blending of philosophical doctrines from different or even opposing schools in an attempt to achieve a unified view.

See also: Greek philosophy; Platonism; Neoplatonism; Socratic philosophy

Further reading
Aristophron, Pan (1934) *Plato's Academy: The Birth of the Idea of Its Rediscovery*, Oxford: Oxford University Press.
Fowler, D.H. (1990) *The Mathematics of Plato's Academy: A New Reconstruction*, Oxford and New York: Clarendon Press.

accent, fallacy of *see* fallacy

access, privileged *see* epistemology

accident A term derived from the Latin *accidens*, present participle of *accidere*: to happen. It has two main uses. The first, in metaphysics, refers to a feature or property of a substance, e.g. to the red color of an apple, without which the substance, i.e. the apple, could still exist. The color of the apple is said to be *per accidens* (a Latin expression meaning by accident), or an accidental property. A *per accidens* predication is one in which an accident is predicated of a substance. An *ens per accidens* is either an accident or an accidental unity of an accident and a substance.

By contrast with any substance, which can exist *per se*, i.e. in and of itself, accidents cannot exist without something in which they are or inhere. To express this notion, philosophers have used the formula *esse est inesse*, meaning that the being of an accident is being in, i.e. in something else. There have been many divergent views on what features are

accidents and what features are not accidents. Some philosophers thought that such things as age, skin color, and moral traits are accidents of a person, while humanity is not. Others, like the French philosopher René Descartes (CE 1596–1650), think that one's several thoughts are accidents of one's soul, while thinking is not. A special case is that of the Judeo-Christian God, which has no accidents, since everything that is true of God necessarily follows from God's nature, or essence, i.e. from the substance It is. In general, then, accidents are modes of being of a substance, or ways in which a substance's essence or nature is specified.

The identity of accidents has been a matter of controversy. If two people, Jane and John, have the same height, say 5 feet and 5 inches, is that height one accident shared by both persons or two accidents, one for Jane and another for John? In the twentieth century, philosophers have lost interest in this and other problems about the relations of accidents to substances, because they have lost interest in the notion of substance. However, questions about contingency and necessity, which used to be formulated by reference to accidents and substances, are still of concern, independently of the accident–substance dichotomy.

It is worth noticing here that, in African thought, Akan thinkers use the term *asiane* to denote accidents. However, these are events restricted to individual persons. Furthermore, for Akan thinkers, accidents also have causes. They are not contrasted with caused events, but with extraordinary events that, by contrast with *asiane*, can also be impersonal, e.g. an unusually long drought.

See also: essentialism; quality

Further reading
Connell, Desmond (1996) *Essays in Metaphysics*, Blackrock, Co. Dublin: Four Courts Press.
Fontaine, Raymond G. (1950) *Subsistent Accident in the Philosophy of Saint Thomas and in His Predecessors*, Washington: Catholic University of America Press.
Hartman, Edwin (1977) *Substance, Body, and Soul: Aristotelian Investigations*, Princeton, NJ: Princeton University Press.

accidental *see* causal law; essentialism; quality

accidentalism A term used in metaphysics with two meanings, one concerning events (presumed to include actions), the other concerning identity.

The first, concerning events, is the term denoting the metaphysical view that at least some events are neither necessitated, nor causally determined, nor predictable. In saying they are not necessitated, it is often meant that no contradiction would be involved in the events' not happening. In saying that some are not determined it is sometimes meant that they do not happen as a result of causes; while, other times, it is meant that even if the events happen as a result of causes, they are still not determined because the causal laws determining them might have been different. As for unpredictable events, some philosophers have argued that there are situations in which events are unpredictable even if they are determined, because no one – except perhaps for an omniscient being – could have good grounds for predicting them.

An example in support of this view concerns motor vehicles. When they were introduced in the United States at the beginning of the twentieth century, no one could have had good grounds for predicting the carnage they were going to bring about on the United States population (let alone that this population was going to get used to it). This was because this carnage was partly the result of the Interstate Highway System built in the 1950s, primarily to ready the United States for a confrontation with the Soviet Union, a world power that did not exist at the beginning of the century.

The second, concerning identity, is the term referring to the view that individuals of the same kind or species are numerically distinct because they have some different non-essential properties. For example, two cats, one white and the other black, differ in color, though, as cats, they are essentially the same. This view presupposes the identity of indiscernibles, but is stronger because it further claims that numerical diversity within a species is entirely the result of differences in non-essential properties.

See also: determinism; identity

Further reading
Berofsky, Bernard (ed.) (1966) *Free Will and Determinism*, New York, Harper & Row.
Strawson, P.F. (1997) *Entity and Identity: And Other Essays*, Oxford and New York: Clarendon Press and Oxford University Press.
—— (1959) *Individuals: An Essay in Descriptive Metaphysics*, London: Methuen.

accounting and finance, ethics of *see* ethics

acculturation *see* diaspora

achievement verb *see* speech act theory

Achilles paradox *see* paradox

acknowledgement *see* knowledge

acosmism A term derived from the Greek *a*, which means "not," and *kosmos*, which means "world." Acosmism was coined by the German philosopher Georg Wilhelm Friedrich Hegel (CE 1770–1831) to denote the view that the world is unreal and that only God exists, a view that he, arguably mistakenly, ascribed to the Amsterdam-born philosopher of Spanish and Portuguese descent Baruch Spinoza (CE 1632–77). A better candidate is the pantheism of Shankara (CE 788–820), the Indian philosopher who founded Advaita-Vedānta Hinduism, and who argued for the monist view that dualism, realism, and theism are illusions, and only *nirguna*, a quality-free Brahman exists.

See also: Advaita; idealism; philosophy of religion

Further reading
Bhattacharyya, Kokileswar, and Pandit (1924) *An Introduction to Adwaita Philosophy Sankara School of Vedanta*, Calcutta: University of Calcutta.
Mason, Richard (1997) *The God of Spinoza: A Philosophical Study*, Cambridge: Cambridge University Press.
Saksena, Lakshmi (1980) *Neo-Hegelian and Neo-Advaitic Monism: A Study in Converging Perspectives*, Delhi: Bharat Bharati Bhandar.

acquired immunodeficiency syndrome (AIDS) *see* ethics

acrasia *see* akrasia

act A term derived from the Latin *agere*: to do. The Greek term is *energeia*, usually translated as *act*, or *actuality*. The Greek philosopher

Aristotle (384–322 BCE) contrasted energeia (*act*) and its near synonym, *entelecheia* (which he associated with form), with *dynamis* (*potentiality*) (which he associated with matter). Entelechy (*entelecheia*) appears in his definition of the soul as the first actuality of the natural body (*On the Soul*, II, 1). For him, a person who does not engage in reflection is potentially wise, so long as he or she has the capacity to reflect. Similarly, someone who does not build is potentially a builder, so long as this person has the capacity to build. In these cases, reflecting and building are acts, the capacity to reflect and the capacity to act are potentialities. Aristotle called any of the latter a *first potentiality* and held that, through experience and practice, it becomes a *first actualization* when the person in our example becomes a wise person or a builder. Aristotle also equates any of these with a *second potentiality*. For now, as a wise person or as a builder, the person can exercise their respective knowledge at will, which is a *second actualization*.

With roughly the same meaning, medieval philosophers contrasted *actus* and *potentia*, and talked of *ens in acto* (*actual being*) and *ens in potentia* (*potential being*); but instead of confining their application to natural processes, as Aristotle had done, they applied them to a clarification of God's nature as *actus purus*, i.e. *pure act*, or *purely actual*. By this they meant that God was a being – indeed, the only being – without potentiality, i.e. completely actualized, which made God the highest or most perfect being. In the process, the act–potentiality distinction became more precise and different species of acts were distinguished, e.g.: pure or absolute, in which no potentiality is involved; not pure, which may give existence to an essence or, alternatively, constitute a substantial or an accidental form.

However there were also other philosophers, mainly during the Renaissance and in modern times, who used the term act with quite different meanings. The Italian philosopher Giovanni Gentile (CE 1875–1944), who characterized his philosophy as ACTUALISM or the philosophy of the pure act, used the term to mean human activity that was supposed to take ontological precedence. The French philo-

sopher Louis Lavelle (CE 1883–1951) accentuated this view; hence, the act–object distinction. The Amsterdam-born philosopher of Spanish and Portuguese descent Baruch Spinoza (CE 1632–77), the French philosopher Henri Bergson (CE 1859–1941), and the British philosopher Alfred North Whitehead (CE 1861–1947) used act in special ways, but, like Gentile and, indeed, Aristotle and medieval philosophers, still thought that act took precedence over potentiality. So did the German philosopher Edmund Husserl (CE 1859–1938), even though he used act in a neutral, non-metaphysical sense, where intentionality was the central feature. Focusing on language from a pragmatic standpoint, the United States philosopher George Herbert Mead (CE 1863–1931) held that the act, beginning with its most basic form, the gesture, was a crucial category of analysis and meaning. Acts can thus be propositional or, more generally, speech acts, and involve intentionality.

In a sense closer to ordinary language, the term act is used as synonymous with action. In this regard, see ACTION, and act utilitarianism under UTILITARIANISM.

See also: action; actualism; ethics; perception; phenomenology; utilitarianism

Further reading
Christensen, J. (1958) "*Actus purus*: An essay on the function and place of the concept of pure act in Aristotelian metaphysics and on its interrelation with some other key concepts," *Classica et Mediaevalia* XIX: 7–40.
Lu, Matthias (1992) *Critical Theoretical Inquiry on the Notion of Act in the Metaphysics of Aristotle and Saint Thomas Aquinas*, New York, NY: P. Lang.
Mead, George Herbert (1964) *The Philosophy of the Act*, Chicago, IL: The University of Chicago Press.

action Generally speaking, an event whereby an agent brings about change(s). It is conceived as physical, psychological, or metaphysical. This has posed many problems concerning the following.

First, action at a distance: see PHILOSOPHY OF SCIENCE.

Second, action theory: also called philosophy of action, this branch of inquiry is the study of the nature, components, structure, and types of explanations of action, especially human action, understood as a kind of event. If actions are events, and these are involved in change, then action theory overlaps with the ontology of change, which deals with the nature, components, and structure of change. One question arising here is whether actions are abstract or concrete. If abstract, an action can have more than one instance, e.g. my using a shovel while planting a tree has more than one instance: a new one each time I use a shovel to plant a tree. On this view, actions are conceived in one of two ways: either as describable by declarative-like sentences such as "my using a shovel" and "your taking a bus"; or as universals, each one of which is called an *act-type* or *action-type*, to be denoted by such adverbial phrases as "using a shovel" and "taking a bus." Each particular instance of any action-type is called an *act-token* or *action-token*. On both interpretations of actions as abstractions, actions are repeatable. By contrast, as concrete, actions are ordinary particulars such as my using this shovel here and now, and your taking a bus here and now; hence, non-repeatable.

Other questions concerning actions are: Since it is possible to do more than one thing in a given performance – say, to plant a tree using a shovel – how are these doings related? Are they all the same or different actions? Are there basic actions? Is, for example, moving my hand when painting a basic action in that I cannot paint without moving my hand but moving my hand does not require my doing anything else to move it? How do deliberate actions differ from reflex movements? How, if at all, can reasons explain actions? Can reasons cause actions? In this regard, externalism is the view that there are reasons for action that are not dependent on motivational features – e.g. desires and aims – of the agents performing the actions, i.e. in this sense *external* to the agent. This view is contrasted with internalism, the view that no reasons for action can be independent of motivational features of the agents. The externalism–internalism controversy is associated with discussions of motivational internalism: the view that certain beliefs – e.g. moral beliefs – entail motives and, hence, are internal reasons for

action. Those who disagree are faced with holding that such beliefs, even when sound, do not always provide reasons for action, or that these reasons are actually external.

Third, action-token: see action theory, above; THEORY OF TYPES.

Fourth, action type: see action theory, above; THEORY OF TYPES.

Fifth, action verb: see SPEECH ACT THEORY.

Sixth, philosophy of action: see action theory, above; ACTIONISM; ACTIVISM; SPIRITUALISM.

See also: metaphysics; theory of types

Further reading
Guttenplan, Samuel (ed.) (1975) *Mind and Language*, Oxford: Oxford University Press.
Melden, A.I. (1961) *Free Action*, London and New York: Routledge & Kegan Paul and Humanities Press.
Whiteley, C.H. (1973) *Mind in Action: An Essay in Philosophical Psychology*, London, Oxford, and New York: Oxford University Press.

actionism Name given to his position by the German philosopher Rudolf Eucken (CE 1846–1926). He held that all philosophy is philosophy of life and argued for using religious inspiration in dealing with social problems. He held that, beyond the facts of human biology and psychology, there was the realm of the human spirit, which was independent of biology and psychology, and should be acknowledged in dealing with social problems. He criticized naturalism as well as socialism for failing to acknowledge this spiritual realm in human beings. Some critics have interpreted this position to be a form of pietism. Others have tried to explore the relations between actionism and other analogous philosophical approaches, for example that of the French philosopher Henri Bergson (CE 1859–1941). One could also explore its relations to philosophical spiritualism, such as that of the French philosopher Maurice Blondel (CE 1861–1949). Rudolf Eucken received the Nobel Prize for literature in 1908 and wrote extensively on the relations between nature, culture, religion, theology, and philosophy. A significant number of his works have been translated into English.

See also: Bergsonianism; spiritualism

Further reading

Eucken, Rudolf (1913) *Knowledge and Life*, London and New York: Williams & Norgate, G.P. Putman [*sic*].

—— (1912) *Naturalism or Idealism? The Nobel Lecture Delivered at Stockholm on March 27th, 1909*, Cambridge, UK: W. Heffer.

Gibson, William Ralph Boyce (1907) *Rudolf Eucken's Philosophy of Life*, 2nd edn, London: A. & C. Black.

Herman, Emily (1913) *Eucken and Bergson: Their Significance for Christian Thought*, Boston and London: Pilgrim Press and J. Clarke & Co.

active *see* euthanasia; understanding

activism A position whereby action takes precedence over contemplation and, in some cases, absorbs all contemplative purpose. This view was hard to develop in classical Western thought and other traditions, where action was at best internal and combined with contemplation in a unified reality. An example of this Classical view is the distinction provided by St Bonaventure (born Giovanni Fidanza, in Bagnorea, Tuscany, in what is now Italy, CE 1217–74) in *De Reductione Art. ad Theol.*, where he distinguishes between the superior light or light of grace, the interior light or light of philosophical knowledge, the inferior light or light of knowledge based on sense perception, and the exterior light or light of the mechanical arts. Once action and contemplation were separated, as they were, for example, in German Idealism, action could and significantly came to be thought prior to contemplation. Various nineteenth- and twentieth-century philosophical positions – from historicism, through Marxism and voluntarisms such as those of the German philosophers Arthur Schopenhauer (CE 1788–1860) and Friedrich Wilhelm Nietzsche (CE 1844–1900), to the pragmatism of the United States philosophers William James (CE 1842–1910) and John Dewey (CE 1859–1952) – have held some version of this view. By contrast, the French philosopher Maurice Blondel (CE 1861–1949) has argued that his philosophy of action does not imply that action is prior to thought, but includes it without eliminating it in the dynamics of living. Arguably, Blondel's position conflicts less with the pragmaticism of the United States

philosopher Charles Sanders Peirce (CE 1839–1914), which places truth and meaning in the practice of inquiry largely understood as scientific inquiry, than with the views of the previously mentioned pragmatists who, in special circumstances, to various degrees, and within various constraints, attributed precedence to emotive or practical concerns over the search for truth.

See also: historicism; idealism; Marxism; pragmatism; voluntarism

Further reading

Bonaventure, Saint John of Fidanza (1996) *On the Reduction of the Arts to Theology*, St Bonaventure, NY: Franciscan Institute.

Festenstein, Matthew (1997) *Pragmatism and Political Theory: from Dewey to Rorty*, Chicago, IL: University of Chicago Press.

Hamilton, Paul D. (1996) *Historicism*, New York: Routledge.

McNeill, John J. (1966) *The Blondelian Synthesis: A Study of the Influence of German Philosophical Sources on the Formation of Blondel's Method and Thought*, Leiden: E.J. Brill.

Vincent, Andrew (1984) *Philosophy, Politics, and Citizenship: The Life and Thought of the British Idealists*, Oxford: B. Blackwell.

activity verb *see* speech act theory

actual A term whose sense varies depending on whether it is used to discuss:

1   The actual–potential distinction: see ACT.
2   Actual–consequence utilitarianism: see UTILITARIANISM.
3   Actual infinite: see INFINITY.
4   Actual occasion: see PROCESS PHILOSOPHY.
5   Actual reality: see METAPHYSICS.

actualism Term used by the Italian philosopher Giovanni Gentile (CE 1875–1944), as shorthand for actual idealism, to characterize his philosophy of the pure act. He used the term act to refer to human activity that, in his view, was supposed to take ontological precedence. Everything real, from nature, through God, to good and evil, and, indeed, empirical subjects, was a result of the pure act of thinking of the transcendental subject. This pure act was to Gentile the only way in which the transcendental subject could undergo a dialectical process. He contraposed this view to that of Hegel's dialectics, which, Gentile thought, turned subjective thinking into an object.

Gentile's actualism influenced his views on education, which he put to work as Italy's minister of education between 1922 and 1924, in the early years of the regime led by the Italian dictator Benito Mussolini (CE 1883–1945). He conceived of education as an act that transcended communication and understanding difficulties between teachers and students into a unity that, to him, took place within the transcendental subject. His influence on Italy's educational system largely disappeared with the fall of Mussolini's regime.

Gentile's philosophy influenced a few Italian thinkers, most notably the contemporary philosopher Michele Sciacca (CE 1908–75), who advocated *integralism*, the view that existence generates itself as act. This self-generation is called objective interiority. Though not very influential in Italy, together with the historicism of another Italian neo-idealist, Benedetto Croce, who did not share Gentile's fascist sympathies, Gentile's actualism was influential outside Italy, for example among such British idealists as Bernard Bosanquet (CE 1848–1923) and Robin George Collinwood (CE 1889–1943).

See also: dialectic; idealism; Kantian philosophy; phenomenology

Further reading
Crespi, Angelo (1926) *Contemporary Thought of Italy*, New York, A.A. Knopf.
Harris, H.S. (1966) *The Social Philosophy of Giovanni Gentile*, Urbana, IL: University of Illinois Press.
Peccorini Letona, Francisco (1981) *From Gentile's "Actualism" to Sciacca's "Idea": Beyond Existentialism and Phenomenology towards the Philosophy of Integrality*, Genoa and Arlington, VA: Studio Editoriale di Cultura and Carrollton Press.
Romanell, Patrick (1982) *Croce versus Gentile*, New York: AMS Press.
Thompson, Merritt Moore (1934) *The Educational Philosophy of Giovanni Gentile*, Los Angeles: University of Southern California.

actualist *see* actualism; logic

actuality *see* act; alethiology; metaphysics

actualization *see* act

actus purus *see* act

ad A Latin preposition widely used in philosophical expressions. Some of these are as follows.

First, *ad aliquid*: an expression meaning *relatively to*, and used in such locutions as "*ad aliquid secundum rationem tantum*" (what is related to something according to the understanding) and "*ad aliquid secundum se*" (what is related to something according to its own being).

Second, *ad baculum*: see FALLACY.

Third, *ad extra*: an expression referring to a transcendent or transitive movement. It is contraposed to *ad intra*, which refers to an immanent movement.

Fourth, *ad feminam*: see FALLACY.

Fifth, *ad hoc*: expression used to refer to an idea, theory, or argument that is supposedly valid only for a particular case, typically without taking other cases into account. See curve-fitting problem, under INDUCTION.

Sixth, *ad hominem*: see FALLACY.

Seventh, *ad humanitatem*: an expression referring to an argument that is supposedly valid for all humans, or independently of any particular human being.

Eighth, *ad ignorantiam*: see FALLACY.

Ninth, *ad quem*: see *ad quod*, below.

Tenth, *ad quod*: also *a quo*, an expression used to refer to the beginning point of a process or, in logic, the premise or premises of an argument. It is contrasted with *ad quem* (also *a quem*), an expression used to signify the end point of a process or, in logic, the conclusion of an argument. The said points are respectively called *terminus a quo* or *terminus ad quod*, and *terminus a quem* or *terminus ad quem*. See FALLACY.

Adam *see* cabala

Adam Kadmon *see* cabala

adaptation *see* evolution

adaptive system *see* cybernetics

addition *see* logic

adequate Term derived from the Latin *ad* (to) and *aequare* (to make equal). Medieval philosophers used it to refer to ideas that correspond exactly to what they are about. Such adequate ideas are supposed to be complete or perfect. Along these lines, the philosopher Aquinas (CE 1225–74) – born near the city of Naples, in what is now Italy – used *adequatio*, the property of being adequate, to define truth, a component of knowledge, as the adequation of thought to thing. Other philosophers – e.g. the German philosopher Leibniz (CE 1646–1716) – made room for degrees of knowledge, some of which involved inadequate ideas, though adequate ideas were present in perfect knowledge. However, there are those who hold that an idea is adequate when its components are completely analyzed and that knowledge, or at least perfect knowledge, is attained only with such analysis. In the twentieth century, the German philosopher Edmund Husserl (CE 1859–1938) used the terms *adequate* and *adequation* to characterize relations between intuitions, such as those we have in sense experience and intentions understood in the sense of what ideas are about. For him, there was adequation whenever an intuition fully fits an empty intention.

See also: Scholasticism

Further reading

Aquinas, Thomas (1992) *Truth: Quaestiones Disputatae de Veritate*, Pittsboro, NC: Inte-Lex Corp.

Waelhens, Alphonse de (1953) *Phenomenologie et Verite*, Paris: Presses Universitaires de France.

Wilson, Margaret Dauler (1990) *Leibniz' Doctrine of Necessary Truth*, New York: Garland Publishing.

adequation *see* adequate

adhibhautika *see* Sāmkhya-Yoga

adhyāsa Sanskrit term meaning "superimposition," "false attribution," "illusion" and, in general, "perceptual error." These are perceptual errors of different kinds. Some are as follows.

First, *artha-adhyāsa* or the mistaken superimposition of an object upon a substratum, e.g. in perceiving an object as material when, in fact, it is a hallucination.

Second, *dharma-adhyāsa* or the mistaken superimposition of attributes or properties, as

when one perceives as heavy what in fact is large but light, such as a large paper cube.

Third, *dharmi-adhyāsa* or the mistaken substantive superimposition or superimposition of objects, e.g. seeing a man's face on the Moon.

Fourth, *jñāna-adhyāsa* or the mistaken superimposition of knowledge of an object – say, my knowing that I am seeing the image of a car on the street – on my knowledge of a substratum such as my knowledge of matter, by thinking that the image is of a material object.

Fifth, *samsarga-adhyāsa* or mistakenly superimposing an attribute, say, the blue color of a blue light on an object, say, a nearby wall.

Sixth, *svarūpa-adhyāsa* or the mistaken superimposition of an illusory object, say, Alice's cat, on an actual one, say, a tree branch outside your window. This situation may not just be an ordinary mistake, but a fundamental one, for example when an empirical object, such as a human body, is ascribed to Brahman.

See also: Hinduism; philosophy of mind

Further reading

Krishna, Daya (1969) *Adhyasa – a non-Advaitic beginning in Samkara Vedanta*, Honolulu: Institute of Advanced Projects, East-West Center, University of Hawaii, pp. 243–9. [Reprinted from *Philosophy East and West* 25(3–4), July–October 1965.]

Scheepers, Alfred Robert (1988) *Adhyasa: een vergelijking tussen de Advaita-Vedanta van Samkara en de fenomenologie van Edmund Husser*, Delft: Eburon. [Text in Dutch and Sanskrit with English translation of Sanskrit; summary in English.]

ādhyātmā A term meaning "personal," "individual," "of the Supreme Self." In monistic systems it means the Supreme Self, the Supreme Spirit, or the soul. In dualist systems, e.g. Dvaita Vedānta, the term *ādhyātmā* means each individual's true soul. The term often appears in the following expressions:

First, *ādhyātmā-Rāmāyana*, an expression used in two ways: first, a spiritual interpretation of Rāmā's life; and second, a work that expands on the *Rāmāyana* by adding non-dualistic concepts and emphasizing Rāmā's divine nature. In this latter use, the expression denotes a part of the Brahmānda-Purāna.

Second, *ādhyātmā-Yoga*, an expression also

used in two ways: The first way denotes the yogic discipline that, through self-knowledge and self-realization, ceases to identify body and mind, leading to the knowledge that a human being is absolute consciousness, hence identical with Brahman. The state of Supraconsciousness thus attained is called *ādhyātmā-prasāda*. In this state, a practitioner of yoga becomes a *jīvanmukta*, a term meaning someone who is liberated while still alive. This liberation is understood to be a freedom from ignorance. The second use of the term ādhyātmā-Yoga sometimes denotes a philosophical school in the tradition of the philosopher Shankara (CE 788–820).

See also: ātman; Hinduism

Further reading
Brahmanandendra Saraswati, Swami (1975) *Adhyatma Yoga Darshana: Rational Intuition of the Supramental State of Unexcelled Bliss*, Sagar, Karnataka State: K.V. Sridhara Rao.
Desjardins, Arnaud (1977) *A la recherche du soi: adhyatma yoga*, Paris: La Table Ronde.
Osho (1994) *Finger Pointing to the Moon: Discourses on the Adhyatma Upanishad*, Shaftesbury, Dorset, and Rockport, MA: Element.
Tapasyananda, Swami (1993) *Adhyatma Ramayana: The Spiritual Version of the Rama Saga*, Madras: Bourne End, Ramakrishna Math; Ramakrishna Vedanta Centre.

ādhyātman *see* ādhyātmā

ādhyātmika *see* Sāmkhya-Yoga

adicity *see* degree

administrative situation *see* philosophy, sociopolitical

Advaita Term meaning "non-duality." It can be ascribed to God or the Absolute Being, which is not accessible through the use of reason because, through the latter, duality is unavoidable. It is also used to refer to one of the six orthodox schools of Indian philosophy, the non-dualistic school of Vedānta, a Sanskrit term meaning *end of the Vedas*, also called Uttara Mīmāmsā, a Sanskrit term meaning *analysis of the scriptures*, and denoting the later portion of the Vedas, the *Upanishads* (virtually all of them dating from the eight to

the fourth century BCE), where the school's roots are found.

Vedānta has no known founders. It holds that the individual soul and Brahman are one, a realization to be attained through an esoteric experience called *moksha*. It also holds that the nature of Brahman is not dual, and the empirical world is not real. Further, it holds that pairs of opposites in nature, or *dvandva*, such as pleasure and pain, and hot and cold, are illusory (*dvandvamoha*). Indeed, one of its doctrines is *ajāta-vāda*, or the theory of non-origination – especially associated with Gaudapāda (see below). According to this doctrine – in a manner that displays an affinity to Zeno's paradoxes (see PARADOX) (named after the Greek philosopher who formulated them, Zeno of Elea (490–430 BCE)) – there is no creation. For that which is non-existent at the beginning and non-existent at the end, is also non-existent in the middle, hence totally non-existent.

As for the evidence that things are otherwise – e.g. that there is a difference between oneself and what one experiences in hearing music or watching the sea, and that there is a difference between one's states and oneself in feeling pleasure or pain – this school of philosophy rejects it on the grounds that such evidence involves drawing distinctions, most notably through the use of language. Critics have claimed that *moksha* must also involve drawing distinctions, because it involves learning or grasping something. However, the followers of Advaita-Vedānta appear to reply that *moksha* is pre-linguistic, and rather in the nature of a non-articulated emotive intuition or gut feeling that refers to the divinity.

A central concept in this school is ignorance (*avidyā māyā*), which helps explain the otherwise paradoxical distinction of a non-dual reality appearing in a dual way, as individuals and as the divinity. This distinction is epistemological, i.e. about how things appear, not metaphysical or about how things are. The main espousers of this school were the philosophers Gaudapāda (sixth or eighth century CE) and Shankara (CE 788–820). Related doctrines are: *anirvācya-vāda*, or the theory of the indefinable; *anirvacanīya-khyāti*, or the theory of error according to which error is neither totally unreal (because its object is perceivable), nor ultimately real (because the false is superimposed on its object); and *anupalabdhi*, or the theory of non-cognition, according to which non-cognition is a valid method of attaining knowledge, namely of non-existence.

The Advaita School has two branches: the Bhāmati and the Vivarana Schools. The latter holds the *bimba-pratibimba-vāda*, a theory of reflection according to which the individual is a reflection of (and identical with) the original intelligence or Brahman.

See also: Brahman; dvaita; Hinduism

Further reading
Sarma, Candradhara (1996) *The Advaita Tradition in Indian Philosophy: A Study of Advaita in Buddhism, Vedanta and Kashmira Shaivism*, Delhi and Oxford: Motilal Banarsidass and Motilal.
Sharma, Arvind (1993) *The Experiential Dimension of Advaita Vedanta*, Delhi: Motilal Banarsidass Publishers.

adventitious *see* idea

adverbial *see* perception

adversarial *see* philosophy, sociopolitical

adwen *see* wisdom

aesthetic *see* aesthetics

aesthetic attitude *see* aesthetics

aesthetic object *see* aesthetics

aesthetic value *see* aesthetics

aesthetics A branch of philosophy whose subject matter is the experience, appreciation, and evaluation of works of art, natural environments, and other objects and events, as well as the identity and kinds of works of art. In so far as it deals with the experience and appreciation of works of art, it is also called philosophy of art. When the notion of art is widely conceived to include works of literature, the aesthetics or the philosophy of art include literary theory, a study of the nature, causes, effects, significance, and criteria for assessing literary works.

Some have held that aesthetics deals with beauty and have tried to answer the question: what is the nature of beauty? Partly in addressing this question, some have distinguished *free beauty*, i.e. an item's beauty based simply on its appearance, not as a kind of item, from *dependent beauty*, which an item has by virtue of its being of a certain kind.

Beauty or the beautiful is sometimes contrasted with the sublime. In *On the Sublime*, by an unknown first-century author (mistakenly thought to be the Greek rhetorician Longinus (*c.* 213–73 CE)), it is argued that the sublime was related to the use of language and gave rules for its expression. The Irish-born statesman and philosopher Edmund Burke (CE 1729–97) distinguished the sublime from the beautiful in psychological terms, arguing that the beautiful is finite and delightful, while the sublime is infinite and involves delight mixed with terror or pain. The German philosopher Immanuel Kant (CE 1724–1804) eliminated the terror or pain component and considered the beautiful as conforming to our faculties, and the sublime as extending beyond their power.

Other philosophers, however, have held that aesthetics does not deal with the items just discussed, and have argued that aesthetics involves an aesthetic attitude, but characterized this attitude in different ways: as disinterested, i.e. devoid of all practical concerns; as detached, i.e. distanced from one's personal concerns; as contemplative and purely sensory, i.e. devoid of any knowledge we may have of the objects we approach with such attitude; or as a combination of these features. However, whether such an attitude exists is controversial, because the existence of the disinterest, detachment, and lack of cognitive content being postulated is controversial. This has led some to conclude that aesthetics is not a separate branch of philosophy. However, this inference supposes that an aesthetic attitude is necessary in aesthetics – a questionable supposition.

A problem in aesthetics is whether *formalism*, the type of theory that emphasizes the form of works of art, rather than such things as what they represent, symbolize, express, evoke, are intended to be, have affinities to, influence or are influenced by, is sound. There are many formalist theories. They are thought most suitable in dealing with the more formal arts, e.g. music; less suitable when dealing with the plastic arts, and least suitable in theories of literature and theater. Formalism arguably is instantiated in Indian aesthetics, where the notion of *sādhāranī-karana*, i.e. idealization, is considered crucial to free the artist's subject matter from faults, mutability, and ugliness. In the Western tradition, a formalist idea is that of unity in diversity, i.e. that the parts of an aesthetic object should significantly differ from each other and, also, contribute to give a significance to the object that would be changed were any of them to be changed.

As an alternative to formalism, philosophers have formulated the doctrine of *expressionism*, or *expression theories of art*, a family of theories sharing the view that centrally art is expression of feeling or emotion, though some consider this to be communication, others intuition, still others clarification, and there are those who associate expression with specific structures or forms of works of art, e.g. of works of music. Still another position is the *mimesis* or *imitation theory of art* (from the Greek *mimesis*, i.e. imitation), also called *mimetic theory of art* or *representational theory of art*, according to which *art imitates nature*, understood as actual or plausible things (though on some conceptions, these can also be merely possible, which makes the theory hardly distinguishable from some formalist ones). This conception points to the notion of an original – in this case nature – and leads to discussion of the value of an original versus the value of its copies or imitations. Should the latter, however accurate, have any less value because they are copies? Is this an artistic or an institutional concern? In this regard, there is also the *institutional theory of art*, which holds that something becomes a work of art by becoming an artifact, and it acquires artifactuality by virtue of occupying a certain position in the context of certain institutions, e.g. by being recognized as a work of art by art critics. However, the question arises: what serves to establish whether a given institution is artistic? So, if not circular, at the very least this theory is incomplete.

Another problem is whether there are aesthetic objects or properties and, if so, what characterizes them. Some have argued that a certain attitude or taste is necessary to appreciate such objects, e.g. to appreciate charm or elegance, while it is not necessary to perceive non-aesthetic objects or properties such as a vase being green or a piece of music being loud. Hence, some have concluded that aesthetic objects or properties cannot be reduced to non-aesthetic ones, though they may, and some have argued they do, supervene on non-aesthetic ones.

Still another problem is whether we can meaningfully judge works of art or literature; if we can, what is the point of doing so? In any case, can the judgments be true or false?, can there be reasons for them?, and can the judgments amount to knowledge? Some Western philosophers answer all of these questions affirmatively, on the grounds that works of art are characterized by aiming to provide aesthetic experiences, i.e. experiences with aesthetic value. Others object that the experiences of works of art have cognitive value, not aesthetic value. Still others hold that works of art have aesthetic value and, sometimes, also cognitive value, but this is not a matter of experience but is, at least in part, instrumental, e.g. in that it is conducive to cultural cohesiveness or flourishing.

Here, there have been Neoplatonic theories that focused on the radiance of beauty, Aristotelian theories focusing on the harmony of beauty, and Thomistic theories that include both and, in addition to physical beauty, talk of spiritual beauty, which derives from the order of spiritual goods.

At any rate, they all agree that there is such a thing as aesthetic discrimination in judgment, whether this involves skills that are cognitive or not. In addition, these theories tend to assume that providing experiences is a central purpose of works of art. However, anthropologists indicate that African art does not have the purpose of providing any experiences. Instead, it has a central practical purpose: the provision of social cohesiveness (which would help answer all the above questions affirmatively).

A related problem is that of the identity of a particular work of art. Is it determined by the author's intentions, as the *author theory* holds, or by something else? It has been argued that the author's intentions are not decisive, if relevant to establish the identity of the work of art. Otherwise, as the Argentine writer Jorge Luis Borges (CE 1899–1986), citing the British author Joseph Rudyard Kipling (CE 1865–1936), indicated, *Gulliver's Travels* would be, as its author intended, a political satire; but, in fact, it historically turned out to be a children's book. This line of reasoning also applies to entire *genra*, i.e. classes or categories of artistic or literary activity having such salient characteristics as a type of technique, content, or form.

An area of aesthetic inquiry attracting lesser but recurrent attention from philosophers concerns humor. The concept derives from the *four-humor theory*, i.e. the view that there are four basic bodily fluids – blood, phlegm, black bile, and yellow bile – and that health is maintained by a balance between these. This theory was held, for example, by the Greek physician Galen (CE 129–*c*. 215) and, through his influence on the Greco-Roman world and the Arabic tradition, was commonly held in the Western world even after the discoveries of the seventeenth century, and, indeed, far into the nineteenth century. At any rate, the concept was extended to such characteristics of people as being in good humor, being of ill humor, and being humorless, and prompted a variety of questions: "What makes a person funny?" "What is it for a person to be witty?" "What is it to have a sense of humor?" "How are these things related to comedy?" Some of the questions also went beyond characteristics of people into the objects of humorous responses: What makes something funny? What makes a remark witty? What is it to have a sense of humor? Answers to these latter questions have been proposed along the lines of the aesthetic theories previously mentioned.

A related matter concerns artistic creation, where some argue inspiration plays a crucial role. The notion of *inspiration* originally meant a divine influence directly exerted upon the mind of an individual. By extension, this concept is also applied to the works of individuals thus influenced, and has acquired an aesthetic use according to which artists are said to be inspired to produce such things as works of art or literature by some divinity, whether God or a Muse. (The Muses were a number of sister goddesses in Greek and Roman mythology, such as Calliope, the Muse of epic poetry, Euterpe, the Muse of music, and Clio, the Muse of history.) In a secular sense, the aesthetic sense of inspiration denotes any influence prompting an individual to create such things as a work of art or literature.

Answers to the previous questions concerning characteristics of persons have not been thoroughly discussed in philosophy, perhaps because they are more complex, involving matters of aesthetics, ethics, the philosophy of language, the philosophy of art, and the philosophy of mind.

A recurrent topic of interest in aesthetics widely understood and other branches of philosophy has been *poetry*. Its study, *poetics*, has also been a topic of discussion in these branches of inquiry. Philosophers have studied both out of a variety of concerns. A concern with truth and reality arguably led to the Platonic conception of poetry as a gift that allows us to share the forms. A concern with truth and reality combined with practical concerns led to the Aristotelian conception of dramatic poetry as mimetic and, in the case of tragedy, cathartic. In modern times, a religious concern has led to conceptions of poetry as a source of revelation.

These conceptions are not unrelated to differing views of language, the relation of poetry to literal meaning and metaphor, and the type of study appropriate to this subject. They are also reflected in different conceptions of the elements of tragedy. The Greek philosopher Aristotle (384–322 BCE), for example, held tragedy to be an imitation of actions by humans superior to us, where the actions had to be serious; where the plot had to include a beginning, a middle, and an end; develop within a single day; involve a reversal of positions and the catastrophic fall of a superior human due to an error in judgment; and involve recognition of the error by this human at the end, when the fall is irreversible. These features, however, were not crucial in Shakespearean theater, where the emphasis was on character development. Nor were they crucial in French neo-classical tragedy, where tragedy was understood as the imitation of a serious action that had to preserve the three unities: of time, place, and action.

See also: empathy; judgment; philosophy of literature

Further reading
Borges, Jorge Luis (1962) "The Argentine writer and tradition," *Labyrinths*, New York: New Directions.
Lyas, Colin (1997) *Aesthetics*, London and Bristol, PA: UCL Press.
Matthews, Patricia M. (1997) *The Significance of Beauty: Kant on Feeling and the System of the Mind*, Dordrecht and Boston: Kluwer Academic Publishers.
Sadler, Simon (1998) *The Situationist City*, Cambridge MA: MIT Press.

affect *see* passion

affectio In medieval philosophy, the result of an impression on the mind. It is therefore an excitation that can take two forms: external, e.g. the impression of sunlight through our vision; or internal, e.g. the impression of a memory on our thinking. The German philosopher Immanuel Kant (CE 1724–1804) understood *affectio* in a manner similar to that of medieval philosophers: the influence, e.g. the sensations, produced by any object on us. In both cases, *affectio* was passive. However, for the Amsterdam-born philosopher of Spanish and Portuguese descent Baruch Spinoza (CE 1632–77), affection was sometimes active, namely when the body was an adequate cause of an *affectio* or, in other words, a cause equal to the *affectio* in that it went hand in hand with the *affectio*. For example, an *affectio* such as a feeling of pain in one's shoulder caused by arthritis, on its turn, affects the body's ability to act, e.g. to raise one's arm, as well as one's idea of such feeling.

A recurrent philosophical problem about the term *affectio* concerns the extent to which affection involves intentions. Sometimes, as in the previously mentioned case of medieval philosophers and Kant, an *affectio* is largely conceived of as a mere sensation. Other times, as is arguably the case in Spinoza's conception, an *affectio* involves at least a minimum of intention, as in the intention not to raise one's arm that accompanies the feeling of pain in one's shoulder.

Affectio is sometimes also used as synonymous with *affect*, which has a meaning closer to emotion or sentiment. For this meaning, see PASSION.

See also: ethics; passion

Further reading
Armon-Jones, Claire (1991) *Varieties of Affect*, Toronto: University of Toronto Press.
Paulhan, Frederic (1930) *The Laws of Feeling*, London and New York: K. Paul, Trench, Trubner & Co. Ltd, and Harcourt, Brace & Company.

affirmative A term used in various branches of philosophy:

First, in traditional logic, the term affirmative is used to characterize kinds of simple propositions: those whereby the subject term is said partly or totally to have the feature of, or belong to, the class denoted by, the predicate term – e.g. "Some cats are black," "All birds are animals," and "The door is open." Propositions such as these are said to have the quality of being affirmative (while negations are said to have the quality of being negative). By analogy with affirmative propositions, one can talk of affirmative judgments or statements. In modern symbolic logic, talk of affirmative propositions, judgments, or statements is largely if not entirely absent.

Second, in ethics and aesthetics, the term "affirmative" has been used, e.g. by the German philosopher Friedrich Nietzsche (CE 1844–1900), to describe an assertive type of attitude that says "yes" to the world as it is, with all that is good and all that is bad in it.

Third, during the second part of the twentieth century and reflecting ordinary United States use, the term "affirmative" has also been used in ethics and sociopolitical philosophy to denote a family of United States policies meant to correct discriminatory practices and social structures that relegate women and minority groups to disadvantageous positions. Various arguments have arisen concerning affirmative action. Some have argued that it establishes quotas (of such things as jobs and places at universities), regardless of qualifications, and that this amounts to reverse discrimination. One reply has been that affirmative action does not establish quotas, but goals, and these are

not supposed to take precedence over qualifications. Instead, it is argued, goals only ensure
that qualified minority and female candidates
are not excluded from positions for which they
are qualified simply on grounds of ethnic
membership of race. This is not reverse discrimination but morally justified preferential
treatment. Concerning this reply, opponents of
affirmative action argue that it amounts to
reverse discrimination, because it uses sex or
ethnic membership, instead of merit as it
should, to ensure that females or minority
members are represented in jobs and education. This has led to discussions, indeed heated
controversy, about whether merit or compensatory justice has ever been or should be a
criterion for hiring or school admissions;
whether instead the common good or, alternatively, principles of distributive justice should
be the used criterion; and, at any rate, whether
affirmative action is supported by any of these
criteria.

See also: argument; categorical; ethics; syllogism

Further reading
Blackstone, William T. and Heslep, Robert D.
   (1977) *Social Justice and Preferential Treat-
   ment: Women and Racial Minorities in
   Education and Business*, Athens: University
   of Georgia Press.
Church, Alonzo (1959) *Elementary Topics in
   Mathematical Logic: 1. The Algebra of
   Classes*, Brooklyn, NY: Galois Institute of
   Mathematics and Art.
Kurtz, Paul W. (1985) *Exuberance: An Affir-
   mative Philosophy of Life*, Buffalo, NY:
   Prometheus Books.
Yovel, Yirmiahu (1986) *Nietzsche as Affirma-
   tive Thinker: Papers Presented at the Fifth
   Jerusalem Philosophical Encounter, April
   1983*, Dordrecht and Boston: M. Nijhoff
   Publishers and Kluwer Academic Publishers.

affirming the consequent *see* fallacy

African philosophy Philosophical inquiry and
resulting philosophical views found in African
thought. In Sub-Saharan Africa, except for
Ethiopia, this inquiry and these ideas have not
until relatively recently taken written form.
None the less, the themes characteristic of the
said inquiry and ideas are philosophical, constituting what has been called *folk-philosophy*

or *cultural thought*, i.e. worldviews predominant among Africans. They are philosophical
because they concern ideas recurrent in philosophy, whether in the Western world, in the
East, or elsewhere: God and other spiritual
entities; the monism–dualism distinction; fate;
morality; the good life; the common good;
legitimacy and consensus; national character,
identity, and culture; development and technology; and social and personal values. These
ideas, and the interest and critical scrutiny they
have elicited in Africa, can be interpreted to
fall under four main categories: *supernaturalism, the individual and the community, social
decision processes and structures*, and *tradition
and modernity*.

A significant number of African philosophers engage in *ethnophilosophy*, which is a
critical examination of implicit notions and
values received from traditional African
thought, both oral and written, as well as of
notions and values diffused into African
thought through the rich interaction that African cultures have had with non-African ones.
Prominent in this context is the negritude
movement, begun in the 1930s by artists and
writers, and eventually formulated into a
coherent political movement by the contemporary philosopher Leopold Senghor, who
became President of Senegal in 1960. Its aim
was to instill a new sense of history and of
their own culture, and a new pride and dignity
in being black, among the many continental
and diasporan Africans who had acquired
Western ways of thinking.

Overall, as the categories listed above suggest, not just curiosity, but substantial practical
concerns have motivated and still motivate
much philosophical inquiry in Africa. Such
inquiry concerns, for example, the justifiability
of governmental structures, and social adaptations to new technologies and development
strategies. Other notable contemporary African
philosophers who have produced works falling
under African ethnophilosophy include Placide
Tempels (who is often considered the creator of
African ethnophilosophy), K.C. Anyanwu,
Kwame Gyekye, Alexis Kagame, and John
Mbiti. Some interpreters would also add Kwasi
Wiredu to this list, though his inclusion is
debatable and, indeed, Wiredu might object.

The ethnophilosophical approach has been criticized by some contemporary African philosophers. Paulin J. Hountondji, for example, argues that its primary aim is to justify European superiority. Others argue that African ethnophilosophy is merely descriptive. This charge, however, is not entirely true of the work of Kagame, Mbiti, Senghor, and Tempels, and does not at all apply to the works of Anyanwu and Gyekye, who engage in a rather critical approach to the subject.

An additional, related, type of approach in African philosophy is what has been called *sagacity philosophy*: the study of the explicitly articulated views of individually identified traditional Africans – i.e. those who explain natural objects and events not only in physical terms, but also in terms of the influences of gods and spirits – who are notable for their wisdom and probity in the eyes of their communities. Most closely associated with this line of thought are the contemporary African philosophers Marcel Griaule, B. Hallen, J.O. Sodipo, and O.H. Oruka. This last author has distinguished between *folk sagacity*, where the sages' thinking remains within the limits of their peoples' traditional thought, and *philosophical sagacity*, where the sages transcend these limits and assess traditional ideas on the basis of self-reflective criticism. This is arguably *philosophy as a branch of inquiry* (see PHILOSOPHY), a notion that covers both ordinary critical inquiry as well as more structured and focused – sometimes called *professional* – critical inquiry about matters of philosophical interest or concern.

A fourth type of approach in African philosophy is sometimes called *nationalist-ideological philosophy*, other times called *liberation philosophy*. It includes some contemporary philosophers, such as Kwame Nkrumah and Julius K. Nyerere, who advocated Pan-Africanism and African Unity. This was hardly a sign of nationalism – a reason sometimes why the liberation philosophy label is preferable. Another reason used is that the present category also includes the thought of the contemporary South African leader Nelson Mandela, which is primarily guided by concerns with individual and national freedom, but not with promoting any particular ideology.

As the preceding discussion makes plain, African philosophy displays a variety of themes, ideas and approaches, whose purposes and circumstances are sometimes distinctive of Africans while, other times, are shared by other human individuals and groups. These are the constraints within which current efforts to develop African philosophy take place.

See also: ethics; metaphysics; philosophy; philosophy of liberation; philosophy of mind; wisdom

Further reading
Griaule, M. (1965) *Conversations with Ogotemmeli: An Introduction to Dogon Religious Ideas*, London: Oxford University Press.
Gyekye, Kwame (1997) *Tradition and Modernity: Philosophical Reflections on the African Experience*, New York: Oxford University Press.
Hallen, B. and Sodipo, J.O. (1986) *Knowledge, Belief and Witchcraft: Analytic Experiment in African Philosophy*, London: Ethnographica Ltd.
Hountondji, Paulin J. (1976) *African Philosophy: Myth and Reality*, Bloomington, IN: Indiana University Press.
Masolo, D.A. (1994) *African Philosophy in Search of Identity*, Edinburgh and Bloomington: Edinburgh University Press and Indiana University Press.
Oruka, O.H. (1990) *Sage Philosophy: Indigenous Thinkers and the Modern Debate on African Philosophy*, Nirobi: Shirikon Publishers.
Tangwa, Godfrey B. (1996) *African Philosophy in a Western Frame*, Bayreuth: Iwalewa-Haus.

African-American philosophy see diaspora; philosophy of liberation

Afrocentricity An approach, in philosophy and other branches of inquiry, aimed at pursuing questions arising from the standpoint of the experience of Africans. This approach is contrasted with standpoints such as that of the European experience, which, Afrocentrists contend, have traditionally peripheralized Africans and peoples from places other than Europe. Afrocentrists for example argue that the view of Ancient Greece as having given the world rational thinking is inaccurate and ethnocentric. When coupled with the view, enhanced if not created during the Renaissance, that Europeans are direct heirs from the Ancient Greeks through Rome, this view becomes Eurocentrism – a form of ethnocen-trism. The question has been raised whether Afrocentricity or Afrocentrism is not also a form of ethnocentrism. Espousers of Afrocentrism have answered that it is not, because it is a pluralistic view that does not seek cultural hegemony. Rather, it seeks to set the record straight, so that when, for example, one talks of classical music or the Middle Ages, it is not automatically assumed that the only classical music and the only Middle Ages are European. To do this would be to peripherialize African history or, for that matter, the history of China or India.

A central assumption of Afrocentrism is that human beings are embedded in culture, whether their own or that of others. Afrocentrists further argue that when, for example, a non-Western author writes from the standpoint of a culture other than his or her own, he or she peripheralizes his or her own culture. To this, it is frequently added that African discourse should be addressed from the standpoint of African conceptual and perceptual realitites, i.e. by indigenous African scholars. To some, these statements suggest that expatriate African writers should come home. Other times, however, it is also added that Eurocentric arrogance needs to be lessened and, hence, Eurocentrism should be reduced by non-Western authors ceasing to write about the West. A number of these points can be found, for example, in Martin Bernal's *Black Athena: The Afroasiatic Roots of Classical Civilization*, a book that galvanized the Afrocentric–Eurocentric controversy in the late 1980s and early 1990s. These views have prompted a great deal of reflection and discussion, controversy, and outright rejection, not just among African philosophers, but also among those involved in the literature of expatriation and exile. Various reasons prompt this resistance to Afrocentrism. One is the awareness that foreigners have contributed many of the most prominent writings about Africa. Another is the enormous range of adaptations African expatriates, like all expatriates, develop, which are not only justified (at least because unavoid-able), but also fruitful in providing a less limited and less conflictive perspective.

See also: culture; diaspora; philosophy, socio-political

Further reading
Alegría, Fernando and Ruffinelli, Jorge (1990) *Paradise Lost or Gained? The Literature of Hispanic Exile*, Houston: Arte Público Press.
Anyamwu, K.C. (1987) "Cultural philosophy as a philosophy of integration and tolerance," *International Philosophical Quarterly* 25, September: 271–87.
Asante, Molefi K. (1988) *Afrocentricity*, Trenton, NJ: Africa World Press.
Bernal, Martin (1987, 1990) *Black Athena: The Afroasiatic Roots of Classical Civilization, Vol. I: The Fabrication of Ancient Greece 1785–1985; Vol. II: The Archeological and Documentary Evidence*, New Brunswick, NJ: Rutgers University Press.
Onyewuenyi, Innocent C. (1993) *The African Origin of Greek Philosophy: An Exercise in Afrocentrism*, Nsukka: University of Nigeria Press.

āgama Sanskrit term meaning: "what has come down from tradition." It denotes an authoritative text of some Indian religion. The *āgamas* are Hindu, Jain, and Buddhist. The Hindu *āgamas* are divided into three classes. The Vaishnava scriptures, *Pāñcarātra* and *Vikhānasa*, deal with the worship of Vishnu. The Saiva scriptures concern the worship of Shiva. The Sakta scriptures deal with the worship of Devī. An *āgama* has four main topics: the making of temples and idols, philosophical doctrines, meditation practices, and worship methods: *kriyā*, *jñāna*, *yoga*, and *caryā*. The latter are subdivided into three groups: *tantra*, which teaches rituals; *mantra*, which teaches the yoga stage of worship; and *upadesha*, which deals with the existence and nature of the three eternal entities, *pashu*, *pāsha*, and *pati*. In Mahāyāna Buddhism, the term *āgama* refers to collections of writings of the earlier Theravāda (or Hīnayāna) School.

See also: Buddhism; Hinduism; Jainism

Further reading
Banerji, Sures Chandra (1988) *A Brief History of Tantra Literature*, Calcutta: Naya Prokash.

Varadachari, V. (1982) *Agamas and South Indian Vaisnavism*, Madras: M.C. Krishnan.

agape *see* love

agapism *see* love; pragmatism

agathon *see* ethics

age of the world A cosmological concept involved in the philosophical thinking of various cultures. For example, among the Nahuas and Mayas of Pre-Hispanic Mexico, who believed we lived in the age of the Fifth Sun. These Suns or Ages were extremely long periods of time from the standpoint of these cultures' conception of what a long time was. The Mayas, for example, measured time not only in days, months, and years, but also in twenty-year periods (*katun*), 400-year periods (*baktun*), 8,000-year periods (*pictun*), 158,000-year periods (*calabtun*), and about a million-year periods (*kincultun*). As for the nature of these Ages, a Nahua version in the *Annals of Cuauhtitlán* says that the four preceding Suns or eras had been tests of types of beings, including the humans who had lived in them. The reported order of these Suns was not always the same. In one version, the First had been the Sun of Earth – of instinctive power, animal energy, instinct; the Second, the Sun of Air – of pure spirit; the Third, which like the Fourth has a less clear meaning than the first two, was the Sun of Fire, upon whose destruction only birds could fly to safety; the Fourth, the Sun of Water, during which fishes in the sea were created, and whose end came about with a flood. Each one of these ages had perished because it was one-sided. In another version, first came the Sun of Water, then of Air, then of Fire, then of Earth. However, in all versions, only our Sun, *Naollin*, which means Four Movements, made it possible for the elements – earth, air, fire, and water – to come together.

Analogous conceptions can be found in the work of the Greek philosopher Heraclitus (*c.* 540–475 BCE), who held the world year or eon to be a vast cycle comprising 360 generations; among the ancient Stoics, who believed in a world year at the end of which the world was destroyed and regenerated by fire; and among thinkers from China and India. In Stoicism, the world year involves the doctrine of eternal return, according to which the world year repeats itself identically each time. The nineteenth-century German philosopher Friedrich Nietzsche (CE 1844–1900) also proposed this view.

In Indian thought, *kalpa* is an extremely long cycle of time equal to 8,640,000,000 years. It is a day of Brahmā and is divided into lesser periods called *manvantara*. One *manvantara* or *mahā-yuga* equals four *yugas*, and 1,000 *mahā-yugas* make a *half-kalpa* or 4,320,000,000 years.

See also: element; myth; Stoicism

Further reading
Allan, Sarah (1991) *The Shape of the Turtle: Myth, Art, and Cosmos in Early China*, Albany, NY: State University of New York Press.
Cunningham, Sir Alexander (1971) *Book of Indian Eras, with Tables for Calculating Indian Dates*, Delhi: Oriental Publishers.
León Portilla, Miguel (1990) *Time and Reality in the Thought of the Maya*, Norman and London: University of Oklahoma Press.
Sandbach, F.H. (1989) *The Stoics*, London and Indianapolis, IN: G. Duckworth and Hackett Pub. Co.
Zeller, Eduard (1951) *Outlines of the History of Greek Philosophy*, 13th edn, rev. Wilhelm Nestle and trans. L.R. Palmer, New York: The Humanities Press.

ageism *see* ethics

agency *see* feminist philosophy

agent Term used in discussions of causation and in ethics. It often appears in two expressions. The first is agent causation, a noun-phrase indicating that a substance, not an event, causes a given event. More narrowly, it was used by the Scottish philosopher Thomas Reid (CE 1710–96) and other philosophers to indicate that an action or event was caused by the exertion of power of some agent having will and understanding. For example, they used agent causation to indicate that a person had done such things as moving a chair or lifting a branch. In this narrower sense, the person had to have the power to both, cause and not cause the event. Also, whatever the agent did had to be up to the agent, not be beyond the agent's control, as is the case with an agent such as a tree that, without having any control over it, falls down thereby smashing a car. That is, this narrow sense of agent causation is akin to that of free will, in that it involves not just freedom of movement, but freedom of decision.

In the *Metaphysics*, the Greek philosopher Aristotle (384–322 BCE) distinguished between two kinds of activities: those where the agent's action affects an object, as in Jane's pushing a mower, where movement is involved; and those in which the agent's action reverts to the agent, as in Jane's thinking about a dream she had, where there is an activity but not movement. Medieval philosophers used this Aristotelian distinction to distinguish between what they called *actio immanens* (or *permanens*), whose English translation is *immanent causation*, which meant the internal activity of the agent, and *actio transiens*, whose English translation is *transeunt causation*, which meant the external event produced by that activity. In a somewhat different sense, the Amsterdam-born philosopher of Spanish and Portuguese descent Baruch Spinoza (CE 1632–77) and other philosophers used this distinction. Spinoza, for example, used it when stating that God is an immanent, but not transitive, cause of all things. The United States philosopher R.M. Chisholm (CE 1916–99) and others used it to distinguish between agent causation and event-causation. According to them, agent causation or immanent causation is an activity internal to the agent causing it, while event causation or transeunt causation is an event external to an agent whose internal activity causes the event.

For the second use of the term, agent-based ethics, see VIRTUE.

See also: act; causal law; determinism

Further reading

Bishop, John (1989) *Natural Agency: An Essay on the Causal Theory of Action*, Cambridge, UK and New York: Cambridge University Press.

Flew, Antony (1987) *Agency and Necessity*, Oxford, UK and New York: B. Blackwell.

aggadah *see* Judaism

aggression *see* war

Agikuyu An African group whose language, like that of the Akamba, has no tense structure expressing the future. This fact led the contemporary African philosopher J.S. Mbiti to conclude that the traditional African concept of time extends only backwards, and that, forwards, it goes no further than six months, at most two years. This view prompted significant controversy. The contemporary African philosopher Kwame Gyekye, for example, objected that, at the very least, Mbiti's view was not true of the Akan people of Ghana. They conceive of God as an infinite being and this presupposes that this being exists in infinite time. Further, Gyekye argued, if Mbiti's view were true only of Eastern African peoples, this would lead to thoroughly significant differences between the religious and philosophical doctrines of Eastern Africans and those of other Africans. However, this is false, hence Mbiti's view is false.

In fairness to Mbiti, it should be said that, in contrast with such European thinkers as the French philosopher Lucien Lévy-Bruhl (CE 1857–1939) and, before him, the German philosopher Georg Wilhelm Friedrich Hegel (CE 1770–1831), Mbiti was not trying to show that the Western conception of time is rational while the African conception is not. Instead, he was trying to show that the African conception of time is pre-industrial, while the Western conception of time is industrial and mechanical. Yet, as the contemporary African philosopher D.A. Masolo states, the fact that the language of the Akamba and Agikuyu has no tense structure to express the concept of the future does not suffice to conclude that the Akamba and Agikuyu, let alone all Africans, have no concept of the future. He argues that the issue is not so much precision or articulation, but how useful given events are for time-related references. According to Masolo, these may involve modes of production characteristic of a period or culture; but not in the general manner in which, according to Marxists, time is not real and its conceptions are always the result of modes of production.

See also: Marxism; metaphysics; myth; philosophy of mind; philosophy of religion

Further reading
Masolo, D.A. (1994) *African Philosophy in Search of Identity*, Edinburgh and Bloomington: Edinburgh University Press and Indiana University Press.
Mbiti, J.S. (1969) *African Religions and Philosophy*, London: Heinemann Educational Books.

agnostic *see* agnosticism

agnosticism From the Greek *a* (not) and *gignoskein* (to know). Term coined by the English biologist and philosopher T.H. Huxley (CE 1825–95) to denote a position of suspended belief. Huxley used it to apply to any ideas concerning which there were insufficient reasons to believe or disbelieve them. Today, however, the term is typically applied to a position of suspended belief about such metaphysical ideas as the existence of God and the existence of an afterlife. This position was, for example, already exemplified by the Greek philosopher Protagoras (490–*c.* 410 BCE) when he held that, with regard to the gods, there is no way of knowing whether they exist or not.
    Agnosticism is a form of skepticism. The English philosopher Leslie Stephen (CE 1832–1904) helped popularize it. In philosophy today, the position is sometimes attributed to the German philosopher Immanuel Kant (CE 1724–1804), who held that we cannot have knowledge of God and immortality, but can only have faith in them. At face value, agnosticism concerning the existence of God, i.e. the position that one does not know or believe whether God does or does not exist, is different from atheism, the position that one knows or believes that God does not exist. Some philosophers, most notably the United States philosopher William James (CE 1842–1910), however, have argued that, in practice, both positions collapse together, because whether terms such as atheism and agnosticism refer to two different things or one is a matter of practice, not merely of language; and agnostics and atheists show no relevant difference in practice: none of them does such things as engaging in worship or praying.

See also: epistemology; ethics; God; metaphysics; philosophy of religion; truth

Further reading
Huxley, Thomas (1986) *Monographs on Religion and Science, Social Science, and History*, Madison, WI: University of Wisconsin, Memorial Library, Collection Preservation Dept.
James, William (1956) *The Will to Believe and Other Essays in Popular Philosophy – Human Immortality: Two Supposed Objections to the Doctrine*, New York: Dover.
Stephen, Leslie (1903) *An Agnostic's Apology, and Other Essays*, London: J. Murray.

agreement and difference, joint method of *see* induction

agreement, method of *see* induction

Agriculture School In Chinese, *Nung Chia*, this term designates a school of philosophy in China, also called the Tillers. Its members held that, originally, there had been a decentralized group of small communities, where all, including their ruler, the Divine Farmer, lived by their own labor, without rewards, punishment, or administration. A representative of this Utopian form of anarchism was Hsü Hsing, who lived around 315 BCE. He criticized the rulers of his time for not working on the fields themselves and, instead, living off the work of others. He also tried to stabilize grain prices by controlling supply, storing grain when the harvest was plentiful and distributing it when it was not.

See also: Chinese philosophy; philosophy, sociopolitical

Further reading
Feng, Yu-lan (1997) *A Short History of Chinese Philosophy*, New York: Free Press.
Shaughnessy, Edward L. (1997) *Before Confucius: Studies in the Creation of the Chinese Classics*, Albany, NY: State University of New York Press.

aha'áná'oo'nííl *see* Native American philosophy

ahamkāra A Sanskrit term meaning "I-maker," "I-crier." In Hindu philosophy, *ahamkāra* denotes individuality and, by extension, egoism, pride, conceit. In the Sāmkhya and Yoga Schools, *ahamkāra* is the third element in the evolution of nature. It is said to evolve from the intellect, buddhi, and lead to the evolution of the phenomenal world, first of the senses, *indriya*, and then, of the essence of the elements, *tanmātra*. The characteristic function of *ahamkāra* is self-assertion. The predicament of human beings consists in mistakenly identifying themselves with nature, rather than with their true self: *ĀTMAN* or *purusha*. Earlier texts reflect the predominance of the Self as a cosmic sense of *ahamkāra* whereby the Creator articulates Himself through speech in order to create the world.

See also: ātman; Hinduism

Further reading

Catalina, Francis V. (1968) *A Study of the Self Concept of Sankhya Yoga Philosophy*, Delhi: Munshiram Manoharlal.

Jacobsen, Knut A. (1997) *Prakrti: The Principle of Matter in the Samkhya and Yoga Systems of Religious Thought*, New York: Peter Lang.

ahantā *see* ātman; Brahman; Hinduism

ahimsā A Sanskrit term meaning "non-violence." In Hindu thought, *ahimsā* means abstinence from injuring any living being through thought, word, or deed. In Jainism, *ahimsā* is the law of compassion in body, mind, and spirit. Negatively, it is the law of not harming any such being in these ways. Positively, it is the practice of love towards all beings. It is formulated in the *mahā-vrata* – great vow – one of the five vows that lead to the liberation of the individual from the limitations of karma. *Ahimsā* is also one of the abstentions or forms of self-control – *yama* – of the Yoga School. Buddhism considers *ahimsā* one of the most important aspects of sound spiritual attitude. Indeed, it is practiced as a precept denying the existence of the ego, on the grounds that injuring another living being is an assertion of egoism. In modern times, Indian thinkers conceive of *ahimsā* as a sense of compassion towards all creatures. Gandhi equated it with self-sacrificial love for all creatures. To him, ahimsā was the first vow of those who held onto the Truth, namely those who exercised non-violent resistance.

See also: Buddhism; Hinduism; Jainism

Further reading

Gandhi, Mahatma (1941) *Ahimsa*, Amadavada: Navajivana Prakasana Mandira.

Sangave, Vilas Adinath (1991) *The Jaina Path of Ahimsa*, Solapur: Bhagawan Mahavir Research Centre.

Ahura Mazda *see* Zoroastrianism

aim *see* intention

aitia *see* causal law

ajahal-laksana *see* meaning

ajāta-vāda *see* Advaita; Hinduism

Akamba *see* Agikuyu

ākāsa Sanskrit term meaning "ether" or "space." Philosophical schools in India conceived of *ākāsa* as a substance. In the Nyāya-Vaiśeṣika School, it was thought to be a substratum of sound. It was described as an all-pervading, infinite, indivisible, permanent, and unperceivable substratum. In Jainism, it provides the ground for all other substances to exist. In Buddhism, it is free from obstructions, and is classified as one kind of non-originated *dharma* – *asamskrta-dharma* – which neither originates nor is destroyed. In Sāmkhya and Advaita, however, *ākāsa* is one of the five elements that are produced and destroyed.

See also: Advaita; Buddhism; Jainism; metaphysics

Further reading

Dasgupta, Surendranath (1961) *A History of Indian Philosophy*, London: Cambridge University Press.

Frauwallner, Erich (1974) *History of Indian Philosophy*, New York: Humanities Press.

Akhbārīs A school of Shī'ite theologians that corresponds to the Sunnīs' ahl al-hadīth. They are traditionalists who eschew speculation. Currently, they are outnumbered by the Uṣūlīs, who favor theological speculation and extrapolation based on religious principles (*uṣūl*). Akhbārīs restrict the authority and prerogatives of individuals recognized as authorities on religion (*ulamā*), such as Imāms of important Mosques, judges, and teachers in the religious faculties of universities. Their reason for this restriction is their belief that jurisprudence should be limited to the application of existing tradition. Though Akhbārīs are Shī'ites, their approach is akin to Ash'arite theology and Sunnī principles of jurisprudence. In accordance with their traditionalist leanings, however, they reject *ijtihād*; that is, reaching original or unprecedented conclusions as the outcome of investigating sources, using reasoning, or attempting to understand. As for sources of religious authority, and by contrast with the Uṣūlīs, they reject consensus (*ijmā'*) and intellect (*'aql*), recognizing only the Quran (i.e. the Scripture) and the Sunna (models of conduct according to authoritative tradition), with the addition that the Quran must be interpreted through the inspired traditions of the Imāms. Also, legal decisions must be based only on relevant traditions of the Imāms.

See also: Arabic philosophy; Neoplatonism; understanding

Further reading
Khan, Qamar-ud-Din (1994) *Conflict of Reason and Tradition in Islam*, Islamabad: Book Trust.
Rahman, Fazlur (1979) *Islam*, 2nd edn, Chicago and London: Chicago University Press.
Whittier, Charles H. (1979) *Islam in Iran: The Shi'ite Faith, its History and Teaching*, Washington, DC: Library of Congress, Congressional Research Service.

akrade *see* determinism

akrasia Also spelled *acrasia*, this is a Greek term meaning "weakness of will," "incontinence," or "lack of self-control," a feature of a person's character displayed in intentional behavior that conflicts with those values, aims, and principles that, upon reflection, the person would uphold. Its opposite is *encrateia* or *enkrateia*: strength of will, continence, or self-control. Both notions arise in the context of decision making, i.e. the process of assessing alternatives that ends in a practical judgment: briefly, a judgment stating the decision we should or will make and the action we should or will take. For the Greek philosopher Socrates (BCE 469–399), who thought a willing error was not an error, *akrasia* posed a paradox: How could one possibly, as the concept of *akrasia* presupposes, act against one's better judgment, be the judgment moral or prudential? The Greek philosopher Aristotle (BCE

384–322) thought that *akrasia* and its opposite, *enkrateia*, were possible when our better judgment conflicted with pleasures and pains and appetites and aversions arising through touch and taste. Today, philosophers conceive of *akrasia* and *enkrateia* as covering a wider scope of mental life than Aristotle thought. At any rate, they are not as interested in *akrasia* and *enkrateia* understood as states of character, as in incontinent and continent actions. The kind of incontinent actions that philosophers most often discuss are those that are uncompelled, i.e. not irresistible, intentional, and in conflict with one's better judgment, e.g. eating a piece of chocolate cake despite the fact that your desire to eat it is not overwhelming, and despite your belief that it is best for you not to eat it. One reason why these actions have received so much attention is that they promise to be instructive concerning the connection between thought and action, which is crucial for explaining intentional behavior in most theories advanced in psychology, the philosophy of mind, and moral philosophy.

See also: action; ethics; intention; philosophy of mind; rationality; reasoning

Further reading
Chappell, T.D.J. (1995) *Aristotle and Augustine on Freedom: Two Theories of Freedom, Voluntary Action, and Akrasia*, New York: St Martin's Press.
Mele, Alfred R. (1992 [1987]) *Irrationality: An Essay on Akrasia, Self-Deception, and Self-Control*, New York: Oxford University Press.
Mortimore, Geoffrey (1971) *Weakness of Will*, London and New York: Macmillan and St Martin's Press.

Aksara *see* Brahman

aku-byōdō *see* Zen

akushu-kū *see* Zen

ālaya-vijñāna Vijñāna A Sanskrit term that, in the early Upanishads, denoted both understanding and wisdom. Through time, its meaning shifted, coming primarily to mean PERCEPTION, while, especially in Buddhism, it meant *moments of consciousness* (that were primarily perceptual), while *jnana* meant "understanding." According to most Buddhist thinkers, these moments of consciousness were intentional in the sense of having an object, i.e. being about something. This conception contributed to the posing of the philosophical problem of how can consciousness continue when a person is not conscious of anything?, e.g. while asleep. The compound term *ālaya-vij-ñāna*, which means "storehouse consciousness," was developed by Buddhist metaphysicians in India to deal with these and other philosophical problems, most notably the problem of delayed karmic effect, and that of causation at a temporal distance. The storehouse consciousness was supposed to store, in potential form, the results of an agent's volitional actions: traces of past experiences and the karmic seeds. These seeds could be actualized at a later time.

See also: Buddhism; Hinduism; perception; philosophy of mind

Further reading
Brown, Brian Edward (1991) *The Buddha Nature: A Study of the Tathagatagarbha and Alayavijnana*, Delhi: Motilal Banarsidass Publishers.
Schmithausen, Lambert (1987) *Alayavijnana, Part 1, Text: On the Origin and the Early Development of a Central Concept of Yogacara Philosophy*, Tokyo: International Institute for Buddhist Studies.
—— (1987) *Alayavijnana. Part 2, Notes, Bibliography and Indices: On the Origin and the Early Development of a Central Concept of Yogacara Philosophy*, Tokyo: International Institute for Buddhist Studies.

alchemy Mystical art and proto-scientific practice that pursued two main aims: changing baser metals into gold, and developing the means to immortality. Western alchemy is said to have originated in Egypt during the first three centuries CE, having been preceded by Chinese alchemy, and followed by variants in India and the Islamic world. Such European figures as the Swiss physician Paracelsus (CE 1490–1541) and the English physicist Isaac Newton (CE 1642–1727) practiced alchemy quite seriously, mostly to pursue the previously mentioned metallurgical and biological aims.

Some of the ideas used in this search were derived from an early Greek theory of relations among the elements and from an allegorical understanding of the transformation of baser metals or mere worldly matter into gold, a paradigm of material perfection, which treated this transmutation as an allegory for the ascent from human toward divine perfection. This process was supposed to involve the search for the *philosopher's stone*, which would transform baser metals into gold and, when combined with alcohol, would produce the elixir of life, a liquid that, if swallowed, was believed to produce immortality or spiritual perfection. Arguably, the basic chemico-theoretical ideas guiding this search were mainly sound, though the means used to apply them were extremely inadequate. In the twentieth century, nuclear fission techniques made it possible to turn baser metals into gold, albeit radioactive gold! As for "the elixir of life," it has not been found; though cloning techniques developed in the twentieth century have opened the door for attaining – at least by reiteration – the means to immortality, yet hardly for the kind of immortality identical with spiritual perfection sought by alchemy. At any rate, both twentieth-century developments have raised a variety of significant problems in moral philosophy.

See also: cabala; ethics

Further reading
Beitchman, Philip (1998) *Alchemy of the Word: Cabala of the Renaissance*, Albany, NY: State University of New York Press.
Hopkins, Arthur John (1934) *Alchemy: Child of Greek Philosophy*, New York, Columbia University Press.
Roob, Alexander (1997) *Alchemy and Mysticism: The Hermetic Museum*, Koln and London: Taschen.

Aleph *see* cabala

aleph null *see* philosophy of mathematics

alethic *see* alethiology

alethiology Based on the Greek term *aletheia*, which is usually translated as "truth," the German mathematician Jonathann Heinrich Lambert (CE 1728–77) coined the term *alethiology* in his *Alethiology or the Doctrine of Truth*, the second part of his *Neues Organon* (1764). In it, Lambert discusses, first, simple concepts, i.e. those that can be thought by themselves; second, the ten principles ruling over concepts: conscience, existence, unity, duration, succession, willing, solidity, extension, movement, and force; and third, the difference between truth and falsity, whereby he discusses concepts, propositions, and relations from the standpoint of principles ruling over them, including the principles of logic. This third part examines which concepts and combinations of concepts are possible, and which ones are impossible. For others, the term *alethiology* designated the study of truth-values by contrast with the study that focuses on the contents of thought.

In contemporary discussions, the adjective alethic is used in modal logic to denote a type of modality, i.e. a type of manner in which a statement describes or applies to its subject matter. By extension, modality denotes the features of items that modal propositions or statements describe or to which they apply. In particular, alethic modality is one of the ways or modes in which a proposition might be true or false: necessity, contingency, possibility, and impossibility. Necessity and possibility are sometimes respectively called apodictic modality and problematic modality. These kinds of propositions, and the ways in which they are mutually related, can be characterized as follows. To say that a proposition is *contingently true* is to say that it is true but could be false, e.g. that Spanish is the dominant language of Argentina. To say that a proposition is *necessarily true* is to say that it is true and could not be false, e.g. that the robbery was the work of thieves. To say that a proposition is *contingently false* is to say that it is false but could be true, e.g. that sparrows do not exist. Finally, to say that a proposition is *necessarily false* is to say that it is false and could not be true, e.g. that a triangle has four sides. As these remarks indicate, any given modality can be defined in terms of any of the others, but most systems of modal logic take necessity or possibility as the basic notion. They differ from each other mainly in the way in which they deal with iterated modalities, as in "it is necessarily true that it is possibly true that there are no clouds."

There are also causal modalities, i.e. modalities involving causal or empirical necessity and contingency; deontic modalities, i.e. those involving obligation and permittedness; epistemic modalities, i.e. those involving knowledge of statements (or knowledge-that); and doxastic modalities, i.e. those involving belief-that.

The significance of these modalities has prompted a number of philosophical doctrines. Necessitarianism, for example, is the doctrine that necessity (in Greek, *ananke*) – as well as any other modality – is an objective feature of the world, which some divide into causal and LOGICAL necessity. While anti-necessitarianism holds either that they are merely verbal, i.e. mere facts of language; or psychological, i.e. entirely explainable in terms of our expectations about the world; or epistemic, i.e. signs of our commitment to whatever is deemed necessary, or merely possible, or even actual but contingent.

Under all the types of possibility previously discussed, one can talk of compossibility or the feature some items have of being capable of existing together. Not all possibilities are compossible. For example, it is possible for the solar system to disappear in one billion years. It is also possible for the solar system to disappear in two billion years. But since these individually possible events exclude each other, they are not compossible. Compossibility is significant for discussions of possible worlds. Here, things are compossible if there is at least one possible world to which all of them belong. Otherwise, they are incompossible. Along these lines, a possible world can be characterized as any combination of compossible possibilities.

See also: logic; philosophy of language; truth

Further reading

Chagrov, Alexander (1997) *Modal Logic*, Oxford and New York: Clarendon Press and Oxford University Press.

Peklo, B.T. (1968) "Deontic and Alethic Modalities," *Analele universitatii bucuresti. Acta logica* 11: 127–32.

Alexandrian School An expression used in two main senses. The first sense relates to any of the intellectual traditions associated with the city of Alexandria between 310 BCE, when Ptolemy Soter (c. 367–283? BCE) founded a school and library in that city, and CE 642, when the city was taken over by Muslim forces. The library of Alexandria was famous and, when it was burned, it is said to have contained 700,000 volumes.

The second sense refers to the Neoplatonic School that developed in Alexandria between CE 430, when the Constantinople-born philosopher Proclus (CE 410–85) settled and taught there, and some time between *c.* CE 610, when Stephanus left to fill the chair of philosophy in Constantinople, and CE 642, when the city was taken over by Muslim forces. The philosophers of the Alexandrian School significantly worked on the interpretation of Aristotle's works. They included its founder and first head, Hierocles (*fl. c.* CE 430), who had studied with Plutarch of Athens; Hermias (*fl. c.* 440); Ammonius (CE 435–517, or CE 445–526); John Philoponus (*c.* CE 490–575); Simplicius (whose writings date beginning in CE 532); Asclepius (mid-sixth century CE); Olympidorus (CE 495/505–after 565); Elias (*fl. c.* CE 540); David (late sixth century CE); and Stephanus (sixth and seventh century CE) – whose departure around CE 610 to take the chair of philosophy at Constantinople roughly marks the end of the school. All of these displayed significant eclecticism, seeking to harmonize what was best of the various philosophies that had come to them. Traditionally, these philosophers have been described as advancing simpler metaphysical views than those advanced by the School of Athens and, besides interpreting the works of the Greek philosopher Aristotle (384–322 BCE), confining themselves to the study of logic and mathematics, thus avoiding controversy with the city's Christian establishment. This view has been criticized by contemporary scholars, according to whom the philosophical differences between the School of Alexandria and that of Athens have become somewhat blurred.

See also: Academy; Neoplatonism

Further reading

Kingsley, Charles (1854) *Alexandria and Her Schools. Four Lectures Delivered at the Philosophical Institution, Edinburgh*, Cambridge: Macmillan and Co.

Malaty, Tadros Y. (1994) *The School of Alexandria*, Jersey City, NJ: St Mark's Coptic Orthodox Church.

Wilder, Alexander (1869) *New Platonism and Alchemy: A Sketch of the Doctrine and Principal Teachers of the Eclectic or Alexandrian School, also, an Outline of the Interior Doctrines of the Alchemists of the Middle Ages*, Albany, NY: Weed, Parsons.

Alexandrianism *see* Alexandrian School; Bologna School; Neoplatonism

algorithm *see* computer theory

alienation *see* idealism; Marxism

Allāh A proper Arabic name of God through which humans call God personally. This name was used before the appearance of the Quran – for example, the name of Mohammed's father was 'Abd Allāh; that is, "servant of God" – and is not used merely by Muslims. Arabic-speaking Christians of the Oriental churches call God by saying Allāh.

In Islam, God is known by ninety-nine other names divided in various ways. A division significant in philosophy is that into Names of the Essence and Names of the Qualities. The name ar-Raḥmān, i.e. "the Compassionate," one of the names by which Allāh is designated, was rejected by the Meccan unbelievers, who refused to recognize it when it was written while drawing the Treaty of Ḥudaybiyyah (CE 628). They had no problem using Allāh, a name known to them and all Arabic speakers. However, ar-Raḥmān was an emblem of the new faith they refused to accept.

See also: Arabic philosophy

Further reading

Asín Palacios, Miguel (1992) *Tres estudios sobre pensamiento y mística hispanomusulmanes*, Madrid: Hiperion.

Fakhry, Majid (1983) *A History of Islamic Philosophy*, 2nd edn, New York and London: Columbia University Press and Longman.

Netton, Ian Richard (1994) *Allah Transcendent: Studies in the Structure and Semiotics of Islamic Philosophy, Theology, and Cosmology*, Surrey, UK: Curzon Press.

Rahman, Fazlur (1979) *Islam*, 2nd edn, Chicago and London: University of Chicago Press.

Wensinck, A.J. (1965) *The Muslim Creed*, London: Frank Cass & Co., Ltd.

allegory *see* Platonism

all-things-considered, reasons *see* justification

alteration *see* change

alternative *see* decision; justification; logic; philosophy, sociopolitical

altruism *see* ethics

ambiguity From the Latin *ambiguitas*: the property of "moving from side to side," this term denotes a feature whereby a term or expression has more than one meaning. It is accordingly said to be ambiguous (from the Latin *ambiguus*: that "moves from side to side"). The opposites of ambiguity and ambiguous respectively are *univocity* (from the Latin *unus*: one, and *vocare*: to call) and *univocal*. A term has univocity or is univocal when it has the same meaning in its several applications.

There are various types of ambiguities. First, when a word is ambiguous, the ambiguity is lexical. It can be a homonymy, i.e. when different terms – called homonymous – have the same sound but different meanings, e.g. pair and pear, or a polysemy, i.e. when the same terms – called polysemous – have different meanings, e.g. fall (the season) and fall (the physical event). Second, besides *lexical* ambiguity, there is *structural* ambiguity; that is, where a component structure (a phrase maker or sequence of phrase makers) of a sentence is associated by the syntax of a language with more than one other component, e.g. John will explain how he lost 220 pounds on Tuesday, September 11. Third, there is also *scope* ambiguity, which results from alternative interpretations of the scope of operators, e.g. Jimmy will run the mile and go swimming only if his parents allow it. Here, the scope of the modifier "only if his parents allow it" can cover only "go swimming" or "Jimmy will run the mile" as well. Fourth, some ambiguities are pragmatic. A *pragmatic* ambiguity is an ambiguity where an expression has more than one meaning as a result of there being more than one function for the expression. For example, "I don't know that she went to the party" may either simply deny knowledge or express doubt.

A philosophically significant ambiguity is the *process–product* ambiguity, which occurs when a noun denotes either a process or activity, or, alternatively, the product of a process or activity. For example, in the sentence "the evaluation was complicated," the term "evaluation" may refer to the activity of evaluating an item or to the judgment passed on the item at the end of the activity.

Questions arise about the relations between *ambiguity*, *obscurity*, and *vagueness* and their respective opposites: univocity, clarity, and precision. Though often confused with each other, they are not mutually equivalent. In the usual, literal sense of its terms, for example, the statement "life is like a deep well" is not clear, but obscure, even if its terms are not used with more than one meaning and its structure is not ambiguous. Also, vague expressions need not be ambiguous. "What a great cup of soup!" is not precise but vague because "great" is used without specification of how great is great; but whatever this specification turns out to be, "great" is not here supposed to have more than one meaning.

Vagueness characteristically includes a reference to cases that fall in the gray area and, in the logical sense of this expression, are called borderline cases or limiting cases and, sometimes, degenerate cases. A borderline or limiting or degenerate case is a case where the vague expression neither definitely applies nor definitely does not apply to a given item. This is characteristically related to lack of precision in the expression, not to lack of information about the item. The latter situation, somewhat misleadingly, is called epistemic vagueness, and is characterized by the fact that, upon acquiring additional information, the vagueness goes away.

Vagueness has often been a source of annoyance to philosophers of logic and language, beginning, perhaps, with the Sorites paradox (see PARADOX) that, generally, can be formulated as follows. A grain of sand does not make a heap of sand. Adding another grain still does not make a heap. In general, adding one more grain does not make a heap. So, by adding grains one by one, a heap is never formed. Attempting to resolve this paradox has led to the formulation of non-classical logics or, more drastically, to (the method of) supervaluation (sometimes called supertruth), i.e. to arbitrarily making a predicate precise, e.g. by first deciding exactly how many grains of sand make a heap; then changing the valuation to a different number; and so on. If a sentence is true in all such valuations, it is said to be really true or supertrue. If false, it is said to be really false or superfalse. All other sentences are considered vague. This method seems to work for vagueness along a scale, as in the Sorites paradox. Yet, it is not clear that it will work equally well for vagueness that involves what has been called a family resemblance (see ESSENTIALISM), as in the traditional case of what makes something a game, where there is no scale involved, but a range of features with varying significance for classifying it in a certain category, say, as being a game.

Going back to ambiguity, besides its significance in logic and the philosophy of language, the notion has been used in existentialist ethics. Here, it denotes human beings' attempts at making moral sense of their lives through situations where the pressures of the social world – e.g. of markets, technology, and politics – seem to condemn such efforts to failure.

See also: fallacy; logic

Further reading
Channell, Joanna (1994) *Vague Language*, Oxford: Oxford University Press.
de Beauvoir, Simone (1968) *The Ethics of Ambiguity*, New York: The Citadel Press.
Eijck, J. van (1996) *Ambiguity and Reasoning*, Amsterdam, The Netherlands: Centrum voor Wiskunde en Informatica.
Walton, Douglas N. (1996) *Fallacies Arising from Ambiguity*, Dordrecht, The Netherlands and Boston: Kluwer Academic Publishers.

American Indians *see* Nahua philosophy; Native American philosophy

Amerindians *see* Nahua philosophy; Native American philosophy

amor dei *see* Jewish philosophy

amor dei intellectualis *see* Jewish philosophy

amoral *see* ethics

amoralist *see* ethics

amphibology *see* fallacy

ampliatio *see* syncategoremata

ampliative *see* induction

an sich *see* idealism

Analects *see* Confucianism

analogical argument *see* philosophy of religion

analogy From the Greek *ana* (according to) and *logos* (ratio, proportion). A similarity between two or more items, e.g. the universe is like an ever-expanding pudding. Analogies such as this one can be used to explain ideas. They can also be used to develop heuristic models, e.g. by saying that an electric current behaves analogously to the water current in a hose, or that the atoms in a molecule behave as if they were holding hands, without thereby claiming any substantial truth for such models. Analogies or similarities are described through comparisons, but the latter are wider in scope in that they can be used to establish differences – the opposite of similarities – as well.

Besides being used to explain ideas, analogies are used in arguments, called arguments by analogy. An example is: "Books and magazines are forms of expression, sold for profit, and covered by the First Amendment. Motion pictures are forms of expression and sold for profit. Hence, motion pictures are also covered by the First Amendment." Arguments of this type have been used in attempting to prove the existence of God. Roughly, from the premise that every artifact, e.g. a watch, is intricate and organized and has a maker, and from the further premise that the universe is intricate and organized too, it is concluded that the universe has a maker as well, namely God. Arguments by analogy have also been used to establish that individuals other than the individual giving the argument have minds, on the grounds that those other individuals behave like the one giving the argument and this individual has a mind.

In this connection, logicians have developed the method of logical analogy, whereby an argument is tested by finding another argument – a counterargument – of the same form. If the latter is not valid, in which case it is a counterargument, then the original argument is not valid either. Though very useful, this method can only establish invalidity. For if one fails to find a counterargument or counter-instance, one never knows whether this is because the original argument is valid or because one's imagination has failed to find an existing counterargument.

Among medieval philosophers, the Analogy of Being provides a way of arguing from one case to another through different levels of being. In the sixteenth century, the Italian Cardinal Cajetan (CE 1468–1524), whose original name was Tommaso de Vio, promoted a renewed interest in analogies. He argued that there is more than one type of analogy, among which he singled out the analogy of proportionality as the basic one, and as that which allowed humans to come to know God.

See also: induction; model; philosophy of religion; philosophy of science

Further reading
McInerny, Ralph M. (1971) *The Logic of Analogy: An Interpretation of St. Thomas*, The Hague: Nijhoff.
Pietarinen, Juhani (1972) *Lawlikeness, Analogy and Inductive Logic*, Amsterdam: North-Holland Pub. Co.

analysandum *see* analysis; definition

analysans *see* analysis; definition

analysis The process of breaking up the *analysandum*, i.e. a concept, sentence, or fact, into its components, the *analysans*. There are many kinds of analysis. One form is used in chemistry to identify the components of a compound substance, by contrast with *synthesis*, whereby a new compound is produced as a result of combining certain components. In philosophy, various philosophers have proposed some type of analysis as a – in the case of some philosophers the – method of philosophy. The German philosopher Edmund Husserl (CE 1859–1938) described and exemplified noematic and noetic analysis, that focused on ideas. The British philosopher G.E. Moore (CE 1873–1958) tried to analyze sense-data. Most often, philosophers have tried to analyze concepts or propositions. This is what is called "conceptual analysis." Others, arguably the Austrian philosopher Ludwig Wittgenstein (CE 1889–1951) in his early work, the *Tractatus*

Logico-Philosophicus, as well as the contemporary English philosopher P.F. Strawson and the English philosopher J.L. Austin (CE 1911–60), have tried to analyze sentences and their kinds. This is what is called "linguistic analysis." Both conceptual and linguistic analysis give rise to a version of the paradox of analysis: every analysis is inadequate either because the *analysans* – say, "unmarried male" – does not analyze the *analysandum* – in our example, "bachelor" – well or completely, or because, if it does, it is uninformative.

Philosophers such as the previously mentioned G.E. Moore and Ludwig Wittgenstein, and the English philosopher Bertrand (Arthur William) Russell (CE 1872–1970), who, at the beginning of the twentieth century, primarily used conceptual or linguistic analysis, most notably logical analysis typically preceded by eduction – i.e. initial clarification of a phenomenon, text, or argument – to do philosophy, are the founders of *analytic philosophy*, or linguistic philosophy, or Oxford School of philosophy, and the followers of Moore and Wittgenstein especially are sometimes called the Cambridge Analytic School (all misleading labels). This is a way of doing philosophy that crucially relies on the said techniques and, given its focus on language, exemplifies the philosophical period characterized by what has been called the linguistic turn. They and their followers are called analytic philosophers.

Besides the United Kingdom, analytic philosophy has been highly influential in the United States and Canada, where it is sometimes also called Anglo-American philosophy, though this latter label is often also used to include, besides analytic philosophy, other philosophical approaches, e.g. pragmatism.

In addition, analytic philosophy has been significantly influential in Australia and New Zealand. Both countries are home to the Australasian Association of Philosophy, which has published the *Australasian Journal of Philosophy* since 1923, where papers in the analytic tradition are regularly published. Philosophy in Australia and New Zealand, however, displays interests that go beyond philosophical analysis, represented by such journals as the *Bulletin of the Australian Society for Legal Philosophy* and, in New

Zealand, *Philosophy and Literature*, and by ethnophilosophy studies, e.g. *Exploring Maori Values*, by the analytically trained New Zealand philosopher John Patterson.

In Continental Europe, analytic philosophy has been overshadowed by other traditions (see CONTINENTAL PHILOSOPHY), though significant work related to philosophical analysis has been published, e.g. in the Netherlands. As for Latin America, analytic philosophy took root late, and has influenced a relatively small group of philosophers who, however, have become very well established in the region. The main centers of analytic philosophy are Buenos Aires in Argentina, Mexico City, and the Brazilian cities of Campinas and São Paulo.

As for the specific views of the founders of analytic philosophy, Moore upheld realism and authored such works as *Principia Ethica*, *Philosophical Studies*, and *Philosophical Papers*. Russell worked in logic, epistemology, and metaphysics. His views were in continuous development, adopting at one time or another such theories as the sense-data theory, and neutral monism. His works were many, most notably *Principia Mathematica* (with the British philosopher Alfred North Whitehead, CE 1861–1947), *An Inquiry into Meaning and Truth,* and *Human Knowledge: Its Scope and Limits*. Wittgenstein's positions are typically classified in two periods: the early or Tractarian period, named after his *Tractatus Logico-Philosophicus*, a book he wrote in the trenches of the First World War and published in 1921, and the later period of the *Philosophical Investigations*, which he wrote between 1936 and 1948 and published in 1953. He came to consider philosophy an analytic, descriptive, therapeutic practice where philosophical puzzles were dismissed upon realizing they resulted from falling into linguistic traps.

By contrast with traditional schools of philosophy, analytic philosophers are not characterized by any shared doctrines. They can however be characterized by, first, a sustained effort to achieve clarity and, second, relying on argument, as well as by their shared methods, i.e. their reliance on some form of conceptual or linguistic analysis in trying to establish what problems are and what problems are not tractable. A significant number of these philosophers' practice also appears to presuppose that philosophy is continuous with science.

In addition, a significant number of analytic philosophers write in English and have tended to address one another rather than the general public. This has prompted criticism on the grounds that analytic philosophy has become a sterile, ivory-tower type of enterprise, and calls for a shift towards pluralistic philosophizing and dialogue with the general public. This criticism, however, presupposes that the provincial manner in which many analytic philosophers have engaged in philosophy points to shortcomings in the methods of analytic philosophy. However, it does not. Analytic philosophers have accordingly replied that analytic techniques and standards are nothing new in philosophy, which, however, does not exonerate the provincial manner in which some have used analytic techniques and standards. The real issue here is how helpful can these techniques be and how applicable the standards when used in more pluralistic and less provincial ways?

Sometimes, the term "analysis" is used in still other ways that, though cognate, are not closely related to those just discussed. Some of these appear in the following expressions:

1 Transcendental analysis: see KANTIAN PHILOSOPHY.
2 Regression analysis: see INDUCTION.
3 Non-standard analysis: see PHILOSOPHY OF MATHEMATICS.
4 Standard analysis: see PHILOSOPHY OF MATHEMATICS.

Similarly, besides being used as an adjective related to the term "analysis" in the senses just discussed, the term "analytic" also appears with significantly different meaning in the following expressions:

1 Analytic Marxism: see MARXISM.
2 Analytic statement: see ANALYTIC–SYNTHETIC DISTINCTION.

See also: analytic–synthetic distinction; Kantian philosophy; phenomenology

Further reading
Ammerman, Robert R. (1965) *Classics of Analytic Philosophy*, New York: McGraw-Hill.

Furberg, Mats (1971) *Saying and Meaning: A Main Theme in J.L. Austin's Philosophy*, Oxford: Blackwell.

Hubbeling, Hubertus Gezinus (1971) *Language, Logic and Criterion: A Defence of Non-Positivistic Logical Empiricism*, Amsterdam: Born N.V.

Rorty, Richard (1967) *The Linguistic Turn*, Chicago and London: The University of Chicago Press.

analytic–synthetic distinction An expression made famous by the German philosopher Immanuel Kant (CE 1724–1804). He said that an affirmative subject–predicate statement (or proposition, or judgment) was analytic whenever the concept denoted by the predicate was contained in that denoted by the subject. Otherwise, it was synthetic. For example, "All tall Italians are Italian" is analytic. While "Some Italians are chess-lovers" is synthetic. A test of analytic statements is that their denial leads to a contradiction. For example, to deny "All tall Italians are Italian" leads to the contradiction "Some tall individuals both are and are not Italian." This type of result does not follow from denying a synthetic statement. The novelty Kant introduced to his predecessors' work on the subject was to separate the logico-linguistic analytic–synthetic distinction from two others: the a priori–a posteriori distinction, which belongs in epistemology, and the necessary–contingent distinction, which belongs in metaphysics.

Since Kant, philosophers have tried to generalize the analytic–synthetic distinction to all statements, while at the same time clarifying it. A current version purported to do this is: to say that a statement is analytic is to say that it is true just in virtue of the meaning of its terms. "Bachelors are unmarried," for example, is analytic. However, this is only correct relative to a system, for example to twentieth-century English. If the meaning of bachelor changed, the said statement could cease to be true. A similar situation arises with the statement "whales are mammals." It is true given the meaning of "whales" and "mammals" in current zoology, a scientific theory. However, it was not true before whales were classified as mammals after the work of the Swedish botanist Carolus Linneaus (CE 1707–78) and the English scientist Charles Darwin (CE 1809–82). In other words, the analyticity of statements stands or falls with the theories or linguistic practices in which they are embedded.

Further, the linguistic practices are contingent and the theories' truth is not an analytic matter, but established through non-deductive reasoning. These and related matters have led some philosophers, most notably the United States philosopher William Van Orman Quine (CE 1908–2000), to reject the analytic–synthetic distinction altogether. However, if these reasons were sufficient for such rejection, the distinction between a logical truth or tautology – a statement that is true just in virtue of its form – e.g. "either this is or is not a cat," and other truths would have to be considered equally dubious – an implication few have found acceptable. By contrast with Quine, the United States philosopher Clarence Irving Lewis (CE 1883–1964), appears to have thought that what he called terminating judgments – giving way to action, experiment, and, hence, to confirmation and disconfirmation – placed both the ordinary meanings as well as the theoretical meanings of terms beyond convention or decision, without displacing logical truths, but freeing them from the ineffability sometimes attributed to them.

See also: empiricism; logic; philosophy of language; rationalism

Further reading
Descartes, R. (1968) *The Philosophical Works*, London: Cambridge University Press. End of "Reply to Objections II," pp. 48–51.
Kant, I. (1965) *Critique of Pure Reason*, New York and Toronto: St Martin's and Macmillan. Introduction, 4, pp. 48–51.
Quine, William Van Orman (1963) "Two Dogmas of Empiricism," in *From a Logical Point of View*, New York and Evanston: Harper & Row, pp. 20–46.

analytical *see* analysis

analytical jurisprudence *see* philosophy of Law

analytical psychology *see* psychoanalysis

anamnesis *see* Platonism

ānanda *see* Hinduism

ananke *see* alethiology; determinism

anaphor *see* reference

anaphora *see* reference

anaphor's antecedent *see* reference

anarchism *see* philosophy, sociopolitical

anarchist *see* philosophy, sociopolitical

anarchy *see* philosophy, sociopolitical

anātman *see* ātman; anattā; Buddhism

anattā Pali term meaning the same as *anātman* (from the Sanskrit *an*, i.e. "not", and *ātman*, i.e. "soul"). In Buddhism, it is sometimes combined with the term *vāda* (theory), to produce *anattā-vāda*, the theory of no-soul or non-I or of *anātman*, attributed to the Buddha (sixth century BCE). This is a corollary of the Buddha's ontology of change where nothing is absolute, substantive, or permanent. According to *anattā-vāda*, a person's self is nothing but a bunch of fleeting sensations. His method to establish this was introspective, not unlike that used many centuries later by the Scottish philosopher David Hume (CE 1711–76). Like Hume, the Buddha found no soul: no substance wherein those sensations could be grounded. However, some interpreters have argued that the Buddha's position was not as definite as Hume's, but aimed only at not introducing concepts that would undermine Buddhist practice. Be this as it may, the no-soul theory became accepted as Buddhism developed. The Hindu philosophical schools criticized the *anattā-vāda* on the grounds that it led to many paradoxical implications; it was unable to explain personal identity, moral responsibility, karma, and rebirth.

See also: ātman; Buddhism

Further reading

Malalasekera, G.P. (1966) *The Truth of Anatta*, Kandy, Ceylon: Buddhist Publication Society.

Nyanaponika, Thera (1959) *Anatta and Nibbana: Egolessness and Deliverance*, Kandy, Ceylon: Buddhist Publication Society.

Wijesekera, Oliver Hector de Alwis (1970) *The Three Signata: Anicca, Dukkha, Anatta*, Kandy, Ceylon: Buddhist Publication Society.

androcentric *see* feminist philosophy

androgyny *see* feminist philosophy

animals *see* ethics

animism From the Latin *anima*, i.e. soul, the term animism in general denotes the belief that things such as pebbles, rivers, planet Earth, and, some would say, the entire universe are animated or at least embody a life-principle. In philosophy, the same doctrine tends to be called *panpsychism*, a term derived from the Greek *pan*, i.e. "all," and *psyche*, i.e. "soul."

In many cultures, this belief is found together with *anthropomorphism*, according to which beings are animated or have life by analogy to human beings. Animism is opposed to materialism. One component of animism is the belief that individual creatures have souls that can continue to exist when, after the individuals' death, their bodies are destroyed. Another component of animism is the belief that spirits are powerful divinities. These components of animism consider the soul to be a vital principle. However, they are not all there is to animism. If they were, and the soul was conceived as a vital principle, guiding, as a final cause, the movements of all bodily movements, it would collapse together with VITALISM.

No doubt, some thinkers have adopted this position. The English psychologist William McDougall (CE 1871–1938), for example, did so and called his psychological theory "animism." However, this is not a prevalent or precise use of the term. The most common uses are the ones described at the outset, which either, narrowly, ascribe a soul to particular material entities like stones and rivers or, in some cases, widely, ascribe a soul or something like it to the entire universe. In this latter sense, some ancient and Western Renaissance thinkers talked of a Soul of the World. A philosophical version of animism is *hylozoism* (from the Greek *hyle*, i.e. "matter", and *zoe*, i.e. "life"), the doctrine that all matter has life. When all life is supposed to involve at least sentience and this is taken to entail that all life involves some soul, then *hylozoism* is a form of panpsychism or animism.

See also: Greek philosophy; anthropomorphism; philosophy of mind; vitalism

Further reading
Clodd, Edward (1993) *Animism*, Thame: Su-hal.
McDougall, William (1911) *Body and Mind: A History and a Defense of Animism*, New York: The Macmillan Company.
Tax, Sol (1988) *Practical Animism: The World of Panajachel. A Guatemala Indian Ethnography*, Chicago: University of Chicago.
Tsurumi, Kazuko (1992) *Animism and Science*, Tokyo: Sophia University.
Tylor, Edward Burnett (1994) *The Collected Works of Edward Burnett Tylor*, London: Routledge/Thoemmes.

anirvacanīya-khyāti *see* Advaita

anirvācya-vāda *see* Advaita

anomalous monism *see* philosophy of mind

ante rem realism *see* Thomism

ante rem universals *see* Thomism

antecedent *see* logic

anthropocentrism From the Greek *anthropos*, i.e. human, and *kentron*, i.e. center, this term (as well as its Latin-derived synonym, homo-centrism, from the Latin *homo*, i.e. "human being," and *centrum*, i.e. "center") denotes the view that, implicitly or explicitly, places humans at the center of the universe, and considers the rest of the universe subservient to and a resource for humans. This view is akin to that expressed by the Greek philosopher Protagoras (490–410 BCE): "man is the measure of all things" (see GREEK PHILOSOPHY). The latter can be interpreted in two ways: first, each individual human being is the measure of all things, and, second, humans as a species are the measure of all things. Anthropocentrism fits the latter interpretation.

This view has been held in much of the history of philosophy, but has acquired particular poignancy in ethics during the twentieth century. In environmental ethics, a traditional anthropocentric (also called homocentric) position has been *conservationism*, the view that the environment – e.g. forests, clean rivers and lakes, clean air – should be conserved for future human use. That is, the environment and its components are purely and simply resources for humans. On this view, whenever conflicts arise between some interest of humans, e.g. to build housing around a city, say, Houston, and the conservation of non-humans, e.g. the conservation of the Houston toad, the conservation of the latter takes precedence if, and only if, it can be shown to constitute a resource for humans and, further, to satisfy an even greater human interest.

This position is opposed to *preservationism*, the view that the environment and its components should be preserved for their own sake. On this view, many accommodations between humans and non-humans are possible; but, if non-humans are endangered by plans aimed at satisfying human interests, these interests do not necessarily take precedence. The question here arises: what criteria for resolving conflicts such as these are sound from a preservationism standpoint?

A range of views, from *ecocentrism*, which invariably gives precedence to non-humans (sometimes even considering humans a plague), to other, more compromising positions, have been advanced. These views are sometimes defended on the grounds that non-humans have rights. Others, however, deny that non-humans have rights, but argue that non-human welfare can, and often does, override human interests or wants. Either way, those holding these views have accused anthropocentric thinkers of *speciesism*, or discrimination against non-human animals. Anthropocentric thinkers reply that, in practice, preservationism is hardly an alternative, because what is good for non-humans must invariably be decided by humans. However, preservationists reply that, even if humans must do this job, from a preservationism standpoint, they should ask questions such as "What is good for the non-humans likely to be affected by human activities in the case, say, of building housing around Houston?" These questions are simply precluded by anthropocentric positions such as conservationism. The question here arises whether preservationism can be practical to any significant extent and whether, to the extent it can, it in effect leads to different results from those likely to be achieved through conservationism. The ethical and sociopolitical aspects of this controversy do not simply concern environmental matters. For example, they also concern the use of non-human animals in scientific experimentation.

See also: ethics

Further reading

Baxter, William F. (1975) *People or Penguins: The Case for Optimal Pollution*, New York and London: Columbia University Press.

LaFollette, Hugh (1996) *Brute Science: Dilemmas of Animal Experimentation*, London and New York: Routledge.

Rodd, Rosemary (1992) *Biology, Ethics, and Animals*, Oxford: Clarendon.

Yi, Jingsheng (1989) *The Practical Aspect of Anthropocentrism: A Comparative Study of Three Major Environmental Ethical Theories*, Ottawa: National Library of Canada.

anthropology A social science or social study, anthropology (from the Greek *anthropos*, i.e. 'human being', and *logia*, i.e. 'theory of') studies humans as psychophysical, social, and biological beings. However, as a philosophical inquiry, also called philosophical anthropology, the study has traditionally attempted to avoid or go beyond considering humans merely as objects for science. Various philosophical schools – e.g. existentialism, personalism, phenomenology – are often cited as exemplifying the aims of philosophical anthropology. A topic that has recurrently attracted the interest of inquirers, both in anthropology as a social study and in philosophy, is the origin and evolution of sex roles. Some founders of anthropology, in the nineteenth century, held that human societies had always been patriarchal. Others held that higher levels of social organization tended to go hand in hand with patriarchy, but less organized social groups were matriarchal. Twentieth-century anthropologists have discounted these simplistic views; however, a growing body of evidence indicates that sex roles are largely shaped by culture. This is of interest to many contemporary anthropologists and philosophers, some of them feminists, who ask: "Which particular cultural factors tend to determine whether a society develops along patriarchal or other lines?" In asking this and related questions, some philosophers are bridging the gap between anthropology as a social study and philosophical anthropology. They are trying to

avoid and go beyond treating humans as mere objects of scientific study, but are building on – not at all ignoring or criticizing as merely scientific – the results of anthropology as a social study.

Anthropological disciplines of particular significance in these endeavors are ethnography (the study of cultures); its subdiscipline, ethnology (the study of cultures through field work, especially participant observation); and ethnomethodology (a phenomenological approach to the study of everyday action and speech).

See also: feminist philosophy; philosophy of science

Further reading

Fitzgerald, Ross (1978) *What It Means to be Human: Essays in Philosophical Anthropology, Political Philosophy, and Social Psychology*, Rushcutters Bay, NSW: Pergamon Press Australia.

Kigunga, Raphael (1996) *The Anthropology of Self-Person and Myth in Africa: A Philosophical Reflection on Man in South-East-Africa*, Frankfurt am Main and New York: P. Lang.

Rescher, Nicholas (1990) *Human Interests: Reflections on Philosophical Anthropology*, Stanford, CA: Stanford University Press.

Rosaldo, Michelle Zimbalist and Lampere, Louise (1974) *Woman, Culture, and Society*, Stanford, CA: Stanford University Press.

anthropomorphism From the Greek *anthropos*, i.e. "human being," and *morphe*, i.e. "form," combined with the ending "-ism," this term used to designate views that attribute human characteristics to non-human entities. Currently, the term is typically used to criticize the attribution. For example, attempts to explain the nature of God in human terms are criticized as anthropomorphic, on the grounds that God is in no way like humans, hence the analogy is inadmissible. In response to these criticisms, some philosophers of religion have argued that, though inadequate to give a true idea of the nature of God, the analogy with humans may be the only way in which humans can approach a semblance of understanding or, at least, relating emotionally to God.

A similar criticism has been advanced against explanations of the physical world in anthropological terms. Here again, the charge is that anthropological notions have nothing to do with the physical world, hence the analogy is inadmissible. This argument could be and has been used to criticize Ancient and Renaissance animistic theories that literally claimed the existence of souls or animating principles in at least certain natural entities. At any rate, the charge of anthropomorphism characteristically implies that either there is a strict separation between – hence dualism of – the human and the non-human that makes the analogy inadmissible because of the radical difference between its terms, or a form of monism – e.g. physicalist monism – which makes that analogy inadmissible because, in effect, there is only one term, hence no room for analogies.

See also: animism; philosophy of mind; philosophy of religion

Further reading
Abrahamov, Binyamin (1996) *Anthropomorphism and Interpretation of the Quran in the Theology of al-Qasim ibn Ibrahim: Kitab al-Mustarshid Kitab al-Mustarshid*, Leiden and New York: E.J. Brill.
Marmorstein, Arthur (1968) *The Doctrine of Merits in Old Rabbinical Literature and the Old Rabbinic Doctrine of God: I. The Names and Attributes of God [and] II. Essays in Anthropomorphism*, New York: Ktav Pub. Co.

anthroposophy *see* mysticism

antinomianism *see* antinomy

antinomy From the Greek *anti*, i.e. against, and *nomos*, i.e. law. In one sense, the term simply means the opposition to each other of two views. Often, these two views are supposed to be conclusions from sound arguments. The German philosopher Immanuel Kant (CE 1724–1804), in *The Critique of Pure Reason*, gave four examples of this kind of situation in the section entitled "Antinomies of Pure Reason." To him, they are positions we take and, upon taking them, we feel that we have to take the opposite position. For example, we may hold that there is freedom in the world, which, for Kant, leads us to say that not everything takes place according to the laws of nature. However, this leads us to state the

opposite, which leads us to deny that there is freedom in the world. A list of fourteen antinomies was offered by the Indian Buddhist philosopher Nagarjuna (CE 100–200). They were: we cannot say whether the world is finite or not or both or neither; or permanent or not or both or neither; or whether the Buddha, after nirvana, is existent or not or both or neither; or whether matter and mind are identical or not.

The same roots of the term antinomy are those of the term *antinomianism*, the name of a recurrent tendency in Christianity to reject the Mosaic, Ecclesiastical, or even moral law, on the grounds that, by grace, Christians are set free from having to obey it. Some groups that displayed antinomianism to various degrees were the Gnostics, the Marcionites, and the Manicheans. During the Reformation, some argued that antinomianism followed from the doctrine of justification by faith alone (see CHRISTIANITY) held by the German churchman and reformer Martin Luther (CE 1483–1546). In this connection, the Familists, the Davidists, and the Adamists displayed some form of antinomianism. Luther and the German theologian Phillipp Melanchthon (CE 1497–1560) were themselves involved in one controversy concerning antinomianism that was settled by the Formula of Concord.

See also: Buddhism; Christianity; Kantian philosophy

Further reading
Borcherding, Alan W Bransen (1992) *Luther's Disputation Theses Against the Antinomians*, Fort Wayne, IN: Concordia Theological Seminary Press.
McLaughlin, Peter (1990) *Kant's Critique of Teleology in Biological Explanation: Antinomy and Teleology*, Lewiston: E. Mellen Press.

anti-realism *see* metaphysics

antisymmetrical *see* ordering; relation

antithesis *see* dialectic

antitypia *see* epistemology

anu *see* atomism; Hinduism; Jainism

anumāna Term meaning "inference," "syllogism," "instrument of inference." It literally

means "after-knowledge," because, in an inference, knowledge is supposed to result from the
use of some other knowledge. The Nyāya
School claims that the syllogism has five
components: thesis, reason, example, subsumptive correlation or generalization of the example, and conclusion. The Mīmāmsā School
holds that a syllogism only needs one of two
sets of three components each: either thesis,
reason, and example, or example, subsumptive
correlation or generalization of the example,
and conclusion. According to Buddhism, only
two members of the syllogism are necessary:
the example and the subjunctive correlation or
generalization of the example. The conclusion
goes without saying (by contrast with the
Western conception of an enthymeme, where
one of the premises, typically the generalization, goes without saying).

Other thinkers have approached inference in
a less formal manner, including such psychological components of inquiry as motives and
purposes. They claimed that there were ten
members of an inference: the desire to know
the truth, doubt concerning the truth of something, capacity of the method used to lead to
knowledge, the purpose of making an inference, removal of all doubt about the soundness
of an inference, thesis, reason, example, subsumptive correlation or generalization of the
example, and conclusion. Specific types of
inferences include various relations between
the terms. One is *anvaya-vyatireka*, or positive
and negative concomitance, e.g. that of the
occurrence of fire whenever smoke occurs and
the non-occurrence of fire whenever smoke
does not occur (an idea analogous to those
found in some of Mill's methods of empirical
investigation).

See also: argument; Hinduism

Further reading
Matilal, Bimal Krishna (1998) *The Character
    of Logic in India*, Albany: State University of
    New York Press.
Phillips, Stephen H. (1995) *Classical Indian
    Metaphysics: Refutations of Realism and the
    Emergence of "New Logic,"* Chicago: Open
    Court.

anupalabdhi *see* Advaita

anvaya-vyatireka *see* anumāna

anvitābhidhānavāda *see* Hinduism

apagoge *see* abduction

apatheia *see* Stoicism

apeiron *see* Greek philosophy; infinity

apellatio *see* syncategoremata

apocatastasis *see* Christianity

apocrypha *see* Jewish philosophy; Judaism

apodictic *see* alethiology

apophantic *see* phenomenology

apophantic analytics *see* phenomenology

aporetic method *see* Socratic philosophy

aporia *see* Socratic philosophy

aporiai *see* Greek philosophy

apotheosis *see* Christianity; Jewish philosophy

appearance *see* metaphysics

appearing *see* metaphysics

apperception *see* Kantian philosophy

appetites *see* human nature

appetition *see* human nature

application *see* applied

applied A term denoting the use, i.e. the
applications, of theoretical results concerning
practical matters. The philosophical usage of
this term, appearing in such expressions as
"applied philosophy" and "applied ethics," is
analogous to, and apparently influenced by, the
use of the term by many members of the
scientific community and the general public
who characterize technology as applied
science.

This characterization of technology has led
to controversy, for example on the grounds
that at least certain technological developments, say, that of superconductors in the
twentieth century, took place before any scientific results were available to explain them.
However, this objection still leaves room for
describing many instances of technology as
applied science, i.e. as using, for practical
purposes, theoretical results of scientific research pursued out of mere curiosity, not with

a practical purpose in mind. Another objection to characterizing technology in this manner has been that instances of scientific research pursued with no practical purpose in mind are not very frequent. Usually, given a country's science policy and the research priorities it embodies, plus the need for grants to pursue scientific research significantly, scientific research projects receiving grants are often understood to have practical applications. There are, no doubt, instances of researchers moved by mere curiosity, but it is at least debatable that their individual intentions are decisive to characterize a collective activity such as scientific research in general and, some would add, their individual scientific research.

An analogous controversy has developed in philosophy concerning the expression "applied philosophy." The controversy can be traced back to the time when the Greek philosopher Aristotle (384–322 BCE) said that all philosophy begins in wonder, attributed a higher value to the contemplative life, and described philosophy, the love of wisdom, as primarily concerned with the knowledge of general principles – a highly theoretical type of knowledge. This conception clashed with conceptions of philosophy, also as the love of wisdom, but understood in a more practical manner or, as it appears to have been the case with the Greek philosopher Pythagoras (570–500 BCE), who reputedly coined the term *philosophia*, understood in a manner that did not, or not sharply, separate practical from contemplative matters.

This type of controversy arises today in philosophy concerning the expression "applied ethics." Some would argue that this expression presupposes a sharp separation between metaethical matters such as the meaning of "good" and "right" and their normative applications. However, the argument goes, such separation is unwarranted, because all ethical inquiry, including so called "metaethics," has practical implications and consequences for people's lives; hence, all ethical inquiry is normative. This is not to say that there is no difference between theoretical and practical aspects of ethics. However, those who object to using the expression "applied ethics" say this expression implies the wrong kind of difference, as if theoretical ethics were not norma-

tive; hence, in that sense, practice oriented. Accordingly, they prefer the theoretical-practical distinction and talk of "theoretical ethics" and "practical ethics," where the difference between the two is only a difference in types of practice-oriented concerns, general if theoretical, and particular if practical. On this view, *theoretical ethics* seeks to develop ethical theories, i.e. generalized devices for formulating, clarifying, and dealing with kinds of moral problems. In the process, it uses actual and plausible practice among other ways of testing the theories. On the other hand, *practical ethics* seeks to resolve particular moral problems concerning particular cases. In the process, it attempts to use ethical theories. In the past, this has sometimes also been called *casuistics* and, by those who thought it amounted to sophistry, *casuistry*.

See also: ethics; knowledge; philosophy of science; wisdom

Further reading
Aristotle (1966) "Metaphysics," in Richard McKeon (ed.) *The Basic Works of Aristotle*, New York: Random House.
De Cusa, Nicholas (1996) *Nicholas de Cusa on Wisdom and Knowledge*, Minneapolis: A.J. Banning Press.
Ferré, Frederick (1988) *Philosophy of Technology*, Englewood Cliffs, NJ: Prentice Hall.
Singer, Marcus G. (1977) *Morals and Values: Readings in Theoretical and Practical Ethics*, New York: Scribner's Sons.

appropriation *see* existentialism

approval *see* ethics

'aql *see* Akhbārīs

Arabic philosophy The philosophical inquiry and resulting views developed largely in Arabic by thinkers of various ethnic and religious backgrounds in societies where Islamic civilization dominated. Arabic philosophy is sometimes called "Islamic philosophy," a misleading label in that it suggests a commitment to Islamic religion, a commitment that was not always present. Arabic philosophy inherited ideas largely characteristic of the post-Plotinian late Greek philosophy, as well as much of the curriculum of Greek philosophy at the time.

With the rise of Islam in the seventh century

CE, and the adoption of Arabic as the language of scholarship during the reign of the Umayyad caliph 'Abd al-Malik (CE 685–705), Greek and Oriental manuscripts began to be translated into Arabic. Initially, this was motivated by practical reasons, which explains why the first translations were limited to works in medicine, alchemy, and astrology. Later, however, an Arabic interest in other works developed. Most significant were the contributions of the Persian convert from Zoroastrianism Abdullah b. al-Muqaffa' (d. CE 757). In literature, from the Pahlevi, he translated the Indian fables known as *Kalilah wa Dimnah*; while, from the Persian, he translated such works as *History of Persian Kings* and the *Book of Mazda*. In philosophy, his interest (or, according to some scholars, that of his son, Muhammad) focused on the works of the Greek philosopher Aristotle (382–322 BCE) and his commentators, from the Greek philosopher Alexander of Aphrodisias (*fl. c.* CE 200) on. For example, Aristotle's *Categories*, *Hermeneutica*, and *Analytica Posteriora*, as well as *Isagoge*, by the Tyre-born Neoplatonic philosopher Porphyry (*c.* CE 232–*c.* 304) were translated into Arabic for the 'Abbāsid caliph al-Manṣūr (CE 754–75). This process accelerated significantly at the beginning of the ninth century, when it was fueled by the unprecedented support of the 'Abbāsid caliph al Ma'mūn (CE 813–33), who regularly presided over unusually bold theological and philosophical disputations, wrote various treatises, and, in CE 830, established the Bait al-Ḥikma (House of Wisdom), also called the School of Baghdad: an institute – including a library – devoted to translation and research.

The resulting translated works became the standard Arabic texts in logic, natural sciences such as physics and biology, metaphysics, and ethics. For ethics, as in Aristotle's works, the focus was on character ethics and its main concern, wisdom, or, in Arabic, *hīkma* – which also means PHILOSOPHY – and the related notion of *hakīm* ("wise"), i.e. someone learned in philosophy and medicine (which at the time was part of philosophy). Other works by the Greco-Roman Neoplatonist Plotinus (CE 204–70) and the Hellenic philosopher Proclus (CE 410–85), as well as the pseudo-Aristotelian

Theologia Aristotelis or *Theology of Aristotle* – which, though its author is unknown, included a paraphrase of various books of Plotinus' *Enneads* (IV, V, and VI according to some scholars, and I through V according to others) – were used to study metaphysics. Mathematics was studied through, among others, the works of two Alexandrians, the *Elements* by Euclid (third century BCE) and the *Almagest* by Claudius Ptolomey (second century CE). Politics was studied primarily through the *Republic* and the *Laws* by the Greek philosopher Plato (428–348 BCE).

The Scholars of the time, the *Mutakallims*, engaged in a deliberate attempt at approaching the data of revelation by relying on reason, though their effort was often motivated by a religious, rather than a rational, concern. The first ones to have started this type of serious theological discussion, which came to be called *kalām* (literally, "word" or "speech"), were the *Mu'tazilites* – whose position was shared by the 'Abbāsid caliph al Ma'mūn, or, at least, their Qadari forerunners. Notable also among the schools of kalām was that of the *Ash'arites*, who developed an atomistic view of time according to which God constantly re-creates the universe, and any regularities in it merely result from God's habits.

The great Arabic philosophers began to appear in the ninth century CE. The first was al-Kindī (d. CE 873), who translated the *Theology of Aristotle* into Arabic. This book, which included the Plotinian theme of emanation from the One, was quite novel in Arabic thought. It is reported to have led al-Kindī to write a commentary, which, like many of the 242 works attributed to him, has been lost, but appears to have formulated the framework for much metaphysical discussion in later Arabic philosophy.

Al-Kindī's works cover a wide range of topics, from logic and metaphysics, through arithmetic and geometry, to music, alchemy, psychology, and politics. This seems to have been what earned him the appelative: "Philosopher of the Arabs." Notable among his philosophical works are *First Philosophy*, *Prostration of the Outermost Heavenly Body and its Submission to God*, and *Proximate Cause of Generation and Corruption*. They are rather eclectic treatises where Aristotelian features predominate. Notable among his theological treatises are *Justice of God's Actions, God's Unity, Refutation of the Manicheans,* and *Capacity and the Moment of its Inception.* Given the themes they explore, even his critics concur that his concern, very much like that of the Mu'tazilah or Mu'tazilites, was to bridge the gap between reason and Islamic dogma – a task he thought he had accomplished leaving Islamic faith intact.

Yet, the study of the rationalist concerns in Greek philosophy prompted religious doubt among others, including al-Kindī's best known disciple, al-Sarakhsī (d. CE 899), who is reputed not only to have formulated them in conversation, but to have written treatises where he argued that the prophets were charlatans.

A naturalistic development of the rationalist thrust just discussed was formulated, first, by Ibn al-Rāwandī (d. *c.* CE 910). His works have not survived. Some interpreters hold that he rejected the possibility of revelation, miracles, rational proofs of God's existence, and the rationality of God. Others, however, hold that he held that revelation was unnecessary, and miracles nonsense, but that reason sufficed to establish God's existence and to tell the difference between good and evil.

Most notable along naturalistic lines, however, is the famous tenth-century physician Abū-Bakr Muḥammad b. Zakariyā al-Rāzī or, in Latin, Rhazes (d. CE 925 or 932), who was an eclectic thinker with strong materialistic leanings. He left no followers. His works were many – he claims 200 in an autobiography – and covered every branch of inquiry except, for some unknown reason, mathematics. His metaphysical works included, among others, *"Plutarch's" Physical Opinions, Commentary on the Timaeus, Refutation of Proclus,* and *Metaphysics According to Plato's Doctrine.* These works evidence that al-Rāzī's position was largely Platonic, espousing a view of five co-eternal principles: matter, space, time, the Soul, and the Creator. As for his ethical thought, most notably formulated in his *Spiritual Physic,* it displays Platonic and Socratic ideas, holding that there are three parts of the soul, and that harmony and balance among these parts is attained through a spiritual physic, i.e. music, and a physical physic, i.e. gymnastics.

The Neoplatonic thrust in the philosophies of al-Kindī – where Aristotelian features tend to predominate – and al-Rāzī – where Platonic features tend to predominate – converged in the work of the philosophers al-Fārābī (*c.* CE 870–950) and Ibn Sīnā – in Latin, Avicenna (CE 980–1037). The former was the first Muslim philosopher to head a school and to come to be known as a teacher. He was the founder of Arab Neoplatonism and the first major Neoplatonic figure after the Constantinople-born Hellenistic philosopher Proclus (CE 233–304). Subsequent philosophers in Islam considered him the founder of philosophy in Islam, and historians of philosophy in Islam called him *the second Master* (Aristotle being considered the first).

Al-Fārābī furthered the development of logic in an unprecedented manner. Notable among his logic works are *Commentary on Analytic Posteria, Commentary on Analytic Priora, Commentary on the Isagoge, Commentary on Topica, Commentary on Sophistica, Commentary on De Interpretatione, Necessary and Existential Premises,* and *Propositions and Syllogisms Employed in all the Sciences.* In addition, his accounts of Aristotelianism and Platonism were far more comprehensive and accurate than other accounts at the time. They can be found in his *Philosophy of Plato, its Parts and the Order of these Parts, Philosophy of Aristotle,* and *Enumeration of the Sciences.*

In these and his other works, al-Fārābī established the authority of Aristotle in logic, physics, and metaphysics, and that of Plato in political philosophy and the inquiry of human and divine laws. As for his *Enumeration of the Sciences,* it clearly and comprehensively conveys al-Fārābī's conception of philosophy and its relation to the sciences, which he classifies as linguistic, logical, mathematical, physical, metaphysical, political, juridical, and theological. On this conception, individual human beings are organically related to other humans, God, and the universe, so that politics and ethics are an extension of metaphysics and, in particular, theology, the highest level of metaphysics. The *Enumeration of the Sciences* became a crucial introduction to the study of the sciences in the Arabic-speaking world, and substantial parts of it were translated into Hebrew by Shemtomb ben Falaquera (CE thirteenth century), who lived in Spain and Provence; to the Hebrew by Kalonymos ben Kalonymos of Arles (CE thirteenth and fourteenth century); and to the Latin by Dominicus Gundisalvi, perhaps with the collaboration of John of Spain (CE twelfth century). The entire book was translated from the Arabic into Latin by Gerard of Cremona in Toledo in the twelfth century CE.

Ibn Sīnā acknowledged his deep indebtedness to al-Fārābī in his coming to understand Neoplatonism. Yet, he was a much clearer and more systematic writer. As a result, he became the most influential exponent of Neoplatonism in the East and Europe. Ibn Sīnā's position – Avicennianism – was transmitted to various Arabic philosophers, including those in what is now Spain (al Andalus). Indeed, Arabic Neoplatonism became identified with Ibn Sīnā among Arabic commentators and critics during the twelfth and thirteenth centuries. Also, in Europe, with the surge in interest in Aristotelianism, he initially became the main Arab expositor of this philosophy, a role later taken over in Europe by Ibn Rushd (see below).

Ibn Sīnā's major philosophical work is *Kitāb al-Shifā'* or *Book of Healing*, whose abridged version – made by Ibn Sīnā himself – is the more widely read *Kitāb al-Najāt* or *Book of Salvation*. Another major work is the *Book of Remarks and Admonitions*. Notable among his other works are *Definitions* and *Divisions of the Theoretical Sciences*. Besides these, he wrote many treatises in linguistics, medicine, and astronomy. Notable among Ibn Sīnā's views is that of the Soul and Reason – both crucial concepts in Neoplatonism – according to which the rational powers of the soul form a hierarchy whereby holy reason is at the top, reason-in-act is subordinated to it and is followed by, in descending order of subordination, habitual reason, material reason, practical reason, the estimative faculty, memory, imagination, etc., until the lowest power, the nutritive, is reached. Ibn Sīnā held that the prophecy belonged with holy reason, by con-

trast with al-Fārābī, who had demoted it to the level of the imagination.

This approach was not without opponents. In the Eastern Islamic world, where he had replaced al-Fārābī as the leading philosopher, he was criticized by the Persian thinker al-Ghazālī (CE 1059–1111) who, after thoroughly studying the doctrines of the philosophers, and while still teaching in or shortly after leaving Baghdad – where he had been appointed a Professor in CE 1091 – wrote his famous *Tahāfut al-Falāsifah*, usually translated as *The Destruction of the Philosophers* or *The Contradiction of the Philosophers*. In this work, assuming the principle of non-contradiction, he attacks the doctrines of the philosophers, e.g. that the world is eternal, and that God cognizes only universals. He also argues that space, not just time, is infinite. His arguments in this regard are aimed at establishing that there is only one kind of causation, that of the Willing Being, i.e. at establishing a thoroughgoing version of OCCASIONALISM. In the process, al-Ghazālī provides a solid refutation of Ibn Sīnā's doctrine of forms and souls. By contrast with the dialecticians and philosophers, he stresses the experience of his own Being as a viable alternative to understanding the world conceptually.

In accordance with this rather mystical and certainly religions resolution, after writing *Tahāfut al-Falāsifah*, and until his death, al-Ghazālī journeyed as a wandering ascetic to Damascus, Jerusalem, Alexandria, Mecca, Medina, back home where he taught for a while at Nishabur (where, in his youth, he had studied theology and begun to write and teach), and then to his native town, Tus, where he died. In his autobiographical analysis of his spiritual growth, *al-Munqidh min aḍ-Dalāl* or *Deliverer from Error*, al-Ghazālī tries to describe an experiential form of human apprehension that is higher than rational apprehension. This mystical path is not exactly that of Ṣūfism, even though al-Ghazālī received personal help from Ṣūfism in his wandering. It is, rather, a mystical path that stays close to the orthodox dogmas of Islam and to the performance of religious duties. It is in this way that al-Ghazālī most influenced the ulterior development of both orthodoxy and mysticism in

Islam. For after him, orthodox theologians tended to be more respectful of mystics and mystics tended to try more carefully to proceed in accordance with Islamic orthodoxy.

As stated, however, by contrast with the mystico-religious developments just described, various philosophers in Western Islam, particularly in what is now Spain, followed Ibn Sīnā's steps. One of these was the tenth-century Jewish philosopher Solomon Ibn Gabirol (in Latin, Avicebron, *c*. CE 1020–*c*. 1057), author of the Arabic Neoplatonic classic *The Fountain of Life* (or *The Source of Life*), originally written in Arabic and preserved only in the Latin *Fons Vitae*, which identified God primarily with potentiality and becoming.

A second one was the twelfth-century philosopher Ibn Bājjah (in Latin, Avempace, d. 1138). In his *The Conduct of the Solitary* and his treatise on conjunction, he formulated a significant view on the conjunction of the intellect with the human. It is based on the progressive abstraction of specific forms – from potentiality to actuality – and the universal character of the active intellect.

A third al Andalus philosopher who received the traditions from Ibn Sīnā and Aristotelianism was a successor of Ibn Bājjah, namely, Ibn Tufayl (in Latin, Abentofail, d. 1186). His only philosophical work was *Living, Son of Wakeful*, an allegorical novel. Ibn Tufail argued for the possibility of discovering, just relying on human reason, Aristotelian explanations of the world and divine truths, but acknowledged the need for religious law and regulation given the imperfect nature of the majority of humans. The analogical principle by which the laws of the Quran and Sunna are applied to cases not explicitly covered in those two sources is called *qiyās*, which literally means "measure" or "exemplar" and, by extension, is used to mean *analogy*.

Two additional and very influential philosophers were Ibn Rushd (in Latin, Averroes; CE 1126–98), and, in the thirteenth century, Ibn Maymūn – whose Jewish name was Moses ben Maimon and whose Latin name was Maimonides (CE 1135–1204) (see JEWISH PHILOSOPHY). Ibn Rushd was an outstanding commentator on Aristotle's works who criticized Ibn Sīnā for straying away from Aristotelianism, and Ibn Rushd formulated his own version, which led to the development of Averroism. His philosophical output was as voluminous as that of the other great Arabic philosophers. He was, however, especially meticulous in his commentaries and invariably focused on the question of the relation between philosophy and Islamic faith. He was also a judge, and wrote treatises on law, medicine, and theology. His philosophical commentaries dealt with all of Aristotle's works as well as with Plato's *Republic* and Porphyry's *Isagoge*. Besides these, he wrote such original works as *The Divergence of al-Fārābī's Approach to Logic...from that of Aristotle, Al-Fārābī's Departure from Aristotle in the Arrangement, Canons of Proof, Definition of Analytica Posteriora, Inquiry into Problems Discussed in Ibn Sīnā's Metaphysics of al- Shifā', and Distinction between the Absolutely Impossible, the Possible in Itself, the Necessary through Another, and the Necessary in Itself.*

All these works earned him in the West a reputation as a commentator who contributed to the understanding of Aristotle. This is no doubt well deserved, but incomplete. For in the Islamic world, he also, and pre-eminently, engaged in the traditional philosophical inquiry concerning the relation between philosophy and Muslim faith. He had a strong commitment both to the infallibility of the Quran and the unity of truth, which he called the *parity of philosophy and scripture*. This commitment made an appeal to interpretation unavoidable. Ibn Rushd systematically formulated this position in his *Tahāfut al Tahāfut* or *Incoherence of the Incoherence*, which is a methodical and comprehensive rebuttal of al-Ghazālī's critique of Greek and Arabic philosophy in *Tahāfut al Falāsifah* or *Incoherence of the Philosophers*. Here, relying on the Quranic passage that says of any Quranic ambiguous verse that "only God and those confirmed in knowledge know its interpretation," Ibn Rushd argues that neither the theologians, be they Mu'tazilites or Ash'arites, nor the literalists, who upheld a literal interpretation of the scriptures, nor the esoterists, whether Ismā'īlīs or Bāṭīnīs; but only the philosophers, were confirmed in knowledge.

As previously indicated, Ibn Rushd was very

influential on the West, first and foremost among Jewish philosophers, from Moses ben Maimon (in Latin, Maimonides; in Arabic, Ibn ben Maymūn, CE 1135–1204), to Levi ben Gershon (in Latin, Gersonides, CE 1288–1344). He was also influential among such Christian philosophers as the Bavaria-born Albertus Magnus (CE 1206–80) and his student, the Naples-born Thomas Aquinas (CE 1225–74). In fact, Ibn Rushd's position, modified by the interpretations of its followers, eventually became a philosophical approach, Averroism, whose best-known advocate was Siger of Brabant (c. CE 1235–c. 1284), born in what is now France. This philosophy had the distinction of being the most frequently condemned by Church leaders and Christian councils (in CE 1209, 1215, 1240, 1270, and 1277) because of such views as the eternity of matter, the absence of personal immortality, and the *double-truth theory* or *twofold-truth theory*. The latter – that true in religion may not be true in philosophy and vice versa – though attributed to Ibn Rushd, was never explicitly formulated in his writings.

After Ibn Sīnā, Shiite philosophers, writing partly in Persian, became influential in Iran. One notable example is that of the philosopher al-Shrīāzī, usually called Mulla Ṣadrā (AD 1572–1640), who was born in Shīrāz, studied in Isfahan, taught in Shīrāz, and founded a school of thought that is still influential in Iran to this day. His works included *Creation in Time, Resurrection, Attribution of Being to Essence, Predestination and Free Will*, and his most influential work, *Kitāb al-Ḥikmah al-Mutʿāliyah* or *Transcendental Wisdom*. He held that existence had primacy over essence and could be intuited but not conceived, and that, in knowing something, the knower's intellect becomes identified with the intelligible form – in this case, the Neoplatonic nous rather than a Platonic form – of the object known. He also argued that, just as there was a *mundus sensibilis* or world of the senses, and a *mundus intelligibilis* or world of ideas or notions capable of being conceived and known, there had to be a *mundus imaginalis* or world of images capable of being imagined.

It is also important to mention that, once the Spanish city of Toledo was overtaken by the forces of the Spanish king Alfonso VI in CE 1096, the translation of works by Arabic and Jewish philosophers, as well as of Arabic versions of works by Greek authors, and their distribution throughout Europe, intensified. A main impulse to this work was provided by Archbishop Don Raimundo or Ramón de Sauvetat, Bishop of Toledo (CE 1126–52) and Bishop Michael in Tarazona. The translators involved in this project have been called the Toledo Translators, the Toledo Translators School, and the Toledo School. However, though they gathered around Bishop Michael and dedicated their works to him, they did not form a school or group in any substantial sense. A few of those notable among them were Domingo Gundisalvo (also called Dominic Gundisalvi, Dominicus Gundisalinus, and Domingo González) (*fl.* CE 1150), Gerardo de Cremona (?), Hispanus (?), Marcos de Toledo (?), and Hermann the German (?).

Another very significant Arabic philosopher was the Tunis-born Ibn Khaldūn (CE 1332–1406), famous for his multi-volume history, which gives an account of the whole range of Islamic knowledge. At present, the entire book has come to be called *Muqaddimah*. Initially, the term *muqaddimah*, which means "introduction," simply denoted the introduction to the multi-volume history. However, during Ibn Khaldūn's lifetime, the history's introduction and first book became an independent work entitled *Muqaddimah*. At any rate, this work became a turning point in the philosophy of history. Ibn Khaldūn argues that nomadic groups such as the Bedouins are closer than sedentary groups to acting in a manner that is good for humans. This is because among nomads the community and group feeling ('asabiyyah) take precedence over individualistic aims. The more urbanized sedentary groups become, the more luxuries they have and, as a result, injustice and aggression prevail, eventually putting an end to civilization. Ibn Khaldūn, however, did not hold that the said historical developments took place merely as a result of a combination of such natural items as geographic, economic, and sociological causes. He held that history was ruled by an extranatural component: the will and plan of God.

With the colonization of the Arab world by Western powers in the nineteenth century, modern European, especially French, philosophy influenced Arab philosophers who, at the same time, engaged in attempts at synthesizing it with traditional Arabic philosophy. They focused on the problem of making room for Islam's conception of life in a modern world dominated by Western concepts and practices. In the nineteenth century, the Persian-born Jamāl al-Dīn al-Afghānī (CE 1839–97), stands out mostly as a revolutionary seeking the liberation and progress of Muslim peoples, but also, in his *Refutation of the Materialists*, as a thinker who criticizes all those thinkers, from Democritus to Darwin, whose views involve denying God's existence. Another important figure is the Egyptian thinker and al-Afghānī's disciple Muḥammad 'Abdu (CE 1849–?). His lectures at Beirut formed the substance of his book, *Risalāt al-Tauḥīd*, where his arguments focus on the necessity of revelation, the superiority of prophecy over truth, and the role of miracles in supporting the statements of the prophets. The approach of these and other thinkers was furthered in the twentieth century by such authors as Sayyid Quṭb, in *Islam and the Problems of Civilization*, and Muḥammad al-Bahī in *Islamic Thought and its Relation to Western Imperialism*, both of whom have advocated a return to Islam. Others have pursued Western philosophical approaches, from positivism, through Marxism, to existentialism. Controversy among these and the previously discussed groups continues within the framework introduced by the role of religion in the Islamic world.

See also: Greek philosophy; Neoplatonism

Further reading

al-Rāzī, Abū-Bakr Muammad b. Zakariyā (1950) *The Spiritual Physick of Rhazes*, trans. Arthur J. Arberry, London: John Murray.

De Boer, T.J. (1967) *The History of Philosophy in Islam*, New York: Dover.

Fakhry, Majid (1983 [1970]) *A History of Islamic Philosophy*, New York and London: Columbia University Press and Longman.

Mahdi, Muhsin and Butterworth, Charles E. (1992) *The Political Aspects of Islamic Philosophy: Essays in Honor of Muhsin S. Mahdi*, Cambridge, MA: Harvard University Press.

Rahman, Falzur (1979 [1966]) *Islam*, 2nd edn, Chicago and London: University of Chicago Press.

Walzer, Richard (1963) *Greek Into Arabic: Essays on Islamic Philosophy*, Oxford: Bruno Cassirer.

Watt, W. Montgomery (1967) *The Faith and Practice of Al-Ghazālī*, London: George Allen & Unwin, Ltd.

arbitration *see* philosophy, sociopolitical

arbor Porphyrii *see* Neoplatonism

archeology of knowledge *see* Continental philosophy

archetype From the Greek *arche*, i.e. *primal*, and *typos*, i.e. pattern. For the Greek philosopher Plato (428–348 BCE), archetypes were the primary forms or ideas in which items participate and of which they are copies. Medieval philosophers inherited a variation of this notion, that only archetypes, e.g. for the philosopher Aquinas (CE 1225–74, born near the city of Naples, in what is now Italy), were supposed to be located in God's mind. On both these views, archetypes were understood from the standpoint of realism, the view according to which abstract entities have independent existence. By contrast, in accordance with his empiricist and nominalist approach to ideas that interpreted the mind to be a *tabula rasa* at birth, the English philosopher John Locke (CE 1632–1704) used the term *archetypes* in a very different sense: as things in the world which are the originals our ideas more or less resemble. By contrast with all the positions just described, the Swiss psychologist Carl Gustav Jung (CE 1875–1961), following the German philosopher Immanuel Kant (CE 1724–1804) and the conceptualist tradition, understood archetypes as a priori structures of humans' mental life which precede the ideas that articulate rational thinking. This conception was central to his analytic psychology, a branch of psychoanalysis different from classical psychoanalysis as formulated by the Austrian neurologist and psychologist Sigmund Freud (CE 1856–1939), in that it emphasizes the notion of a collective unconscious whose primordial forms are the archetypes. For Jung, however, these archetypes were archaic-mythic forms and figures inherited from humanity's past. He inferred their existence and nature from the fact that they recurrently appear in the most diverse cultures and historical periods. He also closely studied the works of the United States philosopher and psychologist William James (CE 1842–1910), which, of particular interest to Jung, included discussions of typologies of the self.

See also: conceptualism; idea; metaphysics; nominalism; Platonism; psychoanalysis

Further reading
Jung, C.G. (1980) *The Archetypes and the Collective Unconscious*, London: Routledge & Kegan Paul.
Stevens, Anthony (1982) *Archetype: A Natural History of the Self*, London: Routledge & K. Paul.

Archimedian ordering *see* ordering

architectonic *see* Kantian philosophy; metaphysics

architecture *see* cognitive

aretaic *see* virtue

arete *see* virtue

argument In logic, a list of statements, some of which, the premises, are regarded as providing a basis for accepting one of them, the conclusion. A term frequently used as synonymous with argument is *inference*, from the Latin *inferre*, i.e. "to bring in," "carry in," and, then, the Middle Latin *inferentia*, also called illation from the Latin *illatio*, i.e. "a carrying in" (the respective adjectives being inferential and illative), this term denotes the process of drawing a conclusion from premises or assumptions. More loosely, it also denotes the conclusion so drawn.

A special case of arguments that are typically called inferences is that of *immediate inference* associated with the categorical propositions of the four main standard forms: *A* or universal affirmative – all *S* are *P*; *E* or Universal negative – no *S* are *P*; *I* or particular affirmative – some *S* are *P*; and *O* or particular negative – some *S* are not *P*. They concern such operations as *conversion* – switching subject and predicate terms of a categorical proposition (which results in the converse of the initial statement), *obversion* – changing from affirmative to negative or vice versa and changing the predicate into its complement (which results in the obverse of the initial statement), and *contraposition* – forming the complements or complement terms of *S* and *P*, and then switching them (which results in the contrapositive of the initial statement). Any inference that is not immediate is a mediate inference, i.e. it requires additional premises to derive the conclusion.

Some help in identifying the premises and conclusion of a given argument or inference is often provided by a logical indicator or logical word such as "for," "because," and "since," which indicate a conclusion preceding and premises following them, and "so," "hence," "it follows that," "thus," and "therefore," which indicate premises preceding and a conclusion following them. The term argument is supposed to apply not only to good, but also to bad, arguments. Hence, to say that the premises are regarded as providing a basis for accepting the conclusion is not to say that they do provide such basis. There are two main kinds of arguments: deductive and non-deductive. A *deductive* argument – a DEDUCTION – is an argument whose premises are regarded as providing a conclusive basis for accepting the conclusion. A *non-deductive* argument is an argument whose premises are regarded as providing a basis, though not a conclusive basis for accepting the conclusion. Non-deductive arguments are often called *inductive*, but this use is less clear. This is because non-deductive arguments include not merely such arguments as induction by enumeration and induction by elimination, but also arguments from analogy and hypothetical arguments (or arguments to the best explanation).

In assessing a deductive argument, two features are crucial: *validity* and *soundness*. In other words, it is first crucial whether the argument is valid, i.e. whether it has a form or structure such that, if the premises were true, the conclusion would have to be true; and, second, it is crucial whether the argument is sound, i.e. whether it both is valid and has only true premises. These are technical senses –

which apply only to deductive arguments – of the terms valid and sound.

In addition, the terms validity and soundness are applied, still in a technical sense, to logical items other than arguments. Validity and valid, for example, are also applied to argument forms or rules of inference; namely, whenever they cannot lead from only true premises to a false conclusion. Also, it is said that a well-formed formula is valid if it is true (or, at least, not false) under every admissible interpretation of its descriptive terms. Along the same lines, it is said that a theorem is valid. Soundness and sound are applied to logical systems. For example, to say that a logical system has *weak soundness* or is weakly sound is to say that every one of its theorems is valid. While to say that a logical system has *strong soundness* or is strongly sound is to say that for every set of sentences in the system, every sentence deducible from this set is a logical consequence of this set.

In ordinary language, the terms valid and sound have various other uses. For example, people say that someone has a sound view or made a valid statement meaning that it is true, or that someone had a sound idea meaning that it is true or, perhaps, useful. It is also said that someone used sound reasoning or has formulated a sound position meaning that the argument(s) used may be good (though they may not be deductive). All these uses are fine, so long as one understands that the context of use is ordinary language, not logic, in which case valid and sound have the technical meanings previously described.

Logicians have also developed the *method of logical analogy*, whereby an argument is tested by finding another argument – a counterargument – of the same form. If the latter is not valid (in which case it is a counterargument), then the original argument is not valid either, i.e., strictly speaking, the rule of inference it involves is invalid. Though very useful, this method can only establish invalidity. For if one fails to find a counterargument or counterinstance, one never knows whether this is because the original argument is valid or because one's imagination has failed to find an existing counterargument. Hence, formal methods have been developed, most notably the method of truth tables to test for validity (see LOGIC).

As for assessing a non-deductive argument, two features are crucial as well: First, whether the argument is *reliable*, i.e. whether, if its premises were true, then the conclusion would be probable, indeed more probable than it would be if the premises were false; and second, whether the premises are true. A non-deductive argument that both is reliable and has only true premises is sometimes called *cogent*. By contrast with deductive arguments, which are valid or not, sound or not, non-deductive arguments can be reliable and cogent to a greater or lesser degree. The degree of probability that the premises of a non-deductive argument, if true, confer on the conclusion, is called *strength*.

In this connection, the *paradigm-case argument* is significant. It is meant to deal with doubts about statements – e.g. about premises in other arguments – of the form "Is *A* really *B*?" by rejecting the doubts. It does so by, first, stating that in typical or paradigmatic situations, part of what is to be *B* involves being *A* and, then, concluding that it is nonsensical to doubt whether *A* is really *B*. This argument has made it into ordinary English parlance through the sarcastic reply "Is the Pope Catholic?" to a question with an obvious answer. The philosophical force of this reply, however, is by itself questionable, if not insufficient, because in dismissing the said skeptical questions, the reply may unjustifiably assume what the question questions.

There are many kinds of arguments, and a list of some follows:

1   A priori: see A PRIORI–A POSTERIORI.
2   From analogy: see ANALOGY; PHILOSOPHY OF RELIGION; SOLIPSISM.
3   From authority: see FALLACY.
4   From design: see PHILOSOPHY OF RELIGION.
5   From dreaming: see CARTESIANISM.
6   From evil: see PHILOSOPHY OF RELIGION.
7   From hallucination: see PERCEPTION; CARTESIANISM.
8   From illusion: see PERCEPTION; CARTESIANISM.
9   Induction by enumeration: see INDUCTION.

10   Induction by elimination: see INDUCTION.
11   To the best explanation: see ABDUCTION.

Sometimes, the name of types of arguments appears in Latin expressions of the type argumentum ad (argument from). A list of these follows:

1   *Ad baculum*: see FALLACY.
2   *Ad hominem*: see FALLACY.
3   *Ad ignorantium*: see FALLACY.
4   *Ad misericordiam*: see FALLACY.
5   *Ad populum*: see FALLACY.
6   *Ad verecundiam*: see FALLACY.

Besides its use in logic, the term argument is sometimes used in ordinary language to mean *quarrel*, and in mathematics, in the expression, argument of a function, which means *mathematical function*.

See also: abduction; deduction; fallacy; induction; logic; philosophy of mathematics

Further reading
Copi, Irving M. (1998) *Introduction to Logic*, Upper Saddle River, NJ: Prentice Hall.
Skyrms, Brian (1975) *Choice and Chance: An Introduction to Inductive Logic*, Belmont, CA: Wadsworth Pub. Co.

argumentative testing *see* Frankfurt School

Arianism   A family of teachings in Early Christianity that subordinated the Son of God to God the Father. It took its name from the Presbyter of Alexandria Arius (CE 256–336), who, during the third and fourth centuries CE, taught in Alexandria. According to him, God, the Father, was transcendent, ungenerated, eternal, immutable, the Creator. The Son was the Logos incarnate in Jesus, was generated by the Father's choice and, as a human being, could suffer, and owed obedience to the Father. Hence, the Son was inferior and subservient to the Father. That is, Arianism concerned the meaning of the incarnation as related to the Christian monotheistic position. Before Arius, thinkers such as Praxeas (?) and the Lybian theologian Sabellius (third century CE) had understood Jesus to be practically a transient manifestation of God. Arius, expanding on this position, led to a controversy that was to end only after eighteen councils. In the controversy, the distinction between being substantially the

same (*homoousias*), and something's having an essence similar to that of something else (*homoiousias*), became crucial. In CE 325, at the Council of Nicea, the Church officially responded to Arianism by condemning Arius and upheld the views of his opponent, the bishop of Alexandria, Athanasius (CE *c.* 297–73). It asserted the Creator nature and full divine character of the Son, who was substantially the same (*homoousias*) with the Father and, indeed, the Holy Spirit. In the process, the Council formulated *Trinitarianism* or the doctrine of the Trinity, according to which the Son, the Father, and the Holy Spirit are three different persons (hypostases) who are ontologically equal, sharing the substance (*ousia*) of God. Arianism did not thereby disappear, but changed, coming to hold that the Son neither had the same substance as the Father, nor was similar to the Father. In CE 381, this position was also condemned by the Church at the Council of Constantinople, which settled the Trinitarian character of Christianity, by contrast with such religions as Islam and Judaism, which exemplify *Unitarianism*, i.e. the doctrine that God consists of only one person.

There are however Unitarians who consider themselves Christian, and there are differences of interpretation between Trinitarians. For example, the Eastern Orthodox Church holds that the Holy Spirit proceeds from the Father *through* the Son; while the Council of Nicea's document says that the Holy Spirit proceeds from the Father *and* the Son, which, in Latin, reads *filoque*, giving its name to the disagreement, that is known as the *filoque* controversy.

A related doctrine, *tritheism* (from the Greek *tri*, i.e. three, and *theos*, i.e. God), says that there are three Gods. In the sixth century CE, the Greek philosopher and theologian Johannes Philoponus (*c.* CE 490–575) (*philoponus*, i.e. workaholic, being his nickname), appeared to have held tritheism in thinking of the *hypostases* of the Trinity as three substances. In the eleventh century CE, the philosopher Roscelin (CE 1050–1120), who studied at Soissons and Rheims, appears to have held tritheism as a result of his extreme nominalism. He stated that, since every existent was an individual, the idea of a whole consisting of parts was a mere word or *flatus vocis*. Hence, were usage to permit it, we could refer to the Trinity as three individual Gods. In CE 1092, the Council of Soissons forced him to renounce these consequences of his nominalism.

See also: abstract; Arabic philosophy; Aristotelianism; nominalism; Thomism

Further reading
Barnes, Michel R. and Williams, Daniel H. (1993) *Arianism After Arius: Essays on the Development of the Fourth Century Trinitarian Conflicts*, Edinburgh: T. & T. Clark.
Maimbourg, Louis (1728, 1729) *The History of Arianism*, London: W. Roberts.

aristocracy *see* philosophy, sociopolitical

aristodemocracy *see* philosophy, sociopolitical

Aristotelianism Also called *peripatetic philosophy*, this term denotes the family of philosophical approaches of those who significantly follow the ideas or methods of the Greek philosopher Aristotle (384–322 BCE), also called the Stagirite because he was born in Stagira. One must say "significantly" because, as in the case of Plato (428–348 BCE), Aristotle's works have exerted such an influence on philosophy that, to some extent, his ideas and methods can be found everywhere. Aristotle's works are subdivided as follows: works on *logic and language* – *Categories*, *On Interpretation*, *Prior Analytics*, *Posterior Analytics*, *Topics*, and *Sophistical Refutations*; works on *the natural world* – *Physics, on the Heavens*, *On Generation and Corruption*, *History of Animals*, *Parts of Animals*, *Generation of Animals*, and *Motion of Animals*; works on *psychology* – *On the Soul* and *The Short Physical Treatises*; works on *metaphysics* – *Metaphysics*; works on *ethics and sociopolitical philosophy* – *Nicomachean Ethics*, *Politics*; Works on *rhetoric* – *Rhetoric*; works on *aesthetics* – *Poetics*.

The first stronghold of Aristotelianism is Aristotle's school, the Lyceum, which existed uninterruptedly from its founding in 339 BCE until about 200 BCE. A second stronghold was the movement centered in Alexandria in the first century BCE. A third area of influence of Aristotelianism can be found in the Neoplatonic schools of Athens and Alexandria, where Aristotle's works were studied together with those of Plato between the fourth and seventh centuries CE.

A fourth, and most important, period of Aristotelianism is represented by philosophical developments in the Islamic world between the ninth and thirteenth centuries CE. The Neoplatonic thrust in the philosophies of the Arabic philosophers al-Kindī (d. CE 873) – where Aristotelian features tend to predominate – and al-Rāzī (d. CE 925 or 932) – where Platonic features tend to predominate – converged in the work of the philosophers al-Fārābī (*c.* CE 870–950) and Ibn Sīnā (in Latin, Avicenna, CE 980–1037). Ibn Sīnā's position, Avicennianism, was transmitted to various Arabic philosophers, including those in what now is Spain (al Andalus). Indeed, Arabic Neoplatonism became identified with Ibn Sīnā among Arabic commentators and critics in the twelfth and thirteenth centuries. Also, in Europe, with the surge in interest in Aristotelianism, he initially became the main Arab expositor of this philosophy, a role later taken over by Ibn Rushd (CE 1126–98). The latter was very influential on the West, first and foremost among Jewish philosophers, from Moses ben Maimon (in Latin, Maimonides; in Arabic, Ibn ben Maymūn, CE 1135–1204), to Levi ben Gershon (in Latin, Gersonides, CE 1288–1344). It was also influential among such Christian philosophers as the Bavaria-born Albertus Magnus (CE 1206–80) and his student, the Naples-born Thomas Aquinas (CE 1225–74).

In fact, Ibn Rushd's position, modified by the interpretations of his followers, led to a philosophical approach, Averroism, whose best known advocate was Siger of Brabant (c. CE 1235–c. 1284), born in what is now France. This philosophy had the distinction of being the most frequently condemned by Church leaders and Christian councils (in CE 1209, 1215, 1240, 1270, and 1277) because of such views as the eternity of matter, the absence of personal immortality, and the double-truth theory or twofold-truth theory. The latter – that true in religion may not be true in philosophy and vice versa – though attributed to Averroes, was never explicitly formulated in his writings.

Finally, Aristotelianism became even more influential with the development of *Thomism*, named after its founder, the philosopher Thomas Aquinas (CE 1225–74), born near Naples, in what is now Italy, a school of philosophy that has come down to our times.

A doctrine Thomism shares with Aristotelianism, for example, is that of *hylomorphism* (from *hyle*, i.e. matter, and *morphe*, i.e. form). It says that all things are composed of matter – the principle of potentiality and passivity – and form – the principle of actuality and activity. A criticism of this view is that hylomorphism treats changes that are not substantial – e.g. that of solid into liquid water – as if they were substantial. Some Aristotelians and Thomists have replied that this is not a problem with hylomorphism, but with how to apply the doctrine. Others have proposed a modification of hylomorphism, namely *hylosystemism*, according to which natural objects are made up of parts that are themselves substantial. Further, the natural objects have generic features that are constant, e.g. that of being water, and specific features that change, e.g. that of being solid. That is, when water liquefies, though there are substantial changes, there are no generic changes and, strictly speaking, the substantial changes are not of homogeneous substances, but of energy systems.

Another notion Thomism shares with Aristotelianism is that of form in the various senses of this term: substantial – the essence of a kind; accidental – an item's feature other than those belonging to its essence; sensible – that of external objects separated from matter through sense-perception; formal – an item's essence as constituent of being; natural – not man-made; ARTIFICIAL – man-made; physical – of a particular thing; metaphysical – of the thing's genus; subsistent – capable of existing without matter; non-subsistent or material – existing only in matter, which was a substrate or substratum constituting the principle of individuation when combined with form.

As Aristotle, Thomist thinkers also used the term substance – the Greek term was *ousia* – to denote the individual existing thing. In his early works, e.g. *Categories*, Aristotle had divided these items into *ousia prote* or first substance or primary substance, i.e. the primary subject of a proposition, and *ousia deutera* or secondary substance, i.e. a genus, which he thought to be less substantial than a species belonging to it and even less substantial than individuals belonging to the species. These distinctions, which Aristotle significantly modified (or even abandoned), e.g. in *Metaphysics*, especially Book Z, were inherited by Thomist philosophers.

Various concepts formulated by Aristotelians have been adopted by other thinkers. Notable among these are *natura naturans* and *natura naturata*. These are best known in association with the work of the Amsterdam-born philosopher of Spanish and Portuguese origin Baruch Spinoza (CE 1632–77), who characterized *natura naturans* as that which is in itself and is conceived by itself, in other words, God as a free cause, and *natura naturata* as everything that follows from God's necessary nature or its attributes, or their modes in so far as they are considered as things that are in God and cannot be conceived without God. Yet, Ibn Rushd (CE 1126–98) had introduced the term *natura naturata* when commenting on Aristotle's *De coelo* I, 1, and further developed the notion of *natura naturans* and that of *natura naturata* in his *Tahāfut al Tahāfut* (*Incoherence of the Incoherence*), disp. 5, dub. 5. This distinction was widely used by later medieval and Renaissance authors.

Aristotle's influence on psychology has been felt far into modern times. In the *Phaedo* (73c–74d), Aristotle's teacher, the Greek philosopher Plato (428–348 BCE) exemplified the principles of contiguity and similarity according to which associations are supposed to occur. These principles were also described by Aristotle with the addition of a third one, contrast, in the *Short Physical Treatises* or *Parva Naturalia* (more specifically, in *On Memory and Reminiscence*, II, 451b, 10 and ff.). If the thought of the Rockies in Alaska reminds one of the southern Andes because of their similarity, then the thought of the Rockies in Alaska has associated with the thought of the southern Andes by *similarity*. If the thought of lettuce reminds one of tomatoes because one has experienced lettuce and tomatoes together in the past, then the thought of lettuce has associated with that of tomatoes by *contiguity*. If the thought of cold weather reminds one of summer time because the latter contrasts with the former, then the thought of cold weather has associated with that of summer time by *contrast* (or *contrariety*).

Several philosophers and psychologists picked up the concept of association where Plato and Aristotle had left it. In the Middle Ages, the Spanish philosopher and humanist Juan Luis Vives (CE 1492?–1540) pursued it in detail in his *De anima et vita*. Sometimes, the laws of association have been thought supplemented by such laws as those of frequency, simultaneity, and intensity. Modern philosophers who discussed association include the English philosopher Thomas Hobbes (CE 1588–1679), the Irish philosopher George Berkeley (CE 1685–1753), the English philosopher John Locke (CE 1632–1704), and the Scottish philosopher David Hume (CE 1711–76) who, motivated by epistemological rather than psychological considerations, argued that the three principles of association were similarity, contiguity, and causation, and that contrast was reducible to a combination of similarity and causation.

A psychological turn became very clear in 1749, in Part I of Hartley's *Observation on Man*, a book where the British physician and philosopher David Hartley (CE 1705–57) tried to formulate an associationist conception of all mental life. He held mental events occurred in parallel to neural events. Mental events were divided into sensations and ideas. Physiological events consisted in transmissions by means of vibrations. When large vibrations occurred in the brain, they caused corresponding sensations. If they were small, vibratiuncles, they caused corresponding ideas. Hartley also distinguished between simultaneous association, which occurs between mental events occurring at the same time, and successive association, which occurs between mental events occurring in close succession. He is considered the father of modern associationism. The Scottish philosopher and psychologist James Mill (CE 1773–1836) furthered this approach in his 1829 *Analysis of the Phenomena of the Human Mind* and, especially, in the two-volume 1869 second edition of this work. The works of James Mill's son, the English philosopher John Stuart Mill (CE 1806–73), and the Scottish philosopher Alexander Bain (CE 1818–1903) were also associationist and, in this regard, displayed Aristotelian influences.

See also: Arabic philosophy; Greek philosophy; Scholasticism

Further reading
Kassim, Husain (1998) *Aristotle and Aristotelianism in Medieval Muslim, Jewish, and Christian Philosophy*, San Francisco: Austin & Winfield.
Stocks, J.L. (1993) *Aristotelianism*, Bristol, UK: Thoemmes Press.

arithmetic hierarchies *see* ordering

arity *see* degree

Arminianism A view initially formulated during the Reformation by the Dutch theologian Jacobus Arminius (CE 1560–1609), who studied at the University of Leiden and then at Geneva, was a professor at the University of Leiden (from 1613 until his death), and a pastor. He was the founder of Armianian theology or Arminianism. According to this school, God's grace is necessary for salvation, but not irresistible, and God's decree is dependent on human free choice, hence on the individual's repentance or lack of repentance. This position is directly opposed to the orthodox doctrine of Calvinism on predestination and free will. Arminius also held the related doctrines that believers may be certain of their salvation and those who regenerate themselves can live without sin. The Dutch Reformed Synod condemned Arminianism. Yet, the debate continued, and was quite heated for many centuries among Protestant theologians of many denominations. Still today, those who, opposing predestination, defend free human choice concerning divine grace are sometimes called "Arminians." The Remonstrant Church of the Reformed theology has its roots in Arminianism.

See also: determinism

Further reading
Rugh, Gilbert W. (1991) *Calvinism and Arminianism*, Lincoln, NB: Sound Words.
Sell, Alan P.F. (1982) *The Great Debate:*

Calvinism, Arminianism, and Salvation, Worthing, West Sussex, UK: Walter.

arrow paradox *see* paradox

Arrow's paradox *see* Arrow's theorem

Arrow's theorem An influential social choice theory result, also called "Arrow's impossibility theorem," and "Arrow's paradox," after the contemporary United States economist Kenneth Arrow, who first formulated it. It goes against the commonsensical supposition that the preferences of individuals in a society can be formulated and then aggregated as an expression of society's preferences, a social choice function. Arrow's paradox states that individual preferences can be smoothly formalized, and can be proven not to be capable of aggregation so as to yield well-formalized social choice functions satisfying four formal conditions. The four conditions are: first, collective rationality – the domain of the social choice functions is unrestricted; that is, any set of individual orderings and alternatives must yield a social ordering; second, Pareto optimality (named after the Swiss-born Italian sociologist and economist Vilfredo Pareto (CE 1848–1923), who first formulated it) – no social ordering is preferable to another if the former cannot make all parties better off than the latter; third, non-dictatorship – the social ordering cannot be identical to a particular individual's ordering; fourth, independence of irrelevant alternatives – the social ordering of any pair of alternatives depends only on the n-tuple of individual orderings of that pair.

Some attempts to resolve the paradox have focused on the first condition, which leads to intransitive orderings. In this regard, it has been argued that preferences can be rational even if they are intransitive. Other attempts have focused on the fourth condition, arguing that cardinal orderings, therefore interpersonal comparisons of the intensity of preferences, are relevant.

See also: decision; philosophy, sociopolitical

Further reading
Arrow, Kenneth (1963) *Social Choice and Individual Values*, 2nd edn, New Haven: Yale University Press.
Harsanyi, John C. (1978) *Bayesian Decision Theory, Rule Utilitarianism, and Arrow's Impossibility Theorem*, Berkeley: Center for Research in Management Science, University of California.

ars Latin term for art, appearing in several philosophical expressions. *Ars combinatoria* is the phrase used by the German philosopher Gottfried Wilhelm Leibniz (CE 1646–1716) to denote the project of building complex concepts from simple ones according to rules. In 1666, he wrote his *De Arte Combinatoria* describing his project for the development of a universal language he called "universal characteristic," and a universal mathematics he called "mathesis universalis." Significant strides towards these goals have been made in the development of symbolic logic during the twentieth century.

Ars conjectandi is the title of a work written by the Swiss mathematician and physicist Jakob Bernoulli (CE 1654–1705) and published posthumously in 1713, where Bernoulli gave the first proof of what came to be known as Bernoulli's Theorem or first-limit theorem. This theorem, also called the *(weak) law of large numbers*, says that, if a series is repeated n times under three conditions: (i) there are two possible outcomes, 0 and 1, on each trial; (ii) the probability p of 0 is the same on each trial; and (iii) this probability is independent of the outcome of other trials; then, for an arbitrary positive number ϵ, as the number n of trials increases, the probability that the absolute value $|r/n - p|$ of the difference between the relative frequency r/n of 0s in n trials and p is less than ϵ approaches 1. Bernoulli thought that this theorem could be used, on the basis of information about r/n, to calculate p when p was unknown. Simplifications of Bernoulli's proof were later produced.

Ars disserendi is the phrase used by the French philosopher Peter Ramus (CE 1515–72) to denote the part of discourse concerned with the discovery and arrangement of arguments. Ramus's position was that logic was better learned from the natural logic of discourse found, for example, in the discussions and practice of persuasion by the Roman statesman, orator, and author Marcus Tullius Cicero (106–43 BCE), than from the artificial logic of the syllogism formulated by the Greek philosopher Aristotle (384–322 BCE). Whatever his logical errors, Ramus used the vernacular and was a great popularizer. His works had more than 700 editions in 100 years, which gave impetus to the Ramist movement in Protestant universities and the colonies of North America.

Ars magna is the phrase used by the Spanish philosopher Raymond Lull (CE 1236–1315) to denote a mechanical method he invented for formulating all the possible combinations for a subject–predicate relation. The method involves three concentric circles divided into compartments. One circle is divided into nine relevant subjects; a second, into nine relevant predicates; a third, into nine questions: whether? what? whence? why? how large? of what kind? when? where? how? One circle is fixed, while the others rotate providing a complete series of questions and related statements. Lull's work, the origin of the approach called Lullism, was a forerunner of Leibniz's *ars combinatoria* and twentieth-century developments in symbolic logic.

See also: argument; logic; rhetoric; syllogism

Further reading
Cardano, Girolamo (1993) *Ars Magna, or, The Rules of Algebra Artis Magnae*, New York and London: Dover and Constable.
Minio-Paluello, L. (1956) *Twelfth Century Logic*, Rome: Editzioni di Storia et Letteratura.
Waite, Arthur Edward (1980) *Raymond Lully, Illuminated Doctor, Alchemist and Christian Mystic*, London: W. Rider & Son, Ltd.

art *see* aesthetics

artifactuality *see* aesthetics

artificial Term indicating the feature of having been made by intelligent beings, which appears in the following philosophical phrases. First, *artificial form* is an expression used in medieval philosophy to denote forms made by humans as opposed to natural forms.

Second, *artificial intelligence* is an expression said to have been coined in 1955 by the contemporary mathematician and computer scientist John McCarthy to denote computer programs designed to simulate human brain functions. It, and its abbreviation, AI, has come to denote the scientific program aimed

at designing and building intelligent artifacts. This conception of artificial intelligence has significant philosophical implications, for example concerning the mind–body problem. For, if successful, the artificial-intelligence program would seem to provide support for some version of materialism. Also, the program has implications for philosophical conceptions of intelligence. Until the 1970s, the predominant conception was heuristic (from the Greek *heuristikos* and the Latin *heuristicus*, which means "to find out" or "discover"): that of intelligence as the ability to search and reason in finding solutions to problems. In this context, *heuristics* is the area of inquiry that studies this ability and describes its rules, though, in general, it studies any rules of discovery. Afterwards, though the conception is still heuristic, the emphasis has shifted to the ability to use common-sense rules of relevance in addressing problems. A less developed, but still current, approach is *connectionism* or *parallel distributed processing*, which is structurally analogous to the microstructure of the brain. In it, the overall decisions of networks of simple components result from the individual decisions made by these components only on the basis of information about their local state.

For *artificial language*, see ARS, LOGIC, COMPUTER THEORY, PHILOSOPHY OF LANGUAGE.

Finally, *artificial life*, as well as its abbreviation, "Alife," is an expression that denotes a research program which studies the general characteristics and processes of life, including such processes as self-organization, self-reproduction, learning, adaptation, and evolution. The artificial-life program is quite analogous to the AI program. Indeed, some scholars have suggested that AI is a branch of Alife. However, given the parallel processing models used in the Alife program, only the parallel processing approach to AI would seem to fall under the umbrella of the artificial-life program.

See also: biology; philosophy of mind

Further reading
Boden, Margaret A. (1996) *The Philosophy of Artificial Life*, Oxford and New York: Oxford University Press.

Haugeland, John (1997) *Mind Design II: Philosophy, Psychology, Artificial Intelligence*, Cambridge, MA and London: MIT Press.

McClintock, A.E. (1995) *The Convergence of Machine and Human Nature: A Critique of the Computer Metaphor of Mind and Artificial Intelligence*, Aldershot, Hants, UK and Brookfield, VT, USA: Avebury.

Wagman, Morton (1998) *Cognitive Science and the Mind–Body Problem: From Philosophy to Psychology to Artificial Intelligence to Imaging of the Brain*, Westport, CT: Praeger.

as if, philosophy of the *see* philosophy of science

'asabiyyah *see* Arabic philosophy

ascent of the soul *see* Jewish philosophy

asceticism From the Greek, *askesis*, which originally meant physical training, but eventually came to mean self-denial, extending its original bodily meaning to a spiritual one. This term now denotes the view, influential in both Western and Eastern thought, that the body should be denied, perhaps made to suffer, in order to purify the soul in its worldly transit towards salvation. That is, asceticism is not mere austerity, which need not lead to spiritual progress, nor identical with mysticism (see MYSTICISM). For though mysticism may arguably imply asceticism, the converse does not hold: spiritual perfection need not entail identification with the divinity. In Hinduism, for example, the third and fourth stages of life should include renunciation, separation from family, and mendication as ways of purifying the soul. Buddhism sought a less drastic path to salvation, but asceticism has nonetheless been influential among Buddhists. Yoga involves techniques for training the body that are quite rigorous. Indeed, in Hatha-Yoga, these techniques are central. Analogously, in early Christianity, asceticism was often overemphasized. Monasticism – from the Greek *monazein*, i.e. "to be alone" – was an attempt at dealing with this problem by setting up ordered communities for withdrawing from the world; but during medieval times, the Flagellants movement gave great impetus to asceticism.

Self-denial has not been restricted to the religious life. In philosophy, asceticism was thought to be a means to salvation among Pythagoreans and Neoplatonists. Also, the Cynics practiced it as a way of rejecting commonly accepted values, and some Stoics praised it and practiced it too. In modern times, the German philosopher Friedrich Wilhelm Nietzsche (CE 1844–1900) discussed the ascetic ideal, arguing that, though it may involve effort and therefore be admirable, it is a form of decadence in that it aims at conserving, not expanding, life. The German philosopher Max Scheler (CE 1874–1928) criticized Nietzsche's interpretation, arguing that Christian asceticism expanded the ability to enjoy by finding joy in the least number of enjoyable and useful objects, while Greek asceticism reduced this capacity. However, according to Scheler, both forms of asceticism are superior to modern asceticism, because they give priority to spiritual over vital values, while modern asceticism gives priority to utility.

See also: Greek philosophy; Hinduism; mysticism; Neoplatonism; Ṣūfism

Further reading
Bouez, Serge (1992) *Ascese et renoncement en Inde, ou, la solitude bien ordonnee*, Paris: Editions L'Harmattan.

Nietzsche, Friedrich (1967) "On the Genealogy of Morals," in Walter Kaufman (ed.) *On the Genealogy of Morals and Ecce Homo*, New York: Vintage, pp. 24–163.

Scheler, Max (1989 [1961]) *Ressentiment*, New York: Marquette University Press.

Wimbush, Vincent L. (1990) *Ascetic Behavior in Greco-Roman Antiquity: A Sourcebook*, Minneapolis: Fortress Press.

ascriptivism *see* ethics

aseity *see ens a se*, under ens

A-series *see* philosophy of science

asiane *see* accident

assertability *see* meaning

assertability conditions *see* meaning

assertability, warranted *see* truth

assertion *see* logic; speech act theory

assertoric *see* alethiology

assessment *see* judgment

assimilation *see* culture

assisted suicide *see* ethics

association *see* associationism; philosophy of mind

associationism Term denoting the view that higher-order mental activities result from combinations of simpler mental activities or external events. In the *Phaedo* (73c–74d), the Greek philosopher Plato (428–348 BCE) exemplified the principles of *contiguity* and *similarity* according to which associations are supposed to occur. These principles were also described by Plato's student, Aristotle (384–322 BCE), with the addition of a third one, *contrast*, in *Parva Naturalia* (specifically, *On Memory and Reminiscence*, II, 451b, 10 and ff.). If the thought of the Rockies in Alaska, reminds one of the southern Andes because of their similarity, then the thought of the Rockies in Alaska has associated with the thought of the southern Andes by similarity. If the thought of lettuce reminds one of tomatoes because one has experienced lettuce and tomatoes together in the past, then the thought of lettuce has associated with that of tomatoes by contiguity. If the thought of cold weather reminds one of summer time because the latter contrasts with the former, then the thought of cold weather has associated with that of summer time by contrast (or contrariety).

Several philosophers and psychologists picked up the concept of association where Plato and Aristotle had left it. In the Middle Ages, the Spanish philosopher and humanist Juan Luis Vives (CE 1492?–1540) pursued it in detail in his *De anima et vita*. Sometimes, the laws of association have been thought supplemented by such laws as those of frequency, simultaneity, and intensity. Modern philosophers who discussed association include the English philosopher Thomas Hobbes (CE 1588–1679), the Irish philosopher George Berkeley (CE 1685–1753), the English philosopher John Locke (CE 1632–1704), and the Scottish philosopher David Hume (CE 1711–76) who, motivated by epistemological rather than psychological considerations, argued that the three principles of association were similarity, contiguity, and causation, and that contrast was reducible to a combination of similarity and causation. A psychological turn became very clear in 1749, in Part I of Hartley's *Observation on Man*, a book where the British physician and philosopher David Hartley (CE 1705–57) tried to formulate an associationist conception of all mental life. He held mental events occurred in parallel to neural events. Mental events were divided into sensations and ideas. Physiological events consisted in transmissions by means of vibrations. When large vibrations occurred in the brain, they caused corresponding sensations. If they were small, vibratiuncles, they caused corresponding ideas. Hartley also distinguished between simultaneous association, which occurs between mental events occurring at the same time, and successive association, which occurs between mental events occurring in close succession. He is considered the father of modern associationism.

The Scottish philosopher and psychologist James Mill (CE 1773–1836) furthered this approach in his 1829 *Analysis of the Phenomena of the Human Mind* and, especially, in the two-volume 1869 second edition of this work. The works of the English philosopher John Stuart Mill (CE 1806–73) and the Scottish philosopher Alexander Bain (CE 1818–1903) were also associationist. In 1885, the German psychologist Hermann Ebbinghaus (CE 1850–1909) propelled associationism even further with his studies of the role of association in learning. Around the turn of the century, the Russian physiologist Ivan Pavlov (CE 1849–1936) shifted the focus of associationism from ideas to stimulus-response and began studying associations in non-human animals.

Associationism is sometimes combined with hedonism to explain why associations occur. The entire associationist approach has been criticized by the English philosopher Francis Herbert Bradley (CE 1846–1924), and the United States philosopher William James (CE 1842–1910). In psychology, representatives of the Würzburg School – e.g. the German psychologist and philosopher Oswald Külpe (CE 1862–1915) and the German philosopher August Messer (CE 1867–1937) – argued that mental processes have a direction and associationism cannot explain it. Along somewhat analogous lines, representatives of Gestalt psychology – e.g. the German psychologist Wolfgang Köhler (CE 1887–1967) and the German and US psychologist Kurt Lewin (CE 1890–1947) – argued that conduct has purposes, and people respond to relations, and associationism cannot explain or make room for any of these facts. They also argued that associationism is discomfirmed by evidence that habits by themselves do not produce action.

See also: philosophy of mind

Further reading
Hartley, David (1998) *Observations on Man*, Washington, DC: Woodstock Books.
Iwasaki, Minoru (1994) *East Asian Associationism and the Logic of Imagination*, Honolulu, HI: East-West Center. Paper no. 12.
Mill, James (1869) *Analysis of The Phenomena of The Human Mind, New Edition with Notes Illustrative and Critical by Alexander Bain, Andrew Findlater, and George Grote; Edited with Additional Notes by John Stuart Mill*, London: Longmans, Green, Reader, & Dyer.
Schultz, Duane P. (1973) *History of Modern Psychology*, New York: Academic Press.
Vives, Juan Luis (1992) *De anima et vita = "El alma y la vida,"* Valencia: Ayuntament de Valencia.

assumption *see* axiomatic method; induction

āstika *see* Hinduism

asymmetrical *see* relation

ataraxia *see* Epicureanism

Atharva-Veda *see* Hinduism

atheism *see* philosophy of religion

atheist *see* philosophy of religion

Athenian School *see* Academy; Neoplatonism

A-theory *see* philosophy of science

ātman Literally meaning "self," this term is used in Hindu thought to refer to the individual, whose relation to Brahman is conceived differently by different schools. In Advaita-Vedānta, *ātman* is the substrate of the individual and identical with Brahman. Since it is the basis of all thought, including doubt, knowledge, and proof, it cannot be doubted to exist,

proven to exist through argument, or its nature and existence known through reflection or the senses.

In the NYĀYA-VAIŚEṢIKA SCHOOL, *ātman* is the substratum of all cognition; but it is not identical with Brahman. Instead, there are two kinds of *ātman*, the Supreme Soul and the individual soul, and the former is revealed to the latter, which can worship it, through the individual soul's inner experiences.

SĀMKHYA-YOGA characterizes *ātman* as an unrelated, self-luminous, omnipresent entity identical with consciousness.

The mental qualities of *ātman* are sometimes construed in Hinduism as belonging to the individual soul. Other times, they are construed as belonging to the composite of *ātman* embodied in a physical body. For ADVAITA, *ātman* merely appears to transmigrate from life to life. For other schools, by contrast, *ātman* actually transmigrates from life to life accumulating *karma* and, sometimes, attaining enlightenment, thereby being released from *samsāra*, the transmigratory wheel. Buddhism, through the doctrine of *anātman*, acknowledges no reality to the self.

See also: Buddhism; Hinduism

Further reading
Jaya Chamaraja Wadiyar, Maharaja of Mysore (1965) *Atman and Brahman in Vedic Religion*, Bombay: Bharatiya Vidya Bhavan.
Narahari, H. Gururaja (1944) *Atman in Pre-Upanisadic Vedic Literature*, Madras: Adyar Library.
Ramanathan, E. Esa (1997) *Vedic Concept of Atman*, Jaipur, India: Rajasthan Patrika.

atom *see* atomism; Abdera, School of

atomic statement *see* logic

atomism Term denoting a family of doctrines, both ancient and modern, Eastern and Western, according to which the universe is constituted by atoms or basic components. The term atom is derived from the Greek *a*, i.e. not, and *tomos*, i.e. cut. The earliest version of atomism can be found in Jainism, a school of Indian philosophy that arose around 800 BCE. In Western thought, atomism initially developed in the city of Abdera, in the Northern Greek region of Thrace, in the fifth century BCE. Its main advocates included the philosophers Leucippus (*fl. c.* CE 440) and his disciple Democritus (460–370 BCE). The Samos-born philosopher Epicurus (CE 341–270) developed it further during the fourth century BCE. So did Heraclides of Pontus (fourth century BCE). At about the same time, atomism was further developed in India by the Nyāya and the Vaiśeṣika Schools, as well as by some Buddhist thinkers. In the third century BCE, the Greek philosopher Strato advanced the view that atoms were infinitely divisible, already pointing to the medieval and modern controversy about the divisibility of atoms. In the first century BCE, the Roman poet and philosopher Lucretius (*c.* 99–55 BCE) formulated a version of atomism that, though largely following the views of Democritus and Epicurus, endowed atoms with the voluntary power to swerve, hence start vortices and thereby worlds.

Some medieval philosophers, e.g. the French philosophers William de Conches (CE 1080–1145) and Nicholas d'Autrecourt (fourteenth century CE), held atomism by appeal to the theory of minimum elements. However, atomism spread in the Western world largely during the Renaissance, with the work of the philosophers Nicholas de Cusa (CE 1401–64), born in the city of Kues (rendered in Italian and other Romance languages as Cusa), in what is now Germany; and Giordano Bruno (CE 1548–1600), born in the city of Naples, in what is now Italy; and that of the astronomer and natural philosopher Galileo Galilei (CE 1564–1642), born in the city of Pisa, in what is now Italy, who found atomism to be consistent with his experiments in physics.

During the seventeenth century, various thinkers, from the French philosophers, Pierre Gassendi (CE 1592–1655) and René Descartes (CE 1596–1650), through the Amsterdam-born philosopher of Spanish and Portuguese descent Baruch Spinoza (CE 1632–1677), to the German philosopher Gottfried Wilhelm Leibniz (CE 1646–1716), developed a variety of atomistic theories. Some postulated atoms that had only extension, while others – e.g., besides Leibniz, the Croatian physicist and philosopher Rudjer Josip Boscovich (CE 1711–87) and the German philosopher Immanuel Kant (CE 1724–1804) – postulated atoms with some interiority, at least with force or tension. After

the seventeenth century, atomism, or the corpuscular model or paradigm, became largely accepted, to the point that, in the twentieth century, it served as a model for the *logical atomism* formulated by the English philosopher Bertrand Russell (CE 1872–1970), whereby certain categories of items were taken as basic and, in accordance with logical rules, more complex items were constructed on their basis. The reaction to such approach led, for example, to the formulation of *semantic holism*, a metaphysical view according to which the meaning of a symbol, say a linguistic expression or a hypothesis, depends on the entire system of representations – a language or a theory – containing it.

See also: Abdera, School of; Greek philosophy; Hinduism; holism

Further reading
Copleston, Frederick, S.J. (1962) *A History of Philosophy, Vol. I, Greece & Rome, Part I*, revised edn, Garden City, NY: Doubleday. Chapter Ten, "The Atomists."
Ganguli, Hemanta Kumar (1963) *Philosophy of Logical Construction, an Examination of Logical Atomism and Logical Positivism in the Light of The Philosophies of Bhartrhari, Dharmakirti and Prajnakaragupta*, Calcutta: Sanskrit Pustak Bhandar.
Peterson, John (1976) *Realism and Logical Atomism: A Critique of Neo-Atomism from the Viewpoint of Classical Realism*, University: University of Alabama Press.
Russell, Bertrand (1972) *Russell's Logical Atomism*, London: Fontana.

atonement *see* Christianity; Jewish philosophy

attention Term typically used by philosophers to denote a kind of mental concentration or focusing on given or expected items. Medieval philosophers already distinguished various kinds of *attention*: potential (*secundum virtutem*) and ACTUAL (*actualis*). Some philosophers have also tried to distinguish between spontaneous and voluntary attention, but this led to controversy in philosophy and psychology. This was because some objected that voluntary attention implies an awareness of one's attention, but such awareness is distracting, thereby doing away with attention. To this, some replied that the voluntary component, hence the awareness of one's paying attention, is present only at the beginning of paying attention. While others have denied that voluntariness necessarily implies continuous, if any, awareness of such voluntariness.

Attention and its kinds have also been a subject of reflection and discussion among modern philosophers such as the French philosophers Antoine Destutt de Tracy (CE 1758–1836) and Étienne Bonnot de Condillac (CE 1715–80), and the Scottish philosopher Thomas Reid (CE 1710–96). However, philosophical discussions of attention became more frequent in the nineteenth century, for example with the criticism by the English philosopher and psychologist James Ward (CE 1843–1925) of the view held by the English philosopher Francis Herbert Bradley (CE 1846–1924) that mental life was an undifferentiated mass, be it a mass of sensations, a primary sentiment, or an immediate experience. Ward argued that attention is what directs our consciousness, and mental life is impossible without it. In the twentieth century, the Spanish philosopher George Santayana (CE 1863–1952) brought this view a step further by arguing that attention is the main, if not the only, way of accessing the realm of essences. Here, attention is seen as a crucial component of reflection. From a different philosophical standpoint, a phenomenological one, the German philosopher Edmund Husserl (CE 1859–1938) investigated the concept of attention especially with reference to various modes of consciousness. He distinguished between the actual mode, where an object is present; the potential mode, where an object merely can be present; and the attentional mode, where the object is, whether present or merely potential, actively focused on by one's conscience. The latter is central in phenomenological reflection (see PHENOMENOLOGY).

See also: philosophy of mind

Further reading
Calabi, Clotilde (1994) The Choosing Mind and the Judging Will: An Analysis of Attention, Frankfurt am Main and New York: P. Lang.
Pillsburg, W.B. (1921) Attention, London: Allen.
Santayana, George (1927) The Realms of

Being, New York: Scribner. Chapter I, "The Realm of Essence."

attentiveness see philosophy of religion

attitude see conscience; ethics; phenomenology; philosophy of mind

attribute see God; quality

attribution theory A social psychology theory dealing with the manner in which, and reasons why, people in everyday situations explain certain events by attributing them to factors they find personally important and not to others. Accordingly, attribution theory attempts to describe common-sense explanations, identify the common-sense criteria by which they are judged, and compare them to scientific explanations. For example, a person whose application for a job or a promotion was rejected may explain it by appeal to such things as his age, ethnic group, sex, or sexual orientation, while dismissing the possibility that he or she may not have been as qualified as others for the job or promotion. In this regard, attribution theory focuses on the function such explanations have for those who give them. For example, in the type of case described, the explanation may have the function of preserving self-esteem, reducing stress, or diminishing the individual's sense of personal responsibility. This has therapeutic implications because attribution theory may recommend such explanations if, for example, they help individuals whose self-esteem is weak. It also may recommend that individuals look elsewhere but in themselves whenever their explanations tend to create or reinforce chronic depression or guilt feelings.

See also: explanation; philosophy of mind

Further reading
Hewstone, Miles (1989) Causal Attribution: From Cognitive Processes to Collective Beliefs, Oxford: Basil Blackwell.
Jaspars, Joseph Maria Franciscus, Fincham, Frank, and Hewstone, Miles D. (1983) Attribution Theory and Research: Conceptual, Developmental, and Social Dimensions, London and New York: Academic Press.

attributive see description; metaphysics

autarkia see Greek philosophy

authenticity *see* existentialism

author *see* aesthetics

authoritarian *see* philosophy, sociopolitical

authoritarianism *see* philosophy, sociopolitical

authoritative *see* epistemology; philosophy, sociopolitical

authority *see* epistemology; philosophy, sociopolitical

autocentric *see* egocentric

autological *see* paradox

automaton *see* computer theory

autonomy *see* determinism; ethics; Kantian philosophy; philosophy, sociopolitical

Averroism *see* Arabic philosophy; Bologna School

aversion therapy *see* philosophy of mind

Avesta *see* Zoroastrianism

Avicennism *see* Arabic philosophy

avidyā Sanskrit term meaning "ignorance," "lack of wisdom." A synonym is *māyā*. It is a central concept in Indian philosophical schools that attempted to address problems concerning suffering and spiritual liberation. Here, a crucial explanation concerning suffering is that it and its cause, karmic bondage, arise from ignorance: from a failure to recognize what is real and the fact that fleeting appearances are mistaken for reality. Specifically, *avidyā* is ignorance of the identity of *ātman* and Brahman, hence ignorance of the spiritual nature of the self. When an individual's wisdom does away with ignorance, the individual is freed from karmic bondage. In fact, karma is one kind of *mala* or "impurity of ignorance," namely that which follows the individual through births and deaths, the other two being *ānava*, which is the main constraint on the individual, and *māyika*, which is the impurity of transmigratory existence.

This conception is at the basis, not only of the ethics developed by Indian schools of philosophy, but of their epistemology and metaphysics as well. For the notion that *avidyā*

caused bondages that trapped individuals in *samsāra*, the transmigratory cycle of life and death, led philosophers to ask epistemologico-metaphysical questions such as "What is the nature of *avidyā*, which permits it to trap individuals in karmic bondage?" "Where does *avidyā* reside?" "Does it come into being?" "How?" Some typical answers given in the Advaita-Vedānta system were: *avidyā* is itself indescribable (*anirvacanīya*), but it is a positive entity (*bhāvarūpta*), and it has two types of powers, that of concealment and that of projection, whose effects are concealing the truth and suggesting the false. *Avidyā* resides either in the individual self or in Brahman. *Avidyā* is beginningless (*anādi*).

See also: Buddhism; Hinduism

Further reading
De, Aditi (1982) *The Development of the Concept of Maya and Avidya with Special Reference to the Concept of Vivarta: An Interpretation of Sankara Philosophy*, Patna: De.

awareness *see* conscience; epistemology

axiology *see* utilitarianism

axiom *see* logic; set; theory of types

axiomata *see* Stoicism

axiomatic method Name given to a method that bases the propositions and concepts of a study on axioms. The term axiom, from the Latin *axioma* and this from the Greek *axioma*, i.e. "something worthy," refers to undemonstrable but necessary propositions on which a given system of knowledge is based. The Greek philosopher Aristotle (CE 384–22) thought of axioms as the primary premises of demonstrations. The Greek geometrician Euclid (*fl. c.* 300 BCE) thought of axioms as common notions that could not be doubted. The German philosopher Christian Wolff (CE 1679–1754), and, largely following Wolff, the German philosopher Immanuel Kant (CE 1724–1804), thought of axioms as indemonstrable, universal propositions. Four features are often attributed to axioms: First, they are indemonstrable; second, they are self-evident to those who carefully reflect about them; third, they are not just subjectively, but objectively true; fourth, they are not derived from, but called forth by experience. The Greek philosopher Plato (428–348 BCE), the French philosopher René Descartes (CE 1596–1650), and the German philosopher Gottfried Wilhelm Leibniz (CE 1646–1716) attributed all four features to axioms. The English philosopher John Locke (CE 1632–1704) attributed only the first three. Kant dropped the third. The English philosophers John Stuart Mill (CE 1806–73) and Bertrand Russell (CE 1872–1970) affirmed the first, thus almost equating an axiom to a postulate (from the Latin *postulatum*, meaning "demand," "request," or "claim"), which usually means a proposition that forms the starting point of an inquiry and is neither a definition, nor a provisional assumption, nor so certain that it can be taken as beyond all reasonable doubt. So did the Scottish philosopher David Hume (CE 1711–76), who may be interpreted to have affirmed the second as well. Besides the previously mentioned term postulate, terms denoting concepts analogous to axiom include DEFINITION, assumption (see INDUCTION), and hypothesis (see INDUCTION).

The axiomatic method became frequently used in science to organize the knowledge of given sciences. It used to be thought to involve five features: first, the identification of the science's subject matter; second, the identification of those of the science's notions that were primitive, i.e. understandable without the help of any definition; third, the formulation of the science's axioms; fourth, definitions of non-primitive concepts in terms of primitive ones; and fifth, proofs of the non-primitive accepted propositions of the science. In modern times, proponents of versions of this method ranged from the French philosopher and mathematician Blaise Pascal (CE 1623–62), to the Polish-American mathematician and logician Alfred Tarski (CE 1901–83) and the United States economist Thorstein Veblen (CE 1857–1929). Attempts at using the method often led to discovering previously unnoticed presuppositions, hence to the formulation of new axioms. Today, the mere organization of a body of knowledge according to the axiomatic method is thought inadequate. What is also required is to present the language and rules of inference involved.

See also: deduction; logic; set; theory of types

Further reading
Fraenkel, Abraham Adolf, and Bar-Hillel, Yehoshua (eds) (1966) *Essays on the Foundations of Mathematics. Dedicated to A.A. Fraenkel on His Seventieth Anniversary*, 2nd edn, Jerusalem, Israel: Magnes Press Hebrew University.
Hintikka, Jaakko, Gruender, C. David, and Agazzi, Evandro (1981) *Theory Change, Ancient Axiomatics, and Galileo's Methodology: Proceedings of the 1978 Pisa Conference on the History and Philosophy of Science*, Vol. 1, Dordrecht and London: Reidel.
Lightstone, A.H. (1964) *The Axiomatic Method: An Introduction to Mathematical Logic*, Englewood Cliffs, NJ: Prentice-Hall.

ayin *see* cabala

aziluth *see* cabala

B

B *see* A

babouvism *see* Marxism

backward causation *see* causal law

Baconian method *see* induction

bad faith *see* existentialism

Baden School *see* Kantian philosophy

Baghdad School *see* Arabic philosophy

balance *see* virtue

balance of terror *see* war

balancing principles and reasons *see* ethics

bamalid *see* syllogism

bambara *see* Bantu

Bantu Several linguistically and culturally interrelated peoples in Central and Southern Africa whose philosophical views have been the subject of many studies since the mid-1940s, when the African philosopher Placide Temples's *Bantu Philosophy* became the center of controversy about the existence and nature of a Bantu philosophy. Some denied any such philosophy existed. Others, for example, the African philosopher Alexis Kagame, argued that, though it existed, Temples had portrayed it in a manner that was based on Western, rather than Bantu, conceptions of science, rationality, logic, and philosophy. This led Kagame, who had studied philosophy at Rome's Gregorian University between 1951 and 1953, and who was an established scholar in Bantu languages, to study Bantu philosophical concepts through the analysis of these languages. Starting with Kinyarwanda, the language of the Bantu of Rwanda, Kagame developed a taxonomy based on eleven grammatical categories. Out of these, he identified four philosophically relevant word-components. Each component is constituted by a prefix and a radical that, combined with one of three article-like vowels (A, I, and U), produces four philosophical categories of being (*ntu*). They are *umuntu*, which means human person or force with intelligence, and includes not just living humans but also spirits and the human dead; *ikintu*, which means all those entities acting under the influence of intelligent forces that are not their own; *ukuntu*, which means mode of being; and *ahantu*, which means place and time.

These categories did not make room for the concept of nothingness as the negation of being. However, Kagame argued that, like the Bambara, the Bantu conceived of nothingness as the negation of specifiable items existing in nature: as non-determined substances – e.g. a non-actualized Temples – and non-concrete existents – e.g. ancestors and spirits – a conception close to the scholastic conception of nothingness as a prelude to creation.

Concerning this latter interpretation, as well as his ranking of kinds of beings, Kagame's heuristic reliance on Aristotelian categories to study Bantu thought has been criticized on the grounds that it led him to formulate too Hellenistic a description of Bantu thought. More centrally, however, the African philosopher D.A. Masolo has criticized Kagame's inference that ordinary use of Bantu language presupposes metaphysical concepts – e.g. that of being with intelligence. Rather, Masolo thinks such use implies merely that a person exists whatever its essential features happen to be – which may not be, and in fact are not, implied by the language's users.

See also: African philosophy

Further reading
Hammond-Tooke, W.D. (1980) *The Bantu-Speaking Peoples of Southern Africa*, London: Routledge & Kegan Paul.
Kagame, Alexis (1976) *La Philosophie bantu comparée*, Paris: Presence Africaine.
Masolo, D.A. (1994) *African Philosophy in Search of Identity*, Edinburgh and Bloomington: Edinburgh University Press and Indiana University Press.
Obenga, Theophile (1989) *Les Peuples Bantu: migrations, expansion et identite culturelle: actes du colloque international (Libreville 1–6 Avril 1985)*, Libreville: CICIBA.
Ruwa'ichi, Thaddeus (1990) *The Constitution of Muntu: An Inquiry into the Eastern Bantus' Metaphysics of Person*, Berne and New York: P. Lang.
Tempels, Placide (1959) *Bantu Philosophy*, Paris: Presence Africaine.

barbara *see* syllogism

barber paradox *see* paradox

Barcelona School A philosophical approach that took root in Barcelona, Spain at the beginning of the nineteenth century and has been characteristic of various philosophers connected with that city since then. These features are a strong sense of reality, a reluctance to reduce philosophy to mere abstractions or to a way of life, an avoidance of the excesses of discourse, a distrust of mere philosophical brilliance, a sense of historical continuity, and a tendency to rely on common sense. The School's activities have been primarily centered at the School of Philosophy and Letters of the University of Barcelona; but its sphere of influence reached beyond that university. Indeed, some of the School of Barcelona's members never taught at the University of Barcelona. They included such authors as Joaquín Llaró Vidal, who taught at the University of Cervera and founded the Philosophical Society in 1815, Jaime Balmes, Joaquín

Carreras Artau, Tomás Carreras Artau, Martí de Eixalá, Antonio Llobet Vallosera, F.X. Llorens i Barba, F. Mirabent, J. Serra Hunter, Ramón Turró, and Joaquín Xirau, who was also connected with the School of Madrid. Some commentators argue that this list should also include Eugenio d'Ors, at least because of his sense of reality and of historical continuity. Others, however, have disagreed with such inclusion.

See also: Madrid School

Further reading
Balmes, Jaime Luciano (1899) *El criterio*, sixth edn, Paris: Garnier Hermanos.
D'Ors, Eugenio (1960) *Eugenio D'Ors: antoloia*, Madrid: Doncel.
Nicol, Eduardo (1961) *El problema de la filosofia hispánica*, Madrid: Editorial Tecnos.
Turró, Ramón (1912) *Orígenes del conocimiento: el hambre*, Barcelona: Editorial Minerva, SA.

bardo *see* Buddhism

bare particular *see* metaphysics

bargaining *see* decision; philosophy, sociopolitical

baroco *see* syllogism

base *see* induction; supervenience

basic action *see* action

basic belief *see* epistemology; justification; knowledge; positivism

basic norm *see* philosophy of law

basic proposition *see* epistemology

basic sentence *see* justification

basic statement *see* justification

basing relation *see* knowledge

basis *see* induction

basis relation *see* knowledge

baskets of knowledge Expression found in a traditional Māori narrative involving a single senior god, Io, who is the source of all knowledge. He sends messengers who tell the sons of Rangi and Papa (the Sky Father and the Earth Mother) that he wants to see one of them.

After being selected and overcoming strong resistance from his brother Whiro, Tāne ascends to the highest heaven and Io gives him three baskets of knowledge. They are the basket of knowledge of peace, goodness, and love; the basket of knowledge of ritual command and ritual; and the basket of knowledge of warfare, agriculture, and the crafts. Tāne brings them down to earth while battling Whiro and his allies and, since then, the baskets of knowledge are said to constitute the basis of Māori traditional knowledge.

This is one of the narratives that attributes knowledge a divine origin and, hence, a status worthy of respect. Also, the image of baskets of knowledge conveys the Māori idea that knowledge is limited and fixed. Hence, though Māori authorities can disagree on the correct version of a given item of traditional knowledge, the disagreement and processes aimed at resolving it are not seen by the Māori as leading to any new knowledge. They only lead to establishing which among the competing versions was correct. Further, non-authorities can only ask informational questions to learn the items of traditional knowledge correctly. They cannot challenge the authorities' claims and have no active role to play when the authorities disagree.

It is also worth noting that the narrative's previously mentioned ranking of the baskets of knowledge places knowledge of peace above knowledge of warfare and, also, above knowledge of ritual.

See also: Māori philosophy

Further reading
Huruata (1979) *Pataka = Storehouse (of Knowledge): Being a Condensation of Books I and II: A Collection of Maori Legend and Lore, Including the Marae Series in Verse and Prose*, Auckland, NZ: Outrigger.
Patterson, John (1992) *Exploring Maori Values*, Palmerston North, New Zealand: The Dunmore Press Ltd.

bātinī *see* esoterism

Bayesian *see* probability

Bayes's theorem *see* probability

beatific vision *see* mysticism

beatitude *see* ethics

beautiful *see* aesthetics

beauty *see* aesthetics

becoming *see* philosophy of science

Bedeutung *see* reference

begging the question *see* fallacy

Begriff *see* idealism

behavior *see* action; behaviorism

behavior therapy *see* behaviorism

behavioral equivalence *see* computer theory; philosophy of mind

behavioral variable *see* decision; philosophy, sociopolitical

behavioralism *see* behaviorism

behaviorism Term applying both to a research program in psychology and to a philosophical position in the philosophy of language and the philosophy of mind. The research program in psychology was first proposed by the United States psychologist J.B. Watson (CE 1878–1958) who coined the term behaviorism in 1913. He argued that psychology should abandon traditional introspective techniques. Instead, it should use the experimental methods of the natural sciences to specify all variables, including behavior, and attempt to explain and predict behavior, where to explain behavior meant to specify the independent variables (stimuli) of which the behavior (response) was lawfully a function. Behaviorism (sometimes called *psychological behaviorism*, *scientific behaviorism*, and *behavioralism*) was adopted by such renowned United States psychologists as C.L. Hull (CE 1884–1952), E.C. Tolman (CE 1886–1959), and B.F. Skinner (CE 1904–90). Some behaviorists included internal neurophysiological conditions among the variables, interpreting these conditions as intervening variables. Others, e.g. Skinner, insisted that only environmental variables should be included, on the grounds that intervening variables – say, the state of thirst – would be a function of environmental ones – say, lack of water.

Behaviorism's model was different from that of reflexology, where the conditioning stimulus does not follow the conditioned response. Here, in *classical* or *Pavlovian*, or *respondent conditioning*, a response or reflex (say, gland secretion) already under the control of a given stimulus (say, the presence of food) would be caused by a new stimulus (say, a bell ringing) if this stimulus were to be repeatedly paired with the old one. By contrast, behaviorism used the *operant conditioning* or *instrumental conditioning* model, where the conditioning stimulus follows the conditioned response. Here, instances of a kind of response (say, a pigeon's pressing a bar), which has repeatedly been followed by instances of a kind of reinforcing stimulus (say, food being dispensed), will occur with greater frequency on future occasions. This process of behavior-modification is called *positive reinforcement* when the reinforcing stimulus is welcome (say, a reward) and *negative reinforcement* when the reinforcing stimulus is unwelcome (say, a punishment). That is, operant conditioning can be used, e.g. in behavior therapy, so that behavior is learned or unlearned.

However, serious difficulties arose concerning the behavioristic program. For the characterization of its basic concepts – say, of the concept of anger – in behavioral terms tended to be circular, uninformative, unable to identify, hence explain, pieces of behavior, and significantly inapplicable to the modification of behavior in actual social circumstances. As a result, it has been displaced by approaches that pay attention to behavior but also include other, e.g. cognitive, components.

As for philosophical behaviorism, it was a family of semantic views. The English philosopher Alfred Ayer (CE 1910–89), and the German philosophers Rudolf Carnap (CE 1891–1970) and Carl Hempel (CE 1905–97), held that the meaning of mentalistic expressions – say, anger – was reducible to publicly testable statements describing behavioral and other processes or dispositions. The English philosopher Gilbert Ryle (CE 1900–76) held that mentalistic terms meant dispositions to behave in typical ways, and disposition-ascribing statements, though lawlike, did not describe actual facts, but only had the function of justifying inferences about

behavior. The Austrian philosopher Ludwig Wittgenstein (CE 1889–1951) also held that mentalistic terms could be applied only by appeal to public, intersubjectively observable behavior, but his position was not committed to reducing mental to non-mental entities. All these positions were sharply criticized in the 1950s and 1960s by the United States philosopher R.M. Chisholm (CE 1916–99), the contemporary United States philosophers J. Fodor and H. Putnam, and the contemporary Canadian philosopher Charles Taylor, and have been modified into forms of functionalism.

See also: action; philosophy of mind; positivism

Further reading
Carrier, Martin (1995) *Mind, Brain, Behavior: The Mind–Body Problem and the Philosophy of Psychology*, Berlin and New York: Walter de Gruyter.
MacKenzie, Brian D. (1977) *Behaviorism and The Limits of Scientific Methods*, London: Routledge & Kegan Paul.
Ryle, Gilbert (1949) *The Concept of Mind*, New York: Barnes & Noble.
Ulrich, Roger E., Stachnik, Thomas J. and Mabry, John (1966) *Control of Human Behavior*, Glenview, IL: Scott, Foresman, and Co.

being *see* existentialism; metaphysics

being-there *see* existentialism

being-toward-death *see* existentialism

belief *see* epistemology; knowledge

belief, basic *see* justification; positivism

belief–desire model *see* intention

belief, ethics of *see* ethics

belief, partial *see* probability

Bell's theorem *see* philosophy of science

beneficence *see* ethics

benefit *see* ethics

benevolence *see* ethics; love; utilitarianism

Bergsonianism Term denoting philosophical and other approaches influenced by, or akin to, the thought of the French philosopher Henri Bergson (CE 1859–1941). In literature, for example, the work of the French novelist Marcel Proust (CE 1871–1922) involves a conception of memory and time analogous to that formulated by Bergson: the future is open and decided moment by moment; time has its own pace; and there is qualitative change through a dynamic, fluid, and continuous process. In philosophy, Bergson's philosophy has influenced or is analogous to those philosophical currents that show a spiritual and evolutionary emphasis, for example that of the French philosopher Édouard Le Roy (CE 1870–1954), who succeeded Bergson at the College of France, and the spiritualized positivism of the Argentine philosopher Alejandro Korn (CE 1860–1936).

There are various salient characteristics of Bergsonianism. A central one is the view that philosophy must start with whatever is given in experience: reason, which provides a static, material view of things, and intuition, which provides access to a dynamic, more basic, spiritual component of reality. For example, reason spatializes time by using concepts, and though to a certain extent we must thus spatialize it, intuition helps us grasp the dynamic nature of time through metaphors. Another central feature of Bergsonianism is that the dynamic nature of time goes together with the dynamic nature of the world, which works through evolution, has a purpose, and is driven by a force, the *Élan Vital*, which is God. Overall, Bergsonianism is characterized by an emphasis on a basic spiritual process that fits well with spiritualistic versions of evolutionary emergentism. This position has often, though by no means always, displayed an anti-intellectualist bent. Indeed, anti-intellectualism is hardly a feature of the last phase of Bergson's thought itself.

See also: evolution

Further reading
Bergson, Henri (1928) *Creative Evolution*, London: Macmillan.
Korn, Alejandro and Pucciarelli, Eugenio (1922) *La libertad creadora*, La Plata: Tall. Graf. Olivieri y Dominguez.
Le Roy, Édouard Louis Emmanuel Julien (1914) *Une philosophie nouvelle, Henri Bergson*, Paris: F. Alcan.
Maritain, Jacques (1955) *Bergsonian Philoso-

phy and Thomism, New York: Philosophical Library.

Berlin Group *see* positivism

Bernoulli's theorem *see ars conjectandi under* ars

Berry's paradox *see* theory of types

best *see* ethics

best-interest standard *see* ethics

Beth's definability theorem *see* model

better *see* ethics

between *see* relation

Bhagavad-Gītā Title of a philosophical poem, meaning *Song of the Blessed One*, in Book Six of the *Mahābhārata*, an Indian epic poem believed to have been composed between the fifth century BCE and the second century CE. The poem includes eighteen chapters and 700 verses relating the dialogue between the reluctant warrior Arjuna, moving into battle at the head of his family against another family, and the god Krishna, who is Arjuna's charioteer. Much of the dialogue is about ethics. In it, Arjuna receives a revelation from Krishna emphasizing selfless deeds and devotion (*bhakti*). Though, strictly speaking, this narrative is considered to be *smṛti*, i.e. fallible tradition, it is often treated as *shruti*, i.e. infallible revelation. Major figures such as the Indian philosophers Shankara (CE 788–820), Rāmānuja (*c.* CE 1055–1137), and Madhva (CE 1199–1278) wrote commentaries about the *Bhagavad Gītā*. Shankara interpreted it to teach that enlightenment can be attained through right knowledge alone. By contrast, Rāmānuja argues that, according to the *Gītā*, enlightenment results from the performance of religious duties, most prominently, devotion to God. Madhva interprets the book to emphasize divine uniqueness and the necessity of loving being attached to God rather than oneself or the results of one's actions. In the poem, the divinity appears in two forms: as Brahman, the impersonal one, and as Krishna, an incarnation of the One in human form.

See also: Hinduism

Further reading

Curtis, Donald (1996) *Understanding and Standing under the Bhagavad Gita*, Los Angeles, CA: Science of Mind Pub.

De Nicolas, Antonio T. (1976) *Avatara, the Humanization of Philosophy through the Bhagavad Gita: A Philosophical Journey through Greek Philosophy, Contemporary Philosophy, and the Bhagavad Gita on Ortega y Gassett's Intercultural Theme, Man and Circumstance: Including a New Translation with Critical Notes of the Bhagavad Gita*, New York: N. Hays.

Feuerstein, Georg (1983 [1974]) *The Bhagavad Gita: Its Philosophy and Cultural Setting*, Wheaton, IL: Theosophical Pub. House.

bhakti Term that, in Hindu theistic thought, means "devotion," involving faith, surrender, love, affection, and attachment. It can assume many forms, for example devotion of servant to master, of friend to friend, of parent to child, of child to parent, of spouse to spouse. Typically, *bhakti* is displayed in worship through offerings (*pūjā*). According to the Indian philosophers Rāmānuja (*c.* CE 1055–1137) and Madhva (CE 1199–1278), *bhakti* is crucial for overcoming the human predicament and thus attaining enlightenment. This is because in response to devotion, the divinity manifests grace and kindness thereby causing those who display devotion to attain *moksha*, that is, liberation, spiritual freedom. In modern times, Indian thinkers, following the Indian philosopher Shankara (CE 788–820) and the modern Indian thinker Swami Vivekānanda (CE 1863–1902), tend to relegate *bhakti* to a lower path than knowledge (*jñāna*) for those who are unable to pursue knowledge. Many theist philosophers, however, consider *bhakti* to be the highest path, where the main obstacle to enlightenment is lack of faith, not ignorance.

See also: Hinduism

Further reading

Pande, Susmita (1989) *Medieval Bhakti Movement, Its History and Philosophy*, Meerut, India: Kusumanjali Prakashan.

Poddar, Hanuman Prasad (1962) *The Philosophy of Love: Bhakti-sutras of Devarsi Narada*, Gorakhpur, India: Gita Press.

bhāvanā *see* Jainism; Nyāya-Vaiśeṣika School

bhayāṅga *see* Buddhism

bias *see* empiricism; ethics

Bible *see* Christianity

biconditional *see* logic

bid'ah Term denoting a practice or belief that did not exist in Islam as it was revealed in the Quran and established by the Sunna on the basis of Prophetic tradition. If a practice or belief lacks this connection with tradition and revelation, there is a presumption against it. From the standpoint of the faithful, most Muslims believe that something new is *bid'ah* only when it contradicts the spirit of Islam, but some Muslims hold that *bid'ah* includes any practice or religious fixture that was absent during early Islamic times, e.g. minarets and mosques are *bid'ah*. From the standpoint of Islamic law, most authorities make room for *bid'ah ḥasanah*, i.e. an innovation that is good in that it does not contradict the essence of Islam. An example of such innovation is the building of an additional story on the Grand Mosque of Mecca so that larger numbers of pilgrims can walk together around the Ka'bah: the large cubic stone structure covered with a black cloth, which stands at the center of the Mosque as the spiritual center for the concentration of consciousness on God.

See also: Arabic philosophy

Further reading

Coulson, N.J. (1964) *A History of Islamic Law*, Edinburgh: Edinburgh University Press.

MacDonald, Duncan Black (1963) *Development of Muslim Theology, Jurisprudence and Constitutional Theory*, Lahore: Premier Book House.

bik'ehgo da'ináanii *see* Native American philosophy

bilā kayfā Term literally meaning "without how" that denotes the Islamic theological principle according to which one should not question revelation when one cannot understand it. This principle was invoked by Abu'l-Ḥasan al-Ash'arī (d. CE 935) and others – e.g. Aḥmad Ibn Ḥanbal (d. CE 855) – regarding the Quran's anthropomorphizing expressions such as "Hand of God," and "Face of God," which attribute human features to God. According to these thinkers, though having a hand and having a face cannot be attributes of God, these expressions have to be taken literally without asking how.

In Islam, the said expressions are isolated and do not reflect an anthropomorphic conception of God. Indeed, they have often been interpreted metaphorically, both in the past and in modern times. The reason al-Ash'arī and others formulated the without-how principle is that they believed if the Quran had metaphorical levels of meaning, it had to be accepted literally to begin with. Further, these philosophers and theologians thought that, since God was assumed to be absolutely incomparable, and the said Quranic expressions, at least metaphorically, involved implicit comparisons, the expressions should be accepted without asking how and, as al-Ash'arī added, without comparison.

This appeal to the *bilā kayfā* principle is analogous to the recourse to *divine mystery* in Catholicism when matters of dogma, e.g. the doctrine of the trinity and unity of God, cannot be reconciled with logic.

See also: Arabic philosophy; Christianity

Further reading
Cohn-Sherbok, Dan (1997) *Islam in a World of Diverse Faiths*, New York: St Martin's.
Reinhart, A. Kevin (1995) *Before Revelation: The Boundaries of Muslim Moral Thought*, Albany, NY: State University of New York Press.

bilateral *see* reductionism

bimba-pratibimba-vāda *see* advaita

bioethics *see* ethics

biological *see* biology

biologism *see* biology

biology From the Greek *bios*, i.e. 'life,' and *logia*, i.e. 'theory of.' Before biology became an independent science, it was treated as a part of philosophical inquiry. This was the case in Ancient Greece among the Pre-Socratics, especially Empedocles (*c.* 490–430 BCE). Indeed, an early philosophical doctrine was *hylozoism*, the view held among others by Thales (640–546 BCE) that all matter is alive.

Biology was also a part of philosophical inquiry for the Greek philosopher Aristotle (384–322 BCE), who began to develop biology as a more independent and less speculative kind of study, but still considered it a part of physics, which, except perhaps for meteorology, he primarily based on an analysis of concepts and considered largely identical with ontology. The Greek term for nature, *physis*, is used by Aristotle primarily to denote the nature or essence of a living thing. He also characterizes *physis* in *Physics II* as a source of movement and rest that belongs to an item in virtue of itself, and tends to identify it with the item's form, not its matter. With Aristotle's disciples, e.g. the Greek philosopher Theophrastus (360–207 BCE), biology became increasingly less speculative, a process that continued in the School of Alexandria. However, though less speculative and making room for such things as dissection and inductive reasoning, biology was still largely theoretical and a far cry from being an experimental science. Indeed, some speculative influences continued to affect its development during the Renaissance and even in modern times, when biology clearly became an independent, experimental science.

As with other sciences, once biology became an independent, experimental science, the question arose: how are philosophy and its spin off, biology, related to each other? The many answers to this question can be classified in various types. First, experimental biologists have held that philosophy and biology are largely unrelated to each other, because biology is a science and uses a strictly cognitive language, while philosophy is not a science and need not use such language.

Many theoretical biologists, historians of biology, and philosophers have criticized this view on the grounds that, at the theoretical level, philosophy of biology, i.e. philosophical inquiry about life overlaps with theoretical biology and uses cognitive language. They accordingly hold, second, that philosophy and biology are somehow related; but disagree on how they are related. Some biologists and many metaphysicians and epistemologists hold that philosophy provides a foundation for biology, whether metaphysical, epistemological, or other. By contrast, many biologists and some philosophers – e.g. those who advocate an inductive metaphysics and a conception of philosophy as a synthesis of the sciences – hold that biology provides results that philosophy can include in a comprehensive view of the universe. Still others hold that philosophy and biology, though not directly related, are indirectly related through some intermediate discipline that, for some of them (e.g. the French philosopher Jacques Maritain, CE 1882–1973), is a metaphysics of the organic world; while for others (e.g. the English biologist J.H. Woodger, CE 1894–1981) is the study of biological language.

These main types of views have combined in a variety of specific positions prompted by questions concerning the status of the organic world in relation to other aspects of reality. One position is REDUCTIONISM, i.e. the view that biological phenomena can be analyzed, explained, and predicted solely on the basis of chemical and physical concepts. A second position is VITALISM, according to which each organism – a term that, in antiquity, used to mean instrument but, in the Middle Ages, came to mean a body equipped with instruments and, since the eighteenth century, means biological body – includes some controlling vital force that cannot be reduced to chemical or physical terms. Many intermediate positions have been formulated between the previous two positions, e.g. *methodological reductionism*, or the view that the analysis, explanation, and prediction of biological phenomena in chemical or physical terms is merely a way of studying them, not a doctrine in metaphysics. Third, *organismic biology* rejects reductionism, vitalism, and their variants on the grounds that the whole organism cannot be reduced to the sum of its parts, whether these are interpreted as merely chemical or physical, or as including a vital force as well.

Other problems have not concerned the ontological status of the organic world in the universe, but such things as the relation between knowledge and biology; the implications of biological inheritance for free will, of biological differences between ethnic groups or sexes for social differences between them, and of biological characteristics of individuals for their own identity. A significant problem that concerns biological taxonomy, i.e. the classification of living beings, is the problem of species posed by the conception of species formulated, among others, by the English biologist Charles Darwin (CE 1809–1882) in the doctrine of *transformism*. This is the view that species evolve. If they do, however, then their boundaries are not clear-cut. However, the traditional conception of a species has clear-cut boundaries. It is very much a traditionally conceived natural kind. This result has a variety of scientific and philosophical implications that biologists and philosophers are still trying to address.

Also, the fact that, in the 1970s, biology ceased to be a merely explanatory science and became a technology through genetic engineering has raised a variety of ethical issues concerning this technology. As well as this, developments in a branch of biology, namely ecology, have led to a variety of other ethical problems and issues, and to applications of ecological concepts and methods in social science and philosophy. These problems, issues and philosophical developments fall under the following headings:

1 Bioethics. See ETHICS; FEMINIST PHILOSOPHY.
2 Biological essentialism. See ETHICS; FEMINIST PHILOSOPHY; PHILOSOPHY, SOCIOPOLITICAL.
3 Ecology. See ECOLOGY; ETHICS.
4 Evolutionary epistemology. See EPISTEMOLOGY.
5 Evolutionary theory. See EVOLUTION.
6 Social ethics. See ETHICS; EVOLUTION; FEMINIST PHILOSOPHY; PHILOSOPHY, SOCIOPOLITICAL.

See also: ecology; epistemology; evolution; feminist philosophy; philosophy, sociopolitical

Further reading
Hull, David L. and Ruse, Michael (1998) *The Philosophy of Biology*, Oxford and New York: Oxford University Press.
Ruse, Michael (1998) *Taking Darwin Seriously: A Naturalistic Approach to Philosophy*, Amherst, NY: Prometheus Books.

bipolarity *see* dialectic

birth control *see* feminist philosophy

bisexuality *see* ethics; feminist philosophy; gender

bit *see* computer theory

bivalence *see* logic

black Athena *see* Afrocentricity

black box Expression referring to a hypothetical item characterized only by its function and used to explain or predict some effect or behavior. It may denote a single item or a system of items whose structure is unknown. It was used, for example, in behavioristic psychology, where the organism is treated as a black box, i.e. without attempting to access its mental components – e.g. motives – through introspection or, in the case of the United States behavioral psychologist B.F. Skinner (CE 1904–90), disregarding also physiological factors. Instead, the focus is on stimulus-response patterns governed by such functions as reinforcement, inhibition, extinction, and arousal. An analogous approach can be found in other branches of inquiry. In cybernetics, for example, though there are no simple input–output rules, the focus is on functional organization and feedback in controlling behavior. Also, a black-box approach to particle behavior is central to quantum physics. In economic theory, the approach to investment theory formulated by the contemporary economist and United States Nobel Prize winner for economics James Tobin is a black-box approach that helps, if not explain, at least predict the behavior of financial markets. In all these cases, the details of underlying structure, mechanism, and dynamics are either unknown or treated as irrelevant.

See also: computer theory; philosophy of economics; philosophy of mind; philosophy of science

Further reading
Catania, A. Charles, Harnad, Stevan R. and Skinner, B.F. (1988) *The Selection of Behavior: The Operant Behaviorism of B.F. Skinner: Comments and Consequences*, Cambridge and New York: Cambridge University Press.
Pylkkanen, Paavo, Pylkko, Pauli, and Hautamaki, Antti (1997) , *Brain, Mind and Physics*, Amsterdam, Washington, DC, and Tokyo: IOS Press and Ohmsha.
Tobin, James (1996) *Essays in Economics*, Cambridge, MA and London: MIT Press.

blindsight *see* perception

bliss *see* ethics

bluffing *see* philosophy, sociopolitical

bocardo *see* syllogism

bodily *see* body

Bodishattva *see* Buddhism

body The concept of body has been discussed from a variety of standpoints in philosophy. However, it has been largely treated as that which appears as a mode of extension. According to the Greek philosopher Aristotle (384–322 BCE), the body is a reality delimited by a surface. It has extension, in so far as it is anything, it is a substance, and it is informed or embedded by a form, hence not mere matter or a mere potentiality. In Ancient Greece and Rome, discussions about the body generally centered around whether a form can be embedded in a body. Contrary to Aristotle, the Pythagoreans had held that the soul was imprisoned in the body. This view was taken up by Platonists who held that the soul – a form – was imprisoned in the body, which, as such, has no form.

Long before Sub-Saharan African peoples had read any Platonists, they conceived of a person as composed of two basic substances. The Akan people, for example, called them *ōkra* (soul), which was conceived as immaterial, and *honam* or *nipadua* (body, flesh), which was considered material. The main philosophical concern in this tradition was that of the connection between *ōkra* and *honam*, analogously to the manner in which the connection between soul and body was a concern for the French philosopher René Descartes (CE 1596–1650) and his followers in the Western world. Indeed, Descartes hypothesized that the connection occurred in the pineal gland. While Akan thinkers, though thinking, like Descartes, that the soul somehow is in the head, formulated the doctrine that *ōkra* is *mogya* (the soul is blood) or *ōkra* is in *mogya*, i.e. the soul is in the blood, to indicate that, ordinarily, they are fused together throughout. One must say ordinarily, because the same thinkers held the notion of disembodied survival or life after death, as made plain by the Akan maxim *onipa wu a na onwui*: when a man dies he is not (really) dead.

Neoplatonists held the body was a level of emanation and, some of them, also considered it as associated with the senses, not with the intellect. By contrast, Epicureans and Stoics sometimes held that only the body existed. On the other hand, early Christian thinkers tended to emphasize the intelligibility or spirituality of the body, a notion transformed by medieval philosophers along Aristotelian lines in treating the body as *formed matter*, a union of form and matter.

In modern times, problems concerning the body have been treated by reference to matter as an object of physical science. For Descartes, body was nothing but filled space. The Amsterdam-born philosopher of Spanish and Portuguese descent Baruch Spinoza (CE 1632–77) retained this geometric conception of the body as a mode of extension. By contrast, the German philosopher Gottfried Wilhelm Leibniz (CE 1646–1716) conceived of the body as ultimately an aggregate of monads that are dynamic and intelligible in nature, so that physical bodies manifested intelligible bodies.

This dynamic conception took a materialistic turn in the English philosopher John Locke (CE 1632–1704), who thought the body itself had a force or active principle. However, the German philosopher Immanuel Kant (CE 1724–1804) distinguished between the dynamic and the phenomenic body, setting the stage for two types of still influential conceptions of the body. One considers the body as simply an external, purely physical, or biological entity, which has an active component, force, or cause. The other considers the body as internal, a sort of resistance to the will of the self (as exemplified by the views of the French philosopher François Pierre Gauthier Maine de Biran, CE 1766–1824), the external appearance of life (as exemplified by the views of the German psychologist Gustav Theodor Fechner, CE 1801–87), or the distention of a reality that, in itself, is tension (as in the position of the French philosopher Henri Louis Bergson, CE 1859–1941).

The German philosopher Edmund Husserl (CE 1859–1938) pursued a middle-ground concerning this dichotomy by arguing that, from a phenomenological standpoint, the body is two, not one: first, the perceiving body, which is dependent on the material body; second, the willing body, which is not reducible to natural entities such as matter and life. Existentialist thinkers – e.g. the French philosophers Gabriel Marcel (CE 1889–1973), Jean-Paul Sartre (CE 1905–80), and Maurice Merleau-Ponty (CE 1908–61) – have further developed this approach that focuses on one's own perception of one's body as a consistent unity and not, as it was for the Austrian physicist and philosopher Ernst Mach (CE 1836–1916) and the English philosopher Bertrand Russell (CE 1872–1970), as something that dissolves into a complex of sensations. Indeed, Merleau-Ponty argues that, however legitimate, considering the body as a mere object is not exhaustive or even primary. By contrast, the phenomenologically described unity of the body is not only primary but supersedes Descartes's separation of body and soul.

This separation, however, has been negated through a different – behavioristic – approach by the British philosopher Gilbert Ryle (CE 1900–76), who argued that Descartes's separation of soul and body, which led to modern psychology's official doctrine of *the ghost in the machine*, is based on the *category mistake* of looking for and hypostasizing an immaterial counterpart of the body in mental life. This amounts to rejecting both materialism and idealism, and, indeed, the public–private distinction in mental life.

See also: behaviorism; phenomenology

Further reading
Heil, John (1998) *Philosophy of Mind: A Contemporary Introduction*, London and New York: Routledge.
Onians, Richard Broxton (1987 [1951]) *The Origins of European Thought*, reprint of Cambridge University Press edn, Salem, NH: Ayer.
Priest, Stephen (1998) *Merleau-Ponty*, London and New York: Routledge.

Ryle, Gilbert (1949) *The Concept of Mind*, New York: Barnes & Noble.

Bologna School A philosophical School developed during the Italian Renaissance as a result of the translation of Book I of the Greek philosopher Alexander of Afrodisia's *De anima* (CE *c*. 200) by the Venetian Hieronimus Donatus (CE *c*. 1457–1511). Though sometimes called the Padua and Bologna School, the Bologna School opposed the ideas attributed to the Arabic philosopher Ibn Rushd (in Latin, Averroes, CE 1126–98), whose influence was mainly felt at the Padua School. The Paduans, often called Averroist Aristotelians, were not interested in theological questions and formulated a kind of naturalistic Aristotelianism. The controversy between Alexandrians and Averroists was recurrent in Renaissance philosophy, which, however, had no body of doctrines, or philosophical methods, or even a philosophical style shared by the philosophers of the time.

In these historical circumstances, the controversy between Alexandrians and Averroists heated up during the early 1500s, centering on the nature of the soul and proofs of its immortality. The leading figures among the Averroists were Agostino Nifo (CE 1473–1546) and Cardinal Gaetano da Thiene (*c*. CE 1387–1465). Nifo was best known for his studies of the methods of attaining knowledge about the natural world. He defended the need to use both methods Ibn Rushd had formulated, from the effect to the cause and from the cause to the effect, and improved upon them. Gaetano da Thiene was influenced by the physicists of the School of Paris, especially by Nicole d'Oresme (in English, Nicholas Oresme, *c*. CE 1325–82), who was best known for his studies on the nature of heat.

The most illustrious Alexandrian involved in the controversy with Nifo and Cardinal Gaetano de Thiene was Pietro Pomponazzi (CE 1462–1525), who, in his *De immortalitate animae*, argued that, from the standpoint of reason, the intellectual soul is as mortal as the sensitive soul, but that the basis of morality is not thereby affected, because the exercise of virtue is a self-sufficient good and, therefore, morality is autonomous, i.e. independent of the threat of eternal punishment or awards for immortal soul. He considered the immortality of the soul to be a matter of faith, not of reason, and held the *theory of the two truths*, namely that though the individual souls could not be proven to be immortal, ordinary people needed to believe in their own immortality so as to obey the rules of morality, by contrast to the wise, who obeyed them for their own sake.

Against Pomponazzi, Gaetano de Thiene argued that, though the individual souls were mortal, the intellect common to all humans was immortal and provided the basis for all eternal truths, whether scientific or moral. Nifo went further and argued that the intellectual soul can be both individuated and act without the body, hence making room for its immortality. This brought him closer to the Thomistic position of the Venezian Cardinal Contarini (CE 1483–1542), and Bologna's Franciscus Silvestrius Ferrariensis (CE 1474–1528).

See also: Arabic philosophy; Greek philosophy; Thomism

Further reading
Copenhaver, Brian P. (1997) *Renaissance Philosophy*, Oxford and New York: Oxford University Press.
Fiorentino, Francesco (1868) *Pietro Pomponazzi studi storici su la scuola bolognese e padovana del secolo XVI, con Molti documenti inediti*, Firenze: Sucessori Le Monnier.
Iorio, Dominick A. (1991) *The Aristotelians of Renaissance Italy: A Philosophical Exposition*, Lewiston: E. Mellen Press.

boniform faculty *see* Cambridge School

bonum *see* ethics

Book of Changes *see* Chinese philosophy; Taoism

book of life *see* determinism

Boolean algebra *see* logic

borderline case *see* ambiguity

bottom-up *see* cognitive; explanation

bound variable *see* logic

boundary situation *see* existentialism

boycotting *see* philosophy, sociopolitical

bracketing *see* phenomenology

Brahmā *see* Brahman

Brahman Sanskrit term of uncertain etymology. Its Sanskrit root, *brh*, means "to grow," "swell," "become great." Initially having a meaning analogous to that of *Mana*, the term came to mean, first, the gaining of magical results from the performance of Hindu rituals; then, in the *Vedas*, the power of the Vedic sacrifices and that of the Brahmins who performed them; and, finally, the holy power of the universe, the ultimate, conscious, blissful, unchanging, eternal being: the original intelligence. On this meaning, together with Vishnu and Shiva, Brahman or rather Brahmā is one of the three divinities in the Hindu trinity. In Vishistādvaita and Dvaita Vedānta, Brahman is conceived as a personal deity or *īshvara* (lord of the universe, from the root *ish*: to rule, reign). However, by contrast with Dvaita, Vishistādvaita use of the term Brahman secondarily denotes the world that depends on Brahman, namely all minds and material things constituting Brahman's body. In Advaita Vedānta, Brahman is apersonal and has no qualities, so that ascriptions of features such as consciousness and bliss to Brahman are interpreted negatively, as negating or excluding such properties as materiality and pain. According to this school, the concept of *īshvara* is merely a superimposition on Brahman. The founder of Advaita Vedānta, the philosopher Shankara (CE 788–820), retained both the personal and impersonal sense of Brahman, distinguishing between Saguna Brahman, or Brahman with qualities, and Nirguna Brahman, or Brahman without qualities. But he considered the former to be merely illusory. While, on the basis of an esoteric enlightened experience (*moksha*) and scripture (*sruti*), he holds that only Nirguna Brahman is real. This is expressed in the Upanishadic statement *Sarvaṃ Kalu idam Brahman*, which means "all is Brahman."

In the sacred scriptures, the *Upanishads* often use the term *idam* (this) to denote this universe as God's revelation in manifest form, by contrast with *tat* (that), to denote Brahman, the undescribable, omnipresent reality that underlies, permeates, and transcends the world of the senses.

See also: Hinduism

Further reading
Griswold, Hervey DeWitt (1900) *Brahman: A Study on the History of Indian Philosophy*, New York: Macmillan.
Tattvabhushana, Sitanath (1983 [1900]) *The Philosophy of Brahmanism Expounded with Reference to Its History*, Madras: Higginbotham.

Brahman-Atman *see* Brahman

Brāhmana *see* Hinduism

Brahmanism *see* Brahman

Brahma-sūtra *see* Hinduism

brain bisection *see* philosophy of mind

Brentano's thesis *see* phenomenology

bridge law *see* reductionism

British empiricists *see* empiricism; rationalism

British moralists *see* ethics

brotherhood A term denoting a society or association. A most notable brotherhood in philosophy was *Ikhwān al-Safā*, Arabic for the *Brotherhood of Purity*. It was a secret society founded in Basra, Iraq, around CE 340. It appears to have been headed by Zayd ibn Rifā'ah, and constituted a forum for discussion and learning. Its members are said to have included Abū Sulaymān Muḥammad al-Bustī, Abū-al-Ḥasan 'Alī al-Zanjānī, Abū Aḥmad al-Mahrajānī, and al-Awfī. They published fifty-one treatises entitled *The Treatises of the Brotherhood of Purity*, which amounted to an encyclopedia of philosophy, theology, metaphysics, cosmology, and the natural sciences (including botany and zoology). These writings displayed great open-mindedness and intellectual interest concerning such cultures as those of Ancient Greece, Persia, and India. Indeed, they argued that there was truth in religions other than Islam. They formulated Neoplatonic ideas and their method consisted in asking questions without answering them except indirectly and by implication. This method, together with the fact that they used to suggest the existence of a higher authority capable of resolving all differences, led some interpreters to characterize the Brotherhood of

Purity as tracing back to the Ismāʿīlīs. Though their ethics involved self-knowledge and liberating the soul from materialism in order to return to God, their discourse displayed strongly humanistic characteristics. The ʿAbbāsid al-Mustanjid, who succeeded to the Caliphate in CE 1160, ordered the burning of the brotherhood's books.

Another notable philosophical brotherhood was the *Brotherhood of the Common Life*, founded by the Dutch religious leader and philosopher Gerhard Groote (CE 1340–84). He was born in Deventer, near Utrecht, taught at Cologne, and, influenced by the Flemish mystic Jan van Ruysbroeck (CE 1293–1381), founded the Brotherhood.

See also: Catholicism; Islam

Further reading
Fuller, Ross (1995) *The Brotherhood of the Common Life and Its Influence*, Albany: State University of New York Press.
Lane-Poole, Stanley (1960) *Brotherhood of Purity*, Lahore: National Book Society.

B-series *see* philosophy of science

B-theory of time *see* philosophy of science

Buchmanism *see* Oxford movements

Buddha *see* Buddhism

Buddhism A religion founded by Siddhārta Gotama Buddha in the sixth century BCE in the eastern provinces of India, far from the Indus Valley, the center of Vedic culture. It became the state religion in the third century BCE but, eventually, it disappeared in India, while it became dominant in China and among other East Asian nations. The Buddha found various ideas already developed in Indian culture such as *karma* (the fruits of action), *samsāra* (the wheel of rebirth or cycle of existence of certain karmic states, not of the soul, and, hence, not to be confused with reincarnation, which, contrary to Buddhist views, presupposes the existence and persistence of the soul) constituted by *gati* (mode of existence) – the various modes of existence within which rebirth takes place, the view that escape from this wheel is the highest good, the open-ended term *dharma* (*hō* in Zen Buddhism) – that which determines our true essence, righteousness, our duties, and

the cosmic rule that gives all things their essence, and the notion of a *guru* (teacher or spiritual master), i.e. a guide through these stages of life. Buddhism teaches that our inability to escape from *samsāra* is the result of our desires or cravings for wealth, pleasure, power, an ever longer existence, and our clinging to such things as ideas, opinions, and philosophical positions, and that these cravings and this clinging can be avoided through the *Madhyamā-pratipad*, literally meaning "middle path," but, in Buddhism, designating *Sādhana* or the *Eightfold Path*: right views, right intentions, right speech, right action, right livelihood, right effort, right mindfulness, and right concentration. It is sometimes cryptically formulated as *shraddhā* (faith), DARSHANA (insight), and *bhāvanā* (contemplation). This path is thought to cultivate *samata*, i.e. tranquility or calmness in the sense of reducing emotive levels so that clear perception and understanding can be attained.

Buddhism is divided into two main groups of schools the *Theravāda* and the *Mahāyāna* Schools. Yet, various views are common to both schools, including:

1 the doctrine that all existence is painful;
2 the doctrine that all existence is impermanent;
3 *nairātmya-vāda* (from *nairātmya*, i.e. no soul or substance, and *vāda*, theory), the doctrine that there is *anātman* or ANATTĀ, or non-I, i.e. no permanent self or ego;
4 the doctrine that everything lasts only a moment;
5 the doctrine that every existing thing depends on other things for its existence.

Also, the *four noble truths, catvāri āryasatyāni*, are central: *duhkha* (the nature and place of suffering and pain), *duhkha-samudaya* (the cause and origin of suffering), *duhkha-nirodha* (the cessation of suffering), and *duhkha-nirodha-mārga* (the path to the cessation of suffering).

The *Theravāda* (or *Hīnayāna*) Schools were the early schools of Buddhism. They held the previously mentioned general Buddhist doctrines, but differed in other respects. For example, the *Sautrāntika* School held that while our sense perceptions justify our belief in the existence of objects independent of our minds, this belief requires an inference, hence we know *indirectly* that they exist. By contrast, the *Vaibhāsika* School held that we know the existence of such objects *directly*. For, first, if our sense perceptions were not entirely reliable in and of themselves to establish the existence of objects independent of our minds, then inference could not establish it. Second, the content of our perceptions is determined by the objects we perceive and the conditions under which we perceive them. Third, idealist arguments, relying on the view that we could have our perceptions in dreams, cannot get off the ground, because they must rely on our perceptually telling the difference between dreams and waking perceptions. As for the *Sarvastivada* School, it held a doctrine of momentariness, the radical view that there were only rapid pulsations of reality that were so infinitesimal as to scarcely exist. In this regard, a notion used by Indian Buddhists is that of *nirodha-samāpatti*, or a state produced by meditation in which no mental events of any kind occur. It raises the question: how can mental events re-emerge from a continuum in which none exists, given the Buddhist view that all existents are momentary? In trying to address this matter, Theravāda Buddhism makes room for one continuous form of being, *bhavānga*, a mode of consciousness in which no mental activity occurs. This form of continuous consciousness, in dreamless sleep or other mental states, guarantees the continuity of an individual's mental life. It is also used to explain the process leading from death to rebirth. Some Buddhists identify *bhavānga* with pure mind, a luminous and radiant entity. A related notion is *vāsanā*: the presence of karmic seeds in continua of passing events, so that, maturing at different times, the seeds may produce tendencies to act this or that way.

A very influential early Buddhist document is the *Dhammapada* (the path of virtue). Framed within the notions of karma and *samāra*, the four noble truths of Buddha and the Eightfold Path, this document presents meditations about the practice of the way to salvation. Among the earliest forms of Buddhism, one can already find the *eight liberations*, meditation exercises associated with the *eight masteries*

involved in overcoming all clinging to corporeal and non-corporeal concerns.

The *Mahāyāna* Schools are the later schools of Buddhism. A notable difference between the Mahāyāna and the Theravāda Schools is that, though the concept of *bodhisattva* (from the Sanskrit, *bodhi*: wisdom and *sattva*: existence in) can be found in Theravāda Buddhism, it is more central to the Mahāyāna Schools. Mahāyāna Buddhism involves rejecting inferior forms of enlightenment and a concern for others. That is, though Theravāda Buddhism is individualistic, Mahāyāna Buddhism involves an ethics of universal compassion (*maitrī-karūna*) or love (*maitrī*) and concern. Indeed, in metaphysics, Mahāyāna Buddhism holds that there are no individuals and we cannot distinguish between individual objects, because everything that exists depends on other things and this is not to be an individual. Epistemologically, the highest knowledge attainable according to this school is *prajnā* or intuitive indeterminate knowledge, which appears to be knowledge unbounded by perceptual, conceptual, or linguistic distinctions. The experiencer of this knowledge is also called *prajnā*.

Various middle positions between the above extremes were sought within the general scope of Mahāyāna Buddhism. For example, the *Mādhyamika* (one of the Mahayana Schools whose name is derived from the Middle Way taught by Buddha), founded by Nāgārjuna (early second century CE), held that our sense perception is characteristically illusory. What really exists, the final truth, is *shūnya* (the void) or *shūnyatā* (voidness), which explains the additional name, *Shūnyavāda*, used to refer to this school (or, according to some, a school that led to the Mādhyamika). It suggests that the phenomenal world is beyond adequate verbal formulation and, hence, in this sense, constitutes ineffable reality that can only be accessed through an esoteric experience; but there is also a conditional truth in everyday language and experience. This middle position is expressed through the eight negations: no elimination, no production, no destruction, no eternity, no unity, no manifoldness, no arriving, no departing.

In addition, another Mahāyāna School, the

Yogācāra, was founded by, among others, Asanga (fourth century CE) and Vasubandhu – or, as it has been argued, if there were two Vasubandhus, by Yogāchārin Vasubandhu or Vasubandhu the Elder (fourth or fifth century CE). It seeks a mid-way between Mādhyamika's and the Theravāda Schools' teachings. It argues that there exist non-substantive minds and the experiences these minds have. On this view, memories of past experiences can become strong, so that we cannot simply experience what we wish – e.g. pain or dullness when we wish to experience pleasure. Critics objected, first, that this was a way of reintroducing substances, and, second, that the Yogācāra could not prove the existence of other minds. A related Yogācāra doctrine is *citta-mātrā*, the view that there are only mental entities, a doctrine that is still controversial within Buddhism.

As stated, Buddhism disappeared in India, but flourished outside India, especially in China, Korea, Japan, and Tibet. Traditionally, there were ten main schools of Buddhism, four of which were significantly involved in the Sinification of Indian Buddhism: *Ch'an* (ZEN), *Hua-yen* or *Flower Garland School*, *T'ien t'ai* or *School of the Celestial Platform*, and *Ching'tu* or *Chinese Pure Land Buddhism* (see below).

T'ien t'ai or School of the Celestial Platform or *Lotus School* (because it is based on the *Lotus Sūtra*) was given its definite form by Chih-I (CE 538–97). It sees the Indian philosopher Nāgārjuna (early second century CE) as its first sage, from whose doctrine that everything that arises conditionally is empty, the T'ien T'ai School derives its doctrine of the three truths. The first truth is that dharmas lack independent reality, hence are empty. The second truth is that dharmas have the passing existence of phenomena and can be perceived by the senses. The third truth, supposed to synthesize the other two, says that the absolute and phenomena are one.

Historically significant for the development of Buddhism in Japan was the *San-lun* School or *School of Three Treatises*, a Chinese form of the Mādhyamika, whose three basic works are indicated in the San-lun School's name. These were introduced in China in the fifth century

CE and the school became most influential under the leadership of Chi-tsang (CE 549–623) in the sixth century. A Korean student of Chi-tsang called Ekwan introduced the school in Japan in CE 625. There, it became the *Sanron* School, though it was never independently organized and its teachings were studied by all sorts of Buddhists. Indeed, the Sanron School strongly influenced Prince Shōtoku (CE 574–622), who unified Japan.

A school of Chinese Buddhism whose appearance was associated with the San-lun School's loss of influence was *Fa-hsiang*, the *Marks of Existence* School, which was founded by Hsüan-tsang (CE 600–64) and his student, K'uei-chi (CE 638–82), continued the teachings of the Yogācāra and was based on the works of Asanga and Vasubandhu. This was the *Hossō* School in Japan.

The Hua-yen School or Flower Garland School was a highly influential Chinese Buddhist School. It traced back to the monks Tu-shun (CE 557–640) and Chic-yen (CE 602–80), though its official founder was Fa-tsang (CE 643–712), and emphasized the equality and mutual dependence of all things. *Lü-tsung*, the discipline school initiated by Tao-hsüan (CE 596–667), was the origin of the *Ritsu* School in Japan, where, though never of great importance, it survives until today. Also worthy of mention is the *San-chieh* School (in Chinese, *San-chieh-chiao*, i.e. *School of Three Stages*), founded by Hsin-hsing (CE 540–94). It holds that the there are three stages to the teaching of Buddhism: first, the period of true dharma, supposed to have lasted for 500 years; second, the period of adulterated dharma, supposed to have lasted 1,000 years; third, the period of degeneration of dharma, supposed to have lasted 10,000 years and to have begun around CE 550. Members of the San-chieh School believed they were the only ones knowledgeable of the teaching appropriate for this third period. They emphasized observance rules, altruism, and asceticism. The School was banned in CE 600 on the grounds that it accused other schools and their rulers of heresy; but actually continued to exist until the mid-800s.

Zen Buddhism also developed in China in the sixth and seventh centuries CE and spread to Japan. Like Mādhyamika, Zen holds that one's usual life (*samsara*) and *nirvana* (or the *tao*) are identical. Enlightenment (*satori*) is so near to us that it is usually overlooked. It distinguishes five degrees of enlightenment, called *go-i*, and the term it uses for karma is *gō*.

In addition, *Mi-tsung*, which meant the School of Secrets, was a tantric school of Buddhism introduced in China in the eighth century. This school, which emphasizes the recitation of mantras, was eventually brought to Japan, where it is known as Shingon.

Ching t'u or Chinese Pure Land Buddhism was another important school that largely constituted the foundation of popular Buddhism. It held that there were a number of transcendent lands or realms each ruled by a buddha. In Japan, it became *jōdo*, Japanese Pure Land Buddhism, which tended to emphasize monotheism. Two terms central to all traditional Japanese forms of Buddhism are *dai-gedatsu*, literally "great liberation," meaning complete enlightenment and also used as synonymous with nirvana, and *daigo-tettei*, meaning a profound enlightenment that involves an experience of emptiness. As for later schools, the *Nichiren* School, or *New Lotus* School or – literally – School of the Lotus of the Sun was named after its founder, Nichiren (CE 1222–82). It teaches that the title of the *Lotus Sūtra* contains the core of Buddhist teachings and that buddhahood can be achieved in an instant simply by, with complete devotion, reciting the formula *Namu myōhō renge-kyō*, i.e. Veneration to the Sūtra of the Lotus of the Good Law. This school is highly nationalistic and, in the twentieth century, various schools of Buddhism, most notably, the *Nichiren-shōshū* School or *True School of Nichiren*, sprouted from it.

Buddhism entered Korea from China in the fourth century CE. It reached its peak between the sixth and ninth centuries CE, when the most influential schools were Chinese Zen Buddhism, Hua-yen, and esoteric Buddhism (*Mi-tsung* being its Chinese name and *Shingon* being its name in Japan). Korean Son Buddhism attempted to synthesize the teachings of *Kyo-hak* (the Doctrinal School of Buddhism) and *Son-ga* (the Meditation School of Buddhism). Son Buddhism held that enlightenment could be achieved without depending upon scriptural teachings, though these teachings provided a philosophical basis for the practice of Buddhism.

Tibetan Buddhism, also called *Lamaism* in Western writings, is a form of Mahāyāna Buddhism practiced in Tibet and neighboring countries. It combines monastic rules and cultic methods, and includes four main schools: *Nyingmapa*, whose main teaching was *dzogchen* (great perfection) or *ati-yoga* (extraordinary yoga), according to which purity of mind is always present and needs only to be recognized; *Sakyapa*, notable for its studies of logic; *Kagyupa*, which emphasizes direct teaching from master to disciple; and *Gelugpa*, the last of the four main schools to be established, which emphasizes the observance of monastic rules and detailed study of authoritative texts. This last school was the first to produce especially concise versions of the *siddhānta*, i.e. in Tibetan Buddhism, the compiled versions of established views formulated by Indian philosophical schools. Other, non-monastic, traditions in Tibetan Buddhism, e.g. *Chöd*, eventually merged with the main schools. Out of a need to overcome sectarian divisions among the schools, a current of thought called *rime* (meaning "unbiased") developed in the nineteenth century. Its influence lasts in the Nyingmapa School and in *Karma Kagyü*, a subdivision of the Kagyupa School. A significant work in Tibetan Buddhism is *The Bardo Tödrol Chenmo*, i.e. *The Great Liberation through Hearing in the Bardo*, a book its Western translator titled *The Tibetan Book of the Dead*. It contains instructions for liberation and is read by a *lama*, i.e. a priest, ideally the dying person's master, to the dying person. *Bardo* is the forty-nine day period between death and rebirth. It has four stages: the natural *bardo* or the onset of death; the painful *bardo* or actual death; the luminous *bardo* or period immediately following death; and the karmic *bardo* or the period in which karmic projections are active. The reading sometimes lasts for forty-nine days and its efficacy consists in leading the dying person to attain, in the luminous *bardo*, the calmness necessary to sense the identity between the luminosity of the person's mind and that of nirvana. The hope of liberation lies in recognizing this identity.

In CE 1390, Tsongkapa (CE 1357–1419) initiated a reform movement that restored celibacy and simple living, and opposed animism and tantric practices. It determined the course of Tibetan Buddhism for about five centuries, until the Chinese invasion of 1959 and the flight of the Dalai Lama to India.

See also: Chinese philosophy; Japanese philosophy; Korean philosophy; metaphysics; philosophy of religion

Further reading

Conze, Edward (1996) *Buddhist Thought in India: Three Phases of Buddhist Philosophy*, New Delhi: Munshiram Manoharlal.

Govinda, Anagarika (1937) *The Psychological Attitude of Early Buddhist Philosophy and Its Systematic Representation According to Abhidhamma Tradition*, Patna: The University.

Huntington, C.W. (1994) *The Emptiness of Emptiness: An Introduction to Early Indian Madhyamika*, Honolulu: University of Hawaii Press.

Lopez, Donald S. (1999) *Prisoners of Shangri-La: Tibetan Buddhism and the West*, Chicago, IL and Chichester: University of Chicago Press and Wiley.

Smith, F. Harold (1951) *The Buddhist Way of Life, Its Philosophy and History*, London: Hutchinson's University Library.

Williams, Paul (1996) *Mahayana Buddhism: The Doctrinal Foundations*, London: Routledge.

bundle theory *see* object

Buridan's ass *see* nominalism

Buridan's School *see* Paris School

bushido *see* Confucianism; Zen

business ethics *see* ethics

bypassing *see* philosophy, sociopolitical

C

C *see* A; logic

cabala From the Hebrew *qabbala*, or *cabbalah*, or *kabbalah*, meaning "the received," or "tradition." This term initially denoted the Prophets and Hagiographs as opposed to the Pentateuch. Then, by extension, it came to denote any emphasis on the spirit rather than the law, or on feeling rather than reason. It is now used to refer to a system of Jewish mysticism and, indeed, theosophy developed during the thirteenth and fourteenth centuries CE, and practiced well into the eighteenth century. The term also loosely refers to all forms of Jewish mysticism that seek to cultivate personal communion between the worshipper and God.

The cabalistic system includes at least nine doctrines. First, there is a doctrine of emanations that relates a transcendent God to the world. The transcendent God is called *Aor Pasot* (i.e. "the Most Simple Light" or "the Purest Light"), *Ayen Soph*, or *Ayin Soph*, or *Ain Soph*, or *En Soph*, meaning "the boundless or limitless," where the terms *Ayen* and *En* derive from *Ayin*, i.e. "nothing." It denotes a deity emanating and extending.

Second, there is the doctrine of the spheres, the *sefiroth*, which mediate between the transcendent and unitary God of rabbinical Judaism and the world of creation. Together, these spheres or emanations constitute the *aziluth* or aziluthic world. They represent God's being and appearance in the cosmos, include active and passive principles, and are akin to the Neoplatonic grades of wisdom. There are ten spheres or *sephiroths*, which are ordered in such a manner that the first contains the remaining nine, the second contains the remaining eight, and so on. They are:

1. *kether* (crown), also called the Supreme Crown, Crown of the Kingdom, and *Corona Summa*, i.e. the first emanation, the seat of the infinite where *Ain Soph*, the Cause of Causes, resides;
2. *chokma* or *hakemah* (wisdom);
3. *binah* (understanding), sometimes referred to as the Supernatural Mother, or as Ihvn Alhim, Jehova Elohim – Elohim being one of the names appearing in Genesis, translated as God or Lord in the Christian Bible, but meaning deities or deity as an aggregate of many infinite forces;
4. *chesed* (mercy), also called *gedulah* (magnanimity or benignity);
5. *gevurah* (austerity, rigor, or severity);
6. *tiphereth* (beauty);
7. *netzach* (victory);
8. *hod* (splendor or glory);
9. *yesod* (foundation or basis);
10. *malkuth* (the Kingdom, rule, reign, royalty, dominion, or power). As for *da'ath* (knowledge), it is the conjunction of chokma (wisdom) and binah (understanding).

The third doctrine is a doctrine of angels and demiurges that help God and humans communicate. The fourth is a doctrine of metempsychosis. The fifth is the doctrine of sin as a separation from the divinity, and perfection as the overcoming of this separation. Humans can help bring about such perfection through knowledge, piety, and observance of the law. Sixth, there is the doctrine of *Adam Kadmon* or *Adam Qadmon*, or *Tikkun*, a primordial human who was of both sexes and from whom all humans are supposed to derive. (As a primordial human, Adam was very different from Adam after his sin, whose size was reduced by God, who also confined Adam's life to the earth on account of Adam's sin.) The seventh doctrine is that each human is a microcosm of the macrocosm. The eighth is the doctrine that synergistic pairs or syzygies – right and left, light and darkness, purity and impurity, male and female – constitute everything and produce harmony in the universe. Finally, the ninth doctrine concerns the use of especially significant amulets, numbers, and letters, the casting of lots for divination, and the changing of one's name when ill or in penance.

Some of these doctrines are interconnected by means of the symbolic use of the *Aleph*, the first letter of the Hebrew alphabet. The Aleph stands for *En Soph*, the pure and boundless godhead. A cabalistic view is that the Aleph takes the shape of a human being pointing both to heaven and earth to indicate that the lower world maps and mirrors the higher. Also, a notion often used in explaining this cabalistic world is that of *nephesh* or breath of life. In Latin, the terms used for breath of life are *anima, mens, vita, appetites*. In Hebrew, the term is *nephesh*. This word is used loosely in the Bible. In the cabala, *nephesh* means the animal passions and the animal soul.

The chief Cabalistic writing is the *Zohar* (*The Book of Splendor*). Written in Aramaic, the *Zohar* is an allegorical commentary on the Pentateuch. It builds on previous Jewish mysticism and is believed to have been written by Moses ben Sheb Tob de León de Guadalajara in the thirteen century, though he attributes it to the second-century Rabbi Simon bar Yohai.

The modern cabala was developed by Isaac Luria (Arl) (CE 1534–72), who lived in Safed, Afghanistan, through graphic descriptions of creation, cosmic rupture, and restoration. He thought of this process in terms of *tzimzum* or *tsimtsum* (contradiction), *shevirat ha'keilin* (breaking of the vessels), and *tikkun* (restoration), a conception that anticipated the thesis–

antithesis–synthesis structure the German philosopher Georg Wilhelm Friedrich Hegel (CE 1770–1831) attributed to the development of human history (see DIALECTIC).

See also: dialectic; idealism; Jewish philosophy

Further reading
Cahn, Zvi (1962) *The Philosophy of Judaism: The Development of Jewish Thought Throughout the Ages, the Bible, the Talmud, the Jewish Philosophers, and the Cabala, until the Present Time*, New York: Macmillan.
Ordine, Nuccio (1996) *Giordano Bruno and the Philosophy of the Ass – Cabala dell'asino*, New Haven: Yale University Press.

cahuitl *see* Nahua philosophy

caitanya, cit *see* Hinduism

calculi of relations *see* logic; relation

calculus A system of symbols by means of which inferences can be made by manipulating its symbols in accordance with its rules. A calculus consists of three main components. The first is an artificial language, which is constituted at least by its *vocabulary* (i.e. symbols and definitions of the type of items they represent), and its *syntax* (i.e. the rules of grammar according to which the symbols can be combined in the calculus). If applied to a given domain of the universe, an artificial language, say, that of mathematics, also includes its *semantics*, i.e. rules of meaning or use for the symbols, say, for the use of differential calculus in physics. The second is rules of inference, sometimes accompanied by axioms (in an axiomatic system or calculus), other times without axioms (in a natural deduction system or calculus). The third is theorems, i.e. sentences that can be deduced in the calculus in accordance with its rules of inference.

Various kinds of calculi are distinguished. They include the following.

First, the *differential calculus*, i.e. a branch of mathematics that deals with the determination of such things as the tangent to a curve, the area between it and some fixed axis, the length of curved lines, and the calculation of volumes. Another name for this type of calculus is *fluxional calculus* – the *fluxion* being the rate of change of a variable quantity (the fluent) relative to time. This was the version of the differential calculus formulated by the English physicist and natural philosopher Sir Isaac Newton (CE 1642–1727), although it was independently developed by the German philosopher Gottfried Wilhelm Leibniz (CE 1646–1716).

Second, the *hedonic calculus*: see UTILITAR-IANISM.

Third, the *lambda-calculus*: see LOGIC.

Fourth, the *propositional calculus*: see LOGIC.

Fifth, the *sentential calculus*: see LOGIC.

Sixth, the *calculus of classes*: see LOGIC.

Seventh, the *calculus of individuals*: see METAPHYSICS (mereology).

Eighth, the *sequential calculus*: see LOGIC (cut-elimination theorem).

Ninth, the *calculus ratiocinator*, Leibniz's name for a formal system of reasoning about scientific facts that were to be recorded by means of a universal notation – *characteristica universalis* or universal characteristic – in developing his program for a *scientia universalis* or universal science. This is related to Leibniz's doctrine of infinite analysis: all concepts may be analyzed into their simple, primitive components via the conjunction or complementation of concepts, except that, in some cases, this analysis is not finite but, instead, converges on the primitive components without ever reaching them.

See also: philosophy of mathematics; set

Further reading
Bernays, Paul (1936) *Logical Calculus*, Princeton, NJ: Institute for Advanced Study.
Boole, George (1951) *The Mathematical Analysis of Logic; Being an Essay Towards a Calculus of Deductive Reasoning*, Oxford: B. Blackwell.

calemes *see* syllogism

Cambridge change *see* change

Cambridge Platonists *see* Cambridge School

Cambridge property *see* change

Cambridge School The name of two different groups. The first denotes a group of philosophers and theologians who flourished at Cambridge University during the seventeenth cen-

tury. They advocated nativism and PLATONISM as modified by the philosopher Augustine, born in the African city of Thagaste (CE 354–430), according to whom our intellectual knowledge is a highly reliable form of illumination we attain through the *lumen naturale* (natural light) or, as it is also called, *lumen naturae*, *lumen connaturale*, or *lumen naturalis rationis*, i.e. the natural light of reason or, for short, the light of reason. In fact, the English empiricist philosopher John Locke (CE 1632–1704) partly addressed his *Essay* against them. Also called the Cambridge Platonists, they included: Nathanael Culverwel (*c*. CE 1618–51), writer of *Discourse of the Light of Nature*; Richard Cumberland (CE 1631–1718), writer of *De legibus nature disquisitio philosophica*; John Smith (*c*. CE 1616–52), writer of *Select Discourses*; Edward Stillingfleet (CE 1635–99), writer of *Origines sacrae*; Benjamin Whichcote (CE 1609–83), writer of *Sermons and Aphorisms*; Henry More (CE 1614–87), writer of *An Explanation of the Grand Mystery of Godliness, Divine Dialogues*, and *Enchiridiom metaphysicum, enchiridiom ethicum*; and, above all, Ralph Cudworth (CE 1617–88), writer of *The True Intellectual System of the Universe* and *A Treatise Concerning Eternal and Immutable Morality*. Cudworth is of significance to later discussions of mechanicism and vitalism in that he argued that to interconnect the spiritual and material orders, one needed to use the notion of a *plastic nature*: an organic principle analogous to the Platonic world-soul, i.e. a self-moved principle of animation in all worldly things.

Also significant is John Smith's study of the interconnections between innate ideas and moral goodness. He thought the development of moral goodness was identical with the attainment of knowledge through spiritual sensations. As for Henry More, he initially favored, but later opposed, Cartesianism, and attempted to reject Cartesian dualism by arguing that spirit is characterized not just by thought but also by extension, and is the sole agent of motion and action, while matter is inert. He used the term *spissitude* to denote the feature of spirit whereby it produces motion or action.

Beyond their uncompromising *innatism* or

nativism, the view that faculties and ideas are present in the human mind since birth, no two of these philosophers shared exactly the same detailed views. However, details apart, they all believed in God's existence; the existence, dignity, and immortality of the human soul; human free will; the primacy of reason; and in the existence of a spiritual entity activating the world of nature. Their views were largely Neoplatonic. Their concerns were primarily religious and theological: Their use of philosophical doctrines was eclectic and aimed at defending Anglican Christianity against such things as Calvinism and its doctrine of predestination, strait-laced Puritanism, the intolerance and fanaticism that followed the Restoration, atheism, and the mechanistic and materialist trends in seventeenth-century science and philosophy that undermined Anglican Christianity.

Second, the name Cambridge School has also been used to refer to the twentieth-century Cambridge Analytic School. (See ANALYSIS.)

See also: Neoplatonism; philosophy of religion; Platonism

Further reading
Colie, Rosalie Littell (1987) *Light and Enlightenment: A Study of the Cambridge Platonists and the Dutch Arminians*, Cambridge, UK: Cambridge University Press.
Rogers, G.A.J., Vienne, Jean-Michel, and Zarka, Yves Charles (1997) *The Cambridge Platonists in Philosophical Context: Politics, Metaphysics, and Religion*, Dordrecht and Boston: Kluwer Academic Publishers.

camera obscura *see* perception

camestres *see* syllogism

canon A Latin term meaning "measuring line," "rule," or "model," derived from the Greek *kanon*, which meant "rule," or "rod." It has been used in philosophy in various senses.

According to the doxographer Diogenes Laertius (*c.* CE 200) and the Greek philosopher Epicurus (341–270 BCE), philosophy is divided into three parts: canonical, physical, and ethical. The canonical part was an introduction to philosophy and was included in a work of Epicurus, *The Canon*, which apparently dealt mainly with matters concerning knowledge and its kinds.

According to the German philosopher Carl Prantl (CE 1820–88), the Byzantine philosopher Michael Psellos (CE 1018–78) used the term "canons" in his *Synopsis of Aristotle's Organon* to designate four rules concerning the equivalence of categorical propositions.

In Chapter II of the *Critique of Pure Reason*'s "Transcendental Methodology," the German philosopher Immanuel Kant (CE 1724–1804) used the term "canon" to designate the a priori principles ruling certain faculties of understanding, e.g. formal logic is a canon ruling the faculties of understanding and reason.

In his *Logic*, the English philosopher John Stuart Mill (CE 1773–1836) proposed various methods of empirical investigation, each one of which is ruled by a canon or regulating principle that formulates the conditions for drawing causal inferences by using the respective method.

In their *The Meaning of Meaning*, the authors Charles Kay Ogden (CE 1889–1957) and Ivor Armstrong Richards (CE 1893–1979) used the term "canon" to designate rules regulating the relations between symbols and their referents.

In late twentieth-century discussions of philosophy and, in general, the humanities, the term "canon" has often been used in its initially religious sense that designates those writings regarded as authoritative: the classics.

In this regard, *classicism* denotes the classical style, or adherence to the principles of art and literature established in Ancient Greece and Rome, and developed in later periods, for example the Renaissance. By extension, classicism also applies to adherence to those principles in the literature of the humanities. Among the features present in classicism are balanced composition and a naturalistic emphasis. By contrast, *romanticism* denotes a reaction against those principles for the sake of individual idealism and emotive expression and attachment, especially in love. A notable romantic movement in Germany was *Sturm und Drang*, i.e. Storm and Stress. It opposed Enlightenment principles and included the philosopher Johann Gottfried von Herder (CE 1744–1803), the poet and philosopher Johan Wolfgang Goethe (CE 1749–1832), and the poet, dramatist, and philosopher Friedrich Schiller (CE 1759–1805).

See also: philosophy

Further reading
Bloom, Harold (1996 [1994]) *The Western Canon: The Books and School of the Ages*, London: Papermac.
Diogenes Laertius (1992) *The Life and Teachings of Epicurus: Book X of the Lives and Opinions of the Famous Philosophers of Diogenes Laertius: To which are Appended the Vatican Sayings and Pertinent Selections from Plato and from Aristotle*, Montreal: Queen-Read.
Herder, Johann Gottfried von (1967 [1800]) *Outlines of a Philosophy of the History of Man*, London: printed for J. Johnson, by Luke Hansard.
Kant, Immanuel (1965) *Critique of Pure Reason*, New York and Toronto: St Martin's and Macmillan.
Mill, John Stuart (1996 [1973]) *A System of Logic, Ratiocinative and Inductive: Being a Connected View of the Principles of Evidence, and the Methods of Scientific Investigation*, London: Routledge.
Ogden, C.K. and Richards, I.A. (1938) *The Meaning of Meaning: A Study of the Influence of Language upon Thought and of the Science of Symbolism*, London, K. Paul, Trench, Trubner & Co., Ltd.
Prantl, Carl (1927) *Geschichte der Logik im Abendlande*, Leipzig: Gustav Fock.

Cantor's paradox *see* set

Cantor's theorem *see* infinity

capacity *see* alethiology; determinism

Capadocians *see* Christianity

capital punishment *see* philosophy of law

capitalism The economic system that emphasizes the role of private ownership of capital and land, and the predominance of the profit motive in guiding market developments. The Classical School of capitalism advocated the free play of a self-regulating market where, given competition, prices would be regulated and labor and capital would shift from less to more profitable activities. This tradition traces back to the Scottish economist and philosopher Adam Smith (CE 1723–90). His first published work, *The Theory of Moral Sentiments* (1759),

was a major contribution to ethics and moral psychology. His work on economics, *An Inquiry into the Nature and Causes of the Wealth of Nations* (1776) – where wealth is understood in wide economic terms as anything that has value in money, exchange, or use – presupposes the work on the ethics of character formulated in his first book. Adam Smith's views have been overly simplified by some interpreters. His position on human motivation, for example, conflicted with the notion held by some twentieth-century economists that, in economic exchanges, we are not tuists. Smith acknowledged this feature of economic exchanges, but held that such exchanges also require co-operation, not merely competition.

The term *laissez-faire* – also *laisser faire* – meaning "let do" or "let make," originated with the *Physiocratic* School that, among other things, was opposed to almost all feudal, mercantilist, or governmental restrictions. Eventually, the term laissez-faire became attached to "capitalism" in the phrase laissez-faire capitalism to mean that economic interests are to be freed from government control and only minimally regulated. Adam Smith clearly advocated personal economic freedom; but he was not a radical individualist because, for him, economic liberty was tied to the rule of law and social order. Indeed, he went beyond the rule of law and merely social order, and tried to show how virtue and liberty, including economic liberty, complement each other in the development of a sound social order. The main critic of capitalism was the German philosopher Karl Marx (CE 1818–83), whose work originated the school of thought and social movement called MARXISM.

See also: decision; Marxism; philosophy, socio-political

Further reading
Oser, Jacob (1963) *The Evolution of Economic Thought*, New York: Harcourt, Brace & World.
Werhane, Patricia H. (1991) *Adam Smith and His Legacy for Modern Capitalism*, Oxford and New York: Oxford University Press.

cardinal *see* decision; virtue

cardinality *see* set

care *see* existentialism

Cartesian circle *see* Cartesianism

Cartesian co-ordinates *see* Cartesianism

Cartesian demon *see* Cartesianism

Cartesian dualism *see* Cartesianism

Cartesian interactionism *see* Cartesianism

Cartesian product *see* set

Cartesianism Term derived from the name of the French philosopher, mathematician, and physicist Renatus Cartesius, the Latinized form of the name René Descartes (CE 1596–1650). It denotes all philosophies that adhered to or further developed some of the basic philosophical doctrines or methods formulated by Descartes. Accordingly, besides including the thought of Descartes, Cartesianism includes, in the first place, the thought of the French philosopher Father Marin Mersenne (CE 1588–1648) and the Mersenne Circle, which conceived of Descartes's mechanicism as a way of attacking atheism. Second, many Jansenists advocated Cartesian views, especially the Oratorians, who understood Cartesianism to be a renewed form of Agustinianism, and whose approach led to the occasionalism of the French philosopher Nicolas Malebranche (CE 1638–1715). Third, the logic of Port Royal was significantly Cartesian. Fourth, the Occasionalists and, to some extent, the Amsterdam-born philosopher of Spanish and Portuguese descent Baruch Spinoza (CE 1632–77) were also influenced by Descartes's thought. At the end of the seventeenth century, the French philosopher Sylvain Régis (CE 1632–1707) defended Cartesianism. Also, the work of the British philosophers Thomas Hobbes (CE 1588–1679) and John Locke (CE 1632–1704), and the German philosopher Gottfried Wilhelm Leibniz (CE 1646–1716) were crucially influenced by Descartes's thought. Finally, Descartes's work became widely known in the Netherlands with Hereboord, Lambert Welthuysen, Heidanus, Volder, Tobie André, and Ruardus Andala; in England with Antoine LeGrand; in Germany with Johann Clauberg; and in Italy with Michele Angelo Fardella (CE 1650–1718) and Giacinto Sigismondo Gerdil (CE 1718–1802). In general, Cartesianism is

any modern philosophy that emphasizes the accessibility of reality to the thinking subject, precision in metaphysics, and the ultimate nature of the dualism of *res cogitans*, i.e. *thought*, and *res extensa*, i.e. *extension*. The conjunction of such dualism with the doctrine of two-way psychophysical causal interaction is called *Cartesian interactionism*.

Descartes lived in the midst of a *scientific revolution*, the period of radical scientific change that spanned the sixteenth and seventeenth centuries. He was a contemporary of the English physician William Harvey (CE 1578–1657), who provided a new understanding of blood circulation and of the heart as a pump; and wrote after the Italian astronomer and natural philosopher Galileo Galilei (CE 1564–1642), whose work on projectiles and falling bodies was already known. Also known was the work of the German astronomer Johannes Kepler (CE 1571–1630) on the movement and dynamics of the planets in the solar system. However, neither the work of the English physicist and natural philosopher Isaac Newton (CE 1642–1727) on the mechanics of terrestrial and celestial bodies, nor the work of the English natural philosopher Robert Boyle (CE 1627–91) on gases had yet appeared.

As stated, Descartes was a scientist as well as a philosopher. He formulated the notion of *Cartesian co-ordinates*, the concept of *imaginary numbers*, and *analytic geometry*, which was crucial for the development of infinitesimal calculus. He also formulated the *laws of optics*, which were independently arrived at by the French mathematician Pierre de Fermat (CE 1601–65). In physics, he partly formulated the *vortex theory*, but died before finishing his work. Newtonian mechanics was soon to become the paradigm for physics during the next three centuries or so. However, it is of interest to notice that the vortex theory had some similarities to the type of relativity theory that superseded Newtonian mechanics in the twentieth century.

Descartes's wider aim was to provide a firm and permanent basis for science, so that the collapse of theories characteristic of scientific revolutions could be avoided. He emphasized the unity of knowledge, the usefulness of philosophy for everyday life, and *foundationalism*:

the view that knowledge must be constructed from the bottom up and that nothing can be accepted until it has been based on first principles. His way of searching for these principles is the *method of universal and systematic doubt*. It is called universal, because, in the search for what is indubitable in the sense of being beyond the possibility of doubt, it attempts to doubt every opinion. It is called systematic, because it attempts to doubt opinions, not one by one, but kind by kind, where the kinds are characterized by the sources of opinion: sense-perception, memory, and reflection. One way of interpreting Descartes's approach has been to say that he offers three arguments, the argument from illusion, the dream argument, and the demon hypotheses, all of which point to a general kind of argument: In believing anything on the basis of sense-perceptions, memories, or judgments about universals, e.g. numbers and figures, I could be mistaken. If so, for the purpose of building science on a firm foundation, I should not trust any such sources of belief and should treat all beliefs thus based as if they were false. Hence, for the purpose of building science on a firm foundation, I should not trust any such sources of belief and should treat all beliefs thus based as if they were false. That is, these considerations did not support the falsity of such beliefs, but only the suspension of judgment concerning the content and sources of those beliefs. After discarding all such opinions as incapable of constituting a firm and permanent basis for knowledge, he came to believe that he could not doubt his own existence, which he formulated in his phrase: *cogito, ergo sum* (I think, I exist), which, as the French philosopher Marin Mersenne (CE 1588–1648) reminded him and Descartes later stated, was very much like the phrase formulated by the philosopher Augustine (CE 354–430, born in the African city of Thagaste) in *De civitate Dei*, i.e. *The City of God* (XI, 26): *si enim fallor sum*, i.e. "if I deceive myself, I exist."

Descartes also found that he could not doubt that he was a thinking thing, and proceeded to develop an inventory of ideas, which he considered innate (mainly those of mathematics). He argued they were implanted in our minds by God, hence were reliable as the basic building blocks of science. This led to the *Cartesian circle*: If the reliability of our innate ideas depends on our knowledge of God, then how can we establish this knowledge? If it follows from some of those ideas, then why are we entitled to rely on them at this stage? Descartes seems to have argued that some ideas – which he called *naturae simplices* (simple natures) – are so *simple, clear, and distinct*, that we can rely on them without any divine guarantee. Indeed, he argues that we can find truth and avoid error when reason proceeds with care, and we adhere to the following doctrine: *idealiter in intellectu*, i.e. the objective is that which is present in thought, while *formaliter in se ipsius*, i.e. the subjective is that which is in the things themselves. In adhering to this principle, Descartes followed a long-standing philosophical tradition characterized by skepticism about evidence of the senses, reliance on abstract perceptions of the intellect, and the belief that intellectual knowledge is a kind of illumination or intellectual intuition derived from a source higher than the human mind, to which Descartes often refers by means of the expression *lumen naturale* (natural light) or, as it is also called, *lumen naturae, lumen connaturale*, or *lumen naturalis rationis*, i.e. the natural light of reason or, for short, the light of reason. This emphasis on clear and distinct ideas and intuition was thoroughly adopted by Spinoza. Beginning with clear and distinct ideas that are self-evident, i.e. warrant their own truth, one aims at unfolding reality by deducing consequences from them. This leads to transcending one's own individual limitations and to living *sub specie aeternitatis*, i.e. under the aspect of eternity, by means of the *scientia intuitiva*, which helps one sense the eternal and universal in all the particulars around, thus making immortality a quality of one's life.

See also: dualism; enlightenment; justification; philosophy of mind; rationalism

Further reading
Doney, Willis (1987) *Eternal Truths and the Cartesian Circle: A Collection of Studies*, New York: Garland.
Nadler, Steven M. (1993) *Causation in Early Modern Philosophy: Cartesianism, Occasionalism, and Preestablished Harmony*, Uni-

versity Park, PA: Pennsylvania State University Press.

Smith, Norman Kemp (1902) *Studies in the Cartesian Philosophy*, London and New York: Macmillan & Co., Limited.

Wilson, Robert A. (1997 [1995]) *Cartesian Psychology and Physical Minds: Individualism and the Sciences of the Mind*, Cambridge and New York: Cambridge University Press.

cārvāka The Indian materialistic schools, both known as *cārvāka* and *lokāyata*, can be traced to the *Rgveda*. Its main development took place in 600 BCE, in the no longer extant *Brhaspati Sutra*. Its various schools share the view that mind is merely the body and its capacities. However, they differ concerning the nature of mental properties. Some hold the doctrine of reductive materialism: all mental properties are physical properties described psychologically. Others advocate emergentism: there are mental properties that, though caused by physical properties, are irreducible to physical properties. In addition, emergentist schools also advocate epiphenomenalism: emergent irreducible mental properties have no causal influence. Critics have argued that all Indian materialistic schools accept sense-perception as the only *pramāṇa* or valid means of knowledge. Yet, some of these schools make room for inference as a valid source of knowledge, at least so far as the conclusions are about items that can be checked through sense-perception. This position is not unlike that of twentieth-century logical positivism (see EMPIRICISM).

Related positions held by some *cārvāka* schools are: to exist is to be perceivable; intelligence is only a certain bodily disposition and soul is only the body in so far as it is intelligent; universal ideas and relations can be understood only through perceptual connections reinforced by memory, which weakens the power of inference; causal connections can be understood only perceptually, and this makes them questionable, because we may perceive two items – say, the two horns of a cow – successively, yet one is not the cause of the other; the existence or non-existence of anything is never certain; all humans aim at pleasure and the avoidance of pain.

See also: Hinduism; holism; philosophy of mind

Further reading
Chattopadhyaya, Debiprasad (1985) *Lokayata, A Study in Ancient Indian Materialism*, New Delhi: People's.

Shastri, Dakshinaranjan (1930) *A Short History of Indian Materialism, Sensationalism and Hedonism*, Calcutta: Book Company.

case *see* ethics

caste From the Latin *castus*, i.e. "pure" or "pious," developed the Spanish and Portuguese term, *casta*, from which caste derives. The term *casta* acquired currency in the Spanish Indies during their maturity period that, in the capital regions and trunk lines, is placed approximately between CE 1580 and 1750, though in more isolated areas developed later and lasted longer. During that period, *casta* began to be used with some frequency to refer to the various groups that had began to develop as a result of social changes which, in part, had been produced by exogamous practices between people of Spanish, Amerindian, and African origin: mestizos – persons of mixed Spanish and Amerindian origin, mulattoes – persons of mixed Spanish and African origin, and Africans. That is, *casta* then referred to everyone not considered a Spaniard or an Indian. In late colonial times, the mixed groupings – mestizos and mulattoes – had grown in numbers and variety, and some subcategories – e.g. zambo for persons who were of mixed Amerindian and African origin – began to be used in some regions.

In social studies, the term caste has been applied to many human and non-human social institutions with meanings that often significantly differ from that of *casta*. Entomologists use it to describe functionally and anatomically different groups – e.g. workers and soldiers – belonging to species of insects such as ants and bees. Social scientists have used the term caste in describing a wide range of societies and, indeed, of social stratification systems. Some have restricted the use of caste to the stratification system influenced by Hinduism in India. Others have used caste in a more general sense, but still to denote groups with three features: endogamy (i.e. compulsory marriage within groups), group membership by birth and for life, and hierarchic ranking of the groups. In India, however, the term caste has been used indiscriminately to denote two very different sets of groups: *varna* and *jati*. There are four *varnas*: *brahmins* (the teachers), *kshatriyas* (the warriors), *vaishyas* (the merchants), and *sudras* (the native untouchable or Dravidians). Each of these is subdivided into many *jati* (birth group or family). The first three *varnas* were called twice born, because they had been born naturally and, then, they had studied the *Vedas*.

The operant groups from the standpoint of stratification appear to be the *jati*, though most Hindu scriptures refer to *varnas*. Hence, the use of caste to refer to both *varna* and *jati* has been criticized as a source of confusion. In addition, it has been suggested that, besides being applied only to *jati* in India, the term caste be used only for rigid, stratified, and endogamous groups when an entire society such as India and, perhaps, South Africa until CE 1994, is divided into such groups. This would permit to describe the *Eta* or *Burakumin* of Japan, or the blacksmiths and praise-singers of some African societies, as pariahs, without thereby implying that their societies are entirely stratified on the basis of castes.

See also: culture; Hinduism; myth

Further reading
Dumont, Louis (1970) *Homo Hierarchicus: An essay on the Caste System*, London: Weidenfeld & Nicolson.
Lockhart, James and Schwartz, Stuart B. (1983) *Early Latin America*, Cambridge, UK and New York: Cambridge University Press. Chapters 5 and 9.
Van den Berghe, Pierre L. (1987 [1981]) *The Ethnic Phenomenon*, New York and London: Praeger.

casuistics *see* applied; ethics

casuistry *see* applied; ethics

catalepsies *see* Stoicism

categorematic *see* syncategoremata

categorematica *see* syncategoremata

categorical A term typically used in such technical phrases as:

1 *categorical grammar*: see PHILOSOPHY OF LANGUAGE;
2 *categorical imperative*: see KANTIAN PHILOSOPHY;
3 *categorical syllogism*: see SYLLOGISM;
4 *categorical theory*: see CATEGORICITY.

Here, we will concentrate on the use of categorical in the expressions categorical statement, categorical proposition, and categorical judgment. The expression *categorical statement* denotes any statements according to which all or some of the members of one class are partially or totally included in, or excluded from, another class. Thus, "Some Italians are young individuals" is a categorical statement meaning that members of one class – that of Italians – are partially included in another class – that of young individuals. This statement is of the form Some *S* are *P*. It is called *particular*, because it is about some members of the class *S*, and AFFIRMATIVE, because it affirms that they belong in the class *P*. It is traditionally designated with the capital letter I. By contrast, "Some Italians are not wealthy" has the form Some *S* are not *P*. This is the form of a categorical and particular, but *negative*, statement, because it asserts that some members of the class *S* are excluded from the class *P*. It is traditionally designated with the capital letter O. Categorical statements can also be *universal*. For example, "All Italians are Europeans" is a universal affirmative statement (traditionally designated with the capital letter *A*), while "No Italians are Tibetans" is a universal negative statement (traditionally designated with the capital letter *E*).

The expression *categorical proposition* is sometimes used in modern logic instead of categorical statement. Also, following Kant, instead of talking of statements, the term categorical is often applied to *judgments* that simply assert or deny a predicate of a subject. In addition, modern logic uses the term categorical in still other senses, for example to describe logical systems (see CATEGORICITY).

See also: logic; syllogism

Further reading
Churchill, Robert P. (1986) *Becoming Logical*, New York: St Martin's Press.
Copi, Irving M. and Cohen, Carl (1994)

Introduction to Logic, New York: Macmillan.

categoricity Term attributed to the United States philosopher John Dewey (CE 1859–1952) denoting a concept that traces back to the German mathematician Julius William Richard Dedekind (CE 1831–1916). It denotes the semantic property of a set of sentences called postulate set, which completely characterizes the structure of its intended interpretation. An example of a set of sentences having such semantic property is the set of postulates for number theory attributed to the Italian mathematician and logician Giuseppe Peano (CE 1858–1932). This set completely characterizes the structure of an arithmetic progression. An example of this structure is the set of natural numbers characterized on the basis of zero as its starting element and the indefinite application of the successor (addition of one) function. Other examples result from selecting an arbitrary integer as its starting element and the indefinite application of a function that consists in adding an arbitrary positive or negative integer.

In a more strictly technical sense, a set of sentences is CATEGORICAL – i.e. is characterized by categoricity – if every two of its interpretations (also called "models" or "realizations") are mutually isomorphic, that is if there exists a one-to-one correspondence between their respective universes of discourse, whereby all such things as the elements, functions, and relations of one universe are exactly mapped onto those of the other. In this connection, a categorical theory is a theory all of whose models are isomorphic. In first-order logic with identity, only theories with a finite model can be categorical; without identity, none can. There are countable discrete orders, not isomorphic to the natural numbers, that have elementary equivalence, i.e. have the same elementary, first-order logic.

See also: completeness; model

Further reading
Makkai, Michael (1989) *Accessible Categories: The Foundations of Categorical Model Theory*, Providence: Ams.
Russell, Bertrand (1993 [1919]) *Introduction to Mathematical Philosophy*, New York: Dover Publications.

categories *see* Kantian philosophy

category From the Greek *kategoria*. Before the Greek philosopher Aristotle (CE 384–22), *kategoria* and related terms had non-philosophical meanings. Quite frequently, *kategoria* meant "accusation" and was the opposite of *apologia*, i.e. defense or praise. Aristotle most frequently used the term meaning predication or attribution, and used it to denote those ultimate terms on the basis of which everything else could be classified. The idea here is that if a set of categories is complete, then each item in the universe will belong to a category. Aristotle listed different sets of categories in different works. In *Categories*, IV, 1b, he listed ten: substance, quantity, quality, relation, place, time, position, condition, action, and passion. In *Topics*, IX, 103b, 23, he also mentions ten; but, instead of substance (*ousia*), he includes what is (*ti esti*). Also, in *Physics* V, 225b, 5–9, he lists eight: position and condition are not mentioned. At any rate, the first set of ten categories was called *praedicamenta* by medieval philosophers. In *Categories* X, Aristotle begins the discussion of the *postpraedicamenta* (in English, postpredicaments), covering opposition, contrariety, priority, simultaneity, movement, and possession. It is here important to mention that some terms or concepts, e.g. being, apply to everything regardless of categories. Any such concept is called a *transcendental* (pl. transcendentals or, in Latin, *transcendentalia*), and the term designating it is called a transcendental term. Besides being, other transcendentals are one or unity, true or TRUTH, good or goodness, and also, according to some medieval philosophers, beautiful or beauty, and thing or something.

The French philosopher Gilbert of Poitiers or Gilbertus Porretanus (CE 1076–1154) divided Aristotle's categories into two groups: primary and secondary. The former included substance and its modes: quantity, QUALITY, and RELATION; the latter – which were thought only adjacent to substances and not, as the primary ones, inherent in them – included time, place, situation, condition, action, and passion.

Other philosophers referred to categories in different senses and claimed to have found a variety of them. The French philosopher René Descartes (CE 1596–1650), for example, divided the universe into mind and matter. The German philosopher Immanuel Kant (CE 1724–1804) characterized twelve categories that constituted an exhaustive classification of judgments. There were four basic divisions – quantity, quality, relation, and modality – each including three categories. The German philosopher Georg Wilhelm Friedrich Hegel (CE 1770–1831) conceived of categories as ideas that serve to explain reality, and claimed there were more than 270 of them.

The English philosopher Alfred North Whitehead (CE 1861–1947) conceived of categories in much the same way, but found only thirty-seven, notable among which was that of eternal objects, which characterize actual occasions and play the role of universals in philosophies that consider universals to be real. Examples of these geometric entities and relationships fall under the *objective species* subcategory, while colors, emotions, pains, and pleasures fall under the *subjective species* subcategory.

The United States philosopher Charles Sanders Peirce (CE 1839–1914) thought of categories in two ways: as the most general ways of classifying experiences, and as the most general ways of subdividing logic. Either way, he claimed there were three categories: quality or firstness – a first-order attribute, relation or secondness – a two-term relation, and representation or thirdness – a three-term relation.

The English philosopher Bertrand Russell (CE 1872–1970) advanced his theory of types instead of the more traditional theories of categories, while the English philosopher Gilbert Ryle (CE 1900–76) conceived of categories as word-types and applied this conception to a characterization of a *category mistake*: the placing of an item in the wrong category, because of some misunderstanding concerning the nature of this entity. For example, upon seeing a university's campus buildings, one may ask: "Which one is the university?", mistakenly implying that the university is one of the buildings that, at best, can be its embodiment or part of its concrete existence.

The term category also appears in the expression *category theory*, which denotes a branch of mathematics that studies the universal properties of structures through their mutual relations. In general, categories are used to classify items in the process of explaining or justifying them. Any classification in such explanatory or justificatory context is called a *taxonomy* or *typology*.

See also: definition; theory of types

Further reading
Edel, Abraham (1950) *Interpretation and the Selection of Categories*, Berkeley: University of California Press.
Rijk, Lambertus Marie de (1952) *The Place of the Categories of Being in Aristotle's Philosophy*, Assen: Van Gorcum.

catharsis *see* aesthetics; philosophy of literature

Catholicism *see* Christianity; creation; determinism; philosophy of religion

catvāriārya-satyāni *see* Buddhism

causa *see* causal law

causal chain *see* causal law

causal-decision theory *see* decision

causal-historical theory of reference *see* philosophy of language

causal immediacy *see* knowledge; philosophy of religion

causal law A regular and invariant connection between one kind of events or states – called causes – and another kind – called effects. For example, the statement "whenever water is heated up to 100 degrees centigrade at one atmosphere of pressure, it boils" formulates a very low-level causal law. While the statement "the water in this kettle boiled because I heated it up to 100 degrees centigrade at one atmosphere of pressure" is a causal statement about particulars; but, though it relies on the previously formulated law, it does not itself formulate a causal law, because it is about particular events, not about kinds of events. Sometimes, a causal law is conceived in accordance with the law of succession, i.e. as connecting events or states that occur at different times, e.g. taking an aspirin causes headaches to disappear in a few minutes. Other times, a causal law is conceived in accordance with the law of coexistence, i.e. as connecting events that occur at the same time, e.g. the gravitational pull of the Moon at noon causes the tide to reach its noon level.

A series of events related as causes to effects is a *causal chain*. A *wayward* causal chain or deviant causal chain is a causal chain used in analyzing a key concept – e.g. reference, action, explanation, artwork – that fails to do the analytic job expected of it. Some causal chains go wrong because the prescribed causal route does not lead to the sought event. Others go wrong because the event does not follow from the prescribed causal chains.

Causal laws contrast with *probabilistic* or *statistical* laws. For causal laws do, while probabilistic or statistical laws do not, denote an invariant connection between kinds of events or states. For example, the laws of classical mechanics are thought to be causal laws in this sense: given the state of a mechanical system at a given time, the laws yield a unique state of the system at any other time. While the laws of quantum mechanics are thought to be probabilistic, i.e. given the state of a system at a given time, they yield only a probability for the occurrence of a state of the system at another time.

The analysis just described is called *regularity analysis* and is associated with the regularity theory of causation. It works well whenever causal relations can be said clearly to involve general laws. Indeed, it is mutually complementary with the covering-law model of explanation (see EXPLANATION). However, it does not serve to account for causal relations between events – that a given storm was caused by the El Niño effect in the Pacific – when we know no general law connecting these events – when we know no law invariably connecting the El Niño effect to specific storms in specific areas. In addition, not all regularities seem to account for causal connections. For example, it is a true generalization, though arguably not one based on a causal law, that no one from the State of Washington has been President of the United States. It is to account for these difficulties that people for-

mulate the counterfactual analysis of causation, according to which what makes an event the cause of another is the fact that, if the *cause* had not occurred, then the other event, its *effect*, would not have occurred. However, problems here arise concerning how to distinguish between causal counterfactuals and noncausal counterfactuals (see CONDITION).

The notion of a causal law is also contrasted with that of a *teleological law*, i.e. a law stating how systems of a certain kind – especially biological organisms – behave so as to attain certain aims. Any of these aims is called a final cause (see backward causation, below).

Sometimes people use the expression *the causal law* meaning the doctrine that every event or state has a cause.

The term cause derives from the Latin *causa*, a term often used in philosophy in the following phrases.

First, *causa cognoscendi*, the cause of our knowledge of something.

Second, *causa essendi*, the cause of that something being what it is.

Third, *causa immanens*, a change produced in something by its own activity.

Fourth, *causa transiens*, a change produced in something by something else.

Fifth, *causa sui*, cause of itself, an expression used by the Amsterdam-born philosopher of Spanish and Portuguese descent Baruch Spinoza (CE 1632–77) (who also used *causa immanens*) to describe God, meaning in part that God owes his existence to nothing but Himself, because God's nature requires that He exist. Spinoza did not use this expression to mean that God brought himself into existence.

Sixth, *vera causa*, true cause, an expression used by the English physicist and natural philosopher Isaac Newton (CE 1642–1727) to denote natural causes that sufficiently explain things.

As for the relation between causes and effects, it is called causation, and is thought to be of different kinds. Some notable ones are as follows.

First, *agent causation*: the action of an agent (a person or object typically understood as substances) in bringing about a change. This is sometimes understood as a kind of event causation – i.e. the causation of one event by another, even if both are immanent to a substance, thereby constituting immanent causation. However, there are those who hold that actions are not events, in which case agent causation and event causation exclude each other. Medieval philosophers distinguished *immanent causation*, i.e. the internal activity of the agent in agent causation, from *transeunt causation*, i.e. the external event produced by that activity.

Second, *backward causation*: the notion that some causes begin to happen after their effects begin to happen, as in the notion of a final cause, i.e. the end for which something happens or towards which something aims. Backward causation should not be confused with the notion of *concurrent causation*, according to which a cause can be simultaneous with its effect – the gravitational attraction of the Moon at a given time and the level of the tides at that time. Nor should either one of these be confused with the notion of *efficient causation*, or *efficient cause*, where the cause begins to happen before its effect begins to happen. The Greek philosopher Aristotle (384–22 BCE) was the first one to distinguish clearly between efficient and final causes. He also characterized *material cause* and *formal cause* as the constituents – matter (*hyle*) and form (*eidos*) – within a substance.

Third, *substantival causation*: the (rather controversial) creation of a radically new substance, not merely the causing of changes in, or rearrangements among, previously existing substances.

Fourth, *causal overdetermination*: the notion that an effect – say, a building's collapse – may be the result of more than one cause – e.g. a bomb and a furnace exploding at the same time. People have argued, however, that these events would have been different had they occurred alone rather than together.

Fifth, *mnemic causation*: the type of causation whereby, in order to explain an organism's behavior, one must specify not only the present state of the organism and the stimuli affecting it, but also the organism's past experiences.

Sixth, *pre-emptive* or *superseding causation*: the notion that an event – say, the furnace's explosion – caused an event a split second before another event – the bomb's explosion –

that would have led to the same result. This notion has often been used in discussions of moral and legal responsibility.

Seventh, *probabilistic causation*: the notion involving the probabilistic law that an event *x* is the probabilistic cause of another event *y*, whenever the probability of *y* increases with the occurrence of *x*. This notion has recently attracted philosophers' interest, but it needs reformulation to rule out the possibility that *x* and *y* are common effects of one cause.

The study of causality, especially of that concerning specific phenomena, is called *etiology* (from the Greek *aitia*, i.e. "cause," and *logos*, i.e. "theory of"), as in, for example, "the etiology of disease."

In Eastern thought, Indian philosophizing has produced a rich variety of causal notions. The term *karana* means "the best cause," "reason," or "origin"; while the term *kārana* means instrument or instrumental cause. There are various types of *kāranas*. *Sādhārana-kāranas* are common causes; *asādhārana-kāranas* are specific causes; *nimittk-kārana* is the efficient cause; *samavāyi-kārana* (also called *upādāna-kārana*) is the material cause; *asamavāyi-kārana* is what produces an effect through the material cause. As for the effect, it is denoted by the term *kārya*; the cause and effect relation is denoted by *kārya-kārana-bhāva*. In Indian philosophy, all but one school hold that all effects have two sets of causes, the material and the efficient cause. The Nyāya-Vaiśeṣika, School, however, holds that, besides the efficient cause and instead of the material cause, there are two causes: the *smavāyi-kārana*, which is a DRAVYA or substance, and the *asamavāyi-kārana*, a *guna* (attribute) or karma. In addition, according to the Yoga School, as the mind associates with the self of an individual, it fills the individual's body. This is denoted by the term *kārya-citta*.

In addition, in Buddhism, *samanantara-pratyaya*, a term derived from *anantara*, i.e. immediately preceding, and *sama*, i.e. similar, denotes a momentary event that cannot exist without being causally connected to an immediately preceding event of the same kind.

See also: determinism

Further reading
Bunge, Mario Augusto (1959) *Causality: The Place of the Causal Principle in Modern Science*, Cambridge, MA: Harvard University Press.
Skyrms, Brian (1980) *Causal Necessity: A Pragmatic Investigation of the Necessity of Laws*, New Haven: Yale University Press.

causal overdetermination *see* causal law

causal relation, singular *see* philosophy of mind

causal statement *see* causal law

causal theory of knowledge *see* epistemology

causal theory of mind *see* philosophy of mind

causal theory of perception *see* perception

causal theory of proper names *see* reference

causal theory of reference *see* philosophy of language

causation *see* causal law

cause *see* causal law

cave, allegory of *see* Platonism

cellular automaton *see* computer theory

cencalli *see* Nahua philosophy

cenoscopic *see* metaphysics

censorship *see* psychoanalysis; philosophy, sociopolitical

central condition *see* condition

central-state materialism *see* philosophy of mind

centralization *see* philosophy, sociopolitical

cenyeliztli *see* Nahua philosophy

certainty From the Latin *cernere*, i.e. "to decide," this term denotes the property of being certain in one of two senses: psychological and epistemic. In the *psychological* certainty sense, certainty is equivalent to certitude and denotes a feature of individuals whereby these have no doubt whatsoever that something is the case: They are *sure* of it. In this sense, one can be certain that something is the case regardless of whether there are any grounds for it, or of how strong they are. In its *epistemic* certainty sense, certainty is a feature of the grounds for being sure that something is the case. These grounds have been variously understood. Some philosophers – e.g. the French philosopher René Descartes (CE 1596–1650) – have held that something – e.g. the truth or falsity of a proposition, statement, or judgment – is epistemically certain if it is impossible to doubt it. On this account, the impossibility of doubting the proposition, statement, or judgment is its self-evidence, i.e. the feature whereby it is plainly true. If knowledge entails epistemic certainty, the rather absolute conception of epistemic certainty just described provides grounds for the skeptical view that little is known. For, at most, tautologies, analytic statements, and a few other propositions whose denial would be self-refuting could be thus certain.

Others – e.g. the United States philosopher Roderick Chisholm (CE 1916–99) – have held that something – e.g. the truth or falsity of a proposition, statement, or judgment – is epistemically certain provided nothing else is more warranted than it. This view, of course, makes room for doubting what is epistemically certain, at least whenever mutually exclusive propositions are equally warranted and nothing else is more warranted than them. Further, if knowing something entails absolute certainty and being absolutely sure of it, the latter conception of epistemic certainty also opens the door to skepticism. However, various philosophers – e.g. the United States philosophers John Dewey (CE 1859–1952), Charles Sanders Peirce (CE 1839–1914), and Chisholm himself – have denied that knowledge requires absolute certainty. By contrast, there are those who, like the English philosopher G.E. Moore (CE 1873–1958), have held that, though knowledge requires absolute certainty, the latter is attainable.

Philosophers have also talked of *moral* certainty, meaning the grounds for something are strong enough to act as if it were true; *metaphysical* certainty, meaning the grounds for something are independent of any particular features of the world but crucial for the world being the kind of world it is; and *logical* certainty, meaning a feature of truths of logic or of propositions derivable from them. In effect, these kinds of certainty involve different degrees of strength on the grounds – moral, metaphysical, or logical – associated with them.

See also: epistemology; explanation; justification; knowledge; skepticism

Further reading
Dewey, John (1988) *The Quest for Certainty: A Study of the Relation of Knowledge and Action*, Carbondale: Southern Illinois University Press.
Kirjavainen, Heikki (1978) *Certainty, Assent and Belief: An Introduction to the Logical and Semantical Analysis of Some Epistemic and Doxastic Notions Especially in the Light of Jaakko Hintikka's Epistemic Logic and Cardinal John Henry Newman's Discussion on Certitude*, Helsinki: Villenpaino.
Trethowan, Illtyd (1948) *Certainty: Philosophical and Logical*, Westminster: Dacre Press.

certitude *see* certainty

cesare *see* syllogism

ceteris paribus *see* philosophy of science

Chabarites *see* Islam

chadō *see* Zen

chain of being Also called the great chain of being, this term denotes the notion that the universe is a hierarchy of beings in which each possible being is actual. In so far as each possible being is supposed to be actual, the notion of the great chain of being involves the principle of plenitude, whose Platonic formulation is: every genuine possibility is actualized. Both the great chain of being and the *principle of plenitude* were discussed by the German-born, United States historian of ideas and philosopher Arthur O. Lovejoy (CE 1873–1962), who established their historical and philosophical significance and uses in light of evolutionary theory. Lovejoy made plain that both notions were commonly assumed throughout the history of Western philosophy. Besides appearing in Platonic discussions, the principle of plenitude was assumed in Neoplatonism, where it was associated with the One's inexhaustible productivity. It eventually led to the medieval hierarchical conception of the universe with its degrees of being. In the works of the philosopher Thomas Aquinas (CE 1225–1274, born near the city of Naples, in what is now Italy), for example and, previously, in the works of the Greek philosopher Aristotle (384–322 BCE), reality is a hierarchical pyramid of beings, unformed matter being at the lowest level, and pure form, i.e. God, being at the top. Between God, the prime mover or unmoved mover, or pure actuality, and prime matter or pure potentiality ranges the world of nature. During the Italian Renaissance, this view led the philosopher Giordano Bruno (CE 1548–1600, born in Naples, which is now in Italy) to formulate his conception of infinite universes. In modern times, it is involved in the *principle of sufficient reason* formulated by the German philosopher Gottfried Wilhelm Leibniz (CE 1646–1716), of which a common formulation is: everything has a sufficient reason (cause or explanation) for its existence or non-existence. This can be reformulated by means of a conjunction of two conditionals: for any item, if it exists, then there is a sufficient reason (cause or explanation) for its existing and, if it does not exist, then there is a sufficient reason (cause or explanation) for its not existing. The first conditional is the positive component, and the second the negative component of the principle of sufficient reason. This negative component is related to the principle of plenitude. For, as stated, the principle of plenitude says: every genuine possibility is actualized. This arguably amounts to stating: for any item, if there is no sufficient reason (cause or explanation) for its not existing, then the item exists. However, this is entailed by the negative component of the principle of sufficient reason.

As for the positive component of the principle of sufficient reason, it is related to a principle also used by philosophers and scientists who preceded Leibniz, going back to the Greek philosopher Anaximander (*c.* 612–545 BCE) and the Greek mathematician, physicist, and inventor Archimedes (*c.* 287–212 BCE). It is the principle of insufficient reason: for any item, if there is no sufficient reason (cause or explanation) for an item's existing, then the item does not exist. This is entailed by the positive component of the principle of sufficient reason: for any item, if it exists, then there is a sufficient reason (cause or explanation) for its existing. In modern times, the principle of plenitude was weakened to state: each possible being will be actual at some time.

See also: evolution; metaphysics

Further reading

Knuuttila, Simo (1981) *Reforging the Great Chain of Being: Studies of the History of Modal Theories*, Dordrecht, Holland and Boston: D. Reidel Pub. Co.

Kuntz, Marion L. and Kuntz, Paul Grimley (1988) *Jacob's Ladder and the Tree of Life: Concepts of Hierarchy and the Great Chain of Being*, New York: P. Lang.

Lovejoy, Arthur O. (1936) *The Great Chain of Being: A Study of the History of an Idea*, Cambridge, MA: Harvard University Press.

challenge and response *see* philosophy of history

Ch'an Buddhism *see* Zen Buddhism

chance *see* determinism

Ch'ang *see* Taoism

Ch'ang-sheng pu-ssu *see* Taoism

change Intuitively, change is the partial or total replacement of one property or thing by another. This notion has been a source of philosophical puzzlement, raising such questions as: What is change really? Is change possible? How? The Greek philosophers Parmenides (*c.* 515–*c.* 450 BCE) and Zeno of Elea (490–430 BCE), and the Indian philosopher Nagarjuna (CE 100–200), held that change was impossible and immutability was an essential property of what is. In Jewish thought, immutability is a feature of the law and God, a conception inherited by Christianity. The Greek philosopher Heraclitus (*c.* 540–475 BCE), on the other hand, held that everything changes continuously. So did the Indian founder of the Buddhist faith, Gautama Siddhartha Buddha (560–477 BCE). The pluralists tried to find a middle ground between these views, arguing that some substances – a few for the Greek philosopher Empedocles (*c.* 490–430 BCE), while infinite for the Greek philosopher Anaxagoras (499–422 BCE) – do not change, but changes can be explained as their combinations and recombinations. The Greek philoso-

pher Democritus (460–370 BCE) also took this position, but while Empedocles and Anaxagoras understood change qualitatively, as a replacement of properties, Democritus understood it quantitatively – as a displacement of atoms, themselves unchanging, against a background of indefinite extension or void. For the Greek philosopher Plato (428–348 BCE), change was largely the replacement of participation in a form by participation in another form, but he began to distinguish kinds of change: alteration and locomotion. The Greek philosopher Aristotle (384–322 BCE) further developed these distinctions. In *Categories* 13, 15a, and 14, for example, he distinguishes six kinds: generation (a change from non-being to being), destruction (which amounts to the opposite of generation, namely corruption: a change from being to non-being), growth, decrease, alteration, and locomotion. In *Physics* III, 1, 201a, 5–7, however, he distinguishes four kinds: substantial, qualitative, quantitative, and local. He points out that there actually are as many kinds of change as meanings of the term "is" and, in *Physics* V, 224a, 21, he provides still another classification. All in all, Aristotle's conception of kinesis or change is the actualization of what is potential.

In modern times, some thinkers – e.g. the German philosophers Georg Wilhelm Friedrich Hegel (CE 1770–1831) and Karl Marx (CE 1818–83), the French philosopher Henri Bergson (CE 1859–1941), the British philosopher Alfred North Whitehead (CE 1861–1947), and the pragmatists – have tended to attribute preeminence to change and process in their conception of the world. Others have held the immutability of some features of the universe, e.g. basic ethical laws or principles or, as in relativity theory and other physical theories, the laws of nature.

In discussions of change, some have formulated the notion of *Cambridge change* in explaining ordinary conceptions of properties. For such notions appear to entail that, if any change happens anywhere in the universe – say, if two faraway galaxies collide – then everything else acquires the property that such an event has occurred. We all become after-collision beings. This leads to the notion of Cambridge change and *Cambridge properties*, which are associated with non-genuine change. For example, if I become taller than I used to be, I acquire a property, that of being taller than I used to be, which involves my undergoing a genuine change. By contrast, if I acquire the property of being when you are taller than you used to be, I undergo no genuine change, only a Cambridge change, and my new property, that of being when you are taller than you used to be, is only a Cambridge property of mine. Cambridge properties are a subclass of extrinsic properties and, together with Cambridge changes, appear to amount to a mere curiosity entailed by some ordinary ways of thinking, but without linguistic, scientific, or philosophical significance.

See also: metaphysics

Further reading
Gallois, Andre (1997) Occasions of Identity: A Study in the Metaphysics of Persistence, Change, and Sameness, New York: Clarendon Press.
Shen, Ching-sung and Van Doan, Tran (1992) Morality, Metaphysics, and Chinese Culture, Washington, DC: Council for Research in Values and Philosophy.
Smith, Quentin (1995) Time, Change, and Freedom: An Introduction to Metaphysics, London and New York: Routledge.
Waterlow, Sarah Nature (1988) Change, and Agency in Aristotle's Physics: A Philosophical Study, Oxford: Clarendon.

chaos see creation; myth; Judaism

chaos theory see philosophy of science

chaotic system see philosophy of science

character see ethics; philosophy of mind

character ethics see ethics; virtue

characteristic see definition

characteristica universalis see calculus

Chartres School see Platonism

charity see ethics; meaning; virtue

Chasidism see Jewish philosophy

chauvinism see feminist philosophy; philosophy, sociopolitical

ch'eng see Confucianism

cheng-i tao see Taoism

cheng-jen see Taoism

cheng ming see Confucianism

Cheng-ta-tao chiao see Taoism

ch'i see Taoism

ch'i-kung see Taoism

ch'ien, k'un see Taoism

chih Chinese term used in more than one sense. The first is as *knowledge*. Various characterizations of this notion were formulated through the ages. Sometimes, *chih* was understood, on the one hand, as the ability to know, and, on the other hand, as actual knowledge, which was identified with wisdom. Later Mohists focused on the connection between names and objects.

The second sense is as *realization*. Confucians, who were mostly interested in *chih*'s moral significance, understood *chih* as being crucially the understanding and appreciation of moral matters. Indeed, one of the central problems in Confucian ethics concerns the realization involved in attaining *chih* and, in this regard, *chih-hsing ho-i*; that is, the unity or harmony of knowledge and action.

Note: The previously discussed term, *chih*, should not be confused with the homophone *chih* as will or purpose. In this sense, *chih* denotes general, as well as specific, goals or intentions in life. These goals or intentions are not beyond individual control: they can be set and attained. Pertaining to the heart/mind, *chih* is sometimes explained by analogy to aiming in archery. While Confucians thought setting the right *chih* to guide one's conduct by it was crucial, Taoists held that we should react to the situations we face, without letting ourselves be constrained by *chih*.

See also: Buddhism; Chinese philosophy; Confucianism; Mohism; Taoism

Further reading
Cua, A.S. (1982) The Unity of Knowledge and Action: A Study in Wang Yang-ming's Moral Psychology, Honolulu: University Press of Hawaii.
Fang, Tung-mei (1981) Chinese Philosophy, Its Spirit and Its Development, Taipei, Taiwan, Republic of China: Linking Pub. Co.

Hall, David L. and Ames, Roger T. (1999) *Thinking through Confucius*, Boulder, CO: NetLibrary, Inc.

Wu, Sen (1979) *Clarification and Enlightenment: Essays in Comparative Philosophy*, Taiwan: Tunghai University Press.

chih-hsing-ho-i *see* chih

chih-jen *see* chih

chih-kuan *see* chih

Chinese Legalism In Chinese, *fa chia*, the Legalist School, also called the School of Laws; that is, the views of Chinese philosophers who upheld the strict application of laws. Their main representatives included Shang Yang (BCE 390–338) and Han Fei Tzu (d. 223 BCE). These philosophers were political realists living during the Warring States period (403–222 BCE), who believed success required organizing the State as if it were a military camp, and failure was equivalent to extinction. They challenged the Confucian model of ritually constituted communities, holding that different times required different approaches. Shang Yang, for example, argued that agriculture and warfare, the two main State concerns at his time, could be carried out successfully by articulating laws clearly and in a detailed manner, and steadfastly enforcing punishments for even minor violations.

On the view of the School of Laws, law and order was to replace morality, not only by articulating and enforcing detailed laws, but also by techniques of statecraft (*shu*) such as accountability (*hsing-ming*) and doing nothing (*wu-wei*): reformulating laws when needed, but resisting the accommodation of particular cases through interpretation. Han Fei Tzu adapted the military conception of *shih* or strategic advantage to government (where *shih* is not to be confused with the term *shih*, which meant scholar-knight and service, and denoted the lower echelon of the official nobility, to which most early philosophers belonged). According to this view, rulers should rely on the collective strength of the empire – not on public acquiescence gained by their personal attributes – in order to impose their will. As for the relations between rulers and their subordinates, the success of a ruler required total distrust.

See also: Chinese philosophy

Further reading

Han, Fei (1959) *The Complete Works of Han Fei tzu A Classic of Chinese Legalism*, London: A. Probsthain.

Levi, Jean (1985) *Dangers du discours: strategies du pouvoir IVe et IIIe siecle avant J.-C.*, Aix-en-Provence: Alinea.

Chinese philosophy Philosophical inquiry and resulting philosophical views found in Chinese thought. They trace back to the sixth century BCE and are still widely represented today. Schools of thought began to appear after the first two centuries of the Spring and Autumn period that extended from 722 BCE to 481 BCE and contended with each other during the Warring States period, from 403 BCE to 222 BCE. Among them, six were predominant:

First, CONFUCIANISM (Ju-chia), whose main representatives were Confucius (551–479 BCE), Mencius (371–289? BCE), and Hsün Tzu (298–238 BCE).

Second, TAOISM (Tao-chia), whose main representatives were Lao Tzu (sixth or fourth century BCE) and Chuang Tzu (399–295 BCE).

Third, MOHISM (Mo-chia), whose main representative was Mo-Tzu (479–438 BCE). This school of Classical Chinese thought is also known as Moism, and as the Mohist School of philosophy. In Moism, li is interpreted as benefit.

Fourth, *Logicians/Dialecticians School* (Pien Che), also called Ming-chia, i.e. School of Names, whose main representatives were Hui Shi (380–305 BCE) and Kung-Sun Lung Tzu (b. 380? BCE).

Fifth, *Yin-yang School* (Yin-yang-chia), whose main representative was Tsou Yen (305–240? BCE)

Sixth, CHINESE LEGALISM (Fa-chia), whose main representatives were Shang Yang (390–338 BCE) and Han Fei Tzu (d. 233 BCE).

Among less predominant schools, it is worth mentioning the third-century BCE *Huang-Lao* (the School of the Yellow Emperor and Lao Tzu), whose teachings were supposed to be based on those of the mythical Yellow Emperor and Lao Tzu. It stressed reliance on rewards and punishments in the task of governing, the power of political and social structures by contrast with that of individuals, and the need for a unifying vision that only the ruler can attain through stillness and *hsü* (tenuousness). These features were supposed to lead to establishing a perfectly organized State that would run smoothly and where the ruler would reign through non-action (*wu wei*), rather than rule. A term co-ordinated with *wu wei* – particularly in the *Tao Te Ching* (see TAOISM) – is *tzu jan*, meaning naturalness, or spontaneity. Also, familial and social obligations are considered *tzu jan* in neo-Confucianism (see below).

Another lesser school that sharply contrasted with Huang-Lao was *Nung Chia*, or *the Agriculture School*, also called the Tillers. Its members held that, originally, there had been a decentralized group of small communities, where all, including their ruler, the Divine Farmer, lived by their own labor, without rewards, punishment, or administration. A representative of this Utopian form of anarchism was Hsü Hsing, who lived around 315 BCE.

The Yin-yang School was significantly interested in cosmology and the interplay between *yin-yang* and *wu-hsing*, i.e. *the five phases*: earth, water, wood, metal and fire. Taoism's dynamic conception of the universe also showed an interest in cosmology: the Taoist notion of *wu* traditionally appears in the pair of opposites *yu* and *wu*, which respectively mean having and nothing. Sometimes, *yu* and *wu* are respectively translated as being and non-being; but it should be kept in mind that *yu* and *wu* are in some kind of dependency relation: they complement each other, and yield to each other in delicate interplay. For example, at one point, the *Tao-te ching* says *yu* and *wu* produce each other; while, at another point, it says the *yu* comes from *wu*. The concept of *wu* was attributed a more fundamental role by later Taoists.

Despite these cosmological interests, the six predominant schools of Chinese philosophy were largely concerned with practical problems and were significantly affected by developments in Chinese society. *Shan* and *o*, i.e. good and evil, were crucial concerns for Chinese philosophers. Confucians sought to do good and eliminate evil, and focused on harmony in human affairs; while Taoists sought to reach a different level of spirituality: beyond good and

evil. Along analogous lines, Taoism, like Confucianism, focused on *sheng* (literally, the sage or sagehood). However, by contrast with Confucianism, it conceived of it as complete attunement to natural and regular, as well as unusual, occurrences, i.e. as harmony with the natural world. Many centuries later, neo-Confucianism also focused on *sheng*, this time as an attainable ideal of the universe as a moral community (a notion foreshadowed in Classical Confucianism's focus on the unity of *t'ien* understood as Heaven (see *t'ien*, below), and human beings' significance in resolving moral problems).

Another example is provided by the Chinese term *ch'ing*. The expression the *ching of x* originally denoted the properties without which *x* would cease to be the kind of thing it is: its essence. That is, it was a term easily applicable to exploring metaphysical or *hsing-erh-shang* (formless) questions (by contrast with *hsing-erh-hsia* (what has form). However, by Hsün Tzu's time – toward the end of the Warring States period – *ch'ing* had acquired its second meaning: human emotions or passions, a term more readily applicable to practical problems. It also acquired a list of emotions – the six emotions – that soon became common: *hao* (fondness), *wu* (aversion or dislike), *hsi* (delight), *nu* (anger), *ai* (sadness), and *le* (joy).

Another significant concept is *yi*, which initially meant a sense of honor, but later came to mean fitting conduct, a commitment to do the right thing or, simply, what is appropriate in the given situation. Still another significant notion is *yü* or desire, which is contrasted with *wu*, a notion that in this case means aversion or dislike (see other meanings, below).

During the Han dynasty, in 136 BCE, a blend of Confucianism with elements of Taoism, Legalism, and the Yin-yang School was adopted as the State ideology. At about this time, the *Huai Nan Tzu* was produced. It is an ancient Chinese syncretic compendium of knowledge, compiled by an academy of scholars under the guidance and support of Liu An, Prince of Huai Nan, and presented to the imperial court of Emperor Wu (circa 140 BCE). It summarizes existing knowledge and, as a political document, it combines Confucian, Legalist, and Taoist elements.

A central Confucian principle already formulated during that period is *ch'eng*, i.e. sincerity (though also translated as authenticity, and truthfulness). It denotes the wholeness or completeness of a person displayed in the sincerity of the person's words. *Ch'eng* was a principle developed in the Confucian *Doctrine of the Mean* formulated in arguably the most philosophical of ancient Chinese documents, the *Chung Yung* (Doctrine of the Mean), which already existed in the early Han dynasty and was to be brought into prominence centuries later by the Chinese Confucian philosopher Chu Hsi (CE 1130–1200). According to the Doctrine of the Mean, the ultimate principle is rather metaphysical in that it is said to be *ch'eng* because totally beyond illusion and delusion, and one's conduct – modeled on *t'ien* (see below) – should strike harmony: the appropriate mean between deficiency and excess. During the Han dynasty, however, creative philosophical inquiry was replaced by the merely backward-looking, detailed study of five works called the *Five Classics*: *Book of Poetry*, *Book of History*, *Book of Changes*, *Book of Rites*, and *Spring and Autumn Annals*.

Another important term in Confucianism is *jen* (variously translated as kindness, humanity, benevolence, altruism, goodness, and perfect virtue), whose literal meaning is "man in society," and which denotes both an ethical ideal for all humans, and the feature of having an affectionate concern for all living things. Confucianism regarded *jen* as the basis of government. Neo-Confucianism expanded the meaning of this term to the entire universe, focusing on human relations from a cosmic standpoint. They also used the term *jen* in the expression *jen-hsin* to denote humans' artificial, selfish desires, by contrast with *tao-hsin*, which denotes humans acting spontaneously in accordance with the Way. In this regard, Hsün Tzu used the term *pi*, i.e. screen, shelter, or cover, as a metaphor for lack of mental clarity or anything that obstructs cognitive tasks. He also used the term *pien* to denote the ability to distinguish mental states and the proper objects of given desires. This ability is crucial in neo-Confucianism, according to which the goal of life is sagehood.

Jen was not only used by Confucian or neo-Confucian thinkers. For example, Mo Tzu (479–381 BCE), who once followed and then opposed Confucius, retained the concept of *jen* in his philosophy of universal love, by arguing that individuals who had *jen* practiced the universal-love principle. He contraposed this principle to partiality or arbitrary preference, and argued for universality as a principle according to which we should treat others' families, cities, and states as if they were our own. In addition, he held that we should act in such a manner as to bring about benefit and prevent harm to the world. With Mo Tzu, the term *pien* came to mean contending over converse claims or disputation, with special emphasis on the analysis and discussion of difficult ethical cases. By contrast, Hsün Tzu arguably upheld a co-operative rather than a disputational model of argumentation.

Pien, in this sense of disputation, eventually became disreputable in Chinese philosophy, apparently because disputation became disputation for disputation's sake. Some have argued that the philosopher Kung-Sun Lung Tzu (b. 380? BC) may have unintentionally contributed to this development by formulating the white-horse paradox in a dialogue where he defends the claim that a white horse is not a horse.

A significant term in the context of the discussions just described is *te*, i.e. moral power or moral virtue. *Te* is a characteristic of a true *wang* or *pa*, i.e. of a king or hegemon. It is the quality whereby the ruled willingly follow the ruler and involves being morally exemplary, though scholars differ on whether this is merely necessary or also sufficient for having *te*. At any rate, the notion of *te* has also been extended to virtue beyond the realm of leadership, i.e. as a disposition that leads to human flourishing or to excellence in any kind of endeavor.

The Han dynasty ended in CE 220 and Wei (CE 220–65), the first Emperor of the Wei-Chin dynasty, ordered the *Five Classics*, except for the *Book of Changes* (*I-Ching*), burned. Han scholars, however, wrote down, in modern script, the texts they remembered. Also, some ancient script texts were found, but the modern-script school rejected them as spurious, which led to recalcitrant disputes between the ancient-script and the modern-script school.

These disputes, however, were significant only to scholars interested in studying the *Five Classics*, a study which did not appeal to Wei-Chin scholars at all. Further, against the Confucian tradition, they tended to disregard ritual, focusing instead on metaphysical problems raised in the *I-Ching* (a key book to understand the Chinese worldview) and by such Taoist philosophers as Lao Tzu and Chuang Tzu. For example, Chuang Tzu had held that *hsü* (void, vacuity, the tenuous) was the ideal state of mind, in which the mind is receptive to all things. Hsiang Hsiu (*fl.* CE 250) and Kuo Hsiang (d. CE 312) wrote *Commentaries on the Chuang Tzu*. Wang Pi (CE 226–49) wrote *Commentaries on the Lao Tzu*, where he concentrated on meanings and principles (*i-li*), and disregarded the traditional forms and numbers (*hsiang shu*) approach to the book's study. He was a leading representative of neo-Taoism together with Ho Yen (third century CE) who, despite being a neo-Taoist, considered Confucius, not Lao Tzu, as the Sage.

Buddhism began to be known in China during the later part of the Han dynasty; but Chinese versions of Buddhism began to develop during the Sui-Tang period (CE 581–907), largely preferring Mahayana to Hinayana Buddhism.

As a response to these developments neo-Confucianism developed, relying on insights found in the *Analects*, *The Great Learning* or *Ta-hsüeh* (a part of the *Book of Rites*), the *Doctrine of the Mean*, and the works of Mencius, and incorporating ideas from Buddhism and Taoism. For example, along Taoist views, neo-Confucian philosophers considered *hsü* the original state of the universe and contrasted it with the Buddhist concept of *k'ung* (emptiness) on the grounds that it made no room for the ultimate reality of the world.

Neo-Confucianism reached its peak during the Sung-(Yüan)-Ming period (CE 960–1126), sometimes described as the Chinese Renaissance. Foreshadowed in the work of Chou Tun-i (CE 1017–73), neo-Confucianism was fully formulated by Ch'eng Hao (CE 1032–85) and his brother Ch'eng Yi (CE 1033–1107). The latter, in his *Commentary to the Book of Changes*, focuses on two terms crucial in metaphysics, the philosophy of mind, and other areas of philosophy: *t'i* or "substance," and *yung*, or "function." Displaying a way of thinking characteristic of Chinese philosophy, he rejects a contraposition between the two and states, instead, that they come from the same source. This approach was applied by Chu Hsi (CE 1130–1200) to the study of human nature, maintaining that *jen*, understood as humanity, is nature or substance (*t'i*), while love, a feeling, is function (*yung*).

Among neo-Confucian philosophers, Shao-Yung (CE 1011–77), like the others, traced the development of multiple things from the Great Ultimate or *t'ai-chi* (mind, reason, and moral law), a principle first formulated in the *I-Ching*, through the *yin* and *yang* modes of action, which are produced by the Great Ultimate without itself engaging in activity. Unlike the others, Shao-Yung used the idea of number in explaining this process.

Also of note was Chang Tsai (CE 1020–77), who wrote an essay entitled "The Western Inscription" where he said that all people were his siblings. Yang Shih (CE 1053–1135), Ch'eng Yi's disciple, criticized Chang Tsai on the grounds that he appeared to be committed to the Mohist doctrine of universal love. Ch'eng Yi then coined the phrase *li-i-fen-shu*, i.e. "principle is one while manifestations are many," in order to clarify Chang Tsai's meaning. Chang Tsai was actually teaching the Confucian doctrine of graded love, according to which while principle (*li*) is one, its manifestations are many.

Confucianism's main representative, however, was Chu Hsi (CE 1130–1200), who systematized neo-Confucianism and developed the Ch'eng-Chu School. Chu Hsi's metaphysics was based on the notions of an incorporeal, unique, eternal, unchanging, and invariably good principle (*li*) and a physical, diverse, transitory, changeable, partly good and partly evil material force (*ch'i*), whose purity is said to explain the existence of good and evil. These notions coexist, unmixed but united. That is, he regarded the Great Ultimate as the principle in its totality, involving principle and material force, but being primarily principle, identical with all things that are simply its manifestations. In fact, Chinese neo-Confucianism considered *li* and *ch'i* to be inseparable.

For Chu, human nature was *li*, while feelings and emotions (*ch'ing*) were *ch'i*, and mind/heart (*hsin*) was also *ch'i*, though very subtle. This position was criticized by Lu Hsiang-shan (CE 1139–93), who held that mind by itself sufficed to harmonize the human and the natural in human nature. This view was revived by Wang Yan-ming (CE 1472–1529) at the end of the Sung-(Yüan)-Ming period, thus originating the *Lu-Wang* School. In formulating his views, Wang refined the notion of *liang-chih*, which had been initially formulated by Meng-tzu or Mencius in the fourth century BCE. For Meng-tzu, *liang-chih* roughly meant "innate knowledge of the good." For Wang, it meant "sense of right and wrong" or "ability to tell right from wrong" that, for him, was the love of good and hate of evil. This ability amounted to a moral consciousness that, according to Wang, involved a vision of *jen* as being *one with the universe* but, given that circumstances change, involved *deliberation*.

During the next dynasty, the Ch'ing (CE 1644–1912), philosophy receded into the background, replaced by historical studies. After that, Marxism soon became the predominant philosophy in mainland China, while other Western philosophy schools – analytic philosophy, existentialism, hermeneutics – became significant in Hong Kong and Taiwan. Also, the New Confucian movement developed not only in Hong-Kong and Taiwan but in mainland China. It was inspired by Hsiung Shih-li (CE 1885–1968), and found most original development in Mou Tsung-san (CE 1909–95), who argued that humans have the capacity for intellectual intuition or personal participation in *tao*, and that Buddhism, Confucianism, and Taoism agree on this point.

See also: Agriculture School; Buddhism; Chinese Legalism; Confucianism; Mohism; Taoism

Further reading
Cua, A.S. (ed.) (forthcoming 2001) *Encyclopedia of Chinese Philosophy*, New York: Garland.
Fang, Tung-mei (1986) *Chinese Philosophy, Its Spirit and Its Development*, Taipei, Taiwan: Linking Pub. Co.
Feng, Yu-lan (1969) *A History of Chinese Philosophy*, Princeton: Princeton University Press.
Graham, A.C. (1995) *Disputers of the Tao: Philosophical Argument in Ancient China*, La Salle, IL: Open Court.
Hall, David L. and Ames, Roger T. (1999) *Thinking through Confucius*, Boulder, CO: NetLibrary, Inc.
Schwartz, Benjamin Isadore (1985) *The World of Thought in Ancient China*, Cambridge, MA: Belknap Press of Harvard University Press.

ching *see* Confucianism

ch'ing *see* Chinese philosophy

Ch'ing-t'an *see* Taoism

Ching-te ch'uan-teng-lu *see* Zen

chit *see* Hinduism

chitta *see* Hinduism

Chöd *see* Buddhism

choice *see* decision; relation; set

Chomsky hierarchy of languages *see* philosophy of language

chosen people *see* Jewish philosophy; Judaism; Nahua philosophy

Christian feminism *see* feminist philosophy

Christianity A religion founded by Jesus Christ (4? BCE–CE 29?), born in Bethlehem or in Nazareth, a town near Jerusalem. It centers around the notions of love and eternal salvation that, intertwined in lasting tension with the Greco-Roman tradition, contributed to shape many characteristics of Western world culture such as the ideal of progress, the ideas of temporal passage, ethical meliorism, and the significant role of rational knowledge in life, together with the associated conceptions and development of science and technology. Christianity's sacred book is the Bible. Its history can be divided into the following periods:

The first is the *Apostolic* period (CE first century). Jesus Christ emerges and, partly through the work of Paul (born in Tarsus, Cilicia, CE first century), it finds its way into the Greco-Roman culture and institutions, and becomes separated from Jewish traditions. During this early period, Christians clashed with the Roman Empire's custom of *apotheosis* – from the Greek *apo* (from), and *theoun* (to deify) – whereby heroes and rulers were thought transformed into divinities. The persecution of Christians during this period largely resulted from their refusal to acknowledge the divinity of the Roman emperor and, by contrast with the pragmatic acquiescence of Roman skeptics, being adamant about it. This was for Christians a matter of religious conscience – quite an incomprehensible notion to most Romans of the time.

The second is the *Consolidation* period (CE 100–313). The Church is developed, becoming stronger in the Roman Empire until Constantine gives it official status. *Patristics* (from the Latin *pater*, i.e. father), the Church fathers and their works, begins. Significant thinkers involved in controversy about Gnosticism (from the Greek *gignoskein*, i.e. to know) – the view that knowledge, not faith, brings salvation, though the said knowledge can be mystical (see below) – were such Greek authors and first Church fathers as Clement of Alexandria (*c.* CE 150–after 215), who was probably born in Athens; Irenaeus (CE 130/140–after 198?), who was probably born in Smyrna, Asia Minor; and Origen (*c.* CE 180–*c.*254), probably born in Alexandria.

Notable among their doctrines is Irenaeus' doctrine of atonement, which became standard during the Middle Ages: that Jesus Christ, in dying on the cross, sacrificed himself for humanity thereby providing vicarious reparation for the sins of humans against God, whose forgiveness could not be elicited by any acts of humans – beings in a state of original sin – alone. Also, Origen was an early proponent of the doctrine of *apocatastasis* or *universalism*, according to which all human beings will be saved.

The Latin author Tertullian (*c.* CE 155–*c.* 240, born in the African city of Carthage), though appearing hostile to philosophy ("What has Athens to do with Jerusalem?") and rationality ("It is certain because it is impossible"), significantly relied on Stoic concepts and arguments beginning to develop the trinitarian conception of God, setting the stage for the trinity conception that would eventually become the official view. Origen and Clement of Alexandria held that there were two roads to salvation: through faith for the masses, and through knowledge for philosophers. In holding these views, they were partial representatives of *Gnosticism*, the view that knowledge, not faith, brings salvation, though the said knowledge can be mystical. This view was especially influential during the second century, under the leadership of two Christian teachers: the Alexandrian Valentinus (CE 100–65), founder of the form of Christian Gnosticism called Valentinianism; and the Syrian Basilides (*c.* CE 120–40), whose philosophical acumen rivaled that of Valentinus, and who further elaborated his doctrine of emanation. Gnosticism threatened what became the orthodox – faith-centered – Church, not just from within, but from without, through the activities of many non-Christian Gnostic sects. Gnostic doctrines are mainly known through refutations. The only known complete Gnostic text is *Pistis Sophia*, a book written in Coptic that was discovered in the eighteenth century and first published in the mid-nineteenth century.

There was a great variety of Gnostic sects, schools, and practices, all related to the mystery religions, and all adhering to such views as: the Great Mother or Sophia descends into the world and gives birth to the seven powers, or angels, the last emanations of God; the Primal Man comes into the world to fight against darkness; and the Soter or Savior is often the Primal Man.

Another movement challenging the early Church was *montanism*, initially led by Montanus who, in CE 156, announced that the dispensation of the Holy Spirit had begun and he was going to be the Holy Spirit's mouthpiece. Montanism was an otherworldly movement that accused the Church of moral laxity and apathy, and taught moral purity, postbiblical revelation, and the imminent end of the world. As a result, the Church became Catholic, i.e. came to terms with the world, adapting to it.

The third is the *Doctrine Formulation* period (CE 313–590) Between the Christian Roman Emperor Constantine the Great (*c.* CE 280–337), and Pope Gregory I, also called Gregory the Great (CE 540–604), many doctrines are developed through a variety of councils that begin to attack as heresies such views as Arianism, Nestorianism, Monophysitism, and Pelagianism. The notion of *heresy* – opinion or doctrine at variance with the accepted one – was crucial in the development of Christianity, a religion based on right opinion or orthodoxy by contrast with Judaism, where the notion of right practice was central.

During and after the Council of Nicea (CE 325), influential Greek authors included Athanasius (*c.* CE 297–373), whose discussions focused on the notions of incarnation and trinity, and who opposed all forms of Arianism; and the three great Capadocians, Gregory of Nazianzus (*c.* CE 330–90), Basil of Cesarea (*c.* CE 330–79), and his brother Gregory of Nyssa (CE 335/340–*c.* 394). They were most notable among Patristic theologians with a philosophical bent, sought a middle way between faith and reason, and developed the notion of nature as God's harmonious creation. Their collective name derives from their having been born in Capadocia.

Among the Latin authors were Ambrose (*c.* CE 340?–397), who was Bishop of Milan and appropriated Neoplatonic doctrines in a manner that anticipated the work of the philosopher Augustine (CE 354–430, born in the African city of Thagaste). Ambrose, besides discussing innumerable theological views, wrote many philosophical works. The latter range from a refutation of skepticism, and a theodicy, to a dialogue on the place of human choice within the universe created by God and ordered by God's providence, and, in his *City of God* (*Civitas Dei*), the nature of human history and the concept of an ideal community of the good. Also, monastic orders developed in response to previous ascetic excesses of the faithful.

Prominent among the doctrines of Judaism accepted by Christianity is that humans were created in the image of God. This notion, as well as that of likeness, played a significant role in Platonic adaptations to Christianity. A different but related doctrine is that of *vestigia Dei*, or God's vestiges. Vestiges are not images, whose likeness is supposed to be reasonably close to the original. By contrast, vestiges could be but slight similarities. For example, triads in the universe were examples of God's vestiges evidencing the Trinity.

The fourth is the *Northern Expansion and Southern and Eastern Retrenchment* period (CE 590–800). Between Gregory I and Charlemagne, the Church expands among Germanic peoples; but it ceases to have influence in much of Spain, and Africa, where Islam dominates. The last Patristic authors – e.g. Maximus the Confessor (CE 579/580–662) and John of Damascus (*c.* CE 650–*c.* 750) – are active during this period.

The fifth is the *Hegemonic Papacy* period (CE 800–1073). Between Charlemagne and Gregory VII, the Pope's power grows, and the Eastern Church separates from the Western Church.

The sixth is the *Militant* period (CE 1073–1294). Between Gregory VII and Boniface VIII, the Papacy's power reaches its peak in Europe and the seven crusades to win the Holy Land back take place (CE 1096–1270). The philosopher Anselm (CE 1033–1109, born in Aosta, in what is now Italy), was a Christian Platonist in metaphysics like Augustine before him, formulates both his cosmological argument for God's existence in the *Monologion*, and his ontological argument for both God's existence and the impossibility of conceiving of God as nonexistent in his *Proslogiom*. In CE 1232, the *Inquisition* is founded, while the *Scholastic method*, originally applied in Bologna's and other law schools and then extended to theology and philosophy, takes hold in Europe through the work of the French philosophers and theologians Peter Abelard (CE 1079–1144) and Peter Lombard (*c.* CE 1095–1160).

Many mutually opposed philosophical views were formulated and heatedly discussed during this period, which later came to be called *Scholasticism*. Among its main figures are the philosopher Thomas Aquinas (CE 1225–74; born near the city of Naples, in what is now Italy), who adapted Aristotle's thought to Christianity in a manner that eventually became the Catholic Church's official doctrine (see THOMISM), and the Scottish philosopher Duns Scotus (CE 1266–1308), who modified along Christian lines the conception of metaphysics formulated by the Arabic philosopher Ibn Sīnā (CE 980–1037) and Augustine's insights, so as to fit with the Aristotelian philosophical and theological mainstream. In Spain, slowly being recovered for the West, King Alfonso the Wise of Castile provided notable support for intellectual and artistic endeavors between CE 1252 and 1284.

The seventh is the *Renaissance and Reformation* period. Between CE 1294 and 1517, European culture undergoes a revolution ranging from the revival of Greco-Roman traditions in philosophy and the arts and sciences, and the beginning of the scientific revolution, through the Fall of Constantinople, the defeat and expulsion of the Moors in Spain, and contact with the Americas, all in the mid-1400s. There is also the publication of the four theses by the German Churchman and Reformer Martin Luther (CE 1483–1546) in CE 1517. These were, first, indulgences cannot remit guilt of punishment for sin – only God can do this; second, indulgences have no effect concerning souls in purgatory: what the pope can do for them must be done through prayer, not through the power of the pope's office; third, the power of the pope concerning indulgences can only apply to the remission of ecclesiastical penalties imposed by the Church; fourth, a truly repentant Christian has already been pardoned by God regardless of indulgences.

The eighth is the period of *Religious Wars*. This period extends between CE 1517 and 1648, i.e. between the publication of Luther's theses and the Peace of Westphalia. During this period, European history was characterized by religious conflict associated with the work of such figures as Luther and the French Protestant theologian John Calvin (CE 1509–64). Also worthy of mention is *Socianism*, a heterodox religious movement originating from the work of the Italian reformer Laelius Socinus or, in Italian, Sozzini (CE 1525–62) and his nephew, Faustus Socinus (CE 1539–1603). Its main document is the *Racovian Catechism* of 1605, which had wide circulation in Europe during the seventeenth century. It was an important influence in the development of Unitarianism and, in England, it influenced the Cambridge Platonists and other philosophers and scientists.

The religious conflicts of the time happened in the context of the strengthening of monarchies in Europe, European expansion in the Americas and, at an ever increasing pace, the development of the scientific revolution. As a response to the latter, the French philosopher René Descartes (CE 1596–1650) developed his philosophical ideas making individual reflection the touchstone of knowledge and existence, which contributed to earn him the title of "Founder of the Modern Age." During this period, *Jansenism* developed among European Roman Catholics. Initiated by the Flemish bishop Cornelius Jansen (CE 1585–1638), this movement included a number of doctrines about grace and free will that emphasized such ideas as predestination, irresistible efficacious grace, and limited atonement. Adopted by the nuns of Port Royal and upheld by Catholic thinkers of the stature of the French philosophers Antoine Arnauld (CE 1612–94) and Blaise Pascal (CE 1623–62), Jansenism was pervasive in Catholicism for about 150 years. It was condemned by Pope Innocent X and the Church of France, but remained influential in the rest of Europe, reappearing in a more rigoristic form in the eighteenth century, when it was condemned again, this time by Pope Clement XI.

The ninth period is the *Modern* one. After 1648, Catholicism and the Protestant Churches or *Protestantism* developed separately. Of significance in Modern philosophy is the development of *pietism*, an eighteenth- and nineteenth-century devotional movement that developed with the Lutheran Church and sought a participation based on religious feeling between members of the church. The family of the German philosopher Immanuel Kant (CE 1724–1804) was pietist. The German philosopher and theologian Friedrich Schleiermacher (CE 1768–1834) gave theological formulation to pietist ideas. So did the German philosopher Rudolf Eucken (CE 1846–1926).

Also worth mentioning is *quietism*, a seventeenth-century mystical and devotional movement within Catholicism. It held that one's entire soul must be devoted to loving God. Hence, waiting for God in meditation became central, because a moment's contemplation was worth a thousand years of good works.

The leaders of the movement were either found to be heretics or censured by the Pope.

Also of significance is *Swedenborgianism*, a worldwide theosophic movement established in London as the Jerusalem Church in CE 1788 and based on the views of the Swedish natural philosopher Emanuel Swedenborg (CE 1688–1772), who adapted Cartesian and British empiricist views so as to argue for a harmony between the mechanistic universe and biblical revelation.

In addition, during the modern period, the Americas freed themselves from European colonial powers. The French Revolution and Napoleonic wars radically altered the map of Europe. The 1869 Vatican Council designated Thomism as the Catholic Church's official philosophical position. Since the 1900s the *Ecumenical Movement* has been growing in strength. Various thinkers voiced a variety of opinions on Christianity. The French philosopher Paul Henri (Baron) D'Holbach (CE 1723–89), for example, held it was a superstition fostered by priests. The German philosopher Johann Gottfried von Herder (CE 1744–1803) held religion was a way in which humans tried to explain the world and Christianity was notable only because of the pre-eminent role of ethics in it. The German philosopher Georg Wilhelm Friedrich Hegel (CE 1770–1831) held Christianity was the absolute truth in pictorial form. The German philosopher Friedrich Wilhelm Nietzsche (CE 1844–1900) compared it to the Antichrist.

See also: creation; determinism; Jewish philosophy; philosophy of religion; Thomism

Further reading
Latourette, Kenneth Scott (1975) *A History of Christianity*, rev. edn, Peabody, MA: Prince Press.
Twesigye, Emmanuel K. (1987) *Common Ground: Christianity, African Religion, and Philosophy*, New York: P. Lang.
Vesey, Godfrey Norman Agmondisham (1989) *The Philosophy in Christianity*, Cambridge, UK, and New York: Cambridge University Press.

ch'üan *see* Confucianism

ch'üan-chen tao *see* Taoism

chung *see* Confucianism

Chung Yung *see* Confucianism

chün-tzu *see* Confucianism

Church fathers *see* Christianity

Church's thesis *see* philosophy of mathematics

Church–Turing thesis *see* philosophy of mind

circle, vicious *see* reasoning

circular reasoning *see* reasoning

circularity *see* reasoning

circulus in definiendo *see* reasoning

circulus in probando *see* reasoning

circulus vitiosus *see* reasoning

circumstance From the Latin *circumstantia*, "what is around something." The term acquired a technical meaning in Spanish – *circunstancia* – as a result of work by the Spanish philosopher José Ortega y Gasset (CE 1883–1955) in *Meditaciones del Quijote* (*Quixote's Meditations*), where he states "I am myself and my circumstance." This means that human individuals are not only surrounded by their circumstances, but also are what and who they are *together with or in connection with* their circumstances. Someone's circumstance, in Ortega's sense, is what the individual experiences as his or her situation in the universe and contributes, together with what we normally called the subject or the I, to characterize that individual. The contemporary Spanish philosopher Julián Marías, in his *Introducción a la filosofía*, further developed Ortega's notion. He characterized it as "everything in my vital horizon." That is, someone's circumstance is everything with which he or she has to deal in life: the physical surroundings, one's own body, other human bodies, social reality, artifacts resulting from human activities, history as experienced, those who have died, the beliefs held by the individual or others, their emotions, expectations, and ultimate ideas or ideals. Though, often, the notion of someone's circumstance is identified with someone's situation, Ortega's and Marías' conception of someone's circumstance is distinct from situation, the latter being narrower and more precise than the former. Here, our situation denotes only those aspects of our circumstance that place us historically, for example our particular projects at a given time.

See also: vitalism

Further reading
Marías, Julián (1969) *Introducción a la filoso-fía*, 10th edn, Madrid: Revista de Occidente.
Ortega y Gasset, José (1963) *Meditations on Quixote*, New York and London: Norton.

citizen *see* philosophy, sociopolitical

citta *see* Hinduism

citta-mātrā *see* Buddhism

City of God *see* Christianity

city-state *see* Greek philosophy; Nahua philosophy; philosophy, sociopolitical

civic humanism *see* philosophy, sociopolitical

civil disobedience *see* philosophy, socio-political

civil rights *see* ethics; philosophy, sociopolitical

civil society *see* ethics; philosophy, sociopolitical

civilization *see* culture

Civitas Dei *see* Christianity

clairvoyance *see* philosophy of mind

clarity *see* ambiguity

class From the Latin *classis*, i.e. division, fleet, army, the term class is used in a variety of senses. The first, in logic and mathematics, is sometimes used as synonymous with the term SET, meaning any consistent list of items whatsoever. When class is distinguished from set, a class is any consistent list of items whatsoever that share a common feature, e.g. a list of red items, while a set is any consistent list of items that, at a given stage of set construction, are non-sets or sets already constructed. In set theory, a *proper class* is a list of sets that are never formed at any stage. An example is the class of all sets, because since there are infinite stages of set construction, there is no stage at which all sets are already formed to be listed into a class. In set theory, an *equivalence class*, also called a *partition*

class, is each subset of a partition or division of a set into mutually exclusive and jointly exhaustive subsets. Equivalence class and partition class are synonymous terms because partitions are closely associated with *equivalence relations*, i.e. with relations that are transitive, symmetric, and reflexive (see RELATION).

A significant concept is also that of the *complement class* C̄ of a given class C: the class of all items in the universe of discourse that are not members of C. It is also called *complementary class* or *complement term*.

The second sense appears in *reference class*, an expression used in the relative-frequency interpretation of probability, according to which probability attaches to sets of events within a reference class, i.e. the class W where n is the number of events in W, say the class of days of the year, and m is the number of events in (or of kind) X, say the kind of rain occurrences in the Connecticut town of Cheshire, within W, so that the probability of X, relative to W – i.e. that it will rain on a given day in Cheshire – is m/n.

For the third, *social class*, see MARXISM.

In Indian philosophy, the term for class is *jāti*, though its philosophical meaning varies from school to school. In BUDDHISM, *jāti* is one of the links in the wheel of empirical existence. In HINDUISM, according to the NYĀYA-VAIŚEṢIKA SCHOOL, which holds the meanings of words refer to classes, *jāti* is defined as that which produces the notion of sameness. Also, by contrast with the Mīmāmsa School, which holds universals do not exist over and above individuals, the Nyāya School holds that class-characters exist apart from individuals, and identifies the highest genus as *sattā* (being), also called *parajāti* (the highest universal), while *aparajāti* is any lower universal.

See also: Marxism; set

Further reading
Boole, George (1965) *The Mathematical Analysis of Logic: Being an Essay Towards a Calculus of Deductive Reasoning*, New York: Barnes & Noble.
Russell, Bertrand and Whitehead, Alfred North (1968) *Principia Mathematica*, London: Cambridge University Press.

class paradox *see* paradox

classic *see* canon; philosophy of literature

classical conditioning *see* behaviorism

classicism *see* canon

clear and distinct *see* Cartesianism

clinamen *see* Epicureanism

cloning *see* ethics

closed formula *see* logic

closed loop *see* cybernetics

closure *see* epistemology

cluster-concept *see* philosophy of science; theory

cluster-law *see* philosophy of science; theory

Coase theorem *see* philosophy of economics

code *see* ethics

coercion *see* philosophy, sociopolitical

cogito *see* Cartesianism

cogito ergo sum *see* Cartesianism

cognition *see* cognitive; epistemology

cognitive Concerning cognition (from the Latin, *cognitio*, i.e. "knowledge" and "recognition"). It appears in a variety of noun-phrases. The first is *cognitive dissonance*, which is mental discomfort that results from one's holding conflicting beliefs or attitudes at the same time. The notion of cognitive dissonance is sometimes used to suggest the dissonance involves motivational features. Suppose an expatriate is considering the likely prospect that he or she might choose to remain an expatriate for life. This person experiences dissonance when thinking of the good features of remaining an expatriate – perhaps economic opportunity or freedom – while also thinking of the bad features of never going back home other than for a visit – staying away from loved family members or friends. The philosophical relevance of cognitive dissonance concerns self-deception, weakness of will, and a variety of moral problems that arise concerning the adaptation or lack of adaptation of expatriates to their foreign environments. Self-

deception may be a response to cognitive dissonance that, for example, may result from realizing the difficulty of staying in a foreign environment forever and the impossibility of returning to a world remembered but gone. A weak will can result from the dissonance caused by realizing the likely undesirable consequences of doing what one should.

The second, *cognitive psychotherapy*, is a noun-phrase coined by the contemporary United States philosopher Richard Brandt to designate a process of assessing and adjusting one's attitudes.

For the third, *cognitive relativism*, see PHILOSOPHY OF SCIENCE.

The fourth is *cognitive science*. This is an interdisciplinary area of research that studies intelligent activity, whether displayed by living organisms (especially human beings) or machines. It combines contributions from a variety of branches of inquiry including anthropology, computer science, linguistics, neuroscience, philosophy, and psychology. One of its main areas of research is that of computational theories of mind. In this regard, a notable approach has been *connectionism*, also called *neural-network model* and *parallel distributed processing*, which aims at modeling cognitive systems using networks of simple processing units by analogy with the structure of the nervous system or a neural net. This approach was influential between the 1940s and 1960s; but, because of technical limitations, ceased to attract interest until the 1980s, when the discovery of ways of overcoming the old limitations of parallel distributed processing – e.g. the back-propagation learning algorithm and the Boltzman-machine learning algorithm – made it appealing again.

Another significant area of cognitive science is the study of *modularity*: the view that psychological organization involves independent and specialized cognitive systems. Modular organization was initially formulated by the neuroanatomist Franz Joseph Gall (CE 1758–1828), later developed by the French physicians Jean-Baptiste Bouilland (CE 1796–1881) and Pierre-Paul Broca (CE 1824–80), and still has advocates in the twentieth century, though it tends to be restricted to such peripheral brain functions as vision, hearing, motor control, and speech. Modularity varies from simple decomposability (where components are independent and an organism's behavior is an additive or aggregative function of the contributions of these independent systems), to what the contemporary social scientist Herbert Simon calls near decomposability, where the short-run behavior of components is independent of other components, and an organism's behavior is a relatively simple function of the contributions of these components.

A model that has been proposed concerning memory is the *holographic model* (by analogy with a hologram, the three-dimensional image of an object, each one of whose parts contains the entire image), according to which memories are distributed holographically across brain areas, perhaps the entire cortex. This model has not gained acceptance. Current theories favor the *cell assembly* view, according to which memories are stored in the connections between groups of neurons.

The fifth is *cognitive value*. This expression was coined by the German mathematician and logician Friedrick Ludwig Gottlob Frege (CE 1848–1925) to denote the difference between logical truths (say "The morning star is the morning star") and other truths (say, the astronomical statement "The morning star is the evening star").

See also: artificial; ethics; intuition; philosophy of language; philosophy of mind; rationality

Further reading
Brandt, Richard B. (1984 [1979]) *A Theory of the Good and the Right*, Oxford: Clarendon.
Festinger, Leon (1957) *A Theory of Cognitive Dissonance*, Stanford: Stanford University Press.
Frege Gottlob (1997) *The Frege Reader*, Oxford and Malden, MA: Blackwell Publishers.
Wagman, Morton (1997) *Cognitive Science and the Symbolic Operations of Human and Artificial Intelligence: Theory and Research into the Intellective Processes*, Westport, CT and London: Praeger.

cognitivism *see* ethics

coherence *see* justification; knowledge; truth

coherentism *see* justification; knowledge; truth

cohuayotl *see* Nahua philosophy

Coimbra commentaries *see* Scholasticism

co-implication In logic, a term sometimes used to denote the biconditional relation between two sentences (see LOGIC). Its Spanish equivalent, *co-implicación*, is sometimes used in this logical sense. However, it was also used by the Spanish philosopher José Ortega y Gassett (CE 1883–1955), who also introduced its contracted form, *complicación* (complication), to designate a relation between thoughts other than that involving an ordinary implication. He held that thoughts can be related in two ways. First, thinking of a concept that can logically imply another, as when thinking of a bachelor, this concept implies that of an unmarried male. This relation is analytic. By contrast, second, thoughts can be related synthetically. Ortega's example is: if we think of a spheroid, we cannot help thinking of it with the space surrounding it, even though the concept of a surrounding space is not logically implied by the concept of a spheroid. The contemporary Spanish philosopher Julián Marías has argued that the idea of essence formulated by the German philosopher Edmund Husserl (CE 1859–1938) involves Ortega's notion of *complicación*, because Husserl's essences are constituted by all items united with each other by their foundation (*Fundierung*). Marías's example is that though the concept of extension is not logically entailed by that of color, it is *complicado* (complicated) in it, because we cannot imagine color without imagining extension.

See also: essentialism

Further reading
Marías, Julián (1969) *Introducción a la filosofía*, 10th edn, Madrid: Revista de Occidente.
Ortega y Gasset, José (1980) *Origen y epílogo de la filosofía*, Madrid: Espasa-Calpe.

coincidentia oppositorum *see* infinity

collective Term appearing in a number of philosophical noun-phrases where it modifies the following terms:

1 choice: see DECISION;
2 conflict: see HOLISM; PHILOSOPHY, SOCIO-POLITICAL;

3 consequences: see ETHICS;
4 decision: see DECISION;
5 representations: see PHILOSOPHY OF SCIENCE;
6 traps: see DECISION;
7 unconscious: see PSYCHOANALYSIS.

collectivism *see* holism; philosophy, sociopolitical

colligation *see* induction

colonialism *see* philosophy, sociopolitical

color realism *see* quality

combat *see* philosophy, sociopolitical; war

combinatory logic *see* logic

comedy *see* aesthetics; philosophy of literature

command *see* ethics; philosophy of language; philosophy of law

commentaries *see* Greek philosophy

commissive *see* speech act theory

commitment, ontological *see* epistemology; metaphysics

common-consent arguments *see* philosophy of religion

common effects *see* causal law

common good *see* ethics; utilitarianism

common ground *see* philosophy, sociopolitical

common notions *see* Stoicism

common sense *see* perception

common-sense philosophy *see* ethics; metaphysics

common-sense realism *see* ethics; metaphysics

communication *see* existentialism; philosophy of language

communism *see* Marxism; philosophy, sociopolitical

communitarianism *see* holism; philosophy, sociopolitical

community *see* epistemology; idealism; pragmatism

commutation *see* logic

commutative *see* logic

compactness *see* deduction; logic

comparison *see* analogy

compassion *see* ethics

compatibilism *see* determinism

compensatory *see* justice

competence, linguistic *see* philosophy of language

competence, moral *see* ethics

competition *see* ethics; philosophy of economics

complement *see* class

complementarity *see* philosophy of science

complementary term *see* class; reasoning

complementation *see* class; logic

complete *see* alethiology; completeness; philosophy of mind

completeness Term used in different senses depending on the fields of inquiry and areas of human activity. It generally indicates that such things as a set of axioms, a language, and a theory are strong enough for some sought purpose.

The first sense of the term appears in formal logic. Among the various notions of completeness used in this area, the most notable are:

1 A set of axioms is *complete* for the logical system L if every theorem of L is provable using axioms of that set.
2 A logical system L has *weak semantic completeness* if every valid sentence of the language of L is a theorem of L.
3 L has *strong semantic completeness* (or is *deductively complete*) if, for every set Γ of sentences, every logical consequences of Γ can be deduced from Γ using L. Also, L is *post-complete* if it is consistent, but no stronger logic for the same language is consistent as well.

The second sense of the term completeness appears in combinatory logic. Combinatory logic includes the following primitive notions:

1 A primitive operation, the application operation (fx), which consists in applying a function f to an argument x.
2 The combinators S and K that involve the rules $Kyx = x$, and $Sxyz = xz(yx)$.

For example, if f and g respectively are two- and one-argument functions, then $Sfgx = f(x,gX)$. Given this, *combinatorial completeness* can be characterized as follows: if the formula $a(x1,...xn)$ is made up of constants and the indicated variables by means of the application operation, then there is a function F made up of constants and the combinators S and K such that $Fx1...xn = a(xl,...xn)$.

The third sense of the term appears in first-order logic. Here, the *completeness theorem* – that all valid sentences are provable – can be formulated as follows: syntactic consistency implies *satisfiability*, where the latter term is analogous to the syntactic notion of *consistency*, i.e. the unprovability of any explicit contradiction. In 1936, the logician Kurt Gödel (CE 1906–78, born in Brünn, Austria–Hungary – now Brno, Czech Republic) proved the *compactness* theorem – if every finite subset of a set of sentences is satisfiable, then the set is satisfiable – that follows directly from the completeness theorem for first-order logic.

The fourth sense of the term appears in symbolic logic. The expression *complete symbols* is used in a manner analogous to the medieval expression *categoremata* – words that have a definite independent meaning – only that it is extended to symbols.

The fifth sense of the term appears in scientific-theory construction. Here, the term completeness denotes a property of theories with regard to which these theories explain their intended subject matter to a greater or lesser extent. This is one of the criteria that contribute to making a case for a theory and against alternative ones. For example, in expanding the laws of electromagnetism to cover open circuits, the Scottish physicist James Clerk Maxwell (CE 1831–79) appealed to considerations of completeness.

The sixth sense of the term appears in philosophy of religion and religious thought (see PERFECTION).

See also: logic; perfection; philosophy of science

Further reading
Manaster, Alfred B. (1975) *Completeness, Compactness, and Undecidability: An Introduction to Mathematical Logic*, Englewood Cliffs, NJ: Prentice-Hall.
Nielson, Hanne Riis (1988) *Functional Completeness of the Mixed [lambda]-Calculus and Combinatory Logic*, Aalborg, Denmark: Aalborg Universitetscenter, Institut for Elektroniske Systemer, Afdeling for Matematik og Datalogi.
Smullyan, Raymond M. (1992) *Godel's Incompleteness Theorems*, New York: Oxford University Press.

complex constructive and destructive dilemma *see* dilemma

complexe significabile *see* complexum significabile

complexity *see* philosophy, sociopolitical

complexum significabile Also called *complexe significabile* (plural: *complexe significabilia*), what is signified by an entire declarative sentence. The Greek philosopher Aristotle (BCE 384–322) had already said in the *Categories* (10, 12b, 6–15) that an assertion was an affirmative proposition, and a negation was a negative proposition, but what fell under an assertion or a negation was not a proposition but a thing. Commenting on this passage in his *Sentences* (I, D2, q. I, a. 1), the philosopher Gregory of Rimini, born in the city of Rimini in what is now Italy (CE *c.* 1300–58), said that the thing Aristotle refers to is not an external reality but something meant by the entire sentence. Since the sentence is a complex, what falls under it can be called *complexum significabile*: that which means by means of a complex. For Gregory of Rimini, *complexe significabilia*, though not existent in the ordinary way, were somehow real. Indeed, they were the proper object of knowledge.

See also: abstract; logic

Further reading
Elie, Hubert (1936) *Le complexe significabile*, Paris: J. Vrin.
Meinong, Alexius (1982) *On Assumptions*, Berkeley, CA: University of California Press.

Complutense *see* Scholasticism

composition *see* fallacy

compossibility *see* alethiology

compound statement *see* logic

comprehension From the Latin *comprehen-dere*, i.e. "to grasp together," this term is used in a variety of philosophical senses. As applied to a term, it denotes the set of attributes implied by the term or, as it is predominantly said today, its intension. For example, the comprehension of the term "triangle" includes such things as being three-sided, being two-dimensional, being a closed figure, and having three angles.

The notion of comprehension was already described by the French philosophers Antoine Arnauld (CE 1612–94) and Pierre Nicole (CE 1625–95) in their *Port-Royal Logic*, published in 1662. It was later discussed by the English philosopher John Stuart Mill (CE 1806–73) in his *Examination of Sir William Hamilton's Philosophy*, published in 1865, where, as it is predominantly done today, he identifies comprehension with intension and contrasts it with extension: the item(s) to which a concept applies. The United States philosopher C.I. Lewis (CE 1883–1964) argued that this distinction was too vague because it did not distinguish between essential and non-essential features. He accordingly distinguished between four aspects of a terms-descriptive meaning. They are *connotation*, i.e. all the features associated with a term; *signification*, i.e. the features that are necessary and sufficient for correctly relating the term to the items to which it applies; *denotation*, i.e. the existent items connoted and signified by the term; and *comprehension*, i.e. the existent and possible items connoted and signified by a term. The notion of comprehension is central in discussions of the *axiom of comprehension* (also called axiom of abstraction, principle of comprehension, and principle of unlimited comprehension), and its relation to the set-theoretic paradoxes. It also has led to discussions concerning the relations between logical concepts and metaphysical views, and to computer science applications.

The German philosopher Wilhelm Dilthey (CE 1833–1911) used the term comprehension (*das Verstehen*) in a very different sense: as a form of apprehension of mental life – which he understood as distinct from nature – by reference to the meaning of its manifestations. In this sense, Dilthey understood the social studies to be hermeneutical. Philosophical discussion of this topic has centered on whether comprehension is ever, if not always, equivalent to explanation. Dilthey thought it never was. Others have adopted a middle-ground position, arguing that it sometimes is thus equivalent. Still others have rejected Dilthey's notion, arguing that comprehension in his sense can provide no knowledge.

See also: meaning; set

Further reading
Dilthey, Wilhelm (1996) *Hermeneutics and the Study of History*, Princeton, NJ: Princeton University Press.
Hofmann, Martin (1997) *Extensional Constructs in Intensional Type Theory*, London: Springer.
Slater, B.H. (1994) *Intensional Logic: An Essay in Analytical Metaphysics*, Aldershot, Hampshire, UK and Brookfield, VT: Avebury.
Tomiyama, Tetsuo (1987) *Representing Knowledge in Two Distinct Descriptions: Extensional vs. Intensional*, Amsterdam, the Netherlands: Stichting Mathematisch Centrum.

comprehensive *see* ethics; philosophy

comprehensiveness *see* ethics; philosophy

compromise *see* philosophy, sociopolitical

computability *see* computer theory

computational *see* cognitive; computer theory

computer modeling *see* computer theory

computer program *see* computer theory

computer theory The study and resulting theories about the design, applications, possibilities, and limitations of computers. A notion central to computer theory is that of *algorithm*: a procedure that, when applied to certain symbolic inputs will, in a finite number of steps, result in a symbolic output. When an algorithm is used to calculate values of a numerical function, the function is said to be algorithmically computable, effectively computable, or, simply, computable. Computers are artifacts that compute. They are complex hierarchical physical systems – i.e. a division of components such as memory boards, processors, and control systems ordered in a manner that reflects their complexity – that use a hierarchy of languages, i.e. a division of languages ordered in a manner that reflect their complexity.

Computer theory has two branches corresponding to the two main types of computer components. One is computer *hardware*, i.e. the computer analogue of an organism's body. It includes memory – where information is stored, a processor – where the arithmetic–logic unit transforms data and the control unit executes programs, and input–output devices for information exchanges between the computer and its environment – or, in the case of feedback and feedforward, through a closed loop, between the computer and the computer, and, in some cases (e.g. floppy disks and magnetic tapes) for additional storage. Memory, processor, and input–output devices communicate with each other through a fast switching system of components.

The other main type of computer component is computer *software*, i.e. the computer analogue of an organism's information processing, i.e. in a wide sense of this term, of its mental life. It is written in a hierarchy of programming languages, i.e. languages that provide instructions for data operations and transfers, transfers of control from one part of a program to another, and modifications of programs.

Theoretically, a computer can be imagined to have an indefinitely expandable storage tape, i.e. to constitute a *Turing machine*, named after the British mathematician and logician Alan Turing (CE 1912–54) who characterized it. This is the physical actualization of a formal logic that has an unlimited number of proofs and theorems. In computer theory, indefinite computability – roughly, the possibility of computation in a Turing machine – is central. In this regard, the halting problem for Turing machines is the problem of devising a Turing machine that computes the function $(h(m,n)=1$ or 0 depending on whether the Turing machine number m ever halts, once started with the number n on its tape. It can be shown that this is an unsolvable problem.

A central concept of the area of computer theory concerned with hardware is that of a *finite automaton*, frequently characterized as an idealized logical network of truth-functional switches and memory components connected to one another. The law governing the behavior of these components is *deterministic* and is defined in a state table that is finite and, hence, can be stored on a tape. When the switches and memory components of a finite automaton are made probabilistic, the outcome is a *probabilistic* automaton.

A finite automaton can also be expanded by adding sensing and behavioral components. A powerful finite automaton capable of executing programs is a *universal computing robot*. When a universal computing robot is expanded so that it can construct robots, it becomes a universal constructing robot or *universal constructor* that, when it can construct itself, is a *self-reproducing automaton*. In developing the logic for self-reproducing automata, the Hungarian born United States mathematician John Von Neumann (CE 1903–57) extended the notion of a finite automaton to that of an *infinite cellular automaton*, which is an infinite checkerboard array of cells where each cell contains the same twenty-nine state finite automaton. These states include: one blank or passive state; twelve switching, storing, and communication states; and sixteen states that simulate construction and destruction. Von Neumann's choice of states makes it possible to activate cells out of a blank area and convert the area into a cellular automaton. This type of automaton is widely used in the study of artificial life (see ARTIFICIAL).

A closed finite automaton would exemplify the so called law of *eternal return* or *eternal recurrence*: its history would be a periodic recurrence of the same series of states or logical machine states. After the invention of modern electronic computers, Turing proposed a test – the *Turing test* – for judging whether a computer is behaviorally equivalent to a human in reasoning and intellect. It consisted in placing a human and a programmed electronic computer in separate rooms and in communication with the person running the test, who does not know which is in what room. If, after communicating with them at length, the experimeter still cannot tell what room holds the machine and which the person, then the behavioral equivalence of person and computer would be confirmed. The doctrine of *logical mechanism* holds that such equivalence is possible: a finite deterministic automaton can perform all human functions.

Two philosophical notions relevant to the area of computer theory concerned with software are that of *calculus ratiocinator*, the name coined by the German philosopher and scientist Gottfried Wilhelm Leibniz (CE 1646–1716) for a formal system of reasoning about scientific facts, and that of *characteristica universalis*, the name he coined for a universal notation by means of which those facts were to be recorded in developing his program for a universal science. The limitations of Leibniz's notions have been made plain by the incompleteness theorems proven by the Austrian logician Kurt Goedel (CE 1906–78). Despite these limitations concerning proof, computers are enormously useful as instruments for discovery through modeling. For example, a computer or system of computers can be used as a universal simulator to model systems that are too complex to study by means of traditional methods.

See also: artificial; calculus

Further reading

Gottlob, Georg, Leitsch, Alexander, and Mundici, Daniele (1997) *Computational Logic and Proof Theory: 5th Kurt Godel Colloquium, Vienna, Austria, August 25–29, 1997 – Proceedings*, Berlin and London: Springer.

Mitcham, Carl and Huning, Alois (1986) *Philosophy and Technology II: Information Technology and Computers in Theory and Practice*, Dordrecht and Boston: Reidel/Kluwer.

conative *see* intention; philosophy of mind

conceivability *see* alethiology

concept *see* conceptualism

conceptual analysis *see* analysis

conceptual immediacy *see* conceptualism

conceptual priority *see* conceptualism

conceptual-role semantics *see* meaning; philosophy of mind

conceptualism A view about the ontological status of universals, e.g. number three, and the property of being a book; that is, of entities supposed to exist over and above the particular items that exemplify or instantiate them, e.g. a particular triad of items, and this particular copy of a book. Conceptualism holds that universals have mental existence, but do not exist outside the mind. It is contrasted with realism, which holds universals have extramental existence, and NOMINALISM, which holds universals are merely general words such as common nouns and adjectives that have no general counterpart in or outside the mind. Conceptualism involves different notions of what a concept is. Some philosophers think concepts are *mental representations or ideas*. Others think they are *brain states*. Still others think they are *rules for the use of general words* such as adjectives, common nouns, and verbs. Next, there are philosophers who think concepts are *abilities to classify items* with or without the assistance of ideas, brain states, or linguistic rules. In addition, some philosophers think concepts are *theoretical constructs*, i.e. classification rules implied in the networks of laws that constitute theories. Whatever the sense of concept used, conceptualization is the application of a concept to items. When, however, the concept is primitive, i.e. either undefinable or treated as undefinable in a theory, or learned simply by acquaintance, the concept exhibits conceptual immediacy. Also, when a concept – say, that of a bachelor – cannot be understood without understanding some other concept – in our case, that of a male, because a bachelor is an unmarried male – then the former exhibits conceptual dependence with regard to the latter, and the latter exhibits conceptual priority with regard to the former.

An example of conceptualism can arguably be found in Kantian philosophy, as well as in the work of Edward Herbert of Cherbury (CE 1583–1648), the English philosopher who founded Deism, and has a family resemblance to Scottish common-sense philosophy, also called common-sense realism. He adopted the Stoic concept of *notiones communes* or *common notions*, i.e. innate and identifiable by having the following features: priority, independence, universality, certainty, necessity, and immediacy. As in Kantian philosophy centuries later, these common notions organize all experience. Next in order of certainty was the *sensus internus* or *internal sense*, which concerned conscience, emotions, and free will. Third, he considered the *sensus externus* or *external sense*, i.e. that which allowed us to intuit external objects. Finally, he treated of *discursis* or *reasoning*, that, to him, was the greatest source of human error.

See also: abstract; metaphysics

Further reading

Katz, Jerrold J. (1989) *Realism vs. Conceptualism in Linguistics*, Yorktown Heights, NY: IBM T.J. Watson Research Center.

Price, Henry Habberley (1962) *Thinking and Experience*, London and New York: Hutchinson.

concern *see* philosophy, sociopolitical

conclusive *see* logic; justification

concomitant variation, method of *see* induction

concrescence *see* process philosophy

concrete *see* abstract; idealism

concrete universal *see* idealism

concretism *see* metaphysics

concurrent cause *see* causal law

concursus dei *see* occasionalism

conditio sine que non *see* condition

condition Term denoting a state of affairs, event, fact, way, or circumstance in which something is. Quite frequently, the term condition is used to denote something that depends on something else, on which something else depends, or both. The dependence implied can be of various kinds. First, it can be metaphysical, as in "God is the ultimate condition on which the universe depends." Second, it can be epistemological, as in "The observer is a crucial condition on which observations in microphysics depend." Third, it can be logical, as in "That something has apple in it is a necessary condition for its being apple pie." To say that an item B is a *necessary condition* (in

Latin, *conditio sine qua non*, i.e. "condition without which not") for another item A is to say that A cannot be or occur without B. While to say that an item A is a *sufficient condition* for another item B is to say that if A is or occurs, then B is or occurs. In this connection, the term *conditional* is used to characterize a kind of statement, namely those of the form "If p, then q," called conditional statements, which describe relations between the conditions denoted by their component statements, its antecedent (in our example, p), and its consequent (in our example, q). For example, the statement "If this is apple pie, then it has apple in it" is a *conditional statement* (also called, with different theoretical implications, a conditional proposition or a conditional sentence). As it is always the case with conditional statements, its antecedent, "this is apple pie," denotes a sufficient condition for what the consequent, "it has apple in it," denotes; conversely, the consequent denotes a necessary condition for what the antecedent denotes.

Some philosophers have discussed conditions that are central but neither necessary nor sufficient for an item – say, a whale – being of a certain kind – say, for its being a mammal. For example, having the basic chromosomic structure whales have (which is very similar to that of mammals and very different from that of fish) is *positively central* – i.e. it has highly significant weight – for classifying them as mammals. It is also *negatively central* – i.e. it has significant weight – for not classifying them as fish. While having the basic chromosomic structure blue fish have (which is very similar to that of fish and very different from that of mammals) is positively central – i.e. it has significant weight – for classifying them as fish, and negatively central – i.e. it has significant weight – for not classifying them as mammals. However, none of these features, however central, are necessary or sufficient conditions for the said classifications. Necessary and sufficient conditions are limiting cases of central conditions.

Logicians have distinguished between different kinds of conditional statements. One is the *material conditional* (also called *material implication*). It is characterized by the fact that it is true so long as either the antecedent is false or the consequent is true. It is false only if the antecedent is true and the consequent is false. In this connection, a *strict implication* or *strict conditional* is characterized by the fact that it is impossible for its antecedent to be true when the consequent is false.

A conditional can also be a *counterfactual* conditional: a *subjunctive* conditional – i.e. a conditional used for hypothetical purposes – that presupposes the falsity of its antecedent, as in the conditional "If this sample of water had been heated up to 100° centigrade at one atmosphere of pressure, then it would have boiled." A special kind of counterfactuals are called *counteridenticals*, e.g. "If I had been you, I would have done the opposite of what you did." Since it is neither a strict nor a material conditional, the problem of counterfactual conditionals arose: What are the truth conditions of counterfactuals and how are they determined by the counterfactuals' components? One response has been to argue for *nomological* conditions (the term *nomological* being derived from the Greek *nomos*, i.e. 'law,' and *logos*, i.e. 'discourse' or 'theory'). This response consists in saying that a counterfactual is true when its antecedent, coupled with laws of nature and statements describing background conditions, logically entails its consequent. On this account, the conditional "If this sample of water had been heated up to 100° centigrade at one atmosphere of pressure, then it would have boiled" is true because the antecedent, plus the relevant laws of nature, entail the consequent. In other words, the antecedent is a *nomologically* sufficient condition for the consequent (and the consequent is a *nomologically necessary* condition for the antecedent). In a parallel manner, when the supposedly involved laws are metaphysical in nature, philosophers have talked of *metaphysically sufficient* and *metaphysically necessary* conditions. The problem here arises of specifying the facts that are fixed without including the denial of the antecedent, of the consequent, or of anything that would not be true if the antecedent were, among the background conditions. This is clearest concerning counteridenticals.

The term conditional is sometimes used in noun phrases among which are: (1) conditional probability (see PROBABILITY) and (2) conditional proof (see LOGIC).

See also: causal law; metaphysics; quality

Further reading
Epstein, Richard L. (1995) *Propositional Logics*, New York: Oxford University Press.
Ferguson, Niall (1997) *Virtual History: Alternatives and Counterfactuals*, London: Picador.
Reichenbach, Hans (1976) *Laws, Modalities, and Counterfactuals: Nomological Statements and Admissible Operations*, Berkeley: University of California Press.

conditioning *see* behaviorism

Condorcet winner *see* decision; paradox

confidentiality *see* ethics

confirmation *see* induction

confirmational holism *see* holism; philosophy of science

conflict *see* philosophy, sociopolitical

confrontation *see* philosophy, sociopolitical

Confucianism A Chinese School and moral teachings thought to be founded by Confucius (sixth–fifth century BCE), a member of a social group, the *Ju*, whose members had an interest in rituals and often were teachers. Confucius retained the interest in rituals, but became concerned with searching for remedies to the then chaotic social and political situation in China. This focus was also characteristic of his followers and constituted the characteristic feature of the school of thought thus developed, Confucianism, whose Chinese name is *Ju-chia* (the School of *Ju*).

Confucianism includes a number of characteristic doctrines and ideals, largely formulated in the *Four Books*, a group of texts including the *Ta-hsüeh* (*Great Learning*) and *Chung Yung* (*Doctrine of the Mean*), which were originally part of the *Book of Rites*, *Lun Yü* (*Analects*), and *Meng Tzu* (*Book of Mencius*). Two of these, the *Great Learning* and the *Doctrine of the Mean*, are included in a classic of Chinese Confucianism, the *Li Chi* or *Record of Rites*, which also includes an essay on learning that emphasizes its interaction with ethical teaching.

Among the central doctrines and ideals in Confucianism are: an affectionate concern for all living beings; reverence towards others – especially *hsiao* (filial piety): the proper treatment of one's parents – manifested through the observance of rules of conduct; an ability to determine when traditional rules should be observed and when one should depart from them; a firm commitment to acting morally even when facing adversity. A central Confucian principle is *ch'eng*, i.e. sincerity. It was developed in the *Chung Yung* or *Doctrine of the Mean*, one of the most philosophical of ancient Chinese documents, which was originally part of the *Book of Rites* and was brought to prominence by the Chinese Confucian philosopher Chu Hsi (CE 1130–1200). According to the Doctrine of the Mean, the ultimate principle is rather metaphysical in that it is said to be *ch'eng* because totally beyond illusion and delusion, and one's conduct should strike the appropriate mean between deficiency and excess. As for strictly practical concerns, crucial concepts are *chung*, meaning loyalty, commitment, and doing one's best, and *shu*, meaning consideration and reciprocity (not to be confused with the term *shu* that meant statecraft and was used by the Chinese Legalism School). In the *Analects*, Confucius explains this latter concept as not doing to another what one would not have wished done to oneself; but he leaves the meaning of *chung* implicit. Interpreters have understood it in various ways: as a commitment to being guided by *shu*, as a commitment to observing rites or the norms of principle (*li*) in a humanized manner, or as strict observance of one's duties toward superiors or equals while being considerate toward equals or inferiors.

Confucian philosophers have often focused on the term *hsin*, one of whose meanings is heart, mind, and feeling. In this sense, *hsin* is both, literally the heart, and the disposition to have appetites, emotions, and cognitions. The problem for Confucian and, in general, Chinese philosophers was that of the nature and role of *hsin*. Meng Tzu or Meng K'o or, in Latin, Mencius (371–289? BCE) talked of four hearts (the four foundations), each associated with a specific virtue and group of cognitive and emotive dispositions. While neo-Confucians argued whether *hsin* was identical with *li* (principle) or *hsing* (nature).

Another Chinese term that is also pronounced *hsin* means trust, faith, and trustworthiness. It came to denote one of the main Confucian virtues, honesty or trustworthiness for the sake of what is right.

Still another important term in Confucianism is *jen* (variously translated as kindness, humanity, benevolence, altruism, goodness, love, and perfect virtue), whose literal meaning is human in society, and which denotes both an ethical ideal for all humans, and the feature of having an affectionate concern for all living things. Confucianism regarded *jen* as the basis of humane government. In the process, it developed the notions of *kung* and *szu*, public and private, in a manner sometimes also found in other schools of Chinese philosophy. Neo-Confucianism (see below) expanded the meaning of the term *jen* to the entire universe, focusing on humans' relations from a cosmic standpoint. They also used the term *jen* in the expression *jen-hsin* to denote humans' artificial, selfish desires, by contrast with *tao-hsin*, which denotes humans acting spontaneously in accordance with the Way.

A related notion in this type of ethics is that of *ming*. In one sense, *ming* means fate, or mandate, or what is beyond human control, because the said virtues involve responsibility and the latter is absence when *ming* is at work. In another sense, however, in *t'ien ming* or the Mandate from Heaven, *ming* means the mandate to rule that issues from *t'ien* understood as the moral endowment of a virtuous human being. In effect, if the emperor does not rule humanely, *t'ien* takes the mandate away.

It should be noted that *t'ien* has a variety of meanings ranging between most and least anthropomorphic. In the sense just discussed, it is conceived highly anthropomorphically, as having desires and engaging in intentional actions. At the other extreme, some thinkers understood it as identical with the natural order. Indeed, it is sometimes used as synonymous with *shang ti*, which means high ancestor or Lord-on-High in the sense of a powerful anthropomorphic entity that is responsible for the State's fate. Also, *t'ien* is used in the expression *t'ien-jen ho-i*, which denotes the relation between *t'ien*, understood as heaven, and human beings. In neo-Confucian ethics, the contrast is conveyed by the polar terms *t'ien li* or heavenly principles, and *jen-yü* or human desires.

Jen was not only used by Confucian or neo-Confucian thinkers. For example, Mo Tzu (479–381 BCE), who once followed and then opposed Confucius, retained the concept of *jen* in his philosophy of universal love, by arguing that individuals who had *jen* practiced the universal-love principle.

In addition, Confucian thinkers used the distinction between *jung* (honor) and *ju* (shame or disgrace). While these notions apply to normal life situations and social positions such as security and danger, and harm and benefit, Confucian thinkers distinguished between honor based merely on external recognition and honor justly deserved (from the standpoint of *jen* – benevolence – and *yi* – rightness), as well as between shame or disgrace resulting from circumstance, e.g. from poverty, and shame and disgrace resulting from one's moral misconduct (i.e. from the standpoint of *jen* and *yi*). The ideal individual (*chün-tzu*) should accept the former, but not be content with the latter form of shame or disgrace.

The various concepts just discussed are part of a virtue-ethics one of whose components, the Doctrine of the Mean, is outlined in the *Chung Yung*. This doctrine involves the notion of *chün-tzu*, i.e. superior human being or exemplary or paradigmatic individual, a practically attainable ideal of excellence characterized by a concern for human beings, proper conduct, and moral rightness. In this regard, Confucianism adopted and further specified two philosophical terms found in the *ta-hsüeh* or *Book of Great Learning*, namely *ko wu* (to correct, arrive at, or oppose some things) and *chih chih* (to expand or reach out for knowledge), which denote two stages of the self-cultivation process. The neo-Confucian philosopher Chu Hsi (CE 1130–1200) used *ko wu* to mean arriving at *li* concerning human matters, and *chih chih* to mean the expansion of knowledge, while Wang Yang-ming (CE 1472–1529), who emphasized the unity of knowledge and action, used *ko wu* to mean correcting the activities of one's *hsin* (heart/mind), and *chi*

chi, the reaching out of *liang chih* (one's innate knowledge of the good). Chu Hsi is credited with having introduced the term *tao-t'ung*, i.e. the orthodox line of transmission of the Way, though the idea can be traced back to Han Yü (CE 768–824) and Mencius (371–289 BCE).

Another key concept in Confucian morality is *ch'üan*, i.e. weighing of circumstances or the comparative assessment of competing considerations concerning a practical problem. It can also denote the assessment of the significance of moral considerations to a practical problem. The upshot of such assessments is a judgment that must be in accordance with principle or reason (*li*), and, when the practical problem addressed involves moral considerations, with rightness (*i*). Sometimes, *ch'üan* denotes a hard case, i.e. one hard to assess given ordinary moral rules.

Though mentioned in the *Analects*, *cheng ming*, the Confucian program correcting the uses of terms (also called *The Rectification of Names*) was especially formulated by Hsün Tzu.

During the Han dynasty, creative philosophical inquiry was replaced by the merely backward-looking, detailed study of five works called the *Five Classics*: *Book of Poetry*, *Book of History*, *Book of Changes*, *Book of Rites*, and *Spring and Autumn Annals*. The Han dynasty ended in CE 220 and Wei (CE 220–65), the first Emperor of the Wei-Chin dynasty, ordered the *Five Classics*, except for the *Book of Changes* (*I-Ching*), burned. As a result, Confucianism was, first, eclipsed by the Wei-Chin School and, then, threatened by the introduction of Buddhism in China. This lasted between the third and sixth centuries CE.

In response to these influences, neo-Confucianism was developed on the basis of insights found in the *Analects*, *The Great Learning*, the *Doctrine of the Mean*, and the works of Mencius (written down in modern script by Han scholars relying on their memories), and incorporating ideas from Buddhism and Taoism. For example, with the Taoist view, neo-Confucian philosophers considered *hsü* (void) the original state of the universe and contrasted it with the Buddhist concept of *k'ung* (emptiness) on the grounds that it made no room for the ultimate reality of the world.

Neo-Confucianism reached its peak during the Sung-(Yüan)-Ming period (CE 960–1126), sometimes described as the Chinese Renaissance. Foreshadowed in the work of Chou Tun-i (CE 1017–73), neo-Confucianism was fully formulated by Ch'eng Hao (CE 1032–85) and his brother Ch'eng Yi (CE 1033–1107). Among neo-Confucian philosophers, Shao-Yung (CE 1011–77), like the others, traced the development of multiple things from the Great Ultimate – mind, reason, and moral law – through the actions of *Yin* and *Yang*, which are produced by the Great Ultimate without itself engaging in activity. Unlike the others, Shao-Yung used the idea of number in explaining this process. Confucianism's main representative, however, was Chu Hsi (CE 1130–1200), who systematized neo-Confucianism and developed the Ch'eng-Chu School. Chu Hsi's metaphysics was based on the notions of an incorporeal, unique, eternal, unchanging, and invariably good principle (*li*) and a physical, diverse, transitory, changeable, partly good and partly evil material force (*ch'i*). These notions coexist, unmixed but united. That is, he regarded the Great Ultimate as the principle in its totality, involving principle and material force, but being primarily principle, identical with all things that are simply its manifestations (though, arguably, this involved the *li* of each thing, so that each thing has both the universal *li* and the *li* that makes it the thing it is). In fact, Chinese neo-Confucianism combined *li* and *ch'i* in the notion of *li-ch'i*.

For Chu, human nature was *li*, while feelings and emotions (*ch'ing*) were *ch'i*, and mind/heart (*ch'ing*) was also *ch'i*, though very subtle. This position was criticized by Lu Hsiang-shan (CE 1139–93), who held that mind by itself sufficed to harmonize the human and the natural in human nature. This view was revived by Wang Yan-ming (CE 1472–1529) at the end of the Sung-(Yüan)-Ming period, thus originating the Lu-Wang School. In formulating his views, Wang refined the notion of *liang-chih*, which had been initially formulated by Meng-tzu or Mencius in the fourth century BCE. For Meng-tzu, *liang-chih* roughly meant innate knowledge of the good. For Wang, it meant sense of right and wrong, or ability to tell right from wrong, which, for

him, was the love of good and hate of evil. This ability amounted to a moral consciousness that, according to Wang, involved a vision of *jen* as being one with the universe but, given that circumstances change, involved deliberation. Hsün Tzu (298–238 BCE) had used the term *pi*, i.e. screen, shelter, or cover, as a metaphor for lack of mental clarity or anything that obstructs cognitive tasks. He also used the term *pien* to denote the ability to distinguish mental states and the proper objects of given desires. This ability is crucial in neo-Confucianism, according to which the goal of life is sagehood.

See also: Chinese philosophy

Further reading
Chan, W.T. (1963) trans. and comp., *A Source Book in Chinese Philosophy*, Princeton, NJ: Princeton University Press.
Cua, A.S. (1998) *Moral Vision and Tradition: Essays in Chinese Ethics*, Washington, DC: Catholic University of America.
—— (1978) *Dimensions of Moral Creativity: Paradigms, Principles, and Ideals*, University Park, PA: Pennsylvania State University Press.
Hall, David L. and Ames, Roger T. (1999) *Thinking through Confucius*, Boulder, CO: NetLibrary, Inc.
Nivison, David S. (1996) *The Ways of Confucianism: Investigations in Chinese Philosophy*, Chicago: Open Court.
Starr, Frederick (1983) *Confucianism Ethics, Philosophy, Religion*, New York: Covici-Friede.

congruence *see* pragmatism

congruism *see* philosophy of religion

Conimbricenses *see* Scholasticism

conjecture *see* induction

conjunction *see* logic

conjunctive normal form *see* logic

connected *see* relation

connectedness *see* relation

connectionism *see* computer theory

connective *see* logic

connexity *see* relation

connotation *see* meaning

conscience From the Latin *con*, i.e. "with" and *scire*, i.e. "to know." The Greek equivalent is *synderesis* that, in the works of the Greek poet Homer (eighth century BCE), meant to be attentively vigilant and, in one of the works of the Greek philosopher Aristotle (384–322 BCE), *De Plantis*, meant to guard, conserve. The origin of the noun form *synderesis* (more precisely *synderesys*) is attributed to the Christian ascetic and biblical scholar Saint Jerome (born in Dalmatia, *c.* CE 340–420), who in his *Commentarium in Ezechielem*, I, 1, xxv, uses it to mean "the spark of conscience" (*scintilla conscientiae*). He thought the conscience's function was to correct the errors of reason and master desires. In English, the term conscience is restricted to moral consciousness. This linguistic specialization can also be found, for example, in German (*Gewissen* by contrast with *Bewusstsein*), but not, for example, in Spanish (*conciencia*), where the identity continues and, to specify one means conscience, the expression moral consciousness (*conciencia moral*) is used. Forerunners of this moral notion of conscience are the Socratic reference to an inner warning voice whose origin traced back to God, and the Stoics' conception of the voice of reason in humans that derives from universal reason and can guide a person's life. During the Middle Ages, Saint Jerome's term, *synderesys*, was used to denote humans' awareness of universally binding rules of conduct, while *conscientia* was used to denote consideration of the relation between universal rules of conduct and particular cases. The latter was referred to in the development of *casuistics* (also called *casuistry*), or the study of the application of general rules of conduct to particular cases. In modern discussions, synderesys ceased to be used, while casuistics fell in disrepute because of a tendency on the part of some of its practitioners to use sophistical arguments in its practice. Also, changes in the conception of human psychology and the nature of general principles prompted an interest in the place, if any, of moral sense. The English bishop, theologian, and moral philosopher Joseph Butler (CE 1692–1752) was most prominent in advancing the view that conscience is the voice of *moral sense* and, as a reflective and rational disposition he characterizes as *self-love* or the disposition to seek one's own overall happiness by regulating one's particular desires (from the desire for particular honors to the desire to benefit another person in particular circumstances), has a central place in human psychology and morality.

See also: ethics

Further reading
Butler, Joseph (1995) *The Works of Joseph Butler*, Bristol, UK: Thoemmes Press.
Gladwin, John W. (1977) *Conscience*, Bramcote: Grove Books.
Shapiro, Ian, and Adams, Robert Merrihew (1998) *Integrity and Conscience*, New York and London: New York University Press.

consciousness *see* philosophy of mind; philosophy, sociopolitical

consensus *see* philosophy, sociopolitical

consensus gentium *see* truth

consent *see* ethics; philosophy, sociopolitical

consequence *see* ethics; logic

consequent *see* condition

consequentia mirabilis *see* logic

consequential property *see* supervenience

consequentialism *see* ethics

consequentialist *see* ethics

conservation *see* ethics; philosophy of science

consilience *see* explanation; induction; theory

consistency *see* logic

constant *see* completeness; logic

constant-sum game *see* decision

constative *see* philosophy of language

constituency *see* philosophy of science; philosophy, sociopolitical

constitution *see* philosophy of law

constitutive principle *see* Kantian philosophy

constraint *see* philosophy, sociopolitical

construct *see* epistemology; ethics; operationalism

constructive dilemma *see* dilemma

constructivism *see* epistemology; ethics; philosophy of mathematics; philosophy, sociopolitical

contact *see* infinity

containment *see* Kantian philosophy

contemplation *see* theory

content *see* fallacy; philosophy of mind; psychoanalysis

context *see* justification; meaning

contextual *see* definition; justification

contextualism *see* justification

contiguity *see* associationism

continence *see* akrasia

Continental philosophy The various and changing philosophical positions developed in Continental Europe since the early to mid-1940s in a manner that diverged from, and often contrasted with, those developed in Great Britain and English-speaking North America. Initially, Continental philosophy mostly meant *PHENOMENOLOGY*, which, at the time, was primarily understood along the ultracartesian lines outlined by the German philosopher Edmund Husserl (CE 1859–1938) as the precise description of the various ways in which material objects, living things, other persons, cultural objects, the past and present, numbers, speech, time and space are given to us in experience.

Later, the name Continental philosophy expanded to cover *EXISTENTIALISM*, a literary and philosophical movement that focused on the uniqueness of each human individual as distinct from abstract human qualities, and whose main exponents were the French philosophers and literary figures Jean-Paul Sartre (CE 1905–80) and Simone de Beauvoir (CE 1908–86). Existentialism is often contrasted with *existential phenomenology* or *existential philosophy*, an approach practiced by a group of thinkers who applied variations of Husserl's phenomenological methods to many philosophical problems. They included, first, the German philosopher Martin Heidegger (CE 1889–1976), who coined the term *hermeneutic phe-*

nomenology for his enterprise of trying to let whatever items we examine show themselves without our pigeonholing them into presupposed categories, which in his later writings, e.g. *Holzwege*, he understood more strongly: as becoming passive in approaching these items. Another representative of this approach (who had first accepted, but later rejected, the label of existentialist) was the French philosopher Gabriel Marcel (CE 1889–1973), whose inquiries focused on intersubjectivity in interpersonal relations. Still another (though sometimes thought to represent existentialism) was the French philosopher Maurice Merleau-Ponty (CE 1908–61), who emphasized the existential bodily nature of the human subject.

Another movement in Continental philosophy was *structuralism*, a range of intellectual activities inspired by the Swiss linguist and Sanskrit scholar Ferdinand de Saussure (CE 1857–1913), founder of structural linguistics, which considered languages as repositories of discursive signs shared by a linguistic community. He called for a science of *semiology*, which would deal with the nature of signs and the laws governing them. His conception of languages as repositories of discursive signs shared by a linguistic community had a forerunner in a contribution by the German philologist Wilhelm von Humboldt (CE 1767–1835): the notion of *Sprachform*, i.e. the inner form each particular language has, which is peculiar to the language and provides a characteristic world outlook for the community of the language's users.

This latter conception, however, begs questions that Saussure's conception did not, e.g. that the *Sprachform* is peculiar to a language and that it provides a characteristic worldview to the language's users.

Saussure's conception of languages as repositories of discursive signs shared by a linguistic community was extended by him and others to social phenomena in general. This way, structuralism evoked new objects by constructing and reconstructing them across disciplines through extrapolation from observations and with the help of ideas borrowed from Marxism and Freudian psychoanalysis. In general, structuralism is the doctrine that all societies share a common and invariant structure that, unconsciously and pre-reflectively, manifests itself in their members' activities. It approaches its research objects from the standpoint of *diachrony*, i.e. through time, and *synchrony*, i.e. as atemporal slices. The latter serves to characterize the objects' structure.

Another distinction drawn by Saussure is that between *langue*, or the structured language, and *parole*, or the speech of an individual language user. This distinction was used by the French structuralist Jacques Lacan (CE 1901–81) to draw a parallel between *parole* and the psychoanalytic concept of ego, and *langue* and the psychoanalytic concept of id (see PSYCHOANALYSIS). On this basis, Lacan proposed a therapy aimed at subverting the ego and giving priority to the many meanings of the linguistic expression of the id, where symbolism plays a crucial role in addressing the self-aggression that, according to Lacan, each of us has as a result of the loss initially felt in infancy and never overcome.

Structuralism developed into *post-structuralism*, a movement of literary criticism that moved away from the structuralist focus on the relation between signs and reality, and, instead, focused on the relations of signs to each other. Two varieties became influential. One is *anti-constructionism*, the doctrine that there is no underlying structure to reveal in a text, hence interpreting the text can only be the task of disentangling its intermingled codes without attempting to decipher them. Its most notable proponent was the French philosopher and literary critic Roland Barthes (CE 1915–80) who, in *S/Z*, a book published in 1970, provided a case study of contrasts between the reading and writing of *Sarrasine*, by the French novelist Honoré de Balzac (CE 1799–1850), which, Barthes held, show that there was no underlying structure but only conflicting codes.

A second form of post-structuralism developed in Continental philosophy is *deconstructionism*, which is characterized by DECONSTRUCTION, an approach that opposes hermeneutics, though it, like hermeneutics, claims Heidegger's transformation of Husserl's phenomenology as its origin. Many deconstructionists acknowledge the French philosopher of science Gaston Bachelard (CE 1884–1962) as the original deconstructionist. Its leading proponent has been the contemporary French philosopher Jaques Derrida, who started as a structuralist. Deconstructionism deconstructs texts, seeking conflicting conceptions of meaning and implication in them, including the linguistic and rhetorical idiosyncrasies of their authors. The point of the interpreter's task is to show how texts undermine the philosophical presuppositions in which they rely. In pursuing this task, deconstructionism tries to overcome modern thinking, hence becoming associated with the range of views that have become associated with the term *postmodernism* (more of a buzz-word than a term with a precise or even clear descriptive meaning), which is used to denote any view or approach that involves a reaction against modern philosophy and some of its predominant doctrines – say, essentialism, foundationalism, and realism – as well as associated ideas and practices in modern culture.

In formulating his position, Derrida has coined the term *différance*, deriving it from the French term *différer*, which means both to differ and to defer. Using the term *différance* in a manner that combines both connotations, Derrida argues that for signifying to occur, there must be a *différance;* that is, first, one sign must be the *signifier* and the other must be the *signified*, i.e. they must differ in function, and, second, since the signifier can only provide a *trace* – i.e. a hint – of the signified, it must defer to the signified so that the latter becomes itself a signifier with regard to another signified, and so on and so forth. From this, Derrida concludes that all words are inaccurate and proposes a new kind of linguistics he calls *grammatology*, whose task is to deconstruct texts.

Another representative of post-structuralism whose position is associated with deconstructionism, though whose approach is quite different from that of Derrida, is the French philosopher and historian of thought Michel Foucault (CE 1926–84). His method, the *archeology of knowledge*, treats systems of thought as structures of discourse that are independent of the intentions and beliefs of their individual authors, yet have a genealogy connecting power and knowledge in that the said systems are understood as systems of control. According to

Foucault, bodies of knowledge – *epistemes* – and, in general systems of thought, are tied but not reducible to structures of power. On this view, an episteme is a contingent system for the production, regulation, distribution, and operation of statements. It is independent of the beliefs and intentions of individual thinkers and, though contingent, creates constraints on thought and action that, to those caught up in them, seem unsurpassable. Given their *epistemic location*, i.e. from the standpoint of what system they engage in discourse, and their *local knowledge*, i.e. the knowledge they have or claim from the historical standpoint of their particular system, they can imagine no alternative to this system.

Still another influential deconstructionist author is the contemporary French philosopher Jean François Lyotard, who has dismissed universal theories as grand narratives, and has argued for little narratives focused on individual human beings. He has also conceived of postmodernism as being characterized by inarticulated beliefs and, accordingly, argued that, in this regard, postmodern philosophy precedes modern philosophy. He argues that judgment is crucially pragmatic and the discourses of individuals are mutually incommensurable, i.e. between any two of them there is a *differend*: an area of differences that, if resolvable, are resolvable only with linguistic innovation.

In sociopolitical philosophy, the expression Continental philosophy is also thought to cover the FRANKFURT SCHOOL and, in particular, the contemporary German philosopher Jürgen Habermas's theory of communicative action aimed at developing a community of communication without alienation and guided only by the sheer force of argument. This approach is quite eclectic, attempting to harmonize ideas from Kantian philosophy, German idealism, Marxism, and the sociology of knowledge and science.

See also: Cartesianism; idealism; Kantian philosophy; Marxism

Further reading
Critchley, Simon, Schroeder, William Ralph, and Berstein, Jay (1998) *A Companion to Continental Philosophy*, Malden, MA: Blackwell.

Derrida, Jacques (1997) *Deconstruction in a Nutshell: A Conversation with Jacques Derrida*, New York: Fordham University Press.
Foucault, Michel (1997) *The Essential Works of Michel Foucault*, New York: New Press, distributed by W.W. Norton & Company.
Hindess, Barry (1996) *Discourses of Power: From Hobbes to Foucault*, Oxford, UK and Cambridge, MA: Blackwell Publishers.
Schirmacher, Wolfgang (1999) *German 20th-Century Philosophy: The Frankfurt School*, New York: Continuum.
Wahl, Jean Andre (1969) *Philosophies of Existence: An Introduction to the Basic Thought of Kierkegaard, Heidegger, Jaspers, Marcel, Sartre*, London: Routledge & K. Paul.
West, David (1996) *An Introduction to Continental Philosophy*, Cambridge: Polity Press.

Continental rationalism *see* rationalism

contingency *see* alethiology

contingent *see* alethiology

contingent being *see* philosophy of religion

continuant *see* philosophy of science

continuity *see* identity

continuum *see* infinity

contract *see* ethics; philosophy, sociopolitical

contractarianism A family of ethical and political theories according to which any ethical or political requirements on individual and group conduct – from moral conceptions, rules, and principles, to policies, practices, and institutions – are ethically or politically justified if, and only if, human beings who are competent to make up their minds about them would agree to abide by them. Such agreement is central to these theories and, given that agreement is a central component of (and sometimes treated as identical with) a contract, it has led to calling the theories contractarian.

Traditionally, such thinkers as the English philosophers Thomas Hobbes (CE 1588–1679) and John Locke (CE 1632–1704), and the French philosopher Jean Jacques Rousseau (CE 1712–78) appealed to the notion of a social contract to justify the State and the features it should have. Some, e.g. Hobbes, argued that the State is justified only to the extent it tends to satisfy the desires or preferences of *actual* individual human beings. This is established, first, by seeing how well actual policies, practices, or institutions – beginning by the institution of the State itself – serve the said interests and, second, by seeing what individuals could agree to if they were to change those actual policies, practices, and institutions. This line of thought has been pursued by the contemporary Canadian philosopher David P. Gauthier.

By contrast with this approach, the German philosopher Immanuel Kant (CE 1724–1804) retained the notion of a contract, but rejected that of justifying moral conceptions, policies, practices, or institutions by reference to the contingent and often non-rational desires of actual human beings. Kant's idea of an original contract is supposed to help determine what policies, practices or institutions are justified, but it is supposed to be agreed upon, not by real, but by *hypothetical* – strictly rational – *human individuals*. They would thus reach hypothetical consent on the matter. The justifying force of such contract was supposed to derive from the rational process these individuals were supposed to follow and the fact that, however pushed or pulled by their desires, human individuals have a settled determination to act in accordance with universal principles and rules of reason.

This approach was further developed, most notably, by the contemporary United States philosopher John Rawls who, in the 1970s, characterized in some detail the hypothetical people who would be in the original position from which moral conceptions and principles of justice would be justified by their agreement. A crucial feature of the original position according to Rawls was that the hypothetical individuals in it were to reach an agreement *behind the veil of ignorance*, i.e. without knowledge of particulars that would allow them to tell whether the moral conceptions and principles of justice they were considering would apply to them by curbing their advantageous, or helping with their disadvantageous, situation in society.

Critics charged that this approach made it impossible for the said individuals to determine what they would want, thus undermining the very notion of a contract and the bargaining involved in the process of reaching it. Rawls later sidestepped this objection: by pursuing his parallel reliance on the considered judgments of rational persons, he later tended to focus on the choices of a hypothetical rational being, rather than on a contract among rational beings. Yet, critics still charged that these hypothetical beings were so far removed from reality as to raise serious questions about the applicability and justifiability of their choices to actual life.

These contractarian approaches have also played a significant role in feminist philosophy, not as ways of attaining, as has traditionally been the focus of discussion, merely a social contract, but a sexual contract.

See also: Kantian philosophy; philosophy, socio-political

Further reading

Rawls, John (1973) *A Theory of Justice*, Cambridge, MA: Harvard University Press.

Vallentyne, Peter (1991) *Contractarianism and Rational Choice: Essays on David Gauthier's Morals by Agreement*, Cambridge, UK: Cambridge University Press.

contradictio in adjecto *see* fallacy

contradiction *see* logic

contradictories *see* syllogism

contraposition *see* argument

contrapositive *see* argument

contraries *see* syllogism

contrariety *see* associationism

contrary-to-duty imperative *see* paradox

contrary-to-fact conditional *see* condition

contrast *see* associationism

contravalid *see* logic

contributive value *see* value

contributory value *see* value

control *see* philosophy of science; philosophy, sociopolitical

controversy *see* philosophy, sociopolitical

convention *see* ethics; philosophy of mathematics; truth

conventional *see* ethics; logic; philosophy of mathematics; truth

conventionalism *see* ethics; philosophy of mathematics; truth

convergence *see* philosophy of science; truth

conversational implicature *see* meaning

converse *see* argument; relation

conversion *see* argument

co-operation *see* ethics; philosophy, sociopolitical

co-ordination problem *see* decision

co-ordinative *see* definition

Copernican Revolution *see* Kantian philosophy

coping *see* philosophy, sociopolitical

copula *see* syncategoremata

copulatio *see* syncategoremata

corner quotes *see* use–mention distinction

corners *see* use–mention distinction

corporate *see* ethics

corporation *see* ethics

Corpus Hermeticum *see* Neoplatonism

corpuscular *see* atomism

corrective justice *see* justice

correlativity theses *see* ethics; philosophy of law

correspondence *see* truth

corrigibility *see* epistemology

corruption *see* change

cosmogony *see* metaphysics; philosophy of science

cosmological *see* philosophy of religion

cosmology *see* metaphysics; philosophy of science

cosmopolis *see* Stoicism

cosmos *see* metaphysics

cost–benefit analysis *see* ethics

cost-effectiveness *see* ethics

count noun *see* natural kinds

countable *see* set

counterargument *see* logic

counterdomain *see* relation

counterexample *see* logic

counterfactual *see* causal law; condition

counteridentical *see* condition

counterinstance *see* logic

counterpart theory *see* alethiology

courage *see* virtue

covering-law model *see* causal law; explanation

Craig's interpolation theorem *see* logic

Craig's theorem *see* logic

creatio ex nihilo *see* creation

creation From the Latin *creare*, i.e. "bring forth," "produce," "beget," this term has at least four philosophical senses. First, it means human production of something – say, a pair of shoes – from something that pre-existed it – say, leather or plastic, and in which it is not necessarily included. Second, it means natural production – e.g. through natural evolution – of something, say, human beings, from something that pre-existed it, say, from a pre-existing line of primates such as prosimians, and in which what was thus produced was neither included nor a necessary result. Third, it means production of something – say, the universe – by a divinity, e.g. Brahman, from something pre-existing – such as Divine Nature or primordial time.

All of the former views find expression in the statement *ex nihilo nihil fit*, which means "nothing comes from nothing." This doctrine makes room only for creation out of some pre-existing reality – e.g. the primeval chaos – and has been variously applied to such things as the creation of the universe, of living beings, and of human artifacts. They contrast with the next and fourth sense: production of something – say, the universe – by a divinity – e.g. the Judeo-Christian God – out of nothing. The

Latin name for this latter sense is *creatio ex nihilo*, an expression that literally means creation from nothing. By contrast with the previous senses that may often involve novelty, or something that did not exist before, this fourth sense involves *radical novelty*. Anticipated by the Syrian Christian Gnostic philosopher Basilides (second century CE), this fourth sense of creation became dominant in the early Christian centuries. It prompted the question "How much does the universe depend on God's sustaining it after its initial creation?" A range of answers has been given to this question. The philosopher Thomas Aquinas (CE 1225–74, born near the city of Naples, in what is now Italy) thought God created a world of substances He sustained in a general way. The French philosopher René Descartes (CE 1596–1650) thought God's sustaining power was so crucial that, each moment, the universe was virtually created anew.

The *creatio ex nihilo* doctrine is variously related to the doctrine of *creationism*. In the Eastern Church and medieval Western Church, this term denoted the doctrine that God creates a soul for each human being. For such thinkers as Bonaventure (CE 1217–74, born Giovanni Fidanza in Bagnorea in what is now Italy), the Arabic philosopher Ibn Sīnā – in Latin, Avicenna (CE 980–1037), and Aquinas, souls were created out of nothing. By contrast with this doctrine, the Latin author Tertullian (*c.* CE 155–*c.* 222, born in the African city of Carthage) held the doctrine of *generationism* or *traducianism*: that souls are created from souls at the time and in the way bodies are generated from bodies. The Egypt-born Christian theologian and biblical scholar Origen (CE 185–253) held the doctrine of pre-existence: that souls pre-exist the body. The German Churchman and Reformer Martin Luther (CE 1483–1546) was undecided concerning traducianism and pre-existence, but Lutherans have tended to adopt traducianism.

In a second sense, creationism is the doctrine that the early chapters of Genesis, according to which God created the universe and all creatures living in it, including humans, in six days, are literally true. This view clashes directly with scientific claims according to which the universe developed for a long time before living beings began to appear in it, and new kinds of living beings kept on appearing through a long process, namely evolution, in which humans are relatively recent newcomers. In the late twentieth century, literalists have argued that Creation science provides scientific backing for the Genesis story, raising the philosophical problem of demarcating science from non-science. Some philosophers think such demarcation is impossible, while others doubt it and, still others, think it is possible and shows that Creation science is clearly a scientific theory, though a thoroughly disconfirmed one.

With regard to the various senses of creation, philosophers and other thinkers have characterized various conceptions of creativity. The English philosopher Alfred North Whitehead (CE 1861–1947), for example, held that creativity, or becoming, is the ultimate category and that the entire universe is continuously involved in creative change. In this sense, creativity involves the first and second above-mentioned senses of creation. The Russian philosopher Nicolas Berdyaev (CE 1874–1948) held that both humans and God are creative and that both humans' and God's creations are out of nothing, a notion that involves the fourth above-mentioned sense of creation.

See also: biology; induction; philosophy of religion; philosophy of science

Further reading
Gunton, Colin E. (1997) *The Doctrine of Creation: Essays in Dogmatics, History and Philosophy*, Edinburgh: T. & T. Clark.
Miller, David Lee (1989) *Philosophy of Creativity*, New York: P. Lang.
Richardson, David Bonner (1968) *Berdyaev's Philosophy of History: An Existentialist Theory of Social Creativity and Eschatology*, The Hague: Martinus Nijhoff.
Ruse, Michael (1998) *Philosophy of Biology*, Amherst, NY: Prometheus Books.

creationism *see* creation; myth

creativity *see* creation

credibility *see* probability

credo quia absurdum *see* faith

credo ut intelligam *see* faith

creed *see* faith

crisis *see* philosophy, sociopolitical; philosophy of science

criteriological *see* epistemology

criteriology *see* epistemology

criterion *see* epistemology

critical Adjective associated to the noun *critic*, a term derived from the Latin *criticus* and the Greek *kritikós* both meaning "skillful at judging," "discriminating." Critical has been used in various noun phrases to denote various philosophical positions.

The first is *critical idealism*, the name the German philosopher Immanuel Kant (CE 1724–1804) gave to his philosophy meaning an idealism based on a critique of the powers of reason.

The second is *critical philosophy*, the name of the type of conceptual analysis the British philosopher C(harlie) D(unbar) Broad (CE 1887–1971) practiced. It focused on basic concepts of ordinary life, and was akin to that practiced by the British philosophers G(eorge) E(dward) Moore (CE 1873–1958) and Bertrand Russell (CE 1872–1970).

The third is *critical legal studies*, inquiry and works by a loosely related group of writers and thinkers in the United States and Great Britain who, since the 1970s, have been formulating a largely negative program in jurisprudence accompanied by an equally negative political ideology. Their views on jurisprudence consist in detecting contradictions in the law and concluding that the law provides no guidance because any case can be defended by appeal to some or other legal authority. The political ideology of this group is akin to that of communitarianism and its critique of liberalism, on the grounds that it overemphasizes individual rights and welfare to the detriment of certain collective goods. However, they stop short of formulating a theory of law or politics because, by and large, they are cognitive relativists.

The fourth is *critical realism*, a philosophical position that holds the independent physical world is the primary object of knowledge and the immediate representations we have are not that world but some corresponding, mediating, mental state.

The fifth is *critical theory*, a critical theory that purports to be simultaneously explanatory, normative, practical, and self-reflexive. It initially was supposed to apply only to the Frankfurt School and its revisionist version of Marxism, but it came to include any theoretical approach with the said features, including liberation theology and at least some forms of feminism. Given its characteristic features, it directly conflicts with any account of science, such as that of positivism, which relies on separating facts and values.

See also: feminist philosophy; idealism; Marxism; philosophy of law; philosophy of science; positivism; philosophy, sociopolitical

Further reading
Ouden, Bernard D. den, and Marcia Moen (1987) *New Essays on Kant*, New York: Peter Lang.
Reus-Smit, Chris (1996) *The Constructivist Turn: Critical Theory after the Cold War*, Canberra: Dept of International Relations, Research School of Pacific and Asian Studies, Australian National University.
Sellars, Roy Wood (1976 [1916]) *Critical Realism: A Study of the Nature and Conditions of Knowledge*, New York: Russell & Russell.
Stirk, Peter M.R. (1999) *Critical Theory, Politics, and Society: An Introduction*, New York: Pinter.

Crown of the Kingdom *see* cabala

crucial experiment *see* induction

cultural *see* culture; feminist philosophy

culture From the Latin *colere*, i.e. "to till" or "cultivate," this term came into use in the eighteenth century and today displays great semantic diversity, prompting discussions in everyday contexts, anthropology, sociopolitical philosophy, and the philosophy of culture or cultural philosophy, i.e. the branch of philosophy that deals with such topics as the notion of culture, its relation to civilization, and the variety of social, scientific, and philosophical problems it poses. This entry itself is an instance, however introductory, of the philosophy of culture.

As for the meanings of culture, there is, for

example, a *collective-heritage* sense in which a culture is developed in the historical experience of social groups and, as social heritage, is intentionally passed on to succeeding generations. What counts as heritage is not just anything that is passed on, however indirectly and inadvertently this may happen. Instead, the group's members must generally endorse what, perhaps inadvertently, is passed on.

For example, even if oedipal complexes turn out to be learned and shared widely in a number of cultures, they would still not be part of these cultures in the collective-heritage sense, because they would not generally be endorsed by the cultures' members. In fact, they would be unrecognized indirect consequences of the learning of other things.

Nor would just anything recognized by the culture's members as an indirect consequence of the learning of other things be part of the culture in the collective-heritage sense. For example, kleptomaniac behavior is recognized across many societies as the indirect consequence of learning other things, but it is not generally endorsed in these societies. Hence, it is not part of their collective heritage.

This collective heritage sense, in which we talk of Southeast Asian, Sub-Saharan, Andean Pre-Colombian, and Native American cultures of North America, by contrast with Western cultures, is different from the *subgroup heritage* sense of culture in which we talk of, say, the jazz musicians' culture or, more accurately, *subculture*. However, the difference is one of scale, because all these groups can be said to have a historically developed, though perhaps more specifically focused, social heritage that they intentionally pass on to succeeding generations.

Other subgroups, however, can arguably be said to have a culture of their own in the sense that they have practices, but no historically developed heritage that they intentionally pass on to succeeding generations. The hippies of the 1960s, and the beatniks before them, for example, can be said to have had a culture in this *practice* sense.

Cultures in this *practice* sense are not typically thought to prompt debate, e.g. in the multiculturalism issue. By contrast, one crucial concern is respect for heritage. However, this respect is both too wide and too narrow to cover all the concerns crucial to the multiculturalism issue. First, it is too wide, because not just any group's heritage is at issue. That of jazz musicians is not. Second, it is too narrow because the culture of such groups as gays and lesbians is also involved in the multiculturalism issue, but not for reasons of heritage. Indeed, these cultures are not, or not predominantly, thought to have a historically developed social heritage of their own that they intentionally pass on to succeeding generations. This suggests that, in fact, there is still another operant sense of culture, the *way of life* or *lifestyle* sense, in which what is at issue is simply the ways in which given groups prefer to live their own lives without in any way treating them as heritage to be passed on.

As for anthropological conceptions of culture, except for agreeing that we all need culture, anthropologists are not entirely of one voice on the subject. First, there is culture *as knowledge* – a conception that identifies culture with the accumulation of information which need not be shared. Second, there is culture *as a cluster of norms and institutions* – a view that identifies culture with group structure. Third, there is culture *as constructed reality* – a position that identifies culture with conceptual structures within which people construct their world assuming it to be shared by other members of a group.

Each one of these conceptions gives prominence to a characteristic function that can also be found in language. Culture as knowledge emphasizes the descriptive function. Culture as a cluster of norms and institutions emphasizes the directive function. Culture as constructed reality emphasizes the emotive, affective, and creative functions of language. It also has been suggested that they all are aspects of an overall conception: that of culture *as a system of meanings*.

The term culture is sometimes used as synonymous with *civilization* (from the English "civilize," and this from the Latin *civil*, a term equivalent to *civis*, "citizen"). Yet, the term *civilization* more frequently designates a societal state characterized by high development of government, science, technology, the arts and letters, and related institutions. The German philosopher of history Oswald Spengler (CE 1880–1936) considered civilization to be the final stage of a society's life cycle, when the cultural possibilities have been actualized and are simply managed while the State expands. He contrasted this stage to culture, a series of stages where the cultural possibilities are still being actualized, i.e. there is novelty.

This view had a forerunner in the Tunis-born Arabic philosopher Ibn Khaldūn (CE 1332–1406), famous for his multi-volume history, which gives an account of the whole range of Islamic knowledge. At present, the entire book has come to be called *Muqaddimah*. Initially, the term *muqaddimah*, which means "introduction," simply denoted the introduction to the multi-volume history. However, during Ibn Khaldūn's lifetime, the history's introduction and first book became an independent work entitled *Muqaddimah*. At any rate, this work became a turning point in the philosophy of history. Ibn Khaldūn argues that nomadic groups such as the Bedouins are closer than sedentary groups to acting in a manner that is good for humans. This is because among nomads the community and group feeling (*'asabiyyah*) take precedence over individualistic aims. The more urbanized sedentary groups become, the more luxuries they have and, as a result, injustice and aggression prevail, eventually putting an end to civilization. Ibn Khaldūn, however, did not hold that the said historical developments took place merely as a result of a combination of such natural items as geographic, economic, and sociological causes. He held that history was ruled by an extranatural component: the will and plan of God.

This concept of the primitive in human beings and society, i.e. *primitivism*, has played a significant role in the thought of the French philosopher Jean Jaques Rousseau (CE 1712–78), Marxism, and other philosophies interested in communal life. Indeed, anthropologists and historians of ideas have studied the idealistic views of primitivism adopted by societies in times of crisis. In parallel with this, there have been negative views where the primitive is equated with backwardness and even barbarism. An associated notion is that of *aborigines* or *aboriginal peoples*, or *native peoples*, such as the Amerindians or Native Americans in the Americas, and the Māori in New Zealand, i.e. peoples who had been living for centuries in the said areas when foreign migrations, e.g. the European migration to the Americas, occurred. Some consider them backward, while others idealize them, and still others, especially today, consider them a significant source of wisdom, e.g. concerning relations between humans and their environment.

Associated with the term culture, which is sometimes also equated with *race* as a group of people connected by common (in some versions, biological) origin, there are such terms as: *multicultural*, which denotes many cultures (sometimes in more than one sense of culture); *cross-cultural*, which denotes items involved in the interaction between two or more cultures and, accordingly, is synonymous with the terms *intercultural* and *interethnic*; and *cultural diversity*, which denotes a variety of cultural groups – sometimes called *ethnic groups* – or items from various cultural groups, i.e. items from groups with different ethnicity; in other words, with different cultural heritage.

This last term sometimes suffers from the ambiguities of the term *diversity*, a term derived from the Latin, *diversitas* (meaning "the feature of being turned in more than one direction or way"). Diversity ordinarily means the property of including many kinds, or varieties. In philosophical and social studies discussions, diversity is most frequently used to denote a variety of cultural, ethnic, racial, or religious groups, and has been applied (sometimes confusedly) in one or more of these ways in such areas of inquiry as ethics, philosophy of education, sociopolitical philosophy, and religious studies.

Useful studies in this regard seem to be rather focused. An example may be to study the similarities, differences, and grounds for each, if any, in guilt-centered cultures versus those in shame-centered cultures. Arguably, the dominant United States culture is guilt-centered when it comes to morals and mores, while many a Latin American culture is shame-based when it comes to morals and mores. In describing and evaluating these differences, it may be useful to keep in mind that, put humorously, in guilt-centered cultures people are morally inner-directed: they feel guilty, i.e. bad about their wrong actions, while they go on shamelessly performing them. However, in shame-centered cultures people are morally other-directed: they feel ashamed, i.e. embarrassed by their wrong actions, while they go on performing them without remorse.

Notable among the various forms of prejudice is *ethnocentrism*: a tendency to regard one's own group or culture as the standard, and all other groups as strange and, usually, inferior. In philosophy, a form of ethnocentrism recently described and criticized has been *Eurocentrism*, a tendency to regard European philosophers and philosophical practice as the standard, and philosophers and philosophical practice in all other groups as peculiar, usually substandard or simply foreign to philosophy. Ethnocentrism has been associated with a whole range of social problems, from discrimination to ethnic cleansing, especially as regards disadvantaged or underprivileged groups and their members.

In this regard, a term that has become entrenched in United States discussions of ethnic relations is *minority*, which is typically used to denote disadvantaged or underprivileged groups and, by extension, individuals. This use of minority, even if unproblematic in the United States, has prompted issues of applicability. For example, the issue has been raised whether Jews and Italian Americans should be considered minorities along with groups already thus identified, such as African-Americans, Amerindians, Hispanics, and Asian-Americans. Second, while African-Americans, Amerindians, and Asian-Americans are defined in ethnic terms, Hispanics are defined both in ethnic terms and in terms of whether Spanish is the predominant language in their country of origin. This has the confusing consequence that when wealthy and socially powerful Latin Americans from predominantly Spanish speaking countries migrate to the United States, they are automatically classified as members of a group that, in the United States, is officially considered disadvantaged, i.e. as Hispanics.

In addition, the term minority in the United States is contraposed to a much larger and diffuse group, White Anglo-Saxon Protestants (WASPs), many of whose members or subgroups – e.g. poor white women – are also disadvantaged. This also has the effect of disguising the fact that, like in all other societies, a small elite largely rules the United States. As for the applicability of the term minority outside the United States, it would be quite confusing, if for no other reason, because ethnic minorities have largely ruled almost all modern colonies of European powers.

See also: ethics

Further reading
Galston, William A. (1991) *Liberal Purposes: Goods, Virtues and Diversity in the Liberal State*, Cambridge, UK: Cambridge University Press.
Geertz, Clifford (1973) *The Interpretation of Cultures: Selected Essays*, New York: Basic Books.
Hick, John and Askari, Hasan (1985) *The Experience of Religious Diversity*, Aldershot, UK and Brookfield, VT: Gower.
Kroeber, A.L. and Clyde Kluckhon (1963) *Culture: A Critical Review of Concepts and Definitions*, New York: Random House.
Milne, A.J.M. (1986) *Human Rights and Human Diversity: An Essay in the Philosophy of Human Rights*, Albany: State University of New York Press.

cum hoc ergo propter hoc *see* fallacy

cursus Coninbricencis *see* Scholasticism

curve-fitting problem *see* induction

custom *see* ethics

customary law *see* ethics

cut *see* philosophy of mathematics

cut-elimination theorem *see* logic

cybernetics Term derived from the Greek *kubernētēs*, i.e. "helmsman," and coined by the contemporary scientist Norbert Wiener in 1947. It denotes the study of the communication and manipulation of information for the control and guidance of physical, chemical, biological, or other systems such as automation-, guidance-, or homeostatic-systems. *Feedback-loops*, and *forward-loops*, widely understood as versions of a *closed-loop* (by contrast with *open-loop*), are circular causal structures (the former feeding information backward, the latter forward), which are crucial to cybernetics and have forerunners in a variety of areas of inquiry, from engineering and formal logic, through economics and biology, to sociology, psychology, and philosophy. The French philosopher René Descartes (CE 1596–1650) implicitly used a feedback loop concept in his *Traité d l'Homme*, when explaining how a rational soul in the brain can respond to external disturbances. The English philosopher John Stuart Mill (CE 1806–73) used one explicitly when he explained the effects of speculation on raising prices as a closed, positive feedback loop: a perceived tendency for the price to raise causes the price to raise, which causes a more widespread perceived tendency for the price to raise, which causes the price to raise even more. At this point, Mill also suggested a negative feedback loop at work: eventually, speculators perceive that the price has become unjustifiably high, they begin to sell, and the price falls.

The United States philosopher John Dewey (CE 1859–1952) explained the effects of a child perceiving the light on its hand as a continuous process that can be interpreted to involve at least a closed, positive feedback loop: the child's perception of the light causes the hand to move towards the light, which causes a sustained perception of the light, the hand, and their relative positions, which causes the hand to keep on moving towards the light. In this process, Dewey can also be interpreted to suggest that a negative loop may become active to keep the hand on course: if and when the hand, however slightly, strays away from the direction leading to the light, a perception of this fact results, and this perception causes the hand to correct its movement so as to stay closer to the path leading to the light. Hence, Dewey's view appears to involve both positive and negative feedback loops as components

of what he describes as a continuous coordination process.

In fact, both cases exemplify an *adaptive system*, i.e. one that incorporates rules or processes for changing in response to outside changes. There is, however, a significant difference between the loops described in Mill's account and those suggested in Dewey's. The latter aim at a particular specified, known target, while the loops on Mill's account do not have fixed, pre-established points at which they begin and end. These represent two different approaches to the role of feedback loops that were explicitly introduced in social studies during the 1940s and 1950s and are still in vogue. One tends to emphasize particular events, communication, and control. It was initially represented in the work of the German psychologist Kurt Lewin (CE 1890–1947) and such contemporary researchers as Norbert Wiener and Karl Deutsch, and is the central concept of the feedback loop in cybernetics. The other approach tends to emphasize the role of closed loops in dynamic behavior. It was originally represented in the work of such contemporary researchers as Arnold Tustin, A.W. Phillips, and Herbert Simon.

See also: computer theory; cybernetics; philosophy of mathematics

Further reading
Deutsch, Karl W. (1948) "Toward a cybernetic model of man and society, from some notes on research on the role of models in the natural and social sciences," *Synthese* 7: 506–33.
Weiner, Norbert (1948) *Cybernetics: or Control and Communication in the Animal and the Machine*, Cambridge, MA: MIT Press.

cynicism *see* Greek philosophy

cyrenaicysm *see* Greek philosophy

D

dai-anjin *see* Zen

dai-funshi *see* Zen

dai-gedatsu *see* Buddhism

dai-gidan *see* Zen

daigo-tettei *see* Buddhism

dai-shinkon *see* Zen

darapti *see* syllogism

darii *see* syllogism

darshana Also *darśana*, a Sanskrit term meaning "vision," "sight," and, in Indian philosophy, "knowledge" and "system." These latter two are meanings where the previous ones are involved, given that the goal of every system of Indian philosophy involves an immediate or intuitive vision of reality. Sometimes darshana is used strictly in the sense of *system* to denote any of the six orthodox systems of Hindu philosophy that present themselves as interpretations of the Vedic scriptures. These schools are Mīmāmsā (also called Pūrva-Mīmāmsā), Sāmkhya, Yoga, Nyāya, Vaiśeṣika, and Vedānta, which is also called Uttara-Mīmāmsā or Advaita, or Advaita-Vedānta. Two pairs of these six schools are connected either historically or conceptually: Sāmkhya-Yoga and Nyāya-Vaiśeṣika. All of these schools seek to liberate the soul from the round of births and deaths and to attain union with the divinity.

In BUDDHISM, *darshana* (in Pali, *dassana*) denotes any insight based on reason that has the capacity to eliminate those passions which are conceptual in nature (*klesha*), false views (*DRISHTI*), doubt (*vichikitsā*), and clinging to rites and rules. *Darshana* is central to the way of seeing (*darshana-mārga*) that leads from having merely blind faith in the four noble truths to actually comprehending them.

See also: drishti; Hinduism; mysticism

Further reading
Aurobindo, Ghose (1971) *Letters on Yoga*, 1st rev. and enl. edn, Pondicherry: Sri Aurobindo Ashram.
—— (1970 [1955]) *The Synthesis of Yoga*, 4th edn, Pondicherry: Sri Aurobindo Ashram.
Radhakrishnan, S. (1966) *Contemporary Indian Philosophy*, 2nd rev. and enl. edn, London and New York: G. Allen – Unwin, Humanities Press.
—— (1948) *Indian Philosophy*, London: George Allen & Unwin Ltd.
Society for the Resuscitation of Indian Literature (1900) *Darshana, or Six Systems of Hindu Philosophy*, Calcutta: H.C. Dass, Elysium Press.

Darwinism *see* evolution

Dasein *see* existentialism

data *see* epistemology; metaphysics; perception; philosophy; philosophy of mind

datisi *see* syllogism

datum *see* epistemology; perception; philosophy; philosophy of mind

de Latin expression meaning "from" or "of," and used philosophically in a variety of locutions including the following:

The first, *de dicto*, is a locution meaning "of what is said" or "of the proposition" and is

---

contrasted with *de re*, which means "of the thing." For example, if interpreted in the *de dicto* sense, the sentence "It is possible that the number of European States is odd" is about the proposition "The number of European States is odd" and means that the proposition can be true. On the other hand, if interpreted in the *de re* sense, the sentence "It is possible that the number of European States is odd" is not about a proposition but about the number of European States and means that the actual number of States that make up Europe has the property of possibly being odd.

The second, *de dicto necessity*, is a locution denoting a property of those propositions – e.g. either it is or it is not raining here and now – that cannot possibly be false. This notion is contrasted to *de re necessity*, a property R that a property F of an object O has, just in case it is impossible for the object O to exist without the property F. For example, the property R of being necessary is a property of the property F, of being identical to itself that the object O has. In this case, F is said to be *de re* necessary, internal, or essential to the object O. Hence, philosophers talk of *de re* necessity as well as of *internal* necessity.

A significant notion related to necessity is that of *indemonstrables* or *apodictic*, which means self-evident and is typically applied to propositions. It is derived from the Greek *apodeitikos*, which was used by the Stoics to denote basic rules of argument of the propositional calculus: *modus ponens*, *modus tollens*, and the *disjunctive syllogism*.

The third is *de facto* (see *de jure*, below).

The fourth is *de inesse*, a Latin phrase derived from *inesse*, i.e. "being in," and used by Scholastic philosophers in two senses. First, *de inesse* denotes the feature of simple categorical propositions whereby, as in "A dog is a canine," the predicate is affirmed of a subject (is in it) or, as in "A dog is not a feline," the predicate is denied of a subject (is not in it). Second, *de inesse* denotes the mode of existence of accidents: since they are not supposed to exist in their own right (*in se*), they exist in something else (*in alio*), namely, substances.

The fifth is *de jure*, a Latin phrase meaning by right and contrasted with *de facto*, which means "in effect." *De jure* is used in a legal

sense meaning "in accordance with positive law," and in a moral sense, meaning "in accordance with morality" or "morally justified."

The sixth is *de re* (see *de dicto*, above).

The seventh is *de re necessity* (see *de dicto necessity*, above).

The eighth is *de se*, a Latin locution meaning "of oneself" and used in contrast with *de dicto* and *de re*. For example, if I notice that someone has spilled soda on one of his shoes and I do not realize that it is I, my belief is *de dicto* if about the proposition describing what I noticed, and *de re* if about the fact that someone has spilled soda on one of his shoes, but not *de se*, even though it is about me, because I do not realize it is about me.

See also: alethiology; justification; knowledge

Further reading
Kripke, Saul A. (1980) *Naming and Necessity*, rev. and enl. edn, Oxford: Blackwell.
Langiulli, Nino (1992) *Possibility, Necessity, and Existence: Abbagnano and His Predecessors*, Philadelphia: Temple University Press.
Plantinga, Alvin (1992) *The Nature of Necessity*, Oxford: Clarendon Press.

De Morgan's laws *see* logic

death Term appearing in the philosophical literature in various locutions including the following. *Death and dying* is a locution denoting an area of ethics (sometimes called *thanatology* from the Greek *thanatos*, i.e. "death," and *logos*, i.e. "discourse," "system," or "body of knowledge") concerned, in general, with the care of the dying patient and, in particular, with the problem of whether euthanasia is ever justified. Some argue that *passive euthanasia* or letting die – i.e. the withdrawal of life-support devices and the omission of heroic measures to keep a patient alive – is justified at least when a terminally ill patient is in great pain and has either explicitly expressed a desire for such treatment or, if unconscious, has left a living will expressing such desire. Others argue that *active euthanasia* – i.e. taking action to hasten the said patient's death – may be also justified, if not required, when trying to keep the patient alive or simply using passive euthanasia would unnecessarily extend the patient's excruciating pain and suffering. Still others argue that the passive–active euthanasia distinction is unclear – e.g. is unplugging a life-supporting device passive or active? – and, at any rate, does not make a significant moral difference concerning the justifiability or unjustifiability of euthanasia. One of the reasons why the active–passive euthanasia distinction is unclear is that, sometimes, it is based on the performance–omission distinction; while, other times, it is based on the continuance or suspension of the use of extraordinary means to keep patients alive.

For *death and immortality*, see BOLOGNA SCHOOL, METAPHYSICS, PHILOSOPHY OF MIND, PHILOSOPHY OF RELIGION.

For *death instinct*, see PSYCHOANALYSIS.

Death of God is a claim reputedly first made by the German philosopher Philipp Mainländer (CE 1841–76), author of *The Philosophy of Redemption*, and according to whom the world begins with the death of God, because God is a principle of unity and the world's appearance shatters it into plurality. The claim was also later made by the German philosopher Georg Wilhelm Friedrich Hegel (CE 1770–1831) in his *Philosophy of Religion* (Part III), referring to God's negation in Christ's death as a necessary moment in the development of the spirit. Afterwards, the German philosopher Friedrich Wilhelm Nietzsche (CE 1844–1900) made it in stating that, since God is Death (and, therefore, the traditional values based on it have lost their reason for being), we must get on living with other alternatives. In the 1960s, a group of United States theologians – including Thomas Altizer and William Hamilton – revived the claim to advance the notion of radical theology: a proposal to be religious without God, while awaiting some new word in what they characterized as a sacred void.

For *death penalty*, see PHILOSOPHY OF LAW.

For *death wish*, see PSYCHOANALYSIS.

See also: abortion; ethics; euthanasia; metaphysics; philosophy of law; philosophy of religion

Further reading

Altizer, Thomas J.J. (1964) *Theology and the Death of God*, East Lansing, MI: Michigan State University.

Charlesworth, M.J. (Maxwell John) (1981)

The Human Condition: Forms of Alienation in Modern Thought and Culture: Nietzsche and the Death of God, Waurn Ponds, Vic.: Deakin University Open Campus Program, School of Humanities.

Urofsky, Melvin I. and Urofsky, Philip E. (1996) *Definitions and Moral Perspectives: Death, Euthanasia, Suicide, and Living Wills*, New York: Garland Pub.

decidability A basic syntactical concept – together with *consistency* and *completeness* – of contemporary metalogic. To say that a well-formed formula of a given logical system *L* is decidable is to say that, in *L*, there is a method of proof or mechanical procedure (called *decision procedure* or *decision method*) whereby, in a finite number of steps, it can be determined whether the said well-formed formula is a theorem of *L*.

The notions of decidable formulas and decidability are involved in the *decision problem*; that is, the problem whether, for a given logical system *L*, there is a decision procedure or method whereby it is possible to determine whether any well-formed formula of *L* is a theorem of *L*. If there is one, the theory – not just each of the formulas – is called decidable. If not, it is called undecidable. A decision method is, for example, that of truth tables (see LOGIC), which serves to determine whether any well-formed formula of propositional (or sentential) logic is a theorem of this logic, hence serves to establish whether propositional logic is decidable. From 1920 to the mid-1930s, logicians tended to think that all logical and mathematical systems were decidable. This view changed when, in 1936, the United States logician Alonzo Church and the British mathematician A.M. Turing (CE 1912–54), independently of each other, proved what came to be known as Church's theorem, according to which the functional first-order calculus was not decidable.

See also: completeness; logic; philosophy of mathematics

Further reading

Gill, R.R. Rockingham (1990) *Deducibility and Decidability*, London and New York: Routledge.

Rozenberg, Grzegorz (1994) *Cornerstones of Undecidability*, New York: Prentice Hall.

decidable *see* decidability

decision A term sometimes connected with, and other times contraposed to, JUDGMENT, and still other times identified with choice. It constitutes a central component of various philosophical conceptions. The contraposition of decision to judgment can be exemplified by the ambiguities of the verb "to approve." It has two senses. In the judgment sense, it means to speak or think favorably of something, pronounce or consider agreeable or good. In the decision sense, it means to confirm or sanction formally, ratify. In the judgment sense, "approve" is often followed by the preposition of, as in: "He approves of the administration's policies." This is the same as saying that he judges favorably of the administration's policies. By contrast, in the decision sense, "approve" is never followed by the preposition "of," as in:"The Senate promptly approved the bill." This is the same as saying that the Senate made a decision and acted accordingly. Its opposite is not "The Senate promptly judged unfavorably of the bill," but "The Senate promptly rejected the bill." Hence, to approve something in this decision sense is to sanction it, i.e. to make a decision and accordingly perform an action that, in this case, creates a legal situation: contributing to make a bill become law.

As for the identification of decision with choice, given the action-oriented nature of decision, it is identified with choice in the sense of a choice one *makes* – i.e. selecting one of a number of available alternative courses of action – not in the sense of a choice someone *has* – i.e. not with the alternative courses of action one has available.

Voluntaristic philosophical traditions tend to emphasize, at least in some contexts, the role of decision over that of judgment. For example, a form of *ethical voluntarism* – the view that the moral value of such things as actions, policies, and traits, or the principles that help establish this value, are somehow dependent on our decisions – is arguably formulated in the contemporary British philosopher J.L. Mackie's *Inventing Right and Wrong*. *Theological voluntarism* includes, first, the view – found in the works of the Danish philosopher Søren Kierkegaard (CE 1813–55) and the Uni-

ted States philosopher William James (CE 1842–1910) – that the truth of such concepts as personal salvation, and the meaning of life to us, is somehow dependent on our decisions, and the medieval view of God's omnipotence goes together with making things good by choosing them.

William James's work in *The Will to Believe* is also an example of *doxastic voluntarism*: the doctrine that, at least in some cases, it is morally permissible to believe as one wishes. *Metaphysical voluntarism* is the doctrine, formulated by the German philosopher Arthur Schopenhauer (CE 1788–1860), that the fundamental organizing factor in the universe is not a principle of rational or moral order, but a blind and meaningless will to be found in living organisms' strife for survival. *Historical voluntarism* – the view that the will of human individuals is a decisive factor in history – can be found in the works of the English philosopher John Stuart Mill (CE 1806–73).

Non-voluntaristic doctrines tend to emphasize the role of judgment over decision. An example is *decision* – or *rational-decision*, or *rational-choice* – *theory*. This theory's basic idea traces back at least to the *Port-Royal Logic* (CE 1662), authored by the French theologian and philosopher Antoine Arnaud (CE 1612–94), where, at the end, it says: "To judge what one must do to obtain a good or avoid an evil one must consider not only the good and the evil in itself but also the probability of its happening or not happening, and view geometrically the proportion that all these things have together." The contemporary standard version of rational-choice theory purports to tell us what to do in order to achieve our aims, but not what these aims should be. It has four main components:

1 the set of feasible courses of action (the *feasible set*); that is, the courses of action that satisfy (or are rationally believed to satisfy) various logical, physical, and social constraints;

2 the causal connections, in the case of *causal-decision theory* (or the set of beliefs about the causal connections in the case of *probabilistic-decision theory*), that determine which courses of action lead to what outcomes;

3 a subjective ranking of the feasible courses of action, typically on the basis of the outcomes they are expected to have; and

4 the notion that to choose rationally is to choose the highest ranked among these courses of action.

The application of rational-choice theory to policy analysis is *social-choice theory*, though it, like rational-choice theory, is also called decision theory and, like rational-choice theory, has two types: causal-decision theory and probabilistic-decision theory (though some versions use preference logics which attempt to sidestep probabilities without committing themselves to the causal version). In its contemporary form, it was initially applied to the study of military operations, logistics, and tactics during the Second World War. In the early 1950s, it was formalized at the Rand Corporation and other policy-oriented institutions. Significantly developed by the contemporary United States economist Kenneth Arrow in his *Social Choice and Individual Values*, social-choice theory was widely used in microeconomics (primarily in the context of market transactions), management science, and military strategy until the 1960s. It was used, for example, to address *free-rider* problems, i.e. problems posed by a person who benefits from a social arrangement without bearing an equitable share of the burdens involved in maintaining such arrangement.

The structure of decisions was supposed to be the same for all cases, which led this methodology to be called *decisionism*. It requires rational policy makers – thought to be the same as rational decision makers – to specify their aims; specify the feasible courses of action to attain these aims – the feasible set; rank them, typically by appeal to the outcomes they are expected to have, and choose that which ranks the highest, i.e. to seek optimizing, or the optimization of the outcome. In addition, it envisions a unitary, consistent policy maker or a group acting consistently as a unit.

This supposition, together with the identification of policy making with decision making, has led critics to argue that decisionism as a normative approach is unrealistic, inaccurate, and hopelessly focused on the short term – a

serious problem, for example, when attempting to establish such long-term policy as foreign policy and science policy. In addition, in attempting to optimize outcomes instead of simply – as in *satisficing* theories – choosing outcomes that are good enough given the circumstances, it is also unrealistic and, not least, it gets involved in the *paradox of perfectionism* (see PARADOX), i.e. it tends to lead to outcomes that are worse than they would have been had not the aim been optimizing them. Concepts significant in social theory are *social traps*, which include collective choice, collective decision, and collective traps. In fact social-choice theory primarily focuses on co-ordination problems concerning choices and decisions. A seminal notion here is that of the *voting paradox*.

As for *traps*, they are situations in which, individually or in groups, people are stuck behaving in a manner they perceive as favorable to their aims when, in fact, it is contrary to them. Some traps result from ignorance; others from more knowledge than one can handle; still others from lack of co-operation; and others from conflict. Ignorance leads to traps in various ways. In a *time-delay* trap, people misperceive the amount of damage their behavior does to their aims because the damage is delayed – as in deficit-building public spending. In a *sliding-reinforcer* trap, the damage is misperceived because it gradually increases over time – as in the use of agricultural methods that cause soil erosion. There are also *total-ignorance* traps, in which the damage, present or future, is not known at all. An example is the 1941–71 use of diethylstilbestrol (DES) in the United States to prevent miscarriages.

As stated, traps may result from things other than ignorance. In an *overload* trap, the damage results from excessive information that the individual or group tries and fails to process – as in the United States court overload. There are also *externality* traps, in which the actions of others or simply the external circumstances cause one's otherwise harmless behavior to damage one's aims. Some of these are *parameter* traps, in which others (e.g. hostage takers) or the circumstances (e.g. natural catastrophes) confront people with desperate choices. Others are *collective* traps, in which the actions of enough others cause one's otherwise harmless behavior to damage one's (and sometimes also their) aims. Some of these are *non-co-operation* traps, and others are *conflict* traps. Overpopulation, where the overall effects but not the individual decisions are interdependent, exemplifies a non-co-operation trap. The arms race, where the decisions themselves are interdependent, exemplifies a conflict trap. Of course, the traps just described, and others, can form hybrid types.

In the 1970s and 1980s, rational-choice theory's offspring, *game theory* (the theory of rational choice as it applies to conflicts), attracted the attention of sociobiologists, philosophers, and even more political scientists. It characterizes conflict situations in terms of four variables (or assumptions) and a set of odds tied to the circumstances: The first is the *motivational* variable: everyone in the situation will act so as to maximize his or her own advantage. The second is the *epistemological* variable: everyone in the situation has roughly equal knowledge and abilities relevant for dealing with the situation. The third is the *resources* variable: resources are limited. The fourth is the *commons* variable, or liberty variable: everyone is at liberty to act as he or she wishes in the situation.

These variables can be used to characterize what, in ethics and sociopolitical philosophy, has been called a *state of nature situation*, i.e. a situation opposite to that of a civil society, in which the rules of civil society cannot be expected to apply and, some would argue, the minimal conditions for the existence of morality are absent or significantly undermined. Such situations are sometimes likened to the *prisoner's dilemma*, a type of problems in game theory and rational-choice theory where any two parties must make simultaneous and independent choices over a range of options whose payoff structure is such that the parties will choose options they rank as worse than other options open to them. This partly results from a fact of strategy (from the Greek *strategia*, i.e. "generalship"), and here is used more widely as the art of combining means to attain overall aims). A strategy rule used in game theory is the *maximin* rule (where max-

imin is derived from the Latin *maximum minimorum* or the greatest of the least), i.e. the rule according to which one should adopt that alternative course of action or policy whose worst outcome to oneself is superior to the worst outcome of other alternatives.

Payoffs were originally measured in *cardinal utility* – typically monetary utility – terms, called *transferable utility*, to avoid the complications of interpersonal utility comparisons, i.e. of comparisons of the respective utilities a course of action would yield to different persons. When cardinal, additive payoffs are involved, games are divided into *constant-sum* games, i.e. games where the sum of all players' payoffs in each outcome remains constant, and *variable-sum* games, where this sum changes. *Zero-sum* games, i.e. where the sum of all players' payoff in each outcome is null, are a special type of constant-sum games. Constant-sum games involving only two players are games of pure conflict, because one player's gain is the other's loss. In constant-sum games with three or more players and in variable-sum games coalitions are possible and often desirable to each player. Games with only ordinal preferences are considered games of pure conflict or co-ordination. The theory of these latter games is still somewhat undeveloped.

Game theory has been criticized on similar grounds to those used to criticize decisionism. It has also been criticized on the grounds that it entirely ignores the political variable in competitive situations, i.e. the constraints created by public response in such situations, which alters the authority and effectiveness of decision makers, as well as the feasibility of alternative courses of action open to them.

See also: Arrow's theorem; intention; voluntarism

Further reading
Arrow, Kenneth (1963) *Social Choice and Individual Values*, 2nd edn, New York: John Wiley & Sons.
Dar, Bashir Ahmad (1956) *Iqbal and Post-Kantian Voluntarism*, Lahore: Bazm-i-Iqbal.
Elster, Jon (1986) *Rational Choice*, New York: New York University Press.
Iannone, A. Pablo (1994) *Philosophy as Diplomacy: Essays in Ethics and Policy Making*, Atlantic Highlands, NJ: Humanities Press.

Stebbing, L. Susan (1914) *Pragmatism and French Voluntarism with Especial Reference to the Notion of Truth in the Development of French Philosophy from Maine de Biran to Professor Bergson*, Cambridge, UK: Cambridge University Press.

decisionism *see* decision

declarations *see* speech act theory

declining marginal utility *see* ethics; philosophy of economics; utilitarianism

decomposability *see* cognitive

deconstruction A method of criticism, a type of internal critique that uses concepts, methods, and rules legitimized or presupposed by a philosophical position, an ideology, or any view or group of views whatsoever, to show the incompleteness or incoherence of such position, ideology, or views. It is central to a literary and philosophical movement, *deconstructionism*, originating in France as a response to another movement of largely French origin, *structuralism*: the view that each linguistic community has a common and invariant structure that, unconsciously and pre-reflectively, manifests itself in their members' activities.

Though many deconstructionists consider the French philosopher of science Gaston Bachelard (CE 1884–1962) as the first practitioner of deconstructionism, the movement was founded by the contemporary French philosopher Jacques Derrida, who developed a notion originally formulated by the Swiss linguist Ferdinand de Saussure (CE 1857–1913) – that speech is a system of differences between signs – into the deconstructionist notion of *différance* (deriving it from the French term *différer*, which means both "to differ" and "to defer"): that, for signs to function, they must differ from each other and, since there is no way of bringing any chain of signification to an end because, invariably, the signifier can only provide a *trace* – i.e. a hint – of the signified, signs must indefinitely defer to one another.

From this radically nominalistic standpoint, Derrida argues that no one can be fully aware of meanings or, as he calls them, *logoi*, because they are characteristically partial and incomplete. Indeed, he claims that in the Western tradition, *logoi* – from Plato's Forms, through ideas as conceived in the empiricist tradition, to Husserl's intentional entities – are supposed to be capable of being fully present to our consciousness and, as such, serve as ground for all our accounts of intention, meaning, truth, and logic. Derrida characterizes these *logoi* or thought-terms as magical and the accounts that include them logocentric. He concludes that such traditional contrasts as those between metaphorical and literal, and rhetoric and logic, lack the foundation their use presupposes. He adds that this false presupposition is involved in ordinary language, thereby affecting not just our theoretical accounts, but our ordinary concepts, that therefore are theory-laden and do not offer an alternative to traditional theoretical thinking, philosophical or otherwise. We can still change our concepts, but – in this Derrida roughly agrees with the Anglo-American philosopher Willard van Orman Quine (CE 1908–2000) – we cannot change our entire theory all at once. From all this, Derrida concludes that all words are inaccurate and proposes a new kind of linguistics he calls *grammatology*, whose task is to deconstruct texts.

Some criticisms of deconstructionism focus on Derrida's notion of *différance*: if this notion has the implications Derrida claims it has, then it too sharply separates deconstructionism from the ordinary concerns from which philosophical reflection originates. As a result, it makes deconstructionism a strictly and merely academic enterprise: irrelevant to life and philosophical inquiry.

Another line of criticism uses deconstruction. It points out that many of the views espoused by deconstructionists have been previously made by such pragmatists as the United States philosophers Charles Sanders Peirce (CE 1839–1914) and John Dewey (CE 1859–1952). Yet, these views do not in and of themselves entail the dramatic implications drawn by deconstructionists. Such dramatic implications follow only if coupled with the positions deconstructionism finds objectionable, for example a definitive view on the meaning of *logoi* (a logos of *logoi*). Hence, deconstructionism can draw those implications only if it refutes itself by assuming what it rejects.

See also: Continental philosophy; nominalism; pragmatism

Further reading
Derrida, Jacques (1997) *Deconstruction in a Nutshell: A Conversation with Jacques Derrida* New York: Fordham University Press.
Melville, Stephen W. (1986) *Philosophy Beside Itself: On Deconstruction and Modernism*, Minneapolis: University of Minnesota Press.
Southwell, Samuel B. (1987) *Kenneth Burke and Martin Heidegger: With a Note against Deconstructionism*, Gainesville: University Presses of Florida, University of Florida Press.

decurtate syllogism *see* syllogism

Dedekind cut *see* philosophy of mathematics

deduction From the Latin *de* ("from") and *ducere* ("to lead"). The Latin term *deductio* was coined as a translation of the Greek *apagoge*, a term used by the Greek philosopher Aristotle (384–322 BCE) in his groundbreaking attempt at systematizing reasoning. Deduction is sometimes called the deductive method. Ordinarily, a deduction is an argument whose premises are regarded as providing a conclusive basis for accepting the conclusion. In modern logic, a deduction is a system-dependent notion: a deduction (also called derivation and, sometimes, demonstration) of a sentence S in the system L is a bounded list of sentences K, each one of which is either an axiom in L, or a component (e.g. a hypothesis in K), or follows from preceding sentences in K by a rule of inference of L, and where the last sentence – the conclusion – is S. When a system has no axioms, it is called a *natural-deduction* system.

The notion of deduction is a generalization of that of proof. A *proof* of a sentence S in the system L is a bounded list of sentences K, each one of which is either an axiom in L, or follows from preceding sentences in K by a rule of inference of L, and where the last sentence (the conclusion), S, is a theorem of L.

Deduction and *consequence* are different things: the former is syntactical, the latter semantic. It was discovered that, given the axioms and rules of inference of classical logic, a sentence s is deducible from a set of sentences K just in case s is deducible from a finite subset of K. From this, it non-trivially follows *com-pacteness*: s is a consequence of K just in case s is a consequence of some finite subset of K.

The German philosopher Immanuel Kant (CE 1724–1804) used the expression transcendental deduction to denote an argument or explanation that makes plain that a principle or concept is necessary for our experience to take place. Accordingly, Kant proposed a *transcendental deduction* of the pure concepts – or categories – of a finite being's understanding – e.g. unity and causality.

See also: argument; logic; Kantian philosophy

Further reading
Goubault-Larrecq, Jean (1997) *Proof Theory and Automated Deduction*, Dordrecht and Boston: Kluwer Academic.
Howell, Robert (1992) *Kant's Transcendental Deduction: An Analysis of Main Themes in His Critical Philosophy*, Dordrecht and Boston: Kluwer Academic Publishers.
Kozy, John (1974) *Understanding Natural Deduction: A Formalist Approach to Introductory Logic*, Encino, CA: Dickenson Pub. Co.

deductive closure *see* epistemology

deductive completeness *see* completeness

deductive explanation *see* explanation

deductive justification *see* justification

deductive–nomological model *see* explanation

deep ecology *see* ecology; ethics

deep grammar *see* philosophy of language

deep structure *see* philosophy of language

default logic *see* logic

defeasibility *see* logic

definiendum *see* definition

definiends *see* definition

definist *see* ethics

definite descriptions *see* description

definition From the Latin *de*, i.e. "from" or "of," and *finire*, i.e. "to limit." Definitions – sometimes called *explications* – are specifications that delimit the meaning or content of terms or expressions, or the way in which these terms or expressions can be used. What a definition defines is called the *definiendum*, while what does the defining is called the *definiens*. When a *definiendum* occurs in the *definiens* (as in "morality is the rules of morality"), or a term is defined by means of a second term that, in turn, is defined by the first term (e.g. "Laws are the rulers' commands and the ruler's commands are the laws"), a definition is called circular or *diallelon* (from the Ancient Greek *di allēlon*, i.e. "through another"). A related concept is *diallelus*: a circular argument, i.e. an argument with at least one premise that cannot be known unless the conclusion is already known.

There are various kinds of definitions, as follows. First, *contextual*, i.e. a definition of an expression as it occurs in a larger expression. For example, a definition of "exactly one" in "there is exactly one number zero," is "there is at least one number zero and it is identical with any number zero."

Second, *in use* (or *directive*), i.e. a definition of an expression's use. For example, "The expression 'boohoo' is used to convey disgust, dislike, or disapproval."

Third, *explicit*, i.e. a definition that makes it clear that it is a definition, identifies its *definiendum*, and completely says what the *definiendum* means or how it is used. An example of an explicit definition is "a sister is by definition a female sibling." Explicit definitions characteristically are about sorts of items or categories. For example, universities – a sort of items – can be defined as institutions of the highest learning in the liberal arts and professions, and authorized to grant degrees. These are defining conditions and, in a broader sense, are some of the identifying conditions or identification conditions that allow us to establish whether a particular item is a university. Often, however, the terms identifying conditions or identification conditions are used in a narrower sense to denote evidence or other grounds that allow us to include an item in the category. For example, in determining whether a particular institution is a university, identifying conditions may be legal documents of its incorporation as a university.

Fourth, *implicit*, i.e. a definition that either does not make it clear that it is a definition, or does not identify its *definiendum*, or does not completely or at all say what the *definiendum* means or how it is used. An example of an implicit definition is that of being soluble in "Under observable conditions of being placed in water, supar is soluble if, and only if, it dissolves."

Fifth, *impredicative*, i.e. a definition of a concept in terms of the totality to which it belongs. When predicating terms of a given type of terms of the same type, e.g. the set of all sets that are not members of themselves, these definitions can lead to paradoxes.

Sixth, *lexical*, i.e. a definition that specifies the conventional meaning of a term or expression, e.g. a dictionary definition.

Seventh, *nominal*, i.e. strictly, a definition of a noun; more generally, a definition of language only, not of what language is about. For example, the expression "the evening star" means the star that is bright at dusk.

Eighth, *ostensive*, i.e. a definition whereby the *definiendum* is specified by pointing to it or, somehow, showing it. For example, a typically ostensive definition of a dog when pointing to a dog is saying "that is a dog."

Ninth, *persuasive*, i.e. a definition aimed at gaining acceptance of a certain view by those being addressed, for example "a tax collector is a heartless bureaucrat."

Tenth, *precising*, i.e. a definition aimed at reducing the vagueness of a term or expression, e.g. "On this street, speeding is going over 35 miles an hour."

Eleventh, *real*, i.e. a definition of the actual item a noun denotes, e.g. "Venus is the second planet of the solar system."

Twelfth, *recursive* (also called by recursion, and inductive), i.e. a definition that defines a basic case, a rule for constructing additional items like it on its basis, and a statement saying nothing else is an item of this kind. For example, a recursive definition of a natural number is: "Zero is a natural number and one is a natural number, any natural number plus one is a natural number, and nothing else is a natural number."

Thirteenth, by *species and genus*, i.e. a definition of a concept – say, a square – according to which the concept applies to only part – a species – of a general type or genus – a rectangle – and is characterized by the *differentia* – having equal sides. While a property independent of a genus differentiates a species that falls under the genus, the English philosopher W.E. Johnson (CE 1858–1931) and his followers argued that there is a kind of property called *determinable* – a term Johnson used instead of universal – that, though analogous to a genus, has no independent property differentiating the determinate that falls under the determinable. For example, color is not a genus but a determinable with regard to the determinate the color blue (where blue is the *determinant* – a term Johnson used instead of particular), because there is no property *P* independent of color such that a color is blue if and only if it is *P*. Medieval philosophers considered genus and species to be the only NATURAL KINDS among the *praedicabilia* (in English, predicables), also called *quinque voces* (literally, "five voices," better translated as "five utterances or forms of speech"), which were the five ways in which general predicates could be predicated: genus, species, difference, proprium, and ACCIDENT. A *proprium* is not just any property or attribute. It is a non-essential peculiarity of a species. An example often given is that the ability to laugh is peculiar to humans but not part of the essential properties of a human defined as a rational animal. This sense of proprium should not be confused with the meaning of proprium as used by the German philosopher and theologian Friedrich Schleiermacher (CE 1768–1834): the inward differentiation of an individual in nature and history. As for genus, if it is not a species of some higher genus, it is called *genus generalissimum* (Latin for "most general genus") and *summun genus* (Latin for "highest genus").

Fourteenth, *stipulative*, i.e. a definition that says what will be meant by a term or expression, regardless of any conventions there may be about its meaning, e.g. "For the purpose of our discussion, ' > ' will mean distracted."

Fifteenth, *theoretical*, i.e. a definition that specifies a concept or kind of item in a theory, and stands or falls with the theory, e.g. "Whales are large marine mammals of the order Cetacea in modern zoology."

In connection with definitions, the notion of

distinction has come to the fore. For example, *fundamentum divisionis*, a Latin expression meaning "foundation of divisions," or "grounds for distinctions," was used in medieval logic and metaphysics. The types of distinctions included the following categories: *real*, meaning that any real distinction has a basis that exists in reality; *mental*, meaning that any mental distinction exists conceptually; *formal* (sometimes used synonymously with mental distinction) – a formal distinction is a notion used in order to deal with problems about the Christian conception of God, and that of identity and especially, thisness or haecceity, by the Scottish philosopher John Duns Scotus (CE 1266–1308), who held the *distinctio formalis a parte re* to mean objective formal distinction, i.e. not merely mental distinction. This was a component of Scotism, and Scotistic realism.

In contemporary discussions, these have been expanded to include talk of: morally significant distinctions, e.g. when it is asked whether that between passive and active euthanasia is relevant for addressing the question "When, if ever, is euthanasia justified?" In reply to questions such as this one, when a distinction is thought to be insubstantial or irrelevant, it is called a distinction without a difference.

See also: logic

Further reading
Gorskii, D.P. (1981) *Definition: Logico-Methodological Problems*, Moscow: Progress.
Tiuryn, Jerzy (1980) *A Survey of the Logic of Effective Definitions*, Cambridge, MA: Massachusetts Institute of Technology, Laboratory for Computer Science.

deflationary theory of truth *see* truth

degenerate case *see* ambiguity

degree A term used in a variety of philosophical phrases, as follows. First, degree of a predicate and function expression: also called *arity*, and *adicity*, it is the number of terms with which the expression needs to be combined in order to yield a well-formed formula. For example, the expression for negation is monadic or of degree one; the expression for conjunction is diadic or of degree two. Any expression of degree at least equal to two is called polyadic.

Second, degree of belief: see PROBABILITY.

Third, degree of confirmation: see PROBABILITY.

Fourth, degree of reality: see METAPHYSICS.

Fifth, degree of unsolvability: a notion relative to a fixed notion of reducibility such as: A is r-equivalent to B if A is r-reducible to B and B is r-reducible to A. Given this, a degree of unsolvability relative to r (an r-degree) is an equivalence class under that equivalence relation, i.e. a maximal class of sets of natural numbers, any two members of which are r-equivalent. In other words, it is a maximal class of equally complex sets of natural numbers. When no constraints are placed on how the algorithm could be used by an imaginary oracle consulting the algorithm, in order to determine whether a given number belongs to a given set, one gets T-reducibility or Turing-reducibility.

See also: logic; philosophy of mathematics

Further reading
Dybvig, R. Kent (1990) *A New Approach to Procedures with Variable Arity*, Bloomington, IN: Computer Science Dept, Indiana University.
Epstein, Richard L. (1975) *Minimal Degrees of Unsolvability and the Full Approximation Construction*, Providence: Ams.

deism *see* philosophy of religion

deity *see* God

deliberation *see* syllogism

deliberative democracy *see* philosophy, sociopolitical

delusion *see* epistemology; ethics

demand *see* ethics; philosophy, sociopolitical

demiurge *see* Neoplatonism; Platonism

democracy *see* philosophy, sociopolitical

demon The Greek philosopher Plato (428–348 BCE), in various dialogues, and the Greek writer and moralist Xenophon (*c.* 430–*c.* 355 BCE), in his *Memorabilia*, often mentioned the demon of the Greek philosopher and Plato's teacher Socrates (469–399 BCE). The noun Plato uses when referring to Socrates' demon is *daimónion*, not *daímon*. Socrates does use the term *daímon* (plural *daímoines*) in a *mythological sense*, e.g. in Plato's *Apology* (27c–d). Here, it refers to those entities that previously had been conceived as divinities and in Socrates' times were considered superhuman beings, i.e. beings that, though the offspring of gods, were neither demi-gods nor heroes. In Plato's *Symposium* (202e and ff.), Socrates uses the term *daímon* to describe LOVE as a being that acts as intermediary between mortals and immortals. By contrast with these, Socrates' demon is described (most notably in *Apology* 31c–d), in what can be called a conduct sense, as a *voice* (*phoné*) or *signal* (*Apology* 41d) that, since he was a child, invariably pushed him to omit what he was about to do: always prohibiting, never encouraging to act. This voice has been variously interpreted: externally, as a divinity's command; internally, as the voice of conscience; existentially, as a vocation unique to each individual human being.

The mythological sense of demon (*daímon*) can also be found among ancient Neopythagorean, eclectic, and Neoplatonic thinkers such as the Syrian Numenius of Apamea (*fl.* mid-second century CE), the Greek Plutarch of Chaeronea (*c.* CE 45–125), and the Egypto-Roman Plotinus (CE 204–70). Their conceptions of demons, though based on Greek mythological traditions, were the result of multiple interpretations. As a result, demons were sometimes conceived as lower divinities, other times as intermediaries, still other times as divine personalities in us.

Another conceptions of demons in the mythological sense can be found in Judaism and later in Christianity, where demons are angels that rebelled against God and became agents of evil.

This mythological sense of demon is sometimes used to refer to *lesser spirits* such as magical forces in ethnic philosophies, where the question has been raised whether they are distinct from deities or linked to them. The Sanskrit term *deva*, meaning bright heavenly one, originally denoted the nature gods of the Vedic religion. Later, it became the term for god in Hinduism and Buddhism. In Zoroastrianism, it denoted the evil spirits (*daevas*), allies of Ahriman. The Indo-European root of this term became *deus* – i.e. god – in Latin, and *theos* – i.e. god – in Greek. The English "devil" proceeds from the Middle English *devel*, and this from the Old English *deofol* that, like *diablo* in Spanish and *diàvolo* in Italian, derives from the Latin *diabolus*, whose Greek counterpart is *diábolos*. The Indo-European root for these is the same as that for *deus* and *theos*.

See also: African philosophy; Māori philosophy; Nahua philosophy; Neoplatonism; Platonism

Further reading
Culianu, Ioan P. (1992) *The Tree of Gnosis: Gnostic Mythology from Early Christianity to Modern Nihilism*, San Francisco: Harper-San Francisco.
Gyekye, Kwame (1987) *An Essay on African Philosophical Thought*, Cambridge, UK and New York: Cambridge University Press.
Rose, Gilbert P. (1989) *Plato's Apology: Text and Commentary*, Bryn Mawr, PA: Thomas Library, Bryn Mawr College.

demonstration *see* deduction

demonstrative *see* logic; philosophy of language; syllogism

denial *see* logic

denotation *see* meaning

denotative meaning *see* meaning

denoting concept *see* meaning

dense ordering *see* ordering

denumerable *see* infinity

denying the antecedent *see* fallacy

denying the consequent *see* fallacy

deontic *see* logic

deontological *see* ethics

deontology *see* ethics

dependence *see* epistemology; logic

dependency relationship *see* feminist philosophy

depth grammar *see* philosophy of language

derivation *see* deduction

derivational logicism *see* philosophy of mathematics

description From the Latin *description*, equivalent to *descriptus*, participle of *describere* (to describe), equivalent to *de* ("from") and *scribere* ("to write"), the term *description* denotes a phrase, statement, or sequence of statements indicating features of an item. In antiquity, descriptions were thought to be incomplete definitions. Even in Port Royal Logic, they were supposed to provide a lower kind of knowledge. Since the nineteenth century, however, descriptions have ceased to be downgraded and, instead, have been studied from a variety of standpoints: as crucial in social studies; as central to the identification and enumeration of the phenomena observed in all scientific inquiry; as a unique tool in the phenomenological study of intentional contents; and as contrasted with mere reports on the one hand and explanations on the other. Indeed, their study led to the *theory of descriptions*: an analysis, initially formulated by the English philosopher Bertrand Russell (CE 1872–1970), of sentences containing descriptions. On Russell's analysis, descriptions include both indefinite descriptions – e.g. "an elephant" – and definite descriptions – e.g. "my father's only uncle." Both, however, are incomplete symbols that are meaningful only in the context of sentences containing them.

Russell argued that descriptions do not have a referential function; hence, various puzzles prompted by descriptions could be solved. For example, the description "the present King of France is not bald" can be true even though there is no present King of France, because, on Russell's analysis, it simply meant "It is not the case that there is exactly one item that is now both King of France and bald." In this rewritten version of the original sentence, the subject is a bare particular ("one item"), and the descriptive phrase in the previous sentence has become a predicate. Also, the statement "The present King of France does not exist" can be true because it does not refer to the present King of France. If it referred or pointed to him, it would thereby entail that he exists, which, given that the statement says he does not exist, would make it contradictory.

The contemporary British philosopher Peter Strawson challenged Russell's analysis, arguing that the statement does not entail but, instead, presupposes that there is a present King of France and that, therefore, the former statement is not false but, instead, has no truth-value. The philosopher Keith Donnellan has recently argued that definite descriptions can be used attributively (in which case Russell's analysis applies), or referentially (in which case Strawson's analysis applies), leading to fruitful discussions about the relations between the meanings and functions of speech acts, and between the areas that respectively study them: semantics and pragmatics.

The term description also appears in such philosophical phrases as:

1 knowledge by description (see KNOWLEDGE);
2 state description (see POSITIVISM);
3 structure description (see POSITIVISM).

See also: knowledge; positivism

Further reading
Katz, Jerrold J. (1974) *An Integrated Theory of Linguistic Descriptions*, Cambridge, MA: MIT Press.
Smiley, T.J. (1983) *The Theory of Descriptions*, London: Oxford University Press.

descriptive emergence *see* holism

descriptive emergentism *see* holism

descriptive individualism *see* holism

descriptive meaning *see* meaning

descriptive metaphysics *see* metaphysics

descriptive psychology *see* phenomenology

descriptive relativism *see* ethics; philosophy of science

descriptivism *see* ethics

descriptivist theory of names *see* reference

desert *see* ethics

design, argument from *see* philosophy of religion

designator, rigid *see* reference

designatum *see* reference

desire *see* ethics; intention

desire–belief model *see* intention

destiny *see* determinism

destructive dilemma *see* dilemma

detachment *see* epistemology; ethics; justification

determinable *see* definition

determinant *see* definition

determinate *see* definition

determinism From the Latin *determinare*, i.e. "to set bounds or limits," this term was first used with a philosophical meaning by the Scottish philosopher Sir William Hamilton (CE 1788–1856), who used it to describe the position of the English philosopher Thomas Hobbes (CE 1588–1679) without confusing it with fatalism (see below). There are various forms of determinism or, as it is sometimes called, the doctrine of determinism. One form is *scientific* determinism, the view that *every event has a cause* and that the event is bound to occur given the occurrence of the cause, plus the standing conditions and laws of nature. So, given the past, only one future is possible. In addition, knowledge of all antecedent conditions and laws of nature would make it possible to predict the entire future. In other words, determinism excludes chance, and conflicts with *indeterminism* – i.e. the view that at least some events occur by accident or, in other words, are not caused – and with various conceptions of a *free will* or *liberum arbitrium*. Along these lines, the United States philosopher Charles Sanders Peirce (CE 1839–1914) formulated the notion of *tychism* (from the Greek *tyché*, i.e. "chance" and the particle "-ism"), according to which chance is a real feature of the universe, i.e. there is real novelty.

Scientific determinism includes various more specific versions. *Biological* determinism is the view that the behavior of all life is bound to occur given heredity and the environment. *Cultural* determinism is the view that individual and group behavior is bound to occur given the individuals' and groups' respective cultures. *Historical* determinism is the doctrine that individual behavior is not decisive in history and that, given historical conditions, historical developments are bound to happen. In other words, if, for example, the Austrian-born, Nazi dictator of Germany Adolf Hitler (CE 1889–1945) had not existed, given the historical conditions in Europe at the time, someone else would have taken his place in the development of the Third Reich.

Sometimes, the term determinism is used in a general way to denote any doctrine according to which, given the past, only one future is possible. This includes not just scientific determinism, but also *theological* determinism, or the doctrine of *predestination*: the view that everything which happens has been predestined to happen by an omniscient, omnipotent divinity. A weaker version holds that, though not predestined to happen, everything that happens has been eternally known by virtue of the divine foreknowledge of an omniscient divinity. If this divinity is also omnipotent, as in the case of Judeo-Christian religions, this weaker version is hard to distinguish from the previous one because, though able to prevent what happens and knowing that it is going to happen, God lets it happen.

To this, advocates of free will reply that God permits it to happen in order to make room for the free will of humans. Indeed, *pelagianism* is the doctrine that humans can attain moral perfection through the exercise of free will. Loosely associated with the teachings of the lay English or Irish theologian Pelagius (*c.* CE 354–*c.* 425), pelagianism was a widespread movement in early Christianity. Though it disappeared as a sect, two periods are identified as instances of *neo-pelagianism*. During the fourteenth century, it was advocated by the English philosopher and theologian Thomas Bradwardine (*c.* CE 1290–1349) and the Italian philosopher Gregory of Rimini (*c.* CE 1300–58). Also, during the sixteenth century, those who emphasized free will in their efforts to oppose the ideas of Protestant thinkers were often considered to represent pelagianism or neo-pelagianism.

The doctrine of theological determinism can be found in a variety of philosophical and cultural traditions. For example, Akan (Ghana) philosophy, uses two terms for destiny. One is *nkrabea* (from *nkra*, "message," and *bea*,

"manner"), which has come to mean the message given by the Supreme Being to the individual soul so as to determine how the individual is to live in the world. The other word for destiny is *hyēbea* (from *hyē*, to "fix," "arrange," and *bea*, "manner"), which means the manner in which the individual is destined to live in the world. As for luck or fortune, it is called *akrade* and, like *asiane*, i.e. accident in Akan thought, it is restricted to individual persons and the result of unknown causes, not pure chance. This conception is widely shared among traditional sub-Saharan Africans.

A particular Western version of theological determinism is the doctrine of *pre-established harmony* formulated by the German philosopher Gottfried Wilhelm Leibniz (CE 1646–1716): each windowless monad that, according to him, constitutes reality develops in harmony with all others because God has established the harmony in choosing to create this world. According to this view and, in general, all theological determinism, the entire history of the universe is like the unrolling of a movie God shot in advance.

Related to this view is the doctrine of *efficacious grace*, originally held by the philosopher Augustine (CE 354–430, born in Thagaste, North Africa) and, in modern times, defended by the French Cartesian Antoine Arnauld (CE 1612–94), according to which salvation is not earned by one's acts but granted by the irresistible grace of God. On the other hand, Thomist philosophers have held the doctrine of *premotio physica*, according to which God intrinsically and physically promotes second causes for action without thereby eliminating the freedom of the causes themselves. The *influxus physicus* (physical influence) of God is necessary for, but not – as held by the Spanish philosopher Luis de Molina (CE 1536–1600) – co-ordinated with, let alone (as in *occasionalism*) suppressing the second causes. Molina and others, however, argued for co-ordinated causation, on the grounds that the intrinsic predetermination in *premotio physica* irresistibly moves the will and, hence, eliminates its freedom. In this context, Molina introduced the notion of *scientia media* or middle knowledge, i.e. God's knowledge of counterfactuals of freedom.

These state, for each free creature God could create, what the creature would do under free-choice conditions in which it could be.

Another related view is *synergism* (from the Greek *synergein*, i.e. "to work together"), according to which there is co-operation or synergy between the human consciousness of free will and the divine grace. This doctrine became the focus of controversy in Protestantism when, influenced by the Dutch humanist Desiderius Erasmus (CE 1467–1536), the German theologian Phillipp Melanchton (CE 1497–1560) argued in his *Commonplaces of Theology* (1521) that the Holy Spirit, the preaching of the Word, and the human will co-operate in the process of conversion and regeneration.

An earlier position aimed at radically upholding free will had been formulated by the English philosopher William of Ockham (*c.* CE 1290–1349), who held that a human being is a *suppositum intellectuale*, i.e. a complete rational being with the power to indifferently and contingently produce effects (so that, even after reaching a given conclusion, the will is free to will it or not), as well as to willing or not willing happiness as one's ultimate aim. Ockham however acknowledged that God knows what we will do; but stated that it is impossible to understand or explain how God can know it.

In addition, there is *logical* determinism, the view that, since whatever will happen in the future can be described by a true proposition, then it is bound to happen. A modal-logic version of this view is the following: since, necessarily, whatever will happen will happen, then, whatever will happen will necessarily happen. However, this is a fallacious use of necessarily. For it is like saying that since, necessarily, if I was born and have not died, then I am alive, then, since I was born and have not died, I am necessarily alive (which implies the false statement that I cannot die).

Some of the latter versions of determinism are sometimes identified with or used as a basis for *fatalism*: the doctrine that whatever happens, happens because of factors – e.g. the stars, the fates, or the forces of biology or history – that are entirely beyond human control. Indeed, the notion that some factors are entirely beyond human control was already deeply entrenched in the ordinary language and conceptions in Ancient Greece and Rome through the concept of *fate*, where the terms for fate respectively were *moira* and *fatum*, both meaning a prophetic declaration or statement. These terms are pre-philosophical, deriving from Greek mythology that, in Greece, identified it as Zeus' decision and, in Rome, with Jupiter's spoken word.

In philosophy, various thinkers upholding forms of determinism have resisted the notion that it implies fatalism, on the grounds that determinism does not rule out the efficacy of human conduct or desire. For example, in Arabic philosophy, the schools that upheld the notion of free will were the Mu'tazilites (from the Arabic *a'tazala*, i.e. "to take one's distance," "remove oneself," or "withdraw") and their forerunners, the Qadarites (from the Arabic *qadar*, i.e. "power" or "will")

This raises the issue of whether determinism is compatible or incompatible with free will, i.e. the view that, generally, individuals could have acted or wished in a manner other than that in which they did. *Incompatibilism* – also called *hard determinism* – is the view that, if determinism is true, then there is no free will. Alternatively, *compatibilism* – or *soft determinism* – is the view that determinism does not rule out free will. In discussions of the free will problem, i.e. the problem of the nature of free will and its relation to conduct, some consider *libertas indifferentiae*, which is to say freedom of indifference or liberty of indifference – i.e. the contingency of alternative courses of action – to be crucial. Others construe such indifference as motivational balance, a notion they consider central to rational choice. Still others emphasize freedom of spontaneity or liberty of spontaneity, i.e. doing as one wants. However, mere wanting may not be enough: one may not be in control of what one wants, because one's wants or one's knowledge of the circumstances are manipulated by others. Those concerned with this point emphasize control. There are those who emphasize not merely control, but autonomy or self-determination, i.e. control based on such things as one's character, and higher values. When that control is exercised from outside the causal chain, as it is the case with those who uphold both incompatibilism and free will, the position is called *metaphysical* libertarianism and those who hold it metaphysical libertarians.

Discussions of the previous problems often include the expression *book of life*, found in Hebrew and Christian scriptures, meaning a record of those destined for eternal happiness that was supposedly kept by God. Medieval philosophers frequently used the phrase book of life in discussing predestination, divine omniscience, foreknowledge, and free will. Some, e.g. the philosopher Augustine (CE 354–430, born in Thagaste, North Africa) and, later, the philosopher Thomas Aquinas (CE 1225–74, born near the city of Naples, in what is now Italy) asked whether the book of life constituted God's unerring foreknowledge or whether items could be added to or deleted from it. Today, some philosophers use this expression to denote a record of all the events in a person's life that, some say, is the person's fate or destiny.

The problem of whether determinism is compatible with free will is relevant to conceptions and applications of responsibility in ethics and the law. For example, the notion of *diminished responsibility*, also called *diminished capacity*, is a concept used in legal defenses of criminal liability cases. It has two variants. In the *mens rea* variant, evidence of mental abnormality – e.g. mental disorder, intoxication, trauma, etc. – is used to argue that, at the time of the crime, the defendant did not have the mental state required for the offense. In the *partial responsibility* variant, it is argued that, even if the defendant had the required mental state, his or her responsibility was diminished and, hence, should be charged with a lesser crime. Either variant, of course, presupposes that responsibility is not diminished in other circumstances.

An incompatibilist determinist, however, would argue that all cases are exactly like the ones just mentioned: that is, according to incompatibilism, responsibility of the decision-making type, i.e. where an agent has the capacity to tell right from wrong, to make decision on this basis, and to act accordingly, is impossible. Of course, the agent can still have causal responsibility or be causally responsible for a given state of affairs, i.e. be the one who caused death, injury, or loss of property. The agent can also have legal responsibility or be legally responsible for it, i.e. be the one the law says should pay for the damages or be punished in specific ways. It is questionable, however, whether the agent has moral responsibility or is morally responsible for the said state of affairs, i.e. whether the person ought to have omitted the action(s) that brought it about. For, otherwise, it would make sense to say that one ought to do or have done something even if one has no control whatsoever over one's own decisions or conduct.

See also: artificial intelligence; causal law; computer theory

Further reading
Berofsky, Bernard (ed.) (1966) *Free Will and Determinism*, New York: Harper & Row.
Valla, Lorenzo (1948) "Dialogue on Free Will," in E. Cassirer, P.O. Kristeller, and J.H. Randall (eds) *The Renaissance Philosophy of Man*, Chicago: University of Chicago Press, pp. 155–82.
Williams, Clifford (1980) *Free Will and Determinism: A Dialogue*, Indianapolis: Hackett Pub. Co.

deterministic automaton *see* computer theory

deterministic law *see* causal law

deterrence *see* philosophy of law; war

Deus Latin term for God appearing in various philosophical phrases including the following. First, *deus absconditus*: meaning hidden God, this Latin phrase was used by German Churchman and Reformer Martin Luther (CE 1483–1546) to convey his view that we should achieve salvation by faith in a universe that was often dark and irrational, and where God was often hidden. This position was in sharp contrast to the enlightened view of the world held by the Dutch Renaissance humanist Desiderius Erasmus (CE 1467–1536).

Second, *deus ex machina*: meaning a god from a machine, this Latin phrase was originally used to denote the frequent practice in classical Greek tragedies whereby a problem of the plot was solved by bringing a god on stage. It denotes anything artificially introduced to

solve a problem, e.g. in a philosophical position, and has been used in the philosophy of
religion to criticize certain conceptions of the
relation of God and the world.

Third, *deus sive natura*: meaning God or
nature, this Latin phrase was used by the
philosopher Baruch Spinoza (CE 1632–77) –
born in Amsterdam of Spanish–Portuguese
descent – to indicate the identification of God
with nature or substance in characterizing
reality; hence, of the goal of religion and the
goal of inquiry.

See also: determinism; philosophy of religion

Further reading
Bonhoeffer, Dietrich (1996) *Act and Being:
Transcendental Philosophy and Ontology in
Systematic Theology*, Minneapolis: Fortress
Press.
Kohler, Rudolf (1955) *Der Deus absconditus in
philosophie und theologie*, Koln: E.J. Brill.
Vuarnet, Jean-Noel (1993) *Frederic Benrath:
Deus sive natura*, Paris: Ed. de L'Amateur.

deva *see* demon

development A term used in a variety of
philosophically significant phrases including
the following. First, *cognitive development*: an
area of psychology and the philosophy of mind
profoundly influenced by the work of the Swiss
psychologist and epistemologist Jean Piaget (CE
1896–1980), who regarded himself as engaged
in *genetic epistemology*: the empirical study of
knowledge by focusing on how our epistemic
relations to the world around us improve.
According to Piaget, these relations are neither
genetically programmed nor learned in the
behaviorist sense. Instead, he held that they
result of interactions involving accommodation
with the world of objects around us, and
assimilation of those objects through children's
cognitive systems. At the core of cognitive
development studies were Piaget's detailed
descriptions and a taxonomy of cognitive
changes from birth to adolescence

Second, *moral development*: an area of
ethics, psychology, and the philosophy of mind
profoundly influenced by the United States
psychologist and moral philosopher Lawrence
Kohlberg (CE 1927–87), who extended Piaget's
study of psychological development to the moral
development of children into adolescence. He
identified three levels – pre-conventional, conventional, and post-conventional – of moral
development, each involving six stages of
motivation: physical punishment, instrumental
self-satisfaction, interpersonal concordance,
conformity to authority, social utility, and universality principles. These stages were criticized
by the contemporary United States psychologist and moral philosopher Carol Gilligan,
who noted that Kohlberg's samples included
only males. She focused on women and concluded that their moral development reflected
an ethics of care by contrast with Kohlberg's
ethics of justice. She distinguished three levels
of motivation in women's moral development:
friendship, empathy, and interdependence.

Third, *socioeconomic development*: an area
of concern and study in the social sciences,
policy studies, and sociopolitical philosophy,
whose roots can be found in such earlier
notions as evolutionary societal progress (in
Social Darwinism), and phased historical sequences (in MARXISM). Socioeconomic development was initially associated with bureaucratic
and technocratic governmental structures
charged with formulating and implementing
programs for social improvement. However,
an emphasis on market forces through privati-
zation, decentralization, and deregulation later
took center-stage. Until the 1960s, socioeconomic development was seen as a series of
stages of growth through which developing
countries had to go, just as industrialized
countries had. This *modernization theory* was
criticized in the 1970s by those who held the
underdevelopment theory, according to which
developing countries cannot leave the periph-
ery of a system centered on industrialized
countries unless the entire system is dis-
mantled. Others have criticized both these
views on the grounds that they assign too
central a role to economic growth, which, in
fact, is significant but not central for development – conditions involving such things as
local cultures and global, as well as local,
environmental concerns are also significant.
There have been attempts at synthesizing all
of these views during the 1980s and 1990s, but
the judgment is still out on the matter.

See also: epistemology; ethics; philosophy of
mind; philosophy, sociopolitical

Further reading
Behar, Joseph E. and Cuzan, Alfred G. (1997) *At the Crossroads of Development: Transnational Challenges to Developed and Developing Societies*, Leiden and New York: E.J. Brill.
Gilligan, Carol (*c.* 1991) *Women's Psychological Development: Implications for Psychotherapy*, New York: Haworth Press.
Piaget, Jean (1997) *The Principles of Genetic Epistemology*, London and New York: Routledge.
Puka, Bill and Kohlberg, Lawrence (1994) *Moral Development: A Compendium*, New York and London: Garland.

deviant causal chain *see* causal law

deviant logic *see* logic

dhammapada *see* Buddhism

dharma From the Sanskrit, *dhr*, i.e. "to sustain," "support," "uphold," *dharma* literally means "what holds together." It is a term with a variety of related meanings including: appropriate ritual, duty, that which is proper, law, righteousness, truth, elements of ontology, property, and fate. In Hinduism, and especially in the Vedas, *dharma* denotes a cosmic rule that assigns things their nature or essence, as well as a set of duties and rules in accordance with which humans ought to act in order to maintain social order, promote social well-being, and be righteous. The pursuit of *dharma* was one of the basic pursuits in life, together with those of wealth (*artha*), pleasure (*kāma*), and spiritual liberation (*moksha*). When *dharmas* belonged to the karmic order, and the goal of life was thought to be spiritual liberation, a conflict arose between *dharma* and *moksha* that was solved in various ways, e.g. by holding the world to be illusory.

Dharma appears in a number of philosophical phrases including:

1 *varna-āsrama-dharma*, i.e. the duties specific to each class and life-stage;
2 *sanātana-dharma*, i.e. the eternal religion;
3 *sva-dharma*, i.e. one's individual duty;
4 *sādhārana-dharma*, i.e. the general duties of each and every individual such as self-control, kindness, and truthfulness.

In JAINISM, *dharma* is the condition of motion and pervades the universe, while *ad-harma*, also a basic component of the universe, is the condition of rest. Liberation is the attainment of *dharma* by the self beyond the world of phenomena.

In BUDDHISM, *dharma* has a normative sense in which *dharmas* are moral duties, and a descriptive sense in which *dharma* is reality and *dharmas* are the many components of reality.

According to the NYĀYA-VAIŚEṢIKA SCHOOL, *dharma* is a quality of the self that can be directly perceived (though with the assistance of yogic power) and denotes merit, not rightness.

In the SĀMKHYA-YOGA School, *dharma* is a mode of the intellect (*buddhi*) and it is a mistake to believe it belongs to the *purusa* or spiritual realm. Hence, morality is an empirical matter.

See also: Buddhism; Hinduism

Further reading
Balbir Singh (1981) *Dharma: Man, Religion and Society*, New Delhi: Arnold–Heinemann.
Hall, Manly Palmer (1925) *The Noble Eightfold Path: The Doctrine of Dharma, the Principles of the Philosophy of the Great Buddha*, Los Angeles, CA: Hall Pub. Co.
Peden, Creighton and Hudson, Yeager (1993) *Freedom, Dharma, and Rights*, Lewiston: E. Mellen Press.

dhāt *see* Ṣūfism

dhyāna Sanskrit term meaning "meditation," "absorption," synonymous with the Pali *jhāna*. In Hinduism, it is one of the three final stages of yoga philosophy according to its founder Patañjali (*c.* second century BCE). At this stage, the mind no longer projects its contents on the object of meditation, but merges with the object. Without this stage, higher stages of consciousness cannot be attained.

In Zen, *dhyāna* is an absorbed state of mind attained by uninterruptedly concentrating on a physical or mental object. In particular, *dhyāna* denotes the four stages of absorption of the world of form that lead to liberation. The first absorption involves relinquishing desire; the second, the attainment of inner calm and joy through stopping conceptualization and discourse; the third involves equanimity, alertness, and, instead of joy, a feeling of well-being; the fourth involves only equanimity and alertness.

In Chinese Buddhism, *dhyāna* includes all meditation practices – even all preparatory practices for *dhyāna* in the previously discussed narrower senses.

See also: Buddhism; Hinduism; Zen

Further reading
Huang Po (1957) *The Huang Po Doctrine of Universal Mind: Being the Teaching of Dhyana Master Hsi Yun as Recorded by Pei Hsiu, a Noted Scholar of the Tang Dynasty Huang Po chuan fa yao*, London: Buddhist Society.
Iyer, T.V. Parameswar Pundit (1977) *Concept of Dhyana: In the Original Sanskrit Texts of the Vedas, Metaphysics, Systems of Philosophy and the Exposition Thereof by Various Modern Thinkers*, presented at the 3rd World Sanskrit Conference: Paris, 20–5 June 1977, Seelisberg, Switzerland: Maharishi European Research University.

diachrony *see* Continental philosophy

diagonal procedure *see* infinity

dialectic From the Greek *dialektos* ("discourse," "debate"), this term is used in a variety of senses. Originally, the art of dialectic was largely the art of engaging in dialogue, typically when the dialogue involved at least two opposing views, often held by individuals – dialecticians – disagreeing and engaging in argument about the matter. In a more technical sense, dialectic was used to refer to a type of indirect argumentation aimed at investigating what would follow from a proposition supposed to be true. Examples of this type of argumentation can be found in the works of the Greek philosophers Zeno of Elea (490–430 BCE), who is reputed to have invented it, and, most notably, Plato (428–348 BCE), who thought dialectic embodied the highest knowledge. For Plato's student, the Greek philosopher Aristotle (384–322 BCE), dialectic had a less positive meaning, because it proceeded from the opinions of human beings and was less reliable than demonstration based on first principles. Yet, it was useful as a method of criticism. Neoplatonic thinkers returned to the positive meaning of dialectic, considering it the way for ascending toward higher realities culminating in the One.

Both of these opposed conceptions of dialectic (as a method for attaining mere pseudo-knowledge vs as a method for discerning truth from falsehood), as well as intermediate conceptions – e.g. merely as an instrument to keep the intellect active – were influential during the European middle ages. In modern times, the Kantian conception of dialectic was that of a misguided attempt at applying the principles governing phenomena to things in themselves. While the Hegelian conception was that all levels of reality developed in accordance with a process involving the triad (which the founder of Hegelianism, the German philosopher Georg Wilhelm Friedrich Hegel (CE 1770–1831) did not use): thesis (from the Greek *tithenai*, i.e. "to set"), antithesis (from the Greek *anti*, i.e. "against," and *tithenai*), and synthesis (from the Greek *syn*, i.e. "together," and *tithenai*).

Hegelian dialectic involved the notion of polarity: an opposition between two terms such as ideas, opinions, and physical forces, a situation that was overcome in the synthesis. This conception of dialectic was adopted by Marxism along the lines of what the German philosopher Friedrich Engels (CE 1820–95) called *dialectical materialism*. On this view, all processes took place in a material world, quantitative changes led to qualitative changes, a sense of history was crucial for understanding reality, and social change occurred through a dialectical process involving class-conflict. During the twentieth century, various alternatives to the Marxist conception of dialectic were formulated, most notably, by the German philosopher Theodor W. Adorno (CE 1903–69), who advanced the notion of *negative dialectics*, according to which every totalizing synthesis – e.g. that in Hegelian and that in Marxist dialectic – is false and pretentious. Yet, the notion of polarity involved in dialectical thinking and processes has been thought important by a number of thinkers who argue that many reflections or processes cannot be fruitful unless they involve opposite balancing components.

Conceptions of dialectic have traditionally been associated with conceptions of reason.

For example, *dialectical reason*, has been used to denote a faculty or way of reasoning or proceeding associated with Hegelian, Marxist, and later conceptions of dialectic. In this sense, dialectical reason has been contraposed to *classical* reason and *analytic* reason – both supposed to be static. Sometimes, the expressions *historical* reason and *concrete* reason are used as synonymous with dialectical reason. However, it should be noticed that some medieval philosophers also used the expression concrete reason by contrast with *abstract* reason, though, for them, both were forms of classical reason. Also, in the original Hegelian works, reason (*Vernunft*) was already concrete (by contrast with *Vernunft* in Kantian philosophy, where it can be pure reason, practical reason or their variants), its abstract counterpart being UNDERSTANDING (*Verstand*). It is also historical in that it develops.

Worthy of note here is the (philosophical) Zürich School, which should not be confused with the (psychoanalytic) Zürich School associated with the work of the Swiss psychoanalyst Carl Gustav Jung (CE 1875–1961). The tenets of the (philosophical) Zürich School were formulated in the journal *Dialectica*, which began publication in the Swiss city of Neuchâtel in 1947. The School's most notable member was the French philosopher of science and literary analyst Gaston Bachelard (CE 1884–1962). The School's approach was a philosophy of *dépassement* (French for transcendence), aimed at moving beyond pure empiricism and pure rationalism; acknowledging that knowledge is crucially unfinished and bodies of belief – however established – are always open to revision; and evaluating dialectic in an effort to apply it to the process where, at each time, opposed beliefs and theories claim finality and closure.

See also: logic; philosophy

Further reading
Erickson, Glenn W. (1990) *Negative Dialectics and the End of Philosophy*, Wolfeboro, NH: Longwood Academic.
Mepham, John and David-Hillel, Ruben (1979) *Dialectics and Method*, Brighton: Harvester Press.

dialectical *see* dialectic

dialecticians *see* dialectic; Chinese philosophy

diallelon *see* definition

diallelus *see* definition

dialogue *see* dialectic

dianoetic *see* understanding; virtue

dianoia *see* understanding

diaspora From the Greek *dia* ("through") and *speirō* ("to sow" or "scatter"), diaspora and its adjective, diasporic, have a variety of meanings, as follows. First, *diaspora as a social category*: this was a sense originally reserved almost exclusively to denote the Jews living in exile from their homeland and scattered all over the planet. Today, the term – as well as the term *hybridity* – is also used in discussions of migration to denote any group of people from the same homeland who are living elsewhere, retain links to their culture of origin, but have to some degree adapted to the culture they inhabit.

Second, *diaspora as a form of consciousness*: in this sense, diaspora denotes individuals' awareness of their being attached to a number of places, of being home away from home or, alternatively, feeling a kind of loneliness or the distance of a stranger everywhere.

This notion has a family resemblance to the notion of *double consciousness* formulated by the United States sociologist and social philosopher W.E.B. Du Bois (CE 1868–1963), a notable representative of the Harlem Renaissance who has had long-standing influence in African-American philosophy with his uncompromising position on equality for African-Americans. He thought the implementation of this end should occur in four ways: through democracy understood as equality of political rights; cultural pluralism understood as an opportunity for African-Americans to become fully conscious of their heritage and talents; Pan-Africanism or the view that African civilization makes a valuable contribution to United States culture while, at the same time, African nations need the help of African-Americans; and socialism. Since 1962 until his death, Du Bois continued fostering Pan-Africanism from Ghana, were he directed the proposed multivolume *Encyclopedia Africana* and, when the

United States failed to renew his passport, became a citizen of Ghana. The question of how to bring about equality for African-Americans continues to shape much of the discussion in African-American philosophy today. So does the notion of double consciousness, which is also significantly discussed among members of other diasporas, most notably the United States Hispanic diaspora, whose members sometimes feel caught between a sense of identity embedded in their culture of origin and the local pressures towards *acculturation*, i.e. the process of adopting the features or patterns of their host culture.

Third, *diaspora as a mode of cultural adaptation*: in this sense, diaspora denotes the fluid, malleable identity that people living away from home develop in adapting to their foreign environments.

Fourth, *diaspora as a problem*: in this sense, diaspora denotes a threat to the host society, usually on the grounds that foreigners' attachments to their homelands and the hybrid cultural identities they develop undermine their loyalty to the society they inhabit. In legal contexts, a member of a disapora is sometimes pinned between the *jus sanguis*, i.e. the member's right to citizenship in the country of his or her ancestors – say, in Italy, so long as one is at most a second-generation Italian descendant and one's Italian father and grandfather never gave up Italian citizenship – and the *jus terris*, i.e. the right – in some countries incompatible with the *jus sanguis* – to be a citizen of the country where one was born. Critics of those who see diasporas as a problem, or of those who argue for a *jus terris* to the exclusion of all *jus sanguis*, point to diasporas as central features of globalization and a source of cultural creativity, however this may change traditional societies.

See also: philosophy, sociopolitical; philosophy and expatriation

Further reading
Cavalli-Sforza, L.L. (1996) *The Great Human Diasporas: The History of Diversity and Evolution*, Reading, MA and Harlow: Addison-Wesley.
Lafaye, Jacques (1977) *The Spanish Diaspora: The Enduring Unity of Hispanic Culture*, Washington, DC: Latin American Program,

Woodrow Wilson International Center for Scholars.
Suleiman, Susan Rubin (1998) *Exile and Creativity: Signposts, Travelers, Outsiders, Backward Glances*, Durham: Duke University Press.

dicent indexical legisign *see* pragmatism

dicent sinsign *see* pragmatism

dicent symbol *see* pragmatism

dichotomous thinking *see* feminist philosophy

dichotomy and gender *see* feminist philosophy

dichotomy paradox *see* paradox

dici de omni et nullo *see* syllogism

dictatorship *see* philosophy, sociopolitical

dicto, modality de *see* de

dictum *see* complexum significabile

dictum de omni et nullo *see* syllogism

différance *see* definition; set; Continental philosophy

difference, method of *see* induction

différend *see* Continental philosophy

differentia *see* definition

dignity *see* ethics

dilemma In logic, an argument whose form is such that one premise is a disjunction. There are two kinds, as follows. The first, a *constructive dilemma* or *simple constructive dilemma*, has the form:

$$\frac{\begin{array}{c} p \supset q \\ r \supset s \\ p \lor r \end{array}}{q \lor s}$$

The second, a *destructive dilemma* or *simple destructive dilemma*, has the form:

$$\frac{\begin{array}{c} p \supset q \\ r \supset s \\ \text{-}q \lor \text{-}s \end{array}}{\text{-}p \lor \text{-}r}$$

A dilemma in which the disjunctive premise

is false is called a *false dilemma*. Some significant problems in logic, for example the relation between the truths of a logical system and the possibility of proving them in the system, can be described in the form of dilemmas. The logician Kurt Gödel (CE 1906–78), born in Brünn, Austria-Hungary – now Brno, Czech Republic, arguably did just that in developing his incompleteness theorems.

In ethics, the expression *moral dilemma* is used in various ways, as follows. The first is in any problem relevant to morality. In this sense, a moral dilemma can be not only a problem involving mutually conflicting moral reasons (e.g. "Should I tell the truth thereby endangering someone's life or should I protect the person's life by telling a lie?"), but also a problem where moral reasons conflict with non-moral reasons (e.g. a Christian Scientist might ask "Should I permit this blood transfusion thereby saving my daughter's life, or should I obey my religion's rule that we should let nature take its course thereby risking my daughter's life?"

The second is in any moral problem where the right answer is not known. In this sense, the moral problem of whether engaging in active euthanasia to prevent a patient's excruciatingly painful death is ever morally permissible is sometimes called a moral dilemma.

Third, and in a more technical sense, a moral dilemma is a situation in which a person ought to perform each of two actions, but cannot do both. Some philosophers argue that, in order to constitute a dilemma, *both these actions should be morally required* in the situation, e.g. my obligation to keep my promise to meet you at noon today and my obligation to get help for an injured person I find on a deserted road on my way to meeting you. They should not be mere conflicts between, say, moral requirements, like those just mentioned, and moral ideals. An example of such a conflict would be that between the obligation to take care of one's children and the moral ideal of becoming a physician and taking care of the sick in some undeveloped area of the planet, where this would undermine one's taking care of one's children. Still other philosophers argue that, even if two moral obligations conflict as in the previously men-

tioned case, they do not constitute a moral dilemma if one of the obligations – say, my obligation to meet you at noon – is overriden by the other. In moral dilemmas, *none of the obligations is overriden*. In addition, to avoid trivial conflicts, some philosophers argue that *the obligations involved must be serious.*

See also: ethics; logic

Further reading
Dawson, John W. (1997) *Logical Dilemmas: The Life and Work of Kurt Gödel*, Wellesley, MA: A.K. Peters.
Sylvan, Richard (1984) *Moral Dilemmas and the Logic of Deontic Notions*, Canberra, Australia: Australian National University.

dimatis *see* syllogism

diminished capacity *see* determinism; philosophy of law

diminished responsibility *see* determinism; philosophy of law

Ding an sich *see* Kantian philosophy

diplomacy *see* philosophy, sociopolitical

direct consequences *see* ethics

direct intention *see* intention

direct knowledge *see* justification; knowledge

direct passions *see* empiricism

direct realism *see* perception

direct reference *see* reference

direct sense *see* opacity

directives *see* speech act theory

disability *see* ethics

disadvantage *see* ethics

disamis *see* syllogism

disciplinary matrix *see* philosophy of science

discipline *see* Continental philosophy

discourse From the Latin, *discursus*, a term used to translate various philosophical terms from the Greek, all of which have been inherited by the term discourse, as follows. First, *as contrasted with intuition*, the term discourse inherited the sense in which *discursus* was used to translate *diánoia* by contrast with, yet without necessarily excluding, *noesis*. Though, in this sense, discourse is contrasted with INTUITION, it is sometimes thought to rely on it to some extent. Arguably, this view was held in various ways and to different extents by the Greek philosopher Plato (428–348 BCE), the Egypto-Roman philosopher Plotinus (CE 204–70), the French philosopher René Descartes (CE 1596–1650), and the Amsterdam-born philosopher of Spanish and Portuguese descent Baruch Spinoza (CE 1632–77. The Greek philosopher Aristotle (384–322 BCE) and the philosopher Thomas Aquinas, born near the city of Naples, in what is now Italy (CE 1225–74), tended to emphasize discursive knowledge. The German philosopher Immanuel Kant (CE 1724–1804), in saying that the central constituents of discourse, concepts, without intuitions are empty and intuitions without concepts are blind, considered both of them to be equally indispensable components of knowledge. At any rate, the term discourse is used by contrast with intuition by all the said authors.

Second, *as propositional speech*, the term discourse proceeds from the Latin translation of the Greek *logos* as *discursus*, which, in this sense, was identified in the European Middle Ages with *oratio*. In this sense, discourse has been divided into direct (or *oratio recta*) – e.g. when one says "My mother said 'You can go to your friend Mary's house and practice your dance; but don't get in the swimming pool'" – and indirect (or *oratio obliqua*) – e.g. when one says "My mother said that I can go to my friend Mary's house to practice our dance but cannot get in the swimming pool." By extension, indirect discourse covers the use of speech to report beliefs.

Third, *in logic*, the expression *universe of discourse* was introduced by the English mathematician and logician Augustus de Morgan (CE 1806–71) in 1845 to denote all the classes of items that, in a given context, are relevant to an argument, e.g. prime numbers when the argument is about what is the largest known prime number. The British logician and mathematician George Boole (CE 1815–64) used the said expression to denote the class of everything; that is, the class of every x such that $x=x$. Today, the expression universe of dis-course and its synonym, domain of discourse, is used largely linguistically to denote all the items about which propositions can be stated.

Fourth, *discourse and power*: this aspect of discourse has been discussed by the French philosopher and psychologist Michael Foucault (CE 1926–84) who, following the German philosopher and philologist Friedrich Nietzsche (CE 1844–1900), held that the search for truth and power are always intermingled and, in effect, there are only regimes of truth empowered and deployed in society through a variety of constraints, including *accepted forms of discourse*, mechanisms for distinguishing true from false statements, and the status granted to those with the authoritativeness – which, in this case, is the same as authority – to determine what is true and what is false.

See also: epistemology; ethics; philosophy, sociopolitical

Further reading
Blythin, Evan (1994) *The Universe of Discourse: Issues and Features*, Lanham: University Press of America.
Hindess, Barry (1996) *Discourses of Power: From Hobbes to Foucault*, Oxford, UK and Cambridge, MA: Blackwell Publishers.
Spisani, Franco (1977) *Implication, Endometry, Universe of Discourse*, Bologna: International Logic Review.

discourse ethics *see* ethics

discovery *see* abduction

discrete *see* metaphysics; philosophy of science

discrimination *see* aesthetics; ethics; perception; philosophy, sociopolitical

discursus *see* discourse

discussion of merits *see* philosophy, sociopolitical

disease *see* ethics; metaphysics; philosophy of science

disembodied *see* metaphysics

disembodiment *see* metaphysics

disinterested *see* ethics

disjointed incrementalism *see* philosophy, sociopolitical

disjunction *see* logic

disjunctive normal form *see* logic

disjunctive proposition *see* logic

disjunctive syllogism *see* syllogism

disjuncts *see* logic

disposition From the Latin *dispositio*, i.e. "distribution," this term has various philosophical uses, including as follows. First, *order*: the way in which the parts of a totality are organized. Second, *way of being*: the manner in which a certain item is, as in *dispositio entis*. Third, *tendency*: a natural or acquired tendency of an object or system to react in characteristic ways in specifiable circumstances. This includes *habits*, especially as applied to persons and their traits, say, generosity, honesty, and a sense of humor. In this sense, a disposition (e.g. the disposition to smoke of a smoker) is contrasted with an *episode* (a particular occasion on which someone smokes, though neither the person is a smoker nor does the person have the disposition to smoke), and so are contrasted the respective adjectives dispositional with episodic. It should be noted that, in Aristotelian ethics, a disposition is not just a habit, but a state of character helping or hindering one's acting between excess and defect in the display of such traits as generosity and courage. What helps or hinders one's acting this way is a *hexis* (from the Greek *hexo*, i.e. "to have," or "to be disposed"), a disposition or state which is not a mere passion (*pathe*) one cannot control, nor a faculty (*dunamis*) of the soul, but a state of character whereby one makes a decision.

The characteristic action, reaction, movement, or other type of change associated with a disposition is called its *manifestation* or *display*. Some manifestations are regular or universal, i.e. invariably associated with a disposition. For example, sugar placed in water under ordinary conditions invariably dissolves. In this case, the disposition is called a *universal* disposition. Other manifestations are probabilistic and the dispositions associated with them are *probabilistic* dispositions. For example, certain atmospheric conditions are likely to cause tornadoes but they do not invariably cause them. In addition, some dispositions have more than one type of manifestation, while others have only one type of manifestation. They are respectively called *multi-track* or *multiply manifested* dispositions, and *single-track* or *singly manifested* dispositions. Irritability, for example, is a multiply manifested disposition, because it may lead to the display of a wide range of behaviors, from withdrawal to fighting. Sugar's water solubility is singly manifested in that it leads to sugar's dissolving in water.

Dispositional claims involve hypothetical or conditional statements that, some argue, capture their entire meaning, e.g. to say that glass is brittle is to say that, if glass were hit under suitable conditions, it would break. That is, dispositional properties are *not occurrent*, which is to say: to have a dispositional property is not thereby to undergo any episode or occurrence. Nor is it to be in any particular state.

Other philosophers, however, take a realistic stand, arguing that talk of dispositions implies the basis of such dispositions and of the truth of the conditionals such talk implies, e.g. the brittleness of glass also implies the molecular structure on which brittleness is based.

See also: condition

Further reading
Armstrong, D.M.(1996) *Dispositions: A Debate*, London and New York: Routledge.
Prior, E.W. (1985) *Dispositions*, Aberdeen: Aberdeen University Press.

dispositional state *see* philosophy of mind

dispositional theory of meaning *see* meaning

dispositional theory of memory *see* memory

disputatio *see* Scholasticism

disputation *see* Scholasticism

disquotation theory of truth *see* truth

distinctio formalis a parte re *see* definition

distinction *see* definition

distributive justice *see* ethics; justice

distributive laws *see* logic

diversity *see* culture

divine attributes *see* God

divine command *see* ethics

divine foreknowledge *see* determinism

divine right *see* philosophy, sociopolitical

divisibility *see* infinity

division, fallacy of *see* fallacy

division of labor *see* Marxism; philosophy of economics

diyah *see* Arabic philosophy

d-n model *see* causal law; explanation

dō *see* Zen

docile bodies *see* Continental philosophy

docta ignorantia Latin expression for "learned ignorance," a characteristic predicated of persons on many an occasion in philosophy, most notably by the Greek philosopher Socrates (469–399 BCE) in his student Plato's *Apology*, when he claimed the only wisdom he could claim for himself was that of knowing that he was not wise. Along this line, the notion of *docta ignorantia* was later formulated as a disposition to know or find wisdom while at the same time claiming not to have it. In an early Christian context, the philosopher Augustine (CE 354–430), born in Thagaste, North Africa, characterized it as a learned disposition of the soul to receive God's spirit (*Letters* 130, c. 15, n. 28). The Italian philosopher Bonaventure (*c.* CE 1221–74) – born Giovanni Fidanza – indicated it was a disposition necessary for our spirit to overcome in its fervent desire for the realm where the *Rex sapientissimus* resides (*Breviloquium*, V iv 7). The expression *docta ignorantia*, however, became widely known through the work of the Renaissance Platonist Nicholas of Cusa (CE 1401–64), born in the city of Kues in what is now Germany, who in his *On Learned Ignorance*, and his *Defense of Learned Ignorance*, held that to know (*scire*) is to be ignorant (*ignorare*), because knowledge begins only when we begin to seek the truth, which entails our acknowledging our ignorance.

Later Renaissance authors, including such skeptics as the French writer Michel de Montaigne (CE 1533–92) and the Portuguese philosopher Francisco Sánches (*c.* CE 1551–1623), used this notion. However, by contrast with Nicholas of Cusa, who sought an ultimate knowledge incapable of being in accordance with the principle of non-contradiction, Montaigne and Sánchez sought, rather, to discard useless opinions in order to better understand empirically the relations between humans and nature. At any rate, whether mystics or empirically minded, all these thinkers sought an original experience and considered the disposition to know to be superior to the attainment of knowledge.

See also: Christianity; Platonism; skepticism

Further reading
Augustine, Saint, Bishop of Hippo (1876 [1872]) *The Works of Aurelius Augustine*, Edinburgh: T. & T. Clark.
Bonaventure, Saint, Cardinal (1970) *Breviloquium*, trans. Erwin Esser Nemmers, Ann Arbor: University Microfilms,
Haydn, Hiram Collins (1960 [1950]) *The Counter-Rennaissance*, New York: Grove Press.
Nicholas, of Cusa, Cardinal (1997) *Selected Spiritual Writings*, New York: Paulist Press.

doctrine of determinism *see* determinism

doctrine of infinite analysis *see* calculus

doctrine of minute perceptions *see* philosophy of mind

doctrine of the king's two bodies *see* philosophy, sociopolitical

doctrine of the mean *see* Chinese philosophy; Confucianism; ethics

doctrine of the two swords *see* philosophy, sociopolitical

dogma From the Latin *dogma*, and this from the Greek *dogma*, i.e. "opinion," associated with the verb *dokein*: "to seem" or "seem good." It has acquired the ordinary meaning of tenet or system of tenets authoritatively laid down (e.g. by a Church), or established by tradition. It also carries the connotation of being unfounded and arrogant assertions and, in this sense, persons who make, or institutions that uphold, such assertions are accused of dogmatism. In philosophy, dogma originally meant opinion and for a position to be dogmatic (*dogmaticēs*) was for it to be *founded* *on principles* or relative to a doctrine. Those philosophers who insisted so much on principles that they disregarded facts or reasons, especially those undermining the principles, were called dogmatic. This latter meaning has largely taken over philosophical discussions since modern times. It is typically used to denote absence of criticism (i.e. the unexamined submission to any views, principles), especially as exemplified in naive realism concerning our knowledge of the world around us, and absolute confidence in a specific source of knowledge, be it sense-perception or reason.

The French philosopher Auguste Comte (CE 1789–1857) discussed dogmatism and skepticism as two opposed life-attitudes, dogmatism being the natural tendency of human intelligence, while the doubts of skepticism and the crises they prompted made it possible for humans to proceed from one dogmatism to the next. This topic was further pursued, for example, by the United States philosopher Charles Sanders Peirce (CE 1839–1914) in his "The Fixation of Belief," where he discussed dogmatic approaches – the methods of tenacity, authority, and the a priori method – as ways of fixing belief that, by contrast with the method of science, were not self-corrective.

See also: epistemology; metaphysics; rationalism

Further reading
Buchler, Justus (1955) *Philosophical Writings of Peirce*, New York: Dover.
Comte, Auguste (1997) *Auguste Comte and Positivism: The Essential Writings*, New Brunswick, NJ: Transaction Publishers.
Wahbah, Murad (1984) *Roots of Dogmatism: Proceedings of the Fourth International Philosophy Conference, 23–26 October 1982*, Cairo, ARE: Anglo-Egyptian Bookshop.

dogmatism *see* dogma

domain *see* discourse; relation

domination and science *see* epistemology; philosophy of science

domination, mechanisms of *see* ethics; philosophy, sociopolitical

domination, philosophy of *see* philosophy, sociopolitical

donkey sentences *see* logic

double-aspect theory *see* philosophy of mind

double consciousness *see* diaspora

double effect, doctrine of *see* abortion; ethics

double negation *see* logic

double-truth theory *see* Arabic philosophy

doubt *see* Cartesianism; epistemology; justification; knowledge; pragmatism; probability

doxa *see* epistemology; knowledge

doxastic holism *see* holism

doxastic voluntarism *see* voluntarism

doxographers An English translation of the modern Latin term meaning "compilers of opinions" coined by the German scholar Hermann Diels (CE 1848–1922) for the title of his book, *Doxographi graeci* (1879). This was the first and still most influential compilation and study of Greek texts by philosophical commentators from the archaic period to around the closing of the School of Athens, whose activities ended when it was dissolved by the Roman Emperor Justinian I (CE 483–565) in CE 529. These works are important not just as sources of information concerning Greek philosophy, but also because ancient, medieval, and modern writers used them as primary materials. Also, the compiling tradition itself is important, tracing back to a lost work by the Greek philosopher Theophrastus (BCE 360–287) supposed to have contained sixteen to eighteen books and cited as *De Physicorum placitis*. After his compilation, and on the basis of how he organized it, doxographies came to be of three main kinds: doctrinal works, which focused on philosophical problems; biographical works, which focused on philosophers; and tradition works, which focused on philosophical schools. These kinds of doxographies are also significant because their approaches have led to three main ways of teaching philosophy. The most accessible one is *Lives and Opinions of Eminent Philosophers*, by the biographer Diogenes Laertius (third century CE) that, as its title indicates, has a biographical emphasis.

See also: Greek philosophy

Further reading

Diels, Hermann (1965) *Doxographi graeci: collegit recensuit prolegomenis indicibusque instruxit*, Berolino: Apud W. de Gruyter et Socios.

Diogenes Laertius (1909) *Lives and Opinions of Eminent Philosophers*, London: G. Bell.

Kirk, G.S., Raven, J.E., and Schofield, Malcolm (1995 [1983]) *The Presocratic Philosophers: A Critical History with a Selection of Texts*, 2nd edn reprinted with additional bibliographical items, Cambridge, UK and New York: Cambridge University Press.

dravya Term denoting "substance" in Indian philosophies. It is the main category according to the Vaiśeṣika School, including all living and non-living beings. It is conceived as a substrate of qualities and activities, and an inherent cause of any product. There are nine categories of substances: earth, water, air, fire, ether, time, space, individuals, and minds. According to JAINISM, the *dravyas* are six: individuals, matter, the principle of motion, the principle of rest, space, and time. All but time have extension, and all but matter are immaterial. In Viśiṣṭādvaita, *dravya* – substance – is one of the two fundamental categories, and there are six substances: primeval matter, time, pure matter, attributive consciousness, individual soul, and God. The first two are material, while the remaining ones are immaterial. According to Dvaita, *dravya* – substance – is one of the ten categories, but it is the most important one, the others being dependent on it. There are twenty substances, one of which – and the only independent one – is God, on which the other nineteen substances depend. As for BUDDHISM, its schools typically deny the existence of substances, holding, instead, that what appear to be substances are merely bundles of states or events.

The term *dravya* appears in a variety of philosophically significant noun phrases:

1 *Dravyārithika-naya*: also called *dravya-naya*, this term means the standpoint of substance, and is used in Jainism to denote the consideration of an object with regard to its substance.

2 *Dravya-āsrava*: here, *dravya* denotes individual. Since *āsrava* denotes the influx of karmic matter, the noun phrase is used to mean that contact of karmic particles with the individual.

3 *Dravya-karma*: actions of body, speech, and mind that, transformed in subtle matter, stick to individuals according to Jainism.

4 *Dravya-nirjarā*: destruction of binding karma particles.

5 *Dravya-paramāṇu*: meaning simple atoms, this is a Buddhist term denoting the subtlest from of matter.

6 *Dravya-sat*: meaning existence as a thing or, less precisely, primary existence, this term denotes a category used in Indian Buddhism, that of the most basic level of existence. It is usually contrasted with *prajñāpti-sat*, the category of things that exist merely as objects of language but, in effect, are composites of primarily existing things. For example, a stone exemplifies *prajñāpti-sat*, while the many items constituting the stone at a given instant exemplify a *dravya-sat*.

See also: Buddhism; Hinduism

Further reading

Herman, A. L. (1991) *A Brief Introduction to Hinduism: Religion, Philosophy, and Ways of Liberation*, Boulder, CO: Westview Press.

Radhakrishnan, S. (1977) *Indian Philosophy*, London and New York: G. Allen & Unwin and Humanities Press.

dravya-sat *see* dravya

dread *see* existentialism

dream argument *see* Cartesianism

drishti Sanskrit term meaning "seeing," "inner light," "vision," "worldview," or "theory." In Buddhism, it means belief, dogma, or false theory, and is applied to crucial false views. On one classification there are seven false views: belief in a self; rejection of the law of karma; belief in a self independent of personality that continues to exist after death and the dissolution of personality; belief in a self independent of personality that ceases to exist after death; observing false ethical guidelines; considering karma that results from wrong acts to be a good thing; and doubting the truths of Buddhism. On another classification, there are three false views: belief in the causelessness of existence, in the inefficacy of existence, and in a self independent of personality that ceases to exist after death.

The term also appears in the noun phrase *drishti-shrshti-vāda*, which means perception is creation and denotes the Advaita theory according to which the entire universe is created by the individual intellect. It holds that the objects of experience do not exist before being perceived.

See also: perception

Further reading
Ganguli, Hemanta Kumar (1988) *Radicalism in Advaita Vedanta: A Comparative Critique of the Theories of Vivarta, Drstisrsti, and Neo-Vedanta of Swami Vivekananda*, Calcutta, India: Indian Publicity Society.
Harvey, Peter (1995) *The Selfless Mind: Personality, Consciousness and Nirvana in Early Buddhism*, Surrey: Curzon Press.

dual-aspect theory *see* philosophy of mind

dual-attribute theory *see* philosophy of mind

dualism According to the German philosopher Rudolf Eucken (CE 1846–1926), the term dualism was introduced by Thomas Hyde in his 1700 *History religionis veterum Persarum* to denote the dualism of Ormazd and Ahriman, the principles of good and evil, in Zoroastrianism. The term was given the same meaning by the French philosopher Pierre Bayle (CE 1647–1706) in the article on Zoroaster in his *Dictionnaire Historique et critique*, and it was thus used by the German philosopher Gottfried Wilhelm Leibniz (CE 1646–1716) in his *Theodicy* (II, 144, 149). By contrast with this, sometimes called *ethical dualism*, the German philosopher Christian Wolff (CE 1679–1754) used it in a metaphysical sense in his *Psychologia rationalis* (34), where he contrasted dualism, the view that reality consists of two separate components, with *monism*, the view that there really exists only one realm of reality. The central notion in *metaphysical dualism* is that there is an unbridgeable separation between two orders of being, be it between eternal Ideas and becoming as in the work of the Greek philosopher Plato (428–348 BCE); or between finite human beings and the infinite divinity as in the thought of the European Middle Ages; or between individual soul and the world on the one hand, and

Brahman on the other, as in Dvaita-Vedānta; or between religious and philosophical truth as in Averroism according to its critics; or between mind and matter as in the work of the French philosopher René Descartes (CE 1596–1650); or between fact and value as in what can be called the *normative dualism* in the work of the Scottish philosopher David Hume (CE 1711–76); or between empirical phenomena and transcendental *noumena* as in the work of the German philosopher Immanuel Kant (CE 1724–1804); or between being and time as in the work of the German philosopher Martin Heidegger (CE 1889–1976), or between being and nothingness as in the work of the French philosopher Jean-Paul Sartre (CE 1905–80). The twentieth century has evidenced sharp reactions against dualism. For example, the United States philosopher John Dewey (CE 1859–1952) argued that all problems of philosophy derive from dualistic thinking and proposes an alternative in his *The Quest for Certainty*. The United States philosopher W.V.O. Quine (CE 1908–2000) has questioned linguistic, epistemological, and ontological dualism in his criticism of the analytic–synthetic distinction. Yet, much of philosophy continues to be dualistic.

See also: metaphysics; philosophy of mind

Further reading
Bayle, Pierre (1734) *A General Dictionary, Historical and Critical*, London: Printed by J. Bettenham.
Dewey, John (1988) *The Quest for Certainty: A Study of the Relation of Knowledge and Action*, Carbondale: Southern Illinois University Press.
Fontaine, Petrus Franciscus Maria (1991–6) *The Light and the Dark: A Cultural History of Dualism*, Amsterdam: J.C. Gieben.
Hyde, Thomas (1700) *Historia religionis veterum Persarum*, Oxonii: e Theatro Sheldoniano.
Quine, W.V. (*c.* 1972) *Two Dogmas of Empiricism*, Englewood Cliffs, NJ: Prentice-Hall.

duck–rabbit *see* perception

Duhem–Quine thesis *see* induction

Duhem thesis *see* induction

duhkha *see* Buddhism

dunamis *see* Greek philosophy; mechanicism

duration *see* philosophy of science

Dutch book *see* probability

duty *see* ethics

dvaita Sanskrit term meaning "duality" and philosophically used to denote the view that separates the human body from the god that created it. In the noun phrase Dvaita-Vedānta, sometimes also called Ekāyana, it designates the third of the major philosophical schools of Vedānta, whose chief representative is the Indian philosopher Madhva (CE 1199–1278), also known as Madhvāchārya and Ananda-tīrtha. He formulated his position in opposition to Advaita-Vedānta, the monist philosophy of the Indian philosopher Shankara (CE 788–820), also known as Shankarāchārya, according to which, though there seem to exist many things and persons, these have only apparent reality status and, in reality, only Brahman exists. By contrast, according to Dvaita, the divinity and the individual soul are eternally separate and the world is no illusion. That is, three separate entities, Brahman, the individual soul, and the world exit eternally. Indeed, each person has his or her own essence, so that some are destined for enlightenment, others for endless transmigration, still others for misery. Despite their reality, however, both the individual soul and the world depend on Brahman.

See also: Advaita; Hinduism

Further reading
Nagaraja Rao, P. (1958) *The Epistemology of Dvaita Vedanta*, Madras: Adyar Library and Research Centre.
Sharma, B.N. Krishnamurti (1996) *Dvaita Philosophy as Expounded by Sri Madhva-carya*, Madras: Radhakrishnan Institute for Advanced Study in Philosophy, University of Madras.
—— (1960) *A History of the Dvaita School of Vedanta and its Literature*, Bombay: Book-seller's Pub. Co.

dvandva *see* Advaita

dvyanuka *see* Hinduism

dyad *see* Academy; Hinduism

dynamis *see* Greek philosophy; mechanicism

dynamism *see* Greek philosophy; mechanicism

dzogchen *see* Buddhism

E

E *see* categorical; logic; syllogism

eclecticism *see* Academy; Alexandrian School; Neoplatonism; spiritualism; Stoicism

ecofeminism *see* ecology; feminist philosophy

ecological *see* ecology

ecology Also – though infrequently – *oecology*, this term derives from the Greek *oiko(s)* – "house" – and *logos* – "discourse," "reason," "body of knowledge" – and was modeled in English after the German *ökologie*. Originally a biological term meaning the branch of biology dealing with organisms and their environment, ecology was extended to other areas, for example sociology, where it means the branch of sociology dealing with the spacing of people and institutions, and the resulting interdependencies. Ecology, whether in biology, sociology, or elsewhere, studies ecologies, that is, relatively settled networks of interactive components.

A term that has acquired some currency in philosophy and social studies is *deep ecology*. It denotes a movement initiated by the contemporary Scandinavian philosopher Arne Naess. Deep ecology is centered, first, on the rejection of the human-in-the environment conception, in favor of a relational, total-field conception, where organisms are conceived of as knots in a field of intrinsic relations; and then, on a prima facie biospherical egalitarianism that places the burden of proof on those who contemplate any killing, exploitation, or suppression of ecological components.

Much of contemporary feminist thought (see FEMINIST PHILOSOPHY) significantly uses the notion of ecology, though different feminists understand it differently. To some, it is a personal value arising from the experience of communing with nature. Indeed, some spiritual and cultural feminists hold that women have a particular affinity with all nature that men lack, whether inherently or because they have lost it.

However, other feminists reject this mysticism and simply stress the practical fact that ecological recklessness is undermining all human and non-human life on planet earth. No doubt, the ecological movement's emphasis on all life by contrast with more traditional contrasts between humans and non-humans, and especially its associated focus on a need for better balance between humans and nature, has some analogies to the emphasis many feminists place on the need for co-operation, a nurturant concern for all life, and a more equitable balance between women and men, and, in general, dominant groups and the traditionally oppressed or disadvantaged. As indicated, these analogies have not escaped feminists; but some of them have criticized the largely male-dominated ecology movement on the grounds that it tends to insist that women subordinate their interests to the greater cause of saving baby seals, whales, or rainforests.

Another aspect of ecological thinking that increasingly influences philosophical and social thought concerns the *ecological conception of the self*. This notion can be traced back to the work of the United States anthropologist Edith Cobb (CE 1895–1977) in *The Ecology* of *Imagination in Childhood*, where she used an ecological approach to analyze children's development of cosmic sense. As the United States anthropologist Margaret Mead (CE 1901–78) commented, however, the method has a wide scope of applicability and "makes it possible to compare the most diverse cultural developments." (Mead had seen Cobb's unpublished manuscript for this book and, as such, cited it in her article.)

This ecological method, however, may help understand not only cross-cultural interactions such as the mutual adaptations – e.g. the internalization or adoption of a group's values – that the expatriate experience involves between individuals and cultures other than their own, but also the adaptations developed between groups in a variety of manners (see DIASPORA; PHILOSOPHY AND EXPATRIATION). It should be noted in this regard that many of these adaptations are instances of *symbiosis*, i.e. the living together of dissimilar organisms, especially, but not exclusively, when mutuality or mutual advantage is involved (besides mutuality, symbiosis may involve predatory and parasitic relations).

A notion that has also gained influence in this context is that of the laws of ecology, which became widely used in the United States and elsewhere after the publication of *The Closing Circle* by the contemporary United States biologist Barry Commoner. They are: first, everything is connected to everything else; second, everything must go somewhere; third, nature knows best; and fourth, there is no such thing as a free lunch. These laws have prompted much controversy, to begin with whether they are laws at all. Nonetheless, they have helped direct the attention of scientists and the general public to significant ecological concerns.

Further reading
Bookchin, Murray (1990) *The Philosophy of Social Ecology: Essays in Dialectical Naturalism*, Montreal and New York: Black Rose Books.
Cobb, Edith (1977) *The Ecology of Imagination in Childhood*, New York: Columbia University Press.
Eaubonne, Francoise d' (1978) *Ecologie, feminisme: revolution ou mutation?*, Paris: Editions ATP.

Iannone, A. Pablo (1999) *Philosophical Ecologies: Essays in Philosophy, Ecology, and Human Life*, Amherst, NY: Humanity Books.
Mead, Margaret (1959) "The cross-cultural approach to the study of personality," in J.L. McCary (ed.) *Personality*, New York and London: Grove Press and Evergreen Books.

economic value *see* value

economics *see* philosophy of economics

economy, principle of *see* nominalism

ecstasy *see* mysticism; philosophy of religion

education *see* philosophy of education

eduction *see* analysis

effect *see* causal law

effective procedure *see* philosophy of mathematics

efficacious grace *see* determinism

efficient cause *see* causal law

effluences *see* perception

effluxes, theory of *see* perception

egalitarianism *see* philosophy, sociopolitical

ego *see* Buddhism; philosophy of mind; psychoanalysis

egocentric From the Latin *ego*, i.e. "self," and *centr(um)*, i.e. "center," literally *having or regarding the self as the center of all things, especially of the known world*, this term was coined by the United States philosopher Ralph Barton Perry (CE 1876–1957) to describe the *egocentric predicament*: the fact that it is impossible for us to eliminate the effects that our becoming aware of an object has on the object, from our awareness of the object. Perry argued on this basis against the idealist inference from the epistemological premise *all that is known is thought*, to the ontological conclusion *there is only thought*.

The phrase egocentric predicament, however, has acquired a second philosophical meaning: each person's position as an experiencing subject who has exclusive access to his or her experiences. This notion poses at least three problems: Can we ever have knowledge of the external world? Can we ever communicate with others? Can we ever have knowledge of what others experience? It is argued that if each one of us is entirely restricted to his or her own experiences, then we can only have knowledge about the world as we experience it, about what others tell us as we interpret it, and about what others experience as we interpret it given our interpretation of what they tell us and our experience of their behavior. In view of these implications, some philosophers have rejected this second notion of egocentric predicament, while others have rejected the notions of knowledge or justified belief presupposed in posing the said problems.

The egocentric – also called autocentric – approach, or egocentrism, in philosophy leading to the problems just described was made particularly influential by the French philosopher René Descartes (CE 1596–1650), who attempted to construct a system of knowledge from the standpoint of the self, indeed, by starting from the subjective awareness of the conscious self. Its influence can be measured at least by the fact that much of contemporary epistemology is a reaction against this approach.

The term egocentric is also used in the phrase *egocentric particular*, coined by the English philosopher Bertrand Russell (CE 1872–1970) – who had previously used the phrase *emphatic particular* – to refer to any word whose denotation is determined by the identity of its user or the time, place, and audience of its use. Examples of these words are "I," "you," "here," "there," "this," "that," "now," "past," "present," and "future." That is, the notion of egocentric particular roughly refers to what today is called an *indexical*: a type of expression whose meaning is in part determined by features of the context of utterance.

Some of the questions arising about egocentric particulars are: Are there some egocentric particulars that can be used to define the others but cannot be themselves defined in terms of the others? Must we use at least some egocentric particulars – say, the term "I" – to give a complete description of the world? Russell argued that all egocentric particulars can be defined in terms of "this," and not vice

versa, and that no egocentric particular was crucial to describe the world completely. A similar suggestion had been made by the German philosopher Hans Reichenbach (CE 1891–1953), when he hypothesized that all expressions whose meaning partly depends on the context of use are *token-reflexive*, i.e. expressions that refer to themselves in linguistic use such as utterance or writing, and could be characterized by means of the phrase "this token." For example, "now" would mean "the time at which this token is used." This hypothesis has been discarded, because the definitions it entails have paradoxical implications.

See also: Cartesianism; philosophy of language; philosophy of mind; reference

Further reading
Perry, Ralph Barton (1912) *The New Realism: Cooperative Studies in Philosophy*, New York: The Macmillan Company.
—— (1912) *Present Philosophical Tendencies: A Critical Survey of Naturalism, Idealism, Pragmatism and Realism, Together with a Synopsis of the Philosophy of William James*, New York: Longmans, Green.
Russell, Bertrand (1940) *An Inquiry into Meaning and Truth*, Baltimore: Penguin Books.

egocentrism *see* egocentric

egoism *see* ethics

eidetic intuition *see* phenomenology

eidetic variation *see* phenomenology

eidola *see* perception

eidology *see* epistemology

eidos *see* Greek philosophy; phenomenology

eight liberations *see* Buddhism

eight masteries *see* Buddhism

eight negations *see* Buddhism

Eightfold Path *see* Buddhism

Einfühlung *see* empathy

ejects *see* philosophy of mind

ekāgra *see* Hinduism

ekayāna *see* Dvaita

élan vital *see* Bergsonianism

Eleatic School *see* Greek philosophy

element From the Latin *elementum*, which meant "first principle," "rudiment." In philosophy, element can be used with at least four meanings:

The first is *basic entities*: i.e. basic components of reality, in particular of material reality. In Greek philosophy, these were conceived in such ways as seeds (*rysomata*), sperm (*spermata*), seminal reasons (*logoi spermatikoi*), and atoms (*atomoi*). These notions connote origin or beginning in a partly chronological, partly metaphysical sense. Philosophers in India, just as the philosopher Empedocles (*c.* 490–430 BCE) in Ancient Greece, talked of four *bhutas* or elements: earth, water, fire, and air. Buddhists thinkers talked of *shandhas* (elements) that unify in creating the illusion of individuality. Chinese thinkers sometimes talked of *wu-hsing*, i.e. five elements or five phases (the basic ones being earth, water, fire, the secondary ones being wood, and metal), or simply of three: earth, water, and fire. In the European Middle Ages, it was normal to present the doctrine of the four elements (earth, water, fire, and air or, better, what is solid, liquid, dry, and gaseous), but a fifth element, ether (the *quinta essentia*) was also mentioned. In Nahua philosophy, the four Suns or World Eras preceding the Fifth Sun in which we live were each associated with one of the four elements: animal energy, air, fire, and water. The present Sun, Naollin – Four Movements – can exist because the four elements can coexist in it.

The second meaning of the term element is *basic components of a doctrine*. For example, the German philosopher Immanuel Kant (CE 1724–1804) divided his *Critique of Pure Reason* into two main parts: the *Transcendental Doctrine of Elements* and the *Transcendental Doctrine of Method*. The *Transcendental Doctrine of the Elements* includes two parts: the *Transcendental Aesthetics* and the *Transcendental Logic*, the latter involving two divisions: the *Transcendental Analytic* and the *Transcendental Dialectic*.

The third meaning is *principles of a study, science, or system*. In this sense, many texts include the term elements in their title, as in *The Elements of Theology*, by the Constantinople-born philosopher Proclus (*c.* CE 410–85).

The fourth is *as a general characteristic of an entity or notion*. In this sense, one could use such sentences as "the element of the negative," and "the hopeful element of the will."

See also: Chinese philosophy; Greek philosophy; Hinduism; metaphysics; philosophy of science

Further reading
Aquinas, Thomas (1983) *On the Mixture of the Elements, to Master Philip*, Stillwater, OK: Translation Clearing House, Dept of Philosophy, Oklahoma State University.
Freudenthal, Gad (1995) *Aristotle's Theory of Material Substance: Heat and Pneuma, Form and Soul*, Oxford and New York: Clarendon Press and Oxford University Press.
Galen (1996) *On the Elements According to Hippocrates*, Berlin: Akademie Verlag.
Proclus (1992) *The Elements of Theology = Diadoxos stoixeiosis theologike*, 2nd edn, Oxford and New York: Clarendon Press and Oxford University Press.

election *see* decision; determinism

elementary equivalence *see* categoricity

elementary quantification theory *see* logic

elenchus *see* Socratic philosophy

eliminability *see* model

eliminative induction *see* induction

eliminative materialism *see* philosophy of mind

eliminativism *see* philosophy of mind

Elohim *see* cabala; God

emanation *see* Neoplatonism

emanationism *see* Neoplatonism

emancipation *see* philosophy, sociopolitical

embodiment *see* abstract; category; phenomenology; philosophy, sociopolitical

emergence *see* evolution; holism

emergent *see* evolution; holism

emergent materialism *see* philosophy of mind

emergentism, descriptive *see* holism

emotion *see* passion

emotions, the seven *see* Korean philosophy

emotions, the six *see* Chinese philosophy

emotive conjugation *see* rhetoric

emotive meaning *see* meaning

emotivism *see* ethics

empathic solipsism *see* solipsism

empathy From the Greek *en* ("in") and *patheia* ("feeling," "emotion," "experience"), this term, like *endopathy* and *introaffection*, translates the German *Einfühlung*, which means "feeling into," and has been used both in aesthetics and psychology. The German philosopher of art Robert Vischer (CE 1847–1933) is credited with having used this term for the first time. His purpose was to explain natural beauty and how it is apprehended by humans. Along these lines, the German philosopher and psychologist Theodor Lipps (CE 1851–1914) used it in his aesthetic theory, according to which empathy is a feeling we experience when we project ourselves into the kind of life aesthetic objects have. The German philosopher and psychologist Wilhelm Worringer (CE 1881–1965) also used the term as a key to aesthetic experience. Here, empathy denotes a state involving identification with, and distance from, the aesthetic object. This notion is to be contrasted with interpretation, or COMPREHENSION (in German, *das Verstehen*), a notion highly developed by the German philosopher Wilhelm Dilthey (CE 1833–1911), who held it involved not just feeling, but all of our mental powers. Nor should empathy be confused with *sympathy*, where one's identity is totally preserved in feeling with another or for another person. However, the notion of empathy has been modified by phenomenologists to account for the manner in which a person reaches the experience of another without having it. Arguably, thus modified, the notion of empathy approaches – though still differs from – the notion of sympathy formulated by the Scottish philosopher David Hume (CE 1711–76).

See also: ethics; phenomenology; philosophy of mind

Further reading

Lipps, Theodor (1926) *Psychological Studies*, 2nd edn, rev. and enl., trans. Herbert Sanborn, London: Bailliere, Tindall & Cox.

Vischer, Robert (1994) *Empathy, Form, and Space: Problems in German Aesthetics*, Santa Monica, CA and Chicago, IL: Getty Center for the History of Art and the Humanities, distributed by the University of Chicago Press,

Worringer, Wilhelm (1997 [1953]) *Abstraction and Empathy: A Contribution to the Psychology of Style*, Chicago: Ivan R. Dee.

empirical *see* a priori–a posteriori

empirical meaning *see* meaning

empirical probability *see* probability

empirical psychology *see* philosophy of mind

empiricism Also called *empirism* (both terms ultimately derived from the Greek *empeirios*: "experienced in," "acquainted with," "skilled at"), a family of theories sharing the view that experience (from the Latin *experior*: "to prove" or "to put to the test"), i.e., briefly, information gained from the senses, is the sole or primary source of knowledge and justified belief attainable by humans and, arguably, other animals. The Latin expression for this view is *nihil est in intellectu quod prius non fuerit in sensu*, i.e. nothing is in the understanding that was not previously in the senses. This family of theories is usually contrasted with RATIONALISM, the family of theories sharing the view that reason is the sole or primary source of knowledge and justified belief attainable by humans and, arguably, other beings. Among empiricist theories, some philosophers distinguish two main types: *concept-centered* (i.e. those theories that, first, identify various concepts applying to experience and, then, claim that all human concepts either are like those identified or are derived from them), and *belief-centered* (i.e. those theories that focus on beliefs and claim that they have no truth-related significance unless they are somehow based on experience).

Along these lines, some philosophers have argued that there is such a thing as *the given*, a brute fact element found through introspection, or presupposed in our perceptual experience. This doctrine was criticized by the United States philosopher Wilfrid Sellars (CE 1912–89), who formulated the *myth of the given*, i.e. the view that the given is a myth. His argument was that knowledge is a kind of conceptualization and, on the typical account of those who argue that there is such a thing as the given, the given cannot be known through conceptualization, hence we cannot know the given and, in other words, it is a myth.

As a matter of emphasis, it is sometimes said that Aristotelianism exemplifies empiricism, while Platonism exemplifies rationalism. It is true that the Greek philosopher Aristotle (384–322 BCE) relied more heavily on inductive studies, while his teacher, the Greek philosopher Plato (428–348 BCE) relied more heavily on mathematics and dialectics; but, in fact, both philosophers, as well as Aristotelianism and Platonism, combined – however differently – empiricism with rationalism. Better historical examples of empiricism can be found in the views of the Greek philosophers Democritus (460–370 BCE) and Epicurus (341–270 BCE), who traced all knowledge to an influx and residue of images of objects perceived.

An example of empiricism in the European Middle Ages can arguably be found in the work of the English philosopher William of Ockham (*c.* CE 1290–1349), who argued that some things were known through themselves (in Latin, *perse nota* or *nota per se* and, in the singular, *per se notum* or *notum per se*), i.e. from the definition of terms or what later came to be called tautologies and analytic statements, while the rest were *nota per experientiam*, i.e. evident from experience. Ockham also used the category of *notitia intuitiva* to denote what we know by immediate awareness, e.g. the world around us.

These distinctions influenced the work of later philosophers. For example, the Italian philosopher Tomasso Campanella (CE 1568–1639), foreshadowing Cartesianism, held that the only empirical datum worthy of trust is that we exist – a datum that withstands any doubt that could be raised about it – and the only trustworthy path to knowledge consists in tracing out the implications of this experience. The most secure part of knowledge is consti-

tuted by *notitia innata* or innate notions, and the knowledge of other things is constituted by *notitia illata* or acquired notions.

As a result of some of the works just mentioned, empiricism developed into a modern movement called British empiricism, whose representatives can be traced back to the English philosopher Roger Bacon (*c.* CE 1214–*c.* 1293), who claimed we should base our beliefs on direct inspection and experimental science. This movement included the English legalist, political figure, and philosopher Francis Bacon (CE 1561–1626), who argued against rationalism, developed the tables of induction, and proposed *eucatalepsia* (the careful accumulation of means to understand reality), as opposed to the skeptics' *acatalepsia* (the suspension of judgment); the Irish philosopher and bishop George Berkeley (CE 1685–1753), who identified being with being perceived, though in his final work, *Siris*, he added the category of *notion* to deal with such ideas as that of God and the soul, which could not be handled by his earlier conception of ideas; the English philosopher John Locke (CE 1632–1704), who argued against innate ideas and traced all ideas to experience, distinguishing between ideas of sensation and ideas of reflection, the latter being derived from the former; and the Scottish philosopher David Hume (CE 1711–76), who drew a sharp distinction between matters of fact and relations of ideas, characterizing *impression* as the material of sensation, and dividing impressions into simple and complex, which respectively led to simple and complex ideas.

It is worth noting here that Locke considered reflection to be an internal sense that allows us to notice our mental operations and is contraposed to sensations. Hume distinguished two kinds of impressions: sensations and reflections, the latter being derived, but not reducible to sensations and leading to impressions of reflection – e.g. aversion or desire, fear or hope – about the ideas derived from sensations such as pain and pleasure. Both Locke's and Hume's views contrast with those authors who thought reflection reducible to sensation, e.g. the French philosopher Etienne Condillac (CE 1715–80).

In the nineteenth century, though empiricism

was not the predominant philosophy, it was upheld by a British philosopher of stature, John Stuart Mill (CE 1806–73), who developed inductive logic, and methods of experimentation or empirical investigation, and used the term *experimentalism* to denote his entire brand of empiricism. Indeed, he went one step further than the previous empiricists and held not only that all concepts are acquired from sense experience (and, hence, there are no innate ideas), but also that all propositions, including the truths of mathematics, are inductively based on experience.

This century also saw the development of *empiriocriticism*, the doctrine formulated by the German Philosopher Richard Avenarius (CE 1843–96). Influenced by the notion of radical empiricism (an approach that required no extra-empirical connective support among our experience's components, which had been formulated by the United States philosopher and psychologist William James, CE 1842–1910), Avenarius argued that we should approach the world through pure experience, i.e. through experience of the given and without assumptions. As a result, dualism is replaced by a conception of self and environment as two aspects of the same experience. This view was also advocated by the Austrian physicist and philosopher Ernst Mach (CE 1836–1916), and criticized by the Russian Marxist Vladimir Ilyich Lenin (CE 1870–1924), who held that Marxism required an epistemological realism in the most literal sense of this term. By contrast, the Russian Marxist revisionist A.A. Malinovski Bogdanov (CE 1873–1928), pen-name of A.A. Malinovski, argued for *empiriomonism*, the view that all was experience: the psychic, individually organized experience; the physical, collectively organized experience. It is also worth mentioning the position of the Austrian philosopher and psychologist Richard Wahle (CE 1857–1935), who advocated the philosophy of occurrences where the given is constituted by neutral, self-dependent images and ideas. He believed this allowed him to avoid dualisms.

An influential type of empiricism has been *fallibilism*, the doctrine that some kinds of beliefs and presuppositions – typically empirical ones – are inherently uncertain and possibly

mistaken. Today, many philosophers advocating some form of fallibilism tend to accept, however, that beliefs about logical principles and one's own current feelings are not among the inherently uncertain and possibly mistaken ones. As for the rest, they argue that beliefs and presuppositions about the existence and nature of entities independent of our minds can only be established by experimental methods and, hence, can only be probable. Indeed, some philosophers – e.g. the United States philosopher W.V.O. Quine (CE 1908–2000) – have raised doubts about the appeal to analyticity to establish certain truths and have pointed out that some beliefs about logical and mathematical principles – e.g. the set theoretical axiom of abstraction – have gone from being thought self-evident to being considered false.

In the twentieth century, empiricism influenced the development of *pragmatism* in the United States and abroad. It also gained new life in *logical positivism*, or, as some of its main proponents called it, *logical empiricism*, a movement aimed at freeing philosophy of its non-empirical elements, sometimes by appeal to a rational reconstruction or logical reconstruction, i.e. the translation of concepts of a certain type, say motivational concepts such as anger and fear, into concepts of another, more perspicuous and testable type such as behavioral concepts. Its main proponents have been the members of the Vienna Circle, which included, among other philosophers, the Austrian Hans Hahn (CE 1879–1934), the Austrian-American Phillip Frank (CE 1884–1966), the Austrian Otto Neurath (CE 1882–1945), the German-Austrian Moritz Schlick (CE 1882–1936), the German-born Rudolf Carnap (CE 1891–1970), and the contemporary Austrian-American philosopher Herbert Feigl, and what has sometimes been called the Helsinki Group, whose most notable members included the contemporary Finnish philosophers Jaakko Hintikka and G.H. von Wright.

By contrast with this movement and, indeed, traditional conceptions of science, there has also developed a type of empiricism within feminist philosophy, *feminist empiricism*. This approach, partly influenced by phenomenology, questions the objectivity of traditional philosophy of science on the grounds that it is caught up in the notion that scientific success is a matter of controlling nature and, as a result, does not pay attention to nature. By contrast, feminist empiricism advocates thorough reliance on concretely experienced facts, even if, as a result, scientific theories are undermined.

See also: nominalism; pragmatism; rationalism

Further reading

Copleston, Frederick Charles (1994 [1966]) *A History of Philosophy, Vol. 8: Modern Philosophy, Empiricism, Idealism, and Pragmatism in Britain and America*, New York: Image Books.

Giere, Ronald N. (1996) *Origins of Logical Empiricism*, Minneapolis and London: University of Minnesota Press.

James, William (1996) *Essays in Radical Empiricism*, Lincoln and London: University of Nebraska Press.

empiriocriticism *see* empiricism

empiriomonism *see* empiricism

empowerment *see* justice

En sof *see* cabala

en soi *see* existentialism

enantiamorphs *see* Kantian philosophy

encrateia *see* akrasia

encyclopedia *see* encyclopedism

encyclopedism The body of doctrines of the encyclopedists, a group of eighteenth-century French philosophers – called *les philosophes*, i.e. the philosophers – who, under the general editorship of Jean Le Rond d'Alembert (CE 1717–83) and Denis Diderot (CE 1713–84), and with the aim of helping eliminate social evils through the spread of knowledge, wrote the thirty five volume French *Encyclopédie* (1751–80), whose entire title is: *Encyclopédie ou Dictionnaire raisonné des sciences des arts et des métiers, receuilli des meilleurs auters at particulièrement des Dictionnaires anglois de Chambers, d'Harris, de Dyche, etc.* Indeed, the *Encyclopedia* was an upshot of an initial project to produce a French translation of Ephraim Chambers's *Cyclopedia: Or, An Universal Dictionary of the Arts and Sciences* (1727).

As the titles of both projects make plain, their authors had a certain ambivalence concerning the distinction between encyclopedia and dictionary, or where among these categories their works fit. Indeed, the distinction is not always easy to draw. To be sure, one significant criterion is that encyclopedias are more extensive – both in the content of their entries and the comprehensiveness of their list of entries – than dictionaries. On this basis, despite its title's ambivalence, the *Encyclopedia*, with its thirty-five volumes, was clearly not a dictionary; but this criterion leaves a large gray area – within which Chambers' two-volume work arguably falls – where it is hard to tell whether a work ceases to be a dictionary and begins to be an encyclopedia.

At any rate the Encyclopedia had a long tradition behind it. Originally, the term encyclopedia was derived from the Greek *enkyklios paideia*, which meant "well rounded education." Eventually, it came to mean a *work involving one or more volumes, including articles on many topics, usually arranged in alphabetical order, covering all areas of knowledge and, less commonly, all areas of a subject.* Already in Antiquity, the *Corpus Aristotelicum* – the body of scientific and philosophical works written by the Greek philosopher Aristotle (384–322 BCE), and, some argue, also by his successor, the Greek philosopher Theophrastus (322–287 BCE) – constituted an encyclopedia. Also, the Roman naturalist and writer Gaius Plinius Secundus-Pliny the Elder-(CE 23–79) produced his 37-volume *Natural History* which, arguably, was an encyclopedia. So was any medieval *Summa*.

What was significant about encyclopedism was a pair of doctrines at the core of the *Encyclopedia*. One was the view that it was both possible and desirable to collect the knowledge dispersed among humans and describe its general system. The other doctrine was that the result was to be a comprehensive, systematic, and descriptive account of the entire body of knowledge of the time, and that this knowledge would help improve humanity. The principle of classification used was based on three sources of ideas: memory, imagination, and reason-prominently experimental reason. The encyclopedists upheld experimental reason and the rule of nature; promoted criticism; prompted the development of new branches of inquiry such as historiography, sociology, economics, and linguistics; attacked fanaticism, obscurantism, and supernaturalism; considered religion to be superstition and theology to be black magic; argued that natural morality was superior to theological morality; supported religious tolerance and individual rights; and promoted more effective approaches to trade and industry.

See also: enlightenment

Further reading

Kafker, Frank A. (1996) *The Encyclopedists as a Group: A Collective Biography of the Authors of the Encyclopedie*, Oxford: Voltaire Foundation.
Morley, John (1923) *Diderot and the Encyclopaedists*, London: Macmillan and Co., Ltd.
Pliny, the Elder (1940 [1986]) *Natural History*, 1st edn; v. 3 and v. 7: 2nd edn, Cambridge, MA and London: Harvard University Press and William Heinemann.

encyclopedists *see* encyclopedism

end in itself *see* Kantian philosophy

endopathy *see* empathy

energeia *see* Greek philosophy; mechanism

energeticism *see* mechanism

energetism *see* mechanism

energism *see* mechanism

energy *see* mechanism; philosophy of science

engineering ethics *see* ethics

enlightenment A term denoting both the attainment of knowledge and the achievement of spiritual or religious insight. In both cases, the word it includes, *light*, is used metaphorically. The latter meaning is predominant in Eastern thought. For example, enlightenment, which involves a release from endless cycles of existence, can be found in all forms of Buddhism, in Hinduism as the way of *jnana* (or knowledge), and in Taoism. However, in the Western world, this sense of the term enlightenment is closely analogous to that of divine illumination, which traces back to light-metaphors in Ancient Greece and the Roman world. This type of metaphor can be found (used for different purposes) in various Platonic passages (e.g. *Timaeus* 68a, and *Republic* 473e, 508d, 515 5, 518a), in Aristotelian comparisons of light with the active intellect, and in the Ciceronian notion of *lumen naturae* or *lumen naturale*, also called *lumen connaturale* or *lumen naturalis rationis*. As divine illumination, it became established especially during the Hellenistic and Patristic periods, when a number of authors formulated the idea of an infinite otherworldly light where souls rest eternally. It is sometimes also called divine revelation or *lumen gratiae*, i.e. the light of grace.

Many other kinds of light – some overlapping with those already mentioned – have been characterized, sometimes also reflecting *Manicheism* – the religion founded by the Babylonian Mānī (CE 216–77) or Manes, where the realm of light is sharply separate from that of darkness. For example, *lumen angelicum* is that of knowledge possessed by angels; *lumen divinae revelationis*, or *lumen fidei*, is that given in divine revelation; *lumen intellectuale*, or *lumen intelligibile*, is that of rational nature; *lumen increatum* is uncreated light containing eternal truths; *lumen interius*, or *lumen cognitionis philosophical*, is that which illuminates us concerning intelligible truths; *lumen exterius*, or *lumen artis mechanichae*, is that which illuminates us concerning artificial shapes; *lumen inferius* is that which illuminates us concerning natural forms; *lumen superius*, or *lumen sacrae scripturae*, is that which illuminates us concerning truths that will help us achieve salvation. In a worldlier sense, the term enlightenment denotes a movement that shaped intellectual life in France as ENCYCLOPEDISM; in England by empiricists and partisans of *deism* understood as the seventeenth- and eighteenth-century movement aimed at replacing theism with the light of reason; and also in Germany. It is still highly influential today; however, it faces the challenges posed by the work of some representatives of the FRANKFURT SCHOOL, e.g. the German philosopher Theodor W. Adorno (CE 1903–69), who held that "the whole is the false" and truth resides only in discrepant details, and Max Horkheimer (CE 1895–1973), who identified positivism – which he opposed – with much of the enlightenment's thought in his *Dialectic of the Enlightenment*. Another challenge is posed by a variety of authors and approaches that fall under the notion of *post-modernism*, discussed under CONTINENTAL PHILOSOPHY.

See also: Buddhism; encyclopedism; Hinduism; Neoplatonism

Further reading

Brown, Stuart (1995) *British Philosophy and the Age of Enlightenment*, New York and London: Routledge.

Hershock, Peter D. (1996) *Liberating Intimacy: Enlightenment and Social Virtuosity in Ch'an Buddhism*, Albany, NY: State University of New York Press.

McCarthy, John C. (1998) *Modern Enlightenment and the Rule of Reason*, Washington, DC: Catholic University of America Press.

Patanjali (1995) *Enlightenment: The Yoga Sutras of Patanjali*, Edmonds, WA: SFA Publications.

Plotinus (1930) *The Enneads*, London: Faber.

ens In Latin, the present participle of the verb *esse*, meaning "to be" or "being," also sometimes used as synonymous with entity, i.e. what is, what exists, thing (though *thing* is often primarily used to denote physical objects, not other existing items such as events or states). *Ens* was used, for example, by the Roman rhetorician Quintilian – Marcus Fabius Quintilianus (*c*. CE 35–*c*. 95) – in his *Institutes of Eloquence* as a translation of the Greek *ontos* (VIII, 3), and *entia* as a translation of the Greek *onta* (II, 14). *Ens* denotes being of any kind and in any mode, whether it exists, or merely can exist, either mentally or outside the mind. In the European Middle Ages, *ens* (*what is* or *thing*) was a common philosophical term and was often used to talk about *esse* (being), because *ens* was considered more readily apprehensible than *esse*. The medieval doctrine of *ens* arguably culminated in the work of the Spanish philosopher Francisco Suárez (CE 1548–1617), whose *Metaphysical Disputations* are, more than anything, ontological disputations. Suárez studied *ens* not only as what is, but also as the condition(s) that make all being possible. In the contemporary world of philosophy, the German philosopher Martin Heidegger (CE 1889–1976) has insisted that thinking about being should be disentangled from thinking about what is or about the world in terms of the entities (*seindes*) that make it up, a kind of thinking he calls *ontic*. The problem remains, however, of how to have access to being if not through what is.

The term *ens* appears in a number of philosophical phrases, most notably as follows. *Ens a se* is a phrase used by medieval philosophers meaning "being from itself." It denotes a being that is completely independent and self-sufficient. Within the Judeo-Christian tradition, God is and must be the only such being.

Ens ex se is a phrase used by Scholastic philosophers meaning "being out of itself." The philosopher Anselm (CE 1033–1109), born in the city of Aosta, in what is now Italy, contrasted it with *ens a se* in his *Monologion*, arguing that *ens a se* is from itself, but not out of itself, because it depends on nothing, while *ens ex se* can depend upon itself for its existence and, hence, would cause itself. Neither *ens a se* nor *ens ex se* are synonymous with *causa sui* (cause of itself), the expression used by the Amsterdam-born philosopher of Spanish–Portuguese descent Baruch Spinoza (CE 1632–77) – who also used *causa immanens* – to describe God. In doing so, Spinoza in part meant that God owes his existence to nothing but himself, because God's nature requires that he exist. Spinoza did not use this expression to mean that God brought himself into existence.

Ens in potentia: see ACT.

Ens in acto: see ACT.

Ens naturae: see *ens rationis*, below.

Ens per accidens: meaning "being by accident," this Latin phrase denotes either an accident, or the accidental unity of a substance and an accident.

Ens perfectissimo: see *ens realissimum*, below.

Ens perfectissimum: see *ens realissimum*, below.

Ens rationis: meaning "being of reason," this Latin phrase denotes an item that depends for its existence upon reason or thought. There are two kinds of beings of reason: those that have a basis in reality but are abstracted from it (e.g. the notion of a human being), and those that have no basis in reality because they are fictional, e.g. unicorns. A distinction already present in the Greek philosopher Aristotle (384–22 BCE), but predominant in the European Middle Ages, is that between what came to be called *ens rationis* (in the plural, *entia rationis*) and *ens reale* (in the plural, *entia reale*), sometimes also called *ens naturae* (plural *entia naturae*): items existing independently of reason or thought.

Ens reale: see *ens rationis*, above.

Ens realissimum: literally, in Latin, "most real being," this phrase is an extension of the notion of *ens perfectissimum* (most perfect being) formulated by the German philosopher Alexander Baumgarten (CE 1714–62). The extension was carried out by the German philosopher Immanuel Kant (CE 1724–1804), who argued that since *ens perfectissimum* denotes God as the sum of all possibilities, and actuality is greater than possibility, God should be preferably referred to as *ens realissimum*, i.e. the sum of all actualities.

See also: metaphysics; Scholasticism

Further reading

Heidegger, Martin (1996) *Being and Time*, Albany, NY: State University of New York Press.

Quintilian (1985) *Institutio Oratoria of Quintilian*, Cambridge: Harvard University Press.

Suárez, Francisco (1935 [1597]) *Disputaciones metafísicas: Sobre el concepto del ente*, trans. Xavier Zubiri, Madrid: Revista de Occidente.

entailment *see* logic

entelechy *see* act; Greek philosophy; mechanicism

enthusiasm From the Greek *enthusiasmos*, equivalent to *enthusia* (possession by a God), this term was used by the Greek philosopher Plato (428–348 BCE) to denote something inspired by a divinity (*Phaedo*, 253a). Plato mentions it when discussing poetic inspiration (*Ion*, 533e), and relates it to *mantike* – divination power (*Timaeus*, 71e). The term has come to mean absorbing or controlling possession of the mind by any interest or pursuit. In this sense, it was used by the English philosopher Anthony Ashley Cooper, Lord Shaftesbury (CE 1671–1713), in his *Letter on Enthusiasm*,

included in the revised second edition of *Characteristics of Men, Manners, Opinions, Times, etc.* (Vol. I, sections 6 and 7), where he argues that not just poets, but philosophers fighting superstition need to display enthusiasm. In the eighteenth century, Enlightenment authors formulated various objections against religious enthusiasm. In the twentieth century, the Spanish philosopher Diego Ruiz (CE 1881–1959) used enthusiasm as a basis for all future ethics.

Further reading

Grean, Stanley (1967) *Shaftesbury's Philosophy of Religion and Ethics: A Study in Enthusiasm*, Athens: Ohio University Press.

Ruiz, Diego (1906) *Teoría del acto entusiasta: Bases de la ética*, Barcelona: Serra hnos. y Russell.

Shaftesbury, Anthony Ashley Cooper, Earl of (1995 [1900]) *Characteristics of Men, Manners, Opinions, Times, etc.: To Which is Prefixed the Preface to the Select Sermons of Dr. Whichcote*, Bristol, UK: Thoemmes Press.

enthymeme *see* syllogism

entia *see* ens

entia non sunt multiplicanda praeter necessitatem *see* nominalism

entitlement *see* ethics

entity *see* abstract; ens; theory

entropy *see* philosophy of science

enumeration *see* definition; induction

environment *see* ecology

environmental *see* ethics

eon *see* age of the world

epagoge *see* induction

epicheirema *see* syllogism

Epicureanism One of the three main schools of philosophy – besides Stoicism and skepticism – during Hellenism (see GREEK PHILOSOPHY), it was founded by the Greek philosopher Epicurus (341–270 BCE), who established Epicurean communities in three cities: Mytilene, Lampsacus, and Athens (306 BCE). At this latter location, Epicurus' school came to be known as *the Garden*. Among doctrines shared by Epicurean philosophers – i.e. besides Epicurus, Metrodorus (*c.* 331–278 BCE), Hemarchus (Epicurus' successor in Athens), and Polyaenus (d. 278 *bc*), were ATOMISM, EMPIRICISM, and hedonism.

Initially, Epicureanism stressed hedonism and the ethics that followed from it. The highest pleasure, whether of soul or body, was *katastematic pleasure*, i.e. a satisfied state. Stimulation pleasures, i.e. *kinetic pleasures*, including those of luxury, can affect our satisfied state, but not increase it. In fact, they make us more vulnerable, hence may undermine our satisfaction. Therefore, our main aim should be to minimize pain through *simplicity in living*, which keeps the body satisfied, and the *study of physics*, which helps the soul attain the highest katastematic pleasure: *ataraxia*, i.e. freedom from disturbance. This latter concept has no known historical connection, but nonetheless a certain family resemblance to Eastern philosophy conceptions of ENLIGHTENMENT and nirvana, even though the latter two involve overcoming concerns with the self, while *ataraxia* is attained through the overcoming of desires for luxury and of beliefs in divine threats and the immortality of the soul, not by overcoming our individuality. Thus understood, Epicureanism is drastically different from the derogatory sense in which the term 'Epicureanism' is used in ordinary language and, also, sometimes used in JEWISH PHILOSOPHY, to denote hedonism.

In the first century BCE, however, a number of Epicurean philosophers appeared who emphasized the other main Epicurean doctrines: empiricism and atomism. Concerning empiricism, the Epicurean theory of knowledge was anti-skeptical, holding that all sensations are true representationally, e.g. through films of atoms (*eidola* in Greek and *simulacra* in Latin) impinging upon our eyes that report them without interpretation. They are not true propositionally. That is, propositions appear only when we interpret those reports and make inferences about external objects. Here, and only here, is error possible. Among the possible interpretations or theories, those which are to be accepted must pass the test of, first, sensations and feelings; second, introspective information and, somehow, a criterion of values; and, third, *prolepsis*, i.e. naturally acquired general conceptions. Epicureans held that, in the case of physics, only one theory passed all these tests.

As for Epicurus' atomism, it had developed from the system the Greek philosopher Democritus (460–370 BCE) had initially formulated. Another Greek philosopher, Aristotle (384–322 BCE), had objected to Democritus' conception of atoms, saying that those which move vertically with the same speed can never meet. It is supposed that Epicurus formulated the doctrine his Roman follower Titus Lucretius Carus (*c.* 99–55 BCE) called *clinamen* or inclination to meet Aristotle's objection. According to this doctrine, atoms experience deviations that allow them to meet.

Without abandoning its interest in logic, epistemology, and cosmology, Epicureanism primarily focused on its initial ethical philosophy towards the end of the first century CE. This emphasis lasted for about two centuries. Its main representatives were the Hellenistic philosophers Diogenianus (second century CE), born in the city of Heraclea, in what is now southern Italy, whose arguments against the Stoic conception of cosmic destiny were later used by the Christian apologist and historian Eusebius of Caeseria (CE 265–340), and Diogenes of Ionoanda (second and third century CE), who offered Epicurean arguments against the fear of death and the gods, and against the Stoic conception of providence.

Epicureanism resurged at different times, though usually with regard to this or that particular aspect of its doctrines. A fuller resurgence, which some have called *neo-Epicureanism*, took place in the seventeenth and eighteenth centuries. Its most notable representatives were the French philosophers Claude Gillermet de Bérigard (CE 1578–1663), Emmanuel Maignan (CE 1601–76), and Pierre Gassendi (CE 1592–1655), who advocated a fuller version of Epicureanism than the others.

See also: atomism; enlightenment; Greek philosophy

Further reading

Preuss, Peter (1994) *Epicurean Ethics: Katastematic Hedonism*, Lewiston: E. Mellen Press.
Sharples, R.W. (1996) *Stoics, Epicureans and*

Sceptics: An Introduction to Hellenistic Philosophy, London and New York: Routledge.

epiphenomenalism *see* philosophy of mind

epiphenomenon *see* philosophy of mind

episodic *see* disposition

episteme *see* Greek philosophy; Continental philosophy

epistemic accessibility *see* epistemology

epistemic certainty *see* certainty

epistemic charity *see* meaning

epistemic community *see* epistemology

epistemic concepts *see* epistemology

epistemic deontologism *see* justification

epistemic dependence *see* epistemology; logic

epistemic holism *see* holism

epistemic immediacy *see* knowledge

epistemic justification *see* epistemology

epistemic logic *see* logic

epistemic operator *see* logic

epistemic possibility *see* logic

epistemic principles *see* epistemology

epistemic priority *see* epistemology; logic

epistemic privacy *see* epistemology

epistemic privilege *see* epistemology

epistemic probability *see* probability

epistemic regress argument *see* justification

epistemic virtue *see* epistemology; justification

epistemological relativism *see* philosophy of science

epistemological solipsism *see* solipsism

epistemological variable *see* decision

epistemology Derived from the Greek *episteme*, i.e. "knowledge," and *logos*, i.e. "discourse," "reason," or "body of knowledge," the term epistemology denotes a branch of philosophy dealing with the nature, kinds, conditions, scope, and mutual relations of belief (or opinion, or *doxa*), doubt, TRUTH, and KNOWLEDGE. The German philosopher Johann Friedrich Herbart (CE 1776–1841) called this branch of philosophy eidology. Epistemology is also called the theory of knowledge. In some languages other than English, a different Greek verb, *gnosco*, i.e., "to know," is combined with *logos* to form a synonym of epistemology. For example, in Spanish, epistemology is called *epistemología, teoría del conocimiento*, i.e. "theory of knowledge," and *gnoseología*. In French, the term *epistemologie* means rather *philosophy of science*.

Epistemology studies epistemic principles applicable to such concepts – called epistemic concepts – as knowledge, belief, doubt, and justification, and include principles of epistemic logic, principles that relate epistemic concepts to one another, and principles that relate epistemic concepts to non-epistemic – e.g. semantic – ones. Some epistemological approaches are *normative*, i.e. aimed at discerning principles that, if followed, will lead one to attain knowledge or, at least, avoid error. Other approaches are *naturalistic*, i.e. empirical investigations – through psychology, other cognitive or social studies, or evolutionary biology – of epistemic concepts, especially knowledge, understood as basic conditions of human life.

A significant epistemic notion is cognition – the act or process of knowing – and its central concept: knowledge, often contrasted with lack of knowledge due, for example, to such perceptual errors as those involved in delusion, illusion, and hallucination.

Kinds of knowledge

Philosophers distinguish various kinds of knowledge. One is *propositional* knowledge – i.e. knowledge of propositions – or *knowledge-that*, e.g. of the proposition 2+2=4. A second kind is knowledge *by acquaintance*, i.e. knowing a person (or some other item) through having met him or her (or having experienced the item). For example, I know my wife's siblings in this sense (I am acquainted with them), because I have met them. A third kind is knowledge of *skills* (i.e. *knowing how* to engage in some or other activity), for example, knowing how to swim.

Conditions of propositional knowledge

Three main individually necessary and jointly sufficient conditions are used to characterize propositional knowledge.

The truth condition

The first condition is the truth condition: if a subject knows the proposition *p*, then *p* is true. This condition is the least controversial, though there is some controversy about the nature of truth (see TRUTH).

The belief condition

The second condition is the belief condition: if a subject knows the proposition *p*, then the subject believes the proposition *p*. There is controversy about the nature of belief. Some philosophers hold that belief (or opinion) is a disposition to utter a proposition under appropriate conditions, while others hold that it is an occurrent or non-occurrent mental state with a content that may be evaluated as true or false. Dispositional accounts of belief, however, have difficulty explaining novel beliefs or utterances, as well as what it could mean to say that a disposition is true or false. At any rate, it is generally agreed that a person's knowledge of a proposition in the ordinary sense of propositional knowledge at least requires that the person have some psychological relation of assent concerning the proposition. Otherwise, it is hard to explain how the person *has* such knowledge.

The justification condition

The third condition, the justification condition, says: the person who knows a proposition has come to believe or accept it in a reliable way. This general formulation has elicited little controversy, but much controversy concerns what it is for a way of coming to believe or accept a proposition to be reliable. In other words, the controversy centers on the nature of *justification*. The various theories of justification, the foundationalism–coherentism controversy, causal theories and the Gettier problem, internalism and externalism, and pragmatic theories are discussed under JUSTIFICATION.

The contrast between normative and naturalistic approaches centers around the justification condition. The normatively oriented United States philosopher Roderick Milton Chisholm (CE 1916–99) and such contemporary philosophers as Laurence BonJour, and Carl Ginet, have held the doctrine of *epistemic deontologism*, according to which being justified in holding a belief implies that one meets such epistemic obligations as those based on the epistemic aim of believing what is true and not what is false.

Other philosophers have developed the notion of *epistemic virtues*: those qualities of persons that are conducive to the discovery of truth. They are to be distinguished from wisdom and good judgment that, though intellectual, are aimed at practical success. On this basis, these philosophers developed the subfield of epistemology called *virtue epistemology*, according to which epistemic virtue is central to understanding justification, knowledge, or both.

Another position is *criteriology*, formulated by the Belgian neo-Thomist philosopher Désiré Mercier (CE 1851–1926) – after CE 1907, Cardinal Mercier. According to criteriology, epistemology is basically psychology, and skepticism is refuted by reference to the motives for judgment. This is one among various types of *naturalized* epistemology, i.e. epistemology explained in naturalistic terms. Another type is *genetic* epistemology, championed by the Swiss psychologist and epistemologist Jean Piaget (CE 1896–1980), namely, the study of what knowledge is through an empirical investigation of how our epistemic relations to objects are improved.

There is also *evolutionary* epistemology, a family of theories that upholds organic evolution and uses it to derive a theory of knowledge. Among these, a subgroup treats evolution as an ANALOGY for explaining the development of knowledge. This subgroup, however, has been challenged on the grounds that biological mutations are random, while scientific development is hardly random. Another subgroup holds that biology literally predisposes as to think in adaptive patterns that happen to involve knowledge. Both have been criticized on the grounds that their view that our mind is biologically adapted to know is an unwarranted hypothesis. The reply, however, has been that evolutionary epistemology must be treated as a research program. Hence, the argument goes, the criticism that the said view is an as yet unsupported hypothesis – even if true – is not damaging, because hypotheses are supposed to be at the center of research programs.

A different view, which tends to equate justification to predictive success, is *instrumentalism*, originally formulated by the United States philosopher John Dewey (CE 1859–1952), according to whom concepts and ideas are instruments aimed at integrating, predicting, and controlling our interactions with the world we experience. A naturalistic version of instrumentalism was formulated by the Czech-born United States philosopher Ernest Nagel (CE 1901–85), who interpreted the principles of logic in instrumental contexts, so that they are freed from any ontological commitment, i.e. from presupposing or implying the existence of any entity whatsoever.

Still another approach involves the notion of *antitypia* (Greek term for resistance, firmness, hardness). Originally formulated by Stoic philosophers, who also talked of resistant matter, *antitypia* is a property different from location. The Stoics used it to characterize bodies. Echoing the Stoics, the German philosopher Gottfried Wilhelm Leibniz (CE 1646–1716) considered it an attribute whereby matter is in space. *Antitypia* was studied and developed to a great degree by the German philosopher Wilhelm Dilthey (CE 1833–1911), who used the term *resistance*, and characterized its descriptive-psychological, and epistemological basis. For Dilthey, resistance is experienced since very early in life as a result of our volitional impulses, in a manner that involves qualitative and spatial constraints. This leads to a pre-analytic apprehension of the external world of physical objects. An analogous view was implied by the United States philosopher Charles Sanders Peirce (CE 1839–1914), when he said that all skeptical doubts about the external world dissolve as soon as a skeptic must face up to a real situation that calls for intervention, e.g. getting out of the way of a fast approaching car. Similarly, the Spanish philosopher José Ortega y Gasset (CE 1883–

1955) held that nothing appears to us as real except to the extent that it is indocile.

Sources of knowledge

Philosophers have distinguished kinds of propositional knowledge depending on the sources of knowledge involved. Notable among these kinds are *a posteriori* knowledge – briefly, knowledge *based on* sensory or perceptual experience – and *a priori* knowledge – briefly, knowledge *not based on* any such experience even if sensory or perceptual experience is involved in our acquiring it (see A PRIORI–A POSTERIORI). This negative construal of a priori knowledge is sometimes criticized as uninformative. Positive accounts rely either on the type of justification a priori knowledge involves, or on the content of a priori knowledge being necessarily true or rationally unrevisable.

The latter type of accounts raises questions concerning the nature and types of necessity and how they relate to knowledge (see ALETHIOLOGY; PHILOSOPHY OF LANGUAGE; TRUTH). Concerning the first type of accounts, some philosophers have argued that, in some cases, it involves *epistemic privacy*, i.e. the notion that a person has *privileged access* to certain propositions. This is understood as direct, non-inferential knowledge of certain propositions, as in a person's knowledge of his or her own mental states. The significance attributed to privileged access cases is that, though the knowledge involved is a posteriori, corrigibility of perceptions in them is thought impossible. By contrast, in such cases, incorrigibility and indubitability of perceptions, and infallibility of perceiving agents are considered necessary.

This view has been criticized by pointing to cases in which agents come to realize that they were, for example, not as tense, or hungry, or unhappy as they had perceived themselves to be. Also, as the Austrian philosopher Ludwig Wittgenstein (CE 1889–1951) put it, a *form of life* in a linguistic community (which he explained as some agreement in the use of language), poses the question whether a private language is possible. Wittgenstein argued that it is not, because a private language would face the *problem of the criterion*, i.e. it would lack a criterion of linguistic use, where a criterion (often used in the plural, criteria), is, roughly, under normal conditions, a sufficient condition for the truth of a statement. This is known as the *private-language argument*. It led Wittgenstein to hold that avowals of mental states to which one supposedly has privileged access are meaningless, since for any inner process (feeling of shame), there must be an observable criterion (reddening of one's face).

The problem of the criterion is sometimes formulated by asking: "How can epistemological requirements be prior to ontological ones?" From a more strictly epistemological standpoint, the problem is formulated by asking: "Can we recognize instances of knowledge without knowing the criteria for knowledge?" and "Can we know the criteria for knowledge without already recognizing some instances of knowledge?" Ancient skeptics answered both questions in the negative. Later philosophers, however, have sometimes held the position called *particularism*, which answers the first question affirmatively but the second negatively. While others hold the position called *methodism*, which answers the second question affirmatively while the first negatively.

Discussion of this question, as well as of the previously mentioned distinction between a priori and a posteriori knowledge, often involves the notion of *epistemic dependence*, a relation whereby some item(s) cannot be known, understood, or exist unless some other item(s) are respectively known, understood, or exist, and that of *independence*, a relation that is not dependence. When the dependence relation concerns knowledge, it is called epistemic dependence. For example, to know that the oak tree smashed the car one must know, say, that the oak tree is large, heavy, and fell on the car. When dependence concerns understanding, it is called *conceptual* dependence. For example, to understand the concept *bachelor*, one must understand the concept *male*. When dependence concerns existence, it is called *ontological* dependence. For example, for a shadow cast on a surface to exist, the surface must exist.

When a dependence relation is not reciprocal – e.g. if a shadow cast on a surface cannot exist without the surface, while the surface can exist without a shadow cast on it – then the relation is called a *priority relation*. The expression *logical priority* is sometimes used to mean either epistemic, conceptual, or ontological dependence. A problem that evidences this type of interface between epistemology and metaphysics is that of *individuation*. In epistemology, it is the problem of identifying the causes of the process whereby a subject discerns an individual. In metaphysics, it is the problem of identifying the basis of the type of process whereby a universal becomes instantiated in a particular or individual.

Knowledge and error

The first two conditions of propositional knowledge are central to a characterization of *error* (from the Latin *error*, i.e. "a wandering about") that denotes, generally, a mistake or inaccuracy which may or may not have to do with action and, concerning mistakes about propositions, the belief in a false proposition. This has led to the development of *error theories*. In ethics, for example, the contemporary British philosopher J.L. Mackie argues that though moral judgments – i.e. statements about the rightness or wrongness of particular actions; the justifiability or unjustifiability of policies, practices, or institutions; or the goodness or badness of attitudes or traits of character – can be supported by appeal to reasons, the principles on which these reasons are based are totally subjective and arbitrary. That is, he advocates an error theory that denies the existence of any moral facts or properties at the level of moral principles and laws.

In Indian thought, an error theory or *khyāti-vāda* can belong to one of three types: *sat-khyāti-vāda* or theories in which the object of error is real, *asat-khyāti-vāda* or theories where the object of error is unreal, and *anirvacanīyakhyāti-vāda* or theories in which the object of error is neither real nor unreal. In Western philosophy, the Greek philosopher Plato (428–348 BCE), in his *Theaetetus*, treated error as misidentification. Also, perceptual errors such as illusions and hallucinations are at the center of philosophical discussions of perception (see PERCEPTION).

Knowledge and the epistemic community

A further question that arises – this time at a social level – concerning the validation of knowledge claims is: "What is the epistemic community within which knowledge claims should be validated and research priorities established?" This has been of particular concern in recent discussions of the politics of knowledge carried out in feminist epistemology and the philosophy of science and technology. For it is thought that social conditions can and do create, first, an epistemic location where knowledge, which is local knowledge, takes place. Second, it is thought they create associated structures of domination reflected in the languages, concepts, and methods – including those for establishing expertise or authoritativeness – that actual epistemic communities find admissible, and embodied in the members of these communities that, in these communities, are considered experts or authorities.

Knowledge and objectivity

In addition, a recurrent related question in epistemology is: "Is knowledge objective or are our beliefs, concepts, and ideas mere constructs or fictions with no objective basis?" In other words: "Is epistemological objectivism justified or is epistemological subjectivism justified?" Already in the Middle Ages, philosophers stating *fictio figura veritatis* assigned a role to fiction in the search for truth. Modern discussions of objectivity and the role of fiction in forming beliefs, concepts, and ideas has given rise to *constructivism*, a family of views sharing the tenet that concepts and ideas are mere constructs, but disagreeing on whether they have no objective basis, or are based on beliefs, concepts, and attitudes that can be involved in a non-relativistic – e.g. considered judgments of competent judges – criterion.

See also: justification; knowledge

Further reading

Peacocke, Christopher (1995) *A Study of Concepts*, Cambridge, MA: MIT Press.

Piaget, Jean (1997) *The Principles of Genetic Epistemology*, London and New York: Routledge.

Wallner, Friedrich (1994) *Constructive Realism: Aspects of a New Epistemological Movement*, Wien: W. Braumuller.

episyllogism *see* syllogism

epoché *see* phenomenology

E-proposition *see* syllogism

equal opportunity *see* ethics; philosophy, sociopolitical

equality *see* ethics; philosophy, sociopolitical

equitability *see* ethics; philosophy, sociopolitical

equity *see* ethics; philosophy, sociopolitical

equilibrium *see* ethics; philosophy, sociopolitical

equipollence *see* skepticism

equipossible *see* probability

equiprobable *see* probability

equivalence *see* logic

equivalence, behavioral *see* computer theory

equivalence class *see* logic

equivalence condition *see* induction

equivalence relation *see* relation

equivocation *see* fallacy

Er, myth of *see* justice; myth

Erfahrung *see* phenomenology

eristic *see* fallacy; syllogism

Erklärung *see* explanation

Erlebnis *see* phenomenology

Eros *see* love; psychoanalysis

erotetic *see* logic

error *see* epistemology; ethics; skepticism

eschatology *see* myth

esoteric *see* esoterism

esoterism In one of its two main senses, this term (derived, like esoteric, from the Greek *esoteros*: "inner," "interior"), denotes some of Ancient Greece's philosophies and schools. Within this general category, there are at least two further subdivisions. First, esoterism denotes philosophies and schools involving doctrines aimed at their members, by contrast with *exoterism* and exoteric doctrines, which are aimed at the general public. A second subdivision is that of schools or philosophies involving doctrines that must be taught only to the initiate. In this case, esoteric means "occult," "secret," or "mystery." Some commentators have stated that PYTHAGOREANISM and, partially, PLATONISM, were esoteric in this latter sense. Others have gone further arguing that even in the Aristotelian corpus, some works – e.g. those in *Metaphysics* – should be considered esoteric, while others – e.g. those in the *Organon* – should be considered exoteric. Among the reasons offered in support of this view are passages in those texts that seem to support this view, the manner in which different Greek philosophical doctrines were transmitted, and the use of esoteric and esoterism in Greek antiquity. Others – e.g. the United States philosopher George Boas (CE 1891–1980) – have argued that the only defensible esoteric–exoteric distinction is that based on the distinction between views formulated in popular language and those that, though not secret, are formulated in technical language.

As for the other main sense in which esoteric and esoterism are used, it goes beyond indicating an emphasis on secret or occult doctrines, denoting a form of, and attitude about, knowledge open only to the elect, the wise, soothsayers, and prophets. In this sense, esoterism has influenced a wide range of cultural expressions, certainly the arts in various – Western or other – traditions. In addition, some who use the terms in this sense (in which is also frequently used in some forms of Eastern philosophy), think the transmission of such knowledge to be undesirable both because it bastardizes it and because it harms the lives of those unprepared to receive it.

See also: Greek philosophy; myth

Further reading
Bhattacharyya, Benoytosh (1932) *An Introduction to Buddhist Esoterism*, London and New York: Oxford University Press.
Godwin, Joscelyn (1995) *Music and the Occult: French Musical Philosophies 1750–1950*, Rochester, NY and Woodbridge: University of Rochester Press.

esprit de finesse *see* faith; intuition

esprit géometrique *see* faith; intuition

esse *see* ens

esse est inesse *see* accident

esse est percipi *see* idealism

essence *see* essentialism

essential property *see* essentialism

essentialism Most typically, this term denotes a family of metaphysical doctrines sharing the view that objects have essences and that there is a distinction between essential properties – briefly, those without which a certain item cannot be what it is – and non-essential properties, those without which the item can still be what it is. Those upholding this distinction might for example say that being a fruit is an essential property of an apple, while being red is a non-essential property of an apple.

Essences are conceived of in various ways. One conception is as *nominal* essences and contrasted with *real* essences. As nominal, essences are said to exist *de dicto*, a locution meaning "of what is said" or "of the proposition" and contrasted with *de re*, which means "of the thing" and is a locution used in connection with real essences. For example, if interpreted in the *de dicto* sense, the proposition "It is possible that the number of European States is odd" is about the proposition "the number of European States is odd" and means that the latter can be true. By contrast, if interpreted in the *de re* sense, the proposition "It is possible that the number of European States is odd" is about the actual number of States that make up Europe and means that this number has the property of being possibly odd. Necessity and possibility as they apply to statements constitute *de dicto* modality. While when they apply to possible worlds, they constitute *de re* modality.

In this regard, philosophers talk of nominal essences having *de dicto* necessity, a locution denoting a property of those propositions – e.g. either it is or it is not raining here and now – that cannot possibly be false. This notion is contrasted to *de re* necessity, a property R that a property F of an object O has just in case it is impossible for the object O to exist without the property F. For example, the property R of being necessary is a property of the property *F* of being identical to itself that the object *O* has. This notion of *de re* necessity is sometimes also called *metaphysical* necessity.

In this regard, the Austrian philosopher Ludwig Wittgenstein (CE 1889–1951) argued that concept words do not denote concepts or essences in the sharply circumscribed sense in which these have been traditionally understood. Such words only point to *family resemblances* between the various items labeled with the words. Along these lines, philosophers have developed *prototype theory*, i.e. a theory that treats human cognition as using categories: indefinitely bounded organizations of items around stereotypical or paradigmatic exemplars, and involving more or less central features for items falling under the concepts.

A variation of metaphysical essentialism is *mereological* essentialism, i.e. the view that every composite is necessarily made up of particular components in a particular configuration so that, if any parts are removed or replaced, it loses its self-identity.

Sometimes, the term essentialism has been used to characterize all philosophies that hold essence to be prior to existence, and contrasts them with those philosophies that hold existence somehow to be prior to essence, namely, EXISTENTIALISM and philosophies of existence.

Specific forms of metaphysical essentialism have been used in discussions of gender differences, and criticized, for example by feminist philosophers, on the grounds that they are unfounded and sources of stereotypes. The same criticisms have been advanced against forms of scientific essentialism used in discussions of human biology and racial or ethnic differences.

See also: *de dicto* and *de re*, under *de*; alethiology

Further reading
Brunner, Diane DuBose (1998) *Between the Masks: Resisting the Politics of Essentialism*, Lanham, MD: Rowman & Littlefield Publishers.
Thom, Paul (1996) *The Logic of Essentialism: An Interpretation of Aristotle's Modal Syllogistic*, Dordrecht and Boston: Kluwer Academic Publishers.

esthetics *see* aesthetics

eternal object *see* category

eternal recurrence *see* computer theory; myth

eternal return *see* computer theory; myth

eternity *see* metaphysics; philosophy of science

ethical absolutism *see* ethics

ethical constructivism *see* ethics

ethical conventionalism *see* ethics

ethical dualism *see* Zoroastrianism

ethical egoism *see* ethics

ethical eudaimonism *see* ethics

ethical hedonism *see* ethics

ethical idealism *see* ethics

ethical intuitionism *see* ethics

ethical naturalism *see* ethics

ethical nihilism *see* ethics

ethical objectivism *see* ethics

ethical pragmatism *see* ethics

ethical relativism *see* ethics

ethical skepticism *see* ethics

ethical subjectivism *see* ethics

ethical values *see* value

ethics A term used in a variety of senses. At least four are significant.

Ethics as morals
In this sense, the term ethics is used in the personal sense: in which a person's ethics (or a person's morals) is a particular person's beliefs and presuppositions about right and wrong, good and bad, justified and unjustified. This – a person's *morals* – is something a particular person *has*. That is, a person's morals include the person's moral beliefs, as well as a variety of things the person takes for granted in everyday life – from morally significant facts to moral rules, laws, principles, values, or ideals displayed in the person's behavior or involved in the person's character. It is in this personal sense that we can say "your ethics are stricter than mine." This sense, in which ethics means

morals, is involved in the notion of a person's being *amoral*, i.e. lacking in morals. This is not to be confused with the notion of an amoral point of view, i.e. a point of view from which moral or ethical considerations are irrelevant, which is contrasted with the *moral point of view*, i.e. the point of view from which moral considerations are relevant and, furthermore, persons' morals, groups' mores, and moral or ethical theories about these are open to critical scrutiny.

As for being *immoral*, it typically means to have features that lead to conduct that is wrong, i.e. impermissible, also called immoral conduct. In this latter sense, not merely persons but actions, decisions, or choices, as well as policies, practices, or institutions, can be called immoral, by contrast with those that are moral. That is, they can be called immoral by contrast:

1 with any person that is morally good, hence in this sense of moral, a moral person;
2 with any action or decision that is morally right, i.e. permissible, hence in this sense of moral, a moral action or a moral decision or a moral choice; and
3 with any policy, practice, or institution that is morally justified, hence in this sense of moral, that is a moral policy, moral practice, or moral institution.

Concerning immorality, the term *evil* is frequently used in ethics as roughly synonymous with *bad*, though evil often has a religious connotation. Both, in ethics and religious thought, bad and evil are associated with the notion of *privation* or *privatio boni*, i.e. an item's lack of good where this good is appropriate for that item to have. In addition, evil typically means bad to a high degree. This is clear, for example, in Akan morality. Here the terms for goodness are *yieyē* and *papayē* or, for short, *papa*, where the last syllable of the full terms, *yē*, means "to do" or "perform." Hence, the terms mean goodness in the sense of good-doing. As for evil, there are two terms with distinct meanings: *bōne*, which denotes ordinary evils such as theft and lying, and *musuo*, which denotes extraordinary evils such as rape and murder. This latter sense of evil

often suggests religious implications such as that of causing the wrath of the deities.

Moral persons, moral responsibility
The term moral, of course, has other senses. For example, in the expression a moral person, it denotes a person who has decision-making responsibility, i.e. has the capacity to tell right from wrong, to make decision on this basis, and to act accordingly. In this sense, a moral person denotes a moral agent by contrast with those items – from mountains and plants to non-human animals – each one of which exemplifies what in environmental ethics has been called a *moral patient*, i.e. an item that undergoes the effects of the actions of moral agents, but is not a moral agent itself because it is incapable of decision-making responsibility.

In this regard, the question has been raised whether a corporation, that is a collective entity, not an individual agent, can be a moral person or have *moral personhood*. The arguments offered in support of an affirmative answer to this question, however, have been largely question-begging, arguing that since corporations display rationality in the same manner individual agents do, by analogy, they can have moral personhood as individual agents can and often do. The question-begging feature of this argument consists in assuming that corporations display rationality (rather than its being displayed only by the members of their boards of directors), a point that is also at issue in establishing whether corporations can have moral personhood.

In this discussion, the notion of decision-making responsibility should not be confused with other notions of responsibility. For example, an agent can have *causal* responsibility or be causally responsible for a given state of affairs, i.e. be the one who caused such things as death, injury, or loss of property. The agent can also have *legal* responsibility or be legally responsible for it, i.e. be the one the law says should pay for the damages or be punished in specific ways.

Without decision-making responsibility, however, it is questionable whether the agent has *moral* responsibility or is morally responsible for the said state of affairs, i.e. whether the agent ought to have omitted the action(s) that brought it about. For, otherwise, it would make sense to say that one ought to do or have done something even if one has no control whatsoever over one's own decisions or conduct. These notions are also relevant concerning the view that social compacts, e.g. Serbia – not merely the Serbian citizens or their leaders – can have collective responsibility for the consequences of decisions made by their leaders, say, the decision to engage in ethnic cleansing in Kosovo in 1999. Answers to this question, however, hinge on answers concerning the moral responsibility of social compacts, e.g., as previously discussed, of corporations.

Ethics as mores

In a second sense, the term ethics goes beyond conduct, applying also to such things as attitudes and practices. In this comprehensive sense, ethics is a group's *mores*: a particular group's predominant beliefs and presuppositions about right and wrong, good and bad, justified and unjustified. Accordingly, ethics in the social sense is something a group – rather that a particular individual – *has*, in that the group has explicitly, however partially, formulated it or predominantly holds it. It is in this sense that we can say "Navajo ethics are different from Western European ethics." It is also in this context that philosophers have used the term *immoralism*, which means indifference or opposition to mores, i.e. to conventional morality, or the morality embodied in customary law, i.e. in the long, continued practices of a group.

Ethics as a branch of inquiry

As soon as a question is raised about the justifiability of a certain person's or group's moral belief or presupposition, ethical or moral inquiry begins. When people engage in critical inquiry about such matters of disagreement, they *do* ethics or moral philosophy, rather than simply have ethics or morals or a moral philosophy that may or may not be shared with most members of their group, thus being in harmony with the group's mores.

In this latter sense, in which people do moral philosophy, rather than simply have a moral philosophy, the latter is an activity, not simply a set of beliefs and presuppositions. The activity is not identical with, but *about* beliefs

and presuppositions, and is often prompted by conflicts among them. Thus ethics here is used in a third sense, as a *branch of inquiry* – sometimes also called ethical theory, moral theory, or reflection on morality. It is a critical study with the goal of soundly dealing with problems of right and wrong conduct; good and bad attitudes, traits, or motives; justified and unjustified policies, practices or institutions that arise in people's lives.

Ethics as a theory or school of thought

In the process of engaging in ethics as a branch of inquiry, people offer different kinds of reasons to support their views. Some, for example, point to the overall consequences of given courses of action to establish that they should (or, alternatively, should not) be pursued, while others point to the rights of individuals. As a result, questions arise about the relevance of these *kinds* of reasons, some for example arguing that consequences are all that matters, others arguing that rights, not consequences, are crucial. In doing this, they are formulating central components of ethical *theories*, i.e. of generalized devices for dealing with moral problems concerning conduct, character, or institutions. These central components are ethical *principles* or moral principles, which are supposed to be invariant and wide in scope, like the golden rule (see below); ethical *laws* or moral laws, which are supposed to be invariant, but narrow in scope, e.g. the rule against lying without good reason; and ethical *rules* or moral rules, which are not invariant but general, and narrow in scope, like the rule that lying is generally wrong.

Scope of ethics

A question that arises about ethics is: "What are its boundaries?" In Ancient Greece, the modern distinction between strictly ethical and other matters was hardly drawn. Even as late as the eighteenth century, ethics as a study was subsumed under the heading of moral philosophy together with what today would be classified as social studies. During the past two centuries, however, various attempts have been made to distinguish ethics from a variety of other areas of human inquiry and activity, addressing the questions: "What is the boundary between aesthetics and ethics?" and "What is the boundary between ethics and etiquette?" As matters of censorship make plain, ethics and aesthetics, however distinct, often overlap. Also, as certain failures of courtesy make plain, some matters of etiquette overlap with ethics, e.g. when being discourteous in ways that amount to treating others in an insensitive or disrespectful manner. Of course, this is not to say that such discourtesy is invariably, if ever, an enormous moral offense, but only that it is both morally significant and, however minimally, morally objectionable.

Ethics arguably covers all areas of human activity – individual and collective conduct, policy-making and convention-settling activities, attitudes, traits, motives and, as proponents of the ethics of belief (see JUSTIFICATION) would add, beliefs – that affect people's lives in non-trivial (even if minimal) ways. This characterization of the scope of ethics has the advantage of avoiding both theoretical conundrums that have plagued ethics for centuries, and a bombastic sense of ethics where the term wrong is invariably understood as highly immoral – a mistake analogous to the view that for some object to have weight it must be heavy.

Applicability of ethics: state of nature situations
A matter related to the scope of ethics is that of the conditions for the applicability of ethics. In this regard, some philosophers argue that at least some of the ordinary rules or principles of morality – e.g. those concerning justice – have no application whenever a *state of nature* exists, i.e. whenever a situation is predominant in which the rules of civil society – of which a state of nature is the opposite – cannot be expected to apply. A state of nature situation can be characterized by means of four variables (or assumptions) and a set of odds tied to the circumstances. The *motivational* variable: everyone in the situation will act so as to maximize his or her own advantage. The *epistemological* variable: everyone in the situation has roughly equal knowledge and abilities relevant for dealing with the situation. The *resources* variable: resources are limited. Last, the *commons* variable or the liberty variable: everyone is at liberty to act as he or she wishes in the situation.

Concerning the commons variable, being at liberty is understood as having a *liberty* or a *weak right*, where to say that a person S is at liberty to do, have, or enjoy x is to say that it is not wrong for S to do, have, or enjoy x. This notion is contrasted with that of a *strong right*, according to which, to say that a person S has a strong right to do, have, or enjoy x is at least to say that, first, it is not wrong for S to do, have, or enjoy x; and second, everyone else has an obligation not to interfere with S's doing, having, or enjoying x. At least when it comes to the rights of citizens – though, on some conceptions of a right, concerning every right – a third condition is arguably required, namely, that S is entitled to claim that everyone else omit interfering with S's doing, having, or enjoying x.

At any rate, even those who argue that at least some of the ordinary rules or principles of morality have no application in a state of nature sometimes add that not all principles cease to apply in such a situation, where our primary obligation is to do all we can in order to get out of such a state. Such a situation, however, can be or become a type of *social trap*, i.e. a type of situation in which individuals or groups are stuck behaving in a manner they perceive as favorable to their aims when, in fact, it is contrary to them. For example, in the midst of the high-tech arms race – arguably an instance of a state of nature situation – a country's leaders may perceive their developing high-tech weapon superiority as favorable to their aim of bringing about a state of civil society out of a state of nature when, in fact, their using such means only leads to further escalation on the part of their opponents and, hence, reinforces their current state of nature. When the aims are moral aims, say, that just mentioned of bringing about a state of civil society out of a predominant state of nature situation, the traps are *moral* traps.

In addition, some philosophers argue that civil society and a state of nature are not merely two extreme types of situations, one where all rules of morality apply, the other where none of them apply. Rather, they argue that civil society and a state of nature are two types of opposite situations, each embodied to a variety of degrees in actual societies. Hence, the problem of the applicability of at least certain moral rules or principles – e.g. those of justice – is always, to some extent and in some respect, at issue, though this does not undermine the applicability of all rules of morality.

Of course, there are exceptions to this type of view. One was, for example, provided by the German philosopher Friedrich Wilhelm Nietzsche (CE 1844–1900), who formulated the notion of a *master morality*, a morality for higher and creative human beings from whom a better type of individual – what he called the *Übermensch*, i.e. the overman or the superman, could emerge. He contrasted *master* morality with *slave/herd* morality, a morality suited to the needs of the mediocre majority, hence predominant in the world. To Nietzsche, they both were manifestations of humans' basic drive: the *will to power*. These notions are at the core of Nietzschean philosophy and display elements of human *perfectibility* and human *flourishing* (if not perfectionism) that trace back to Aristotelian conceptions of human excellence, and Renaissance and modern conceptions of HUMANISM curbed by the Hobbesian conception of human nature.

In addition to the matters just discussed, the sort of problem outlined in contrasting state of nature situations with civil society situations often leads to discussions of cases and the sorts of moral rules, laws, or principles that take precedence when dealing with them.

Practical or applied ethics
An increasingly influential area of ethics is *practical* or *applied ethics*. It has been understood in at least three ways. First, it has been understood as the area of ethics where ethical theories are applied to concrete ethical problems.

Second, it has been understood as a modern version of *casuistics* (called *casuistry* by its detractors), which was the medieval branch of ethics concerned with the application of ethical principles to particular cases. It should be noted, however, that medieval casuistics operated against the background of Catholic religion and worldview. By contrast, in the contemporary – pluralistic – world, casuistics is a rather inductivist approach that starts with paradigmatic cases and, by analogy, extrapolates features of those cases to other cases

being examined. Either way, practical ethics is a sub-branch of ethical inquiry contrasted with, though related to – indeed, arguably prompting the discussion of problems that belong in – theoretical ethics (see below).

Third, practical ethics has been understood as philosophical inquiry concerning, not merely the examination of cases or the application of ethical theories to concrete moral problems, but also as the theoretical inquiry these prompt, e.g. about the performance–omission distinction, and the notion of a person. A problem concerning this interpretation is whether practical ethics thus understood still denotes a sub-branch of ethical inquiry or whether, by including the said theoretical problems, it has no distinctive meaning and, instead, becomes synonymous with the term ethics.

Problems in practical ethics arise concerning, to mention just a few, such things as ABORTION, access to health care, acquired immunodeficiency syndrome (AIDS), advanced directives and the related topic of EUTHANASIA, assisted suicide, gene-splicing or genetic engineering, cloning, research on human subjects, environmental deterioration, animal welfare and rights, energy production and use, punishment, and WAR. Discussions about many of these topics often involve an appeal to the notion of *reverence for life*, a final value in the thought of the philosopher, theologian, and medical missionary Albert Schweitzer (CE 1875–1965). A sub-branch of practical ethics is *professional* ethics, which deals with ethical problems arising in the professions, e.g. in the health care and legal profession. Also, a part of practical ethics that includes professional ethics is *social* ethics, i.e. the part of ethics dealing with moral problems raised by people's mutual interactions.

A problem often arising in *health care ethics* – but not only in this area – is that of *confidentiality*. It is formulated in questions such as the following: "Should a physician inform the parents of a teenage patient who requests a prescription to use contraceptives, and who, having had various abortions, visits the doctor?" "Should a cancer patient's health records be made available to insurance companies?"

Less widely addressed, but significant, is the problem of the notion of health itself. In health care, conceptions of *disease* and *health* are crucial for treatment decisions. These conceptions vary from country to country. United States physicians, for example, treat high blood pressure but, except in extreme cases, not moderately low blood pressure. In Germany, by contrast, moderately low blood pressure was also treated until a few decades ago, though German practice appears now to approach United States practice. Perhaps a more pressing problem area concerning the notion of health is that of defining genetic illnesses. Should these cover such things as a low but normal IQ, aging, and being relatively short in stature? Expanding the concept of genetic illnesses would lead to greater use of medication and to treating as pathological conditions traditionally considered normal. On the other hand, it would make room for treatment and possibly insurance coverage concerning these conditions whose exclusion is thought unfair to those who suffer them.

Another area of applied ethics is *engineering ethics* and the related – wider – field, *technology ethics* or the *ethics of technology*, which deals with ethical problems and issues in and about technology. Paramount among its subdivisions are those concerned with genetic engineering, computers, energy and, at a higher level, social engineering generally. These are all paradigmatic examples of *technology*, a term derived from the Greek *techne*, i.e. "art" or "craft" or the skill involved in either art or craft, and *logos*, i.e. "discourse," "reason," or "body of knowledge," and currently used with this body of knowledge emphasis, by contrast with *technique* that also derives from *techne*, but denotes a specific manner, procedure, or skill used in a particular endeavor.

Here, as in other areas of applied ethics, the question arises: "Who is to tell?" Answers to this question sometimes involve appeals to experts or authorities. However, objections have been raised on the grounds that social conditions can and do create structures of domination reflected in the languages, concepts, and methods – including those involved in establishing expertise or authoritativeness – that actual epistemic communities find admissible, and embodied in the members of these communities that, in these communities, are considered experts or authorities. That is, concerns have been raised about *technocracy* or the rule of the experts.

Various suggestions have been made to address this problem, among them the *science court*, whose members would be competent, impartial scientists from disciplines adjacent to the subject of dispute, not from the discipline directly involved in the dispute. The procedure would involve three stages. First, the court would identify the scientific and technological – not the ethical, political, and policy – question at issue. Second, scientist-advocates would engage in adversarial proceedings on the model of a court of law. Third, the judges would decide what the scientific facts actually are. This approach was criticized on the grounds that it presupposed something untenable: a sharp separation between facts and values, and also on the grounds that it would merely help proliferate opinion. As a result, philosophers have proposed the *technology tribunal*, which would expand the scope of issues beyond merely factual ones, and the court's membership beyond scientists. Yet, this suggestion is also open to the criticism that it would contribute to proliferation of opinion.

One might be inclined to take a skeptical stand on these matters. Yet, it should be noticed that even these disagreements make plain, as the contemporary Belgian philosopher Gilbert Hottois states, that, of late, the technological conscience has developed, however diffusedly, its moral sensitivity concerning recent results and new possibilities in biotechnology.

Still another area of applied ethics is *environmental ethics*. Two traditions have developed in this area. They involve contrasting conceptions of the land and, in general, the environment or the biota, and of the relations between humans and the land, the environment, or the biota. One, *conservationism*, emphasizes conservation of the biota for future human use. Since it gives priority to human use, it is *anthropocentric*. Since it is concerned with human use, it is often – though not invariably – utilitarian (see UTILITARIANISM). The other tradition, *preservationism*, emphasizes preservation of the biota for its own sake. Hence, it is not anthropocentric. Nor is it, in most cases, utilitarian. In its predominant non-utilitarian form, preservationists have often appealed to a subgroup of the rights of non-humans (which include those of non-human individuals): the rights of the land, the environment, or the biota (which are rights of collectives) to emphasize that the biota is not just an instrument for the attainment of human aims.

A related area of inquiry that includes or overlaps with environmental ethics, but is wider and, indeed goes beyond ethics, is that of *environmental philosophy*. A concept that has acquired some currency in this area of philosophy is that of *deep ecology*: a movement initiated by the contemporary Scandinavian philosopher Arne Naess. It is centered, first, on the rejection of the human-in-the-environment conception, in favor of a relational, total-field conception, where organisms are conceived of as knots in a field of intrinsic relations; and, then, on a prima facie biospherical egalitarianism that places the burden of proof on those who contemplate any killing, exploitation, or suppression of ecological components.

The various problems addressed by environmental ethics range from some that overlap with those of technology ethics (e.g. those concerning energy sources and environmental deterioration), to some that overlap with health care ethics (e.g. those concerning various forms of pollution as they affect public health). Also, since all or nearly of them are associated with business and economic concerns, they overlap with problems also addressed by *business ethics*: the area of applied or practical ethics concerned with moral problems – problems of right and wrong conduct; good and bad traits or attitudes; and justified policies, practices, or institutions – that arise concerning business, i.e. concerning business management, marketing and advertising, accounting and finance, international business, any business organization or firm, and the institution of business as a whole. This originates subfields of business ethics such as management ethics, the ethics of accounting and finance, and the ethics of marketing and

advertising. They deal with problems ranging from the priority criteria for resolving conflicts of obligations accountants have to their clients, the public, and others, and to the glass ceiling: the discriminatory barriers women executives find in the corporate world.

Business ethics also deals with problems concerning the very notion of a *market* and its characteristic features. One of them is *exchange* or the giving of something in return for something else, by contrast, for example, with a *gift* or the giving of something in return for nothing. Another such feature is *competition* or the rivalry or struggle between two or more individuals or organizations concerning something that, in markets, is often market share (see CAPITALISM; PHILOSOPHY OF ECONOMICS). Still another is their *social dependence*, i.e. dependence on some form of civil society where there are common ways of doing things or, in other words, however incipiently, on a state.

Some ethical problems in business arise in some cultural or religious traditions, but not in others. For example, in Islam, interest is forbidden. As a result, Islamic groups have developed the *mudārabah*: the type of business arrangement whereby one person puts up the capital and another the labor. With the approval of various Islamic religious authorities, the *mudārabah* is used by some Middle East banks that treat deposits of money as the invested capital in a *mudārabah*, whereby the depositor becomes a limited partner in the bank's ventures, thus earning a return on the investment.

Issues in business ethics, especially in international business, prompt questions about the justification of economic aid and, more recently, about international commerce policies addressing the *globalization* of business activities and markets. Significant in this regard has been the work of the contemporary Indian economist and Nobel Prize winner Amartya Sen, who questions traditional notions of rationality in economic theory and reformulates the relations between ethics and economics.

Moral problems and moral issues
The moral problems addressed in the various areas of ethics just discussed typically involve opposed moral beliefs, rules, rights, duties and

obligations, and principles, and sometimes develop into moral issues. Central to *issues* is *heated conflict*, whether *of beliefs, demands, or both*, whose varieties are *controversy* – when, however heated the conflict, reliance on reason and meaningful dialogue have a predominant role in it – and *confrontation* – when reliance on reason and meaningful dialogue take a back seat.

Detachment, a feature often thought to characterize objectivity in persons, is typically absent among those caught up in the controversies and confrontations characteristic of issues. This attitude need not involve selfishness, though, granted, selfish motives – a type of reasons of expediency – can and often lead people to engage in the issues. People may also be led by reasons of *moral expediency*, in which case, even though not selfish, their aims – say, the upholding of presumed individual rights – are treated as if they were overriding and above critical scrutiny.

The question then often arises, especially when policy making is concerned: "What should be done about this issue, e.g. the abortion issue, given that there is heated conflict about it?" Some argue that such conflict is a *moral externality*, i.e. a mere matter of politics and not morally relevant. However, others reply that, since the political circumstance of conflict significantly affects people's lives and sets constraints on what policies or decisions are feasible, it is not a mere matter of politics, but ethically relevant as well.

Theoretical ethics

The immediate and pressing concerns addressed in practical ethics characteristically lead to problems in theoretical ethics. Some of these problems are about the nature of the good and the right, and their mutual relations. They typically belong under a subfield of theoretical ethics called moral epistemology (see below). Other problems of theoretical ethics concern whether presumed moral standards are actually *moral rules*, which have narrow scope and general validity (e.g. the injunction against lying); *moral laws*, which have narrow scope but universal validity (e.g. the injunction against lying without good reason); or *moral principles*, which have wide scope and universal validity (e.g. the principle

of formal justice, according to which, everyone should be treated equally unless there are good reasons to the contrary). Their products are ethical theories (see below). We will next survey some main subfield or problem areas in theoretical ethics.

Moral epistemology

As stated, some problems of theoretical ethics concern matters of moral epistemology. One is formulated by the questions: "Are ethical expressions – say, 'he is good' – capable of being true or false, and is any ethical rule or principle – as in *descriptivism* or *cognitivism* – descriptive, hence capable of being true or false, and of being known?" Or, instead, are they expressions of emotion as in *emotivism*, the doctrine that moral expressions are very much like saying "helping others: hurrah!" or "murder: boohoo!"? Or are they recommendations or commands – as in *prescriptivism*, the doctrine that moral expressions are very much like saying "I recommend helping others" and "I advise against murder," or "Help others!" and "Don't commit murder!"? Both emotivism and prescriptivism are forms of *non-cognitivism*. In defending these views, some philosophers have held *ascriptivism*, i.e. the view that moral judgments have, as previously explained, an emotive or prescriptive meaning, and then a descriptive meaning denoting the non-moral properties of what is judged, and that ascriptions of truth to these judgments fit a redundancy account as merely expressing agreement with the attitudes expressed in the judgments. However, this still precludes moral mistakes, a view to which cognitivists and ordinary moral thought and language are committed.

Some of the said philosophers have also held that ethical expressions express attitudes and that changing one's position on matters of attitude would involve, not reason, but a Gestalt-shift, very much like a conversion. Discussion of whether this is so often involves arguments about the *fact–value distinction*, i.e. between how things are and how they should be, and one origin of this distinction, namely, the inference the Scottish philosopher David Hume (CE 1711–76) drew from it: that you cannot derive an "ought" from an "is" or, to use contemporary philosophical language, ethical language is, if not merely expressive, prescriptive, not descriptive, and you cannot derive prescriptions from descriptions.

Another problem in moral epistemology is whether moral concepts and ideas are mere constructs with no objective basis or, as in *ethical constructivism*, based on moral beliefs, concepts, and attitudes, which makes room for the view that they involve a non-relativistic – e.g. considered judgments of competent judges – criterion, or for the view that they involve relativistic presuppositions (see ethical relativism, below).

Some have argued that if ethical constructivism is based on the considered moral judgments of competent judges and simply aims at a reflective equilibrium among these, then it is merely a form of a coherence view of moral truth and, indeed, a form of ethical or moral idealism.

This depends on how the notion of *reflective equilibrium* is understood. It was first formulated by the United States philosopher Nelson Goodman (CE 1906–98) in *Fact, Fiction, and Forecast*, and was further developed with regard to ethics by the contemporary philosopher John Rawls. Rawls distinguished *narrow reflective equilibrium*, i.e. the outcome of a process of mutual adjustment between ethical principles and our considered moral judgments, from *wide reflective equilibrium*, the outcome of a process like that just described where the moral conception accepted in narrow equilibrium is assessed on the basis of moral arguments by comparison with other moral conceptions.

If this is all there is to reflective equilibrium in ethics, then, as the previous criticism suggests, it arguably amounts to a form of a coherence view of moral truth and, indeed, a form of ethical or moral idealism. However, need reflective equilibrium be restricted to moral discourse? Instead, some propose ethical or moral *pragmatism*: the view that moral problems, like any other problems, are the occasion for inquiry, and moral judgments made in response to moral problems are simply moral hypotheses to be confirmed or disconfirmed depending on how well they address the problems. The manner in which they are to be tested serves to distinguish a variety of ethical

pragmatism approaches. These range from *discourse ethics*, where only the force of the better argument is supposed to prevail, to approaches where constraints of time and politics are also crucial, such as the approach called *philosophy as diplomacy*.

In making issues, issue-overload, and conflict some of its main subjects of reflection, philosophy as diplomacy investigates *social decision procedures* that range from discussion of merits and negotiation, through bargaining, to arbitration and mediation (whose religious forerunner is *intercession*, i.e. a prayer or pleading to God on behalf of another or others), and, when confrontation is a significant part of the picture, other procedures ranging from insulation, through peaceful disobedience, to strikes and combat. In any case, pragmatic approaches or pragmatic theories, i.e. approaches or theories exemplifying what has been called moral pragmatism, have the feature – to some, the advantage; to others, the disadvantage – of by-passing the fact–value distinction and its implications. They also have the feature of focusing on the process of forming such things as moral judgments, decisions, policies, and conventions. This is an ongoing process whereby, if constrained in a sound way, the outcomes – say, the judgments, decisions, policies, or conventions – would be justified.

Problems of the type just described are sometimes called problems of *metaethics*, as if they were outside of and above ethics. However, they lead to positions that have consequences for people's lives, hence, arguably, however epistemological or semantic, are also normative. Indeed, failure to realize this fact has led some philosophers to advocate some forms of ethical relativism (see below) under the heading of metaethical relativism.

Still other problems of theoretical ethics are openly normative. They are about right and wrong conduct; good and bad traits or attitudes, or character; justified or unjustified policies, practices, or institutions. Among these, there are problems of practical ethics, such as those previously discussed that arise in or about business, health care, technology, and the like. Solutions to problems in these areas often rely on different concepts. For example, informed consent has been central in problems of conduct arising in health care ethics. Tacit consent has been widely used in policy problems. Corporate responsibility and the moral status of corporations – whether a corporation can be a moral agent, i.e. capable of moral decision-making or have moral agency, i.e. have the said capacity – has been central to some problems addressed in business ethics.

Conceptions of ethics as a branch of inquiry

A view some hold concerning ethics as a branch of inquiry is that it is *autonomous*, i.e. that, in some sense, it follows its own principles. Sometimes, the autonomy of ethics is defended by appeal to the *naturalistic fallacy* or, more generally, the *definist fallacy*. A definist is someone who holds that normative moral terms such as "good" and "right" can be defined in non-normative terms, e.g. a person's interest – in the subjective sense of what the person is interested in, or in the objective sense of what is to the person's advantage or benefit – or God's command. In other words, that there are non-normative characteristics that are good-making or right-making characteristics. This is not to say that whoever is a definist concerning a normative term must also be a definist concerning all other normative terms. The English philosopher G.E. Moore (CE 1873–1958), for example, was a definist regarding the term "right," but not regarding the term "good."

Usually, definists are also ethical naturalists; that is, they hold that normative moral terms can be defined by means of terms denoting natural properties, e.g. as in the case of ethical hedonism, that of being conducive to pleasure. *Ethical naturalism* – sometimes in the form of evolutionary ethics – is characteristically contrasted with *ethical conventionalism*, the view that the done thing – the mores in a particular group – is the right thing. In this context, discussion of such concepts as co-operation and competition, their role in social life and whether they have an evolutionary basis are central.

Ethical conventionalism is a form of *ethical relativism* (sometimes also called normative relativism), the view that such things as actions are right and wrong, traits are good and bad, and policies are justified and unjustified depending on what individuals believe (which is a version of *ethical subjectivism* or *moral subjectivism*), on what groups predominantly believe (i.e. ethical conventionalism), and the like. An example of ethical conventionalism is the view that, when in Rome, one should do as the Romans do. An example of ethical subjectivism has been *situation ethics*, a somewhat anti-theoretical doctrine fashionable in Europe and English- and French-speaking North America between the mid-1940s and the 1960s. It is the view that what one should do is entirely dependent on the particular context or circumstances in which one must decide, and there are no general guidelines or universal moral laws or principles that can be of any help in making such a decision.

Ethical relativism is sometimes thought supported by the obvious fact of *cultural relativism* (also called *descriptive relativism*, *cultural relativity*, and *ethical relativity*), i.e. that morals vary between individuals and mores vary between groups. However, this cultural fact does not by itself entail ethical relativism. For differences in morals and mores are superficial and often involve agreement on deeper moral principles or, at least, on the belief that the points of disagreement are open to assessment on the basis of reasons, i.e., in this sense, objective. At any rate, ethical relativism is itself a form of ethical skepticism – the view that there are hardly any, or hardly any knowable, ethical truths or, as in *ethical nihilism*, that there are none.

The German philosopher Arthur Schopenhauer (CE 1788–1860), for example, came close to holding ethical nihilism in his ethics of pessimism, where the only value judgment retaining validity concerns renunciation. Partly influenced by and reacting against Schopenhauer, the German philosopher Friedrich Nietzsche (CE 1844–1900) argued for the stronger view that traditional ways of thinking – from the belief in God to all metaphysical and religious interpretations of the world and ourselves – were untenable because expressions of *slave/herd morality*: the social devices whereby the weak and mediocre defend themselves and retaliate against stronger, higher forms of human life. Nietzsche argued this situation faced humans with a radical form of ethical nihilism and, indeed, value nihilism, because it concerned all – ethical and non-ethical – values. Some of Nietzsche's interpreters see this as only a moment, the negative nihilism moment in Nietzsche's thought, and argue that he also proposed *positive nihilism*. This was a form of nihilism that led to a transvaluation of all values, through an affirmation of life that involved a version of ethical naturalism understood in evolutionary terms and aimed at the development of a master morality or morality of a higher humanity. Such morality was creative, risk-taking, and enhancing of cultural life by analogy with the manner in which such enhancement is brought about in the artistic life.

Sometimes, philosophers argue for restricted versions of ethical nihilism. For example, the contemporary philosopher J.L. Mackie argues that though moral judgments, i.e. statements about particular actions, policies, practices, institutions, or traits of character, can be supported by appeal to reasons, the principles on which these reasons are based are totally subjective and arbitrary. That is, ethical relativism arises at the theoretical level in the form of an *error theory* that denies the existence of any moral facts or properties at the level of moral principles and laws. Among those who draw the ethics–metaethics distinction (see above), this form of relativism is sometimes called *metaethical relativism*.

Ethical relativism is the opposite of *ethical objectivism* or *moral objectivism*, the view that such things as actions are right and wrong, traits are good and bad, and policies are justified and unjustified, at least partly independently of what individuals or groups believe. Some versions of ethical objectivism are committed to the notion of objective rightness, i.e. the feature of an action whereby the action is right independently of whether anyone believes it is right, by contrast with the action's subjective rightness, i.e. the feature of an action whereby the action is believed (or justifiably believed) to be objectively right.

There are various kinds of ethical objectivism. *Strong ethical objectivism*, sometimes called *ethical absolutism*, holds that there is one true set of moral rules, laws, and principles. While *weak ethical objectivism* holds that

there is a core set of moral rules, laws, and principles that are shared by actual moralities and universally valid, while recognizing that there are areas of conduct – e.g. sexual mores – where no moral rules, laws, or principles are universally valid.

One version of ethical absolutism is *ethical* or *moral rigorism*: the view that some ethical injunctions, e.g. the injunction not to lie, hold invariably and regardless of the circumstances. One can reject moral rigorism without rejecting ethical absolutism, e.g. by holding that, though there are invariant moral laws or principles, their injunctions vary depending on the circumstances. This amounts to acknowledging the fact of ethical relativity and its moral significance, without accepting ethical relativism. One tradition falling under this category is the previously mentioned ethical or moral objectivism, the view that there are moral truths that can be objectively determined.

Some versions of moral objectivism exemplify *moral realism*, i.e. the view that there are moral facts and properties, that statements about them can be known, and that some of our beliefs about moral facts and properties are both true and justifiable. Some ethical realists uphold *moral rationalism*, i.e. hold that moral facts and properties are known *entirely* (some would merely say *primarily*) through reason. Among proponents of moral rationalism (i.e. among moral rationalists), there are also ethical or moral intuitionists or proponents of *ethical* or *moral intuitionism*, i.e. those who hold that at least some truths of ethics are known through intuition. Various versions of moral intuitionism have been formulated. One is part of Scottish common-sense philosophy, a comprehensive philosophical position formulated by Thomas Reid (CE 1710–96), whose central tenet is that perception involves both sensation and intuitively known general principles or truths – concerning external objects as well as morality – that are available to all human beings and, together with sensations, yield knowledge. Also, the English philosopher Harold Arthur Prichard (CE 1871–1974), who founded the Oxford School of intuitionism, argued that only by direct intuitions can we tell what we ought to do. While the English philosopher G.E. Moore (CE 1873–1958) held that we intuit non-natural properties such as goodness. And the Scottish philosopher W.D. Ross (CE 1877–1971) advocated intuitive induction, a process whereby one goes from particular instances to moral principles. Other moral realists, however, disagree with moral rationalism and hold the *moral sense theory of ethics*, according to which moral feelings of pleasure or pain are part of moral perceptions, indicative of a person's character, and a crucial component of coming to know moral facts and properties (further specifications or narrower versions of this approach focus, for example, on a sense of justice or a sense of fairness). Still other moral objectivists are ethical naturalists (see above).

There are many characterizations of both the definist fallacy and its narrower form, the naturalistic fallacy. To expand on what was previously indicated, the *definist fallacy* can be characterized as falsely presupposing that normative or, more generally, value terms – e.g. good, a feature of good items, or the good, the items that are good – can be defined in non-normative or non-value terms – e.g. in terms of interests – or, on a stronger version, that value terms are definable at all. While the *naturalistic fallacy* (of which there are many interpretations and versions) can be characterized as falsely presupposing that a statement of fact involves or entails a statement of value.

There has been a great deal of controversy, not only concerning what the characterization of these fallacies should be, but whether they are actually fallacies. For example, the English philosopher G.E. Moore proposed the *open-question test* or *open-question argument*, according to which, if the question "But is it good?" makes sense of any such definition of good, then the definition is unfounded, and since the question always makes sense, any such definition is unfounded. However, this may be interpreted to show that a fallacy is involved or, alternatively, that a central characteristic of moral discourse is its *openness* (i.e. that its statements are always open to scrutiny), so that, even if statements of fact can entail statements of value, and arguments establishing it can be highly confirmed, moral discourse about it never achieves closure.

This makes room for a type of objectivity that is neither *personal* (i.e. not objectivity as a person's detachment), nor *institutional* (i.e. not objectivity as an institution's practice of omitting to bias reports, as in omitting to editorialize the news). This third type is objectivity in the *social testing* sense, whereby reports, statements, ideas, and any social arrangements affected by them are open to critical scrutiny by anyone, and, in addition, the arrangements are open to the test of actual social practice and interaction with anyone. That is, in the social-testing sense, objectivity is the fact that it is always possible for anyone to give reasons for or against reports, statements, ideas, and any social arrangements affected by them, as well as test these arrangements in actual social practice.

Who's to tell?
A question that characteristically arises in both practical and theoretical ethics is: "Who is to tell whether actions are right or wrong, motives good or bad, and the like?" In practical ethics, this question is sometimes addressed by appeal to an institutional reviewing board such as an *ethics committee*, especially where hard cases – i.e. cases where the answers are not easy to find – and hard choices – i.e. choices that are difficult because of the sacrifices involved in each available option – are concerned. Used most often in health care ethics, this sort of organization – often patterned on the ideal notion of a jury system – has been extended to other areas, such as the ethical evaluation or moral evaluation of science and technology policy. In general, *ethical evaluation* or *moral evaluation* is an assessment based on ethical or moral rules, laws, principles, or other criteria. In institutional reviewing board cases, the said evaluation relies on conceptions of character ethics, as well as on other traditional theoretical approaches aimed at dealing with the valid moral question: "Who's to tell what is right, wrong, good, bad, justified or not?"

With regard to this question, some theorists simply answer that God is to tell. On this, the *divine-command theory*, moral obligations are, or are based on, God's commands. By contrast, other – non-supernatural – theories appeal to crucial moral concepts instead, most notably those of a *disinterested judge*, a *disinterested observer*, and an *ideal observer*, whose characteristic features – such as fairness, and authoritativeness on the matters at hand – are to help in identifying who should tell. Still others – e.g. philosophers who advocate some form of feminist ethics – question simplistic or lopsided appeals to the notion of moral competence sometimes also called moral sense and tied to the notion of common morality. Instead, they argue that members of given groups – e.g. lesbians in lesbian ethics approaches – are to tell at least concerning ethical matters of significance to them.

Types of ethical theories

Of course, whoever turns out to be in the group of people who are to tell could benefit from general guidelines for addressing the problems about which they are supposed to make decisions. This is where traditional ethical criteria, standards, rules, laws, and principles, which are at the core of many, if not all, ethical theories, are crucial. There are various kinds of such theories. Three prominent types – teleological, deontological, and character ethics theories – will be discussed next.

Teleological theories

Consequentialist or *teleological* theories of ethics (where teleological is the adjective corresponding to *teleology*, which is derived from the Greek *telos*, i.e. "end," and *logos*, i.e. "discourse," "reason," or "body of knowledge") hold that whether actions are right or wrong; persons or their features are good or bad; and policies, practices, and institutions are justified or unjustified, is solely or crucially based on the value of the consequences or, in ordinary terms, the happiness or felicity they bring about or lead to.

There are various notions of happiness. Some understand happiness to be *pleasure and the absence of pain*, which, when considered to be the overriding aim of conduct, is the doctrine of *hedonism*. Others consider happiness to be the satisfaction of any wants or desires – typically understood as dispositions to have, do, or experience something – without reducing their objects to pleasure or pain and, on some versions, without their having only self-regarding objects. Still others – typically

Aristotelians – consider happiness to be *eudaimonia* ("flourishing"), which, when considered to be the overriding aim of conduct, amounts to *eudaemonism*, which, like hedonism, has an ethical version, *ethical eudaemonism*, and a psychological version, *psychological eudaemonism*. It should be noted that, unlike modern notions of happiness, eudaemonia is objective, i.e. it is a kind of mental activity; it has little to do with subjective states of contentment; and constitutes the life-goal of human development.

Besides, there are those that consider happiness to be *well-being*, i.e. a combination of health, prosperity, and satisfaction of ordinary wants or desires. Also, there are those who consider happiness to be supreme happiness or *bliss*, a notion that usually carries religious connotations and then is used as synonymous with *beatitude*. Whatever one's position about these doctrines, they share the view that happiness is good or the good or, as the Greek philosophers called it, *agathon*. They also exemplify the concept of an overriding reason or, alternatively, as some have argued, the concept of overridingness as a feature of moral judgments. For on the views just discussed, other considerations are overriden by those of happiness.

Consequentialist theories make room for all these conceptions of happiness. Hence, there are various kinds of consequentialist theories or consequentialism. One is *ethical egoism*, which should not be confused with *psychological egoism*, the psychological doctrine that any individual in fact acts so as to maximize his or her own balance of favorable over unfavorable consequences. A characteristic version of ethical egoism holds that the consequences which matter for their own sake concern the individual's self-interest, i.e. are the consequences for the individual assessing prospective actions, policies, or features of persons, while the consequences for others count only instrumentally for the sake of the said individual. *Enlightened ethical egoism*, a version of egoism that involves assessing consequences in the long run, especially as it concerns the long-run consequences to the agent of taking advantage of others, amounts to what is traditionally called *prudence*. In this sense, it is sometimes equated with self-interest in a narrow sense of the term where self-interest contrasts with *selfishness*, which is not enlightened and can be irrational. A form of ethical egoism was held by the German philosopher Max Stirner (CE 1806–56), who argued that a union of egoists could have strength while preserving individual freedom. Yet, against Stirner's claim that this would not increase conflict, the rule of aiming at dominating others would institute conflict as a rule, i.e. even when avoidable, and increase it, e.g. in the arms race and analogous situations.

Another form of consequentialism is *altruism*, where the consequences that matter are those affecting others. Still another is UTILITARIANISM, according to which the consequences that matter are those affecting the common good, i.e. the general well-being of those affected by them.

The principle involved in altruism, as well as that involved in utilitarianism is a principle of *beneficence*, also called a principle of *benevolence*, by extension from the background attitudes and traits involved, which are forms of benevolence. These principles constitute positive versions of the associated theories, in that they aim at bringing about good. By contrast, they are principles of *non-maleficence* in the negative versions that only aim at avoiding harm or misery. Some further subdivisions are those of *act-utilitarianism*, where the consequences of the particular act in question are all that is taken into account in evaluating an act. This theory contrasts with *rule-utilitarianism*, sometimes also called *indirect utilitarianism* or *indirect consequentialism*, where the consequences of generally following the rule of performing a certain act are taken into account to assess the rule, but only rules thus established are used to assess acts regardless of the acts' consequences. Act-utilitarians sometimes accuse rule-utilitarians of *rule fetishism*, i.e. of treating moral rules as fetishes: objects eliciting unquestioning reverence, respect, or devotion. While rule-utilitarians accuse act-utilitarians of immorality in that their views make room, for example, for framing the innocent when this would bring about the greatest happiness of the greatest number.

A notion crucial to all these approaches is

that of the *collective consequences*, i.e. the consequences brought about by the joint occurrence of individually performed actions. They are sometimes called *indirect consequences* – or *side-effects* – and are contrasted with *direct consequences*, i.e. those consequences of an act that are not the result of any contributions by any other acts.

As it is plain by now, there are many versions of utilitarianism. One difference between them concerns the manner in which the value of the consequences is determined. In the earlier version of utilitarianism formulated by the English philosopher Jeremy Bentham (CE 1748–1832), they were assessed by means of the *hedonic calculus*, also called *felicific calculus*. It involved assessing – to the extent possible, measuring – the intensity, duration, certainty or uncertainty, propinquity or remoteness, fecundity, purity, and extent of the pleasures or pains constituting the consequences. That is, Bentham's version of utilitarianism was committed to ethical hedonism, i.e. the doctrine that pleasure, including the absence of pain, is the only good. As stated, this should not be confused with the psychological doctrine called psychological hedonism, according to which agents in fact pursue only pleasure, including the absence of pain.

Later versions focused on the good or happiness understood in a variety of ways, from the satisfaction of personal preferences (that are merely subjective) to the satisfaction of needs (where the concept of need is understood as objective, somehow based on humans' nature and aims, and its satisfaction measurable by reference to census data), thus significantly broadening utilitarianism. In any case, such calculations of happiness involve, first, *intrapersonal utility comparison*, i.e., briefly, comparison of the various degrees in which alternative consequences would tend to make a given person happier or unhappier. Second, since in most ethical problems of significance, more than one person is affected, the said calculations also involve *interpersonal utility comparison*, i.e., briefly, comparison of the various degrees in which alternative consequences would tend to make affected persons happier or unhappier than others.

In addition to the previous types of

utilitarianism, there is *ideal utilitarianism*, the view that certain things such as knowledge or being autonomous are good whether or not people value them. In this connection, the English philosopher William Paley (CE 1743–1805) formulated *theological utilitarianism*, according to which the common good is the will of God and, in the long run, egoism and altruism would coincide.

At a worldlier level, there is also a version of utilitarianism often used in business and policy making: *cost–benefit analysis*, whereby the desirable consequences of each course of action are quantified in monetary terms thus becoming benefits, the undesirable consequences are quantified thus becoming costs, the benefit over cost ratio is calculated for each course of action, and that action (or, if there is more than one, any of these) is chosen that has the highest ratio. This is sometimes also called *cost-effectiveness analysis*. Most often, however, the latter expression denotes a procedure whereby the aims to be pursued are decided independently of benefit-to-cost ratios – e.g. by selecting those that accord with principles of justice (see JUSTICE) – and, only then, cost–benefit analysis is used to select the cheapest way of reaching those aims. In this latter sense, cost-effectiveness analysis is a combined, not strictly utilitarian, approach.

An economic notion that has played a significant role in ethics – especially in utilitarianism – and the philosophy of economics is that of *expected utility*. This is a notion understood in such ways as likely, probable or, at least, not unlikely satisfaction of demand, and, in particular, that of *declining marginal utility*, i.e. that equal marginal increments of money tend to bring about less satisfaction – less utility, less happiness – to people, the more money these people have. Often, this notion is used to argue for equality of income distribution.

Finally, there have been attempts at formulating versions of utilitarianism that do not rely on the hedonic calculus or, for that matter, on any calculus at all. Instead, as previously indicated, they rely on census information to determine whether alternative courses of action being assessed would satisfy a minimum standard of provisions characterized by the needs of those affected.

Deontological theories

An alternative approach to ethical theory is *deontological*, i.e. based not on the value of consequences, but on features that such things as actions, persons, practices, institutions, and traits have apart from the value of their consequences. Persons, for example, are said to have *dignity* because of the mere fact that they are persons, hence to be worthy of esteem, respect, or honor and, accordingly, to have rights suitable to this status, e.g. the right of privacy. An example of this is claimed to be the right of women to their own bodies and to make choices entirely on their own and without outside interference about whether or not to have abortions. In this context, discussions of self-esteem or self-respect and their relation to self-determination or *autonomy* (from the Greek *autos* ("self") and *nomos* ("law"), meaning "self-rule"), or *positive freedom*, i.e. the ability to control one's own choices without being carried away by passion or desire, have received much attention from philosophers.

The notion of autonomy has a special – stronger – meaning in *Kantian ethics*. For Kantian philosophy is deontological, i.e. its practical principle or principle to assess conduct, the *categorical imperative*, focuses on features of the actions it serves to evaluate, not on the value of their consequences. These features involve an unconditional end, autonomy, a concept Kantian philosophy uses to characterize ethical theories whose principles derive from sources in the person as involving autonomy or being autonomous. They are contrasted with those that are heteronomous or have *heteronomy*, from the Greek *heteros* ("other") and *nomos* ("law"), meaning "the rule of another," by which Kantian philosophy means that their principles derive from sources outside the person. These typically involve some *hypothetical imperative(s)*; that is, principles or maxims or actions involving conditional ends, not, as the categorical imperative, an unconditional one. In this context, it should be mentioned that the German theologian Paul Tillich (CE 1886–1965) recommended *theonomy* (from the Greek *theos*, i.e. "God," and *nomos*, i.e. "rule" or "law") or *theonomous reason*, i.e. the state of being subject to the rule of God, because it is founded on being itself.

From the standpoint of Kantian ethics, however, theonomy is a form of heteronomy.

Discussions aimed at assessing the relative merits of right-based versus duty-based theories have sometimes focused on the relations between rights and duties, and have given rise to various *correlativity* theses concerning the correlativity of rights and duties. A *duty* or moral duty is a requirement of morality. Some are *perfect* duties or *strict* duties – e.g. the duty to keep my promise to return your ten dollars tomorrow – in that the object and circumstances for the performance of these duties are definite. A perfect duty need not involve only a performance. It can also involve an omission, say, the duty to omit divulging a specific piece of sensitive information.

Others duties are *imperfect* duties (e.g. the duty to give to charity), in that their objects and circumstances are indefinite. Other distinctions are: *negative* duty, i.e. the duty to omit an act, versus *positive* duty, i.e. the duty to perform an act; *prima facie* duty, i.e. what appears to be a duty, versus *actual* duty, i.e. what in fact, in the circumstances, is a duty.

Another consideration involved in assessing the relative merits of right-based versus duty-based theories concerns the applicability of rights versus that of duties. For example, there is little argument about adults having duties concerning infants. Yet, it is a matter of debate whether there are *rights of children*, given that children cannot claim them. Of course, a *guardian* or a *trustee* – i.e., in general, a person, usually one of a group of persons, appointed to administer the affairs of another person, or of such organizations as a company and an institution – could and does often take care of claiming the rights for a child. Yet, this makes the right-based approach more cumbersome than the duty-based-approach – a non-decisive shortcoming, but nonetheless a shortcoming of the theory.

Duties may conflict with other practical considerations, some non-moral (e.g. inclination), which sometimes moves us to do the opposite of our duty; others moral, such as loyalty and mercy, which sometimes move us to do the opposite of what duties of justice require. In the latter cases, we may go ahead and do what justice requires; but even if we do, there remains a moral residue of regret about the unfortunate circumstances that may lead to the moral cost of sacrificing loyalty or mercy to duty. This is not, or not a well-grounded moral residue of guilt, because we did our duty. Yet, there is a residue that undermines our happiness even if what really mattered took precedence in our actions. The latter is one way in which the notion of *moral luck* comes into play in ethics. Besides being prompted, as described, by circumstance, it can also come into play through the ability we happen to have to try to do our duty, and to succeed in doing our duty – an ability we do not develop entirely as a matter of choice. In these regards, some human beings are simply luckier than others, and the relevant notion of luck is moral luck because it makes a moral difference in action. In addition, there are moral actions that, perhaps motivated also by loyalty, or by love, go beyond the call of duty. That is, though morally admirable, these actions are not required by duty (perfect or imperfect), but merely recommended or encouraged by moral ideals. They are called *meritorious* or *supererogatory*. Here again, a certain kind of moral luck may be relevant concerning the circumstances which make such actions possible and the personal characteristics that make it possible for some – but not just any – persons to perform them. In this sense, the notion of moral luck is akin to the religious conception of *grace*.

As for rights, they are conceived as either the other side of the coin of a duty (if I have a duty to return your ten dollars, you have a right to my returning your ten dollars to you), or involve more than that. For example, consider the concept of a citizen, i.e. someone whose dignity as a person in a civil society establishes a variety of entitlements or moral rights or moral claims – from that not to be wantonly killed to that of tap-dancing in his or her property. In this sense, a person is said to have a right (i.e. a moral right or a moral claim) when the person is free to exercise it, everyone else is required to omit interfering with this exercise, and – if a right is more than simply the other side of a duty – the person is entitled to claim that none thus interfere. In a manner somewhat analogous to the distinction between perfect and imperfect duties, the Dutch humanist Hugo Grotius (CE 1583–1645) distinguished between *perfect rights*, i.e. the precise rights of justice that can be enforced, and *imperfect rights*, i.e. imprecise rights that cannot be enforced. As with duties, a right can be a *prima facie* right, i.e. what appears to be a right, or an *actual* right or *absolute* right, i.e. what in fact, in the circumstances, is a right.

These notions, like many concepts in ethics, were based on the *jus naturale* or *natural law*: an objective set of moral norms governing all humans and somehow built into the very structure of the universe (on the laws of nature), depending on the particular writers or schools involved, through such things as a supernatural legislator, through features shared by all humans, or through the structure of human communities. The natural law is the basis of any *natural right*, e.g. the right to life and the right to liberty, as well as of any natural duty correlated to a natural right, e.g. the duty not to kill or take someone's freedom away, unless there are overriding reasons to the contrary, e.g. self-defense. Besides natural rights and duties, there are *acquired* rights and duties, e.g. those created by making a promise; *special* rights and duties, e.g. those created by the parent–child or teacher–student relations; and, some argue, also *welfare* rights, i.e. those to a minimum standard of provisions, and their correlative duties. Some thinkers have also talked of *inalienable* rights, i.e. rights that cannot be transferred to others, by contrast with *alienable* rights, i.e. rights that can be so transferred, thereby being lost by the transferee. On this view, *property* rights (i.e. rights in or to possessing, enjoying, and disposing of something), for example, are alienable, while the rights to be treated with respect, and not to be murdered, are considered inalienable.

When rights are violated, people are sometimes said to be treated unfairly or discriminated against. This implies some notion of *justice*. A traditional one is the *golden rule* – do unto others as you would have them do unto you – whose intent, philosophers have argued, is to formulate the notion involved in the principle of *formal justice*: No one should be treated differently from anyone else, despite the various differences between individuals, except when one or more of these differences constitutes a good reason for doing so. Of course, the question arises: "What reasons are good reasons for treating people differently?" Even consequentialist principles can be seen as answers to this question, but, among deontological principles, the answers come in the form of principles of *substantial justice*. For example, a principle of substantial justice is involved when one argues that people can be discriminated against by not being treated as they deserve given their qualifications – a failure according to the principle of *compensatory justice*, one of whose versions says that everyone should be treated in accordance with what they deserve or their merit given their qualifications. Another principle of substantial justice is involved when one argues that people are discriminated against when they are not allotted their due share of opportunities – a failure according to the principle of *distributive justice*, of which there also are various versions, e.g. that of justice as fairness described below. Various forms of discrimination have been identified and described such as *ageism* or age discrimination (based on age), *racism* or racial discrimination (based on race), and *sexism* or sexual discrimination (based on sex). These can be displayed in conduct constituting behavioral discrimination (as in a waiter's refusing to serve a customer because of the customer's race), embedded in the structure of institutions constituting institutional discrimination – as in the case of institutional racism embedded in former apartheid institutions in South Africa – or entrenched in people's character constituting attitudinal discrimination – a form of prejudice. Various views and movements have developed to oppose them, such as the civil rights movement, and *ableism*, the view and movement that opposes discrimination against individuals suffering from any form of disability. These are generally advanced on grounds of fairness, of which various principles have been formulated. Highly influential among them are those formulated by the contemporary philosopher John Rawls. Briefly, the first, the *liberty principle*, says: everyone is entitled to as much liberty as is compatible with equal liberty for all.

In this regard, the notion of *tolerance* or *toleration* (from the Greek *tlenai*, i.e. "to bear" or "endure") is relevant. Some philosophers have set the limits of toleration where one individual's liberty threatens that of another. Of course, the question arises: "On what basis should it be decided which liberty should be restricted?" Addressing this question is a crucial purpose of Rawls's second principle, the *difference principle*. It says: differences are justified when they are to the advantage of each. In this context, among notions associated – sometimes nearly synonymous – with fairness are *equality*, whether formal, substantive, or of opportunity, and the more flexible notions of *equity* and *equitability*. However, they all share an emphasis on the lot of *each* particular individual, not merely, as in utilitarian approaches, on society overall (see JUSTICE).

In this regard, some would argue that giving precedence to members of traditionally disadvantaged groups in hirings, promotions, or school admissions – i.e. using preferential-treatment approaches – is justified because it works to the advantage of each. Of course, those individuals who think they are thereby being put at a disadvantage concerning their chances for being hired, promoted, or admitted to schools argue that preferential treatment is partial, a form of *partiality*, i.e. a form of reverse discrimination, because in no way to the advantage of each. In addition, they will often adopt the standpoint of compensatory justice and emphasize merit based on qualifications as taking precedence over all other considerations. Anyone taking such a position is a meritarian, i.e. a partisan of *meritarianism*, the view that, as a matter of justice, merit and only merit should be used in deciding who is to occupy what positions in society. If a society were entirely structured along meritarianism's criteria, it would be a *meritocracy*.

Whether concerning merit or not, the problem often arises of how to determine what right or duty takes precedence in given circumstances when two or more conflict. Here, *balancing* principles and reasons come into play. Their central function is to serve to determine priorities in given circumstances

and, since priority questions also arise concerning the relative value of consequences of alternative courses of action, balancing principles and reasons not only play a role in deontological theories, but also can, and – some argue – must, play a role in combined theories, i.e. theories that combine deontological and consequentialist considerations.

An example of a balancing principle is the *principle of double effect*. Traditionally, this principle says that one may act in ways that foreseeably lead to deadly results, so long as: first, one's action has a good result; second, one did not intend the deadly result to occur as an end or as a means; third, one did not bring about the good result by means of the deadly one; and fourth, the good result was sufficiently significant to outweigh the deadly one. The modern modification occurs in the third and fourth conditions. In the case of abortion, this means that the aim of saving the mother's life can be achieved so long as one does not intend to kill the fetus, even if it has been foreseen that this will happen. Also, weighing the life of a mother against that of the fetus is no longer required (on the grounds that weighing incommensurable goods is impossible).

Another notion that cuts across all types of theories and is often involved in health care ethics and, in general, practical ethics arguments is that of the *best-interest standard*, according to which, for example, health care practitioners should make decisions informed by what is in a patient's best interest. This is usually supposed to be established on the basis of such evidence as that provided by people who can form an informed judgment or opinion, and can make an informed decision on the matter, e.g. those who know the patient closely or who were present in the process leading to advanced directives formulating the patient's wishes.

Character ethics theories

Still another approach is that of *character ethics* or *agent-based ethics*, or *virtue ethics*, which focuses primarily on the kind of persons we should be, and character traits, attitudes, and motives for action we should have, and assesses actions and policies from the standpoint of what those persons would judge or do. In this connection, some authors have used the term *ethology* (from the Greek *ethos* – "character," "habit," "custom" – and *logos* – in this case, "study") to denote the study of character from a primarily descriptive and explanatory – not, as in character ethics, primarily normative – standpoint. This is useful for starters. For example, one may study the similarities, differences, and grounds for each, if any, in guilt-centered cultures versus those in shame-centered cultures. One might for example think that the dominant United States culture is guilt-centered when it comes to morals and mores, while many a Latin American culture is shame-based when it comes to morals and mores. In describing and evaluating these differences, it may be useful to keep in mind that, put humorously, in guilt-centered cultures people are morally inner-directed: they feel guilty or bad about their wrong actions, while they go on shamelessly performing them; while in shame-centered cultures people are morally other-directed: they feel ashamed or embarrassed by their wrong actions, while they go on performing them without remorse.

In traditional moralities, that of the Akan people (in Ghana) is an example of character ethics with its emphasis on *suban*, i.e. character. In philosophy, Aristotelian ethics is an example of character ethics or virtue ethics, or virtue theory. It crucially distinguishes between *extrinsic* or *instrumental* desires (desires of items for the sake of something else), and *intrinsic* desires (desires of items for their own sake). It holds that the desire for happiness is intrinsic and the goal of life, and characterizes happiness dynamically, as an activity of the soul whereby humans flourish by acting in accordance with the mean: a form of *harmony* (from the Greek *harmos* – a "fitting" or "joining"), lying somewhere between excess and defect in the display of such traits as benevolence, generosity, and courage. It accordingly is an ethics of self-realization that, in the Greek context where individuals were hardly conceivable outside of the body-politic where they developed, involved social as well as individual concerns.

What helps or hinders their acting this way is a *hexis* (from the Greek *hexo*, "to have," or "to be disposed"), i.e. a disposition or state that is not a mere passion (*pathe*) one cannot

control, nor a faculty (*dunamis*) of the soul, but a state of character whereby one makes a decision. The development of *phronesis*, i.e. practical wisdom, helps in determining *the mean*. The corresponding practice is the exercise of the virtues that, for the founder of Aristotelianism, the Greek philosopher Aristotle (384–22 BCE), since it is done for its own sake, cannot be theoretical knowledge or even the knowledge involved in *poiēsis*, i.e. production, an activity characteristic of crafts.

An analogous doctrine of the mean can also be found in Chinese philosophy. It was formulated in arguably the most philosophical of ancient Chinese documents, the *Chung-Yung* (*Doctrine of the Mean*), which already existed in the early Hahn dynasty (206 BCE–CE 220) and was brought into prominence by the Chinese Confucian philosopher Chu Hsi (CE 1130–1200). According to the Chinese *Doctrine of the Mean*, the ultimate principle is rather metaphysical in that it is said to be *ch'eng* (or *sincerity*) because it is totally beyond illusion and delusion, and one's conduct should strike harmony: the appropriate mean between deficiency and excess.

In modern times, the British philosopher Bishop Joseph Butler (CE 1692–1752) characterized happiness or *self-love* in terms of harmony: as the harmonious satisfaction of one's basic desires, where these basic desires need not be narrowly self-regarding but include, e.g. the desire to help another person (which gives a not merely self-regarding meaning to self-love or self-interest). At any rate, it is in the context of character ethics where the often-used notion of personal *integrity*, and the related notion of a *fault of character* (which constitutes a breakdown of a person's integrity) belong. It is also in this context that the notion of moral agency is studied in terms of moral development understood as character development or, alternatively or concurrently, as the development of conscience or the characteristic whereby moral considerations such as moral principles are used to make moral decisions.

This is the subject matter of *moral psychology*, which also aims at establishing the moral status of persons as moral agents rather than moral patients, in terms of their decision-making traits: rationality, understood as the ability to deliberate and make decisions on the basis of reasons; moral sense or moral sensitivity, or conscience, which in medieval thought was called *synderesis* and *scintilla conscientiae*, i.e. spark of conscience, understood as the ability to tell right from wrong, perceive moral significant facts and features, and judge or decide on the basis of, and in accordance with, sound moral considerations; and fortitude or at least practical rationality, i.e. the ability to do what one decided to do as a result of moral deliberation.

These features are thought valuable and worth developing by a variety of thinkers. Sometimes, movements develop on this basis. An example is the Moral Rearmament Movement or Buchmanism, or the Oxford Group that gained influence in the United States and the United Kingdom in the early twentieth century. It was founded by the United States Lutheran minister Buchman (CE 1878–1961) as an international movement aimed at promoting universal brotherhood through a commitment to an objective moral system largely patterned on moral views expressed in the Gospels.

A topic of certain interest in connection with character ethics and the notion of harmony or balance is that of *humor*. The concept derives from the four-humor theory, i.e. the view that there are four basic bodily fluids – blood, phlegm, black bile, and yellow bile – and that health is maintained in a balance between these. This theory was held, for example, by the Greek physician and philosopher Galen (CE 129–*c.* 215) and, through his influence on the Greco-Roman world and the Arabic tradition, was commonly held in the Western world even after the discoveries of the seventeenth century, and, indeed, far into the nineteenth century. At any rate, the concept was extended to such characteristics of people as being in good humor, being of ill humor, and being humorless, and prompted questions a variety of questions: "What makes a person funny?" "What is it for a person to be witty?" "What is it to have a sense of humor?" Answers to these questions have not been thoroughly discussed in philosophy, perhaps because they are more complex involving matters of aesthetics, ethics, the philosophy of language, the philo-sophy of art, and the philosophy of mind. At any rate, it is significant to notice that one can be witty – i.e. amusing or clever in perception and expression – and, yet, have no sense of humor, because one takes oneself or one's ideas, ideals, or causes too seriously, and a central feature of *a sense of humor* is having a balanced, not overly exaggerated, conception of oneself. That is, a sense of humor arguably excludes all traditional forms of what in Ancient Greece was called *hubris*, which meant insolence as involved in excessive pride or self-confidence and arrogance, and which can be found in such things as pompousness, fanaticism, and, first and foremost, egoism, where one takes oneself so seriously that no one else matters except as a means to one's own advantage. Hence, a sense of humor is morally, not just aesthetically, significant.

Combined theories of ethics

The various approaches or theories just discussed can be combined in many ways. An example of a combined theory is that formulated by the contemporary United States philosopher Marcus G. Singer. Like in the deontological theory formulated by the German philosopher Immanuel Kant (CE 1724–1804), the principles in Singer's theory lead one to ask of a particular piece of behavior at issue: "What would happen if everyone did that?" That is, *universality* or *universalizability*, or *generalizability* or *generic consistency*, is crucial for the piece of behavior to be permissible. Indeed, a crucial principle for Singer, the *generalization principle*, arguably states in the active voice what the previously stated principle of formal justice states in the passive voice: what is right (or wrong) for one person is right (or wrong) for any similar person in similar circumstances. However, unlike Kant's, Singer's principles do not stay at the largely formal level, and lead one to consider the value of the consequences of everyone's doing what is at issue. To this end, Singer formulates the *generalization argument*, which also involves the *principle of consequences*: if the consequences of *A*'s doing *x* would be undesirable, then *A* ought not to do *x*. The generalization argument is: if the consequences of everyone's doing *x* would be undesirable, while the consequences of no one's doing *x* would not be, it follows that no one ought to do x without a justifying reason.

This argument and the associated generalization principle have originated much discussion concerning, for example, what features are relevant for establishing the similarity of persons and circumstances, and under what descriptions the generalization argument enjoins or fails to enjoin given actions. Singer has formulated conditions for determining whether or not given descriptions are adequate for generalization purposes. One feature that makes them inadequate is *invertibility*, i.e. where the consequences of doing something are as undesirable as those of not doing it, which indicates the description is too general. Another is *reiterability*, i.e. where the action described is arbitrarily specified as taking place at some particular time, or at some particular place, or by some particular person, or in relation to some particular person or thing, as in "If everyone were to eat at six o'clock, then there would be no one to perform certain essential functions, hence no one ought to eat at six o'clock." This argument is reiterable because one could as well say at seven o'clock or at any and every other time with the same result. Once these conditions that the argument be neither invertible nor reiterable are met, the said principles, as in Kant's theory, are supposed to entail what is not permissible and what is permissible, the latter including a range of alternative courses of action, not necessarily just one. This is why theories such as Kant's and Singer's can be said to provide *limiting conditions* for action rather than, as optimizing forms of consequentialism, required single actions. Accordingly, the former are sometimes called *limiting-conditions theories*.

Challenges against the centrality of universalizability in all moral discourse and moral reasons has been sometimes based on appeals to the belief that personal relations, say, *friendship*, involve clear moral cases where the reasons used by those involved are not of a general nature, but strictly particular. It is argued that a friend could appropriately say, in justifying his or her self-sacrifice for the sake of his or her friend: "I did it for you," while such reasons as "I did it to bring about the greatest happiness of the greatest number" and

"I did it because the consequences of everyone failing to do such a thing would be disastrous" would not be appropriate reasons of friendship. This has prompted a still on-going discussion of the kinds of reasons that can be motives for moral action and whether any justifying reasons can or must always be included among them.

See also: epistemology; justice; philosophy of language; philosophy, sociopolitical; utilitarianism; virtue

Further reading
Broad, C.D. (1971 [1930]) *Five Types of Ethical Theory*, London and New York: Routledge & Kegan Paul and Humanities Press.
Cortina, Adela (1998) *Democracia participativa y sociedad civil: Una ética empresarial*, Santafé de Bogotá, Colombia: Siglo del Hombre Editores.
Gert, Bernard (1996) *Morality and the New Genetics: A Guide for Health Care Providers*, Sudbury, MA and London, UK: Jones and Bartlett Publishers.
Hottois, Gilbert (1990) *Le Paradigme bioéthique: Une éthique pour la technoscience*, Bruxelles: De Boeck.
Jonsen, Albert R. and Toulmin, Stephen Edelston (1988) *The Abuse of Casuistry: A History of Moral Reasoning*, Berkeley: University of California Press.
Lecourt, Dominique (1999) *Contre la peur: de la science à l'éthique, une aventure infinie*, Paris: PUF.
Rogers, A.K. (1971) *Morals in Review*, New York: AMS Press.
Sen, Amartya (1990 [1987]) *On Ethics and Economics*, Oxford: Basil Blackwell.
Singer, Marcus G. (1971 [1961]) *Generalization in Ethics: An Essay in the Logic of Ethics with the Rudiments of a System of Moral Philosophy*, New York: Atheneum.

ethnic cleansing *see* philosophy, sociopolitical

ethnic group *see* culture

ethnicity *see* culture

ethnocentrism *see* culture

ethnography *see* anthropology

ethnology *see* anthropology

ethnomethodology *see* anthropology

euthanasia From the Greek *eu* ("good") and *thanatos* ("death"), this term broadly denotes killing or letting a sick individual die on the grounds that death is better for that individual than staying alive. In an extended sense, the sick individual in question can be a human or a non-human animal; but the controversy about euthanasia typically focuses on euthanizing humans. It should be noted that euthanasia is not the same as, nor does it include, *assisted suicide*. In the latter, the patient ends his or her own death by means of some medication prescribed by a physician or of some other procedure set in motion by the patient. In *euthanasia*, someone other than the patient sets the procedure in motion.

Various distinctions have been drawn in dealing with problems of euthanasia. Notable among them is the active–passive euthanasia distinction. *Active* euthanasia is taking steps to end a sick individual's – typically a patient's – life, while *passive* euthanasia is the omission or termination of the means for prolonging that individual's life. Various questions arise concerning this distinction. First, why is it drawn where it is drawn rather than, for example, considering the termination of life-prolonging means to be active? Second, and most signifi-

cantly, is the active–passive euthanasia distinction morally significant, or is the dying person's good and dignity – even if it involves taking steps to end the person's life – what crucially matters?

Other distinctions drawn in the euthanasia issue are the voluntary–non-voluntary distinction, and the voluntary–involuntary distinction. *Voluntary* euthanasia means that the sick person has consented to having his or her life ended. It contrasts with the wide sense of *non-voluntary* euthanasia: that the sick person has not made the decision. However, this includes both persons who are in no position to consent, and those who, though in a position to consent, do not consent, which leads to distinguishing between involuntary and non-voluntary euthanasia. Though, in this regard, the meaning of these terms is sometimes switched, *involuntary* euthanasia is frequently used to mean that the person's death is brought about over the person's objections, while *non-voluntary* euthanasia is often used to mean that the person's death is brought about when the person is not competent to consent.

Arguments for euthanasia often appeal to the dying person's pain and indignity that death can bring to an end. These are often associated with a variety of claims. One is the claim that insisting on the prolongation of pain is mere sadism. Another is the claim that the right to life understood as one's having a right to do as one pleases with one's life involves the right to die, a right that is often supported on grounds of individual autonomy. A third is the claim that what should be prolonged is not merely life but the quality of life. A fourth is that, if passive euthanasia is accepted, then active euthanasia must be accepted, because there is no real difference between the two. Traditional morality, however, forbids the taking of such a person's life. In addition, some who object to euthanasia on non-traditional grounds often focus on policies permitting euthanasia and argue that, once they are in place, their scope of application risks expansion to an ever-widening group of people. They also argue that, even if no such risk materializes, as a result of the large number of euthanasia cases arising in contemporary society, euthanasia practices will involve a bureaucratization of death and, hence, become perfunctory. They further argue that this prospect is likely given the widespread bureaucratization and perfunctory nature of much health care, say, in the United States, where concerns with health care costs sometimes arguably undermine its quality.

See also: death; ethics; philosophy, socio-political

Further reading

Baird, Robert M. and Rosenbaum, Stuart E. (1989) *Euthanasia: The Moral Issues*, Buffalo, NY: Prometheus Books.

McMillan, Richard C., Engelhardt, H. Tristram, and Spicker, Stuart F. (1987) *Euthanasia and the Newborn: Conflicts Regarding Saving Lives*, Dordrecht and Lancaster: Reidel.

evaluation *see* judgment

evambhātanaya *see* Jainism

Evemerism *see* philosophy of religion

event *see* causal law; metaphysics

everlasting *see* philosophy of religion; metaphysics

evidence *see* justification

evidential reason *see* justification

evidentialism *see* philosophy of religion

evidentiality *see* philosophy of religion

evil *see* ethics; philosophy of religion

evolution From the Latin *e* ("out") and *volvere* ("to roll"), the general idea of evolution can be found in many philosophical traditions, usually when discussing aspects of the problem of the one and the many, and of that of change and permanence. For example, philosophers in India, most notably those in the Sāmkhya School (see HINDUISM), used evolutionary ideas in cosmology, when discussing the relation between Brahman and the development of the universe. So too did, in Greece (see GREEK PHILOSOPHY), Pre-Socratic philosophers – most notably Anaximander (*c.* 612–545 BCE) and Empedocles (*c.* 495–435 BCE) – when discussing orders of progression among living organisms. So too did, to some extent, Democritus (*c.* 460–*c.* 370 BCE) and the Epicureans, when

hypothesizing mechanical atomic processes to explain the formation of increasingly complex entities (see EPICUREANISM). Ideas such as these remained influential until modern times when, for example, the Encyclopedists formulated evolutionary ideas of a materialistic nature (see ENCYCLOPEDISM). The Italian philosopher Giambattista Vico (CE 1668–1774) formulated a spiral version – non-mechanicist – of evolution to explain cultural and historical change (see PHILOSOPHY OF HISTORY). The German philosopher Johann Gottfried von Herder (CE 1776–1841) – one of the most notable representatives of romanticism and the *Sturm und Drang* (see CANON) – suggested that evolution depends on adaptation, and formulated a notion of progress implying that higher and later stages depended on lower and earlier ones. Like Herder, the French philosopher Auguste Comte (CE 1798–1857) – who, by contrast with Herder, was the leading representative of positivism – applied evolutionary ideas to the study of cultural and historical change, suggesting that the highest and latest stage was scientific (see POSITIVISM).

As for the modern concept of evolution in strictly biological terms, it has at least two senses. In a narrow sense, this term denotes the processes described by the theories of organic evolution proposed by the British scientist Charles Darwin (CE 1809–82) and others, i.e. by theories that, in a narrow sense, are called *Darwinism*. In a broader sense, evolution denotes the processes described by those views influenced by Darwin's theory. These are also, in a broader sense, called Darwinism. That is, in this broader sense, Darwinism includes the views of the English naturalist Alfred R. Wallace (CE 1823–1913), the English philosopher Herbert Spencer (CE 1820–1903), the English biologist and philosopher T.H. Huxley (CE 1825–95), the German biologist and philosopher Ernst Haeckel (CE 1834–1919), the United States sociologist William Graham Sumner (CE 1840–1910), and, arguably, the United States pragmatic philosophers Charles Sanders Peirce (CE 1839–1914) and John Dewey (CE 1859–1952).

At the core of Darwinism is the view that biological species evolve primarily through chance variation and natural selection. Darwin talked of chance variation, not to indicate that variations were not caused, but to contrast his views with those of the French naturalist Jean Baptiste Pierre Antoine de Monet de Lamarck (CE 1744–1829). According to the Lamarckian conception of evolution, or Lamarckism, there is a general correlation between the variations an organism needs and those it has. Indeed, Lamarck, like most evolutionary thinkers at Darwin's time, thought that the evolution of species was induced by the environment. By contrast, Darwin thought that all sorts of variations occur, but the organisms that proliferate are the *fittest*, i.e. those that succeed in the struggle for existence or struggle for survival because they happen to have features needed to survive and reproduce. Hence, the struggle's outcome is called *survival of the fittest*, a phrase coined by Alfred R. Wallace (CE 1823–1913) and either used soon thereafter or independently coined by Herbert Spencer (CE 1820–1903).

This is a notion of biological survival, which has been extended to other contexts in such phrases as cultural survival and linguistic survival, and their correlates, cultural extinction and linguistic extinction. Indeed, the latter two notions became a growing concern – and prompted calls for the preservation of linguistic diversity – towards the end of the twentieth century, when faster globalization processes increased assimilation pressures on many local cultures leading to a growing demise of their traditional languages.

Going back to Darwin, another contrast between his work and that of his contemporaries is that Darwin was open to the possibility that evolution generally occurred gradually though, in particular cases, it might occur quite rapidly, i.e. in accordance with the Lamarckian evolutionary model. However, many of Darwin's followers were strict gradualists.

Despite these contrasts, after Darwin, an adaptation ceased to be conceived as any trait that makes a species fit to its environment, and became limited to just those features that are crucial for survival and reproduction, and were acquired through natural selection. For example, after Darwin, though the sutures in the skulls of animals that give birth to live offspring facilitate this process in those species whose offspring are born live, they ceased to be considered adaptations, because of their having existed in ancestors that did not give birth to live offspring.

Eventually, Darwinism merged with Mendelian genetics, giving rise to *neo-Darwinism*. The genetic constitution of a living being, its genotype, controls enzymes and in that way controls that being's physical characteristics which, to that extent, are hereditary. Some writers have stressed the importance of these factors, thereby being called hereditarians, and their position being called *hereditarianism*, by contrast with *environmentalist theories*, i.e. theories that stress environmental influences. In discussions of these theories, the notion of *heritability* – a measure of genetic inheritance – is often used. It denotes an estimate of the proportion of a given trait's variation that can be attributed to genetic variation in a population.

At present, except for the naturalistic aspects of this view, all other aspects of neo-Darwinism are being challenged. For example, neo-Darwinists held that any inferior organism, however minutely inferior it might be, was sure to become extinct, and that almost all variations led to extinction. However, current evolutionists acknowledge that many molecular changes may be evolutionarily neutral and, indeed, over 95 percent of an organism's genes may have no function whatsoever.

A related matter is that of the relation of evolutionary processes to features of humans and societies that are not biological in nature. An influential position in this regard is *emergent evolution*: the doctrine that instances of novelty, i.e. novel qualities, not reducible to their antecedents, appear in the course of evolution. Versions of this view were held, among others, by the English scientist and philosopher C. Lloyd Morgan (CE 1852–1936), the United States philosopher (born in Sweden) John Elof Boodin (CE 1869–1950), the British philosopher (born in Australia) Samuel Alexander (CE 1859–1938), and the South African philosopher and statesmen Jan Christian Smuts (CE 1870–1950). In formulating emergent evolution, Alexander used the term *nisus*, which in English means "striving," to denote the evolutionary tendency to move toward higher levels. More radically, the French philosopher Pierre Teilhard de Chardin (CE 1881–1955) argued that evolution extends to the *noosphere* (the sphere of the mind), which, eventually, will lead to world culture and the *omega point*: a hyperpersonal consciousness that will be God in history.

As for the influence of Darwinism on social thought, Spencer was influential in developing a view of how the social world should be, given the facts of evolution. Sometimes, this view is interpreted to involve an unbridled social competition for existence and extreme *laissez-faire* economics. Arguably, Spencer did not uphold this position, even though he used the notion of organismic analogy to attribute features of organisms – understood as biological bodies – to social structures and, indeed, societies, e.g. to argue that, like organisms, societies have birth to death cycles. However, Sumner did: he formulated an initial version of *Social Darwinism* centered on the notion of social survival, according to which the socially fittest – who he identified with the wealthy – survive or become socially powerful.

Evolutionary ideas have been applied to develop such fields of inquiry as evolutionary ethics (see ETHICS) and evolutionary epistemology (see EPISTEMOLOGY). They have also prompted social movements, e.g. the *eugenics* movement, originated by the English scientist Francis Galton (CE 1822–1911), who argued that mental ability was inherited differentially by individuals, groups, and races. This view was associated with eugenic Darwinism: the movement aimed at using evolutionary ideas to improve humans as a matter of national interest, a position that displayed its worst excesses during the rise of fascist and nazi ideologies in the early to mid-twentieth century. At present, eugenics is more modestly described as an applied science aimed at improving genetic potentialities of humans; but it is still highly controversial, especially as it concerns racial relations. It has also been opposed by feminist thinkers on the grounds that the eugenics movement (which, ironically, was called eugenic feminism in nineteenth-century England) opposed any real independence for women as a threat to motherhood.

Arguably, eugenics has at present been significantly replaced by the scientific study of social behavior from a biological standpoint – or *sociobiology* or *social biology* – pioneered by the Harvard biologist Edward O. Wilson in his *Sociobiology: The New Synthesis*, and further developed in *Consilience: The Unity of Knowledge*. This, however, has not brought all related social issues to an end. Even though today's concerns do not focus on governmental eugenic projects, they focus on policies regulating genetic engineering and, most dramatically, the cloning of humans. Some of the questions asked are: "Should this new technology be used only for therapeutic purposes or should it also be permitted for enhancements, say, so that parents can improve the intellectual abilities of their offspring?" "How should the therapeutic-enhancement distinction be drawn?" "Should, for example, the genetically engineered development of a pituitary gland replacement, which helps children attain normal height, be considered therapeutic or an enhancement?"

See also: ethics; explanation; mechanicism; metaphysics

Further reading

Barthélemy-Madaule, Madeleine (1982) *Lamarck, the Mythical Precursor: A Study of the Relations between Science and Ideology*, Cambridge, MA: MIT Press.

Bratchell, D.F. (1986) *The Impact of Darwinism: Texts and Commentary Illustrating Nineteenth Century Religious, Scientific and Literary Attitudes*, Aldershot: Gower.

Dawkins, Richard (1976) *The Selfish Gene*, New York: Oxford University Press.

Lecourt, Dominique (1995) *Lyssenko: Histoire réelle d'une science prolétarienne*, Paris: Presses Universitaires de France.

Sober, Elliot (ed.) (1984) *Conceptual Issues in Evolutionary Biology*, Cambridge, MA and London, UK: MIT Press.

—— (1984) *The Nature of Selection: Evolutionary Theory in Philosophical Focus*, Cambridge, MA and London, UK: MIT Press.

Wilson, Edward Osborne (1998) *Consilience: The Unity of Knowledge*, New York: Knopf, distributed by Random House.

—— (1977 [1975]) *Sociobiology: The New Synthesis*, Cambridge, MA: Belknap Press of Harvard University Press.

evolutionary epistemology *see* epistemology

evolutionary ethics *see* ethics

evolutionary theory *see* evolution

ex cathedra *see* philosophy of religion

ex nihilo *see* creation

exact similarity *see* identity

examination, paradox of the unexpected *see* paradox

exchange *see* philosophy of economics

exciting reason *see* explanation; justification

excluded middle, principle of *see* logic

exclusive disjunction *see* logic

excuse *see* justification

exegesis *see* hermeneutics

exemplar *see* Platonism

exemplarism *see* Platonism

exemplification *see* abstract

exile *see* diaspora

existence *see* phenomenology

existential generalization *see* logic

existential graph *see* logic

existential import *see* metaphysics

existential instantiation *see* logic

existential philosophy *see* existentialism

existential proposition *see* logic

existential quantifier *see* logic

existentialism A philosophical and literary movement that became influential in Europe, especially in France and Germany around mid-twentieth century, and then spread to other geographical areas, for example the Americas, challenging ESSENTIALISM and focusing on the unique situation of the individual – and only in this particularized sense, on the human condition or human predicament – by contrast with abstract universal features of human beings. Existentialism can be said to emphasize the question "Who am I?" instead of the questions "What am I?" or "What is it to be human?"

Some of the views formulated by existentialist thinkers trace back to those of the French thinker Blaise Pascal (CE 1623–62), whose Catholic fideism questioned the power of reason and upheld faith. More recent forerunners are such literary figures as the Russian novelist (and, given the closeness between literature and philosophy in Russian philosophy, philosopher) Feodor Mikhailovich Dostoevsky (CE 1821–81) and the novelist and short-story writer Franz Kafka (CE 1883–1924), born in Prague, which is now in the Czech Republic but was then in Austria-Hungary.

A most important forerunner of existentialism is the Danish devotional, literary, and philosophical writer Søren Aaby Kierkegaard (CE 1813–55), whose Protestant fideism resisted conceptions that placed God or the individual's relation to God in any system; he advocated an irony of indirect communication that rules out alternatives to a void needing revelation, and conceived of life as involving levels that, in ascending importance, are the aesthetic, the ethical, and the religious. He understood the commands of the aesthetic as taking the form of inevitability: "Do what you must," while those of the ethical take the form of a generalized code: "These are the things that you must and must not do." By contrast with these, the commands of the religious, uttered by God, involve choice and apply to particular cases, where the generalized commands of ethics may be suspended: "Choose to do what here and now, in these particular circumstances, I am telling you to do." It is at this stage where repetition – the work of freedom – allows one to make the leap of faith and reach the eternal moment again and again, and where fear and trembling are the appropriate attitude because the teleological suspension of the ethical, i.e. the suspension of moral requirements, can occur. He advocated an appropriation of truth, which he contrasted with the infinite approximation to truth practiced by science.

Still another forerunner of existentialism is the Spanish philosopher Miguel de Unamuno (CE 1864–1936), who was influenced by Kierkegaard and aimed at describing life, not merely scientifically, but as a complex of emotional and intellectual components where the word was the most intimate expression of a person's life. Finally, an additional forerunner is the German philosopher Friedrich Wilhelm Nietzsche (CE 1844–1900), an atheistic thinker who also rejected systematic thought.

There are various recurrent themes that tend to unite various authors under the existentialism heading. Among these are those that focus on aspects of our *facticity* (how we find ourselves to exist): the individual's awareness of him or herself and on his or her own body in the world; the individual's freedom of choice; the contingency of the individual's situation, options, and of any decision's results; anguish about this situation; our finitude, and authenticity in making one's unavoidable choices. One of existentialism's central problems is that of communication, which this school understands as not merely linguistic, but as taking place within a certain context that involves attitudes, an awareness of possibilities, and the like.

Among influential French existentialists are Jean-Paul Sartre (CE 1905–80), whose literary works – e.g. *Nausea* – and philosophical works – e.g. *Being and Nothingness* – emphasized human reality as a *pour soi* (for oneself) rather than, as in science, an *en soi* (in itself)). In this regard, he explored – especially in his novel *Nausea* – the notion of nausea: one of the ways in which one becomes aware of the contingency of the mass of existing things, and – in various works – the notion of *bad faith*, sometimes also called *false consciousness*, as a particular form of self-deception in its derogatory sense that, in this case, involves a cowardly refusal to admit our facticity, and its manifestation in various human relations, e.g. in intimacy. A related notion formulated, for example, by Nietzsche is that of *vital lies*, i.e, instances of lying to oneself or to others, or holding or advocating false beliefs, in order respectively to foster such things as health, self-esteem, the ability to cope, hope, and creativity in oneself or others.

Sartre thought that, though humans and the world are given, humans invent a nature for themselves and for the world. This is what he meant in defining humans as *noughting nought*. Also influential was Sartre's friend, the Algerian-born poet, journalist, and philosopher Albert Camus (CE 1913–60), whose works – e.g. *The Myth of Sisyphus*, *The Stranger*, and *The Fall* – focused on the absurd – the confrontation between ourselves and an indifferent universe – and the options we have about this fact. He held human solidarity to be a final value entailing the unjustifiability of metaphysical revolt that he considered exemplified in nihilism, suicide, and, as he added later in the development of his thought, capital punishment. In addition, Sartre's friend and companion of many years, the French philosopher and feminist thinker Simone de Beauvoir (CE 1908–86), was also influential through such works as *The Second Sex* and *The Ethics of Ambiguity*, where she focused on the condition in which all humans find themselves and the experience of women in it.

Sometimes also characterized as an existentialist, though perhaps more accurately characterized as a representative of *existential philosophy* (see CONTINENTAL PHILOSOPHY), is the French philosopher Maurice Merleau-Ponty (CE 1908–61), whose works – e.g. *Phenomenology of Perception* and *The Structure of Behavior* – emphasized not just the existential but the bodily nature of the individual human being and developed an alternative to dualism by distinguishing between the objective body or the body conceived from a physiological standpoint, and the phenomenal body, which is not just some or other body, but my body or your body as experienced. He thought he had thus overcome the solipsism he saw as a consequence of Cartesian dualism, by focusing on an intersubjectivity conceived as intercorporeity. All of these authors are representatives of *atheistic existentialism*.

Another French thinker who initially accepted but later rejected the label existentialism was Gabriel Marcel (CE 1889–1973). By contrast with Sartre, Camus, Simone de Beauvoir, and Merleau-Ponty, Marcel focused on communion with God and loved ones who have died, a theme he addressed in a number of his thirty plays as well as in his *Presence and Immortality*. This concern tends to place his work within an approach sometimes called *philosophy of existence*, which, focusing on being, gives more predominance to metaphysical concerns. Notable among this approach's representatives is the German Jewish philosopher Martin Buber (CE 1878–1965), who described two primary relationships: I and Thou (or I-Thou), characterized by openness, reciprocity, and a sense of being involved personally, and I and It (or I-It), characterized by the tendency to treat something or someone as an impersonal object, merely as governed by causal forces.

A German philosopher in this tradition who more clearly emphasizes metaphysical concerns is Martin Heidegger (CE 1884–1976), whose works – e.g. *Being and Time*, *What is Thinking?*, and *An Introduction to Metaphysics* – primarily focus on the recovery of being (*Sein*), whose conception, he thought, had been lost through thinking of it as a property or essence of entities (*seindes*) that make it up, a kind of thinking he calls *ontic*. Heidegger proposes to look at it from the standpoint of existence, i.e. as *Dasein* or being there, which is an individual position stretching from birth to death, where one finds oneself thrown into the world, is always taking a stand about it in a future-oriented manner, and is always involved in discourse about it, which crucially involves *Mitsein*, i.e. communicating with others. Further, Heidegger holds that, in focusing on Dasein, one also focuses on *das Nichts*, i.e. nothingness, which he interprets to be that of one's past and one's future. In fact, Heidegger claims that nothingness has ontological status, and underlines this claim in stating *Das Nichts nichtet*, i.e. nothingness nots.

In proposing to look at Dasein from the standpoint of existence, Heidegger sought non-metaphysical ways of coming to think of being – the ultimate category and final reality – since he thought the word, i.e. the logos, to be present in all discourse, through poetry. He also developed the notion of *language-game*, which is not merely to play with language, but a way of seeing what language actually says when used, and the notion of a *world-game*, where in thinking of things as things, we let them be so that their being approaches us. For Heidegger, this amounts to a thinking jump – a notion presumably analogous to a quantum jump in thinking – whereby we play with that on which being rests, and with our own human being.

By contrast with Heidegger, the contemporary Spanish existential philosopher Julián Marías argues that life, not being, is the ultimate and final reality. This position would dissolve or, at least, downgrade Heidegger's as well as all approaches focused on being. Indeed, it would also weaken deconstructionist accounts of *the other* or *otherness* (understood as a transcendence beyond being that elevates this notion to a category analogous to nothingness in Heidegger's account); while it might reinforce those conceptions that see the meaning of our world resulting from the fact that we are with others – who constitute the other – in the world.

Along these lines, the contemporary Spanish philosopher José Luis L. Aranguren has elaborated on the notion denoted by the Spanish term *temple*, i.e. emotive state of mind, whereby one feels in a certain way regarding oneself or others. Such a state of mind can and does change; but it need not change radically and, hence, involve settled dispositions displayed in how we approach the world around us and ourselves. The term Heidegger has used in this regard is *Stimmung*, which he understands as a way of being. Yet, the question arises: "How should this notion be interpreted: physiologically, psychologically, existentially?" Rather than in answering this question, Aranguren is interested in how the notion of *temple* applies to different ways of approaching religion. His example is that of Catholic versus Protestant attitudes towards religion. He argues that these involve a total disposition affecting all the previously mentioned aspects. Aranguren uses the Spanish term *talante* to refer to this total disposition.

Sometimes contrasted with French existentialism or Heideggerian philosophy of existence types, there is also an approach called *existential philosophy* or *Existenz philosophy*, or *existence philosophy*, a term coined by the philosopher Karl Theodor Jaspers (CE 1883–1969), whose works – e.g. *Existence Philosophy*, *Reason and Anti-Reason in Our Time*, and *Ciphers of Transcendence* – focus on the notion of existence as normative. Jaspers focuses on *Grenzsituationen*, i.e. ultimate situations or limiting situations – death, suffering, struggle, and guilt – that set limits to individual freedom, and individuals' historical being or historicity. In this context, Jaspers reasons that an understanding of being can be only partially attained through signs, not concepts, in a manner that involves indirect communication, similar to intuition but ambiguous. Jaspers has used the term *Scheitern*, i.e. failure (in his *Philosophie, III*), to denote the failure of the empirical approach from the standpoint of existential clarification. This, he argues, is made plain by the fact that the various empirical realities cannot sustain themselves.

Along the same lines, the Spanish philosopher José Ortega y Gasset (CE 1883–1955) has used the Spanish term *naufragio*, i.e. shipwreck, to argue that human existence is actually a *naufragio*, a state of affairs where humans find themselves lost and in need of knowing what to expect or believe about their existence. They need to know *a qué atenerse*, i.e. what to count on. This leads Ortega to use the term *raciovitalismo*, which can be translated as *ratiovitalism*, by which he means the integration of vitalism with rationalism, for our existence is rooted in life but, as indicated, as humans we need to know what to count on; in other words, we need reasons. This involves Ortega's notion of *razón vital*, i.e. vital reason, or *razón viviente*, or *living reason*: that life itself functions as reason. He and his followers – e.g. the contemporary philosopher Julián Marías – hold that only from this standpoint can we understand anything human.

Ortega also argues that culture does not sustain itself but only in so far as it helps humans to stay afloat in the shipwreck of existence in which they find themselves. In this context, Ortega's conception of personal identity is crucial to his conception of identity. He identifies a particular person's life with reality, and conceives of the person's identity as including the person's circumstances. That is, each personal life results from an interaction between the individual person and the person's circumstances. This leads Ortega to advocate *perspectivism*, a term coined by the German philosopher Gustav Teichmüller (CE 1832–88), who argued reality is complex and each system is a partial, however true, version of reality. A version of this view, which has a family resemblance to the doctrine of *monadology*

advocated by the German philosopher Gottfried Wilhelm Leibniz (CE 1646–1716) (see METAPHYSICS), was also advocated by the German philosopher Friedrich Wilhelm Nietzsche (CE 1844–1900). As for Ortega's perspectivism, it is the doctrine that each person has a unique standpoint and perspective. Ortega went on to claim that all perspectives are true except when they claim exclusivity.

Within the context of the ideas just discussed, one can give one's life worth and significance – others use the term meaning – by developing a *vocation* (in Spanish, *una vocación*), from the Latin *vocatio*, i.e. "to call"; in other words, a calling or life project in terms of which one becomes one's authentic self.

See also: Continental philosophy; essentialism; philosophy of religion

Further reading
Copleston, Frederick Charles (1973) *Contemporary Philosophy: Studies of Logical Positivism and Existentialism*, new and revised edn, London: Search Press.
Solomon, Robert C. (1979) *Phenomenology and Existentialism*, Washington: University Press of America.
Wahl, Jean Andre (1969) *Philosophies of Existence: An Introduction to the Basic Thought of Kierkegaard, Heidegger, Jaspers, Marcel, Sartre*, London: Routledge & K. Paul.

Existenz philosophy *see* existentialism

exoteric *see* esoterism

exoterism *see* esoterism

expatriation *see* diaspora; philosophy and expatriation

expected return *see* paradox; philosophy of economics

expected utility *see* paradox; philosophy of economics

expediency *see* ethics

experience *see* empiricism

experientialism *see* philosophy of religion

experimental investigation, methods of *see* induction

experimentalism *see* empiricism

experimentation *see* empiricism

experimentum crusis *see* induction

expert *see* epistemology; ethics; philosophy of science; philosophy, sociopolitical

expertise *see* epistemology; ethics; philosophy of science; philosophy, sociopolitical

explaining reason *see* explanation

explanandum *see* explanation

explanans *see* explanation

explanation From the Latin *ex* ("out") and *planare* ("to level" or "make plain"), the act of making something clear or understandable. That which provides the explanation is called the *explanans*, while that which is explained is called the *explanandum*.

There are various kinds of explanations. For example, a *causal* explanation – say, the car is smashed because the tree fell on it – identifies a particular factor (in this case an event) as the decisive one (the cause) in bringing about an event: the effect. Though there is general agreement that causal explanations can apply to events, it is controversial whether, even if actions are events, they can be explained simply by means of causal explanations, or whether reasons must be involved and, if they must, whether they can be causes. What would, for example, explain someone's smoking a cigarette? That this person is addicted to it (a physiological condition), wanted to smoke a cigarette (a psychological event), or, upon reflection, thought it would be fine for him or her to smoke a cigarette (a reason)? All answers may be appropriate depending on the context: the first candidate may be a reply to a request for a physiological explanation; the second, to a request for a psychological explanation; the third, to a request for an ordinary explanation. This has led philosophers to say that "the cause" is context-dependent.

Others have argued that, even if context-dependent, this notion of cause is that of *efficient* cause, hence inadequate, because actions, if not other occurrences, can often be explained only in terms of a purposive or *teleological explanation*, where the aims pursued are paramount. In this regard, one position is *teleology*: the philosophical doctrine that everything is, or at least intentional agents are, goal-directed or functionally organized. Its most extreme opposite is MECHANICISM, the doctrine that any event and, arguably, even any action of an intentional agent can be explained by means of a mechanistic explanation. In one – extreme – sense, this means that everything can be explained entirely in terms of masses in motion. However, this is false because, even in physics, many ordinary events – e.g. in optics or acoustics – cannot be explained that way. In a more frequent sense, however, a *mechanistic explanation* simply means a non-teleological explanation. Arguably, contemporary science primarily, if not exclusively, uses mechanistic explanations in this latter sense.

As for teleology, it includes two versions. One is *external* teleology, i.e. the view that the natural world can be explained by analogy to an intentional agent. *Internal* teleology is the view that the natural world is goal-directed. Natural theologians have attributed this goal to God. Today's philosophers talk of *teleological function*, as in cybernetics, in terms of persistence towards a goal under changing conditions. In this regard, a significant area of philosophical discussion is that of the relation between *explanation* or *explanatory reasons* or, as the Scottish philosopher Francis Hutcheson (CE 1694–1746) called them, *exciting reasons* (such as an agent's affections or desires that help to explain the agent's behavior), and JUSTIFICATION, or *justificatory reasons*, which serve to establish why the agent's beliefs or behavior are justified.

Another question raised is: "Does reference to particular factors suffice to constitute an explanation, or should such factors fall under general laws?" An influential position in reply to this question is the *covering-law model* or *deductive–nomological model* of explanation (the term nomological being derived from the Greek *nomos*, i.e. "law," and *logos*, i.e. "discourse," "reason," or "body of knowledge"). This model is also called the *Hempel model*, *Hempel–Oppenheim model*, *Popper–Hempel model*, and the *subsumption theory of explanation*. Some of these names make plain that the model has been especially associated with the German philosophers Carl Hempel (CE 1905–97) and Paul Oppenheim (CE 1884 or 5–1977), and the Anglo-Austrian philosopher Karl Popper (1902–94). The model attempts to represent the general form of explanations as involving a subsumption of the identified causal factors under a law. For example, on this account, simply saying that a sample of water boiled because it was heated up to 100° centigrade at one atmosphere of pressure is not all there is to the explanation. It also involves implicit reference to a law, say, that whenever a sample of water is heated up to 100° centigrade at one atmosphere of pressure, it boils. On this account, an explanation is understood as a deductive argument. That is why the model is called the deductive–nomological model of explanation. However, the covering law can be probabilistic, therefore providing an *inductive* explanation or *inductive–probabilistic* explanation.

One objection against this model has been that the model hardly applies to scientific or ordinary explanations, because these involve statistically true, not universally invariable, generalizations. Explaining why Jimmy contracted chicken pox may at best involve reference to a generalization of the form: whenever children who have not had chicken pox are exposed to those who have it, they are highly likely to contract it. One could of course use this generalization in a deductive argument, which would be involved in an inductive–statistical explanation (or, simply, statistical explanation), and which has a form whereby an inference is drawn from statistical generalizations and observations about particular cases. Yet, its conclusion would then be an *explanandum* like "It was highly probable that Jimmy would contract chicken pox," not the original *explanandum*: "Jimmy contracted chicken pox."

Other objections involve explanation in the social sciences and history. For example, historians often offer explanations of the form: "The United States Revolution happened because of taxation without representation." This is a singular causal statement. However, it is arguably difficult, if at all possible, to formulate a covering law about taxation without representation that would deductively entail the *explanandum*: the United States revolution happened. Further, such a law would provide a sufficient condition or a set of jointly sufficient conditions for the occurrence of the *explanandum*, i.e. a condition or set of conditions given which the *explanandum* must occur. Yet, in offering explanations of the type indicated, historians seem keen on pointing to a necessary condition or a set of individually necessary conditions, i.e. a condition or set of conditions without which the *explanandum* cannot occur. In other words, they are keen on pointing out that without the taxation without representation issue, the United States Revolution would not have happened. This would make the covering-law model irrelevant. One could reply that this is not all they do and that they are actually trying to formulate a condition or set of conditions that is both necessary and sufficient for the occurrence of the *explanandum*, i.e. without which the *explanandum* could not occur, and given which the *explanandum* must occur. However, this interpretation is not supported by evidence from historians' works.

Philosophers have also argued that at least some explanations are best understood as *arguments to the best explanation*. In this connection, the notion of *consilience* is significant. According to the English philosopher William Whewell (CE 1794–1866), who first formulated this notion, the best inductions are those in which grounds for various hypotheses, previously thought to explain discrete sets of data, are found to converge together. Consilience is a characteristic of theories that significantly display such features as simplicity, generality, unification of knowledge, and explanatory strength. Since, on these counts, they provide the best explanation, it is concluded (by arguments to the best explanation) that these theories are true.

Sometimes, the German term for explanation, *Erklärung*, is used in contrast with *das Verstehen* (comprehension, or understanding), in arguing about the nature of social studies. In von Schiel's translation of the English philosopher John Stuart Mill's *Logic*, social studies were for the first time called *Geisteswissenschaften*, i.e. *sciences of the spirit*, as a translation of what Mill had called *moral sciences*. The issue here is whether social studies should merely aim at comprehending: reconstructing meanings instead of discovering causes. In this regard, people sometimes talk of explanation as *explication*, or *clarification*, in the manner, say, in which an anthropologist engaged in participant observation might attempt to explain an until then unknown practice of a newly discovered group of humans.

The German philosophers Wilhelm Dilthey (CE 1833–1911) and Rudolf Eucken (CE 1846–1926) spearheaded the conception of the social sciences as interpretive rather than explanatory branches of inquiry. They advocated a *Lebensphilosophie* or *philosophy of life*, which consisted in beginning by acknowledging the variety and complexity of concrete and meaningful human experiences as they are lived, and recognizing that they are immersed in a historical context. They proceeded to attempt to understand (*verstehen*), describe, and sometimes change them without reduction or abstraction. This approach also influenced the development of the concept of *Lebenswelt* in phenomenology.

Finally, the question has been raised whether there are ultimate principles of explanation. The English philosopher Herbert Spencer (CE 1820–1903) thought there were, though he held they were beyond human reach and called them the *Unknowable*. This notion had been foreshadowed by the German poet, dramatist, and philosopher Friedrich Schiller (CE 1759–1805), who thought the world was unknowable; hence, we were free to formulate conjectures about its nature. Schiller thought poets provided conjectures about first principles for philosophers – a notion tracing back to Platonic discussions about the relation between poetry and philosophy.

See also: causal law; definition; description; empathy; justification; phenomenology

Further reading
Hempel, Carl Gustav and Oppenheim, Paul (1948) *Studies in the Logic of Explanation*, Indianapolis, IN: Bobbs-Merrill.
Henderson, David K. (1996) *Explanation in the Human Sciences*, Memphis, TN: Dept of Philosophy, University of Memphis.
Körner, Stephan (1975) *Explanation: Papers and Discussions* New Haven: Yale University Press.
Van Fraassen, Bas C. (1980) *The Scientific Image*, Oxford and New York: Clarendon Press and Oxford University Press.

explanatory emergence *see* holism

explanatory reductionism *see* holism

explication *see* definition

explicit definition *see* definition

exploitation *see* philosophy of economics; philosophy, sociopolitical

exponible *see* logic

exportation *see* logic

expositio *see* Scholasticism

expressibility logicism *see* philosophy of mathematics

expression *see* aesthetics; logic

expressionism *see* aesthetics

expressive *see* model; speech act theory

extension *see* Cartesianism; reference

extensionalism *see* metaphysics

extensionality, axiom of *see* set

extensionality thesis *see* metaphysics

extensive magnitude *see* measurement

external negation *see* logic

external reason *see* epistemology; justification

external relation *see* relation

external world *see* metaphysics

externalism *see* justification

externality *see* ethics; philosophy of economics

exteroception *see* perception

extrasensory perception *see* philosophy of mind

extrinsic desire *see* intention

extrinsic value *see* intention

F

F *see* logic; syllogism

fa *see* Chinese philosophy

face and heart *see* Nahua philosophy

fa-chia *see* Chinese Legalism

fa-hsiang *see* Buddhism

fact *see* metaphysics

fact–value distinction *see* ethics

facticity *see* existentialism

faculty psychology *see* philosophy of mind

fair *see* ethics

fairness *see* ethics

faith From the Latin *fidere* ("to trust"), this term denotes either an attitude of believing in – i.e. trusting or having hope in the future assistance of – someone or something, or a different attitude of believing that something is, was, or will be the case, regardless of, and sometimes in the face of, evidence or proof about the truth of what one believes to be the case. There are both religious forms of faith, such as faith in God and in personal immortality, and non-religious forms of faith, such as people's faith in their country's eventual solution of its political conflicts, and a student's faith in his or her eventually receiving a university degree.

A body of belief held on faith is also called *a faith* or *a creed*. Different attitudes have been held concerning faith and its relation to reason. One, for example, is manifest in the phrase *credo quia absurdum* ("I believe because it is absurd") and the related *Credo quia impossibile est* ("I believe because it is impossible"), both derived from the thought of the Christian apologist Tertullian (*c.* CE 155–*c.* 222; born in the African city of Carthage), who opposed the Greek philosophers for whom reason was the single means of determining what should be believed. Another example is manifest in the sentence *credo ut intelligentiam* ("I believe in order to understand"), stated by the Christian philosopher Augustine (CE 354–430; born in the African city of Thagaste), to convey the view, also accepted by the philosopher Anselm (CE 1033–1109; born in Aosta, a city in what is now Italy), and many other medieval authors, that belief must precede knowledge.

Referring to intuition in an intellectual sense, the French philosopher and mathematician Blaise Pascal (CE 1623–62) used the expression *esprit de finesse* – i.e. "spirit of finesse," or a balancing capacity to deal with complicated matters not reducible to simple principles – that he contrasted with the *esprit géometrique*, i.e. spirit of geometry, or reason. He believed that faith related more closely to the *esprit de finesse* and its reasons of the heart, of which, according to him, reason knows nothing. In this regard, he formulated *Pascal's wager*, an application of his work on probability to the question of God's existence. It can be formulated as follows: 1. If I believe in God and God exists, then I can attain infinite happiness. 2. If I believe in God and God does not exist, then nothing or not much is lost. 3. If I do not believe in God and God exists, then I will attain infinite misery. 4. If I do not believe in God and God does not exist, then not much, if anything, is gained. Hence, because the potential winnings are far greater, I should believe that God exists.

These contrasts reached the twentieth century. For example, the Spanish philosopher Miguel de Unamuno (CE 1864–1936) saw the conflict between faith and reason at the center of the *tragic sense of life*, whereby we live claiming that we should have a place in the universe that reason cannot support and also claiming that, in addressing our place in the universe, we should rely on reason and reason alone.

Also, the United States philosopher William James (CE 1842–1910) discussed faith in the context of the *ethics of belief*. In the background of this discussion is a notion of justification that involves either evidential reasons (i.e. reasons for the truth of the belief, which can be evidence, or proof); or non-evidential reasons (i.e. reasons other than those for the truth of the belief). James argued that one is justified in believing what one prefers when a conjunction of three conditions is satisfied. First, one faces a *genuine option*, that is, a choice between hypotheses that itself has three features: it is *forced* (i.e. one must believe one of the hypotheses); *living* (i.e. each hypothesis is plausible and has value, positive or negative, but never neutral, to the agent facing the choice); and *momentous* (i.e. what one chooses is significant, e.g. because unique, to one's life). Second, the option cannot be solved on intellectual grounds, i.e. evidence or proof are absent or mixed. Third, one's happiness is contingent on believing one of the hypotheses (e.g. believing in God would make one happy), while one's misery is contingent on believing any of the others. For James, these conditions provided a justification of belief, not of the truth of what thereby was believed. Also, his account left the possibility open that one might be justified in believing regardless of evidential reasons in still other types of cases. However, as presented, James appears to justify too much. For example, he would appear to justify the belief held by the parents of a child needing a blood transfusion that, because of the parents' religious beliefs in letting nature take its course and that believing otherwise in this case

would make them miserable, no such transfusion should be administered. Of course, in defense of James' position, one might reply that the belief is justified so long as it does not lead to action. However, critics reply that all belief tends to lead to action (even when it fails to do so); hence, either the parents have no such belief or their belief is as questionable as the action itself because, if left unimpeded, it would lead to a questionable act.

Various replies to this and other criticisms, as well as counter-replies, have continued to be formulated. In addition, some philosophers have advocated *vital lies*, i.e. instances of lying to oneself or to others, or holding or advocating false beliefs, in order to foster such things as health, self-esteem, the ability to cope, hope, and creativity in oneself or others.

See also: epistemology; justification

Further reading
James, William (1956) "The Will to Believe," in *The Will to Believe and Other Essays in Popular Philosophy*, and *Human Immortality*, New York: Dover.
Price, Henry Habberley (1969) *Belief: The Gifford Lectures Delivered at the University of Aberdeen in 1960*, London and New York: Allen & Unwin and Humanities Press.
Unamuno, Miguel de (1990) *The Tragic Sense of Life in Men and Nations*, Princeton, NJ: Princeton University Press.

fallacy From the Latin *fallacia* ("deceit," "trick," or "fraud"), this term means bad or faulty reasoning, and is often also called *non sequitur*, a Latin phrase meaning "it does not follow," and, less often, *paralogism*, from the Greek *para* ("beside") and *logos* ("reason"). With a narrower focus on the use of argument for the purpose of *refutation*, i.e. to prove opposed views wrong, a fallacy is sometimes also called a *sophistic refutation* or an *apparent refutation*.

There is an indefinitely large number of ways in which reasoning can be faulty; but, among those most notable, are as follows.

Formal fallacies
These are faulty or erroneous inferences relatively to a system of formal logic (see LOGIC). Some are erroneous simply given their form and without any regard to the content of their

sentences. Others are erroneous in a system because they use rules of inference not included in the system. Notable among these are the fallacies of propositional logic (or sentential logic, or the logic of statements). They are the fallacy of *affirming the consequent,*

If *p* then *q*
and *q*
Hence *p*

For example,

If this is apple pie then it has apple in it
and it has apple in it
Hence, it is apple pie

and the fallacy of *denying the antecedent,*

If *p* then *q*
and not *p*
Hence not *q*

For example,

If this is apple pie then it has apple in it
and it is not apple pie
Hence, it does not have apple in it

Informal fallacies
These are fallacies resulting from errors concerning the meanings, relevance, or pragmatic use of terms or sentences involved. Notable among them are as follows.

Ad baculum is a type of argument that appeals to a threat or fear in support of a conclusion. For example, a jury member could say to the other jury members: you should find the defendant guilty because, otherwise, you will be stuck in this jury for a long time. Though, as exemplified, this type of argument is fallacious when it unduly appeals to threats, it arguably is not fallacious when it permissibly appeals to threats, as in cases invoking punishment to justify obedience to the law, e.g. you should not break the law because, otherwise, you will be likely to be punished.

Ad hominem (literally, "argument against the man") is a type of argument that attacks a person's views or reasons by appeal to characteristics of the person. One subtype relies on attacks on the person's character, e.g. "what he says cannot be believed because he's a liar." In evaluating legal testimony, such an attack may be valid in establishing the lack of credibility of

a witness. So can it be in political debate, for example in establishing the trustworthiness of a candidate to public office. However, such attacks on character are often fallacious, for example when the attack is clearly undeserved, or when it is used to distract from other, more significant matters.

A second subtype of *ad hominem* arguments relies on attacks on the *relation between the person's views and his or her actions*, e.g. "You don't practice what you preach." It is fallacious to infer, from the fact that one fails to act in accordance with the views one advocates, that these views are false. However, this version of the argument may not be fallacious when it is used to point out that the circumstances make the advocated views unjustified, e.g. because what they advocate cannot be generally, if ever, done.

Other subtypes are the *tu quoque* (you-too) version, and the *bias* (what you advocate is to your advantage) version, which can be fallacious or not depending on conditions such as those just discussed concerning the previous versions. A morally significant version of the *ad hominem* argument is what can be called the *ad naturam* argument, whereby one's views are discounted merely because of the kind of person one is, as in the reply "because you are a woman" (argument *ad feminam*).

Ad ignorantiam is an argument inferring that a proposition is true from the premise that the proposition is not known to be false. These arguments could be easily abused, for example when a person must be guilty of a crime because we do not have much or any evidence disproving that the person is guilty. However, when evidence is inconclusive, they may be acceptably used to establish certain presumptions. For example, in police investigations, a person's unexpected and out of character disappearance from the person's usual whereabouts for a number of years, plus the absence of any evidence that the person is alive – i.e. plus ignorance concerning whether or not the person is alive – can serve as an acceptable basis to presume the person may very well have died.

Ad misericordiam is any argument appealing to pity, sympathy, or compassion in support of a conclusion in a manner that tends to hide strong evidence against the conclusion, or puts undue emotional pressure on those to whom it is addressed.

Ad populum, also called fallacy of slanting, is any argument appealing to popular sentiment or belief in support of a conclusion in a manner that exaggerates the evidential support provided by such sentiment, or tends to hide strong evidence against the conclusion. A related fallacy is the *argumentum consensus gentium*, where the popular sentiment or belief being appealed to is that of all, most, or a great many human beings.

Ad verecundiam is any argument pointing out that, if one did not accept a certain opinion, one would fail to respect the expert that formulated it, e.g. you should believe the experts' opinion that the city water is safe because it would be arrogant and disrespectful for you not to believe their opinion. This may be an acceptable ground to establish a presumption or shift the burden of proof so long as it does not tend to hide or distract people from paying attention to relevant evidence; however, it is fallacious when it is used to bring closure to an argument or to treat respect for experts as always overriding the examination of evidence.

Argument *from authority* is any argument that uses expert opinion to support a conclusion. It is a practical, though fallible, way of presumptively establishing a conclusion and shifting the burden of evidence; however, it is fallacious if used to bring closure to an argument on the basis of the respect due to experts, or if treating expert opinion as always taking precedence over the examination of evidence (as in the previously described *ad verecundiam* fallacy and, arguably, into *argumentum consensus gentium* too).

Begging the question (*petitio principii*) or, in general, *circular reasoning* are fallacies in that the conclusion, though involving different words, is not, as in good deductive arguments, contained in the premises. Instead, it has exactly the same content, i.e. merely repeats or says exactly the same thing, as the premises. Arguably a related version – because it also assumes or presupposes what is or should be at issue – is the *black-or-white* fallacy, i.e. any argument that insists on selecting one of two alternatives when at least a third one, i.e. a *tertium quid* – a Latin phrase used by medieval logicians to mean "a third something" – is available.

Contradictio in adjecto is a Latin expression meaning "a contradiction in what is added," which denotes a fallacy involving a contradiction between, for example, a noun and an adjective modifying it, e.g. a dimensionless cube.

Cum hoc ergo propter hoc is sometimes called the fallacy of *false cause*; this fallacy involves the error of arguing that, simply because two events are correlated (eleven Argentine players and eleven blue and white shirts are present on the field at the beginning of a World Cup game involving Argentina's team), one of them – say, the blue shirts' being present – is the cause of the other – the players' being present.

Gambler's fallacy, also called *Monte Carlo* fallacy, consists in supposing, of a sequence of independent events, that the probabilities of later outcomes must decrease or increase to compensate for earlier outcomes.

Genetic fallacy argues from the goodness or badness of an item's origin to the goodness or badness of the item. A particular case of this fallacy is the *ad hominem* fallacy discussed above.

Ignoratio elenchi, also called the fallacy of irrelevant conclusion or missing the point, is a type of argument involving a failure of relevance, say, by arguing that theft is wrong during a trial aimed at determining whether a defendant is guilty of theft.

Infinite regress (in Latin, *regressus ad infinitum*) is a ground used to consider a view defective because thought to generate an infinite series of such things as explanatory reasons, and justifying reasons, and either no such series is thought to exist or the series, though existing, is thought not to have its explanatory or justificatory role. When the views thus criticized are indeed unwarranted, it is not simply, if at all, because they generate an infinite series. For not every infinite series is vicious. The views are often unwarranted because of other features, e.g. that they try to provide justification or explanation when all such things are precluded.

Lazy reason – *argos logos* in Greek and *ignava ratio* in Latin – fallacy is to suspend all inquiry on the grounds that it is useless or that nothing not already known can be discovered. Also called *lazy sophism*, this was often characterized as a fallacy in Ancient Greece and Rome. A variety of versions were formulated. One was: either what is sought is known or it is unknown. If known, then it is useless to seek it, because one already knows it. If unknown, then it makes no sense to seek it, because one knows not what to seek. Either way – either because one already knows it or because one knows not what to seek – it is worthless to seek anything.

In a different sense, the German philosopher Immanuel Kant (CE 1724–1804) used the expression *lazy reason* (*faule Vernunft*) to denote the view that all inquiry has ended, which leads reason to rest rather than continuing to inquire.

Non causa pro causa is also called the fallacy of *false cause*; this type of fallacy consists in taking for the cause of something what is not its cause.

The fallacy of *accent* is any argument involving a shift in emphasis as a means of establishing a proposition.

The fallacy of *amphibology* is any argument relying on its components being capable of more than one interpretation, e.g. come to the meeting, because Mary will tell everyone how she lost 80 pounds at City Hall on Tuesday, May 3.

The fallacy of *composition* is any argument inferring that a whole has a certain feature simply because its parts have it, e.g. the book is thin because the book pages are thin.

The fallacy of *division* is any argument inferring that a part has a certain feature simply because the whole it belongs to does, e.g. the book pages are thick because the book is thick.

The fallacy of *equivocation* is the use of an expression in two different senses operant in the same argument. Arguably a form of equivocation is *subreption* (from the Low Latin *subreption*, noun for *subreptio*, "to steal"; hence, "a stealing"), the fallacy consisting in the subreptitious introduction of a proposition or a change in meaning.

The fallacy of *four terms* is any syllogism appearing to involve three but, in fact, involving four, e.g. what is right is useful, only one of your arms is right, hence only one of your arms is useful.

The fallacy of *hypostatization* is also called of *reification*; this fallacy consists in an argument postulating a thing on the basis of features that do not require it, e.g. plants have souls, because they grow well when they are watered, hence they like being watered, and liking is a feature of souls.

The fallacy of *hasty generalization* is any argument drawing an inductive conclusion from limited evidence, e.g. he will never learn how to swim, because he tried twice and failed.

The fallacy of *many questions* is the tactic of asking questions by packing presuppositions in them that will be implied by any yes or no answer to the questions, e.g. "Have you quit beating your little brother?"

The fallacy of *secundum quid* is the failure to take a statement in its proper restricted sense, where *secundum quid* – Latin for "according to something" – was used in medieval philosophy to mean in a qualified, restricted, or secondary sense.

Post hoc ergo propter hoc a Latin phrase meaning "after this, therefore because of this"; it is the name of one of the fallacies of relevance, also known as the fallacy of *false cause*.

An additional shortcoming that can be attributed to an argument is that of being a *slippery-slope* argument, or *wedge* argument, i.e. that a reason the argument uses to justify something would, if good, entail the justification of another thing, and then another and another, all considered unjustified. Hence, it is concluded the argument is not good. These and many other informal fallacies had already been studied in Antiquity and used by the sophists who thoroughly developed eristic (from the Greek *eris*, i.e. "strife"), the art of controversy, often involving fallacious but persuasive arguments.

See also: logic

Further reading
Barry, Vincent E. and Soccio, Douglas J. (1988) *Practical Logic*, New York: Holt, Rinehart & Winston.

Copi, Irving M. (1986) *Informal Logic*, New York and London: Macmillan and Collier Macmillan.

fallibilism *see* epistemology

false *see* logic; truth

false cause, fallacy of *see* fallacy

false consciousness *see* existentialism; Marxism

false dilemma *see* dilemma

falsifiability *see* induction

falsifiable *see* induction

falsification *see* induction

falsity *see* logic; truth

family *see* feminist philosophy

family resemblance *see* essentialism

fanā' *see* Ṣūfism

fantasy *see* imagination; Frankfurt School

faqr *see* Ṣūfism

farḍ *see* illumination; philosophy of religion

fascism *see* philosophy, sociopolitical

fatalism *see* determinism; dharma

fate *see* determinism; dharma

fatwa *see* philosophy of religion

feasible set *see* decision

Fechner's law *see* philosophy of mind

feedback *see* computer theory; cybernetics

feedforward *see* cybernetics

feeling *see* aesthetics; ethics

felapton *see* syllogism

felicific calculus *see* ethics

felicity *see* ethics

felicity conditions *see* speech act theory

female future *see* feminist philosophy

feminine *see* gender

feminism *see* feminist philosophy

feminist criticism *see* feminist philosophy

feminist philosophy Feminist is a term derived from the Latin *femina* ("woman") and the suffix *-ist*. The related term, feminism, is derived from the Latin *femina* and the Latin suffix *-ismus* (used to form action nouns denoting such things as action or practice, state or condition, principles, doctrines, usage, and characteristic). These terms were imported into English shortly after the term *féminisme* (also derived from the Latin) acquired wide circulation in French during the late nineteenth-century women's campaigns. These advocated the right to vote and to have access to education and the professions, and the right of married women to own property and have custody of their children. Soon they spread to the rest of Continental Europe, the American continent, Australia, and New Zealand. It should here be noted, however, that *womanism*, a term synonymous with feminism, has been preferred by some, though not many, contemporary African-American feminists on the grounds that it is rooted in African-American culture, while feminism, to them, is a foreign term.

In general, *feminism* is a perspective that refuses to identify the entire human experience with that of males, and is associated with the belief that women are unjustifiably disadvantaged or even oppressed, while men are not or are less so. As for *feminist philosophy*, it can be characterized as a philosophical approach that expresses the same refusal and is associated with the same belief. There are various forms of feminisms and feminist philosophy that include cultural, radical, liberal, socialist, Marxist, psychoanalytic, existentialist, and others. Some of these mutually overlap, while others exclude each other.

Forerunners of feminism and feminist philosophy
Various authors are characterized as early forerunners of feminist thought. They include the French author Christine de Pizan (*c.* CE 1364–*c.* 1431), who, in *The Book of the City of Ladies*, argued for the advantage of educating women; the French authors Marie de Gournay (CE 1565–1645), who, in her *Equality of Men and Women*, upheld the equality of women and men, and François Poulain de la Barre (CE 1647–1723), who, in *The Equality of*

the Sexes, formulated Cartesian arguments for the same view and advocated the equal right of men and women to knowledge.

This appeal to rights was deepened by the English author Mary Wollstonecraft (CE 1759–97), who, in *A Vindication of the Rights of Women*, argued for the right of women to an education and their concomitant political emancipation, on the grounds that women and men were essentially rational – and did not have different natures as the French philosopher Jean Jacques Rousseau (CE 1712–78) held. Wollstonecraft argued that granting women such right would allow them to become better wives and mothers.

An attempt at finding a balance between the claims of equality and difference can be found in *The Subjection of Women*, by the English philosopher John Stuart Mill (CE 1806–73), and, in a more radical form, in *The Enfranchisement of Women*, by Mill's intellectual companion (and wife from 1851, when her existing husband died, until her death), the English author Harriet Hardy Taylor (CE 1807–58). In advocating equality, however, Taylor unsystematically focused on the gender differences associated with the mother–child relation and with motherhood understood as the female reproductive process of gestation, giving birth, and lactation, and the social institution whereby mothers bear the primary responsibility for the care of their own children way past these children's infancy.

Modern and contemporary feminist philosophies

The latter three forerunners of feminism – Wollstonecraft, Taylor, and Mill – formulated the main ideas guiding *liberal* feminism: an emphasis on rationality as common to women and men, on equality in social arrangements, and on the legal rights of women to pursue their own aims. To the previously mentioned rights to vote, to an education, and to own property, twentieth-century liberal feminists have added concerns with women's rights to equal pay and equal opportunities. A criticism raised against this approach is that, by focusing on rationality, it disregards gender differences that, in the case of women, are closely associated with their child-bearing and child-rearing roles. Some contemporary feminists – e.g. Susan

Okin – have argued that the liberal conception of justice can be sensitive to these differences in sex roles and gender. Others, however, have argued that such conception cannot be sensitive to these differences. Still others have argued that liberalism places an undue emphasis on justice by contrast with deeper social factors associated with oppression, such as class and gender.

Two closely related, indeed influential, approaches offered as an alternative to liberal feminism have been *Marxist* feminism and *socialist* feminism. These approaches are sometimes treated as identical, other times as different from each other. In either case, Marxist feminism seeks to apply Marxist notions to the situation of women and holds that this situation can be understood according to the model of class analysis, and that women's liberation is contingent on the transformation of the socioeconomic system towards a classless society. This was the position advocated by the Russian thinker Alexandra Kollontai (CE 1872–1952) in her *The Social Basis of the Woman Question*: proletarian women should cease collaborating with bourgeois (e.g. liberal) feminism and attack the root of their oppression – the capitalist system.

Critics of this position have argued that the beneficiaries of the oppression of women are not only capitalists, but men generally. Hence, they conclude that orthodox Marxist feminism, which considers all exploitation to be class-rooted and typically sees women as belonging to the class of the men they belong to, cannot account for this apparent double exploitation of women: one based on class, the other on gender. In the sense in which it is contrasted with Marxist feminism, the term *socialist* feminism is used to denote the approach that makes room for both class-based and gender-based oppression.

By contrast with the previous positions, *radical* feminism treats all oppression as based on gender and, accordingly, focuses on patriarchy as the crux of the oppressed status of women. The institution of *patriarchy* covers any social system based on the government and economic control exercised by the *paterfamilias* (father of the family) or other senior male member(s) of the family. *Patriarchal* systems are *patrilineal*, i.e. they determine descent through the male line. They contrast with those that are *matriarchal* or instances of *matriarchy*, i.e. any social system based on the government and economic control exercised by the mother of the family or other senior female member(s) of the family. These latter systems are *matrilineal* or instances of *matriliny* or *matrilocality*, i.e. they determine descent through the female line. Given the facts of patriarchy, radical feminists consider legal inequality as only one aspect of male domination of women that also occurs within family structures, thus leading to radical feminism's motto: "the personal is political."

An expression feminists used to employ, and sometimes still employ (though rarely in current feminist philosophy), to refer to views and attitudes that uphold male superiority is male chauvinism or, for short, *chauvinism*. This term traditionally denoted excessive patriotism or nationalism, and derived from the name of Nicolas Chauvin – a soldier in the army of the French General and Emperor of France between CE 1804 and 1815, Napoleon Bonaparte (CE 1769–1821) – noted for loud-mouthed patriotism. In its extreme form, male chauvinism becomes *misogyny*, i.e. the attitude of hating women.

As previously indicated, a significant feminist concern is the dependency relations developed in patriarchal social structures (e.g. the father-based family), which place or tend to place such things as sex, procreation, and political and economic power under the significant if not total control of men. In fact, the doctrine of coverture, a principle of English common law, was that upon forming a family through marriage (the institution whereby two individuals, typically a man and a woman, establish an intimate social union involving legal or religious commitments, through a legal or religious ceremony), a woman forfeited any of her previous rights. Since the 1820s, this doctrine has been the focus of many criticisms by feminist as well as non-feminist women's rights advocates.

A few of these criticisms have pointed to historical instances of matriarchy as evidence of the natural equality of the sexes, if not of the superiority of women. This is a view related to *matriarchy theory*, a branch of inquiry whose initial theorists, who argued that the fall of matriarchies was inevitable and a necessary component of the rise of civilization, were not feminists. Matriarchy theory approaches significantly focus on the *male–female dichotomy*, i.e. a division into two groups that, in a variety of ways, are seen as mutually exclusive, or at least in mutual tension.

Whatever position representatives of radical feminism take on the latter matters, they face the question: "If women's oppression is crucially caused by patriarchy and its various manifestations, what should be done about it?" Some think that women's biological condition undermines women. For example, the contemporary author Shulamith Firestone, in *The Dialectic of Sex*, held that women's role as child-bearers was oppressive and should be eliminated with the help of modern reproductive technologies. By contrast, the contemporary author Sarah Ruddick, in *Maternal Thinking. Towards a Politics of Peace*, sees women's reproductive and child-rearing functions as valuable and a source of distinctive ways of thinking, e.g. in dealing with conflict. Those adopting this latter stance propose a re-evaluation and expansion of those roles and the concomitant institutions.

At any rate, writing from the variety of perspectives previously mentioned, feminist philosophers challenge various traditional philosophical approaches on the grounds that they do not take women's concerns, identities, and problems seriously, and fail to acknowledge women's ways of being, thinking, and acting as just as valuable as those of men. This involves *feminist criticism*, i.e. a criticism of male-dominated views, attitudes, and social structures characterized by male bias and male privilege.

As an alternative to the previous positions, which often involve definitional arguments, still other feminist thinkers have argued that there are only working definitions of feminism and feminist philosophy because these are dynamic. Arguably, this approach is partly exemplified by *existentialist* feminism's view that women's subordination is to a large extent the result of their being defined by men, and that the subordination will be overcome when women accept responsibility for defining themselves and become more autonomous subjects.

Influential among existentialist feminists has been the French philosopher Simone de Beauvoir (CE 1908–86). In *The Second Sex*, she criticized the previously mentioned Marxist account of women's subordination to men, as well as the account found in Freudian psychoanalysis, according to which the different status attributed to men and women is based on patterns of sex-related psychological development. She argues that the subordination of women results from the multiplicity of evaluations and social practices that shape people's understanding of themselves as males or females, and that women have colluded in accepting this status of being defined in relation to men.

Influential among contemporary philosophers who have pursued the questions raised by de Beauvoir is the French philosopher Luce Irigaray who, for example, has discussed the psychoanalytic view that all theory results from unconscious determinants. She points out that, in trying to establish the relation between a postulated drive and a representation – a fantasy, an image, a word – one can only experience the representation. This claim is relevant for *psychoanalytic* feminism, which seeks to use psychoanalysis to study the origin of philosophical categories such as rationality and emotion but, at the same time, raises questions about specific concepts used in traditional psychoanalysis.

Feminist spirituality

The feminist approaches just discussed are echoed in the development of various types of feminist spirituality. For example, *cultural* feminism, a position analogous to that of the peace movement, concentrates on the development of an identifiable woman-culture, largely through individual and community efforts and often with an emphasis on intimacy. Cultural feminism is compatible with, though does not require, *spiritual* feminism, a religious movement involving a criticism of male-centered religious conceptions and proposing alternative women-friendly conceptions. An influential example of this approach is found in the work of the feminist theologian Mary Daly, for instance

in *Beyond God the Father*. Here, Daly characterizes the original sin as stolen energy, and salvation as women's reclaiming this energy stolen by men and forming a sisterhood of humanity whose ideal is a community of women living in harmony with nature and non-human animals.

Some spiritual feminists have also displayed an interest in such things as Goddess worship, witchcraft, and divination. This conception of the divinity has been shared by various – some quite unrelated – cultural traditions. It is that of the Great Mother (Mater Deum Magna), the central figure of a religious cult that made its way from Phrygia into Greece and Rome and, eventually, together with Mithras and Isis, became one of the three most important cults in the Roman Empire. The Great Mother, also called Cybele, Dindymene, Mater Idaea, Sipylene, Agdistis, Ammas, Rhea, Gaia, Demeter, Maia, Ops, Tellus, or Ceres was the parent of gods and humans, the All-begetter, the All-nourisher, the fertile Mother Earth. The cult ceased to be widespread in Antiquity around CE 394. However, as indicated, it has awakened an interest among contemporary spiritual feminists.

The label cultural feminism was coined by representatives of socialist feminism and Marxist feminism in the 1970s to emphasize the preoccupation of some feminists with largely personal concerns and their lack of enthusiasm for mass reforms, a preoccupation that socialist feminists found unacceptable. Along similar lines, representatives of socialist and Marxist feminism have criticized spiritual feminism as escapist, and a distraction from the actual material struggle women face today. At any rate, all these varieties of feminism sharply criticize many traditional social structures, especially the patriarchal institutions of the various main world religions such as those of Christianity and Islam.

Cultural feminism tends to uphold the differences between the sexes – i.e. the male–female and masculinity–femininity dichotomies – and to imply that they are unchangeable, accepting the view that women are by nature less violent, more co-operative, and more caring than men. To be sure, cultural feminism opposes the inference from women being more caring than men to women being more emotional, let alone less rational than men. Yet, the position of cultural feminism may involve an element of ESSENTIALISM, which can also be found in less congenial brands of feminism, such as female *supremacism*. This latter term is sometimes used as a synonym of *gynocentrism* (which other times simply means a woman-centered conception of the world), a position according to which a feminist revolution would (and should) bring about, not equality, but a gynocentric world: a power structure instituting female supremacy. A version of this position envisages a female future, where features considered feminine would be generally affirmed, species responsibility would be in the hands of females, and the number of males would be kept down to about 10 percent of the population.

Feminist philosophy and traditional philosophical approaches

Some feminists have also criticized dichotomous thinking in theorizing about gender, on the grounds that it involves a conception of gender as a dichotomy where males and characteristics supposedly essential to them – e.g. aggressiveness and rationality – and females and characteristics supposed to be essential to them – e.g. maternal instinct, maternal thinking, and emotion – are considered to be exhaustive and mutually exclusive.

Along these lines, some feminist philosophers have attacked traditional epistemology and the philosophy of science, holding that rationality and emotion are mutually integrated and equal sources of knowledge. This position, however, is still considered too abstract in pursuing epistemology from a feminist standpoint. So is a mere reference to objectivity as lack of bias where the latter is understood as excluding all particularity, e.g. historical, or gendered. In an attempt at formulating more concrete alternatives, feminist philosophers have accordingly focused on objectivity. For example, the contemporary philosopher Sandra Harding has formulated the notion of *strong objectivity*, which is politically informed.

Another area of concern has been the extent to which empiricism can serve to address feminist concerns. In this regard, the contemporary philosopher Lynn Nelson has advocated a form of non-individualistic empiricism characterized by webs of belief that can be tested against the experiences of the community of knowers. Also along empiricist lines, the contemporary philosopher Helen Longino has argued that evidential reasoning is context-dependent but objectivity is ensured by social criticism. These and other non-traditional empiricist positions have been criticized as inadequate by various philosophers, from Sandra Harding to philosophers who rely on genealogy and interpretation, e.g. Linda Alcoff.

In metaphysics, some feminist philosophers have attacked traditional metaphysics, holding that mind and body mutually constitute each other, hence mind–body dualism is false. Still others have attacked traditional sharp separations between self and others, holding that empathy helps individuals reach others, so that the problem of other minds does not arise. Feminist discussions have also led to criticisms of scientific concepts, methods, and practices, as evidenced, for example, in Sandra Harding's collection entitled *Discovering Reality: Feminist Perspectives on Epistemology, Methodology, and Philosophy of Science*.

In this latter regard, feminist philosophers have raised the previously mentioned criticisms of scientific essentialism and the implications and stereotypes drawn from it concerning women – a charge given credence by the fact that a number of philosophers have held that only males fully display human nature. This self-serving view has lost currency in contemporary philosophy and has been criticized on various grounds. Feminist philosophers have argued that it only espouses a patriarchal ideology without any basis on fact. They have also pointed out that such a conception tends to be associated with describing women as "the weaker sex" and, in some cases, this has been taken to mean psychologically weaker, as evidenced by many nineteenth- and early twentieth-century studies of hysteria.

In addition, some feminists have applied, and further developed in a feminist context, ideas formulated by the French philosopher Michel Foucault (CE 1926–84), who argued that bodies of knowledge – *epistemes* – and, in general, systems of thought are tied but not reducible to structures of power. On this view, an episteme is a contingent system for the production, regulation, distribution, and operation of statements. It is independent of the beliefs and intentions of individual thinkers and, though contingent, it creates constraints on thought and action – e.g. concerning the nature of gender, the existing types of gender, and the social options associated with them – that, to those caught up in them, seem unsurpassable.

As for ethics and sociopolitical philosophy, some feminist philosophers have criticized masculinist emphasis on rules and principles. Instead, they have advocated an ethics of care focused on personal relations and responsibilities, as involved in particular circumstances. Most influential here has been the work of the contemporary psychologist Carol Gilligan in her *In a Different Voice*.

Whatever their differences, feminist philosophical approaches aim at explaining why women are subordinate and at suggesting ways in which this subordination can be overcome. Recent feminist thinkers, however, have objected that earlier feminists have approached such an overall purpose in too systematic and unified a fashion. Indeed, they have argued that this is an instance of the type of male-thinking that feminists have criticized. By contrast, these more recent philosophers advocate *feminist diversity* on the grounds that the concerns of women vary by class, race, and culture. This suggestion, however, has met with criticism by other feminist philosophers, who are concerned that an emphasis on feminist diversity may lead to the disintegration of both feminist philosophy and the feminist movement.

See also: philosophy of science; philosophy, sociopolitical

Further reading

Beauvoir, Simone de (1972) *The Second Sex*, Harmondsworth: Penguin.
Daly, Mary (1968) *Beyond God the Father*, Boston: Beacon Press.
De Gournays, Marie (1989) *Égalité des hommes et des femmes*, Paris: Côté-Femme.
Firestone, S. (1979) *The Dialectic of Sex*, London: The Women's Press.
Fletcher, John and Benjamin, Andrew E. (1990) *Abjection, Melancholia, and Love:* *The Work of Julia Kristeva*, London and New York: Routledge.
Fraser, Nancy, and Bartky, Sandra Lee (1992) *Revaluing French Feminism: Critical Essays on Difference, Agency, and Culture*, Bloomington: Indiana University Press.
Frye, Marylin (1983) *The Politics of Reality: Essays in Feminist Theory*, Trumansburg, NY: The Crossing Press.
Gilligan, Carol (1982) *In a Different Voice*, Cambridge, MA: Harvard University Press.
Harding, Sandra (1983) *Discovering Reality: Feminist Perspectives on Epistemology, Methodology, and Philosophy of Science*, Dordrecht, Netherlands: Reidel.
Irigaray, Luce (1995 [1993]) *An Ethics of Sexual Difference*, Ithaca, NY: Cornell University Press.
Lugones, María C. and Spellman, Elizabeth V. (1983) "Have we got a theory for you! Feminist theory, cultural imperialism and the demand for 'the woman's voice'," *Women's Studies International Forum* 6(6): 573–81.
Mill, John Stuart (1906) *Subjection of Women*, London and New York: Longmans and Green.
Poulain de la Barre, François (1990) *The Equality of the Sexes*, Manchester: Manchester University Press.
Spellman, Elizabeth V. (1988) *Inessential Woman*, Boston: Beacon Press.
Taylor, Harriet (1983) *The Enfranchisement of Women*, London: Virago.
Wollstonecraft, M. (1995) *A Vindication of the Rights of Women*, in S. Tomaselli (ed.) *A Vindication of the Rights of Man and a Vindication of the Rights of Women*, Cambridge, UK: Cambridge University Press.

feminist spirituality *see* feminist philosophy

ferio *see* syllogism

ferison *see* syllogism

fesapo *see* syllogism

festino *see* syllogism

fetishism *see* ethics; Marxism; myth; psychoanalysis

fetus *see* abortion

fiction *see* imagination; philosophy of law; philosophy of science; psychoanalysis

fictionalism *see* philosophy of science

fideism *see* existentialism; philosophy of religion

fidens quaerens intellectum *see* philosophy of religion

field *see* relation

field theory *see* philosophy of science

figure *see* logic; syllogism

figure-ground *see* perception

final cause *see* causal law

finitary *see* philosophy of mathematics

finite *see* infinity

finite automaton *see* computer theory; cybernetics

finitism *see* philosophy of mathematics

finitude *see* existentialism; philosophy of religion

first actualization *see* act

first-cause argument *see* philosophy of religion

first imposition *see* philosophy of language

first intention *see* philosophy of language

first law of thermodynamics *see* philosophy of science

first-limit theorem *see* ars conjectandi, under ars

first order *see* logic

first-order policy problems *see* philosophy, sociopolitical

first philosophy *see* metaphysics

first potentiality *see* act

firstness *see* metaphysics

fitness *see* evolution

Five divine presences *see* metaphysics

five elements *see* element

five phases *see* element

Five Pillars of Islam *see* Arabic philosophy

five suns *see* Nahua philosophy

five ways *see* Scholasticism

Florence Academy *see* Neoplatonism

Florentine Academy *see* Neoplatonism

fluent *see* calculus

fluxion *see* calculus

focal meaning *see* metaphysics

folk philosophy *see* philosophy

folk psychology *see* philosophy of mind

fons vitae *see* Arabic philosophy

for itself *see* existentialism

force, idea- *see* idea; voluntarism

force, illocutionary *see* speech act theory

force in physics *see* philosophy of science

force, thought- *see* idea; voluntarism

forcing *see* logic

foreknowledge, divine *see* determinism

forgiveness *see* Christianity; Judaism

form, aesthetic *see* aesthetics

form, grammatical *see* logic

form, logical *see* logic

form, metaphysical *see* Platonism

form of life *see* philosophy of language; philosophy, sociopolitical

form, Platonic *see* Platonism

form, substantial *see* Thomism

formal arts *see* aesthetics

formal cause *see* causal law

formal distinction *see* definition

formal fallacy *see* fallacy

formal justice *see* ethics

formal language *see* logic

formal learnability theory *see* philosophy of language

formal logic *see* logic

formal ontology *see* phenomenology

formal semantics *see* philosophy of language

formalism, aesthetic *see* aesthetics

formalism, ethical *see* ethics

formalism in mathematics *see* philosophy of mathematics

formalism, jurisprudential *see* philosophy of law

formalization *see* logic

formation rule *see* logic

forms, theory of *see* abstract; Academy; Aristotelianism; Platonism; Thomism

formula *see* logic

fortitude *see* ethics; Kantian philosophy; virtue

foundation axiom *see* set

foundationalism *see* justification

fountain of life *see* Arabic philosophy

four books *see* Confucianism; Islam

four causes *see* causal law

four elements *see* Greek philosophy; Nahua philosophy

four noble truths *see* Buddhism

fourth condition *see* epistemology

fractals, theory of *see* philosophy of mathematics

fragmentation *see* Frankfurt School; philosophy, sociopolitical

Frankfurt School A group of philosophers, social scientists, and cultural critics associated with the University of Frankfurt, some of whom founded the Institute of Social Research at that university during the 1920s, around the beginning of the Weimar Republic. Among its first-generation members were the German philosophers Max Horkheimer (CE 1895–1973), Theodor W. Adorno (CE 1903–69), and Herbert Marcuse (CE 1898–1979), the German psychoanalyst Erich Fromm (CE 1900–80), and the German literary critic Walter Benjamin (CE 1892–1940). Most prominent among its second-generation members was the contempor-

ary German philosopher Jürgen Habermas, who studied with Adorno in the 1950s and, though resigning from the Institute in the early 1970s to join the Max Planck Institute, continued to pursue the Institute's interests afterwards.

One purpose guiding the members' efforts was to rethink Marxism in the aftermath of the Russian Revolution. In the process, they developed a critical theory of society, i.e. an effort to continue the Marxist transformation of moral philosophy into a social and political critique while rejecting the dogmatic aspect of orthodox Marxism. Three stages are usually distinguished in the School's development. The first, from its beginning to around the mid-1930s, concentrated on combining, through interdisciplinary efforts, empirical analysis with historical materialism. The second stage began around the time when, with Adolf Hitler (CE 1889–1945) as Chancellor of Germany, the School relocated first in Geneva (in 1933) and, then, in New York City (in 1935), when it affiliated with Columbia University. This period marked a shift towards a lesser emphasis on – or the abandonment of – Marxism. The third stage began around 1945 and focused on a critique of instrumental reason that was seen as exploiting nature, dehumanizing and exploiting human beings in a bureaucratic, manipulated, commodity-oriented culture.

A point already formulated by Benjamin, largely in connection with aesthetics, and then developed by Adorno during the second and third stages, in connection with contemporary societies, concerns fragmentation, which he considered inescapable and a more realistic alternative to the traditional one-sided social conceptions and arrangements. "The whole is the false," he said, and he sought a non-instrumental, non-dominating relation to nature and others in fragmentary – mostly aesthetic – experiences, where freedom can be achieved, so long as they remain fragmentary – a prospect Adorno thought eventually bound to fail.

In the process, Adorno explored the mimetic and imaginative elements of art, which, through *fiction*, the product of *fantasy* (sometimes used as synonymous with IMAGINATION but, more often, as imagination that is extravagant or unrestrained), helps fantasize or imagine others without becoming identical or identified with them.

The work of Habermas was significantly developed in response to the views just discussed. He proposed a recasting of critical theory by developing an interdisciplinary research program in the social sciences and again emphasizing normative concerns. The potential for freedom, Habermas argued, lies in communicative or discursive rationality based on argumentative testing, where the force of the better argument prevails, norms for non-dominating relations can be developed, and a broader notion of reason can be formulated and actualized.

See also: aesthetics; Continental philosophy; Marxism; philosophy of science; philosophy, sociopolitical

Further reading
Jay, Martin (1996) *The Dialectical Imagination: A History of the Frankfurt School and the Institute of Social Research, 1923–1950*, Berkeley and London: University of California Press.
Schirmacher, Wolfgang (1999) *German 20th-Century Philosophy: The Frankfurt School*, New York: Continuum.
Wiggershaus, Rolf (1995) *The Frankfurt School: Its History, Theories, and Political Significance*, Cambridge, MA: MIT Press.

free beauty *see* aesthetics

free enterprise *see* philosophy of economics

free logic *see* logic

free rider *see* decision

free variable *see* logic

free will *see* determinism; philosophy of religion

free-will defense *see* philosophy of religion

free-will problem *see* determinism

freedom *see* existentialism; philosophy, sociopolitical

frequency *see* associationism; probability

friendship *see* ethics

frisesomorum *see* syllogism

function, mathematical *see* logic

function, propositional *see* logic

function, state *see* philosophy of science

function, teleological *see* explanation

function, truth- *see* logic

functional abstraction *see* logic

functional calculus *see* logic

functional completeness *see* completeness

functional dependence *see* logic

functional explanation *see* explanation

functional jurisprudence *see* philosophy of law

functionalism *see* philosophy of mind

functor *see* logic

fundamental distribution of terms *see* syllogism

fundamentalism *see* philosophy of religion

fundamentum divisionis *see* definition

fusion of horizons *see* hermeneutics

future *see* metaphysics; philosophy of science

future contingents *see* logic

future generations *see* ethics

futuribilia *see* logic

fuzzy logic *see* ambiguity; logic

fuzzy set *see* ambiguity; set

G

G *see* logic

Galenian figure *see* syllogism

gambler's fallacy *see* fallacy

game *see* play

game theory *see* decision

Garden of Eden *see* myth

Garden, the *see* Epicureanism

Gathas *see* Zoroastrianism

gati *see* Buddhism

gedatsu *see* Zen

gehenna *see* myth

Geist *see* idealism

Geisteswissenschaften *see* explanation; philosophy of science

Gelugpa *see* Buddhism

gemara *see* Judaism

Gemeinschaft *see* holism; philosophy, sociopolitical

gender From the Middle English *gendre* or *gender*, which derived from the Middle French *gendre*, which derived from the Latin *gener-* (genus) meaning "kind," "sort," or "class." In contemporary English, gender is often used as synonymous with the sex of an individual, i.e. meaning *biologically a male or a female*. However, it is also used in a *social* or *cultural sense*, to denote features, roles, and character traits socially considered to belong to the traditionally thought dichotomous categories feminine and masculine.

A number of contemporary social scientists and philosophers have challenged gender essentialism (see ESSENTIALISM). One way of doing this has been to denounce as stereotypical the purported *fixed status* of the characteristics assigned to the concepts of femininity or masculinity. This type of criticism focuses on language and gender. Seminal among works in this area is *Language and Woman's Place*, by the linguist Robin Lakoff, who argues that, to sound feminine, women are faced with having to use forms of speech, e.g. rising intonation, which are considered ineffective in public life, e.g. because they are interpreted as evidence of insecurity. One of Lakoff's influential critics has been linguist Janet Holmes, who in *Women, Men and Politeness*, argues that one and the same linguistic expression typically has various functions, not necessarily those subject to victimization on which Lakoff focused. Other critics have argued that the speech styles Lakoff identifies are specific only to white, or even white middle-class women, and not to African-American women; and that gender-differentiated linguistic conventions are not arbitrary, but strategic responses to social constraints and specific communicative context. These latter thinkers have been investigating women as linguistic agents, not merely as victims.

A different approach is displayed by French thinkers who address language as an open, non-neutral system for representing the world, ourselves, and others. Notable among their representatives has been the French philosopher Luce Irigaray, who has explored the possibility of linguistic usage, especially by women, which could undermine predominantly male-centered linguistic conventions and open linguistic access to women's experiences. She speculates about "*parler femme*," i.e. woman-speech, something that does not yet exist.

The previous approaches have led some thinkers concerned with gender to question the categories masculine and feminine. One way of doing this has been to question the widespread assumption that the categories masculine and feminine, and the specific items each names, are directly and primarily determined by biology. This is not to say that biology has no influence on gender differences: the social features, roles, and traits associated with one of the said categories, by contrast with those associated with the other. Instead, it is to caution against gender stereotyping. The grounds for such a cautionary view are that, first, such influence is not as direct and invulnerable to change as that between, say, biology and sleeping habits. Second, given substantial empirical evidence, whatever the influence of biology on gender, it is not uniform throughout cultures; but different cultures identify different features, roles, and traits as belonging in the feminine and masculine categories.

In addition, the feminine–masculine dichotomy itself has been questioned by philosophers who have, for example, asked: "How natural is heterosexuality?" "How natural is the existence of only two polarized gender categories?" "How natural is the hierarchy traditionally associated with them?" (See FEMINIST PHILOSOPHY.) Influenced by Irigaray, who had questioned such conceptions, these critics noted that linguistic abstractions and related linguistic practices serve to construct categories of sex, sexuality, and gender. As a response, they have developed *queer theory*, which emphasizes the instability of such categories. For example, the contemporary theorist Judith P. Butler, in *Gender Trouble*, proposes a gender theory that makes room for non-traditional forms of sexuality and gender, including also gender-neutral categories or, alternatively, gender-bending conceptions. In the process, such notions are discussed as that of compulsory heterosexuality, and compulsory sexual identity, as exemplified in some surgical procedures currently performed on newborns – typically to make them female – when the sexual organs of newborns are unclear. In the process, the related categories of homosexuality, heterosexuality, and homophobia also come under scrutiny. Analogous interests and concerns have arisen as a result of psychological and sociological studies of female – by contrast with male – moral, intellectual, and physical development, which have significant implications concerning gender sensitivity (see FEMINIST PHILOSOPHY).

See also: biology; ethics; evolution; feminist philosophy

Further reading
Butler, Judith P. (1990) *Gender Trouble*, London and New York: Routledge.
Chanter, Tina (1996) *Rethinking Sex and Gender: Spindel Conference 1996*, Memphis, TN: Dept of Philosophy, University of Memphis.
Goodwin, M.H. (1990) *He-Said-She-Said: Talk as Social Organization among Black Children*, Bloomington, IN: Indiana University Press.
Holmes, Janet (1995) *Women, Men and Politeness*, London: Longman.
Irigaray, Luce (1985) *This Sex Which Is Not One*, Ithaca, NY: Cornell University Press.
Lakoff, Robin (1975) *Language and Woman's Place*, New York: Harper & Row.
Zack, Naomi, Shrage, Lauie, and Sartwell, Crispin (1998) *Race, Class, Gender, and Sexuality: The Big Questions*, Malden, MA: Blackwell Publishers.

genealogy *see* historicism

general jurisprudence *see* philosophy of law

general relativity *see* philosophy of science

general-systems theory *see* philosophy of mathematics

general term *see* description

general will *see* philosophy, sociopolitical

generalizability *see* ethics

generalization argument *see* ethics

generalization, existential *see* logic

generalization principle *see* ethics

generalization, universal *see* logic

generation *see* change; creation; historicism

generationism *see* creation

generative grammar *see* philosophy of language

generic consistency, principle of *see* ethics

generic image *see* perception

gene-splicing *see* ethics

genesis *see* creation; historicism

genetic engineering *see* ethics

genetic epistemology *see* epistemology

genetic fallacy *see* fallacy

genetic psychology *see* philosophy of mind

genocide *see* philosophy, sociopolitical

genotype *see* evolution

genra *see* aesthetics

genus *see* definition

genus generalissimum *see* definition

genus summun *see* definition

geometric conventionalism *see* philosophy of mathematics

geometric method *see* Cartesianism

geometry, Euclidean *see* philosophy of mathematics

geometry, non-Eucledian *see* philosophy of mathematics

German Idealism *see* idealism

German Philosophy, the *see* idealism

Gesellschaft *see* philosophy, sociopolitical

Gestalt conception of personal identity *see* identity

Gestalt, figure-ground *see* perception

Gestalt psychology *see* perception; philosophy of mind

Gestalt shift *see* ethics

Gettier problem *see* epistemology; justification; knowledge

ghaybah *see* Ṣūfism

given, myth of the *see* empiricism

given, the *see* epistemology

glass ceiling *see* ethics

Gleason's theorem *see* logic

global problems *see* philosophy, sociopolitical

global supervenience *see* supervenience

glory *see* philosophy of religion

glossae *see* Scholasticism

glossogonus metaphysics *see* metaphysics

gnoseology *see* epistemology

gnosis *see* Christianity; Neoplatonism

Gnostic *see* Christianity; Neoplatonism

Gnosticism *see* Christianity; Neoplatonism

go *see* Buddhism; Japanese philosophy

goal-directed behavior *see* intention; philosophy of mind

goal-directed system *see* cybernetics

God An Anglo-Saxon name, originally Teutonic. There are many conceptions of God and the gods. In the singular, the concept can be found in monotheistic religions ranging from the Egyptian sun god Ra, through the Indian BRAHMAN, to the Jewish YAHWEH, and the Arabic ALLĀH.

The names of God in JUDAISM vary. They include Ihvn Alhim and Jehovah Elohim. Elohim is a name thought too sacred to write about (and is one of the names appearing in Genesis, translated as God or Lord in the Christian Bible, but meaning deities or deity as an aggregate of many infinite forces), and referred to as *binah* (understanding), the third sphere of the cabalistic universe, sometimes also referred to as the Supernatural Mother.

In philosophy, conceptions of God have wavered between absoluteness and relativity. In the Vedas, Brahman is said to reside in all things and be, and be reached by means of, intuition. In the Upanishads, Brahman is the

One and the Self or Soul of all things. While in the same religious tradition, the conception of the god Shiva has ranged from that of a god among others, to that of a dual male–female divinity, to still that of many goddesses, to finally that of an ineffable being very much like the One of the Upanishads.

Though Ancient Greece was largely polytheistic (where *polytheism* is the view that there is more than one god), a significant number of Greek philosophers were monotheistic (where *monotheism* is the view that there exists one and only one god). For example, Xenophanes (*c.* 570–*c.* 475 BCE) considered God as unmoving and the One. Plato (428–348 BCE) stressed God's absolute nature in the early dialogues; but became increasingly concerned with God's relation to the world of change in the middle and later ones. Aristotle (CE 384–322) formulated the idea of the unmoved mover, which was strongly monotheistic. For the Egypto-Roman philosopher Plotinus (CE 204–70), God was the One, superior to all existence and ideas, and the source from which all these emanated.

In addition, *pantheism*, the doctrine that the world is identical with God, has many philosophical instances ranging from some of the Stoics, through Renaissance philosophers, to Hegelians. In this regard, *Pantheismusstreit* – literally, dispute over Pantheism – is a German term denoting an eighteenth-century debate among German philosophers about the nature of pantheism and whether a pantheist must be an atheist, i.e. someone who believes there is no God. Finally, *panentheism*, the doctrine that all reality is part of God, has had proponents in Western philosophy – beginning with the thinker who coined the term: the German philosopher Karl Christian Friedrich Krause (CE 1781–1832) – as well as in Eastern thought, e.g. the Pakistani philosopher Muḥammad Iqbal (CE 1877–1938).

The divine attributes of the Judeo-Christian God involve, most notably, omnipotence, i.e. God is all-powerful; omniscience, i.e. God is all knowing; omnibenevolence and absolute justice, i.e. God is absolutely benevolent and just; omnipresence, i.e. God is everywhere; personhood, i.e. God is perfect; INFINITY, i.e. God is infinite; eternity, i.e. God is eternal; and

uniqueness, i.e. God is the only God. Christian philosophers emphasized these attributes too, sometimes formulating paradoxes. For example, the philosopher Augustine (CE 354–430; born in the African city of Thagaste) held God's infinity was such that contradictory propositions could be true of God. Others formulated the *paradoxes of omnipotence*. These start with questions: "Can God perform logically contradictory tasks?" "Can God cease to be omnipotent?" "Can God create another omnipotent being?" "Can God create a stone He cannot then move (paradox of the stone)?" In each case, either God can, in which case God's power would become limited, or God cannot, in which case God's power is limited.

As for Islam, the term for attribute is ṣifāt. In this tradition, God's attributes are closely akin to those in Christianity. They include life, power, knowledge, will, hearing, seeing, and speech (see ISLAM).

There is also a fact about – if not an attribute of – God, namely, that God is the Creator of the universe. In explaining this relation, some medieval philosophers – e.g. Augustine, the philosopher Giovanni Fidanza Bonaventure (CE 1217–74; born in the city of Bagnorea, in what is now Italy), and the philosopher Thomas Aquinas (CE 1225–74; born near the city of Naples, in what is now Italy) – argued that there are *rationes seminales*, i.e. seminal reasons or a group of virtual forms in God, and that these activate the creation.

As for the other attributes, the philosopher Anselm (CE 1033–1109; born in the city of Aosta, in what is now Italy), defined God as the absolute and all-knowing Supreme Being. So did Aquinas, who adopted the doctrine of one of the most influential philosophers of the Islamic world, Ibn Sīnā (in Latin, Avicenna; CE 980–1037), that God has an identity of essence and existence. Another influential philosopher in this tradition was the Arabic philosopher Ibn Rushd (in Latin, Averroes; CE 1126–98), who conceived of God as eternal and absolute. Together with Ibn Sīnā and al-Fārābī (CE *c.* 870–950), he was especially influential among Jewish philosophers, for example Moses ben Maimon or Maimonides, or Ibn Maymūm (CE 1135–1204), and even more so his follower

Levi ben Gershon or Gersonides (CE 1288–1344), both of whom followed Aristotle and Ibn Rushd in characterizing God as the unmoved mover.

By contrast with these notions, among polytheistic views of the gods, Ancient Greeks often said that humans existed to entertain the gods. In philosophy, however, this view was not common if at all existent. The Greek philosopher Epicurus (341–271 BCE) held that the gods existed in perfect bliss and were indifferent to humans. This view influenced that of the Roman poet and philosopher Titus Lucretius Carus (*c.* 99–55 BCE), who held that the gods existed in the interspace between naturally created worlds, and were self-sufficient and indifferent to humans.

Other traditions have shown analogous ambivalence concerning the conception and functions of God/the gods. To mention just one, among the Pre-Hispanic Nahuas of the Americas, Toltec doctrine referred to a supreme divinity by many names: Tloque Nahuaque (Possessor of the Near and Close), Moyocoyatzin (He Who Invents Himself), and, less univocally, Ometeotl (the Supreme Dual God). However, the designs of this God were not accessible to humans. Indeed, this divinity is somewhat indifferent to humans or, at best, treats humans as mere objects of amusement and mockery.

Some of these themes can also be found among the Mayans. One of their books, the *Chilam Balam of Chumayel*, espouses a monotheistic conception of God, where the word of God preceded heaven and earth. Another Mayan book, the *Popol Vuh*, refers to more than one god deliberating and proceeding to create the universe where they require that humans care about them; indeed, they destroy trial versions of humans who failed to do so.

As for Africa, the ontology of the Akan people (in Ghana), for example, is henotheist – i.e. it upholds *henotheism*: the view that one god is supreme, while not denying that there are other gods. It includes Onyame or Onyankopōn (the Supreme Being) at the apex, abosom (lesser deities or spirits) next, nsamanfo (ancestral spirits) after these, and the phenomenal world at the bottom of this hierarchy.

Another conception of the divinity shared by various – some quite unrelated – cultural traditions is that of the Great Mother (Mater Deum Magna), the central figure of a religious cult that made its way from Phrygia into Greece and Rome and, eventually, together with Mithras and Isis, became one of the three most important cults in the Roman Empire. The Great Mother, also called Cybele, Dindymene, Mater Idaea, Sipylene, Agolistis, Ammas, Rhea, Gaia, Demeter, Maia, Ops, Tellus, and Ceres was the parent of gods and humans, the All-begetter, the All-nourisher, the fertile Mother Earth. The cult ceased to be widespread in Antiquity around CE 394. However, it has awakened an interest among contemporary spiritual feminists. Also, one can still find a reverenced figure of this type in the South American Pachamama, and her likeness can sometimes be found in some corner of this or that Catholic Church in northwestern Argentina, Bolivia, and Peru. A related figure is Ts'its'tsi'nako, the creator deity among the Keres (a Pueblo people of New Mexico, the United States), who is represented as Thought-Woman or Spider Grandmother and creates by thinking and speaking.

As for New Zealand, Māori religious beliefs, for example, include the great god Tāne or Tāne-mahuta. He separated his father Rangi or Rangi-nui (the sky) from his mother Papa or Papatuanuku (the earth), separated himself from them, and clothed his mother with trees and other plants. Accordingly, he is the god of the forests, common ancestor of all plant life. He, like Tangaroa, another one of the great Maori gods, is ever-present and all-seeing, and also creator of the first woman, hence of the origin of the Māori people who, therefore, are related to all plant life. Another great god is his brother, Tū or Tū-mata-uenga (the warlike ancestor of humans), who fought with Tāne and defeated him and his other brothers (including Whiro, who is bad), thus attaining humans' right to use plant life; but, since it is related to the Māori, not to abuse it. In addition, everything has its patupaiarehe (protecting or guardian spirit). In short, there is a hierarchy of divinities related to humans and the natural world so that humans and the natural world are kin.

In Japan, Shintō, meaning "way of the gods," was originally a pantheistic religion that worshipped nature deities. From Confucianism, it adopted the veneration of ancestors, and was also influenced by Buddhism. Its central myth is that Amaterasu Omikami – the heaven-radiant Great Divinity – was sent to the sky to rule over the sun and, from there, sent her grandson to earth. He founded an eternal dynasty in the islands that constitute Japan. In CE 1868, Shintō became the State religion where the emperor was worshipped as a god. In CE 1945, Shintō lost this status and, the next year, the emperor renounced all claims to divinity.

In modern times, atheism – the doctrine that no God exists – has become a rather common position in philosophy (though there still are many philosophers who uphold some form of monotheism), and, indeed, in theology, among Death of God theologians who seem to view traditional conceptions of the divinity as losing their credibility and force.

See also: Arabic philosophy; Christianity; Jewish philosophy; philosophy of religion

Further reading
Bailey, John (1983) *Gods and Men: Myths and Legends from the World's Religions*, Oxford and New York: Oxford University Press.
Johnson, Paul G. (1997) *God and World Religions: Basic Beliefs and Themes*, Shippensburg, PA: Ragged Edge Press.
Neusner, Jacob (1997) *God*, Cleveland, OH: Pilgrim Press.
Patterson, John (1992) *Exploring Maori Values*, Palmerston North, New Zealand: The Dunmore Press.

God, arguments about the existence of *see* philosophy of religion

God, biblical *see* Jewish philosophy; Judaism

God, names of *see* Yahweh

God of Abraham *see* Jewish philosophy; Judaism

God of Abraham, Isaac, and Jacob *see* Jewish philosophy; Judaism

God of Aristotle *see* Jewish philosophy; Judaism

Gödel numbering *see* philosophy of mathematics

Gödel's incompleteness theorems *see* philosophy of mathematics

Goke-shichishū *see* Zen

golden age *see* myth

golden mean *see* ethics

golden rule *see* ethics

good *see* ethics; supervenience

good, common *see* ethics; utilitarianism

good-making characteristic *see* ethics; supervenience

good, the *see* ethics

goseki *see* Zen

Göttingen Circle *see* Kantian philosophy

government *see* philosophy, sociopolitical

Gozu School *see* Zen

grace *see* philosophy of religion

grammar *see* logic; philosophy of language

grammar, logical *see* logic

grammar, speculative *see* philosophy of language

grammatical form *see* logic; philosophy of language

grammaticality intuition *see* intuition

gratia praeveniens *see* philosophy of religion

great chain of being *see* chain of being

great instauration *see* philosophy of science

great learning *see* Chinese philosophy

great-man theory *see* philosophy, sociopolitical

Great Mother, the *see* God

great skepticism *see* skepticism

great ultimate, the *see* Chinese philosophy

greatest-happiness principle *see* ethics

Greek philosophy This flourished for a period of more than 1,000 years, from before 600 BCE to soon after CE 600, by when all or nearly all the philosophical approaches of the Western world, and many of the scientific theories that have become accepted since then – among them, the atomic theory, the heliocentric view of the solar system, and the theory of organic evolution – had been outlined.

These developments took place in Schools of philosophy that developed in Ancient Greece or *Hellas*, a culturally cohesive but politically fragmented area in what is now Greece and some of the surrounding countries. Each governmental unit in this area was a *polis* or city-state, whose internal organization varied widely from *polis* to *polis*, and from time to time. Athens, for example, was a direct democracy at one time, but not at most other times. Sparta always had a governmental organization widely different from that of Athens, with which it was frequently at war.

The schools of philosophy developed in this area are grouped in the following main categories.

The Pre-Socratics
These were the early Greek philosophers who were not influenced by Socrates (469–399 BCE) – most of whom lived before he was born. The first in this category were the Milesians or Ionian philosophers, who focused on the question: "What is there really?" They understood it to ask for a basic substance. The astronomer, mathematician, engineer, and philosopher Thales (640–546 BCE) answered that it was water. The geographer, alleged inventor of the sun dial, and philosopher Anaximander (612–545 BCE) answered that it was the *apeiron*, the indefinite boundless that came into and went out of existence according to a principle of cosmic justice. His reported pupil, Anaximenes (CE 588–524), said that it was air understood in a somewhat psychical way, because he identified it with the breath of life. Change occurred through condensation and rarefaction.

The Pythagoreans
A School initiated by the philosopher and religious-sect leader Pythagoras (570–500 BCE), who, as recent scholarship suggests, was

not, as traditionally thought, a systematic thinker, scientist, and mathematician. He is, however, credited with coining the term *philosophia*, Greek for the English PHILOSOPHY (from the Greek *philos*: "lover" or "friend of," and *sophia*: "wisdom"). The School's reflection centered on the application of numbers to reality (particularly in astronomy), the development of geometry, and the analysis of *harmony* (from the Greek *harmos*: "a fitting or joining"), which was applied especially to health, but also to astronomy in the notion of the *harmony of the spheres*. Pythagoras was famous in Ancient Greece for introducing the doctrine of *metempsychosis*, i.e. the doctrine that the soul is immortal and is reborn in human and animal reincarnations. Pythagoreanism lasted from 550 to 430 BCE and exercised an influence for centuries.

Heraclitus (*c.* 540–475 BCE), born in Ephesus, rejected popular religion and the works of the Greek poets, and opposed democracy as a pretense. He considered the main feature of reality to be CHANGE, considered it to be basically fire, and explained it by appeal to the *logos*, a pattern amounting to operant justice whereby opposites in conflict such as day and night, birth and death, and good and evil produce change. Accordingly, though Heraclitus apparently had no disciples or close followers, the term Heraclitean is used to denote philosophies or approaches that emphasize change.

The Eleatics
This included the lawmaker and philosopher Parmenides (*c.* 515 –*c.* 450 BCE), who stressed monism and the unity of all things based on logical arguments founded on a conception of meaning that amounted only to reference, and Zeno of Elea (490–430 BCE.), who shared with Parmenides the view that all is one and plurality and change are unreal. Zeno is reputed to have invented dialectics and argued for the view of reality as a changeless being by formulating paradoxes of space, time, motion, and change he considered implicit in the common-sense conception of a world of changing multiplicity (see PARADOX).

Besides the previous philosophers, others came to be associated with this School, most notably: the admiral and philosopher Melissus of Samos (mid-fifth century BCE), who formulated arguments analogous to those of Zeno; and the philosopher and exiled wandering-minstrel Xenophanes (570–c. 470 BCE), who, like Parmenides, held that all is one, though more as an assumption than, as for Parmenides, a logical consequence of views on meaning.

The Pluralists

These were philosophers who solved the problem of change by combining permanence of the parts or elements of things with changes in the manner in which the parts were combined. They included Empedocles of Agrigentum (c. 490–430 BCE), who identified earth, air, fire, and water as the unchangeable elements that mixed to form all else; Anaxagoras of Clazomene (499–422 BCE), who postulated small particles he called seeds mixed to produce all else; and the atomists Leucippus (fl. c. 440 BCE) and his disciple Democritus of Abdera (460–370 BCE), who held that the basic parts were atoms (the uncuttable), i.e. solid, simple, homogeneous, and without void, which were in perpetual motion, separated from each other by the void, and different from each other in size, shape, and velocity – quantitative differences from which all qualitative differences derive (see ABDERA, SCHOOL OF; ATOMISM).

The Sophists

From the Greek sophistes ("one who professes to make people wise"), this term denotes a number of itinerant thinkers who, during the second half of the fifth century BCE, traveled throughout the Greek world professing to teach, for a fee, rhetoric, philosophy, and how to succeed in life. The Sophists did not form a school or share a body of opinion. They have sometimes been portrayed as charlatans (hence the pejorative term sophism) and other times as high-minded moralists and educators. The truth of the matter is more complex than that. The Sophists included a great variety of individuals who, as a social movement, constituted a response to the expansion of Greek learning, changes in Greek culture where traditional informal teaching approaches had become inadequate and formal teaching required some form of standard economic support, exposure to cultures other than those of Greece

(e.g. brought in by the Persian invasions), and the growing litigiousness of Athenian society, which called for instruction in the art of speaking well and convincingly. They were typically concerned with ethics and individual life, by contrast with traditional philosophers who had been concerned with cosmological questions and the life of the collective, a concern that can also be found in the contemporary tragedies authored, for example, by Euripides (c. 480–406? BCE), but not, or less so, in the earlier tragedies authored by Sophocles (495–406 BCE) and, especially, in those by Aeschylus (525–456 BCE).

Notable among the Sophists was Protagoras of Abdera (c. 490–c. 420 BCE), the most famous, and in all likelihood the first, who held that humans are the measure of all things (in Latin, homo mensura), i.e. that there was no objective truth. Also notable was Gorgias (c. 483–376 BCE), a student of Empedocles. He denied that he taught ethics, asserting instead that he trained clever speakers. Little remains from what he wrote, and it is hard to determine the force of these fragments. According to some interpreters, he argued for metaphysical nihilism, as well as for epistemological nihilism as follows: nothing exists; even if it did, it could not be known; and even if it existed and could be known, it could not be communicated. Other interpreters, however, suggested these arguments were a parody of Parmenides' argument that only one thing exists. Other notable sophists were Antiphon (fifth century BCE), who argued law and custom should be followed only when witnessed by others and, otherwise, one should follow nature; Hippias (fifth century BCE), reputed to have discovered the quadratrix, the first curve other than the circle known to the Greeks; and Prodicus (fifth century BCE), who held the naturalistic view that conceptions of the gods resulted from the usefulness of things and was praised by Socrates for his emphasis on using words correctly and distinguishing the different meanings of terms.

The classic period

This period includes the works of Socrates (469–399 BCE), his student, Plato (428–348 BCE), who founded the ACADEMY, and Plato's student Aristotle (384–322 BCE), who founded the Lyceum (see ARISTOTELIANISM), all of whom contributed to synthetizing the natural philosophy of the Pre-Socratics, and the ethical and cultural concerns of the Sophists, so that philosophy came to be conceived as being crucially concerned with the place of humans in the universe.

The influence of Socratic philosophy, with its emphasis on the irony (in Greek, *eironeia*, i.e. "dissembler") of claiming to be wise only in knowing that no one has attained wisdom, was felt not only on Plato's work, but also on the minor Socratic schools. One such was the Megarian School (*c*. 400–*c*. 300 BCE), also called the Megarians or Megarics, which stressed dialectics, and was influenced by Zeno of Elea. It included an associate of Socrates, Euclid of Megara (450–374 BCE), and Didorus Cronos (fourth century BCE), who, apparently in upholding determinism, argued that the possible does not exist. He is credited with having added temporal variables to modal propositions so that possibility, impossibility, necessity, and non-necessity are always relative to a given time. His disciple, Philo of Megara (fourth century BCE), who anticipated the propositional calculus characterizing the material conditional as a conditional that is true if, and only if, it is false that its antecedent is true and its consequent false (see CONDITION). Philo was also the author of the Master Argument or Ruling Argument, apparently aimed at defining possibility by showing that denying the proposition "some things are possible that neither are nor will be true" is inconsistent with the conjunction of the propositions "every truth about the past is necessary" and "nothing impossible follows from something possible," both of which he appears to have considered obvious.

Another Megarian was Stilpo of Megara (fourth century BCE), who urged *apatheia* or resigned self-control. The Megarians also included, or had affinities with, the Elean–Eretrian School, founded by Phaedo of Elis (fourth century BCE) the early Cynic School, which included Antisthenes (*c*. 445–360 BCE), who argued that only individuals exist, and Diogenes (400–*c*. 325 BCE), who held asceticism was the way to freedom; and the Cyrenaic School or Cyrenaicism. This was a classical

Greek philosophical school founded by Aristippus (435–356 BCE) who, like Antisthenes, believed that universals were just names, taught that good and evil are reducible to pleasure and pain, the end of life is self-gratification, and philosophy is the study of how best to attain it. Though its members dealt with other topics, Cyrenaicism was mostly noted for its hedonism. After its foundation by Aristippus, the Cyrenaic school lasted for a couple of centuries. It appears to have been superseded by Epicureanism. The influence of Socrates, Plato, and Aristotle are primarily discussed in this dictionary in the SOCRATIC PHILOSOPHY, PLATONISM, ARISTOTELIANISM, and ACADEMY entries.

In response to Plato's and Aristotle's works, a large body of commentaries developed. Concerning Plato, Crantor (fourth century BCE), a member of the first Academy, composed the first known commentary (*hypomnema*) on the *Timaeus*. This practice soon became a tradition in Alexandria, where Eudorus (fourth century BCE) also commented on the *Timaeus* and, possibly, on the *Theaetetus*. By the second century BCE, the tradition of Platonic commentary was flourishing. It consisted in selecting *lemmata*, i.e. portions of text for general and, then, adding detailed commentary, which included raising *aporiai*, i.e. problems, and addressing them, refuting previous authors, and clarifying matters of language and doctrine.

Concerning Aristotle, the commentaries include, first, those of Peripatetic scholars of the second to fourth centuries CE, most notably Alexander of Aphrodisias (*fl. c*. 200). Second, they include the Neoplatonists up to the seventh and especially during the sixth century CE, beginning with Porphyry (CE 232–*c*. 309) and ending with Stephanus, leaving for Constantinople around CE 610. Third, they include Byzantine thinkers, most notably Eustratius (*c*. CE 1050–1120) and Michael of Ephesus (*fl. c*. CE 1130). Concerning Plato, commentaries may go back to the Old Academy, but certainly begin with Eudorus in the first century BCE in Alexandria and continue far into the Neoplatonic period.

Various ideas were prominent throughout the thousand years of Ancient Greek philosophy. Notable among them was *dynamis* (or *dunamis*), meaning power or energy. It was used by various Greek philosophers – e.g. Anaximander and Anaxagoras – to explain the origins of the elements. Aristotle used it to mean potentiality, in contrast to actuality (*energeia* or its near-synonym *entelecheia*).

After the classic period, Greek philosophy schools initially developed during the Hellenistic age or Hellenism (323–30 BCE, though some prefer 311–87 BCE) constitute *Hellenistic* philosophy: EPICUREANISM, STOICISM, and SKEPTICISM. They were to be followed by NEOPLATONISM and, to some extent, Eclecticism. All, except Eclecticism, are discussed in the entries bearing their names. As for Eclecticism in Ancient Greek philosophy, it is discussed in the following entries: ACADEMY, ALEXANDRIAN SCHOOL, NEOPLATONISM, and STOICISM.

See also: Aristotelianism; Epicureanism; Platonism; skepticism; Socratic philosophy; Stoicism

Further reading

Copleston, S.J., Frederick (1962) *A History of Philosophy: Volume I, Greece and Rome, Part I and Part II*, Garden City, NY: Omage Books.

Guthrie, William Keith Chambers (1962) *A History of Greek Philosophy*, Cambridge, UK: Cambridge University Press.

Greek skepticism *see* skepticism

Grelling paradox *see* theory of types

Grenzbegriff *see* Kantian philosophy

Grenzsituationen *see* existentialism

grihastha *see* Hinduism

grue paradox *see* induction

Grundnorm *see* philosophy of law

gufu-shogyō-zen *see* Zen

guilt *see* culture; ethics

guise theory *see* logic

guna *see* Hinduism

guru *see* Buddhism; Hinduism

gynocentric *see* feminist philosophy

gynocentrism *see* feminist philosophy

gyō-jù-za-ga *see* Zen

gyulü *see* Buddhism

H

H *see* logic

Háá'ayį́įh, sihasin dóó hodílzin *see* Native American philosophy

habit *see* disposition

Hades *see* myth

Ḥadīth *see* Islam

hadrah *see* metaphysics

haecceity *see* definition; identity

Haggadah *see* Jewish philosophy; Judaism

hakīm *see* Arabic philosophy

hāl *see* Sufism

Halakha *see* Jewish philosophy; Judaism

Halakhah *see* Jewish philosophy; Judaism

Halldén-complete *see* model

hallucination *see* perception

halting problems *see* computer theory

hangman, paradox of the *see* paradox

happiness *see* ethics

ḥaqīkah *see* esoterism

Haqq *see* esoterism

hard cases *see* ethics

hard choices *see* ethics

hard determinism *see* determinism

hardware *see* computer theory

harmony *see* Chinese philosophy; ethics; Greek philosophy; philosophy, sociopolitical

harmony, pre-established *see* determinism

harassment, sexual *see* ethics; feminist philosophy

Hasidism *see* Jewish philosophy; Judaism

hasty generalization, fallacy of *see* fallacy

health *see* ethics; metaphysics; philosophy of science

heap paradox *see* paradox

heart *see* Chinese philosophy

Heaven *see* myth

Hebraism *see* Jewish philosophy

hedonic calculus *see* ethics; utilitarianism

hedonism *see* ethics

Hegelian *see* idealism

Hegelianism *see* idealism

Hegelians, Young *see* idealism; Marxism

hegemonic *see* Marxism

hegemony *see* Marxism

Heideggerian *see* existentialism

Heidelberg School *see* Kantian philosophy

Heisenberg *see* philosophy of science

Hell *see* myth

Hellenism *see* Greek philosophy

Hellenistic philosophy *see* Greek philosophy

Helsinki, Group of *see* empiricism

Hempel–Oppenheim model *see* explanation

Hempelian *see* explanation

henads, doctrine of *see* Neoplatonism

Henkin semantics *see* logic

henotheism *see* God

Heraclitean *see* Greek philosophy

hereditarianism *see* evolution

hereditary *see* evolution

heredity *see* evolution

heresy *see* Christianity; Jewish philosophy; Judaism

heritability *see* evolution

hermeneutic circle *see* hermeneutics

hermeneutics This term is derived from the Greek word *hermeneia* (interpretation or explanation) and its adjectival form, *hermeneuticos*. It denotes the art or theory of interpretation, as well as any inquiry (including a philosophical inquiry) that starts with questions of interpretation.

Originally signifying only the interpretation of religious texts, hermeneutics has come to be used in a much broader scope, initially in philosophical and social-science discussions among German thinkers and, later, among thinkers of other traditions. As for the initial linguistic promptings of this type of discussion, the German term for explanation, *Erklärung*, is sometimes used in contrast with *das Verstehen* (comprehension, or understanding) in arguing about the nature of social studies. The issue here is whether social studies should merely aim at comprehending: reconstructing meanings instead of discovering causes. In this regard, people sometimes talk of explanation as *explication*, or *clarification*, or even *interpretation*, in the manner, say, in which an anthropologist engaged in participant observation might attempt to understand or interpret an, until then, unknown practice of a newly discovered group of humans.

The German philosopher Martin Heidegger (CE 1884–1976) extended the notion of hermeneutics and the *hermeneutic circle* to cover all knowledge and activity. The contemporary German philosopher Hans-Georg Gadamer has focused on hermeneutics in a manner that involves a conception of language as the *horizon* of a hermeneutic ontology: hermeneutics as an unending process. He has applied it to the understanding of others as individuals or groups, by appeal to the *fusion of horizons* that can and does occur when we enter a hermeneutic situation with an open mind. Examples of such fusion can be found in encounters that lead to mutual understanding between people from different cultural traditions. In these, their horizons fuse to the extent that their translations of each other's concepts do not just overlap, but, sometimes, converge towards a shared understanding.

See also: existentialism; philosophy of religion; philosophy of science

Further reading
Gadamer, Hans Georg and Silverman, Hugh J. (1991) *Gadamer and Hermeneutics: Science, Culture, Literature: Plato, Heidegger, Barthes, Ricoeur, Habermas, Derrida*, New York, NY and London: Routledge.
Schleiermacher, Friedrich (1998) *Hermeneutics and Criticism and Other Writings*, Cambridge, UK and New York: Cambridge University Press.
Vattimo, Gianni (1997) *Beyond Interpretation: The Meaning of Hermeneutics for Philosophy*, Stanford, CA: Stanford University Press.

hermeticism *see* Neoplatonism

hermeticum, corpus *see* Neoplatonism

hermetism *see* Neoplatonism

heterological *see* paradox

heteronomy *see* Kantian philosophy

heterosexism *see* gender

heterosexuality *see* gender

hetu *see* logic

hetvābhāpsa *see* logic

heuristic *see* abduction; artificial; induction

heuristics *see* abduction; artificial

hexis *see* disposition; ethics

hidden variable *see* philosophy of science

hierarchical system *see* computer theory

hierarchy *see* ordering; set

higher-order logic *see* logic

hīkma *see* Arabic philosophy; wisdom

himma *see* mysticism

Hinayana Buddhism *see* Buddhism

Hinduism The group of native religions and philosophical traditions of India that accepts the doctrinal authority of the *Vedas*, scriptures whose name means "knowledge." These scriptures have various parts. The first, the *Samhitās*, i.e. *collections*, includes the *Ṛgveda*, a set of hymns praising the gods; the *Sāmaveda*, which contains, among other things, the music associated with these hymns; the *Yajurveda*, or sacrificial formulas; and the *Atharvaveda*, or magical formulas. The Second, the *Brāhmanas*, is a set of texts devoted to describing and explaining the significance and value of ritual practices – *nitya-karma* or Vedic duties – and sacrifices. Each of the Vedas includes a *brāhmana*, a manual providing instructions for the practical use of the contents of the *Samhitā*. Appended to these manuals are various explanatory texts that have provided the starting point for philosophical discussions. The third, the *Upanishads*, is a set of largely philosophical texts, which includes the four *mahāvākya* or great sayings: consciousness is Brahman; this Self is Brahman; that thou art; and I am Brahman.

A later stage of Vedic works is constituted by the *Sutras* (from the Sanskrit *sūtra*, i.e. thread or precept) – collections of aphorisms formulating the requirements of the Vedic religion. They include the *Brahma-Sūtras*, which are regarded as authoritative by the *Vedānta* School of philosophy. However, they are variously interpreted by philosophers such as Shankara (CE 788–820), Rāmānuja (eleventh century CE), and Madhva (CE 1197–1276). Of significance among the *Sūtras* are also the *Dharma Sutras*, which formulate social duties.

The *Brahma-Sūtras* are a collection of aphorisms and verses on the philosophy of the Vedānta formulated in the Upanishads. It has various other names: *Vedānta-sūtra*, *Śārīraka-sūtra*, *Bhiksu-sūtra*, and *Uttara-Mīmāmsā-sū-tra*, and is basic only to the Vedānta School. Its aim is to present the teachings of the Vedānta in a logical order. It has four chapters, each divided into various sections. The first chapter, entitled *harmony* (*samanvaya*), explains how apparently doubtful statements in the Upanishads make sense. The second chapter, entitled *non-conflict* (*avirodha*), presents the Vedānta position as it relates to other philosophical systems. The third chapter, entitled *the means* (*sādhana*), outlines the spiritual path to liberation. The fourth chapter, entitled *the fruit* (*phala*), discusses the goal sought through this path.

Chief among all the previously mentioned works is *The Laws of Manu*, the primary ancient Hindu legal code. *Manu* – a term meaning "man" in Sanskrit – denotes a series of progenitors of humans, each of whom was said to have ruled the world for a period of time. The seventh one is said to be the individual from whom all currently existing humans descend. Like Noah, he is reputed to have survived the deluge in an ark. He is also reputed to have authored *The Laws of Manu*.

Besides the Vedas, the Hindu tradition includes two epic works, the *Rāmāyana* and the *Mahābārata*, both developed during the first millennium BCE and probably compiled around CE 200. These works are comparable, though wider in their scope of influence, to the *Iliad* and *Odyssey* in Ancient Greece. The *Rāmāyana* is the story of the kind Rama, whose wife is taken by the king of Ceylon and later rescued. It includes moral and religious teachings, as well as the doctrine of divine incarnation. The *Mahābarata* is the story of the struggle between two families, the Kurus and the Pāndavas, both with claims upon the throne. It includes the *Bhagavad-Gītā*, i.e. *Song of the Lord*, a discussion between the incarnate Krishna and the warrior Arjuna (one of the Pāndavas), when the battle with the Kurus is about to begin. It deals with conflicts between individual and social ethics, the value of duty, and the immortality of the soul. In addition to the *Bhagavad-Gītā*, the *Mahābhārata* includes an account of the four *Āshramas* or the four stations of life – student, householder, forest-dweller, and ascetic – and their duties, as well as a discussion of the four castes: *Brahmin* or priest and teacher; *Kshatriya* or warrior; *Vaishya* or merchant; and *Shudra* or worker (see CASTE).

As well as the previously mentioned works, Hindu literature includes the *purānas*, or ancient narratives written in verse, which constitute a kind of encyclopedia of Hindu religions and traditions. As for ethical teachings, they are included in the scriptures called *Nīti-Shāstras*.

A religion without a known founder, Hinduism reflects the cultural history and social arrangements of the Indian people from the time civilization flourished in the Indus Valley to our day, i.e. from about 1500 BCE to the present. Indeed, it is sometimes said that Hinduism is *dharma* (right action) rather than a religion. At the very least, in Hinduism, conduct and belief are thoroughly intertwined.

Reverence was a significant component of traditional Indian society's way of life. Elders, especially one's parents and teachers, were held in godlike esteem. They were *ārādhya*, i.e. objects of reverence. So it was for all form of life, which is divided into four stages or *Āshramas* each with its own rules and entitlements, which explains why non-violence (*Ahimsā*) and vegetarianism are also important components of Indian society's way of life. In the Hindu polytheistic tradition, the older Vedic deities as well as the later gods and goddesses were, and still are, *Ārādhya*. It is common to find them in the household, very much as the *lares* in Roman religion. Yet, there is a basic Hindu trinity constituted by Brahmā, the creator of the universe (which belongs to the realm of *māyā*; and should not be confused with Brahman, the eternal being of the Upanishads); *Shiva* (Rudra in the Vedas), whose feminine, active power is *Sakti*, which in Hindu means force, power, or energy, or Natarāja, king of the dance, god of the world stage, the god of destruction, creation, embodiment, maintenance, and liberation; and *Vishnu*, the worker, the sun god. In the *purānas*, a synthesis was formulated whereby Vishnu was the sustainer, Brahma the creator, and Shiva the destroyer. This trinity is called *Trimūrti*, literally, three forms, and is an instance of *triadism*, a term denoting any doctrine according to which reality or a part thereof has three parts. Other instances are *triloka* (literally, "three worlds"), i.e. the three worlds of Hindu cosmology – *svarga* or heaven, *bhūmi* or earth, and *pātāla* or the underworld. Outside Hinduism, triadism can be found in the Christian trinity and, in philosophy, in conceptions of human beings as being constituted by body, vital principle, and soul; or by body, soul, and spirit.

Indian philosophizing significantly concerns itself with the notion of consciousness or mind, *citta* (also *chitta*), with different meanings in different traditions. These include the Hindu philosophy schools, which take the Vedas to be authoritative, and the *nāstika*, i.e. the unorthodox philosophical schools – BUDDHISM and CĀRVĀKA, and JAINISM, which do not. Within Buddhism, e.g. in the *Vaibhāshika Buddhism*, consciousness is born out of the interaction of the senses with their objects, while in *Yogācāra-Buddhism*, consciousness is the primary and, basically, the only DHARMA. By contrast, in Hinduism, more specifically in the SĀMKHYA-YOGA system, *buddhi* (the intellect), *ahankāra* (the ego), and *indriyas* (the senses) are often called *citta*; but, more precisely, *citta* is the mind, which involves various mental processes and has various stages. One of the stages of *citta* is *ekāgra*, where one concentrates steadily on one object for a long time.

Six philosophical schools are developed as part of Hinduism, though two pairs of them are connected, either historically or conceptually. The schools are *Mīmāmsā* or *Pūrva-Mīmāmsā*, Sāmkhya-Yoga, *Nyāya-Vaiśesika*, and *Vedānta* or *Uttara-Mīmāmsā* or ADVAITA, or *Advaita-Vedānta*. Their discussions address almost all of the same problems addressed in Western philosophy. However, there is no term exactly equivalent to philosophy in Hinduism. The closest one is *darśana* (seeing), which is achieved by embracing and being changed by the content of the sacred texts. Another term, though only applicable to the logical philosophies, is *ānvīkṣi*.

Also, the purpose of the discussions and practice of Hinduism is not simply knowledge or wisdom, but *moksha* ("enlightenment/-liberation"), which includes escape from karma and the *reincarnation* cycle. Whoever attains *moksha* is a perfected person: *siddha* (a term that, in the *purānas*, denotes a semi-divine being of great purity and power). The Sāmkhya-Yoga School refers to this liberation as *kaivalya* ("aloofness," "aloneness," or "isolation"), meaning a complete detachment – immediately caused by *viveka* ("knowledge") – from matter and from transmigration. As for the sorrows overcome in liberation, the Sāmkhya School distinguishes three types. One is *ādhibhautika*, miseries caused by extrinsic, natural influences, such as other individuals, animals, and inanimate objects. Another is *ādhyātmika*, miseries caused by internal influences, generated by illness of the body, which may lead to dangerous levels of bile, or unsatisfied passions of the mind, such as desire and anger.

All of the previously mentioned schools share the doctrine that the individual *ĀTMAN* ("soul") has been indefinitely transmigrating and continues to do so until it attains enlightenment/liberation through the cumulative consequences of its actions in succeeding lifetimes (*karma*). However, some schools, most notably Advaita-Vedānta, formulate metaphysical interpretations of karma and transmigration that significantly alter the meaning of these notions. For example, the doctrine of *ajāta-vāda* or *non-origination* – held by the philosopher Gaudapāda (CE sixth or eighth century) but not by the philosopher Śamkara (CE 788–820) – holds that there is no causal change: that which does not exist at the beginning does not exist at the end, nor does it exist in the middle; hence it is utterly non-existent.

Also, some schools – Sāmkhya, Advaita, and Saiva Siddhānta – hold the doctrine of *jīvanmukta* (liberated while living), according to which an individual may be liberated while living in a physical body. For Sāmkhya, this happens when there is an experiential discrimination between two *tattvas* or categories: *purusha* (eternal spirits) and *prakriti* (the basis of the natural world). For Advaita, liberation occurs with *AVIDYĀ*, i.e. the destruction of ignorance, the path of knowledge involving three steps: *shravana* or study, *manana* or reflection (which removes an aspirant's doubts about the nature of the object to be contemplated, namely Brahman), and *nididhyāsana* or contemplation. It should be noted that, for

Advaita-Vedānta, the One or the Absolute is called *Nirguna-Brahman* or Brahman without qualities, and this ultimate reality cannot be described positively because it is infinite and our thought is finite. Hence, the most appropriate way to describe it is through a formula such as *neti-neti*, i.e. "not this, not this"; in other words, only through negations.

For Saiva Siddhānta, the individual soul is freed by enjoying bliss while in a physical body. It distinguishes four ways of (or paths for) attuning the body, the sense organs, and the mind to worship. One such *way* or *path* (*mārga*) is *dāsa-mārga*, i.e. the way of the servant; another is *putra mārga*, i.e. the way of the son; a third is *sakhā mārga*, i.e. the way of the friend; the fourth is *sanmārga*, i.e. beyond a path.

The Mīmāmsa School (a name that literally means *inquiry* or *investigation* and is short for the Pārva Mīmāmsa School) is centrally concerned with the correct interpretation of the Vedas. It holds significant views in the PHILOSOPHY OF LANGUAGE. For example, *anvitābhidhānavāda* denotes the *Prābhākara Mīmīmsa* theory, according to which the meaning of any word is always related to the meanings of the other words in a sentence. This is akin to *ABHIHITĀNVAYA-VĀDA*, the Bhātta Mīmāmsa theory, according to which uttered words have their own separate meanings that combine to produce the meaning of an uttered sentence. In the *philosophy of knowledge*, the Mīmāmsa School distinguishes three sources of knowledge: perception, inference, and testimony or authority. As regards Hinduism, the Mīmāmsa School holds that there are everlasting souls or minds that do not necessarily involve consciousness. It also holds that there are everlasting material atoms and that atoms attracted each other, producing physical objects that are independent of any minds. Also, the Mīmāmsa School accepts the transmigration of the souls and the doctrine of karma but, by contrast with other orthodox schools of Hinduism, it sometimes denies the existence of God and, at other times, simply rejects the theistic arguments of Nyāya-Vaiśesika, letting the Vedas be the only source of knowledge of God.

In Indian philosophy generally, an atom, understood as the smallest, indivisible particle of matter, is called *paramānu*. Two atoms combine to form a *dyad* (*dvyanuka*), and three dyads form a triad, i.e. the smallest visible substance. A notion of interest here is *rju-sūtra-naya*: the standpoint of momentariness or the mathematical, momentary present. It could be interpreted as the standpoint of an atom of time; yet, it is supposed to be fleeting. The question arises whether it can be fleeting but discrete or whether, because fleeting, it must involve continuity, and hence not be atomic. This question is ascribed by the Jainas to Buddhism.

The Sāmkhya-Yoga School upholds two basic categories: *purusha* (eternal spirits), and *prakriti* (the basis of the natural world). The world evolves out of the latter with the help of the former through a kind of causation where the effect pre-exists in the cause. It thus results in the production of *mahat*, i.e. the cosmic intelligence, *buddhi*, which is the substance of all mental processes, and AHAMKĀRA, i.e. the principle of individuation. Three aspects of *ahamkāra* originate specific developmental lines: *sattva* leads to *manah* or the mind, the sense-organs, and the five means of action; *rajas* produces the energy that empowers all developments; and *tamas* leads to the *mahā-bhūta* or five subtle (also called great) elements. These are *śabda* or sound, *sparsha* or touch, *rūpa* or color, *rasa* or taste, and *gandha* or smell. It is from these that the coarser ones – *ākāsha* or ether, *vāyu* or air, *tejas* or fire, *ap* or water, and *pthivī* or earth – respectively follow. The *Bhagavad-Gitā* sometimes considers *sattva*, *rajas*, and *tamas* to be three *gunas*; other times, it considers them to be three types of *tapas* (From the Sanskrit *tap*, i.e. "heat"), a term that initially applied to the heat of the sun but later came to mean emotional fervor, primal energy, and ascetic power. The gods both create and destroy by means of *tapas*. According to the *Bhagavad-Gitā*, *sattva* is virtuous, *rajas* is ambitious, and *tamas* is perverted.

The Nyāya-Vaiśeṣika School deals primarily with logic, epistemology, and metaphysics. It admits four sources of knowledge: perception, inference, analogy, and credible testimony. According to this school, one must suppose that there is a *nirvikalpaka-pratyaksha*, or indeterminate perception of simple entities, constituting the complex things we perceive. (By contrast, the Mīmāmsā School holds that, though quite vague and indefinite, our perception of simple entities is actual and not a mere supposition.) The Nyāya-Vaiśeṣika School also includes *samshaya*, i.e. doubt, as one of its categories.

As for metaphysics, the Nyāya-Vaiśeṣika School holds that there are nine substances: the four atoms, space, time, ether, mind, and self. The atoms are eternal and contained in space. Their four kinds are earth, air, fire, and water. Their combinations, whose properties are explained in terms of properties of their components, are not eternal.

These combinations include, in addition to material entities, immaterial persons. Each is a substantial and enduring self, characterized by being conscious, feeling pleasure and pain, feeling love and aversion, and having the capacity to make choices. Persons differ from each other in that they are different centers of consciousness, and not merely in having been through different transmigratory lines.

As the preceding outline indicates, the philosophical schools of Hinduism produced rich views in metaphysics, epistemology, ethics, and logic. The discussions they prompted ranged from arguments concerning the problem of evil, through those about the nature of identity, to those about evidence understood as a valid source of knowledge. Discussions in logic, just as those in much of Western philosophy – perhaps with the exception only of some medieval philosophers and contemporary symbolic logicians – did not sharply distinguish deductive and non-deductive inferences from epistemology, though they did distinguish them from psychological processes.

A variety of other schools developed in India, some within Hinduism and very close to Vedānta, and others that were quite unorthodox. An example of the former is *Vishis-tādvaita-Vedānta* or *qualified non-dualism*, the school founded by the philosopher Rāmānuja (CE eleventh century), whose main doctrine was that the world is founded on a spiritual principle, Brahman, which is real and independent. The individual soul and inanimate nature are also real, and distinct from Brahman, but they are dependent on Brahman in that their reality resides entirely in and cannot be without Brahman. Vishistādvaita refers to three main aspects of philosophy: *tattva* ("reality"), *hita* ("means"), and *purushārtha* ("goal of life"). This school grants that personal values are subordinate to the impersonal and abstract supreme reality postulated by Advaita; but holds against Advaita that truth, beauty, and goodness have a reality that conflicts with Advaita's impersonal abstraction. This difference led to the establishment of Vishistādvaita-Vedānta.

As for sharply unorthodox schools, the most notable are the CĀRVĀKA or *lokāyata* schools, which shared the view that mind is merely the body and its capacities, but differed concerning the nature of mental properties. Related positions held by some cârvâka schools are:

- to exist is to be perceivable;
- intelligence is only a certain bodily disposition and soul is only the body in so far as it is intelligent;
- universal ideas and relations can be understood only through perceptual connections reinforced by memory, which weaken the power of inference;
- causal connections can be understood only perceptually, and this makes them questionable, because we may perceive two items – say, the two horns of a cow – successively, yet one is not the cause of the other;
- the existence or non-existence of anything is never certain;
- all humans aim at pleasure and the avoidance of pain.

Also notable is *Sikhism*, a religion founded by Guru Nānak (CE 1469–1538) with the aim of synthesizing Hinduism and the teachings of Islam, introduced by invading Muslims. It accepted reincarnation, rejected mere ritual and renunciation, and emphasized that liberation is possible only through human efforts.

As for the tradition and practice of Hinduism, both Brahman and Vishnu have *sat* ("being"). Brahman is described as the embodiment of *sat* ("existence"), as well as *chit* ("consciousness/intelligence"), and *ānanda* ("bliss"). The fundamental qualities, *guna*, which make up *prakriti*, all the objects of the

sensible world are three: *sattva*, the embodiments of what is pure and subtle, e.g. sunlight; *rajas*, the embodiments of activity, e.g. a volcanic eruption; and *tamas*, the embodiments of heaviness and immobility, e.g. a boulder. Since they are qualities of *māyā* (also called *nāmarūpa*) or of the *power to assume material forms*, and because they are objects of appearance or deception (i.e. worldly), they veil the reality of Brahman even though they depend on Brahman for their existence. There are various stages in this process. One, for example, is *nirdvamda*, the state in which the mind no longer conceives of opposites. Another is *nirodha*, a state of intense concentration in which the subject–object distinction is annihilated. Still another is *nirodha-smāpatti*, a state in which all mental activity is suspended.

Whoever overcomes the *gunas* becomes *gunātīta*, and realized Brahman, therefore attaining *moksha*, i.e. ENLIGHTENMENT/liberation. In Advaita-Vedānta, the identity with Brahman is realized through *naishkarmya-siddhi*, i.e. inactivity or non-doing. Those said to have reached a high level of enlightenment are said to perceive the *Nāda-Brahman* (from *Nāda*, the vibratory energy of sound, and Brahman), a term denoting the symbol *OM* (also *AUM*), which symbolizes the sound of Brahman. Except for Śankara's conception, the primal or original vibration from which the universe is said to have arisen is called *Nāda-bindu*, while the inner, indivisible, constant is called *nitya-vāk*.

In Hinduism, sound is associated with the spoken word and uttered testimony in the term *śabda*. In the Nyāya School, *śabda* is a trustworthy person's testimony, while the Advaita School considers *śabda* the means through which the basic unity of being is revealed. A number of related and philosophically relevant terms are: *śabda-bohda*, i.e. verbal cognition; *śabda jñāna* or *śabdamiti*, i.e. verbal knowledge; *śabda-tanmātra*, i.e. the subtle sound or element of ether; and *śabda-vṛtti*, i.e. significant force.

As indicated previously, in Hinduism, also, the ideal life requires a series of stages or *āshramas* to be mastered one at a time. First, there is *brahmacarin*, the life of discipline and education, which focuses on knowledge (the term *sādhana*, which means self-effort or spiritual discipline, is used by different schools of Hinduism with different meanings, from discrimination in Sāmkhya to contemplation in Sivādvaita). Second, there is *gṛhasta*, the life of the householder and active worker, which is the most important stage, where one leads a married life discharging social responsibilities and contributing to society. Third, there is *vānaprashta*, a period of retreat where one's social bonds are loosened. Fourth, there is *sannyāsin*, the life of the hermit or renouncer, where renunciation helps break the hold of existence and attain fullness and freedom. Throughout the process, various things hinder *nivritti-mârga*, the path of turning away from activity and to spiritual recollection, and, hence, the attainment of complete concentration or *samādhi*: AVIDYĀ or desire, *pradosha* or ill-will, *styāna* or sloth, *middha* or torpor; *anuddhatya* or restlessness, *kaukrītya* or compunction; and *vichikitsā* or doubt.

A guide through the stages of life is a *guru* (teacher or spiritual master). There are different gurus depending on the stage of life: First, there are parents, who give us a body and teach us about life and its problems; second, there are all kinds of teachers, who give us instruction; third, there are spiritual masters, who teach us the meaning of life, the way to self-realization, and the dangers and obstacles involved; fourth and finally, there is the cosmic guru, the fully enlightened divine incarnation to whom the spiritual master leads us.

See also: Advaita; Buddhism; cārvāka; Jainism; Nyāya-Vaiśeṣika School; Sāmkhya-Yoga

Further reading
Bernard, Cyril (1977) *Hinduism: Religion and Philosophy*, Alwaye: Pontifical Institute of Theology and Philosophy.
Chatterjee, Satischandra (1950) *An Introduction to Indian Philosophy*, 4th edn, rev. and enl., Calcutta: University of Calcutta.
Hiriyanna, Mysore (1996) *The Essentials of Indian Philosophy*, London: Diamond.

Hinnon *see* myth

Hintikka set *see* set

Hispanic philosophy *see* Latin American philosophy

ḥiss *see* mysticism

historical determinism *see* determinism

historical jurisprudence *see* philosophy of law

historical materialism *see* Marxism

historical theory of reference *see* reference

historicism From the German word, *Historismus*; in its general sense, this term denotes any doctrine that emphasizes an irreducibly historical character of knowledge, society, or human nature. It was originally introduced by the Hungarian-born sociologist Karl Mannheim (CE 1893–1947) and the German Protestant theologian Ernst Troeltsch (CE 1865–1923), and was an ambiguous term from the outset, sometimes used honorifically, other times pejoratively. It is typically applied to the views of thinkers ranging from the Italian philosopher Giovanni Battista Vico (CE 1688–1744), who argued that everything is history, through such neo-Kantian German philosophers as Wilhelm Dilthey (CE 1833–1911) and Wilhelm Windelband (CE 1848–1915), who held that the social studies and history are caught up in the presuppositions of their time, to various Hegelian and Marxist authors. Quite often, historicism is associated with the view that what is needed is a historical *explication* of the items – whether knowledge, society, or human nature – being investigated.

An approach that overlaps with or is included in historicism is *genealogical* or *genetic*, and sometimes involves a significant reliance on the concepts of *generation* and *a generation*.

In Jean Beaufret's Preface to the French translation of *Der Satz vom Grund*, by the German philosopher Martin Heidegger (CE 1884–1976), we find the notion of *genealogical thinking* described as a going back to the origin(s) or its *genesis* (Greek for origin), meaning not simply a history, but, more crucially, what it is from the outset to be human as a historical being. An example of this type of thinking can be found in the writings of the German philosopher Friedrich Wilhelm Nietzsche (CE 1844–1900), most notably in his *Genealogy of Morals*, where he acknowledges that this approach could also be found among English writers.

Nietzsche's approach has influenced the

French philosopher and historian of thought Michel Foucault (CE 1926–84), whose method, the *archeology of knowledge*, treats systems of thought as structures of discourse that are independent of the intentions and beliefs of their individual authors, yet have a genealogy connecting power and knowledge in that the said systems are understood as systems of control. According to Foucault, bodies of knowledge – *epistemes* – and, in general, systems of thought are tied but not reducible to structures of power. On this view, an episteme is a contingent system for the production, regulation, distribution, and operation of statements. It is independent of the beliefs and intentions of individual thinkers and, though contingent, creates constraints on thought and action that seem unsurpassable to those caught up in them. Given their *epistemic location*, i.e. from the standpoint of whatever system they engage in discourse, and their *local knowledge*, i.e. the knowledge they have or claim from the historical standpoint of their particular system, they can imagine no alternative to this system.

See also: explanation

Further reading
Page, Carl (1995) *Philosophical Historicism and the Betrayal of First Philosophy*, University Park, PA: University of Pennsylvania Press.
Reill, Peter Hanns (1975) *The German Enlightenment and the Rise of Historicism*, Berkeley: University of California Press.

historicity *see* existentialism; historicism

historiography *see* philosophy of history

historism *see* historicism

history *see* philosophy of history

hita *see* Hinduism

hō *see* Buddhism; Zen

Hobbesian *see* philosophy, sociopolitical

holism This term, as well as its synonym, *wholism*, denotes any of a number of views stating that the whole of some system (i.e. a *holistic system*), or of the properties of a system as a whole (i.e. *holistic properties*), has *organic unity*, i.e. equal or greater reality than the system's parts or its individual properties, or a necessary explanatory role unavailable at the level of the system's parts or its individual properties.

This type of conception is most common in biology and social studies. Among the concepts crucial to holism are *descriptive emergence* and the associated doctrine of *descriptive emergentism*: the view that properties of wholes emerge in wholes and cannot be defined by properties of their parts. This approach conflicts with *descriptive individualism*, i.e. the view that all properties of wholes can be defined in terms of properties of their parts.

Recently, *doxastic* or *epistemic holism* has acquired currency. This is the view that a person's – some would say a rational person's – beliefs are so interwoven that any change in any one of them may affect the content of any other(s). This is related to *semantic* or *meaning holism*, the view that the meaning of all terms or sentences are so interwoven that changes in one (or in one belief) may change any other meaning(s). *Methodological* (also called *metaphysical*) *holism* arises in the context of explanation. It holds that the laws of more complex cases in a system or object (e.g. laws of collective behavior in society) are not deducible in any way from laws of less complex cases (e.g. from laws of individual behavior in society). Its opposite is *methodological individualism*, the view that such deducibility is possible. This latter approach usually appeals to the notions of *descriptive individualism*, previously characterized.

In political thought, *individualism*, which justifies coercive institutions only to the extent that they protect the rights or good of individuals, is typically opposed to *collectivism* or *communitarianism*, a family of positions – ranging from *communism*, through *fascism*, to *corporativism* – that upholds the precedence and independent justification of the collective over the good or rights of individuals.

In biology and the philosophy of biology, holism is sometimes also called VITALISM. In psychology, the notion of *Gestalt* is holistic. As for other social studies, classical German sociologists distinguished between the individualistic concept of *Gesellshaft*, a social group whose members intentionally join it in order to pursue its purposes, e.g. a club, and the (at least partly) holistic concept of *Gemeinshaft*, a social group in which its members find their identity, or a significant feature of their identity, e.g. a nation.

See also: philosophy of science

Further reading
Kaldis, Byron (1993) *Holism, Language, and Persons: An Essay on the Ontology of the Social World*, Aldershot and Brookfield, USA: Avebury.
Peacocke, Christopher (1979) *Holistic Explanation: Action, Space, Interpretation*, Oxford and New York: Clarendon Press and Oxford University Press.

holistic properties *see* holism

holistic system *see* holism

Holocaust *see* philosophy, sociopolitical

hologram *see* cognitive

homo ludens *see* play

homo mensura *see* Greek philosophy

homocentrism *see* anthropocentrism

homoeomeric *see* natural kinds

homoeomerity *see* natural kinds

homoeomerous *see* natural kinds

homogeneity *see* natural kinds

homogeneous *see* natural kinds

homoiomeres *see* natural kinds

homoiousias *see* Arianism

homomorphic *see* model

homomorphism *see* model

homonymous *see* ambiguity

homonymy *see* ambiguity

homoousias *see* Arianism

homophobia *see* gender

homosexuality *see* gender

homuncular functionalism *see* philosophy of mind

homunculus *see* philosophy of mind

honam *see* body

honesty *see* ethics

honor *see* ethics

hope *see* faith

horizon *see* hermeneutics

hormic psychology *see* philosophy of mind

Hossō School *see* Buddhism

Hózhó *see* Native American philosophy

hsiao *see* Confucianism

hsin *see* Confucianism

hsing *see* Confucianism

hsing-erh-hsia *see* Chinese philosophy

hsing-erh-shang *see* Chinese philosophy

hsü *see* Chinese philosophy

Huai Nan Tzu *see* Chinese philosophy

Huang-Lao *see* Chinese philosophy

Hua-Yen School *see* Buddhism

hubris *see* ethics

Huexotzinco *see* Nahua philosophy

ḥull *see* Arabic philosophy

human-centered *see* anthropocentrism

human condition *see* existentialism

human existence's nature and value *see* existentialism

human nature From the Latin *humanus* ("human") and *natura* ("blood-kinship," "character," "quality," "world"), this term denotes the feature(s) shared by all and only humans that explain(s) the kinds of beings humans are. A term sometimes used as synonymous with human nature is *humanity*, from the Latin *humanitas*: "human nature," "feeling," "kindness." The belief that there is a human nature is part of the wider view that all natural kinds have essences. There is controversy about this, as well as about what constitutes human nature if there is one. Some – e.g. the English philosopher Thomas Hobbes (CE 1588–1679) – have held that human nature involves basic selfish *appetites* such as that for *self-preservation* and that for *glory*, all of which come to be forms of *appetition* for power. Others – e.g. the British philosopher Bishop Joseph Butler (CE 1692–1752) – have replied that it is compatible with benevolence, distinguishing *basic desires* or *basic appetites* that can be for self-preservation as well as for doing good to someone or other, and self-love, which is a cool desire for the harmonious satisfaction of one's basic desires. Still others have argued that human nature is sociability – the ability to use language or laugh, or tell stories – or the desire for immortality.

There is also controversy about how to discover human nature, some arguing that this requires intuition, others that it requires biological or social-science studies; there is controversy, too, about the implications, if any, of human nature for morality; and about the extent to which all humans display human nature. Indeed, a number of philosophers – most of them male – have held that only males fully display human nature. This self-serving view has lost currency in contemporary philosophy and has been criticized on various grounds. Feminist philosophers have argued that it only espouses a patriarchal ideology without any basis in fact. Indeed, they have argued that the term *man* should not be used as synonymous with the term *humanity* and have significantly succeeded in undermining the currency of such usage. Other philosophers, whether feminist or not, have argued that though males and females share biological features, these do not constitute our nature. Some – existentialists and others – further argue that no such nature exists, because no human essence exists. Similar discussions can be found concerning human nature as it concerns different ethnic groups. Specific conceptions of human nature, their uses, and the forms of scientific essentialism with which they are associated have been criticized, on the grounds that they are unfounded and sources of *stereotypes*.

See also: essentialism; existentialism

Further reading

Asselin, Don (1989) *Human Nature and Eudaimonia in Aristotle*, New York: Lang.
Cannel, Ward (1974) *The Human Nature Industry: How Human Nature is Manufactured, Distributed, Advertised and Consumed in the United States and Parts of Canada*, Garden City, NY: Anchor Press.
Jaggar, Alison M. (1988) *Feminist Politics and Human Nature*, Totowa, NJ: Rowman & Littlefield.
Rouner, Leroy S. (1997) *Is there a Human Nature?*, Notre Dame, IN: University of Notre Dame Press.

human predicament *see* existentialism

human relation with the deities *see* God; philosophy of religion

human rights *see* ethics

human sciences *see* philosophy of science

humanism This term came into use in English after *Humanismus* was introduced in German in the early nineteenth century to emphasize the importance of studying classical languages and authors; however, a number of cognate terms had been used in various European languages for centuries. In Italy, for example, *umanista* had been used since the Renaissance – by contrast with such terms as *giurista* ("jurist"), *legista* ("teacher of law"), and *artista* ("artist") – to denote those who devoted themselves to the *studia humanitatis*, i.e. to the study of the humanities or branches of inquiry that were thought to deal with the general characteristics and situations of human beings: history, literature, moral philosophy, grammar, and rhetoric. To be sure, jurists, teachers of law, and others dealt with human matters; but, as Greco-Roman authors had already stated, they did so as *professionals* for specific purposes and within specific practices, not simply as human beings, which is what humanists were thought to do. The study of the humanities was a *liberal*, not a *professional* study.

The question has been asked whether humanism is philosophically significant. Some have answered negatively, arguing that it is, rather, guided by literary, not philosophical, concerns. Others have answered positively, arguing that humanism is a philosophy – indeed, the Renaissance philosophy that opposed Scholasticism. Both positions are exaggerations. Renaissance humanists such as the

Dutch man of letters Desiderius Erasmus (CE 1466?–1536), the French philosopher and essayist Michel de Montaigne (CE 1533–92), the philosopher Nicholas of Cusa (CE 1401–64) (born in what is now Germany), the philosophers Marsilio Ficino (CE 1433–99), Giovanni Pico della Mirandola (CE 1463–94), and Lorenzo Valla (c. CE 1407–57) (all three born in what is now Italy), and the French philosopher Petrus Ramus (CE 1515–72) were significantly guided by a concern with ethics and were engaged in extensive philosophical discussions concerning ethical and related topics, e.g. that of free will.

At the same time, however, there is no body of doctrines, or philosophical methods, or even a philosophical style shared by the authors just mentioned. That is, they do not constitute a philosophical school or period. Yet, their discernment and celebration of human capacities deserving unbounded cultivation helped constitute a unique intellectual environment that influenced philosophical and related inquiries, and provided a model of human self-reliance – sometimes, though not invariably, in opposition to theism – in Europe, much of the Americas and Australasia, and other areas of Western influence until today.

Arguably, humanistic ideas, especially that of the *perfectibility of humans*, shaped much of eighteenth-century philosophical thought in the Western world. Even since the nineteenth and twentieth centuries, when industrialization, urban growth and decay, nationalism, ideology-driven conflicts, and mass society seem to reduce humanistic ideals to ashes, humanist thinking has been influential. It emphasizes endurance, nobility, moderation, flexibility, sympathy, co-operation, education, and, first and foremost, intelligence aided by freedom of thought and expression in enhancing human creativity, promoting scientific and technological research, instituting wise and equitable social arrangements, and, in general, furthering human flourishing.

See also: Arabic philosophy; Aristotelianism; Greek philosophy; philosophy of education; Platonism

Further reading
Dukor, Maduabuchi F. (1994) *Theistic Humanism: Philosophy of Scientific Africanism*, Lagos, Nigeria: Noble Communications Network.
Kristeller, Paul Oskar (1962) *Renaissance Thought: The Classic, Scholastic, and Humanistic Strains*, New York: Harper & Row.
Lamont, Corliss (1990) *The Philosophy of Humanism*, seventh edn, rev. and enl., New York: Continuum.

humanism, civic *see* political philosophy

humanity *see* human nature

Humean philosophy *see* empiricism

humor *see* aesthetics; ethics; philosophy of science

humors *see* philosophy of science

Husserlian *see* phenomenology

ḥuzn *see* Ṣufism

hybridity *see* diaspora

hyēbea *see* determinism

hyle *see* Aristotelianism; causal law

hyletic *see* phenomenology

hylomorphism *see* Aristotelianism

hylosystemism *see* Aristotelianism

hylozoism *see* animism; biology

hypostasis *see* metaphysics

hyposthasize *see* metaphysics

hypothesis *see* induction

hypothetical consent *see* contractarianism

hypothetical construct *see* operationalism

hypothetical imperative *see* Kantian philosophy

hypothetical syllogism *see* syllogism

hypothetico-deductive method *see* induction

hysteria *see* feminist philosophy

I

I *see* categorical; logic; syllogism

I and It *see* existentialism

I and Thou *see* existentialism

ichiji-fusetsu *see* Zen

I-ching *see* Chinese philosophy; Taoism

icon *see* philosophy of language; pragmatism

id *see* psychoanalysis

idam *see* Brahman

idea From the Greek *idea*, which originally meant "vision" or "contemplation," the term *idea* has the same root as eidos – "form," "shape," "figure" – and often the same meaning. In Ancient Greek atomism, which stressed the role of ideation in sense perception, ideas were *eidola*, i.e. images. In Platonism, where *idea* and *eidos* were used, ideas were the structural elements of things-as-thought-of, while sense perception at best provided clues towards forming ideas. In the Aristotelian and Thomistic traditions, both approaches are used: any thinking starts with a *phantasma*, a Latin term derived from the Greek *phantasma* (akin to *phatazein*: "to bring before the mind"), which meant mental image (i.e. a sense-datum); and the formal component of thought is attained by abstraction from the initial mental image. In discussions of these matters, philosophers sometimes use the term *ideatum*, which has two meanings: first, the object of an idea, and second, that which is represented in the mind by an idea.

The seventeenth- and eighteenth-century empiricists generally followed the view of Ancient Greek atomism, holding ideas to be, or be very intimately associated with, sense-images. In the Middle Ages, the philosopher Giovanni Fidanza Bonaventure (1217–74; born in the city of Bagnorea, in what is now Italy) held that, with regard to our experience of the world around us, the mind begins as a *tabula rasa* (Latin for "blank tablet"); however, certain ideas of things beyond our ordinary world, e.g. that of God, are innate. This position was echoed by the Scottish philosopher John Duns Scotus (CE 1266–1308), though he used the expression *tabula nuda* (Latin for "naked tablet") to convey the idea.

By contrast, seventeenth- and eighteenth-century rationalists followed the views of Platonism in various ways. Indeed, Cartesian philosophers distinguished between *innate* ideas (i.e. general truths that were in the mind from birth), *adventitious* ideas (i.e. images or concepts that are or seem to be acquired through the senses and are accompanied by a judgment about their non-mental cause), and *factitious* ideas, which are made up from the elements of ideas of other things. The Cartesian criterion for the truth of ideas was that they be *clear*, i.e. recognizable in various contexts, and *distinct*, i.e. never confused with other ideas.

The notion that there were no innate ideas was revived by the English philosopher John Locke (CE 1632–1704), who placed the notion that the mind begins as a *tabula rasa* at the center of his empiricist approach. Indeed, the expression *tabula rasa* has come to be associated with Locke's philosophy. His views were sharply opposed by the German philosopher Gottfried Wilhelm Leibniz (CE 1646–1716).

In the centuries that followed, the German philosopher Immanuel Kant (CE 1724–1804) and his followers argued that some formal elements in experience were contributed by the mind, and distinguished between *ideas of pure reason* – such as those of the unity of the subject, the complete systematic organization of experience, and the unity of all existence – that make our experience possible, and *ideas of practical reason* – those of God, freedom, and immortality – that are not based on experience but give practical guidance and significance to our lives. Hegelian philosophers adopted the latter distinction but focused on the *Absolute Idea* or *Absolute Spirit*, a dialectically developing unity of the rational and the real.

Various nineteenth- and twentieth-century philosophers focused on the power of thinking. For example, the French philosopher Alfred Fouillée (1838–1912) argued for the reality of human freedom by appeal to the voluntaristic notion of *idea-force* or *thought-force*, which is the effectiveness of the mind evidenced by the tendency of ideas to become actualized. Along similarly voluntaristic lines, pragmatist philosophers thought of ideas as the sum of their practical consequences, or this sum plus the consequences of holding the ideas, or as instruments and plans of action.

In a more Kantian and Humean vein, the Spanish philosopher José Ortega y Gasset (CE 1883–1955) distinguished between *ideomas*, i.e. ideas as merely formulated, which are abstract, and *draomas*, i.e. beliefs that are concrete and affect human action in everyday life. Also, philosophers advocating phenomenology attempted to combine the rationalist and empiricist traditions in the notion that the essence of an idea could be directly seen.

See also: Aristotelianism; atomism; Cartesianism; empiricism; phenomenology; Platonism; pragmatism; rationalism

Further reading

Jolley, Nicholas (1990) *The Light of the Soul: Theories of Ideas in Leibniz, Malebranche, and Descartes*, Oxford and New York: Clarendon Press and Oxford University Press.

Watson, Richard A. (1995) *Representational Ideas: From Plato to Patricia Churchland*, Dordrecht and Boston: Kluwer Academic Publishers.

idea theory of meaning *see* meaning

ideal *see* idealism

ideal conditions *see* philosophy of economics; philosophy of science

ideal market *see* philosophy of economics

ideal mathematics *see* philosophy of mathematics

ideal observer *see* ethics

ideal proposition *see* logic

ideal-realism *see* idealism

ideal, the *see* logic

ideal type *see* philosophy, sociopolitical

ideal types *see* theory of types

ideal utilitarianism *see* ethics; utilitarianism

idealism From the Greek *idea* ("vision" or "contemplation"), and its English derivatives, IDEA and ideal, the term idealism was first used philosophically by the German philosopher and mathematician Gottfried Wilhelm Leibniz (CE 1646–1716) to denote Platonic thought and contrast it with empiricism. In ordinary usage, idealism has discarded this epistemological connotation of ideal, but retained its valuational reference to some form of perfection. In philosophy, the term idealism denotes a family of doctrines sharing the view that, somehow, reality is not independent of cognizing minds, but exists as a correlate of mental operations. These doctrines sometimes retain not only the epistemological but also the valuational connotation of ideal and idealism, indicating that reality somehow is, shares, or reflects perfection. There are various kinds of idealisms in philosophy, as follows.

One is *German idealism*, whose stages are characterized primarily by the views of three philosophers. The first, its founder, was Johann Gottlieb Fichte (CE 1762–1814), who advocated *subjective idealism*, i.e. the doctrine that the world is posited by the judging subject. In the valuational sense of ideal, Fichte saw the ideal providing the teleological determining factor of the real. On this view, which the German philosopher and physiologist Wilhelm Wundt (CE 1832–1900) called *ideal-realism*, the real is not the knowledge attained through current science, but the knowledge to be attained by ideal, perfect science.

The second was Friedrich Wilhelm Joseph Schelling (CE 1775–1854) who, following Fichte in his middle stage of philosophical development, advocated *objective idealism*: the doctrine that nature is visible intelligence and there is an absolute awareness whose development is the revelation of the Absolute in history. Some interpreters argue that this absolute awareness includes feeling. However, if this position is interpreted merely to identify reality with idea, reason, or spirit, then it includes *panpsychism* and such empiricist views as that formulated by the Irish philosopher and bishop George Berkeley (CE 1685–1753) that *esse est percipi*: "to be is to be perceived."

Objective idealism was also sometimes called *transcendental idealism* by Schelling. Yet, this doctrine should not be confused with the Kantian position called *transcendental idealism*, *critical idealism*, and, more recently, *epistemological idealism* where, by contrast with Schelling's identification of nature with intelligence, the contents of direct sense-experience are not supposed to be things in themselves

The culmination of German idealism took place with the third and chief member of this tradition, Georg Wilhelm Friedrich Hegel (CE 1770–1831), who originated a school of thought reaching beyond idealism, e.g. into Marxist and other forms of dialectic, called *Hegelianism*. By extension, some of its main figures, even if they rejected central tenets of Hegel thought, are called Hegelian. Hegel formulated the doctrine of *absolute idealism*, a synthesis of subjective and objective idealism. Among the notions central to Hegel's philosophy is that of the concrete universal, a type of concept that cannot be understood as merely a generalization or abstraction from particulars, because particulars cannot be apprehended without such concepts. In this regard, Hegel

used the term *notion* to denote any idea of reason, which is at once implicitly universal, particular, and singular.

Central to all these position is the interpretation of the Absolute as spirit (*Geist*), a conception that connected German idealism with religious thought. The spirit could exist in different ways. The subjective spirit exists, e.g. in personal morality, while the objective spirit exists in abstract right, and the absolute spirit overcomes the dualisms of morality (*Sittlichkeit*), because it is the unity of both in social ethics and the institutions. Indeed, Hegel claimed not only that opposites could be shown to be compatible in some higher notion that involved the *resolution* or *sublation* – in German, *Aufhebung*, i.e. "to preserve," "to raise up," and "to cancel" – of their opposition; but he also at times claimed that one opposite implied or required the other.

Along these lines, shortly after Hegel's death, most of his followers were interested in adapting his views to Christian thinking. Notable among them was Ferdinand Christian Baur (CE 1792–1860), founder of the Tübingen School, the validity of whose radical critique of Chrisitian texts, and whose methods, still prompt controversy The emphasis on Christianity began to change with the works of the so called *Young Hegelians*, D.F. Strauss (CE 1808–74), Ludwig Feuerbach (CE 1804–72), Bruno Bauer (CE 1809–82), and Arnold Ruge (CE 1803–80), who focused on Hegel's historical accounts of religion, and expanded Hegel's account of human productivity and, with the most famous Young Hegelian, Karl Marx (CE 1818–83), eventually focusing on labor.

The many subdivisions among Hegelian schools of thought and the increasing skepticism about Hegelianism's absolutist claims led to a strong anti-Hegelian reaction towards the end of the nineteenth century. However, a variety of concerns led a variety of philosophers and historians – Ernest Renan (CE 1823–93) and Hippolite Adolphe Taine (CE 1828–93) in France, Benedetto Croce (CE 1866–1952) and Giovanni Gentile (CE 1875–1944) in Italy, Francis Herbert Bradley (CE 1846–1924) and John M'Taggart Ellis (CE 1866–1925) in England – to adopt a Hegelian approach that came to be called *neo-Hegelianism*.

Most notable among neo-Hegelians in the United States was the philosopher Josiah Royce (CE 1855–1916), who became one of the main exponent of idealism in his time. He broadened the conception of a community of inquiry formulated by Charles Sanders Peirce (CE 1839–1914) with regard to science. For Royce, the entire world is a community of interpretation that includes all the social communities of the empirical world. Indeed, in this community even physical objects relate to each other through physical communication whose forms are the laws of nature. Royce, however, stresses that individuality and existence go together as part of an infinite unity. This is but one example of the nineteenth-century idealism's emphasis on individuality that appears to have resulted from a reaction to an overemphasis on the absolute and the organic nature of society found in previous forms of idealism.

An influential group between CE 1858 and 1900 was the *Kant Club*, which then became the *Saint Louis Hegelians* and, eventually, was called the *Philosophical Society of Saint Louis*, and founded *The Journal of Speculative Philosophy*, in which Peirce, other pragmatists, and some idealists published their work.

There were also parallel developments, e.g. that represented by the position of the Italian philosopher and statesman Vincenzo Gioberti (CE 1801–52). He called it *ontologism*, and characterized it as a dialectics that involved only Being. He identified God with creation. He saw his position as the opposite of what he called *psychologism*: seeking truth from the human subject instead of from Being and its revelation. Various versions of idealism have been formulated in philosophical areas other than epistemology and metaphysics, where the ones just discussed primarily belong. For example, in ethics, the Scottish philosopher William R. Sorley (CE 1855–1935) upheld *ethical idealism*, the view that value is crucial to reality, persons having intrinsic value, while things having merely instrumental value. Also, the German philosopher August Messer (CE 1867–1937) upheld the doctrine of ethical idealism, which he argued served to resolve not only ethical but also epistemological problems. In ethics and the philosophy of religion (besides metaphysics), the United States philo-sopher Borden Parker Bowne (CE 1845–1910) advanced the doctrine of *personalism*, arguing that personality is embedded in experience, hence crucial for explaining experience not only as that of the human person but also as that of the divine. This position was also advanced, among Bowne's students, by Albert Knudson (CE 1873–1953), Ralph Flewelling (CE 1871–1960), founder of *The Personalist*, and Edgar Sheffield Brightman (CE 1884–1953). In France, a version of personalism was formulated by authors influenced by Thomism, most notably by Emmanuel Mounier (CE 1905–50), Jacques Maritain (CE 1882–1972), and Étienne Gilson (CE 1884–1978).

Against personalism, the German philosopher Dietrich Heinrich Kerler (CE 1882–1921) proposed a kind of collective or intersubjective idealism: the doctrine of *impersonalism*, according to which not only one's own person, but all persons, including God, constitute the basis for values and their apprehension. Finally, the term idealism is sometimes also used to denote positions that stress the ideal in the sense of perfection, e.g. Utopian ideals in political philosophy.

See also: metaphysics; philosophy, sociopolitical; Platonism; rationalism

Further reading
Baur, Michael and Dahlstrom, Daniel O. (1999) *The Emergence of German Idealism*, Washington, DC: Catholic University of America Press.
Copleston, Frederick Charles (1994) *A History of Philosophy, Vol. 8, Modern Philosophy: Empiricism, Idealism, and Pragmatism in Britain and America*, New York: Image Books.
Rodríguez Huéscar, Antonio (1995) *José Ortega y Gasset's Metaphysical Innovation: A Critique and Overcoming of Idealism*, Albany: State University of New York Press.
Pippin, Robert B. (1997) *Idealism as Modernism: Hegelian Variations*, Cambridge and New York: Cambridge University Press.

idealiter in intellectu *see* Cartesianism

ideality *see* metaphysics

ideas of practical reason *see* idea; Kantian philosophy

ideas of pure reason *see* idea; Kantian philosophy

ideas of reflection *see* empiricism

ideas of sensation *see* empiricism

ideational theory of meaning *see* meaning

ideatum *see* idealism

identification *see* identity

identification conditions *see* definition

identifying conditions *see* definition

identifying description *see* reference

identity From the late Latin *identitas* and equivalent to the Latin *identidem* ("sameness"), which resulted from combining *idem* ("same") with *-ti-* (?) – yielding *identi-* – and *-tas* (suffix equivalent to the English "-ty"), this term denotes the relation each thing bears just to itself.

Identity *proper* or *strict* identity is *numerical* identity, typically distinguished from *exact similarity*, which is *qualitative* identity, whereby two or more exactly similar objects are copies of each other, yet are more than one; hence, not identical. The notion of numerical identity is also different from *haecceity*, from the Latin *hacceitas*, "thisness" or "specificity," which means either the fundamental actuality of an existent entity, or an individual essence, i.e. a feature an object has necessarily, and without which it would cease to exist. This idea originated with the work of the Scottish philosopher John Duns Scotus (CE 1266–1308), who raised questions about the *principium individuationis*, i.e. the cause or basis of individuality in individuals, and argued that prime matter is indeterminate and a formal difference is necessary. Haecceity adds no qualitative determination, but it is because of it that a being is *this* being. By contrast, the individualized nature of each creature, in abstraction of its haecceity, is objectively real as well as potentially universal, hence providing the basis for scientific knowledge. This is what the United States philosopher Charles Sanders Peirce (CE 1839–1914) called *Scotistic realism*.

Duns Scotus denied that haecceity was a form or universal, holding that it only applied to contingently existing entities in the actual world. However, the German philosopher Gottfried Wilhelm Leibniz (CE 1646–1716), turned haecceitas into an *individual essence or nature*: a set of features that uniquely identify the individual given the principle of identity of indiscernibles. A corollary of this view is the doctrine of *mereological essentialism*: every composite being is necessarily constituted by its particular parts in their particular configuration, and loses its identity if any parts are removed or replaced or their particular configuration altered. This doctrine has the questionable implication that if a human being has a tooth removed, then the human being's haecceity is lost. Leibniz seems not to have discussed this implication, but he did accept the also controversial implication that only the counterparts of individuals can exist in logically distinct possible worlds.

In logic, the notion of identity appears in the *law of identity*, also called the *principle of identity*, which holds that a proposition or thing is identical with itself and implies itself, or that, as formulated in medieval logic, A is A, and, in modern logic, if p then p, and p if and only if p. It is one of the three basic laws of classical logic together with the principle or law of contradiction (contradictories cannot both be true, i.e. it is not the case that p and not p), and the principle or law of excluded middle (contradictories cannot be both false, or either p or not p).

The notion of identity has raised a variety of philosophical problems prompted by the fact of change. A copper weather vane ceases to be a weather vane when melted, even if all the copper that constituted it (and no other matter did) remains. Also, it remains a weather vane even if part of it is dissolved by acid rain. This has led philosophers to talk of *tensed* identity: the weather vane and the copper are identical when they share all time-bound properties – i.e. those that characterize a weather vane – at time t_1, and *relative* identity: the weather vane is the same lump of metal as the copper, but not the same artifact.

In trying to specify criteria for the identity of items, philosophers have formulated various principles that come under the heading of the *identity of indiscernibles*. One of these principles says that any two items are identical if they share all of their properties. Against this principle, it is argued that it is trivial, because one of the properties shared by each of the items will be that of being identical with the other. Accordingly, a second principle has been suggested: any two items are identical if they share all of their *qualitative* properties, i.e., briefly, all those properties – e.g. that of being green – that more than one item can have and that do not involve being related to any particular object.

Against this second principle, philosophers have described counterexamples of possible worlds where only two identical objects exist. They have argued that these worlds are conceivable; but the said objects would share all qualitative relational qualities, and, hence, on the basis of the said principle, they would be one, not two items. Some have replied that these counterexamples involve hidden qualitative relational properties – e.g. their relation to the person imagining the items, say, one to the left, the other to the right – that differentiate the items.

Other philosophers, however, have formulated a third principle: any two items are identical if they share all of their *non-relational* qualitative properties. However, this principle has been criticized on the grounds that it is possible to conceive of possible worlds constituted by only two items that share all of their non-relational qualitative properties, e.g. two balloons sharing such things as the same color, shape, size, and composition. Indeed, some have argued that elementary particles in physics are counterexamples to this third principle.

The converse of the principle of identity of indiscernibles is the *indiscernibility of identicals* principle, also called *Leibniz's law*, most often formulated as the converse of the first version just formulated: if an item denoted by the term *A* is the same item denoted by the term *B*, then there is no difference between the item denoted by *A* and the item denoted by *B*. A contraposed form of this principle is the *distinctness of discernibles* principle: if there is a difference between two items, then they are not identical. This is used to argue against identity claims such as that the mental and the

physical are identical, for example by claiming that the physical is spatial and temporal, while the mental is only temporal, not spatial.

A particular area of traditional philosophical interest is that of *personal* identity. This notion is not that of *psychological* identity, which involves such things as values or goals structuring a person's life. Nor is it the notion of *social- or role-related* identity, which involves such thing as patterns of behavior that are socially expected because a person is, say, a male, a female, a physician, or a lawyer. Nor is the notion of personal identity the same as that of a person's *cultural* identity, or the related group notion of *national* identity, which involve patterns of thought and behavior that form part of the heritage of a social group with which their members are educationally connected, e.g. by having grown up in that group. Such heritage is constituted by intentionally passing down features of the group that may be, but need not be, involved in the wider notion of *group* identity that, as arguably evidenced by the case of gays and lesbians, have group identity based only on a currently shared way of life.

All the latter notions are involved in the *politics of identity*: a policy process where policies, practices, and institutions are assessed, and political action is taken about them, on the basis of the advantages or disadvantages the policies, practices, or institutions, and taking political action about them, has for given social groups such as (in the United States) African-Americans, Hispanics, women, the elderly, gays and lesbians, and the handicapped. Also, individuals often engage in such assessment and action motivated by their identification, i.e. with what group(s) they identify, or of what group(s) they consider themselves to be members.

This identification often involves some form of *kinship*. Two persons have a kinship relation (or are kin) when one descends from the other or when both descend from a common ancestor. When the purpose of identification based on kinship goes beyond acknowledgement of group membership, involving claims, say, rights-claims, then it requires some form of social recognition. Conflicts arise when recognition is not given and, sometimes, when it is given. For example, a result of the politics of identity has been that United States law defines a Hispanic as a person of Hispanic descent or from a country whose predominant language is Spanish. Further, immigration forms used to list a variety of categories – one being Hispanic, another being Caucasian or white – out of which new immigrants had to check one only, and the said definition of Hispanic appeared on the form. This could be at least a source of puzzlement, if not annoyance, to an immigrant from Argentina who was of Italian descent and had grown up believing that he was a Caucasian who happened to have been born in Argentina. Given the definition on the form, he was now Hispanic. This was the beginning of a process that some scholars have called *racialization* (i.e. the forced classification of persons in artificial and inaccurate racial or ethnic categories), which has been recurrent, and a source of criticism and conflict in identity politics.

By contrast with all these latter notions of identity, that of *personal* identity is simply that of the *numerical* identity of persons through time. In the Western tradition, the philosophical problem of personal identity is not primarily that of whether persons have identities. Humans typically remember their past histories as their own and have little, if any, need for establishing that they are their own, except when forgetfulness and imagination undermine their memory. Rather, the philosophical problem of personal identity is that of characterizing the conditions given when a person existing at one time, and a person existing at another time, turns out to be one and the same person. Some philosophers have attributed permanence to the soul and change to the body, so that personal identity amounts to that of an immaterial substance. Others have associated personal identity with a principle of development in the body. Still others – David Hume (CE 1711–76), Buddhist thinkers, (arguably) deconstructionist philosophers – have denied the possibility of the self, hence of identity. Still others, from the philosopher Augustine (CE 354–430; born in the North African city of Thagaste), through the English philosopher John Locke (CE 1632–1704), to the French philosopher Henri Bergson (CE 1859–1941)

have associated the psychological continuity or psychological persistence through time characteristic of personal identity with memory. Also, some philosophers have associated personal identity with the physical continuity of a person's living organism or the person's brain. In the late twentieth century, philosophical discussions of personal identity have shifted towards a consideration of the significance of personal identity.

Involved in the notions of personal identity, psychological identity, and other types of identity that apply to persons is the notion of a *person*, i.e. an individual having decision-making capabilities, whether potential or actual, or, as the respective property is called, *personhood*. This conception is relevant in moral philosophy, especially in agent-morality or character ethics (see ETHICS), and in METAPHYSICS (see AGENT).

See also: dualism; philosophy of mind

Further reading
Alexander, Ronald G. (1997) *The Self, Supervenience and Personal Identity*, Aldershot: Ashgate.
Garrett, Brian (1998) *Personal Identity and Self-Consciousness*, London and New York: Routledge.

identity of indiscernibles *see* identity

identity, principle of *see* logic

identity, psychophysical *see* philosophy of science

identity, theoretical *see* philosophy of mind

identity theory *see* philosophy of mind

identity thesis *see* philosophy of mind

ideographic *see* philosophy of science

ideology *see* philosophy, sociopolitical

ideoma *see* idealism

ideo-motor action theory *see* intention

ideoscopic *see* metaphysics

idols of the cave *see* induction

idols of the marketplace *see* induction

idols of the theater *see* induction

idols of the tribe *see* induction

if *see* logic

ignorance *see* knowledge

ignorantia, docta *see* docta ignorantia

ignoratio elenchi *see* fallacy

Igyō School *see* Zen

illation *see* argument

illative *see* argument

illative sense *see* reasoning

illicit process of the major *see* syllogism

illicit process of the minor *see* syllogism

illocutionary *see* speech act theory

illumination In the history of philosophy, truth and God have been described by reference to light and, often, all three notions are combined into a single one. In Western thought, truth and light appear associated, for example, in the myth of the cave described by the Greek philosopher Plato (428–348 BCE) in Book VII of the *Republic*, according to which humans are in a natural state of darkness concerning reality, truth is luminous, and humans find fragments of the truth through flashes of illumination. The identification of light, not just with truth, but with God, can be found in the Gospels, especially in the Gospel of John, and later in Neoplatonic writings that regarded light as both physical and spiritual, as in the works of the philosopher Augustine (354–430; born in the North African city of Thagaste) and, throughout the European Middle Ages, in many works falling in the Augustinian tradition.

In Islam, the Israqiyah School, from *ishraq*, i.e. "illumination," blended exoteric elements of classical Greek philosophy and the esoteric Zoroastrian identification of light with one of the divine forces (see ESOTERISM). In fact, the Islamic world not only made room for illumination through mystical practices, but even made room for the esoteric possibility that a human being be illuminated spontaneously with a transcendental spiritual truth, without having followed the path traced by a master. This possibility is *fard*, whose literal meaning is "solitary," and need not be associated with a traditional religion. If outside traditional reli-

gion, however, such revelation is not transmissible. If within the tradition, it is still not capable of being fully transmitted because no specific way of attaining it was followed, though the individual who achieved this revelation is considered a witness. This doctrine of *fard* is analogous to the Catholic doctrine of *spontaneous baptism*, or *baptism by the Holy Spirit*, without human intervention.

Doctrines of illumination can also be found in Eastern thought. For example, in Hinduism, illumination removes ignorance, hence suffering and limitation. Also, in Buddhism, especially in early Buddhism, one of the ten stages of bodhisattvahood, or the deferring of Buddhahood for the sake of others, is brightness of intellect (see BUDDHISM; HINDUISM).

In modern Europe, the doctrine of illumination can be found in Protestantism, especially among Quakers, whose founder, the English Churchman George Fox (CE 1624–91), formulated the doctrine of the *inner light*, i.e. a special relationship to God that granted an authority no institution could match.

See also: intuition; truth

Further reading

Engel, S. Morris (1969) *Language and Illumination. Studies in the History of Philosophy*, The Hague: Martinus Nijhoff.

Walbridge, John (1992) *The Science of Mystic Lights: Qutb al-Din Shirazi and the Illuminationist Tradition in Islamic philosophy*, Cambridge, MA: distributed for the Center for Middle Eastern Studies of Harvard University by Harvard University Press.

illusion, argument from *see* perception

illusion, concept of *see* perception

image *see* idea

image of God *see* Christianity; Judaism

image theory of meaning *see* meaning

image theory of memory *see* memory

imaginary *see* imagination

imagination From the Latin *imaginatio* ("fancy"), a term equivalent to *imaginatus* ("imagined"), the term imagination denotes the mental disposition to think about items that are novel, contrary to fact, or not currently perceived. Imagination is always imagination of some object even when the object does not exist. This intentionality of imagination needs to be explained by theories of imagination. Some philosophers have suggested that to imagine is to be conscious of a mental image. Others have held the doctrine of *irrealism*, according to which, all irreal objects – which need not be identical with ideal objects – are those that exist only within the boundaries of a reflecting consciousness. Still other philosophers, however, have argued that the existence, properties, and nature of any such image is questionable, and have proposed an *adverbial theory of imagination* whereby to imagine something that has a certain property, say, that of being green, is interpreted as imagining greenly.

The term *fantasy* (from the Greek *phantasia*, i.e. "imaging") is sometimes used as synonymous with imagination; but, more often, it denotes imagination that is extravagant or unrestrained. In this context, the product of imagination is *fiction*: something feigned, invented, imagined, a made-up story. This is not to say that fiction has no function. Indeed, the French physicist Pierre-Maurice-Marie Duhem (CE 1861–1916) held that fiction had a central role in science, in particular in physics. His view, *fictionalism*, is that physical theories are not explanatory but representations that do not reveal the nature of matter. They do provide general rules (of which physical laws are particular cases), yet are neither true nor false but convenient or inconvenient fictions – useful or useless fantasies – whereby the physical world is treated as if it were, or behaved in, accordance with these fictions. The same has been said of *social ideologies*: they are neither true nor false, but fictions whose symbolic and motivational functions make them useful or useless for a variety of social purposes, such as the attainment of social cohesiveness or the securing of support for policies, practices, or institutions. In this context, philosophers sometimes use the noun *the imaginary*, meaning a social, political, institutional, or philosophical construction with often morally significant functions.

See also: Frankfurt School; philosophy

Further reading
Cartwright, Nancy (1983) *How the Laws of Physics Lie*, Oxford and New York: Clarendon Press and Oxford University Press.
Eldridge, Richard Thomas (1996) *Beyond Representation: Philosophy and Poetic Imagination*, Cambridge and New York: Cambridge University Press.
Scruton, Roger (1998) *Art and Imagination: A Study in the Philosophy of Mind*, South Bend, IN: St Augustine's Press.

imitation *see* aesthetics; metaphysics

imitationism *see* philosophy of mind

immanence *see* transcendent

immanent causation *see* agent

immaterial *see* metaphysics

immaterialism *see* metaphysics

immediacy *see* knowledge; philosophy of religion

immediate *see* knowledge; philosophy of religion

immediate inference *see* argument

immoralism *see* ethics

immortality *see* metaphysics

immutability *see* change

impenetrability *see* philosophy of science

imperative, categorical *see* Kantian philosophy

imperative, hypothetical *see* Kantian philosophy

imperative of modernity *see* philosophy

imperatives *see* speech act theory

imperfect duties *see* ethics

imperfect rights *see* ethics

imperialism *see* philosophy, sociopolitical

impersonalism *see* idealism

impetus *see* Arabic philosophy; Neoplatonism; philosophy of science

implication *see* logic

implicature *see* logic

implicit definition *see* definition

imposition *see* intention; meaning

impossibilia *see* paradox

impredicative definition *see* definition

impredicative property *see* theory of types

impression *see* empiricism

improper symbol *see* syncategoremata

in Term appearing in a variety of sentences that pose significant philosophical problems. Consider, for example, the sentences "physical objects are in space," "consciousness is in the world," "the world is in consciousness," "the absolute is in itself," "the predicate is in the subject," "the accident is in the substance," "the part is in the whole," "a human individual is in the world." These at least pose the problem of the meaning of *in* depending on the sentence used. They also pose the problem of whether there are various modes of *being in*. In the entry for accident, for example, it was mentioned that philosophers have coined the formula *esse est inesse*, meaning that the being of an accident is *being in*, i.e. in something else. Is this also how a physical object is in a place? Is it how a predicate is in a subject? Medieval and other philosophers have distinguished between various modes of being in such cases as a thing being in a place or an accident being in a subject; a species being in a genus; an attribute being in a substance; and an object or fact being capable of being or even actually being in a knower's consciousness. Others have tried to characterize the term *in* as indicating a diadic asymmetric relation that can sometimes, but not always, be transitive as in "if the tree is in the yard and the yard is in the town, then the tree is in the town." In addition, philosophers sometimes use the Latin expression *in se* (in itself) to mean standing alone by contrast with *in alio* (in another), and apply *in se* to substances and *in alio* to accidents.

Various philosophical positions have been associated with the meanings and modes of *in*. One of them, influential in the Western as well as other philosophical traditions, is *in rebus realism* or *in re realism* or *metaphysical realism*, the view that there are real – usually conceived as spatiotemporal, though in certain philosophical discussions as universal – objects; that they exist independently of our experience, and that they have relations and properties independently of the concepts we use to understand them. This view is widely held in philosophy, science, and common sense. Yet, it has been criticized on the grounds that we cannot know real objects or facts, because we can know them only through our concepts. As a result, some have proposed the opposite of this view, *anti-realism*: the doctrine that denies one or more of metaphysical realism's three tenets. However, the reply has been that anti-realism's objection amounts to a disguised tautology (we can know facts and objects only as we can know them), hence does not entail anti-realism nor does it rule out the possibility that we can know facts and objects even if metaphysical realism is true.

See also: metaphysics; Thomism

Further reading
Katz, Jerrold J. (1998) *Realistic Rationalism*, Cambridge, MA: MIT.
McCormick, Peter J. (1996) *Starmaking Realism, Anti-Realism, and Irrealism*, Cambridge, MA: MIT.
Putnam, Hilary (2000) *The Threefold Cord: Mind, Body, and World*, New York and Chichester: Columbia University Press.

in re realism *see* in; Thomism

in re universals *see* Thomism

inalienable rights *see* ethics

inclusive disjunction *see* logic

incoherence, self-referential *see* theory of types

incommensurability *see* philosophy of science

incompatible *see* determinism

incompatibilism *see* determinism

incomplete symbol *see* logic

incomplete system *see* model

incompleteness theorem *see* philosophy of mathematics

incompossible *see* alethiology; *de re*, under de

inconsistency *see* logic

inconsistent triad *see* syllogism

incontinence *see* akrasia

incorporeal *see* metaphysics

incorrigibility *see* epistemology

indecidability *see* philosophy of mathematics

indefectibility *see* perfection

indefinite descriptions *see* description

indemonstrables *see* alethiology; *de re,* under de

indenumerable *see* infinity

independence *see* epistemology; logic; probability

indeterminacy argument *see* skepticism

indeterminacy of translation *see* philosophy of language

indeterminacy principle *see* philosophy of science

indeterminate *see* ambiguity

indeterminism *see* determinism

index *see* pragmatism

indexical *see* logic; philosophy of language

Indian philosophy *see* Advaita; Buddhism; carvākā; Hinduism; Jainism; Nyāya-Vaiśeṣika School; Sāmkhya-Yoga;

indicator, logical *see* argument

indicator word *see* argument

indifference, liberty of *see* determinism

indifference, principle of *see* probability

indifferentism *see* metaphysics

indirect communication *see* existentialism

indirect consequentialism *see* ethics

indirect discourse *see* reference

indirect intention *see* intention

indirect knowledge *see* knowledge

indirect passions *see* intention

indirect proof *see* logic

indirect sense *see* reference

indirect-speech act *see* speech act theory

indiscernibles, principle of the *see* identity

indiscernibility of identicals *see* identity

individual *see* metaphysics

individualism *see* holism; philosophy, sociopolitical

individuality *see* idealism

individuation *see* epistemology; metaphysics

indriya *see* knowledge

indubitability *see* Cartesianism; epistemology

indubitable *see* Cartesianism; epistemology

induction From the Latin *inductio,* a term reputedly coined by the Roman eclectic philosopher Marcus Tullius Cicero (106–43 BCE) from *in* ("in") and *ducere* ("to lead"), i.e. to lead in, in order to translate the Aristotelian term *epagoge* ("bringing in"), the term induction, sometimes also called the *inductive method,* is used in various senses. In a traditional sense, it denotes an argument that goes from instances to a generalization, a type of argument also called induction *by enumeration.* In a more modern sense, it denotes any argument where the premises provide a basis, though not a conclusive basis, for accepting the conclusion. This type of argument is sometimes also called *ampliative inference* and, besides induction by enumeration, it also includes such types of non-deductive arguments as induction *by elimination, arguments by analogy,* and *reduction.* Indeed, in this sense, induction is sometimes used as synonymous with *nondeductive argument,* thus also including *arguments to the best explanation* and all aspects of *confirmation.* In addition, there is a third – deductive – sense of induction, namely that found in *mathematical* induction or *proof by recursion,* where the premises of the argument provide conclusive reasons for accepting the conclusion. It involves, first, a basic clause that says a member of a collection has a certain feature *F*; and, second, an inductive clause, that says that, for any member of the collection with the feature *F*, its successor has the feature *F*.

Typically, induction is guided by a hypothesis or set of hypotheses, where a *hypothesis* –

from the Greek *hypo* ("under") and *hitasthai* ("to stand") – means a provisional explanation that, if sufficiently confirmed, may come to be considered a law or theory. This is the sense in which hypothesis is used in the *hypothetico-deductive method*, a method most often associated with mathematics and the natural sciences. It consists in using hypotheses, together with other confirmed premises, to infer *observation sentences*, i.e. sentences stating something capable of being observed. The degree of confirmation of the hypotheses significantly depends on whether the said observation sentences are found to be true and interesting. In any case, the hypotheses can be useful *heuristically* or have *heuristic value* – i.e. in leading to discoveries – even when they turn out to be false. Sometimes, the term *assumption* – from the Latin *ad*, i.e. "to," and *sumere*, i.e. "take," and meaning "to take for granted" – is used as synonymous with hypothesis in the sense just discussed; though, most frequently, assumption is used to designate the starting point of a deductive argument (see ARGUMENT; LOGIC). In deductive logic, hypothesis is sometimes used as synonymous with this latter sense of assumption.

Induction was strongly recommended by the English legalist, political figure, and philosopher Francis Bacon (CE 1561–1626) as a basis for science. He found various *idols* or erroneous ways of forming opinions. He classified them into groups. One group was that of the *idola tribus* or idols of the tribe, i.e. ways characteristic of humans, such as the tendency to generalize on the basis of too few instances. Another group was that of the *idola specus* or idols of the cave, i.e. ways affected by individual bias. A third was that of the *idola fori* or idols of the market place, i.e. ways resulting from the influence of mere words on our thinking. A fourth group was that of *idola theatri* or idols of the theater, i.e. ways of forming opinions that result from traditions of reasoning. Bacon recommended to fight these errors by means of induction as a combination of induction by enumeration and other forms of inductive reasoning.

Bacon believed that to know anything is to know its cause(s). Accordingly, he suggested that empirical inquiry be conducted by means of *tables of induction*, which foreshadowed the methods of empirical investigation later formulated by the English philosopher John Stuart Mill (CE 1806–73) (see below). These tables included the table of *essence and presence*, i.e. a list of cases where the feature being investigated occurred. Bacon also mentioned the table of *absence in proximity*, i.e. a list of cases that where generally alike, yet where the feature being investigated did not occur. There was also the table of *degrees or comparison*, i.e. a list of cases where the feature being investigated occurs in different degrees. Bacon thought these tables helped exclude irrelevant data, thus leading to the discovery of causes.

An influential view of confirmation is *colligation*. It was first formulated by the English philosopher William Whewell (CE 1794–1866), who held that colligations are ways of seeing facts in a new light and generalize over data in accordance with three criteria. First, they account for the given data. Second, they provide successful *predictions*, i.e. inferences to the future based on the data. Third, they involve a *consilience* of inductions, whereby evidence for inductions concerning events, previously thought unrelated, converge. Consilience is characteristic of theories involving high degrees of simplicity, generality, unification, and deductive strength. These, sometimes thought to be merely pragmatic advantages of theories, were, for Whewell, criteria for the theories' truth.

John Stuart Mill's *methods of empirical investigation* (for finding causes given the effects or, alternatively, for finding effects, given the causes) were described in his 1843 *A System of Logic* and are widely used today. First, the method of *agreement* says that if two or more instances of a given phenomenon have only one condition in common, that condition is the cause or effect of the phenomenon. This method, like the others, presupposes that each relevant condition or combination thereof has been taken into account and sufficiently analyzed so that no hidden circumstances were missed, and that they occurred at different times. For example, if cholera is predominant in a certain area, but some villages in the area show a comparatively low rate of cholera, we may want to find the cause. If, as researchers found out, the people in these villages have only one antecedent condition in common, that they regularly drink a tea made with fruits and leaves of the *maesa lanceolata* bush, then this tea is or involves the cause that prevents cholera.

Some contemporary logicians distinguish between the *direct* method of agreement, which is the method just described, and the *inverse* method of agreement, which goes from the non-occurrence of instances of a given phenomenon, to the absence of conditions normally expected to be present. It concludes the invariably absent condition is causally related to the phenomenon whose instances did not then occur.

Another method is the method of *difference*, also called the *laboratory method* because it is often used in laboratory experiments. It says: if an instance in which the phenomenon occurs, and an instance in which it does not occur, all have conditions in common save one, that one occurring only in the former is the effect, or cause, or part of the effect or cause of the phenomenon.

A third method is the *joint method of agreement and difference*, which normally involves the direct method of agreement and the method of difference. For example, one could start with the previous cholera example, then analyze the leaves and fruits of the *maesa lanceolata* bush and find that the active ingredient is maesanin, and then apply the method of difference: expose two groups of otherwise identical mice to the germs that cause cholera, but give maesanin only to the members of one of these groups. If these do not, while the others do, get cholera, then one could conclude that maesanin prevents cholera relatively to the conditions kept unchanged – i.e. *controlled* for – in both groups.

A fourth method is the method of *concomitant variation*, used specifically in cases in which the phenomenon under investigation and the conditions causally related to it are simultaneous. It says: if a condition or part thereof (e.g. the gravitational attraction of the moon in a certain shoreline area) varies as a phenomenon varies (e.g. as the level of the tide changes), this condition or its part, i.e. the gravitational pull of the moon, is causally related to the phenomenon; that is, to the tides.

A fifth method Mill described is the method of *residues*: to take away from a phenomenon what is known by previous inductions to be the effect of certain antecedent conditions, and what remains is the effect of the remaining antecedents. This, however, relies on the assumption that single factors cause single effects, an atomistic principle that is not free from controversy. Logicians today tend to consider this latter method a method for suggesting research questions (e.g. are the remaining effects caused by the remaining antecedents or by these in combination with others?), not for inferring causal connections.

An additional method some logicians describe today is the *joint method of agreement*, which combines the direct and the inverse method of agreement. This method combines the said two methods, none of which involves control between different groups. Hence, it is different from the joint method of agreement and difference in that the method of difference the latter includes characteristically involves control, i.e. the invariance of given conditions when the phenomenon occurs and when it does not.

All of Mill's methods involve the principle of *limited variety* (i.e. that the range of alternative conditions is limited), the principle of *determinism* (i.e. that the causally decisive factor is among the conditions considered), or some principles analogous to these. In order for Mill's methods to work, these background principles as well as the *relevance condition* (that the conditions considered be relevant to that being investigated) need to have been independently supported.

A problem arising in connection with induction is the *curve-fitting problem*, i.e. the problem of making predictions from past observations by fitting curves to the data, in particular of justifying the family of curves – too complex or overly simplified? – from which one will be fit to the data. This type of problem appears in *regression analysis*, i.e. the part of statistical theory concerned with the analysis of data in order to infer a linear-function relation between an assumed independent variable, the *regressor variable*, and a dependent variable, the *response variable*. One method for inferring the best fitting line in a scatter diagram that results from regression analysis is to find the line that minimizes the average absolute distance between a line and the points in the diagram. A more frequently used method, the least squares method, minimized the average of the squares of these distances. When more than one independent variable is hypothesized, then the *theory of multiple regression*, which involves multiple regressors, is used.

Also significant is the work of the Austrian philosopher Karl Raimund Popper (CE 1902–94), who agreed that scientific theories should have *testability*, i.e. the capacity to undergo experimental testing, but proposed to replace logical positivism's *verifiability criterion* of cognitive significance – that a sentence is meaningful provided there is a method for verifying it – with *falsificationism*, or error elimination, through the positing of unjustifiable conjectures or hypotheses, and their refutation or falsification through critically and relentlessly testing their deductive implications.

Falsifiability, however, turned out to be dependent on hypotheses involved in its tests, hence less decisive than Popper thought, making room for approaches that rely on disconfirmation (and confirmation), where *confirmation* is an evidential relation between evidence and a statement the evidence supports, and *disconfirmation* is an evidential relation between evidence and a statement whose falsity the evidence supports. Confirmation can be incremental, i.e. involving some degree of support, and absolute, i.e. providing high degree of support. However, the support is never identical with certainty. In this regard, the Vienna born, Austrian-English philosopher Friedrich Waismann (CE 1896–1959), coined the notion of *open texture*, i.e. the possibility of vagueness, arguing that vagueness always remains regardless of how many efforts are made to make expressions precise, because, for example, not all possible vagueness is foreseen or foreseeable at the time of such efforts. He concluded that this explains why empirical statements are not conclusively verifiable.

Sometimes, rival theories provide parallel explanations of a broad set of phenomena and conflict with each other only regarding a particular prediction. This is supposed to be resolved by a *crucial experiment* (also called *experimentum crusis*): an experiment that establishes which theory is correct concerning that prediction. However, the French physicist Pierre Maurice Marie Duhem (CE 1861–1916) argued that no crucial experiment was possible. For experiments in physics are observations of phenomena accompanied by interpretations and, therefore, physicists submit whole groups of hypotheses – not a single hypothesis – to experimental tests, and experimental evidence alone cannot conclusively falsify hypotheses. This is known as the *Duhem thesis*, also called the *Duhem–Quine thesis* because it was revived by the United States philosopher W.V.O. Quine (CE 1908–2000) in 1953.

Studies of induction and confirmation have lead to the formulation of various *paradoxes of confirmation*. Notable among them is the paradox of the *ravens*: Arguably, the hypothesis "All ravens are black" is incrementally confirmed by observing one black raven. This hypothesis is logically equivalent to "All non-black things are non-ravens." This is confirmed by observing the instance of a non-black non-raven, e.g. a rose. However, by the equivalence condition (whatever confirms a hypothesis must equally confirm any statement logically equivalent to it), observing a rose confirms the hypothesis "All ravens are black." This paradox is supposed to raise questions, if not about induction generally, about the equivalence condition it or what its traditional interpretation presupposes.

Another puzzling presupposition of induction is the *principle of the uniformity of nature*. Philosophers have found it difficult to formulate this principle in a coherent and useful manner. For nature is not uniform in all respects, and, however true, it is uninformative to say simply that nature is uniform in some respects. As a result, in order to establish which uniformities support projections to the future, philosophers have sought to rely on confirmation criteria such as those mentioned elsewhere in this entry.

Another influential paradox is *the new riddle of induction* or *grue paradox* formulated in the book *Fact, Fiction, and Forecast* by the United States philosopher Nelson Goodman (CE 1906–98). He argued that for every intuitively acceptable inductive argument, there are indefinitely many other analogous inductive arguments, which therefore seem acceptable, yet are intuitively unacceptable. For example, consider the argument: all emeralds so far observed are green; hence, all emeralds are green. It is intuitively acceptable. Now introduce the predicate "grue" where, for some yet entirely future time *T*, an object is grue, provided it has the property of being green and first examined before *T*, or blue and not first examined before *T*. Given this, consider the argument: all emeralds so far observed are grue; hence, all emeralds are grue. Though this has the same structure as the previous argument, it is intuitively unacceptable, because it entails all emeralds unexamined before *T* are blue, while the first argument entails they are green. This riddle challenges us to justify our preference for one group of inductions – say using "green" rather than "grue" – over the other, and formulate the restrictions that demarcate the acceptable from the unacceptable arguments.

One suggested solution has been to distinguish between a qualitative predicate and a non-qualitative predicate. A *qualitative predicate* is defined *syntactically* as a more or less simple predicate requiring no definition. *Semantically*, a qualitative predicate is – while a non-qualitative predicate is not – a predicate designating a property that, to us, is natural. *Ontologically*, a qualitative predicate is – while a non-qualitative predicate is not – a predicate that is embedded in the causal or modal structure of the actual world. The syntactical version, however, makes qualitative predicates dependent on our historically accidental use of language; while the semantic version makes them depend on our historically accidental conceptual habits. As for the ontological version, it makes them dependent on the causal and modal structure of the world; but this does not settle which structure this is, which, after all, we establish by starting with qualitative predicates based on our accidental use of language and conceptual habits, or on theoretical concepts or views inductively dependent by

using such predicates. This appears to make the suggested solution question-begging.

Another suggestion has been that only the first type of arguments lead to conclusions that can legitimately project, involve projectible predicates, and involve projectible hypotheses. However, this solution is too drastic, as evidenced by predicates applying to solid, liquid, and gaseous states of water, such as "solid and less than 0°, or liquid and between 0° and 100°, or gaseous and more than 100°" which would as a consequence fall under the category of statements that cannot legitimately project. Still another suggestion has been to require evidentially supported translations of grue-like hypotheses into conjunctions of ordinary inductive hypotheses. Discussion continues on this topic.

Finally, there is the *problem of induction*, i.e. the problem of whether we are justified in placing any degree of confidence in the conclusions of non-deductive inferences. Philosophers have addressed this problem in various ways. Kantian philosophers, for example, have invoked synthetic a priori principles. In the twentieth century, some philosophers have rejected the problem of induction as a pseudo-problem. Others – e.g. the German philosopher Rudolf Carnap (CE 1891–1970) – have invoked an inductive intuition so that one would see that induction is sound. Still others – e.g. the German philosopher Hans Reichenbach (CE 1891–1953) – have attempted to provide a pragmatic *vindication* of induction, i.e., briefly, evidence that it works. Also, Nelson Goodman proposed the previously described new riddle of induction as a replacement for the old problem of induction. Yet, none of these positions have secured much acceptance.

See also: abduction; argument

Further reading
Baird, Davis (1992) *Inductive Logic: Probability and Statistics*, Englewood Cliffs, NJ: Prentice Hall.
Barker, Stephen Francis (1969) *Induction and Hypothesis: A Study of the Logic of Confirmation*, Ithaca, NY: Cornell University Press.

inductive clause *see* induction

inductive definition *see* definition

inductive explanation *see* explanation; justification

inductive justification *see* justification

inductive probability *see* probability

inductive reasoning *see* induction

inductivism *see* philosophy of science

inexistence, intentional *see* meaning; phenomenology

infallibility *see* epistemology

inference *see* argument

inferential justification *see* justification

inferential knowledge *see* knowledge

infima species *see* definition

infinitary logic *see* logic

infinite *see* infinity

infinite, actual *see* infinity

infinite analysis, doctrine of *see* infinity

infinite being *see* infinity

infinite, potential *see* infinity

infinite regress argument *see* fallacy

infinity The property of being infinite, a term derived from the Latin *in* ("not") and *finis* ("boundary," "limit," "end"). In Ancient Greece, the concept of infinity was already present among the Pre-Socratics and centrally used by a disciple of Parmenides (*c.* 515–*c.* 450 BCE), Zeno of Elea (490–430 BCE), whose paradoxes attacked the notion of divisibility, apparently in attempting to support the Parmenidean doctrine of the One, the only, homogenous, indivisible Being. The concept of infinity, however, was mostly developed during the classical period, especially by Aristotle (384–322 BCE), who distinguished kinds of infinity. *Potential infinity* or *a potential infinite* is a property of that which has the capacity of being divided, augmented, or diminished unendingly; while *actual infinity* or *an actual infinite* is an unendingly divided, augmented, or diminished actual series. Aristotle argued that Zeno's paradoxes involved the mistake of treating all infinity as actual.

After the Classical period, while mathematicians began working on methods of analysis that foreshadowed calculus, philosophers came to identify positive or actual infinity with the divinity (the infinite being), and potential infinity with matter. The notion of actual infinity became even more strongly associated with perfection during the Middle Ages, when potential infinity was considered relative and restricted to created things. This dichotomy, however, was somehow weakened during the Renaissance, when the traditional, non-mathematical notion of infinity, as for example described by the philosopher Nicholas de Cusa (CE 1401–64; born in the city of Kues (in Italian, Cusa) in what is now Germany), was the *coincidentia oppositorum* ("coincidence of the opposites") doctrine, according to which what could be opposites, to finite beings like us, united in God's infinity. That is, though Aristotle's principle of non-contradiction applies reasonably well to finite beings, the opposite principle applies to infinite beings.

As for the mathematical conception of infinity, a distinction related to that drawn during the Classical Greek philosophy period between actual and potential infinity can be found in the modern doctrine of *infinite analysis* formulated by the German philosopher, mathematician, and diplomat Gottfried Wilhelm Leibniz (CE 1646–1716). It says that, in some cases, there is no finite analysis of a notion into its primitive components, but there is an analysis that converges on the primitive components without ever reaching them.

In contemporary set theory, infinity is the property of a set – e.g. the set of natural numbers – whereby it has a proper subset – e.g. that of even integers – whose members can be placed in one-to-one correspondence with all the members of the set. If the members of a set can be placed in a one-to-one correspondence with the natural numbers, then the set is *denumerable*; otherwise, it is *indenumerable*. By means of the *diagonal procedure*, the Russian-born German mathematician Georg Cantor (CE 1845–1918) showed that there are infinite sets that cannot be put in a one-to-one correspondence with the set of natural numbers. The axiom of set theory involved here is the *infinity axiom* or *axiom of infinity*: the infinite set ω exists.

The notion of infinity plays a crucial role in logic through the notion of an *infinite regress argument*. This is a type of argument meant to establish that a certain position is unjustified because it leads to an infinite series where either none exists or, if one were to exist, the position's justification would be substantially if not totally undermined. Yet, as discussed elsewhere, this conclusion is questionable (see FALLACY).

See also: act; paradox; set

Further reading
Moore, A.W. (1993) *Infinity*, Aldershot and Brookfield, VT: Dartmouth.
Rucker, Rudolf v. B. (1995) *Infinity and the Mind: The Science and Philosophy of the Infinite*, Princeton, NJ: Princeton University Press.

influxus physicus *see* determinism

informal fallacy *see* fallacy

informal logic *see* logic

information-theoretic semantics *see* meaning

information theory *see* meaning

informed consent *see* ethics

informed decision *see* ethics

informed judgment *see* ethics

inherent value *see* value

innate ideas *see* empiricism

innatism *see* Cambridge School

inner speech *see* philosophy of mind

inquiry *see* reasoning

insanity *see* rationality

inscrutability of reference *see* philosophy of language

insolubilia *see* paradox

inspiration *see* aesthetics; philosophy of religion

instance *see* metaphysics

instant *see* metaphysics; philosophy of science

instantiation *see* metaphysics

instantiation, universal *see* logic

instinct *see* philosophy of mind

institution *see* ethics; philosophy, sociopolitical

institutional discrimination *see* ethics

institutional economics *see* philosophy of economics

institutional ethics *see* ethics

institutional objectivity *see* empiricism; ethics

institutional racism *see* ethics

institutional reviewing board *see* ethics

institutional theory of art *see* aesthetics

instrumental conditioning *see* behaviorism

instrumental desires *see* ethics

instrumental rationality *see* rationality

instrumental reason *see* rationality

instrumental value *see* ethics

instrumentalism *see* epistemology; philosophy of science

insufficient reason *see* chain of being

insulation *see* philosophy, sociopolitical

integracionismo In English, *integrationism*, this Spanish term denotes a philosophical approach or, rather, a *philosophical program* proposed by the Spanish philosopher José Ferrater Mora (CE 1912–91). It consists in attempting to combine opposite concepts characteristic of traditionally opposed philosophical doctrines. Ferrater Mora suggests that this can be done either by formulating positions that involve passing from one to the other and vice versa, or by combining the opposite concepts somewhere along the line of oscillation between the said poles. He describes various areas of application for integrationism. First, concerning views on universals and particulars, he sees conceptualism as an integrationist position between the extremes of realism and nominalism, so long as it is understood as a constant intellectual movement from realism to nominalism and back in the process of understanding particulars, their features, and their mutual relations. Second, concerning views on being and becoming, he suggests an integrationist position where, for any item one picks, it shares both on being and becoming, though to different degrees. Third, concerning epistemological views on appearance and reality, he suggests an integrationist approach that would not reduce the objects of knowledge to mere bunches of qualities, nor to a mere existence in itself. Instead, the approach would assume that actually existing objects of knowledge have some properties – hence are not merely noumenal – even if they are not reducible to them. Fourth, concerning views on MECHANICISM and organicism, he argues that no real entity is purely mechanical or purely organic, but integrates both aspects to different degrees depending on the entity. Fifth, concerning views of history as nature or spirit, where particular stages in human history should not be seen as mere natural developments, or as mere spiritual developments, but as humans' efforts to emerge from and raise themselves above nature and form societies of persons.

Integrationism was criticized as an empty theory, on the grounds that it gets caught up in an unending dialectics between opposite poles, without going beyond the assertion that they should be integrated. Ferrater Mora replied that this was a danger that integrationism shared with all other philosophical views and, besides, did not need to happen. Indeed, he argued that, for example, concerning views on human history, integrationism was in no way empty because it led to seeing historical developments as humans' efforts to emerge from nature and form societies of persons.

See also: abstract; epistemology; evolution; metaphysics; philosophy of history

Further reading

Ferrater Mora, José (1988) *El ser y la muerte: bosquejo de filosofía integracionista*, Madrid: Alianza.

Giner, Salvador y Esperanza Guisán (1994) *José Ferrater Mora: El hombre y su obra*, Santiago de Compostela: Universidad de Santiago de Compostela.

integralism *see* actualism

integration *see* integracionismo

integrity *see* ethics

intellect *see* understanding

intellectual *see* epistemology; philosophy, sociopolitical

intellectual virtues *see* virtue

intellectualism *see* voluntarism

intelligence *see* artificial; philosophy of mind

intelligibilia *see* Neoplatonism

intelligible world *see* Kantian philosophy; voluntarism

intension *see* meaning; reference

intensional *see* meaning; reference

intensional logic *see* logic

intensive magnitude *see* measurement

intention From the Latin *intentio* and this, like *intentus* ("intent"), from *intendere* ("to stretch toward," "aim at"), the term intention has two senses: first, in an *episodic sense*, it means a feature of a particular action, namely its aim, as when one acts intentionally or aiming at bringing about some event, state of affairs, or object; second, in a *habitual sense*, a feature of one's mind or, at least, of one's pattern of actions, namely its aim, as when one aims at or has the aim or end of acting in a certain way, now and later.

Some philosophers conceive of intentions on a *desire–belief model*: For Jim to cross the street with the intention of buying tomatoes at the market across the street is explainable by his desire to buy tomatoes and his belief that he can get tomatoes at the market. This is an example of the intention of a particular action. Some philosophers argue that it can also be applied to the sense in which intention is a feature of one's mind or of one's pattern of action. For example, for Mary to act kindly towards others with the intention of doing good to them – both now and later – is explainable by her settled desire to do good to them and her belief that she can do this by acting kindly.

In this regard, philosophers have largely understood *desire* or *want* as a felt disposition to have, do, or experience something, and have characterized various types. For example, an *extrinsic* or *instrumental* desire is the desire one has for something because it is conducive to something else one desires. When, and only when, this is the only reason, the desire is *strictly extrinsic*. *Intrinsic* desire is the desire of something for its own sake. When, and only when, this is the only reason, the desire is *strictly intrinsic*.

Returning to the desire–belief model view of intentions, some philosophers argue that at least some intentions involve distinctive attitudes that are not reducible to desires, believes, or their combinations. In this regard, the Scottish philosopher David Hume (CE 1711–76) argued that some passions, e.g. pride, humility, love, and hate, are *indirect passions*, i.e. they have assignable causes such as qualities of a person who is in love, and indirect objects, e.g. the said person. He contrasted them with *direct passions* such as desire, aversion, hope, and fear, which are feelings immediately caused by pleasure, pain, or the prospect of any of these, and have things or events as their objects. The English philosopher Jeremy Bentham (CE 1748–1832) expanded on this by distinguishing between *direct intentions*, i.e. intended events, objects, or states of affairs directly brought about by one's actions or in performing one's actions, and *indirect* or *oblique intentions*, i.e. intended results partly caused by the events, states of affairs, or objects directly brought about by one's actions or in performing one's actions. An example of an indirect intention is the intention to interrupt a conversation between two people at a party by directly intending to sing loudly. Here, the intention to sing loudly at the party is an example of a direct intention.

A distinction relating intentions to reflection and communication is that between *first intentions*, i.e. thoughts aiming at, hence about, entities other than thoughts, and *second intentions*, i.e. thoughts about thoughts. It has been influential in doctrines of intentionality and the philosophy of language.

Associated with intention is the notion of *volition*, i.e. a complex mental event that includes cognitive, affective, and conative components, and is involved in the beginning of an action. The conative component is the *motivation* or *impetus* that, if not strong enough to cause action, is called a *velleity*. Some philosophers consider volitions to result from the *will*, i.e. the faculty or set of abilities involved in initiating an action. Other philosophers neither postulate a will nor consider volition to be associated with intention. Instead, they consider volition to be associated with combinations of beliefs and desires.

Three main accounts of volition have been formulated. One attempts to reduce the action to the entire causal chain constituting the mental event (the volition) that yields bodily movement(s). It has been criticized on the grounds that when one tries to distinguish the mental event from its resulting bodily movements, the notion of action becomes necessary, hence undermining the attempted reduction.

A second account identifies the action with the volition, so that bodily movements are its effects. This account has been criticized as obscurantist on the grounds that it postulates an entirely *ad hoc* concept – that of volition – that, because *ad hoc*, has no explanatory use.

A third, the causal theory of action, identifies the action with the volition's effects. This account is also open to the charge of obscurantism. In addition, it needs to formulate a satisfactory account of the conative component in volition and needs to address a variety of counterexamples.

A related conception of the will is the *ideomotor action theory* according to which every representation of a movement awakens in some degree the actual movement represented. This conception, perfected and defended by the United States pragmatic philosopher William James (CE 1842–1910), was meant to provide the psychological basis of volition: actions tend to occur when thought, so long as unopposed by contrary thoughts that, by the same theory, would tend to lead to opposite actions. The development of BEHAVIORISM in the early twentieth century led to sharply, if not entirely, reducing the use of the concept of will in psychology.

See also: phenomenology; philosophy of mind

Further reading

Audi, Robert (1986) *Action, Decision, and*

Intention: Studies in the Foundations of Action Theory as an Approach to Understanding Rationality and Decision, Dordrecht and Boston, Hingham, MA: D. Reidel Pub., distributed in the USA and Canada by Kluwer Academic Publishers.

Bratman, Michael (1998) *Faces of Intention: Selected Essays on Intention and Agency*, Cambridge, UK and New York: Cambridge University Press.

Rundle, Bede (1997) *Mind in Action*, Oxford and New York: Clarendon Press and Oxford University Press.

intentional object *see* phenomenology

intentionality *see* meaning; phenomenology

interactionism *see* philosophy of mind

intercession *see* ethics; philosophy of religion; philosophy, sociopolitical

interchangeability, salva veritate *see* opacity

interdefinability, of connectives *see* logic

interdependence *see* ecology; philosophy, sociopolitical

interdisciplinary inquiry *see* philosophy of science

interest *see* ethics; philosophy, sociopolitical

interethnic *see* culture

intermediate value *see* value

internal necessity *see* alethiology

internal negation *see* logic

internal realism *see* philosophy of science

internal reason *see* justification

internal relation *see* relation

internalism, epistemological *see* justification

internalism, motivational *see* justification

internalism, reasons *see* justification

internalization *see* ecology

international terrorism *see* war

interoception *see* perception

interpersonal utility *see* ethics; utilitarianism

interpretant *see* pragmatism

interpretation *see* hermeneutics; logic

interpretation, non-standard *see* logic; philosophy of language

interpretation, standard *see* logic; philosophy of language

interpretive system *see* operationalism

intersection *see* set

intersubjective *see* epistemology; ethics; existentialism

intersubjectivity *see* epistemology; ethics; existentialism

intersubstitutivity, salva veritate *see* opacity

interval scale *see* measurement

intervening variable *see* philosophy of mind

intimacy *see* existentialism; feminist philosophy

intransitivity *see* relation

intrapersonal utility *see* ethics; utilitarianism

intrinsic desires *see* ethics

intrinsic property *see* relation

intrinsic value *see* ethics

introaffection *see* empathy

introjection *see* psychoanalysis

introspection *see* philosophy of mind

intuition From the Latin *in* and *tueri* ("to look at"), the term intuition denotes a direct – i.e. non-inferential or sense-perceptual or introspective, or based on memory – insight into, apprehension of, grasp, or knowledge of either a proposition such as "2+2=4," and "Torture for the sake of torture is always wrong," or a concept, e.g. that of the color green; or an entity, e.g. God. *Self-evidence* is a feature of self-evident propositions, i.e. the feature whereby they are plainly true. It is, for example, a feature of those propositions such as "'either it is or it is not raining here and now," and "bachelors are unmarried," that one can see non-inferentially that they are true once one understands them, they are said to be known, or they are capable of being known, by intuition. Some philosophers hold that contradictions, e.g. "It is and it is not raining here and now," are also said to be known, or to be capable of being known by intuition.

In Western philosophy, intuition is often related to innate ideas at least in so far as these are understood along the lines of Aristotelianism and Stoicism as dispositions or tendencies. Sometimes, intuition is also contrasted with discursive reasoning. For example, referring to intuition in an intellectual sense, the French philosopher and mathematician Blaise Pascal (CE 1623–62) used the expression *esprit de finesse* – i.e. spirit of finesse, or a balancing capacity able to deal with complicated matters not reducible to simple principles – that he contrasted with the *esprit géométrique*, i.e. spirit of geometry, or reason. In addition, Cartesian and other thinkers have distinguished between *intelligible* intuition by which we intuit truths of reason and *sensible* intuition by which we intuit truths of fact. In ethics, some philosophers have held that some ethical truths – e.g. the above-mentioned "Torture for the sake of torture is always wrong" – and concepts – e.g. that of the good – are known through intuition. Along these lines, the German philosopher and mathematician Edmund Husserl (CE 1859–1938) distinguished between *empirical* intuition, attained through the senses, and *eidetic* intuition that, starting with but going beyond the previous ones, apprehends essences. In addition, philosophers and others have talked of *grammatical* intuition: the ability whereby some competent language-users know immediately whether given sentences are grammatical or not.

In Eastern philosophy, intuition is often related to *moksha*, i.e. spiritual enlightenment and liberation. All orthodox schools of HINDU-ISM, i.e. schools of Indian philosophy that accept the scriptural authority of the Vedas, besides this authority and inference, rely on intuition as a source of knowledge, and treat intuition as more reliable than inference. The Nyāya School, for example, treated it as the most important source of knowledge and distinguished between *perceptual* intuition or intuition attained through the senses, and *yogic* intuition, which was independent of the senses.

In all of the schools, intuition is thought to support a direct relation between self-consciousness and super-consciousness. In interpreting the end of the Vedas, namely, the Upanishads, the Vedānta School holds that *anubhava* or intuition of the self reveals BRAHMAN or the One in unity with *ātman*, the soul. Indeed, along these lines, some twentieth-century followers of this school assert that the highest state of knowledge is self-luminous intuitional knowledge.

Outside Hinduism, Buddhism is another Eastern philosophical tradition using a notion of intuition, namely that of *prajñā* (transcendental wisdom or existential intuition), whereby one knows things in their totality and as unities. The state of those who attain this knowledge is prajnaparamita (*prajñā* awakened or attained), i.e. the perfect enlightenment of Buddha, which is also the aim of *satori* in Zen.

See also: Buddhism; Cambridge School; Cartesianism; empiricism; Hinduism; phenomenology

Further reading
Bergson, Henri (1992) *The Creative Mind: An Introduction to Metaphysics*, New York, NY: Carol Publishing Group.
Falkenstein, Lorne (1995) *Kant's Intuitionism: A Commentary on the Transcendental Aesthetic*, Toronto and Buffalo: University of Toronto Press.
Lévinas, Emmanuel (1995) *The Theory of Intuition in Husserl's Phenomenology*, 2nd edn, Evanston, IL: Northwestern University Press.

intuitionism, ethical *see* ethics

intuitionism, logical *see* logic

intuitionism, mathematical *see* logic

intuitionism, Oxford School of *see* ethics

intuitionist logic *see* logic

intuitions *see* theory

intuitive induction *see* ethics

inversion spectrum *see* philosophy of mind

inverted qualia *see* philosophy of mind

invertibility *see* ethics

invisible hand *see* philosophy of economics

involuntary euthanasia *see* euthanasia

Ionian philosophy *see* Greek philosophy

I-proposition *see* syllogism

irony *see* existentialism; Greek philosophy

irrational *see* rationality

irrationality *see* rationality

irrealism *see* imagination

irredundant *see* epistemology; logic; probability

irreflexive *see* relation

irrelevance *see* ethics; logic

irrelevant conclusion, fallacy of *see* fallacy

īshvara *see* Brahman

Islam This term, meaning "submission to God," is the name of the religion founded by Muḥammad (CE 570–632), who, beginning when he was about forty years old, received revelations he recorded for twenty-two years. These now constitute the sacred book of Islam that, for some time now, has been standard practice to call the *Quran* (though it is still sometimes called the *Koran* or *Qur'ān*). Also, the *hadīth*, i.e. reports of the deeds and sayings of the Prophet as recounted by his companions, were compiled, and, by the beginning of the tenth century CE, various collections had been produced. Six of these are known as the *The Six Genuine Ones*, on account of their being regarded as especially authoritative in conveying the *Sunna* or model patterns of behavior.

The Islamic faith is characterized by monotheism. Besides the enormous influence of Muḥammad himself, Islam shows influences from various religious traditions. Notable among these are Judaism and Christianity, from which Islam has inherited the notion that we must be resurrected with 'living bodies of flesh," and accepted such individuals as Adam, Noah, Abraham, Moses, and Jesus as prophets who prepared the way for Muḥammad.

The basic tenets or requirements of Islam are called the *Five Pillars of Islam*. The crucial one is the *Shahādah*, from *shahida*, i.e. to observe, to witness, to testify, as well as perceiving and testifying, which is the affirmation that Allāh is the only God and Muḥammad is the messenger of God. The remaining four Pillars are the *Salāh*, i.e. the five daily ritual prayers; the *Zakāh* or giving of alms; the *Sawm*, i.e. fasting during the month of Ramadan; and the *Hajj* or the pilgrimage to Mecca at least once in a lifetime.

The practice of Islam proceeds from Muḥammad's saying that Islam is to believe in God and the Prophet, to say the prescribed prayers, to give alms, to observe the feast of Ramadan, and to make the pilgrimage to Mecca. The duties of Islam's members accordingly include daily restatements of faith, five prayers facing in the direction of Mecca each day, fasting during the month of Ramadan, one pilgrimage to the holy city of Mecca (from which Muḥammad was expelled and had to flee to Medina when he first tried to free Mecca from its idols), and payment of a tax.

From an ethical standpoint, Islam emphasizes retributive justice, though mercy was evidenced in Muḥammad's elimination of the traditional Arabian practice of infanticide in the case of female infants. Legally, the Quran and the Sunna are at the core of Islamic law. In addition, Muslim jurisprudence is based on the *qiyās* or analogical reasoning, and the *ijmā* or popular consensus (though the scope of the latter varies from group to group). Politically, the Islamic concept of *jihād*, which means to surrender one's property and oneself in Allāh's path, was aimed at establishing the Islamic socio-moral order. Except for the Khārijites, who held *jihād* to be one of the Pillars of Faith, Muslim schools have downplayed it for a variety of reasons, from the need to consolidate the Community of the Faith to the need to coexist with other groups.

As for theological doctrines, the greatest contrast concerns free will. The Mutazilites and Qadarites upheld free will while their orthodox opponents upheld absolute fatalism. This contraposition soon came to be involved in the wider theological issue of *God's justice*, concerning which the Mutazilites subsumed the idea of God under that of human justice, while the orthodox subsumed the idea of justice under that of God.

Another point of theological contention was the relation of faith to deeds. The Khārijites considered a grave sinner to be an infidel. By contrast, most Muslims considered such a person to be a Muslim, though a sinner-Muslim. In this regard, the Mutazilites formulated the doctrine of the *intermediate state*, according to which a grave sinner was neither a Muslim nor a non-Muslim.

A further matter of theological controversy concerned the Divine Attributes. In an attempt to safeguard the notion of *tanzīh* or divine transcendence, the Mutazilites explained away all anthropomorphic expressions in the Scriptures and the Ḥadīth. This approach eventually led them to reject all Divine Attributes and hold that God is pure Essence and has no eternal names or qualities. This implied the rejection of the view that the Speech of God was an Attribute of God. Accordingly, the Mutazilites held that the Quran was a created work, not the eternal word of God. They were criticized for emptying God of content in a manner inadequate for religious consciousness. The Mutazilite reply was to accuse the orthodox thinkers of likening God to humans.

The upshot of these controversies was to create an orthodox reaction against the Mutazilite position on God's reason and justice, and human free will. This led to an emphasis on Divine Power, God's Will, grace, and fatalism. As a result, the orthodoxy risked losing the initial comprehensive nature of the Islamic faith.

Attempts at reaching a synthesis between the Mutazilite and orthodox positions were formulated in *Ash'arism*, whose founder was Abu'l-Ḥassan al-Ash'arī (d. CE 942), and *Māturīdism*, founded by Abū Manūr al-Māturīdī (d. CE 945). Though quite analogous to Ash'arism, Maturidism held a more flexible position concerning human free will, by emphasizing God's omnipotence but making room for the efficacy of the human will. Though these synthesizing systems became recognized in Islam, their tensions with their more radical orthodox opponents have continued.

In the late medieval period, Islam was significantly affected by tensions between orthodox Islam and *Ṣūfism* – which claimed the privilege of leading individuals' inner development – as well as by many cross-currents. For centuries, an orthodox reaction had been developing against the religious corruption and moral laxity prevalent in India and the out-laying provinces of the Ottoman Empire. It finally took form in the *Wahhābī* movement's orthodox revival of the nineteenth century. Also in the nineteenth century, African reform movements developed, most notably, *neo-Ṣūfism*, which gave up medieval views concerning its exclusive role in leading individuals' inner development.

Other movements starting in the nineteenth century have been modernist in emphasis, addressing the tensions between reason and tradition, or reason and traditionalized faith. They have revisited doctrinal discussions and considered institutional challenges, for example about the development of an interest-free though modern banking system, and about the role of women in modern Islamic societies.

Some African-American thinkers have been associated or in dialogue with Islam through the *Nation of Islam*, a sect also known as the *Black Muslims of America*. The original sect advocated anti-white and separatist doctrines. It changed significantly upon the death of its founder, Elijah Muhammad in 1975. Most of its members, guided by Muhammad's son, Wallace, formed the orthodox group named *American Muslim Mission* in Chicago. A dissident faction, led by Louis Farrakhan, retains the name Nation of Islam as well as the original doctrines.

See also: Arabic philosophy; Aristotelianism; Neoplatonism

Further reading

Fasi, Muhammad (1988) "Stages in the development of Islam and its dissemination in Africa," in M. El Fasi (ed.) *General History of Africa*, Vol. 3, Berkeley: University of California Press, pp. 56–91.

Haq, S. Moinul (1997) *Muhammad, Life and Times: A Historical Interpretation*, Karachi: Hamdard Foundation Pakistan.

Kenny, Joseph (1997) *Early Islam: Background, the Life of Muhammad, the Umayyyad [sic] and 'Abbāsid Caliphates, Echoes Today*, Nigeria: Dominican Publications.

Rahman, Fazlur (1979 [1966]) *Islam*, 2nd edn, Chicago and London: University of Chicago Press.

Wensinck, A.J. (1965) *The Muslim Creed*, London: Frank Cass.

Islamic Neoplatonism *see* Arabic philosophy; Aristotelianism; Neoplatonism

Islamic philosophy *see* Arabic philosophy; Aristotelianism; Neoplatonism

Islamic Scholasticism *see* philosophy of education

isolation argument *see* epistemology

isomorphism *see* model

is-ought *see* ethics

issue *see* philosophy, sociopolitical

iterated modality *see* alethiology; *de re,* under de

iterative hierarchy *see* set

J

J *see* logic

jahad *see* meaning

Jainism One of the heterodox schools in Indian philosophy. Though it rejects the authority of the Vedas, it is influenced by one of the Vedas, the *Yajurveda*, a highly ritualistic book systematized by the philosopher and religious thinker Vardhamana (599–527 BCE), also called Mahavira, who, however, appealed to logic and experience, not to the book's authority, in formulating his views.

Among the central doctrines of Jainism are ATOMISM and mind–body dualism. These doctrines involve two overall categories or *tattvas* of items in the universe: *jiva*, i.e. the conscious, and *ajiva*, i.e. the unconscious, which includes space, time, matter, rest, and motion. All of these except time are thought to be physical in nature, in that they have extension and parts. They are called *astikāya dravyas* and their physical features are called *gunas*. Time, by contrast, is thought to have neither extension nor parts and, as such, to belong in the category of the non-physical, or *anastikāya dravya*.

According to Jainism, *loka* – the world – has three parts: *ūrdhva-loka*, i.e. where the divinities reside, *madhya-loka*, i.e. earth, and *adho-loka*, i.e. the place where happiness and misery are experienced depending on one's virtues or vices. Perfect individuals go beyond *ūrdhva-loka*, to *lokākāsha*, where they stay motionless.

Jainism also holds that time repeats itself in six vast epochs, only two of which permit *moksha* or release of the soul from its embedd-edness in the body, which is due to karmic matter formed by our passions. *Moksha* can be attained through the *tri-ratna* or *sādhana*, i.e. right faith, right knowledge, and right conduct, which means the belief in the doctrine of Jainism, knowledge of nature (which Jainism holds can only be probable and partial because the universe is multiple), and behavior, which involves five virtues: non-violence, truthfulness, omitting to steal, chastity, and lack of worldly attachment. Non-violence is especially significant in Jainism, which sees violence as incompatible with achieving enlightenment and accordingly stresses the practice of avoiding injury to all living beings.

A concept significant to the ethics and philosophy of language of this school is *evambhūtanaya*, i.e. the such-like standpoint: the standpoint concerned with the performance of a certain function suggested by the etymology of a term. This term introduces linguistic requirements, so that for a term to be properly used in accordance with *evambhūtanaya*, it must apply to an item that does what the term implies e.g. to a strong person when the term implies strength. In determining this, the interpretational standpoint becomes crucial. According to Jainism, a *naya* is a particular standpoint in considering an individual's behavior, for example, from one standpoint, the individual is cooking, while from another the individual is cutting vegetables, heating water, etc. The former standpoint, from which all pieces of behavior are controlled by a single purpose, is called *naigama-naya*. It is sometimes interpreted also as the teleological standpoint that synthesizes the universal and the particular aspects of a series of events. Yet, Jainism holds the *naya-vāda* or relative pluralism theory, that any point of view that regards itself as absolutely true to the exclusion of all others commits the fallacy of point of view or *nayābhāsa*. What can, however, be attained is *naya-nishcaya*: perfect vision or knowledge of an item in a particular context.

The branch of inquiry that studies words in Jainism is *nikshepa*. It is supposed to analyze and understand the content of words with regard to proper names (*nāma-nikshepa*), the meaning of an object in relation to time (*dravya-nikshepa*), the meaning a word (*sthāpana-nikshepa*), and the meaning of the nature of an object (*bhāva-nikshepa*).

See also: Buddhism; Hinduism

Further reading
Latthe, Anna Babaji (1950) *An Introduction to Jainism*, Bombay: Natha Rangaji.
Nyayavijaya, Muni (1998) *Jaina Philosophy and Religion*, Delhi: Motilal Banarsidass Publishers, Bhogilal Lehar Chand Institute of Indology and Mahattara Sadhvi Shree Mrigavatiji Foundation.

jakumetsu *see* Zen

jalpa *see* rhetoric

James–Lange theory *see* philosophy of mind

Jannah, al- *see* myth

Jansenism *see* Christianity

Japanese philosophy In Japan, just as in India and China, the distinction between philosophy and religious thought was not sharply drawn for centuries. Indeed, *tetsugaku*, literally "learning" or "studies of wisdom," did not appear in Japan until after the Meiji restoration of CE 1868, when Japan was opened to Western influences.

A much earlier, though somewhat analogous, phenomenon concerns the Japanese need for drawing distinctions between religious traditions: the native religion of Japan, *Shinto*, which existed for at least two millennia, was not named until the sixth century CE, when BUDDHISM was imported from China. CONFUCIANISM had been introduced together with

Chinese script one century earlier; but it had not by itself sufficed to bring about the self-reflective task of naming Japan's traditional religion. At any rate, Confucianism did not reach the peak of its influence in Japan until the Tokugawa era (CE 1603–1867), with the work of neo-Confucian philosophers.

Notable among Chinese neo-Confucian philosophers was Chu Hsi (CE 1130–1200), who synthesized principle and actualization as requiring each other, e.g. in regarding *jen*, "benevolence," as both the principle of love and a human character trait, though he made investigation of things, say, of the principle's applications, primary. A Japanese philosopher who pursued the approach of the Chu Hsi School was Hayashi Razan (CE 1583–1657). Another neo-Confucian Chinese philosopher was Wang Yang-Ming (CE 1472–1529), who argued against Chu Hsi that sincerity of the will should precede the investigation of things because the principle existed in the mind. A Japanese philosopher who pursued Wang Yang-Ming's approach was Nakae Tōju (CE 1608–48).

Before Confucianism could attain such influence in Japan, however, Buddhism was most influential during the Heian and Kamamura periods. The former followed the establishment of the *Tendai* School of Buddhism by Dengyō Daishi at Mount Hiei, near the city of Kyoto in the early ninth century CE. The Kamakura period lasted between CE 1185 and 1335. During this period, Japan saw the rise of the *Shōguns*, a line of military men who ruled Japan from CE 1192 to 1868. They turned Kamakura, a city on the sea to the south of Tokyo, into a second capital and attracted teachers and artists from the Emperor's city of Kyoto.

All major Buddhist Schools developed in China took hold in Japan. The two most influential, however, were the T'ien-T'ai (in Japanese, *Tendai* School) and the Ch'an School (in Japanese, *Zen* School), a meditation School. In China, these schools developed in a parallel manner. In Japan, along with Pure Land Buddhism, they jointly led to the development of the *Nichiren*, a most powerful Japanese sect, and of *Zen Buddhism*. All Buddhist terms, which had been translated into Chinese, were also translated into Japanese. For example, *gō* became Japanese for *karma*.

Like Confucianism, Buddhism involved philosophical thought. Among its foremost representatives in Japan were Saichō of *Tendai* (CE 767–835), Kūkai of *Shingon* (CE 774–835), Shinran of *Jōdo Shinshū* (CE 1173–1262), Dōgen of *Sōtō Zen* (CE 1200–53), and Nichiren of *Nichiren Buddhism* (CE 1222–82). While each school of Buddhism upheld its characteristic doctrines in Japan, all schools of Japanese Buddhism share an emphasis on *mujō*: the impermanence or transitoriness of phenomena. This was made plain in the path of *Geidō*, a Zen-influenced tradition that involved aesthetic and religious components whose main notions included: *aware* or sad beauty, *yūgen* or profundity, *ma* or interval, *wabi* or poverty, *sabi* or solitude, and *shibui* or understatement.

The Bushidō or "Way to Knightly Virtue" tradition of the Samurai developed from both Confucianism and Zen Buddhism. It was a warrior ethic based on the duties of loyalty and self-sacrifice. It blended soldiery and priesthood, and involved mental and physical training aimed at applying, in the service of the Samurai's Lord or Emperor, the virtues of bravery, chivalry, honor, and contempt for death. In the twentieth century, the Samurai code has received philosophical discussion in the works of such contemporary thinkers as Takuan Soho and Nitobe Inazo.

As previously stated, tetsugaku, literally "learning" or "studies of wisdom," did not appear in Japan until after the Meiji restoration of CE 1868, when Japan was opened to Western influences. As a result, first Hegelianism and neo-Kantianism, then Pragmatism and Marxism, and later existentialism have exercised significant influence in Japanese academic philosophy. Pivotal in this process have been Nishida Kitarō (CE 1870–1945) and the *Kyoto School*. Nishida attempted to develop an East–West philosophical dialogue, as well as an interfaith dialogue, within a Buddhist framework centered on the notions of *kū* or emptiness, and *mu* or nothingness. In the process, in his earlier work, *A Study of Good*, Nishida formulated and often reworked the notion of *junsui keiken* or pure experience, which was influenced by the thought of the United States

philosopher William James (CE 1842–1910) and, most notably, by Zen Buddhism. He is also, especially, known for his philosophy of the "place" (*basho*) of nothingness.

A modern Buddhism mass movement in Japan is *Sōka Gakkai* or *Scientific Society for the Creation of Values*. It was founded by Makiguchi Tsunesaburō (CE 1871–1944) in 1930 and followed the thought of Nichiren. At the end of the twentieth century, it remains a very influential movement. Still other new philosophical religions in Japan are *Omotokyo* and a Nichiren derivative: *Rissho Kosekai*.

Twentieth-century philosophical efforts in Japan have attempted to criticize and replace, or further develop, Nishida's thought. The main opponents of the work of Nishida and the Kyoto School have been Marxist philosophers, most notably Tosaka Jun (CE 1900–45). By contrast with these critics, the philosopher Nishitani Keiji (CE 1900–c. 1989), for example, used Zen logic to formulate a way of overcoming nihilism, a notion he understands relatively to specifiable features or values (which in nihilism are undermined), i.e. as *relative nothingness*. He attempted this by relying on the notion of *absolute nothingness* found in Buddhism and in the Christian notion of *kenosis* or emptiness, where the features or values relative to which nihilism is understood are overcome or excluded. A parallel contemporary effort is that of Hisamatu Shin'ichi, who studies Japanese aesthetics by reference to Nishida's thought on absolute nothingness. Other important Kyoto School thinkers are Watsuji Tetsuro (CE 1889–1960), who formulated a communitarian ethical theory, and Kuki Shūzō (CE 1888–1943), who discussed Japanese traditional aesthetic concepts such as that of *iki* or chic.

See also: Buddhism; Confucianism; Zen

Further reading

Li, Lincoln (1996) *The China Factor in Modern Japanese Thought: The Case of Tachibana Shiraki, 1881–1945*, Albany: State University of New York Press.

Mortensen, Finn Hauberg (1996) *Keierkegaard Made in Japan*, Odense: Odense University Press.

Piovesana, Gino K. (1997) *Recent Japanese*

Philosophical Thought 1862–1996: A Survey, 3rd rev. edn, Richmond: Japan Library.
Ryusaku Tsunoda, de Bary, Wm. Theodore and Keene, Donald (eds) (1958) *Sources of Japanese Tradition*, two vols, New York: Columbia University Press.

jāti *see* class

Jehovah *see* Yahweh

jen *see* Chinese philosophy; Confucianism

jen-hsin *see* Chinese philosophy; Confucianism

Jewish feminism *see* Jewish philosophy

Jewish philosophy In a wider sense, this term denotes philosophical works created by Jewish philosophers and informed by the texts, traditions, and experiences of the Jewish people; while in a narrower sense, it denotes philosophical inquiry aimed at developing or justifying concepts involved in Jewish religion and tradition.

Jewish philosophy began with Philo Judaeus of Alexandria (*c.* 20 BCE–CE 40). His aim was to interpret Jewish theology by appeal to concepts and methods of Greek philosophy. Using allegory in the manner the Stoics used it, Philo developed a conception where biblical persons and places became universal symbols. Despite his efforts, however, Philo had little if any influence on Jewish thought. Indeed, his philosophical theology approach was not accepted in Judaism until the ninth century CE, after it had been accepted in the Islamic world, where Jews lived at the time.

Saadiah ben Joseph al-Fayyumi (CE 882–942) or Saadiah Gaon, who lived in Baghdad, was the first notable Jewish philosopher to aim at harmonizing philosophy and religion after Philo. His *Book of Critically Chosen Beliefs and Convictions* was produced in response to the Karaites, who wished to return to the tradition of the *Torah* as the only authority. He defended the *Talmudic* and *Rabbinic* tradition and reason, rejecting atomistic occasionalism, arguing for a natural order created by God, and providing a classification of the commandments by reference to their greater and lesser rationality.

By contrast with Saadiah, his contemporary Isaac Israeli (CE 850–950), who lived in Qayrawan, North Africa, had no interest in religious ideas. Instead, he pursued a strictly philosophical, largely Neoplatonic, line of thought that was later further enhanced by the thought of Solomon Ibn Gabirol or Avicebron (*c.* CE 1020–*c.* 1057). The latter lived in Málaga, in what is now Spain and, without concern for religious ideas, formulated a philosophy where form and matter had precedence over nous, the universal mind. Long recognized as a Hebrew poet of stature, in the nineteenth century, Ibn Gabirol was discovered to have authored the famous Neoplatonic work entitled *The Fountain of Life* (or *The Source of Life*), originally written in Arabic and preserved only in the Latin *Fons Vitae*, which identified God primarily with potentiality and becoming.

Also significant for his poetic and philosophical contributions was Moses Ibn Ezra (*c.* CE 1055–after 1135). Highly notable among the critics of the Karaites was Abraham Ibn Ezra (*c.* CE 1089–1164), a native of Toledo, Spain. He was admired by his younger contemporary Abraham Ibn Daud (*c.* CE 1110–80), a historian and philosopher who relied on historiography to argue for the providential continuity of the Jewish intellectual and religious tradition, and who led the foundation for the work of the great Jewish philosopher (discussed below): Moses ben Maimon or Maimonides (CE 1138–1204).

Abraham Ibn Ezra's influence as a commentator on the Scriptures (he was the first to suggest that the Book of Job was a translation) reached even the Jewish philosopher of Spanish and Portuguese descent Baruch Spinoza (CE 1632–77), whose work is also discussed below and who, in his *Theological Political Tractate*, mentioned Abraham Ibn Ezra's work as an authoritative source. Besides being a philosopher, Abraham Ibn Ezra wrote poetry (for a long time, and for unknown reasons, under a pseudonym), was an eminent mathematician and naturalist, and a warm and sympathetic character. Despite undergoing many hardships and suffering a long exile, in which he died, he always considered himself a Spaniard and wrote whimsically about his destiny, arguably foreshadowing in a variety of ways some Golden Age Spanish authors, e.g, Franciso de Quevedo y Villegas (CE 1580–1645).

Also during the eleventh and twelfth centuries, in what is now Spain, the problem of harmonizing faith and knowledge based on reason had attained prominent interest. In this regard, the philosopher Bahya ben Joseph ibn Paquda (early twelfth century CE), from Saragosa, formulated a rational theology that culminated in an ethic of gratitude towards God. Also, there were still other thinkers who opposed Aristotelian trends. For example, in the book known as *The Kuzari*; which was formally entitled *In Defense of the Despised Faith*, Judah Ha-Levi (CE 1075–1141) sharply criticized Aristotelian ideas.

Yet, the tide in medieval Jewish philosophy was steadily moving toward a predominance of Aristotelianism. It became clear in *The Exalted Faith*, by the previously mentioned Abraham Ibn Daud, where Neoplatonic concepts such as emanation and the unknowable unity of God are kept, but embedded in an Aristotelian framework. This approach had been developed by Arabic philosophers, most notably al-Fārābī (*c.* CE 870–950), and Ibn Sīnā (in Latin, Avicenna; CE 980–1037), and perfected by Ibn Daud's contemporary, Ibn Rushd (in Latin, Averroes; CE 1126–98).

At the peak of this period, in the major work of medieval Jewish philosophy, the *Guide to the Perplexed*, Moses ben Maimon or Maimonides (CE 1135–1204) of Córdoba (but who wrote the book while in Egypt) supported both reason and revelation against Gnostic mysticism as already present in the Haggadah, i.e. in traditional free interpretations and parables based on scripture. In his book, which he wrote in order to enlighten his disciple Rabbi Joseph Ibn Aknin on *Maaseh Bereshith* and *Maaseh Merkabah* (the history of creation and the history concerning the celestial chariot), Maimonides generally agreed with the philosophers, a fact that, together with his tendency to omit discussion of matters of Jewish faith, led many to question his orthodoxy and, even today, seek esoteric interpretations of his work. At any rate, he argued that philosophers should contribute to the welfare of their community, even if personal happiness was to be attained in the contemplation of God.

As for *Gnostic mysticism*, it involved a rejection of logic and an emphasis on pursuing perfection, seeking self-purification, and engaging in a set of practices called the *cabala*. It spread throughout what is now Spain as well as in other areas of what is now Europe, and, in 1305, a synod gathered in Barcelona banished secular study and Maimonides' works. However, synods had only local jurisdiction. Subsequently, another synod gathered at Montpellier and excommunicated those who prevented the study of science or abused Maimonides.

The controversy continued. In Provence, the astronomer, mathematician, exegete, and philosopher Levi ben Gershon (known in Latin as Gersonides; CE 1288–1344) published his *Wars of the Lord*, where he criticized both Ibn Rushd and, in part, Maimonides, and proposed a rigorously rationalistic position that also denied the personal providence of popular faith, arguing that it is impossible for God to know particulars *as particulars*. In the process, he discussed the question of reward and punishment and, concerning the Book of Job, he argued that when a good and just person like Job is punished, this is not actually irrational when one understands that this person's judgment and punishment are based on the person's unfulfilled potential, not on the person's actual deeds, however right and good these might be.

This rationalistic position led Hasdai ben Abraham Crescas (CE 1340–1410) to attempt to demonstrate the insufficiency of reason, hence the failure of Aristotelianism, and the need for revelation. Against the notion of intelligence, he advanced the notion of *amor dei* or love of God as the basis for understanding oneself and God. He was an ardent defendant of Judaism against Christianity's pressures to convert. His student, Joseph Albo (*c.* CE 1360–1444) sought to formulate Jewish theology as an axiomatic system in what he thought would help defend Jewish thought against its critics.

The controversy between advocates of the Talmud and those of the Cabala continued far into the seventeenth century, spreading throughout Jewish communities in Europe and Asia. This led to extremisms, especially of the Cabalists and, as a result, to some skepticism, for example, in the deism of Uriel da Costa (CE

1585–1647), and in the thought of Baruch Spinoza, who believed Judaism should have ended with the fall of the Temple. His philosophy centrally uses a notion already invoked by Maimonides, *amor dei intellectualis* or intellectual love of God, which for Spinoza was the third and highest stage in the ascent of the soul towards intellectual salvation – where one can see the universal in all the particulars of one's life. This approach continues to influence Jewish thought today.

Modern developments in Jewish philosophy are often dated back to the work of the German philosopher Moses Mendelssohn (CE 1729–86), who upheld conformity to ceremonial law while trying to remove theocracy from Judaism. Under the influence of the Enlightenment, this position issued in a reform movement that stressed reason, instituted the conducting of services in the vernacular, and emphasized scientific interpretations of Scripture and Oral Law. On the other hand, the eighteenth and nineteenth centuries saw the development of *Hasidism*, a mystical movement that sharply influenced Jewish culture.

Parallel developments took place in philosophy. The German philosopher Hermann Cohen (CE 1842–1918) followed Kant and Hegel in emphasizing universal rational teachings of Judaism; while David Baumgardt (CE 1890–1963) sought to reconcile ethical naturalism with traditional religious ideas. The German philosopher, theologian, and political leader Martin Buber (CE 1878–1965) advocated an existential personalism, while the German philosopher Franz Rosenweig (CE 1886–1929), who collaborated with Buber on a new German translation of the Hebrew Bible, tried to find a balance between existential concerns and universal conceptions of Judaism by emphasizing the existential efficacy of traditional beliefs and practices.

The ideas and social processes leading to the Second World War and beyond undermined the universal optimism that had been predominant among Jewish thinkers. As a result, many of these began to focus, if not less on the universal, at least more on the particular, attempting to develop philosophies that paid careful attention to national concerns. Along these lines, Asher Ginzberg (CE 1856–1927), whose pen name was Ahad Ha'Am, argued the creation of a spiritual center of Jewish culture in Palestine would help preserve the Diaspora Jewry from assimilation. Mordecai Kaplan (CE 1881–1981) sought to formulate a social mission and a collective identity for Jews independently of many beliefs and practices traditionally associated with Jewish identity. Abraham Joshua Heshcel (CE 1907–72) sought to preserve the spiritual aspects of the Jewish experience in ritual, ethical and social action. Joseph Soloveitchik (CE 1903–93) pursued a return to Orthodox ideals, while Yeshayahu Leibowitz (CE 1903–94) argued for the independence of Jewish religious observance from State mandates without disregarding the reality of the State of Israel. Also, the contemporary thinker Emil Fackenheim argues for the need to find individualized ways of keeping Jewish ideas, practices, and commitments alive.

In addition, contemporary feminist concerns have prompted the development of Jewish feminism, a philosophical approach aimed at dealing with tensions between those concerns and Jewish traditions.

See also: Arabic philosophy; existentialism; Neoplatonism

Further reading
Efros, Israel (1974) *Studies in Medieval Jewish Philosophy*, New York: Columbia University Press.
Geras, Norman (1998) *The Contract of Mutual Indifference: Political Philosophy after the Holocaust*, London and New York: Verso.
Ha-Levi, Judah (1998) *The Kuzari: In Defense of the Despised Faith*, trans. N. Daniel Korobkin, Northvale, NJ: J. Aronson.
Rosenfeld, Max (1997) *Festivals, Folklore and Philosophy: A Secularist Revisits Jewish Traditions*, Philadelphia, PA: Sholom Aleichem Club.
Zank, Michael (1996)"*The Individual as I*" in *Hermann Cohen's Jewish Thought*, Amsterdam: Harwood Academic Publishers.

jhāna *see* dhyāna

jihād *see* Islam

Jinn *see* metaphysics

jiriki *see* Zen

jìvanmukta *see* Hinduism

jñāna *see* knowledge

jñānendriya *see* knowledge

Job, Book of *see* Jewish philosophy

joint method of agreement and difference *see* induction

jōriki *see* Zen

jouissance *see* feminist philosophy

ju-chia *see* Chinese philosophy; Confucianism

Judaism The religion of the Jewish people. It is the origin of both Christianity and Islam. From a religious standpoint, Judaism is said to originate in a compact between God and Abraham whereby God would help the development of His chosen people, the people of Israel, in exchange for their devotion. Its main tenets, which initially existed in traditional ritual and Mosaic law, include monotheism, the belief that humans were created in the image of God, the belief that God revealed Himself to humans, that the people of Israel's divine obligation is to teach the universal Fatherhood of the God of Israel, that humans are responsible for their misconduct, that right actions are the way to salvation, that the right will triumph in the world, and that humans will be judged in terms of justice in the world to come.

Notable among the concepts of Judaism is the belief in the absolute unity and uniqueness of God (associated to the belief that Jewish people are the chosen people of God), which led to rejecting the Roman Empire's custom of *apotheosis* – from the Greek *apo* ("from"), and *theoun* ("to deify") – whereby heroes and rulers were thought transformed into divinities. This, on its turn, led to the persecution of the heirs of Judaism, the early Christians, because of their refusal to acknowledge the divinity of the Roman emperor and, by contrast with the pragmatic acquiescence of Roman skeptics and others, being adamant about it. Their position was a matter of religious conscience – quite an incomprehensible notion to most Romans of the time. It seriously affected Christianity and not Judaism because, as the French historian and linguist Ernest Renan (CE 1823–92) indi-

cated, Christianity's cohesiveness was based on shared beliefs, while Judaism's cohesiveness was based on shared practices. The beliefs, not the practices, made it obligatory for Christians not to say publicly that they acknowledged the divinity of the Roman emperor. This emphasis on belief is why the notion of *heresy* – opinion or doctrine at variance with the accepted one – was crucial in the development of Christianity.

By contrast, in Judaism, the notion of heresy acquired prominence during the fifteenth century, when the foremost espousers of Jewish philosophy, the Spanish Jewry, underwent enormous pressures and persecution. It was then that Profiat Duran (d. *c.* CE 1414), also known as Efodi, criticized Christianity from a Jewish standpoint seeking to balance the practical with the intellectual aspects of the *Torah*. It was also then that Simeon ben Tzemach Duran (CE 1361–1444) aimed at fixing the boundaries within which a thinker might still be considered Jewish, i.e. the boundaries of orthodoxy or right opinion, thereby fixing the boundaries of heresy. This was an original contribution to – and implicit criticism of – the project of Jewish dogmatics, and arguably marked the historical beginnings of Orthodox Judaism and conservative Judaism.

A central conception in Judaism is that of God. From its inception, Judaism conceived of God as a Lord of history, a history rooted in a covenant between Yahweh and His chosen people: Israel. This was the biblical God, the God of Abraham. With the prophets, God became the God of Abraham, Isaac, and Jacob, a conception that raised the history of the people of Israel to the level of world history. These conceptions are quite different from the God of the philosophers, which provided an explanation for the universe but did not take upon itself to satisfy human wishes or look after the destiny of His chosen people. Indeed, the God of Aristotle which, as the final cause of change, found the first substance, matter (*hyle*) and, out of it, got the world started, was eventually seen by some Jewish philosophers as inadequate in that this conception made matter God's partner in creating the world, instead of giving God the prominence He was supposed to have.

Another central concept was that of *sin* and the need for *atonement*, a ceremony aimed at cleansing the temple, priesthood, and people of their sins by renewing their special relationship with God, and thereby attaining God's forgiveness for those sins. The atonement ritual included abstinence and sacrifice. The custom is still in practice today, on Yom Kippur, a day set aside as the holiest of the year, when confession of sins and repentance are stressed.

The canonical books of Judaism (the Old Testament according to Christianity) included the *Torah*, or the *Mosaic Law*. Its text was interpreted in two bodies of writings: the *Talmud* and the *Midrash*. In one sense, the Talmud is made up of the *Mishnah*, which sums up the law from the fifth century BCE to the second century CE, and the *Gemara* (an Aramaic term meaning completion), which amplifies and explains the Mishnah. In another sense, the Talmud can be divided into the *Palestinian Talmud*, completed by the fifth century CE when, persecuted by Constantine, the Palestinian schools decayed; and the *Babylonian Talmud*, completed by the seventh century CE. As for the Midrash, it includes the *Halakha* or *Halakhah*, or *Halacha* (literally "custom," "rule"), a compilation of Jewish traditional law and minor precepts, and the *Haggadah* or *Aggadah*, or *Agada* (literally "narration"), a set of free interpretations and parables based on Scripture and aimed at edification.

By contrast with these, the *apocrypha* – from the Greek *apocruphos* ("secret") – are writings concerning whose authority there was disagreement at the time the canon of the Bible was established. They include fourteen books dealing with history and doctrine, and which often emphasize the apocalypse. In the Catholic tradition, these same books are called *deuterocanonical*.

There was disagreement over the apocrypha because some influential thinkers believed them to involve flights of fantasy, even though some of their subject matter – e.g. the creation of the universe by God – was not questioned in Judaism. Indeed, Jewish and, under its influence, Christian tradition upheld notions of creation, primeval chaos, and nothingness that deeply influenced the development of Jewish

and Christian philosophical thought. In Genesis 1, for example, primeval chaos was the earth without form and void. Further, the Jewish conception of the creation of the universe is that of its production by a divinity out of nothing. The Latin name for this latter sense is *creatio ex nihilo*, an expression that literally means "creation from nothing." This led to questions about whether it was rational to believe that reality was everlasting – a notion decisive for the philosopher Baruch Spinoza (born in Amsterdam of Spanish-Portuguese descent; CE 1632–77) (see JEWISH PHILOSOPHY) – or created; and whether, if created, the world or its creatures were somehow created at each new moment – an occasionalist doctrine that found its first proponents in the Islamic world and its full formulation in Spinoza's century – or once for all.

Law was central to Judaism and led to the development of a special hierarchy. It included *Rabbis*, who were both religious teachers and civil judges; the *Sanhedrin*, which was formed by priests with both religious and civil power; *scribes*, who fixed the text of the law; and *Pharisees*, who devoted their lives to the tradition of the law.

Judaism went through various stages of development. The periods of exile and restoration led to the fixing of the law in writing. Roman rule and the Diaspora led to the internal development of Judaism. The fall of the Temple originated the oral law, the Talmud, and the final universalization of Judaism. A specially notable concept in this process has been that of the *Kingdom of God*, according to which God's rule over humanity was to be fulfilled in the future. This notion was associated with *messianism*, the doctrine that a personal Messiah (meaning "the anointed one"), would lead to the Kingdom of God. This idea gained force among Jews especially during the first century BCE. It was influential in the development of Christianity beginning with Jesus, a messianic figure who started by announcing that the Kingdom of God was at hand, both in the sense of being already present and in the sense of being imminent.

During the long development of Judaism, various influential doctrines were formulated, among them the coming of the Messiah, the age of universal peace, and the return to Zion. Under the influence of the Enlightenment, a reform movement – *Reform Judaism* – developed. It stressed reason, instituted the conducting of services in the vernacular, and emphasized scientific interpretations of Scripture and Oral Law. *Homiletics* – the art of preaching – adapted to these changes. On the other hand, the eighteenth and nineteenth centuries saw the development of *Hasidism*, a mystical movement that has sharply influenced Jewish culture. With the advent of the State of Israel in the twentieth century, the contrast between traditional European forms of Judaism and African forms of Judaism such as Ethiopian Judaism and, for example, its claim to have originated from one of the lost tribes of Israel, has been a source of conflict and religious as well as historical debate.

See also: Christianity; Islam; Jewish philosophy

Further reading

Davies, William David (1984) *Cambridge History of Judaism*, London: Cambridge University Press.

Eisen, Arnold (1998) *Rethinking Modern Judaism: Ritual, Commandment, Community*, Chicago, IL and London: University of Chicago Press.

judgment From the Latin *jus* ("right") and *dicere* ("to determine" or "say"), this term is used in various philosophical senses. Most frequent among these are:

1 a mental act or process whereby one forms an opinion about something;
2 the opinion resulting from the said mental act or process;
3 a speech act whereby one states something; and
4 the statement resulting from the said speech act.

All of these senses emphasize the fact that judgment involves the use of thought or language in *upholding* or *assenting to* (rather than, for example, merely entertaining) one or more propositions or declarative sentences. That is, a judgment in any of the previous senses is different from, but involves, one or more propositions or declarative sentences.

Hence, since these propositions or declarative sentences are true or false, the judgment upholding or assenting to them is by extension also said to be true or false.

The Greek philosopher Aristotle (384–322 BCE), in *De Interpretatione*, said that a proposition is a true or false assertion resulting from a judgment. Also, representatives of THOMISM, who focused on the union or division of concepts involved in judgments, held that judgments are second-order operations, while apprehensions of concepts are first-order operations, and that the basic unity of knowledge is judgments, in that they formulate assertions or denials that characterize unions or divisions between apprehended concepts. Along these lines, Port Royal logicians held that judgments are mental activities whereby, of two ideas, one affirms or denies that one is the other. In KANTIAN PHILOSOPHY, judgments became central for structuring the world of phenomena, appreciating beauty, and finding purpose in nature.

In reply to these views, some philosophers have argued that judgments thus understood were merely psychological (indeed, faculties constituting the subject matter of faculty psychology), and obscured the logical relations involved. They accordingly argued that though judgments are assertions or denials, their character does not merely depend on their being assented to or not, but on the logical structure of judgments themselves. Among these, some proceeded to investigate the phenomenology of judgment-structures; while others concluded that, devoid of their psychological components, judgments merely amounted to propositions or declarative sentences and these were the appropriate subject of study. Still others, however, objected that declarative sentences where not declarative until used with declarative functions, hence they should be approached pragmatically and studied in use, i.e. as declarative speech acts.

The term judgment is sometimes also used in ways that contrast, overlap, or coincide with other terms. For examples, see the entries on *decision* and *myth*. In addition, the term judgment is sometimes used when talking of a moral judgment or, more generally, of a judgment of value. The latter is an *evaluation*, i.e.

judgment to the effect that an item has such features as that of being beautiful or not, humorous or not, and, in ethics, good or bad, right or wrong, justified or not. Evaluation, however, like *assessment*, may refer to the process of considering the pros and cons of alternative courses of action (e.g. in risk assessment, the risks and benefits involved with alternative courses of actions), or to the product resulting from such process: the actual judgment that a given course of action is preferable to the alternative ones. Despite using the term judgment in these contexts, not all philosophers agree that it denotes any item capable of being true or false. For discussions of this and related topics, see the entries on DECISION and ETHICS.

See also: analytic–synthetic distinction; decision; ethics; Kantian philosophy; philosophy of mind

Further reading
Bosanquet, Bernard (1999 [1895]) *The Essentials of Logic: Being Ten Lectures on Judgment and Inference; Implication and Linear Inference*, Bristol, UK: Thoemmes.
Henrich, Dieter (1992) *Aesthetic Judgment and the Moral Image of the World: Studies in Kant*, Stanford, CA: Stanford University Press.
Husserl, Edmund (1973) *Experience and Judgment: Investigations in a Genealogy of Logic*, London: Routledge & K. Paul.
Steinberger, Peter J. (1993) *The Concept of Political Judgment*, Chicago: University of Chicago Press.

judgments, terminating *see* analytic–synthetic distinction

jūjūkai *see* Zen

jung, ju *see* Confucianism

jurisprudence *see* philosophy of law

jury theorem *see* paradox

jus ad bellum *see* war

jus civile *see* philosophy of law

jus divinum *see* philosophy of law

jus gentium *see* philosophy of law

jus in bello *see* war

jus naturale *see* ethics; philosophy of law; Stoicism

jus sanguis *see* diaspora

jus terram *see* diaspora

just *see* justice

just cause *see* war

just in case *see* logic

just-war theory *see* war

justice From the Latin *jus* ("right," or "law"), this term denotes a variety of conceptions accounting for what each is due. One such conception is that of *formal* justice, which can be formulated as follows: no one ought to be treated differently from anyone else, despite the various differences between individuals, except when one or more of these reasons constitute a good reason for doing so. However defensible and necessary, this principle points to another conception of justice, namely *substantial* justice, which concerns the specification of what reasons are good reasons for treating some people differently from others.

One conception of substantial justice is that of *compensatory* justice, of which there are many applications. One of these is *corrective* justice: Whenever an injustice has been committed, just compensation or reparation is owed to injured parties. A related one, that of *retributive* justice, applies to the punishment of those who commit injustices: Whenever an injustice has been committed, just retribution is owed to the injuring parties. This concept is historically related, but different from – because more flexible than – the *lex talionis* principle, according to which, when an offense has been committed, the punishment inflicted should correspond in degree and kind to the offense of the wrongdoer, as in an eye for an eye, a tooth for a tooth.

Still another conception of substantial justice is *commutative* justice, which can be understood as a matter of desert (or fitness). A principle of justice as desert or merit is: people should be treated in a manner that fits their personal qualities, e.g. given such things as positions, wage increases, and educational opportunities in accordance with such things as their abilities, performance, and other qualifications.

Finally, there is the notion of *distributive justice*, whose characteristic principle may be formulated as follows: differences in the treatment of individual persons are justified if they work to the benefit of each.

Discussions of justice are prominent concerning issues of age, GENDER, income, racial, or other forms of inequality or discrimination, the most blatant being segregation *de jure*, i.e. segregation by law, while other forms – e.g. segregation in housing – simply constitute segregation *de facto*, i.e. segregation in effect. In this connection, conflicts between commutative and distributive justice are thought to arise. For what, from the standpoint of distributive justice, may work to the advantage of each (e.g. wages exactly sufficient to meet a minimum of provisions for each), from the standpoint of commutative justice may not provide each with what he or she deserves – e.g. some individuals being more highly rewarded than others, given that they are more productive.

Highly influential among principles of justice today are those formulated by the contemporary United States philosopher John Rawls. His first principle, the *liberty principle*, says: everyone is entitled to as much liberty as is compatible with equal liberty for all. The second, the *difference principle*, says: differences are justified when they are to the advantage of each. In this context, among notions associated – sometimes nearly synonymous – with fairness are equality, whether formal, substantive, or of opportunity; and the more flexible notions of equity and equitability. However, they all share an emphasis on the lot of each particular individual, not merely, as in utilitarian approaches, on society overall.

Rawls argued for these principles of justice in two ways. On the one hand, he imagined an original position in which individuals choosing the principles of justice would do so *behind the veil of ignorance*, i.e. with knowledge of the general features, desires, abilities, and need of humans, but with no particular knowledge of where anyone would stand in relation to other humans. From this standpoint, these individuals would use the *maximin* rule of game theory (where maximin is derived from the Latin from *maximum minimorum* or "the greatest of the least"), i.e. the rule according to which we are to adopt that alternative course of action or policy whose worst outcome is superior to the worst outcome of all others. In this way, each individual would omit to choose any strategy that, however beneficial to society at large, would involve a benefit below the social minimum for some who, given the veil of ignorance, could include the individual making the choice. In addition, Rawls supported the principles of justice he formulated by arguing that they were in accord with the considered judgments of competent judges of moral matters. With the years, he tended to emphasize this latter approach and de-emphasize the former.

Let us consider an application. Using Rawls's principles, some would argue that giving precedence to members of traditionally disadvantaged groups in hirings, promotions, or school admissions – i.e. using preferential-treatment approaches – is justified because it works to the advantage of each. Of course, those individuals who think they are thereby being put at a disadvantage concerning their chances for being hired, promoted, or admitted to schools argue that preferential treatment is in no way to the advantage of each. In addition, they will often adopt the standpoint of compensatory justice and emphasize merit based on qualifications as taking precedence over all other considerations. Anyone taking such a position is a *meritarian*, i.e. a partisan of *meritarianism*, the view that, as a matter of justice, merit and only merit should be used in deciding who is to occupy what positions in society. If a society were entirely structured along meritarianism's criteria, it would be a *meritocracy*.

Some philosophers have tried to resolve conflicts concerning what criteria should take precedence in assigning positions or burdens in society, by relying on the market. Still others have tried to combine market and other considerations to resolve the equity problems that arise. Some of these combinations – for example, as discussed above, that pursued by John Rawls – involve an appeal to the previously mentioned maximin rule.

In this regard, United States policy-making discussions have increasingly used the term *empowerment* with a variety of meanings, from simply that of winning elections, to that of political mobilization aimed at challenging inequitable relations. Besides focusing the discussion on the role of power in the implementation of justice, however, empowerment has been a buzz word rather than a useful concept.

The problem also arises of whether justice pays. This problem traces back to ancient times, when Plato (428–348 BCE), in the *Republic*, used the *myth of Er* (a warrior who revived shortly after death to report on the fate of the souls of the dead) to argue that justice pays, usually in this life and certainly in the afterlife. Of course, this is not satisfactory for those who do not believe in an afterlife. Some philosophers, however, have tried to dissolve rather than resolve the problem. One such attempt involves arguing that the question of whether justice pays is trivial, because, whether justice is understood as a social practice or a general rule of individual conduct, the question has a trivial affirmative answer. Another attempt argues that questioning whether justice pays involves confusion about the nature of justice, its relation to benefit, and the kind of reasons that would justify justice (instead of merely showing it to be beneficial), which amount to a category mistake or to a practical contradiction like that of rejecting the use of reasons and then asking for reasons that would justify the use of reasons.

See also: ethics; philosophy, sociopolitical

Further reading

Barry, Brian (1989) *Theories of Justice*, London: Harvester Wheatsheaf.
Habermas, Jürgen (1988) "Law and Morality," in Sterling M. McMurrin (ed.) *The Tanner Lectures on Human Values VIII*, Salt Lake City, USA and Cambridge, UK: University of Utah Press and Cambridge University Press.
Kolm, Serge-Christophe (1996) *Modern Theories of Justice*, Cambridge, MA: MIT Press.
Quinn, Michael (1991) *Justice and Egalitarianism: Formal and Substantive Equality in Some Recent Theories of Justice*, New York: Garland Pub. Inc.
Rawls, John (1971) *A Theory of Justice*, Cambridge, MA: Harvard University Press.
Walzer, Michael (1983) *Spheres of Justice: A Defense of Pluralism and Equality*, New York: Basic Books.

justificatio actionis *see* justification

justificatio cognitionis *see* justification

justification The notion of justification involves reference to reasons – justifying reasons – or grounds – justifying grounds – that can be of various kinds and justify a wide range of items, from beliefs, actions, motives, and attitudes, to policies, practices, institutions, social movements, and aesthetic movements. These items are said to be justified whenever there are good justifying reasons or grounds for them. Among those concerning the justification of belief (which some call the *ethics of belief* because they consider it to be a moral justification), some are *evidential* reasons, i.e. reasons for the truth of the belief that can be evidence, i.e. observation, or proof; while others are *non-evidential reasons*, i.e. reasons other than those for the truth of the belief.

Concerning evidential reasons, the Austrian philosopher Alexius Meinong (CE 1853–1920) distinguishes three types of evidence: *a priori* evidence, i.e. any tautology or analytic statement; direct, certain, *a posteriori* evidence, i.e. any veridical report of introspective observation; and *Vermutungsevidenz* (German for surmise evidence), any direct, but not certain, a posteriori evidence. The last is significant in studying memory, perception, and induction.

Among non-evidential reasons are reasons involved in such notions as *justification by faith*, and *justification by works*. For example, in his "The Ethics of Belief," the British mathematician and philosopher William Kingdom Clifford (CE 1845–79) argued that it is always wrong, everywhere, and for anyone, to believe anything upon insufficient reason. In saying this, he seems to have used the expression "insufficient reason" as reasons that are neither proof nor predominant evidence (or even evidence so unmixed that it raises no reasonable doubt). He argued for this on largely utilitarian grounds (see below), stating that all beliefs based on insufficient reason lead to undesirable consequences regarding our character (they make us gullible), and to actions that themselves have undesirable consequences concerning ourselves and others. This position was criticized by the United States philosopher William James (CE 1842–1910) in his essay, "The Will to Believe." He argued that, sometimes, a person is justified in believing a certain proposition *p* on non-evidential reasons, though, of course, these reasons do not in any way establish the truth of the said proposition. He specified a set of three jointly sufficient conditions for the person to be thus justified. First, intellectual grounds – proof or evidence – for the truth of the proposition believed are mixed or absent. Second, the happiness of the person believing the proposition is contingent on the person's believing it. Third, the person must be facing a *genuine option*, i.e. a set of alternative propositions the person could believe, which has the following three features. First, the option is *forced* (not avoidable), i.e. either one or the other proposition is believed: there is no additional alternative. Second, the option is *living* (not dead), i.e. each alternative proposition involves some plausibility to the person, and also matters to the person in the sense that it carries positive or negative value – it is neither epistemologically nor valuationally indifferent. Third, the option is *momentous* (not trivial), i.e. it is significant to the person's life, e.g. because it is unique.

The Russian-born United States philosopher Morris Cohen (CE 1880–1947) argued against James concerning one of the applications of James's position: the belief in God, in an afterlife, or in a given religion (rather than none at all). Cohen argued that one often, if not always, has the option of working on one's detachment so that one's option between two propositions need not be forced. The question arises whether sometimes, however, an option is so momentous that working on one's detachment is not an option. On the other hand, even if James is correct on this, do his conditions justify too much or too little? These are some of the questions that contemporary treatments of the topic have addressed.

Some philosophers have held that evidential reasons must be somehow conclusive, whether they be deductive, inductive, or epistemic. In this context, to say that reasons are *conclusive* is to say that they support the item being justified so much that one might as well stop deliberation or inquiry. This support can be in the form of deductive reasons that constitute a sound deductive argument. Or it can be in the form of inductive reasons that constitute a highly reliable and cogent inductive argument. Moreover, it can be in the form of epistemic reasons highly supported by the available body of knowledge. Other philosophers, however, have defended weaker notions of justification. For example, they have argued that the reasons in a justification must merely be *prima facie*, i.e. reasons in favor of the item justified that, however, can be outweighed by other considerations. They are called *prima-facie evidence*, or *prima-facie reasons*, and are said to constitute *prima-facie justification*.

A traditional theory of justification has been *foundationalism*, the view that knowledge and knowledge-relevant (epistemic) justification involves two tiers. First, some instances of knowledge and justification are non-inferential or foundational: they are basic beliefs that are self-justifying or intrinsically credible, and belonging to few and narrow kinds. These instances are formulated in *protocol statements*. Second, all other instances are inferentially derived from the basic beliefs, i.e. they are instances of inferential justification. On *radical* foundationalism, the basic beliefs must be certain and the second-tier beliefs must be deductively derived from the former. On *modest* foundationalism, none of these two features are required. As for the non-inferential justification involved here, it can be of three kinds. First, by self-justification (e.g. the belief in the law of non-contradiction), whereby the belief justifies itself with no evidential support. Second, by non-belief, non-propositional experiences – e.g. our seeing the janitor in the aisle justifies our believing that the janitor is in the aisle. Third, by a non-belief reliable origin – e.g. by relying on processes that tend to lead to true beliefs such as perception, memory, or introspection. However, even this view is faced with showing how second-tier beliefs follow from first-tier beliefs.

In this regard, an argument tracing back to Ancient Greece is the *epistemic regress argument*. It can be outlined as follows: any justified belief occurs in a chain including at least two links – the supporting link (evidence) and the supported link (justified belief). However, these chains are either circular, endless, based on unjustified beliefs, or based on foundational beliefs that need no other beliefs for their own justification. Hence, only chains based on foundational beliefs lead to justified beliefs.

Another influential theory is *coherentism*, which sharply opposes foundationalism. It concerns the structure of knowledge or justified beliefs and holds that all beliefs which amount to knowledge are justified in virtue of their relations to other beliefs, specifically in virtue of their belonging to a coherent – i.e. free from contradictions – system of beliefs. This system, overall, is better than alternative systems with regard to such criteria as clarity, comprehensiveness, and explanatory power. However, on this view, certain beliefs, such as the belief that the Soviet Union ceased to exist in the early 1990s, clearly and practically can only have the degree of truth of the system to which they belong – a degree that is far from certainty. Also, there is no known system to which all beliefs taken to be true belong.

A middle ground is that of *contextualism*. This is the view that justification always takes place within a background of beliefs and presuppositions that need not be, and often are not, supported by means of evidence, proof, or any way of establishing basic beliefs. It is closely related to the *relevant-alternatives* conception of justification whereby knowledge claims are justified, not by ruling out all logically possible alternatives, but by excluding relevant or plausible alternatives; for example, because of specific shortcomings identified on the basis of criteria actually presupposed in widespread scientific and, to some extent, everyday practice. Contextualism does not attempt to address the skeptical questions that prompt foundationalism or coherentism. Instead, it rejects such questions as misguided, for example, on the grounds that they arise under imaginary conceptions of knowledge and justification – conceptions that are sharply in conflict with those presupposed by the knowledge claims and challenges asking for their justification that ordinary people and scientists make.

Some philosophers, e.g. the United States philosopher Roderick Chisholm (CE 1916–99), and the contemporary philosophers Laurence

BonJour and Carl Ginet, have held the doctrine of *epistemic deontologism*: that the concept of justification is normative and can be analyzed, with regard to knowledge, using such moral terms as "ought," "obligatory," "permissible," and "forbidden." That is, being justified in holding a belief implies that one meets such epistemic obligations as those based on the epistemic aim of believing what is true and not what is false.

Other philosophers have developed the notion of *epistemic virtues*: those qualities of persons that are conducive to the discovery of truth. They are to be distinguished from wisdom and good judgment that, though intellectual, are aimed at practical success. On this basis, these philosophers developed the subfield of epistemology called *virtue epistemology*, according to which epistemic virtue is central to understanding justification, knowledge, or both.

A related position is that of philosophers who hold the traditional justification condition for knowledge, which centers on evidence, should be discarded and, instead, recommend a causal condition. This approach was partly prompted by the *Gettier problem*, i.e. a type of case offered by the contemporary philosopher Edmund Gettier whereby, though an agent has justified true belief that p, the agent does not know that p. For example, suppose Peter believes the false proposition Cliff lives in Meriden, Connecticut. On this basis, Peter infers (by disjunction introduction), hence is justified in believing that Cliff lives in Meriden, Connecticut, or the CEO of Olin Corporation is in Spain. It so happens that the CEO of Olin Corporation is in Spain. However, Peter does not know this. Yet, on traditional accounts of justification, he is justified in believing the previous disjunction. On the causal account, this situation is avoided because, according to this account, if an agent knows that p if p is true, the agent believes that p, and the agent's belief – the causal condition – is causally produced and sustained by the fact that makes p true. The philosophical debate on this topic is still unsettled (see KNOWLEDGE).

A theory related to the position just discussed is *reliabilism*, the doctrine that a belief amounts to knowledge or is epistemically justified when it is connected to the truth through a reliable process or combination of processes. On this view, a belief amounts to knowledge if a lawlike connection existing in nature guarantees that the belief is true. This connection makes the process(es) reliable.

The previous discussion of justification largely, if not only, concerns knowledge, i.e. it is *justificatio cognitionis* ("justification of knowledge"). By contrast with it, in ethics, there is *justificatio actionis* ("justification of actions"). For example, the contemporary Austrian-American philosopher Herbert Feigl distinguished between two classes of justification. One is *validation* or *justificatio cognitionis*, which is involved in the application of inductive, deductive, or other principles to infer consequences from them. The other, *vindication* or *justificatio actionis*, applies to the principles themselves and takes and should take pragmatic considerations into account.

In this regard, *externalism* is the view that there are reasons for action that are not dependent on motivational features or motives of the agents performing the actions, i.e. on thoughts such as desires and aims that the agent uses as reasons for acting. The reasons mentioned by externalism are external reasons or reasons external to the agent. This view is contrasted with *internalism*, the view that no reasons for action can be independent of motivational features of the agents, i.e., in this sense, all reasons are internal reasons or reasons internal to the agent. The externalism–internalism controversy is associated with discussions of *motivational internalism*: the view that certain beliefs – e.g. moral beliefs – entail motives and, hence, are internal reasons for action. Those who disagree are faced with holding that such beliefs, even when sound, do not always provide reasons for action, or that these reasons are actually external. This controversy carries over to the notions of *epistemological internalism*, which requires access to what provides justification for a belief, and *epistemological externalism*, which rejects any such requirement.

A significant area of philosophical discussion is that of the relation between *explanation* or *explanatory reasons* or explaining reasons, or, as the Scottish philosopher Francis Hutch-

eson (CE 1694–1746) called them, *exciting reasons* (such as an agent's affections or desires that help to explain the agent's behavior), and *justification*, or *justificatory reasons*, which serve to establish why the agent's beliefs or behavior are justified. For example, John might give one of his kidneys to his daughter Joan so that she will be able to live a life free from dialysis machines, and a person at the hospital might ask John: "Why did you do that?" He might reply: "Because I love her." This explains his act. It may not be the only reason he has. He may for example also recognize and be distraught at the fact that his daughter's husband would be desolate if she continued to need dialysis. Yet, he gave his kidney only because he loves her. It is his motive or reason for action. Does it however justify his act?

One might reply that the act did not need justification because, though not morally required, it was not morally forbidden. However, though an action may not require or be in need of justification (in that there is no reason to think that it is wrong, hence no presumption against it), it does not follow that it may not be justified or that it is nonsense to talk of justifying it in the sense of giving reasons why it is right. Some philosophers have accordingly distinguished between a *strong sense* of justification, i.e. in response to a challenge or presumption, and a *weak sense* of justification, i.e. merely in response to an unchallenging question about the reasons for an act. In the latter case, all one has to do is give reasons for the act, and these may be motives, hence provide an explanation as well as a justification. However, if the strong sense of justification is required, then, besides giving reasons for the act, one needs also to show these reasons outweigh alternative ones, i.e. that they are overriding reasons or, when a comprehensive approach is presupposed, reasons *all-things-considered*.

It should be noted that some *overriding* reasons or some reasons all-things-considered may not be subjective reasons or reasons the agent can understand, even if they are objective reasons, i.e. reasons that support a course of action whether the agent understands it or not. Further, those philosophers and psychologists allowing for subconscious motivation hold the cause of an action need not be the agent's motives for the action. For example, John may cross the street and, if asked why, say he crossed it to see a picture inside a shop, while the subconscious motive could be that he had an urge to buy chocolates at the shop.

Not entirely unrelated to this discussion is that of how the concept of *excuse* relates to that of justification. One view is that an excuse implies that the behavior being justified, given the particular circumstances in a particular case, is typically morally wrong or objectionable. That is, an excuse is a justification in response to a strong moral challenge – not merely, say, to curiosity – which is characteristic of situations in which a justification in the strong sense is required.

The question has been asked: can justifications in the strong sense use particular reasons such as "Because I love her" or must they use general or generalizable reasons such as "Because the act led to the greatest happiness of the greatest number," "Because the act was in accordance with the categorical imperative," and, arguably, "Because she is my daughter" (in which case she would be treated in a non-particular manner, merely as an item in the general class of individuals who are daughters of whoever gives the reason)? The problem is that, in the case previously described, John might defensibly say the reason justifying and not just explaining his kidney donation is purely particular: "Because I love her," and makes room for no generalizable version without implying a change in his relation with his daughter.

One might reply that the said reason, though explanatory, does not justify his act. Also, John might then say that he sees no reason why no justifications for his act, because they are generalizable, involve reasons he could – consistently with his relation to his daughter – use as a motive for acting. At least in this case, he takes the stand of motivational internalism, while those who consider his demand misplaced take that of motivational externalism.

Discussions of justification have prompted various paradoxes, one being the *lottery paradox*. It concerns a lottery involving n tickets, where n is a large number, and it involves two assumptions: first, that exactly one ticket will win and, second, the *rule of detachment*, i.e. if the probability of a proposition p, relatively to one's evidence, is less than 1 but within a high threshold, then one is justified in believing that p (and not merely that p is highly probable). However, if the number n of tickets is large enough, the rule of detachment implies that the first ticket, T1, will lose, because its probability equals $(n-1)/n$ that, for a sufficiently large n, will exceed the said threshold. By parallel reasoning, it follows that all other tickets will lose too. Hence, against the first assumption, no ticket will win.

Finally, an area of special interest in matters of justification is that of *legal evidence*, which overlaps, but is not identical with, epistemic evidence. For example, in criminal law cases, the rule of evidence is that, in order to judge a person to be guilty, the evidence must be such as to show the person to be guilty beyond all reasonable doubt. So epistemic evidence making it highly likely that the person is guilty, however sufficient to conclude it in ordinary life or science, is insufficient to conclude it in a criminal law case.

By contrast, in the civil law, the rule is that of the *preponderance of the evidence*. That is, if the evidence makes it more likely than not that a person is guilty, then that suffices to conclude it, even if in ordinary life or science it would be insufficient to draw such conclusion.

See also: epistemology; ethics

Further reading
Clifford, W.K. (1879) *Lectures and Essays*, London: Macmillan.
Corrado, Michael Louis (1994) *Justification and Excuse in the Criminal Law: A Collection of Essays*, New York: Garland Pub.
Habermas, Jürgen (1994) *Justification and Application: Remarks on Discourse Ethics*, Cambridge, MA: MIT Press.
James, William (1956) *The Will to Believe and Other Essays in Popular Philosophy, and Human Immortality*, New York: Dover.
Sosa, Ernest (1994) *Knowledge and Justification*, Aldershot, UK and Brookfield, VT: Dartmouth.

justified *see* justification

justifying reasons *see* justification

K

K *see* logic

kabbala *see* cabala

kaivalya *see* Hinduism

kāla *see* philosophy of science

kalām *see* Arabic philosophy

kālika-sambandha *see* philosophy of science

kālika-viseshanatā *see* philosophy of science

kalpa *see* age of the world

Kantian philosophy A philosophical approach, sometimes also called *Kantianism*, tracing back to the work of the German philosopher Immanuel Kant (CE 1724–1804). Kant aimed at vindicating the authority of reason by bringing about a Copernican Revolution in philosophy. He asked not how our representations can accord with objects, but how objects can accord with our representations. Accordingly, he treated epistemology as *first philosophy*, an approach that eventually led him to advance the doctrine of *transcendental idealism*: that all our theoretical knowledge is only the systematization of spatiotemporal appearances or phenomena. This position, also called *formal idealism* and *critical idealism*, was formulated by Kant in the first – 1781 – edition of his *Critique of Pure Reason*, in his 1783 *Prolegomena to any Future Metaphysics*, where he replied to critiques of the previous book, and in the second – 1787 – significantly revised edition of the *Critique of Pure Reason*. These and later works are often contrasted with his earlier, pre-critical works, where his position on idealism was not fully developed.

Transcendental idealism
Transcendental idealism makes room for formulating the necessary principles ruling over spatiotemporal appearances, but also implies that the reality of spatiotemporal appearances did not exhaust reality, i.e. Kant distinguished between the *phenomenal world*, to which we had access, and the *noumenal world*, the world of the *Ding an sich* (German for thing in itself) or *noumenon*, to which we were conceptually committed, but had no access. For Kant, the concept of the noumenon was a *Grenzbegriff*, a limiting concept or – by analogy with the concept of limit in the calculus used in the Newtonian physics of which Kant was so keenly aware – a limit in that what appears to us points to it, arguably infinitely approaches it, but does not include or reach it.

Kant divided the intellect into the faculties of sensibility or *Sinnlichkeit*, and those of thought or *Denken* (though experience is connected through the *unity of apperception*, i.e. the presence of the "I think" in each experience). In investigating – or engaging in *Überlegung* or reflection about – the necessary principles ruling over spatiotemporal appearances, Kant sought to uncover two types of things. First, concerning the faculties of sensibility, he sought to uncover the space–time *schemata* that structure the manifold of sense. He treated this in the section of his *Critique of Pure Reason* entitled *Transcendental Aesthetic*. Second, he sought to uncover the *conceptual forms* or *pure concepts of the understanding*, or *categories of the understanding* – which had been previously called *Reflexionsbegriffe*, i.e. concepts of reflection – which, in attaining knowledge, he held were required by our constitution. His position was that while concepts without intuitions – all of which, for humans, are sensible intuitions, i.e. acquired through the senses – were empty, intuitions without concepts were blind, leaving us with a mere manifold or multiplicity of unintelligibly scattered impressions.

Here, transcendental reflection makes it possible to determine the conceptual or sensory origin of given representations. This was the *transcendental deduction of the categories*, i.e. an argument – called in general a transcendental argument – whereby it is shown which they are, given the undoubted assumption that we have representations. This is treated in the section of Kant's *Critique of Pure Reason* called *Transcendental Analytic*. In the third part of the *Critique*, the *Transcendental Dialectic*, Kant treats of the *transcendental paralogisms* or *paralogisms of pure reason,* or *psychological paralogisms*, which involve the fallacy of assuming a substantial self whenever we say "I think."

Kant held that everything sensed has quality, quantity, relation, and modality, and, using these headings, outlined his *table of judgments* (a list of the necessary forms of judgments needed for any finite understanding), from which he derived his *table of categories* (the concepts involved in such judgments) listing twelve categories, three under each heading. Under quality, were reality (or the positive), negation, and limitation. Under quantity, he listed unity, plurality, and totality. Relation covered inherence and subsistence, causality and dependence, and community. Modality included possibility–impossibility, existence–non-existence, and necessity–contingency. Necessity and possibility are now sometimes respectively called *apodictic modality* and *problematic modality*. For Kant, they corresponded to apodictic judgments and problematic judgments.

In Kantian philosophy, these categories of the understanding are *constitutive*; while other concepts are *regulatory* or *regulative*, i.e. direct our thinking. Examples of the latter are heuristic or methodological principles aimed at providing teleological explanations (see EXPLANATION). It should be noted that these categories of the understanding, especially the relational ones that apply to spatiotemporal relations, rather than helping us formulate particular and fully specified judgments, help us formulate *schemata* (from the Greek *schema*, meaning "form" or "diagram"), i.e. the analogies of experience, which are principles for making the said specifications. The schema of quantity is number; that of reality is the continuous production of varying degrees of sensation; that of substance is permanence through time; that of causality is succession through time; and that of reciprocity is coexistence in time. These schemata bring sense and understanding together in particular ways and thus constitute the schematism of the pure understanding. As for colors and sounds, though they, like time and space, are dependent on the said subjective conditions of experience, Kant assigns them a different status and warns against the *subreption* (from the Low Latin *subreption*, noun for *subreptio*, "to steal," hence "a stealing"), i.e. the concealment, of such sensations. After all, they are not relational as the schemata discussed. Given the procedure just described for deriving the categories, Kant called his philosophy *architectonic*.

A significant forerunner of this approach is that of the English philosopher Edward Herbert of Cherbury (CE 1583–1648), who founded Deism. This approach has a family resemblance to Scottish common-sense philosophy, also called common-sense realism. He adopted the Stoic concept of *notiones communes* or *common notions*, i.e. innate and identifiable by having the following features: priority, independence, universality, certainty, necessity, and immediacy. As in Kantian philosophy centuries later, these common notions organize all experience. Next in order of certainty was the *sensus internus* or internal sense, which concerned conscience, emotions, and free will. Third, he considered the *sensus externus* or external sense, i.e. that which allowed us to intuit external objects. Finally, he treated of *discursis* or REASONING.

A crucial concept in Kant is that of containment, which he used to characterize an *analytic* judgment (in more recent terminology, an analytic proposition or statement) as one whose predicate is contained in the subject, e.g. "every dog is a canine" and, in the form Kant called a *limitative* judgment (every *A* is not a *B*), "every dog is not a cat." He contrasted an analytic judgment with a *synthetic* judgment (or, as is said today, a synthetic proposition or statement), i.e. one whose predicate is not contained in its subject, e.g. "Jim is sleeping right now." This distinction was not new. The German philosopher Gottfried Wilhelm Leibniz (CE 1646–1716) had already formulated it. However, Kant asked whether there could be synthetic judgments that were known a priori, i.e. independently of any particular experience. He answered affirmatively claiming that mathematical and metaphysical characterizations of our notions of space and time involved various *synthetic a priori judgments*, e.g. the judgment formulated by means of the proposition "there is one infinite space."

Kant held a theory of space that agreed with the Newtonian one in holding that space is absolute, not relative (i.e. not dependent on relations between physical objects), as the Leibnizian theory held. Kant based his argument on the existence of *enantiamorphs*, objects whose shapes differ, as do those of a right and left hand. He argued that, since a member of a pair of enantiamorphs can be made to look like the other by looking at it in a mirror, but not by changing its spatial orientation, it followed that there was absolute space.

By contrast with the Newtonian view that made space God-dependent, however, Kant held that space was mind-dependent, and that some facts about space could be apprehended only intuitively. However, as previously stated, he cautioned against the fallacies of rational psychology or the psychological paralogism, or the paralogisms of pure reason that, from premises that begin with the modifier "I think," conclude that human beings have a substantial, continuous, and separable soul.

In the process of formulating transcendental idealism, Kant characterized various notions of reason. First, reason itself is the faculty of superior knowledge and, as such, contrasts with experience. *Pure* reason is the faculty that provides us with the principles of a priori knowledge and, as pure reason, contrasts not only with *experience* but also with *understanding*. The latter is the faculty that organizes the data of the senses into categories, while the former is the faculty that unifies the various categories of knowledge attained by means of the understanding. Pure reason is *theoretical* reason or *speculative* reason when it concerns the a priori principles of knowledge, while it is *practical* reason or *pure practical* reason (*Wille*) when it concerns the a priori principles of action.

Kant's moral philosophy

In ethics, the realm of practical reason, Kantian philosophy is deontological, i.e. its practical principle or principle to assess conduct, the *categorical imperative*, focuses on features of the actions it serves to evaluate, not on the value of their consequences. These features involve an unconditional end, *autonomy*, from the Greek *autos* ("self") and *nomos* ("law"), meaning "self-rule," a concept Kant used to characterize ethical theories whose principles derive from sources in the person as being autonomous. He contrasted them with those that were heteronomous, where *heteronomy*, from the Greek *heteros* ("other") and *nomos* ("law"), means the rule of another, by which Kant meant that their principles derived from sources outside the person. These typically involve some *hypothetical imperative(s)*; that is, principles or maxims of actions involving conditional ends, not, as the categorical imperative, an unconditional one.

The categorical imperative is the *moral law* when applied to imperfect beings like humans, who are often driven at least partly by their inclinations, not by what Kantian ethics considers the only source of moral worth: the *good will*, i.e. the settled determination to do one's duty. Indeed, the *morality* or *moral worth* of an action is for Kant entirely a matter of whether the person performing it has the motive of duty (hence good will), while its *legality* or *rightness* is simply a matter of whether the action accords with the moral law. In order to act from the motive of duty, human beings often need to exercise *fortitude*, or strength of will, which is the central Kantian moral virtue. As for the categorical imperative,

Kant considered it one principle, though he gave various formulations of it. The main three are: the principle of *universality*, "act only according to that maxim by which you can at the same time will that it should become a universal law" – the principle of *humanity* (or *personality*); "act so that you treat humanity, whether in your own person or in that of another, always as an end and never as a means only"; and the principle of the *kingdom of ends*, "act only so that the will through its maxims could regard itself at the same time as universally lawgiving." Each formulation is meant to bring out an aspect of what the moral law involves. Yet, questions have been raised about whether these formulations are indeed of one or, rather, of more than one principle.

Kant's moral philosophy implies a particular conception of practical reason or practical rationality, i.e. of the capacity for reasoning aimed at prescribing or choosing conduct. It is that of *autonomous reason*, i.e. as a source of rules of conduct independent of one's desires or preferences, which contrasts with *instrumental reason*: the conception that reason is only a way of maximizing the attainment of our goals as these are determined by such things as our desires and aversions.

Kant's position was aimed at circumscribing theoretical knowledge in such a manner that practical knowledge would be possible. This was not only evidenced in his moral philosophy, but also in his aesthetics. Accordingly, in his *Critique of Judgment*, he argued for limited principles in this area.

Kant's influence

Kant's philosophy has influenced many philosophical developments falling under the heading of *neo-Kantianism* or *neo-criticism*. One of them was *Krausism*, the philosophy originated in the work of the German philosopher Karl Christian Friedrich Krause (CE 1781–1832), who developed Kant's views along pantheistic and mystical lines. He eventually formulated a position called *panentheism*, according to which human consciousness and nature are part of but not identical with the Absolute Being, and do not exhaust it. He envisioned an end of history in which the finite realm of human activity would unite with the infinite essence in a universal spiritual and moral order.

Another neo-Kantian school was the *Marburg School*, characterized by a logistic-methodological approach. Its founder, the German philosopher Hermann Cohen (CE 1842–1918), formulated an idealistic position concerning the natural sciences. He held that physical objects are known only by means of the laws these sciences formulate and that these laws presuppose a priori principles and concepts of the type advocated by Kant. Yet, he rejected Kant's conception of space and time, which involved both the sensibility of intuitions and the formal component of concepts. He argued that space and time are construction methods of thought, not – as Kant had held – a priori forms of perception, and that talk of intuitions prior to or independently of conceptualization was nonsense. In fact, Cohen concluded the thinking of the scientific community constituted scientific reality.

Other members of the Marburg School were: the German philosophers Paul Natorp (CE 1854–1924), who extended Cohen's views into psychology; Ernst Cassirer (CE 1874–1945), who generalized them to all symbolic forms such as myth and religion; Karl Vorländer (CE 1860–1928), who advocated Kantian ethics as a corrective to Marxism; and Rudolf Stammler (CE 1856–1938), who applied Kantian ideas to the philosophy of law, holding that law was to society as mathematics is to the physical world – a universally applicable formal scheme independent from its subject matter.

Many other forms of neo-Kantianism or neo-criticism have existed. Among those developed by German philosophers, one is that represented by the philosopher Emil Lask (CE 1875–1915), who formulated the notion of an *Urform*, a category of categories from which the transcendental logic could be derived. Another form of neo-Kantianism in Germany was the *Physiological School* of Hermann von Helmholtz (CE 1821–94) and Friedrich Albert Lange (CE 1828–75), who argued physiology developed and corrected Kantian ideas. Another is the *Psychological School* or *Göttingen School* originated by Leonard Nelson (CE

1882–1927) and Jakob Friedrich Fries (CE 1773–1843), hence sometimes also called *neo-Friesianism*, who argued for the introspective approach to discovering Kantian principles. Still another is the *Axiological School* or *Baden neo-Kantianism* of Wilhelm Windelband (CE 1848–1915) and Heinrich Rickert (CE 1863–1936), who placed values at the center of Kantian philosophy and made significant contributions to the history of philosophy and the methodology of history.

Windelband is noted for his distinction between the *nomothetic knowledge*, i.e. the knowledge of laws sought by the natural sciences and the *ideographic* knowledge, i.e. the knowledge of particulars sought by history. There is also the version of Kantian philosophy formulated by Georg Simmel (CE 1858–1918), who argued that Kantian categories are relative to individuals and cultures. Also, there was the *Back to Kant School* of Otto Liebmann (CE 1840–1912), who argued for a Kantian metaphysics that would formulate hypotheses about essences.

In addition, there were neo-Kantian thinkers in France and Italy who tended to prefer neo-criticism as a label for their approach. Notable among them was the French philosopher Charles Renouvier (CE 1815–1903), who accepted Kantian phenomenalism, but rejected the notion of a thing-in-itself. Renouvier opposed such absolutes as the unconditioned and the infinite, proposing instead the view that things were relative to each other, which he called the *principle of relativity*. He supported the antimetaphysical aspect of Comtian positivism and, opposing determinism, stressed chance and the accidental character of much of history. To emphasize this, he coined the term *uchronie* (Greek for "out of time"). It denoted any imaginary slight change at a historical juncture whose occurrence might have led to vast differences in ulterior historical developments.

See also: conceptualism; empiricism; rationalism

Further reading

Abbott, Thomas Kingsmill (1967) *Kant's Critique of Practical Reason, and Other Works on the Theory of Ethics*, 6th edn, London: Longmans.

Kneller, Jane and Axinn, Sidney (1998) *Autonomy and Community: Readings in Contemporary Kantian Social Philosophy*, Albany: State University of New York Press.

Ouden, Bernard D. den and Moen, Marcia (1987) *New Essays on Kant*, New York: Peter Lang.

Sellars, Wilfrid (1982) *Science and Metaphysics: Variations on Kantian Themes*, New York: Humanities Press.

Smith, Norman Kemp (1953) *Immanuel Kant's Critique of Pure Reason*, London: Macmillan.

Kantianism *see* Kantian philosophy

kārana *see* causal law

karma *see* Buddhism; Hinduism; Jainism

karmic *see* Buddhism; Hinduism; Jainism

kārya *see* causal law

kārya-citta *see* causal law

kārya-kāla *see* metaphysics

kārya-kārana-bhāva *see* causal law

katastematic pleasure *see* Epicureanism

katharsis *see* philosophy of literature

k'e *see* Native American philosophy

Kerry's paradox *see* paradox

kevala *see* knowledge

kevala-jnāna *see* knowledge

kevala-laksana *see* meaning

kevala-pramāna *see* knowledge

Khorda Avesta *see* Zoroastrianism

khyāti *see* knowledge

khyāti vāda *see* truth

killing and letting die *see* euthanasia

kinds *see* natural kinds

kinesis *see* change

kinetic pleasure *see* Epicureanism

kingdom of ends *see* Kantian philosophy

kingdom of God *see* Judaism

kinship *see* identity

knower *see* knowledge

knower, paradox of the *see* paradox

knowledge From the Greek *gignoskein* ("to decide upon," "determine," "decree"), this term has both descriptive and practical connotations. Descriptively, it stands in contrast to mere opinion and, also, to ignorance understood as either the absence of opinions on a certain matter, or an erroneous opinion on that matter. Practically, it stands in opposition to ignorance as inability – not knowing how – to do something.

Kinds of knowledge
Philosophers have distinguished various kinds of knowledge. One is *propositional* knowledge (i.e. knowledge of propositions), for example that 2+2=4, and that the moon circles the earth.

A second kind is knowledge *by acquaintance*, i.e. knowing an item through having experienced it, say, knowing a person through having met him or her. For example, I know my wife's ten siblings in this sense, because I have met each one of them. This is related to the question: "What type of knowledge by acquaintance must be involved in recognition, i.e. in identifying an individual item – a person, a cathedral in a foreign land – as being who or what the item is?" Recognition often occurs without having physically encountered, but having seen a picture of, the item in question. As a result, one for example recognizes the Iguazú Falls (situated in the border between Argentina, Brazil, and Paraguay) as those one saw in a picture. Yet, one did not have full-fledged knowledge, i.e. *primary* or *direct* knowledge by acquaintance, but only what can be called *secondary* or *indirect* knowledge by acquaintance of the falls. If the item in question were a person, having direct knowledge by acquaintance because one met the person, is part of what puts one in a position to introduce the person to another. While merely having seen the person in pictures does no such thing. At any rate, if the latter type of case exemplifies knowledge, then it seems reasonable to consider it a case of knowledge by acquaintance, because the examples just discussed of recognizing the falls or a person one saw only in pictures do not at all fit the

other types of knowledge described. The situation is different in cases of acknowledgement, which often involves some proposition or fact, e.g. one's acknowledgement that one was late for an appointment.

Some philosophers, however, have argued that the only kinds of knowledge by acquaintance are knowledge of the contents of our minds, self-consciousness or knowledge of ourselves, and knowledge of universals. In this regard, the Austrian philosopher Alexius Meinong (CE 1853–1920) held that all mental states have the feature of being *self-presenting*, i.e. of being immediately present to our thought, and that no mental state can be presented to our thought in any other way. In other words, we can only experience mental states by living through them.

In any case, the notion of knowledge by acquaintance involves *epistemic immediacy*, i.e. one of the types, together with causal, psychological, and logical immediacy, of the general notion of immediacy. Epistemic immediacy is a presence to the mind without intermediaries, a notion widely used in philosophy through the ages. *Logical* immediacy denotes either *conceptual immediacy*, i.e. the feature a concept has of being definitionally primitive, or *inferential* immediacy, i.e. that the inference from a premise to a conclusion depends on no other premises. As for *psychological* immediacy, it denotes the feature some processes – e.g. of belief formation – have of involving no other psychological processes.

In Indian thought, a notion analogous to that of immediacy is *kevala-jnāna* (from *kevala*, "oneness" and *jnāna*, "knowledge"), i.e. direct knowledge, immediate perception and, especially in JAINISM, omniscience. As for *kevala-pramāna* (from *kevala*, "oneness" and *pramāna*, i.e. "means of valid knowledge"), it means "knowledge of an object as it is," and designates the form of valid knowledge in Dvaita Vedānta. All these terms fall under the general category of *khyāti*, i.e. apprehension, discernment, or knowledge

A third kind is *knowledge of skills* (i.e. knowing how to engage in some or other activity), for example knowing how to swim, how to drive, how to sing, or, for that matter, how to engage in philosophical inquiry.

Philosophers have also distinguished various kinds of propositional knowledge, most notably, *a posteriori* knowledge – briefly, knowledge based on sensory or perceptual experience – and *a priori* knowledge – briefly, knowledge not based on any such experience even if sensory or perceptual experience is involved in our acquiring it (see A PRIORI–A POSTERIORI).

As for the characterization of propositional knowledge, three main individually necessary and jointly sufficient conditions have been formulated. The first, which has not been controversial, is the *truth condition*: if a subject knows the proposition *p*, then *p* is true.

A second condition is the *belief condition*: if a subject knows the proposition *p*, then the subject believes the proposition *p*. A few philosophers have challenged this condition arguing that belief is a disposition, while knowledge of a proposition only requires its acceptance, i.e. an act, not a proposition. As other philosophers have indicated, however, whether belief or mere acceptance is involved, a person's knowledge of a proposition in the ordinary sense of propositional knowledge at least requires that the person have some psychological relation of assent concerning the proposition. Otherwise, it is hard to explain how the person has such knowledge.

The third is the *justification condition*: the person who knows a proposition has come to believe or accept it in a reliable way. This general formulation has elicited little controversy. However, a great deal of controversy concerns what it is for a way of coming to believe or accept a proposition to be reliable. In other words, the controversy centers on the meaning of JUSTIFICATION.

Propositional knowledge and justification
Foundationalism is the view that the structure of justification in knowledge has two levels. First, some instances of knowledge and justification are non-inferential, or foundational. All other instances are of inferential knowledge or justification; that is, they follow from foundational knowledge or justification.

An alternative and influential theory is *coherentism*. It concerns the structure of knowledge or justified beliefs and holds that all beliefs that amount to knowledge are justified in virtue of their relations to other beliefs, specifically in virtue of their belonging to a coherent – i.e. free from contradictions – system of beliefs that, overall, is better than alternative systems with regard to such criteria as clarity, comprehensiveness, and explanatory power.

As for the *causal theory of knowledge*, it involves the view that the traditional justification condition for knowledge, which centers on evidence, should be dismissed and, instead, a causal condition should be used. This approach was partly prompted by the *Gettier problem*, i.e. a type of case offered by the contemporary philosopher Edmund Gettier whereby, though an agent has justified true belief that *p*, the agent does not know that *p*, i.e. is not a knower in this case. For example, suppose Peter believes the false proposition Cliff lives in Meriden, Connecticut. On this basis, Peter infers (by disjunction introduction), hence is justified in believing, that Cliff lives in Meriden, Connecticut or the CEO of Olin Corporation is in Spain. It so happens that the CEO of Olin Corporation is in Spain. However, Peter does not know this. Yet, on traditional accounts of justification, he is justified in believing the previous true disjunction. On the causal account, this situation is avoided because, according to this account, an agent knows that *p* if *p* is true, the agent believes that *p*, and – the causal condition – the agent's belief is causally produced and sustained by the fact that makes *p* true. The philosophical debate on this topic is still unsettled (see JUSTIFICATION).

A notion that has been significant concerning the latter conception of knowledge (because it is involved in the Gettier problem) is that of *closure*: a property a set of objects has under a given relation *R*, whenever *x* is a member of the set and *x* is in the relation *R* to an object *y*, then *y* is also a member of the set. This is because, to a large extent, the Gettier problem depends on an affirmative answer to the question: "Is the set of justified propositions closed under deduction?"

In addition, there are various versions of the *pragmatic theory of knowledge*, most notably that formulated by the United States philosopher Charles Sanders Peirce (CE 1839–1914). This is an evolutionary theory. According to

Peirce, belief is a state characterized by a satisfactory feeling of relief at the absence of doubt and an action-guiding function. While doubt is like an itch: a state characterized by a feeling of dissatisfaction at the irritation of doubt and no action-guiding function. Inquiry (like scratching in the case of an itch) is the struggle to get rid of doubt and attain a state of belief. All inquiry aims at such settlement of opinion though, of course, various circumstances unsettle opinions by raising doubts. In any case, for Peirce, knowledge, by contrast with mere belief or opinion, is indefinitely stable opinion, and the truth involved in knowledge is the set of those opinions that would survive the indefinitely prolonged test of critical scrutiny carried out by potential inquirers. On this view, though we can know something by holding an opinion that happens to be bound to survive the indefinite test of critical scrutiny, we cannot know that we know it, because we have no access to the total indefinite series such test would constitute.

Various additional locutions are applied to characterize knowledge, for example *de dicto*, a locution meaning of what is said or of the proposition and contrasted with *de re*, which means of the thing. Accordingly, if two persons know that one student has received the Presidential Award but only one of them knows who the student is, the latter has *de re* knowledge, while the former has only *de dicto* knowledge of this matter. In this connection, a locution also applied to knowledge is *de se*, a Latin locution meaning of oneself and used in contrast with *de dicto* and *de re*. For example, if I know that someone has spilled soda on one of his shoes and I do not realize that it is I, my knowledge is *de dicto* if about the proposition describing what I noticed, and *de re* if about the fact that someone has spilled soda on one of his shoes, but not *de se*, even though it is about me, because I do not realize it is about me.

Also, the previously mentioned distinction between direct and indirect knowledge is drawn, in general, in terms of belief. Here, indirect knowledge is the kind of knowledge that involves a belief based on another belief, i.e. a *basing relation*, also called *basis relation*.

Otherwise, it is direct knowledge. A species of indirect knowledge is inferential knowledge, i.e. knowledge based on, or resulting from, an inference.

Knowledge and society

Besides epistemology, knowledge has been studied in the *sociology of knowledge* or *social epistemology* (the study of the social causes of belief rather than of the reasons for having the beliefs, in order to apply its results to social planning), whose founder was the Hungarian-born, German social scientist Karl Mannheim (CE 1893–1947). He also held the doctrine of the relativity of knowledge, which he thought followed from his studies. The term *relativity of knowledge* is used to mean that knowledge and, in particular, the truth it involves is subjective either in that it is entirely dependent on individual beliefs or, as Mannheim seems to have believed, on social beliefs. However, this view is self-refuting if it involves the claim to be true and known and it undermines the possibility of attaining what Mannheim's sociology of knowledge sought: knowledge of the social causes of belief. Instead, it landed it in the situation of merely amounting to a set of arbitrary, entirely subjective beliefs. Some thinkers interpreting knowledge as a form of power have pursued this line of thought during the twentieth century.

Philosophy of knowledge outside the Western tradition

Notions analogous to those previously discussed in this entry can be found in philosophical traditions that developed independently of Western philosophy. In Indian philosophy, for example, the notion of *indriya* – sense organ – has a central role concerning knowledge, but various interpretations, both of the sense organs and of the senses, depending on the school involved. The *Nyāya-Vaiśeṣika School*, for example, considers a sense organ to be the seat of contacts with the mind that cause cognitions. The Dvaita School recognizes five external senses but adds *manas*, the mind, and *sāksin*, the witness consciousness.

At any rate, the term for knowledge is *jñāna*, which is also the term for WISDOM and COMPREHENSION. It has been variously understood in different schools of Indian philosophy.

For example, in Jainism, this is a knowledge of details; Nyāya-Vaiśeṣika emphasizes its self-reflexive character – *jñāna* is not only about objects but about itself; and in Saiva Siddhānta, it is the path to liberation.

Various terms involving knowledge in the sense just described are: *jñāna-karma-samuccaya*, which is the combination of knowledge and action, a combination some thinkers held to be the means to liberation; *jñāna-lakshāna*, which is a special kind of knowledge involving perception based on past experience; and *jñāna-shakti*, the ability to know, while *jñānendriya* are the organs of knowledge. JAINISM recognizes five such organs: *srotra* (hearing), *tvak* (touch), *caksus* (sight), *rasana* (taste), and *ghrāna* (smell); while the Samkhya School and Nyāya-Vaiśeṣika also recognize *manas* ("the mind") as a sense organ or one of the *indriyas*.

A notion often used in Indian philosophy concerning knowledge is that of *kalpāna*, a term denoting presumptive knowledge or assumption (usually applied to the association of name and permanence with objects), and involving IMAGINATION and CREATION.

Characterizations of knowledge, its kinds, and instruments were not pursued in other traditions to the same extent as in those just discussed. To be sure, Chinese philosophy includes discussions of knowledge; however, these are always subservient to its more primary concerns: ethics and, in relation to it, metaphysics. For example, in Chinese neo-Confucianism, Lu Hsiang-shan (CE 1139–93) held that mind by itself sufficed to harmonize the human and the natural in human nature. This view was revived by Wang Yan-ming (CE 1472–1529) at the end of the Sung-(Yüan)-Ming period, thus originating the Lu-Wang School. In formulating his views, Wang refined the notion of *liang-chih*, which had been initially formulated by Meng-tzu or Mencius in the fourth century BCE. For Meng-tzu, *liang-chih* roughly meant "innate knowledge of the good." For Wang, it meant "sense of right and wrong" or "ability to tell right from wrong," which, for him, was the love of good and hate of evil. This ability amounted to a moral consciousness that, according to Wang, involved a vision of *jen* as being *one with the universe* but, given that circumstances change, involved *deliberation*.

See also: epistemology; justification

Further reading
Cover, J.A. (1994) *Theories of Knowledge and Reality: An Introduction to the Problems and Arguments of Philosophy*, New York: McGraw-Hill.
Pasnau, Robert (1997) *Theories of Cognition in the Later Middle Ages*, Cambridge, UK and New York, NY: Cambridge University Press.
Subbaravu, Veluri (1998) *Theories of Knowledge: Its Validity and Its Sources*, Delhi: Sri Satguru Publications.

Koran *see* Islam

Korean philosophy Philosophical reflection in Korea was, from its early stages of development, subject to significant Chinese influence. These influences began to make themselves felt during the Three Kingdoms era (57 BCE to CE 558). They included BUDDHISM, CONFUCIANISM, and TAOISM. Yet, the native tradition of *shamanism* – an animistic conception of humans and nature – remained a significant influence in Korea, and contributed to modify the previously mentioned exogenous traditions.

Buddhism influenced Korean philosophical reflection especially through the Mahāyāna group of schools, which mixed with shamanism to produce a shamanic polytheism. This syncretic tendency led to recurrent attempts to reconcile conflicting doctrines. Most notable among the philosophers who flourished within this tradition are Wonhyo (CE 617–86), and Chinul (CE 1158–1210). Wonhyo devoted his efforts to reconciling the views of the Mādhyamika School, which denied existence and the possibility of worldly instead of transcendental truth, and the Vijnaptinatrata-vadin School that affirmed both existence and the possibility of worldly truth. In his *Tae-seung Kishin-non* (*The Awakening of Faith in Mahayana*), he formulated his *Hwajaeng-non* or theory of reconciliation of dispute. Chinul, the founder of Korean Sŏn Buddhism, attempted a reconciliation between Kyo-hak, the Doctrinal School of Buddhism, which emphasized enlightenment through scriptural interpretation, and Sŏn-ga, the Meditation School of Buddhism, which emphasized enlightenment through activities independent of scriptural interpretation. Chinul's position provided a philosophical basis for applying the doctrines of the Scriptural School to the practices of the Son School.

According to the *Samguk Sagi* or *Chronicle of the Three Kingdoms*, Confucianism became highly official in Korea in CE 372 with the establishment of a national university, *Taehak*, devoted to Confucian education. It is therefore reasonable to believe that Confucianism's presence in Korea significantly predated Taehak, possibly going as far back as three centuries earlier, during the early days of the Koguryo dynasty in the kingdom of the same name, which adjoined the Chinese mainland and the Chinese colony of Lolang. Also, the Kingdom of Paekche had established a doctoral program in the study of Confucian scriptures, and apparently a national Confucian university, at about the same time that Taehak was founded. Also, under the rule of King Kunch'ogo (CE 346–74), Pekche scholars went to Japan to teach Confucianism to the Japanese nobility. As for the Kingdom of Silla, it followed the same path slightly later. Indeed, although Buddhism was the state religion of the Unified Silla period (CE 668–918), Confucianism constituted its philosophical and institutional basis. When a national university was established in the Unified Silla kingdom in CE 682, its curriculum consisted primarily of Confucian and other Chinese texts.

This pre-eminence of Confucianism in Korea was strengthened when the founders of the Choson dynasty (CE 1392–1910) adopted Confucianism, or rather neo-Confucianism – a synthesis of Confucianism, Taoism, and Buddhism formulated by the Chinese philosopher Chu Hsi (CE 1130–1200) – as the national ideology, which led it to flourish for about five centuries. Among the philosophers who contributed to this development was Yi Hwang (whose pen name was T'oegye; CE 1501–70), who interpreted the origin of the four cardinal virtues – benevolence, righteousness, propriety, and knowledge – and the seven emotions – pleasure, anger, sorrow, joy, love, hate, and desire – in a way that gave priority to *i* (*li*), the principle, over *ki* (*ch'i*), the material force. He went further than his Sung mentor, Chu Hsi, in

claiming that the principle includes the generative power or activity. T'oegye's views were influential in spreading neo-Confucianism to Japan, and were criticized by Yi I (whose pen name was Yulgok; CE 1536–84), who claimed that the source of generative power in the universe resided in material force. From either standpoint, however, the emphasis was on self-cultivation – an emphasis that remained through the various stages of Korean Confucianism's development.

Neo-Confucianism, however, became excessively speculative and abstract during later periods, evolving into somewhat of a national orthodoxy around the mid-seventeenth century. Dissatisfaction with it was prompted by the need for social reform that followed the CE 1592–7 Japanese invasion, and by the influence of Western science and Christianity, which began reaching Korea through China around the early seventeenth century.

Reacting to this situation, a group of Confucian thinkers began emphasizing the need for *Sirhak* or "Practical Learning" by discarding abstract speculations in favor of inquiry aimed at improving social conditions. This philosophical approach, called the Sirhak movement, spanned from the seventeenth to the nineteenth century CE, when the work of Chŏn Yag-yong (CE 1762–1836) became highly influential formulating a new Confucian synthesis based on utility, practicality, and reliance on evidence.

During the later part of the Yi dynasty (after the mid-1850s), however, fear of interaction with Europeans led the government to impose a closed-doors policy. This involved a persecution of Catholicism and the banning of Catholic writings. The ban was also extended to the philosophies of the Chinese Confucian thinkers Wang Yang-ming (CE 1472–1529), who had argued for *chih-hsing ho-i* or the unity of knowledge and action, and *liang-chih* or humans' innate knowledge of the good, and Lu Hsiang-san (CE 1139–93), who had argued for *t'ien-jen ho-i* or the unity of Heaven and humans, and advocated following the moral nature of humans.

As a result, the Practical Learning movement declined and neo-Confucianism, which had been on the upswing, took center stage again. Already in the eighteenth century, Im Sŏng-ju

(CE 1711–88), formulated an absolute monism of *ki*, defining principle as basically nothing more than material force. According to him, human nature is *ki*, which is restricted to sense-experience, and is good. The role of *i*, or principle expressing itself in various ways, was eliminated on the grounds that it was redundant since it could occur only through *ki*. By contrast with the previous thinker, in the nineteenth century, Ki Jŏng-jin (CE 1798–1876) asserted the absolute monism of *i*.

The influence of Confucian philosophy is still very strong in Korean thought. Indeed, even movements developed against Confucianism manifest its influence. For example, since its founding by Ch'oe Suun in CE 1860, Ch'ŏndogyo has significantly influenced Korean society. It was originally formulated as a reaction against Confucianism, Buddhism, Taoism, and Christianity; but it retained concepts from some of these traditions. Notable among them is the Confucian concept of *chuntzu* or superior man. As for influences from other traditions, one example is the Taoist concept of *wu-wei* or natural life. The Ch'ondogyo concept of the dignity and equality of all humans is somewhat analogous to the Christian concept of humans, though disanalogous in that this concept implies a difference between humans and God while Ch'ondogyo holds that humans are divine in original nature.

See also: Buddhism; Confucianism; philosophy of religion

Further reading

Chung, Edward Y.J. (1995) *The Korean Neo-Confucianism of Yi T'oegye and Yi Yulgok: A Reappraisal of the "Four-Seven Thesis" and Its Practical Implications for Self-Cultivation*, Albany: State University of New York Press.

Korean National Commission for UNESCO (1983) *Main Currents of Korean Thought*, Seoul, Korea and Arch Cape, Oregon, US: The Si-sa-yong-o-sa Publishers, Inc. and Pace International Research, Inc.

Yong Choon Kim (1978) *The Ch'ondogyo Concept of Man*, Seoul, Korea: Pan Korea Book Corporation.

ko-wu, chih-chih *see* Confucianism

Krausism *see* Kantian philosophy

Kripke semantics *see* logic

Kulturwelt *see* phenomenology

k'un *see* Taoism

Kundalini Yoga *see* Sāmkhya-Yoga

kung, szu *see* Confucianism

kyo-hak Buddhism *see* Buddhism

Kyoto School *see* Japanese philosophy

L

L *see* logic

labor *see* Marxism; philosophy of economics

lāhūt *see* Ṣūfism

laissez-faire *see* capitalism; philosophy of economics

laksana *see* meaning

laksita-laksana *see* meaning

Lamaism *see* Buddhism

Lamarckism *see* evolution

lambda abstraction *see* logic

lambda calculus *see* logic

lambda operator *see* logic

lambda term *see* logic

land *see* Agriculture School; capitalism; Chinese philosophy; ethics; Native American philosophy

language *see* logic; philosophy of language; play

language-game *see* existentialism

language, philosophy of *see* philosophy

language, social effects of *see* philosophy of language

large numbers, law of *see* ars conjectandi, under ars

latent content *see* psychoanalysis

Latin American philosophy Philosophical inquiry and resulting philosophical views found in Latin America. Pre-Hispanic indigenous cultures developed ideas about the universe and discussed them in ways that, arguably, qualify as philosophical (see NAHUA PHILOSOPHY). Yet, philosophical inquiry and views since the Conquest of the Americas have shown little if any direct influence from those pre-Hispanic ideas and discussions.

Philosophers sometimes talk of Ibero-American philosophy, meaning philosophy practiced or philosophical ideas and concerns found in predominantly Spanish- or Portuguese-speaking countries of Europe and the Americas. Hispanic philosophy is subsumed under Ibero-American philosophy, being philosophy practiced or philosophical ideas and concerns found in predominantly Spanish-speaking countries of Europe and the Americas. Latin American philosophy overlaps with the previous two categories, being philosophy practiced or philosophical ideas and concerns found in countries of the Americas other than the United States and Canada, whether their predominant language is Spanish as in many of them, Portuguese as in Brazil, or Guaraní (together with Spanish) as in Paraguay. In short, the term Latin American philosophy applies to Western-influenced philosophy and philosophies developed since the Conquest that are typically – though not necessarily always – formulated in Spanish or Portuguese.

In this regard, it should be mentioned that though Guyana (whose predominant languages are English and East Indian), Surinam (where Dutch is predominant), and French Guyana (where the predominant language is French) are geographically part of Latin America, not many consider them to be part of Latin America from a cultural or philosophical standpoint.

At any rate, the main influence on philosophy in Latin America has been Western, indeed, until recently, primarily European. To be sure, the ideas and philosophical approaches of North American philosophers such as William James (CE 1842–1910) and Ralph Waldo Emerson (CE 1803–82) have influenced Latin American philosophical thought; but most Western influences have proceeded from Europe.

A note of caution: though predominantly Hispanic, the Latin American world is not as homogeneous as it is sometimes believed. This is evidenced in its linguistic variety. Spanish dialects differ sharply from region to region in Latin America, often within the same country. As already mentioned, Brazil's official language is Portuguese, while the official languages in Paraguay are Spanish and a pre-Hispanic language: Guaraní. Quechua is a major language in Ecuador, Peru, Bolivia, and northwestern Argentina, and Guaraní, not Spanish, is the predominant language in the Argentinean provinces of Misiones and Corrientes. The main languages of Guyana are, as previously indicated, English and East Indian; while the language of Surinam is Dutch and that of French Guyana French.

Latin America also displays significant religious variety. Catholicism is the predominant religion in the region as a whole; but Hinduism and Islam are predominant in Surinam. More significantly, even in those countries where Catholicism is the official religion, there is the question of who converted whom. Anthropologists have reported observing Mayan ceremonies in the main area of a Guatemalan Catholic church while mass was being conducted in a corner. In Bolivia, statues of the Pachamama (Mother Earth) have been found with those of Catholic saints in Catholic churches. That is, the post-Conquest linguistic and cultural world of the Americas is neither merely Hispanic, nor merely Western, but includes other influences. In some Latin American countries, these are largely Eastern influences. In others, most notably in Brazil, they are African. Yet, those non-European influences that most significantly contribute to the Latin American world's being less than homogenous are languages, cultures, and ways of thinking characteristic of the pre-Hispanic world.

Given the cultural and linguistic background just described, not to mention the more than 500 years of post-Conquest history in the Americas, and the large number and variety of countries in Latin America, it is predictably difficult to find any predominant feature in the region's philosophical activity. Yet, a strong human and social interest, primarily displayed in a concern with education and politics, has been quite recurrent in Latin American philosophy. So has the influence of Catholic thought in much of the philosophy in the region. In addition, philosophical discussions in Latin America have frequently focused on questions of national identity.

It is customary among students of Latin American philosophy to divide its history into four periods. First, the *colonial period* (c. CE 1550–c. 1750), is characterized by the type of philosophy practiced in Spain and Portugal at the time. Notable among Iberian figures were the Spaniards Francisco de Vitoria (c. CE 1492–1546) and Domingo de Soto (CE 1494–1560), the Portuguese Pedro da Fonseca (CE 1528–99) and, most prominently, the Spaniard Francisco Suárez (CE 1548–1617). They discussed logical and metaphysical problems that had occupied the attention of Thomist authors and commentators, such as the problem of universals and particulars, and that of the logic of terms and propositions (see SYNCATEGOREMATA; THOMISM). They also discussed ethical, legal, and sociopolitical problems such as the rights of Amerindians and the relation of Amerindians to their conquerors. The most notable figure of this period in the region was the Mexican philosopher Alonso de la Vera Cruz (c. CE 1504–84), an Augustinian who had studied with Soto and was the first to teach philosophy at the Royal Pontifical University of Mexico founded in 1553. He was an eclectic and didactic author and composed various treatises, two on logic, one on physics, another on theology and the law, and still another on marriage, the last dealing with the status of Indian marriages pre-dating the Spanish Conquest. Other authors of note were the Peruvian Thomist Juan Pérez Menacho (CE 1565–1626), who, for example, wrote a *Treatise on Theology and Morals*, and the Scotistic Augustinian Chilean Alfonso Briceño (*c.* CE 1587–1669), who carried out most of his philosophical activities in Peru and published, for example, *On Scotus' First Book of the Sentences*.

During this period, some authors were also influenced by humanist writers. They included the advocate for the Indians Bartolomé de las Casas (CE 1474–1566) and the famous Mexican poet, now thought to be a precursor of feminism, Sor Juana Inés de la Cruz (born Juana Ineés de Asbaje; CE 1648–95). Another notable writer of the period was the Spanish-Incan historian Garcilaso de la Vega (*c.* CE 1539–1616) (son of a Spanish conquistador and an Incan Princess, Isabel Chimpu Oelloa), who was an Inca apologist, and arguably a precursor of the philosophy of culture and ethnophilosophy in trying to explain and justify the Inca traditions and worldview to the Spanish conquerors. This period declined with the expulsion in CE 1767 of the Jesuits from the Americas, where their cities had thrived, and ended shortly before the wars of independence that began in the early nineteenth century.

The *independence period* (*c.* 1750–*c.* 1850) is characterized by a turning away from things Spanish and a growing interest in social and political questions, and in such philosophical positions as Cartesianism, those characteristic of the French Enlightenment, the contractarian ideas predominant in France, those formulated by British empiricists, and those characteristic of early utilitarianism.

In Mexico, Juan Benito Díaz de Gamarra y Dávalos (CE 1745–83) advocated modern philosophy in his *Errors of Human Understanding*. In Cuba, this development became prominent with the work of Félix Varela (CE 1788–1853) who, for example in his *Lessons in Philosophy*, upheld reason and sense-experience as sources of knowledge without rejecting the Church's authority concerning matters of dogma. This type of change took longer in Brazil, where Francisco de Mont'Alverne (CE 1784–1858) formulated modern philosophical ideas in *Compêndio de filosofia*.

These initial attempts were followed by many others produced by authors who participated in the independence movements and who spread the liberal ideals that supported these movements. Notable among them was Simón Bolívar (CE 1783–1830), leader of the rebellion against Spain that began from a Venezuelan base, took over much of Venezuela and New Granada, and then spread southwards towards Peru, reaching Lima in CE 1823. In Argentina, where the revolution began in 1810 prompted by the imprisonment of the Spanish King and takeover of Spain by Napoleonic forces in CE 1808, the revolutionary armies led by General José de San Martín (CE 1778–1850) crossed the Andes into Chile in CE 1817 and then moved on to Peru in CE 1820, taking Lima in CE 1821, some notable liberal authors were Mariano Moreno (CE 1778–1811) and Juan Crisóstomo Lafinur (CE 1797–1824).

The *positivist period* (*c.* CE 1850–*c.* 1910) developed after the wars of independence had largely ended and the new countries of the region faced a variety of socially destabilizing conditions, from collapsing colonial economies, through unsettled territorial claims, to internal anarchy. As a result, order, justice, and progress became the buzz-words of the day among Latin American thinkers who found themselves drawn to positivism, a position that typically advocated social progress by applying science to the practical resolution of social problems. The primary concern of this group of intellectuals was the rejection of all metaphysics in a sense in which, arguably, also much theoretical (even if not metaphysical) thinking was rejected. In fact, theories came to be measured by their practical use in dealing with social problems. The Brazilian flag has actually preserved this period's ideal in its motto: Order and Progress.

Among the early, transitional figures of this period, the Argentine writer Esteban Echeverría (CE 1805–51), author of *Socialist Dogma*, was influenced by French socialist writers. Juan Bautista Alberdi (CE 1812–84), also an Argentine, was the first one to argue, in his *Ideas*, that Latin America should develop a philosophy adequate to its needs. Alberdi's work was also influential in establishing the text for the Argentine constitution of 1853, a document that, in a number of respects, was analogous to that of the United States, and which served as a basis for Argentina's enormous economic and demographic growth under liberal institutions between 1853 and 1912 and, with the introduction of universal suffrage in 1912, under liberal and democratic institutions until the military *coup* of 1930, when illegitimacy embraced the country until the democratic stabilization that began in 1983. Another transitional author was the Venezuelan Andrés Bello (CE 1781–1865), who lived in Chile from 1829 until his death, and whose *Philosophy of Understanding* constituted an outstanding exposition of an empirical, logical, and psychological approach to philosophy where metaphysics was reduced to psychology.

The writers that followed were mostly positivists. Notable among them were the Cuban Enrique José Varona (CE 1849–1933) and the Argentine José Ingenieros (CE 1877–1925). Varona published *Philosophical Lectures* where, by contrast with his positivistic contemporaries, he offered explanations of behavior that were not merely mechanistic. Ingenieros did not entirely reject metaphysics, which he characterized as the realm of that yet to be experienced. His main works were *Towards a Morality Without Dogmas*, which reflects both transcendentalist ideas as well as some ideas found in Schopenhauerian thought; *The Mediocre Man*, an inspirational book emphasizing the ideal of character development and aspiring for greatness, and *Principles of Psychology*, where he formulates a reductionist conception of psychology.

In Mexico, under President Juárez, Gabino Barreda (CE 1818–81) reorganized Mexican education in accordance with Comtean positivistic principles. His critic, Justo Sierra (CE 1848–1912), advocated a Darwinian version of positivism. In Brazil, the most influential positivists were Comtean positivists, in particular Miguel Lemos (CE 1854–1916), and Raimundo Teixeira Mendes (CE 1855–1927). All these thinkers were characterized by various degrees of dogmatism and an emphasis on mechanistic explanations and narrowly conceived practical concerns.

The *contemporary period* (*c.* 1910–present) began with a generalized rebellion against the narrow dogmatism and mechanistic explanations of the Latin American positivists. Notable among its founding figures (who developed parallel views though apparently interacted very little if at all) was the Argentine Alejandro Korn (CE 1860–1936), a practicing psychiatrist and professor of anatomy at the National University of La Plata. He philosophized along the lines of Bergsonianism, Kantian philosophy, and what he called "autochthonous positivism" attempting to formulate a spiritualized version of positivism in such works as *Creative Liberty*, where he defended a concept of freedom as creative, and *Axiology*, where he formulated a subjectivist philosophy of values. He eventually became professor of philosophy at the national university of Buenos Aires.

Another notable of the period was the Peruvian Alejandro Octavio Deústua (CE 1849–1945), who criticized positivism in his *The Ideas of Order and Freedom in the History of Human Thought*, and also advocated a philosophy of creative liberty. Along parallel lines to those of Korn and Deústua, the Chilean Enrique Molina (CE 1871–1964) produced *Bergson's Philosophy*. Also notable was the Mexican Antonio Caso (CE 1883–1946), whose conception of humans as spiritual beings who surpass nature through love was formulated in his *Existence as Economy, Disinterestedness, and Charity*. Another Mexican philosopher, José Vasconcelos (CE 1882–1959), continued Caso's work, combining it with Neoplatonic and Pythagorean influences in *Aesthetic Monism*, and pointing to a philosophical awareness of Latin American cultures in *Cosmic Race*. The Uruguayan Carlos Vas Ferreira (CE 1872–1958) advocated a dynamic logic based on experience in his *Living Logic*. The Brazilian Raimundo Farias Brito (CE 1862–1917) formulated an arguably Neoplatonic alternative to positivism in his *The World's Goal*, where he characterized the world as a unifying intellectual activity.

The next generation of contemporary philosophers felt the influence of such European philosophical traditions as Hegelianism, Marxism, pessimism, nihilism, and existentialism. The most important figure of this generation is Francisco Romero (CE 1891–1962), whose

Theory of Man formulated a philosophical anthropology based on a metaphysics of transcendence. Also significant was the work of the Mexican Samuel Ramos (CE 1897–1959), who further developed Vascocelos's work in *Cosmic Race* in his *Profile of Man and Culture in Mexico*, awakening a philosophical interest in Latin American cultures that has since been strong and has motivated a great deal of philosophical discussion about national and regional identity. This was a later interest of the Argentine Carlos Astrada (CE 1894–1970), who studied in Germany, initially formulated existentialist ideas in *The Existential Game*, but then gave them a Marxist, Hegelian, and anthropological emphasis in *Existentialism and the Crisis of Philosophy* and, even more so, in *Land and Figure*. Marxism had its most articulate representative of the period in the Peruvian José Carlos Mariátegui (CE 1895–1930), who produced a Marxist analysis of Peru in his *Seven Essays on the Interpretation of Peruvian Reality*.

As a consequence of the Spanish Civil War, many Spanish philosophers moved to Latin America, most notably José Gaos (CE 1900–69), who advocated the Unamunean idea of *hispanidad* or *Hispanicness* and, accordingly, promoted communication among Hispanic philosophers. Another important influence was that of European intellectuals other than Spaniards who emigrated to Argentina as a result of the impending beginning of the Second World War. Notable among these was the Italian philosopher Rodolfo Mondolfo (CE 1877–1976). He was a highly revered historian of philosophy in Italy and Latin America, whose work focused on Ancient Greek philosophy, modern philosophy, and Marxism. He conceived of Greek thought as dynamic and argued that, though there is an unavoidable subjective element in philosophizing, progress is none the less made through the deepening of philosophical understanding.

The influence exerted by this European philosophical diaspora was felt by the generation of 1910, which attained the professionalization of philosophy as a reputable branch of inquiry in Latin America. Perhaps most notable among them was the Argentine Risieri Frondizi (CE 1910–83), who was influenced by the neo-Kantian and Anglo-American traditions, formulating, in *The Nature of the Self*, a functional conception of the self and, in *What is Value?*, a conception of value as a Gestalt quality.

At the same time, following Ramos, the Mexican Leopoldo Zea raised questions concerning the possibility and identity of Latin American philosophy, which originated a still ongoing controversy. Others – e.g. the Mexican Oswaldo Robles, and the Argentine Octavio Nicolás Derisi – have pursued a neo-Thomist approach, though, besides traditional Thomist questions of logic and metaphysics, they also pursued questions in axiology and philosophical anthropology. Still others – the Argentine Astrada, the Mexican Eli de Gortary, and the Brazilian Caio Prado Júnior (CE 1909–86) – pursued Marxist approaches, sometimes, as in Astrada's case, combined with existentialism. A special mention needs to be made of the Argentine Vicente Fatone (CE 1903–62), who studied the nature of mystic experience and held that human reality involves dialogue through which one liberates oneself and others from irrationality, fear, and hate, leading oneself and others towards rationality, effort, and love. A central notion in Fatone's position is that of freedom, which he conceived in an existentialist fashion. He was a careful student of Indian philosophies. His publications included *Existentialism and Creative Freedom*, *Philosophy and Poetry*, *Essays on Hinduism and Buddhism*, and *The Philosophy of Nāgārjuna*.

Partly influenced by Marxism, partly by the problematic of the contemporary Mexican philosopher Leopoldo Zea, partly by traditional Catholic ideas, Latin American thinkers in the 1970s developed the PHILOSOPHY OF LIBERATION movement. This is an autochthonous Latin American philosophical movement influenced by the *theology of liberation* movement. The latter started in the 1960s and was aimed at improving the situation of the oppressed. Its initial formulations included *The Pedagogy of the Oppressed*, published in 1970 by the contemporary Brazilian author Paulo Freire, and *Theology of Liberation*, published the next year by the contemporary Peruvian author Gustavo Gutiérrez. This movement also influenced theologians outside Latin America. An example is the contemporary United States author James H. Cone, whose *A Black Theology of Liberation*, published in 1970, conceived of oppression as black oppression and of Christianity as the religion of the oppressed through which they were to achieve their true liberation or emancipation.

In the late 1970s and early 1980s, the liberation theology movement developed increasingly closer ties to Marxist thought and, as a result, in his 1980–5 visits to Latin America, Pope John Paul II denounced social injustice while cautioning against the excesses of liberation theology. Gustavo Gutiérrez was summoned to Rome to explain his views, other prominent figures of the movement were suspended from the priesthood or had their right to teach suspended, and the movement declined. So did the philosophy of liberation movement that the theological movement had inspired, not before producing such works as: *Philosophy of Liberation*, published in 1977 by the contemporary Argentine philosopher Enrique Dussel, who, since then, has been active in Mexico; *Latin American Philosophy of Liberation*, whose second edition was published in 1992; and *Philosophies for Liberation: The Liberation of Philosophizing?*, published in 1997 by the contemporary Argentine philosopher Horacio Cerutti Guldberg, who has also been active in Mexico.

As for philosophical analysis, it took root late in Latin America, and has influenced a relatively small group of philosophers who, however, have become very well established in the region. The main centers of analytic philosophy are Buenos Aires, Mexico City, and the Brazilian cities of Campinas and São Paulo. Among its most important practitioners are the Argentines Genaro R. Carrió, Gregorio Klimovsky, and Thomas Moro Simpson, the Peruvian Francisco Miró Quesada, and the Spanish-born Luis Villoro in Mexico. Some Latin American analytic philosophers left Latin America but kept an ongoing dialogue with those who remained. Among these are the Chilean Roberto Torretti, who has been active in Puerto Rico, and the Guatemalan Héctor-Neri Castañeda (CE 1924–91), who was active in the United States. A cognate philosopher

and physicist who practices not just analytic but, as he states, synthetic philosophy, is the Argentine Mario Bunge, who has been active in Canada.

In addition, in Latin America today, there are many philosophers acquainted with both the analytic, the Kantian, and the existentialist traditions who, to various degrees, combine them rather than, as in the past, engage in intellectual or institutional wars between schools. One of them is Enrique E. Marí, who teaches philosophy of law and sociopolitical philosophy at the Argentinean National University of Buenos Aires. Another is Osvaldo Guariglia, the Director of the Institute of Philosophy at the same university. Also, a growing number of professional philosophers in Latin America today engage in areas of practical ethics such as health care ethics and the ethics of technology. One of them is Florencia Luna, founder of the first bioethics journal in Latin America: *Perspectivas Bioéticas en las Américas*. The main concern of these philosophers is not, as it often was in the past, to import the latest philosophical ideas from Europe or elsewhere. Nor is it, as it often was in the past, to cut off dialogue with representatives of philosophical traditions other than the one they advocate. Nor are they blandly eclectic. Instead, while open to all ideas whatever their origin, they seek to adapt them and use them to develop new ones that are applicable to Latin America's realities.

Finally, it needs saying that Latin American philosophy uses a variety of expressions, for example literature. Notable among those who have philosophized through literature is the Argentine writer Jorge Luis Borges (CE 1899–1986). His "Funes, the Memorious," for example, explores the Lockian case of a person who, instead of memory, has continuous immediate perception. Another example is Borges's "A New Refutation of Time," a critique of empiricist as well as rationalist conceptions of time. Also, his "Pierre Menard, Author of the Quixote," and "Kafka and His Precursors" test and examine current conceptions of the identity of artworks. In addition, *The Book of Imaginary Beings* does not merely include descriptions of metaphysical beings, but also of beings such at the double – i.e. a person's duplicate or counterpart – which, especially when one is thought to meet oneself, raises current questions concerning identity. *The Book of Imaginary Beings* is itself an instance of an open-ended, infinite book, even though one can hold a finite copy of it, hence a literary case of relevance to issues in logic and computer theory. Another author who has pursued philosophical inquiry through literature is the Belgium-born, naturalized Argentine, and then French writer Julio Cortázar, whose *Bestiarios*, for example, explores matters of identity with a biological emphasis. Still another is the Argentine physicist and writer Ernesto Sábato, whose *One and the Universe* ranges over the entire spectrum of philosophical categories. More recently, similar attempts, but adding a social emphasis to previous metaphysical concerns as the nature of personal identity and such epistemological concerns as the reliability of memory, can be found in the literature in exile movement that has developed within the Hispanic diasporas of Europe and North America.

See also: analysis; Cartesianism; empiricism; existentialism; idealism; Kantian philosophy; Marxism; positivism; Thomism

Further reading
Alegría, Fernando and Ruffinelli, Jorge (1990) *Paradise Lost or Gained? The Literature of Hispanic Exile*, Houston, TX: Arte Público.
Gracia, Jorge J.E. (1989) *Philosophy and Literature in Latin America: A Critical Assessment of the Current Situation*, Albany, NY: State University of New York Press.
Roig, Arturo Andrés (1994) *El pensamiento latinoamericano y su aventura*, Buenos Aires: Centro Editor de América Latina.
Sáenz, Mario (1999) *The Identity of Liberation in Latin American Thought: Latin American Historicism and the Phenomenology of Leopoldo Zea*, Lanham, MD: Lexington Books.

latina *see* feminist philosophy

lattice theory *see* philosophy of mathematics

law and social order *see* philosophy of law

law, bridge *see* reductionism

law, customary *see* ethics

law, legitimacy of *see* philosophy of law

law, moral *see* ethics

law, Mosaic *see* Judaism

law, natural *see* ethics

law of coexistence *see* causal law

law of double negation *see* logic

law of eternal return *see* age of the world; computer theory

law of identity *see* identity

law of large numbers *see* ars conjectandi, under ars

law of succession *see* causal law

law of trichotomy *see* relation

law, positive *see* philosophy of law

laws of ecology *see* ecology

laws of nature *see* ethics; philosophy of science

laws of thought *see* logic; syllogism

lazy sophism *see* fallacy

leap of faith *see* existentialism

least squares method *see* induction

Lebensphilosophie *see* explanation

Lebenswelt *see* explanation; phenomenology

lectio *see* Scholasticism

legal disability *see* philosophy of law

legal duty *see* philosophy of law

legal formalism *see* philosophy of law

legal immunity *see* philosophy of law

legal liability *see* philosophy of law

legal moralism *see* philosophy of law

legal no-right *see* philosophy of law

legal positivism *see* philosophy of law

legal power *see* philosophy of law

legal privilege *see* philosophy of law

legal realism *see* philosophy of law

legal right *see* philosophy of law

legalism, Chinese *see* Chinese philosophy

legality *see* Kantian philosophy

legisign *see* pragmatism

legitimacy *see* philosophy, sociopolitical

Leibniz's law *see* identity

lekton *see* Stoicism

lemmata *see* Greek philosophy

Leninism *see* Marxism

lesbian *see* feminist philosophy; gender

letter *see* logic

level *see* theory of types

lex talionis *see* ethics; philosophy of law

lexical ambiguity *see* ambiguity

lexical definition *see* definition

lexical ordering *see* ordering

li *see* Chinese philosophy; Confucianism; Mohism

liang-chih *see* Chinese philosophy

liar paradox *see* paradox

Liber de Causis *see* Neoplatonism

liberal *see* philosophy of economics; philosophy, sociopolitical

liberal feminism *see* feminist philosophy

liberalism *see* philosophy of economics; philosophy, sociopolitical

liberation *see* Latin American philosophy; philosophy, sociopolitical

libertarian *see* determinism; philosophy, sociopolitical

libertarianism *see* determinism; philosophy, sociopolitical

libertas indifferentiae *see* determinism

liberty *see* determinism; philosophy of law; philosophy, sociopolitical

liberty variable *see* decision

liberum arbitrium *see* determinism

Li Chi *see* Confucianism

li-ch'i *see* Chinese philosophy; Confucianism

life *see* biology; body; ecology; evolution; existentialism; Hinduism

life game *see* play

life, philosophy of *see* explanation

life plans *see* ethics

life, reverence for *see* ethics

life space *see* perception

life style *see* culture

life world *see* phenomenology

light *see* enlightenment

li-i-fen-shu *see* Chinese philosophy

limit *see* Kantian philosophy; logic

limitative judgment *see* Kantian philosophy

limited variety, principle of *see* induction

limiting case *see* ambiguity; philosophy

limiting conditions *see* ethics; philosophy of science

limiting-conditions theories *see* ethics; philosophy of science

line simile *see* Platonism

linear order *see* relation

linguistic analysis *see* analysis

linguistic competence *see* philosophy of language

linguistic performance *see* speech act theory

linguistic philosophy *see* analysis

linguistic semantics *see* philosophy of language

linguistic theory of logical truth *see* logic; truth

linguistic turn *see* analysis

linguistics, philosophy of *see* philosophy of language

literal meaning *see* meaning

literary theory *see* aesthetics

literary work *see* aesthetics

literature *see* philosophy of literature

local knowledge *see* epistemology

locality assumption *see* philosophy of science

location, epistemic *see* epistemology

locutionary act *see* speech act theory

logic A branch of inquiry concerned, first, with *arguments*, their kinds (i.e. deductive, and non-deductive), and the features that serve to establish whether given arguments are good or not, e.g. validity and soundness in the case of deductive arguments. Second, logic is concerned with the *laws* or *principles of logic* (originally considered *laws of thought*) in accordance with which good arguments must proceed, e.g. the law or principle of identity, that of non-contradiction, and that of excluded middle or *tertium non datur*. Third, logic is concerned with the system (from the Greek *sys*, i.e. "together" and *stenai*, i.e. "to stand up"), also called *logical system*, *logistic system*, *logical calculus* or simply *calculus*, *logical system*, and *a logic* – e.g. sentential logic, or predicate logic – that serves to characterize any such arguments, their structure, and the nature, structure, and meaning of their components.

Most influential in logical inquiry as pursued in the Western world have been the logical treatises of the Greek philosopher Aristotle (384–322 BCE), whose collection is called *Organon*, which, in Greek, means "instrument." It included the following treatises: *Categories*, *About Interpretation*, *First Analytics*, *Second Analytics*, *Topics*, and the *Refutations of the Sophists*.

A basic premise of Aristotle's work on logic is that an important aspect of arguments that helps assess them is their structure or logical form. This led to a type of study that traditionally focused on the syllogism and, today, is embodied in *symbolic logic* or *mathematical logic*, i.e. a study of inference in formal languages understood as models of fragments of natural languages. There are two kinds of logical systems created in symbolic logic. Some, called *axiomatic* systems, are constituted by a language, rules of inference or rules of reasoning, axioms, and theorems, which follow from the rules of inference and the axioms. Others, called *natural-deduction* systems, are constituted by all such components except axioms.

Validity and soundness

In assessing a deductive argument, two features are crucial: *validity* and *soundness*. In other words, it is first crucial whether the argument is *valid*, i.e. whether it has a form or structure such that, if the premises were true, the conclusion would have to be true; and second, it is crucial whether the argument is *sound*, i.e. whether it both is valid and has only true premises. These are technical senses – which apply only to deductive arguments – of the terms valid and sound.

With regard to validity, the British philosopher Arthur N. Prior (CE 1914–69) introduced a sentential connective he called tonk, characterized by the rules or axioms:

1 $\{[\ p{\rightarrow}(p \text{ tonk } q)]$; and
2 $[(p \text{ tonk } q){\rightarrow}q]$.

Of course, in any system with these rules, every q follows from any p. Prior's point was to show that validity should not be conceived as entirely dependent on arbitrarily defined syntactical rules or axioms. The question arises: "On what grounds can one rule out such rules or axioms?" Two types of grounds have been suggested. One is that they are not natural notions. The other appeals to specific relations between the sentences connected by proposed rules or axioms.

In addition to their technical uses, the terms validity and soundness are applied, still in a technical sense, to logical items other than arguments. Validity and valid, for example, are also applied to argument forms or rules of inference, namely whenever they cannot lead from only true premises to a false conclusion. Also, it is said that a well-formed formula is valid if it is true (or, at least, not false) under every admissible interpretation of its descriptive terms. Along the same lines, it is said that a theorem is valid. Also, soundness and sound are applied to logical systems. For example, *soundness* is the system's property of being not too strong in a certain regard. To say that a logical system has *weak soundness* or is *weakly sound* is to say that every one of its theorems is valid. While to say that a logical system has *strong soundness* or is *strongly sound* is to say that for every set of sentences in the system, every sentence deducible from this set is a logical consequence of this set.

In ordinary language, the terms valid and sound have various other uses. For example, people say that someone has a sound view or made a valid statement meaning that it is true, or that someone had a sound idea meaning that it is true or, perhaps, useful. It is also said that someone used sound reasoning or has formulated a sound position meaning that the argument(s) used may be good (though they may not be deductive). All these uses are fine, so long as one understands that the context of use is ordinary language, not logic, in which case valid and sound have the technical meanings previously described.

Implication and its cognates
As the preceding characterization makes plain, a concept central in logic is that of *logical implication*: a relation that holds between two statements when the truth of one (which can be the conjunction of a number of statements) ensures the truth of the other. The logical notion of implication should not be confused with the conversational notion of implication, which is technically called the pragmatic notion of *implicature*, and was studied by the contemporary philosopher H.P. Grice in *Studies in the Ways of Words* (1989). It can be conversational, as in: "there is an ice cream shop two blocks from here," which may conversationally implicate, though logically does not imply, say, "let's have ice cream there." It can also be conventional, as in "He is old but healthy," where the contrast between being old and being healthy is not said, but implicated by the meaning of the terms involved.

These implicatures involve the conversational *maxim of relevance* to which co-operative speakers can be expected to conform, i.e. make your contribution relevant to what prompts it. For example, if someone asks "What did you have at the restaurant?," answering "We had food" – unless it is a joke or it is meant to implicate the non-descript nature of the food – irrelevantly implicates that the person asking the question does not know that one typically has food at restaurants. Here, the maxim of relevance is associated with what can be called the *maxim of fairness*, i.e., at least for starters,

adopt the best interpretation you can imagine of others' sentences.

In applying truth conditional theories of meaning to natural languages, the contemporary philosopher Donald Davidson introduced an analogous – though narrower in scope – maxim he called the *principle of charity* that, like the maxim of fairness, applies to interpretations: interpreting a person means making the best possible sense of that person, and this means assigning meanings to what the person says that maximize its overall truth. This *epistemic charity* implies that, if a sentence *s* is true in a person's language if, and only if, some chicken swim, then that tells us the meaning of the sentence *s* in that person's language. Another maxim is the *maxim of quantity*, i.e. make your contribution as informative as required. This maxim is associated with *scalar* implicatures, e.g. if they say "some of the water spilled," they exclude most or all of the water spilling. There are also *conventional* implicatures, i.e. those in sentences whose meaning commits their users to some view. For example, in saying "he is tired but not sick," the sentence's user is committed to the view that there is a contrast between being tired and being sick.

Going back to inference, the notion of a *consequence* appears in a number of noun phrases. One is *logical* consequence: the proposition, sentence, or other information that follows logically from one or more declarative sentences (which can themselves not be true). Another is *semantic* consequence: the information that follows from the meaning of a term. A third is a consequence *relation*, which means the same as implication.

Implication conditions in Indian logic
Indian philosophy developed logic as much as Western philosophies and significantly more than any other non-Western philosophical tradition. The conditions for implication are different in Indian logic from the Western notions just discussed. *Hetu* (meaning "reason," "probes," "middle term") is a term in Indian logic denoting the *reason on whose basis something is inferred*. It must meet five conditions: there must be knowledge of the universal and invariable concomitance between the middle and the major term or *sādhya*

(meaning *that which is to be proved, the probandum*); it must be considered necessarily and unconditionally present in the minor term; it must not be found where the major term is not found; it must not be related to something absurd; and it must not be contradicted by an equally strong middle term.

The Nyāya School distinguishes three kinds of middle terms: *anvaya-vyatireka* (positive and negative); *kevalānvaya* (merely positive); and *kevala-vyatireka* (merely negative). AD-VAITA only acknowledges merely positive middle terms. As for the conclusion or *nigamana*, it is the last member of a five-member syllogism.

As for fallacious reasoning or *hetvābhāsa*, the Nyāya School distinguishes five kinds resulting from a reason's shortcomings. First, *savyabhicāra* or *anaikāntika*: the reason is inconsistent or irrelevant. Second, *viruddha*: the reason is contradictory or in conflict with the conclusion. Third, *prakaranasama* or *sat-pratipaksha*: the reason is contradicted by a counterargument or opposite reason. Fourth, *sādhyasama* or *asiddha*: the reason is not established; and fifth, a rhetorical condition: *kālātīta* or *bādhita*: the reason is mis-timed or somehow inopportune. These concepts are used in *nigraha-sthāna* or refutations.

Implication in modern logic

As for the modern logic notion of implication, it applies to conditional statements. Material implication has the form: if *p* then *q*, and is symbolized as $p \supset q$ or as $p \rightarrow q$. This is true whenever *p* is false or *q* is true. Strict implication can also have the form: if *p* then *q*, but it is formulated differently (e.g. $p \Rightarrow q$) and it is true when, and only when, the corresponding material implication is necessarily true or, in other words, when *p* cannot be true if *q* is false.

Formal paradoxes

The notions of implication just discussed have given rise to various paradoxes – the paradoxes of material implication and the paradoxes of strict implication – resulting from the principles involved, which had already been noticed in the Middle Ages. One such principle was called consequentia mirabilis (the astonishing implication) by medieval philosophers. It is the principle that if a statement follows from its own negation, then it must be true. Strict *consequentia mirabilis* is the principle that if a statement logically follows from its own negation it must be true. Since the negation of a tautology is a contradiction, and any statement follows from a contradiction, every tautology follows from its own negation. This and other such implications are unexceptionable, hence so is *consequentia mirabilis*. In modern logic, the following valid forms of argument are paradoxes of material implication:

$$q$$
$$\therefore p \supset q$$

and

$$\text{not-}p$$
$$\therefore p \supset q$$

The paradoxes of strict implication are:

$$\text{Necessarily } q$$

$$\therefore p \Rightarrow q$$

and

$$\text{Impossibly } p$$

$$\therefore p \Rightarrow q$$

Consistency

Depending on the particular type of logic involved, various notions of consistency (from the Latin *con*, i.e. "with," and *sistere*, i.e. "to stand" or "cause to stand") are used. In Aristotelian logic, consistency was *semantic* consistency: two or more sentences are consistent if they are simultaneously true under some interpretation. In modern logic, *consistency* is the unprovability of a contradiction in a logical system. Its opposite, *inconsistency*, is the provability of a contradiction in a logical system, and the *axiom of consistency* is an axiom stating that a given set of sentences in a logical system is consistent. With regard to inconsistency, the notion of a *contravalid proposition* is sometimes used to mean a proposition *p* that belongs to a logical system and from which all propositions in the system follow. In most typical systems, contravalidity coincides with self-contradictoriness.

Completeness

In first-order logic, the *completeness theorem* – that all valid sentences are provable – can be formulated in consistency terms: syntactic consistency implies satisfiability. Here, the term *satisfiability* is analogous to the notion of *syntactical consistency*, i.e. the unprovability of any explicit contradiction. In 1915, the German logician Leopold Löwenheim (CE 1878–1957) proved that for finite sets of first-order predicate logic, if there is an interpretation which makes them true, then there is an interpretation that can be put on a one-to-one correspondence with the domain of natural numbers and which makes the sets true as well. In 1919, the Norwegian logician Albert Thoralf Skolem (CE 1887–1963) generalized this result to infinite sets of sentences and made clear that the proof used the *axiom of choice*, i.e. that given any family of sets, including infinite sets, one can simultaneously choose a member of each set, thus constructing a set that has just those members. In 1922, he offered a proof of the theorem that did not use the axiom of choice and where the second interpretation's domain was – rather than merely being mapped on – the domain of natural numbers. This came to be known as the *Löwenheim–Skolem theorem*.

Using these results, in 1931, the logician Kurt Gödel (CE 1906–78; born in Brünn, Austria-Hungary – now Brno, Czech Republic) proved the *incompleteness theorem*, establishing that any system rich enough to express the theory of natural numbers is consistent only if incomplete and, if complete, then it is inconsistent. In 1936, Gödel also proved his *compactness theorem* (if every finite subset of a set of sentences is satisfiable, then the set is satisfiable), which follows directly from the completeness theorem for first-order logic.

Laws of logic

The preceding discussion centrally involves the notion of a *contradiction* that, from the standpoint of ordinary language, can be rather semantically characterized as the assertion and denial of the same thing at the same time. Syntactically, a contradiction can be characterized as a declarative sentence that is false just in virtue of its form. A principle associated to the notion of a contradiction is the *principle of non-contradiction* (also called the *principle of contradiction*): It is not the case that a declarative sentence and its negation are both true. This is formally formulated as: $\sim(p\,\&\sim p)$. Traditionally, this principle has been formulated as: the same property cannot both belong and not belong to the same item in the same respect and at the same time. Another traditional formulation is: the same things cannot both be and not be in the same respect at the same time.

This principle is one of the three *laws* or *principles of logic* (or *laws* or *principles of thought*). A second such principle – which some logical intuitionists reject – is the *principle of excluded middle* or *tertium non datur*: Either a declarative sentence is true, or its contradictory is true. In other words: contradictories cannot both be false. This is formally formulated as: $p\,v\sim p$. The third principle is the principle of identity, traditionally formulated as: whatever is, is, and formally formulated as $p{\supset}p$. Some logicians have argued that the principle of excluded middle or *tertium non datur* should be stated as: it is true that either a declarative sentence or its opposite is the case, which they would formalize as $T(pv{-}p)$. They have also argued that this should be distinguished from the *principle of bivalence*: any significant statement is either true or false, which they would formalize as: $Tp\,v\,T{-}p$. Standard truth-functional logic cannot distinguish between the principle of excluded middle and that of bivalence, and other logicians have argued that there is no difference between the two.

Pragmatic contradicion

In addition, there is the notion of a *pragmatic contradiction*, often characterized as a contradiction between what is said and what is done. An example is: "I am not denying anything right now." Also, when uttered, "I am not uttering anything right now" is an example of a pragmatic contradiction; but, if written in silence, it is not. Also, the statement "No statement should be taken seriously" is a pragmatic contradiction if meant to be taken seriously, but not otherwise. In general, one can characterize a pragmatic contradiction as a statement that leads to a contradiction through the description of the kind of statement it is –

e.g. a denial, an utterance, or a statement meant to be taken seriously – and what it says or implies. An analogous notion at the level of an inference or argument is that of a *self-defeating position*, i.e. an argument or set of arguments (or a position) such that at least one of the conclusions reached in the set of arguments undermines at least one of the premises used to derive one of the said conclusions. An example of a self-defeating position is:

1 Any reason is as good as any other.
2 If so, then there is no good reason for concluding anything.

Hence, there is no good reason for concluding anything.

Here, the conclusion, if true, undermines the premises used to reach it. Besides, arguably, the conclusion is self-refuting.

Sometimes, the logical principles just discussed as well as studies in proof theory are said to constitute the subject matter of *metalogic*, though, arguably, they are highly theoretical subjects of logic, studied at the theoretical level where logic merges with the philosophy of logic.

Types of logic
There are various kinds or types of logic, depending on the types of linguistic expressions whose logic is being studied. Typically, in logic and semiotics, the term *expression* is used when one wants to omit being unnecessarily specific. Examples of expressions can be declarative sentences of various types, questions, or commands. An equivalent of the term expression is the term *sentence* understood as a well-formed and grammatically complete string of symbols in a language. In this sense of sentence, questions, commands, expressions of desire are sentences, though questions and expressions of desire are not declarative sentences, because they do not have a primary descriptive function. Sometimes, the term *declarative sentence* is used as synonymous with *proposition* though, strictly speaking, a proposition is the meaning of a sentence or, as some authors would say, the state of affairs designated by a declarative sentence, where state of affairs denotes a possibility, actuality, or impossibility expressed by the sentence. Other

philosophers prefer to talk of *statements*, i.e. declarative sentences used by language users in certain circumstances. Accordingly, they talk not of the meaning of the sentence, but of what the statement means.

As for the types of logic, they include such things as the *logic of statements*, *logic of questions*, and *logic of commands*, many of which fall under the general category of formal logic or symbolic logic, or mathematical logic.

Logical form and its applications
Formal logic is concerned with focusing on the *logical form* of statements and arguments, i.e. the result of replacing variable terms – which stand for *variables*: roughly, types of items, e.g. propositions – or other symbols available in a given logical system for all of a proposition's or argument's content terms, in accordance with the system's *formation rules*, i.e. rules for formulating the system's well-formed formulas (see below).

Formal logic is not concerned merely with their *grammatical form*, i.e. the form the statements or arguments may have given the syntax of a particular natural language such as English or Spanish. For example, in propositional logic, the lowest level of analysis is *simple* or *atomic propositions*, i.e., semantically speaking, propositions that neither have propositions as components nor can be rephrased without redundancy by means of at least one component proposition. They contrast with *compound* or *molecular propositions*, i.e. those that have at least one component proposition or can be rephrased without redundancy by means of at least one component proposition. In this type of logic, the form of the proposition "All Greeks are human" is p. In predicate logic, which also investigates relations between some of the terms making up simple propositions – e.g. descriptive terms such as "Greeks" and "human," the form of the said proposition is $(x) (Gx {\supset} Mx)$. This is the form of a rephrasing of "All Greeks are human" – namely, "for anything, if it is a Greek, then it is human" – that is closer to its logical form: the form it would have in a language where all relevant relations of concern to the particular logical system are made plain.

One of the motivations for developing formal logic concerns *validity*, i.e. that feature of good deductive arguments whereby their form has the following characteristic: if all of the premises are true, then the conclusion must be true (see above). To be sure, logicians have developed the *method of logical analogy*, whereby an argument is tested by finding another argument that is of the same form but which is invalid. For, if the latter is not valid (in which case it is a *counterargument* or *counterinstance*), then the original argument is not valid either. Though very useful, however, this method *can only establish invalidity*. For if one fails to find a counterargument or counterinstance, one never knows whether this is because the original argument is valid or because one's imagination has failed to find an existing counterargument. By contrast, in formal logic, this limitation can be overcome, because formal logic devises methods for considering all possible counterarguments, most notably the *method of truth tables* (see below), which involves rules of combinatorial algebra. In doing this, formal logic develops in accordance with the *principle of logical form*: an argument is valid or invalid in virtue of its logical form (which is determined by the logical form of its constituent sentences).

Formulas

In formal logic, a formula is any combination of symbols in a logical system, and a well-formed formula (wff or woof) has the following characteristics: Either it is one of the individual formulas of a given logical system (e.g. *p*, *q*, *r*, and other such letters, with or without subscripts, designating individual propositions in propositional logic), or it is the result of combining those individual formulas by means of connectives of the system in accordance with the relevant rules of the system (e.g. $-p$, $p \& q$, pvq, and $p \supset q$ in propositional logic), or it is the result of combining any of the previously mentioned by means of the said connectives and such punctuation symbols as parenthesis and brackets in accordance with the relevant rules of the system, e.g. in propositional logic, one wff would be $p \supset (q \& r)$. A formula, sometimes also called a logical construction, may not be well formed, e.g. because it is an incomplete symbol or set of symbols, as in *pq* remains the same

when the order of the products is reversed resulting in *q&p*. This is made plain by truth tables: tabular displays associating arrangements of truth values – i.e. the values (in classical logic, two: T for true and F for false; but, broadly, also others, say, I for indeterminate) – with declarative sentences. Some basic

Negation	Conjunction
$-p$	$p \& q$
F T	T T T
T F	F F T
	T F F
	F F F

Inclusive disjunction	Material conditional
$p \lor q$	$p \supset q$
T T T	T T T
F T T	F T T
T T F	T F F
F F F	F T F

truth tables are:

Propositional logic

A kind of formal logic where truth tables play a central role is propositional logic (also called *sentential logic*, *sentential calculus*, and the *logic of statements*). It is that type of logic that deals with declarative sentences – or statements or declarative linguistic expressions, or propositions – whose basic components are themselves declarative sentences, statements, or expressions. It involves the distinction between atomic (or simple) statements or propositions and molecular (or compound) statements or propositions (see above).

Its grammar includes *connectives* (also called *sentential connectives* and *sentential operators*) (typically "and," "or," "if... then... ," and "not"); individual propositions symbolically designated with such letters as *p*, *q*, *r*, *s*, and *t* with or without subscripts, which stand for simple propositions (or, syntactically speaking, for propositions considered in disregard of their internal structure); and combinations of these with connectives or truth functional connectives to produce compound propositions (or, syntactically speaking, propositions whose internal structure is at least partially reproduced). Examples are: −*p* (*negation* or *denial*) – which stands for the ordinary language internal negation appearing inside a sentence as in "John is not sick" and the external negation as in "It is not the case that John is sick;" *p*&*q* (*conjunction*, also called *logical product*); *p*v*q* (*inclusive disjunction*, sometimes also called *logical sum*, though the British logician and mathematician George Boole (CE 1815–64) used the expression logical sum to denote the *exclusive disjunction*: either *p* or *q*, not both, and not neither; and *p*⊃*q* (*material conditional*, also called *material implication*), which stands for "if *p* then *q*," or "*p* only if *q*."

Also used are the *biconditional*, *p*≡*q*, which stands for "*p* if and only if *q*," or "*p* just in case *q*," or "*p* if *q*," and the *Sheffer stroke* (also called *Stroke notation*): *p*|*q*, which stands for the *Stroke function*: −(*p*&*q*), which is equivalent to −*p*&−*q*. The Stroke function, formulated by the Russian-born United States philosopher H.M. Stroke (CE 1883–1964), provided a symbol for an insight the United States philosopher Charles Sanders Peirce (CE 1839–1914) had and Stroke rediscovered: that the entire Boolean structure could be formulated by means of the single primitive "neither...nor...."

These connectives are called *truth-functional* connectives by analogy with the notion of a *mathematical function*: an operation such as *y*=*f*(*x*) that, when applied to an entity or set of entities called its argument(s) (e.g. *f*(*x*) where the argument is *x*), yields an entity – in our example, *y* – called the value of the function for that argument. It can be a *partial* function when it applies to some but not all, and a *total* function when it applies to all of the set or entities. A *truth function* is a *propositional function*, i.e. an operation that, when applied to an argument, yields a truth value as the value of that function for that argument. In all of these cases, there is a functional dependence between the arguments' values and the respective functions' values.

As indicated, truth values in classical logic are two: false (or falsity) and true (or truth). Other logics make room for additional truth values, e.g. undetermined, originating three-valued, or, if more (or, some would say, three or more) truth values are involved, multi-valued logics. In (classical) propositional logic, two sentences are materially equivalent provided they have the same truth value (i.e. are both true, or are both false), and logically equivalent provided each can be deduced from the other.

In propositional logic, the truth-functional connectives are associated with truth tables: tabular displays of truth values that the truth functions associated with the connectives take, given the truth values assigned to their arguments (see above). Given the definition of validity, for any argument in this logic, one can construct an associated conditional to the argument's from, i.e. a conditional resulting from placing, between brackets, the propositional form of each premise in conjunction with all the others, followed by the material conditional connective, and this by the form of the argument's conclusion.

Since, in a valid argument, when all premises are true, then the conclusion must be true, it follows that the associated conditional of a valid argument is true, regardless of what particular truth values each component proposition has, i.e. its is formally true or a tautology. This relation has elicited the method of truth tables for determining validity. It consists in finding the associated conditional for an argument's form, and then constructing a truth table for that conditional. The argument is valid when, and only when, the associated conditional is a tautology. For example, consider an argument of the form

p&*q*

hence *p*

Its associated conditional is (*p*&*q*)⊃*p*

This conditional's table is

(p & q) ⊃ p

T T T T T

F F T T F

T F F T T

F F F T F

1 2 3 4 5

Here, the truth values for the conjunction symbol are listed under the conjunction symbol (column 2), and are the values a conjunction would have given the respective values of its constituents (listed in columns 1 and 3). The values for the conditional are listed under the material conditional symbol (column 4), and are the values a material conditional would have given the respective values of their components (listed in columns 2 and 5). As column 5 indicates, the conditional is a tautology. Hence, the original argument is valid. Among the main laws of propositional logic are logical equivalences called *De Morgan's laws*, also called *De Morgan's theorems* and *distributive laws*. They are:

$$\sim (p \ \& \ q) \supset (\sim p \ v \sim q),$$
$$\sim (p \ v \ q) \supset (\sim p \ \& \sim q),$$
$$\sim (\sim p \sim q) \equiv (p \ v \ q),$$

and $\sim (\sim p \ v \sim q) \equiv (p \ \& \ q)$; but, sometimes, only the first two are thus called.

These equivalences concern syntax and make plain the *interdefinability of connectives*, i.e. that any one connective can be defined in terms of combinations of others. They should not be confused with examples of *semantic equivalence*, the feature statements have when they can replace each other without changes in meaning.

The *rules of inference* or *rules of reasoning* – i.e. rules for proceeding validly from premises to conclusions – of propositional logic apply to particular connectives. They include:

double negation introduction (or rule of double negation): p, hence $--p$
double negation elimination (also called *rule of double negation*): $--p$, hence p
conjunction introduction (or rule of conjunction): p, q, hence $p\&q$
conjunction elimination (or rule of simplification): $p\&q$, hence p;
also, $p\&q$, hence q
disjunction introduction (or rule of addition): p, hence pvq
disjunction elimination: pvq, $p\supset r$, $q\supset r$, hence r
material conditional introduction: p therefore q, hence $p\supset q$
material conditional elimination in two forms: (1) *modus ponens*: $p\supset q$, p, hence q; and (2) *modus tollens*: $p\supset q$, $-q$, hence $-p$
negation introduction: p therefore $r\&-r$, hence $-p$
negation elimination: $-p$ therefore $r\&-r$, hence p

A more complex principle is, for example, *exportation*: $[(p\&q)\supset r] \equiv [p\supset (q\supset r)]$. Another is *Peirce's law*: $((p\supset q)\supset p)\supset q$.

Negation elimination and negation introduction exemplify what is called, following Aristotle (384–322 BCE) an *indirect proof*, i.e. a proof using a subproof and, in particular, of *reductio ad absurdum*, i.e. a proof that assumes a hypothesis in the subproof, infers a contradiction from it, and, on this basis, concludes, on the main proof, that the subproof's hypothesis must be false and its contradictory true. A related type of indirect proof – which some consider a particular version of *reductio ad absurdum* (on the assumption that the impossible can be shown only by showing it is or involves a contradiction) – is *reductio ad impossibile* (Latin for "reduction to the impossible"), i.e. a proof that assumes a hypothesis in the subproof, infers the impossible from it, and, on this basis, concludes, on the main proof, that the subproof's hypothesis must be false and its contradictory true. By contrast with indirect proof, Aristotle talked of *ostensive syllogism* or *ostensive proof*. Today, the expression *direct proof* is used to denote ostensive syllogisms and any other proofs that do not include a subproof.

Predicate logic
A logic modernly developed through an enrichment of propositional logic with additional vocabulary, syntax, and rules of inference is predicate logic, also called *functional calculus* and the *logic of classes* (or, when it concerns only one-variable formulas, *lower functional calculus*, *first-order logic*, *elementary-quantification logic*, and *restricted-quantification logic*). In Antiquity, the logic of classes was first developed by the Greek philosopher Aristotle, who studied the syllogism. The theory of the syllogism was further developed by ancient as well as medieval logicians and, in this work, is treated as an independent entry (see SYLLO-GISM).

Predicate logic focuses on declarative sentences – or declarative linguistic expressions – that include such connectives as "all," "any," "every," "a," "each," "some," "there is," and "there exists." These terms are rendered through the use of two quantifiers: the *universal quantifier* – (x), meaning for all x – and the *existential quantifier* – $(\exists x)$, meaning there is at least one x. Predicate logic also uses individual variables such as v, w, x, y, z with or without subscripts; individual constants a, b, c with or without subscripts; and predicate letters, $A, B, \ldots, F, \ldots Z$ with or without subscripts. Each such letter with or without subscript stands for a *predicate*, which here is not, as in Aristotelian logic, what is affirmed or denied of a subject; but, as in modern logic, what is affirmed or denied of an individual (in first-order predicate logic) and, in higher-order predicate logic, what stands for properties, relations, functions, or classes of individual objects. All of these symbols can be combined to formulate universal propositions or propositions of a universal form (e.g. $(\exists x)Ax$), and existential propositions or propositions of the existential form (e.g. $(\exists x)Ax$).

The individual constants just mentioned should not be confused with logical constants, i.e. with symbols denoting connectives such as $-, v, \&$. These are contraposed to those symbols that constitute expressions such as terms and predicates, which stand for content.

A *closed sentence* (whose opposite is an *open sentence*) is also called a *closed formula* (whose opposite is an *open formula*). It is characterized on the basis of the notion of a *free occurrence*, i.e. an occurrence of a variable such that assigning a value to the variable is necessary for the formula containing the variable to acquire meaning (where a *value* of a variable is an entity assigned to it). Given this, to say that a sentence or formula is closed is to say that it has no free occurrences of variables. To say that it is open is to say that it has at least one such free occurrence or that there is a free variable – i.e. a variable not falling under the scope of a quantifier – in it. Predicate logic is also called functional calculus because its formulas are regarded as representing functions in the calculus. In this regard, the variables in these formulas are called *functors*, i.e. that which functions.

Quantification, i.e. the application of one or more quantifiers to an open sentence, can be referential and substitutional. In *referential* quantification, only referential terms such as nouns and pronouns can be replaced by variables. While in *substitutional* quantification, any terms – e.g. also terms denoting relations – can be replaced by variables. Referential quantification is a kind of objectual quantification, where the truth of a quantification sentence depends on the values of the variables bound by its quantifiers. While in substitutable quantification, the truth of a quantification sentence depends on whether the sentences resulting from replacing its variables by their substituends are true.

Predicate logic includes the rules of inference of propositional logic plus:

existential generalization (also called *existential introduction*): from Aa, infer $(\exists x)\,Ax$;
existential instantiation (also called *existential elimination*): from $(\exists x)\,Ax$, infer Aa, if Aa can be inferred from an instance Ay of $(\exists x)\,Ax$, provided that the constant a does not occur in any premise or in any previous A-formula of the argument;
universal instantiation (also called *universal elimination*): from $(x)\,Ax$, infer Aa;
universal generalization (also called *universal introduction*): infer $(x)\,Ax$ from Aa, provided that the formula Aa can be inferred when the variable a does not previously occur in the argument (hence it could be any individual).

Logic and philosophy of logic
Logics are divided into *first-* and *higher-order* logics. The former are logics that contain only variables for individual object; while second- and higher-order logics also contain variables for properties, relations, functions, or classes of individual objects. The study of the relation between and respective implications of first- and higher-order logics falls under the *philosophy of logic*, or *philosophical logic*, a study whose subject matter is very close to that of formal logic, but goes beyond codifying valid arguments and supplying logical systems or logistic systems, or combinations of artificial languages (the logical grammar of each one of which is constituted by its vocabulary or primitive – i.e. underived – symbols, rules of syntax, and rules of semantics), axioms, and

rules of inference for assessing complex arguments. Philosophical logic also examines the basic elements of such systems and attempts to clarify and assess the formalizations they involve.

An important theorem in first-order logic is the *compactness theorem*: if every finite subset of a given theory T is consistent, then the whole theory is consistent. This is an immediate result from the *completeness theorem*, because if the theory were not consistent, then a contradiction could be proved in it, and since proofs are finite, it would use a finite subset of axioms from the theory.

Another significant theorem is *Craig's interpolation theorem*, according to which, if a sentence Φ of first-order logic entails a sentence Ψ, then there is an *interpolant*, a sentence Φ in the vocabulary common to Φ and Ψ that entails Φ and is entailed by Ψ.

An additional theorem is the *cut-elimination theorem*, according to which a certain type of inference rule – which includes *modus ponens* – is unnecessary in classical logic. This was proved with a *sequent calculus*, i.e. a deductive system including rules for statements about derivability. It includes the *cut-rule*: " Given that C yields D or M, and that C together with M yields D, we can infer that C yields D," which was called the cut-rule because it cuts the middle formula M. The proof involved showing that the predicate calculus – of which the sequent calculus was an adequate formalization – did everything the sequent calculus did, hence the cut rule was unnecessary.

Additional logical systems

Additional logics can be developed by further enriching the previously discussed logical systems. For example, a logic that expands the syntax of first-order logic by adding operators of various degrees, and that also expands the corresponding semantics accordingly, is the *operator theory of adverbs*. This theory treats adverbs and other predicate modifiers as operators that form predicates of predicates. For example, in "the stone falls rapidly to the ground," there is a one-place predicate, "falls," which applies to the stone, a zero-place operator, "rapidly" and a one-place operator "to ( )," which applies to "the ground" (which fills the area between parentheses). Formulated in terms of its logical structure, the sentence reads: [to (the floor) [rapidly [falls (the stone)]]].

Another type of logic is *modal logic*, characterized by including the operators "it is possible that," symbolized by $\Diamond$, and "it is necessary that," symbolized by $\Box$. To say that what a declarative sentence means is possible, or $\Diamond p$, is to say that it is not necessarily false, or $-\Box-p$. Also, to say that what a declarative sentence means is necessary, or $\Box p$, is to say that its negation is not possible, or $-\Diamond-p$.

In scholastic discussions of modal propositions, a distinction was drawn between *modus*, i.e. what today is called a *modal operator*, and *dictum*, i.e. the proposition modified by the modus. For example, in "It is impossible that Socrates is not Greek," the modus is "It is impossible that" and the dictum is "Socrates is not Greek." In this case, the modus is affirmative, while the dictum is negative. Accordingly, scholastic logicians classified modal propositions in four categories: A, i.e. affirmative modus and affirmative dictum; E, i.e. affirmative modus and negative dictum; I, i.e. negative modus and affirmative dictum; and U (or O), i.e. negative modus and negative dictum.

The United States philosopher Charles Sanders Peirce (CE 1839–1914) invented a system of logic graphs called *existential graphs* involving some notions of possible worlds used in the semantics of modal logic. Between the 1930s and 1950s, various axiomatic systems for necessity and possibility were proposed in this general area of possible-worlds semantics; but it was very difficult to answer questions about these systems. The contemporary United States philosopher Saul Kripke formulated an alternative approach now called *Kripke semantics* or *relational semantics*. It was more natural than the other systems and conceived of the relation of *accessibility* or *relative possibility* – a binary relation R on the non-empty set W of possible worlds, so that a pair (W,R) is a frame for a sentential language with the operators for necessity and possibility – as a relation among mathematically primitive possible worlds. It led to interpretations of a variety of modal systems, becoming standard. In this type of logic, *semantic consequence* is defined as follows: to say that a set of sentences S semantically entails a sentence s, is to say that no interpretation I makes all members of the set S true and, yet, makes the sentence s false.

A kind of expressions largely ignored in traditional logic but extensively studied in modern semantics is that of *indexicals*: expressions whose meaning is partly determined by characteristics of the context of utterance. Examples of indexicals are personal pronouns such as "I" and "you," and demonstratives such as "now" and "today." The contemporary United States philosoper David Kaplan, for example, has argued that indexical singular terms are directly referential and a species of rigid designator (see REFERENCE).

Another type of formal logic is *epistemic logic*: the logic that studies such concepts as knowledge, reasonable belief, justification, and evidence. It has been formalized on the model of modal logic by means of such epistemic operators as the epistemic plausibility operator "it is plausible that," and the knowledge operator "it is known that." Adding the notion of *epistemic possibility* (that of being compatible with all that someone knows), the related epistemic possibility operator "it is compatible with all that someone knows," and the knowledge operator to quantificational logic with identity, makes it possible to study the relations between quantifiers and epistemic operators.

Next, there is *erotetic logic*, i.e. the logic of questions. Various approaches exist, among them: the *Platonic* approach – questions exist independently of interrogatives; the *possible-world* approach – questions as functions of possible worlds; and the *epistemic-imperative* approach – questions combine epistemic with imperative sentences of the form "make it the case that I know...." In a broader sense, "erotetic" denotes what concerns speech act and response, including not just question and answer, but such combinations as assertion and agreement or denial; and command and compliance or non-compliance.

There is also *free logic*, a special form of predicate logic, with or without identity, where not all singular terms – i.e. free variables and individual constants – need to denote something. This is done because applying a classical predicate logic to ordinary language leads to the counterintuitive result that apparently non-denoting terms such as Pegasus and the King of Argentina would denote something. Various proposals have been made to avoid this result. The German mathematician and philosopher Gottlob Frege (CE 1848–1925), for example, proposed the *chosen-object theory*: to assign an arbitrary denotation to each non-denoting term in a natural language. The English philosopher and mathematician Bertrand (Arthur Williams) Russell (CE 1872–1970) proposed the *description theory*: deny singular term status to most non-denoting terms in a natural language. Also, it has been proposed that the existential import of the existential quantifier be weakened, so that denotations are possible but not necessarily to actual objects. Free logic involves a more radical solution: to make room for non-denoting singular terms while preserving the existential import of the existential quantifier. This leads to the rejection of the existential generalization rule, so that, in free logic, one cannot infer that there exists a King of Argentina from the statement: "The King of Argentina plays polo."

Free logic also leads to changes in the truth conditions for sentences that include non-denoting terms. For example, a free logic may include *conventional semantics*, where the truth values of atomic sentences containing non-denoting terms are assigned by convention. It may include *outer-domain semantics*, where the non-denoting terms are treated separately as having non-existent denotations. Or it may include *supervaluational semantics*, where though the atomic components of a sentence may have no truth value, the sentence none the less has a truth value. For example, "The King of Argentina plays polo" and "The King of Argentina does not play polo" have no truth value; however, "The King of Argentina plays polo and the King of Argentina does not play polo" is false regardless of what specific truth value its component sentences have.

Further, formal logics traditionally disregarded such phenomena as vagueness, ambiguity, and time. Some formal logics have sought to take them into account. For example, *fuzzy logic* includes ambiguous or vague terms and a sentence can take any real number between 0 and 1 as a truth-value (against which the method of supervaluations or arbitrarily precising vague predicates has been advanced); *tense logic* (or dynamic logic, originally called the modal logic of programs) takes temporal differences into account. In this regard, the notion of future contingents or *futuribilia*, singular events or states of affairs that may, and, again, may not occur in the future, is discussed. In Ancient philosophy (e.g. in Aristotle's sea-battle example), they were thought to establish that not everything is fated to happen. In the Middle Ages, the Boethian–Thomistic position was that God could know future contingents because the flux of time was eternally present to him. Others, e.g. the Scottish philosopher John Duns Scotus (CE 1266–1308) argued that God contingently foreknew free acts. Still others – e.g. the Spanish philosopher Luis de Molina (CE 1535–1600) – argued that God knew what possible creatures would do in any possible situation. This line of inquiry remains alive in the philosophy of religion and logic today.

There is also *deontic logic*, i.e. the logic of obligation and permission, of which there are three main types. One is *standard* deontic logic, which results from adding the operators O, or "it ought to be that," and P, or "it is permissible that," to sentential logic, with the addition of the following axioms: $Op \equiv -P-p$, e.g. it is obligatory that I keep my word, if and only if it is not permissible that I do not keep it; $Op \supset -O-p$, e.g. if it is obligatory that I keep my word, then it is not obligatory that I do not keep it; $O(p \supset q) \supset (Op \supset Oq)$, e.g. if it is obligatory that if I keep my word then I be treated as undeserving punishment, then, if it is obligatory that I keep my word, then it is obligatory that I be treated as undeserving punishment; and OT, where T denotes any tautology.

A second type is dyadic deontic logic, whose operators are O, or "it ought to be that..., given that..." and P, or "it is permissible that..., given that...." These, plus the formalization of a statement of obligation $O(p/q)$ – understood as absolute if the conditions q describes are tautologous and as conditional if these conditions are better than they would ever be with p – plus a variety of axioms

involving the previous operators and relations, are added to sentential logic

A third type is *two-sorted* deontic logic, a type proposed by the Guatemalan philosopher Héctor Neri Castañeda (CE 1924–91), who distinguished between propositions – which can have truth values – and *practitions*, the contents of such things as commands, imperatives, and requests. Its operators are Oi, or "it is obligatory i that," Pi, or "it is permissible i that," Wi, or "it is wrong i that," and Li, or "it is optional i that," where i refers to any prima-facie obligatory, permissible, or optional action. Accordingly, for a certain practition A, $PiA \equiv -OiA$; $WiA \equiv Oi-A$; and $LiA \equiv (-OiA \& -Oi-A)$. Ol stands for an overriding obligation, i.e. not just prima facie but actual obligation.

Of particular interest here are the *paradoxes* of deontic logic, which result from using standard deontic logic formalizations to represent consistent English sentences expressing obligations or permissions. Consider the seemingly true and mutually consistent sentences:

1 Jim breaks a business contract.
2 If Jim breaks a business contract, then the courts ought to punish Jim for breaking a business contract.
3 It is obligatory that if Jim does not break a business contract, then the courts do not punish him for breaking it.
4 Jim ought not to break a business contract.

In standard deontic logic, they are formalized as follows:

1') p
2') $p \supset Oq$
3') $O(-p \supset -q)$
4') $O-p$

Here, 1') and 2') entail Oq. Also, 3') and one of the axioms of standard deontic theory previously mentioned entail $O-p \supset O-q$, which, together with 4'), entails $O-q$, which contradicts the previously derived Oq. Most logicians agree that this undermines standard deontic logic; however, it is still an open question whether and, if so, which other deontic logic can avoid the contradictory results just exemplified.

Hyperdeontic logics (or *logics of rules*) and other logics use *forcing*, i.e. a method of separating sets of sentences to ensure, for example, that a sentence A is not deducible from B, not-A is consistent with B, or a model B is not a model of A (all of this having for example the purpose of avoiding contradictions in the logic).

Another logic is *combinatory logic*: a branch of formal logic that studies the operations suitable to the construction and manipulation of functions as rules, e.g. as calculation rules, which can, but need not, have a limit, i.e. a maximum and/or a minimum value. Though originally developed with the aim of resolving foundational problems, combinatory logic is now studied because of its applications to computer science and linguistics. All systems of combinatory logic include the *application operation*: an operation whereby if f is a function and x a possible argument, then (f x) – a more convenient notation than f(x) in combinatory logic – is the result of the application operation. Once functions of one variable are introduced, and functions can be arguments, then the application operation serves to cover functions of more than one variable. In one combinatorial logic system, the new functions of the *lambda calculus*, also λ calculus (a system that has no constants and is equational, i.e. its only predicate is "="), can also be built by functional abstraction: If $a(x)$ is an expression built by application from constants and the variable x, then $a(x)$ defines a function – $(\lambda x.a(x))b=a(b)$. In this system, λ is the lambda operator and a lambda-term or λ term is always defined inductively by means of such clauses as: infinitely many variables are terms, any two of these combined are terms, and the application of λ to a term and a variable is a term, namely a lambda term.

A list of additional logics or names of logics already discussed follows.

Default logic is a formal system for reasoning developed by Raymond Reiter in 1980. Its defaults have the form "$P:MQ1,\ldots,MQn/R$" and read: "If P is believed and $Q1\ldots Qn$ are consistent with one's beliefs, then R may be believed." Discussions of default logic have addressed the concept of *defeasibility*: a property that some rules, principles, arguments, or pieces of reasoning have of being capable of being defeated by some alternative rule, princi-

ple, argument, or piece of reasoning. For example, the moral rule "One ought not to lie" is defeatable when another moral rule – say, "One ought not to help commit murder" – overrides it, say, because if one did not lie in the circumstances, one would help commit murder.

Deviant logic is an area of logic whose systems differ from classical or standard logic while dealing with the same subject matter. For example, *intuitionist logic* rejects the law of excluded middle or *tertium non datur* and the interdefinability of quantifiers. *Infinitary logic* is the logic of expressions of infinite length, prompted, for example, by the fact that a notion as central to mathematics as finitude cannot be formulated by means of first-order logic, which is finitary.

Informal logic, or *practical logic*, is the area of logic that evaluates arguments in the context of everyday uses in natural languages.

Intensional logic is at part of deductive logic that deals with the validity or invalidity of arguments where this depends on strict difference or identity of meaning.

Logic of discovery: see ABDUCTION.

Logic of relations or *relational*: see RELATION.

Logic of validation: see ABDUCTION.

Many-valued logic is any logic that rejects the principle of excluded middle or *tertium non datur*.

Mathematical logic is another name for formal logic.

Matrix logic is the type of logic that attempts to extend the computational capabilities of logic bringing it closer to mathematics. It interprets Boolean logic connectives as matrix operators acting in two adjoining spaces of logic vectors. Also, it provides a mathematical formulation that makes room for many-valued logics.

Monotonic logic is any logic that meets the condition that for all statements p_1, p_2, $\ldots p_n r$, s, if $p_1, \ldots, p_n$ entails r, then, for any s, $p_1, \ldots p_n$, s entails r. *Non-monotonic logic* is any logic that does not meet this condition.

Ordinal logic is a means of associating a formal axiomatic system Sn with each constructive ordinal notation n in an effective and uniform manner. It was developed as an attempt at overcoming the incompleteness of formal systems; but it was proven that though an ordinal logic can be complete for true universal statements, it cannot at the same time be invariant in the sense that if the ordinal a is equal to the ordinal b, then the formal system S_a has the same consequences as the formal system S_b, where S_a and S_b respectively satisfy $S_{sc(a)}=S'_a$ and $S_{sc(b)}=S'_b$ and the union of the $S_{\{f\}(n)}$ where $\{f\}$ is an effective function for $n=0, 1, 2, \ldots$.

Quantum logic is the logic that has, as models, certain non-Boolean algebras derived from the mathematical representation of quantum mechanical systems. Quantum logics are different from classical logics depending on their formulation. Important in this area is *Gleason's theorem*, which entails that algebraic structure is not preserved by any partition of the dynamical features of a quantum system.

Relevance logic is a type of logic where contradictions are isolated in such a manner that they do not lead to questionable inferences. That is, *paraconsistency* – the property that one cannot derive all statements from a contradiction – characterizes relevance logic. This is of interest because inconsistent theories sometimes keep on being developed even after their inconsistencies have been recognized. At the same time, it brings out the contrast with classical logic, e.g. with the *spread law*: that from a contradiction anything follows.

Terminist logic was developed in European universities during the thirteenth century CE. Its aim was to help find the logical form of declarative sentences used in philosophical disputations, focusing on the properties of terms (see SYNCATEGOREMATA). An important tradition or school in logic is that of *Polish logic*. It uses distinctive – and very simple and clear – notation. For example, the Polish logician Jan Lukasiewicz (CE 1878–1956) uses the letter A to denote the inclusive disjunction, as in Apq. In the notation devised by the English philosopher Bertrand Russell (CE 1872–1970), this is formulated as $p \lor q$. Lukasiewicz uses the letter C to denote the material conditional, as in Cpq. In Russell's notation, this is formulated as $p \supset q$. Lukasiewicz uses the letter K to denote the conjunction, as in Kpq; while in Russell's notation, this is formulated as $p \& q$. Lukasiewicz uses the letter N to denote the negation, as in Np; while in Russell's notation, this is formulated as $\sim q$.

See also: argument; philosophy of mathematics; set; syllogism

Further reading
Braybrooke, David, Brown, Bryson, and Schotch, Peter K. (1996) *Logic on the Track of Social Change*, Oxford, UK: Clarendon Press.

Castañeda, Héctor-Neri (1975) *Thinking and Doing*, Dordrecht, Holland and Boston, USA: Reidel.

Copi, Irving M. and Cohen, Carl (1994) *Introduction to Logic*, New York: Macmillan.

Haller, Rudolf (1986) *Non-existence and Predication*, Amsterdam: Rodopi.

Jacquette, Dale (1996) *Meinongian Logic: the Semantics of Existence and Nonexistence*, Berlin and New York: W. de Gruyter.

Kneale, William and Kneale, Martha (1962) *The Development of Logic*, Oxford: Oxford University Press.

Lukasiewicz, Jan (1988 [1851]) *Aristotle's Syllogistic from the Standpoint of Modern Formal Logic*, Oxford: Clarendon Press.

NMELP '96 (1997) *Non-Monotonic Extensions of Logic Programming: Second International Workshop, NMELP '96, Bad Honnef, Germany, September 5–6, 1996: Selected Papers*, Berlin and New York: Springer.

Quine, W.V. (1970) *Philosophy of Logic*, Englewood Cliffs, NJ: Prentice Hall.

Scholz, Heinrich (1961) *Concise History of Logic*, New York: Philosophical Library.

Stern, August (1988) *Matrix Logic*, Amsterdam, Holland and New York, USA: North Holland.

Strawson, P.F. (1952) *Introduction to Logical Theory*, London: Methuen.

Wolfram, Sybil (1989) *Philosophical Logic: An Introduction*, London and New York: Routledge.

logical A good number of noun-phrases involving the adjective *logical* designate notions involved in one or more logics and accounts involving applications of one or more aspects of logic. Among them are as follows.

Logical atomism: see EMPIRICISM.

Logical behaviorism: see BEHAVIORISM; PHILOSOPHY OF MIND.

Logical certainty: see CERTAINTY.

Logical consequence: see LOGIC.

Logical constant: see LOGIC.

Logical construction: see LOGIC.

Logical dependence is a relation whereby some item(s) cannot be known, understood, or exist unless some other item(s) are respectively known, understood, or exist. Otherwise, it is independence. A special case of independence is that of a set of hypotheses being *irredundant*, i.e. each hypothesis in the set is independent of the others. When the dependence relation concerns knowledge, it is called *epistemic* dependence. For example, to know that the oak tree smashed the car one must know, say, that the oak tree is large, heavy, and fell on the car. When dependence concerns understanding, it is called *conceptual* dependence. For example, to understand the concept bachelor, one must understand the concept male. When dependence concerns existence, it is called *ontological* dependence. For example, for a shadow cast on a surface to exist, the surface must exist. When a dependence relation is not reciprocal – e.g. a shadow cast on a surface cannot exist without the surface, while the surface can exist without a shadow cast on it – then the relation is called a *priority relation*. The expression logical priority is sometimes used to mean either epistemic, conceptual, or ontological dependence.

Logical empiricism: see EMPIRICISM.

Logical form: see LOGIC.

Logical form, principle of: see LOGIC.

Logical forms as essences: see PHENOMENOLOGY.

Logical grammar: see LOGIC; PHILOSOPHY OF LANGUAGE.

Logical graph: see LOGIC.

Logical immediacy: see KNOWLEDGE.

Logical implication: see LOGIC.

Logical independence: see EPISTEMOLOGY; logical dependence (above); PROBABILITY.

Logical indicator: see ARGUMENT.

Logical proper name: see REFERENCE.

Logical mechanism: see COMPUTER THEORY.

Logical necessity: see ANALYTIC–SYNTHETIC DISTINCTION; *de re* (under *de*).

Logical notation: see LOGIC.

Logical paradoxes: see LOGIC.

Logical positivism: see EMPIRICISM.

Logical priority: see EPISTEMOLOGY; LOGIC.

Logical probability: see PROBABILITY.

Logical product: see LOGIC.

Logical reconstruction: see EMPIRICISM.

Logical sum: see LOGIC.

Logical syntax: see LOGIC.

Logical system: see LOGIC.

Logical table of judgments: see KANTIAN PHILOSOPHY.

Logical truth, linguistic theory of: see TRUTH.

See also: logic

Further reading

Faudree, Ralph (1995) *Independence, Domination, Irredundance, and Forbidden Pairs*, Orsay, France: Université Paris-Sud, Centre d'Orsay, Laboratoire de Recherche en Informatique.

Geiger, Dan (1989) *Logical and Algorithmic Properties of Independence and Their Application to Bayesian Networks*, Los Angeles, CA: UCLA, Computer Science Dept.

Golumbic, Martin Charles (1990) *Advances in Artificial Intelligence: Natural Language and Knowledge-Based Systems*, New York: Springer-Verlag.

Logicians/Dialecticians School *see* Chinese philosophy

logicism *see* philosophy of mathematics

logistic system *see* logic

logocentric *see* deconstruction

logoi *see* deconstruction

logos *see* Greek philosophy

loka *see* Jainism

lokayāta *see* cārvāka

loneliness *see* diaspora

loop *see* computer theory; cybernetics

Lorenz attractor *see* philosophy of mathematics

lottery paradox *see* justification; paradox

love From the Middle English *lov(i)en* and this, from the Old English *lufian*, a cognate of the Old Frigian *luvia*, the Old High German *lobōn*, and the Latin *lubēre*, which later became *libēre*: "to please." In Latin, the terms for love are *amor* and *caritas*. In Greek, the main terms for love are *philia*, *eros*, and *agape*. *Philia* came to be understood as the type of love involved in friendship. In Chinese, the term for love is, in some of its senses, the term *jen*, variously translated as kindness, humanity, benevolence, altruism, goodness, and perfect virtue; but whose literal meaning is "man in society." Mohism in China advocated the doctrine of universal love, where love was understood as love for the world. While Confucianism's notion of love denotes both an ethical ideal for all humans, and the feature of having an emotive concern for all living things. In this latter sense, *jen* is aimed to humans generally, and is arguably stronger than *philia*, which is directed to particular persons involved in the interpersonal relation of friendship where they, as individuals, are crucial both as objects and subjects of the love friendship involves. On the other hand, *jen* is not identical with *caritas* and *agape*, which denote a higher or selfless type of love: a freely given gift. As for *amor* and *eros*, they are the type of love involving desire.

The Greek philosopher Empedocles (*c.* 495–*c.* 435 BCE) was the first philosopher to use the notion of love in a cosmic sense, in introducing the complementary notions of *philia* (in this case, love understood merely as a principle of attraction) and *neixos* (strife understood as a principle of repulsion) in order to explain motion and the universe. However, the Greek philosopher Plato (428–348 BCE) gave the notion of love wide philosophical currency, referring to it in many dialogues. For example, he had his teacher, the Greek philosopher Socrates, say in the *Symposium* (177e) that all love (*eros*) is love of beauty and its perfect form is the love of the abstract form of beauty itself. That is, Plato envisioned a range of instances of love, from the mere love of a beautiful body, through the love of a beautiful body and its form, what since the Renaissance came to be called *Platonic love*: the perfect love where a beautiful body is loved for the sake of its form, beauty. The Greek philosopher Aristotle (384–322 BCE) continued this line of thought as the desire of the imperfect for the perfect. Also, in his ethical works,

Aristotle developed the notion of love as friendship based on rationality and noetic actualization, but also engaging the emotions of friends that concern the pleasant, and the useful.

As for love in the sense of *agape* and *caritas*, it appears to have originated in the common meals or love feasts of early Christians, and means a freely given gift or unselfish love for all people. It led to the doctrine of *agapism*, i.e. that love is the chief virtue and actions are good or right to the extent they manifest it. The paradigmatic case of *agape* is that of God becoming human and allowing for His own sacrifice – a gift constituting a favor humans could not possibly return – in order to lift them from the state of original sin from which they could not lift themselves by anything they could do. This is not, as in the Platonic and Aristotelian views previously discussed, simply the seeking of perfection by the imperfect. Rather, it is more of a dialectical act whereby what is perfect, God, seeks the imperfection of becoming human, in order to make room for the hope of perfection for humans, though some would argue that, in doing this, God is actualizing His own perfection to the utmost. In return, love and awe is what humans should feel for God.

Later Christian writers also incorporated the Greek notion of love as *philia* or as a special kind of *eros*: a desire for perfection in the form of the love of God. This can be found in the writings of the philosopher Augustine (CE 354–430; born in the North African city of Thagaste) and in those of the philosopher Aquinas (CE 1225–74; born near the city of Naples, in what is now Italy), though the latter made room for *caritas*, a kind of supernatural love that required something like the grace of God to be displayed.

During the Italian Renaissance, members of the *Florentine Academy* – e.g. the Figine-born Marcilio Ficino (CE 1433–99), Lisbon-born Leon Hebreo (*c.* CE 1460–1520), and the Naples-born Giordano Bruno (CE 1548–1600) – showed an increased interest in the Platonic version of love with regard to persons other than God. Later, the Jewish philosopher of Spanish and Portuguese descent Baruch Spinoza (CE 1632–77) kept the notion of the love for God alive with his view that the intellectual love of God is the highest end of humans and allows them to live under the aspect of eternity.

In modern and contemporary times, there have been various attempts at characterizing love. One view – e.g. that of the French writer Stendhal or Marie Henri Beyle (CE 1783–1842) – characterizes love as a merely subjective phenomenon taking place in the individual who loves and not necessarily related to any features of the person loved. This is the modern version of love in the expression "love is blind." Another view – e.g. that of the Spanish philosopher José Ortega y Gasset (CE 1883–1953) – characterizes love as a human, indeed a literary, invention. There are, however, other, less subjectivist views of love. One is that love results from psychophysiological or merely physiological processes. Arguably, this view has a family resemblance to that of the medical psychologist and founder of modern psychoanalysis Sigmund Freud (CE 1856–1939), who held that *eros*, or sexual satisfaction, is the core of love, and that human history is a struggle between *eros* or the wish for sexual satisfaction, and *thanatos*, or the death wish (see PSYCHOANALYSIS).

Finally, there have been phenomenological interpretations of love. Notable among these is the position of the German philosopher Max Scheler (CE 1874–1928), who held that love is an intentional process whereby an individual values a loved one as a personal act of selection, not as an arbitrary act and, hence, cannot be reduced to, or explained merely by, appeal to physiological or psychological events. This position has been generalized to many aspects of human life by the Spanish philosopher Joaquín Xirau (CE 1895–1946), who considered love to be the highest genus and basis of the universe's structure. By contrast, the French philosopher Jean-Paul Sartre (CE 1905–80) focused on what he took to be the conflict central to love: one wants to be loved freely but, at the same time, not contingently by another person. Sartre holds that this absence of contingency would undermine the freedom of the loved one. However, this is a problem only if one does not accept the

contingent – however strong and permanent – character of love. Finally, along less dramatic or metaphysical or strictly personal lines, the Mexican philosopher Antonio Caso (CE 1883–1946), who pursued a phenomenological approach in expanding the positivist conception of experience, argued that love understood as charity is a governing principle of human existence that builds on other principles, such as that of economy and that of disinterest. This ties in with discussions of love one finds in ethics, for example in Aristotelian ethics, as well as in such consequentialist ethical theories as *altruism*, which invariably gives priority to the good of others over one's own, and *utilitarianism*, whose central principle is one of beneficence and whose motivating factor arguably is, at least historically, benevolence.

See also: ethics; Greek philosophy; philosophy; pragmatism

Further reading

Caso, Antonio (1987) *La existencia como economía, como disinterés y como caridad*, Mexico: Universidad Nacional Autonóma de México: Instituto Politécnico Nacional.

Lear, Jonathan (1998 [1990]) *Love and Its Place in Nature: A Philosophical Interpretation of Freudian Psychoanalysis*, New Haven, CT: Yale University Press.

Liang, Sheng (1997) *Chien ai: Hsin Mo hsüeh = Universal Love: Neo-Mohism*, Livingston, NJ: HEYE.

Price, A.W. (1997 [1989]) *Love and Friendship in Plato and Aristotle*, Oxford and New York: Clarendon Press and Oxford University Press.

Sartre, Jean-Paul (1993) *Being and Nothingness: A Phenomenological Essay on Ontology*, New York: Washington Square Press.

Scheler, Max (1985) *Wesen und Formen der Sympathie*, Bonn: Bouvier Verlag.

Stern-Gillet, Suzanne (1995) *Aristotle's Philosophy of Friendship*, Albany: SUNY Press.

Löwenheim–Skolem theorem *see* logic

lower functional calculus *see* logic

luddites *see* philosophy, sociopolitical

Lullism *see* ars *magna*, under ars

lumen gratiae *see* enlightenment

lumen naturae *see* Cartesianism; enlightenment

lumen naturale *see* Cartesianism; enlightenment

Lyceum *see* Aristotelianism

M

M *see* syllogism

Ma'ase Bereshith *see* Jewish philosophy

Ma'ase Merkabah *see* Jewish philosophy

Machiavellianism *see* philosophy, sociopolitical

machine-state functionalism *see* computer theory; philosophy of mind

Mach's principle *see* philosophy of science

M'Naghten rule *see* philosophy of law

macrocosm *see* metaphysics

macrolevel *see* philosophy, sociopolitical

macrosocietal *see* philosophy, sociopolitical

madhhab *see* Arabic philosophy

madhyamā-pratipad *see* Buddhism

Mā-dhyamika *see* Buddhism

madrasah Literally meaning a "place of study," this term designated a school of higher study in the Islamic world. Its higher-study ranking presupposed that its students had memorized the entire Quran. Its curriculum included the liberal arts *trivium* (grammar, logic, and rhetoric), as well as law, mathematics, literature, history, higher-level grammar, and subjects of specific Islamic concern such as the calculation of prayer times, Quranic exegesis, and chanting. Sometimes, the curriculum also included medicine and agronomy.

In practice, the *madrasah* was largely a place where students resided, because instruction was normally given in the mosque. The typical layout of a *madrasah* included a central courtyard, a prayer hall, and small rooms that the students occupied.

The *madrasah* was a model for the development of universities in Europe. Indeed, in the *madrasah*, such traditions originated as the undergraduate–graduate studies division, the practice of giving a certificate to students at the end of their years of studies, and the practice of wearing black university gowns (which were worn in learned disputations in Fāṭimid Egypt).

The funds required to build *madrasahs* (the Arabic plural is *madāris*) came from different sources. Some were built with money from political leaders, who also provided small pensions for students. Others were built with funds from merchant and craft guilds. One of the earliest and most famous was founded by the 'Abbāsid caliph al Ma'mūn (CE 813–33), who regularly presided over unusually bold theological and philosophical disputations, himself wrote various treatises and, in CE 830, established the *Bait al-Ḥikma* ("House of Wisdom"), also called the *School of Baghdad*: an institute – including a library – devoted to translation and research.

In later times, the Fāṭimids – under whose aegis, the Shī'a movement had attained open political success – promoted the building of *madrasahs* for propagandist purposes, thus founding, for example, the mosque-school al-Azhar in Cairo, which later turned into a Sunnī institution and, until today, is reputed to be the greatest traditional Islamic university in the world. On the other hand, Sunnī Muslims counteracted the Fāṭimid theological threat by establishing *madrasas* of their own.

See also: philosophy of education

Further reading
Al-Radi, Selma M.S. (1997) *The "Amiriya in Rada": The History and Restoration of a Sixteenth-Century Madrasa in the Yemen*, Oxford and New York: Oxford University Press for the Board of the Faculty of Oriental Studies.
Makdisi, George (1991) *Religion, Law and Learning in Classical Islam*, Hampshire, UK and Brookfield, UT: Variorum.
Nashshabah, Hisham (1989) *Muslim Educational Institutions: A General Survey Followed by a Monographic Study of al- Madrasah al-Mustansiriyah in Baghdad*, Beirut: Librairie du Liban.
Walls, Archibald G. (1990) *Geometry and Architecture in Islamic Jerusalem: A Study of the Ashrafiyya*, London, UK: Scorpion Publishing Ltd, World of Islam Festival Trust.

Madrid School A group of philosophical authors that the contemporary Spanish philosopher Julián Marías proposed be called *Escuela de Madrid* ("Madrid School") and characterized as having been produced in response to the thought of the Spanish philosopher José Ortega y Gasset (CE 1883–1955). This response need not be one of agreement or further development of Ortega's ideas. The only requirement to count as part of the Madrid School is that of having taken part in the movement of philosophical renovation initiated and advocated by Ortega y Gasset, and having held, as he did, that Spanish philosophical thought should be brought up to the level of the times. Besides Julián Marías himself, various philosophers are cited as part of the Madrid School. One is Manuel García Morente (CE 1888–1942), who initially upheld a position influenced by the Marburg neo-Kantian tradition but, later, under Ortega's influence, moved closer to the philosophy of vital reason. In criticizing Hegelianism, as well as positivism and naturalism, he elaborated a distinction between *process*, as merely mechanical and natural, and *progress*, as involving value discovery and appropriation. He also

attempted to overcome the realism–idealism dichotomy.

Another philosopher mentioned as a member of the Madrid School is Xavier Zubiri (CE 1898–1983), who held largely existentialist views, introducing the notion of *religación*, which has been transliterated into English as *religation* – an inborn sense of obligation to fulfill a certain task in the world – as a replacement for the Heideggerian notion of *being hurled* (*geworfen*) into the world. Still another is José Gaos (CE 1900–69), who, after teaching in Madrid, moved to Mexico. He focused on philosophical activity and, in particular, on the philosophy of philosophy, which he characterizes as not a branch of philosophy, but a part of philosophical inquiry that makes plain the personal nature of philosophizing. As well as these, there is the contemporary philosopher José Luis Aranguren, who formulated the notions of *temple*, understood as the emotive state whereby one feels in a certain way concerning oneself and the world (which can be manifested physiologically, psychologically, or existentially), and *talante*, a more comprehensive emotive state that affects all the manifestations of *temple* in a person. There is also the contemporary philosopher Pedro Laín Entralgo, who taught and wrote about the history of medicine and, in philosophy, formulated conceptions of hope and the other that include but are not reducible to mere biology or psychology.

The Madrid School also includes other philosophers who also were active elsewhere. One is Joaquín Xirau (CE 1895–1946), who was also a member of the *School of Barcelona*. In studying the relation between being and value, he argued that they do not exist as merely objective or merely subjective, but in a reality, where, as in the intimacy of love, which is also factual, subjectivity does not exclude objectivity.

See also: existentialism; Kantian philosophy; Latin American philosophy

Further reading
Gray, Rockwell (1989) *The Imperative of Modernity: An Intellectual Biography of José Ortega y Gasset*, Berkeley: University of California Press.
Marías, Julián (1959) *La escuela de Madrid:*

estudios de filosofía española, Buenos Aires: Emecé.

magic *see* theurgy

magnitude *see* measurement

Mahābhārata *see* Hinduism

mahā-bhūta *see* Hinduism

mahat *see* Hinduism

mahāvākya *see* Hinduism

Mahāyāna Buddhism *see* Buddhism

maieutic *see* Socratic philosophy

maitrī *see* Buddhism

maitrī-karunā *see* Buddhism

major premise *see* syllogism

major term *see* syllogism

mala *see* avidyā

male bias *see* feminist philosophy

male–female dichotomy *see* feminist philosophy

male privilege *see* feminist philosophy

man *see* human nature

mana *see* Māori philosophy

management *see* ethics

manaḥ *see* Hinduism

manana *see* Hinduism

mandala *see* theurgy

Mani *see* myth

Manichaeanism *see* myth

manifest content *see* psychoanalysis

manifold *see* Kantian philosophy

manipulation *see* philosophy, sociopolitical

manu *see* Hinduism; myth

many questions, fallacy of *see* fallacy

many-valued logic *see* logic

Māori philosophy The philosophical ideas of the Māori people about ethics and metaphysics as they are recorded and transmitted in tradi-tional Māori narratives and proverbs, whose philosophical significance has attracted the attention of practitioners of ethnophilosophy and anthropology. The Māori philosophical ideas and the manner in which they are recorded and transmitted make plain the close association existing between Māori literature – i.e. oral literature – and Māori ethics and metaphysics.

Notable among Māori ideas is that of balancing opposing interests and ideals. Māori ideas recurrently point to equally real and significant polar opposites in the areas of ethics and metaphysics, and to the fact or, in ethics, the need for finding some mode of coexistence between these opposites. Some of these pairs of polar opposites are: light and dark, life and death, male and female. They, as pairs, are part and parcel of human perfection. Whenever conflicts arise (in or among people, or between people and their environment), they are attrib-uted to a lack of balance between the opposites belonging to a pair. Accordingly, the resolution of the conflict is conceived as a way of bring-ing about the missing balance, never as a way of eliminating one component of the pair for the sake of the other.

A crucial concept in achieving this balance among the Māori is *tapu*, which functions as a protective device. Something becomes *tapu* as a result of being imbued with *mana* or status (some would say spiritual status), hence there is a prohibition against defiling it – e.g. through alcohol abuse – and an obligation to treat it with respect. One's body is *tapu*; strictly speaking, it is personal *tapu*. This means that, ideally, no one can be simply dismissed as worthless, even though seniority and rank are part of the Māori conception of social life. In fact, just as in Western societies, Māori society often fell far short of treating others with such respect, certainly between, and sometimes even within, tribal groups.

Entities other than persons are *tapu* as well, and deserve respect. For example, the harakeke (*Phormium tenax*), or New Zealand flax, is a material traditionally used by the Māori in weaving, and treated as deserving respect. In the case of weaving, the respect for the materials is to be manifested in creating a beautiful object.

The basis for this respect is associated with the fact that harakeke is believed to descend from the great god Tāne-mahuta, from which the Māori also descend through Tāne's breathing life into the first woman and producing the Māori with her. This association is a basis for Māori self-esteem or *Maoritanga*, and is interpreted in such a way that not just the Māori or all humans, but all materials, have *mauri* or a *wairua*, i.e. a sort of life force – though in no way implying animism – or character in them. In fact, all components of the environment – from plants and animals, through humans (both individually and through *whanaunga-tanga*, i.e. as bound together by tribal ties, kinship, and family responsibility), to houses, harbors, rivers, canoes, and mountains – share this character. Given this, though using them is permissible, the use must be respectful, i.e. a worthy use that, according to the Māori, must enhance them. Among the Māori, this belief in a life force in non-humans manifests itself in a spiritual conception of work, while the belief in a life force in all humans and, especially, in those around us, manifests itself in whanaungatanga. Indeed, for the Māori, one is responsible not just for what is under one's control, but for all of one's kin. Thus, those in positions of authority, the *rangatira*, can discharge their individual and collective responsibility the most.

The belief in mauri in all non-human entities is taken to entail a radical obligation. In fact, even hostile things, such as disease-causing organisms, must be respected. Here again, the notion of balance comes in. If Dutch Elm disease attacks – as it did – the elms in New Haven, Connecticut (the Elm City), then attacking the organism causing the disease is not right. What is right, or *tika*, is to attempt to restore the balance, e.g. as it was also done by developing elms resistant to the disease and planting them where the old ones used to be.

This notion of balance is also present in the manner in which the Māori deal with *kino*, i.e. ugly situations, and *pai*, good situations. Balance is here manifested in terms of reciprocity or fitting responses. When there is peace, one should act peacefully; but, when at war, one will have to face up to the ugliness of the situation and do some ugly things oneself. In the latter type of situation, *utu*, which is not identical with, but, in this case, would take the form of retaliation, is often considered unavoidable. Indeed, since there are many degrees of conflict, though *utu* may be unavoidable or the only fitting response to an offense, it need not always or for the most part involve bloodshed.

See also: baskets of knowledge

Further reading
Patterson, John (1992) *Exploring Maori Values*, Palmerston North, New Zealand: The Dunmore Press.
Sharp, Andrew (1997) *Justice and the Maori: The Philosophy and Practice of Maori Claims in New Zealand since the 1970s*, 2nd edn, Auckland and New York: Oxford University Press.

Maoritanga *see* Māori philosophy

maqām *see* Ṣūfism

Marburg School *see* Kantian philosophy

mārga *see* Hinduism

marginal utility *see* philosophy of economics; utilitarianism

market *see* ethics; philosophy of economics

marriage *see* feminist philosophy

Marxism A family of philosophies derived from the writings of the German philosopher Karl Marx (CE 1818–83). It has become common practice to extend use of the term Marxism to cover the writings of Karl Marx as well – an extension Marx would have rejected, since he considered his writings to be scientific, not philosophical. Yet, Marx's conception of what counts as scientific appears to have fallen significantly outside of what counts as scientific today. At any rate, aware of the ideas of certain French writers who described their works as Marxist, Marx declared himself not to be a Marxist.

As for the developments that led to Marxism, after the death of the German philosopher Georg Wilhelm Friedrich Hegel, most of his followers were interested in adapting his views to Christian thinking. This began to change with the works of the so called Young Hegelians, D.F. Strauss (CE 1808–74), Ludwig

Feuerbach (CE 1804–72), Bruno Bauer (CE 1809–82), and Arnold Ruge (CE 1803–80), who focused on Hegel's historical accounts of religion, and expanded Hegel's account of human productivity, eventually, with the most famous Young Hegelian, Karl Marx, focusing on labor. Marx, however, distanced himself from the Post-Hegelian approaches of other Young Hegelians. This is evident in such books as *The Holy Family*, where he favors the radicalism of the labor movement; *The German Ideology*, where he emphasizes the importance of class distinctions; and *The Poverty of Philosophy*, where he points out the limitations of philosophy in helping formulate workable rather than abstract and irrelevant conceptions of socialism. In referring to this period in Marx's development, some scholars talk of *the young Marx*, whom they consider more philosophically alert, though doctrinally less independent than the later Marx, the author of *Capital*. This exegetical approach was adopted in various publications, for example, by the Algeria-born French philosopher Louis Althusser (CE 1918–90), and constitutes one of the great variety of exegetical approaches (see below) that Marx's followers have adopted.

At any rate, Marx never wrote a systematic account of his thought, which changed significantly through time and was not merely philosophical but also partly economic, sociological and historical in nature. Further, Marx's writings were specifically concerned with Western capitalist developments of his time and, in one of his letters, he expressly warned against interpreting his writings as accounting for the necessary development of every society. Within the said interpretive constraints, however, there are core components of Marx's thought.

One of these is the understanding of human labor as the source of economic value, and *labor power* as a special type of commodity in a commodity exchange system, hence contrasted with work: the exertion of effort to produce something whether or not in an exchange system. In this system, given the established division of labor, labor produces more exchange value than it costs employers as subsistence wages. This is the *theory of surplus value*, which brings out the fact that treating

humans as sources of profit-generating commodities may, and sometimes does, conflict with treating them as persons.

Such situations in which people were treated merely as means to economic ends were a source of indignation for Marx not just in his early writings, but even in his less moralistic *Capital*, as well as a reason for proposing the alternative socialist, and communist forms of social organization. He saw workers in a capitalist system suffering from three forms of *alienation*. First, they are alienated from the products of their labor, which are commodities alien to them. This and workers' isolation as egoistic market agents, prompts workers to seek to control commodities by acquiring them, though, in effect, commodities take control of workers lives – a phenomenon Marx called the *fetishism of commodities*. Second, workers are alienated from their basic activity in life, labor, which they have sold for wages. Third, workers are alienated from other humans in being reduced to isolated individuals seeking to satisfy their own self-interested wants alone.

In searching for a way out of the previous situation, Marx formulated a variety of views. Predominant among them is the doctrine of *historical materialism*. This is the doctrine that the economic structure of society is the foundation of society and that, as the productive forces develop, the economic structure changes, thereby changing such other aspects of society as political, legal, moral, religious, and philosophical ideas, which constitute society's superstructure. Though it has become a central part of Marxism that the said changes occur through a process of *class-struggle* (in particular, a struggle between the proletariat or underclass and other classes), Marx only briefly commented on this mechanism. However, by contrast with societies with familiar forms of government, Marxism advocates the eventual institution of *communism* – the self-perpetuating party rule in a class-less society.

Marx's influence has been extensive though, as previously indicated, not always welcomed by Marx himself. Even his contemporary, Friedrich Engels (CE 1820–95), who co-authored with Marx such books as *The German Ideology* and *The Communist Manifesto*, independently authored works that significantly depart from Marx's ideas. One such work is *Dialectics of Nature*, a book published after Engels's death that, though considered a Marxist text, is highly concerned with the articulation of the dialectical method in nature, a topic largely, if not entirely, absent in Marx's works. Indeed, Engels, not Marx, articulated the dialectical method. Also, later in his life, Vladimir Ilich Lenin (CE 1870–1924), the Russian political leader and creator of Soviet *dialectical materialism*, a significant influence in Russian philosophy, concluded in his *Philosophical Notebooks* that, given the until then unacknowledged connections between Hegel's *Science of Logic* and Marx's *Capital*, Marxists had misunderstood Marx.

At any rate, Marxism developed in Revolutionary Russia and, later, in the Soviet Union, around the notion that Marxism was the uniquely true worldview. This position, called *Orthodox Marxism*, was supported by Lenin in his *Materialism and Empiriocriticism*, where he also advocated the copy theory of knowledge according to which true concepts, like photographs, mirror reality. This position became entrenched when Joseph V. Stalin (CE 1879–1953) ruled as Secretary General of the Soviet Communist Party, which, under Stalin's rule, was designated as the supreme interpreter of the interests of the working class, hence instituting totalitarian rule.

Many thinkers, though sympathetic to Marx's and Marxist ideas, rejected Orthodox Marxism, constituting what is sometimes called *Western Marxism* or *neo-Marxism*: a range of approaches whose fidelity to Marx's thought varies greatly from one approach to another. Among them were the Hungarian Georg Lukács (CE 1885–1971), the members of the FRANKFURT SCHOOL, the Praxis School of Yugoslav philosophers, the existentialist French philosopher Jean-Paul Sartre (CE 1905–80) in his later period, and the Italian philosopher Antonio Gramsci (CE 1891–1937).

The latter is noted for emphasizing the role of cultural factors in determining what is dominant at given times. Along these lines, he developed the concept of *hegemony*, from the Greek *hegemon* ("leader" or "ruler"). It denotes the total domination of the middle class,

not only politically and economically but in the realm of ideas: people's minds. Hence, they take the dominant social order to be a matter of common sense and never question it. According to Gramsci, this hegemonic control is never totally secure; there is always room for resistance and subversive cultural work.

The *Frankfurt School* aimed at rethinking Marxism in the aftermath of the Russian Revolution. In the process, its members developed a *critical theory of society*, i.e. an effort to continue the Marxist transformation of moral philosophy into a social and political critique while rejecting the dogmatic aspect of Orthodox Marxism.

As for the *Praxis School* mentioned above, it received its name from its journal *Praxis*. This term derives from the Greek, *prasso* (i.e. "doing," "acting"), and was initially used in philosophy by the Greek philosopher Aristotle (BCE 384–322), for whom praxis denoted the sphere of thought and action involving the ethical and political life. It contrasted with *theoria*, i.e. the inquiry into matters of epistemology and logic. This is how praxis came to mean practice by contrast with THEORY.

In Marxism, these two spheres are not radically separate. Instead, praxis denotes the interactions and interconnections between practical and theoretical concerns and activities. Its starting point is that of practical concerns that precede both theoretical inquiry and the mere application of theory to the world. Further, in explaining historical developments Marxism traditionally appealed to forms of production. The Praxis School focused on this theory–practice relationship and the way in which and extent to which forms of production help explain historical developments.

See also: Frankfurt School; idealism; Marxism

Further reading

Althusser, Louis (1997) *Reading Capital*, London and New York: Verso.
Mandel, Ernest (1994) *The Place of Marxism in History*, Atlantic Highlands, NJ: Humanities Press.
Schirmacher, Wolfgang (1999) *German 20th-Century Philosophy: The Frankfurt School*, New York: Continuum.

Tucker, Robert (1972) *The Marx–Engels Reader*, New York: Norton.
—— (1967) *Philosophy and Myth in Karl Marx*, Cambridge, UK: Cambridge University Press.

masculine *see* gender

mass noun *see* natural kind

master argument *see* Greek philosophy

master morality *see* ethics

material cause *see* causal law

material conditional *see* logic

material equivalence *see* logic

material implication *see* logic

materialism, central-state *see* philosophy of mind

materialism, dialectical *see* Marxism

materialism, emergent *see* philosophy of mind

materialism, historical *see* Marxism

materialism, non-reductive *see* philosophy of mind

maternal thinking *see* feminist philosophy

mathematical analysis *see* philosophy of mathematics

mathematical constructivism *see* philosophy of mathematics

mathematical function *see* logic

mathematical induction *see* induction

mathematical intuitionism *see* logic

mathematical logic *see* logic

mathematical space *see* philosophy of science

mathematics, philosophy of *see* logic; philosophy of mathematics

matriarchal *see* feminist philosophy

matriarchy *see* feminist philosophy

matrilineal *see* feminist philosophy

matrilocality *see* feminist philosophy

matrix mechanics *see* philosophy of science

matter *see* metaphysics; philosophy of science

matter, prime *see* Aristotelianism

matter, principle of the conservation of *see* philosophy of science

mauri *see* Māori philosophy

maxim *see* ethics; Kantian philosophy

maximal consistent set *see* set

maximin rule *see* justice

maximization *see* decision

māyā *see* Hinduism

mean *see* Chinese philosophy; ethics

meaning In a communication context, a purport, sense, or significance of a symbol or combination of symbols in a language or of non-linguistic symbols, or signals. In a non-communication context, the importance or significance of something, as in the meaning of life. Meaningfulness is the feature of being meaningful, i.e. of having meaning in one of the previously described senses of meaning. When a term has more than one meaning, it is frequently said that it has more than one sense.

Kinds of meaning
There are various kinds of meaning. *Conventional* meaning is the meaning an expression or sentence commonly has in a language under given-use conditions. Its opposite is *stipulative* meaning, i.e. the non-conventional meaning an expression or sentence is given regardless of any use conditions. *Literal* meaning is the non-figurative meaning an expression or sentence commonly has in a language under given-use conditions. *Synonymy* is sameness of literal meaning between two or more terms or sentences. The opposite of literal meaning is *figurative* or *metaphorical* meaning, where metaphorical is the adjective associated with metaphor, from the Greek *meta* ("beyond" or "over") and *pherein* ("to bring," "bear," or "carry"). Specifically, *metaphor* is one of the four figures of speech. The other three involve some type of non-literal substitution: *metonymy* (the effect for the cause); *synecdoche* (the part of the whole or vice versa); and *irony* (the contrary meaning to that intended). A metaphor, rather than substitutions, involves

non-literal identifications, e.g. "the clouds slept madly."

The term meaning is sometimes used to denote a *language user's* meaning or *speaker's* meaning, or *utterer's* meaning; that is, what the person means to communicate in using a particular linguistic expression. This may or may not coincide with the expression's conventional meaning(s). In formulating, say, moral problems, and proposed solutions to them, some philosophers use the expression *operant* meaning to denote the meaning – whether conventional or not – terms being used have in the context in which the problems addressed arise.

A distinction widely used in ethics is that between *cognitive* meaning, i.e. what a term or sentence denotes or describes (e.g. an object, fact, event, or state of affairs) and *emotive* meaning or *expressive* meaning, i.e. what a term or sentence expresses (e.g. a feeling or an attitude). In addition, there is *prescriptive* meaning, i.e. what a term or sentence prescribes, recommends, or commands.

Some philosophers have argued that ethical terms and sentences have only emotive or prescriptive, never cognitive meaning. On this view, for example, the sentence "murder is wrong," would mean only something like "Murdering: boohoo!" or "Murdering: never do it!" Others acknowledge the emotive element in ethical language, but argue that it is accompanied by a cognitive component as well. Against this view, it is argued that such a situation is peculiar to ethics or, at most, to evaluative language, but not part of descriptive sentences such as those of science. Yet, this reply is countered with analysis of descriptive language where both components are present. For example, the sentence "Neutrinos exist" is interpreted as including an emotive and a cognitive component in the expression "Neutrinos existing: yes!"

Meaning and reference

Various theories of meaning have been formulated to characterize the general nature and scope of meaning. The oldest is the *idea theory* of meaning or *ideational theory* of meaning, or *image theory* of meaning. It holds that the meaning of words in public language derives from the ideas or mental images that words are used to express. Some of these theories locate the meaning of terms or sentences entirely in thought as mental content. Others, by contrast, at least partly locate the meaning of terms or sentences in overt speech or even in social practices as linguistic conventions. Among those holding the latter, some argue that mental content is entirely unnecessary, while others hold that both mental content and linguistic conventions are necessary and none can exist without the other.

In the 1970s, the contemporary United States philosopher Hilary Putnam argued against such theories of meaning by means of the *Twin-Earth case*, which is about a planet just like Earth, except that there is no H_2O on Twin-Earth but, instead, XYZ. So, even if Twin-Earth inhabitants use the term water, they mean XYZ: Twin-water, not H_2O by it. By means of this case, Putnam argued against the idea theory of meaning (or ideational theory of meaning or image theory of meaning). For, according to Putnam, the case showed that at least some meanings are partly determined by things other than those, like concepts or ideas, that belong in our mental life.

An equally old theory of meaning is the *referential* theory of meaning, according to which the meaning of a linguistic expression is somehow connected to what the expression is about or its reference. To understand this view, one must keep in mind that meaning is sometimes divided into two contrasting notions: *reference* or *denotative meaning* or *denotation*, or extension – what terms are about or that to which terms point – and *descriptive meaning* or *connotation*, or *intention* – what terms describe or the set of attributes implied by the term.

These are not recent distinctions. Arabic philosophers distinguished between *first understanding* – that is of things – and *second understanding* – that is of the understanding of things – and, later, scholastic philosophers distinguished between *terms of first intention*, which refer to things, and *terms of second intention*, which refer to terms of first intention. In the twentieth century, this distinction was revived in the notion of *intentionality*, whereby all mental phenomena point to objects whose mode of existence, since some of them are mythical, is intentional inexistence, i.e. they exist only as purported objects of intentions. There are, of course, mixed uses of the notions just discussed. The English philosopher Bertrand Russell (CE 1872–1970), for example, used the expression denoting concept to indicate something with a meaning that also denotes.

In the context of the relations between meaning and reference, philosophers have formulated the notion of a *meaning postulate*: a sentence that specifies the entire, or part of the, meaning of a predicate by specifying how the referents of predicates are interconnected as a result of the meaning of those predicates. Such sentences include, but are not restricted to, contextual, recursive, and explicit definitions, as well as reduction sentences for such predicates as soluble.

Meaning and truth

Whatever the general nature of meaning turns out to be, there are different theories concerning the way in which the meaning of a particular term or sentence should be specified. Tarskian semantics, for example, which was formulated by the Polish-American mathematician and logician Alfred Tarski (CE 1901–83), regards semantics or the theory of meaning as the study of a language's expressions and the objects to which they refer. This theory deals with the problem of truth through an analysis of the truth predicate *true* that is used to characterize sentences. The resulting type of theory – *truth-conditional theory of meaning* or *truth-conditional semantics*, or *truth value semantics* – holds (on one of the various versions of these theories) that specifying the meaning of a term or sentence must involve the specification of truth conditions. For example, in specifying the meaning of the sentence "some birds fly," one must specify, by means of a corresponding Tarskian biconditional, that "some birds fly" is true if and only if some birds indeed fly (see TRUTH; USE–MENTION DISTINCTION).

On another version, truth conditional theories of meaning hold that the proposition expressed by the term or sentence must be specified, e.g. it must be specified that the meaning of the sentence "some birds fly" is

that some birds fly. The contemporary United States philosopher Donald Davidson has followed Tarski in formulating the convention *T* as follows: the sentence s of *L* is true if and only if *p*. Here, *s* is a sentence of a language *L* and *p* is a statement to be verified in the object language, e.g. that birds fly. Davidson calls a sentence governed by the said convention a *T*-sentence.

Tarski also used the notion of satisfaction in order to define truth recursively for languages that include quantifiers. *Satisfaction* is a relation holding between an open formula such as chimpanzee$_x$ and an object – say, the chimpanzee called Washa – whenever the formula applies to an object. Now, an open formula cannot be true or false and, therefore, its truth or falsity cannot be used to characterize the truth or falsity of sentences whose quantifiers range over the open formula. However, its being in a satisfaction relation with an object can be used for this purpose.

In applying truth-conditional theories of meaning to natural languages, Donald Davidson introduced a *principle of charity* that applies to interpretations: interpreting a person means making the best possible sense of that person, and this means assigning meanings to what the person says that maximize its overall truth. Thus, *epistemic charity* implies that, if a sentence *s* is true in a person's language if, and only if, some chicken swim, then that tells us the meaning of the sentence *s* in that person's language.

Meaning and use

By contrast with truth-conditional theories of meaning, such as those just described, other philosophers have formulated *assertability theories of meaning* and *conceptual-role theories of meaning* or *conceptual-role semantics*. The former require that assertability conditions must be specified, e.g. it must be specified that one can assert the sentence "birds fly" if and only if one sees some birds flying, hears reports of some birds flying, or the like. This is a descendant of the early twentieth-century *verification theory of meaning*, which said the meaning of a sentence is the conditions under which it can be verified or established to be true.

Finally, conceptual-role theories of meaning require a translation based on identity of use or conceptual role in one's own language, e.g. if one's own language were Spanish, "some birds fly" could be accordingly translated by means of the sentence "*algunos pájaros vuelan.*" However, the conceptual-role theory of meaning or conceptual-role semantics typically supposes that we think in the language of thought and the said translation is between the language of thought and the public language, say English.

Both assertibility-condition and conceptual-role theories of meaning are often called *use theories of meaning*. A concept that has become influential in discussions of use theories is that of a *language game*, which involves a wide variety of interpersonal uses of language between which there are family resemblances, but which do not involve sets of necessary and sufficient conditions that make a language game precisely definable.

Meaning, holism, atomism, and nihilism

The preceding discussion raises a question that concerns meaning-construction: Can terms have meanings independently of other terms in the sentence where they appear, of the entire sentence where they appear, or even of other terms and sentences in the language to which they belong? Whether they can is a problem about which opinions have differed. Theories that specify meanings in the first two ways just described tend to adopt the doctrine of the *compositionality of meaning* or *semantic compositionality*: the meaning of a sentence entirely results from the meaning of its components and its structure. Further, concerning the meaning of the terms, those who think they can have meaning independently of other terms in the sentences where they appear, the entire sentences where they appear, and other terms and sentences in the language, believe that the basic semantic relation is between a term or concept and the item to which it applies. This position is called *semantic atomism* and is held by such contemporary United States philosophers as Fred Dretske, Jerry Fodor, Ruth Millikan, and Dennis Stampe.

One of its opposites is *semantic holism*: the doctrine that the meaning of an expression in a language is determined by the meaning of every other expression in that language. Another is *semantic molecularism*: the doctrine

that the meaning of an expression in a language is determined by the meaning of other expressions – but not of every other expression – in that language. In addition, opposed to all these views is *semantic nihilism*: the doctrine that words lack meanings and there are no mental states, hence, strictly speaking, agents do not mean anything in using words.

Going back to the compositionality of meaning, one explanation of it was provided by the *picture theory of meaning*, according to which a declarative sentence is a picture of a possible state of affairs, where the sentence's terms correspond to components of the state of affairs and the sentence's structure corresponds to the arrangement of components in the state of affairs the sentence pictures.

A different view was formulated by the German mathematician and logician (Friedrich Ludwig) Gottlob Frege (CE 1848–1925) in *The Foundations of Arithmetic*, where he cryptically stated his *context principle*: only in the context of a sentence does a word have a meaning. This leans toward meaning holism or semantic holism. In general, conceptual-role theories lean in the direction of meaning holism or semantic holism.

Meaning and translation

A question meaning holism prompts is: "Can different persons' use of the same words have the same meaning?" Another question is: "Can terms common to different theories have the same meaning?" The answer to these questions depends on whether some of a term's conceptual connections are more significant for determining its meaning than others. On a radical meaning-holism view, they are not.

This has led to formulating the *indeterminacy of translation thesis*, which has two versions, both applying to *radical translation*, i.e. a situation in which a field linguist has to translate an until now entirely unknown language. The *strong thesis* concerns the indeterminacy of theoretical sentences as wholes. It says that, in the radical translation situation, one could construct manuals for translating the new, source-language into the translator's target-language, in a manner consistent with all behavioral data; however, the manuals could still diverge in the target-language sentences chosen to the extent of these being mutually inconsistent. The *weak thesis* concerns the indeterminacy of reference or inscrutability of reference. It says that, given all possible behavioral data, divergent target-language interpretations of source-language words could offset one another so as to support different target-language translations, and no further data of any kind could serve to establish that one such interpretation is the correct one.

Speaker's meaning, disposition, implicature, and presupposition

As previously stated, the term meaning is sometimes used to denote a language user's (or speaker's) meaning; that is, what the person means to communicate in using a particular linguistic expression. Since this does not always coincide with the conventional meaning of linguistic expressions or, for that matter, with what normally the speaker would mean to communicate in using the expression, some philosophers have formulated a *dispositional theory of meaning*. On it, an expression's meaning is what the speaker would mean to communicate with it given such conditions as the speaker's state of mind, and knowledge.

Along these lines, others have formulated a *pragmatic theory of meaning* that goes beyond what is sometimes called *teacherese*: book cases of grammatically and logically impeccable linguistic constructions. The pragmatic theory of meaning thus makes room for *conversational implicature*. This is the linguistic performance whereby, in response to "I'm out of flour," one says "There is a grocery store around the corner." Though the latter does not entail that the grocery store is open and has flour for sale, it can be said that it conversationally implies it.

This notion is different from that of *presupposition*, which has two meanings: one semantic, the other pragmatic. Semantically, to say that a sentence *S* presupposes another sentence *S'* is to say two things. First, if the sentence is a statement (e.g. "the King of Argentina is old"), then it and its negation entail *S'* (there is a king of Argentina). Second, if the sentence is a question (e.g. "did you bring your little brother?", then both an affirmative and a negative answer to it entail *S'* ("you have a little brother"). Pragmatically, not sentences, but sentence-users make presup-

positions in using them. To say that the user of a sentence *S* presupposes *B* in using it is to say that *B* is a belief or set of beliefs the user holds in using the sentence. For example, in asking others "Isn't the king of Argentina unusual?", the believer believes both that there is a king of Argentina and knows some of the king's features, and that the others also believe there is one and know some of his features. This notion of pragmatic presupposition, like that of conversational implicature, displays a concern with formulating a theory of meaning that is true to the richness of linguistic usage. This concern has also led to the *phenomenological theory of meaning*, where the emphasis is placed on linguistic and communication experiences.

Meaning and information

Rather than focusing on the speaker, some philosophers and linguists have focused on information and its conveyance in the *information theory* or *communication theory*. This is mainly a mathematical theory of communication, but has been applied by various contemporary philosophers, most notably Fred Dretske, to develop a semantic theory of information and meaning or information-theoretic semantics. This focuses on how events (signals) acquire meaning understood as a message or messages, and how the latter – which can be understood as mental states – can be traced to their origin(s) in the environment.

Non-Western theories of meaning

Theories of meaning have not been confined to Western philosophy. In Indian philosophy, various types of meaning are discussed. An important concept in this regard is that of *lakṣaṇā* or secondary meaning, which replaces the primary meaning of a term when it does not fit well in the context. One type, for example, is *jahdad-ajahal-lakṣaṇā* (exclusive-nonexclusive implication), a linguistic use in which only part of the primary meaning of a term is retained. For example, in the identity statement "this is that dog," the term "this" refers to an item and connotes present time and place, while the term "that" refers to the same item and connotes some other time or place; however, both connotations are left out, retaining only the reference to the item denoted in the identity statement. This is how Advaita-Vedānta philosophers obtain the meaning of identity statements.

Another type is *jahdad-lakṣaṇā* (exclusive implication), sometimes also called *kevala-lakṣaṇā* (bare implication), a linguistic use in which a meaning entirely other than the primary meaning of a term is retained. For example, in saying "the cottage on the creek," the primary meaning of "creek" is entirely replaced by, for example, shore, which, none the less, is an actual component of the creek.

A third type is *ajahal-lakṣaṇā* (non-exclusive implication), a linguistic use where the primary meaning is retained with the addition of a secondary one, as when "the red is cozy" is used meaning "the red house is cozy," thus retaining the primary meaning of "red" but adds that of "house" as its secondary meaning.

Finally, a fourth type is *lakṣita-lakṣaṇā* (implied implication), as in "the girl is a gazelle," where "gazelle" is used metaphorically to indicate speed and slenderness, features that are not components of a gazelle, though they can be attributed to some, indeed, frequently, to most of them.

These notions are connected with that of *sāmānya*, i.e. generality, class, concept, or genus, in *sāmānya-lakṣaṇā*, or relation by generality or class nature, a kind of implication whereby, in perceiving a particular patch, say, a green patch, one perceives the general property, in the said example, greenness, associated with it.

See also: philosophy of language; reference

Further reading

Black, Max (1954) *Models and Metaphor*, Ithaca: Cornell University Press.

Erwin, Edward (1970) *The Concept of Meaninglessness*, Baltimore and London: The Johns Hopkins University Press.

Ganeri, Jonardon (1999) *Semantic Powers: Meaning and the Means of Knowing in Classical Indian Philosophy*, New York: Clarendon Press.

Hare, R.M. (1964) *The Language of Morals*, New York: Oxford University Press.

Johnson, Mark (ed.) (1981) *Philosophical Perspectives on Metaphor*, Minneapolis: University of Minnesota Press.

Kazmi, Ali A. (1998) *Meaning and Reference*, Calgary, Alberta: University of Calgary Press.

Searle, John R. (1998) *Mind, Language and Society: Philosophy in the Real World*, New York, NY: Basic Books.

Urmson, J.O. (1968) *The Emotive Theory of Ethics*, London: Hutchinson.

meaningful *see* meaning

meaningfulness *see* meaning

means–ends continuum *see* pragmatism

measurement The assignment of numbers to variable properties of objects or processes in such a manner that the numbers correspond to degrees of the said properties. A measurable property or *magnitude* (or dimension or, in what can be called the *indefinite sense* of the term quantity, its quantity), say, length, can be ordered by a comparative relation, so that an object having this property can be said to be longer than (or shorter than, or as long as) another. That is, the object can be said to have more length than (or less length than, or as much length as) another. Its particular length is, in what can be called the *particular sense* of the term quantity, the particular quantity of its length.

Not all properties are measurable. For example, blue and red are both colors, but they are not degrees of color: It makes no sense to say that red has more color than blue. To be sure, colors can have measurable properties such as brightness, but though this makes color brightness a measurable property, it does not make color a measurable property.

The theory of measurement studies the conditions of measurement. Measurement is of magnitudes. Older writings on this subject distinguish between two types of magnitude: *intensive* magnitude, which involves no operation corresponding to addition, and *extensive* magnitude, which involves addition. In a somewhat parallel manner, contemporary works distinguish between the *topological* and the *metrical* conditions of measurement. Topologically, the measurement of a magnitude M must satisfy the relations of *asymmetry*, transitivity, and C-connectedness. To say that two items a and b are in a relation of asymmetry with regard to the magnitude M is to say that if aMb, then it is not the case that bMa. To say that three items *a*, *b*, and *c* are in a *transitivity* relation with regard to the magnitude *M* is to say that if *aMb* and *bMc*, then *aMc*. To say that two objects *a* and *b* are in a *C-connectedness* relation with regard to the magnitude *M* is to say that either *aMb* or *bMa*, or *aCb*, where *C* means that *a* and *b* coincide with regard to the measured magnitude.

As for the metrical conditions of measurement, they include the previous ones plus the condition that the magnitude measured be *additive*, i.e. that there is a physical joining operation of objects *a* and *b* whereby the value of the magnitude *M* resulting from the joining of *a* and *b* be equal to the arithmetic sum of the value of *M* that *a* has and the value of *M* that *b* has.

If these conditions are satisfied for a given *empirical relational system* (i.e. a system defined by an operation, say, weighing two objects with the same scale), then, according to the representation theorem, there is a corresponding numerical relational system which is a numerical image of the empirical system. Also, according to the *uniqueness theorem*, for a specific empirical relational system, there is a specific type of numerical image, e.g. on a ratio scale or on an interval scale (see below).

An additional concept crucial to measurement is *derived* measurement, i.e. the measurement of additive magnitudes on the basis of laws whereby the derived magnitude – say density – is explicitly definable in terms of the values of the dependent and independent variables in an associated functional equation, e.g. *W/V* in the case of density, where *W* denotes weight and *V* denotes volume.

In order to measure, various scale types are used – e.g. ratio scales, and interval scales – each one of which is characterized by specific scale transformations. A measurement is on a *ratio scale* whenever, for any measurement functions *f* and *g* for an empirical relational system *E*, there exists a real number $n > 0$ such that for any number *x* in the domain *D*, $f(x)=ng(x)$. Here, the function $h(x)=nx$ is the *scale transformation*.

By contrast, a measurement is on an *interval scale* whenever, for any measurement functions *f* and *g* for an empirical relational system *E*,

there is a number $n > 0$ and a number *m* in the domain *D* of real numbers, such that the functions are related by $f=ng+m$. Here, the function $h(x)=nx+m$ is the scale transformation.

For example, measurements of temperature without an absolute zero are on an interval scale, while measurements of one variable in relation to another – say, of density by reference to weight and volume – are on a ratio scale. Not all magnitudes are additive. Hence, with regard to them, only orderings based on topological conditions are possible.

See also: induction; philosophy of science

Further reading
Pap, Arthur (1969) *An Introduction to the Philosophy of Science*, New York: Free Press, Chapter 8.

mechanical jurisprudence *see* philosophy of law

mechanicism Derived from the Greek term *mechanē* ("machine"), in its philosophical use, this term has come to denote a wide family of views characterized by a commitment to one or more forms of naturalistic explanations, characteristically called mechanistic explanations (typically, though not always, because they are in terms of masses in motion like those in Newtonian mechanics). At one extreme of these views' range, there are those holding that only one type of naturalistic explanations is valid: those that explain phenomena by reference to masses in motion. These are exemplified by the type of explanations characterizing Newtonian physics, which has led to using the term Newtonian in general, as denoting the view that nature is a mechanical system structured in accordance with mathematical reason. At the other extreme, there are those holding that though valid explanations must be naturalistic, they may take many forms.

The main point of mechanicism is that of eliminating all forms of teleological explanations, in particular those pointing to final causes or vital causes. Views opposed to mechanicism go under the heading of *dynamism* from *dynamis* (or *dunamis*), meaning "power" or "energy," a notion used by various Greek philosophers. For example, Anaximander (*c.* 612–545 BCE) and Anaxagoras (*c.* 500–428 BCE) used it to explain the origins of the elements, while Aristotle (380–322 BCE) used it meaning potentiality in contrast to actuality (*energeia* or its near synonym *entelecheia*). More specifically, the term dynamism applies to the philosophy formulated by the Croatian physicist and philosopher Rudjer Josip Boscovich (CE 1711–87) in his *Theory of Natural Philosophy*, where he replaced atoms with point-like centers of force, thus removing any vestiges of mechanicism from Newtonian physics.

Towards the end of the nineteenth century, the German physical chemist Wilhelm Ostwald (CE 1853–1932) criticized predominant materialism and mechanicism, and formulated the doctrine of *energeticism*, also called *energism* and *energetism*: that energy is the fundamental substance underlying all change. Accordingly, he proposed the unified science of *energetics*, which could be based only on the notion of energy. A related position is that formulated by the United States philosopher J. Mark Baldwin (CE 1861–1934), who argued that the seeming irreducibility between the agenetic methods of mechanicism and the genetic methods of vitalism needs to be overcome and this can be done in aesthetics, where all aspects are included. This position was called *pancalism*.

The appeal of non-mechanistic explanations is that mechanicism appears to conflict with deeply entrenched beliefs scientists and non-scientists alike share about the intentional nature of human action. However, current studies of feedback mechanisms and their applications to the ecology of social behavior and individual development – e.g. the development of imagination in childhood – suggest ways of combining mechanistic and non-mechanistic views into a conception of nature and human action that gives its due to all concerns involved.

See also: biology; holism; philosophy of science; vitalism

Further reading
Cobb, Edith (1977) *The Ecology of Imagination in Childhood*, New York: Columbia University Press.
Iannone, A. Pablo (1999) *Philosophical Ecologies: Essays in Philosophy, Ecology, and Human Life*, Amherst, NY: Humanity Books.

Nagel, Ernest (1979) *Teleology Revisited and Other Essays in the Philosophy and History of Science*, New York: Columbia University Press.

mechanics *see* philosophy of science

mechanism, logical *see* computer theory

mechanistic explanation *see* explanation

media ethics *see* ethics

mediate inference *see* argument

mediation *see* philosophy, sociopolitical

medical ethics *see* ethics

medieval philosophy *see* Arabic philosophy; Aristotelianism; Jewish philosophy; Neoplatonism; Platonism; Scholasticism; Thomism

meditation *see* Buddhism; Hinduism; Zen

Megarians *see* Greek philosophy

meliorism *see* pragmatism

memory From the Middle English *memorie*, and this from the Latin *memoria*, this term still denotes – as it did in Latin – the state of retaining, or the capacity, faculty, or disposition of retaining or recalling items previously thought, perceived, or, in general, experienced. The act of recalling my first day in first grade is a *memory occurrence* or an *occurrent memory*, while the state of retaining and being able to recall it under suitable conditions is a *memory state*. This distinction was already present in the work of the Greek philosopher Plato (428–348 BCE), who discussed the difference between *mneme* ("memory") and *anamnesis* ("the act of recalling").

Two main questions arise concerning memory: "What type of entity is it?" "And can it be a basis for knowledge?" Different theories have been formulated concerning the first question. One is the *image theory* of memory. One version of it is that recalling a certain item is the same as having a mental image of a past experience, which has a special feature – perhaps its being a decayed image – which marks it off as being a *past* experience. This theory, however, cannot account for the experience people frequently have of recalling something, without being in any way aware of any feature in what they recall that helps them determine whether they are recalling or merely imagining it.

A contemporary successor of the image theory of memory is the *representational theory* of memory. It holds that to recall a certain item is to have some type of mental or even linguistic representation of it and, in addition, to have stored the information acquired about the said item without interruption since it was initially acquired. Yet, in recalling an e-mail address when one types it, one often does not have any mental or even linguistic representation of it in mind. One just types it, very much in the same way in which, in driving a car, one does not have – indeed, one better not have! – a mental or linguistic representation of each thing involved in driving it. Further, prompted by suitable circumstances (say a picture of a long forgotten toy), one might recall the toy after having ceased to store much, if not all, of the information initially acquired about it.

By contrast with theories of the previous types, some philosophers have advanced the *dispositional theory* of memory, according to which no representation of any kind is needed in order to recall. Dispositional theories, however, differ concerning whether the information recalled must have been continuously retained since initially acquired.

As for the previously formulated second question – i.e. whether memory can be a basis for knowledge – a variety of answers have been given. Some have argued that one must not only remember correctly, and be sure of it, but also know that one's memory of the particular item recalled is reliable. Others have argued that only accurate recall and certainty of recall are needed. Still others have argued that, besides accurate recall and certainty of recall, one must also not have any reason specific to the particular case of recall that raises questions about the reliability of one's memory of it.

However, the question arises whether one need have any such reason because there are none; or, though they exist, because one is unaware of them; or, though aware of them, because one does not recognize their force. The last two alternatives would seem to entail that one can recall an item so long as one is ignorant of available reasons for distrusting one's memory in the particular case. While the first alternative suggests one cannot recall an item unless there exist no reasons at all for distrusting one's memory in the particular case, however hard to discover they might be. A possibly fruitful line of inquiry in this regard would be that of studying the criteria the legal system uses to question the reliability of witnesses' memories. Another would be that of studying the criteria psychologists use to question the reliability of their human subject's memories.

In addition to the previously discussed and most influential theories of memory, there have been attempts at characterizing memory by appeal to machine models from computer theory and related areas of inquiry. This family of theories sometimes goes under the heading of the *machine theory* of memory.

The significance of the concept of memory is not exhausted by its relevance to knowledge. After all, memory is crucially associated with conceptions of personal identity. For example, they involve memory in the case of expatriates who, after many years abroad, may have no way of checking whether what they take to be memories about their homeland are fantasies or, indeed, memories. Memory is also crucial concerning the personal identity of the elderly who, like temporal expatriates of sorts, may have no way of checking what are their memories and what are their fantasies about, say, their childhood. These issues are not merely epistemological or metaphysical, but also moral, for example concerning matters of self-image, self-reliance, and self-esteem.

See also: knowledge; perception; philosophy of mind

Further reading

Bursen, Howard Alexander (1978) *Dismantling the Memory Machine: A Philosophical Investigation of Machine Theories of Memory*, Dordrecht and Boston: D. Reidel Pub. Co.

Malcolm, Norman (1975 [1963]) *Knowledge and Certainty: Essays and Lectures*, Ithaca: Cornell University Press.

Wyer, Robert S. (1995) *Knowledge and Memory: The Real Story*, Hillsdale,

New Jersey and Hove, UK: L. Erlbaum Associates.

Mendelian genetics *see* evolution

mens rea *see* philosophy of law

mental distinction *see* definition

mental representation *see* perception

mentalese *see* philosophy of mind

mentalism *see* philosophy of mind

mention *see* use–mention distinction

mercy *see* ethics

mereological essentialism *see* identity

mereological sum *see* metaphysics

mereology *see* metaphysics

merit *see* ethics; justice

meritarian *see* ethics; justice

meritarianism *see* ethics; justice

meritocracy *see* ethics; justice

meritorious *see* ethics

Merton School *see* Oxford movements

messianic *see* Judaism

messianism *see* Judaism

metaethical relativism *see* ethics

metaethics *see* ethics

metahistory *see* philosophy of history

metalanguage *see* use–mention distinction

metalogic *see* logic; philosophy of mathematics

metamathematics *see* philosophy of mathematics

metaphilosophy *see* philosophy

metaphor *see* meaning

metaphysical *see* metaphysics

metaphysical certainty *see* certainty

metaphysical holism *see* holism

metaphysical idealism *see* metaphysics

metaphysical libertarianism *see* determinism

metaphysical naturalism *see* metaphysics

metaphysical necessity *see* essentialism

metaphysical realism *see* metaphysics

metaphysics This term came from the position of an untitled book by the Greek philosopher Aristotle (384–322 BCE) in the classification of his works made by the Hellenic philosopher (see ARISTOTELIANISM) Andronicus of Rhodes (first century BCE). It meant "beyond physics," because the book appeared after Aristotle's *Physics*. It now means the philosophical study of the nature, constitution, and structure of reality, or of how things actually are, as contrasted with appearance, or how things seem to be to a particular perceiver or set of perceivers.

Reality and appearance
Sometimes, it is argued that reality is *objective* reality, i.e. first, agreement on its nature, however universal, does not rule out the possibility that reality is other than the people agreeing perceive it to be; second, reality can exist regardless of appearances and our ability to investigate. These features of objective reality are sometimes described by saying the reality is *two-way independent* of appearance. The French philosopher René Descartes (CE 1596–1650), however, used the phrase objective reality to refer to any given idea in contrast with *formal* or *actual* reality, which he ascribed to the cause of that idea, and held that thought had to be as real as the former.

When the Classical Greek philosopher Plato (428–348 BCE) said that time is the moving image of reality in the *Timaeus*, he was formulating a metaphysical doctrine: the *imitation* or *mimesis theory* of the relation between reality – the Forms – and appearance. This is a theory that he also applied to aesthetics as a version of the mimetic or imitation theory of art, according to which he held that art is an imitation of an imitation, and imitates not just actual things but probable or possible things (see AESTHETICS).

According to Plato's theory of Forms (which he kept on reworking throughout his life), there was no form for simply being a particular, hence particulars had no reality. Plato's student, Aristotle (384–322 BCE), in contrast with Plato, held that only particulars, or primary substances, were genuinely real, and abstract entities or universals had no existence apart from particulars but (though there has been controversy about this) existed in them, i.e. they were immanent; in other words, in the particulars. This was a version of substantialism that became most influential in the history of philosophy. Aristotle used the term *ousia*, i.e. "substance," to denote the individual existing thing. He initially divided these items into *ousia prote* or first substance, i.e. the primary subject of a proposition, and *ousia deutera*, or secondary substance, i.e. a genus, which he thought to be less substantial than a species belonging to it and even less substantial than individuals belonging to the species. It should, however, be noted that he drew the distinction between primary and secondary substance in his youthful *Categories*, but, later, significantly modified – arguably abandoned – his position in his *Metaphysics* (especially Z).

Unity and multiplicity
Philosophers have often followed Plato's example, concentrating on cases where the entities abstracted are *general* or *universals* such as numbers, sets, geometrical figures, propositions, properties, and relations. These abstractions (e.g. the square) are said to be abstracted from *particulars* (e.g. from particular squares), but include no feature peculiar to any of these particulars. In one sense, they help bring a modicum of unity in the multiplicity of individuals in our experience. This has led to wondering whether, at some level, there is overall unity to the *world* (from the Old English *weorold*: "all") or *universe* (from the Latin *universus* and this from *unus*: "one," and *versus*: "turned into," the Greek term being *to dorr*, "the whole"), i.e. everything that exists, while the physical world or physical universe (in Latin: *summa rerum*: "the sum of all things") is everything that exists in space and time. If so, multiplicity is somehow overcome as merely a perspectival appearance or a superficial appearance. This problem is called the *one–many problem*, or *one-and-many problem*, and, sometimes, it is also called the *one over many problem*.

Monism is the view that, at some level, all things are one. *Pluralism* is the view that there are many principles or many types of principles, though each one of these has unity. That is, pluralism is opposed not only to monism, but also to *dualism*, the doctrine that there are two and only two kinds of existing things: mental and material. Within pluralism, there are subcategories. Some are metaphysical. One version, *substantival* pluralism, holds that there is a plurality of substances. Another, *attributive* pluralism, holds that there is a plurality of attributes. Still other versions of pluralism are methodological. One version is *explanatory* pluralism, the doctrine that many explanatory principles and frameworks are necessary to account for the range of events and experiences in the universe. However methodological, this version involves ontological commitments, and, hence, has metaphysical implications. As for the monism versus dualism disagreement, in modern times, it largely belongs in the PHILOSOPHY OF MIND, focusing on whether the mental and the physical are one or two things and, if one, what is its nature.

Universals and particulars
By contrast with universals, in metaphysics, *individuation* or *instantiation* is the process whereby a universal – whether a property or a law – is instantiated in a particular or individual, or instance. As a result, certain notions were developed that took slightly different meanings in different traditions. It was for example argued that, in knowing something, the knower's intellect becomes identified with the *intelligible form* – a Platonic form in Platonism, the Neoplatonic *nous* in Neoplatonism, or, during the medieval period, the *rationes aeternas*, i.e. eternal ideas in God's mind – of the object known. It was also argued that, in addition, there was a *mundus sensibilis*. Also, in the Islamic world, the philosopher al-Shriāzī, usually called Mulla Ṣadrā (CE 1572–1640) argued that, just as there was a *mundus intelligibilis* and a *mundis sensibilis*, there had to be a *mundus imaginalis* or world of images capable of being imagined.

A doctrine related to the universals–particulars distinction is that of *indifferentism*: the view that species are defined as the indifference of individuals (so that individuals are not the same essentially but are the same indifferently), and universals are conceived as *indifferenter*, i.e. not making a difference or non-essential, which arguably constitutes a form of attenuated realism. Metaphysical indifferentism should not be confused with the Kantian doctrine of *epistemological indifferentism*, a doctrine that oscillates between dogmatism and skepticism.

Metaphysics, its kinds, its cognates, and philosophy

As Plato's example also indicates, traditional metaphysics was speculative. Indeed, seventeenth-century thinkers coined the Latin word *noologia* to denote an even more speculative study: that of the supreme principles or principles from which metaphysics infers its conclusions. The Italian mathematician, physicist, and philosopher Ermenegildo Pini (CE 1739–1825) coined the term *protologia* (proto-reason) to denote a fundamental knowledge, residing in the Supreme Unity or God, which would provide the basis for all knowledge, including science, by making intellection possible. This knowledge, however, was transcendent to humans and consisted in the Supreme Being understanding itself. By contrast, the same term, *protologia*, was adopted by the Italian philosopher Vincenzo Gioberti (CE 1801–1852) to designate the study of the intelligible being that is intuited through thought immanent to humans where psychological, ontological, and philosophical thought occurred united. At any rate, the critics of metaphysics, let alone even more speculative subjects, argued that it dealt with entirely unresolvable problems, a view that positivism brought to an extreme by arguing that metaphysical statements were cognitively meaningless.

Analogous attempts at delineating new areas of philosophical inquiry above or within metaphysics had been taking place at least since the mid-seventeenth century. Some, for example, divided metaphysics into *ontologia* and *pneumatologia*, the latter studying *pneumata*, i.e. spirits, and being divided into *theologia*, which studied God, *angelographia*, which studied angels, and *psychologia*, which studied the soul. Others talked of *pneumatica*, *pneumatologia*, or *pneumatosophia* as the study of spiritual or mental substance as such. Later, it became usual to equate pneumatologia with

metaphysics. Though the term pneumatologia has lost philosophical currency in the twentieth century, there have been a few attempts – e.g. by the German philosopher Gustav Class (CE 1836–1908) and the Austrian philosopher Othmar Spann (CE 1878–1950) – to use it to denote a study or theory of the spirit.

In addition, the German philosopher Johann Friedrich Herbart (CE 1776–1841) characterized metaphysics as having the goal of ordering and reordering knowledge. He divided it into four areas: *methodology*, which aimed at reducing the contradictions present in the given; *ontology*, which is the study of being and, he thought, non-contradictory by definition and explained by appealing to the doctrine of *pluralistic reism*, i.e. that reality is basically constituted by simple qualitative units called *reals* (a version of *concretism* or *reism*, the view that the basic entities are concrete objects); *synechiology*, which aims at providing the basis of natural science; and *eidology*, by which he meant epistemology.

An attempt at establishing the role of metaphysics in contemporary philosophy that might have been acceptable to some of metaphysics' critics can be found in the work of the Austrian philosopher Adolf Stöhr (CE 1855–1921), who argued that there were three types of metaphysics. *Pathogonous* metaphysics was prompted by pain and the suffering heart. *Glossogonous* metaphysics was the result of linguistic confusion. *Theorogonous* metaphysics was prompted by wonder and issued in imaginative construction. He rejected the first two types, and upheld the third on the grounds that it satisfied an aesthetic propensity.

A more recent attempt in favor of a role for metaphysics can be found in the work of the contemporary British philosopher P.F. Strawson, who formulated the notion of *descriptive* metaphysics: the philosophical study that describes the actual structure of our thought about the world. Strawson developed descriptive metaphysics by distinguishing *m-predicates* or material body-predicates from *p-predicates* or person-predicates, and characterizing descriptive metaphysics as the study of predicates such as these. He contrasted this study with *revisionary* metaphysics, the study that attempts to produce a better structure.

Even descriptive metaphysics, however, can be open to the charge often advanced against metaphysics: that it is guilty of *hypostasis* or *reification*, i.e. regarding a concept or abstraction as an independent reality. The term hypostasize, like reify, denotes the positing of objects for the purposes of one's theory. This, some argue, is a fallacy. Though others reply that there is no fallacy if the positing is in accordance with valid criteria for *ontological commitment*. This commitment, significantly characterized by the United States philosopher W.V.O. Quine (CE 1908–2000), is relative to specifiable theories, denoting the object(s) or class(es) of objects without whose existence a theory cannot be true. Hence, the issue becomes whether a concept or set of concepts involves ontological commitment in a theory and whether this theory is more defensible than alternative ones.

An alternative position assumes that there is at least a part of nature that is knowable only through the methods of the sciences. This, itself a metaphysical position, is sometimes called *naturalistic metaphysics*. Quine uses the term *ontic theories* to denote these as well as all other metaphysical theories. They are very general descriptions of the universe and must be compatible with, if not knowable through, the sciences. Yet, Quine thinks a variety of such conceptual schemes can be formulated and defended through various adjustments based on a variety of criteria, not the least of which is conceptual economy.

This position is not unrelated to that of the United States philosopher Charles Sanders Peirce (CE 1839–1914), who advocated the doctrine of *tychism* (from the Greek, *tyche*, i.e. "chance"), according to which the universe is one of chance and its basic laws are probabilistic and only approximate. Yet, all things tend to develop habits, hence the associated doctrine of *synechism* (from the Greek *synecheia*, i.e. "continuity"), according to which continuity is a significant component of the universe and philosophy should accordingly try to formulate hypotheses that embody it.

It is also worth noting that metaphysical notions are often involved, through their associated semantics, in non-metaphysical inquiries. For example, the concept of *health*, which in metaphysics has sometimes been equated with that of being, is involved in inquiries in health care, health care ethics, and philosophy of science. In health care ethics, for example, conceptions of disease and health, which are crucial for sound treatment decisions, are subjects of discussion. United States physicians, for example, treat high blood pressure but, except in extreme cases, not low blood pressure. In Germany, by contrast, at least until recently, low blood pressure also has been treated.

Ontology

A central area of metaphysics is ontology (called by a few philosophers *ontosophy*), which today is typically conceived as the branch of metaphysics that studies what entities or kinds of entities constitute the universe. Among the candidates are individuals (e.g. a tree), persons (e.g. Aristotle), properties (e.g. that of being green), modes (e.g. that of having extension), relations (e.g. parenthood), events (the tree's falling), states of affairs (the tree's having fallen), facts (e.g. the fact that the tree fell), and sets (e.g. the set of all trees). The question arises: which, if any, take priority over others? *Objective relativism*, for example, is the name coined by the United States philosopher Arthur E. Murphy (CE 1901–62) to denote the conception whereby events have primacy over objects. At any rate, by contrast with all these species of items, philosophers have also talked of *being as being* and of *nothing* or *nothingness* as the absence of particular beings or of being in general.

This area of metaphysics includes *first philosophy* in the Aristotelian sense of this term (in Latin, *philosophia prima*), also called *metaphysical theology*; that is, the study of being as being or being *qua* being, by contrast with *ouk on*, i.e. non-being or nothing at all as well as particular entities, even those that are nothing in the sense of *me on*, i.e. of having no actual but potential being. The expression first philosophy, however, was used in CARTESIANISM with a different meaning: to embrace the topics of the existence of God, the immortality of the soul, and the nature of mind and matter.

The Aristotelian conception of first philosophy is related to the notion of *focal meaning*, whereby all different senses of being relate to the primary kind of being, just as all different health related conditions – such as exercise, diet, medicine, climate – relate to the single item: health.

Ontology, its kinds, and traditions

Ontology has been divided in a variety of ways. The English philosopher Jeremy Bentham (CE 1748–1832), for example, distinguished between *cenoscopic* and *idioscopic* ontology, The former studies the properties common to all individuals while the latter studies the properties common to all individuals of given classes. This distinction is not unlike that proposed by medieval philosophers and, later, the German philosopher Christian Wolff (CE 1679–1754), between *general* and *special* metaphysics or, by even later philosophers – e.g. Edmund Husserl – between *general* and *regional* ontology. The United States philosopher Charles Sanders Peirce (CE 1839–1914) formulated a classification of sciences into cenoscopic and idioscopic, which is reminiscent of the distinctions just described.

Notable among ontologies is *extensionalism*, a family of ontologies restricted to existent entities. In extensionalist semantics, all references to such imaginary items as Pegasus, the winged horse, or round squares, are explained away. This approach has been used, for example, to attempt to reduce mental states formulated by means of intensional language to extensional descriptions of physiological states.

Extensionalism is also displayed by *mereological* theories formulated from the standpoint of the approach called *merology*. These derive their name from the Greek *meros* – i.e. part – and focus on such things as part, proper part, improper part, mereological sum or a collection of parts, universal sum, and atom or that which has no proper parts. When formalized, mereological theories are axiomatic systems, e.g. those formulated by the Russian-born Polish philosopher and logician Stanislaw Lesniewski (CE 1884–1939) and by the United States philosopher Nelson Goodman (CE 1906–98). Both systems are compatible with *nominalism*, i.e. the view that abstract entities such as sets and properties have no existence in reality and are, at best, shorthand for bunches of individuals.

Their extensionalism, however, conflicts with some deeply entrenched common-sense views. For example, it conflicts with the view that an object, say a tree, can acquire or lose a part, say a branch. It also conflicts with the view that a copper vase is different from the copper used to make it, even though the copper and the resulting vase have the same parts. Further, mereology implies *collectivism*, i.e. the view that any individuals, however scattered, constitute a mereological sum, hence an object. This view also conflicts with other well-established common-sense beliefs, e.g. the belief that when a ceramic vase falls and breaks into pieces it ceases to exist. Collectivism holds that it continues to exist, however scattered the vase's pieces.

Discussions concerning the existence of individuals versus that of universals are part of the realism versus anti-realism controversy, a controversy that has also covered the spatiotemporal world. Those who uphold metaphysical *realism* maintain, for example, that a spatiotemporal world – and, in more traditional versions, that universals such as Plato's Forms – exist. There are two kinds of realism that apply to qualities or properties: realism *ante rem* holds a property can exist even if it has no instances, while realism *in rebus* holds properties exist only if they have instances. An influential version of the latter is Scottish common-sense philosophy, a comprehensive philosophical position formulated by Thomas Reid (CE 1710–96). It holds each creature has a unique *haecceity* or particularity that is formally distinct from its individualized nature. A central tenet of this position is that perception involves both sensation and intuitively known general principles or truths – concerning external objects as well as morality – which are available to all human beings and, together with sensations, yield knowledge.

An alternative to these positions is CONCEPTUALISM, which can arguably be found in Kantian philosophy, as well as in the work of Edward Herbert of Cherbury (CE 1583–1648), the English philosopher who founded Deism. He adopted the Stoic concept of *notiones communes* or *common notions*, i.e. notions that are innate and identifiable by having the following features: priority, independence, universality, certainty, necessity, and immediacy. As in Kantian philosophy centuries later, these common notions organize all experience. Next in order of certainty was the *sensus internus* or internal sense, which concerned conscience, emotions, and free will. Third, he considered the *sensus externus* or external sense, i.e. that which allowed us to intuit external objects. Finally, he treated of *discursis* or REASONING, which, to him, was the greatest source of human error. Sometimes, all contemporary forms of realism are called *neo-realism*. The many positions opposed to realism are called *anti-realism*.

A contemporary United States philosopher who has advocated a return to metaphysics as traditionally conceived is Paul Weiss. He argues that reality has four modes: actuality, ideality, existence, and God, whose interrelations constitute the structure and function of the cosmos. They are mutually irreducible and all, as well as their interrelations, have to be explored to understand the universe. Accordingly, he criticizes specific philosophies whose metaphysics, if any, focus merely on one mode of reality (e.g. extensionalism on existence and, arguably, descriptive metaphysics on actuality), on the grounds that they are incomplete. He has extended this approach to sociopolitical philosophy and the philosophy of language.

The relations between semantics and ontology were investigated by the United States philosopher Charles Sanders Peirce. He described three types of features concerning signs: the character of the sign itself, the relation of the sign to its object, and the way in which the interpretant (which determines how the sign represents the object) represents the object. These semantic categories reflect three ontological categories: *quality* or *firstness* – a first-order attribute; *relation* or *secondness* – a two-term relation; and *representation* or *thirdness* – a three-term relation. Peirce thought the metaphysical and other conflicts between past philosophies resulted from one-sided approaches. Instead, he proposed an *architectonic*, i.e. letting the system rise from an adequate and many-sided analysis of experience. Along these lines, though with an active rather than passive emphasis, the Russian philosopher A.A. Malinovski (who used

the pseudonym A. Bogdanov; CE 1873–1928), proposed *tectologia* (a term derived from the Greek *tectainomai*, i.e. "to make"), a science aimed at constructing the universe on the basis of neutral components that have not yet been structured by experience.

Some additional problems in ontology are as follows. First, whether there is an external world, i.e. a world of items whose existence is independent of our perceiving them.

Second, whether there are degrees of reality. That there are is a doctrine one finds, for example, in Neoplatonism and, through Neoplatonic influences, in ARABIC PHILOSOPHY, under the heading *al-ḥaḍārāt al-ilāhiyyah al-khams*, i.e. the Five Divine Presences. The doctrine of the Five Divine Presences is prominent in Ṣūfism, whose sacred dance is popularly called *haḍrah* (presence). Notable for its systematic nature is the conception the Five Divine Presences formulated by Abū Ṭālib al-Makkī (d. CE 996), according to which, in descending order, each *haḍrah* (presence) is: *hāhūt* (Ipseity, the Essence, the Godhead, Absolute Reality), *Lāhūt* (the Reality of Being, the Divinity, the Personal God), *malakūt* (the subtle world of Angels), and *nāsūt* (the human world).

There are analogous doctrines in HINDUISM, TAOISM, and BUDDHISM, as well as in Greek philosophy. For example, the term *hāhūt* is analogous to what, in Plato's *Parmenides*, is called "The One Who is One" and, in Vedānta, is called *Parabrahman* or *nirquna Brahma* (Brahman beyond qualities). By contrast, *Lāhūt* is analogous to what, in Platonic terms, is described as "The One Who Is" and, in Vedānta, as *saquna Brahma* (Brahman qualified).

As for *malakūt*, it is the world of such items as exemplars, and archetypes. In Islam, the inhabitants of *malakūt*, *Jinn* (related to the English word 'genie'), are divided into non-central beings – e.g. all non-humans in our everyday world – and central beings, i.e. human beings, who are central because they are able to grasp reality and, hence, to be saved. An analogous notion to that of *malakūt* in Vedānta is *vijñānamaya-kosha*, the sheath of the intellect that, together with *manomaya-kosha* (the mental sheath), and the *prānamaya-kosha* (the sheath of vital air) – the second sheath encasing the body – constitutes the subtle body. As for *nāsūt*, it is the sensible, corporeal world, what in Vedānta is called *sthūla sharīra*.

A third problem in ontology is whether individuals can survive their corporeal death and even be immortal. A central term here is *incorporeal*. From the Late Latin *incorporeous* (and this from *in*, i.e. "not," and *corporeous*, i.e. "corporeal"), incorporeal means not corporeal, immaterial. It denotes the immaterial state of existence of a person who has no body. A particular case of incorporeal is *disembodied*, i.e. the immaterial state of existence of a person who used to have a body. For example, human beings, if they survive their death, are supposed then to be disembodied; while such beings as God and angels are not supposed to be disembodied, though they are supposed to be incorporeal. That is, the notion of disembodiment or non-embodiment, and disembodied or non-embodied beings, characteristically concerns problems of survival after death and immortality, which arise not just in Western thought, but in ethnic philosophies and philosophy. For example, the Akan (Ghana) word *sunsum* ("spirit") is generally used by Akans to denote a non-physical part of a human, derived from the individual's father, which is responsible for the degree of impact this individual has on other people. For the Akan, humans are partly spiritual, the physical world is animated, and spiritual beings play important roles in the thought and conduct of living persons. In short, Akan ontology is significantly spiritual.

This notion of immaterial should not be confused with that of immaterial involved in the doctrine of *immaterialism*: that objects are best characterized as mere collections of qualities. Further, this notion of immaterialism should not be confused with *epistemological* or *metaphysical idealism*, because the latter two, but not the former, imply that the existence of objects and their features is dependent on their being objects of cognizing minds.

A notion that played an important role in discussions of immortality and the related mind–body problem is that of *mode* (from the Latin term *modus*, i.e. "manner," "way," or "fashion"). Among Ancient Greek philosophers, the notion of a mode was used, first, in logic, to denote the arrangement of statements in a categorical syllogism. In this sense, it is translated as "mood" in English. Mode was also used among medieval philosophers who distinguished modes of signifying (*modi significandi*), modes of understanding (*modi intelligendi*), and modes of being (*modi essendi*). Modern philosophers used the notion of mode very centrally. In Cartesianism, modes are particular ways of having extension or thought, hence features of a substance, i.e. analogous to accidents. This use influenced empiricist philosophers who considered modes to be ideas representing the complex properties of things.

Cosmogony

Cosmogony – from the Greek *kosmos* ("world") and *gignesthai* ("to be born") – is the study and accounts of the origins of the universe. It overlaps with metaphysics when non-physical accounts of the origin of the world are given, and with the natural sciences – especially physics – and the PHILOSOPHY OF SCIENCE otherwise.

Cosmology

Cosmogony is part of *cosmology* (from the Greek kosmos, i.e. "world" and logos, i.e. "reason regarding"): the branch of metaphysics that partly overlaps with the philosophy of science and studies the origin and structure of the universe, as well as its basic components, e.g. space, time, causality, and the laws of nature.

There are various types of cosmologies that are sometimes classified by the basic components they include. For example, in Hinduism, *Trimūrti* – literally, three forms – is an instance of *triadism*, which is any doctrine, e.g. a cosmology, according to which reality or a part thereof has three parts. Other instances are *triloka* (literally, "three worlds"), i.e. the three worlds of Hindu cosmology: *svarga* or heaven, *bhūmi* or earth, and *pātāla* or the underworld. In addition, there are versions of triadism that do not constitute entire cosmologies, e.g. the Christian trinity and, in philosophy, such conceptions of a human being as that which considers it constituted by body, vital principle, and soul; or that which conceives of it as constituted by body, soul, and spirit; and the Platonic division of the human person or soul into impulse or instinct, courage or assertiveness, and intelligence or reason.

As previously indicated, the categories just discussed are not only the subject matter of metaphysics, but also the subject matter of the natural sciences and the philosophy of science (see CAUSAL LAW; PHILOSOPHY OF SCIENCE). Here, it may be useful simply to give an idea of the scope of theories associated with these various notions by listing some conceptions of time and eternity traditionally discussed in metaphysics, science, and, more recently, in the philosophy of science.

The term *time* is derived from the Latin *tempus*, which was derived from the Greek *temno*, i.e. "cut off." However, the Greek terms for time were *chronos* and *aion*. The Greek philosopher Plato (428–348 BCE) described time as a moving image of eternity (see PLATONISM). His student, the Greek philosopher Aristotle (384–322 BCE) thought of time in terms of duration, characterizing it as the number of movement with regard to the before and after (see ARISTOTELIANISM). The Egypto-Roman philosopher Plotinus (CE 204–70) followed Plato, but held that time was the reason for the restless energy of the world soul (see NEOPLATONISM). In Hinduism, some works take the view that time is the generator of all things, including Brahman, and that it will be the source of their destruction as well (see BRAHMAN; HINDUISM).

The philosopher Augustine (CE 354–430; born in the African city of Thagaste) claimed to know only that time is present in us and measured in the mind. He, however, ventured to elaborate that it is a present of things past (memory), a present of things present (sight), and a present of things future (expectation), the latter feature being echoed centuries later by the Argentine poet José Hernández (CE 1834–86) in his *Martín Fierro*, when the main character, the gaucho Martín Fierro, says that time is expectation of what is to be.

The Roman philosopher Anicius Manlius Severinus Boethius (c. CE 480–525) used the expression *totum simul* (Latin for "the whole at the same time") to characterize eternity. This characterization was used throughout the Middle Ages and, as late as the twentieth century,

it was also used by the United States philosopher Josiah Royce (CE 1855–1916). The English philosopher Thomas Hobbes (CE 1588–1679) thought, like Augustine, that the past is in memory; but, for Hobbes, the present was not in us but in nature, while the future was not at all. The Jewish philosopher of Spanish and Portuguese descent Baruch Spinoza (CE 1632–77), echoing a Platonic theme, thought time was simply a limited perception of eternity which, accordingly, was more fundamental.

Also, the English physicist and philosopher Isaac Newton (CE 1642–1727) argued that, despite all relativities of measurement and perception, there is absolute time; while the German philosopher Gottfried Wilhelm Leibniz (CE 1646–1716) held that time was relative: the order of successive existence. The German philosopher Immanuel Kant (CE 1724–1804) though it was a basic conceptual constituent of our perception of the natural world. Also, in the twentieth century, the physicist Albert Einstein (CE 1879–1955) characterized time as the fourth dimension of the space–time continuum where future and past occurrences are all fixed in world lines. The question, of course, arises, "Why adopt any of these views?" Some of the criteria used are discussed in the PHILOSOPHY OF SCIENCE entry.

As for *space*, Ancient Greek atomists considered it to be the void, that in which atoms move. Plato considered it to be a receptacle in which Forms are instantiated. Aristotle understood space in terms of place, for which he used the term *pou*, i.e. "where." He used *topos* to denote place. The Latin terms used were *locus* for place, *situ* for position, and *ubi* for the presence of something somewhere. Regarding *ubi*, medieval philosophers distinguished between *circumscriptive ubi*, i.e. as the presence of a body in a place, and *non-circumscriptive ubi*, i.e. as being present in a non-extended manner. This latter sense of *ubi* led to the notions of ubiquity or omnipresence and to the view that God is ubiquitous, i.e. present everywhere in the sense of operant everywhere; but, since this is non-circumscriptive presence, not in the sense of localized everywhere.

In discussing the structure of the universe, the twin notions of macrocosm – from the

Greek *makros* ("great") and *kosmos* ("world") – and microcosm – from the Greek *mikros* ("small") and *kosmos* ("world") – have been developed. *Macrocosm* typically denotes the universe, while *microcosm* typically denotes any human being understood as a small universe. This type of conception can be found in Indian philosophy, e.g. in the Vedānta identification of Brahman, the all-encompassing divinity or soul of the universe, with *ātman*, the individual soul. In China, a similar conception was formulated by some branches of early Confucianism.

In the Western world, there are indications of the macrocosm–microcosm analogy among early and classical philosophers; however, the Stoics clearly formulated it. They held that the world-soul is to the universe as the individual soul is to the individual's body, and that the rational part of the individual soul is analogous to universal reason. This type of idea was often formulated in the Middle Ages (e.g. among mystics), and was widespread in the Rennaissance – e.g. in the thought of the philosophers Nicholas de Cusa (CE 1401–64; born in the city of Kues (Cusa in Italian), in what is now Germany) and Giordano Bruno (CE 1548–1600; born in the city of Naples, in what is now Italy); and the Swiss physician Paracelsus (CE 1490–1541). It can be found in modern philosophy, e.g. in the conception of a monad formulated by the German philosopher Gottfried Wilhelm Leibniz (CE 1646–1716).

According to Leibniz's account in his *Monadology*, each monad mirrors the universe through a *pre-established harmony*, i.e. a synchronous operation of all monads since the moment of their creation by God. Monads were the basic individual components of a viable ontology: immaterial entities without spatial parts and whose basic properties were a function of their perceptions and appetites. Leibniz held that monads perceive other monads with various degrees of clarity. Only God perceived all monads with absolute clarity. In this regard, he also held the doctrine of *minute perceptions*, namely that each created substance has some perceptions of which it is not aware.

Among nineteenth- and twentieth-century philosophers, the macrocosm–microcosm ana-logy is found in the work of the United States philosopher Ralph Waldo Emerson (CE 1803–82), who held the individual soul involved a correspondence to everything in the world; the German philosopher Rudolf Hermann Lotze (CE 1817–81), who developed the twin notions in the three volumes of his *Microcosmus*; and the English philosopher Alfred North Whitehead (CE 1861–1947), who held that, from its own standpoint, each actual occasion or actual entity – items that replaced the old category of substance – reflects the entire universe.

See also: abstract; alethiology; analysis; Arabic philosophy; Aristotelianism; conceptualism; description; Epicureanism; epistemology; essentialism; logic; nominalism; quality; philosophy of language; philosophy of mathematics; philosophy of mind; philosophy of science; Platonism; Scholasticism; set; skepticism; Stoicism; theory of types; Thomism

Further reading
Oderberg, David S. (1999) *Form and Matter: Themes in Contemporary Metaphysics*, Malden, MA: Blackwell Publishers.
Sprague, Elmer (1978) *Metaphysical Thinking*, New York: Oxford University Press.
Strawson, P.F. (1963) *Individuals*, Garden City, NY: Anchor.

metapsychology *see* philosophy of mind

metascience *see* philosophy of science

metatheorem *see* use–mention distinction

metatheory *see* theory

metempsychosis *see* Greek philosophy

method, abductive *see* abduction

method, axiomatic *see* axiomatic method

method, deductive *see* deduction

method, hypothetico-deductive *see* induction

method, inductive *see* induction

method of agreement *see* induction

method of agreement and difference *see* induction

method of concomitant variation *see* induction

method of difference *see* induction

method of hypothesis *see* abduction

method of residues *see* induction

method of supervaluations *see* logic

methodism *see* epistemology

methodological conservatism *see* philosophy of science

methodological holism *see* holism

methodological individualism *see* holism

methodological naturalism *see* naturalism

methodological skepticism *see* skepticism

methodological solipsism *see* solipsism

methodology *see* philosophy of science

metonymy *see* meaning

microcosm *see* metaphysics

microlevel *see* philosophy, sociopolitical

microsocietal *see* philosophy, sociopolitical

middle knowledge *see* determinism

middle-Platonism *see* Platonism

middle-Stoicism *see* Stoicism

middle term *see* syllogism

middle way *see* Buddhism

migration *see* diaspora

Milano School *see* Thomism

Milesians *see* Greek philosophy

Millenarianism *see* philosophy of religion

Mill's methods *see* induction

Mīmāṃsā *see* Hinduism

Mīmāṃsā, pūrva *see* Hinduism

mimesis *see* aesthetics

mimetic theory of art *see* aesthetics

mind *see* philosophy of mind

mind–body problem *see* philosophy of mind

mind, causal theory of *see* philosophy of mind

mind, momentary *see* philosophy of mind

mind, philosophy of *see* philosophy of mind

mind-stuff *see* philosophy of mind

ming *see* Chinese philosophy

ming chia *see* Chinese philosophy

minimalist theory of truth *see* truth

minimum standard of provisions *see* ethics; utilitarianism

Minkowski space–time *see* philosophy of science

minor premise *see* syllogism

minor term *see* syllogism

minority *see* culture

minute perceptions, doctrine of *see* philosophy of mind

miracle *see* philosophy of religion

misogyny *see* feminist philosophy

misplaced concreteness, fallacy of *see* process philosophy

Mitakuye Oyasin *see* Native American philosophy

Mitsein *see* existentialism

Mi-tsung *see* Buddhism

mixed hypothetical syllogism *see* syllogism

mnemic causation *see* causal law

modal logic *see* logic

modal logic of programs *see* logic

modal square of opposition *see* syllogism

modalities, alethic *see* alethiology

modalities, apodictic *see* alethiology

modalities, deontic *see* alethiology

modalities, doxastic *see* alethiology

modalities, epistemic *see* alethiology

modalities, iterated *see* alethiology

modalities, problematic *see* alethiology

modality *see* alethiology

modality, de dicto *see* essentialism

modality, de re *see* essentialism

mode *see* metaphysics

model A term (which earlier was *modell*) derived from the Italian *modell(o)*, the result of combining the Italian term *modo*, i.e. "mode," plus the diminutive ending "-ello," a combination derived from the Latin *modus* plus the diminutive ending *-ellus*. Though, in ordinary English, model has different nuances of meaning, all of these tend to share the common notion of a standard or example for imitation or comparison.

As for scientific uses, though the term model is used in a variety of senses, three main types can be distinguished: representational, theoretical, and imaginary. A *representational* model is a physical representation of an object – e.g. an architect's model of a proposed building – used to explain or describe features of the object by examining its representation. There are four subtypes of representational models. First, a *true* representational model is a representation where all significant characteristics of the object are reproduced on a set scale. For example, all minute details of a proposed building and even the trees surrounding it are reproduced on such a scale. Second, an *adequate* representational model is a representation where only some significant characteristics of the object – say, a building's doors, windows, and corridors, but not its light switches – are reproduced on a set scale. Third, a *distorted* representational model is a representation where all or some features of the object are reproduced with different scales, say, its width and depth are reduced by twice the amount by which its length is reduced. Fourth, an *analogue* representational model is a representation where the features of an object are not themselves reproduced, but the representation (say, palm trees holding up the sky) is used to draw an analogy meant to help explain or describe the object, e.g. in explaining that, seen from inside the building, the columns of the Johnson Wax building in Racine, Wisconsin, hold up the building roof as if they were palm trees holding up the sky (which is, in fact, what its designer, the United States architect Frank Lloyd Wright (CE 1869–1959) intended).

By contrast with representational models, *theoretical* models are assumptions about an object being explained or described. They do this by attributing features of established theories to the structure of the object being explained, in a manner that need only approximate the object's actual structure. Examples of these are the corpuscular model of light, and feedback-system models of social behavior.

By contrast with representational and theoretical models, *imaginary* models are much more tentative. They may use representational features or theoretical assumptions, but do not involve any commitment to their being true of the object studied. Instead, they only aim at explaining what the object studied would be like if it were to satisfy certain conditions. An example would be that of imagining how the molecules in a gas would move if there were little beings opening and closing minuscule doors between different minisections of a volume of the said gas.

Sometimes, theoretical models are called *mathematical* models and are studied in *model theory*, a branch of mathematics that studies the connections between languages and their interpretations or structures. Developed during the first part of the twentieth century, model theory produced various important results and led to a model-theoretic view of science.

Some significant concepts in model theory are as follows. *Structure*: a domain of objects together with a function specifying interpretations, with regard to that domain, of the relation, function, and individual symbols of a given language.

Homomorphism: a structure-preserving mapping from one structure to another. To say that a mapping is structure-preserving is to say:

1 that if objects in the first structure bear a certain relation to one another, then those in the other structure bear the same relation to one another;
2 that the value of a function for a given object or n-tuple of objects in the first structure is the same as the function for the corresponding object or objects in the other structure; and
3 that the image in a structure of an object in the first is the corresponding object.

Isomorphism: a one-to-one homomorphism whose converse is also an homomorphism.

Some significant results in model theory are follows.

Beth's definability theorem: a theorem of first-order logic that says: a theory defines a term t implicitly if and only if an explicit definition of the term, on the basis of the other primitive concepts, is entailed by the theory.

Ramsey-eliminability is the name given in the philosophy of science to the failure of a term of a theory to be explicitly definable in terms of the remaining vocabulary of a theory.

Completeness is a property something – e.g. a model, a logic, a theory – has when it is strong enough in some desirable respect. For example, a language is *expressively complete* if each of a class of items is expressible in the language. A set of axioms is complete relatively to a given logical system L if each theorem of this system is provable by using those axioms. A logical system L has *weak* semantical completeness if each valid sentence of the language of this system is a theorem of the system, while the logical system L has *strong* semantical completeness (or is deductively complete) if, for every set of sentences S, every logical consequence of this set is deducible from it by using the said system L. A propositional logic system L is *Halldén-complete* if, whenever $p \ v \ q$ is a theorem of the system and p and q share no variable, then either p or q is a theorem of the system. A logical system L is *post-complete* if it, but no stronger logical system, is consistent for the language of L. Finally, a logical system L is *negation-complete* if, for every sentence of this system, either it or its negation is provable in the system. Incompleteness is characterized as a failure of completeness in one or other of the previously described senses.

A relatively recent development in model theory is *situation theory*, i.e. a theory of semantics whose central notion is not the truth in a given structure, but the information carried by a statement about a situation (where the situation is, for example, a state of affairs).

See also: explanation; logic; philosophy of mathematics; philosophy of science

Further reading
Achinstein, Peter (1968) *Concepts of Science: A Philosophical Analysis*, Baltimore and London: The Johns Hopkins University Press.
Black, Max (1962) *Models and Metaphors: Studies in Language and Philosophy*, Ithaca, NY: Cornell University Press.
Chang, Chen Chung and Keisler, H. Jerome (1973) *Model Theory*, Amsterdam, New York, and Oxford: North-Holland Publishing Company.

modern *see* philosophy of history; Continental philosophy

modern philosophy *see* Cartesianism; empiricism; idealism; Kantian philosophy

modernism *see* philosophy

modernity *see* philosophy

modest foundationalism *see* justification

modularity *see* cognitive

modus ponendo ponens *see* logic

modus ponens *see* logic

modus tollendo tollens *see* logic

modus tollens *see* logic

Mohism Chinese philosophical school that constituted the main alternative to CONFUCIANISM between the fifth and the third century BCE. It was based on the doctrine of *universal love*, formulated in the writings of Mo Tzu (fifth century BCE), also known as Mo Ti. His doctrines are included in a text entitled MoTzu that was probably compiled by some of his followers.

Mo Tzu initially studied Confucian doctrines; but was unable to agree with their definition of morality as *li* or ritual. Mo Tzu argued that the greatest harms come from partiality and that, hence, partiality should be replaced with universality, by which he means a state of affairs where one would treat the states, cities, and families of others as one would treat one's own.

We might be tempted to interpret Mo Tzu's conception of universality as a version of the Golden Rule of the Judeo-Christian tradition, usually phrased as "Do unto others as you would have them do unto you." Yet, the touchstone of the Golden Rule is what the individual would have others do to himself or herself. This is not so in Mo Tzu's universality.

Here, the touchstone is what the *individual* would have others *do to the state, city, or family to which the individual belongs*. In other words, Mo Tzu's concept of morality is community-oriented rather than individualistic. Indeed, the term Mo Tzu uses to denote the type of love he advocates is *jen* (variously translated as kindness, humanity, benevolence, altruism, goodness, and perfect virtue), whose literal meaning is *man in society*, and which denotes both an ethical ideal for all humans, and the feature of having an emotive concern for all living things. Whatever conduct fits this ideal, Mohism considers *yi*, i.e. right or one's duty.

Other views of Mo Tzu included the belief in the existence of spirits and demons who reward those who do and punish those who do not live in accordance with *jen*; the belief in a supreme being – Heaven personified – who also punishes those who do not love each other; the belief that offensive warfare is unjustified; that Confucian rituals were too complex; and apparently also that music was a waste of time.

Mo Tzu's followers were well organized and studied problems in logic, epistemology, and technological applications of science that led to the formulation of some Mohist materialistic doctrines. Apparently, these followers fell into disrepute because of their attempts at forcing people to love each other.

See also: Chinese philosophy

Further reading
Chai, Chih-ch'eng (1986) *"Propriety as Right-eousness" versus "the Beneficial as Right-eousness": A Comparative Study of the yi-li [Righteousness-Benefit] Theories of the Pre-Qin Confucian and Mohist School*, Kent Ridge, Singapore: Institute of East Asian Philosophies.
Graham, A.C. (1985) *Divisions in Early Moh-ism Reflected in the Core Chapters of Motzu*, Singapore: Institute of East Asian Philosophies.
Mo Tzu (1929) *The Ethical and Political Works of Mo Tzu*, trans. Y.P. Mei, London: Arthur Probsthain,

moksha *see* Hinduism

moku-funi *see* Zen

Mokushō Zen *see* Zen

molecular statement *see* logic

Molyneux question *see* perception

momentariness, doctrine of *see* Buddhism

monad *see* metaphysics

Monadology *see* metaphysics

monarchy *see* philosophy, sociopolitical

monasticism *see* asceticism

mondō *see* Zen

monism *see* philosophy of mind

monism, anomalous *see* philosophy of mind

monism, neutral *see* philosophy of mind

monotheism *see* philosophy of religion

monotonic *see* logic

Montague grammar *see* philosophy of language

Montanism *see* Christianity

Monte Carlo fallacy *see* fallacy

moods, syllogistic *see* syllogism

moral action *see* ethics

moral agency *see* ethics

moral agents *see* ethics

moral argument for God's existence *see* philosophy of religion

moral certainty *see* certainty

moral choice *see* ethics

moral claim *see* ethics

moral decision *see* ethics

moral development *see* ethics

moral dilemma *see* dilemma

moral duty *see* ethics

moral epistemology *see* ethics

moral evaluation *see* ethics

moral evil *see* philosophy of religion

moral expediency *see* ethics

moral hypotheses *see* ethics

moral issues *see* ethics; philosophy, sociopolitical

moral judgments *see* ethics

moral laws *see* ethics

moral luck *see* ethics

moral patient *see* ethics

moral person *see* ethics

moral personhood *see* ethics

moral point of view *see* ethics

moral pragmatism *see* ethics

moral principles *see* ethics

moral problems *see* ethics

moral psychology *see* ethics

moral rationalism *see* ethics

moral realism *see* ethics

Moral Rearmament Movement *see* ethics

moral relativism *see* ethics

moral relativity *see* ethics

moral reasoning *see* ethics

moral right *see* ethics

moral rules *see* ethics

moral sense *see* ethics

moral sensitivity *see* ethics

moral status *see* ethics

moral subjectivism *see* ethics

moral theory *see* ethics

moral trap *see* ethics

moral values *see* value

morality *see* ethics

morals *see* ethics

mores *see* ethics

mother–child relation *see* feminist philosophy

Mother Earth *see* feminist philosophy; God

motherhood *see* feminist philosophy

motion *see* philosophy of science

motivation *see* perception; philosophy of mind

motivational explanation *see* justification

motivational internalism *see* justification

motivational variable in competitive situations *see* ethics; philosophy, sociopolitical

motive *see* ethics; justification

moving-rows paradox *see* paradox

m-predicate *see* metaphysics

mu *see* Zen

mudārabah *see* ethics

muddling through, method of *see* pragmatism

mu-ichimotsu *see* Zen

multicultural *see* culture

multiculturalism *see* culture

multiple realizability *see* philosophy of mind

multiple-relation theory *see* perception

multiplicity *see* metaphysics

multiracial *see* culture

mundus imaginalis *see* Arabic philosophy

mundus intelligibilis *see* Arabic philosophy

mundus sensibilis *see* Arabic philosophy

muntu *see* rationality

music *see* Academy; aesthetics

music of the spheres *see* Pythagoreanism

Muslim philosophy *see* Arabic philosophy

musuo *see* ethics

Mutakallims *see* Arabic philosophy

Mu'tazilah *see* Arabic philosophy

Mu'tazilites *see* Arabic philosophy

mutuality *see* ecology

mysterium fascinosum *see* philosophy of religion

mysterium tremendum *see* philosophy of religion

mystery *see* philosophy of religion

mystical experience *see* mysticism

mystical theology *see* mysticism

mysticism From the Greek *mystes*, i.e. "one initiated in the mysteries," the term mysticism can be traced back to the Greek mystery religions whose initiates were called *mystes*. Today, the term mysticism denotes a way of attaining knowledge of reality by means other than sense-perception or discursive or conceptual thought. When mysticism, despite its non-discursive way of proceeding, purports to be compatible with discursive procedures by having a mathematical, scientific or, conceptual basis, it is called *theosophy*. Arguably, Gnosticism, NEOPLATONISM, PYTHAGOREANISM, and some elements of HINDUISM, BUDDHISM, TAO-ISM, and ṢŪFISM are theosophical (see below).

Often, mysticism involves reference to somehow enhanced psychological states. For example, a concept frequently used in discussions of mysticism is that of *ecstasy*, from the Greek *ex* ("out") and *histanai* ("to stand"), meaning "to stand outside oneself." It denotes a psychological state of intense mental absorption, often identified with enlightenment and a union of the soul with a higher reality.

Mysticism can be found in Western thought and in other traditions. In the Upanishads, for example, BRAHMAN is identified with *ātman* and the utmost attainment in life is to become aware of this through a mystical identification with the deity. This points to an *introversive* form of mysticism, i.e. a form that proceeds through an inward path. A similar approach is evidenced in a pair of notions invoked in Islamic mysticism: *al-himma*, literally "concentration" or "resolve," which denotes the *quality of perseverance striving towards God*, and its opposite, *al-ḥiss*, literally, "noise" or "sensation," which is ordinarily used to mean sensation, but, in mysticism, denotes the distractions that drive the soul away from contemplating God, and the state of being thus distracted.

By contrast with this approach, some forms of mysticism are *extraversive*, i.e. forms where mystical union (in Latin, *unio mystica*), i.e. the

union of a human being's soul with God, is attained through an outward path in which the individual feels at one with the entire universe. Arguably, pantheism is a culmination of this approach.

A third approach can be found in Buddhism. It does not aim at union with or knowledge of reality, but merely at the attainment of a state of being.

Within the Judeo Christian tradition, mysticism can be found in the Gnosticism of early Christianity; some versions of Neoplatonism (including some in Arabic philosophy); the Ṣūfism of the Islamic world; the Jewish traditions of the CABALA that, since the nineteenth century, has been revived in Hasidism; the mystics of Catholicism and Protestantism; and a variety of contemporary authors from the United States philosopher William James (CE 1842–1910) to the Austrian philosopher Martin Buber (CE 1878–1965).

A notable mystic in the Middle Ages was the philosopher Bonaventure (*c.* CE 1221–74), born Giovanni Fidanza in the Tuscan city of Bangorea, in what is now Italy. He wrote and preached on the relation between philosophy and theology, and subscribed to such doctrines as hylomorphism, the plurality of forms, and that to know is to perceive the truth directly, i.e. without argument. His mystico-theological works include *Itinerarium mentis ad deum* or *The Mind's Journey onto God*, where he describes a seven-stage journey towards peaceful repose in which our minds are transformed into God. His central theme in this regard is the three ways. One is the *purgative* way, whereby conscience leads us to repel sin. A second is the *illuminative* way, whereby the intellect leads us to imitate Christ. The third is the *unitive* way, whereby wisdom unites us to God through love.

Also notable in the Middle Ages was the German mystic Meister Eckhart (CE 1260–1327), who formulated a Neoplatonic version of mysticism: God is pure being; by comparison with God, all else is nothing; one must empty oneself in order to unite with God; the basis of conscience and religious awareness is the *Seelenfünklein* or spark of the soul, which makes union with God happen; when it happens, the Son is begotten by the Father and the procession of the Holy Spirit occurs in the soul (as it is occurring eternally).

In the Renaissance, Spain contributed various notable mystics. One was Teresa de Ávila, born Teresa de Cepeda y Ahumada, and also known as Teresa of Jesús (CE 1515–82), one of the founders of the Reformed or Discalced (i.e. barefoot) Carmelite nuns. Her works include a spiritual biography, *Life*; an account of the origins of the Discalced Carmelites, *The Foundations*; a book of advice to her nuns, *The Way of Perfection*; and a description of the contemplative life, *The Interior Castle*. They are masterpieces of Spanish prose and formulate a number of ideas about the passions, faculties, activities, and basis of mental life.

Another significant Spanish mystic was the co-founder of the Reformed or Discalced Carmelites, John of the Cross, born Juan de Yepes y Álvarez (CE 1542–91). His reformist activities landed him in prison between 1576 and 1577, where he began to compose some of his best works. They include some of the finest poems in Spanish mystical literature, e.g. "Spiritual Canticle," "Living Flame of Love," and, most notably, "Dark Night of the Soul," where he described the soul's journey towards its final union with God along lines parallel to those of Jesus's crucifixion and glory.

A third, equally significant Spanish mystic was Luis Ponce de León (1527?–91 CE), a teacher of theology and philosophy at the University of Salamanca and famous as a Hebrew scholar. He was a Vicar-general and provincial of the Augustinian order and, as a result of theological disputes with the Dominican order, was imprisoned for four years by the Inquisition. There is an anecdote that, upon returning to class from his four-year imprisonment, Friar Luis's opening remarks were: "As we were saying yesterday," after which he continued with the lectures interrupted by the Inquisition. Only twenty-four of his lyric poems have survived. They display his humanism, knowledge of the classics and the Bible, and, some of them, the influence of the Roman poet Horace, i.e. Quintus Horatius Flaccus (68–8 BCE). Among his most notable poems are "Retired Life," "Prophecy of the Tajo," and "To Francisco Salinas." His prose works, which display a significant interest in language, poetry in prose, and knowledge of what today is called stylistics, include *The Names of Christ* and *The Perfect Wife*.

Outside Spain, the German mystic and philosopher Jacob Boehme (1575–1624 CE) held that behind the world, there is an *Ungrund* (German for "groundless") or Abyss that is God and is the source and explanation of the world. This notion was very influential in later religious thought down to the twentieth century when the Russian philosopher Nicolas Berdyaev (1874–1948 CE) said that humans, like God, are creative and all creation is out of nothing: besides God, there is an *Ungrund* out of which all creation comes.

As for theosophic mystical positions associated with Christianity, at least three are worth mentioning. One is *Swedenborgianism*, which has become a worldwide theosophic movement, established in London as the Jerusalem Church in 1788 CE and based on the views of the Swedish natural philosopher Emanuel Swedenborg (1688–1772 CE), who adapted Cartesian and British empiricist views so as to argue for a harmony between the mechanistic universe and biblical revelation. A second one is *anthroposophy*, a mystical system seeking the development of spiritual awareness. It is based on the views of the German philosopher Rudolf Steiner (1861–1925 CE) and has established centers in Europe and the United States. A third is the position of the Russian thinker Madame Helena Petrovna Blavatskaya, née Hahn, ordinarily called Madame Helena Petrovna Blavatsky (CE 1831–91), the founder of the Theosophical Society, whose views were influenced by mystical elements of Indian thought.

See also: Arabic philosophy; Buddhism; cabala; Christianity; Greek philosophy; Hinduism; Jewish philosophy; Judaism; Neoplatonism; Ṣūfism

Further reading

Fakhry, Majid (1997) *A Short Introduction to Islamic Philosophy, Theology and Mysticism*, Oxford, UK and Rockport, MA: Oneworld.

Kesavan, Hiremaglur K. (1997) *Science and Mysticism: The Essence of Vedic Philosophy*, New Dehli: New Age International.

Merlan, Philip (1963) *Monopsychism,*

Mysticism, Metaconsciousness: Problems of the Soul in the Neoaristotelian and Neoplatonic Tradition, The Hague: Martinus Nijhoff.

Weinstock, Israel (1969) *Studies in Jewish Philosophy and Mysticism*, Jerusalem: Mossad Harav Kook.

myth From the Greek *mythos*, i.e. "legend," the term myth ordinarily denotes a narrative account, taken, but not known, to be true, about something that occurred in the remote past or in far away places. By extension, however, the term myth has come to denote any narrative account or concept taken, but not known, to be true.

Myths are often associated with the presumed origins of a nation, culture, or religious tradition. It is no coincidence, then, that the founder of modern PHILOSOPHY OF HISTORY, the Italian philosopher Giambattista Vico (CE 1668–1744) was also the founder of the philosophy of culture and the philosophy of mythology. Let us consider examples of myths related to the presumed origins of nations, cultures, or religious traditions.

Various cultural and religious traditions include a *myth of creation*. Some views on creation find expression in the statement *ex nihilo nihil fit*, which means "nothing comes from nothing." This doctrine makes room only for creation out of some pre-existing reality – e.g. the primeval chaos – and has been variously applied to such things as the creation of the universe, of living beings, and of human artifacts. The notion of chaos itself in this context is also a myth. *Chaos*, a Greek term meaning "space" as well as "gulf," "chasm," and "abyss," was for the Greek poet Hesiod (eighth century BCE) an unformed mass of primeval existence. In Genesis 1, primeval chaos was the Earth without form and void.

The previous views on creation contrast with those presupposing the production of something – say, the universe – by a divinity – e.g. the Judeo-Christian God – out of nothing. The Latin name for this latter sense is *creatio ex nihilo*, an expression that literally means "creation from nothing." Anticipated by the Syrian Gnostic Basilides (second century CE), this fourth sense of CREATION became dominant in the early Christian centuries. It

prompted the question: "How much does the universe depend on God's sustaining it after its initial creation?" A range of answers have been given to this question. The philosopher Thomas Aquinas (CE 1225–74; born near Naples in what is now Italy) thought God created a world of substances which He sustained in a general way.

In Hinduism, *Manu* – a term meaning man in Sanskrit – denotes a series of progenitors of humans, each one of which was said to have ruled the world for a period of time. The seventh one is said to be that from whom all currently existing humans descend. Like Noah, he is reputed to have survived the deluge in an ark. He is also reputed to have authored the chief ancient Hindu legal code: *The Laws of Manu*.

Another creationist myth, formulated in the Semitic-Babylonian world, is that of Tiamat, the primeval mother understood as undifferentiated darkness and the personification of darkness and chaos. In union with *Apsu*, she begets the gods and the universe. Tiamat is related to other similar divinities shared by various – some quite unrelated – cultural traditions. One such divinity is the Great Mother (*Mater Deum Magna*), the central figure of a religious cult that made its way from Phrygia into Greece and Rome and, eventually, became one of the the most important cults in the Roman Empire, together with those of Mithras and Isis. The Great Mother, also called Cybele, Dindymene, Mater Idaea, Sipylene, Agolistis, Ammas, Rhea, Gaia, Demeter, Maia, Ops, Tellus, and Ceres was the parent of gods and humans, the All-begetter, the All-nourisher, the fertile Mother Earth. In the Americas, one finds a related figure: *Ts'its'tsi'nako*, the creator deity among the Keres (a Pueblo people of New Mexico, United States), who is represented as Thought-Woman or Spider Grandmother and creates by thinking and speaking, and the South American *Pachamama*, Mother Earth.

Just as a nation, culture, or religion frequently has myths concerning its origins or its connection to the origins of humans, it often also has an *eschatology*: myths concerning such final matters as death, the end of the world, and the state of humans after such things as death and the end of the world. One can find eschatologies of philosophical significance in Hinduism; the Greco-Roman world; Zoroastrianism; Chinese, Japanese, and Korean thought; the Judeo-Christian tradition, Pre-Hispanic cultures; and in a variety of schools of thought developed within these traditions. Indeed, one finds forms of these myths at work within modern or contemporary schools of Eastern and Western thought, from Zen Buddhism, and Advaita Vedānta in the East, to German idealism, and popular forms of Marxism in the Western world.

According to the eschatology of ZOROASTRIANISM, there were originally two powerful divinities, the good spirit, Ahura Mazda or Ormazd, and the evil spirit, Ahriman or Angra Mainyu. The history of the world is the struggle between these two divinities; however, Ahura Mazda will eventually triumph, bringing about the *kingdom of heaven*. There will be a *final judgment*, and the wicked, i.e. those who, according to the accounting of their actions, have done more evil than good, will be plunged into hell. While the righteous, i.e. those who have done more good than evil, will eternally live in Ahura Mazda's kingdom in fellowship with each other and Ahura Mazda's angels.

In the Greco-Roman eschatology, there is *Hades*, i.e. the underworld. In Hinduism, there is *naraka*, a place of torture where the souls of the evil go. Indeed, Manu mentions twelve hells. Some hells common in Indian philosophy are *put*, a hell without children; *avīci*, a hell for those awaiting reincarnation; *kudmala*, the worst hell for those who will be reincarnated; *samhāta*, a hell for evil-doers; and *talātala*, the worst hell, which is where those without hope of reincarnation go. By contrast, in the Judeo-Christian eschatology there is one hell, where sinners eternally pay for their sins. The New Testament calls it *gehenna*, from the Hebrew *Ge Hinnom*, the Valley of Hinnom. According to some authors, the reason for this is that Jerusalem's dump was in the valley where fires burned constantly. In addition, it was considered a place of abomination because, according to tradition, children had been sacrificed there to the Canaanite deity Moloch, which demanded the first born. Gehenna is active, while

Sheol is a region of inactivity and stillness. This eschatology also includes *Heaven*.

Among the religions influenced by the previous tradition is Manichaeism, the syncretistic religion founded by the Babylonian prophet Mani in the third century CE and lasting until the thirteenth-century Mongol invasions. Mani claimed that God had revealed Himself through Buddha in India, Zoroaster in Persia, Jesus in Israel, and Mani himself in Babylon. His myths postulated the good kingdom of God or kingdom of light, and the evil kingdom of Satan or kingdom of darkness, which were in a constant struggle successively involving the Primal Man, Adam and Eve, and Jesus. God's aim and that of his messengers – Primal Man, the Living Spirit, and Jesus – was to free light that, for example, was captured in the form of human souls. The way to attain this salvation or liberation, understood as an escape from embodiment, was – as in Buddhism and Hinduism – through asceticism and esoteric knowledge.

Sometimes, myths acquire symbolic significance. The myth of the *Garden of Eden* or Paradise, *al-Jannah*, for example, is the most frequent Koranic symbol for paradise, and a very frequent symbol in Christianity as well. In Christianity, the name Garden of Eden or simply Eden (from the Hebrew *Eden*, i.e. "delight" or "pleasure") is also used to denote the place where Adam and Eve lived before the fall.

Another myth that has come to be used also, if not only, for its symbolic meaning, or test of the value of one's existence, is the myth of *eternal return*, which, together with reincarnation and other notions is a form of *palingenesis* (from the Greek *palin*, i.e. "again," and *genesis*, i.e. "origin," "beginning," or "creation"), a term denoting the periodic recurrence of the same things or events. The myth of eternal return, in one of its modern versions, was formulated by the German philosopher Friedrich Nietzsche (CE 1844–1900). It involves the so-called law of eternal return or eternal recurrence, which a closed finite automaton would exemplify: its history would be a periodic recurrence of the same series of states. Nietzsche used this notion to test whether one's attitude affirms one's existence and the world or rejects them. The test consists in asking: "Would I want to go through this series – my existence and that of my world – over and over again?" Of course, when the entire universe is supposed to develop in accordance with the law of eternal return or eternal recurrence, the question arises: "In what way can one series of states be distinguished from any other identical series of states?" Even if there were only one series, however, it would still be possible to test its significance by asking: "Would I want this series to be any different?"

This use of a myth to test the value of one's existence belongs to a long philosophical tradition. For example, already in Ancient Greece, the philosopher Plato (428–348 BCE) tells the *myth of Er* at the end of *Republic* to dramatize the rewards of justice in this life, and certainly in the afterlife. Er is a warrior who comes back to life shortly after his death, whereupon he describes reincarnation – i.e. the embodiment of the souls that leave their prior, separate, state of pre-existence – and how the souls of the just are sent to heaven, while those of the unjust are sent to the underworld. The notion of *pre-existence* is traditionally distinguished from *creationism* or *theological creationism*, i.e. according to which the souls of persons are directly created by God, and *traducianism*, according to which each person's soul is created by a parental soul.

A myth that, in part, has the same symbolic function is *Somnium Scipionis*, which appears in Book VI of *De re publica* by the Roman philosopher Marcus Tullius Cicero (106–43 BCE). It is the story – told by the Roman general Publius Cornelius Scipio Aemilianus Africanus Minor or Scipio the Younger (*c.* 185–129 BCE), who defeated Carthage – of a dream in which his adoptive grandfather, Publius Cornelius Scipio Africanus Major or Scipio the Elder (237–183 BCE), the Roman general who defeated Hannibal (247–183 BCE), who had invaded Italy, tells him he will defeat Carthage in two years and Numantia later. His ancestor also tells him he will return to a city in disarray and will need the light of the soul, of intelligence and prudence, to address the situation. In order to encourage his grandson, he shows him the fate of souls that served their fatherland and practiced compassion and justice. The description displays a vision of the universe as a harmonious temple constituted by nine spheres. The supreme rational deity that governs it, through decisions that become natural law and provide the standard by which to judge human laws, lives in the outermost and first – celestial – sphere. Virtuous souls are citizens living in the next seven spheres above the moon. To attain compassion and justice, one must turn one's aim towards these spheres, and forget all earthly goods, instead of focusing on the ninth, sublunar world of earth, where everything perishes except human souls. The story expands on Platonic notions of the immortality and simplicity of the soul, and emphasizes that the souls should be trained in noble activities, noblest among them being those aimed at saving one's own country.

Finally, a myth that has been adapted to psychoanalysis is that involved in the Polynesian notion of *taboo* (or tabu), which denotes a mysterious power thought to involve danger to oneself or one's group. Some taboos involve death and items associated with it such as corpses, and murderers; and blood and items associated with it such as childbirth and menstruation. Other taboos involve sex and items associated with it, e.g. incest. Still other taboos involve strangers, chiefs, and priests.

Myths are closely related to the notion of *fetishism*, i.e. of treating objects as *fetishes*: objects eliciting unquestioning reverence, respect, or devotion. This practice is significant in religious practices throughout the world, from Judaism, Christianity, and Islam, to Sub-Saharan and Asian religions. Sometimes, fetishism is associated with *totemism* (from the Ojibwa, *ototeman*, i.e. "brother–sister kinship"), a view according to which a group regards itself as having a blood-relationship to a kind of living non-human animals or plants.

The significance of myths has also been studied for historical or anthropological purposes, even by authors such as the eighteenth-century French Ecyclopedists, who were committed to debunking myths. Indeed, philosophers of history have been interested in myths as repositories of human ideas, as evidence for preliterate human histories, and as indicators of the structure of human consciousness. Also, contemporary authors – e.g. arguably, some deconstructionists – have argued that even the most deeply entrenched categories of human knowledge, however different in degree of sophistication, are not different in nature from traditional myths. The question of course arises whether this interpretation is self-refuting. It would seem to be so if not meant to be itself merely another myth. If, however, it is itself meant to be merely another myth, the question arises: "Why advocate it at all instead of simply not caring?" After all, on this version, it is merely a myth.

See also: metaphysics; philosophy of religion

Further reading
Gusdorf, Georges (1968) *Mythe et métaphysique. Introduction á la philosophie*, Paris: Flammarion.
Schlagel, Richard H. (1996 [1995]) *From Myth to Modern Mind: A Study of the Origins and Growth of Scientific Thought. Volume 1, Theogony through Ptolemy; Volume 2, Copernicus through Quantum Mechanics*, New York: P. Lang.
Segal, Robert Alan (1966) *Theories of Myth*, New York: Garland.

myth of the given *see* empiricism

myth of the neutral man *see* feminist philosophy

N

N *see* logic

Nāda *see* Hinduism

nafas-al-Raḥmān *see* Ṣūfism

Nahua philosophy Nahua philosophy, a significant form of thought developed during the
Pre-Hispanic period in areas of what is Mexico
today, used individual, social, and metaphysical concepts associated with Nahua society.

Nahua society was divided into independent
city-states that, like the city-states of Ancient
Greece and those of the Italian Renaissance,
were often at war with one another. Each city-
state was called *tlatocayotl* or *yelitzli*. The
structure the state was made up of units,
including the *cohuayotl* (community), the *cencalli* (the group of all who live in a residential
compound), and *cenyelitzli* (the family dwelling).

The Nahuas had a highly developed system
of universal and obligatory education. A guiding educational ideal among them was that of
face and heart, which is interpreted in a somewhat stoic fashion to mean wisdom and firmness, though the particular interpretation of
this ideal varied among groups. For example, it
was different between the Mexicas, whose
culture upheld martial mysticism, and other
groups, who advocated a return to *huehuehtlamatiliztli*, the ancient wisdom of the Nahua
world embodied in Toltec art and ideas, and
symbolized by the figure and cult of Quetzalcoatl, the plumed serpent. At any rate, a view
shared by all groups was that the human
predicament involved living in a place of
painful joy and that, in this place, wisdom

and firmness were crucial for individuals to
fulfill their individual destiny in a manner that
provided glory to their elders and ancestors.

As already indicated, the cultural heritage of
the Nahuas was Toltec. Indeed, it was part of
their tradition that nobility, the right to rule,
and the political power to exercise this right
came from *Tula*, the mythical Quetzalcoatl's
Toltec city. This helps explain why the Mexica,
a Nahua-speaking group that had traditionally
been a tributary of other Nahua-speaking
groups believed to have Toltec descendants as
rulers, sought to link itself to the Toltecs by
installing a similar ruler and so shed their
tributary position. In the process, the Mexica
developed a mystico-militaristic conception of
the universe whereby they were the chosen
people of *Huitzilopochtli*, the sun god.

This latter conception – of the Mexica – was
one but by no means the only or a predominant conception in Nahua cosmology; though
all Nahuas expressed the implicit concern with
transcending instability and death. Indeed, the
mexicas attempted to transcend it by conceiving of themselves, as their original leader
Tlacaelel had suggested, as the cosmic colla-
borators of the sun. Their role was to ensure
that the blood of human sacrifices kept the sun
going – a role that became part and parcel of
their militaristic expansion.

A related myth present in Nahua – and,
indeed Maya – thought was that of the five
suns. In one of the Nahua standing texts, the
Annals of Cuauhtitlán, one Nahua version is
that the history of the world is divided into *five
suns* or eras. The inhabitants of each of the

first four suns became extinct, and the suns died, each to make room for the next, with us living in the fifth Sun. The first Sun, symbolized by the ocelot (in some versions called the Sun of earth), was ruled by instinct or animal energy. The second, the Sun of air, was the era of pure spirit. The third was the Sun of rain or fire, survived only by birds. The fourth, the Sun of water, was destroyed by a flood.

In other Nahua versions, the order of the Suns is changed, the first being the Sun of water, then of air, then of fire, and then of earth. At any rate, each Sun was associated with an element: animal energy, air, fire, and water. Only when the fifth Sun – *Naollin* or Four Movements – came into existence, was it possible for the elements to come together to form it. However, this Sun can also come to an end, which can be prevented only by humans climbing the ladder of redemption, a regenerative process represented in Nahua symbolism and in the twenty days of the Maya calendar. This symbolism involves a rhetoric of color in Nahua texts, which is not unlike that in Navajo thought (see NATIVE AMERICAN PHILOSOPHY).

The Nahua intellectual world involved *tlamatinimeh* or sages, whom the Spanish historian and ethnologist Fray Bernardino de Sahagún (*c.* CE 1499–1590), the compiler of the *Florentine Codex* and main compiler of their works, unabashedly called philosophers. They were not aloof and were held in high regard by the general population. Also, they held a wide variety of views. A center for their development was Huexotzinco, whose ruler, Lord Tecayehuatzin, organized a gathering of poets and sages in CE 1490. Its aim was to clarify the purpose and significance of poetry. After the discussion had been exhaustively carried out, one of the sages, Ayocuan, exalted the city of Huexotzinco as a center of the arts and letters – as the house of music, painted books, and butterflies. He advocated its predominant doctrine of peace by contrast with cities like Mexico-Tenochtitlan, which had founded their glory on weapons and war. That is, not all or even most of these sages shared the militaristic-cosmological Mexica views.

The intellectual center of the Nahua world, however, was the city of Tezcoco, whose rulers,

Nezahualcoyotl (who reigned between CE 1418 and 1472), and his son Nezahualpilli (who reigned between CE 1472 and 1516) had become political, but not intellectual allies of the Mexicas. Indeed, after Nezahualcoyotl was obligated to erect a temple to Huitzilopotchli by the Mexicas, he built a more sumptuous temple – devoid of imagery – to the unknown god of the Toltecs right across from the former.

These views were formulated by various sages between CE 1430 and 1519, and can be found in the collection entitled *Cantares Mexicanos*, which include the "Dialogue on Flower and Song," believed to be a record of the actual dialogue that took place among the sages at Tecayehuatzin's palace in CE 1490. Among these sages who, as a rule, formulated their thoughts in poems (or songs), were Nezahuacoyotl of Tezcoco, Tecayehuatzin of Huexotzinco, Ayocuan of Tecamachalco, Tochihuitzin of Tlatelolco, and Totoquihuatzin of the Tacuba area.

Concerning their divinities, they often mentioned a supreme divinity called *Tloque Nahuaque* or the Possessor of the Near and Close, *Moyocoyatzin* or He Who Invents Himself, and *Ometeotl* or the Dual God. The said Nahua thinkers conceived of this divinity as the *Ipalnemohuani* or Giver of Life who, none the less, was somewhat indifferent and made decisions inaccessible to humans. Indeed, some of these sages suspected human beings were an object of mockery and amusement to this supreme being, the god-above-all-gods who lived in *Omeyocan*, the highest heaven.

This raised questions about the significance of human existence. Some held that life on *tlalticpac*, i.e. the surface of the earth, was only a dream and *cahuitl*, i.e. time, was continuously abandoning humans. In addition, as Nezahualcoyotl often repeats in his poems, life on earth is transitory and ephemeral, and, as Ayocuan Cuetzpaltzin of Tecamachalco is said to have indicated everywhere he went, even the earth is impermanent. Yet, given that we were unable to reach beyond, Nezahualcoyotl adopted a somewhat hedonistic or at least Epicurean stand holding we might as well enjoy the world around us (see EPICUREANISM). While Ayocuan Cuetzpaltzin, upon raising the question "Are we here in vain?" proceeds to adopt a more transcendent position: flowers and songs, i.e. symbols and poems, endure in the supreme divinity – the Giver of Life – and this divinity makes itself manifest in them.

In the process of discussing the said philosophical topics – indeed, at the beginning of the dialogue – Tecayehuatzin himself and the Nahua sages with him asked whether flower and song can provide the only *neltiliztli*, i.e. "truth," or *nelhuayotl*, i.e. "basis," for humanity on earth. It is worth noting that both these Nahua terms derive from *tla-nelhatl*, i.e. "root," which indicates that the Nahua term for truth connoted the feature of being well established, firm, or rooted. The Nahua sages concluded that, indeed, the only way of attaining truth, hence being rooted for humans is through flowers and songs, i.e. symbols and poems. They differed, however, on whether such truth was of significance to and lasted in the Supreme Being.

See also: age of the world; Native American philosophy

Further reading
Adams, Richard E.W. (1977) *Prehistoric Mesoamerica*, Boston: Little, Brown.
León-Portilla, Miguel (1992) *The Aztec Image of Self and Society*, Salt Lake City, US: University of Utah Press.
Nicholson, Irene (1967) *Mexican and Central American Mythology*, London and New York: Paul Hamlyn.

Nahuas *see* Nahua philosophy

naigama-naya *see* Jainism

nairātmya *see* Buddhism

nairātmya-vada *see* Buddhism

naishkarmya-siddhi *see* Hinduism

naive realism *see* perception

nāma *see* Buddhism; Hinduism

nāman *see* Hinduism

nāmarūpa *see* Buddhism; Hinduism

names *see* reference

nara *see* Hinduism

naraka *see* myth

nārāyana *see* Hinduism

narrow content *see* philosophy of mind

narrow reflective equilibrium *see* ethics

nāstika *see* Hinduism

nāsūt *see* Ṣūfism

Natarāja *see* Hinduism

nation *see* culture; philosophy, sociopolitical

Nation of Islam *see* Islam

nationalism *see* philosophy, sociopolitical

Native American philosophy Widely understood, this term denotes the philosophical reflection and philosophies of the *Native Americans* (also called *Amerindians* and *American Indians*), i.e. the descendants of groups from Asia (and, some argue, other areas) who, beginning more (some say much earlier) than 40,000 years ago, migrated first into present-day Alaska and then into areas of what are now Canada, the United States and, eventually, other areas of North, Central, and South America.

Among these groups, some – e.g. the Incas of what is now Peru, Bolivia, northern Chile and northwestern Argentina, the Mayas of Mexico and Guatemala, and the Nahuas of Mexico – developed outstanding settlements, cultivating corn, building large cities with plazas, parks, and public buildings, as well as pyramids, and roads used for extensive trade. In addition, a good many other groups engaged in analogous activities to a somewhat smaller scale and developed their own forms of art, oral and, in some cases (e.g. that of the Nahuas), written literature that described their myths, and formulated their cosmological ideas and, indeed, conceptions of truth, personal value, and life's significance. An example of these is discussed elsewhere in this dictionary (see NAHUA PHILOSOPHY).

Besides those already mentioned, many groups in what is now the United States and Canada – e.g. the Navajo, the Hopi, and the Lakota – have shown significant resilience and, today, are widely recognized for the philosophical value of their ideas, especially those concerning the interconnection between human settlements and their natural environment.

This interconnection is reflected even in the manner in which these groups conceived of knowledge. For example, in Navajo philosophy, *aha'áná'oo'nííl* or "the gathering of family," is one of the four categories of KNOWLEDGE. It focuses on family ties and emotive connections, and is associated with the yellow evening twilight. A second category is *bik'ehgo da'iináanii* or "that which gives direction to life." It focuses on character development and moral deliberation, and is associated with the dawn. A third category is *háá'ayį́įh, sihasin dóó hodílzin* or "rest, contentment, and respect for creation." It focuses on the interconnected character of all life and *k'e*, i.e. love or reverence for nature, and is associated with darkness. A fourth is *nihigáál* or "sustenance." It focuses on self-reliance and becoming a contributing member of one's community, and is associated with the blue twilight. As for the significance of all these categories and the types of interconnections they reflect, Navajo philosophy holds that the ultimate aim of knowing and living is *hózhó* or the beauty way of life.

The Navajo knowledge system, like that of many Native American peoples, is based on metaphysical principles. For the Hopi, *navoti*, i.e. abstract knowledge, has – like Navajo speech – causal effectiveness in engaging supernatural factors that involve conscious and animate force. Among Navajo metaphysical views, the central notion is that of *nílch'i*, a term sometimes translated as wind, though it denotes the air or atmosphere in its entirety. Nílch'i is thought to be holy; to suffuse all nature; to give life, thought, speech, and the ability to move to all living things; and to serve as means of communication between all components of the living world.

In Navajo thought, the world existing on the earth's surface is the result of nílch'i's emerging from the underworlds it had created. This type of emergence, together, with the various characteristics attributed to nílch'i, makes this conception quite unlike much, if not all, of Western thought. Perhaps the only likely affinity is with the notion of the One found in emanationism (see NEOPLATONISM).

At any rate, the Navajos' use of the category k'e, i.e. love or reverence for nature, has influenced various contemporary authors who discuss ecological problems and propose solu-tions involving a change in the manner in which humans conceive of their relation with the land, the environment, or, in general, the biota.

As indicated, though the philosophies of Native American peoples display many differences; they share some similarities, certainly in the United States and Canada. For example, among the Lakota, *Mitakuye Oyasin*, meaning "we are all related," is an expression used in greetings and ceremonies to point out that all life forms are interconnected. Also, the Navajo concept of the holy wind is analogous to the Dakota concept of *Skan*, the Great Spirit. Indeed, scholars have suggested that this concept may be quite widespread among other native North Americans. The animating force of the universe is called *wakan* among the Siouan, *orenda* among the Iroquoian, *manitou* among the Algonquian, and *nawalak* among the Kwakiutl.

See also: myth; Nahua philosophy

Further reading
Brandt, R.B. (1954) *Hopi Ethics: A Theoretical Analysis*, Chicago: University of Chicago Press.
De Mallie, R.J. and Lavenda, R.H. (1977) "Wakan: Plains Siouan concepts of power," in R.D. Fogelson and R.N. Adams (eds) *The Anthropology of Power: Ethnographic Studies from Asia, Oceania and the New World*, New York: Academic Press.
Farella, John R. (1984) *The Main Stalk: A Synthesis of Navajo Philosophy*, Tucson, AZ: The University of Arizona Press.
Ladd, J. (1957) *The Structure of a Moral Code: A Philosophical Analysis of Ethical Discourse Applied to the Ethics of the Navajo Indians*, Cambridge, MA: Harvard University Press.
McNeley, James Kale (1981) *Holy Wind in Navajo Philosophy*, Tucson, AZ: The University of Arizona Press.
Sturtevant, W. (ed.) (1979–) *Handbook of North American Indians*, twenty vols, Washington, DC: Smithsonian Institution Press.

native forms *see* Platonism

nativism *see* Cambridge School

natura naturans *see* Aristotelianism

natura naturata *see* Aristotelianism

naturae simplices *see* Cartesianism

natural deduction *see* logic

natural duty *see* ethics

natural evil *see* philosophy of religion

natural forms *see* Aristotelianism

natural kinds Also simply called kinds, these are categories of entities traditionally thought to have modal implications. For example, if an individual is a member of the natural kind "human being," then that individual is necessarily a human being.

With regard to natural kinds, and the sortal predicates that traditionally are thought to serve to characterize natural kinds by designating sortal properties, the Aristotelian concept of *homoeomerity* or the property of being *homoeomerous* (from the Greek *homoiomeres*, "of like parts"), is significant. It denotes a property of some things – some offer the example of blood – whose parts, no matter how small, share properties of the whole – e.g. are still blood. This term is stricter than homogeneous and uniform (and the associated nouns homogeneity and uniformity), for the latter can be applied to things at some level, without implying that it applies to them throughout. For example, the color of the sky can be uniformly or homogeneously, but not homoeomereously, blue. The opposite of homoeomerous is *anhomoeomerous*.

Count nouns and mass nouns are significant concerning sortals or natural kinds. From a *syntactical standpoint*, a *count noun* such as "stone(s)" and "chair(s)" can occur syntactically in the plural, with the indefinite article "a(n)," or with quantifiers "each," every," "many," "few," "several," and numerals. A *mass noun* such as "water" (in, for example, "water is fluid") and "literature" (in, for example, "literature is fascinating") cannot, but it, while not a count noun, can occur with the quantifiers "much," and "little." While both count nouns and mass nouns can occur with the quantifiers "all," "most," and "some." From a *semantical standpoint*, count nouns but not mass nouns can refer distributively.

These syntactic and semantic features produce different classifications and pose the problem of finding logical forms and formulating the truth conditions for sentences including mass nouns. Some contemporaries – e.g. the Indian philosopher Anil Gupta – have argued that sortal properties should be distinguished from properties denoted by certain predicates – e.g. "red" – by including criteria for individuating the particulars – i.e. the bits or amounts for mass nouns – that fall under such predicates and, also, by including criteria for sorting these particulars into the class. Other philosophers – e.g. the United States philosopher Willard V.O. Quine (CE 1908–2000) – have argued that natural kinds and their modal implications should be replaced with scientific theories that have no such implications. While still other contemporary philosophers – e.g. the United States philosophers Hilary Putnam and Saul Kripke – have argued that scientific theories indeed have such modal implications.

See also: essentialism; philosophy of science

Further reading
Riggs, Peter J. (ed.) (1996) *Natural Kinds, Laws of Nature and Scientific Methodology*, Dordrecht and Boston: Kluwer Academic Publishers.
Schwartz, Stephen P. (1977) *Naming, Necessity, and Natural Kinds*, Ithaca, NY: Cornell University Press.

natural language *see* logic; philosophy of language

natural law *see* ethics

natural light *see* Cambridge School; Cartesianism

natural religion *see* philosophy of religion

natural rights *see* ethics

natural selection *see* evolution

natural theology *see* philosophy of religion

naturalism A doctrine encompassing metaphysical or ontological naturalism and methodological or epistemological naturalism. *Metaphysical* naturalism holds that everything is constituted by natural entities. In modern times, natural entities are often understood to be entities existing in space–time and studied by the sciences (on some versions, only by the natural sciences), though, throughout the history of philosophy, the conception of nature, or the set of natural entities, hence of naturalism, has varied a great deal. *Methodological* naturalism holds that acceptable methods of explanation are somehow cognate to those of the sciences. These views should not be confused with materialism, because naturalism does not hold either that all natural entities are material or that all naturalistic explanations must be reducible to material entities. When extended to ethics, naturalism is called *ethical naturalism*.

In the nineteenth century, ethical naturalism became associated with *ethical nihilism*: the view that there are no knowable ethical truths or valid moral judgments. The German philosopher Arthur Schopenhauer (CE 1788–1860), for example, came close to holding ethical nihilism in his ethics of pessimism, where the only value judgment retaining validity concerns renunciation. Partly influenced by and reacting against Schopenhauer, the German philosopher Friedrich Nietzsche (CE 1844–1900) argued for the stronger view that traditional ways of thinking – from the belief in God to all metaphysical and religious interpretations of the world and ourselves – were untenable because expressions of slave/herd morality: the social devices whereby the weak and mediocre defend themselves and retaliate against stronger, higher forms of human life. Nietzsche argued this situation faced humans with a radical form of ethical nihilism and, indeed, *value nihilism*, because it concerned all – ethical and non-ethical – values. Some of Nietzsche's interpreters see this as only a moment – the *negative* nihilism – in Nietzsche's thought. They argue that Nietzsche also proposed *positive* nihilism, a form of nihilism that led to a transvaluation of all values, through an affirmation of life. Positive nihilism as conceived in Nitzschean philosophy involves a version of ethical naturalism understood in evolutionary terms and aimed at the development of a *master morality* or morality of a higher humanity, which was creative, risk-taking, and enhancing of cultural life by analogy with the manner in which such enhancement is brought about in the artistic life.

By contrast with these positions, in the later part of the twentieth century, ethical naturalism has been associated with *moral realism*,

which sometimes has also included evolutionary components, only that these explain the developments of such characteristics of persons and human interactions as reciprocal altruism and fairness.

Widely conceived, the concept of nature would cover such notions as that of *lumen naturale* (natural light) or *lumen naturalis rationis*, i.e. the natural light of reason or, for short, the light of reason. It would also cover the doctrine that gives priority to the *ius naturale* (natural right) and *lex naturale* (natural law), e.g. on the Thomist and other Christian conceptions where the natural right and the natural law depend on the divine law and are known through the natural light of reason. Some philosophers, however, have argued that the conceptions just discussed should not come under naturalism because, if they did, the notion of naturalism would be unnecessarily diluted.

Yet, even with these restrictions, naturalism would include positions as disparate as Aristotelianism, atomism, Stoicism, materialism, and pragmatism. For this reason, still other philosophers – e.g. the German thinker Wilhelm Dilthey (CE 1833–1911) – have proposed the additional restriction that the term naturalism be used in contraposition to supernaturalism (i.e. to any doctrines that postulate other worlds), and to those diluted versions of *supernaturalism* that place freedom and values in a world beyond our own.

This use of naturalism, however, would still make room for certain conceptions of reason, spirit, and Platonic ideas in the world of nature. This is why other thinkers – e.g. the United States philosopher John Dewey (CE 1859–1952), a notable representative of naturalism himself – have gone further and argued that additional restrictions are needed on the term naturalism so that it becomes a useful while not excessively narrow term. Dewey proposed that such doctrines as metaphysical spiritualism and idealism be also excluded because, though perhaps anti-supernaturalist, they are diluted historical versions of supernaturalism. He draws the line on the basis of conceptions of humanity: supernaturalism presupposes that humans need some kind of salvation, while naturalism does not presuppose any such thing. However, it would arguably not exclude Epicureanism – so long as seeking *ataraxia* is not to seek salvation – or the conception of the nature of things (*rerum natura*) that the Roman poet and philosopher Lucretius (99 or 94–55 BCE) formulated (see EPICUREANISM).

During the second part of the twentieth century, naturalism became very influential, especially among philosophers of mind, in the United States. Elsewhere, its influence has not been as significant. The question has been raised: "Can naturalism make room for natural properties that determine other properties without being equivalent to them, or must all naturalism be *reductive* naturalism?" (See REDUCTIONISM.) Some philosophers argue that it can, meaning that the supervenience of emergent properties is compatible with every thing being composed of natural entities (from which the emergent properties arise).

See also: evolution; holism; metaphysics; reductionism; supervenience

Further reading
Almeder, Robert F. (1998) *Harmless Naturalism: The Limits of Science and the Nature of Philosophy*, Chicago: Open Court.
Bhaskar, Roy (1998) *The Possibility of Naturalism: A Philosophical Critique of the Contemporary Human Sciences*, 3rd edn, London and New York: Routledge.
Kornblith, Hilary (ed.) (1985) *Naturalizing Epistemology*, Cambridge, MA: MIT.
Krikorian, Yervant Hovhannes (ed.) (1946 [1944]) *Naturalism and the Human Spirit*, New York: Columbia University Press.

naturalistic fallacy *see* ethics

nature *see* naturalism

natures, simple *see* Cartesianism

naufragio *see* existentialism

nausea *see* existentialism

Navaho philosophy *see* Native American philosophy

naya *see* Jainism

nayābhāsa *see* Jainism

naya-nishcaya *see* Jainism

naya-vāda *see* Jainism

Nazism *see* philosophy, sociopolitical

necessary and sufficient condition *see* explanation

necessary condition *see* explanation

necessitarianism *see* alethiology; *de re*, under de

necessity *see* alethiology; *de re*, under de

need *see* ethics

negation *see* logic

negation-complete *see* model

negative duty *see* ethics

negative feedback *see* cybernetics

negative freedom *see* philosophy, sociopolitical

negative liberty *see* philosophy, sociopolitical

negative theology *see* Neoplatonism

negotiation *see* philosophy, sociopolitical

negritude *see* African philosophy

nei-ch'i *see* Taoism

nen *see* Zen

neo-colonialism *see* philosophy, sociopolitical

neo-Confucianism *see* Confucianism

neo-criticism *see* Kantian philosophy

neo-Epicureanism *see* Epicureanism

neo-Friesianism *see* Kantian philosophy

neo-Hegelianism *see* idealism

neo-Kantianism *see* Kantian philosophy

neo-Marxism *see* Marxism

neo-Nazism *see* philosophy, sociopolitical

neo-orthodoxy *see* philosophy of religion

neo-paganism *see* philosophy of religion

neo-pelagianism *see* determinism

Neoplatonism In a narrow sense, this term denotes the period of Platonism that started with the philosophical thought of the Egypto-Roman philosopher Plotinus (CE 204–70) and ended in CE 529, when the Platonic School of

Athens was closed by the Byzantine emperor Flavius Anicius Justinianus – Justinian I or Justinian the Great (CE 483–565). In a wide sense, Neoplatonism is a most persistent strand of Western philosophy, with representatives still flourishing as late as in the nineteenth century.

A significant doctrine in Neoplatonism was *Gnosticism*, the view that knowledge, not faith, brings salvation. This view was especially influential during the second century, under the leadership of two Christian teachers: the Syrian Basilides (*c.* CE 120–140) and the Alexandrian Valentinus (CE 100–165). It threatened what became the orthodox – faith-centered – Church, not just from within, but from without, through the activities of many non-Christian Gnostic sects. In Gnosticism, the demiurge is the ignorant, weak, and either evil or morally limited cause of the cosmos.

As previously indicated, most influential among Neoplatonists was the Egypto-Roman philosopher Plotinus, the author of the *Enneads*, a collection of his essays collected and edited by his disciple, Porphyry (CE 234–*c.* 305), after Plotinus' death. Plotinus is most often associated with the doctrine of emanationism, according to which everything else that exists is an emanation from a primordial unity that Plotinus called the *One*, which was ineffable because total unity. A second principle, the *Nous*, i.e. intelligence or understanding, is a plurality. It is the realm of the Platonic forms that, in medieval philosophy, became the *rationes aeternas* or *eternal reasons* or *exemplars*. A third principle, the *Soul* or *psyche* is the agency through which the higher world bears on or in-forms the lower sensible world of body. Plotinus and his disciples argued fiercely against the Gnostics. The main doctrinal difference was that the Gnostics thought matter – i.e. the principle of evil, ugliness, and all things bad – was antithetic to, and independent from, the One. Plotinus and his disciples, on the other hand, viewed matter as, ultimately, descended from the One through a procession of hypostases, especially the incarnate soul that needs to defer to the needs of the body. That is, Plotinus' ontology is monist, while that of the Gnostics is dualist.

Plotinus' disciples were the Etruria-born Amelius (*c.* CE 225–90) and the Tyre-born Porphyry. The latter was widely influential in the Latin West, the Greek East, and, through translations, in the Arabic world as the founder of Neoplatonic commentaries on the works of Plato and Aristotle. Like Plotinus, Porphyry was not a Christian. Indeed, he wrote a book – no longer extant except in fragments, entitled *Against the Christians*. His pupil, the Syrian philosopher Iamblichus (*c.* CE 245–325) started the Syrian School, which emphasized *theurgy* – from *theos*: "God" and *ergon*: "work," i.e. "a work of god" – as a complement to philosophical reasoning in the search for enlightenment (see THEURGY).

Worth noting is Porphyry's illustration of the relations between genus, species, and individuals by means of the Tree of Porphyry or *Arbor Porphyrii*. In characterizing them, he used the category of *substance* (which is a genus and not a species), terms that are both genus and species, and the *differentiae* associated with these terms, down to the narrowest species and the individuals. The complements of the differential terms are to the right of the diagram (see below).

In the late Greek and Roman periods, *hermetism* (also *hermeticism*), a doctrine derived from the fourth century BCE *Corpus Hermeticum* – a body of Neoplatonic, astrological, and alchemical writings falsely attributed to Hermes Trismegistus, a Greco-Egyptian version of the Egyptian god Thoth – became influential. It was a philosophical theology based on the assumption that human salvation depended on the revealed knowledge (*gnosis*) of God.

An important Neoplatonic School was the *School of Alexandria*, developed in Alexandria between CE 430, when Proclus (CE 410–84) studied with Olimpiodorus (CE 495/505–after 565) and sometime between *c.* CE 610, when Stephanus left to fill the chair of philosophy in Constantinople, and CE 642, when the city was taken over by Muslim forces. The philosophers of the ALEXANDRIAN SCHOOL significantly worked on the interpretation of Aristotle's works. They included its founder and first head, Hierocles (*fl. c.* CE 430), who had studied with Plutarch of Athens; Hermias (*fl. c.* CE 440); Ammonius (CE 435–517, or 445–526);

Tree of Porphyry

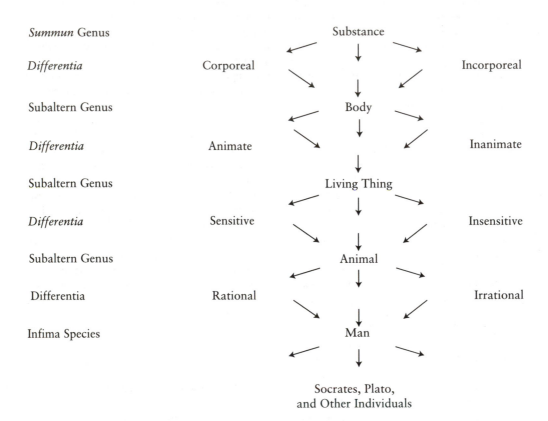

Summun Genus		Substance
Differentia	Corporeal	Incorporeal
Subaltern Genus		Body
Differentia	Animate	Inanimate
Subaltern Genus		Living Thing
Differentia	Sensitive	Insensitive
Subaltern Genus		Animal
Differentia	Rational	Irrational
Infima Species		Man

Socrates, Plato,
and Other Individuals

John Philoponus (*c.* CE 490–575), Simplicius (whose writings date beginning in CE 532), Asclepius (mid-sixth century CE), Olympiodorus, Elias (*fl. c.* 540), David (late sixth century CE), and Stephanus, all of whom displayed significant *eclecticism*, seeking to harmonize what was best of the various philosophies that had come to them. A term sometimes used in this context is *syncretism* (from the Greek *synkretizein*, i.e. "to combine"), which denotes the blending of philosophical doctrines from different or even opposing schools in an attempt to achieve a unified view.

Traditionally, these philosophers have been described as advancing simpler metaphysical views than those advanced by the School of Athens (see below) and, besides interpreting Aristotle's works, confining themselves to the study of logic and mathematics, thus avoiding controversy with the city's Christian establishment. This view has been criticized by contemporary scholars, according to whom the philosophical differences between the School of Alexandria and that of Athens have become somewhat blurred. Some evidence for this claim is provided by the intellectual exchanges and interactions between the schools. For example, Proclus did study at the Alexandrian School but then with Syrianus (fifth century CE) at the School of Athens.

At any rate, at the School of Athens, Proclus developed, among other doctrines, that of the *henads*, according to which the One contains all diversity in itself and the inferior beings mirror the superior reality, so that the members of the hierarchical series of the One, Being, Life, Intelligence, and Soul reflect one another.

This doctrine led Proclus to believe that the universe is full of divinities or levels of divinity: the intelligible-intellectual gods (in Latin, *intelligibilia*, i.e. "things capable of being understood"), which were parts of reality accessible through reason, though Proclus thought THEURGY superseded all human wisdom. At any rate, the henads arguably were forerunners of the *intelligible spheres*, and their hierarchy foreshadowed the monadology formulated in modern times by the German philosopher Gottfried Wilhelm Leibniz (CE 1646–1716).

Also worthy of mention is the unidentified author called *Pseudo-Dionysius* (end of the fourth or beginning of the fifth century CE), who used Proclus' works as the basis of various treatises on God and mystical theology. He argued that *positive theology* rests on the scriptures, because we can know of God only what God has revealed to us in them. Yet, *negative theology* shows we cannot understand the names of God we find in the scriptures. We could, along the lines of *superlative theology*, call God a Super-Being, Super-Unity, and Super-Goodness, but we could not understand what we are saying. This opens the way to *mystical theology*, which relies on our supreme ignorance of God to help us acquire supreme knowledge.

In addition, Neoplatonism influenced ARABIC PHILOSOPHY. Among the various sources of this influence is *Liber de Causis*, a ninth-century CE Neoplatonic treatise on God and the world, which was translated from Greek into Arabic and then into Latin. Frequently attributed to Aristotle, the influence of this work lasted until the fourteenth century, most notably in the work of the German mystic Meister Eckhart (CE 1260–1327). In addition, the Neoplatonic doctrine of Gnosticism appears to have influenced Arabic thought through the *Seveners* (an early offshoot of which were the *Qarmatians*), which constituted a resurgent Gnosticism in Islamic guise.

During the Italian Renaissance, an attempt was made in Florence to reproduce Ancient Greece's Academy of Athens. The Byzantine Neoplatonic philosopher Giorgius Gemistos Plethon (*c.* CE 1355–1440) was brought to Florence where his lectures were very well received and he inspired the Italian banker,

statesman, and patron of the arts and literature Cosimo de' Medici, the Elder (CE 1389–1464) to support the founding of the *Florentine Academy* or *Florence Academy*. Marsilio Ficino (CE 1433–99) was appointed head of the Academy. His conception of Platonic love as the perfect love, where a beautiful body is loved for the sake of its form, influenced European literature in the late fifteenth and sixteenth century. Ficino also adopted the notion of *prisca theological*: that there was an ancient philosophical and religious wisdom that had been received by Plato and later validated by Christian revelation. The Academy included various additional influential members, most notably Pico della Mirandola (CE 1463–94), who argued for the unity of knowledge and the validity of sources ranging from the cabala to tradition.

The authors just discussed shared the characteristic feature of Renaissance philosophy: a discernment and celebration of human capacities deserving unbounded cultivation. This helped constitute a unique intellectual environment that influenced philosophical and related inquiries, and provided a model of human self-reliance – sometimes, though not invariably, in opposition to theism.

See also: Arabic philosophy; cabala; Platonism

Further reading
Cleary, John J. (ed.) (1997) *The Perennial Tradition of Neoplatonism*, Leuven, Belgium: Leuven University Press.
Lloyd, A.C. (1998 [1990]) *The Anatomy of Neoplatonism*, Oxford: Clarendon Press.
O'Meara, Dominic J. (1995) *Plotinus: An Introduction to the Enneads*, Oxford and New York: Clarendon Press and Oxford University Press.
Rappe, Sara (1999) *Reading Neoplatonism: Non-Discursive Thinking in the Texts of Plotinus, Proclus, and Damascius*, Cambridge and New York: Cambridge University Press.
Wallis, Richard T. (1995) *Neoplatonism*, London and Indianapolis: Duckworth and Hackett Pub.

neo-positivism *see* positivism

neo-Pythagoreanism *see* Pythagoreanism

neo-rationalism *see* rationalism

neo-realism *see* realism

neo-Scholasticism *see* Thomism

neo-spiritualism *see* spiritualism

neo-Stoicism *see* Stoicism

neo-Taoism *see* Chinese philosophy; Taoism

neo-Thomism *see* Thomism

neo-vitalism *see* vitalism

nephesh *see* cabala; philosophy of religion

neti-neti *see* Hinduism

neural net *see* cognitive; computer theory

neurosis *see* psychoanalysis

neustic *see* speech act theory

neutral impressions *see* philosophy of science

neutral monism *see* philosophy of mind

neutral philosophy *see* phenomenology

Neutralism *see* phenomenology; philosophy of mind

neutralization *see* phenomenology

New England Transcendentalism *see* transcendent

New Philosophers, the *see* philosophy, sociopolitical

New Realism *see* philosophy of mind

Newcomb's paradox *see* paradox

Newcomb's problem *see* paradox

Newtonian *see* mechanicism; philosophy of science

nexus *see* process philosophy

Nichiren School *see* Buddhism

Nichts, das *see* existentialism

Nichts nichtet, das *see* existentialism

nididhyāsana *see* Hinduism

Nietzschean philosophy *see* ethics; naturalism

nigamana *see* logic

nigraha-sthāna *see* logic

nihigáál *see* Native American philosophy

nihil est in intellectu quod prius non fuerit in sensu *see* empiricism

nihilism *see* ethics; Greek philosophy; philosophy, sociopolitical; philosophy of religion; skepticism

Nijūshi-ryū *see* Zen

nikshepa *see* Jainism

ninkyō-funi *see* Zen

nipadua *see* body

nirdesha *see* Hinduism

nirdvamda *see* Hinduism

Nirguna Brahman *see* Hinduism

nirodha *see* Hinduism

nirodha-samāpatti *see* Buddhism; Hinduism

nirvāna *see* Buddhism

Nirvāna School *see* Buddhism

nirvikalpaka-pratyaksha *see* Hinduism

nisus *see* evolution

nīti-shāstras *see* Hinduism

nitya *see* Hinduism

nitya-karma *see* Hinduism

nitya-vak *see* Hinduism

nīvarana *see* Hinduism

nivritti-mārga *see* Hinduism

nkrabea *see* determinism

nō *see* Zen

noema *see* phenomenology

noematic *see* phenomenology

noesis *see* phenomenology

noetic *see* phenomenology

noetic synthesis *see* perception

noetics *see* phenomenology

nominal definition *see* definition

nominal essence *see* essentialism

nominalism From the Latin, *nomen*, i.e. "name," this term denotes a doctrine concerning universals: briefly, that universals do not exist except in name. Nominalism is sometimes hard to distinguish from *conceptualism*, which holds that universals have mental existence, but do not exist outside the mind. It is also contrasted with *realism*, which holds universals have extra-mental existence.

Nominalism was significantly developed in Arabic philosophy and during the European Middle Ages. It can arguably be found in the *Tahāfut al-Falāsifah*, usually translated as *The Destruction of the Philosophers* or *The Contradiction of the Philosophers* (see ARABIC PHILOSOPHY), by the Persian philosopher, theologian, and mystic al-Ghazālī (CE 1059–1111). He argued that there are only definite phenomena of one kind regularly succeeding definite phenomena of another kind. Though his arguments were aimed at establishing that there is only one kind of causation: that of the Willing Being (i.e. to establishing theistic OCCASIONALISM), they entailed a somewhat restricted version of nominalism. For now, from the standpoint of the infinite power of the Willing Being, every real entity is in effect contingent, hence possible, but in a position of complete indeterminateness. The ground of its modal determinations lies entirely with the free decision of the Willing Being. The only necessity al-Ghazālī accepted was that implied by logical absurdities. That is, he rejected the view of some dialecticians that the power of the Willing Being included the power to do or bring about the logically impossible. Here, besides modern discussions of causality, one finds a foreshadowing of the ANALYTIC–SYNTHETIC DISTINCTION.

In the European Middle Ages, nominalism was advocated by the English philosopher William of Ockham (*c.* CE 1290–1349). He also foreshadowed the analytic–synthetic distinction in arguing that some things were known through themselves (in Latin, *perse nota* or *nota per se* and, in the singular, *per se notum* or *notum per se*, i.e. from the definition of terms or what later came to be called tautologies and analytic statements), while the rest were *nota per experientiam*, i.e. evident from experience. In addition, Ockham used the category of *notitia intuitiva* to denote what we

know by immediate awareness, e.g. the world around us.

His and his followers' philosophical position – Ockhamism – was characterized by the *principle of parsimony*, i.e. a preference for simplicity in theory construction. Also called the *principle of economy*, this principle has various senses: intellectual, where simplicity of concepts is sought; ontological, where simplicity of entities is sought; and practical, where simplicity in action is sought. A famous version of this principle is *entia non sunt multiplicanda praeter necessitatem* attributed to Ockham. He never actually formulated it in his writings, though he did say things like: *pluralitas non est ponenda sine necessitate* (a plurality should not be unnecessarily introduced), and *frustra fit per plura quod potets fieri per pauciora* (it is pointless to do with more what can be done with less). This is perhaps why the principle of parsimony came to be called *Ockham's razor*.

The United States philosopher W.V.O. Quine (CE 1908–2000), the United States philosopher Nelson Goodman (CE 1906–98), and others have arguably advocated versions of nominalism. Indeed, Quine has gone as far as raising doubts even about the appeal to analyticity to establish certain truths and has pointed out that some beliefs about logical and mathematical principles – e.g. the set theoretical axiom of abstraction – have gone from being thought self-evident to being considered false.

See also: alethiology; conceptualism; *de re*, under de; empiricism; essentialism; Platonism

Further reading

Gosselin, Mia (1990) *Nominalism and Contemporary Nominalism: Ontological and Epistemological Implications of the work of W.V.O. Quine and of N. Goodman*, Dordrecht and Boston: Kluwer Academic Publishers.
Tooley, Michael (1999) (ed.) *The Nature of Properties: Nominalism, Realism, and Trope Theory*, New York: Garland Pub.

nomological *see* condition; explanation

nomology *see* phenomenology; philosophy of law

nomos *see* condition; explanation; phenomenology; philosophy of law

nomotetic *see* Kantian philosophy

non-action *see* Taoism

non causa pro causa *see* fallacy

non-cognitivism *see* cognitive; ethics

non-contradiction, principle of *see* logic

non-embodiment *see* metaphysics

non-epistemic *see* perception

non-Euclidean geometry *see* philosophy of mathematics

non-I *see* anattā; Buddhism

non-monotonic logic *see* logic

non-natural properties *see* ethics

non-predicative property *see* theory of types

non-reductive materialism *see* philosophy of mind

non-reflexive *see* relation

non sequitur *see* fallacy

non-standard analysis *see* philosophy of mathematics

non-standard interpretation *see* logic; philosophy of language

non-standard model *see* philosophy of mathematics

non-standard semantics *see* logic; philosophy of language

non-subsistent form *see* Thomism

non-symmetric *see* relation

non-transitive *see* relation

non-violence *see* philosophy, sociopolitical

noologia *see* metaphysics

norm *see* philosophy of law

normal form *see* logic

normative ethics *see* ethics

normative relativism *see* ethics

nota notae est nota rei ipsius *see* syllogism

nota per experientiam *see* empiricism

nota per se *see* syllogism

notation, logical *see* logic

nothing *see* existentialism; metaphysics; myth

nothingness *see* existentialism

notion *see* empiricism; idealism

notional assent *see* reasoning

notions, common *see* Stoicism

notitia *see* empiricism; idealism

notitia illata *see* empiricism

notitia innata *see* empiricism

notitia intuitiva *see* empiricism

notitiae communes *see* Stoicism

notum per se *see* syllogism

noughting nought *see* existentialism

noumenal world *see* Kantian philosophy

noumenon *see* Kantian philosophy

nous *see* Neoplatonism; understanding

novelty *see* creation; evolution

n-tuple *see* set

null class *see* set

null relation *see* relation

number *see* philosophy of mathematics

number theory *see* philosophy of mathematics

numbers, law of large *see* ars conjectandi, under ars

numerical identity *see* identity

numinous *see* philosophy of religion

nyansa *see* wisdom

nyāya *see* Hinduism; Nyāya-Vaiśeṣika School

Nyāya-Vaiśeṣika School One of the six orthodox schools of Hinduism, supposed to have been founded by Gotama (*fl.* between the sixth and third century BCE, though some reports place him in the CE). It is also called *Tarkavidyā* or "the science of debate," and *Vādavidyā* or "the science of discussion." The *Nyāya* School of philosophy is named after the term *nyāya* ("method"), understood as method of proof, hence the translation of the School's name, "the science of logical proof." It is a system for the investigation of the world and human knowledge.

Vaiśeṣika derives its name from the term *Viśeṣa*, i.e. "distinction." It is a philosophy of nature that focuses on the comprehensive identification and listing of all distinct and irreducible constituents of the universe. The Nyāya and Vaiśeṣika Schools influenced each other to the point that they eventually came to form the syncretistic Nyāya-Vaiśeṣika School. In this synthesis, Nyāya contributed the logic and epistemology, while Vaiśeṣika provided the metaphysics.

The Nyāya-Vaiśeṣika School admits four sources of knowledge: perception, inference, analogy, and credible testimony. According to this school, one must suppose that there is a *nirvikalpaka-pratyaksha* or indeterminate perception of simple entities constituting the complex things we perceive. (By contrast, the Mīmāmsā School holds that, though quite vague and indefinite, our perception of simple entities is actual and not a mere supposition.) The Nyāya-Vaiśeṣika School also includes *samshaya*, i.e. "doubt," as one of its categories.

As for metaphysics, the Nyāya-Vaiśeṣika School holds that there are nine substances: the four atoms, space, time, ether, mind, and self. The atoms are eternal and contained in space. Their four kinds are earth, air, fire, and water. Their combinations, whose properties are explained in terms of properties of their components, are not eternal.

These combinations include, in addition to material entities, immaterial persons, each being a substantial and enduring self characterized by being conscious; feeling pleasure and pain, love and aversion; and having the capacity to make choices. Persons differ from each other in that they are different centers of consciousness, not merely in that they have been through different transmigratory lines. Finally, Nyāya-Vaiśeṣika School is monotheistic.

See also: Hinduism

Further reading
Chatterjee, Satischandra (1950) *An Introduction to Indian Philosophy*, 4th edn, rev. and enl., Calcutta: University of Calcutta.
Hiriyanna, Mysore (1996) *The Essentials of Indian Philosophy*, London: Diamond.

Nyingmapa *see* Buddhism

O

O *see* categorical; logic; syllogism

Obaku School *see* Zen

object From the Latin *objectum*, the past participle of *objicio* (its infinitive being *objicere*), and this from *ob*, i.e. "over," "against," and *jacere*, i.e. "to throw." Literally, *objicio* meant to throw forward, to be offered, exposed to something, presented to one's eyes. Figuratively, it meant to propose, cause, inspire, interpose, and oppose. These various meanings of *objicio* and its derivative, *objectum*, help clarify the various meanings of the term object. The ordinary current meaning of object is that which exists outside of, or independently of, mental activities. This, however, was the original meaning of subject, from *subjacio* and its infinitive *subjacere*, and the latter from *sub*, i.e. "under," and *jacere*, "to throw."

The term object acquired wide philosophical currency in the European Middle Ages, though its meaning was different in metaphysics, where it meant an end or final cause; in epistemology, where it meant the end of an act of knowing; and ethics, where it meant purpose. From this, arguably, all such senses of object shared a core meaning: whatever is subject to some power or condition, whether cognitive, volitional, or emotive.

In epistemology, object later came to mean whatever is thought, i.e. whatever is designated by an intentional cognitive reference. This usage was the predominant one in Cartesianism and Empiricism, yet, in Kantian philosophy, it changed so that object came to mean what is at least partly outside awareness, i.e. reality; by contrast with the subject, which is the center of awareness. This subject–object distinction, which some consider a subject–object dichotomy, originated the modern use of *subjective* as what is in the subject, i.e. judgments in the cognizing subject, or mental entities in the psychological subject. In phenomenology, there has been an attempt at moving towards the traditional use of object as intentional object, i.e. as whatever a judgment can be about. This is very close to the logical meaning of subject as that of which something can be affirmed or denied.

In metaphysics, today, a concrete particular object is often understood as a complex of two kinds of components: *properties*, which can be exemplified in many instances and account for the object's qualitative identity; and a *substratum*, on which rest the properties belonging to a particular object and accounting for its numerical identity. By contrast, *bundle theory* holds that a concrete object is a complex of properties which all stand in a contingent relation of *co-instantiation* to each other. Critics have argued that this makes all objects have their properties essentially, hence cannot change. However, bundle theorists reply that, at most, momentary objects have their properties essentially, that enduring concrete objects are series of momentary objects in some contingent relation with each other, and that the enduring objects' properties can change.

Critics have also said that, according to bundle theory, two different momentary objects could have all properties in common.

However, proponents reply that this is a problem only if the thesis that a momentary object is a complex of co-instantiated properties is a necessary truth, not if it is a contingent truth. Since, in this latter case, two different momentary objects could happen momentarily to have all their properties in common, the proponents of bundle theory would seem to imply that this possibility is, at worst, an oddity, not a problem for the theory. Other proponents, however, defend bundle theory by simply rejecting as inconceivable the critics' claim that two different momentary objects could happen to have all properties in common.

Discussions of bundle theory have sometimes centered around the notion of *compresence*, an unanalyzable relation that can serve to analyze particular objects as complexes of qualities which, for example, in psychology, are simultaneous in one experience, and, in physics, overlap in space and time.

See also: epistemology; ethics; metaphysics; phenomenology

Further reading
Denkel, Arda (1996) *Object and Property*, Cambridge and New York: Cambridge University Press.
Dougherty, Kenneth Francis (1951) *The Subject, Object, and Method of the Philosophy of Nature According to Thomas Aquinas*, Washington: Catholic University of America Press.
Hill, Claire Ortiz (1991) *Word and Object in Husserl, Frege, and Russell: The Roots of Twentieth-Century Philosophy*, Athens, OH: Ohio University Press.

object, eternal *see* category; metaphysics; process philosophy

object, intentional *see* object; phenomenology

object language *see* use–mention distinction

object, propositional *see* philosophy of language

objective body *see* abstract; category; phenomenology; philosophy, sociopolitical

objective interiority *see* actualism

objective probability *see* probability

objective reality *see* metaphysics

objective reason *see* justification

objective relativism *see* metaphysics

objective rightness *see* ethics

objective spirit *see* idealism

objectivism, ethical *see* ethics

objectivism, moral *see* ethics

objectivity *see* epistemology; ethics

objectual quantification *see* logic

Objektiv *see* philosophy of language

obligation *see* ethics; logic

oblique context *see* opacity; reference

oblique intention *see* intention

observation *see* empiricism

observation language *see* philosophy of science

observation sentence *see* reductionism

observation term *see* philosophy of science; reductionism

obverse *see* argument

obversion *see* argument

occasionalism In its strict sense, this term denotes the seventeenth-century doctrine, prompted by the mind–body dualism formulated in CARTESIANISM, that God is the intermediary between mind and body. Though prompted by the aforementioned dualism, this doctrine was not *ad hoc*, but based on criticisms of such conceptions of causality as that minds can have an effect on bodies, and that motion can be produced by the passive extension ascribed to bodies in Cartesianism. Its advocates included the German philosopher Johannes Clauberg (CE 1622–65), the Belgian philosopher Arnold Geulincx (CE 1624–69), and the French philosophers Gérard de Cordemoy (CE 1626–84), Louis de la Forge (CE 1632–66) and, perhaps most notably, Nicolas Malebranche (CE 1638–1715).

Occasionalism is related to, and arguably influenced by, but not identical with, the ancient, medieval, and modern doctrine of *concursus dei* ("God's concurrence") or divine concurrence. The latter is a particular case of the medieval view that any causation involving created substances must also involve both the substances' causal powers and God's causal activity. For example, a person's actions result from both the person's causal powers and God's causal support. This support is *divine concurrence*. So, the doctrine of divine concurrence, like occasionalism, holds God's causal power to be necessary for any event to occur. Yet, by contrast with occasionalism, which reserves all causal power to God, it holds creatures have some causal power, thus constituting an attempt at solving the problem of free will.

Philosophers in the Islamic world had already formulated a generalized version of occasionalism. Notable among them is the Persian philosopher, theologian and mystic al-Ghazālī (CE 1059–1111), who argued along occasionalist lines in his *Tahāfut al-Falāsifah*, usually translated as *The Destruction of the Philosophers* or *The Contradiction of the Philosophers* (see ARABIC PHILOSOPHY). Al-Ghazālī argued that definite phenomena of one kind regularly succeeding definite phenomena of another kind is all there is. His arguments were aimed at establishing that there is only one kind of causation: that of the Willing Being – i.e. at establishing theistic occasionalism. This also entailed a somewhat restricted version of nominalism. For now, from the standpoint of the infinite power of the Willing Being, every real entity is in effect contingent, hence possible, but in a position of complete indeterminateness. The ground of its modal determinations lies entirely with the free decision of the Willing Being.

See also: Arabic philosophy; atomism; Cartesianism; empiricism

Further reading
Fakhry, Majid (1958) *Islamic Occasionalism and its Critique by Averroes and Aquinas*, London: George Allen & Unwin.
Nadler, Steven M. (1993) *Causation in Early Modern Philosophy: Cartesianism, Occasionalism, and Preestablished Harmony*, University Park, PA: Pennsylvania State University Press.

occurrences, philosophy of *see* empiricism

occurrent *see* disposition

occurrent memory *see* memory

Ockham's razor *see* nominalism

Ockhamism *see* nominalism

Oedipus complex *see* psychoanalysis

ōkra *see* philosophy of mind

oligarchy *see* philosophy, sociopolitical

OM *see* Hinduism

omega-completeness *see* philosophy of mathematics

omega-consistency *see* philosophy of mathematics

omega-point *see* evolution

omega rule *see* philosophy of mathematics

omega-valued *see* philosophy of mathematics

Ometeotl *see* Nahua philosophy

Omeyocan *see* Nahua philosophy

omission *see* ethics

omnibenevolence *see* God

omnipotence *see* God

omnipotence, paradoxes of *see* God

omnipresence *see* God

omniscience *see* God

One, the *see* Hinduism; Neoplatonism

one–many problem *see* metaphysics

one over many *see* metaphysics

one-sword theory *see* philosophy, sociopolitical

one-way reduction sentences *see* reductionism

onipa *see* body

ontic *see* ens; existentialism

ontic theories *see* metaphysics

ontological argument *see* philosophy of religion

ontological commitment *see* epistemology; metaphysics

ontological dependence *see* epistemology; logic

ontological principle *see* process philosophy

ontological priority *see* epistemology; logic

ontological solipsism *see* solipsism

ontologism *see* idealism

ontology *see* metaphysics

ontosophy *see* metaphysics

Onyame *see* God

opacity The feature some linguistic constructions – called *opaque* constructions – have of resisting substitutivity of identicals. For example, consider the knowledge claim formulated by the sentence "I know that the man in the gray suit is the one who robbed the bank." Suppose that the claim is true and the man's name is John; but that the person making the claim does not know that John is the man's name. Even though John is identical with the man in the gray suit, replacing the phrase "the man in the gray suit" with the name "John" will turn the claim into a false one. This substitution procedure falls under a general procedure called *quantifying in*, i.e. using a quantifier outside an opaque construction in trying to bind a variable within the construction. This can happen with propositional attitude verbs, e.g. "to believe," and "to know," as well as with modal operators. For example, another instance of quantifying in would be to attempt to infer from the true sentence "Necessarily, if I have been born and I am not dead I am alive," which does not rule out that I can one day die, the false sentence "If I have been born and I am not dead, then I am necessarily alive," which entails it is impossible for me to die.

That is, the sentence resists substitutivity of identicals, and, in the first example, the phrase "the man in the gray suit" is said to be *referentially opaque* or to be characterized by *referential opacity*, i.e. it occurs in a sentence whose truth value depends on something other than whether the phrase "the man in the gray suit" refers to the same item as the name "John" in the given example. A term's occurrence is *referentially transparent* when it is not referentially opaque. Accordingly, the criterion relevant in this case is that traditionally called *interchangeability salva veritate*, or *substitutivity salva veritate*, where *salva veritate* is a Latin phrase meaning "with truth saved." An *opaque context*, e.g. that of sentences including epistemic operators such as believe, desire, know, possibly, and necessarily, does not satisfy the criterion.

The notion of opaque context is related to that of *oblique context* or *oratio obliqua* or *indirect discourse*. It is a linguistic context where one of its expressions indicates a sense other than its customary one. For example, in (1) "Socrates died from the effects of drinking the hemlock," the context of the noun "Socrates" is direct. In other words, the noun "Socrates" is used in its direct sense or customary sense whereby it denotes the Greek philosopher who drank the hemlock, namely Socrates. By contrast, in (2) "'Socrates' is an eight-letter word, the context of the term "Socrates" is oblique, because it denotes a word, not its customary sense of the Greek philosopher who drank the hemlock. The type of oblique context related to opacity is exemplified by the context of the term "Socrates" in the sentence (3) "Historians believe that Socrates died from the effects of drinking the hemlock." For in this sentence, the dependent clause "Socrates died from the effects of drinking the hemlock" designates a proposition, i.e. that which historians believe, while in sentence (1), "Socrates died from the effects of drinking the hemlock" designates what makes the proposition true, i.e. a truth value.

See also: logic; reference

Further reading
Humphreys, Paul and Fetzer, James H. (1998) *The New Theory of Reference: Kripke, Marcus, and Its Origins*, Dordrecht and Boston: Kluwer Academic Publishers.
Munitz, Milton Karl and Unger, Peter K. (eds) (1974) *Semantics and Philosophy*, New York: New York University Press.

opaque construction *see* opacity

opaque context *see* opacity

open formula *see* logic

open loop *see* cybernetics

open-question argument *see* ethics

open sentence *see* logic

open society *see* philosophy, sociopolitical

open texture *see* induction

openness *see* ethics

operant conditioning *see* behaviorism

operant meaning *see* meaning

operational definition *see* operationalism

operationalism Also called *operationism*, a philosophy of science program aimed at interpreting scientific concepts through experimental procedures or operations and observational results. The United States physicist P.W. Bridgman (CE 1882–1963) formulated this program, arguing that the meaning of any concept is the set of operations one uses in fixing that concept. For example, the concept of length is identical with the operations of measuring. More abstract concepts involve mental or written operations that fix them. With regard to theoretical terms, operationalism adopted the positivistic requirement that theoretical terms be explicitly defined through directly observable conditions. All of these ways of characterizing meanings on the basis of the said operations constituted *operational definitions* of the terms.

However, since alternative measurement procedures could be used for the same concept, explicit definitions were found impossible. Instead, *reduction sentences* were used to define concepts partially by means of sentences that included them as intervening variables, in sentences of the form "Under observable conditions *C*, *x* is *T* if and only if *O*," as in "Under the observable condition of being placed in water, sugar is soluble if and only if it dissolves." This was later weakened to make room for clusters of theoretical concepts (hypothetical constructs or theoretical constructs), by making them definable through an interpretive system predicting collective rather than individual effects of the concepts. Whenever a scientific concept is, as just described, only partially defined, observational consequences do not exhaust its content. Hence, more than one theoretical statement will be compatible with all the observational consequences. This situation is called *theoretical underdetermination*.

See also: empiricism; measurement; theory

Further reading
Benjamin, A. Cornelius (1955) *Operationism*, Springfield, IL: Thomas.
Goldberg, Stanley (1984) "Being Operational vs. Operationism: Bridgman on Relativity," *Rivista di storia della scienza* 1(3), November.

operations *see* operationalism

operator, deontic *see* logic

operator, scope of *see* logic

operator, sentential *see* logic

operator theory of adverbs *see* logic

opinion *see* epistemology; knowledge

opposites *see* infinity

O-proposition *see* syllogism

optimal state of affairs *see* philosophy of economics

optimality, Pareto *see* philosophy of economics

optimization *see* decision

optimizing *see* decision

option, genuine *see* justification

oracles, Chaldean *see* philosophy of religion

oracula chaldaica *see* philosophy of religion

oratio obliqua *see* opacity

order *see* logic; ordering; philosophy, sociopolitical

ordered n-tuple *see* logic

ordered pair *see* logic

ordering An arrangement of elements of a set whereby some of them precede others. In set theory, an ordering is an arrangement of the items of a set so that some of them come before others.

There are various kinds of orderings. One of them is a *dense* ordering, i.e. an ordering where, between any two items, there is a third.

There are three jointly minimal conditions a relation R must meet to be an ordering – *reflexivity*: $(x)\ Rxx$, *antisymmetry*: $(x)(y)\ ((Rxy$ & $Ryx) \supset x=y)$, and *transitivity*: $(x)(y)(z)\ ((Rxy$ & $Ryz) \supset (Rxz))$. When a relation is reflexive, antisymmetrical, and transitive, it is called a *partial* ordering. If reflexivity is replaced by *irreflexivity*: $(x)\ -Rxx$, then the relation is called a *strict partial* ordering. In addition, a *total* ordering or *strict linear* ordering on X is a partial ordering that, in addition, satisfies the *connectedness* condition: $(x)(y)\ (Rxy\ v\ Ryx)$. Finally, a set X is a well-ordered set (or is said to be in a well-ordering relation) by R if R is a total ordering of X and every non-empty subset of Y of X has an R-least member: $((y) \subseteq X)(y \neq \Phi \supset (\exists z \varepsilon Y)((w)\varepsilon Y)Rzw)$. Without the antisymmetry condition, this becomes a *weak linear* ordering. Also, a *well-ordering relation* excludes infinite descending sequences; while a *strict well-ordering relation* is irreflexive instead of reflexive, thus excluding loops.

Different from any of the former is a *lexical* ordering or *lexicographic* ordering (sometimes also called and *Archimedian* ordering), a method whereby, given a finite ordered set of symbols (e.g. the letters of the alphabet), all finite sequences of those symbols are ordered through a recursive process. First, all single letters are listed alphabetically; then, all pairs are listed in the order aa...az; ba...bz, Za...ZZ; then all triplets are similarly ordered, and so on.

These various types of orderings, as indicated by some of the examples, have applications in mathematics and logic. They originate *hierarchies*, i.e. divisions of mathematical or logical objects in accordance with given orderings which reflect the complexity of the objects they involve. For example, there are hierarchies of real numbers (arithmetic hierarchies), of sets of real numbers, and of formulas (involving predicate hierarchy), defined as *first order* when they apply to individual variables and *higher order* when they apply to more than one individual variable.

The types of orderings mentioned also have applications in ordering-policy alternatives in economics and other policy studies, as well as in other fields of inquiry.

Further reading

Reinelt, G. (1985) *The Linear Ordering Problem: Algorithms and Applications*, Berlin: Heldermann.

Riecan, Beloslav (1997) *Integral, Measure, and Ordering*, Dordrecht, Boston, and Bratislava: Kluwer Academic Publishers and Ister Science.

Stork, P. (1991) *Policy Optimization Using a Lexicographic Preference Ordering*, Rotterdam, Netherlands: Erasmus University.

ordinal logic *see* logic

ordinary-language philosophy *see* perception

ordinary rational agent *see* rationality

organic *see* biology

organic unity *see* biology; ethics

organicism *see* ethics

organism *see* biology

organismic analogy biology *see* philosophy, sociopolitical

organismic biology *see* biology

organismic metaphor *see* biology; philosophy, sociopolitical

organization *see* ethics; philosophy, sociopolitical

organon *see* logic

origin *see* element

original *see* aesthetics

original intelligence *see* Advaita; Brahman

original sin *see* myth; philosophy of religion

orphic mysteries *see* philosophy of religion

Orphism *see* philosophy of religion

Orthodox Marxism *see* Marxism

orthodoxy *see* philosophy of religion

Oryō-ha *see* Zen

Oryō School *see* Zen

Osiris *see* philosophy of religion

Oslo Group *see* positivism

ostensive definition *see* definition

ostensive proof *see* logic

other, the *see* existentialism

other minds, problem of *see* philosophy of mind; solipsism

othering *see* Platonism

otherness *see* existentialism

ought-is problem *see* ethics

ouk on *see* metaphysics; philosophy of religion

ousia *see* metaphysics

outer-domain semantics *see* logic

outflanking *see* philosophy, sociopolitical

overdetermination *see* causal law

overman *see* ethics

overriding reason *see* ethics

overridingness *see* ethics

over-soul *see* transcendent

Oxford calculators *see* Oxford movements

Oxford Group *see* ethics

Oxford movements Philosophical and related movements developed at Oxford University. One of them was that started with the arrival of the Franciscans in the thirteenth century CE. Its most notable members were the English philosophers Robert Grosseteste (*c.* CE 1168–1253) and Roger Bacon (*c.* CE 1214–*c.* 1293), and the Scottish philosopher John Duns Scotus (CE 1266–1308), the originator of the type of philosophical approach – partly Augustinian, partly Aristotelian – called Scotism.

Another movement was that of the *Oxford Calculators*, also called the *Merton School* because many of them were at Oxford University's Merton College. These were an early to mid-fourteenth-century group of natural philosophers, logicians, and mathematicians.

They were called calculators after the title of a book written by one of the group's members, who was probably called Richard Swineshead, and who published *Liber Calculationum* or *Book of Calculations* a few years before CE 1350. This book discussed a range of topics concerning the quantification and measurement of motion and other forms of change.

There is also the *Oxford Movement*, a nineteenth-century Catholic movement of spiritual renewal. Notable among its leaders was the English churchman John Henry Newman (CE 1801–90), whose works aimed at characterizing a reasonable basis for religious faith as related to various conceptions of reasoning (see INDUCTION).

In addition, there is the *Oxford Group*, also called *Buchmanism* and *Moral Rearmament*, a twentieth-century movement of moral revival founded by the United States Lutheran minister Frank Buchman (CE 1878–1961). This movement sought to bring about universal brotherhood through an objective system of morality that was largely derived from Christianity. It should be noticed that the name the Oxford Group is sometimes also used to denote a twentieth-century group of analytic philosophers. This latter group is discussed under ANALYSIS in this dictionary.

See also: analysis; ethics; Christianity

Further reading
Ollard, S.L. (1933) *A Short History of the Oxford Movement*, London and Milwaukee, USA: A.R. Mowbray & Co. Ltd and The Morehouse Publishing Co.
Sylla, Edith Dudley (1991) *The Oxford Calculators and the Mathematics of Motion, 1320–1350: Physics and Measurement by Latitudes*, New York: Garland Pub.

Oxford philosophy *see* analysis

Oxford School of Intuitionism *see* ethics

P

P *see* logic; syllogism

pacifism *see* philosophy, sociopolitical

pact *see* philosophy, sociopolitical

Padua School *see* Bologna School

pai *see* Māori philosophy

palingenesis *see* myth

Pan-Africanism *see* diaspora

pancalism *see* mechanicism

panentheism *see* God

panlogism *see* idealism

panpsychism *see* animism

pansomatism *see* positivism

pantheism *see* God; philosophy of religion

Pantheismusstreit *see* God

paraconsistency *see* logic

paradigm *see* philosophy of science

paradigm-case argument *see* argument

paradox From the Greek *paradoxa*, which means "contrary to received opinion" and was derived from *para*, i.e. "contrary to," and *doxa*, i.e. "opinion." The term paradox has come to mean *seeming contrary to common sense* or a *seemingly sound piece of reasoning that leads to a contradiction or a plainly false conclusion*. In the Middle Ages, many paradoxes and other difficult to resolve problems were classified as *impossibilia* or *insolubilia*,

the latter but not the former involving real or apparent contradictions.

There is a great variety of paradoxes. Some notable examples are as follows. The deontic paradoxes arise when a set of sentences about obligation or permission in a natural language, say English, appears to involve no contradictions; but, when represented in a system of *deontic* logic, the resulting set of sentences involves at least one contradiction. An example is the *contrary-to-duty imperative paradox*. Suppose John steals Jim's car, but is caught and brought to court, where Jane is the judge. The following declarative sentences appear true:

1 John steals Jim's car.
2 If John steals Jim's car, then Jane should punish John for stealing Jim's car.
3 It is obligatory that, if John does not steal Jim's car, then Jane does not punish John for stealing Jim's car.
4 John ought not to steal Jim's car.

The following are formalizations of the previous sentences in standard deontic logic:

1'. s
2'. $s \supset Op$
3'. $O(-s \supset -p)$
4'. $O-s$

Given these premises, various inferences follow. First, Op follows from premises 1' and 2', by *modus ponens*. Second, the standard deontic logic axiom $O(A \supset B) \supset (OA \supset OB)$ has $O(-s \supset -p) \supset (O-s \supset O-p)$ as an instance that, by *modus ponens* and together with premise 3' implies $O -s \supset O -p$, and the latter, together with premise 4', entails $O -p$ by *modus ponens*. However, this contradicts the previously inferred Op. Logicians have generally agreed that standard deontic logic is thus inconsistent and their inquiry focuses on what alternative approach to adopt.

Another deontic paradox is the *paradox of the knower*, which arises out of assuming that some people – e.g. petty thieves – sometimes do what they know they should not do – e.g. shoplift – and that some people – e.g. storeguards – are obligated to know of any such wrongdoing being performed. For example, if A shoplifts and B is the shop's guard on duty, then, given the previous assumptions, B is obligated to know that A shoplifted. Also, it seems both true and consistent with the previous statements to say: (1) A ought not to shoplift.

On the other hand, the notion of knowledge entails the theorem: if B knows that A shoplifted, then A shoplifted. However, the following is a standard deontic logic theorem: if $p \supset q$ is a theorem, then $Op \supset Oq$ is a theorem. From these two statements, it follows that if B is obligated to know that A shoplifted, then A ought to shoplift. However, this conditional, together with the above statement that B is obligated to know that A shoplifted, entails: (2) A ought to shoplift; this contradicts (1).

For the *grue* paradox, see INDUCTION.

The *hedonistic paradox* can be formulated as follows. The principle of hedonism states that we should aim at maximizing pleasure in whatever we decide to do. In order thus to maximize pleasure, for each decision we face (even if we are deciding what dish to request when dining at a fancy restaurant), we need to calculate all alternative courses of action, the pleasures attached to each, and decide accordingly. Such calculations are long, cumbersome, and dreary, hence painful, not pleasant. Also, when time is of the essence, they result in missing opportunities out of faithfulness to the hedonist principle. As a result, the application of the principle of hedonism leads to less pleasure than we would have attained had we not applied it. The hedonistic paradox is but a particular case of the *perfectionist paradox*, which can be formulated as follows. The principle of perfectionism states that we should aim at maximizing good in whatever we decide to do. In order thus to maximize good, for each decision we face (even if we are deciding what dish to request when dining at a fancy restaurant), we need to calculate all alternative courses of action, the good attached to each, and decide accordingly. Such calculations are long, cumbersome, and dreary, hence painful, not good. Also, when time is of the essence, they result in missing opportunities out of faithfulness to the perfectionist principle. As a result, the application of the principle of perfectionism leads to less good than we would have attained had we not applied it.

Newcomb's paradox or *Newcomb's problem* is a conflict between the *principle of maximizing expected utility*: one should choose the option whose expected utility is greatest (where the expected utility is obtained by adding the product of multiplying the utility of each possible outcome by its probability), and the *principle of dominance*: if the states determining the outcomes of options are causally independent of the options, and there is one option that is better than the others in each state, one should choose it.

For example, suppose Peter can choose the first or both of two boxes where the first contains a billion dollars or nothing, and the other contains two thousand dollars. Suppose further that Jane is a very reliable predictor who has predicted Peter's choice and arranged the boxes' contents as follows. If Jane has predicted that Peter will take only the first box, she has placed one billion dollars in the box; while if she has predicted that Peter will take both boxes, she has left the first box empty. Given Jane's high reliability, the probability that Peter will get a billion dollars by taking only the first box is high; but the probability that he will get one billion, two thousand dollars by taking both boxes is low. That is, the expected utility of taking only the first box is greater than that of taking both boxes. So, on the basis of the principle of maximizing expected utility, Peter should take only the first box; however, on the basis of the principle of dominance, Peter should take both boxes, because his choice does not causally influence the contents of the boxes, and choosing both would yield him two thousand dollars plus whatever the contents of the first box happen to be.

Philosophers have proposed to solve the paradox by changing the definition of expected utility so that it becomes sensitive to the causal, but not the evidential, influence of options on the states determining their outcomes.

The *paradox of analysis* can be formulated as follows. For a linguistic analysis to be adequate, the *analysans* and the *analysandum* must be synonymous. That is, if "unmarried male" is the *analysandum* of "bachelor," both expressions must mean the same. However, if they do, then the sentence "A bachelor is an unmarried male" is synonymous with the sentence "A bachelor is a bachelor." Yet, the latter two sentences do not appear to be synonymous. This can also be formulated as a dilemma: either an analysis is not adequate (whenever the *analysans* and the *analysandum* are not synonymous) or it is not informative (when they are synonymous).

A common formulation of the *paradox of self-deception* is as follows: if one deceives oneself, one lies to oneself, and succeeds in getting oneself to believe the lie. However, in lying to oneself, one knows one is telling a lie, hence one does not believe the lie. This has been put in the form of the dilemma: either an individual is not an individual, or self-deception is impossible.

The *paradox of the unexpected future event* is often formulated as the *paradox of the unexpected examination*, the *class paradox*, or the *paradox of the unexpected execution*. Its general form is: one day of the coming week, the event *x* will happen (e.g. *A* will be given an examination, or *B* will be executed), but at breakfast time on that day, *A* (or *B*) will have no good reason to expect it. However, the event cannot happen on the last day of the week, because it will then be expected. For the same reason, it cannot happen on the day before the last day of the week. And so on. Hence, it will never happen.

For the *paradox of the ravens*, see INDUCTION.

For the *paradox of the stone*, see GOD.

For the *paradoxes of confirmation*, see INDUCTION.

For the *paradoxes of material implication*, see LOGIC.

For the *paradoxes of omnipotence*, see GOD.

For the *paradoxes of self-reference*, see THEORY OF TYPES.

For the *paradoxes of strict implication*, see LOGIC.

For the *postcard paradox*, see THEORY OF TYPES.

For the *preface paradox*, see THEORY OF TYPES.

For the *semantic paradoxes*, see THEORY OF TYPES.

For the *paradoxes of set theory*, see SET.

The *Sorites*: from the Greek *soros*, i.e. "heap" (hence its other name, the *heap paradox*), this term denotes a paradox that concerns gradations. Generally, it can be formulated as follows: a grain of sand does not make a heap of sand. Adding another grain still does not make a heap. In general, adding one more grain does not make a heap. So, by adding grains one by one, a heap is never formed. A reply to this paradoxical result has been to reject the assumption that if a heap cannot be made with a number n of grains, then it cannot be made with $n+1$ grains. However, this reply assumes that there is a sharp cutoff point after which a bunch of grains becomes a heap. This might seem plausible for heaps, but not for other items involving gradations, say, shades of color, tadpoles gradually turning into frogs, and infants gradually turning into toddlers. Another reply has been to say that a single grain does not make a difference at any point, hence vaguely defined bunches of grains, ranges of color, age-ranges, and the like are the basic elements to use in talking of gradations. This however appears to require the formulation of a logical system involving no sharp cutoffs – an enterprise that is still in its infancy (see fuzzy logic, under LOGIC).

The *Saint Petersburg paradox* was originally formulated as a puzzle about gambling by the Netherlands-born Swiss mathematician and physicist Daniel Bernoulli (CE 1700–82) to argue that expected utilities, not expected returns, govern rational preferences. The gamble pays $2 if heads turn up on a coin's first toss, $4 if heads first turn up on the second, $8 if heads first turn up on the third, etc. The expected return is $(½)2+(¼)4+(1/8)8+\ldots$, i.e. infinite. Yet, no one would find such a gamble worth much money. Bernoulli argued that the utility of wealth is proportional to the logarithm of the wealth a prospective gambler has which, together with Bernoulli's other assumptions about the gamble, gives the gamble a finite expected utility. The Austrian economist Karl Menger (CE 1840–1921) formulated a version of this paradox where utility payoffs replaced monetary payoffs. This gave the gamble infinite expected utility, which would suggest that, even with infinite expected utilities, no one would find the gamble worth much money. This paradox is still being debated.

The *voting paradox* was discovered by the French philosopher Marie-Jean-Antoine-Nicolas de Caritat, Marquis de Condorcet (CE 1743–94), who thereby started what today is called *social-choice theory* (see DECISION). Suppose voters A, B, and C rank proposals x, y, and z as follows: $A – xyz$; $B – yzx$; $C – zxy$. It follows that, in majoritarian voting, x beats y, y beats z, but z beats x. This state of affairs is called *cyclical* to indicate that collective preferences are not transitive. Condorcet argued that any satisfactory voting system must ensure the selection of a proposal that beats all alternative proposals in majoritarian competition. Such a proposal is called a *Condorcet winner*. In this connection, Condorcet also formulated the *jury theorem*: if voters register their opinions about something and the probabilities of these individuals being correct are greater than 1/2, equal, and independent, then the majority of voters is more likely to be correct than any minority or any one voter.

Zeno's paradoxes are paradoxes attributed to the Greek philosopher Zeno of Elea (490–430 BCE). The paradoxes concern space, time, motion, and change, and some interpreters have argued that, as a set, they help support the view that reality is a changeless and indivisible being. They include at least four paradoxes:

First, the *racetrack paradox* – a runner trying to reach the end of a track must first get to the midpoint; then, the midpoint between the midpoint and the end; next, the midpoint between the latter and the end; and so on. These points are infinite, hence the runner cannot reach the end of the track.

Second, the *paradox of Achilles and the tortoise* – the tortoise is given a lead when racing against Achilles, the fastest runner in Greece. In trying to pass the tortoise, Achilles must first get to the point where the tortoise starts. However, when he gets there, the tortoise has advanced to point 2. Achilles must then reach point 2; but, when he gets there, the tortoise has advanced to point 3. Achilles must now try to reach point 3; but when he does, the tortoise has reached point 4. Indeed, whenever Achilles reaches a point at which the tortoise just was, the tortoise has moved a bit – however infinitesimally – further. Hence, so long as the tortoise does not stop, Achilles never reaches the tortoise.

Third, the *paradox of the stadium* – consider three equal rows of bodies, A, B, and C, lined up in front of you. One row, B, is at rest, and A and C move perpendicularly to the initial line up, an equal distance L in opposite directions at the same time and at the same rate. It takes the same time for A to travel $L/2$ relatively to B, as it takes A to travel L relatively to C. Hence, double the time equals its half.

1 Initial positions:
AA
BB
CC

2 Positions after A and C move:
AA
 BB
  CC

Fourth, the *flying arrow paradox* – at any instant, a flying arrow is at a particular place, hence it is not moving. For if it were moving, it would not be at the place where it is.

Some scholars also mention the *dichotomy paradox*, which apparently can be formulated as follows. For any division of a whole (e.g.

space, the line *xy*, time, or reality), either the whole has a finite or an infinite number of parts that either have or lack magnitude. If divisible into a finite number of parts that lack magnitude, the whole cannot be reconstituted. If divisible into an infinite number of parts that lack magnitude, the whole cannot be reconstituted. If divisible into an infinite number of parts that have magnitude, the whole can be reconstituted but will be much larger than the original. If divisible into a finite number of parts that have magnitude, then their magnitude must be finite and, therefore, will disappear in a finite number of divisions. Hence, no whole is divisible.

Versions of at least some of these paradoxes were also formulated by the Chinese philosopher Hui Shi (*c.* 380–*c.* 305 BCE) AND, LATER, BY THE INDIAN PHILOSOPHER NAGARJUNA (CE 100–200).

For the *unexpected examination paradox*, see the paradox of the *unexpected future event*, above.

See also: decision; logic; induction; set; theory of types

Further reading
Copi, Irving M. (1971) *The Theory of Logical Types*, London: Routledge & Kegan Paul.
Faris, J.A. (1996) *The Paradoxes of Zeno*, Aldershot, UK and Brookfield, VT: Avebury.
Quine, W.V. (1966) *The Ways of Paradox and Other Essays*, New York: Random House.

parallel distributed processing *see* computer theory

parallelism, psychophysical *see* philosophy of mind

paralogism *see* fallacy; Kantian philosophy

paramānu *see* Hinduism

paramilitary terrorism *see* war

paranormal *see* philosophy of mind; philosophy of science

parapsychology *see* philosophy of mind; philosophy of science

Pareto efficiency *see* philosophy of economics

Pareto optimality *see* philosophy of economics

Pareto superior *see* philosophy of economics

Paris School Term used to refer to two sharply different and historically quite separate groups of philosophers active in Paris. The most recent one was largely an existentialism school that flourished after the Second World War and was led by the French philosopher Jean-Paul Sartre (CE 1905–80) and Simone de Beauvoir (CE 1908–86), and included various other thinkers (see EXISTENTIALISM).

The name *Paris School*, or *the Parisians*, however, has also been traditionally used to refer to a group of thinkers who flourished in Paris in the fourteenth century CE. Its is sometimes also called *Buridan's School* because its most notable member was the French philosopher John Buridan (*c.* CE 1295–1356), a moderate nominalist who distinguished between denotation and connotation, studied the modal syllogism, and discussed problems concerning the relation between reason and the will.

Another notable member was the French ecclesiastic, philosopher, and scientist Nicole d'Oresme (*c.* CE 1325–82), one of the first Western philosophers to write philosophy in the vernacular. He anticipated the mean-speed and distance theorems later formulated by the physicist and astronomer Galileo Galilei (CE 1564–1642), born in Pisa, in what is now Italy. In mathematics, d'Oresme formulated the notion of irrational exponent.

Still other notable members were Marsilius of Inghen (*c.* CE 1330–96), who held quantity and extension were not identical, and formulated the impetus theory. Another was Albert of Saxony (CE 1316–90), a terminist logic philosopher (see SYNCATEGOREMATA) who also wrote treatises on geometry. The French physicist, historian and philosopher of science Pierre-Maurice-Marie Duhem (CE 1861–1916) argued that the Paris School members have been wrongly interpreted to be nominalists. Though influenced by nominalism, they also, according to Duhem, displayed Thomist and Scotist views. Also, he held them to have offered the main, if not the only, late Middle Ages precedent for modern physics, especially for the principle of inertia. Other historians, however, have argued that besides, and sometimes before, the Paris School, the Oxford Calculators, also called the Merton School (see OXFORD MOVEMENTS) anticipated modern physical principles.

See also: definition; identity; nominalism; Scholasticism; Thomism; philosophy of science; syncategoremata

Further reading
Duhem, Pierre-Maurice Marie (1909) *Un Précurseur français de Copernic: Nicole Oresme (1377)*, Paris: Librairie Armand Colin.
—— (1974 [1905]) *Les Origines de la statique*, Paris: A. Hermann.
Wahl, Jean Andre (1969) *Philosophies of Existence: An Introduction to the Basic Thought of Kierkegaard, Heidegger, Jaspers, Marcel, Sartre*, London: Routledge & K. Paul.

parousia *see* Platonism

parse tree *see* philosophy of language

parsimony, principle of *see* nominalism

parsing *see* philosophy of language

part *see* holism

partial *see* Chinese philosophy; ethics

partial belief *see* probability

partial function *see* logic

partial ordering *see* ordering

partiality *see* Chinese philosophy; ethics

participation *see* philosophy, sociopolitical

participatory *see* philosophy, sociopolitical

particular, bare *see* description

particular proposition *see* syllogism

particularism *see* epistemology

particularization *see* ethics

particulars *see* abstract

partition *see* set

parva naturalia *see* Aristotelianism; associationism

Pascal's wager *see* faith; philosophy of religion

passion From the Latin *passio*, and this from the Greek *pathos* (a passive state), this term contrasts with action and denotes something

passive or the condition whereby something is acted upon by other things. With Cartesianism, and along Platonist lines, it came to mean *affect* (from the Latin *affect[are]*: "to strive after," "to do to"), i.e. a family of mental states – such as anger, fear, sadness, and elation – that, though they amount to dispositions in that they often lead us to act, are nonetheless passive in that they are partly caused by states or events, e.g. we may be sad because a relative is ill, or elated because we won the lottery, or irritated for reasons we cannot definitely identify.

The term passion has various synonyms. For example, *emotion*, from the Latin *emotus* ("moving away"), is used in philosophy and psychology in a manner hardly distinguishable from passion and even feeling, though it is applied in a more restricted range of contexts than passion and feeling. The question has arisen whether we flee as a consequence of feeling afraid or feel afraid as a consequence of fleeing. The United States philosopher William James (CE 1842–1910) argued that an arousing stimulus caused internal physiological processes and external expressive and motor actions, and that emotions were the feelings of these physiological and behavioral processes. Independently, a few years later, the Danish physician Carl Georg Lange (CE 1834–1900) argued that emotion is a function of the perception of changes in the visceral organs innervated by the autonomic nervous system. These different though related views have been associated by psychologists in a *functional theory of emotions*: the *James–Lange theory*, which is interpreted to hold that emotions are feelings of bodily states, hence follow rather than precede, and so do not produce these states.

The Scottish philosopher David Hume (CE 1711–76) argued that some passions, e.g. pride, humility, love, and hate, are *indirect* passions, i.e. they have assignable causes such as qualities of a person who is loved, and indirect objects, e.g. the said person. He contrasted them with *direct* passions such as desire, aversion, hope, and fear, which are feelings immediately caused by pleasure, pain, or the prospect of any of these, and have things or events as their objects.

The study of passion and its cognates, emotion and feeling, is thought to be involved in moral development, whose study belongs in the subdiscipline of psychology called *moral psychology*, an extension to morals of the work of the Swiss psychologist Jean Piaget (CE 1896–1980). He developed *genetic epistemology*, a study that focuses on intellectual development, tracing the growth of concepts – from shape and space, through time and causality, to logical concepts – out of random activity in children. According to Piaget, intellectual development requires adaptation and structural change so as to achieve various forms of equilibrium both with the organism and the surrounding world.

Moral psychology's most notable proponents are the United States psychologist Lawrence Kohlberg (CE 1927–87), and the contemporary United States psychologist Carol Gilligan. Kohlberg formulated a theory of moral development that involves three levels – including two stages each – characterized by specific ways in which individuals understand right and wrong. The most basic is the *Preconventional Level*. Its first stage involves a conception of right and wrong based on punishment and obedience. In its second stage, right and wrong are conceived in terms of what satisfies one's own needs and, occasionally, those of others. The second, *Conventional Level*, involves a first stage where right and wrong are understood in terms of what pleases or helps others and gains their approval. In its second stage, rights and wrong are understood as what conforms to authority and maintains social order. As for the third, *Post-Conventional Principled* or *Autonomous Level*, its first stage involves a conception of morality centered on social utility, while its second stage involves a conception of morality based on a universal moral principle such as the Kantian categorical imperative. Kohlberg thought this sequence proceeded from less to more sophisticated morals.

Gilligan, by contrast, has focused on the relation between moral development, gender, and values, concluding that Kohlberg stages at best apply to male, not to female, moral development. After all, Kohlberg's research sample involved only males. Gilligan's study led her to conclude that women were characterized by an *ethic of care* that she contrasted to Kohlberg's *ethic of justice*. She distinguished three stages in the development of an ethic of care. The first is egocentric and based on likes and dislikes. The second involves identification with others and is based on hurting or not hurting. The third, where the self re-emerges, places equal stress on oneself and others through interdependence.

A central doctrine of moral psychology related to the passions has been *projectivism*, i.e. the view that the supposed moral properties of things are mere projections of our sentiments onto them.

See also: ethics; philosophy of mind

Further reading

Green, O.H. (1992) *The Emotions: A Philosophical Theory*, Dordrecht and Boston: Kluwer.

James, Susan (1997) *Passion and Action: The Emotions in Seventeenth-Century Philosophy*, Oxford and New York: Clarendon Press and Oxford University Press.

Kenny, Anthony (1963) *Action, Emotion, and Will*, London and Henley: Routledge & Kegan Paul.

Lickona, Thomas (ed.) (1976) *Moral Development and Behavior*, New York: Holt, Rinehart & Winston.

Peters, R.S. (1958) *The Concept of Motivation*, London and New York: Routledge – Kegan Paul and Humanities Press.

passive *see* passion

passive euthanasia *see* ethics

paternalism *see* ethics; feminist philosophy; philosophy, sociopolitical

patriarchal *see* feminist philosophy

patriarchalism *see* feminist philosophy

patriarchy *see* feminist philosophy

patristic authors *see* Christianity

payoff matrix *see* decision

peace *see* philosophy, sociopolitical

Peano's postulates *see* philosophy of mathematics

pedagogy *see* philosophy of education

Peirce's law *see* logic

Pelagianism *see* determinism

per accidens *see* accident

per se *see* accident

per se nota *see* empiricism; nominalism

percept *see* perception

perception From the Latin *percipio* (both "gaining knowledge through the senses" and "apprehension with the mind"), this term denotes the act or ability of discriminating between different data of the senses – sometimes called *percepts* – or, according to some thinkers, also of the intellect, in which case *concepts*, the content of intellectual conception, would also be included. If it extracts information about one's environment, it is *exteroception*; if about oneself, *interoception*. A particular form of interoception is *proprioception*: the perception of one's own body through stimuli arising in such subcutaneous tissues as muscles, tendons, and joints.

In Ancient Greece, an influential theory of perception was the *theory of effluxes*, held by Democritus (*c.* 460–*c* 370 BCE). It accounted for taste by appeal to shapes of atoms, and for sight by appeal to effluences, i.e. moving films of atoms supposed to impinge on the eye. This theory was also held by the Greek philosopher Epicurus (341–270 BCE), who used the term *eidola* to indicate the said films of atoms were images or detached outlines of the perceived objects. Sometimes, eidola is translated by means of the term *image* (from the Latin *imago*, which means "imitation"). The term image, as well as the term *phantasm*, translate the Greek *phantasma*, a notion used in the Aristotelian-Thomistic tradition to denote an idea in potentiality (*dynamis*). As for the objects of perception (*aisthesis* in Greek), Aristotelian thinking divides them into three kinds. Some, the *special sensibles*, have special senses exclusively associated with them, i.e. they are directly perceived by one sense only, be it sight, hearing, smell, taste, or touch. Others, the *common sensibles*, are directly perceived by more than one special sense, e.g. shape by sight and touch; movement (in certain circumstances) by sight and touch. Both special and common sensibles are collectively called *proper sensibles* and contrasted with *incidental sensibles*, which are perceived as a consequence of properly perceiving something else, e.g. something white as a result of perceiving a falling snowflake. Aristotelians held that, to recognize the common sensibles, a common mental faculty or power is needed because, otherwise, they could not be mutually compared. In the Middle Ages, this power was called *sensus communis*, i.e. common sense.

An experience relevant in assessing the validity and scope of application of the distinctions just discussed is *synaesthesia* or *synesthesia*, i.e. the experience in which one sensory modality – say, warmth – is or appears to be sensed in another – say, sound – in experiencing a warm sound. Can one have a tactile feeling like warmth of something normally perceived with the sense of hearing?

Something similar to images, i.e. simple ideas, was used by the British empiricists. The English scientist Francis Galton (CE 1822–1911) introduced the term *generic image* as a bridge between sensations and concepts. It was a composite of a variety of sensations, analogous to a photograph.

The *Molyneux question* or *Molineux problem* was posed by the Dublin lawyer William Molineaux (CE 1656–98), who asked whether a person blind from birth but taught through touch to distinguish a globe from a cube would be able to tell a globe from a cube visually upon acquiring eyesight. This question serves to understand the different conceptions of perception advanced by different theories, by distinguishing those that answer affirmatively from those than answer negatively.

The study of visual perception was revolutionized by the adoption of the *camera obscura model*, where a camera obscura is a darkened enclosure that focuses light from an external object by a pinpoint hole instead of a lens, creating an inverted, reverse image on the opposite wall. This model rendered previous theories – e.g. the *emanation theory* that explained perception as resulting from emanated copy-images of objects entering the eye – obsolete. It shifted the location of the sensation from the lens – where some theories placed it – to the retina, thus helping support the distinction between primary and secondary qualities, undermining the medieval realist view of perception, and furthering the view that consciousness is separated from the world. Arguments about the existence of, conceptual need for, and significance of images have persisted in contemporary discussions of sense-data.

Some perceptions of interest to Gestalt psychologists are generically called *duck–rabbit* or *figure–ground* perceptions. They consist in the discrimination of an object or figure from the background against which it is set. For example, a picture of a given vase can be alternately seen as a picture of a pair of faces. This led to the conclusion that complex perceptions are not the sum of simpler ones – in other words, that there is underdetermination of perception by sensory stimuli – but involve interpretation or, in other words, hypotheses.

A related perceptual phenomenon is *blindsight*, i.e. residual visual capacity associated with brain lesions that, however, do not prevent test subjects from identifying features of items situated in the regions where they cannot see or, at least, are convinced they cannot see.

Among the advocates of Gestalt psychology, the German and United States psychologist Kurt Lewin (CE 1890–1947) was perhaps the most influential in the United States. His central concept was that of *life-space*, which includes the person and the person's psychological environment, and which he diagrammed by using topological methods. He focused on motivation, which he explained by saying that, in a person's life-space, life-space objects had *valences*, or *vectors of force*, acting on the person just like physical vectors of force act on physical objects.

Discussions of perception often make reference to the concept of *hallucination*, i.e. of subjective experiences – e.g. of a live pink elephant walking in the yard – which have no counterpart in reality – e.g. no live pink elephant in the yard or elsewhere. It is worth noting that a hallucination need not be deceptive. It can be a pseudohallucination, i.e. a subjective experience that has no counterpart in reality, and the individual undergoing it recognizes at the time as having no counterpart

in reality. At any rate, the concept of hallucination is used in the *argument from hallucination* for such things as sensations, percepts, sense-data, representations or mental representations (sometimes also called by their German name: *Vorstellung* or, in the plural, *Vorstellungen*), and merely mental images. The argument can be outlined as follows: sometimes we have subjective experiences of items that are just like those of the real thing – e.g. of a live pink elephant walking in the yard – when that item is not out there – i.e. there is no such elephant in the yard. Hence, it is reasonable to suppose that, when we perceive an item and do not undergo a hallucination (e.g. when we see a car coming and, indeed, a car is coming), we also have a mental representation of that item in our mind.

Illusions – e.g. perceiving a stick in a glass of water to be bent when, in fact, the stick is not bent at all, or perceiving a moving star in the sky when, in fact, it is an airplane light – are used in discussions of perception to indicate that certain forms of perception are *non-epistemic*. That is, they are used to establish that one can perceive an object or event without knowing or believing that it is that object or event one is seeing. Other cases of perception, however, are *epistemic*, e.g. perceiving that one is seeing an airplane light in the sky when, in fact, that is what one is perceiving. Perceiving facts is always epistemic.

Our perception of objects, as distinct from our perception of facts, is used to argue against the possibility of *perceptual relativity*: the view that what we perceive is relative to our language, conceptual framework, or theories we use to interpret the world. For one can see, smell, hear, touch a tapir even if one does not know the word "tapir" or have the concept of a tapir, or have knowledge of how to classify a tapir. In such a situation, one could see, smell, hear, and even touch it; but one could not say that it was a tapir, or that it was a hoofed quadruped, somewhat resembling swine, with a long, flexible stout, and belonging to the family *Tapiridae* of South and Central America, the Malay Peninsula, and Sumatra. These are facts, and perception of facts is much more affected by words, concepts, and scientific theories available to the perceiver, hence originating perceptual relativity, though not thereby entailing *perceptual relativism*, the doctrine that perceptions of facts are true or false depending entirely on the linguistic, conceptual, or theoretical framework available to the perceiver. The question remains whether the said conceptual and theoretical frameworks are relevant and accurate accounts of their subject matter.

The arguments based on illusions and hallucinations have been used to criticize *direct or naive realism* (sometimes called the *theory of appearing* – the doctrine that we directly perceive external objects as they are, and that this is not further analyzable), and establish *representative realism*: the doctrine that we do not directly perceive external objects but, instead, perceive representations or *sense data* (singular: *sense-datum*) or *sensa* (singular *sensum*) – i.e. representations immediately given in perception – of external objects, which is associated with the *representative theory of ideas*, i.e. that we know reality only through the mediation of ideas. Both these theories are forms of *perceptual realism*, the doctrine that, directly or not, we perceive external objects. Direct realists need only deny that we perceive intermediary objects rather than the actual external objects. That is, they could even agree to the *causal theory of perception*: the theory that external objects not only cause our experiences and beliefs but also cause the sort of experiences we have. The English philosopher H.H. Price (CE 1899–1984) accepted the sense-data view, but argued against the causal theory of perception, emphasizing that every family of sense-data converges in a standard solid that, therefore, is not caused by the external object but is a projection based on sense-data (though it has some of the properties of the external object).

A sophisticated version of perceptual realism can also be found in ordinary-language philosophy, one of whose aims is to develop a highly sophisticated version of the realistic view that sense-data – i.e. mental intermediaries between us and the world – are not given in our experience, but the world itself is a datum (given in our experience), though this may happen through complex causal chains.

In this context, some philosophers have used the term *sensibilia* to denote entities of which no one is perceptually aware at the moment, but that, in all other respects, are just as the objects of perceptual awareness. For direct realism sensibilia are simply physical bodies. For representative realism, however, they are unsensed sense-data. The question arises whether any such mental entity can exist when it is not part of anyone's mental activity.

It should be mentioned that the term *sensation* – from the Latin *sentire*, i.e. "to feel," or "perceive" – which is involved in these discussions, has various uses, though it is most frequently used to denote a mental event more closely tied to an external or physiological stimulus than the term perception connotes. Sensation is independent of reflection or any kind of mental structuring of stimuli and, for that reason, it was central to the doctrine of *sensationalism* – held by such thinkers as the English philosopher Thomas Hobbes (CE 1588–1679), the French philosopher Etienne Condillac (CE 1715–80), and the English philosopher and psychologist David Hartley (1705–57) – that all mental states, especially cognitive states, are derived from sensations by composition or association.

A number of philosophers have argued against representational realism. For example, the English philosopher Gilbert Ryle (CE 1900–76) formulated the *problem of the speckled hen*. He argued that a sense-data analysis implies that whenever one sees a speckled hen one does so through the apprehension of a speckled-hen sense-datum, and that it should be immediately obvious how many speckles the hen has. However, I can apprehend that it has more than 100 speckles without being able to tell, as the sense-data analysis requires, that it be immediately obvious to me how many they are.

Along with such criticisms, philosophers have argued for a theory that avoids positing intermediary objects in the analysis of perception. It is the *adverbial theory of perception*, i.e. that even in hallucinations, illusions, and the like, to perceive is to perceive in a certain manner, not to have an experience of such things as ideas, representations, and sense-data. They have further argued that to postulate the latter entities not only unnecessarily complicates our universe, but, also, and more significantly, it shifts rather than solves the problem. This is because it turns it into the problem of accounting for what it is to have an experience of ideas, representations, or sense-data in our mind.

Still other philosophers have argued for the *multiple-relation theory of perception*, where relations are a crucial component of perception that help connect sensations and ideas by reference to the particular situations encountered by perceiving agents. On this view, perceiving such things as a cat, a bus, a falling star, and an ocean wave breaking is not radically different from perceiving the fact that a cat is at the door, that the bus is leaving, that a falling star is crossing the southern sky at a certain time and from a certain standpoint, and that a wave is breaking against the rock under my feet. A related view was that held by the English philosopher G.F. Stout (CE 1860–1944), who held that the representations of thought reflect a noetic synthesis that contains both *sensa* or the data from the senses, and an unbreakable reference to the external world that keeps us in direct contact with this world.

A traditional theory that, most frequently, has been associated with some form of the sense-datum theory is *phenomenalism*. This doctrine, whose name derives from the Greek *phainomenon*, i.e. "appearance," traditionally asserted that we know only phenomena or appearances, and that there is nothing behind the phenomena which causes their appearance. Versions of it were formulated by some of the British Empiricists, arguably by the British philosopher John Stuart Mill (CE 1806–73) when he conceived of matter as a permanent possibility of sensation, and by many representatives of Kantian philosophy. In the twentieth century, phenomenalism has been identified with the view that propositions asserting the existence of physical objects mean the same thing as propositions asserting that observers would have certain complicated series of sensations, say, seeing a bird eat from a feeder, turn its head, fly away, were they to have certain other sensations, say, first seeing a bird land on the feeder. In this sense, and by contrast with its traditional versions, phenomenalism is com-patible with the appearance, causal, adverbial, and other theories.

See also: empiricism; imagination; philosophy of mind

Further reading
Dretske, Fred I. (2000) *Perception, Knowledge, and Belief: Selected Essays*, Cambridge, UK and New York: Cambridge University Press.
Swartz, Robert J. (1965) *Perceiving, Sensing, and Knowing*, Garden City, NY: Doubleday.

perceptual realism *see* perception

perceptual relativism *see* perception

perceptual relativity *see* perception

percipient events *see* process philosophy

perfect competition *see* philosophy of economics

perfect duty *see* ethics

perfect rights *see* ethics

perfectibility *see* perfection

perfectihabia *see* perfection

perfection From the Latin *perfectio* (i.e. "completeness," "completion," or "indefectibility"), this term has initially been used to denote a characteristic of God, as in divine perfection, divine completeness or divine indefectibility, all features indicating that God is without fault or imperfection, hence, among other things, unfailing. This feature has often been identified with the *summun bonum* (Latin for "the highest good"), i.e. that with regard to which all other things or combinations of things are wanting.

This notion of perfection as involving completeness has been related to the *principle of plenitude* or *perfection*, whose Platonic formulation is: "every genuine possibility is actualized." In this regard, the German philosopher Gottfried Wilhelm Leibniz (CE 1646–1716) used this principle and the associated *principle of sufficient reason* – a common formulation of which is: "Everything has a sufficient reason (cause or explanation) for its existence or non-existence" – to establish that a perfect being is possible, a step for him in proving God's existence by means of the ontological argument. He argued that perfections are simple properties that make room for superlative degrees and do not exclude each other. Hence, it is possible that some being has all of them or, in other words, a perfect being – God – is possible. Leibniz also used the principle of sufficient reason in trying to establish that the actual world is the best possible world. However, he tried to avoid the implication that the actual world was necessarily actual, by arguing that the statement "this is the best possible world" involves a comparison with infinitely many other worlds hence, if true, it is contingent.

The notion of perfection has also been applied to human affairs, especially in the Christian tradition that emphasizes human *perfectibility* or capacity for improvement and, as some would say, unbounded improvement. This feature can also be found in the thought of the French philosopher Jean Jacques Rousseau (CE 1712–78) and other secular philosophies such as positivism, Marxism, and Nietzschean philosophy.

See also: chain of being; ethics; metaphysics

Further reading
Lovejoy, Arthur O. (1936) *The Great Chain of Being: A Study of the History of an Idea*, Cambridge, MA: Harvard University Press.
Passmore, John (1970) *The Perfectibility of Man*, New York: C. Scribner's Sons.

perfectionism *see* ethics; paradox

perfectionism, paradox of *see* ethics; paradox

performance *see* ethics; speech act theory

performative *see* speech act theory

perifilosofía *see* philosophy

Peripatetics *see* Aristotelianism

perlocutionary act *see* speech act theory

person *see* identity

person stage *see* identity

personal identity *see* identity

personal matter *see* ethics

personal problem *see* ethics

personal sense of "philosophy" *see* philosophy

personal supposition *see* reference

personalism *see* idealism

personality *see* ethics; philosophy of mind

personhood *see* ethics; identity

perspectivism *see* existentialism

persuasive definition *see* definition

pessimism *see* ethics

petitio principii *see* fallacy

phalanx *see* philosophy, sociopolitical

phantasia *see* imagination

phantasma *see* perception

phase-space *see* philosophy of mathematics

phenomenal body *see* existentialism

phenomenal property *see* philosophy of mind; quality

phenomenal world *see* Kantian philosophy

phenomenalism *see* positivism

phenomenological attitude *see* phenomenology

phenomenological reduction *see* phenomenology

phenomenology A philosophical family of methods, all of which involve some form of intuitionism, and made notable in one of its initial versions by the German mathematician, logician, and philosopher Edmund Husserl (CE 1859–1938) Among the notions in Husserl's phenomenology the concept of intentionality is central. *Intentionality* is a term coined by philosophers in the Middle Ages meaning the feature of being about something, e.g. someone's belief that there is a tooth fairy displays intentionality in being about something, even though the tooth fairy does not exist. Arabic philosophers distinguished between *first understanding* – that is of things – and *second understanding* – that is of the understanding of things – and, later, scholastic philosophers distinguished between *terms of first intention*, which refer to things, and *terms of second intention*, which refer to terms of first intention. These distinctions are related to Husserl's distinction between the *natural attitude*, i.e. our ordinary involvement with items in our world, and the *phenomenological attitude*, a reflective attitude about the said ordinary involvement. The phenomenological attitude is the standpoint from which intentions present in the natural attitude and their objects are analyzed. From this standpoint, *reflection*, i.e. phenomenological reflection, leads to the apprehension of essences.

In the nineteenth and twentieth centuries, this distinction was revived in the notion of intentionality, whereby, as indicated, all mental phenomena point to objects whose mode of existence, since some of them are mythical, is *intentional inexistence*, i.e. they exist only as purported objects of intentions. It was the nineteenth-century philosopher Franz Brentano (CE 1838–1917) who revived the term intentionality in developing his descriptive psychology, a study of mental phenomena that focuses on what Brentano took to be characteristic of them: precisely their intentionality. His student, the Austrian philosopher Alexius Meinong (CE 1853–1920), established an influential Institute of Psychology in the Austrian city of Graz. He formulated a theory of objects – the doctrine of *Aussersein* – according to which the being (*Sein*) of an object is different from the object's character, i.e. its *Sosein*. For example, neither a unicorn nor a round square have any being (*Sein*), but each has a character (*Sosein*) that is different from that of the other. He also contributed to the influence of the notion of *subsistence* (a translation of the German *Bestand*), which denotes the kind of being characteristic of ideal objects, such as mathematical objects and other abstractions. It is contrasted with the kind of being characteristic of the objects studied by the sciences except psychology and mathematics, which is called *existence* (*Existenz*). In this regard, Brentano, like a number of contemporary philosophers, had denied that existence is a predicate. Instead, he said existence is a *synsemantic term*, i.e. it expresses our acceptance or rejection of any given items.

Husserl's concept of intentionality developed along the lines of the approaches just discussed. It has two components: the processes of intending or *noesis*, and the item intended or *noema*. Related adjectives are *noetic* for the processes of intending, *noematic* or *hyletic* for the items intended, *noematic analysis* for the description of the object intended, *noetic analysis* for the subjective intentions, *noetics* (Husserl's term is *Noetik*) for the phenomenology of reason and, as other authors have suggested, for the study of all thought.

The said descriptions are worked out through *eidetic intuition*, i.e. intuition of the essence – the *eidos* – or form in our mental images, which is reached through *eidetic variations*. These are variations we can bring about in those mental images, which are supposed to be approached through *epoché*, i.e. by the suspension of judgment concerning particular features of those mental images. This is a form of the neutrality or neutralism, or neutral philosophy that German philosophers have traditionally called *Voraussetzunglossigkeit*.

In Husserl's case, the neutrality involved is neutralization – Husserl's term was *Neutralisierung* – of our assumptions or presuppositions by disconnecting them from all views concerning the natural world. Initially, Husserl, opposing *psychologism* – the doctrine that the categories of psychology can be used in the understanding of the abstract concepts of mathematics, logic, and philosophy – sought to understand numbers in terms of the essences found through eidetic intuition in our numbering thoughts. Then, he attempted to use the same method to find logical forms as essences and, in his *Formal and Transcendental Logic*, he used the term *nomology* (from the Greek *nomos*, i.e. "law," and *logos*, i.e. "discourse or theory") to denote the most general aspects of mathematical studies and systems. Afterwards, he generalized this approach to all metaphysical problems.

Using the methods just discussed issues in an *eidetic reduction* or *phenomenological reduction*. This reduction, in general, amplifies the notion of intentionality. Husserl's Cartesian discovery comes about in this process. It is not the discovery of the individual self, but that of *transcendental subjectivity* or the *transcendental ego* as a first and basic datum that includes objectivity giving us both the individual self and the *Umwelt* or world surrounding the self's subjectivity. Both sides invariably interact, thus resolving or, rather, dissolving the problem of other minds, making communication possible, and suggesting the existence of a *Kulturwelt* or world resulting from the community of individuals. In his later work, Husserl distinguished between the scientific world and the *Lebenswelt*, i.e. lived world or life world, considered the latter prior to the former, and thought the task of phenomenology was the analysis of the *Lebenswelt*. Also, the term transcendental grew in prominence in his writings. He began to talk of transcendental phenomenology and of transcendental-phenomenological idealism, a standpoint from which phenomenology yielded the subjective structures out of which the concrete individual world is formed.

Central in the preceding discussion is Husserl's distinction between the *apophantic*, i.e. the realm of sensory experience and propositions or judgments, and the *ontological*. According to Husserl's terminology, the study of formal structures in the apophantic domain is *apophantic analytics*, while the study of formal structures in the ontological domain is *formal ontology*.

A central theme in European phenomenology is that of embodiment, especially studied by the French philosopher Maurice Merleau-Ponty (CE 1908–61), who distinguished between the *objective body* – i.e. the body as a physiological entity – and the *phenomenal body* – i.e. a particular person's own body as this person experiences it. The phenomenal body is crucial for understanding the phenomenological concept of *embodiment*, i.e. that experience whereby, without needing to understand the physiology of one's body, one can have a sense of one's body and confidence in one's capacity to do such things as walking, scratching, writing a sentence, and dancing.

This contrast can also be found in Husserl's contrasting use of *Erfahrung*, i.e. "experience," which can be the subject of methodological description and analysis, and *Erlebnis*: experience that is lived through and never quite capable of being analyzed. The latter term had been introduced by the German philosopher Wilhelm Dilthey (CE 1833–1911) and the Spanish philosopher José Ortega y Gasset (CE 1883–1955), who, translating it into Spanish as *vivencia*, made it a pivotal term in many of his works.

See also: Continental philosophy; essentialism; existentialism; metaphysics; pragmatism

Further reading

Husserl, Edmund (1962) *Ideas*, London and New York: Collier–Macmillan and Collier Books.

Kockelmans, Joseph J. (1967) *Phenomenology*, Garden City, NY: Doubleday.

philosopher's stone *see* alchemy

philosophes *see* encyclopedism

philosophia perennis *see* philosophy

philosophia prima *see* philosophy

philosophical anthropology *see* anthropology

philosophical behaviorism *see* behaviorism

philosophical psychology *see* philosophy of mind

philosophical theology *see* philosophy of religion

philosophy From the Greek *philos* ("love of") and *sophia* ("wisdom"), this term is used in a variety of senses.

Senses of the term "philosophy"

In its *personal* sense, the term philosophy denotes a particular person's beliefs and presuppositions about the world. It is that person's worldview or outlook on things. Some believe, for example, that the universe had a beginning and will have an end. Others hold that it always was and will be. At any rate, the notion of *worldview* was given philosophical currency by the German philosopher Wilhelm Dilthey (CE 1833–1911), who used the German for worldview, i.e. *Weltanschauung*, to denote a comprehensive view of the universe and of humans' place in it that includes factual beliefs, judgments of value, and ultimate goals.

In its *social* or *group* sense, the term philosophy denotes a particular group's predominant beliefs and presuppositions about the world. In attempting to resolve differences in personal outlooks, people sometimes appeal to philosophy in this social sense. i.e. to the philosophy or predominant worldview of a particular church, ethnic group, society, or group of societies. In this social sense, one can talk, for example, of Western philosophy by contrast, say, with East Asian philosophy.

A group's philosophy can be and often is criticized by members of the group or of other groups in more than one way. Most commonly, the criticism expresses views opposite to those being criticized. Thus, critics thinking that time is linear might simply state this belief in criticizing the views of Hopi Indians in the United States or Aymará Indians in Bolivia who think time is circular. Other times, however, a group's philosophy might be criticized on the grounds that, on a certain matter (say, whether humans are complex physical and chemical systems), the group's philosophy is unclear or silent. In either case, the criticisms indicate the philosophical problem formulated by the question: "What is the right view on these matters?"

One might reject this question, and criticize the philosophies just mentioned and any other attempts at resolving philosophical puzzlements as irrelevant, a waste of time, or a pointless exercise. However, this in itself would be to formulate *a philosophy*. So, unless one refuses to think about these matters at all, having a philosophy is inescapable.

To say that having a philosophy is inescapable is to formulate a philosophical view that is part of philosophy and, like any other philosophical views, is open to question. To subject a philosophical view to critical scrutiny and try to assess its soundness by appealing to reason is to engage in philosophical inquiry. When people engage in this inquiry, they *do* philosophy, rather than simply *have* a philosophy as in the personal and social senses. In this sense, *philosophy* is *about* beliefs and presuppositions and contrasts with *a philosophy*, which is made up of beliefs and presuppositions. That is, philosophy, in this *activity* sense or *philosophy as a branch of inquiry*, is a critical and – as a joint enterprise – comprehensive study of the various aspects of the world: reality, knowledge, reasoning, norms, and values.

A special form of philosophy as a branch of inquiry is *ethnophilosophy* or *folk philosophy*, which is not merely an anthropological or historical study, but a type of philosophical inquiry, i.e. a critical and comprehensive study focused on philosophies predominant in parti-

cular ethnic groups. Hence, it is closely associated with the philosophy of culture or cultural philosophy (see CULTURE), and has been significantly developed concerning – and by – philosophical inquiry in Sub-Saharan Africa, where it has long been largely oral (see AFRICAN PHILOSOPHY), in New Zealand (see MĀORI PHILOSOPHY), in the Americas (see NAHUA PHILOSOPHY; NATIVE AMERICAN PHILOSOPHY), and elsewhere.

When pursued in a sustained manner, philosophy as a branch of inquiry typically produces philosophies in the *theory* sense of the term philosophy, i.e. generalized devices for dealing with problems concerning personal or social philosophies, or concerning other, alternative devices that may have or could be formulated for dealing with these problems. When philosophical theories become historically influential, they are called philosophies in the *school* sense of philosophy. Aristotelian philosophy, for example, is a philosophy in both the theory and the school sense of the term, because it is not only a generalized device for dealing with the said problems, but also historically influential.

Philosophical problems and methods
Philosophy deals with problems about such areas of human activity as science, morality, art, literature, religion, life, and the physical world, sometimes comprehensively denoted by the expression *the social and natural worlds*. These are philosophical problems, i.e. problems that characteristically involve conflicting ideas about such things as the existence, nature, explanation, and justification of aspects of the world, and about what individual or collective course(s) of action are accordingly called for.

As for philosophical methods for dealing with the problems, in a sense, there are as many as philosophers. Yet, various methods can be mentioned and are discussed when appropriate in the specific areas of philosophy, e.g. PHILOSOPHY OF SCIENCE, discussed below, especially as it concerns methods for establishing or confirming theories, and in such entries as INDUCTION and LOGIC in this dictionary. One method, however, that is shared by philosophers and theoreticians in such branches of inquiry as physics and psychology, is the *thought-experiment* method, which consists in testing a hypothesis by imagining a situation and what would be said about it or happens in it.

Philosophy and philosophies

The question arises whether, given the great number of arguments and counterarguments generated by philosophies and schools of philosophy, any agreement can ever be reached. In this regard, some have used the expression *philosophia perennis*, which initially appeared in the title of *De perenni philosophia*, a book published by the Renaissance philosopher Agostino Steuco of Gubbio, or Steuchen (CE 1497?–1548), in CE 1540. The book held that the differences between medieval philosophers and the School of Padua were immaterial and that there was significant common ground uniting these traditions (see BOLOGNA SCHOOL). Afterwards, the expression was also used in other senses, for example, to designate the truths shared by all Thomists; those shared by Greek and medieval philosophers; and, as in the case of the German philosopher Gottfried Wilhelm Leibniz (CE 1646–1716), to denote all valid elements of the history of philosophy. Today, *philosophia perennis* primarily denotes a supposed body of truths that can be found in the writings of influential philosophers or which are common to opposing schools of philosophy.

Whether there is such a thing is a valid question in philosophy itself. Some philosophers would argue that it is a question in *metaphilosophy* or *periphilosophy* (or *perifilosofia*), because it is about philosophy. Yet, there is no good reason to believe that questions and inquiry about philosophy should not be considered part of philosophy. After all, philosophy is a characteristically self-critical, hence self-referential, enterprise. We will later return to the question whether there is or can be philosophical common ground through the history of philosophy.

A related doctrine is that of *problematicismo* (Italian term that can be translated as *problematicism*), formulated as an alternative to actualism and neo-scholasticism, most notably by the Italian philosopher Antonio Banfi (CE 1886–1957). Problematicism is the doctrine that philosophy is a branch of inquiry aimed only at clarifying problems and examining their significance and that of their components, but not at solving them. It is thus incapable of becoming a science. As a study of problems and their components problematicism is a form of analysis. As a study of the significance of problems, indeed, of the entire range of problems we face in life, beginning by the very problem posed by our finding ourselves alive in the world, problematicism dovetailed with EXISTENTIALISM and HISTORICISM.

This suggestion points to a conception of philosophy that emphasizes wisdom as an activity more than a resulting body of knowledge. This dichotomy can be traced back to the Greek philosopher and religious-sect leader Pythagoras (570–500 BCE), who is credited with coining the term *philosophia*, Greek for the English *philosophy* (as previously stated, from the Greek *philos*: "lover or friend of," and *sophia*: "wisdom"). The question was left open at Pythagoras' time whether this wisdom should be primarily an activity or primarily a body of knowledge, and different philosophers emphasized one or the other. In some cultures other than that of Ancient Greece, the equivalent terms for wisdom involve analogous differences in emphasis if not meaning. One example is arguably the Arabic word for wisdom (which also means philosophy): *ḥikma*, though this may be a result of the word's having been selected to translate Greek philosophical works. In one African language (that of the Akan people), the word for wisdom is *nyansa* (or its possible equivalent, *adwen*, which means thinking), and denotes the capacity for philosophical thinking understood as an inborn mental faculty. In fact, *nyansa* has some of the same additional connotations as the Greek term for wisdom, *sophia*: "skill," "learning," "practical knowledge."

Philosophy's motivation

Whatever the specific characteristics of philosophy as a branch of inquiry turn out to be, as previously indicated, this activity is prompted by motives of at least two main types. One is curiosity or, as the Greek philosopher Aristotle (384–322 BCE) said, wonder about our world, quite often about what we take for granted in it. For example, such curiosity may lead us to wonder about the nature of infinity or whether numbers exist over and above the mental life that conceives of them. The other type of motives is concern, which typically prompts problems in ethics and sociopolitical philosophy such as whether punishment is justified and, if so, how, and whence do governments have the right to govern.

Philosophy's scope
There can be a philosophical inquiry about anything, for philosophy deals with everything. In order to focus inquiry, however, Western philosophy has been traditionally divided into branches. The most frequently used classification is: METAPHYSICS, EPISTEMOLOGY, LOGIC, ETHICS, PHILOSOPHY, SOCIOPOLITICAL and AESTHETICS (see the respective entries in this dictionary). This classification is a matter of emphasis rather than mutually exclusive categories.

Philosophy, its branches, and other branches of inquiry
A matter of recurrent reflection and philosophical significance concerns the relations between philosophy and fields other than philosophy. A question arising in this context is: "Is philosophy a science, a branch of literature, an extension of religion, a form of education, or something else?" Even within the Western tradition, views on this matter are far from unanimous. Some philosophers – especially in the twentieth century, e.g. the German philosopher Hans Reichenbach (CE 1891–1953) – have thought of philosophy as a *science*. Others – e.g. the English philosopher and historian Robin George Collinwood (CE 1889–1943) – have thought of philosophy as analogous to, if not identical with, *literature*, a notion articulated or, at least, embedded in the practice of various Spanish-speaking writers – e.g. the Argentine author Jorge Luis Borges (CE 1899–1986) – as well as in the Chinese and Indian philosophical traditions. Still others – e.g. the Roman Consul Anicius Manlius Severinus Boethius (*c*. CE 480–525) – thought of it as an extension of *religion*, providing consolation to those faced with misfortunes. Earlier in Ancient Greece, philosophers believed that philosophy was a form of education leading to the good life. Another notion has been that of philosophy as the *handmaiden of the sciences* or an *underlaborer* dispelling conceptual confusions arising from everyday life or science. It is also possible to conceive of philosophy as *diplomacy* – a conception that focuses on the often unsettled and conflictive nature of concerns contributing to pose everyday, scientific, and philosophical problems, and on open-ended social decision procedures that may help settle the concerns and deal with the problems.

More on philosophy's methods
The conceptions just discussed make room for a variety of methods. One, *conceptual analysis* or *linguistic analysis*, has been briefly described. It consists in dispelling conceptual confusions arising from everyday life or science (see ANALYSIS). Another widely used method is the method of *dialectic*, which involves proposing a conceptual thesis and then dealing with objections (see DIALECTIC). It should be noted that these methods, though not generally recognized as such, are significantly empirical, because, at least in part, they rest on empirical information about language. Moreover, the empirical nature of these methods lends empirical features to any philosophical inquiry that uses them.

Philosophical problems and philosophical issues
Whatever the overall conception of philosophy at work, the nature and extent of the common ground – i.e. the shared beliefs and presuppositions among those involved in a conflict posing a problem or issue – is significant for dealing with the problems or, when these become socially heated, the *issues*. Such common ground, however, is often very limited and threatened by conflict. Indeed, the complexity of contemporary life that partly results from rapid and varied technological developments, associated at least in some countries with controversy and confrontation, has led to a largely new phenomenon: *issue-overload*.

Issues are collective events characterized by collective conflicts: sharp oppositions of beliefs and attitudes between those involved in the conflicts. They are prompted by concerns involved in these beliefs and attitudes, and pose sociopolitical problems that are the subject matter of various social studies – e.g.

policy studies and, generally, political science – as well as sociopolitical philosophy. Discussions of issues characteristically involve doubtful, arguable, and disputed cases or, as they are generally called in this pragmatic sense, *borderline cases* in the application of ideas, or *hard cases*.

See also: Cartesianism; Greek philosophy; historicism; idealism; Kantian philosophy

Further reading
Iannone, A. Pablo (1994) *Philosophy as Diplomacy: Essays in Ethics and Policy Making*, Atlantic Highlands, NJ: Humanities Press.
Shusterman, Richard (1997) *Internationalism in Philosophy*, Oxford: Blackwell Publishers.
Windelband, W. (1979) *A History of Philosophy: With Especial Reference to the Formation and Development of its Problems and Conceptions*, 2nd edn, rev. and enl., Westport, CT: Greenwood Press.

philosophy, African *see* African philosophy

philosophy, African-American *see* diaspora; Islam; philosophy of liberation

philosophy, analytic *see* analysis

philosophy and expatriation Traditionally, philosophers have approached their times and cultures with a critical, distant eye. This is no accident and it holds true even of philosophers who had the purpose of providing, or whose positions amounted to, a justification of their times, cultures, faiths, Churches, or States. It is no accident, because a critical, hence detached, approach is crucial to philosophy and the wonder with which it is supposed to begin. This is a wonder about the familiar that everyone takes for granted and, thereby, turns philosophers into strangers in their times and cultures. They are a bit marginal, partly because they critically approach what these times and cultures assume to be known by everybody.

This marginal place and critical role of philosophers is quite analogous to the marginal place and critical role of many expatriates. For expatriates characteristically wonder at what everyone takes for granted. It is, for example, a common experience for recent expatriates who have come to the United States from Europe, Latin America, or Asia to wonder why, upon running into United States acquaintances on the street or at a mall or campus, being asked "How are you?" and, accordingly, beginning to answer the question, the acquaintances often show a sort of restlessness, as if they had not meant to learn how the expatriate was after all. Of course, in the United States, casually asking, "How are you?" in the said circumstances is largely equivalent to saying, "Hi." Everybody knows this, takes it for granted and, accordingly, gives a short answer – say, "Fine. And you?" For recently arrived expatriates, however, this is a source of wonder and, often, of criticism. They get the initial feeling that their acquaintances – perhaps all United States persons – simply do not care about others and cannot understand why they take the trouble to pretend to care by saying, "How are you?"

Granted, this is an example of a superficial misunderstanding that a little bit of time and listening can easily resolve. However, the example does exemplify the type of critical wonder that gets the inquiry started and begins to create feelings of estrangement. Further, the analogy goes deeper. Just as with expatriates, philosophers often experience a mixture of melancholy and exhilaration in doing philosophy; they develop adaptations to worlds they find, at least in some respects, foreign or, to them, unfamiliar enough to deserve examination; and, given this concern, they rely significantly on convention-settling processes – from proposing new social arrangements and ways of thinking about the world to suggesting and practicing ways of changing it. That is, just as individual expatriates, as well as entire cultures, make use of these processes in building a place for themselves in a foreign world, so too philosophy involves the use of the same kind of processes, in so far as it aims at bringing about conceptual and practical changes in the world in which we live.

These features provide a certain commonality with those involved in cross-cultural conflicts caused by cross-cultural fragmentation and interactions. Hence, they provide a way in which philosophy can find a common ground that can help it to interlock with non-philosophical activities. It can also help philosophers to communicate and engage in meaningful dialogue and convention-settling interactions with non-philosophers involved in various social issues (see ETHICS; PHILOSOPHY, SOCIO-POLITICAL).

The role here envisioned for philosophy can proceed in accordance with the conception of *philosophy as diplomacy*, which is a branch of inquiry aimed at dealing with a variety of problems and issues – e.g. cross-cultural problems and issues – in ways that are feasible, effective, and crucially sensitive both to the often unsettled and conflictive nature of the concerns that contribute to pose the problems and issues, and to the variety of open-ended social decision procedures and processes that may help settle these concerns. These procedures and processes may deal with the problems and issues in such ways as negotiation, arbitration, mediation, and a variety of interactions that build familiarity if not a common ground of attitudes and reasons between the individuals and groups involved.

An example of philosophy as diplomacy in action could, for example, involve taking a middle ground between the excesses of separatism and integrationism in cross-cultural conflicts. This middle ground is a sounder alternative, because it does not close in to dialogue (as separatism does), nor does it require convergent, generalized agreement on matters of belief and value (as integrationism does). Instead, the only common ground this more parsimonious alternative requires is that which furthers meaningful cross-cultural dialogue and social interactions between the groups and individuals involved in the intercultural conflicts that prompt the issue.

This emphasis on a parsimonious approach through open-ended dialogue and social interactions evidences two crucial features of philosophy as diplomacy. The first feature is that philosophy as diplomacy deals with problems in ways that are sensitive to the often unsettled and conflictive nature of the concerns that pose the problems and issues. The second feature is that philosophy as diplomacy is also sensitive to the variety of social decision procedures and processes involved in dealing with social problems and issues such as those concerning cross-cultural interactions (see PHILOSOPHY, SOCIOPOLITICAL).

To say that philosophy as diplomacy aims at avoiding ill might lead one to think that philosophy as diplomacy is primarily a consequentialist notion – that is, that it takes the justifiability of policies and decisions to depend only on the value of their consequences. However, it does not. For ill may consist in the violation of a right or failure to act in accordance with a duty or with principles of justice. These are deontological considerations – that is, they take the justifiability of policies and decisions to depend only on their accordance with rights, duties, or principles of justice (see ETHICS).

Nor is the conception of philosophy as diplomacy primarily deontological. It does not rule out the possibility that in certain cases – arguably in cases of widespread community deterioration – the social consequences are so catastrophic as to take precedence. This need not be so because other deontological considerations take precedence. For the situations envisioned approach state of nature situations; and in any such situation, it is at least questionable whether deontological considerations such as rights or the obligations correlated with them carry much, if any, weight (see ETHICS). At any rate, the relative weight of these various considerations is at issue in such situations, and its determination needs to be worked out through policy-making and convention-settling processes such as those previously mentioned.

See also: diaspora; ethics; philosophy of literature; philosophy, sociopolitical

Further reading
Cavalli-Sforza, L.L. (1996) *The Great Human Diasporas: The History of Diversity and Evolution*, Reading, MA and Harlow: Addison-Wesley.
Iannone, A. Pablo (1999) *Philosophical Ecologies: Essays in Philosophy, Ecology, and Human Life*, Amherst, NY: Humanity Books.
—— (1994) *Philosophy as Diplomacy: Essays in Ethics and Policy Making*, Atlantic Highlands, NJ: Humanities Press.
Lafaye, Jacques (1977) *The Spanish Diaspora: The Enduring Unity of Hispanic Culture*, Washington, DC: Latin American Program,

Woodrow Wilson International Center for Scholars.

Suleiman, Susan Rubin (1998) *Exile and Creativity: Signposts, Travelers, Outsiders, Backward Glances*, Durham: Duke University Press.

philosophy, Anglo-American *see* analysis

philosophy, Arabic *see* Arabic philosophy; Aristotelianism; Neoplatonism

philosophy as diplomacy *see* philosophy, sociopolitical

philosophy, Chinese *see* Agriculture School; Buddhism; Chinese Legalism; Confucianism; Mohism; Taoism

philosophy, Continental *see* Continental philosophy

philosophy, critical *see* Kantian philosophy

philosophy, cultural *see* culture

philosophy, ethno- *see* philosophy

philosophy, Hispanic *see* Latin American philosophy

philosophy, Ibero-American *see* Latin American philosophy

philosophy, in Australia and New Zealand *see* analysis; Māori philosophy

philosophy, Indian *see* Advaita; Buddhism; cārvāka; Hinduism; Jainism; Sāmhya-Yoga; Nyāya-Vaiśeṣika School

philosophy, Islamic *see* Arabic philosophy; Aristotelianism; Neoplatonism

philosophy, Latin American *see* Latin American philosophy

philosophy, Nahua *see* Nahua philosophy

philosophy, Native American *see* Native American philosophy

philosophy of action *see* action

philosophy of art *see* aesthetics

philosophy of biology *see* biology

philosophy of culture *see* culture

philosophy of economics The study of methodological and normative problems and concepts involved in economics. This term – formed by combining the English suffix "-s" with the adjective "economic," which derives from the Latin *oeconomic(us)*, and this from the Greek *oikonomikós* (relating to household management) equivalent to *oikonómos* ("steward"), derived from *oikos* ("house") and *nomos* ("law") – designates the study dealing with the production, distribution, and consumption of goods and services, and the behavior of money markets, as well as how they affect individuals, organizations, and even entire societies in or concerning which they take place.

Accordingly, the philosophy of economics concerns economic theory, economic theories, and their relations to matters of policy and social life. One such concept is that of a *market*, whose characterization involves at least two features. One is *exchange* or the giving of something in return for something else, by contrast, for example, with a *gift* or the giving of something with nothing demanded in return (though, to be sure, givers generally expect reciprocity). Another feature is *competition* or the rivalry or struggle between two or more individuals or organizations concerning something that, in markets, is often market share, which takes various forms:

1 *overall market share*, i.e. the percentage of total sales they make;
2 *served-market share*, i.e. the percentage of total sales they make in their targeted market;
3 *relative market share (to top three competitors)*, i.e. the percentage of sales they make relatively to the combined sales of their three largest competitors; and
4 *relative market share (to leading competitor)*, i.e. the percentage of sales they make relatively to the sales of their leading competitor.

It should be noted that, arguably, competition is present even in highly directed economies, though it may be competition for resources that would facilitate meeting set quotas in the corresponding market, or even competition for power in the bureaucracy directing the economy and controlling planned market operations.

The exchange feature of markets has been the crucial focus of *exchange theory*, an attempt at explaining individual behavior in terms of market exchanges. In this area, for example, the *Coase theorem*, named after the contemporary English economist and economics Nobel Prize winner Ronald H. Coase who formulated it, is the informal insight that, assuming no transaction costs involved in exchanging rights for money (i.e. no costs resulting from the transaction itself) then, regardless of how rights are initially distributed, rational agents will buy and sell them so as to maximize individual returns. In jurisprudence, this theorem has been used as the basis for claiming that, even though transaction costs in rights distribution are usually high, laws should confer rights on those who would purchase them, were they for sale in markets free from transaction costs.

A concept hinted at in the conditions of the Coase theorem – which are ideal conditions, i.e. never quite actualized conditions – is that of an *ideal market*, i.e. a hypothetical market in which all economic agents are perfectly informed of the price of goods and services, and the cost of their production and transaction costs are nil.

Another concept applying to an ideal market is that of *perfect competition*. This is a state of affairs in which, for a given good, first, every consumer is a perfectly rational maximizer of utility; second, every producer is a perfectly rational maximizer of profits; third, there are enough producers of the goods in question to prevent any producer from setting the price of the goods; and fourth, there are no differences between instances of the same goods from different producers. This notion of perfect competition results in Pareto optimality (see below), which has led some philosophers to conclude that it has normative implications.

A related economic notion that has played a significant role in the philosophy of economics and ethics is that of *expected utility* – variously conceived as the likely, probable, or not unlikely satisfaction of demand – and, some argued, in particular that of *declining marginal utility*, i.e. that equal marginal increments of money tend to bring about less satisfaction – less utility, less happiness – to people, the more money these people have. This notion is used by some utilitarian philosophers to argue for

equality of income distribution on the grounds that it prevents money from accumulating into the hands of a group of people and, as a result, it tends to prevent declining marginal utility from making these less happy than otherwise they will be.

Another notion of significance is that of an *economic externality*, i.e. a circumstance such as a governmental policy that is not in itself economic. Some argue that any such circumstance should be disregarded in economic assessments; while others argue that doing so turns economic analysis, however precise, into the analysis of economic problems, policies, and decisions in ideal worlds too far removed from reality.

Still others argue for *liberalism* in economics, which is crucially characterized by extensive freedom for individual economic agents through significant absence of regulation, and absence, too, of centralization of economic activities. Centralization and regulation are the opposite of economic liberalism, characterize directed economies, and are often associated with the public ownership of the means for economic activity. There is a range of types of economic liberalism, the extreme form of which is *laissez-faire* – also *laisser faire* – meaning "let do" or "let make." This theory originated with the *physiocratic school* that, among other things, was opposed to almost all feudal, mercantilist, or governmental restrictions. Eventually, the term *laissez-faire* became attached to "capitalism" in the phrase *laissez-faire capitalism* to mean that economic interests are freed from government control and only minimally regulated.

A related notion is that of *equilibrium*, which has also been used in sociopolitical philosophy understood as individual and social harmony. As individual harmony, it can be found in accounts of good character, e.g. in the ethical theory formulated by the Greek philosopher Aristotle (384–322 BCE). This theory, first, crucially distinguishes between *extrinsic* or *instrumental desires* – desires of items for the sake of something else – and *intrinsic desires* – desires of items for their own sake. Second, it holds that the desire for happiness is intrinsic and the goal of life. Third, it characterizes happiness dynamically, as an activity of the soul whereby humans flourish by acting in accordance with the mean, which Aristotle characterized as a form of harmony – from the Greek *harmos* (a "fitting" or "joining") – lying somewhere between excess and defect in the display of such traits as generosity and courage.

An analogous doctrine of the mean can also be found in Chinese philosophy. It was formulated in arguably the most philosophical of ancient Chinese documents, the *Chung Yung* (*Doctrine of the Mean*), which already existed in the early Han dynasty (206 BCE–CE 220) and was brought into prominence by the Chinese Confucian philosopher Chu Hsi (CE 1130–1200). According to the Chinese Doctrine of the Mean, the ultimate principle is rather metaphysical in that it is said to be *ch'eng* (or sincerity) because totally beyond illusion and delusion, and one's conduct should reach harmony: the appropriate mean between deficiency and excess.

In modern times, the British philosopher Bishop Joseph Butler (CE 1692–1752) characterized happiness or self-love in terms of harmony: as the harmonious satisfaction of one's basic desires. This led to the view, pursued by authors of utilitarian and contractarian persuasions, that social harmony was the harmonious satisfaction of the self-love of everyone (or most) in society. Indeed, in contemporary contractarian approaches (say, that of the contemporary United States philosopher John Rawls), it has come to be understood in terms of *equilibrium* (Latin term for balance), as a balance between a range of considered judgments of individuals (see ETHICS).

Equilibrium is also a notion involved in *production theory*, the economic theory dealing with the conversion of labor, capital, and raw materials into consumer goods by business firms so that their profit is maximized. Some market participants have a tendency to focus on one of these components, say, on capital, to the detriment of the others. This is sometimes taken to be a ground for arguing that those associated with that component, say, investors, should have a greater income than others. Such a position, however, appears implausible when one considers that it results from focusing on

just one component, capital, in a one-sided and blinkered manner.

An influential movement concerned with equality of income distribution is MARXISM, whose emphasis has been on greater income being deserved by laborers. One of its important aspects in this regard is its understanding of *human labor as the source of economic value*, and *labor power* as a special type of commodity in a commodity exchange system, hence contrasted with *work*, which is the exertion of effort to produce something whether or not in an exchange system. In this system, given the established division of labor, labor produces more exchange value than it costs employers as subsistence wages. This theory of surplus value brings out the fact that treating humans as sources of profit-generating commodities may, and sometimes does, conflict with treating them as persons. Such situations in which people were treated merely as means to economic ends were a source of indignation for the originator of Marxism, the German philosopher Karl Marx (CE 1818–83) not just in his early writings, but even in his less moralistic *Capital*, as well as a reason for his proposing the alternative socialist and communist forms of social organization.

Conceiving of the market as a feedback system (see COMPUTER THEORY), which involves such components as labor, capital, and consumer constituencies, provides a starting point to limit capitalist, Marxist, or consumerist exaggerations. The question however remains: "How much income should each sector get?" In this regard, a very different approach has been pursued along the lines proposed by the Italian economist Vilfredo Pareto (CE 1848–1923). He coined the term *Pareto efficiency* – though the term that acquired predominance is *Pareto optimality* or *Pareto optimum* – to denote a state of affairs where no one can be made better off without making someone worse off. The optimal state of affairs was that in which Pareto optimality was achieved.

Pareto optimality is at the center of welfare economics, the branch of economics concerned with formulating criteria that help establish the equity, fairness, or justice of economic arrangements. The *basic theorem of welfare economics* has two forms: direct and converse. The *direct* form roughly asserts that every competitive equilibrium is a Pareto optimum. The *converse* form says that every Pareto optimum is a competitive equilibrium. As the contemporary Indian economist and economics Nobel Prize winner Amartya Sen has stated, however, the direct form of the theorem makes room for highly inequitable and possibly disastrous situations, namely whenever the utility of those who are extremely poor cannot be improved without diminishing the utility of those who are extremely rich. This is a point at which, against *laissez-faire* economics, proponents of welfare economics try to formulate equity criteria that will help reach an economically and morally sound situation. As for the converse form, as Sen has also pointed out, it is used to make Pareto optimality a necessary, but not by itself sufficient, condition of morally acceptable competitive situations. Other conditions, e.g. the initial distribution of resources, are also crucial. Hence, this version is nothing especially favored by *laissez-faire* economists, though it can be used by those concerned with reform or even more radical change.

See also: ethics; philosophy, sociopolitical; utilitarianism

Further reading

Hausman, Daniel M. (1981) *Capital, Profits, and Prices: An Essay in the Philosophy of Economics*, New York: Columbia University Press.

Stark, Werner (1998) *The Ideal Foundations of Economic Thought: Three Essays on the Philosophy of Economics*, London: Routledge.

Wilber, Charles K. (1998) *Economics, Ethics, and Public Policy*, Lanham, MD: Rowman & Littlefield.

philosophy of education Philosophical inquiry dealing with the ends and ideals of education, as well as with pedagogy, which focuses on educational methods and procedures. In Ancient Greece, the predominant educational ideal was *kalós kaì agathós*, which is variously translated as "right and good," "just and good," and "beautiful and good." The philosophers of the classical period tried to specify this ideal and formulate the methods for attaining

it. Socrates (469–399 BCE), for example, formulated the doctrine of *Socratic intellectualism*, according to which goodness, virtue, or wisdom is simply a kind of knowledge and, once one knows what is good and what is evil, one is bound to do the right thing. This doctrine was most strikingly expressed by Plato (428–348 BCE) in the *Protagoras*, where Socrates plays games with an earnest Protagoras.

The doctrine was abandoned by Aristotle (384–322 BCE) who argued that moral character included knowledge of good and evil, but also had an emotive component that resulted from training the passions. It should be mentioned that, along these lines, Plato, in the *Republic*, had already introduced the tripartite soul, from which a psychology of emotion follows that seems to invalidate the ethical consequences of Socratic intellectualism. For there, Plato considered training of the passions to be crucial for developing the ideal state.

These initial ideas prompted a range of questions that have since formulated problems central to the philosophy of education: "What are the aims of education?" "Is the attainment of wisdom one of them?" "What about the attainment of virtue?" "What is wisdom?" "What is virtue?" "How are wisdom, virtue, and knowledge related?" "Are there kinds of wisdom?" "How is virtue related to the virtues?" "Can wisdom be taught?" "Can virtue be taught?" "How?" "What is teaching?" "Is teaching at all possible?"

Though STOICISM later revived Socratic intellectualism and, during its third phase, that of Roman Stoicism, accordingly implemented educational processes that, in effect, amounted to the education of the Roman leaders, the Aristotelian conception, to which all Stoics were indebted, remained influential. As for curricular coverage, the standard subjects were, first, the *trivium* (from the Latin *tres*, i.e. "three," and *viae*, i.e. "ways"): grammar, rhetoric, and dialectic; and then the *quadrivium* (from the Latin *quatuor*, i.e. "four," and *viae*, i.e. "ways"): geometry, arithmetic, astronomy, and music, a set of subjects that the Carthage-born author Martianus Capella (fifth century CE) solidified by means of an allegory, thus influencing the curriculum of medieval universities.

Following the example set in Alexandria, the most vigorous remnant of Greek culture until its fall in the seventh century CE, advanced studies among the Hellenized peoples of Egypt, the Middle East, and Iran in the sixth century already included a philosophical curriculum based on Aristotle's works. With the rise of Islam in the seventh century CE, and the adoption of Arabic as the language of scholarship during the reign of the Umayyad caliph 'Abd al-Malik (CE 685–705), Greek and Oriental manuscripts began to be translated into Arabic. Initially, this was motivated by practical reasons, which explains why the first translations were limited to works in medicine, alchemy, and astrology. Later, however, an Arabic interest in other works developed. Most significant were the contributions of the Persian convert from Zoroastrianism Abdullah b. al-Muqaffa' (d. CE 757). In literature, from the Pahlevi, he translated the Indian fables known as *Kalilah wa Dimnah*; while, from the Persian, he translated such works as *History of Persian Kings* and the *Book of Mazda*. In philosophy, his interest (or, according to some scholars, that of his son, Muḥammad) focused on the works of the Greek philosopher Aristotle and his commentators, from Alexander of Aphrodisias (*fl. c.* CE 200) on. For example, Aristotle's *Categories*, *Hermeneutica*, and *Analytica Posteriora*, as well as *Isagoge*, by the Tyre-born Neoplatonic philosopher Porphyry (*c.* CE 232–*c.* 304) were translated into Arabic for the 'Abbāsid caliph al-Manṣūr (CE 754–75). This process accelerated significantly at the beginning of the ninth century, when it was fueled by the unprecedented support of the 'Abbāsid caliph al Ma'mūn (CE 813–33), who regularly presided over unusually bold theological and philosophical disputations, himself wrote various treatises and, in CE 830, established the *Bait al-Ḥikma* (House of Wisdom), also called the *School of Baghdad*: an institute – including a library – devoted to translation and research.

The resulting translated works became the standard Arabic texts in logic; natural sciences such as physics and biology; metaphysics; and ethics where, as in Aristotle's works, the focus was on character ethics and its main concern: wisdom or, in Arabic, *ḥikma* – which also

means PHILOSOPHY – and the related notion of *hakīm* ("wise"), i.e. someone learned in philosophy and medicine (which at the time was part of philosophy). Other works by the Greco-Roman Neoplatonist Plotinus (CE 204–70) and the Hellenic philosopher Proclus (CE 410–85), as well as the pseudo-Aristotelian *Theologia Aristotelis* or *Theology of Aristotle* – which, though its author is unknown, included a paraphrase of various books of Plotinus' *Enneads* (IV, V, and VI according to some scholars, and I through V according to others) were used to study metaphysics. Mathematics was studied through, among others, the works of two Alexandrians, the *Elements* by Euclid (third century BCE) and the *Almagest* by Claudius Ptolomey (second century CE). Politics was studied primarily through the *Republic* and the *Laws* by the Greek philosopher Plato (428–348 BCE).

These works were approached through a variety of dialectical methods by the Scholars of the time, the Mutakallims, who were engaged in a deliberate attempt at approaching the data of revelation by relying on reason, though their effort was often motivated by a religious, rather than a rational, concern. The first ones to have started this type of serious theological discussion that came to be called *kalām* (literally, "word" or "speech"), were the Mu'tazilites – whose position was shared by the 'Abbāsid caliph al Ma'mūn – or, at least, their Qadari forerunners. Notable also among the schools of *kalām* was that of the Ash'arites, who developed an atomistic view of time according to which God constantly re-creates the universe and any regularities in it merely result from God's habits. At any rate, technically, *kalām*, initially meant an argumentative response to a perceived deviation on matters of doctrine; later, the use of syllogistic methods in assessing philosophical views; and, eventually, also the speculative and defensive use of reason. In this sense, *kalām* became a name for what is sometimes described as *Islamic Scholasticism*. These practices and institutions had a significant influence in the eventual development of universities in Europe (see below).

With the arrival of large numbers of Europeans in the American continent in the fifteenth century, scholars accompanying the expeditions recognized the sophistication of some native educational ideals and methods. For example, the Nahuas of what is now Mexico had a highly developed system of universal and obligatory education. A guiding educational ideal among them was that of *face and heart*, which is interpreted in a somewhat stoic fashion to mean wisdom and firmness, though the particular interpretation of this ideal varied among groups. For example, it was different between the Mexicas (from which Mexico and Mexicans inherited their names), whose culture upheld martial mysticism, and other groups, which advocated a return to *huehuehtlamatiliztli*, the ancient wisdom of the Nahua world embodied in Toltec art and ideas, and symbolized by the figure and cult of Quetzalcoatl, the plumed serpent. At any rate, a view shared by all groups was that the human predicament involved living in a place of painful joy, and that, in this place, wisdom and firmness were crucial for individuals to fulfill their individual destiny in a manner that provided glory to their elders and ancestors.

With the changes brought by these discoveries, the Renaissance interest in the Ancient Greco-Roman world, and the development of Protestantism, changes in education were seen as necessary. Some Renaissance and humanistic ideals concerned the notion of an institution whose conception was largely settled in the late Middle Ages and Renaissance periods, and apparently derived from the Arabic institution of the *madrasah*: that of a university (a term ultimately derived from the Latin *universitas*, equivalent to *univers(us)*, i.e. "universe," plus the appropriate particles, universe being derived from *uni*: "one," and *versus*: "turned"). Also, in Low Latin, the term *universitas* (from which the Old and Middle French *universite* and, then the English university developed), meant guild or corporation. The guiding notion here appears to have partly been the formalist idea that all parts constitute the whole to one purpose. Indeed, one finds a similar principle in aesthetics (a significant Renaissance concern), in the principle of *unity in diversity*, i.e. that the parts of an aesthetic object should significantly differ from each

other and contribute a significance to the object that would be changed were any of them to be changed.

Besides the concern with the structure of knowledge (when not of the universe) and how it should be reflected in educational institutions, there were concerns that focused on teaching practices. The Moravian philosopher John Amos Comenius (CE 1592–1671), for example, emphasized student participation, logical interconnection of different subject matters, and the need for a close correlation between curricular content and student intellectual maturity. These ideas were echoed by the French philosopher Jean Jaques Rousseau (CE 1712–78), who, believing humans were naturally good and the good in human nature was liable to be spoiled by society, argued for an educational approach that would fit the nature of the students, letting them follow their feelings, and which would discard artificial and impractical components of traditional – scholastic – education.

Along these lines, an emphasis on individual moral development and the primary education years was proposed by the Swiss philosopher of education J.H. Pestalozzi (CE 1746–1827). Like Pestalozzi and Comenius, the German philosopher of education Friedrich Wilhelm August Froebel (CE 1782–1852) held that education was a natural development of human abilities and emphasized that the teacher's role was to stimulate voluntary activity.

A concern with the fact that the inner impulse or ability to learn was not equally distributed throughout the population, accompanied by a concern with nurturing natural talent, led the third President of the United States, Thomas Jefferson (CE 1743–1826) to propose a system of public education aimed at discovering and developing naturally talented individuals so that knowledge could be furthered and diffused.

A century later, with systems of public education clearly in place, Rousseau's proposal took a positivistic turn in Latin America with the educational reform movement – the *Reforma* – of the early 1900s, where scientific experimentation was proposed as an alternative to scholastic lecturing. In the United States, this emphasis on experimentation was associated with an emphasis on individual development in the work of the philosopher John Dewey (CE 1859–1952). For him, inquiry is a problem-solving activity, and education focuses on inquiry and continuous experimentation aimed at furthering the development of individuals and at helping them meet their individual needs.

As for educational ideals in other traditions, the Indian philosopher and religious and political leader Mohandas K. Gandhi (CE 1869–1948) recurrently advocated the ideal of *organic education*, i.e. of educating individuals as indivisible wholes of physical and spiritual features. The means to attain this aim was centered on the learning of a craft. For Gandhi, this craft was spinning and weaving, which he considered the core of village life.

Contemporary discussions in the philosophy of education have been largely isolated from the philosophical mainstream in the United States and other countries. However, of late, they have focused on critical and creative thinking, on the relations between education and cultural diversity, and on education and moral development, in a manner that appears to dovetail with a variety of mainstream philosophical discussions in logic, ethics, and sociopolitical philosophy. In addition, they have fitted together with moral development studies carried out in moral psychology, a significant area of psychology and mainstream philosophy. The most notable proponents of such studies are the United States psychologist Lawrence Kohlberg (CE 1927–87), and the contemporary United States psychologist Carol Gilligan (see PASSION). Kohlberg formulated a theory of moral development that involves the attainment of various stages, most conspicuously where one uses principles largely understood as principles of justice or, at least, as principles constituting perfect obligations. Gilligan, by contrast, has focused on the relation between moral development, gender, and values, concluding that Kohlberg stages at best apply to male, not to female, moral development. A forerunner of this work was the Swiss psychologist Jean Piaget (CE 1896–1980), who focused on intellectual development (see PASSION).

See also: ethics; madrasah; philosophy of mind; philosophy, sociopolitical

Further reading
Noddings, Nel (1998) *Philosophy of Education*, Boulder, CO: Westview Press.
Winch, Christopher (1999) *Key Concepts in the Philosophy of Education*, London: Routledge.

philosophy of history The philosophy of history is that branch of philosophy which studies human history (from the Greek *historia*, i.e. "information" or "inquiry"), attempts at recording and interpreting it, and the methods used in doing so. The philosophy of history inquires what, if any, is the nature, significance, and justifiability of history as a study – in which case it is called *critical* philosophy of history – and of history as a series of social events – in which case it is called *substantive* philosophy of history. Substantive philosophy of history asks whether there is any aim or goal toward, or pattern according to which, the events of history develop; whether there is liberty in history; and how human history relates to metaphysical problems. Critical philosophy of history asks how the study of history relates to anthropology; and how it relates to philosophy.

Since these questions are about history and lead to theories of history, they are sometimes called *metahistorical* and the inquiry leading to them, the philosophy of history, is also called *metahistory*. However, the difference between history and metahistory is one of levels of inquiry, not a sharp difference in kind where engaging in metahistory would be historically neutral, historically detached, or independent from engaging in historical inquiry.

The founder of modern philosophy of history, as well as of philosophy of culture and philosophy of mythology, was the Italian philosopher Giambattista Vico (CE 1668–1744). Among philosophies of history (i.e. among particular philosophical theories about history), some make room for *progress*, i.e. change for the better, while others do not. Progress is only apparent or momentary if one assumes the Stoic doctrine of eternal return, according to which the world year repeats itself identically each time. Vico's view was not so much a cyclical, but a helicoidal, conception of history. That is, all nations rise and fall in cycles, but within an overall linear history governed by providence. Each cycle passes through three ages: an age of gods, when people think primarily in terms of the gods; an age of heroes, when virtues and institutions are established by reference to the personalities of heroes; and an age of humans, when the sense of the divine is lost, luxury and falseness overcomes life, and thought becomes abstract and ineffective.

This view had a partial forerunner in the Tunis-born Arabic philosopher Ibn Khaldūn (CE 1332–1406), famous for his multi-volume history, which gives an account of the whole range of Islamic knowledge. At present, the entire book has come to be called *Muqaddimah*. Initially, however, the term *muqaddimah*, which means "introduction," simply denoted the introduction to the multi-volume history. Also, during Ibn Khaldūn's lifetime, the history's introduction and first book became an independent work entitled *Muqaddimah*. At any rate, this work became a turning point in the philosophy of history. Ibn Khaldūn argues that nomadic groups such as the Bedouins are closer than sedentary groups to acting in a manner that is good for humans. For among nomads the community and group feeling (*'asabiyyah*) take precedence over individualistic aims. The more urbanized sedentary groups become, the more luxuries they have and, as a result, injustice and aggression prevail, eventually putting an end to civilization. Ibn Khaldūn, however, did not hold that the said historical developments took place merely as a result of a combination of such natural items as geographic, economic, and sociological causes. He held that history was ruled by an extranatural component: the will and plan of God.

Against cyclical views, the German philosopher Johann Gottfried von Herder (CE 1776–1841) held that evolution depends on adaptation, and formulated a notion of progress suggesting that higher and later stages depended on lower and earlier ones. Like him, the French philosopher and founder of positivism Auguste Comte (CE 1798–1857) applied evolutionary ideas to the study of cultural and historical change, suggesting that the highest and latest stage was scientific.

As for our knowledge of history, Vico proposed the formula *verum ipsum factum*, by which he meant one can know only what one has done. This points to a genetic conception of knowledge, and raises methodological questions about humans' ability to know anything but the components of their history.

The development of late nineteenth- and early twentieth-century positivism, however, with its emphasis on a conception of knowledge based on empirical data and inferences to the future based on these data, i.e. predictions whose content is observable, raised additional methodological questions about history. For history studies the past and, if anything, makes *retrodictions*, i.e. inferences to the past based on current data. The problem is that the content of these retrodictions is not observable.

Given this situation, some historians and philosophers of history concluded that history's methods include such confirmation methods used in other studies as clarity, consistency, and explanatory power; but that prediction (or retrodiction) is not one of – or not one of the main – methods of history. History's emphasis is narrative and the type of explanation characteristic of its narratives involves an emphasis on crucial conditions without which the data we have from given historical events, periods, or figures would not be present. In other words, history uses the method of hypothesis or ABDUCTION, or arguments to the best explanation to explain received data (see EXPLANATION).

Other philosophers reverted to the speculative approach to history. The nineteenth-century German philosopher Friedrich Nietzsche (CE 1844–1900), for example, revived the Stoic notion of eternal return. The German philosopher of history Oswald Spengler (CE 1880–1936), echoing some of Vico's ideas, considered *civilization* to be the final stage of a society's life cycle, when the cultural possibilities have been actualized and are simply managed or administered rather than further developed, while the State expands. He contrasted this stage to *culture*, a series of stages where the cultural possibilities are still being actualized, i.e. there is novelty.

The English philosopher of history Arnold Toynbee (CE 1889–1975) formulated a position analogous to that of Spengler, though, on Toynbee's view, the societies' cycles are less rigid than on Spengler's. Toynbee's view involves a biological challenge and response mechanism: societies decline when they fail to respond to the challenges they face. Any response occurs through a creative minority that follows a withdrawal and return pattern: it withdraws under the challenge and returns with a response. If the transmissive majority does not respect the creative minority and accordingly fails to accept the proposed response, then the society is in danger.

The best-known figure in the philosophy of history in the Anglo-Saxon world was the historian and philosopher R(obin) G(eorge) Collingwood (CE 1889–1943). In his often reprinted *The Idea of History*, he formulates the view that all history is history of thought.

The wide-vistas approach to the philosophy of history was denounced by such neo-Kantian German philosophers as Wilhelm Dilthey (CE 1833–1911) and Wilhelm Windelband (CE 1848–1915), who held that history, the social studies, and, indeed, the philosophy of history are caught up in the presuppositions of their time. This criticism was echoed by twentieth century neo-positivists and analytic philosophers, though not on the same grounds. Put briefly, their point was rather historiographic, hence methodological: sound methodology – and, indeed, intellectual modesty – precludes such wide-vistas exaggerations. To give an accurate historical account, one must cautiously proceed paying attention to each aspect of historical inquiry: review the sources, identify the relevant data they contain, formulate hypotheses, critically examine the hypotheses given the data and their interpretation, combine these data while assessing how, if at all, they support the said or alternative hypotheses, and formulate the final product in narrative form. This process typically issues in much richer, and varied narratives that are hardly reducible to the procrustean patterns of the said wide generalizations.

A revival of the exaggerations of substantive philosophy of history can arguably be found in the debate concerning modernism and postmodernism. The term *postmodernism* – more of a buzz-word than a term with a precise or even clear descriptive meaning – is used to denote any view or approach that involves a reaction against modernism (see CONTINENTAL PHILOSOPHY). As for *modernism*, some philosophers associated with postmodernism – e.g. the French philosopher and historian of thought Michel Foucault (CE 1926–84) and the French philosopher Jean François Lyotard – have described it as a period extending from the Enlightenment and Romanticism to the present that is committed to grand historical narratives where progress – whether Marxist, capitalist, or positivist – is a central component, and humanity is the hero of the story. However, this characterization, which postmodernists use to reject the said modernist grand narrative, is itself a grand narrative about patterns in large-scale historical periods, hence also exemplifies a substantive philosophy of history. It is therefore open to the same methodological objections previously mentioned.

See also: abduction; evolution; explanation; historicism; metaphysics; myth

Further reading
Aron, Raymond (1961) *Introduction to the Philosophy of History*, Boston: Beacon.
Danto, Arthur Coleman (1985) *Narration and Knowledge: Including the Integral Text of Analytical Philosophy of History*, New York: Columbia University Press.
Fain, Haskell (1970) *Between Philosophy and History: The Resurrection of Speculative Philosophy of History Within the Analytic Tradition*, Princeton, NJ: Princeton.
Gallie, W.B. (1964) *Philosophy and the Historical Understanding*, Berkeley: University of California.
Gardiner, Patrick (1959) *Theories of History*, Glencoe, IL: The Free Press.

philosophy of language The philosophical study of language: its kinds, e.g. natural, like English or Spanish; or artificial, like Basic or Pascal among computer languages; its main constituents, e.g. grammatical form, vocabulary, meaning, and function; its practice, e.g. whether used in poetry, science, or business transactions; and its relation to related studies, e.g. linguistics.

Traditional studies in the philosophy of language were significantly linked to metaphysics. Some distinctions have come down to us: an *imposition*, for example, is a linguistic convention whereby a term denotes something.

It is a *first imposition* if it designates extra-linguistic items such as trains and stars. It is a *second imposition* if it designates linguistic items such as nouns, adjectives, and declensions. A parallel distinction is drawn between *first intentions*, i.e. any thoughts about non-mental items such as trains and stars, and *second intentions*, i.e. any thoughts about first intentions.

Syntax, semantics, and pragmatics

Philosophers of language traditionally distinguish three main areas of language. One is *syntax*, i.e. the structure of well-formed strings of symbols – such as letters and or other characters or marks – in languages, e.g. "All *S* are *P*" is the structure of the sentence "All cats are mammals." The study of linguistic structure was emphasized by the members of the Prague School of linguistics, which was active in the 1920s and 1930s, and has become a significant component of linguistics and the philosophy of language.

A second area is *semantics* in the product-sense of semantics, i.e. the meanings of the said strings of symbols, rather than the activity-sense of semantics in which semantics denotes a branch of inquiry that is carried out about meanings. In the product-sense, for example, "All cats are mammals" ordinarily has a descriptive meaning asserting, say, that all items which are cats are also items that are mammals. The third area is *pragmatics*, i.e. the use of such strings of symbols in languages and the conditions attending to such use. These conditions include, for example, the ordinary conditions under which "All cats are mammals" has descriptive meaning, by contrast with the special conditions under which "All cats are mammals" would have emotive meaning, say, when a student has had enough of listening to the "All cats are mammals" example in a philosophy class over and over again and, angrily, shouts it, interrupting the teacher and, immediately, leaving the room and slamming the door behind. This latter example indicates how normally descriptive sentences could have an exclusively or primarily, emotive use, hence, arguably, semantics is dependent on pragmatics. Similar examples – e.g. poets' use of bad syntax to attain certain linguistic effects – can be given to indicate the dependence of syntax on pragmatics.

Declarative sentences, propositions, and statements

In this regard, philosophers concerned with semantics have argued that to make sense of such items of syntax as declarative sentences in different languages – say "it rains" in English and "*llueve*" in Spanish – one must postulate a proposition, i.e. the shared meaning of the sentences and, indeed, of all sentences synonymous with them. Analogously, the Austrian philosopher Alexius Meinong (CE 1853–1920) postulated the *Objectiv*, i.e. what is signified by a declarative sentence, a notion that the English philosopher Bertrand Russell (CE 1872–1970) considered quite similar to what he called a *proposition*. That is, propositions are abstract objects concerning which one can have the *psychological attitude* or *propositional attitude* – i.e. a psychological state – of believing it, entertaining it, doubting it, denying it, or the like.

However, critics argue that one need not say that synonymous declarative sentences have the same meaning – a noun that leads to hyposthasizing an infinity of unnecessary entities, i.e. propositions. Rather, they hold all one needs is to say that synonymous declarative sentences are identical in what they mean – a verb that can be understood in terms of identity of linguistic conventions or use. And when the sentences are thus used in specifiable circumstances, they belong to a category of pragmatics: *statements*.

Concepts and problems of semantics

The topics just discussed belong in the general area of logic and the philosophy of language called *semantics* (in the activity-sense of semantics), which studies the interpretations of languages (i.e. what their symbols mean), more specifically, in *formal semantics*, which studies the interpretations of formal languages.

An *interpretation* – or a semantics in the product-sense of semantics – of a formal language is the assignment of meanings to its symbols and truth conditions to its sentences. Usually a distinction is made between a standard interpretation and a non-standard interpretation of a formal language. A *standard* interpretation is an interpretation that involves usual rules concerning such things as correlations of symbols with the elements in the interpretation's domain, e.g. one-to-one correlations of numerals with the domain elements in the case of the language of arithmetic, say "0" with zero, "−" with subtraction, etc. Other standard interpretations are isomorphic with the one just described.

A *non-standard* interpretation is an interpretation that does not follow the usual correlation and related rules. In respect to second-order logic, for example, a standard semantics is an interpretation where the model for the language is the same as that for the corresponding first-order language, and the variables of each kind – e.g. relation variables, function variables – range over every item of that kind in the domain of discourse. Non-standard semantics, also called *Henkin* semantics, is a semantics where each model is constituted by a domain of discourse and a specified – not necessarily exhaustive – collection of the relations in the domain. The specified collections are the second-order variables in the model. This type of semantics regards second-order languages as multi-sorted first-order languages.

Of relevance here is *extensionalist* semantics, where all references to such items as Pegasus the winged horse or round squares are explained away. This approach has been used, for example, to attempt to reduce mental states formulated by means of intensional language to extensional descriptions of physiological states.

Sometimes, the term semantics is used in the more specialized sense of *linguistic* semantics, an area in the philosophy of linguistics: the study of particular types of constructions within a natural language. Montague grammars (see below) provide a framework for such studies.

Concepts and problems of pragmatics

Philosophical concerns with the pragmatics of language have led to the study of such *speech acts* as requests and commands by contrast with descriptions. They also lead to the study of *propositional attitudes* – attitudes about propositions, say, believing or disbelieving propositions – and their objects. For example, John may believe that he is sick and Mary may also believe that she is sick. Both can formulate this belief by saying "I am sick." However, suppose that John's belief is true while Mary's belief is false. Since their belief is formulated by the same declarative sentence – "I am sick" – which, arguably, expresses the same proposition, it must involve different *propositional objects* or *referents* in conjunction with the proposition. Otherwise, it could not have, as it does, opposite truth values.

A related topic is the logical theory of *reduplication*, which concerns sentences where the subject is duplicated by using such terms as the Latin *qua* and its English translation "as." An example is "a person, *qua* person, deserves respect." Such reduplicative use of a sentence's subject typically has the function of explaining why the subject has the predicate used in the sentence

Communication theories

A crucial problem in the philosophy of language is that of communication. Communication failures are one reason why philosophers have discussed the notion of *linguistic competence*. In this regard, some have been impressed by the fact that it takes *only* about two years for a child to acquire linguistic competence, while others have been impressed by the fact that it takes *no less* than about two years for a child to acquire linguistic competence. Those who think it less than it should be expected, have focused, following the contemporary United States philosopher and linguist Noam Chomsky, on *grammar* – the system of rules specifying a language – and, in particular, on the *depth grammar* or *deep structure* of a language's grammar, from which actual grammatical uses of the language can be derived. This is done through a series of transformations carried out in accordance with *transformation rules* that constitute *generative grammars* or *generative devices*, i.e. precisely formulated deductive systems specifying all and only the well-formed sentences of a language and their relevant structural properties. On this approach, the syntactic structure of a sentence results from a series of trees connected by operations called transformations, where the initial tree – the deep structure or deep grammar – is generated by a vocabulary and a phrase structure, and the final tree – the surface structure or surface grammar – contains the meaning units of the sentence in their proper order.

Philosophers and linguists upholding this theory have argued that children are somehow born with meaning and other postulates that allow them to acquire linguistic competence relatively quickly. This inborn competence is invested in a *universal grammar*, i.e. what the grammar of all natural languages must share because of the innate linguistic competence of humans.

An alternative approach has emphasized statistical approaches to linguistic usage, using them to explain why children do not normally take less than two years to acquire linguistic competence. This approach is associated with behaviorism, a position that Chomsky attacked on the basis of the poverty of the stimulus: a psychological event displayed when behavior is not entirely controlled by concurrent or preceding stimuli. Chomsky argued that stimuli do not control or suffice to predict much of human, especially verbal, behavior.

Still another approach has been that of the United States mathematician and philosopher Richard Montague (CE 1930–71): a *Montague grammar*, which uses a categorical grammar as its syntactical component. The possibility of merging this approach with that of Chomsky's has elicited much discussion. A notion that is used in the process is that of *parsing*, i.e. the process of determining the syntactical structure of a sentence on the basis of the rules of a given grammar by means of a *parse tree*, a tree-like structure constructed through a sequence of steps.

Still another approach sidesteps the disagreement just mentioned between Chomsky and behaviorism through an emphasis on strategies (and away from merely statistical or merely transformational approaches). It is *formal learnability theory*, the study of human language learning through the formulation of formal models that use artificial languages and simplified learning strategies. This approach has led to closer approximations to actual language learning.

Whatever stand one takes on this matter, appeals to the learning of conventions and, as the Austrian philosopher Ludwig Wittgenstein (CE 1889–1951) put it, a *form of life* of a linguistic community – which he explained as some agreement in the use of language – posed a variety of questions. Notable among them is whether a *private language* is possible. Wittgenstein argued that this is impossible, because a private language would face the *problem of the criterion*, i.e. it would lack a criterion of linguistic use, because linguistic use is a matter of social convention, not, as a private language, of individual decision. In other words: an individual can give a word a meaning – by stipulation (see stipulative definition under DEFINITION), but no individual can give a word a use, because others have an influence on this.

Translation problems

Another question, which Wittgenstein suggested but never substantially addressed, was whether communication was possible between different linguistic communities with different criteria for linguistic usage or, to use an analogy he and his followers have used, between different linguistic communities that play different language games.

This points to the *indeterminacy of translation* theses first propounded by the United States philosopher W.V.O. Quine (CE 1908–2000) in the context of *radical translation*: an imaginary situation in which a field linguist is faced with translating a language entirely unknown to others until now. The *strong thesis* concerns the indeterminacy of theoretical sentences as wholes. It says that, in the radical translation situation, one could construct manuals for translating the new source-language into the translator's target-language, in a manner consistent with all behavioral data; but the manuals could still diverge in the target-language sentences chosen to the extent of these being mutually inconsistent. The *weak thesis* concerns the *indeterminacy of reference* or *inscrutability of reference*. It says that, given all possible behavioral data, divergent target-language interpretations of source-language words could offset one another so as to support different target-language translations, and no further data of any kind could serve to establish that one such interpretation is the correct one.

Quine initially proposed the radical translation program to test his conception that synonymous statements and analytic statements could be reduced to behavioral dispositions of a verbal sort. On this account, synonymy was understood as sameness of stimulus meaning, where stimulus meaning was the stimuli leading one to assent to a sentence. As for analyticity, this was the disposition whereby one assents to a sentence whatever the stimulus. The radical translation program, however, suggested that incompatible translation manuals could fit all these dispositions, hence undermined the said conceptions of analyticity and synonymity as well.

Language and culture

The questions posed by Wittgenstein also point to the problem of communication – and, in a very concrete sense, translatability – between communities having different, sometimes widely different, cultures. In the multicultural societies of the twentieth century, these are serious social problems that, sometimes – as in issues concerning speech codes – concern the social effects of language, e.g. the effects on members of disadvantaged groups when language stereotypes them, or the socially divisive effects of stereotyping language.

Various historical discussions in philosophy include the term *speculative grammar*. In the European Middle Ages, this term meant philosophical discussions of language. In modern times, speculative grammar was used by the United States philosopher Charles Sanders Peirce (CE 1839–1914) to mean his analysis of the classification of *signs* or *representamens* that, on his account, is separate from the other two areas of semiotics: critical logic and speculative rhetoric. In this regard, Peirce characterized logic as *semiotic* – a term originally introduced by the English philosopher John Locke (CE 1632–1704) for the study of signs and signification – sometimes spelling it as *semeiotic*, and *semeotic*, i.e. the quasi-necessary or formal theory of signs. This theory is now divided into areas parallel to those of the philosophy of language discussed at this entry's outset: syntax (also called syntactics) or the study of syntactical structure, semantics or the study of meaning, and pragmatics or the study of linguistic use and function.

A similar type of study was characterized by the Swiss linguist and Sanskrit scholar Ferdinand de Saussure (CE 1857–1913), founder of *structural linguistics*, which considered languages as repositories of discursive signs shared by a linguistic community. He called for a science of *semiology*, which would deal with the nature of signs and the laws governing them. His conception of languages as repositories of discursive signs shared by a linguistic community had a forerunner in a contribution by the German philologist Wilhelm von Humboldt (CE 1767–1835): the notion of *Sprachform*, i.e. the inner form each particular language has, which is peculiar to the language and provides a characteristic worldview or outlook on things for the community of language's users.

This latter conception, however, begs questions that Saussure's conception did not, e.g. that the *Sprachform* is peculiar to a language, and that it provides a characteristic worldview for the language's users. At any rate, Saussure's conception of languages as repositories of discursive signs, shared by a linguistic community, was extended by him and others to social phenomena in general. This work had significant influence in the development of structuralism and philosophical approaches associated with Continental philosophy (see CONTINENTAL PHILOSOPHY).

As for approaches associated with Anglo-American philosophy (see ANALYSIS), the work of Peirce and his follower, Charles W. Morris (CE 1901–79), led the theory of signs or semiotic to attain wide recognition as the philosophical and scientific study of any items carrying information, as well as communication or the transmission of information.

According to the theory of signs, a *sign* is any item that carries information, e.g. linguistic and other animal behavior aimed at conveying information, maps, road signs, diagrams, and pictures. A sign can be a *conventional sign*, i.e. a sign that has no significant physical correspondence or similarity to those items it denotes, e.g. signs in natural languages. By contrast, an *index* or *natural sign* is a sign whose occurrences are causally or statistically correlated with those of its referents, e.g. fever is a natural sign of infection. And there is also the notion of an *icon*, i.e. a sign that resembles its referent or a feature of its referent, e.g. onomatopoeias.

A related set of distinctions was formulated by the Hungarian scientist and philosopher Michael Polanyi (CE 1891–1976). He called a word being used a *subsidiary* and held that a subsidiary refers to something he called *focal matter*. According to Polanyi, this affects not only much of knowledge generally, but also our *tacit knowledge*, i.e. something we grasp by dwelling in a range of contexts that involve from theories to tools. This way, symbols, e.g. the flag, can be contrasted with signs, e.g. a street sign. For in a *symbol*, what becomes its focal matter does so through our projecting a variety of features on it; while we do not do this with *signs*.

The association between mental activity and language was also investigated by the British philosopher Alfred North Whitehead (CE 1861–1947), who held humans perceive in two main ways: first, in terms of causal efficacy, which stresses temporal relations, e.g. a glass is perceived as causally related to my having just quenched my thirst; second, in terms of presentational immediacy, which stresses spatial relations, e.g. a patch of green. They combine in a particular perception, e.g. that of a green glass. According to Whitehead, by itself, the word "green" refers to a quality spread in space, while, by itself, the word "glass" refers to its causal efficacy in my experience. When they combine in the sentence "I can see a green glass," Whitehead calls the combination a symbolic reference.

See also: logic; meaning; reference; speech act theory

Further reading

Lycan, William G. (2000) *Philosophy of Language: A Contemporary Introduction*, New York: Routledge.
Martinich, A.P. (ed.) (1990) *The Philosophy of Language*, 2nd edn, New York and Oxford: Oxford University Press.
Searle, John R. (1998) *Mind, Language and Society: Philosophy in the Real World*, New York, NY: Basic Books.

philosophy of law Also called *jurisprudence* (from the Latin *juris prudentia*, i.e. "knowledge of the law" or "wisdom concerning the law"), the philosophy of law is the study of the concepts and principles involved in a legal system or, in *general* jurisprudence (sometimes also called *nomology* – from the Greek *nomos*, i.e. "law," and "logos," i.e. "discourse" or "theory"), in all legal systems, as well as the relation between law and morality. Branches of jurisprudence are *analytical* jurisprudence, which focuses on the meaning and interconnections of legal concepts; *functional* jurisprudence, which focuses on the relation between legal rules and social needs and interests as well as other moral concerns; *historical* jurisprudence, which focuses on the historical development of legal concepts or principles; and *sociological* jurisprudence, which focuses on the relation between legal rules and positive morality, i.e. institutional and individual group behavior.

Various philosophical questions arise about the law: "What is a valid law?" "How is it related to social order?" "Under what conditions is a system of law legitimate?" There are three main traditions concerning these questions in the philosophy of law: legal positivism, the natural law tradition, and legal realism or proceduralism.

Among the various theories under the heading of *legal positivism* – i.e. the view that there is no necessary connection between law and morality – is the *command theory of law*, formulated, for example, by the English philosopher John Austin (CE 1790–1859). According to the command theory, laws properly so called are commands, hence entail a purpose and a power to sanction those who disobey them. Those laws constituting what is called *positive law* entail a sovereign and an independent society that usually obeys the sovereign.

Other types of legal positivism – e.g. that upheld by the German philosopher Hans Kelsen (CE 1881–1973) – consider the law to be not essentially coercive, as for Austin, but *normative*. Kelsen holds that a *Grundnorm* or *basic norm* is the norm, i.e. the rule, which gives validity to the whole system, e.g. by specifying what can and what cannot be a law. The validity of the basic norm, however, cannot be established by a social fact such as public acceptance. Instead, it must be presupposed by the validity of the norms it legitimates as laws. At any rate, all forms of legal positivism constitute examples of *jurisprudential formalism*, or *legal formalism*, or *mechanical jurisprudence*, in that they give formal – i.e. procedural and content-independent – solutions to legal questions, i.e. by merely analyzing stated legal rules and concepts. Another version involves the notion of the *rule of recognition* and related rules formulated by the English philosopher H.L.A. Hart (CE 1907–92), according to whom the law is a union of two sets of rules: the *primary* rules that formulate our duties; and the *secondary* rules, which give guidance on how to recognize, change, and adjudicate primary rules.

As for the *jus naturale* or *natural law* tradition, i.e. natural law theory, it rejects as artificial legal positivism's radical separation between the validity of legal rules creating legal rights – i.e. rights specified by those rules – and the moral status of such rights or, in short, between law and morality. For example, natural law theory makes the question of a law's validity partly or entirely dependent on whether it is in accordance with practical reason – the application of morality. An issue arising here about the relation between law and morality is whether the law may be used to enforce morality. The position of those answering in the affirmative, who often are concerned with enforcing sexual morality, is the doctrine of *legal moralism*.

In contrast with both positivism and natural law theory, *legal realism* or *proceduralism* focuses on what the courts and citizens actually do, and on the law's claim to legitimizing certain group interests. In doing so, it studies the functioning and political power of the law or legal systems.

Various central concepts of the philosophy of law that cut across the theories just outlined were perspicuously formulated by the United States jurist Wesley Newcomb Hohfeld (CE 1879–1918). He identified eight fundamental legal notions – among which are rights that, thus defined, are called *Hohfeldian rights* – which have been later adopted by philosophers and others:

A person S has a legal *duty* to another person P to perform some act A when the law requires that S do A for P.

A person S has a legal *privilege* (or liberty) relatively to another person P to perform some act A when S has no legal duty to P not to do A.

A person S has a legal *right* against another person P that P perform some act A when P has a legal duty to S to do A.

A person S has a legal *no-right* against another person P that P not perform some act A when P has a legal liberty relatively to S to do A.

A person S has a legal *power* over another person P to effect some consequence C for P when there is some voluntary action of S that will bring about C for P.

A person S has a legal *disability* relatively to another person P to effect some consequence C for P when there is no action S can perform that will bring about C for P.

A person S has a legal *liability* relatively to another person P to effect some consequence C when P has a legal power to effect C for X.

A person S has a legal *immunity* against another person P from C when P has no legal power over S to effect C.

These notions are crucial for the moral doctrine of the *correlativity of rights and duties*, which has various formulations. One is: a person S has a moral right against another person P that P perform some act A when P has a moral duty to S to do A. Here, S's right is a correlative right to P's duty and P's duty is a correlative duty to P's right.

Significant in the philosophy of law is the problem of the nature and justification of punishment. *Punishment* has three features: first, it is painful or unpleasant to whoever receives it; second, it is applied to a legally defined person – an ordinary individual or a corporate person – found to qualify as an offender, i.e. as having broken a law or, in other words, committed a crime; third, this finding is reached through legally established procedures. A particularly significant type of punishment is *capital* punishment, also called the *death penalty*, where the sanction applied to the offender is death.

The notion of punishment is often contrasted with that of a *sanction* or *social sanction*, i.e. an extra-legal pressure exerted upon agents by others either to encourage the agent's displaying, or to discourage agents' failure to display conduct that is customary, desirable, or morally required. There are also *internal sanctions*, i.e. either negative feelings such as *guilt* or *shame* for having failed to display the said conduct, or positive feelings such as those of *gratification* or *self-esteem* for having displayed the said conduct. In addition, there are *religious sanctions*, which are divine or human, which can be called *ministerial*. Divine sanctions are rewards or punishments given to humans by divinities either before or after the humans' death, on account of the accordance or lack of accordance between the humans' behavior or thoughts and religious requirements or ideals. *Ministerial sanctions* are rewards or punishments given to humans by representatives of the divinities on the said grounds.

A question arising about punishment in general is: "Is punishment ever justified?" In reply to this question, various theories have been formulated. One type of theories aimed at formulating a justification for punishment is constituted by *retributivist theories* or *retributivism*: the view that punishment is justified by the moral desert of the offender. This theory is different from *vengeance* because the latter, but not retributivism, aims at satisfying the feelings solely of those harmed by the offender or their sympathizers. Nor is it to be confused with the *lex talionis* (typically formulated as: an eye for an eye, and a tooth for a tooth), which is about the type of punishment fitting a given offense.

By contrast with retributivism, philosophers have formulated non-retributive theories aimed at justifying punishment. These are *consequentialist theories*, i.e. based on the consequences of punishment. Notable among them are *deterrence* (or *telishment*) *theories*, i.e. those that hold punishment is justified because the painful or unpleasant sanctions which constitute it tend to prevent future crime. Other consequentialist theories of punishment are *rehabilitation theories*, i.e. those that hold punishment is justified because it involves re-educating criminals in ways that tend to prevent future crime.

Deterrence theories have been criticized on the grounds that, given that many, especially serious crimes are committed in a rage, punishment is not an effective deterrent, hence its deterrent features can hardly justify it. Other reasons of ineffectiveness have been formulated against rehabilitation theories. On the other hand, retributivist theories have been criticized as attempts at legislating morality by ensuring that people get what they deserve, hence as involving an authoritarian conception of the law which, critics argue, is morally objectionable and tends to undermine morality and society.

As for the actual features in adjudicating cases, the Anglo-American legal system includes the notion of *mens rea* (which in Latin meant "guilty mind"). This notion denotes a culpable state of mind in committing a wrongful act (*actus reus*). This state may be: motivational, e.g. the purpose to perform a wrongful act; cognitive, e.g. the belief that the act is wrong; or behavioral, e.g. negligence. In addition, Anglo-American criminal law uses the *M'Naghten rule*, which defines legal insanity for purposes of creating a defense of criminal liability. According to this rule, legal insanity is any defect of reason, due to disease of the mind, which causes an accused criminal either not to know the nature and quality of his or her act, or not to know that this act was legally or morally wrong. Today, this rule – or the reason of insanity – is either taken to establish that the accused is not a moral agent or, alternatively, that though a moral agent, the insanity of the accused is an instance of the accepted moral excuse of mistake or ignorance.

Also, the notion of *diminished responsibility*, also called *diminished capacity*, is a concept used in legal defenses of criminal liability cases. It has two forms. The first is the *mens rea* variant, in which evidence of mental abnormality – e.g. mental disorder, intoxication, trauma, etc. – is used to argue that, at the time of the crime, the defendant did not have the mental state required for the offense. The second is the *partial-responsibility* variant, where it is argued that, even if the defendant had the required mental state, his or her responsibility was diminished and, hence, should be charged with a lesser crime.

A special kind of law is the *constitution*, a term derived from the Latin *constitutio* that meant "arrangement," "organization," "order," and, in a juridical sense, "law," "statute," "decree." From a philosophical standpoint, *constitution* has been used to translate the Greek *katabolē*, which meant "foundation," "principle," or "beginning." The Latin *constitutio* accordingly implied the creation or beginning of a society.

See also: ethics; philosophy, sociopolitical

Further reading
Austin, John (1999 [1832]) *The Province of Jurisprudence Determined*, Union, NJ: Lawbook Exchange.
Feinberg, Joel and Coleman, Jules L. (1999) *Philosophy of Law*, 6th edn, Belmont, CA: Wadsworth Pub.
Hart, H.L.A. (1998 [1968]) *Punishment and Responsibility: Essays in the Philosophy of Law*, Oxford and New York: Clarendon Press and Oxford University Press.
Hohfeld, Wesley Newcomb (1923) *Fundamental Legal Conceptions as Applied in Judicial Reasoning and Other Legal Essays*, New Haven: Yale University Press.
Kelsen, Hans (1999 [1945]) *General Theory of Law and State*, Union, NJ: Lawbook Exchange.

philosophy of liberation A Latin American philosophical movement influenced by the theology of liberation movement. The latter started in the 1960s and was aimed at improving the situation of the oppressed. Its initial formulations included *The Pedagogy of the Oppressed*, published in 1970 by the contemporary Brazilian author Paulo Freire, and *Theology of Liberation*, published the next year by the contemporary Peruvian author Gustavo Gutiérrez. This movement also influenced theologians outside Latin America. An example is the contemporary United States author James H. Cone, whose *A Black Theology of Liberation*, published in 1970, conceived of oppression as black oppression and of Christianity as the religion of the oppressed through which they were to achieve their true liberation or emancipation.

In the late 1970s and early 1980s, the liberation theology movement developed increasingly closer ties to Marxist thought and, as a result, in his 1980–5 visits to Latin America, Pope John Paul II denounced social injustice while cautioning against the excesses of liberation theology. Gustavo Gutiérrez was summoned to Rome to explain his views, other

prominent figures of the movement were suspended from the priesthood or had their right to teach suspended, and the movement declined. So did the philosophy of liberation movement that the theological movement had inspired, not before producing such works as *Philosophy of Liberation*, published in 1977 by the contemporary Argentine philosopher Enrique Dussel, who, since then, has been active in Mexico, *Latin American Philosophy of Liberation*, whose second edition was published in 1992, and *Philosophies for Liberation: The Liberation of Philosophizing?*, published in 1997 by the contemporary Argentine philosopher Horacio Cerutti Guldberg, who has been active in Mexico as well.

See also: Latin American philosophy; philosophy of religion; philosophy, sociopolitical

Further reading
Cerutti Guldberg, Horacio (1997) *Filosofias para la liberacion: Liberación del filosofar?*, Mexico: Universidad Autonoma del Estado de Mexico.
—— (1983) *Filosofía de la liberación latinoamericana*, Mexico: Fondo de Cultura Económica.
Dussel, Enrique D. (1996) *The Underside of Modernity: Apel, Ricoeur, Rorty, Taylor, and the Philosophy of Liberation*, Atlantic Highlands, NJ: Humanities Press.
—— (1985) *Philosophy of Liberation*, Maryknoll, NY: Orbis Books.
McLaren, Peter and Lankshear, Colin (1994) *Politics of Liberation: Paths from Freire*, London and New York: Routledge.

philosophy of linguistics *see* philosophy of language; philosophy of science

philosophy of literature Also called *literary theory*, this is a philosophical reflection addressing such topics as the nature of literature; its relation to art; the differences between poetry, narrative, and such forms of drama as comedy and tragedy; the relations of these to life; the nature and grounds of philosophical ideas involved in literary works; the role of criticism in literature; the nature of literary understanding; the locus of interpretation in literature (text, author, critics, reader as in the *Rezeptionsaesthetik School* that, in English, is the *reader-response theory*); and the identity of a work of literature.

Sometimes, philosophy of literature is understood as *literature in philosophy*, i.e. the inquiry aimed at placing literature in the context of *a particular philosophy*, so that it is understood in terms of the philosophy in question. This task is different from that pursued in aesthetics, in that the latter need not be, and often is not, pursued with a preconceived commitment to a particular philosophy, while literature in philosophy involves such a commitment. Indeed, philosophers have frequently pursued the literature in philosophy project. Already Plato (428–348 BCE) in his discussions of poetry, and Aristotle (384–322 BCE) in his *Poetics*, engaged in this type of project that has many instances throughout the history of philosophy.

At other times, philosophy of literature is approached as *philosophy in literature*, i.e. the study of ideas of philosophical interest found in literary works. It has been stated that this presupposes philosophy and literature are simply different forms of the same content. Perhaps it is better to say that this presupposes some of the content of literary works also can be – and indeed is – philosophical and open to philosophical assessment. Some authors have also argued that, in any case, the philosophical examination of ideas found in literary works implies the superiority of philosophical over literary discourse, at least when dealing with that shared content. Yet this is not implied by the examination itself, though it may be implied or assumed by philosophers who are set on clarifying ideas that – they presume – literary works can only imperfectly express.

As an alternative to the presumptuous approach just described, philosophy of literature can be conceived as *philosophy through literature*, i.e. philosophical inquiry pursued through literary works. This is to say that, in creating literary works, one can philosophically address individual, social, or other problems and ways of dealing with them. Indeed, the Danish philosopher and theologian Søren Kierkegaard (CE 1813–1855) appears to have done just that in reacting, throughout his work, against the philosophical arrogance that he found displayed by the German philosopher Georg Wilhelm Friedrich Hegel (CE 1770–1831) in his *Phenomenology of Spirit*, which treats art

and religion as but imperfect adumbrations of ideas that can be fully and accurately formulated only in philosophical discourse. A notable example of philosophy through literature can also be found in Russian philosophy, in the works of Feodor Mikhailovich Dostoevsky (CE 1821–81), Leo Nikolaevich Tolstoy (CE 1828–1910), and others, as well as in the works of such Latin American writers as the Argentine writer Jorge Luis Borges (CE 1899–1986); the Belgium-born, naturalized Argentine and then French writer Julio Cortázar (1914–84); and the contemporary Argentine author Ernesto Sábato.

Finally, philosophy of literature can be conceived, quite comprehensively, though in a more detached manner, as *philosophy and literature*, i.e. an inquiry in which philosophy and literature are taken to be distinct and self-guided activities that, none the less, relate to each other in various ways. Some authors take this to imply a merely reflective, somewhat detached, task: that is, merely an inquiry into what, if anything, distinguishes philosophy and literature from each other; to what extent and under what circumstances it does so; and, in general, how these two areas of human activity relate to each other. The relations between philosophy and literature may include overlapping with each other in certain pursuits; coinciding in their purposes, content, social, or individual functions; or taking precedence over, or even conflicting with, each other.

Indeed, the various relations between philosophical and literary discourse in their wide variety of forms prompt philosophical as well as literary inquiry about the role of fiction in exploring fact, or the relation between fiction and memory. This leads, for example, to questions of philosophical and literary significance concerning the place, if any, of truth in fiction. It also raises, in connection with memory, questions of philosophical and literary interest concerning, for example, personal identity, especially in the literature in exile movement of the late twentieth and twenty-first century.

See also: anthropology; Continental philosophy; culture; metaphysics; myth; philosophy and expatriation; philosophy of history; philosophy of language

Further reading

Alegría, Fernando and Ruffinelli, Jorge (1990) *Paradise Lost or Gained? The Literature of Hispanic Exile*, Houston, TX: Arte Público Press.

Bruns, Gerald L. (1999) *Tragic Thoughts at the End of Philosophy: Language, Literature, and Ethical Theory*, Evanston, IL: Northwestern University Press.

Buchler, Justus (1974) *The Main of Light: On the Concept of Poetry*, London and New York: Oxford University Press.

Jones, Peter (1975) *Philosophy and the Novel*, London and New York: Oxford University Press.

philosophy of logic *see* logic; philosophy of mathematics

philosophy of mathematics The branch of philosophy that deals with the nature, scope, and ontological status of the subject matter of mathematics; the grounds of mathematical knowledge; and the relation of mathematical knowledge to its applications.

Early Greek mathematicians and philosophers – traditionally associated with the Pythagoreans – held two basic beliefs. First, they thought it possible to measure all relations by using natural numbers or their exact ratios, i.e. that *rational* numbers sufficed for this purpose. Second, given the previous belief, and the fact that they did not sharply, if at all, distinguish physics from mathematics, these mathematicians further believed that space, time, and motion could be measured on the basis of discrete, atomic units. The discovery of *irrational* numbers such as the square root of two shattered the first belief. Zeno's paradoxes (see PARADOX), formulated by the Greek philosopher Zeno of Elea (490–430 BCE), dramatized the collapse of the second belief.

As a result, Greek mathematicians and philosophers began to draw distinctions between mathematics and physics that eventually led to what has come to be known as *Euclidean geometry*, because it was formulated in *The Elements* by the Greek mathematician Euclid of Alexandria (third century BCE). This work used definitions, postulates, axioms, and theorems, and its proofs of the theorems used only potentially infinite geometric and arithmetic procedures. It set much of the research agenda for mathematical investigations for

more than two thousand years, first during the Alexandrian age – e.g. in works by the Greek mathematician, physicist, and inventor Archimedes (*c.* 287–212 BCE) on topics ranging from the measurement of circles to the quadrature of the parabola; then in the Greco-Roman world, where Hipparcus (*c.* 190–*c.* 125 BCE) invented trigonometry, which Menelaus (first century CE) further developed. These results were accompanied by the work of Diophantus (*fl. c.* CE 250), who, in *Arithmetica*, codified algebra. Also, Arabic and Persian mathematicians and philosophers further developed algebra by introducing the concept of zero as a number, and formulating Arabic notation, which enormously facilitated calculations until then carried out with Roman numerals.

The sharp separation between geometry and algebra remained until the French mathematician and philosopher René Descartes (CE 1596–1650) developed *analytic geometry*, which established the equivalence between geometric figures and algebraic formulas, thus making *differential calculus* possible. This is a branch of mathematics that deals with the determination of such things as the tangent to a curve, the area between it and some fixed axis, the length of curved lines, and the calculation of volumes. It has also been called the *fluxional calculus* – the *fluxion* being the rate of change of a variable quantity (the *fluent*) relative to time (see CALCULUS). This was the version of the differential calculus formulated by one of the two people who developed it independently from each other, the English physicist Sir Isaac Newton (CE 1642–1727), the other being the German philosopher Gottfried Wilhelm Leibniz (CE 1646–1716). The differential calculus helped unify and mathematize physics in an unprecedented manner. Yet, it involved a philosophically puzzling and mathematically vague notion: that of infinitesimal spatial and temporal increments. This led to the formulation of *constructivism* (see below) in attempts at providing a solid ontological basis for the differential calculus.

Among current ontological issues, various positions are advanced about the objects of mathematics. One, *simple realism*, would associate a *standard model* – i.e. a theory that systematizes some or all of our knowledge of mathematics – made up of independent objects with classical theories formulated in first-order language. Other forms of realism would involve a *non-standard model*, i.e. a model that is non-isomorphic to the standard model, e.g. of all true first-order sentences about natural numbers. There are also models where the objects are constructs, explicitly definable stage-by-stage. This position – mathematical *constructivism* – sometimes coincides with *conventionalism*, the view that mathematical truths are truths we create by adopting certain conventions concerning language, definitions, rules of inference, and axioms. However, constructivism need not be subjective as conventionalism is.

Another version of constructivism is mathematical *intuitionism*, a position formulated by the Dutch mathematician L.E.J. Brouwer (CE 1881–1966), according to which there are no unexperienced mathematical truths, and mathematical constructs are generated on the basis of the *Urintuition* or primitive intuition of temporal counting, a conception analogous to the Kantian conception of a priori time. This posed the problem of generating the *continuum*, i.e. the non-denumerable set of real numbers or points of a line that, by its very non-denumerable nature, cannot be generated by counting. Intuitionism's best attempt at circumventing this problem was Brouwer's notion of an *infinite choice sequence* of rational numbers. Though generated by a rule, such a sequence is non-denumerable and leaves some room for choice concerning the successive terms of the sequence, e.g. by merely formulating parameters within which these terms should be. A consequence of Brouwer's position is the rejection of the law of excluded middle. For, given the construction requirement, the truth of a proposition is not generally equivalent to the falsity of its contradictory.

Conventionalism was put into question by the discovery that arithmetic is incomplete if consistent (see LOGIC). For if, according to this, a sentence in a system is true but undecidable, i.e. has neither proof nor disproof, then it would appear it is not true by convention, i.e.

just because of the axioms, rules of inference, and definitions of the system. For, if it were true because of these, it could be proved. However, if it were not true, its negation would be true by convention, hence, likewise, provable. Of course, a conventionalist could, like the constructionist previously indicated, say that neither the said sentence nor its negation is true if the sentence is undecidable, i.e. that arithmetic has truth value gaps.

A related issue concerns the character of *magnitudes. Analysis*, for example, is considered a mathematics of continuous magnitudes, by contrast with *arithmetic*, which is considered a mathematics of discrete magnitudes. Traditionally, analysis is formulated in a second- or higher-order language. This is *standard analysis*. When carried out in a first-order language, it is possible to formulate a model of *non-standard* analysis, i.e. a model not isomorphic to standard analysis, but where the axiom set is none the less satisfied.

In this regard, the work of the Italian mathematician Giuseppe Peano (CE 1858–1932) is significant. He formulated what is now known as *Peano's axioms*, or *Peano's postulates*, a list of assumptions from which the natural numbers can be derived. The postulates are formulated in various ways. One such way is: 0 is a number; 1 is a number; the successor of any number n is $n+1$ and is also a number; no two numbers have the same successor; 0 is not the successor of any number; and a principle of mathematical induction: if 0 has a property P, and if, if n has P then $n+1$ has P, then every number has P.

The continuous character of real numbers was addressed by the German mathematician Julius Wilhelm Richard Dedekind (CE 1831–1916), when, in 1872, he characterized a *Dedekind-cut* and suggested that the essence of continuity is the following. If, whenever a line is divided into two sets A and A' such that if p belongs to A and q belongs to A', then p is lesser than q; if p belongs to A and q is lesser than p, then q belongs to a; and if p belongs to A' and q is greater than p, then q also belongs to A', then there is a real number r that produces this cut. That is, A is the set of all numbers lesser than r, and A' is the set of all numbers greater than r.

As the preceding discussion makes plain, a significant area of the philosophy of mathematics concerns the concept of *number* and its *kinds* (e.g. natural, rational, real, and complex, which include imaginary, numbers), and overlaps with *number theory. Mathematical* analysis or *standard* analysis is the branch of number theory that studies real numbers. These include, as increasingly comprehensive proper subclasses of natural numbers, the integers (positive, negative, and zero), the rational numbers or fractions, the algebraic numbers such as the square root of two, and non-algebraic or transcendental irrational numbers, or simply transcendental numbers, e.g. pi.

A related family of issues concerns the *foundations of mathematics*. A significant attempt in this regard was the program developed by the German mathematician and philosopher David Hilbert (CE 1862–1943), who in doing so founded *proof theory*, the branch of mathematics pursuing this program. It aimed at securing the ideal, i.e. infinitary, parts of mathematics by formalizing them and then proving the resulting systems to be extensions of *finitary systems*, i.e. systems using only proof-finitary reasoning or numerical calculations. Ideal mathematics was thus supposed to regulate real mathematics, which consisted of the meaningful and true propositions, i.e. real propositions, of mathematics and their proofs. Foundational approaches like this one eventually failed, partly because of Gödel's theorems (see below). These were problems in the area of inquiry that came to be called *metamathematics* and *metalogic*.

There are also ontological concerns regarding, for example, the scope of mathematics. Here, some views, as already indicated, are infinitary; others are finitary, either making room for future objects to be constructed or, in the case of strict finitists, rejecting even these.

Still another influential concern in the philosophy of mathematics is that of the place and significance of Euclidean geometry, where parallels on a plane never meet; non-Euclidian geometry, where they can meet; and neo-Euclidian geometry, where they never meet but the metric is non-traditional.

The latter topic is related to *chaos theory*, the branch of mathematics that tries to formulate aspects of the universe that involve less – or less straightforward – predictability such as meteorological phenomena, the boiling of water, and processes of social change. These involve phases of transition each of which, mathematically, can be understood as a *phase space* or *phase state*, or *state space*, and the *Lorenz attractor* or *strange attractor*, i.e. the most stable point in phase space, a notion that, in quantum physics, can be used to represent a physical system's possible states. These can include a state at a given time, i.e. an instantaneous state, and a variable state, i.e. a state whose values vary through time and, hence, involve state variables.

Involved in chaos theory is the *theory of fractals*, a branch of geometry that studies figures in terms of dimensions that range between natural-number-based dimensions. For example, on this conception, a line that goes to infinity and then, leaving little space in between, goes back, parallel to the previous section of the line, to minus infinity, and continues to go back and forth between plus- and minus-infinity (let us call it *the infinite folded spaghetti space*) would have a dimension greater than 1 (the dimension of a line) but short of 2 (the dimension of the plane). The theory of fractals has been applied with significant success to such purposes as the computerization of some musical, architectural, and painting styles. Indeed, some chaos and fractals theorists believe that much of nature – from weather patterns, to DNA structure – is fractal.

Another theory that has had a variety of applications in biology, the social sciences, and computer theory is *systems theory*, i.e. the study of the abstract organization of objects and processes, regardless of their particular or special nature. It focuses on the arrangement of, and interconnections between, a system's parts, avoiding reductionism. A related, though independently developed, branch of inquiry is *systems analysis*, which applies principles about systems to decision-making that involves multiple aims, constraints, risks, costs, benefits, and other variables.

Among notable twentieth-century results are

Gödel's *incompleteness* theorems, two theorems formulated and proven by the Austrian logician Kurt Gödel (CE 1906–78) in the early 1930s. The first shows that, for any member of a class of formal systems, there is at least one true sentence that cannot be proven in that system. The second theorem shows that, for any member of a class of formal systems, there is a sentence that expresses its consistency and cannot be proven in the system. The proofs of these theorems are based on three main ideas: first, Gödel numbering, i.e. an assignment of natural numbers to each of the objects belonging to the syntactical categories of the system T considered; second, a representational scheme, i.e. the use of the said numbering to codify properties of the system, and the selection of a theory S in which those properties are formulated as theorems; third, a diagonal or fixed point construction within the said theory for the notion of unprovability in the formal system T. These results tended to undermine not only Hegelian and related notions of a self-grounding system of all knowledge (see IDEALISM), but also *logicism*, i.e. the view that mathematics or some crucial part of mathematics is part of logic. This view, advanced by the British logicians and philosophers Bertrand Russell (CE 1872–1970) and Alfred North Whitehead (CE 1861–1947) in their *Principia Mathematica*, combines two theses: *expressibility* logicism, i.e. the view that mathematical propositions are (or are equivalent expressions to) logical propositions, and *derivational* logicism, i.e. the view that the axioms and theorems of mathematics can be derived from logic.

In order to overcome incompleteness, mathematicians use *proof-theoretic reflection principles*, which are formulated for systems containing enough number theory to arithmetize their own syntax. One such principle is a collection of statements in a system S, according to which, if a formula A is provable in S, then A is true. There are also *set-theoretic reflection principles*, according to which any property A in S that holds of the universe of all sets, also holds of some portion of that universe which is coextensive with a given set x.

The German mathematician Georg Cantor (CE 1845–1918) had used the last letter of the alphabet, ω, i.e. omega, as a proper name for the first infinite ordinal number. This usage has been extended to designate the set of finite ordinals and the set of natural numbers. The term omega is also used as a prefix to denote properties of sets of sentences. Notable among these properties are omega-completeness and omega-consistency. *Omega-completeness* is the property a set of sentences has of entailing every universal sentence whose particular instantiations it also entails. *Omega-consistency* is the property a set of sentences has of not entailing the negation of any universal sentence whose particulars it entails. In addition, the term omega appears in two additional phrases. One is *omega rule*, which denotes a non-effective rule for inferring a universal sentence from its instances. The other is *omega-valued*, which denotes a many-valued logic whose set of truth tables is as large as, or identical with, the set of natural numbers.

Finally, *Church's thesis* or *Church's theorem* is highly significant for the development of modern mathematics, artificial intelligence, and computer theory. Its 1935 formulation by the contemporary United States logician Alonzo Church was: the notion of an effectively calculable function of positive integers should be identified with that of a recursive function. This meant that to say a class of problems was solvable in a strictly mechanical manner by following fixed elementary rules (i.e. that there was an effective procedure for solving problems of that class), was to say that it was solvable by appeal to recursiveness. In 1936, Church argued that such identification should be accepted because other plausible explanations of the informal notion of an effectively calculable function were weaker than or equivalent to those identifying it with recursiveness. Church's thesis – i.e. every calculable function is recursive – has been a working hypothesis, if not an axiom, of the branch of contemporary mathematics called *recursive function theory*.

See also: epistemology; metaphysics; philosophy of language; philosophy of science

Further reading
Korner, S. (1968) *The Philosophy of Mathematics*, New York: Dover.

Lucas, J.R. (1999) *Conceptual Roots of Mathematics*, London: Routledge.

Maddy, Penelope (1995) *Philosophy of Mathematics*, Dettelbach: Josef H. Röll.

philosophy of mind This area is sometimes also called philosophical psychology. Its central concepts concern the content and nature of mental events or states (where some thinkers construe a state as a DISPOSITION), in particular, consciousness, the concept of the self or ego (one instance of which is self-consciousness or awareness of oneself), and the structure of mind or mental life. The philosophy of mind deals with thought, both as mental activity – whether cognitive or emotive – and as the product of such activity, whether these are ideas, aims, or other mental items.

The mind–body problem

Concerning the content and nature of mental events or states, a traditional problem is the mind–body problem, i.e. the problem of whether mental events or states are physical events or states. Mind–body *dualism* is the doctrine that they are different from each other, a position that leads to questions about the structure of the mind or mental life. It is asked whether the mind is unified and has one function, i.e. does one kind of thing (as in Cartesian as well as associationist views), whether it is unified but has many functions, i.e. does many kinds of things (as in the Ockhamist position), or whether it is subdivided in various departments, as in faculty psychology.

Faculty psychology

Faculty psychology traces back to the Greek philosopher Aristotle (384–322 BCE), who divided the human soul into five special senses: three inner senses – common sense, IMAGINATION, and MEMORY – and two additional senses: active (a term Aristotle did not use but which has become customary to use) and passive mind. This view was influential in the Middle Ages. European philosophers further subdivided Aristotle's three inner senses into seven. Philosopher-physicians in the Islamic world – e.g. Ibn Sīnā or, in Latin, Avicenna (CE 980–1037) – combined Aristotelian faculty psychology with the physiology of the Greek philosopher and physician Galen (CE 129–*c.*

215), by proposing brain locations for the faculties, thus starting a line of inquiry that continues today.

The Greek term for soul was *psyche*, a term that stood for a principle of animation or life. The Latin term for soul was *anima*. In addition, Latin has the term *spiritus* (i.e. "breath"), which was also used to translate *psyche* but, by the Renaissance, has come to be used to denote something different from the soul. For example, the Italian philosopher Bernardino Telesio (CE 1509–88), who thought matter capable of feeling, used spirit to denote *subtle matter*, the principle of all movement in the universe. Another Italian philosopher, Giovanni Batista Vico (CE 1668–1744), argued that humans can understand only what they make, thus foreshadowing some tenets of idealism and later notions of the sciences of the spirit (see EXPLANATION; PHILOSOPHY OF HISTORY). In the twentieth century, the German philosopher Max Scheler (CE 1874–1928) used the term *spirit* to denote an individual's development as a person. This view was further articulated by the Argentine philosopher Francisco Romero (CE 1891–1962), who held that to be is to transcend (arguably, such things as a condition, a state, or a moment) and being a person was the highest order of transcendence because it involved *spiritual* transcendence. An analogous position was formulated by the German philosopher Nicolai Hartmann (CE 1882–1950), who, however, was closer to faculty psychology in holding that the *spirit* was a component of persons whereby they could grasp values and discern their nature.

Faculty psychology was subject to criticism by Cartesian thinkers, who held various kinds of mind–body dualism, i.e. the view previously characterized for Cartesians that the mental and the physical are two different substances, the former unextended, the latter extended. One version was *interactionism*, according to which these substances somehow have effects on each other. This position raised the question of how states of an extended substance can causally affect states of an unextended substance. Another was *epiphenomenalism*, the doctrine that physical states cause mental states but not vice versa. This doctrine also raised the previous question, and also made it hard, if not impossible, to explain how we could have intentions, let alone effective intentions.

Still another was *occasionalism*. Briefly, in its strict sense, the term denotes the seventeenth-century doctrine prompted by the mind–body dualism formulated in Cartesianism that God is the intermediary between mind and body. Though prompted by the aforementioned dualism, this doctrine was not *ad hoc*, but based on criticisms of such conceptions of causality as that minds can have an effect on bodies, and that motion can be produced by the passive extension ascribed to bodies in Cartesianism. Its advocates included the German philosopher Johannes Clauberg (CE 1622–65), the Belgian philosopher Arnold Geulincx (CE 1624–69), and the French philosophers Gérard de Cordemoy (CE 1626–84), Louis de la Forge (CE 1632–66), and, perhaps most notably, Nicolas Malebranche (CE 1638–1715).

An additional position was *parallelism*, sometimes also called *psychophysical parallelism*, the view that the mental and the physical never causally interact, but co-occur, typically because of God's creation. This view raised questions about the possibility of our acting freely, plus the obscurity of the hypotheses – such as that God exists and created the world – used to support it.

As a result, many philosophers rejected the Cartesian division of the world into mental and physical but, instead of adopting faculty psychology, adopted other positions. The German philosopher Gottfried Wilhelm Leibniz (CE 1646–1716), for example, argued that the universe was made up of monads or extensionless centers of force endowed with feeling, perception, and appetition, and that there was a hierarchy of monads (from those infinitely close to insentience, to God), and that the soul was a higher-level monad controlling colonies of lower-level monads, which entailed the soul–body distinction was a matter of degree. He suggested that any physical configuration was a momentary mind that lacked memory, and formulated the theory of minute perceptions, i.e. that each created substance has some perceptions of which it is not aware.

Other philosophers, instead, advocated *monism*, which holds some type of *identity theory*, sometimes also called *psychophysical identity theory*, i.e. any theory that, somehow, identifies the mental with the physical, an identity sometimes called *theoretical identity*. The Jewish philosopher of Spanish and Portuguese descent Baruch Spinoza (CE 1632–77), for example, held a *dual-attribute* theory, also called *dual-aspect* theory, according to which the mental and the physical are two modes of a single substance, God. A stronger stand along these lines is taken by *eliminative* materialism, according to which there is no such thing as the mental. This is itself a form of monism, because a form of materialism. *Central-state* materialism is a special version of eliminative materialism holding that all mental states are states of the brain or central nervous system. A related notion suggested by the contemporary Australian philosopher J.J.C. Smart is that of a *topic-neutral linguistic expression*, namely an expression that is noncommittal between two different interpretations of it. For example, the description of a perceptual image one had as "something was going on which is typical of what happens when I am awake and look around me" is topic-neutral concerning whether what was going on was material or not.

During the seventeenth and eighteenth centuries, some psychologists used the notion of a *sensorium*, i.e. the seat and cause of sensation – and, according to some thinkers, also of muscular activity and motion – in the brain of humans and other animals. This term has lost currency in contemporary psychology.

Conceptions somewhat analogous to those just discussed can be found in other cultures. For example, the Akan people from Ghana use the term *ōkra*, which is usually translated as soul, to denote either a physical-like entity free from spatial constraints and unobservable by means of ordinary perception or, alternatively, not a physical-like, but a spiritual, i.e. immaterial, entity that, however, thoroughly interacts with the body.

Against these positions, various philosophers argued for an opposite type of monism, namely, *idealism*, thus totally eliminating the material. The English philosopher W.K. Clifford (CE 1845–79) formulated a position that eliminated the material component, yet amounted, arguably, to a kind of identity theory. He distinguished between *objects*, by which he meant items that may be part of one's consciousness, and *ejects*, which were mind-stuff, had the quality of feeling, made up the world around us, and could not be part of one's consciousness. In addition, there is *neutral monism*, sometimes also called *neutralism*: the view developed by the New Realism movement in the early twentieth century. It included such figures as the United States philosophers E.B. Holt (CE 1873–1946), W.P. Montague (CE 1873–1953), and Ralph Barton Perry (CE 1876–1957), all of whom shared the view that all of reality is of one kind that is neither mental nor physical.

Later in the twentieth century, with successes in physically explaining chemistry and chemically explaining biology, *materialism*, the form of monism according to which everything is material or physical – hence also called *physicalism* or the *doctrine of psychophysical identity* – has gained support, though perhaps more as a promise than as a reality. One type of physicalism formulated by the contemporary United States philosopher Donald Davidson is *anomalous monism*, the doctrine that events can be intentional under one description and non-intentional under another description; but while all events are physical, not all events may be mental. He further denies that, strictly speaking, there are psychological or psychophysical laws. The principle of the anomalism of the mental is both the position constituted by the latter thesis and what Davidson calls his position on irreducibility.

Physicalism has led to distinguishing between *type* physicalism, i.e. the view that every type or kind of entity is physical, and *token* physicalism, i.e. the view that every particular is physical, with physicalism's identity theory being a type–type identity theory, i.e. about types, not tokens. Given type physicalism, every token falls under some type, hence each token is in a relation of token–token identity with some token of a physical type. The type–token distinction has also been applied to epiphenomenalism.

Along the lines of the latter materialistic theories, the Polish philosopher Tadeuz Kotarbinski (CE 1886–1981) formulated the doctrine of *concretism* or *reism*, which, as *ontological* reism, said that all objects are physical or sentient things and, as *semantic* reism, said that only names of concrete objects are genuine. He also formulated the doctrine of *imitationism*, according to which psychological propositions are reducible to the basic form: individual so-and-so experiences thus, such-and-such is so. Once reduced to this form, psychological propositions can be understood, and judged to be true or false, not by introspection, but by imitating the behavior of others. He used the term *praxiology* to denote the applications of these doctrines to matters of value and conduct.

Associationism

In modern times, the most notable alternative to faculty psychology was *associationism*: the view that higher-order mental activities result from combinations of simpler mental activities or external events. In the *Phaedo* (73c–74d), Plato already held the associationist principles of *contiguity* and *similarity* according to which associations are supposed to occur. These principles were also described by Aristotle, with the addition of a third one, *contrast*, in *Parva Naturalia* (*On Memory and Reminiscence*, II, 451b, 10 and ff.). In the Middle Ages, the Spanish philosopher and humanist Juan Luis Vives (CE 1492?–1540) pursued the same approach in detail in his *De anima et vita*.

Modern philosophers who discussed association were empiricists who, motivated by epistemological rather than psychological considerations, argued that the three principles of association were *similarity*, *contiguity*, and *causation*, and that contrast was reducible to a combination of similarity and causation. A psychological turn became very clear in 1749, in Part I of *Observation on Man*, a book where the British physician and philosopher David Hartley (CE 1705–57) tried to formulate an associationist conception of all mental life. He held mental events occurred in parallel to neural events. Mental events were divided into sensations and ideas. Physiological events consisted in transmissions by means of vibrations. When large vibrations occurred in the brain, they caused corresponding sensations. If they were small, *vibratiuncles*, they caused corresponding ideas. Hartley also distinguished between *simultaneous* association, which occurs between mental events occurring at the same time, and *successive* association, which occurs between mental events occurring in close succession. He is considered the father of modern associationism.

The concept of *empirical psychology*, by contrast with *rational psychology*, was formulated by the German philosopher Christian Wolff (CE 1679–1754), who understood the latter to be the metaphysical analysis of the soul, and the former to be a study of the soul's powers or faculties as revealed to our inner sense. Eventually, empirical psychology became *associationism* or *associationalism*, or *associational psychology* through the works of Hartley, the Scottish philosopher David Hume (CE 1711–76), the Scottish philosopher James Mill (CE 1773–1836), and his son, the English philosopher John Stuart Mill (CE 1806–73).

Experimental psychology

Psychology began to separate from philosophy as experimental psychology, leading to a process that ended in the twentieth century when the autonomy of psychology was attained through the establishment of independent psychology departments. *Experimental psychology* was developed by the German physicist and philosopher Gustav Theodor Fechner (CE 1801–87), who invented the science of *psychophysics* and advanced an identity theory according to which every object is both mental and physical. He followed on the path of the German physiologist Ernst Heinrich Weber (CE 1795–1878), who had shown that there is a constant ratio between the *relative threshold* – the strength that must be added to a stimulus for a just noticeable difference to be perceived – and the magnitude of the stimulus. The *absolute threshold* is the stimulus strength needed to create a conscious sensation. In the process, Fechner eventually formulated *Fechner's law* (also called the *Weber–Fechner law*), according to which $S = C \times \log R$, i.e. the intensity of sensation S equals the logarithm of the stimulus S multiplied by a constant C. Later, psychophysicists replaced this law with the power law $R = C \times S^n$, where n depends on the kind of stimulus. At any rate, psychophysics

made plain that experience, a mental phenomenon, could be quantified in physical terms.

A school that combined associationism and experimental psychology was the *Würzburg School*, whose founding is attributed to the German psychologist and philosopher Oswald Külpe (CE 1862–1915). It continued Fechner's experimental research in aesthetics. The work developed within the framework of associationist hypotheses, though these were used as heuristic devices rather than presumed truths. The School studied conative processes such as willing, and the process of thinking. One of its initial results was the formulation of a notion until then not recognized by Western philosophers or psychologists: that of *Bewusstseinslage* or *state of consciousness*, i.e. a psychological process without sensory content. The School ceased activities in the 1920s; however, years later, the notion of state of consciousness was independently revived by the Austrian-born British philosopher Ludwig Wittgenstein (CE 1889–1951). The School also made contributions to the formulation and clarification of the notions of *Vorstellung* or representation, which it interpreted as an individual's way of perceiving and responding to the surrounding world; and *Aufgabe* or task.

Genetic psychology

In opposition to associationism, the English philosopher and psychologist James Ward (CE 1843–1925) advocated *genetic psychology*, distinguishing phases in the process from sensations to ideas which takes place within a continuum of presentations, the *psychoplasm*. The English psychologist William McDougall (CE 1871–1938) founded *hormic psychology* (from the Greek *hormē*, i.e. "impulse"), according to which striving for goals is a basic category of psychology that cannot be explained mechanistically and from which behavior derives. However, psychology and the philosophy of mind soon underwent significant methodological changes moving away from presentations and attacking *mentalism*, i.e. any theory committed to the existence of mental events and processes, i.e. to events and processes that, though not necessarily immaterial or non-physical, none the less exhibit intentionality.

Behaviorism

These changes occurred with the advent of *behaviorism*, which was both a research program in psychology and a philosophical position in the philosophy of language and the philosophy of mind. The research program in psychology was first proposed by the United States psychologist J.B. Watson (CE 1878–1958), who coined the term behaviorism in 1913. He argued that psychology should abandon traditional introspective techniques. Instead, it should use the experimental methods of the natural sciences to specify all variables, including behavior, and attempt to explain and predict behavior, where to explain behavior meant to specify the independent variables (*stimuli*) of which the behavior (*response*) was lawfully a function. Behaviorism (sometimes called *behavioralism*) was adopted by such renowned United States psychologists as C.L. Hull (CE 1884–1952), E.C. Tolman (CE 1886–1959), and B.F. Skinner (CE 1904–90). Some behaviorists included internal neurophysiological conditions among the variables, interpreting these conditions as intervening variables, where an *intervening variable* is a state of an organism or person that is hypothesized to explain behavior and is defined in terms of its causes and effects, not in terms of its own features. Others, e.g. Skinner, insisted that only environmental variables should be included, on the grounds that intervening variables – say, the state of thirst – would be a function of environmental ones – say, lack of water.

Behaviorism's model was different from that of *reflexology*. Here, in *classical* or, after the Russian physiologist Ivan Petrovich Pavlov (CE 1849–1936), who first described it, *Pavlovian*, also called *respondent conditioning*, a response or *reflex* – say, gland secretion – already under the control of a given stimulus – say, the presence of food – would be caused by a new stimulus – say, a bell ringing – if this stimulus were to be repeatedly paired with the old one. A process of current use in behavior therapy that either involves or is analogous to classical conditioning is *redintegration*, whereby a feature of a situation, e.g. a smell of gas, causes an individual to remember or imagine the whole situation visually, e.g. the catastrophic events that can transpire from a gas leak.

Other related forms of behavior therapy include *aversion therapy* and *desensitization*.

By contrast with classical conditioning, behaviorism used the *operant conditioning model*, where the conditioning stimulus follows the conditioned response. Here, instances of a kind of response – say, a pigeon's pressing a bar – which has repeatedly been followed by instances of a kind of reinforcing stimulus – say, food being dispensed – will occur with greater frequency on future occasions. This process of behavior modification is called *positive reinforcement* when the reinforcing stimulus is welcome – say, a reward – and *negative reinforcement* when the reinforcing stimulus is unwelcome – say, a punishment. That is, operant conditioning can be used, e.g. in behavior therapy, so that behavior is learned or unlearned.

However, serious difficulties arose concerning the behavioristic program. For the characterization of its basic concepts – say, of the concept of anger – in behavioral terms tended to be circular; uninformative; unable to identify, hence explain, pieces of behavior; and significantly inapplicable to the modification of behavior in actual social circumstances. As a result, it has been displaced by approaches that pay attention to behavior but also include other, e.g. cognitive, components.

As for *philosophical behaviorism*, it is a family of semantic views. The English philosopher Alfred J. Ayer (CE 1910–89), and the German-born philosophers Rudolf Carnap (CE 1891–1970) and Carl Hempel (CE 1905–97) held that the meaning of mentalistic expressions – say, anger – was reducible to publicly testable statements describing behavioral and other processes or dispositions. The English philosopher Gilbert Ryle (CE 1900–76) held that mentalistic terms meant dispositions to behave in typical ways, and disposition-ascribing statements, though lawlike, did not describe actual facts, but only had the function of justifying inferences about behavior. Ludwig Wittgenstein also held that mentalistic terms could be applied only by appeal to public, intersubjectively observable behavior; however, his position was not committed to reducing mental to non-mental entities.

Functionalism

All these positions were sharply criticized in the 1950s and 1960s by the United States philosopher R.M. Chisholm (CE 1916–99), the contemporary United States philosophers J. Fodor and H. Putnam, and the contemporary Canadian philosopher Charles Taylor, and have been modified into forms of *functionalism*, the view that mental states are defined by their causes and effects, so that what makes them mental (e.g. what makes an itch unlike a bite mental) is not an intrinsic property, but relations to inputs (e.g. sensory stimuli such as a bite), other mental states (e.g. worrying about the bite's effects), and output (e.g. behavior such as applying an antibiotic cream on the bite). These studies include theories of personality, i.e. of the overall psychological make-up of persons. They study such notions as that of *instinct* – i.e. of any untrained disposition to act in pursuit of certain aims without having to be aware of or foresee these aims – and that of psychological *trait* – i.e. of any disposition to act in pursuit of specific conscious aims. The studies also include *localizationist theories* of the brain.

The development of computers assisted the development of functionalism in at least two ways. First, the distinction between *hardware* and *software* is analogous to that between *function* or *role*, on the basis of which particular mental states are characterized, and *structure* or *occupant*, i.e. the particular item that occupies or has a role. These functions or roles have *multiple realizability*, i.e. in different types of entities, the same causal role, i.e. a singular causal relation, may have different occupants. For example, in a human being, a neural state may be the occupant that performs the causal role characteristic of the human's applying cream on a surface. In a robot, a computer state may be the occupant that performs the causal role characteristic of the robot's applying cream on a surface.

Second, the automated nature of computers helps explain how inner states can produce output without appeal to a *homunculus* (a little human being directing the output intelligently). This approach, primarily spearheaded by Hilary Putnam, is called *Turing machine functionalism* or *machine-state functionalism*.

Putnam himself, together with the contemporary United States philosophers Ned Block and Jerry Fodor, criticized this view on the grounds, for example, that minor differences in output – e.g. one person saying, as in English, "Ouch!" and another saying, as in Spanish, "¡Ay!" – would entail that their mental states were different even though both were in pain.

Along behaviorist lines, the United States philosopher Wilfrid Sellars (CE 1912–89) proposed the notion of *inner speech* and, along non-behaviorist lines, Jerry Fodor formulated the cognate notion of *mentalese* or *brain writing* to explain how their respective alternatives to functionalism were free from the problem besetting functionalism just mentioned. *Inner speech* or *mentalese* is supposed to be a language-like way of expressing or recording the contents of mental events in the appropriate place in one's brain or mind. However, critics have argued that such a system of expression or recording is not close enough to a language for the analogy to work, or that there are no such contents to be expressed or recorded in mental life, or that even if there were such recording or expression systems, there is no reason – as advocates of mentalese themselves acknowledged – to think that all brains or minds use the same system.

Another version of functionalism, associated with the contemporary United States philosophers William G. Lycan and Daniel C. Dennett, is *teleological* or *homuncular functionalism*, which likens a person to a corporation constituted by different departments performing different jobs, plus sub-departments of these, and so on up to the neurological level.

The most influential version is the *causal theory of mind*, which holds any mental-state term is defined by the common-sense sentences in which it appears. These are analyzed by philosophers, while scientists determine what physical state is the cause of such a mental state. If no such physical state is found, then the supposed mental state denoted by a given mental-state term does not exist. Of interest in this regard is the notion of a *subdoxastic state* formulated by the contemporary United States philosopher Stephen P. Stich. He characterizes it as a state similar to beliefs in that it can have intentional content, guide behavior, and serve to justify beliefs; but, by contrast with beliefs, it is not fully accessible through introspection, and its basis – i.e. cues that lead me to the state, say, of believing that you are irritated – cannot be articulated.

All forms of functionalism (and physicalism too) are open to various criticisms, most notably that they identify mental states in relational terms, while mental states appear to have content constituted by non-relational qualitative features also called *phenomenal properties* or *qualia* such as the odor of a fishing harbor, and the traffic noise in the Argentine city of Buenos Aires. Another criticism is that the said theories cannot account for spectrum inversion – where one person's experiences of blue are qualitatively just like another person's experiences of yellow and vice versa – and other types of *qualia* inversion. This is thought to suggest that content depends on extrinsic contextual factors. If so, then a theory explaining the connection between mental symbols and the contextual factors is needed.

Some philosophers have proposed that psychology focus on narrow content by concerning itself only with the syntax of mental sentences, hence foregoing the aim of explaining intentional contents such as wants and desires – sometimes also called *pro attitudes* – used in explaining behavior. Others, however, stick to wide content and try to provide a naturalistic account of all mental content. Along these lines, the contemporary United States philosopher Fred Dretske has also tried to explain how, though content depends on a causal-historical context, it can be causally significant.

Current trends
A view sometimes criticized by representatives of associationism, behaviorism, or functionalism is *folk psychology* – a common-sense theory supposedly presupposed by common-sense explanations of human behavior. Its critics uphold *eliminativism*, the view that folk psychology is both an empirical theory and probably largely false. A number of contemporary United States philosophers, however, argue against eliminativism. For example, as previously stated, Daniel C. Dennett and Wil-

liam G. Lycan uphold functionalism in proposing functional explanations of consciousness. David Rosenthal considers consciousness a kind of intentionality, namely states we somehow come to believe we are in. John R. Searle argues that consciousness can be explained by appeal to microphysical properties of the brain. Others, who hold the doctrine of *emergent materialism* (also called *non-reductive materialism*), think that, though originating in material systems, consciousness is irreducible and emergent; still others, that it is epiphenomenal; and there are those who think it is explainable only by appeal to still undiscovered, properties neither mental nor physical.

An area that has caused much controversy in psychology and philosophical psychology alike concerns the concept, measurement, and sources of intelligence. In the first place, this term is used to translate the Latin *intelligentia*, a term that has been used with many meanings such as understanding or intellect, reason, that which is intelligible (*nous*), and the intelligible spheres or angels. In contemporary psychology, intelligence denotes a faculty or family of faculties, or a function or family of functions, aimed at resolving theoretical or practical problems individual organisms – e.g. but not exclusively, human beings – face. Besides controversies concerning the concept of intelligence, there are controversies concerning its measurement and sources, most notably the controversy concerning the extent to which intelligence is inherited and whether there are group differences in intelligence that are caused by genetic factors.

Parapsychology
In addition to mainstream areas of inquiry dealing with the previous topics and theories, the philosophy of mind includes other studies. One example is parapsychology, the study of the *paranormal*, i.e. anomalous phenomena neither recognized nor rejected by science, such as: extrasensory perception (ESP), e.g. telepathy or communication without sensory perception, and clairvoyance or seeing objects or actions beyond the range of normal vision, both of which can be interpreted as including cases of precognition or knowledge of future events through extrasensory means; telekinesis, i.e. the production of motion in a body with-

out applying material force; and psychokinesis (PK), e.g. materializations. In the philosophy of religion, this type of phenomena, and the dispositions or virtues presumed to be associated with them, are also called *preternatural* (from the Middle Latin *praeternaturalis*, an adjective for the Latin phrase *praeter naturam*, i.e. "beyond nature"), and also *supernatural* (derived from the Latin phrase *supra naturam*, i.e. "above nature").

Philosophy of mind in India

As for Eastern thought, philosophical discussion of mental phenomena and their interpretation has been very significant in Indian philosophy. In this tradition, the term for soul is *jīva*, which derives from the root *jīv*: "to continue breathing." The soul is also called *bhoktā* (experient), *kartā* (agent), and *purusha* (what lies in the citadel of the body). A great variety of conceptions of the soul can be found in Indian philosophy. For example, JAINISM characterizes *jīva* as involving consciousness, life, immateriality, and spatial extension; BUDDHISM denies the existence of *jīva*; the Nyāya, School considers *jīva* to have no parts and be both pervasive and eternal; according to its epistemological correlate, the Vaiśeṣika School, *jīva* is pervasive, eternal, imperceptible and spiritual; for the SĀMKHYA-YOGA School, *jīva* is an eternal, immutable, conscious being; Advaita-Vedānta considers it a blend of the Self and the non-Self; while DVAITA holds that there are infinite individual souls that are atomic in nature; and for Vishistādvaita-Vedānta, individual souls are real, eternal, spiritual, knowing and cognitive in nature.

Further reading

Baker, Lynne Rudder (1995) *Explaining Attitudes: A Practical Approach to The Mind*, Cambridge and New York: Cambridge University Press.

Lowe, E.J. (1999) *An Introduction to the Philosophy of Mind*, Cambridge, UK and New York: Cambridge University Press.

Searle, John R. (1998 [1996]) *The Philosophy of Mind*, Springfield, VA: The Teaching Company.

philosophy of mythology *see* myth

philosophy of physics *see* philosophy of science

philosophy of religion A central cluster of questions in the philosophy of religion includes: "Does at least one divinity exist?" "What is it (are they) like?" "What arguments are there for or against its (their) existence?" These questions have sometimes been classified as belonging to METAPHYSICS, more specifically in the area of ontology called *first philosophy* in the Aristotelian sense of this term (in Latin, *philosophia prima*); that is, the study of *being as being*, by contrast with *ouk on*, i.e. non-being or nothing at all as well as the study of particular entities, even those that are nothing in the sense of *me on*, i.e. of having no actual but only potential being. The reason for this has been that the subject matter of first philosophy is those objects that are separate and unmovable; if there is a GOD, He must be among such objects.

At any rate, the inquiry into the nature and existence of God often involves a characterization of the attributes of the said divinity or divinities. For example, the divine attributes of the Judeo-Christian God involve, most notably, omnipotence, i.e. God is all-powerful; omniscience, i.e. God is all knowing; omnibenevolence and absolute justice, i.e. God is absolutely benevolent and just; omnipresence, i.e. God is everywhere; personhood, i.e. God is perfect; infinity, i.e. God is infinite; eternity, i.e. God is eternal; and uniqueness, i.e. God is the only God.

Three main views have been characterized concerning the existence of God (or gods): *agnosticism*, i.e. the view that one does not know or believe whether God (or any god) does or does not exist; *atheism*, i.e. the view that no God exists; and *theism*, i.e. the view that at least one God exists. Theism may collapse together with *monotheism*, i.e. the view that there is only one god, which contrasts with *pantheism*, the view that everything – typically the natural universe – is identical with God, as well as with *polytheism*, the view that there is more than one god. Associated with polytheism is *shamanism*, i.e. any religion based on the person of a *shaman*, who is a religious leader in many hunting and gathering groups and societies who embodies the traditions of those groups and societies. Vestiges of shamanism can be found in the Americas,

India, Australia and Asia; however, they are remarkably common in northern Asia. Shamans are believed to communicate directly with and be assisted by spirits that are supernatural, i.e. exist outside our world. This communication is said to occur through possession or wandering ecstasy. In the case of possession, the spirits are supposed to speak through the shaman. While in wandering ecstasy, the shaman is supposed to travel to the world of the spirits while only the shaman's body remains in our world.

The ontological argument

As for the Judeo-Christian tradition, there is a wide variety of arguments for God's existence. A notable type of argument is the ontological argument, of which there is a great variety of formulations. The most famous formulation of the ontological argument is that of the philosopher Anselm of Canterbury (CE 1033–1109), born in the city of Aosta, which is now in Italy. He gave two versions of the argument, the first for God's existence, the second for the impossibility of conceiving that God does not exist. Both arguments are partly based on a presumed distinction between two conceptions of God. In one conception, God is characterized as having all the divine attributes commonly ascribed to God in Anselm's religious environment: omnipotence, omniscience, personhood, absolute benevolence and justice, uniqueness, and eternalness. In the second conception, God has all these features plus existence. Anselm subscribed to what can be called the *perfection hypothesis*: God in the second conception was greater or more perfect than God in the first conception. Given this, the first version of Anselm's ontological argument can be formulated as follows:

1 God is that than which nothing greater can be conceived (by definition).
2 God exists in the understanding (because we understand the previous definition).
3 If God exists only in the understanding and not also in reality, then something greater than God can be conceived (by the perfection hypothesis).
4 God exists only in the understanding and not also in reality (hypothesis).
5 Something greater than God can be con-

ceived (from steps 3 and 4 by a valid rule of inference: *modus ponens*).
6 Something greater than that than which nothing greater can be conceived, can be conceived (from steps 1 and 5, by replacing the definition of "God" for the term "God").
7 God exists not only in the understanding but also in reality (because step 6 is a contradiction, hence step 4, which led to it, is false, and its opposite, step 7, is true).

Anselm's second argument parallels the first:

1 God is that than which nothing greater can be conceived (by definition).
2 God exists in the understanding and can be conceived in the understanding (because we understand the previous definition).
3 If God can be conceived to exist only in the understanding and not also in reality, then something greater than God can be conceived (by the perfection hypothesis).
4 God can be conceived to exist only in the understanding and not also in reality (hypothesis).
5 Something greater than God can be conceived (from steps 3 and 4 by a valid rule of inference: *modus ponens*).
6 Something greater than that which nothing greater can be conceived, can be conceived (from steps 1 and 5, by replacing the definition of "God" for the term "God").
7 God cannot be conceived to exist only in the understanding and not also in reality (because step 6 is a contradiction, hence step 4, which led to it, is false, and its opposite, step 7, is true).

A prominent criticism of this argument has been to point out that the perfection hypothesis presupposes that existence is a predicate, and this presupposition is false. For a real predicate adds content to a concept, and simply saying that an item falls under a concept – as saying that an item exists – does not add any content to the concept. Some philosophers have replied that existence is a predicate only in the case of God; however, this makes Anselm's argument *ad hoc*.

Another objection suggested by the Italian philosopher Thomas Aquinas (CE 1225–74), born near Naples, in what is now Italy, is that Anselm confuses a proposition that is self-evident *per se nota*, i.e. in and of itself, and a proposition that is evident *quoad nos*, i.e. for us. For, Aquinas adds, what Anselm claims to be the concept of God – i.e. that than which nothing greater can be conceived – is not the concept of God, but merely the concept of a property that the concept of God must have, if there is such a concept. This property is that nothing greater than this concept can be thought.

The five ways

After criticizing Anselm's argument, Aquinas proceeded to offer five arguments, the *quinque viae* or *five ways*: from motion, from the nature of efficient cause, from possibility and necessity (or from contingent beings), from gradation, and from the governance of the world. The first three are versions of the *cosmological* argument. The first version, for example, starts by acknowledging that there are now things undergoing change as a result of things that cause it. If any cause of change must itself be the result of a cause, then there is an infinitely long chain of causes. However, it is argued, this is impossible and, therefore, something is a first cause, namely God.

This, as well as the other versions of the cosmological argument, however, rest on at least two presuppositions. The first is that change presupposes an ultimate, unchanging source of change. The second is that the fact that there is a world at all demands an explanation. Yet, at least this latter supposition begs the question, for it is precisely what an atheist and arguably also an agnostic will deny.

The argument *from gradation* involves the presupposition that our judgments of degree are made about things by reference to some maximum they resemble. It also presupposes that the maximum of every genus is its cause. Aquinas concludes that there must be a maximum that is the cause of every being and all perfections of all beings, namely God. This can be interpreted as an argument to the best explanation of our judgments of degree. The first presupposition of this argument, however, is not obvious. Our judgments of degree could as well be made by comparison with other items to which the predicates involved apply in different degrees. Further, even if the argument were sound, there is no reason to believe that

the maximum involved has all the divine attributes God is supposed to have.

The argument *from the governance of the world* is one of various versions of the teleological argument, i.e. arguments relying on the world's goal-directedness. In this particular case, the argument relies on an analogy between the world and a machine in their respective intricate features. It concludes that, since machines have makers, the world must have a maker as well, namely God. Given its reliance on an analogy, this argument is also called the *analogical* argument. Also, given its reliance on goal-directedness, it is called the argument *from design*. It has been widely criticized, first, on the grounds that it in no way establishes the existence of a divinity with the attributes the Judeo-Christian God is supposed to have; and second, on the grounds that evolution offers a viable alternative explanation for the analogies between the world and machines.

These *viae*, i.e. ways, as Aquinas called them, were methods of proof, which fit general usage. The terms *via* and *viae* were also used for approaches to understanding, e.g. *via nominalium* or the way of nominalism; for historical periods, e.g. *via antiqua* or the old way, and *via moderna* or the modern way; and realms of the universe, e.g. *via spiritualis* or the realm of the spirit and *via naturae*, the natural course of things. In addition to methods of proof, Aquinas and others also referred to other ways of discovering God. One was *via eminentiae* (Latin for "the way of eminence"), which was a positive way of discovering God; while another was *via negationis* (Latin for "the negative way"), which meant that, since God was radically other than the world, God and God's characteristics could be discovered by negating those of the world.

Other arguments for God's existence

Another notable type of arguments is *moral* arguments, some of which are arguments to the best explanation for the objectivity of moral obligations. The best known version is the Kantian formulation of this argument, which was anticipated by the Spanish neo-Scholastic philosopher Gabriel Vásquez (CE 1549–1604). In the Kantian version, the argument characterizes complete goodness as perfect virtue rewarded with perfect happiness, and holds that its attainment must be a real possibility if reason is to agree with morality. However, the natural world does not – while God would – ensure the real possibility of perfect goodness. Hence, the argument concludes, we are entitled to postulate the existence of God. Critics of this argument have been prompt to point out that we need not postulate perfect goodness in order to have reasons to be moral and that, in fact, such a postulate would tend to undermine our moral sense, by making it subservient to the search for personal happiness.

A related argument for God's existence is the *common-consent* argument espoused, for example, by the British philosopher James Martineau (CE 1805–1900). He argued, along Kantian lines, that we all have the experience of an inner moral demand to act in terms of the higher – moral – motive, and that, since it is not explainable in naturalistic terms, this is an experience of divine revelation available to all.

There is also *Pascal's wager*, an application of the work on probability carried out by the French philosopher Blaise Pascal (CE 1623–62) to the question of God's existence. It can be formulated as follows: (1) If I believe in God and God exists, then I can attain infinite happiness. (2) If I believe in God and God does not exist, then nothing or not much is lost. (3) If I do not believe in God and God exists, then I will attain infinite misery. (4) If I do not believe in God and God does not exist, then not much, if anything, is gained. Hence, because the potential winnings are far greater, I should believe that God exists. This, however, if cogent, justifies one's belief in God, but hardly proves its truth.

Also, there are arguments *from mystery*, which rely on the notion of the Holy and the worshipper's attitudes about it. These attitudes were characterized by the German philosopher Rudolf Otto (CE 1869–1937), who coined the terms *mysterium tremendum* to denote the utter mystery beyond all rational analysis that is associated with the sacred being, and *mysterium fascinosum* to denote the deep fascination of the worshipper with the sacred being. A related attitude, the *numinous*, is the feeling of awe worshippers feel in sacred places or before sacred objects. As for the term *sacred* (derived, through the Middle English, from the Latin *sacrare* ("to devote"), which is equivalent of the Latin *sacer*: "holy"), it denotes anything held worthy of veneration. It is contrasted with *secular* (derived from the Latin *saeculum*: "long period of time," which means worldly or temporal).

In addition, there are the arguments of *natural theology* (in Latin, *theologia naturalis*) or *natural religion* (by contrast with *supernatural theology* or *theologia supernaturalis*) – present in Aquinas, but whose most notable proponent was the English philosopher-theologian William Paley (CE 1743–1805) – which aim at establishing God's existence on reason and knowledge of the natural world instead of revelation. A twentieth-century teleological version of these arguments was formulated by the French biophysicist and philosopher Pierre A. Lecomte du Noüy (CE 1883–1947), who, adopting an evolutionary framework, argued that the earth is too recent a development for life to have appeared accidentally, and that the upward course of evolution contradicts the law of entropy or second law of thermodynamics, which includes the fact that, if a large physical system is isolated exchanging no energy with its environment, then the entropy – or measure of disorder – of the system continuously increases, which means the system decays. He concluded that the only explanation for these processes was *telefinalism*, i.e. the hypothesis that the universe is achieving ultimate ends and this entails the existence of God.

A position opposite to natural theology was espoused by members of the *neo-orthodoxy* movement. Among these are the Swiss theologian Karl Barth (CE 1886–1968), the leading exponent of *crisis theology*, a dialectical theology that emphasizes the contradictions between God and the world; the Swiss theologian Emil Brunner (CE 1899–1966), who held – against liberal theology – that humans cannot provide their own salvation, but – against crisis theology – that humans none the less have certain powers of responding to God; and two United States theologians (both from Wright City, Missouri): the opponent of pragmatism Helmut Richard Niebuhr

(CE 1894–1962), and the pacifist and labor supporter Reinhold Niebuhr (CE 1892–1971).

Still a different view is *speculative theism*, which, against Hegelian pantheism, avoids identifying God with the Absolute; however, it sees humans as free, finite persons whose center is the infinite person of God. Its main advocates were the German philosopher Christian H. Weisse (CE 1801–66) and the German philosopher Hermann Fichte (CE 1796–1879), the son of the German philosopher Johann Gottlieb Fichte (CE 1762–1814), the founder of German idealism.

There have been thinkers who identify God with a being beyond human comprehension and point to faith as the only way for humans to believe. For example, the Scottish philosopher William Hamilton (CE 1788–1856) argued that objects are known through their relations to other objects, i.e. as conditioned, hence the infinite is unknowable. This, he argued, is the realm of faith or the *Unconditioned*.

Involved in the preceding discussions are the opposing notions of *supernaturalism*, i.e. the view that God is spiritual and causally independent of the natural world, and *theological naturalism*, the view that a rational conception of God is not only consistent with, but an integral part of, the natural world (see NATURALISM).

The problem of evil

There are also various arguments against God's existence. Prominent among them is the argument from evil, which can be formulated as follows. If God were omniscient, omnipotent, and absolutely benevolent and just, then there would be no evil in the world. However, there is evil in the world. Hence, God is not omnipotent, or not omniscient, or not absolutely benevolent and just.

Various replies have been formulated, especially by thinkers who, unconvinced by the argument from evil, prefer to talk of the *problem* of evil, and propose various solutions to it. These solutions fall under the general category of *theodicy* (from the Greek *theos*, i.e. "God," and *dike*, i.e. "justice"), a term coined by the German philosopher Gottfried Wilhelm Leibniz (CE 1646–1716) to denote the justification of God's ways to humans. First, it has

been said that some evil is necessary to recognize the good. However, critics ask: "Why so much?" "Do we need so long a night to appreciate the light of day?" Second, it has been suggested that what we take to be evil is actually good. However, critics reply that this is a possibility we cannot understand, hence it cannot serve as a reason for us. Third, it has been argued that this is the best of all possible worlds. One reply has been that such a view is implausible. We can easily imagine another, better, world in which an infant murdered in this one would live happily and make others happier. Fourth, it has been argued that it is not God, but we ourselves, acting on our own free will, who bring about evil in the world. Yet, critics reply that this does not explain the widespread death and suffering brought about by floods, earthquakes, and other natural disasters, many of whose victims are innocent children.

Here, it is important to have in mind that, though the term evil is frequently used in ethics as roughly synonymous with bad, it often has a religious connotation. Both, in ethics and religious thought, *bad* and *evil* are associated with the notion of *privation* or *privatio boni*, i.e. an item's lack of good where this good is appropriate for that item to have. In addition, evil typically means bad to a high degree. This is clear in some African thought where, for example, in Akan morality, there are two terms for evil: *bōne*, which denotes ordinary evils such as theft and lying, and *musuo*, which denotes extraordinary evils such as rape and murder. This latter sense of evil often suggests religious implications such as that of causing the wrath of the deities.

In the 1960s, some United States theologians called the *Death of God theologians*, most notably Thomas Altizer and William Hamilton, formulated *radical theology* or *theological nihilism*, or the *Death of God movement*: a movement according to which the concept of God had lost its validity, but worship was still possible where the sacred void replaced God.

Other arguments against God's existence take a sociologico-historical form concerning the origin of the divinities. One is *Euhemerism* (also called *Evemerism*), the doctrine held by Euhemerus, also Evemerus (third century BCE), a Greek philosopher born in Sicily, according to whom the gods originated from popular heroes who gradually became the object of common veneration. This doctrine was very influential and Christians used it to debunk the Greek and Roman gods.

Grace

Besides God's existence, the philosophy of religion deals with a variety of topics. One concerns the reason why God created the universe, including humans. Is it for the *glory* – understood as a state of splendor – of God? Did God need to be glorified by humans? Or would God have achieved perfection without them? Another topic concerns the manner in which the faithful obey God. Some think all such acting involves God's *grace*: a term derived from the Latin *gratus* ("beloved," "agreeable"), which is the favor, related to salvation, from God to humans. This position, called *congruism*, was advocated by the Spanish philosopher and theologian nicknamed *Doctor Eximius*: Francisco Suárez (CE 1548–1617). Since early Christian times, this doctrine was associated with that of *gratia praeveniens* ("prevenient grace"), that God not only provides grace but the will to receive it. Significant in this regard is the discussion among Cartesian philosophers such as Antoine Arnauld (CE 1612–94) and Nicolas Malebranche (CE 1638–1715) about *efficacious grace*, i.e. whether God always acts by general, never by particular, volitions, e.g. whether God wills the laws of nature in general and each natural event occurs according to them, or whether God directly wills each natural event.

Inspiration

A notion relevant in the context of divine grace is that of *inspiration* (from the Latin *inspiratio*, the act of *inspirare*: "to breathe upon or into"): a divine influence directly exerted upon the mind of an individual. By extension, this concept is also applied to the works of individuals thus influenced. It has also acquired an aesthetic use according to which artists are said to be inspired to produce such things as works of art or literature by some divinity, whether God or a Muse, i.e. any of a number of sister goddesses in Greek and Roman mythology such as Calliope, the Muse of epic poetry, Euterpe, the Muse of music, and Clio, the Muse of history. Other notions relevant in the context of grace are that of *prayer* – pleading to a divinity on behalf of oneself or others – and that of *intercession*, i.e. a prayer or pleading to God on behalf of another or others.

Soul and matter

A related notion to that of inspiration (the act of breathing in) is that of *breath of life*. In Latin, the terms used for breath of life are *anima, mens, vita, appetites*, hence they are associated with soul. In Hebrew, the term is *nephesh*. This word is used loosely in the Bible. In the cabala, *nephesh* means the animal passions and the animal soul. A related problem in the philosophy of religion is that of the relation between the soul and matter. This is discussed in the *Chaldean oracles* or *oracula chaldaica*, a second century CE poem that describes the descent of the soul into matter and its possible rise through the concentric circles of the universe towards heaven. The poem displays Platonic, Neoplatonic, and neo-Pythagorean influences and is believed to express views from the neo-Pythagorean mystery religion.

The latter is one of the various *mystery religions* or religious cults that flourished in the Hellenic and Roman periods. They involved esoteric knowledge and rituals supposed to purify the initiate and secure union with the divinity and personal immortality. There were various mysteries. For example, the *Eleusian* mysteries – from Eleusis, near Athens, where the respective shrine was located – were initially about the myth of Demeter and Persephone that was supposed to explain the seasons. Afterwards, they focused on personal rebirth. This was also the final stage of the myths of Isis-Osiris, Cybele-Attis, and Aphrodite-Adonis, which had originally been about ways of ensuring fertile crops. The *Orphic* mysteries involved Orpheus and Eurydice, the latter having to return to the underworld because, when Orpheus was leading her out of it, he failed to follow instructions and turned to look at her. An analogous tale can be found in the Judeo-Christian tradition's story of Lot, Abraham's nephew, whose wife was turned into a pillar of salt for looking back during their flight from Sodom. *Mithraism* centered on the slaying of bulls in the name of the hero-god Mithra. Its initiates had to rise through seven levels of purification analogous to the seven heavens those bound for paradise must pass. It primarily attracted Roman soldiers and it had affinities with – if did not in fact influence – the practice of bullfighting in Spain and some Latin American countries where bulls are tested and tired by *banderilleros* and mounted picadors, and then fought and killed in a highly ritualistic way by a matador using only a cape and a sword. In the later years of the Roman Empire, a sun god was imported into Rome from the Near East. It was called *sol invictus* or invincible sun, and was identified with Mithra, the God of Mithraism. The December festival of this god became Christmas in Christianity.

Finally, and by contrast with all previous mysteries, *Dionysian* mysteries involve an ecstatic celebration of the deity through song, dance, wine drinking, and full participation in slaughtering and savoring sacrificial animals. They offer some parallels with the ritual practices of *Voodoo* (also called Vodun), the West Indian religion derived from African cults that contains elements of Catholicism, and the *Macumba*, a similar cult largely derived from Africa and practiced in Brazil, which uses fetishes and sorcery.

Religious obligations

Various religions acknowledge obligations that God places upon humans. In Islam, for example, these are called *farḍ* and, just as in Christian religions and Judaism, include witnessing to the truth, prayer, and fasting. In addition, within these religions, some groups – the Hanafīs in Islam – distinguish between divinely instituted obligations whose omission is a sin – what the Hanafīs call *farḍ* – and religious obligations imposed by law – what the Hanafīs call *wājib* – whose omission may not be a sin.

Religious obligations imposed by law are often enacted by religious authorities, just as matters of religious doctrine are often formally settled by religious authorities, thus constituting orthodoxy, though Western religions are stricter on this matter than Eastern and other religions. In Islam, for example, each opinion

or decision regarding religious doctrine or law made by a recognized authority (often called a *muftī*) is called *fatwa*. Sometimes the latter are codified constituting precedents to guide judges in resolving legal cases. An example is the *Fatāwā ʿAlamgīriyyah*, collected in India under the Moghul Empire.

The matters just discussed relate to the question of the relation between individual reason and Church authority on matters of doctrine and morals. In Catholicism, for example, this relation has been officially established, and the phrase *ex cathedra*, literally "from the chair," is used to denote statements issued by the Pope on a doctrine of faith or morals that, according to Catholic doctrine, are infallible due to the Pope's supreme apostolic authority.

In this regard, some hold the doctrine of *evidentialism* or *evidentiality*, i.e. that religious beliefs can be rationally accepted only if they are supported by all the other propositions one knows or justifiably believes. By contrast, others uphold *fideism*, i.e. that one's religious beliefs have authority that cannot be discredited by reason. This position has given rise to *fundamentalism* in twentieth-century United States Protestantism. This version of fundamentalism reacted against modernism and emphasized the inerrancy of the Bible not only concerning matters of doctrine and morals, but also concerning the Christian historical record, which the Bible is supposed to reflect literally. Analogous forms of fundamentalism can be found in Judaism and Islam. A fundamentalist position often found in Christianity and Judaism is *millenarianism*: the belief in the *millennium*, a period of general righteousness and happiness in the indefinite future.

Still others hold the view – which has been called *experientialism* – that some religious beliefs are directly justified by religious experience and, hence, rational, without need to rely on inferences from other propositions one knows or on justified beliefs one holds. This position is not unrelated to the view that religious experience involves a relation of immediacy – i.e. presence to the mind without intermediaries – between a human being and the divinity, hence one of the strongest possible sources of knowledge.

Sometimes, the latter positions invoke a *miracle* – that which cause wonder – or a series of them, in support of their claims. The issue here becomes whether miracles, which by their very nature are exceptions to the laws of nature, can be established to occur and, if so, how. Some thinkers have attempted to combine these notions by arguing that, though the cause of miracles may be involved in the laws of nature, the miraculous events themselves occur only when a divinity calls them forth.

See also: a priori–a posteriori; Buddhism; Christianity; epistemology; faith; Hinduism; Islam; Judaism; metaphysics; myth

Further reading
Clack, Beverley (1998) *The Philosophy of Religion: A Critical Introduction*, Cambridge: Polity Press.
Hick, John (1990) *Philosophy of Religion*, Englewood Cliffs, NJ: Prentice Hall.
—— (1964) *The Existence of God*, New York and London: Macmillan and Collier–Macmillan.
Weil, Simone (1997 [1992]) *Waiting for God*, New York: Harper & Row.

philosophy of science The branch of philosophy that critically examines the concepts, problems, methods, scope, fields, practice, and results of science. These results often include scientific *laws*, i.e. generalized devices for dealing with scientific problems, and scientific *theories*, i.e. networks of these devices. Often, new scientific *concepts* – i.e. ideas about the world and its components formulated in scientific practice – are involved in these laws and theories, and new scientific *methods* – i.e. ways of addressing scientific problems – are formulated in accordance with the concepts. As for scientific *problems*, they are puzzles about the world and its various components often prompted by conflicts between ordinary or scientific concepts about these matters.

Science and control
A traditional notion of science is that it provides control of or power over nature. This was the aim of the English philosopher Francis Bacon (CE 1561–1626) in his writings, especially the *New Organon*, where he argued for and outlined the empirical method, and the posthumously published *The New Atlantis*. He sought the *Great Instauration*, i.e. leading humans to acquire power over nature, and a society where science was considered the key to happiness and was promoted under State guidance and control.

In this regard, it has also been argued that science provides control or power over people. A question that arises on this subject concerning the validation of knowledge claims is: "What is the epistemic community within which knowledge claims should be validated and research priorities established?" This has been of particular concern in recent feminist discussions in epistemology and the philosophy of science and technology, on the grounds that social conditions can and do create structures of domination reflected in the languages, concepts, and methods actual epistemic communities find admissible. These structures of domination have been discussed by the French philosopher Michel Foucault (CE 1926–84), who argued that bodies of knowledge – *epistemes* – and, in general systems of thought, are tied but not reducible to structures of power. On this view, an *episteme* is a contingent system for the production, regulation, distribution, and operation of statements. It is independent of the beliefs and intentions of individual thinkers and, though contingent, creates constraints on thought and action that seem unsurpassable to those caught up in them.

This is a frequent stumbling-block in the development of fields of *interdisciplinary* inquiry (also called interdisciplinary studies), i.e. of fields of inquiry that bring together the concepts, methods, and research practices of different disciplines (though such studies were far from Foucault's concerns). An example of this type of study is the combination of chemistry and biology to study the chemistry of biological organisms and processes at the molecular level. It was so successful that, eventually, a new discipline resulted: molecular biology. However, such success does not come about without overcoming the participants' misgivings concerning changes in methods, concepts, or research practices associated with the combination of research efforts in more than one discipline.

Not unrelated to matters of power, or, at the very least, to the practical consequences of concepts widely held by scientific and related communities, are the implications of different conceptions of *disease* and *health* in health care. In this area, conceptions of disease and health are crucial for treatment decisions and, to some extent, vary from society to society. To be sure, some conceptions of health and disease predominate through societies and the centuries. For example, a long-standing conception of health in physiology and philosophy was held by the Greek physiologist Galen (CE 129–215) and, through his influence on the Greco-Roman world and the Arabic tradition, also in the Western world even after the discoveries of the seventeenth century, indeed, far into the nineteenth century. It is the four-humor theory, i.e. the view that there are four basic bodily fluids – blood, phlegm, black bile, and yellow bile – and that health consists in a balance between these. This conception has now been superseded by modern physiological conceptions. Yet, differences of detail remain. United States physicians, for example, treat high blood pressure but, except in extreme cases, not low blood pressure. In Germany, by contrast, low blood pressure has also been treated in the past (though apparently this practice is receding). These differences and their practical consequences are more pronounced when conceptions of mental illness and mental health come into play. Indeed, they go beyond practice, affecting overall conceptions of what it is to be a human being, through which health and being have sometimes been associated in metaphysics.

Science and truth

Aside from matters of power, the question arises whether scientific concepts and theories can be true or false and what their nature is. *Fictionalism* has been an influential position in this regard. It was proposed as a general philosophical approach by the German philosopher Hans Vaihinger (CE 1852–1933) who called it *idealistic positivism*, but whose position came to be called the *philosophy of the as if* or *fictionalism*. In physics, fictionalism was advocated by the French physicist Pierre-Maurice Marie Duhem (CE 1861–1916), who held that fiction had a central role in science, in particular in physics. His position is that physical theories are not explanatory but representa-

tions that do not reveal the nature of matter. They do provide general rules, of which physical laws are particular cases; yet, they are neither true nor false but convenient or inconvenient *fictions* – useful or useless fantasies – whereby the physical world is treated as if it were or behaved in accordance with these fictions.

There is a certain connection between this view and that of Foucault's. After all, what Duhem said of physical theories has also been said of social ideologies: they are neither true nor false, but fictions whose symbolic and motivational functions make them useful or useless for a variety of social purposes such as the attainment of social cohesiveness or the securing of support for policies, practices, or institutions. These fictions are not to be confused with physical states of affairs, or even with events in *ideal conditions*, i.e. never quite actualized, though not physically impossible, conditions. For the latter are hypothetical conditions describing limiting – though possibly attainable – cases, while on the views being discussed fictions are assumed to be inexistent and unattainable. An example of what Duhem and Foucault had in mind is the notion of a *social fact*. According to the French sociologist Émile Durkheim (CE 1858–1917), social facts included collective representations: the symbols that made social cohesiveness possible. In fact, they led to a collective conscience in society.

An alternative view on these matters, *instrumentalism*, has been formulated by pragmatic philosophers during the first part of the twentieth century. For example, the United States philosopher John Dewey (CE 1859–1952), who first formulated it, held that concepts and ideas are instruments aimed at integrating, predicting, and controlling our interactions with the world we experience.

A naturalistic version of instrumentalism was formulated by the Czech-born United States philosopher Ernest Nagel (CE 1901–85), who interpreted the principles of logic, as well as scientific theories, in instrumental contexts, so that they were freed from ontological commitments. On this view, theories are simply calculating devices or instruments for proceeding from one set of observed data to another set of predicted observations. Accordingly, a *theoretical statement* – any statement including one or more *theoretical terms*, i.e. terms denoting theoretical entities, theoretical concepts, or clusters of theoretical concepts called *hypothetical* or *theoretical constructs* – has no referent and cannot be true or false, while an *observational statement* or *observation statement* – a statement including only *observational terms* or *observation terms*, i.e. terms describing data and predictions, which are inferences to the future based on the data – has referent(s), and can be true or false. This particular way of distinguishing between theoretical and observational statements lost favor for some decades, but has recently been revived in response to the perplexing features of quantum physics.

Concepts and methods of science
Opposed to the previous positions is *scientific realism*, which claims that developed scientific theories typically refer to real features of the world, discomfirmation of past theories provides no good grounds for skepticism concerning the truth of contemporary scientific theories, and theoretical terms meant to denote unobservable items should be interpreted to refer to these items in the real world, not instrumentally. *Internal realism* accepts the second and, on an indefinitely warranted assertibility sense, the third, but not the first of these claims.

From the standpoint of *methodology*, i.e. that branch of the philosophy of science (closely related to epistemology) which describes and assesses the methods scientists use to establish scientific views, various ways have been formulated in which theories can gain confirmation. Some are inductive. Others, as in the case of the Austrian philosopher Karl Popper (CE 1902–94), involve *conjectures* and *refutations* (see INDUCTION).

Still other ways of confirming theories, as in the case of the English philosopher William Whewell (CE 1794–1866), involve *consilience* and *colligation* (see INDUCTION). There is also *semantic holism*: all theoretical terms have their meaning given as a group in a theory, and the related doctrine is *confirmational holism*: confirmation is gained by whole theories, not by their individual component statements. In addition, *methodological conservatism* holds that the scientific community favors theories that both are compatible with the data and only minimally change previously held scientific beliefs. There are also those who hold simplicity is the overriding factor in accepting theories, though they often advance different conceptions of simplicity. What in fact the scientific community appears to do, however, is to favor theories for which, given the data and the particular science's purpose(s), a better case can be formulated on the basis of such considerations as the theories' clarity, internal consistency, external consistency (i.e. consistency with currently accepted scientific beliefs), explanatory power, predictability, simplicity, completeness, fecundity, and applicability.

As for concepts central to science and the philosophy of science, *conservation* and *symmetry* have been connected with important principles in physics and the *philosophy of physics*, the branch of philosophy of science concerned with physics. Old conservation principles were about matter, energy, and momentum, such as the principle of conservation of matter. Associated concepts were, for example, about matter and impenetrability, a feature attributed to physical bodies that somehow presupposed the distinction between fullness and the void, and concerning which it was often pondered whether it was identical with extension. They are all now part of the relativistic principle of conservation of momentum-energy. Also, in particle physics, one conservation law is the conservation of byron number. That is, contemporary conservation principles still state, like old conservation principles, that some physical quantity is conserved, even though the quantity in question may be different. The German mathematician Emmy Amalie Noether (CE 1832–1935) showed that each conservation law can be derived from an associated underlying symmetry that expresses the invariance of some structural feature of the world relatively to some transformation.

Other significant concepts in physics belong in *thermodynamics*, the area of physics that describes and correlates the physical properties of macroscopic systems of matter and energy. One is that of heat, which is characterized in the *first law of thermodynamics*, which assumes the *principle of conservation of energy*: energy cannot be created or destroyed (leaving aside transformations of mass into energy and vice versa). The first law says that the amount of heat transferred to a system plus the amount of work done on the system equals the increase in internal energy in the system.

Another concept is *entropy*, i.e. the disorder or lack of structure, or (in a wide sense of this term) disarray in a system of elements such as the organic molecules of an organism isolated from its environment. The *law of entropy* or *second law of thermodynamics* says that the entropy, i.e. the disorder, of an isolated system can never decrease. It leads to the conclusion that, if a large physical system is isolated exchanging no energy with its environment, then the entropy – or measure of disorder – of the system continuously increases, which means the order in the system decays. The second law suggests that there is an absolute temperature scale, hence an absolute zero; but the *third law of thermodynamics* says that the absolute zero can be infinitely approached but never reached.

As for theoretical tensions in contemporary physics, that between quantum physics and relativity theories is most notable. *Special relativity*, formulated by the German-born physicist Albert Einstein (CE 1879–1955), applies to electrodynamics, while *general relativity*, also formulated by Einstein, applies to gravitation. Both special and general relativity are often called the *theory of relativity*. These are actually invariance theories; however, they have been called relativity theories because, given the invariance of the laws of nature, then certain properties – e.g. spatio-temporal properties – previously presumed to be independent of observations, e.g. simultaneity, actually turn out to be relative to the state of motion of the observer. Thus, they embody the doctrine of *relationism* or *relationalism* concerning time and space, i.e. the doctrine that time and space are not ABSOLUTE, which is to say independent of objects, but relative or relational, which is to say they must be conceived as a set of temporal and spatial relations that hold between material components of the universe.

Special relativity is an invariance theory in that it can be briefly stated as saying that the laws of nature are invariant from all frames of reference for all non-accelerated systems. *General relativity*, in a parallel manner, can be briefly stated as saying that the laws of nature are invariant from all frames of reference for all mechanical systems, whether accelerated or not. The mathematical ideas that made the general theory of relativity possible were formulated by the Russian-born and German-naturalized mathematician and physicist Hermann Minkowski (CE 1864–1909). In 1908, he showed that the observer-independent structure of special relativity could be represented by means of a four-dimensional metric. Using this metric, the *Minkowski space–time*, general relativity could describe gravity as a curvature of space–time in the presence of mass, and the paths of falling bodies as worldlines in curved space–time.

Critics point out that, in avoiding action at a distance, contemporary physics widely uses *field theory* or *unified field theory*, a theory which assigns values of physical qualities to space points or space–time points, and then formulates laws associated with these values. They further argue that this is a strong reason for concluding that space–time points, and the worldlines constituted by these points and representing dynamic histories of moving particles, actually exist. If so, relationism, which holds there are only spatio-temporal relations and no space–time points, is false. It may be fruitful to explore the implications of this point for the views of a philosopher traditionally associated with relationism: the German philosopher Gottfried Wilhelm Leibniz (CE 1646–1716), who defined *time* as the order of succession or possibilities that cannot coexist, in contrast with *space*, which he defined as the order of possible coexistences.

Space–time
A significant notion concerning relativity theory is that of *mathematical space*, which is often conceived as *continuous*, i.e. for any two points in it, there is at least one point in between. By contrast, some thinkers have imagined it to be *discrete*, i.e. this is typically

the view that for any two contiguous points in it there is no point in between, though space could have degrees of discreteness, so that at least two – but possibly more – pairs of points in it have no points in between.

Analogously, *mathematical time* is often conceived as *continuous*, i.e. for any two moments in it, there is at least one (shorter) moment in between. By contrast, some thinkers have imagined it to be *discrete*, i.e. this is typically the view that for any two contiguous moments in it there is no moment in between, though time could have degrees of discreteness, so that at least two – but possibly more – pairs of moments in it have no moments in between. The notion of a *time-slice* as a temporal stage of a continuous particular object, or *continuant* fits well with the continuous notion of mathematical time. If time were discrete, however, each moment would be a time-slice and, though we might think of a time-slice as a time-segment longer than a moment, this would only be a conceptual construction: no time-slices would in fact be longer segments of time.

Whether in traditional terms or in relativity-physics terms, however, the present and the associated notion of *duration* as a measurement of time elapsed, as first conceived by the Greek philosopher Aristotle (384–322 BCE), is relative to an observer's frame of reference. Indeed, the present was called the *specious present* by various authors, most notably by the United States philosopher William James (CE 1842–1910), to denote the span of duration we grasp in a moment by applying conceptual divisions to what he thought was a continuous flow – or becoming – of experiences.

There are two theories of becoming, the A-theory and the B-theory. According to the *B-theory*, time is a fixed series of events going from earlier to later, called a B-series. While the *A-theory* holds that time is a series of events that, in addition, go from the future through the present into the past, i.e. an A-series. This latter notion, called temporal becoming of time, raises many puzzles. For if a moment of time can shift into the past, then it will become another moment of time. However, this entails that a moment is not identical

to itself! This result has led to various attempts – both linguistic, and psychological or experiential – at reducing the A-series to the B-series; however, these attempts have been found inadequate.

A focus on experience such as that displayed by James has also often led to a relationist position. For example, a general form of relationism is *Mach's principle*, formulated by the Austrian physicist and philosopher Ernst Mach (CE 1836–1916). According to it, all physical events or states – including the inertial forces Newtonians used to argue against relationism – are to be explained in relationist terms. He thought that in explaining the movement of the water rotating within a bucket, one needed not say, as the English physicist and mathematician Isaac Newton (CE 1642–1727) had, that it rotated with respect to space itself, but only that it rotated with respect to the rest of the universe. This view went along with Mach's conception that all scientific concepts – e.g. that of relative space – by contrast with metaphysical concepts – e.g. that of absolute space – were summaries of sensations or neutral impressions that are related to further such experiences.

It is worth noticing also that the invariance theories described are *limiting-conditions theories* because, at their core, they simply state what types of things cannot happen, e.g. that the laws of nature cannot change, while making room for a wide range of events to occur or states to exist within these constraints. By contrast, Newtonian physics specifically describes series of events – e.g. the trajectory of a projectile – given their initial conditions.

Space and time in Indian thought

A comparison with conceptions of time in Indian philosophy shows significant analogies (and disanalogies) with some of the notions just discussed. The term for time is *kāla* (while *kalā* is a unit of time, as well as a part, and a limited agency). In JAINISM, time is immaterial, continuous, has no beginning, and involves two types: absolute time or *dravya-kāla*, and relative or perceived time, or *vyavahāra-kāla*, also called *samaya*. As for the SĀMKHYA-YOGA School, there is no time separate from atoms and their movement, being the duration of an atom's traversing a unit of space. By contrast, the NYĀYA-VAIŚEṢIKA SCHOOL considers time to be everywhere, have a separate existence, and have no parts even if perceptions of changes makes it appear to have parts. However, in order to explain any time relation (*kālika-sambandha*) embodied in such common empirical notions as minutes, hours, and days, the Nyāya-Vaiśeṣika, School uses the concept of *kālika-viseshanatā* or temporal attibutiveness, a relation through which all things are supposed to exist in time. The Vishistādvaita-Vedānta School holds time to be eternal, dependent on BRAHMAN, and correlative with *praktri* (matter). According to the Advaita Vedānta School, time is the relation between Brahman, which is real, and *māyā*, the non-real. Finally, in Dvaita Vedānta, time is one of the substances, with a beginning and an end, and consisting of everflowing units.

Quantum theory
Going back to contemporary physics, relativity theories, however revolutionary, arguably did not break with classical physics to the extent *quantum theory* (also called *quantum physics* and *quantum mechanics*) did. Developed independently by the German physicist Werner Karl Heisenberg (CE 1901–76) as *matrix mechanics*, and the German philosopher Erwin Schrödinger (CE 1887–1961) as *wave mechanics*, this theory introduces probabilities and irreducible acts of measurement in dealing with motion – i.e. with physical objects' spatial changes – and the interactions of physical objects. Heisenberg, for example, formulated the *indeterminacy principle* or *uncertainty principle* that bears his name: certain pairs of observables (e.g. linear momentum and position of an electron) cannot be measured simultaneously. This has the constraining consequence that the product of the uncertainty of the two measurements cannot be greater than h, where h is a constant known as *Planck's constant*. For his part, Schrödinger associated with each physical system, a time-dependent probabilistic function, the *state function* or *state vector*, or Ψ *function*, which changes through time in accordance with a master equation called the *Schrödinger equation*, and provides a way of calculating the probability that, for a given observable – say, momentum – and a given value that observable can take, a

measurement of the observable will yield that value. In the Schrödinger version, the state function or state vector, or Ψ function is a time-dependent function associated with each physical system. Accordingly, in quantum physics, a *state* – i.e. the way an object or system is, its basic properties, or the basis of its properties – does not fix the values of observable occurrences. Instead, it yields the probabilities of these observable occurrences given particular values in particular measurement situations.

Einstein argued that quantum physics was incomplete, and this raised other problems. One was Schrödinger's cat paradox. There are various versions of this paradox. According to one, a cat is in a cage and is being aimed at by a shotgun connected at point p to a paraffin screen towards which particles – say, electrons – are being shot by a cyclotron. If a particle hits point p on the screen, the shotgun's trigger is released and the cat is shot dead. Yet, the state function has no definite result, hence, according to it, the shotgun is neither triggered nor not triggered and the cat is neither dead nor alive. This is the quantum measurement problem.

A related concept in the philosophy of physics is that of *complementarity*, a term coined by the Danish physicist Niels Bohr (CE 1885–1962) to describe the fact that magnitudes – e.g. position and momentum – occur in conjugate pairs subject to the uncertainty principle according to which they cannot be simultaneously determined.

A mathematical result relevant to quantum theory is *Bell's theorem*, named after the Irish physicist John Stewart Bell (CE 1928–90), who formulated it. It shows that the explanation of statistical correlations existing between causally non-interactive systems cannot always presuppose hidden variables, i.e. independent features of the systems whose fixed past values determined the correlations. In establishing this theorem, Bell formulated a locality assumption that constrains hidden variables which might be used in describing the state of a system. This applies to the 1935 Einstein example, later – in 1951 – simplified by the contemporary physicist David Bohm, according to which a pair of systems interact briefly and then separate, but later measurements performed separately in each show high correlations. The *locality assumption* does not allow the measurement performed on one of the said systems immediately to influence the outcome from measuring the other system. Bell showed that the locality assumption, together with other assumptions about hidden variables, does not just restrict the probabilities in measuring outcomes according to a system of inequalities he formulated (*Bell inequalities*), but also that, as a result, the probabilities of some quantum systems violate these inequalities. This is Bell's theorem.

In the process of trying to bridge the gaps between quantum physics and relativity physics at the subparticle level, physicists have been led to raise questions about the origin of the universe. *Cosmogony*, a branch of inquiry traditionally attracting philosophical reflection, overlaps with science when physical accounts of the origin of the world are given. When these accounts are of the basic constitution of the world, then science overlaps with another area of inquiry traditionally attracting philosophical reflection: *cosmology*.

Scientific change

Sometimes, in the context of confirmation, philosophers – e.g. as some have understood him, the United States philosopher Charles Sanders Peirce (CE 1839–1914) – claim that science is characterized by convergence toward a final, unified theory. Others – most notably the United States contemporary philosopher and historian Thomas Kuhn – claim that science develops through mutually discrete stages divided by crises. Each *crisis* is a period during which no prevalent rules for doing science are followed by recognized members of the scientific community. Kuhn initially held that after a crisis, *normal science* developed around a basic *paradigm*, i.e. a model or instance of importance, say, the solar system model of the atom, whose features are shared by new scientific developments in normal science so as to form a disciplinary matrix. Later in his career, Kuhn has made the notion of a paradigm less central to the practice of normal science.

A related notion has been that of *incommensurability*, a property of scientific theories and, according to Kuhn, paradigms, whereby, though they may not contradict each other, there is no common body of data to which they refer. Indeed, some philosophers have argued that all *observational language* or *observation language*, beginning by each *observational term* or *observation term* – i.e. any term denoting observed or observable data – is theory-laden, hence not neutral. That is, they have argued for *scientific relativism*, a form of cognitive or epistemological relativism, according to which there are no universal truths about the world. They have further argued that scientific progress is possible only if theories are introduced that are incommensurable with older ones because, otherwise, falsehoods will never be uncovered. Yet, the question arises: "How could falsehoods be uncovered if there is no way of comparing incommensurable theories by reference to shared data?" Indeed, this would make the position self-refuting.

These relativist thinkers hold that criteria such as simplicity, completeness, explanatory power, applicability, and fruitfulness can be and are used. However, some argue that, at least on the relativistic positions they advocate, these criteria are irretrievably subjective involving not merely expectations of the scientific community, but raw social pressures, hence threatening the development of sound methods for science.

The latter points are frequently formulated in the *social sciences* (or, as some prefer to call them, the social studies), which include at least economics, psychology, sociology, political science, and linguistics, and which differ from the natural sciences in some of their methods and purposes, e.g. concerning (sometimes) the type of EXPLANATION they seek (see PHILOSOPHY OF HISTORY). How much and in what regards they so differ is a topic in the subareas of the philosophy of science dealing with the said specific studies: the PHILOSOPHY OF ECONOMICS, of psychology, and the like. One subject of significant contemporary interest among social scientists and philosophers of science alike is that, from a societal and pragmatic point of view, the constituency of science – i.e. the scientific community together, to some extent, with non-scientists interested in scientific results or processes – is significant if science is to provide explanations addressing the questions they have. The issue arises: "What constraints does this constituency create on scientific inquiry?" This has been of particular concern in recent discussions carried on in feminist epistemology and the philosophy of science and technology of the politics of knowledge, on the grounds that social conditions can and do create structures of domination reflected in the languages, concepts, and methods – including those for establishing expertise or authoritativeness – that actual epistemic communities find admissible, and embodied in the members of these communities who, in these communities, are considered experts or authorities.

Scientific explanation
A recurrent point of contention about the social sciences concerns the type of explanation they can and should give. In this regard, sometimes, the German term for explanation, *Erklärung*, is used in contrast with *Verstehen* (a noun whose technical meaning is COMPREHENSION, UNDERSTANDING, or interpretation, and which is derived from the verb *verstehen*, i.e. to understand). This contrast appears in discussions of the nature of social studies, which, in von Schiel's translation of John Stuart Mill's *Logic*, were for the first time called *Geisteswissenschaften*, i.e. sciences of the spirit, as a translation of what Mill had called moral sciences. The issue here is whether social studies should merely aim at comprehending, i.e. reconstructing meanings instead of discovering causes. In this regard, people sometimes talk of explanation as *explication*, or clarification, in the manner, say, in which an anthropologist engaged in participant observation might attempt to explain an until then unknown practice of a newly discovered group of humans.

In this regard, classical German sociologists distinguished between the individualistic concept of *Gesellshaft*, a social group whose members intentionally join it in order to pursue its purposes, e.g. a club, and the at least partly holistic concept of *Gemeinshaft*, a social group in which its members find their, or a significant feature of their, identity, e.g. a nation. Items falling under the latter, holistic concept were sometimes said to need explication, not explanation. A related approach was that proposed by the German philosopher Wilhelm Windelband (CE 1848–1915), who distinguished between the *natural* or *nomothetic* sciences, i.e. sciences based on law, and the *cultural* or *ideographic* sciences, i.e. sciences based on particular individuals. He held that nomothetic sciences sought laws governing particular individuals, and ideographic sciences sought the form of particular individuals.

See also: epistemology; explanation; holism; induction; justification; logic; metaphysics

Further reading
Ackerman, Robert (1970) *The Philosophy of Science: An Introduction*, New York: Pegasus.
Brodbeck, May (1968) *Readings in the Philosophy of the Social Sciences*, New York and London: Macmillan and Collier–Macmillan.
Pap, Arthur (1962) *An Introduction to the Philosophy of Science*, New York and London: The Free Press and Collier–Macmillan.
Potter, Garry (1999) *The Philosophy of Social Science: New Perspectives*, Harlow, Essex, UK and New York: Longman.

philosophy, Russian *see* existentialism; Marxism; philosophy of literature; philosophy, sociopolitical

philosophy, sociopolitical Sometimes also called *political philosophy*, *social philosophy*, and *social and political philosophy*, this branch of philosophy deals with concepts and problems posed by social life. It overlaps with *political theory*, the branch of political science that, historically, embraced the whole of political science, but is now largely confined to studies of normative and conceptual aspects of government involving its principles and conduct. In addition, political science pursues empirical studies of states and their interactions, and policy-making processes involved in government and the interactions between states, i.e. in *politics* or *political life*.

Policy-making and its spheres
Policy-making itself is the introduction of policies, i.e. of laws or administrative regulations to be followed by social groups. Laws and administrative regulations enacted by governmental

agencies are *public policies*, i.e. to be followed by members of society at large. Administrative regulations introduced by non-governmental entities, say, business firms, are *private policies*, i.e. to be followed by the said entities' members and those seeking their products or services alone.

Contemporary social problems and issues, and policy-making

A central concept in sociopolitical philosophy is that of *conflict*, e.g. as in *rebellion* or the opposition of an individual to the State; as in *revolution*, or the opposition of enough influential individuals to the State so that drastic *social change*, i.e. change at the societal and not just the individual or interpersonal levels, ensues; and as in the wide range of instances of *reform*, where social change, though not drastic, occurs. So is that of its opposite, *consensus*. Either way, a crucial social problem arises: "What social decision procedures are effective and justified under what circumstances?" *Social-decision procedures*, sometimes also called *social-decision processes*, range from discussion of merits and negotiation; through bargaining; to arbitration, mediation (whose religious forerunner is intercession, i.e. a prayer or pleading to God on behalf of another or others), and voting (all of which are typically proactive, i.e. aimed at preventing confrontation or otherwise avoidable and undesirable or objectionable states of affairs). When confrontation is a significant part of the picture, other procedures are crucial, ranging from insulation and outflanking, through bluffing, manipulation, and civil disobedience, to strikes and combat.

These procedures are often discussed in connection with *disjointed incrementalism*, a significant social-decision procedure consisting in incremental changes brought about by social groups or individuals whose activities are not mutually co-ordinated. It was substantially characterized by the contemporary political scientist Charles Lindblom and the contemporary philosopher and political scientist David Braybrooke in *A Strategy of Decision: Policy Making as a Social Process*. Lindblom formulated a comparable approach that he called the *science of muddling through*. This type of procedure has been incorporated in the ap-

proach called *philosophy as diplomacy*, which also covers situations where incrementalism is unsuitable and more drastic violent action involving various forms of violence – from hostage-taking to combat – may be thought needed.

It is in this context that adherents of *pacifism* and non-violence come into play. They take the view that only non-violent social-decision procedures are justified. Relevant to establishing the nature and limitations, if any, of pacifism, is the said conception of philosophy as diplomacy. Briefly, it focuses on the often unsettled and conflictive nature of concerns contributing to pose everyday, scientific, and philosophical problems, and on open-ended social-decision procedures that may help settle the concerns and deal with the problems. In addition, philosophy as diplomacy addresses the fact that contemporary policy-making is often intractable because of the complexity of contemporary life that partly results from rapid and varied technological developments, associated at least in some countries with controversy and confrontation. This widespread situation has led to a largely new phenomenon: *issue-overload*, which is also a subject for philosophy as diplomacy.

That is, philosophy as diplomacy focuses on a central feature of issues and issue-overload: heated conflict – whether of beliefs, demands, or both. The varieties of conflict are *controversy* – when, however heated the conflict, reliance on reason and meaningful dialogue have a predominant role in it – and *confrontation* – when reliance on reason and meaningful dialogue take a back seat.

Also significant in this regard is the role of co-operation and competition in dealing with problems and issues. Concerning them, the following areas have attracted much philosophical discussion: *social traps* (see DECISION) and *fairness* or *equity* or *equitability*, and its relation to equality, whether formal, substantial, or of opportunity (see ETHICS). All of these notions come into play in the concept of a *social crisis*, especially as the crisis poses *global* problems, i.e. problems prompted by a variety of factors ranging all over the planet such as those prompted by global warming, ozone layer depletion, high-tech weapons, and the globalization of business. This also evidences the fact that some problems – e.g. those posed by global warming – arise at the macrolevel of social life, i.e. are *macrosocietal*, while others – e.g. whether or not to support the building of a new town swimming pool – arise at the microlevel of social life, i.e. are *microsocietal*. These are examples of the varieties in the scope of social problems, which are correlated with varieties in the scope of policies.

In addition, about a given matter of conflict, say abortion, one can ask the first-order question: "What, if any, abortions are morally permissible and what abortion policies are accordingly justified, regardless of any controversy or confrontation there may be about it?" In trying to address the issue about abortion, however, one may need to ask a second-order question: "What abortion policies are justified, given that there is a societally disruptive controversy and even confrontation about it?" In considering both the first- and the second-order question, however, one may need to ask a third-order question: "Should the policy question be asked at the first-order or second-order level?" That is, as these questions make plain, there are at least *first-order*, *second-order*, and *third-order policy problems*.

Consciousness and policy-making

The notion of consciousness also has a special meaning in this context. It is not just any kind of awareness as consciousness is often understood in psychology and the philosophy of mind, but awareness of one's own interests or the rules of conduct one should follow given such things as one's interest group and class. That is, though still connected to the philosophy of mind sense, the notion of consciousness here is closer to the moral notion of conscience in that it is aimed at guiding conduct. However, though it can overlap with it, it is not identical to the latter notion, where the conduct is supposed to be governed by moral rules, laws, or principles. In the political sense of consciousness, though admissible, and arguably desirable, such governing criteria are not required.

Policy-making and its constituencies

The question in all these cases arises: "What constraints on policy-making are or should be created by the constituencies of policy makers?" Such constraints, i.e. limitations on what policy makers can effectively do to introduce policy, are political constraints, i.e. limitations having to do with politics or the policy-making processes arising in government and the interactions between states. Other types of constraints are not political but, for example, technological, or economic constraints. At any rate, even with the best of moral intentions, policy makers – i.e., most generally, those persons, whether elected or not, private or public, who have an influence in the creation of laws or administrative regulations to be followed by social groups, typically by societies – at least need the acquiescence of their constituencies, if not also their votes, to continue their work.

Now, since constituencies are often concerned with the immediate, can policy-makers approach policy requiring long-term approaches – e.g. foreign policy – in a sound manner? In this situation, appeals to experts or authorities is often made. This appeal, however, has been of particular concern in recent discussions of the politics of knowledge carried out in feminist epistemology and the philosophy of science and technology, on the grounds that social conditions can and do create structures of domination reflected in the languages, concepts, and methods – including those for establishing expertise or authoritativeness – that actual epistemic communities find admissible, and embodied in the members of these communities that, in these communities, are considered experts or authorities.

As an alternative to domination and, indeed, to lack of constituency acquiescence, various participatory process have been advocated and, sometimes, introduced. Some are the previously mentioned social-decision procedures. All of them can constitute a political evaluation process, i.e. a process whereby alternative policy options are assessed and further explored or discarded. This process calls for a great deal of political savvy or *savoir-faire*, i.e. practical wisdom about how to address the political circumstances developed in the process.

Policy-making objectivity

A related problem that, however, is not specific to sociopolitical philosophy concerns *objectivity*: whether moral concepts and ideas are objective (i.e. totally independent of all or, at least, of any one of our moral beliefs, concepts, and ideas); whether they are utterly subjective (mere constructs with no objective basis); or whether, as in constructivism, they are based on moral beliefs, concepts and attitudes, which makes room for the view that they involve a non-relativistic – e.g. considered judgments of competent judges – criterion or, alternatively, for the view that they involve relativistic presuppositions.

A related position can be traced to what the Austrian philosopher Ludwig Wittgenstein (CE 1889–1951) called a *form of life* of a linguistic community, which he explained as some agreement in the use of language. Wittgenstein posed a variety of questions about it, among them, whether a private language is possible. He argued that this was impossible, because a private language would face the *problem of the criterion*, i.e. it would lack a criterion of linguistic use. In this regard, a question, which Wittgenstein suggested but never substantially addressed, was whether communication was possible between different linguistic communities with different forms of life, hence criteria for linguistic usage. This line of thought has been significantly pursued by the British social and political philosopher Peter Winch (CE 1926–97), who has argued for a significant breakdown of communication between communities with different forms of life in Wittgenstein's sense.

The notions of form of life and communication failures between communities with different forms of life have affinities to issues of *fragmentation* discussed by members of the FRANKFURT SCHOOL and later philosophers writing independently of that school. This, for example, arises in dealing with issues, most notably technology-related issues, where the concepts, methods, traditions, and conventions of the various constituencies involved are highly fragmented, making communication and mutual social adaptations difficult to say the least.

Policy-making and legitimacy

Part of sociopolitical philosophy deals with the nature and justification of institutions and any social organization such as a business firm and a state. These have an abstract nature, as the views of the English philosopher Gilbert Ryle (CE 1900–76) make plain. He conceived of categories as word-types and applied this conception to a characterization of a *category mistake*: the placing of an item in the wrong category, because of some misunderstanding concerning the nature of this entity. He gave the following example concerning the institution of the university (which can be extended to other institutions as well): upon seeing a university's campus buildings, one may ask: "Which one is the university?", mistakenly implying that the university is one of the buildings that, at best, can be its embodiment or part of its concrete existence.

As regards the justification of institutions (their legitimacy), a central concern has been *freedom*, which has been understood in two main ways: *positive freedom* or *autonomy*, or *self-determination*, i.e. the ability to control one's own choices without being carried away by passion or desire, and *negative freedom* or *negative liberty*, i.e. the absence of interference by others.

These concepts are central in *anarchism*, where all forms of freedom are paramount and the very notion of control, hence any institution that exercises it, is suspect, pointing to the sociopolitical philosophy questions: "Is control ever justified?" "When and why?" In this regard, *political nihilism* is the doctrine that the destruction of the inherited social order has positive value. Indeed, *Russian nihilism*, a position influential in Russian philosophy and, indeed, Russian society, during the 1860s, held that the annihilation of the past and present, i.e. of all social and cultural values realized in current institutions and practices, were desirable for the sake of the future understood as social and cultural values yet to be realized. Notable among Russian nihilists was the Russian philosopher Mikhail Bakunin (CE 1814–76), who argued the destruction of all political and economic privilege was a constructive act because all privileged people were intellectually and emotionally depraved.

As previously stated, concerns with control are sometimes applied to science and, indeed, all validations of knowledge. A question that arises here is: "What is the epistemic community within which knowledge claims should be validated and priorities established?" As indicated elsewhere, this has been of particular concern in recent feminist discussions in epistemology and the philosophy of science and technology, as well as in philosophy of domination and related – sometimes called *Hobbesian* – approaches from that of Thomas Hobbes (CE 1588–1679) to that of Michel Foucault (CE 1926–84), on the grounds that social conditions can and do create structures of domination reflected in the languages, concepts, and methods actual epistemic communities find admissible (see CONTINENTAL PHILOSOPHY; PHILOSOPHY OF SCIENCE).

Forms of government: their characteristics and purported justifications

With regard to structures of domination, various conceptions of *imperialism* have developed in the late twentieth century. The traditional notion was that of *geopolitical* imperialism, which was an all-dominant phase of geopolitical *colonialism*: the practices, theories, and attitudes involved in establishing an empire or large group of colonies. Its historical examples ranged from that of the Roman Empire, through the sixteen-century imperial powers (primarily Spain, Portugal, Britain, and France), to the latest twentieth-century colonial power: Russia, with its Soviet area of influence in Eastern Europe, Cuba, and Afghanistan.

Upon the breakdown of the twentieth-century imperial powers (with Britain's evolving and Russia's simply breaking up), new notions of imperialism were developed by extension from the traditional one. Though not focused on military might or territorial spread, they still reflect a reaction against the influence of such countries as the United States, and the old European colonial powers. Such new notions include *cultural* imperialism – the striving towards cultural domination – and *epistemic* imperialism – the striving towards domination of information and the ways of conveying and evaluating it in understanding or practically dealing with the world. These positions sometimes – though not necessarily always – lead to advocating *egalitarianism*, the view that distribution of opportunities and burdens in society should, at least in principle, be equal.

A problem that has arisen is whether, with the growth of transnational corporations and the globalization of business, states or businesses are the main culprits for these influences. If businesses are, labeling them forms of neocolonialism may be a complete misnomer.

Another topic of interest in this area is that of the nature, kinds, and legitimacy or justification of different forms of government. Typically, the focus is on *democracy* (from the Greek *democratía*, i.e. government by the people), a form of government analogous to what the Greek philosopher Aristotle (384–322 BCE) called *polity* – in particular, *deliberative democracy*, as contrasted with other forms of government and their claims to legitimacy. An example of these other forms of government is *monarchy* (from the Greek *monarchía*, and this from the Greek *monárches*, i.e. "ruling alone"), the rule by a hereditary sovereign, and the associated *divine-right theory* or *divine right of kings* theory that aims at legitimizing monarchic rule. This theory, also called the *one-sword theory*, was derived from the medieval *doctrine of the two swords*, which traced all authority to God. By contrast, the divine-right theory held that both temporal and spiritual authority belong to the monarch, having been granted to the monarch by God.

A related medieval metaphor meant to suggest the fiction that the monarch never dies is the *doctrine of the king's two bodies*, according to which one of these bodies is the king's natural body, while the other is the body politic, which cannot be invalidated or frustrated by the natural body's limitations.

A second form of non-democratic government is *fascism* (from the Italian *fascio*, i.e. "bundle," and "-ism") – the authoritarian capitalist-class rule – and the associated *overriding national interest theory* that aims at legitimizing such rule. Still another is *communism* (from the Latin *commun(is)*, i.e. "common," and "-ism") – the self-perpetuating party rule in a class-less society – and the family of professedly Marxist and other theories that aim at legitimizing it. Yet another is *Nazism* (from the German *Nazi(onalsozialist)*, i.e. "National Socialist," and "-ism") – the authoritarian ethnic-group rule – and the family of doctrines and organizations falling under the heading of *neo-Nazism* – e.g. the Ku Klux Klan, the Order, and the Aryan Nation Church affiliates, including the Michigan Militia and similar extremist groups – that aim at legitimizing such practices as ethnic cleansing, apartheid, and various forms of separatism.

There are classifications of government that largely cut across the previous ones, and hence contribute to forming subcategories of the ones just listed. One is *aristocracy* (from the Greek *aristokratía*, i.e. "rule of the best"), a form of government consisting in the rule by an elite. The Greek philosopher Plato (428–348 BCE) added the condition that the elite should rule in the interest of what is best for society. According to him, there were lower forms of government. Second to aristocracy, there was *timocracy* (from *timokratía*, "rule by the honorable"). Third, there was *oligarchy* (from the Greek *oligarchía*, i.e. "the rule of the few"), a form of government consisting in the rule by a relatively small group or a dominant class of society; but characterized by Plato as the rule of the wealthy. The fourth was *democracy* where, according to Plato, the criterion for governing was popularity. The last was *tyranny* (from the Latin *tyrannia*, a term combining *tyrannus*, from the Greek *tyrannos*, "despot," with *-ia*), which for Plato meant government by raw power.

In practice, some of these terms have acquired different meanings in addition or to the exclusion of their original ones. The term aristocracy has come to designate the rule by a group of people holding special rank and privileges such as the nobility. Since, by contrast with the rest of society, these groups are comparatively small, the term aristocracy is often used as equivalent with oligarchy, in the sense of a form of government consisting in the rule by a relatively small group or a dominant class of society.

There are also traditional, but largely post Greco-Roman terms. One is *theocracy* (from the Greek *theocratía*, i.e. "the rule of God"), a form of government organized on the basis of divine laws or commands. Usually, theocracy is associated with absolute monarchies, e.g. those in Ancient Egypt, which were tightly associated with the priesthood. At any rate, a theocracy based on Catholic Church control was what was advocated by *traditionalism* or *ultramontanism*, an eighteenth-century theory of history formulated by counter-revolutionary intellectuals in France and Spain after the French Revolution.

Examples of more participatory theocratic governments were Geneva under Calvinism, the New England colonies under Puritanism, Florence under the Italian monk Jerome Savonarola (CE 1452–98), early Judaism, and, some would argue, twentieth-century Israel, though others would justifiably consider it a democracy, and still others would say it is a combination of both. Such combinations, though infrequent, are not impossible because, as indicated, the categories cut across the previous ones. Hence, they can give rise to hybrid forms of government; indeed, though rare, *aristodemocracy* or, at least, *oligodemocracy* has existed. Arguably, Athenian democracy, which excluded all women, was an oligodemocracy. Also arguably, Calvinist Geneva and Puritan New England were democracies in the manner they were run and, since they were organized on the basis of divine laws, they were theocracies as well. Though there is no special traditional term for this governmental combination, perhaps they should be called *theodemocracies*.

Among notions relevant here are the public good, the public interest, and the related notions of public debate (which is central to deliberative democracy); public participation (which is central to *participatory* democracy, but not as central to *representative* democracy, where government occurs through elected representatives); public opinion, public adaptability, and the policy-making influence of the public. As for public good, a concept relevant to it is that of *voluntarism* in its social sense, also called *voluntaryism* or, more frequently, *the non-profit sector*, i.e. the social sector constituted by all organizations aimed at providing goods or services but not at making a profit, so that their earnings are used only for operational costs or to fund the goods or services they provide.

Society, government, and nature
Some of the twentieth-century positions discussed in this entry have been influenced by nineteenth- and early twentieth-century appli-

cations of Darwinian ideas to society. For example, the English philosopher Herbert Spencer (CE 1820–1903) was influential in developing a view of how the social world should be, given the facts of evolution. Sometimes, this view is interpreted to involve an unbridled social competition for existence and extreme *laissez-faire* economics. Arguably, Spencer did not uphold this position, even though he used the notion of *organismic analogy* or *organismic metaphor* to attribute features of *organisms* – understood as biological bodies – to social structures and, indeed, societies, e.g. to argue that, like organisms, societies have birth to death cycles. However, the United States sociologist William Graham Sumner (CE 1840–1910) did hold the view. He formulated an initial version of *Social Darwinism*, according to which the socially fittest – who he identified with the wealthy – survive or become socially powerful.

Various concepts are salient concerning the *legitimacy* of social structures. One is the notion of the *general will*, which the French philosopher Jean Jacques Rousseau (CE 1712–78) used meaning both the ideal judgment of a society reached when individuals, as citizens, judge from the standpoint of the common good and, simultaneously, having given up their rights to the community through a social contract or pact, from the standpoint of the sovereign power of a society. This contract need not be explicit but only involve tacit consent. However, what constitutes *tacit consent* is controversial. Some social-contract theorists believe that merely receiving benefits from society is enough to assume such consent. Others hold that no such consent exists unless the benefits were requested. Also, the question arises whether those who request benefits should be competent and, if so, in what respects. This is particularly significant in modern societies, where governmental structures are complex and explicit consent and requests are difficult to implement.

Of relevance to discussions of the structure of government is Rousseau's belief that, since all power came from the people, *separation of powers* was impossible. By contrast, such separation, already recommended during the Renaissance by the French philosopher and essayist Michel de Montaigne (CE 1533–92), and further advocated by the French philosophical writer Montesquieu (born Charles Louis de Secondat, whose title was Baron de la Brède et de Montesquieu; CE 1689–1755), was instituted in the United States Constitution.

Another salient concept is that of an *interest*, which can be that of a person, a group, or a state. In the case of a person's interest, it can be used in the subjective sense of what the person is interested in, or in the objective sense of what is to the person's advantage or benefit. In the case of a group's or state's interest, the sense used tends to be the objective one of what is to the group's or state's advantage or benefit.

Rousseau thought human nature was basically good, but went astray as a result of instituting the wrong social arrangements. A range of Utopian thinkers followed on these or analogous steps, originating more than one *Utopia* (from the Greek *ou*, i.e. "not," and *topos*, i.e. "place"), a term coined by the English statesman and essayist Thomas More (CE 1478–1535) as the name for his ideal society, and now used to denote an ideal, unactualizable social arrangement.

A notable Utopian thinker was the French social theorist and critic François-Marie-Charles Fourier (CE 1772–1837). He argued that a full person was attainable only in unity with others; that, historically, members of societies were mutually antagonistic; and that this could be overcome in a *state of harmony*. Such a state could be attained by organizing society on the basis of the *phalanx*, or 300 to 400 families amounting to about 1,600 to 1,800 people, whose characters were blended scientifically so as to produce harmony. This vision of co-operation was *Utopian socialism*, a type of social organization which places the ownership or control of the means of production in the community as a whole. Fourier's idea influenced later proponents of *anarchism* (which tried to attain community control of the means of production by restricting or eliminating government controls), *syndicalism* (which tried to attain community control of the means of production through worker federations), and other community-oriented social movements.

In the process of discussing the various forms of government, various ideal types have been developed, most notably by the Italian political scientist Gaetano Mosca (CE 1838–1941). He distinguished four ideal types based on how authority flows and whether classes are open or closed: In *autocracy*, authority from the rulers to the ruled; in *liberalism*, from the ruled to the rulers; in *democracy*, the ruling class can be renewed with members of other classes; in *aristocracy*, the ruling class is closed to members of other classes. These types have been widely used to characterize such notions as that of the theory of the state, e.g. liberalism in characterizing the liberal theory of the state. Mosca held that every society is ruled by an elite, i.e. an organized minority, but also held the normative principle that political developments and arrangements are to be judged by whether and how they prevent one person, class, force, institution, etc. from dominating all others.

A question often arising in this context and leading to a focus on forms of government that fall under the heading of autocracy is that of the nature of the *state* or *civil society* by contrast with its opposite, a *state of nature*. Some philosophers, most notably, Thomas Hobbes (CE 1588–1679) have argued that at least some of the ordinary rules or principles of morality (e.g. those concerning justice) have no application at all wherever a state of nature exists, i.e. wherever a situation is predominant in which the rules of civil society cannot be expected to apply. This type of situation is obviously opposite to that of a civil society and can be characterized by means of four variables (or assumptions) and a set of odds tied to the circumstances. The *motivational* variable: everyone in the situation will act so as to maximize his or her own advantage, which, at the very least, includes ensuring his or her own survival or self-preservation and all competitive advantages that would help secure it. The *epistemological* variable: everyone in the situation has roughly equal knowledge and abilities relevant for dealing with the situation. The *resources* variable: resources are limited. Last, the *liberty* variable: everyone is at liberty to act as he or she wishes in the situation. This is also called the *commons* variable, because every-one's being thus at liberty defines a *commons*, i.e. a realm where there are no strong rights, e.g. no property rights, but only liberties (or weak rights) (see ETHICS).

Here, being at liberty is understood as having a *liberty* or a *weak right*, where to say that a person S is at liberty to do, have, or enjoy x is to say that it is not wrong for S to do, have, or enjoy x. This notion is contrasted with that of a *strong right*, according to which, to say that a person S has a strong right to do, have, or enjoy x is at least to say that, first, it is not wrong for S to do, have, or enjoy x; and second, everyone else has an obligation not to interfere with S's doing, having, or enjoying x. At least when it comes to the rights of a citizen – though, on some conceptions of a right, concerning every right – a third condition is arguably required, namely, that S is *entitled to claim* that everyone else omit interfering with S's doing, having, or enjoying x.

It is useful here to notice that, by contrast with a citizen, a political subject or, simply, a *subject*, e.g. anyone living under an absolute monarchy, is not entitled to any such claim. In international situations, where the relations are from state to state and there is no overall government, the commons variable is dominant and, therefore, at that level, persons are subjects, not citizens. *Citizenship* is a relation some of them – those who live under governments other than those excluding the said entitlement to claim – have with regard to their own respective governments concerning political participation, say, voting rights that immigrants who remain aliens do not have.

The commons variable is exemplified in international waters; while the jurisdictional waters of a country involve sovereignty claims, i.e. strong rights of the country to the corresponding area or, in other words, a country's property rights to the area. It should be noted in this connection that the term *sovereignty*, coined by the French political philosopher Jean Bodin (CE 1530–96), derives from the French *souverain*, i.e. the chief or supreme power of the State. The question, of course, has arisen: "Who does or should have sovereignty: the ruler or the ruled?" Hobbes, like Bodin, attributed it to the ruler. Others, e.g. Rousseau (see above), attributed it to the people.

Even those who argue that at least some of the ordinary rules or principles of morality have no application in a state of nature, however, sometimes add that not all principles cease to apply in such a situation. Hobbes himself held that, in a state of nature, our primary purpose should be to do all we can in order to get out of such a state. Others, however, often called *Machiavellians* or advocates of *Machiavellianism* – also called *Realpolitik* or *political realism* – hold that even in civil society it all comes down only to power relations. This position takes its name from the Renaissance Italy author Niccolò di Bernardo Machiavelli (CE 1611–77), who, following Roman historians, developed a position called *civic humanism* or *classical republicanism*, which also addressed the question of the division of power within the power elite. Machiavelli's classical republicanism held that the only way a state could do well was if its citizens were devoted to its well-being. They would take turns ruling and would have a secular virtue – *virtù* – which was political in nature. This position was also advanced by the British author James Harrington (CE 1611–77) in the seventeenth century and modified by eighteenth-century British and Continental writers in ways that influenced, for example, the United States founding fathers. Harrington opposed Hobbes's authoritarian views and, like Machiavelli, argued for an elected form of government whereby well-to-do males would rotate at the top for limited periods of time.

In addition to the positions just described, some philosophers argue that civil society and a state of nature are two types of opposite situations, each embodied to a variety of degrees in actual societies; hence, the problem of the applicability of at least certain moral rules or principles – e.g. those of justice – is always, to some extent and in some respect, at issue, though this does not undermine the applicability of all rules of morality. In other words (at least as a transition from a state of nature to a civil society situation) there is a possible function and, indeed, a moral justification for autocracy.

Others argue, however, that such a justification is, at best, only for the transitional period, and has no force once civil society is established. These thinkers characteristically advocate some form of *liberalism*, a notion covering a wide range of views concerning what coercive institutions are justified. *Classical liberalism* (today often called *libertarianism*), holds that constraints on liberty are only commissions, i.e. positive acts that prevent individuals from doing what otherwise they could do. Failing to help them, on the other hand, are omissions, hence not constraints to their liberty. Classical liberalism is different from anarchism: the doctrine that no coercive institutions are justified. By contrast with classical liberalism, another form of liberalism, *welfare liberalism* conceives of constraints on liberty as including omissions, namely those to provide a minimum of provisions.

Ideal types have also been used for purposes other than those pursued by Mosca. The German sociologist Max Weber (CE 1864–1920), for example, held that explanations of large-scale, macrosocial phenomena, require ideal types such as authority, and the Protestant ethic.

Genocide

A relatively modern notion in sociopolitical philosophy is that of *genocide* (from the Greek *genos*, "tribe," and the Latin *-cide*, "killing"), briefly, the deliberate and systematic extermination of a national, ethnic, racial, or religious group, such as the Jewish Holocaust during Germany's Third Reich. In the present United Nations Convention on Genocide, the term genocide covers any of the following activities:

1 killing members of the group;
2 causing serious bodily or mental harm to members of the group;
3 deliberately inflicting on the group conditions aimed at bringing about its partial or total destruction;
4 imposing measures aimed at preventing births within the group;
5 forcibly transferring children from the group to another group.

Globalization issues

As for emerging issues in sociopolitical philosophy, some concern globalization of such things as technology, e.g. computer technology; business practices and organization, e.g. financial markets; the courts, e.g. in trials of ex-dictators outside the countries where they once ruled; and culture, e.g. in the creation of world-wide outlets for Hollywood movies. The globalization of computer technology, coupled with that of financial markets, has prompted a variety of social concerns and even a certain resurgence of the attitudes and practices of the *luddites*, the various bands of workmen in England who, between CE 1811 and 1816, organized to destroy manufacturing machinery they believed responsible for increased unemployment.

Similar concerns have arisen about the related topic of global markets and, in general, globalization. In this regard, some thinkers – e.g. the contemporary influential financier George Soros in his "Toward a Global Open Society," *The Atlantic Monthly* (January 1998), pp. 20–4, 32 – have proposed to develop the needed institutions by appeal to the notion of an *open society*, a term coined by the Austrian philosopher Karl Raimund Popper (CE 1902–94). It is related to the openness Popper proposed in epistemology to replace logical positivism's verifiability criterion of cognitive significance with *falsificationism*, or error elimination, through the positing of unjustifiable conjectures or hypotheses, and their refutation or falsification through critically and relentlessly testing their deductive implications. Analogously, the open society is a society open to improvement by making room for trying a wide range of policy-hypotheses aimed at attaining the greatest degree of economic and non-economic freedom for all, through such things as the implementation of the rule of law, division of powers, free enterprise, respect for individual rights, and substantial opportunity to minorities and other disadvantaged groups. Late-year 2000 public discussions and demonstrations centered on this opportunity and environmental concerns.

Also worthy of mention are the New Philosophers, a group of French sociopolitical philosophers who flourished as a result of the May 1968 student and worker uprising, becoming influential in the 1970s. They advocated anti-establishment, anti-Marxist, and anti-ideological views. Notable in this group are André Glucksmann, Jean Marie Benoist, Phillipe Nemo, and Bernard-Henry Lévy.

See also: ethics; explanation; holism; induction; justification; philosophy of history

Further reading
Barry, Brian (1965) *Political Argument*, London and New York: Routledge & Kegan Paul and Humanities Press.
Bowie, Norman E. (1998) *The Individual and the Political Order: An Introduction to Social and Political Philosophy*, 3rd edn, Lanham, MD: Rowman & Littlefield.
Braybrooke, David and Lindblom, Charles E. (1963) *A Strategy of Decision: Policy Evaluation as a Social Process*, London and New York: Collier Macmillan Publishers and The Free Press.
Dunn, John (1985) *Rethinking Modern Political Philosophy*, Cambridge, UK and New York, US: Cambridge University Press.
Foucault, Michel (1997) *The Essential Works of Michel Foucault*, New York: New Press, distributed by W.W. Norton & Company.
Giddens, Anthony and Hutton, Will (2000) *On the Edge: Living with Global Capitalism*, London: Jonathan Cape.
Iannone, A. Pablo (1994) *Philosophy as Diplomacy: Essays in Ethics and Policy Making*, Atlantic Highlands, NJ: Humanities Press.
Jacobs, Lesley A. (1997) *An Introduction to Modern Political Philosophy: The Democratic Vision of Politics*, Upper Saddle River, NJ: Prentice Hall.
Tannenbaum, Donald G. (1997) *Inventors of Ideas: An Introduction to Western Political Philosophy*, New York: St Martin's Press.

phrase marker *see* ambiguity

phrastic *see* speech act theory

phronesis *see* ethics

physicalism *see* philosophy of mind; reductionism

physis *see* biology

pi *see* Chinese philosophy

pictorial theory of truth *see* truth

pien *see* Chinese philosophy

pien che *see* Chinese philosophy

pietism *see* Christianity

pistis sophia *see* Christianity

Planck's constant *see* philosophy of science

plastic arts *see* aesthetics

plastic natures *see* Cambridge School

Platonic form *see* Platonism

Platonic love *see* love; Neoplatonism

Platonism In a wide sense, the range of philosophies influenced by the thought of the Greek philosopher Plato (428–348 BCE), whose views or those of his teacher, the Greek philosopher Socrates (469–399 BCE), were formulated in dialogues. On the basis of linguistic similarities, internal historical evidence, and alleged doctrinal progression many – though not all – historians of philosophy today divide these dialogues into three periods. One is the *Socratic* or *Early Dialogues Period*, which, on the basis of linguistic similarities, scholars believe to include the *Apology*, *Charmides*, *Crito*, *Euthypro*, *Hippias Minor*, *Ion*, *Laches*, *Protagoras*, and, arguably, Book I of the *Republic*. The *Middle Period* includes all but Book I of the *Republic*, *Phaedo*, *Symposium*, and *Phaedrus*. The *Late Period*, according to Ancient sources, includes the *Laws* – reportedly the last dialogue Plato wrote – and, given linguistic similarities, also the *Sophist*, *Statesman*, and *Philebus*. Stylistically, the *Timaeus* should also belong to this late period. Yet, some scholars think it should be placed in the Middle Period because they believe its doctrines were later discarded by Plato.

Some influential Platonic doctrines
Various influential doctrines were formulated by Plato in these dialogues. One is the doctrine of *anamnesis*, i.e. reminiscence or recollection, according to which the soul has knowledge before entering the body and learning is nothing but recollecting what one once knew but then forgot. Another is the *doctrine of the Forms* or *theory of the Forms*, sometimes also called *Ideas*. These are eternal, changeless, incorporeal, imperceptible entities – e.g. number three by contrast with any particular triad, or any numeral or sign for number three – that we can know only though reflection.

Plato's thought on this matter evolved through the years. Indeed, in one of his later dialogues, the *Parmenides*, he formulated various criticisms of the Forms, the most famous of which has come to be called *the third-man argument*. A later version of this argument is this: if the group of particular human beings, *the first man*, provides good reason to posit the existence of a Form Man, *the second man*, then the group constituted by the first man and the second man provides equally good reason to posit yet another Form, *the third man* (in Greek, *trítos ánthropos*). Since this argument can be reiterated indefinitely, it leads to positing indefinitely many Forms of Man, which would undermine the theory of Forms, because the theory was partly meant to explain *unity in diversity* (what the many distinct men have in common). Some scholars claim that this argument led Plato to abandon his theory of Forms; others, that it led him to modify the theory; still others, that his position was unaffected because the argument made assumptions Plato's theory did not make.

The Forms are a source of religious or moral motivation in that, upon being discovered by any person, the person feels LOVE for them. Plato affirmed *love* as a transcendent force in human life, ascending from merely bodily attraction to mental and spiritual attraction. Since the Renaissance, this highest form of love came to be called *Platonic love*, which some – but not all or even most – interpreters have conceived as the perfect love where a beautiful body is loved for the sake of its form, beauty.

As for the moral and social implications of the doctrine of the Forms, in depicting the ideal city in the *Republic*, Plato argues that it should be ruled by philosophers who have gained special understanding of the Form of the Good. To help them gain this understanding, they should receive an education that Plato describes in the *allegory of the cave*: they will be like prisoners who, having seen only shadows in the cave in which they were imprisoned, are freed, leave the cave, and eventually become able to see the sun, hence acquiring the ability to return to the cave and see the shadows for what they really are.

Plato often used comparisons to clarify his points. Besides the previously discussed allegory of the cave, he uses the *ascent of Eros* or *heavenly ladder*, or *stairs of beauty* mentioned in the *Symposium* to indicate that there is a hierarchy of beauty. Another notable comparison is the *line of truth* simile appearing in the

Republic. The line of truth is a twice-divided vertical line. Its main division is that between opinion and knowledge. The opinion segment is divided into imagination and sense-perception, while the knowledge segment is divided on the one hand into the knowledge of mathematics and logic, and on the other hand, at the highest level, the knowledge of the Forms.

In the *Timaeus*, Plato introduced the *demiurge*, a deity who shaped the cosmos from the pre-existing chaos. Plato's demiurge, by contrast with later conceptions of this deity, is perfectly good and, using the Forms or Ideas (eternal, changeless, incorporeal, transcendent entities), shapes chaos into the best possible image of the Forms.

Platonism after Plato

As stated, the Platonic doctrine of the Forms was criticized – arguably by Plato himself in the *Parmenides* (132A), and also by others – on the basis of the previously mentioned third-man argument. The argument was also later used by Plato's student, the Greek philosopher Aristotle (384–322 BCE) in various passages of the *Metaphysics* and *Sophistical Refutations*. In fact, there were various versions of this argument: Plato's (which uses the Form of the Large), the Sophists', and Aristotle's. This latter version is that previously stated. One of the foremost commentators on Aristotle, the Greek philosopher Alexander of Aphrodisias (*fl. c.* CE 200), added – echoing Plato's remarks in the *Parmenides* – that the argument does not stop with the third man, because the question then arises what is common to the third and the other two, and so on and so forth, so that an *infinite regress* or *regressus ad infinitum* or, as has been suggested, an *indefinite regress* or *regressus ad indefinitum* originates (see FALLACY). Aristotle, however, seemed concerned, not so much with the regress, but with the unnecessary multiplication of entities. To avoid it, it suffices to say – as, according to some, but by no means all or even most interpreters, Aristotle did, and as others have held since then – that no Idea exists separately from individuals, but that it is a universal that manifests itself in particular entities. It should be mentioned that the said separability is common among Platonists, but that it is controversial whether it is part of Plato's views.

Also, various Christianized versions were formulated of Plato's simile of the heavenly ladder, most notably, by the philosopher Augustine (CE 354–430; born in Thagaste, North Africa). Also, the heavenly-ladder simile influenced the thought of Neoplatonic thinkers, most notably the Egypto-Roman philosopher Plotinus (CE 204–70).

During the Western Middle Ages, there were a number of intellectual groups imbued with the spirit of Platonism. One of them was the *School of Chartres* that, rather than a school or a movement, was a community of thinkers mostly from cities in what is now France, who shared interests and aspirations initially formulated by the philosopher Gerbert of Aurillac (d. CE 1003), who was born in the city of Auvergne, studied in Rheims and became Bishop of Rheims, eventually being elected to the Papacy under the name Sylvester II. This community of interests and aspirations is variously characterized as *Christian Platonism*, *Christian Rationalism*, and *Christian Humanism*. Gerbert's disciple, Fulbert (d. CE 1028), about whom not much is known except that he also became Bishop of Rheims, is credited with having founded the School of Chartres, focusing on a greater understanding of Ancient authors within the boundaries of the Christian faith.

Notable among the members of this group was Bernard of Chartres (*c.* CE 1080–1167), who held ideas are eternally real in God's mind and coined the expression *formae nativae* or native forms to denote the copies of those ideas. Also notable was William of Conches (CE 1080–1145), who incorporated most of the science of the day into his work and interpreted the doctrine of the trinity in Platonic terms. This, plus the fact that he followed the Brittany-born philosopher Peter Abelard (CE 1079–1142) made him the target of criticism. Perhaps most notable was Gilbert of Poitiers (CE 1076–1154), whose doctrine of the trinity – which distinguished God as pure being and God as triune – also made him the target of criticism. Indeed, in CE 1148, it was pronounced heterodox by the Synod of Rheims, whereupon Gilbert withdrew the material found objectionable. He also distinguished between the *native forms*, which are the same for all individuals of the same species or genus, and the *individualized essence* of a thing. He had many followers, some of whom published the school's views in the *Sententiae divinitatis*.

Other members included Theodoric (Thierry) of Chartres (twelfth century CE), who advocated a realist doctrine of universals, and Clarembaud of Arras (*fl. c.* CE 1155), who shared Theodoric's position on universals and conceived of God as *forma essendi* in the sense of pure form or pure act. Some scholars consider the English philosopher John of Salisbury (*c.* CE 1115–80) a member of the School of Chartres, while others consider him less closely associated with it. Indeed, he arguably was a conceptualist concerning universals, claiming that genera and species are *figurae rationis* or mental constructs, whose existence is not in things, though we acquire them by abstracting from things and in the comparison of things.

Another influential School was the *School of Saint Victor* or the *Victorines*, an Augustinian school located outside Paris that remained active between CE 1108 and CE 1789, when the French Revolution contributed to its demise. Founded by William of Champeaux (CE 1070–1120), the school reached its peak during its first century of existence. Champeaux was particularly interested in the problem of universals. He initially advocated the *identity theory*: that the individuals of a species all have the same common nature, hence their individual differences are only accidental. Under the influence of Abelard, however, Champeaux shifted to an *indifference theory* of universals, according to which, though the essences of the individuals of a species were not the same, they were similar, and their species was based on this similarity. Other notable members of the school were philosophico-mystical thinkers concerned with the soul's ascent: Hugh of Saint Victor (CE 1096–1141) and Richard of Saint Victor (late twelfth century CE).

For much of Platonism's history, an influential Platonist doctrine – e.g. held by Bonaventure (*c.* CE 1221–74), who was born Giovanni Fidanza in the Tuscan city of Bangorea, in what is now Italy – has been *exemplarism*: the view that all existing items are copies of, or patterned after exemplars (from the Latin

exemplum: "model" or "example"), i.e. after causes or ideas in God's mind. In this regard, Plato had formulated the notion of *parousia* – a Greek term meaning "a being present" or "arrival" – to mean the presence of a Form in an item. In Christianity, the term *parousia* has been used to denote Jesus's return.

Platonism has been influential down to the modern period (see IDEA; RATIONALISM). Indeed, even in the twentieth century, for example with the notion of eternal objects in process philosophy and, as a significant tradition, in the philosophy of mathematics.

See also: Greek philosophy; Neoplatonism

Further reading

Balaguer, Mark (1998) *Platonism and Anti-Platonism in Mathematics*, New York: Oxford University Press.
Cleary, John J. (1999) *Traditions of Platonism*, Aldershot: Ashgate.
Merlam, Philip (1975) *From Platonism to Neoplatonism*, The Hague: Nijhoff.
Moline, Jon (1981) *Plato's Theory of Understanding*, Madison, WI: University of Wisconsin Press.
O'Meara, Dominic J. (1998) *The Structure of Being and the Search for the Good: Essays on Ancient and Early Medieval Platonism*, Aldershot: Ashgate.

plausibility *see* logic; probability

plausible *see* probability

play The concept of play has been widely used in aesthetics, other areas of philosophy, and psychology. The term *play* – and its translations, e.g. *Spiel* in German, *giòco* in Italian, *juego* in Spanish – is used in a variety of senses. However, in the sense in which it is used in aesthetics, other areas of philosophy, and psychology, it means *fun* or *jest*, as opposed to earnest; a *pun*, i.e. a play on words; and *amusement* or *recreation*. In the latter sense, *play* denotes a function of exercise or activity, e.g. of a *sport* or a game, where *game* is applied to items that range widely from card games, through language games, to the game of existence or life-game and to that of CREATION, be that an artist's or God's creation. A sense of play relevant to the previous ones is that of a dramatic performance. Another one is that of freedom of movement (typically applied to objects), and freedom of action or thought, as in "the full play of the mind." Still another is that of ACTION, activity, or operation, as in "the play of fancy."

The notion of *language-game* is discussed in this dictionary under EXISTENTIALISM, together with that of *world-game*, in discussing the views of the German philosopher Martin Heidegger (CE 1889–1976). As for that of the *game of existence* or *life game*, it was significantly developed by the Dutch philosopher and historian of culture Johan Huizinga (CE 1872–1945), who held that play is an independent function, not only of humans, but also of all living entities. He argues that play is something free, superfluous, that tends to create order (hence its association with beauty), separate from ordinary life (from which it seeks to escape), hence springing from tension and accompanied by uncertainty. Huizinga also holds that these features make play a cultural phenomenon displayed in institutions ranging from art, through the law, to war, and in such activities as philosophy and science. This all-encompassing nature of play makes it possible to talk of cultures that displayed a greater or lesser degree of play. For example, the significance of play was high in medieval life, reaching its peak in the Renaissance. Arguably, it grew in significance during the twentieth century, but its significance was low in the nineteenth century, which Huizinga considered an essentially serious century.

See also: aesthetics; metaphysics; myth; philosophy of religion

Further reading

Huizinga, Johan (1998) *Homo Ludens: A Study of the Play-Element in Culture*, reprint, London: Routledge.

Marin, Louis (1990 [1984]) *Utopics: The Semiological Play of Textual Spaces*, Atlantic Highlands, NJ: Humanities Press International.

Vyas, Ramnarayan (1992) *Philosophy, Physics, and the Cosmic Play*, Delhi: Ajanta Books International.

pleasure *see* Epicureanism; ethics

pleasure, katastematic *see* Epicureanism

pleasure, kinetic *see* Epicureanism

pleasure, principle of *see* ethics

plenitude, principle of *see* chain of being

pluralism *see* metaphysics

plurality of causes *see* causal law

plurality of forms *see* Thomism

pneuma *see* Stoicism

pneumata *see* metaphysics

pneumatica *see* metaphysics

pneumatologia *see* metaphysics

pneumatosophia *see* metaphysics

poetics *see* aesthetics

poetry *see* aesthetics

poiesis *see* ethics

point events *see* process philosophy

polarity *see* dialectic

policies *see* philosophy, sociopolitical

policy-makers *see* philosophy, sociopolitical

policy-making *see* philosophy, sociopolitical

polis *see* Greek philosophy

Polish logic *see* logic

Polish notation *see* logic

political constraints *see* philosophy, sociopolitical

political evaluation process *see* philosophy, sociopolitical

political philosophy *see* philosophy, sociopolitical

political savvy *see* philosophy, sociopolitical

political theory *see* philosophy, sociopolitical

political variable in competitive situations *see* decision

politics *see* philosophy, sociopolitical

polity *see* philosophy, sociopolitical

polyadic *see* degree

polysemy *see* ambiguity

polysyllogism *see* syllogism

pons asinorum *see* syllogism

Port Royal logic *see* Cartesianism

position, self-defeating *see* logic

positional qualities *see* quality

positive duty *see* ethics

positive feedback *see* cybernetics

positive freedom *see* philosophy, sociopolitical

positive law *see* philosophy of law

positive morality *see* philosophy of law

positivism A family of philosophies that gives precedence to science and its methods. Like the German philosopher Johann Gottfried von Herder (CE 1776–1841), who had held that evolution depends on adaptation, and formulated a notion of progress suggesting that higher and later stages depended on lower and earlier ones, the French philosopher and founder of positivism Auguste Comte (CE 1798–1857) applied evolutionary ideas to the study of cultural and historical change, suggesting that the highest and latest stage was scientific.

In the twentieth century, however, there was a rebirth of positivism, but the type of positivism that flourished then was *empirical* or *logical positivism*, which, to distinguish it from nineteenth-century – especially *Comtean* – positivism, is sometimes called *neo-positivism*. A criterion closely associated with twentieth-century positivism and central to the *verifiability theory of meaning* and to *verificationism* or the *doctrine of verification* – the doctrine that the meaning of a statement is its method(s) of verification – is the *verifiability criterion of meaning* (also called the *principle of verifiability*) according to which sentences are meaningful if, and only if, they can be empirically verified. It should be noted that while early verificationism was reductionist, contemporary verificationism is neutral on whether verification is holistic or not. Also, as formulated by the contemporary philosopher Michael Dummett, verificationism is a constraint on the notion of truth, not a criterion of meaningfulness.

Neo-positivist formulations of verificationism at the beginning of the twentieth century

led to a revival of *phenomenalism*. This doctrine, whose name derives from the Greek *phainomenon*, i.e. "appearance," traditionally asserted that we know only phenomena or appearances, and that there is nothing behind the phenomena which causes their appearance. Versions of it were formulated by some of the British Empiricists, arguably by the British philosopher John Stuart Mill (CE 1806–73) when he conceived of matter as a permanent possibility of sensation, and by many representatives of Kantian philosophy. In the twentieth century, with the verifiability criterion of meaning, positivism became associated with the doctrine that propositions asserting the existence of physical objects mean the same thing as propositions asserting that observers would have certain complicated series of sensations – say, seeing a bird eat from a feeder, turn its head, fly away – were they to have certain other sensations – say, first seeing a bird land on the feeder.

Twentieth-century positivism, both empirical and logical, has been developed primarily at the Vienna Circle, the Warsaw School or Warsaw Circle, and, in Scandinavia, at the Oslo School or Oslo Group and the Uppsala School. The Argentine philosopher Alejandro Korn (CE 1860–1936) – who in many ways followed the thought of an opponent of positivism, the French philosopher Henri Bergson (CE 1859–1941) – tried to synthesize positivism with the idea of freedom and value upheld by its opponents. Korn considered this *spiritualized positivism* to be a refinement on native Argentine versions of positivism developed after independence (see BERGSONIANISM; LATIN AMERICAN PHILOSOPHY).

The Vienna Circle was most influential in twentieth-century positivism. It was constituted by philosophers who met periodically in Vienna between 1922 and 1938. Most notable among its members were the German philosopher Rudolf Carnap (CE 1891–1970), the Austro-Hungarian philosopher Herbert Feigl (CE 1902–88), the Austrian philosopher Otto Neurath (CE 1882–1945), the German-Austrian philosopher Moritz Schlick (CE 1882–1936), and the Vienna-born Austrian-English philosopher Friedrich Waismann (CE 1896–1959).

The Vienna Circle proposed a conception of scientific knowledge that was free from the need to receive justification from a philosophical epistemology. It conceived of empirical theories as logical structures of statements that were empirically accountable by reference to their predictions (i.e. inferences to the future based on present data), which could be checked by observations.

Reviving an interest in the unity of science that could be traced back to Ancient atomism and the Enlightenment, the Vienna Circle held that these theories formed a coherent system called *unified science*. Also, it held that the analysis of the logical form of expressions made it possible to determine their combined value, and it adopted the verifiability criterion or principle. Along these lines, for example, Carnap introduced the notions of a *state description*, i.e. the linguistic counterpart of a possible world, and a *structure description*, i.e. a set of state descriptions.

The verifiability principle, however, was not sufficiently precise, which eventually led Waismann to coin the notion of *open texture*, i.e. the possibility of vagueness, arguing that vagueness always remains regardless of how many efforts are made to make expressions precise, because, for example, not all possible vagueness is foreseen or foreseeable at the time of such efforts. He concluded that this explains why empirical statements are not conclusively verifiable. Analogously, the German philosopher Hans Reichenbach (CE 1891–1953), who originally had been a member of the Berlin Group (which included such philosophers as Kurt Grelling, Richard von Mises, and Walther Dubislav), distanced himself from the more radical positivist tenets, arguing that those propositions that are verified indirectly have surplus meaning, i.e. meaning over and above any traceable, observable consequences.

The Warsaw Circle was centered in Warsaw and Lvov and maintained relations with the Vienna Circle. Notable among its members were the Polish logician Jan Lukasiewicz (CE 1878–1956), the Russian philosopher and logician Stanislaw Lesniewski (CE 1884–1939), and the Polish philosopher Tadeusz Kotarbinski (CE 1886–1981). The last advocated *reism* or *concretism*, i.e. the doctrine that there are only concrete individual objects. In the philosophy of language, this takes the form of *semantic* reism, i.e. only the names of concrete objects point to real objects. In the philosophy of mind, the doctrine is *ontological* reism or *physicalism*, but Kotarbinski called it *somatism*. It is also called *pansomatism*. Lesniewski formulated a logic based on the *prototethic*, i.e. a theory of first principles where equivalence is the only undefined term. The protothetic led to a propositional logic enriched with quantifiers and functorial variables, and this led to a theory of name variables, and a theory of part–whole relations. Lukasiewicz formulated a three-valued logic, developed Polish notation, and used modern logic to study Aristotelian and Stoic logic.

Members of the Uppsala School – most notably, Axel Hägerström (CE 1868–1939) – have primarily focused on the concepts of science, while philosophers at the Oslo Group – most notably, the contemporary philosopher Arne Naess – have focused on the development of a theory of interpretation.

See also: empiricism;   epistemology;   logic; philosophy of science

Further reading
Comte, Auguste (1957) *A General View of Positivism*, New York: R. Speller.
Friedman, Michael (1999) *Reconsidering Logical Positivism*, Cambridge: Cambridge University Press.
Weinberg, Julius Rudolph (1950 [1936]) *An Examination of Logical Positivism*, London: Routledge & Kegan Paul.

positivism, legal *see* philosophy of law

possibility *see* alethiology; *de re*, under de

possible-world semantics *see* alethiology; *de re*, under de

possible worlds *see* alethiology; *de re*, under de

post hoc, ergo propter hoc *see* fallacy

post rem realism *see* Thomism

post rem universals *see* Thomism

postcard paradox *see* paradox

post-complete *see* completeness

postmodern *see* Continental philosophy

postmodernism *see* Continental philosophy

postpraedicamenta *see* category

postpredicaments *see* category

poststructuralism *see* Continental philosophy; deconstruction

postulate *see* axiom

postulate set *see* categoricity

potential *see* act

potentiality *see* act

potentiality, first *see* act

potentiality, second *see* act

pour soi *see* existentialism

poverty of philosophy *see* Marxism

poverty of the stimulus *see* philosophy of language

power set *see* set

power, will to *see* ethics

p-predicates *see* metaphysics

practical attitude *see* syllogism

practical ethics *see* ethics

practical imperative *see* Kantian philosophy

practical judgment *see* akrasia

practical logic *see* logic

practical rationality *see* Kantian philosophy; rationality

practical reason *see* Kantian philosophy

practical reasoning *see* syllogism

practical syllogism *see* syllogism

practical wisdom *see* ethics

practition *see* logic

practitioners and practical ethics *see* ethics

praedicabilia *see* definition

praedicamenta *see* category

pragmatic ambiguity *see* ambiguity

pragmatic contradiction *see* logic

pragmatic maxim *see* pragmatism

pragmatic theory of truth *see* truth

pragmatics *see* philosophy of language

pragmatism The United States philosopher Charles Sanders Peirce (CE 1839–1914) introduced the term *pragmatism* in 1878 to designate the name of his theory of meaning, whose criterion of meaning was the pragmatic maxim. Initially, the maxim said that the meaning of a conception was the sum of the consequences that might conceivably result by necessity from the conception's truth. Later, Peirce revised it to allow for counterfactual conceptions such as sugar never put to the test of solubility in water. Also, he later changed the name of his philosophy to *pragmaticism*, because the previous term had been extended by the United States philosopher William James (CE 1842–1910) to a theory of action, instead of being used for a theory of meaning as Peirce intended.

Peirce's conception emphasizes the notion of a *community of inquiry*, i.e. the unlimited community constituted by the unlimited or indefinite generations of inquirers who would engage in the, in principle, unending critical scrutiny of views formulated for testing in science. Even though individual humans and groups are fallible, humans need not give up hope of finding truth, goodness, and beauty. For inquiry, especially scientific inquiry, is self-corrective and, in the long run, falsities; wrong actions; morally objectionable traits of character; faulty policies, practices, and institutions; and ugliness will be recognized and discarded in favor of believing TRUTH (where the real or the fact or the truth is what is then believed), upholding goodness, and sensing beauty. This is Peirce's doctrine of *agapism*.

Some important concepts in Peirce's characterization of this process are based on his notion that sign relations are triadic, involving the *sign* or *representamen*, its OBJECT (or what it stands for), and an *interpretant* (or meaning) that determines how the sign stands for the object. Peirce distinguished three divisions of signs based on the character of the sign, the relation between the sign and its object, and how the interpretant represents the object. The first division includes a *qualisign* or *First*, i.e. a mere appearance; a *sinsign* or *token*, or *Second*, i.e. an individual object or event; and a *legisign* or *Third*, i.e. a general type. According to the second division, a sign can be an *icon* by denoting an object on the basis of its similarity to it; and *index* by being in some causal or dynamic relation to the object; or a *symbol* by being based on convention. In the third division, signs are *rhemes*, i.e. predicative; *propositional*, i.e. propositions; and *arguments*. Ten classes of signs are characterized: qualisign (any sensation); icon sinsign (a diagram); rhematic indexical sinsign (for example, a sudden cry); dicent sinsign (say, a weathervane); iconic legisign (a diagram abstracted from its embodiment); rhematic symbol (a common noun); rhematic indexical legisign (a demonstrative pronoun); dicent indexical legisign (a street cry); dicent symbol (a proposition); argument (a syllogism).

The United States philosopher Clarence Irving Lewis (CE 1883–1964) formulated a version of pragmatism and empiricism strongly influenced by Kantian ideas. Significant in this regard is his concept of *congruence*: the relation of a certain empirical judgment (e.g. that the janitor is on the other side of the door) with a collection of justified judgments (e.g. that one just saw the janitor, and that he said he was waiting for us to leave in order to clean the room), whereby the said empirical judgment acquires a degree of justification.

In ethics and the philosophy of religion, the United States philosopher William James (CE 1842–1910) formulated pragmatic approaches to the ethics of belief that have been discussed elsewhere in this dictionary (see FAITH).

A form of pragmatism has been *fictionalism*, which holds the sciences provide general rules (of which physical laws are particular cases), but are neither true nor false but convenient or inconvenient *fictions* – useful or useless fantasies – whereby the physical world is treated as if it were or behaved in accordance with these fictions (see PHILOSOPHY OF SCIENCE).

There is a certain connection between this view and that of the French philosopher and historian of science Michel Foucault (CE 1926–84). He said that social ideologies are neither true nor false, but fictions whose symbolic and motivational functions make them useful or useless for a variety of social purposes such as the attainment of social cohesiveness or the securing of support for policies, practices, or institutions. These fictions are not to be confused with physical states of affairs or events in ideal conditions, i.e. never quite actualized, though not physically impossible conditions. For the latter are hypothetical conditions describing limiting cases – perhaps infinitely approached but never completely actualized – conditions, while fictions are assumed not to be part of the physical world at all.

The United States philosopher John Dewey (CE 1859–1952) first formulated *instrumentalism*, a type of pragmatism, during the first part of the twentieth century. He held that concepts and ideas are instruments aimed at integrating, predicting, and controlling our interactions with the world we experience. Inquiry begins when the situations we experience are conflictive, disturbing, confusing, unclear, ambiguous, or indeterminate. Inquiry aims at dealing with these features of the situation. However, with experience we begin, and to experience we return. There is no final end in nature or by convention. Instead, there is a *means–ends continuum*, where the ends we pursue are final until achieved, then becoming means for further projected ends.

Sometimes, pragmatism has been associated with *meliorism* (from the Latin *melior*, i.e. "better"), the doctrine that human beings, while incapable of perfection, are capable of an unending series of improvements. This doctrine had been advocated by the United States philosopher Paul Carus (CE 1852–1919) in his *Monism and Meliorism*, where he suggests humans' mission is to improve the world. It is hard to find texts of pragmatist philosophers upholding this view, except perhaps for some works of William James, where he, like Carus, advocates the human mission to improve the world. These texts appear to have been the reason for characterizing pragmatism as meliorism.

Various contemporary versions of pragmatism have been formulated, perhaps most notably by the United States philosopher Richard Rorty in his *Consequences of Pragmatism* and other works where he discusses modern philosophy's features and shortcomings, and seeks to outline new prospects for philosophy and, in general, intellectual activities.

See also: empiricism; epistemology; ethics; faith; logic; meaning; philosophy of language; positivism; truth

Further reading

Buchler, Justus (1955) *Philosophical Writings of Peirce*, New York: Dover.
Copleston, Frederick Charles (1994) *Empiricism, Idealism, and Pragmatism in Britain and America*, New York: Doubleday.
Gouinlock, James (1976) *The Moral Writings of John Dewey*, London and New York: Collier Macmillan and Hafner Press.
James, William (1956) *The Will to Believe and Other Essays in Popular Philosophy, and Human Immortality*, New York: Dover.
Kennedy, Gail (1950) *Pragmatism and American Culture*, Boston: C.D. Heath.
Rescher, Nicholas (2000) *Realistic Pragmatism: An Introduction to Pragmatic Philosophy*, Albany, NY: State University of New York Press.
Rorty, Richard (1982) *Consequences of Pragmatism*, Minneapolis: University of Minnesota Press.

Prague School of linguistics *see* philosophy of language

Prajna *see* Buddhism

prakriti *see* Hinduism

praxiology *see* philosophy of mind

praxis *see* Marxism

Praxis School *see* Marxism

preanalytic *see* theory

precising definition *see* definition

precision *see* ambiguity

precognition *see* philosophy of mind

preconscious *see* psychoanalysis

pre-critical *see* Kantian philosophy

predestination *see* determinism

predicables *see* definition

predicaments *see* category

predicate *see* logic

predicate calculus *see* logic

predicate hierarchy *see* ordering

predicate logic *see* logic

predication *see* quality

predicative *see* theory of types

prediction paradox *see* paradox

predictions *see* philosophy of history; philosophy of science; positivism

pre-emptive causation *see* causal law

pre-established harmony *see* metaphysics

pre-existence *see* myth

preface paradox *see* paradox

preference *see* ethics

preference logics *see* decision

preferential treatment *see* ethics

prehensions *see* process philosophy

prejudice *see* culture; ethics

premise *see* logic

premise, major *see* syllogism

premise, minor *see* syllogism

prenex normal form *see* logic

prepredicative *see* phenomenology

prescriptive meaning *see* meaning

prescriptivism *see* ethics

present *see* philosophy of science

Presocratics *see* Greek philosophy

presupposition *see* meaning

preternatural *see* philosophy of mind

pretheoretical *see* theory

prima-facie duty *see* ethics

prima-facie evidence *see* justification

prima-facie justification *see* justification

prima-facie reasons *see* justification

prima-facie right *see* ethics

primary process *see* psychoanalysis

primary qualities *see* quality

primary substances *see* abstract

prime matter *see* chain of being

prime mover *see* chain of being

primitive *see* culture

primitive concept *see* theory

primitive symbol *see* logic; theory

primitivism *see* culture

principium individuationis *see* identity

principle, difference *see* ethics; justice

principle, generalization *see* ethics

principle, liberty *see* ethics; justice

principle of beneficence *see* ethics

principle of bivalence *see* logic

principle of charity *see* meaning

principle of compensatory justice *see* ethics

principle of consequences *see* ethics

principle of conservation *see* philosophy of science

principle of contributive justice *see* ethics

principle of determinism *see* induction

principle of distributive justice *see* ethics

principle of dominance *see* paradox

principle of double effect *see* abortion; war

principle of economy *see* nominalism

principle of formal justice *see* ethics; justice

principle of generic consistency *see* ethics

principle of indifference *see* probability

principle of insufficient reason *see* chain of being

principle of limited variety *see* induction

principle of logical form *see* logic

principle of maximizing expected utility *see* ethics; utilitarianism

principle of non-contradiction *see* logic

principle of parsimony *see* nominalism

principle of perfection *see* perfection

principle of plenitude *see* chain of being

principle of proportionality *see* war

principle of sufficient reason *see* chain of being

principle of the anomalism of the mental *see* philosophy of mind

principle of the conservation of matter *see* philosophy of science

principle of uncertainty *see* philosophy of science

principle of universality *see* ethics

principle of universalizability *see* ethics

principle of unlimited comprehension *see* set

principle of utility *see* ethics; utilitarianism

principle of verifiability *see* positivism

principles, ethical *see* ethics

prior probability *see* probability

priority, conceptual *see* conceptualism

prisca theologica *see* Neoplatonism

prisoner's dilemma *see* decision

privacy *see* ethics

privacy, epistemic *see* epistemology

private language *see* philosophy of language; epistemology

privation *see* ethics; philosophy of religion

privilege *see* philosophy of law

privileged access *see* epistemology

pro attitudes *see* philosophy of mind

proactive *see* philosophy, sociopolitical

probabilism *see* probability

probabilistic automaton *see* computer theory

probabilistic causation *see* causal law

probabilistic disposition *see* disposition

probabilistic independence *see* probability

probabilistic law *see* causal law

probability From the Latin *probabilitas*, and this from the Latin *probabilis* ("capable of standing a test") and the particle *-tas*, where *probabilis* derived from *probāre* ("to test" or "to prove"), the term probability denotes a measure of the degree to which items such as events, states of affairs, objects and propositions should be expected to occur (if events), take place (if states of affairs), exist (if objects), or be true (if propositions).

There are abstract formalizations of probability and interpretations of probability. The most common abstract formulation involves three axioms for the probability functions Pr. First, $Pr(x) \geqslant 0$ for all x. Second, $Pr(x)=1$ if x is necessary. Third, $Pr(x \text{ v } y)=Pr(x)+Pr(y)$, where '$v$' means the inclusive disjunction of logic or union as in set theory. The third axiom, called *finite additivity*, can be generalized to *countable additivity*, where the function Pr ranges over infinite disjunctions or unions. *Conditional* probability, or $Pr(x/y)$, is the quotient $Pr(x\&y)/Pr(y)$. An item x is *positively statistically* (or *probabilistically*) correlated with an item y if $Pr(x/y)$ is greater than $Pr(x/-y)$, where $-y$ is the negation of a proposition y, the non-occurrence of an event y, or the complement of y in set theory. An item x is *negatively statistically* (or *probabilistically*) *correlated* with an item y if $Pr(x/y)$ is less than $Pr(x/-y)$, where, as before, $-y$ is the negation of a proposition y, the non-occurrence of an event y, or the complement of y in set theory. As for *probabilistic independence* (or *statistical independence*), if $Pr(x/y)=Pr(x/-y)$, then x is statistically (or probabilistically) independent of y. This abstract formulation leads to a variety of theorems, e.g. $Pr(-x)=1-Pr(x)$. An important probability theorem is the *first-limit theorem* (see *ars conjectandi* under ARS).

There are various interpretations of probability: classical, relative frequency, propensity, logical, and subjective. The *classical* interpretation holds that the probability of an event e is equal to a ratio: the number of *equipossibilities*, or *equipossible* or *equiprobable events* – i.e. events having the same probability – that are favorable to the event e divided by the total number of relevant equipossibilities. Here, as in other versions of probability that apply to particular events, the *principle of indifference*

is assumed: if the weight of reasons favoring one event is equal to the weight of reasons favoring another, then both events have the same probability. This principle can be extended even when probabilities are supposed to apply to sets of events: if the weight of reasons favoring one set of events equals the weight of reasons favoring another set of events, then both sets of events have the same probability.

The *relative-frequency* interpretation or relative-frequency theory applies not to particular events but to sets of events in a class called the reference class as follows: if R is the reference class, and n is the number of events in R, and m is the number of events of a kind K within R, then the probability of K relative to R is m/n. A problem arising here is the *problem of the single case*, i.e. that single items are often supposed to be probable, yet the relative frequency interpretation applies only to sets of items. This has prompted the *propensity* interpretation, which holds that probability is a somewhat primitive measure of the propensity or disposition of a kind of conditions to yield an outcome of a given type, or a frequency of such type of outcome in the long run. Since dispositions are not identical with – indeed, can exist in the absence of – corresponding outcomes, and serve to explain any outcomes and their frequencies: the problem of the single case is avoided.

The classical, relative-frequency, and propensity interpretations are sometimes called *objective* or *statistical*, or *empirical* probability. They all involve a concept of probability according to which the values of probability depend on what actually happens. It is contrasted with *subjective* probability (also called *epistemic* probability), i.e. where the probability of a proposition is the degree of belief or partial belief in it given our background knowledge, and with *logical* probability, where the probability of a proposition q given a proposition p is the degree to which p logically entails q, where the non-traditional notion of degrees of entailment is introduced. In addition, there is the notion of *plausibility* (from the Latin *plausibilis*, i.e. "deserving applause"), which does not entail an actual, not even partial, degree of belief but merely semblance of truth

– or truthlikeness or verisimilitude – or possibility of belief, given our background beliefs. That is, to say that a person, object, or event is plausible is to say that its existence or occurrence fits well with our background beliefs about the world, regardless of whether it is indeed real or of how likely it is to exist or happen. This is why fictional characters and events in literature (or for that matter in cases used in philosophical discussions) can be plausible, thereby making the fictional works in which they appear believable (and the philosophical examples convincing). *Plausibility* or *verisimilitude*, or, as the Austrian philosopher Karl Popper (CE 1902–94) called it, *truthlikeness*, combines truth with information content, hence is different from probability, which increases with lack of content. Popper tried to characterize truthlikeness by means of set theory. More recent attempts have been based on the notion of similarity of a statement, understood as the distance from a state of affairs allowed or assumed to be true by the statement.

The interrelated notions of *prior* probability and *posterior* probability are used to update probabilities given new data. They are involved in *Bayes' theorem*, a set of relations between prior and posterior probabilities or odds, where prior probabilities are supposed to be established on the basis of observed frequencies. The applicability of these relations has been criticized on the grounds that prior probabilities are either inaccessible or insignificant. The German logician and philosopher Rudolf Carnap (CE 1891–1970) thought along these lines, but added that, in conditioning on the evidence, one should do so on one's total evidence. This is known as the *rule of total evidence*.

In applying probabilities, the nature of a *sample* – a subclass of the general class about which probability statements are made – is crucial. One wants a *fair* or *representative* sample, i.e. a sequence of items – the sample members – that mirrors the said general class. There is no certainty that one has a fair sample, but there are tests for making it likely that one does. For example, one can use *randomization*, which is to try to get a *random* sample, i.e. a sample such that each member of the general class has an equal chance of being

in the sample (see randomness, below). Also, one can try to increase sample size. One can also use *stratification*, i.e. subdivide the observational information by reference to different significant features, say, age, marital status, and religious denomination in studying attitudes about abortion.

The concept of randomization implies that of randomness. Subjectivist interpretations of randomness focus on an individual's inability to predict future occurrences on the basis of the sample available to the individual. Objectivist interpretations require that the probability be the same in the general class and any samples of this class that are selected through a mechanical procedure. Indeed, some characterize the randomness of such samples as passing every effective statistical test for randomness. Besides, there have been attempts to characterize the objective randomness of a sample on the basis of the following feature: the computer programs needed to generate the sample are made up of sequences of steps that are as long as the sequence of sample members.

A *random* process or *stochastic* process is a process that changes probabilistically, not deterministically, through time. This mathematical notion has been applied to the study of epidemics, soil erosion, and metal fatigue, i.e. the spread of cracks in metals.

In addition to these notions, there is the doctrine of *probabilism*, which is often attributed to the Spanish theologian Bartolomeo Medina (CE 1527–89), who held that, for an opinion to be probable, it is not enough that there are seemingly good reasons and many people supporting it, because, otherwise, all errors would be probable. He held that for an opinion to be probable, wise persons must support it with excellent reasons.

A frequently mentioned puzzle concerning probabilities is the *Dutch book*: a bet or combination of bets whereby the bettor is bound to suffer a net loss regardless of the outcome. An example is the bet that the horse Penny Post will win the race at odds 3:2 combined with a bet that the horse Penny Post will lose the race at the same odds. Either way, the bettor would lose one dollar.

This concept has been used in the *Dutch-book argument* that a rational person's degrees of belief must be in accordance with the axioms of the probability calculus because, otherwise, the person would be vulnerable to a Dutch book, i.e. to an incoherent set of odds whereby the person would lose come what may. The notion is also used in the related *Dutch-book theorem*: a person who both bets on proposition *p* as fair if the odds conform to the person's degree of belief in *p*, and is also willing to make any combination of bets that would individually be considered fair, is vulnerable to a Dutch book.

See also: epistemology; logic; philosophy of mathematics

Further reading

Harper, William L. (1987) *Foundations of Probability Theory, Statistical Inference, and Statistical Theories of Science*, Boston, MA: Kluwer Academic.

Von Plato, Jan (1998) *Creating Modern Probability: Its Mathematics, Physics, and Philosophy in Historical Perspective*, Cambridge, UK and New York: Cambridge University Press.

Weatherford, Roy (1982) *Philosophical Foundations of Probability Theory*, London and Boston: Routledge & K. Paul.

problem of evil *see* philosophy of religion

problem of induction *see* induction

problem of other minds *see* philosophy of mind; solipsism

problem of the criterion *see* epistemology

problem of the single case *see* probability

problem of the speckled hen *see* perception

problematic judgment *see* Kantian philosophy

problematic modality *see* alethiology

problematicismo *see* philosophy

procedural justice *see* justice

procedural principles *see* ethics; justice

proceduralism *see* philosophy of law

procedure, social decision *see* philosophy, sociopolitical

process *see* process philosophy

process philosophy A philosophical position formulated by the British philosopher Alfred North Whitehead (CE 1861–1947), in its final form in his *Process and Reality*, which has influenced not just philosophical inquiry but theology, where any position strongly influenced by process philosophy is called *process theology*. Whitehead himself called this position *philosophy of organism*. Central to this position is the philosophical category Whitehead calls *actual occasion* or *actual entity* (e.g. God or any existing item), understood not as an enduring, substantial entity, but as a process whereby our unconscious registering of the immediate past is woven together. Whitehead identified each actual entity with this process, which he called *concrescence*. He coined the term *fallacy of misplaced concreteness* to denote the mistake of considering mind and matter to be ontological ultimates.

For Whitehead, a *connection* or *nexus* is an emergent actual occasion that combines other actual occasions through *prehensions* or primitive acts of feeling, or taking account of the universe, which involve not-conscious awareness. Whitehead classifies such prehensions in four categories: *physical*, i.e. by an actual occasion of another actual occasion; *conceptual*, i.e. by an actual occasion of an eternal object; *positive*, i.e. an actual occasion's making what is prehended part of itself; or *negative*, reflecting the universe from the standpoint of the actual occasion.

In the process, actual occasions atomize the *extensive continuum* (the four-dimensional space–time manifold where events occur and objects interrelate), but also add to it. In fact, besides division and aggregation so that, for example, the space–time manifold's ultimate particles are *point-events*, i.e. points of instantaneous space, the extensive continuum also includes qualitative changes that amount to novelty. To account for such a novelty, as well as on the retention of novelties, and relying on the ontological principle – actual entities are the only reasons – Whitehead posited a divine being, God, whose nature, he argued, accounted for the fact that the world always involves new possibilities.

Part of Whitehead's aim in formulating process philosophy is to derive scientific concepts from nature, by which he means the world as presented to our awareness. He does talk of percipient events meaning the relevant states of the percipients' bodies; however, the percipients' minds, as well as values, are excluded from this project.

See also: logic; metaphysics; philosophy of religion

Further reading
Emmet, Dorothy (1966) *Whitehead's Philosophy of Organism*, 2nd edn, London: Macmillan.
Kraus, Elizabeth M. (1998) *The Metaphysics of Experience: A Companion to Whitehead's Process and Reality*, 2nd edn, New York: Fordham University Press.
Rescher, Nicholas (1996) *Process Metaphysics: An Introduction to Process Philosophy*, Albany: State University of New York Press.

process–product ambiguity *see* ambiguity

process theology *see* process philosophy

process, social decision *see* philosophy, sociopolitical

production theory *see* philosophy of economics

productive reason *see* reason

professional ethics *see* ethics

programming languages *see* computer theory

programs, modal logic of *see* logic

progress *see* philosophy of history

projectible predicates *see* induction

projection *see* psychoanalysis

projectivism *see* passion

prolepsis *see* Epicureanism; Stoicism

proof and inference *see* deduction

proof by recursion *see* induction

proof, direct *see* logic

proof, finitary *see* philosophy of mathematics

proof, indirect *see* logic

proof-theoretic reflection principles *see* philosophy of mathematics

proof theory *see* philosophy of mathematics

propensity *see* probability

proper class *see* class

proper names, causal theory of *see* reference

proper sensibles *see* perception

proper symbol *see* syncategoremata

properties of terms, doctrine of *see* syncategoremata

property *see* quality

property, accidental *see* accident

property, Cambridge *see* change

property, consequential *see* supervenience

property, extrinsic *see* relation

property, impredicative *see* theory of types

property, intrinsic *see* relation

property, non-predicative *see* theory of types

property, phenomenal *see* quality

property, predicative *see* theory of types

proportionality, principle of *see* war

proposition *see* logic; philosophy of language

proposition, modal *see* alethiology

propositional attitude *see* philosophy of language

propositional calculus *see* logic

propositional knowledge *see* epistemology; knowledge

proprietates terminorum *see* syncategoremata

proprioception *see* perception

proprium *see* definition

prosyllogism *see* syllogism

Protestantism *see* Christianity

protocol statements *see* justification

protologia *see* metaphysics

proton pseudos *see* syllogism

protophilosophy *see* philosophy

protothetic *see* positivism

prototype theory *see* essentialism

providence *see* determinism; philosophy of religion

prudence *see* ethics

psychoanalysis A method invented by the Austrian medical psychologist Sigmund Freud (CE 1856–1939), aimed at determining the cause of neuroses and the means to their cure. Freud formulated a hypothesis about human nature – now called *deep psychology* – which, at least initially, characterized the psychological structure of a human being as involving three factors: the *id*, the source of the flow of the *libido* – i.e. sexual energy or drives – into our mental life; the *ego*, the center of rational awareness, self-preservation, and effective action; and the *superego*, the individual's conception – *internalization* – of society's pressures and requirements. That is, in Freud's theory, the term ego has a special meaning. It is an orderly self-image contrasted with the id – the set of often subconscious drives in an individual – and the superego – the social dos and don'ts an individual has internalized.

The *pleasure principle* or *Eros* guides the primary process of uninhibited discharge of energy from the id. Since tension is unpleasant, Freud sometimes writes as if what is sought is the absence of tension, hence the *Nirvana principle* associated with *Thanatos*, i.e. the death instinct or death wish he postulated in later writings. When the id and the superego strongly conflict in an individual – a matter established through the *reality principle* that calls attention to the actual constraints on the person's options – the ego and the superego get rid of the id's demands through an act of repression called the *censor*. That is, the reality principle guides this secondary process of repression and censorship.

The repressed drives are thus pushed into the person's *subconscious*, i.e. mental activity the person has but does not register, part of which is *preconscious*, i.e. absent from but capable of being readily brought into consciousness. The drives, however, retain their energy, influencing the person's conscious life in a variety of ways. Sometimes, *sublimation*, i.e. the channeling of these drives into socially acceptable displays, occurs. *Rationalization*,

the act of ascribing such things as one's acts and opinions to seemingly reasonable and conscious causes, where subconscious or preconscious causes actually operate, is another mechanism whose results are ambiguous. For Freud, these mechanisms all lead to creativity. When the repression–sublimation mechanism does not work, neurosis occurs. Among the most frequent examples of neuroses, Freud mentions the *Oedipus complex* or the sexual desire of a son for his mother, and the *Electra complex* or the sexual desire of a daughter for her father. Neuroses are supposed to be cured through psychoanalysis, a method whereby, with the help of an analyst, a person's subconscious is probed so that the content of the repressed drive is brought into consciousness. The assumption is that, once this happens, the content ceases to interfere with the person's thinking and behavior.

Freud often used the language of myths to formulate his theories. A myth that he adapted to psychoanalysis is that involved in the Polynesian notion of *taboo* (or *tabu*), which denotes a mysterious power thought to involve danger to oneself or one's group. Some taboos involve death and items associated with it, such as corpses and murderers; others blood and items associated with it, such as childbirth and menstruation. Other taboos involve sex and items associated with it, e.g. incest. Still other taboos involve strangers, chiefs, and priests. As indicated, Freud focused on death or the death instinct, which he mythologically called Thanatos, and on pleasure or the life instinct, which he mythologically called Eros.

One version of psychoanalysis, *analytical psychology*, is that founded by the Swiss psychologist Carl Gustav Jung (CE 1865–1961), according to whom there existed a *collective unconscious* – an inherited archive of archaic-mythic forms and figures – that was shared by all humans and on which the particular individual's unconscious that preoccupied Freud was based. These archetypal patterns are used in any *projection*, i.e. an individual's application of the archetypal patterns to the individual's world, and explain the relations of the individual to this world. Besides the archetypes, Jung points to unconscious pictorial elements such as the sun, the star, the snake, and the mandala, which he considers a symbol of the sought for unity of the self. Accordingly, since mandalas typically have four parts, Jung considers the *quaternium* – not the trinity – to be the symbol of wholeness. These doctrines did not easily fit the classical psychoanalytic framework and Jung's followers soon abandoned classical or Freudian psychoanalysis. They are sometimes called the (*psychoanalytic*) *Zürich School*, not to be confused with the (*philosophical*) *Zürich School*, whose most notable member was the French philosopher of science and literary analyst Gaston Bachelard (CE 1884–1962), and whose tenets were formulated in the journal *Dialectica*, which began publication in the Swiss city of Neuchâtel in 1947.

Freud's conception of the unconscious was most thoroughly formulated in his analysis of dreams where he distinguishes between the manifest content of a dream (the dream as dreamt or as remembered in waking) and its latent content (the unconscious dream-thoughts that, for Freud, could be made conscious through free association).

A notion predominant in psychoanalysis that has attained wide use in psychology and psychiatry is that of *fetish*. Its original meaning is religious, denoting any object regarded with awe, as having magical potency, or housing a powerful being. In psychoanalysis, as well as psychology and psychiatry, the term fetish has a sexual connotation, denoting any object – from a part of the body, to locks of hair, shoes, and underclothes – that causes an erotic response or fixation. The compulsion to use any object as a fetish in this sense is called *fetishism*.

Psychotherapy is the application of psychoanalytic principles and concepts to the identification of the causes of, and the treatment of, psychological disorders, including interrogation, the interpretation of gestures, signs, and symbols (which was associated with his work on humor and its relation to the unconscious), and the analysis of dreams.

Among contemporary writers, the French philosopher Jacques Lacan is notable for his conception of fiction as it relates to psychoanalysis. He holds the unconscious is structured like a language and the conscious ego is a fiction, the *image* – *imago* or *specular ego* – that begins to be developed early in childhood and, lacking the negative features of the actual ego, is an ideal, often what the mother wishes for the child. This symbolic stage is superseded by a stage dominated by apprehension towards the father as law-maker and speech-giver, leading to the child's aggressive tendencies engendered by the failure to come up to the ideal, which leads in turn to self-aggression, which needs to be subverted by therapy.

See also: Continental philosophy; epistemology; philosophy of mind; philosophy of science

Further reading
Farrell, B.A. (1994) *Philosophy and Psychoanalysis*, Toronto and New York: Macmillan College Pub. Co., Maxwell Macmillan Canada, and Maxwell Macmillan International.
Feigl, Herbert (ed.) (1964) *The Foundations of Science and the Concepts of Psychology and Psychoanalysis*, Minneapolis: University of Minnesota Press.
Grünbaum, Adolf (1993) *Validation in the Clinical Theory of Psychoanalysis: A Study in the Philosophy of Psychoanalysis*, Madison, CT: International Universities Press, Inc.
Levine, Michael P. (1999) *The Analytic Freud: Philosophy and Psychoanalysis*, London and New York: Routledge.

psychological behaviorism *see* behaviorism

psychological certainty *see* certainty

psychological continuity *see* identity

psychological eudaimonism *see* ethics

psychological hedonism *see* ethics

psychological immediacy *see* knowledge; philosophy of religion

psychological solipsism *see* solipsism

psychologism *see* phenomenology

psychology *see* philosophy of mind

psychology, analytical *see* psychoanalysis

psychology, philosophy of *see* philosophy of science

psychophysical identity *see* philosophy of science

psychophysical parallelism *see* philosophy of mind

psychophysics *see* philosophy of mind

public *see* philosophy, sociopolitical

punishment *see* philosophy of law

pure concept *see* Kantian philosophy

pure reason *see* Kantian philosophy

purusha *see* Hinduism

pūrva-mīmāṃsā *see* Hinduism

Pyrrhonism *see* skepticism

Pythagoreanism A term derived from the famous pre-Socratic philosopher Pythagoras (570?-495? BCE), which denotes pre-Socratic philosophers and scientists who tried to interpret the universe in terms of numbers.

Ancient Pythagoreans – or, simply Pythagoreans – are traditionally associated with the *School of Croton*, in what is now Southern Italy, flourishing during the sixth and fifth centuries BCE. Pythagoras had migrated there from the island of Samos off Asia Minor in 530 BCE. and, once in Croton, founded a school or sect that included esoteric initiation ceremonies, strict vows, a communal sharing of goods, a hierarchy of ranks through which one could progress from novitiate to full member, sexual equality in that both men and women could be members, and, apparently, among some of them, the practice of some form of vegetarianism. In a surge of populism or democratic feeling, the initial school was destroyed by angry townspeople sometime in the fifth century BCE, but the Pythagoreans founded new, widely separated communities, and became stronger than before.

Despite the fact that Pythagoras' fame grew exponentially as time went by, modern scholars have concluded that he was neither a mathematician, nor a scientist, nor a philosopher in any systematic sense of this term. He apparently, like the Greek philosopher Socrates (470–400 BCE), wrote nothing. Among the ideas Pythagoras is likely to have held, one, which he seems to have introduced, is the doctrine of *metempsychosis* or *transmigration of the soul*, or *reincarnation*, i.e. that the soul is immortal and is reborn in humans and other animals. He also seems to have believed that salvation was attained through metempsychosis in so far as one sought the truth. Such truth seekers were characterized by *philosophia*, from *philos*, i.e. "love of" (and this from *philia*: "the love associated with friendship"), and *sophia*, i.e. "wisdom." Indeed, Pythagoras is credited with having coined the term *philosophia*.

Concerning mathematics, he seems to have believed in the mythical power of number, as indicated by his school's apparent veneration for the *tetractys*, i.e. the tetrad constituted by the numbers one through four, which add up to the sacred number ten. He also seems to have held the doctrine of the *harmony of the spheres*, i.e. that the heavens move in accordance with numbers and produce music where the progression of tones is in accordance with numerical ratios. Given the startling properties of numbers, Pythagoreans sought analogies between their relations, and relations between other items. As a result, a Pythagorean table would be formulated listing basic principles or pairs of opposites. One such table included: limited–unlimited; even–odd; one–many; right–left; male–female; rest–movement; straight–curve; light–darkness; good–evil; square–oblong.

The Ancient Pythagoreans were mathematicians and philosophers who held two basic beliefs. First, they thought it possible to measure all relations by using natural numbers or their ratios. Second, given the previous belief, and the fact that they did not sharply, if at all, distinguish physics from mathematics, these mathematicians further believed that space, time, and motion could be measured on the basis of discrete, atomic units.

The discovery of irrational numbers such as the square root of two shattered the first belief. The paradoxes formulated by the Greek philosopher Zeno (see PARADOX) dramatized the collapse of the second belief. As a result, around the end of the fifth century, Greek mathematicians and philosophers began to draw distinctions between mathematics and physics that eventually led to what has come to be known as Euclidean geometry, because it was formulated in *The Elements* by the mathematician Euclid of Alexandria (third century BCE).

There was a resurgence of Pythagorean thought in the first century BCE, which also involved Platonic, Aristotelian, and Stoic ideas. It is traditionally called *neo-Pythagoreanism*, and lasted until the end of the second century CE. Various philosophers proceeded along these lines. One was the Greco-Roman philosopher Nigidius Figulus (first century BCE), who combined mystical and astrological ideas. Another was Apollonius of Tyana (CE first century), who considered humans to be citizens of the universe and in popularizing Pythagoreanism argued that there was a supreme god above all gods and that it did not require any sacrifices. A third was the Greek philosopher Moderatus of Gades (first century CE), who held numbers were principles. A fourth philosopher was the Arabia-born Nichomachus of Gerasa (second century CE), who held ideas were numbers that pre-existed in God's mind, and the One was the principle of reason and the divinity; and whose treatise on arithmetic was still used as late as the Renaissance. Finally, there was the Syrian philosopher Numenius of Apamea (second century CE), who is sometimes regarded as the founder of Neoplatonism and whose ideas include most of those later formulated by the Egypto-Roman philosopher and main Neoplatonic figure, Plotinus (CE 204–70). In any case, the philosophers of the Academy had been interpreting Platonism as an unfolding of Pythagoras' insights and, by the late third century CE – by the time of the Neoplatonist Iamblichus (c. CE 270–330), the main representative of the Syrian School – Pythagoreanism had become identified with Platonism. Eventually, any thinker who believed the universe was ordered in accordance with mathematical relations came to be called a Pythagorean or a neo-Pythagorean.

See also: esoterism; Greek philosophy; Neoplatonism; philosophy of mathematics; Platonism

Further reading

Boudouris, K.I. (1992) *Pythagorean Philosophy*, Athens: International Center for Greek Philosophy and Culture.

Kingsley, Peter (1995) *Ancient Philosophy, Mystery, and Magic: Empedocles and Pythagorean Tradition*, Oxford and New York: Clarendon Press and Oxford University Press.

Q

Q *see* logic

Qadarites *see* determinism

qarmatians *see* Neoplatonism

qiyās *see* Arabic philosophy

quadrivium *see* philosophy of education

quaestio *see* Scholasticism

quaestiones disputatae *see* Scholasticism

quaestiones quodlibetales *see* Scholasticism

quale *see* quality

qualia *see* quality

qualisign *see* pragmatism

qualitas ipsa cognitionis *see* quality

qualitative identity *see* identity

qualitative predicate *see* induction

quality A term derived the Middle English *qualityē*, and this, through Old French, from the Latin *quālitās*, a term equivalent to *qualis*, which meant "of what sort" or "of what kind." It is used, in general, as synonymous with property or attribute or, in the plural, *qualia*, which is the plural of *qualis* – from which *quale* is derived – a termed coined by the Roman philosopher Marcus Tullius Cicero (106–43 BCE) to translate the Greek *poion*.

The term quality has a variety of specific meanings. Sometimes, quality or qualis is used as synonymous with phenomenal property or qualitative feature. A related notion is that formulated as *qualitas ipsa cognitionis* by the Spanish neo-Scholastic philosopher Gabriel Vásquez (CE 1549–1604). *Qualitas ipsa cognitionis* is the quality of a conception (with emphasis on the idea) by contrast with *res cognita*, i.e. the thing known (with emphasis on the thing or reality). This distinction anticipated the modern distinction between idea and reality.

Qualities are divided into:

1 *primary*: physical properties or logical constructions of physical properties;
2 *secondary*: dispositions to produce sensory experiences of certain sorts under appropriate conditions;
3 *tertiary*: dispositions that are not secondary qualities, e.g. fragility.

Some thinkers, e.g. the English philosopher John Locke (CE 1632–1704), have held that colors, tastes, smells, sounds, and warmth and cold are secondary qualities; that is, not real in the sense of being independent of how they look under any circumstances. By contrast, *color realism* is the view that colors are either primary or tertiary qualities, i.e. that *x* is red is independent of whether it looks red under appropriate circumstances.

The notion is also advanced of *positional* qualities, i.e. qualities characterized by the relative positions of points in objects and their surroundings. Shape, size, motion, and rest are positional qualities.

One and the same quality can be described by means of more than one predication, i.e. by applying different predicates to the items supposed to have the quality. This is frequently exemplified by saying that one can say of the same item "this is water" and "this is H_2O." As a result, it makes sense to ask whether a certain quality is correctly described by means of a given predication, e.g. whether one should predicate of an item that it is water in the ordinary sense, or that it is H_2O in the chemistry sense. This is a matter of significance, not only because different predications are appropriate in different contexts, but also because, in some cases (e.g. sugar's disposition to dissolve in water), qualities (e.g. sugar's solubility) are defined on the basis of characteristics of predications used to describe them (e.g. the counterfactual conditional "if this sugar cube were placed in water, it would dissolve").

None of the preceding senses of the term quality should be confused with the sense it has in the SYLLOGISM.

See also: empiricism; epistemology; essentialism; metaphysics

Further reading
Bealer, George (1983 [1982]) *Quality and Concept*, Oxford: Clarendon.
Clark, Austen (1993) *Sensory Qualities*, Oxford and New York: Clarendon Press and Oxford University Press.
Goodman, Nelson (1990) *A Study of Qualities*, New York: Garland.

quantification *see* logic

quantification theory *see* logic

quantificational logic *see* logic

quantifier *see* logic

quantifier inference rules *see* logic

quantifier shift fallacy *see* fallacy

quantifying in *see* opacity

quantity *see* measurement; syllogism

quantum logic *see* logic

quantum physics *see* philosophy of science

quasi-indicator *see* reference

quasi-quotes *see* use–mention distinction

quaternio terminorum *see* syllogism

quaternity *see* psychoanalysis

queer theory *see* gender

quiddity *see* essentialism

quietism *see* Christianity

quinque viae *see* philosophy of religion

quinque voces *see* definition

quoad nos *see a parte rei*, under a; philosophy of religion

quodlibet *see* Scholasticism

Quran *see* Islam

R

R *see* relation

race *see* culture

racetrack paradox *see* paradox

racial discrimination *see* justice

racialization *see* identity

raciovitalismo *see* existentialism

racism *see* ethics

radical empiricism *see* empiricism

radical feminism *see* feminist philosophy

radical translation *see* philosophy of language

rajas *see* Hinduism

Rāmāyana *see* Hinduism

ramified type theory *see* theory of types

Ramist movement *see* ars disserendi, under ars

Ramsey-eliminability *see* model

Ramsey sentence *see* theory

random process *see* probability

randomization *see* probability

randomness *see* probability

rangatira *see* Māori philosophy

range *see* relation

rasa *see* Hinduism

ratio scales *see* measurement

rational agent *see* rationality

rational being *see* rationality

rational-choice theory *see* decision

rational number *see* philosophy of mathematics

rational person *see* rationality

rational psychology *see* philosophy of mind

rational reconstruction *see* empiricism

rationalism From the Latin *ratio*, i.e. "reason," the term *rationalism* denotes either an epistemological, a psychologico-evaluative, or a metaphysical doctrine; or, quite frequently, a combination of these. *Epistemologically*, rationalism holds that reason either supersedes other things – e.g. sense-experience – or, more radically, is the only way, in the acquisition of knowledge and formulation of sound explanations and justifications. In this sense, rationalism is contrasted with EMPIRICISM understood as the doctrine that information gained from the senses is the sole or primary source of knowledge and justified belief attainable by humans and, arguably, other animals.

The latter notion of empiricism is different from that of empiricism understood as the doctrine that there are no innate ideas, i.e. general truths that are in the mind from birth. Rationalists can hold, and some have held, that there are no innate ideas.

Psychologically, rationalism holds that reason, understood as the ability to reflect and understand, i.e. the intellectual side of some agents, is superior to emotion or the will in evaluation and decision-making. In this psychologico-evaluative sense, rationalism is identified with intellectualism and contrasted with voluntarism and emotivism (see VOLUNTARISM; ETHICS).

Metaphysically, rationalism is the doctrine that reality is basically structured according to rational principles. In this sense, it is usually contrasted with *irrationalism* understood as the doctrine that all or part of reality either lacks any logic, i.e. it is sheer chaos; or is unknowable, e.g. in the case of items purportedly incapable of being apprehended through any means; or both lacks any logic and is unknowable.

When used concerning Ancient Greece's philosophers, rationalism is used to characterize, for example, the Platonic and Neoplatonic doctrine that knowledge is knowledge of the Forms, not of the imperfect actualization of those Forms we can attain in the ordinary world. In this sense, rationalism is used at least epistemologically and metaphysically. Epistemologically, it is contrasted with a kind of empiricism that was much less radical than later empiricist positions, for example with the Aristotelian view that, however non-exclusively, knowledge to some extent relies on experience. While metaphysically, it is contrasted with irrationalism or, in Platonic terms, chaos.

There are modified uses of the term rationalism that restrict its scope. For example, the expression *continental rationalism* uses the term rationalism epistemologically to denote seventeenth-century CARTESIANISM. Similarly, the phrase *Continental rationalists* denotes all Cartesian philosophers, most notably René Descartes (CE 1596–1650), Baruch Spinoza (CE 1632–77), Nicolas Malebranche (CE 1638–1715), and Gottfried Wilhelm Leibniz (CE 1646–1716).

In addition, the philosophers of the ENLIGHTENMENT were called rationalists, and their philosophy was considered an instance of rationalism in the epistemological sense, though, in this case, the meaning was somewhat different, namely that of following new rather than traditional knowledge and methods.

In the nineteenth century, as a result of Hegelian influences, rationalism became largely associated with idealism. Some twentieth-century philosophers, especially certain Italian

thinkers whose philosophical approaches can be characterized as positivistic, empiricist, or analytic, have used the term neo-rationalism to denote their approach. Notable among these is Ludovico Geymonat in his *Studi per un nuovo razionalismo* (CE 1945) and *Saggi di filosofia neorazionalistica* (CE 1953). In addition to these, other philosophers have been thought to exemplify neo-rationalism. Some are neo-Kantians – especially neo-Friesians – by contrast with phenomenologists. Others are Western Marxists, who opposed contemporary irrationalist tendencies, e.g. Georg Lukács (CE 1885–1971) and Antonio Gramsci (CE 1891–1937).

Rationalism is also used in the PHILOSOPHY OF RELIGION to denote those thinkers who oppose the view that revelation is the only or primary source of religious knowledge.

Also, in ethics, rationalism appears in the expression *moral rationalism*, which denotes the view that moral facts and properties are known entirely through reasons. Among proponents of moral rationalism – i.e. among moral rationalists – there are also ethical or moral intuitionists, or proponents of ethical or *moral intuitionism*, i.e. those who hold that at least some truths of ethics are known through intuition. Various versions of moral intuitionism have been formulated. The English philosopher G.E. Moore (CE 1873–1958), for example, held that we intuit non-natural properties such as good. While the Scottish philosopher W.D. Ross (CE 1877–1971) advocated intuitive induction, a process whereby one goes from particular instances to moral principles. Other moral realists, however, disagree with moral rationalism and hold the moral sense theory of ethics, according to which moral feelings of pleasure or pain are part of moral perceptions, indicative of a person's character, and a crucial component of coming to know moral facts and properties.

See also: decision; empiricism; enlightenment; epistemology; ethics; metaphysics; philosophy of mind; rationality

Further reading

Boas, George (1980 [1961]) *Rationalism in Greek Philosophy*, Baltimore: Johns Hopkins Press.

Copleston, Frederick, S.J. (1963) *A History of*

Philosophy, Volume 4, Modern Philosophy: Descartes to Leibniz, Garden City, NY: Doubleday.

Cottingham, John (1997 [1984]) *Rationalism*, Bristol: Thoemmes Press.

De Santillana, Giorgio (1968 [1941]) *The Development of Rationalism and Empiricism*, Chicago: UCP.

rationality A term derived from the Latin *rationalitas*, i.e. "reasonableness," which is used in descriptive and normative senses. *Descriptively*, rationality primarily denotes the intellectual features – e.g. the ability to use language – that allow one to reach beliefs or decisions through reflection. Some philosophers consider this, i.e. *theoretical* rationality, to be all that rationality descriptively means. Others think rationality also denotes *practical* rationality: the practical features – e.g. good driving habits – that allow one to make correct decisions when not much, if any, reflection is possible or useful.

Theoretical rationality involves *theoretical reason*, the feature whereby agents engage in theoretical inquiry or theoretical reasoning aimed at acquiring theoretical knowledge – i.e. knowledge of the kinds of reasons or explanations that serve to account for such things as types of events, and types of states of affairs in the universe, which is formulated in a theoretical statement or theoretical judgment, or in a series of these – or, more broadly, the feature whereby agents engage in inquiry or reasoning aimed at acquiring knowledge of any truths.

Theoretical rationality is contrasted with practical rationality, which involves *practical reason*, i.e. the feature whereby agents engage in inquiry aimed at acquiring practical knowledge, i.e. knowledge of guides to good conduct and the justification of practices, policies, and institutions. In the Aristotelian tradition, both theoretical and practical reason are contrasted with *productive reason*, which is narrowly practical, i.e. a feature of agents whereby they make objects such as buildings, ships, and sculptures, or bring about particular results, such as restored health.

The preceding notions of reason, just as any other notions of reason – e.g. abstract, concrete, dialectical, vital (see DIALECTIC; KANTIAN PHILOSOPHY) – involve a recurrent process–product ambiguity: that between *constituting reason* and *constituted reason*. The former is an activity based on appeal to reasons that can, but need not always be, subjective reasons either in the sense of mere reasons for action an agent has and understands, or in the sense of reasons the agent has that, however, have no basis in reality. While constituted reason is the end product of the activity successfully carried out: the rational truths resulting from the activity.

In modern times, the German philosopher Immanuel Kant (CE 1724–1804) conceived of practical reason or practical rationality as a special capacity for reasoning aimed at prescribing or choosing conduct. It is that of *autonomous reason*, i.e. a source of rules of conduct independent of one's desires or preferences, and contrasts with *instrumental reason*: the conception that reason is only a way of maximizing the attainment of our goals as these are determined by such things as our desires and aversions.

Sometimes, the normative uses of rationality are divided into theoretical and practical, but emphasizing the thinking process, not the faculty involved. On this approach, theoretical rationality is a feature primarily of the process whereby beliefs are reached. As for the feature the beliefs must have, some argue that the beliefs must be self-evident or derived from self-evident beliefs in reliable ways. Others argue that the beliefs must be consistent with most of one's beliefs. Still others argue that the process whereby the beliefs are reached must be reliable, e.g. by using scientific methods. All these criteria involve different conceptions of JUSTIFICATION and none has secured general agreement.

Practically, *normative* rationality is sometimes understood as instrumental rationality, the characteristic feature of instrumental reason: acting in such a manner that it maximizes the achievement of one's own goals. Others have questioned this notion on the grounds that the said goals must be compatible or in harmony with all of one's other goals. Still others have argued that they must be morally acceptable goals, e.g. because they are universalizable, i.e. a reason for everyone, not just for you or me. The attribute of rationality is often applied to persons, e.g. in the expressions rational being and rational agent. A rational agent is a rational being in so far as it concerns action. There are various characterizations of the concept of rational agent. One is that used in economics and rational choice theory (see DECISION). Another is that of an ordinary rational agent. With some variations, this notion appears in a variety of cultures. For example, in the thought of the Akan people of Ghana, the term for rational being is *muntu*, which designates both the living and the dead, and implies a greater degree of the intimate interaction between all beings presupposed in African thought.

As for applications of rationality to social processes, the work of the German social theorist and sociologist Max Weber (CE 1864–1920) has been very influential. He conceived of the rationality of action as *Zweckrationalität*, i.e. as means–ends rationality. As for the rationality of value or *Wertrationalität*, he understood it as consisting of actions aimed to ultimate ends, regardless of the consequences. However, he considered the adoption of such ends to be arbitrary, hence politics to be a mere struggle between mutually irreducible competing ends. This led him to characterize rationality as the disenchantment of the world, a conception that significantly influenced critical theory (see CRITICAL).

See also: decision; empiricism; enlightenment; epistemology; ethics; metaphysics; philosophy of mind; rationalism

Further reading
Bennet, Jonathan (1964) *Rationality*, London and New York: Routledge & Kegan Paul and The Humanities Press.
Schmid, Walter T. (1998) *Plato's Charmides and the Socratic Ideal of Rationality*, Albany, NY: State University of New York Press.
Stein, Edward (1996) *Without Good Reason: The Rationality Debate in Philosophy and Cognitive Science*, Oxford and New York: Clarendon Press and Oxford University Press.

rationalization *see* psychoanalysis

rationes aeternas *see* metaphysics; Neoplatonism

rationes seminales *see* God; Stoicism

ravens paradox *see* induction

re, modality de *see de dicto*, under de

real assent *see* reasoning

real definition *see* definition

real distinction *see* definition

real essences *see* essentialism

real mathematics *see* philosophy of mathematics

real numbers *see* philosophy of mathematics

real proposition *see* philosophy of mathematics

realism, ante rem *see* metaphysics

realism, direct *see* perception

realism, in rebus *see* metaphysics

realism, internal *see* philosophy of science

realism, metaphysical *see* metaphysics

realism, moral *see* ethics

realism, naive *see* perception

realism, perceptual *see* perception

realism, scientific *see* philosophy of science

realism, Scotistic *see* identity

reality *see* metaphysics

reality principle *see* psychoanalysis

realizability, multiple *see* philosophy of mind

realization, physical *see* reductionism

realpolitik *see* philosophy, sociopolitical

reals *see* metaphysics

reason *see* Kantian philosophy; rationalism; rationality

reason, abstract *see* dialectic

reason, analytic *see* dialectic

reason, concrete *see* dialectic

reason, constituted *see* rationality

reason, constituting *see* rationality

reason, dialectical *see* dialectic

reason, for action *see* justification

reason, historical *see* dialectic

reason, lazy *see* fallacy

reason, normative *see* rationality

reason, objective *see* justification

reason of insanity *see* philosophy of law

reason, practical *see* rationality; Kantian philosophy

reason, principle of insufficient *see* chain of being

reason, principle of sufficient *see* chain of being

reason, productive *see* rationality

reason, pure *see* Kantian philosophy

reason, speculative *see* Kantian philosophy

reason, subjective *see* justification; rationality

reason, theoretical *see* Kantian philosophy; rationality

reason, vital *see* existentialism

reasoning Using reason in one of two senses: *psychological*, i.e. as a process of thinking aimed at answering certain explicit or implicit questions, and *logical*, i.e. as a formal process aimed at answering certain questions by means of deductive conclusions, inductive conclusions, or discoveries guided by heuristic strategies. In either sense, reasoning is included in inquiry widely understood as an intellectual or practical process of seeking answers to explicit or implicit questions (e.g. in trying to understand the physical universe or, alternatively, in science or everyday life, the motivation of a person's behavior), or of seeking fitting responses to given situations (as in trying to come up with a fitting reply to a joke, or with a poem one simply envisions).

The English churchman John Henry Newman (CE 1801–90) argued that, in any case of reasoning, an individual mind does the reasoning and, therefore, concrete reasoning is more basic than abstract reasoning. All good reasoning results from the *illative sense* – i.e. the faculty of drawing logical conclusions – which humans have. According to Newman, the illative sense is the final criterion of the validity of any instance of concrete reasoning. This sense can lead to certainty in a psychological, though not logical, sense. Along these lines, Newman characterized a type of informal inference whereby, by virtue of the illative sense, one reaches certitude or real assent concerning the way things are. He contrasted it with formal inferences or formal reasoning, which is conditioned by the certainty or probability of the premises, hence can only attain a thus conditioned conclusion or nominal assent.

As for the concept of circularity, it can be applied to definitions or to reasoning. Concerning definitions, when a *definiendum*, i.e. what a definition defines, occurs in the *definiens*, i.e. what does the defining (as in "morality is the rules of morality"), or when a term is defined by means of a second term that, in turn, is defined by the first term (e.g. "Laws are the rulers' commands and the ruler's commands are the laws"), a definition is called circular or *diallelon* (from the ancient Greek *di allēlon*, i.e. "through another"). The Latin term for this is *circulus in definiendo*, i.e. circle in defining.

With regard to reasoning, the relevant concept is *diallelus*: a circular argument, i.e. an argument with at least one premise that cannot be known unless the conclusion is already known. This type of argument is also called *circulus in probando* (Latin for circular reasoning) because it involves a *circulus vitiosus* (Latin for a vicious circle).

In addition, philosophers have discussed the notion of *practical reasoning*, i.e. the inferential process of deliberation whereby alternative courses of action are assessed on the basis of various considerations and, as a result, a decision is made and one or more actions are performed. That is, practical reasoning is carried out with a *practical attitude*: an attitude aimed at taking action. Traditionally, the logic involved in this process is called *practical syllogism*; in modern logic, it falls under the general categories of deontic logic and nomic or hyperdeontic logic (see SYLLOGISM; LOGIC).

See also: argument; decision; fallacy; logic; syllogism

Further reading
Clark, Andy, Ezquerro, Jesús, and Larrazábal, Jesús M. (1996) *Philosophy and Cognitive Science: Categories, Consciousness, and Reasoning: Proceedings of the Second International Colloquium on Cognitive Science*, Dordrecht and Boston: Kluwer Academic Publishers.
Harding, Carol Gibb (1985) *Moral Dilemmas: Philosophical and Psychological Issues in the Development of Moral Reasoning*, Chicago and New Brunswick: Precedent Pub., distributed by Transaction Books.
Passmore, John Arthur (1962 [1961]) *Philosophical Reasoning*, New York: Scribner.

reasons, all-things-considered *see* justification

reasons, evidential *see* justification

reasons, exciting *see* justification

reasons, explaining *see* justification

reasons, explanatory *see* justification

reasons for belief *see* faith

reasons, justifying *see* justification

reasons, non-evidential *see* justification

reasons of the heart *see* faith

reasons, overriding *see* justification

rebellion *see* philosophy, sociopolitical

rebirth, wheel of *see* Buddhism

recognition *see* knowledge

recognition, rule of *see* philosophy of law

recollection *see* Platonism

reconstruction, logical *see* empiricism

reconstruction, rational *see* empiricism

Rectification of Names *see* Confucianism

recurrence, eternal *see* computer theory; myth

recursion, definition by *see* definition

recursion, proof by *see* induction

recursive definition *see* definition

recursive function theory *see* philosophy of mathematics

recursive proof *see* induction

redintegration *see* philosophy of mind

reducibility, axiom of *see* theory of types

reduct *see* logic

reductio ad absurdum *see* logic

reductio ad impossibile *see* logic

reduction *see* reductionism

reduction base *see* reductionism

reduction bridge law *see* reductionism

reduction, eidetic *see* phenomenology

reduction, phenomenological *see* phenomenology

reduction, psychological *see* phenomenology

reduction sentence *see* reductionism

reductionism The attempt to carry out a *reduction*: the characterization of concepts and laws of one kind, by means of a *reduction base* or *reductive base*: concepts and laws of another kind. In philosophy, an example of reductionism is *physicalism*, i.e. the attempt to characterize psychological concepts and laws entirely by means of physical or physiological concepts and laws. Another example is provided by early twentieth-century attempts at characterizing physical objects entirely in terms of sense-data. Still another is that of *logicism*, the attempt at formulating all of mathematics entirely in terms of the vocabulary and theorems of logic. In science and the philosophy of science, there have also been reductionist attempts, e.g. that aimed at characterizing theoretical concepts entirely in terms of observational terms. In this context, the concept of a *reduction sentence* was introduced by the German-born philosopher Rudolf Carnap (CE 1891–1970). Any such sentence used a test condition predicate *T* such as "is placed in water" and a display predicate *D* such as "dissolves" – each one of which was an *observa-tion term* or *observational term* in that it denoted what was observed or observable – to characterize a dispositional or non-observational predicate such as "is water soluble." The sentence's form was:

$$(x)[Tx \supset (Dx \supset Sx)]$$

A substitution instance of this sentence form for the previously mentioned predicates would be: for any x, if $>x$ is placed in water, then, if x dissolves, then x is water soluble. Associated with the latter, there were reduction sentence forms for the non-occurrence of the non-observational predicate: $(x)[NTx \supset (DNx \supset -Sx)]$, and bilateral reduction sentences, which contrasted with the previously discussed or one-way-reduction sentences, and whose form was: $(x)[Tx \supset (Dx \equiv Sx)]$. Reduction sentences, however, failed to help in applying the predicate S when the test condition failed to apply, say, when x – be it sugar or chalk – is not placed in water.

Along these lines, Carnap distinguished between *syntactical* sentences, i.e. those describing a language; *object* sentences, i.e. those describing physical object; and *pseudo-object* sentences, i.e. those purported to be object sentences but that, in effect, are syntactical. Pseudo-object sentences, he argued, are used in philosophy and cause much confusion. To avoid it, he suggested that questions be *internal*, not external, i.e. that they be asked within an identifiable framework, say, that of numbers, where one can follow the *principle of tolerance*, i.e. choose any linguistic form one wishes.

Not unrelated to the previous reductionist attempt is that of *explanatory reductionism* or *methodological individualism* (see HOLISM). Methodological individualism arises in the context of explanation. It holds that the laws of more complex cases in a system or object (e.g. laws of collective behavior in society) are somehow deducible from laws of less complex cases (e.g. from laws of individual behavior in society). As a general view, this may simply turn out to be a form of the fallacy of composition, e.g. of arguing that if all French citizens have good taste then France, the state, has good taste (even though the state arguably has no sense of taste or ability to judge for it to have taste at all, let alone good taste). The question then arises: "When can one infer from properties of the whole's components to properties of the whole itself?" This is an empirical question that requires empirical investigation

in order for it to be settled by empirically establishing reduction *bridge laws*. These are laws that identify or connect features of wholes with those of their parts. For example, by stating that the structure of water is HOH, or that temperature is mean-translational kinetic energy.

In many, if not all, cases in which theory reduction is maintained to have taken place, there is no identity, but *physical realization*, i.e. the instantiation of the properties reduced in more than one physical process.

See also: explanation; holism; philosophy of mind; philosophy of science

Further reading
Clark, Austen (1980) *Psychological Models and Neural Mechanisms: An Examination of Reductionism in Psychology*, Oxford and New York: Clarendon Press and Oxford University Press.
Hoyningen-Huene, Paul and Wuketits, Frank M. (1989) *Reductionism and Systems Theory in the Life Sciences: Some Problems and Perspectives*, Dordrecht and Boston: Kluwer Academic Publishers.

reductive naturalism *see* naturalism

redundancy theory of truth *see* truth

reduplication *see* philosophy of language

reduplicative *see* philosophy of language

reference The characteristic some terms or expressions have of pointing to something, or being about something. It is also called *denotation*, or *extension* of a term or expression, in contrast to the expression or term's *connotation* or *intension*. What a term or expression points or refers to is its *referent* (sometimes also called its *extension*). The referent of a term or expression is also called *designatum* (from the Latin *designo*: "to mark out" or "trace").

Terms used in reference are *indexicals*, e.g. such personal pronouns as "I," and "she," such demonstratives as "this," and "that," such temporal modifiers as "now," and "tomorrow," and such locative modifiers as "here," and "there." The contribution of an indexical – e.g. "I" in "I know how to skate" – to what is said is called its *content*, which, of course, varies with who or what the indexical denotes, though the indexical has a single meaning – its *character* – in a language. The Guatemalan philosopher Héctor Neri-Castañeda (CE 1924–91) formulated the notion of a *quasi-indicator* in discussing indexical reference. For example, the sentence "Paul claims that Paul is tired" does not represent the indexical element of Paul's having said "I am tired." To represent it, one must add "he himself" as in "Paul claims that he himself is tired." This phrase, "he himself," is a quasi-indicator that denotes Paul's reference to himself as himself.

Indexicals, say, pronouns, typically function in an *anaphora*, i.e. a device in which a term (called *anaphor*) has its semantic properties determined by a preceding term or noun phrase called the anaphor's *antecedent*.

The medieval term for reference was *suppositio* that, in Latin, meant supposition. At its core, the theory had the notion of *proprietates terminorum* (Latin for "properties of terms"), which serves to characterize three types of reference on the basis of the terms involved. The first is *personal* supposition, which involves reference to individuals (which need not be persons). For example, in "every cat is an animal," the term "cat" has personal supposition. A second type is *simple* supposition, which involves reference to species. For example, in "feline is a species," the term "feline" has simple supposition. The third type is *material* supposition, which involves reference to linguistic expressions. For example, in "character is a three-syllable word," the term "character" has material supposition.

Personal supposition is further divided concerning quantification. The personal supposition of the term "John" is *discrete* in "John is a physician." That of the term "Greek" is *determinate* in "Some Greek is mortal." That of the term "feline" is *confused* and *distributive* in "Every feline is an animal."

Controversy has arisen concerning proper names. The English philosopher Bertrand Arthur William Russell (CE 1872–1970), for example, held, similarly to the German mathematician and logician Friedrich Ludwig Gottlob Frege (CE 1848–1925), that ordinary proper names, such as "Socrates," abbreviate definite descriptions such as "The Ancient Athenian philosopher who was condemned to drink the hemlock." This leaves open the possibility that someone else might have been condemned to drink the hemlock. The contemporary United States philosopher Saul Kripke rejected the Russell–Frege interpretation. Instead, he argued that the reference of a proper name is determined, not by a descriptive condition, but by a causal chain. Accordingly, a proper name is a *rigid designator*: Any sentence of the form "Socrates is..." expresses a proposition that is true in a given possible world (or set of circumstances) if and only if our actual Socrates satisfies, in that world, the condition...."

The theories in the background of this controversy are the *causal* (or *causal-historical*, or *historical*) *theory of proper names*, or the *causal* (or *causal-historical*, or *historical*) *theory of reference*, i.e. the view that proper names designate what they name by virtue of a causal connection or historical causal chain to it – a view sometimes confused with the *direct-reference theory* of proper names, according to which these denote the individuals called by them, without indicating or implying any attributes of those individuals – and the *descriptive or description theory* of proper names, or descriptive or description theory of reference: the view that names are associated with something like a definition, and refer by expressing descriptive features or properties, the referent(s) being the item(s) with those features or properties.

That is, some philosophers – from the Greek philosopher Plato (428–348 BCE) in the *Theaetetus* 201d, through the English philosopher John Stuart Mill (CE 1806–73) in *Logic* I, 2, sec. 5, to the Austrian philosopher Ludwig Wittgenstein (CE 1889–1951) in the *Tractatus Logico-Philosophicus* 3.203 – have held that proper names have reference or denotation, but not connotation. As previously indicated, other philosophers – e.g. Frege – have held that proper names have both *Bedeutung*, i.e. reference or denotation, and *Sinn*, i.e. connotation. Along these lines, some – e.g. Russell – have argued that so-called proper names, say, "Socrates," are really concealed descriptions and that, in the strictly logical sense, proper names, like the pronoun "it," refer to objects apart from any descriptions. While others, e.g. the contemporary United States philosopher John R. Searle, have argued that proper names cannot refer or denote apart from descriptions, each proper name having an identifying description that is the inclusive disjunction of properties commonly attributed to the item denoted by the proper name.

As for Frege, he elaborated on his initial notions in three papers he wrote between 1891 and 1892: "Function and Concept," "On Concept and Object," and "On Sense and Meaning." In the first of these, Frege introduced the notion of two truth values: The Truth and The False and characterized sentences as names for these objects, while concepts are functions that map sentences to these objects. Frege said that functions are unsaturated or incomplete, while objects are saturated.

An additional problem arises concerning reference in indirect discourse or *oratio obliqua*, i.e. in oblique contexts, where, for example, by means of a subordinate sentence, one can say "John believes that the bank thief was the man in the gray suit," "John claimed to know that the bank thief was the man in the gray suit," or other similar statements that roughly convey John's meaning. In these expressions, the phrase "the bank thief" is used in the indirect sense, since there is a verb of propositional attitude – "believes," "claimed" – involved. A problem is: what substitutions, if any, are permissible in this context for inferential purposes? This referential opacity characteristic of referentially *opaque contexts*, is contrasted with that of reference in direct discourse or *oratio recta*, i.e. in referentially *transparent contexts* or simply transparent contexts where one directly quotes: John said "The bank thief was the man in the gray suit."

See also: essentialism; meaning; opacity; philosophy of language

Further reading
Carl, Wolfgang (1994) *Frege's Theory of Sense and Reference: Its Origins and Scope*, Cambridge and New York: Cambridge University Press.
Kazmi, Ali A. (1998) *Meaning and Reference*, Calgary, Alberta: University of Calgary Press.
Vergauwen, Roger (1993) *A Metalogical Theory of Reference: Realism and Essentialism*

in Semantics, Lanham, MD: University Press of America.

reference class *see* probability

reference, inscrutability of *see* philosophy of language

referent *see* reference

referential opacity *see* opacity; reference

referential quantification *see* logic

referential theory of meaning *see* meaning

referentially transparent *see* opacity; reference

reflection *see* attention; empiricism; Kantian philosophy; phenomenology

reflection principles *see* philosophy of mathematics

reflective equilibrium *see* ethics

reflex *see* philosophy of mind

reflexive *see* relation

reflexivity *see* relation

reflexology *see* behaviorism; philosophy of mind

Reforma *see* philosophy of education

Reformation *see* Christianity

refutation, sophistic *see* fallacy

regional supervenience *see* supervenience

regress, infinite *see* fallacy

regress argument, epistemic *see* justification

regress argument, infinite *see* fallacy

regression analysis *see* induction

regressor variable *see* induction

regularity analysis *see* causal law

regularity theory of causation *see* causal law

regulative principle *see* Kantian philosophy

reification *see* metaphysics

reify *see* metaphysics

reincarnation *see* Buddhism; Hinduism; Pythagoreanism

reism *see* metaphysics

reiterability *see* ethics

relation A two-or-more-place property such as *older than*, and *between*. Relations are studied in various branches of inquiry, most notably in the *logic of relations*: the part of logic concerned with the formulation and implications of relational concepts. In set theory, a relation is understood as any set of ordered pairs (or triplets etc., though they can be reduced to pairs). The terms of a relation are the members of the pairs, the first term being the *referent* and the second the *relatum*. Its *domain* is the set of all first terms. Its *counterdomain* (or *range*, or *converse domain*) is the set of all second terms. The field of a relation is the union of its domain and counterdomain.

A significant relation is that of *connectedness*, also called *connexity*. The relation R is said to be *connected* (or *trychotomous*, or *total* (*trychotomy*)) if, for any two distinct elements x and y in a given domain, either xRy or yRx. The relation is said to be *strongly connected* if, for any two distinct elements x and y in a given domain, either xRy or yRx, even if x and y are identical. In the domain of positive integers, the relation $>$ is connected, because for any two integers a and b, either $a > b$ or $b > a$. However, it is not strongly connected, because when $a=b$ it is not the case that $a > b$ or $b > a$.

By contrast with all these, the inclusion relation is not connected, because it is not true that, given any two sets A and B, either B is included in A or A is included in B. They could simply exclude each other.

A relation can be: *reflexive* or that of *reflexivity*: for all a, aRa;
symmetrical or that of *symmetry*: for all a and b, if aRb, then bRa;
transitive or that of *transitivity*: for all a, b, and c, if aRb and bRc, then aRc

Intransitivity is a relation that amounts to the opposite of transitivity. The relation is then intransitive or non-transitive. *Asymmetry* is a relation that amounts to the opposite of symmetry. The relation is then asymmetrical or non-symmetric. *Non-reflexivity* is a relation that amounts to the opposite of reflexivity. The relation is then non-reflexive. All serial rela-

tions – e.g. older than – are non-reflexive, asymmetrical, and transitive.

The conjunction of the previous three relations characterizes an *equivalence relation*. A class of objects in an equivalence relation to each other is an equivalence class. Reflexivity, transitivity, and *antisymmetry* – i.e. for all a and b, if a is in relation R to b and b is in relation R to a, then $a=b$ – characterize a *partial order*; while transitivity, connectedness, and asymmetry – i.e. a is in relation R to b and b is in relation R to a, holds for no a and b – characterize a *linear order*.

Other significant notions are the *converse* of a relation aRb, i.e. the set where the domain and counterdomain of the relation are switched; the *complement* of a relation aRb, i.e. the set of all pairs (a,b) for which it is not the case that aRb; and the *ancestral* of a relation aRb, i.e. the set of all pairs (a,b) for which either the relation aRb holds, or the infinite series of relations aRc_1 and c_1Rc_2 and...c_nRb holds. Finally, the *universal* relation is the relation everything has to everything else.

Philosophical discussions of relations typically involve relations as related to properties, especially to the distinction between essential and accidental properties. In this regard, an item i bears an *internal* relation to another item j provided that this relation is an essential or intrinsic property of i. Otherwise, when the relation is a non-essential, accidental, extrinsic property of i, i bears an *external* relation to j.

There have also been philosophical discussions questioning whether relations exist, or whether only one-place properties, attributes, or qualities exist. These views have been largely, if not entirely, rejected, on the grounds that relations are a crucial component of modern logic and mathematics.

Concerning the role of relations in mathematics, a notion significant to that of intuition, namely that of choice sequence, was introduced by the Dutch mathematician L.E.J. Brouwer (CE 1881–1966), in order to express the non-classical properties of the continuum within intuitionism. A *choice sequence* is the result of an initial finite segment and a rule for continuing it stage-by-stage, which, at the same time, can leave open the exact location in the continuum of a number towards which others converge. In other words, this number would violate the classical *law of trichotomy*: given any pair of real numbers, they are in such a relation to each other that the first is either less than, equal to, or greater than the second.

See also: logic; set

Further reading
Fraissé, R. (1986) *Theory of Relations*, Amsterdam and Oxford: North-Holland.
Merrill, Daniel D. (1990) *Augustus De Morgan and the Logic of Relations*, Dordrecht and Boston: Kluwer Academic Publishers.

relational logic *see* logic

relational semantics *see* logic

relationalism *see* philosophy of science

relationism *see* philosophy of science

relative identity *see* identity

relative time *see* philosophy of science

relativism, cognitive *see* philosophy of science

relativism, cultural *see* ethics

relativism, descriptive *see* ethics

relativism, ethical *see* ethics

relativism, objective *see* metaphysics

relativism, perceptual *see* perception

relativism, scientific *see* philosophy of science

relativity, cultural *see* culture; ethics

relativity, ethical *see* ethics

relativity of knowledge *see* knowledge

relativity, perceptual *see* perception

relativity, theory of *see* philosophy of science

relatum *see* relation

relevance condition *see* induction

relevance logic *see* logic

relevant alternatives *see* justification

reliabilism *see* justification

religación *see* Madrid School

religion *see* philosophy of religion

religion, natural *see* philosophy of religion

religion of humanity *see* humanism; philosophy of religion

religion, philosophy of *see* philosophy of religion

reminiscence *see* Platonism

Renaissance philosophy *see* Bologna School; Neoplatonism

repetition *see* existentialism

replacement, axiom of *see* set

representamen *see* philosophy of language; pragmatism

representation theorem *see* measurement

representational theory of art *see* aesthetics

representational theory of memory *see* memory

representations, mental *see* conceptualism; perception

representative democracy *see* philosophy, sociopolitical

representative realism *see* perception

representative theory of ideas *see* perception

representatives *see* speech act theory

repression *see* psychoanalysis

republicanism, classical *see* philosophy, sociopolitical

rerum natura *see* naturalism

res cogitans *see* Cartesianism

res extensa *see* Cartesianism

resemblance, family *see* essentialism

residues, method of *see* induction

resistance *see* epistemology

resources variable *see* ethics; philosophy, sociopolitical

respondent conditioning *see* behaviorism; philosophy of mind

response variable *see* induction

responsibility *see* determinism; ethics; philosophy of law

restricted quantification *see* logic

resultant attribute *see* supervenience

retributive justice *see* justice; philosophy of law

retributivism *see* philosophy of law

retrodiction *see* induction

retroduction *see* abduction; philosophy of history

return, eternal *see* myth

reverence for life *see* ethics

revolt, metaphysical *see* existentialism

revelation *see* philosophy of religion

reverse discrimination *see* ethics; justice

reverse racism *see* ethics; justice

reversibility racism *see* ethics; justice

revisionary metaphysics *see* metaphysics

revolution *see* philosophy, sociopolitical

revolution, scientific *see* Cartesianism

Ṛgveda *see* Hinduism

rhematic indexical legisign *see* pragmatism

rhematic indexical sinsign *see* pragmatism

rhematic symbol *see* pragmatism

rhetoric From the Greek *rhetor* ("orator"), this term denotes the art and study of dealing with the principles of persuasion. In the Aristotelian tradition, it was associated with philosophy. However, there were already Ancient authors who considered it an essentially practical activity aimed at winning arguments. These differences in emphasis, if not in kind, can also be found in Indian philosophy and tradition, where rhetoric is practiced, among other things, in the study of *jalpa*: arguing constructively or destructively for the purpose of winning a debate.

In medieval times, rhetoric was part of the trivium (see PHILOSOPHY OF EDUCATION); however, its use became more confrontational during the Renaissance, when it was primarily seen as a tool – an Aristotelian tool at that – for attacking Aristotelian logic. In the twentieth century, rhetoric began to reappear in philosophical discussions, e.g. in the 1936 *The Philosophy of Rhetoric*, by the British poet and philosopher I.A. Richards (CE 1893–1979), followed by the 1952 *Rhetoric and Philosophy*, by the contemporary Belgian philosopher Chaïm Perelman, and, in late century, came to be given primary attention in the policy-making context in Giandomenico Majone's 1989 *Evidence, Argument and Persuasion in the Policy Process*, and my 1994 *Philosophy as Diplomacy: Essays in Ethics and Policy Making*.

Topics of interest in rhetoric are also relevant to the philosophy of language. An example is that of emotive conjugation: a humorous verbal conjugation that mocks first-person bias by describing the same action in successively more pejorative terms through first, second, and third persons, as in "I am well informed, you believe hearsay, he believes whatever he hears on TV."

See also: philosophy of language; philosophy, sociopolitical

Further reading
Black, Deborah L. (1990) *Logic and Aristotle's Rhetoric and Poetics in Medieval Arabic Philosophy*, Leiden and New York: E.J. Brill.
Iannone, A. Pablo (1994) *Philosophy as Diplomacy: Essays in Ethics and Policy Making*, Atlantic Highlands, NJ: Humanities Press.
Majone, Giandomenico (1989) *Evidence, Argument, and Persuasion in the Policy Process*, New Haven and London: Yale University Press.
Perelman, Chaïm (1968) *Rhetoric and Philosophy*, University Station: The Pennsylvania State University Press.
Seigel, Jerrold E. (1968) *Rhetoric and Philosophy in Renaissance Humanism: The Union of Eloquence and Wisdom, Petrarch to Valla*, Princeton, NJ: Princeton University Press.
Wardy, Robert (1998) *The Birth of Rhetoric: Gorgias, Plato, and their Successors*, London and New York: Routledge.

Rhodes School *see* Stoicism

ri-bi *see* Zen

Richard's paradox *see* theory of types

right (adjective) *see* ethics

right, strong *see* ethics

right, weak *see* ethics

rightness, objective *see* ethics

rightness, subjective *see* ethics

rights, absolute *see* ethics

rights, acquired *see* ethics

rights, actual *see* ethics

rights, alienable *see* ethics

rights, correlative *see* ethics; philosophy of law

rights, Hohfeldian *see* philosophy of law

rights, imperfect *see* ethics

rights, inalienable *see* ethics

rights, legal *see* philosophy of law

rights, moral *see* ethics; philosophy of law

rights, natural *see* ethics

rights of children *see* ethics

rights of citizens *see* ethics

rights of non-humans *see* ethics

rights of the land *see* ethics

rights, perfect *see* ethics

rights, property *see* ethics

rights, special *see* ethics

rigid designator *see* reference

rigorism *see* ethics

rime *see* Buddhism

rinne *see* Zen

Rinzai School *see* Zen

Rinzai-shū *see* Zen

risk assessment *see* judgment

Ritsu School *see* Buddhism

rju-sūtra-naya *see* Hinduism; philosophy of science

robot *see* computer theory

romanticism *see* canon

rule of addition *see* logic

rule of conjunction *see* logic

rule of detachment *see* justification

rule of double negation *see* logic

rule of law *see* philosophy of law

rule of reasoning *see* logic

rule of recognition *see* philosophy of law

rule of simplification *see* logic

rule of total evidence *see* probability

rule utilitarianism *see* ethics; utilitarianism

rules of inference *see* logic

rules of reasoning *see* logic

ruling argument *see* Greek philosophy

rūpa *see* Hinduism

Russell's paradox *see* theory of types

Russian nihilism *see* philosophy, sociopolitical

Russian philosophy *see* existentialism; Marxism; philosophy of literature; philosophy, sociopolitical

S

S see logic; syllogism

śabda-bohda *see* Hinduism

śabda-jñāna *see* Hinduism

śabda-tanmātra *see* Hinduism

sacred being *see* philosophy of religion

sacred void *see* philosophy of religion

sacrifice *see* ethics; philosophy of religion

sādhana *see* Buddhism; Hinduism; Jainism

Sādhārana-kāranas *see* causal law

sādhāranī-karana *see* aesthetics

sādhya *see* logic

sagacity *see* African philosophy

sagehood *see* Chinese philosophy; Confucianism

Saint Louis, Philosophical Society of *see* idealism

Saint Petersburg paradox *see* paradox

Sakti *see* Hinduism

salva veritate *see* opacity

samādhi *see* Hinduism

samanantara-pratyaya *see* causal law

sāmānya *see* meaning

sāmānya-lakshana *see* meaning

samatha *see* Buddhism

samavāyi-kārana *see* causal law

samhitas *see* Hinduism

Sāmkhya-Yoga Also called *Sānkhya-Yoga*, this is one of the six orthodox schools of HINDU-ISM, supposed to have been founded by Kapila, whose works have been lost and about whose life no details are known. The Sāmkhya-Yoga School upholds two basic categories: *purusha* (eternal spirits), and *prakṛti* (physical stuff that is the basis of the natural world). The world evolves out of the latter with the help of the former through a kind of causation where the effect pre-exists in the cause. It thus results in the production of *mahat*, i.e. the cosmic intelligence, *buddhi*, i.e. the substance of all mental processes, and *ahankara*, i.e. the principle of individuation. Three aspects of *ahankara* originate specific developmental lines: *sattva*, what is lightweight and fine-grained, which leads to *manah* or the mind, the sense-organs, and the five means of action; *rajas* or what is active, which produces the energy that empowers all developments; and *tamas* or what is heavy and coarse, which leads to the *mahā-bhūta* or five subtle (also called great) elements – *śabda* or "sound," *sparsha* or "touch," *rūpa* or "color," *rasa* or "taste," and *gandha* or "smell" – from which the coarser ones – *ākāsha* or "ether," *vāyu* or "air," *tejas* or "fire," *ap* or "water," and *pthivī* or "earth" – respectively follow.

The *Bhagavad-Gita* sometimes considers *sattva*, *rajas*, and *tamas* to be three *guṇas*; other times, it considers them to be three types of *tapas* (from the Sanskrit *tap*, i.e. "heat"), a term that initially applied to the heat of the sun but later came to mean emotional fervor, primal energy, and ascetic power. The gods both create and destroy by means of *tapas*. According to the *Bhagavad-Gītā*, *sattva* is virtuous, *rajas* is ambitious, and *tamas* is perverted.

According to the Sāmkhya-Yoga School, *sattva*, *rajas*, and *tamas* are unmixed at some points in the development of the physical universe, and mixed at other points. When they are mixed, they make up physical bodies, some of which embody bits of *purusha*. When this mixing takes place, transmigration occurs. Also, mental properties exist only in such combinations of *prakṛti* and *purusha*, which raises the question: "What distinguishes different minds when *purusha* is not embodied?" The School's answer was that each bit of *purusha* had a transmigratory history that was different from that of every other bit of *purusha*. This rather *ad hoc* position was criticized, for example, by members of the NYĀYA-VAIŚEṢIKA SCHOOL. As a result, some thinkers formulated Advaita-Vedānta, according to which all *purusha* distinctions are illusory. Other thinkers held that minds have inherent, not merely embodied, mental properties such as consciousness, e.g. in Vishistād-vaita-Vedānta or qualified non-dualism, and in the non-orthodox, dualist School, DVAITA.

As with the other schools, for Sāmkhya-Yoga, the purpose of the discussions and practice of Hinduism is not simply knowledge or wisdom, but *moksha* (enlightenment/liberation), which includes escape from karma and the reincarnation cycle. The Sāmkhya-Yoga School refers to this liberation as *kaivalya* (aloofness, aloneness, isolation), meaning a complete detachment – immediately caused by *viveka* (knowledge) – from matter and from transmigration. As for the sorrows overcome in liberation, the Sāmkhya-Yoga School, distinguishes various types. One is *ādhibhautika*, miseries caused by extrinsic, natural influences, such as other individuals, animals, and inanimate objects. Another is *ādhyātmika*, miseries caused by internal influences, generated by illness of the body which may lead to dangerous levels of bile, or unsatisfied passions of the mind, such as desire and anger.

See also: Hinduism

Further reading

Chatterjee, Satischandra (1950) *An Introduction to Indian Philosophy*, 4th edn, rev. and enl., Calcutta: University of Calcutta.
Hiriyanna, Mysore (1996) *The Essentials of Indian Philosophy*, London: Diamond.

samsāra *see* Hinduism

samsaya *see* Hinduism

San-chieh School *see* Buddhism

sanction *see* philosophy of law

Sānkhya *see* Sāmkhya-Yoga

San-lun School *see* Buddhism

Sanron School *see* Buddhism

Sarvāstivāda *see* Buddhism

sat/chit/ānanda *see* Hinduism

satisfaction *see* ethics; truth

satisfiability *see* logic

satisficing theories *see* decision

sattva *see* Hinduism; Sāmkhya-Yoga

Sautrāntika *see* Buddhism

save the appearances, to *see* philosophy of science

scalar *see* logic

scepticism *see* skepticism

schema *see* Kantian philosophy

schemata *see* Kantian philosophy

schematic *see* Kantian philosophy

schematism *see* Kantian philosophy

scholastic methods *see* Scholasticism

Scholasticism A variety of scholarly and instructional techniques – commentaries and disputations – introduced in Western Europe during the late Middle Ages. Scholasticism is sometimes mistakenly used to refer to all medieval philosophy; but the latter included, for example, mystics, who hardly used scholastic methods. Also, Scholasticism is sometimes mistakenly used to imply that it denotes a unified set of doctrines. Yet, no such set of doctrines existed. Instead, there were only scholastic methods – *lectio*, i.e. neutral reading of the text; *meditatio*, i.e. reflection on the text; *quaestio*, i.e. questions about the text; *expositio*, i.e. interpretation of the text; and *disputatio*, i.e. disputation or discussion regarding the text – whose initial formulation is attributed to law schools, notably that at Bologna. Around the exposition, the *quaestio* (pl. *quaestiones*) was structured.

At first, the *quaestiones* were but another manifestation of the *lectio* widely understood as *expositio*. During the thirteenth century, when the *disputatio* developed, the *quaestiones disputatae*, i.e. the questions being discussed, were conceived. A subgroup of these were the *quaestiones quodlibetales*, i.e. the questions to be discussed in *disputatio quodlibetal*, which resulted from the fact that, on certain days, those listening could choose the questions in any order. In all these cases, the *disputatio* involved a *defendans*, who asserted a thesis, and an *arguens*, who denied it and tried to prove the denial by means of syllogisms. The terms used to accept premises in the process were *concedo* or *transeat*; while to deny them, the term was *nego*, and to point out their ambiguity, the term was *distingo* in the case of the major premise, and *contradistingo* in the case of the minor premise.

These methods were then extended to theology and philosophy through the works of such authors as the French philosopher and theologian Peter Abelard (CE 1079–1142) and the Lombardy-born theologian Peter Lombard (CE 1100–60), and remained dominant until the beginning of the sixteenth century, when educational changes pushed them aside. Both Abelard and Peter Lombard published *summae* – plural of the Latin *summa*, i.e. "compendium" – a form of investigation developed in the twelfth century that, first, was books of sentences formulating theological and philosophical opinions, but, later, became organized discussions of philosophical and theological problems.

There was a return of Scholasticism in the late sixteenth century, called *Second Scholasticism*, which is represented, for example, by the works of the Portuguese philosopher Pedro da Fonseca (CE 1528–99), whose *Coimbra Commentaries* were widely discussed during the seventeenth century, and whose logic text,

Institutes of Dialect, saw many editions. A complementary body of work is constituted by the *Conimbricenses*, the teachings of the Jesuit philosophers who, beginning in CE 1555, imparted them at the University of Coimbra. They were the basis for the *Cursus philosophicus conimbricensis*, or *Cursus conimbricensis*, a very influential text not just in Portugal and Spain but also in central and Western Europe. Among those who contributed to this eight-volume text were Manuel de Goes, Cosme de Magallanes, Baltasar Alvarez, and Sebastián de Couto. Some of these were published in Lyon, others in Coimbra, one in Lisbon. They mainly deal with Aristotle's logic and physics texts, including the Greek text and Latin translation. The works on ethics are hardly discussed. As for metaphysics, the works of Pedro da Fonseca, who had the idea for the *Cursus conimbricensis*, were supposed to complement the latter. An idea the *Conimbricenses* formulated that was later adopted by the German philosopher Gottfried Wilhelm Leibniz (CE 1646–1716) was that of *vinculum substantiale* or substantial vinculum, i.e. a type of relation between simple substances that leads to the creation of a substantial compound, which adds something over and above the sum of the simple substances conjoined in the compound.

A related and partly competing body of work is the *Collegium Complutense philosophicum discalceatorum fratrum Ord. B.M. de monte Carmeli*, a four-volume work published by Carmelite friars of Alcalá, Spain, between CE 1624 and 1647. This group is sometimes called the *Collegium Complutense* (the Complutense School) and is regarded as an equal of the *Collegium Salmanticense* (the Salamanca School) and others in attempting to spread Thomism during the seventeenth century.

See also: Aristotelianism; Cambridge School; Neoplatonism; Platonism; Thomism

Further reading

Kretzmann, Norman, Kenny, Anthony John Patrick, and Pinborg, JanSee (1997 [1982]) *The Cambridge History of Later Medieval Philosophy: From the Rediscovery of Aristotle to the Disintegration of Scholasticism, 1100–1600*, Cambridge, UK and New York: Cambridge University Press.

Pieper, Josef (1961 [1960]) *Scholasticism: Per-*

sonalities and Problems of Medieval Philosophy, London: Faber & Faber.

Scholasticism, Islamic *see* philosophy of education

School of Athens *see* Academy; Neoplatonism

School of Bologna *see* Bologna School

School of Laws *see* Chinese Legalism; Chinese philosophy

School of Names *see* Chinese philosophy

School of Padua *see* Bologna School

School of Salamanca *see* Scholasticism

Schröder–Bernstein theorem *see* set

Schrödinger cat paradox *see* philosophy of science

Schrödinger equation *see* philosophy of science

science *see* philosophy of science

science court *see* ethics

science, philosophy of *see* philosophy of science

scientia intuitiva *see* Cartesianism

scientia media *see* determinism

scientia universalis *see* calculus

scientific behaviorism *see* behaviorism

scientific concepts *see* philosophy of science

scientific laws *see* philosophy of science

scientific methods *see* philosophy of science

scientific practice *see* philosophy of science

scientific problems *see* philosophy of science

scientific realism *see* philosophy of science

scientific relativism *see* philosophy of science

scientific results *see* philosophy of science

scientific revolution *see* Cartesianism

scientific theories *see* philosophy of science

scintilla conscientiae *see* ethics

scope ambiguity *see* ambiguity

scope of operators *see* ambiguity

scope of policies *see* philosophy, sociopolitical

scope of social problems *see* philosophy, sociopolitical

Scotism *see* definition; identity

Scotistic realism *see* definition; identity

Scottish common-sense philosophy *see* ethics; metaphysics

sea-battle *see* logic

second actualization *see* Aristotelianism

second imposition *see* meaning

second intention, terms of *see* intention

second-order logic *see* logic

second-order policy problems *see* philosophy, sociopolitical

second potentiality *see* Aristotelianism

second Thomism *see* Thomism

secondary process *see* psychoanalysis

secondary qualities *see* quality

secondary substance *see* metaphysics

secondness *see* metaphysics

secret *see* esoterism

secular *see* philosophy of religion

secundum quid *see* fallacy

Seelenfünklein *see* mysticism

sefiroth *see* cabala

segregation de facto *see* justice

segregation de jure *see* justice

selection, natural *see* evolution

self *see* identity

self-consciousness *see* knowledge; philosophy of mind

self-deception *see* existentialism; paradox

self-determination *see* ethics; philosophy, sociopolitical

self-esteem *see* ethics

self-evidence *see* certainty

self-interest *see* ethics

self-knowledge *see* Socratic philosophy

self-love *see* ethics

self-presenting *see* knowledge

self-preservation *see* philosophy, sociopolitical

self-realization *see* ethics

self-reference *see* theory of types

self-referential incoherence *see* theory of types

self-reliance *see* transcendent

self-reproducing automaton *see* computer theory

self-respect *see* ethics

semantic atomism *see* meaning

semantic completeness, strong *see* completeness

semantic completeness, weak *see* completeness

semantic compositionality *see* meaning

semantic consequence *see* logic

semantic consistency *see* logic

semantic holism *see* meaning

semantic molecularism *see* meaning

semantic nihilism *see* meaning

semantic paradoxes *see* theory of types

semantic solipsism *see* solipsism

semantic theory of truth *see* truth

semantic truth *see* truth

semantics *see* logic; philosophy of language

semantics, conceptual role *see* meaning

semantics, extensionalist *see* philosophy of language

semantics, Kripke *see* logic

semantics, linguistic *see* philosophy of language

semantics, non-standard *see* philosophy of language

semantics, outer domain *see* logic

semantics, possible worlds *see* logic

semantics, standard *see* philosophy of language

semantics, supervaluational *see* logic

semantics, Tarskian *see* meaning

semantics, truth-conditional *see* meaning

seminal reasons *see* God; Stoicism

semiology *see* Continental philosophy

semiotic *see* philosophy of language

semiotics *see* philosophy of language

sengyo *see* Zen

sensa *see* perception

sensation *see* perception

sensationalism *see* perception

sense *see* meaning

sense, common *see* perception

sense-data *see* perception

sense datum-theory *see* perception

sense, direct *see* opacity

sense, external *see* metaphysics

sense, indirect *see* opacity

sense, internal *see* metaphysics

sense, moral *see* ethics

sense of fairness *see* ethics

sense of humor *see* aesthetics; ethics

sense of justice *see* ethics

senses, special *see* philosophy of mind

sensibilia *see* perception

sensible form *see* Thomism

sensible intuitions *see* Kantian philosophy

sensibles, common *see* perception

sensibles, proper *see* perception

sensibles, special *see* perception

sensorium *see* philosophy of mind

sensum *see* perception

sensus communis *see* perception

sensus externus *see* metaphysics

sensus internus *see* metaphysics

sentence *see* logic; meaning; philosophy of language

sentence, basic *see* justification

sententiae divinitatis *see* Platonism

sentential calculus *see* logic

sentential connective *see* logic

sentential operator *see* logic

sentiment *see* ethics

separation, axiom of *see* set

separation of powers *see* philosophy, sociopolitical

sequent calculus *see* logic

serial relations *see* relation

sermo *see* abstract

set Any collection or list. Such collections are studied in *set theory*. The notion of sets was significantly developed by the English mathematician and logician George Boole (CE 1815–64) when formulating what has come to be known as Boolean algebra. It led to a theory of such algebras, specifically to lattice theory.

According to set theory, the items listed in any collection are said to be members of the corresponding set. The membership relation is symbolized by means of the symbol ε, as in: 5 ε {*x* |*x* is a natural number} or, in English: five is a member of the set of natural numbers. Also, the *identity* of a set is entirely determined by its members. Two set-denoting terms *A* and *B* denote the same set when what *A* denotes has the same members as what *B* denotes. The smallest possible set is the *empty* set (or empty class), most often symbolized by the symbol ø, or by the combination of symbols {}.

Sets can be in various relations such as *union*: the union of sets *A* and *B* is the set whose members are the addition of the members of *A* plus the members of *B*; *intersection*: the intersection of sets *A* and *B* is the set whose members are both members of *A* and members of *B*; *inclusion*: the inclusion of set *B* in *A* is the set whose members are, some, members of *A*, and all members of *B*.

Various notions are based on the relations just described. For example, whenever every member of a set *B* is also a member of another set *A*, the first is a *subset* of the second and the second is a *superset* of the first, which is symbolized as follows: $B \subseteq A$. Two sets whose intersection is empty are *disjoint* sets. A *partition* of a set is the complete division of a set into mutually disjoint subsets. The *difference* between two sets *A* and *B* is the set whose members are members of *A* but not of *B*. Finally, the *singleton* set is the intersection of the set of even natural numbers with that of the prime natural numbers. It is called singleton because its only member is number two. Any set or class that has exactly one member is called the *unit class*. Sets or classes are delineated within a *universe of discourse* or *domain of discourse* (usually symbolized by *U* or *D*), i.e. all those items within which a given class fits (in traditional logic, a *genus*), e.g. gems are a universe of discourse for the class of emeralds (and so are stones). Boole also talked of the *universal class*, i.e. that class to which everything belongs. He symbolized it by the numeral 1. Another symbol for it is *V*. The *complement* class of a given class *x*, or 1−*x*, is the class of everything in the universe but the members of *x*.

The notion of *ordering* was introduced in set theory, where an ordering is an arrangement of the items of a set so that some of them come before others. This is done by means of the notion of an *ordered pair* of items *a* and *b*, which is frequently symbolized as follows: (*a,b*). The Cartesian product of two sets *A* and *B* is the set of all ordered pairs whose first entry is a member of *A* and whose second entry is a member of *B*. These notions, together with those previously discussed, serve to construct classical mathematics within set theory. For example, natural numbers can be represented as sequences of sets where 0=ø; 1={ø}; 2={ø,{ø}}; 3={ø,{ø}, {ø,{ø}}}, etc. Also, by taking the existence of one-to-one correspondence between two sets to be, by definition, what makes two sets be of the same size, the Russian-born German mathematician Georg Cantor (CE 1845–1918) showed that it follows that the set of all natural numbers, the set of all even natural numbers, and many more sets have all the same size. Such infinite sets are called *countable* because they can be put in a one-to-one correspondence with the set of natural numbers. The number of their elements is the first infinite *cardinal* number. Since, in addition, the set of all subsets of a set is larger than the set, there are infinite cardinal numbers greater than the first. This series of infinite cardinal numbers has sometimes been called *Cantor's paradise*. The general term for an infinite cardinal or ordinal number is *transfinite* number. In the process, Cantor showed that there are at least two kinds of infinity involved in ordinary mathematics, and that a mathematical treatment of these infinities is needed. This result is often formulated by saying that the continuum is *uncountable*.

Early versions of set theory involved paradoxes called the *paradoxes of set theory* or *set-theoretic paradoxes*. The most famous is *Russell's paradox*, which involves the set of all sets that are not members of themselves. If it is, it isn't, and if it isn't, it is. The culprit seems to have been the *principle of unlimited comprehension*: for any property, there is a set that has it.

During the twentieth century, set theory was systematized so as to ensure that its earlier paradoxical versions were avoided. This was accomplished by means of a number of axioms such as the *extensionality axiom* – A and B denote the same set when the members of the set that A denotes and B denotes are the same; the *pairing axiom* – for any items a and b there is a set {a;b}; the *separation axiom*: for any set A and property P there is an item x that is a member of A and has P; the *power set axiom* – for any set A there is a set B such that all of its members are included in A and either A has or does not have still other members; the *infinity axiom* or *axiom of infinity* – the infinite set ω exists; the *choice axiom* – for any set of non-empty sets there is a set that contains exactly one member from each; the *replacement axiom* – if A is a set and every member a of A is replaced by some b, then there is a set containing all the b's; the *foundation axiom* – sets are formed in stages called the *iterative hierarchy* whereby one begins with non-sets, then forms all possible sets of these, then forms all possible sets of the latter, and so on.

An influential notion in set theory is that of a *hierarchy*, i.e. a division of objects ordered in such a manner that it reflects its complexity. It is applicable in technology, e.g. in car production lines, where higher-order machines (higher-order computers) regulate the functions (say, to paint or to tighten screws) that lower-order machines (robots) perform. It is also applicable in logic and mathematics, whose formulas – e.g. atomic sentences and, at a higher order of complexity, molecular sentences – are iteratively defined to reflect their degrees of complexity in some ordering. Analogously, the notion of hierarchy is applicable to many other branches of inquiry from biology to social science.

Also worthy of mention is the *Schröder–Bernstein theorem*, according to which *mutually* dominant sets are *equinumerous*, where to say that a set A is *dominated* by a set B is to say each member of A can be mapped to a unique member of B, so that no two members of A are mapped to the same member of B. To say that A and B are *equinumerous* is to say that they have the same number of members.

Among various other notable concepts in set theory are as follows. First, a *Hintikka* set (named after the contemporary Finnish philosopher Jaakko Hintikka), also called *model* set, or *downward saturated* set, i.e. a set of well-formed formulas that are all true under a certain interpretation of their non-logical symbols. In other words, it is a set of well-formed formulas that sufficiently describe a state of affairs – e.g. by ruling out mutually exclusive propositions – to make plain that it is possible.

Second, a *maximal consistent* set, i.e. in formal logic, a set of sentences S that is consistent and which has the following characteristic which makes it maximally consistent: if a certain set V is consistent and S is included in or identical with V, then S is identical with V. A maximally consistent set is complete.

See also: logic; paradox; philosophy of mathematics; relation; theory of types

Further reading

Ferreirós Domínguez, José (1999) *Labyrinth of Thought: A History of Set Theory and its Role in Modern Mathematics*, Boston, MA: Birkhäuser Verlag.

Tiles, Mary (1989) *The Philosophy of Set Theory: An Historical Introduction to Cantor's Paradise*, Oxford, UK and Cambridge, MA, US: B. Blackwell.

seven emotions, the *see* Korean philosophy

sex *see* gender

sexism *see* ethics

sexuality *see* psychoanalysis

shabda-vṛtti *see* Hinduism

shahādah *see* Islam

shaman *see* philosophy of religion

shamanism *see* philosophy of religion

shan, o *see* Chinese philosophy

shang ti *see* Chinese philosophy

shaykh *see* Ṣūfism

Sheffer stroke *see* logic

Shen *see* Chinese philosophy

sheng *see* Chinese philosophy

Sheol *see* myth

Shih *see* Chinese Legalism

shiki *see* Zen

Shingon School *see* Buddhism

shinnyo *see* Zen

Shintō *see* God

Shiva *see* Hinduism

shu *see* Chinese Legalism; Confucianism

shūnya *see* Buddhism

shūnyatā *see* Buddhism

Shunyavānda *see* Buddhism

si enim fallor, sum *see* Cartesianism

siddha *see* Hinduism

siddhānta *see* Buddhism

side-effects *see* ethics; utilitarianism

sifah *see* God; quality

sign, conventional *see* philosophy of language

sign, natural *see* philosophy of language

signate matter *see* Thomism

significatio *see* syncategoremata

signification *see* syncategoremata

significatum *see* syncategoremata

signified *see* Continental philosophy

signifier *see* Continental philosophy

signs *see* philosophy of language

signs, theory of *see* philosophy of language

Sikhism *see* Hinduism

similarity, exact *see* identity

simple constructive dilemma *see* dilemma

simple destructive dilemma *see* dilemma

simple natures *see* Cartesianism

simple statement *see* logic

simple supposition *see* syncategoremata

simple theory of types *see* theory of types

simplicity *see* induction

simplification, rule of *see* logic

simulator, universal *see* computer theory

simultaneity *see* philosophy of science

sin *see* philosophy of religion

sincerity *see* Chinese philosophy; Confucianism

sine qua non *see* condition

single case, problem of the *see* probability

singleton set *see* set

singular causal relation *see* philosophy of mind

singular causal statement *see* explanation

singular statement *see* syllogism

singular term *see* syllogism

Sinn *see* reference

sinsign *see* pragmatism

Sirhak *see* Korean philosophy

Sittlichkeit *see* idealism

situation ethics *see* ethics

situation theory *see* model

six emotions, the *see* Chinese philosophy

skepticism From the Greek *skepsis* ("consideration" or "doubt"), in the broadest sense, the doctrine that there is no knowledge or justification concerning at least certain types of beliefs or propositions, or the refusal to accept that there is such knowledge or justification. Skepticism can be partial or total. *Partial* skepticism applies only to some types of beliefs or propositions. There are various versions of partial skepticism depending on which types of beliefs or propositions they cover. *Total* skepticism applies to all types of beliefs or propositions.

Partial, as well as total, skepticism have also been subdivided into practical and theoretical. *Practical* skepticism is an attitude of suspending belief and disbelief that may, but need not, be accompanied by a general recommendation that everybody do likewise. While *theoretical* skepticism holds that there is no knowledge of a specifiable kind or set of kinds. It has been subdivided into moderate and radical. Theoretical skepticism is *moderate* when it applies only to knowledge supposed to be attained through science, mathematics, logic, or introspection. It is *radical* when it applies to all purported knowledge, including ordinary knowledge.

Partial and moderate skepticism can involve a *theory of error*, e.g. holding that the belief that there are moral facts, principles, or laws is erroneous. Total and radical skepticism, however, cannot typically involve a theory of error, because total skepticism applies to all beliefs and propositions, while radical skepticism applies to all purported knowledge, and theories of error are claimed to be true and known to be true about erroneous beliefs.

There is also a particular form of skepticism that cuts across the previous categories, namely *methodological* skepticism. It is related to a concept central to epistemology: that of *criterion* (often used in the plural, *criteria*), i.e. roughly, under normal conditions, a sufficient condition for the truth of a statement or belief, hence for the justifiability of holding such belief. Some, for example, have argued that, for any inner process (say, a feeling of shame), there must be an observable criterion (reddening of one's face). This has originated the *problem of the criterion* (see EPISTEMOLOGY). This problem is sometimes formulated by means of the question: "How can epistemological requirements be prior to ontological ones?" From a more strictly epistemological standpoint, the problem is formulated by means of two questions: "Can we recognize instances of knowledge without knowing the criteria for knowledge?" "Can we know the criteria for knowledge without already recognizing some instances of knowledge?" Ancient skeptics answered both questions in the negative. Later philosophers, however, have sometimes held the position called *particularism*, which answers the first question affirmatively but the second negatively. While others hold the position called *methodism*, which answers the second question affirmatively while the first negatively.

Concerning *ancient* skepticism, it can be traced back to modest Socratic claims concerning wisdom. After the Platonic and Aristotelian periods, Greek philosophy experienced the development of *Pyrrhonism*, also called *epistemological nihilism*, according to which no knowledge is possible. Its founder was the Greek philosopher Pyrrho (*c.* 360–270 BCE), who wrote nothing. According to his disciple, Timon of Phlius (*c.* 320–230 BCE), who was less extreme than his teacher, Pyrrho held that it was impossible to know anything and, in arguing for it, introduced the notion of *equipollence*: that there are arguments of equal strength on all sides of any question and therefore we should practice *epoché*, i.e. suspend judgment on every question. In practice, one should withdraw into oneself and develop *ataraxia*: an attitude of imperturbable serenity or calmness. Ancient skeptics, mostly Pyrrho's followers, formulated each argument under a particular heading called a *trope*, from the Greek *tropos*, i.e. heading.

Skepticism influenced the Second Academy, which emphasized probability and shifted its position towards skepticism. Indeed, its founder, the Greek philosopher Arcesilaus (*c*. 315–242 BCE), held the doctrine of *eulogon*: that the guide to life was to be probability. Yet, this version of skepticism was much more moderate than the previous ones. A return to a more radical skepticism was displayed by the Third Academy.

The Greek philosopher Sextus Empiricus (CE second and third century) summarized Pyrrhonism in his *Outlines of Pyrrhonism* and *Adversus mathematicus*. His work is a main source for our knowledge of Pyrrhonism – and Greek philosophy in general – and the neo-Pyrrhonist position he formulated that, however, he preferred to call methodical.

After this, Ancient Greek skepticism as a school ended. It appeared in India, as part of the *cārvāka* or *lokayata* schools, in the seventh or eight century CE, and reappeared in the fifteenth century in Italy, then expanding to Europe as a means of making room for the life of faith. Cartesianism enlivened skepticism and made it part and parcel of modern philosophy's discussions, where it has been influential up to the present in such philosophical approaches as *deconstructionism* (see CONTINENTAL PHILOSOPHY), the *incommensurability thesis* in the philosophy of science (see PHILOSOPHY OF SCIENCE), the *indeterminacy of translation* thesis in the philosophy of language (see PHILOSOPHY OF LANGUAGE), and elsewhere.

Some of these discussions have gone as far as claiming that we do not know that we are not now dreaming; yet they claim we can know our surroundings. The paradoxical nature of these claims has led some philosophers to formulate the notion of *tracking*. This is a relation between one's belief and the truth of what one believes according to which the belief or its mode of acquisition must somehow indicate or be connected to the truth of what is believed. On this view, to explain how one knows that there is a car coming, one can appeal to one's tracking the truth of the proposition "there is a car coming," for example through a specific visual experience one has

of seeing a car coming, which would not occur if a car were not coming.

The proposition "there is a car coming" may entail the further proposition that one is not dreaming; but, if one cannot track the truth of this latter proposition, then one would not know that one is not dreaming, even if one knew that there is a car coming. An implication such as this one is still paradoxical and has undermined the tracking account. As a result, contemporary skeptics have attempted to reformulate the Cartesian dream argument (see CARTESIANISM), an attempt that has revived the epistemological version of the problem of the criterion (see above and EPISTEMOLOGY). The alternatives, however, need not only be particularism, methodism, or skepticism, all of which address the dichotomy between particular cases of knowledge and general criteria for knowledge. Other alternatives have been suggested, most notably those focusing on *epistemic virtue*, i.e. the disposition individuals have to come to know things in practice (see EPISTEMOLOGY), on *confirmation* (see INDUCTION), or on a combination of both.

See also: Academy; Cartesianism; epistemology; justification

Further reading
Bosley, Richard (1993) *On Knowing that One Knows: The Logic of Skepticism and Theory*, New York: P. Lang.
Stough, Charlotte L. (1969) *Greek Skepticism: A Study in Epistemology*, Berkeley: University of California Press.
Unger, Peter K. (1975) *Ignorance: A Case for Scepticism*, Oxford, UK: Clarendon Press.

Skeptics *see* skepticism

Skolem-Löwenheim theorem *see* logic

Skolem-normal form *see* logic

Skolem's paradox *see* paradox

slave morality *see* ethics

sliding-reinforcer trap *see* decision

slippery-slope argument *see* fallacy

social action *see* decision

social and political philosophy *see* philosophy, sociopolitical

social biology *see* evolution

social change *see* philosophy, sociopolitical

social choice in conflict situations *see* decision

social-choice theory *see* decision

social contract *see* philosophy, sociopolitical

social Darwinism *see* evolution

social-decision procedures *see* philosophy, sociopolitical

social-decision processes *see* philosophy, sociopolitical

social epistemology *see* knowledge

social ethics *see* ethics

social fact *see* philosophy of science

socialism *see* philosophy, sociopolitical

sociobiology *see* evolution

sociological jurisprudence *see* philosophy of law

sociology of knowledge *see* knowledge

Socinianism *see* Christianity

Socratic intellectualism *see* Socratic philosophy

Socratic method *see* Socratic philosophy

Socratic paradoxes *see* Socratic philosophy

Socratic philosophy The thought and methods of the Greek philosopher Socrates (469–399 BCE), and the development and influence of his approach in later centuries. He is well known by his dictum that only the examined life is worth living, which gives predominance to the famous maxim of the oracle at Delphi "Know thyself!" and places self-knowledge at the center of his philosophy.

A few things are known about Socrates and his family. His father, Sophroniscus, was a sculptor. His mother, Phaenarete, was a midwife, a fact Socrates appears to have mentioned frequently in relation to his considering himself a *midwife of ideas*. Socrates' wife was Xanthippe, with whom he seems to have had a number of children. Until the beginning of the Peloponnesian war between Athens and Sparta

(431–404 BCE), if no later, he seems to have had at least middle-class means. However, the start of the war seems to have created or heightened a sense of personal mission in Socrates who, being slightly over forty years old, began talking to anyone he could at the *agora* – the public square – or elsewhere, concerning the need to find oneself and its interconnection with the salvation of Athens.

In the process, he seems to have neglected his patrimony, a matter that may be related to the fact that his wife has been perceived as trying Socrates' patience. Indeed, the name Xanthippe has become synonymous with a scolding and ill tempered wife. Yet, since women were entirely dependent on their husbands in Ancient Greece, and she apparently had children to feed, she may deserve a more charitable interpretation than has been cast upon her. Perhaps the only exception is the charitable interpretation in the twentieth-century novella by Alfredo Panzini, *Santippe*.

His philosophical zeal and the manner in which he carried his conversations with the citizens of Athens brought Socrates some followers (typically well-to-do bright young citizens who still had not attained fame or notoriety), and many enemies, typically intellectually or politically established citizens who felt threatened by Socrates' ideas. Among these were those who eventually brought him to trial, an event that resulted in Socrates being condemned to drink a potion of poisonous hemlock, which he did rather than leave Athens because, as reported by his disciples, of the obligation he felt as a citizen to obey the laws of his city-state.

Socrates wrote nothing; but the Platonic dialogues, especially the early ones (see PLATONISM) are thought to represent Socrates' ideas with some accuracy, though this involves the *Socratic problem*, i.e. the problem of distinguishing between Socrates' ideas and those of Plato (428–348 BCE), his disciple, who wrote the dialogues.

The Socratic method, also called *elenchus* or *cross-examination*, is substantially identical with the *aporetic* method (from the Greek *aporia*, i.e. "puzzle" – pl. *aporiai*), which consists in the raising of questions without offering solutions. In the Socratic-Platonic tradition, this method is described as a *maieutic* method (from the Greek *maia*, i.e. "midwife"), because it is meant to be a way of delivering an individual's ideas, which individuals are supposed to know through *recollection* or *reminiscence* from an eternal existence, and which are thought to have been obscured by the trauma of birth. At the very least, it involves a challenge to the use of a word or to the formulation of a belief; an examination of particular cases involving the word or notions used in order to discover what they have in common; and a search for a definition that would cover these cases or the results of examining them.

Given these features of Socrates' method, the Greek philosopher Aristotle (CE 384–322) credited Socrates for his contributions to inductive arguments and universal definition. Aristotle also correctly credited Socrates with a concern for ethical matters. Most notable in this regard is *Socratic intellectualism*, i.e. the view that moral goodness or virtue is a kind of knowledge, and that if one knows what is good or evil, then one cannot but act so as to do or bring about what is good, and omit or prevent what is evil. A corollary is the Socratic view that there is no *akrasia* or weakness of the will (see AKRASIA). Socrates thought that thinking otherwise would pose what has come to be called the *Socratic paradox*, and is frequently formulated as a problem: "How could one possibly, as the concept of *akrasia* presupposes, act against one's better judgment, be the judgment moral or prudential?"

Socrates' view on *akrasia* has been interpreted to imply one of two things: either that all desires are rational, or that knowledge of the good has more motivational power than any non-rational desires might have. Plato and Aristotle disagreed with Socrates on *akrasia* (though Socrates' doctrine was later revived by Stoic philosophers). Yet, Plato and Aristotle agreed with Socrates that the soul is not, as in the Homeric tradition, a mere ghost that continues to exist in the underworld, but the core of a human being, and that a certain kind of knowledge or wisdom leads to right conduct. To attain this end, the passions, which are part of the soul, must be trained in accordance with what reason requires. In addi-

tion to remaining influential in Platonism and Aristotelianism, Socratic philosophy was also influential among the Cynic, Megarian, and Cyrenaic schools (see GREEK PHILOSOPHY).

See also: Academy; Greek philosophy; Platonism

Further reading
Benson, Hugh H. (1992) *Essays on the Philosophy of Socrates*, New York and Oxford: Oxford University Press.
Gower, Barry and Stokes, Michael C. (1992) *Socratic Questions: New Essays on the Philosophy of Socrates and its Significance*, London and New York: Routledge.
Matthews, Gareth B. (1999) *Socratic Perplexity and the Nature of Philosophy*, Oxford and New York: Oxford University Press.
Panzini, Alfredo (1954) *Santippe*, Verona: Mondadori.
Vlastos, Gregory (ed.) (1971) *The Philosophy of Socrates*, Garden City, NY: Doubleday.

Socratic schools *see* Academy; Greek philosophy

soft determinism *see* determinism

software *see* computer theory

Sōka Gakkai *see* Japanese philosophy

sol invictus *see* philosophy of religion

solipsism From the Latin *solus*, i.e. "alone" and *ipse*, i.e. "self," this term denotes the doctrine that the individual person stands in various forms of isolation from any other person or sentient being that may exist. This view is associated, though not identical, with *egocentrism*, the view that individuals are or should be *egocentric* (from the Latin *ego*, i.e. "self," and centr(um), i.e. "center"), literally having or regarding the self as the center of all things, especially of the known world.

There is a range of variants of solipsism. One is *empathic* solipsism, according to which we are isolated from other sentient beings because we can never understand their experience well enough. Another is *semantic* solipsism, i.e. the view that all words mean or denote mental entities accessible only to the user of those words. A kind of semantic solipsism is *psychological* solipsism, i.e. the view that states ascribed to ourselves (e.g. I am happy) have a meaning radically different from states ascribed to others (e.g. you are happy). There is also *methodological* solipsism, i.e. the view that, in explaining the behavior of sentient beings, we should refer only to states or events occurring in their minds or brains. In addition, there is *epistemological* solipsism, the view that any individual can only claim his or her own existence and that of his or her own states. This view is often associated with SCEPTICISM. Finally, there is *ontological* or *metaphysical* solipsism, i.e. an individual's view that he or she and his or her own states are all that exists. Sometimes, this is called *metaphysical egoism* to emphasize its negative moral implications through total self-absorption. The Austrian-born British philosopher Ludwig Wittgenstein (CE 1889–1951) argued that there can be no private language, a view that undermined solipsism.

See also: Cartesianism; egocentric; philosophy of mind; skepticism

Further reading
Addis, Mark (1999) *Wittgenstein: Making Sense of Other Minds*, Aldershot: Ashgate.
Hanfling, Oswald (1976) *Solipsism and the Self*, Milton Keynes, UK: Open University Press.

somatism *see* positivism

somnium Scipionis *see* myth

Son Buddhism *see* Buddhism

sophia *see* philosophy

sophism *see* fallacy

sophism, lazy *see* fallacy

Sophists *see* Greek philosophy

Sorites *see* syllogism

sorites paradox *see* paradox

sortal predicates *see* natural kinds

sortal properties *see* natural kinds

sortals *see* natural kinds

Sosein *see* phenomenology

Soter *see* Christianity

Sōtō School *see* Zen

soul *see* philosophy of mind

soul of the world *see* Stoicism

sound argument *see* argument; logic

sound position *see* argument; logic

sound reasoning *see* argument; logic

sound view *see* argument; logic

soundness *see* argument; logic

soundness, strong *see* argument; logic

soundness, weak *see* argument; logic

Southern School *see* Zen

sovereignty *see* philosophy, sociopolitical

space *see* metaphysics; philosophy of science

space, absolute *see* philosophy of science

space, life- *see* philosophy of mind

space, mathematical *see* philosophy of science

space, phase- *see* philosophy of science

space, relative *see* philosophy of science

space, state- *see* philosophy of science

space–time *see* philosophy of science

spaciotemporal continuity *see* philosophy of science

speaker's meaning *see* meaning

special relativity *see* philosophy of science

special senses *see* philosophy of mind

special sensibles *see* philosophy of mind

species *see* definition

species, problem of *see* biology

speciesism *see* anthropocentrism

specious present *see* philosophy of science

speckled hen *see* perception

spectrum inversion *see* philosophy of mind

speculative grammar *see* philosophy of language

speculative philosophy *see* philosophy

speculative reason *see* Kantian philosophy

speculative rhetoric *see* philosophy of language

speculative theism *see* philosophy of religion

speech act theory The theory of language, sometimes called *pragmatics*, which emphasizes linguistic performance or the use of sentences – i.e. what can be done with them – rather than merely the meaning of the sentences used. A seminal influence in the development of speech act theory was that of the English philosopher J.L. Austin (CE 1911–60), who distinguished between a *locutionary act* (i.e. the use of a certain sentence), an *illocutionary act* (i.e. the kind and intention of the sentence given the context in which it was used in the locutionary act containing it), and a *perlocutionary* act (i.e. the act a speaker successfully elicits by means of a locutionary act and the illocutionary act it contains). For example, using the sentence "I have no chocolate" is a locutionary act that, as its related illocutionary act, may involve a mere report or, alternatively, a request for chocolate. The related perlocutionary act would be someone's acknowledgement of my lack of chocolate if the illocutionary act was a report, and someone giving me chocolate if the illocutionary act was a request.

A sentence can be used with more then one illocutionary force. For example, one can say "The car is outside" as a description or as a request. The force or forces with which a sentence can be used is its illocutionary force potential. The *felicity conditions* – i.e. those that contribute to the illocutionary success – of an illocutionary act consist not merely in its communicative or institutional success but also in its appropriateness as a linguistic performance (was "sorry" or "I apologize" appropriate?), effectiveness (was it taken as a sincere apology?), and sincerity (was it meant?). In this regard, the contemporary English philosopher R.M. Hare has distinguished the *phrastic* component – i.e. the referential or indicative component – of a sentence, from the *neustic* component – i.e. the assenting aspect – of a sentence. In terms of these notions, "Please bring me candy" can be formulated by means of the expression "Bringing me candy: please," where "Bringing me candy" is the phrastic

indicating the event, and "please" is the neustic indicating the speaker's attitude about the event. While in "You bring me candy," though the phrastic is the same – "Bringing me candy," the neustic is different: "yes," because the type of assent involved is different.

Speech act theory focuses on the characterization and classification of illocutionary acts, which have been classified into various (in some cases overlapping) kinds and subkinds. *Representatives* are such acts as reports and descriptions that commit the act's performers to the truth of what is being represented by the performers. They fall under the more general category of *constatives*, which includes statements (whether assertions or denials), predictions, and answers. *Directives* are such acts as requests and commands or imperatives that attempt to commit the acts' recipients to a course of action, and permissions, which make way for the act's recipients taking a course of action. *Commissives* are such acts as promises, offers, and bets that attempt to commit the acts' performers to a course of action. *Expressives* are such acts as expressions of feelings or wishes that express psychological states of the acts' performers. *Acknowledgements* are such acts as greetings, apologies, congratulations, and condolences. *Declarations* are acts that involve an intrinsic guarantee of performance. They include some commissives, but also predictions and, arguably, such conventional illocutionary acts as resignations, sentences, adjournments, acquittals, and certifications.

Various kinds of verbs have been distinguished in speech act theory. An *activity* verb denotes an activity that goes on for some time and need not have an end point, e.g. to reflect. An *accomplishment* verb denotes an activity that goes on for some time and aims at a definite end that characterizes it, e.g. to write (a novel) or pursue (an education). An *achievement* verb denotes either the attainment of an activity's end point, e.g. attain (a goal); or effecting a change, e.g. start (a speech); or undergoing a change, e.g. forget (an address). A *task* verb denotes an activity aimed at attaining something denoted by an achievement verb. A *state* verb denotes a condition, disposition, or habit (e.g. know (how to drive), love (to cook), or swim (regularly)), by contrast with what just happens to go on or a mere episode.

See also: meaning; philosophy of language

Further reading
Searle, John R., Kiefer, Ferenc, and Bierwisch, Manfred (1980) *Speech Act Theory and Pragmatics*, Dordrecht, Holland and Boston: Hingham, MA: D. Reidel and Kluwer Boston.
Tsohatzidis, Savas L. (1994) *Foundations of Speech Act Theory: Philosophical and Linguistic Perspectives*, London and New York: Routledge.

spirit *see* philosophy of mind

spirit, absolute *see* idealism

spirit of finesse *see* faith; intuition

spirit of geometry *see* faith; intuition

spirits *see* philosophy of religion

spiritual *see* philosophy of mind

spiritual beauty *see* aesthetics

spiritual feminism *see* feminist philosophy

spiritual sensations *see* Cambridge School

spiritualism From the Middle Latin *spiritualis*, i.e. "pertaining to or consisting of spirit" and "-ism" (and *spiritualis* from the Latin *spiritus*, i.e. "breath"), the term spiritualism has both philosophical and religious connotations. In philosophy, it is often associated with idealism; while in religion, it is sometimes used to denote the indwelling of the Holy Spirit (see CHRISTIANITY), and other times to denote views or attitudes that involve a belief in the Christian God and a life imbued with Christian practices.

Spiritualism is also a term associated with the nineteenth-century French reaction against Comtian positivism. It was largely initiated by the French philosopher Victor Cousin (CE 1792–1867), who advocated the notion of the *juste milieu*, a term that, in his case, meant a form of eclecticism where he included elements of Scottish common-sense philosophy, Hegelianism, and many other traditions. He considered spontaneity to be its own cause and the basis of both individual freedom and knowledge. He argued that spontaneity was present

in the act of creation. Also, through a spontaneous apperception, we can attain knowledge about the universe, primarily about the laws concerning substance and causality.

A particular form of spiritualism, frequently called *neo-spiritualism*, is that formulated by the French philosopher Jules Lachelier (CE 1834–1918), who was the teacher of the French philosophers Emile Boutroux (CE 1845–1921) and Henri Bergson (CE 1859–1941), both of whom are often also considered to exemplify neo-spiritualism. Lachelier advocated a form of spiritual realism whereby the spirit and spontaneity of humans provided an alternative to both idealism and materialism.

In the twentieth century, the Argentine philosopher Alejandro Korn (CE 1860–1936), who in many ways followed the thought of Bergson, tried to synthesize both positions. He formulated a philosophy he meant to be both positivistic and compatible with human freedom and value, and which he considered a refinement on native Argentine versions of positivism developed after independence.

See also: idealism; positivism

Further reading
Krikorian, Yervant Hovhannes (ed.) (1946 [1944]) *Naturalism and the Human Spirit*, New York: Columbia University Press.
Olson, Alan M. (1992) *Hegel and the Spirit: Philosophy as Pneumatology*, Princeton, NJ: Princeton University Press.

spissitude *see* Cambridge School

split brain effects *see* philosophy of mind

spontaneity *see* spiritualism

spontaneity, freedom of *see* determinism

spontaneity, liberty of *see* determinism

spontaneous apperception *see* spiritualism

Sprachform *see* Continental philosophy; philosophy of language

spread law *see* logic

square of opposition *see* syllogism

square of opposition, modal *see* syllogism

square of opposition, modern *see* syllogism

square of opposition, traditional *see* syllogism

stadium, paradox of the *see* paradox

Stagirite *see* Aristotelianism

standard analysis *see* philosophy of mathematics

standard interpretation *see* philosophy of language

standard model *see* philosophy of mathematics

standard semantics *see* philosophy of language

standard solid *see* perception

state *see* philosophy of mind; philosophy of science

state, city- *see* Greek philosophy; Nahua philosophy

state description *see* positivism

state, dispositional *see* philosophy of mind

state function *see* philosophy of science

state functionalism, machine- *see* philosophy of mind

state, instantaneous *see* philosophy of mathematics

State, liberal theory of the *see* philosophy, sociopolitical

state, mental *see* philosophy of mind

state of affairs *see* logic

state of nature *see* ethics; philosophy, sociopolitical

state, physical *see* philosophy of mind; philosophy of science

state, political *see* philosophy, sociopolitical

state space *see* philosophy of mathematics

state table *see* computer theory

state term, mental *see* philosophy of mind

state terrorism *see* war

state variables *see* philosophy of mathematics

state verb *see* speech act theory

statement *see* logic; meaning; philosophy of language

statistical explanation *see* explanation

statistical independence *see* probability

statistical law *see* causal law

statistical probability *see* probability

stereotypes *see* essentialism; feminist philosophy

stimulus *see* behaviorism; philosophy of mind

stimulus-meaning *see* philosophy of language

stipulative definition *see* definition

stochastic process *see* probability

Stoicism From the Greek *stoa*, i.e. "porch," this term denotes a Greco-Roman school of thought founded by the Cyprus-born Greek philosopher Zeno of Citium (*c*. 334–262 BCE) in Athens. The school's name derives from the place in Athens at which the school first met. The school formulated various doctrines in logic and epistemology, physics and metaphysics, and ethics (which included a theology). Its development is usually divided into three periods: Ancient Stoicism, the Middle School of Stoicism, and the New Stoicism.

Ancient Stoicism formulated propositional logic, deriving logical connections from reason through some sort of necessity. In epistemology, Ancient Stoicism formulated the doctrine of *common notions* (from the Latin *notiones comunes* and this from the Greek, *koinai ennoiai*, though the term *prolepsis*, i.e. naturally acquired general conceptions, was also used in this regard): basic ideas constituting the starting points of knowledge. In physics, Stoic philosophers of this period stressed the corporeal nature of the world, and emphasized fate, though its effects were supposed to take place through a world soul or *pneuma*, which in Greek means air. A mental principle of this type also called *pneuma* had been postulated by the Greek philosopher Anaximenes (588–524 BCE), who maintained air held the world together and embedded all life. Analogously, for the Stoics, *pneuma* was supposed to control all matter in accordance with *logos*, i.e. with reason. In addition, Stoic philosophers formulated the notion of *logos spermatikos*, which was translated into Latin as *rationes seminales*, i.e. seminal reasons, and denoted forces of nature that were present in matter and through which effects occurred. In ethics, the area in which Stoicism is best known, the school emphasized *apatheia*, i.e. resignation, an attitude of acceptance of one's situation in the world based on the acknowledgement that it reflects the logos. Notable among the representatives of Ancient Stoicism were its already mentioned founder, Zeno of Citium, and two other Greek philosophers, the Assos-born Cleanthes (331–232 BCE), and the Cilicia-born Chrysippus (*c.* 280–206 BCE).

The Middle and New Schools of Stoicism displayed significant eclecticism, especially the Middle School with its encyclopedic, syncretistic, and pantheistic emphasis. The *Middle School* of Stoicism or Middle Stoicism developed primarily in Rhodes. Its main representatives were two Greek philosophers: the Rhodes-born Panaetius (*c.* 185–110 BCE), who formulated a more pragmatic ethics than that of Ancient Stoicism; and the Apamea, Syria-born Posidonius (*c.* 135–50 BCE), who revived the Platonic inclusion of irrational components of the soul, hence undermining the predominant Stoic view that *akrasia* was impossible. The New Schools of Stoicism, also called the *New* Stoicism or *Roman* Stoicism, developed under the Roman Empire. Their main representatives were the Roman philosopher and writer of tragedies Lucius Annaeus Seneca (*c.* CE 1–65), born in Córdoba, in what is now Spain, the Greek philosopher and teacher Epictetus (*c.* CE 55–*c.* 135), born in Hierapolis (who began as a slave but was eventually freed), and the philosopher, writer, and Emperor of Rome Marcus Aurelius (CE 121–80). The emphasis during this period was primarily on ethics, where the idea of the control of life by reason led to a greater emphasis on public duty.

A related Stoic notion to that of logos is that of *jus naturale* or natural law, which actually was originated by Stoic thinkers and adopted by Roman lawyers, many of whom were Stoic as well. The notion of natural law as a standard of right and wrong beyond positive law became possible as a result of the Stoic conception of a universal reason at work in the world processes. Another notion that became possible is that of *Cosmopolis*, the city of the universe, whence the term *cosmopolitan*, i.e. people of the cosmos rather than merely of a given area.

In their discussions of knowledge, the Stoics talked of *cataleptic representations* (*kataleptike phantasia*), or, as others translate the Greek expression, *comprehensive representation*, *direct apprehension*, *immediate evidence*. All of them have something to do with perception (*catalepsis*), are a component of knowledge, and are supposed to be shared by all humans. They were not innate and included ideas of good, evil, and the existence of God.

As for the philosophy of language, the Stoics characterized a *lekton* (*lekta* in the plural) as the meaning of an utterance, i.e. as what an utterance signifies. *Lekta* were supposed to be associated, not just with declarative sentences (whose associated *lekta* were *axiomata* or propositions in that, though tensed, they could be true or false), but also with other, non-declarative, sentences including questions, commands, requests, and promises. The acceptance of a proposition was called *synkatathesis*.

In logic, the Stoics not only began to formulate propositional logic, but, also, motivated by their interest in fate, explored questions in modal logic. In this connection, the Greek term *apodeitikos*, a term derived from *apo* ("from") and *deiknymai* ("to show"), and applied to propositions or judgments meaning they are necessary, was used by the Stoics to denote basic rules of argument of the propositional calculus: *modus ponens*, *modus tollens*, and the *disjuntive syllogism*.

Like other Ancient philosophies, Stoicism underwent a rebirth – sometimes called *neo-Stoicism* – beginning with the Renaissance. A proponent of neo-Stoicism was the Flemish writer Justus Lipsius (CE 1547–1606), who argued that constancy was the highest value and consisted in an inner force developed through reflection and patient effort, and unaffected by outward circumstances that, none the less, was not identical with obstinacy. His work influenced writers in the Spanish Golden Age, most notably Francisco de Quevedo y

Villegas (ce 1580–1645). Another proponent was the French thinker Guillaume Du Vair (ce 1556–1621), who interpreted Stoic maxims in Christian terms.

The Stoic position concerning common notions was also adopted by the English philosopher Herbert of Cherbury (ce 1583–1648), who founded Deism. The common-notions view has a family resemblance to *Scottish common-sense philosophy*, also called *common-sense realism*. These common notions are innate and identifiable by having the following features: priority, independence, universality, certainty, necessity, and immediacy. Also, as in Kantian philosophy later, these common notions organize all experience.

See also: Greek philosophy

Further reading
Sharples, R.W. (1996) *Stoics, Epicureans and Sceptics: An Introduction to Hellenistic Philosophy*, London and New York: Routledge.
Zeller, Eduard (1967 [1892]) *The Stoics, Epicureans and Sceptics*, new and revised edn, London and New York: Longmans and Green.

stone, paradox of the *see* God

strange attractor *see* philosophy of mathematics

stranger *see* diaspora

strategy *see* decision

strategy rule *see* decision

strict conditional *see* condition

strict duties *see* ethics

strict identity *see* identity

strict implication *see* condition

strict liability *see* ethics; philosophy of law

strict partial ordering *see* ordering

striking *see* philosophy, sociopolitical

stroke function *see* logic

stroke notation *see* logic

strong right *see* ethics

strong semantic completeness *see* completeness

strong soundness *see* logic

strong supervenience *see* supervenience

structural ambiguity *see* ambiguity

structuralism *see* Continental philosophy

structure *see* Marxism

structure, deep *see* philosophy of language

structure description *see* philosophy of language

struggle, class *see* Marxism

struggle for existence *see* evolution

struggle for survival *see* evolution

stuff, mind- *see* philosophy of mind

Sturm und Drang *see* canon

sub specie aeternitatis *see* Cartesianism

subaltern *see* syllogism

suban *see* ethics

subconscious *see* psychoanalysis

subcontrary *see* syllogism

subdoxastic *see* philosophy of mind

subimplication *see* syllogism

subject *see* object

subject–object dichotomy *see* object

subject–object distinction *see* object

subject, political *see* philosophy, sociopolitical

subject–predicate logic *see* logic

subjective *see* epistemology; philosophy of science

subjective probability *see* probability

subjective ranking *see* decision

subjective reasons *see* justification; rationality

subjective rightness *see* ethics

subjectivism, epistemological *see* epistemology

subjectivism, ethical *see* ethics

subjectivism, moral *see* ethics

subjunctive conditional *see* logic

sublation *see* idealism

sublimation *see* psychoanalysis

sublime *see* aesthetics

subreption *see* fallacy; Kantian philosophy

subset *see* set

subsidiary *see* philosophy of language

subsistence *see* phenomenology

substance *see* abstract; Arabic philosophy; Aristotelianism; Thomism

substance, primary *see* abstract; Arabic philosophy; Aristotelianism; Thomism

substance, secondary *see* abstract; Arabic philosophy; Aristotelianism; Thomism

substantial form *see* Thomism

substantialism *see* abstract; metaphysics

substantival causation *see* causal law

substantival pluralism *see* metaphysics

substitutability salva veritate *see* opacity

substitutivity salva veritate *see* opacity

substrate *see* Aristotelianism; Thomism

substratum *see* Aristotelianism; Thomism

subsumption *see* syllogism

subsumption theory *see* explanation

succession *see* philosophy of mathematics

suchness *see* Zen

sufficient condition *see* explanation

sufficient reason, principle of *see* chain of being

Ṣūfism From the Arabic *ṣūfī*, i.e. "mystic," and "-ism," the term Ṣūfism denotes a mystical movement developed in the Islamic world. It sought union with Allah through love and renunciation. More specifically, the aim of the Ṣūfist spiritual journey is to die before one dies so that one can subsist in God alone. This latter state of illumination, which is said to be undefinable, is called *baqā*, which means "subsisting" or "immortality," while the end of the spiritual journey is *fanā* or "extinction," which is analogous to the Buddhist nirvana. In this regard, Sufis distinguish between *Ḥāl* ("state" or "condition"), i.e. a transitory state of illumination, and *maqām* ("station"), a permanent state of illumination. As in other similar movements, the practice of Ṣūfism leads to the development of spiritual masters called *shaykh* as well as *murshid* (i.e. "guide") and, in Iran and India, *pīr*.

A crucial philosophical term used in Ṣūfism is *dhāt* (i.e. essence, quiddity, ipseity). It was derived from the Arabic particle *dhū* (which means "possession of"), of which it is the feminine form. Just as the Latin term essentia, the term *dhāt* was derived in an attempt at making it correspond to the Greek *ousia*. In Arabic philosophy, *adh-dhāt* denotes the essence of something in itself, by contrast with the quality (*sifah*) it has. Sufis use the phrase *jannat adh-dhāt*, meaning paradise of the essence, to refer to the divinity itself.

Another technical term of Ṣūfism is *ghaybah* (i.e. "absence" or "being concealed"), which denotes absence from the world or withdrawal from all things except the worship and awareness of God. This term also denotes the Shī'ite *doctrine of occultation*, or *disappearance* from human view (some say from the world altogether) of the Twelfth Imam or Twelve Imam Shī'ism. This is analogous to the Quran's saying that Jesus was not killed on the cross, but was raised to a higher state of being from which he will return at the end of the world. Other groups, e.g. the Druzes, hold similar beliefs about some of their members.

A related concept is *huzn* ("sadness," "grief"), which in Ṣūfism means sacred nostalgia and is used to denote a longing for Reality, which is hidden beyond the veil of separation and, with regard to which, we are all in exile: the world is exile (see PHILOSOPHY AND EXPATRIATION). Indeed, Ṣūfism sharply contrasts *nāsūt*, the sphere of what is human and mortal, with *lāhūt*, the sphere of the divinity.

Ṣūfī thinkers often use metaphorical expressions to convey their doctrines. One such expression is *nafas-al-Raḥmān*, i.e. the breath of the Merciful. It is used in Ṣūfī metaphysics to denote the actualization of possibilities, in particular the creation of the world by God who, figuratively, breathes it out, very much as, in speaking, a speaker breathes out what is in his or her mind. In a different sense, *nafas-al-Raḥmān* denotes the celebration held when a pupil in a traditional Quranic school has memorized the Quran, from its beginning up to the 55th *Sūrah* (i.e. chapter), entitled *ar-Raḥmān*.

Ṣūfism was initially suspect in Islam; but it gained acceptance primarily as a result of the work of the Persian thinker al-Ghazālī (CE 1059–1111), whose mission was not only to re-orient orthodox Islam, but also to reform Ṣūfism. Though, through the philosophical inquiry into the ultimate nature of God, he had attained no results, he did not turn to Ṣūfism as an alternative source of this knowledge. Indeed, he rejected Ṣūfī theosophic mysticism and criticized those who dwelled on extatic mysticism as a source of knowledge. Instead, he used the Ṣūfī experiential journey to test Islamic faith and concluded that faith could be acquired only through the life of the heart. His position was that mysticism could yield no extra facts about reality, but only a meaningful way of approaching reality as a unity.

All earlier Ṣūfī traditions as well as Neoplatonic emanationist doctrines held in Arabic philosophy were incorporated in the works produced by the philosopher Ibn al-'Arabī (in Latin, Abenarabi; CE 1164–1240), born in what is now Murcia, Spain. He held that Absolute Reality is transcendent and nameless, and its only attribute is self-existence. Accordingly, he denied the possibility of any analogy between God and creation, hence the possibility of knowing God. However, this Absolute, by a process of descent, becomes aware of its attributes of perfection. They exist only in God's mind, but are the attributes of which the world is made. The world's creation is the projection of these attributes from God's mind into real existence, most notably the essence of the prophet Muḥammad, which is the highest essence, manifests itself into the prophet's historical person. This descent opens up the possibility of mystical ascent. Central in Ibn al-'Arabī's thought is the notion of *degrees of love*, which range from mere sympathy, to pure love of a person as such and regardless of circumstances. The thought of Ibn al-'Arabī has influenced poetry throughout the Islamic world and became again part of philosophy during the *Ṣafawids dynasty* that ruled Persia from the sixteenth to the early eighteenth century.

See also: Arabic philosophy; Buddhism

Further reading
Arberry, A.J. (1942) *An Introduction to the History of Sufism*, London and New York: Longmans and Green and Co.
Corbin, Henry (1998) *Alone with the Alone: Creative Imagination in the Sufism of Ibn 'Arabi*, Princeton, NJ: Princeton University Press.

suicide, assisted *see* ethics; euthanasia

summae *see* Scholasticism

summum bonum *see* perfection

summum genus *see* definition

sumption *see* syllogism

sun *see* God; Nahua philosophy; philosophy of religion; Platonism

sunsum *see* metaphysics

sūnya *see* Buddhism

sūnya-vāda *see* Buddhism

superaltern *see* syllogism

superalternation *see* syllogism

superego *see* psychoanalysis

supererogation *see* ethics

superimplication *see* syllogism

superman *see* ethics

supernatural *see* philosophy of mind; philosophy of religion

supernatural theology *see* philosophy of religion

supernaturalism *see* philosophy of religion

superseding cause *see* causal law

superset *see* set

superstructure *see* Marxism

supersubstantial *see* Thomism

supervaluation *see* ambiguity; logic

supervaluation, method of *see* ambiguity; logic

supervaluational semantics *see* logic

supervenience Typically, a dependence and emergence relation between attributes, properties, or facts of one type – e.g. moral – and attributes, properties, or facts of another type – e.g. non-moral. This is as when one says that the intrinsic value of an ecosystem depends on and emerges from the nature and functions of the ecosystem, thereby being a resultant attribute or property of, or fact about, the ecosystem.

Sometimes, supervenience is also used as a dependence relation between given judgments or language of one type (e.g. describing a person's action under certain circumstances) and judgments or language of another type (e.g. evaluating that person's action as being right), whereby one is committed also to saying that any other person in exactly the same circumstances acted rightly, because this judgment or language is supervenient on the previous descriptive judgment or language regardless of who it is about.

In some cases, supervenience is claimed in areas other than ethics or aesthetics, for example in the philosophy of mind, when giving a naturalistic but not reductionist account of mental attributes, properties, or facts by saying that they are dependent on and emergent from neurophysiological facts or properties.

Much attention has centered on the nature of such dependence. Some argue for *weak* supervenience, i.e. the view that if, in any single possible world, any two of its individuals x and y differ in attributes, properties, or facts of type A, then they also differ in attributes, properties, or facts of type B (where attributes, facts, or properties of type A are supervenient of those of type B). Others uphold *strong* supervenience, i.e. the view that if any two distinct individuals, whether in a single possible or in two distinct worlds, differ in attributes, properties, or facts of type A, then they also differ in attributes, properties, or facts of type B (where attributes, facts, or properties of type A are supervenient of those of type B).

In addition, the view that the physical facts, attributes, or properties determine all the facts is called *global* supervenience. *Regional* supervenience is the view that if any two spatiotemporal regions a and b, whether in a single possible or two distinct worlds, differ in some respect, then they also differ in some physical respect.

Discussions of supervenience involve the distinction between intrinsic or essential and extrinsic or accidental properties (see RELATION). For example, the property of being a university associated with the physical buildings of the University of Wisconsin-Madison is not simply (if at all) supervenient on intrinsic properties of those physical buildings. If supervenience is involved in this case, it is the result of a wide range of facts and properties called the supervenience base. This is a situation where global supervenience or, alternatively, regional supervenience is invoked.

See also: holism; quality

Further reading
Alexander, Ronald G. (1997) *The Self, Supervenience, and Personal Identity*, Aldershot, Hants, UK and Brookfield, VT: Ashgate.
Drai, Dalia (1999) *Supervenience and Realism*, Aldershot and Brookfield, USA: Ashgate.
Kim, Jaegwon (1993) *Supervenience and Mind: Selected Philosophical Essays*, New York: Cambridge University Press.

suppositio *see* syncategoremata

supposition *see* syncategoremata

suppositum intellectuale *see* determinism

supreme being *see* God

surface structure *see* philosophy of language

surplus meaning *see* positivism

surplus value *see* Marxism; philosophy of economics

survival, biological *see* evolution

survival, cultural *see* evolution

survival, linguistic *see* evolution

survival of the fittest *see* evolution

survival, social *see* evolution

suspension of judgment *see* Cartesianism; phenomenology

sustaining cause *see* causal law; occasionalism

sūtra *see* Buddhism; Hinduism

Swedenborgianism *see* Christianity

syllogism From the Greek *syn*, i.e. "together," and *logizesthai*, i.e. "to reckon" or "to conclude by reasoning," the term syllogism denotes a form of deductive argument where the conclusion follows from two premises. In Aristotelian works, syllogism is opposed to *epagogē*, the Greek term for INDUCTION, on the point that the syllogism is demonstrative. There are three main types of syllogisms: categorical, hypothetical, and disjunctive.

A *categorical syllogism* is a deductive argument including three categorical statements, two of them the premises, and the other the conclusion. It has exactly three class denoting terms, each occurring twice, but never twice in the same statement. As for the concept of categorical statements just mentioned, let us consider two examples: "Every Italian is a European" and "Some Europeans are not French." They can be generally characterized as follows: a *categorical statement* is a statement to the effect that one class is partially or totally included in or excluded from another class. Every categorical statement can be formulated in a *standard form*. There are four which, traditionally, are formulated using the capital letter *S* for the subject and the capital letter *P* for the predicate: "All *S* are *P*," also called *universal affirmative* or *A*; "No *S* are *P*," also called *universal negative* or *E*; "Some *S* are *P*," also called *particular affirmative* or *I*; and "Some *S* are not *P*," also called *particular negative* or *O*. *A*, as well as *E*, is called a universal statement or universal proposition, while *I*, as well as *O*, is called a particular statement or particular proposition.

These statements constitute the *traditional square of opposition*, a graphic representation of logical relations between categorical statements:

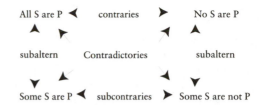

Contradictories are those statements than cannot be both true or both false. *Contraries* are those statements that cannot be both true, though they can be both false. *Subcontraries* are statements such that at least one of them must be true, though both can be true. A *subaltern* is a statement in a relation of *subalternation* to another statement, the *superaltern* (that is in a relation of *superalternation* to the former), if the superaltern implies the other, but not vice versa. For these relations to hold, it must be assumed that the subject terms – of the statements involved denote non-empty classes or categories. This is what was assumed in the traditional square of opposition. It is not assumed in the *modern square of opposition* where, as a result, only contradictories remain.

Along these lines, logicians have formulated the *modal square of opposition*:

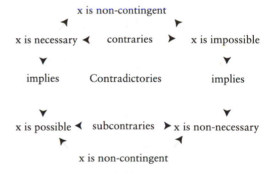

The three class-denoting terms in a categorical syllogism are called *major* (usually designated by the capital letter *P*), *minor* (usually designated by the capital letter *S*), and *middle* (usually designated by the capital letter *M*).

These terms are associated with given premises. The *major premise* is that including the predicate term of the conclusion. The *minor premise* is that including the subject term of the conclusion. In medieval logic, the minor premise was called the *subsumption* (from the Latin *sub*, i.e. "under" and *sumere*, i.e. "to take" or "include") of the major premise, which was called the *sumption*.

The terms and kinds of categorical statements just described serve to characterize the figure and mood of a syllogism, whose combination constitutes the *form* of a syllogism. The *figure* of a categorical syllogism is the schema determined by the position of the middle term in relation to the minor term:

Figure 1:	Figure 2:
M is *P*	*P* is *M*
S is *M*	*S* is *M*
Hence, *S* is *P*	Hence, *S* is *P*

Figure 3:	Figure 4:
M is *P*	*P* is *M*
M is *S*	*M* is *S*
Hence, *S* is *P*	Hence, *S* is *P*

The fourth figure, also called *Galenian* figure, can be reduced to the first three (by switching the terms taken to be major and minor).

The *mood* of a categorical syllogism is the configuration of types of categorical statements that constitute it, e.g. *AAA*, and *AEE*.

Various valid forms of the syllogism are barbara (first figure in *AAA* mood), celarent (first figure in *EAE* mood), darapti (third figure in *AAI* mood), darii (first figure in *AII* mood), datisi (third figure in *AII* mood), felapton (third figure in *EAO* mood), ferio (first figure in *EIO* mood), ferison (third figure in *EIO* mood), fesapo (fourth figure in *EAO* mood), fresison (fourth figure in *EIO* mood), and others.

In modern times, spatial representations – called *Euler diagrams* – of class relations were formulated by the Swiss mathematician Leonhard Euler (CE 1707–83) for the categorical statement forms: every *A* is *B*; no *A* is *B*; some

A is *B*; and some *A* is not *B* (see Figure 1). The British logician John Venn (CE 1834–1923) introduced a different spatial representation of the same forms – called *Venn diagrams* – which made it possible to check the validity of syllogisms representing any syllogism by three overlapping circles, one for each class-denoting term the syllogism contains (see Figure 2).

Aristotelian logicians used the phrase *proton pseudos*, Greek for "first error," to denote a false major premise in a syllogism. Some have extended this notion to mean any false initial statement in a deductive system. Still others use *proton pseudos* to mean any false basic proposition.

Some arguments are interpreted to be syllogisms with a suppressed premise. Any such argument is called *enthymeme* or *decurtate syllogism*. In addition, there are *polysyllogisms*, i.e. series of syllogisms connected by the fact that the conclusion of one is the premise of another. If this other is the next, they are called *prosyllogisms*. While those in which the conclusion of another syllogism within the chain is used as a premise are called *episyllogisms*. In addition, syllogisms in which each premise represents an enthymematic syllogism are called *epicheirema*.

In this connection, the problem arises of discovering the middle term of a syllogism. Medieval logicians developed a diagram called *pons asinorum*, i.e. the donkeys' bridge, meant to help find all middle terms (see Figure 3).

Medieval logicians believed two principles or laws of thought lie under all valid syllogisms. These were formulated as *dictum de omni et nullo* (also *dici de omni et nullo*), a Latin phrase meaning "said of all and none." *Dictum de omni* naturally applies to universal affirmative statements, e.g. in "every dog is a canine," whatever is denoted by "dog" is included under "canine." While *dictum de nullo* naturally applies to universal negative statements, e.g. in "no bird is a mammal," whatever is denoted by "bird" is not included under "mammal." A related Latin phrase was *nota notae est nota rei ipsius* or "the note of a note is a note of the thing itself," used to mean that whatever is the understanding of a component of some item falls under the understanding of the item.

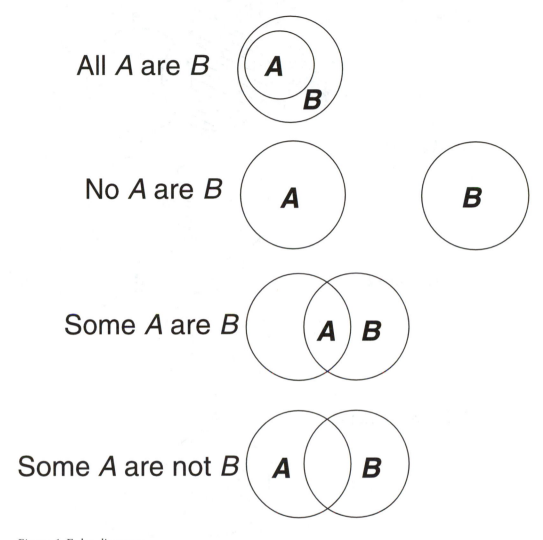

Figure 1 Euler diagrams

Besides Euler diagrams and Venn diagrams, other procedures have been invented to establish whether syllogisms are valid or not. One involves an *inconsistent triad*, i.e. in general, any three propositions that cannot all be true; however, as applied to the syllogism, any three categorical propositions that cannot all be true. The method of inconsistent triads relies on the fact that a syllogism is valid provided that its premises and the negation of its conclusion are an inconsistent triad.

As for the *hypothetical* syllogism, in a narrow sense, it has the form:

If *p* then *q*.
If *q* then *r*.
Hence, If *p* then *r*.

A substitution instance of this form of argument is

If Jimmy is a healthy infant, then Jimmy is curious.

All *A* are *B*

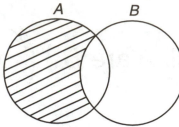

No *A* are *B*

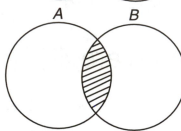

Some *A* are *B*

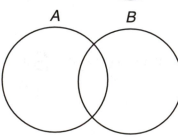

Some *A* are not *B*

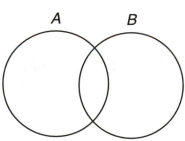

Valid Argument Diagram:

All *A* are *B*

All *B* are *C*

Hence, all *A* are *C*

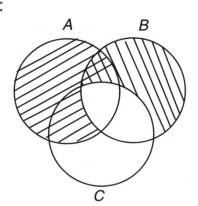

Figure 2 Venn diagrams

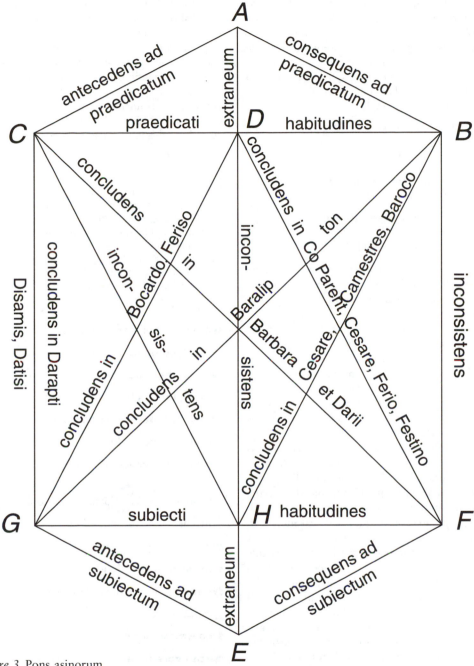

Figure 3 Pons asinorum

If Jimmy is curious, then Jimmy sometimes causes mischief.

Hence, if Jimmy is a healthy infant, then Jimmy sometimes causes mischief.

In a wider sense, the hypothetical syllogism is any form of reasoning – e.g. *modus ponens* and *modus tollens* (see LOGIC) – whose major premise is composite and whose minor premise affirms or denies one of the parts.

Finally, the *disjunctive* syllogism has two forms. The weaker one uses the *inclusive* disjunction. For example:

Either I am sick or I am tired.
I am not sick.
Hence, I am tired.

The *stronger* form uses the *exclusive* disjunction. For example:

Either he is five or he is six years old.
He is not five.
Hence, he is six years old.

Another relevant concept is that of *sorites* (from the Greek *soros*, i.e. "heap"), which denotes an argument made up of categorical statements and that can be interpreted as a series of categorical syllogisms, so that the conclusion of each but the last syllogism in the series is a premise of the next.

Philosophers have discussed the notion of *practical syllogism* and its associated notion of *practical reasoning*. Practical reasoning is the inferential process whereby alternative courses of action are assessed on the basis of various considerations and, as a result, a decision is made and one or more actions are performed. That is, practical reasoning is carried out with a *practical attitude*: an attitude aimed at taking action. Practical syllogism denotes the type of arguments involved in practical reasoning. On a narrow conception of practical syllogism, it is an argument whose premises are statements and whose conclusion is a statement serving as a ground for decision and action. On a wider conception of a practical syllogism, the argument's conclusion is not a statement, but the content of the decision made and action(s) taken at the end of the process of practical reasoning.

Philosophers have argued for the latter, wider, conception, on the grounds that, on the narrower conception, beliefs can be formed without any intention to act in accordance with them being formed. However, when the wider conception is adopted, familiar logical criteria for assessing arguments do not suffice,

and additional evaluation criteria need to be established. Some of these criteria concern such things as the timeliness of the decision, the relevance of the alternatives considered, and the exhaustiveness of these alternatives. Others concern the compatibility or incompatibility of the decisions or actions to be taken. Still others concern the prudence or morality of the said decisions or actions. All these matters are discussed in ethics and sociopolitical philosophy.

See also: logic

Further reading

Lukasiewicz, Jan (1988 [1851]) *Aristotle's Syllogistic from the Standpoint of Modern Formal Logic*, Oxford: Clarendon Press.
Thom, Paul (1981) *The Syllogism*, München: Philosophia.
Thompson, Bruce E.R. (1992) *An Introduction to the Syllogism and the Logic of Proportional Quantifiers*, New York: P. Lang.

symbiosis *see* ecology

symbol *see* philosophy of language

symbol, complete *see* syncategoremata

symbol, improper *see* syncategoremata

symbol, incomplete *see* syncategoremata

symbol, proper *see* syncategoremata

symbolic logic *see* logic

symbolic reference *see* philosophy of language

symbolism *see* Continental philosophy

symbols *see* philosophy of language

symbols, primitive *see* logic; theory

symmetrical *see* relation

symmetry *see* relation; philosophy of science

sympathy *see* ethics

synaesthesia *see* perception

syncategoremata From the Greek *syn*, i.e. "together," and *categorema*, i.e. "predicate," the term *syncategoremata* (or syncategorematic terms as opposed to *categoremata* or categorematic terms) has been used in at least two senses. First, syntactically, the term *syncategoremata* denotes those terms that cannot by themselves serve as subjects or predicates of propositions. For example, "and," "or," "if," "each," and "therefore" are *syncategoremata*. Second, *syncategoremata* were characterized semantically in the Middle Ages by such authors as the English philosopher William Sherwood (1200/10–66/71), the Lisbon-born philosopher Peter of Spain (*c*. CE 1205–77), the French philosopher Lambert of Auxerre (mid-thirteenth century CE), and the English philosopher William of Ockham (*c*. CE 1290–1349). They formulated the doctrine of properties of terms (*proprietates terminorum*) – a central component of their *logica moderna*, i.e. modern logic, also called *terminist logic* because it focused on the logical features of terms. They contrasted *logica moderna* or terminist logic with Aristotelian logic. According to terminist logic, *syncategoremata* are terms without, while *categoremata* are terms with, definite independent meaning. That is, *categoramata* are descriptive terms such as "dog," "table," and "water," while *syncategoremata* are logical or non-descriptive terms such as "and," "or," and "some." In the Middle Ages, these senses applied to terms in natural languages, while in modern logic, they are extended to terms in artificial languages. In this extended usage, *syncategoremata* are also called *improper symbols* and incomplete symbols, while *categoremata* are also called *proper symbols* and complete symbols.

In addition, medieval logicians also distinguished between syncategorematic and categorematic *uses* of terms. For example, in "God is," the term "is" is used to claim that God exists; hence, if, as they thought, it asserts a fact about the universe, it is used categorematically. While in "my dog is black," the term "is" is merely combining terms, hence used syncategorematically.

Another example was that of terms – e.g. "nothing" – which could be subjects or predicates of propositions but included the use of the syncategorematic term "not" in them. They were classified as syncategorematic because, otherwise, they led to invalid inferences. For example, even if nothing is better than a Caribbean vacation, and burnt coffee is better than nothing, it does not follow that burnt coffee is better than a Caribbean vacation.

Another contribution of terminist logic was the formulation and study of the distinction between the *significatio*, i.e. meaning or signification, of a term, and the *suppositio*, i.e. the particular items or *significata* (singular: *significatum*) denoted by, a term. Today, this distinction is roughly the distinction between intensional and extensional meaning of a term (see MEANING).

The kinds of suppositions were variously characterized by different authors. According to Peter of Spain, for example, *suppositio* could be discrete (*suppositio discreta*), when a single individual is denoted, as in "Plato is an animal", and common (*suppositio communis*), when universals are denoted, as in "Beauty is a Form." Common supposition is divided into natural (*suppositio naturalis*), when a term's supposition depends only on the term, as in "Fish are animals," and accidental (*suppositio accidentalis*), when the supposition depends on what is added to the term, as in "Brightly colored fish are collectors' items." Accidental supposition is divided into simple (*suppositio simplex*), i.e. when species or genera are denoted, as in "Brightly colored fish are collectors' items," and personal (*suppositio personalis*), i.e. when the term denotes any of its logically dependent items, typically any individuals, whether persons or not, as in "Fido is Alice's fish."

Other philosophers distinguished between formal supposition (*suppositio formalis*), when a non-linguistic item is denoted, e.g. "Socrates" in "Socrates died in Athens", and material supposition (*suppositio materialis*), when the item's name is denoted, e.g. "Socrates" in "Socrates has three syllables." This was the medieval version of the use–mention or metalanguage–object language distinction.

See also: logic

Further reading
Rijk, Lambertus Marie de (1967 [1962]) *Logica modernorum: A Contribution to the History of Early Terminist Logic*, Assen: Van Gorcum.
William of Shyreswood (1968 [1941]) *Treatise on Syncategorematic Words: Translated [from the Latin] with an Introduction and Notes by Norman Kretzmann*, Minneapolis

and London: University of Minnesota Press and Oxford University Press.

syncategorematic terms *see* syncategoremata

synchrony *see* Continental philosophy

syncretism *see* Academy; Neoplatonism

synderesis *see* conscience

syndicalism *see* philosophy, sociopolitical

synecdoche *see* meaning

synechiology *see* metaphysics

synechism *see* metaphysics

synergism *see* determinism

synergy *see* determinism

synkatathesis *see* Stoicism

synonymous definition *see* definition

synonymy *see* meaning; philosophy of language

synsemantic *see* phenomenology

syntactic ambiguity *see* ambiguity

syntactic consistency *see* logic

syntactics *see* philosophy of language

syntax *see* logic; philosophy of language

synthesis *see* dialectic

synthetic *see* analytic–synthetic distinction

synthetic a priori *see* Kantian philosophy

Syrian School *see* Neoplatonism

system, axiomatic *see* logic

system, interpretive *see* operationalism

system, logical *see* logic

systems analysis *see* philosophy of mathematics

systems theory *see* philosophy of mathematics

syzygies *see* cabala

T

T *see* meaning

table of categories *see* Kantian philosophy

table of judgments *see* Kantian philosophy

table, Pythagorean *see* Pythagoreanism

tables of induction *see* induction

taboo *see* myth; psychoanalysis

tabu *see* myth; psychoanalysis

tabula nuda *see* idea

tabula rasa *see* idea

tacit consent *see* philosophy, sociopolitical

tacit knowledge *see* philosophy of language

tahafut *see* Arabic philosophy

Ta-hsüeh *see* Chinese philosophy; Confucianism

t'ai-chi *see* Chinese philosophy

t'ai-p'ing ching *see* Taoism

t'ai-p'ing tao *see* Taoism

t'ai-shang kan-ying p'ien *see* Taoism

talante *see* existentialism

Talmud *see* Jewish philosophy; Judaism

tamas *see* Hinduism

Tāne-mahuta *see* Māori philosophy

tantras *see* theurgy

tanzīh *see* Islam

tao *see* Taoism

tao-chia *see* Taoism

tao-chiao *see* Taoism

tao-hsin *see* Chinese philosophy; Confucianism

Tao-te ching *see* Chinese philosophy; Taoism

tao-tsang *see* Taoism

tao-t'ung *see* Confucianism

Taoism A term used in the Western world to describe both philosophical Taoism, *tao-chia* or School of the Way, and religious Taoism, *tao-chiao*, a diverse collection of religious movements and schools among which the main were the Way of the Realization of Truth (*ch'üan-chen tao*), and the Way of Right Unity (*cheng-I tao*).

An important concept in Taoism is *ch'ang*, i.e. the property of being constant, enduring, eternal. The *Tao-te Ching* (*Classic of the Way and Its Virtue*), Taoism's main document, attributes this property to all universal laws. As regards practical matters, the central goal of Taoism is the attainment of *ch'ang-sheng pu-ssu*, i.e. immortality. This is conceived as physical in most schools of religious Taoism; but philosophical Taoism conceives immortality as spiritual and explains it as enlightenment and oneness with the highest principle, the *Tao*. A person who has attained this end is called *chen-jen*, i.e. a pure human being.

The main Taoist figures were Lao-Tzu (sixth century BCE) and Chuang-Tzu or Chuang-Chou (fourth century BCE). They are notable for having characterized the notion of *wu wei* or non-action alongside the previous notions. In Lao-Tzu, it is the absence of striving towards goals and a form of government that does not impose any type of conduct on people. In Chuang-Tzu, *wu wei* denotes a type of existence where one is not guided by preconceived aims, projects, or ideals.

The conceptions of *wu wei* found in Lao-Tzu and Chuang-Tzu include *wu*, a term that traditionally appears in the pair of opposites *yu* and *wu*, which respectively mean "having" and "nothing." Sometimes, *yu* and *wu* are respectively translated as "being" and "non-being"; however, it should be kept in mind that *yu* and *wu* are in some kind of dependency relation. For example, at one point, the Tao-te ching says *yu* and *wu* produce each other; while, at another point, it says the *yu* comes from *wu*. The concept of *wu* was attributed a more fundamental role by later Taoists (see below).

Though similar to each other, the positions held by Lao-Tzu and Chuang-Tzu have significant differences. The former recommends a return to the simple life of small agrarian communities where people do not care about what happens in neighboring communities. However, Chuang-Tzu focuses on changing oneself rather than changing society so as to lead a life free from friction.

Ch'ing-t'an, a term meaning pure conversation, denotes a method used by the *Hsüan hsüeh* (the Mysterious Learning School), a neo-Taoist school originated in the third century CE that focused on a refined form of conversation used to reinterpret the works of Lao-Tzu and Chuang-Tzu. Its main representatives were Wang Pi (CE 226–49), Kuo Hsiang (*fl. c.* CE 312), Hsiang Hsiu (CE 221–300), and Ho Yen (third century CE). Both Wang and Kuo considered Confucius to be a true sage, for he embodied non-being, while Lao Tzu and Chuang Tzu only discussed it. But while Kuo believed the universe to generate itself, Wang held it arose from a unified state called *wu* (non-being). Wang is significant for developing the notion of pattern (*li*) and pairing such concepts as substance (*t'i*) and function (*yung*). His commentary on the *Tao-te Ching* was very influential in Chinese thought. As for Ho Yen (third century CE), he considered the Tao to be the ultimate reality, incapable of being described

or named, yet at work in and shaping all things. Despite being a neo-Taoist, Ho Yen considered Confucius, not Lao Tzu, as the sage.

Ch'i, a term literally meaning air, vapor, breath, ether, corporeal vital energy, strength, and the "atmosphere" of a season, person, event, or work, denotes a central concept in Taoism and Chinese medicine. In Taoism, *ch'i* is the life force, primordial force, cosmic spirit, or psycho-physical energy that pervades and gives life to everything. *Ch'i* can be pure or impure, active or still. It is high in health and low in illness. In human bodies, it is supposed to gather in an area surrounding the navel called the ocean of breath, and is to be carefully tended by means of breathing exercises that aim at developing a variety of abilities also central in martial arts. *Ch'i* has been co-ordinated with *li* (pattern), constituting the medium in which *li* is embedded and through which it can be experienced. It is a concept akin to that of matter in Western thought, except that, by contrast with matter, *ch'i* is active and dynamic, which has raised questions different from those raised by matter.

The term *ch'i* appears in the expression *ch'i-kung*, which roughly means "working the energy," and denotes physical exercises central to Chinese medicine. They have Buddhist and Taoist components and apply to body, mind, and breath. Widely understood, the martial arts – *wushu* – are forms of *ch'i-kung*. *Ch'i* also appears in the expressions *nei-ch'i* or inner breath, which denotes the primordial vital energy stored within the body since birth, and is contrasted with *wai-ch'i* or outer breath, which denotes the air we exhale. Taoists try to conserve and reinforce their *nei-ch'i*, so as to bring it back to the state in which it was at the time of birth. If any of a person's *nei-ch'i* escapes during exhalation, it is believed that the person's life will be shorter.

Ch'ien and *k'un* are the names of the first and second hexagram or two of the eight trigrams in the *I-Ching* or *Book of Changes*. *Chi'en*, composed of three undivided lines ($\equiv$) symbolizes *yang*, and means heaven, the father, creativity; while *k'un*, composed of three divided lines ($\equiv\ \equiv$), symbolizes *yin*, and means earth, the mother, endurance. Together, they constitute the cosmic order.

Besides those already mentioned, various additional Taoist texts exist. One is *t'ai-p'ing ching* or *Book of Supreme Peace*, a text having various versions, which was the basis of *t'ai-p'ing tao* or *Way of Supreme Peace*, a Taoism school founded between CE 172 and 178, which emphasized magic, mass ceremonies where public confessions led to healing. It became politically powerful and, in CE 184, thousands of its followers, led by the school's founder, Chang Chüeh (d. CE 184), who aimed at establishing peace and equality among individuals, revolted against the central government. They wore yellow head bands, hence the revolt's name: *The Rising of the Yellow Turbans*. They failed, and Chang Chüeh and his brothers, Chang Pao and Chang Liang, who fought by his side, were killed; but the school remained politically influential for quite some time.

Another Taoist text is *t'ai-shang kan-ying p'ien* or *Treatise on Action and Recompense*, which can be traced back to the Sung dynasty (CE 960–1279) and focuses on morals, especially on rewards and punishments. It appears to have been influenced by Buddhism and Confucianism.

The Taoist canon is the *Tao-tsang*. Its oldest section traces back to the fifth century CE; while the Tao-tsang reached its final form between CE 1111 and 1118. Its complete version was compiled during the Ming dynasty (CE 1368–1644).

See also: Chinese philosophy

Further reading
Chang, Chung-Yuan (1975 [1963]) *Creativity and Taoism: A Study of Chinese Philosophy, Art and Poetry*, London: Wildwood House.
Fang, Tung-mei (1986) *Chinese Philosophy, Its Spirit and Its Development*, Taipei, Taiwan: Linking Pub. Co.
Graham, A.C. (1995) *Disputers of the Tao: Philosophical Argument in Ancient China*, La Salle, IL: Open Court.
Kohn, Livia (1999) *Taoist Mystical Philosophy: The Scripture of Western Ascension*, Boulder, CO: NetLibrary, Inc.

Taoistic Confucianism *see* Confucianism

tapas *see* Hinduism

tapu *see* Māori philosophy

Tarskian biconditional *see* meaning

Tarskian satisfaction *see* meaning

Tarskian semantics *see* meaning

Tarskian theory of truth *see* truth

Tarski's (T) schema *see* truth

Tarski's theorem *see* truth

task verb *see* speech act theory

tattva *see* Hinduism; Jainism; Sāmkhya-Yoga

tautology *see* analytic–synthetic distinction

taxonomy *see* biology; category

te *see* Chinese philosophy

techne *see* ethics

technique *see* ethics

technocracy *see* ethics

technology ethics *see* ethics

technology tribunal *see* ethics

tectologia *see* metaphysics

telefinalism *see* philosophy of religion

telekinesis *see* philosophy of mind

teleological argument *see* philosophy of religion

teleological explanation *see* explanation

teleological law *see* causal law

teleological suspension of the ethical *see* existentialism

teleological theories of ethics *see* ethics

teleology *see* explanation

telepathy *see* philosophy of mind

telishment *see* philosophy of law

telos *see* ethics

temperance *see* virtue

temple *see* existentialism

temporal becoming *see* philosophy of science

Tendai School *see* Chinese philosophy; Japanese philosophy

tense logic *see* logic

tensed identity *see* identity

term, major *see* syllogism

term, minor *see* syllogism

term, transcendental *see* category

terminating judgments *see* analytic–synthetic distinction

terminist logic *see* logic; syncategoremata

terminus a quem *see* *ad quod*, under ad

terminus a quo *see* *ad quod*, under ad

terminus ad quem *see* *ad quod*, under ad

terminus ad quod *see* *ad quod*, under ad

terms, observational *see* philosophy of science

terms, theoretical *see* philosophy of science

terror *see* war

terrorism *see* war

tertiary qualities *see* quality

tertium non datur *see* logic

tertium quid *see* fallacy

testability *see* induction

thanatos *see* death; euthanasia; psychoanalysis

theism *see* philosophy of religion

theocracy *see* philosophy, sociopolitical

theodemocracy *see* philosophy, sociopolitical

theodicy *see* philosophy of religion

theologia naturalis *see* philosophy of religion

theological creationism *see* myth

theological naturalism *see* philosophy of religion

theological utilitarianism *see* ethics; utilitarianism

theological virtues *see* Thomism

theological voluntarism *see* voluntarism

theology *see* philosophy of religion

theology, natural *see* philosophy of religion

Theology of Aristotle *see* Arabic philosophy

theology of liberation *see* Latin American philosophy

theology, philosophical *see* metaphysics

theology, supernatural *see* philosophy of religion

theonomy *see* ethics

theorems *see* logic

theoretical concepts *see* philosophy of science

theoretical constructs *see* philosophy of science

theoretical entities *see* philosophy of science

theoretical identity *see* philosophy of mind

theoretical inquiry *see* rationality

theoretical judgment *see* rationality

theoretical rationality *see* rationality

theoretical reason *see* rationality

theoretical reasoning *see* rationality

theoretical statement *see* philosophy of science

theoretical terms *see* philosophy of science

theoretical underdetermination *see* operationalism

theoria *see* theory

theory The term theory is derived from the Greek *theoria*, which meant vision and implied careful or attentive (*horao*) observing (*thea*). Latin writers related *theoria* to *contemplatio* and tended to use it and the related verb *contemplor* in a religious sense (e.g. Cicero, *De re publica*, Book VI, Somnium Scipionis), meaning the contemplation of the temple (*templum*). However, this is not the sense in which, for example, the Greek philosopher Aristotle (BCE 384–322) discussed contemplation as involved in the highest form of life pursued by philosophy. He meant the aim of that curiosity which starts with wonder, not about the colossal, unusual or freakish, but about the familiar, the ordinary we take for granted in everyday life: a vision or attentive, careful observation.

Various criteria have been formulated for theory construction. A notable one is that advanced by the English philosopher William Whewell (CE 1794–1866), namely *consilience*. According to him, the best inductions are those in which grounds for various hypotheses, previously thought to explain discrete sets of data, are found to converge together. Consilience is a characteristic of theories that significantly display such features as simplicity, generality, unification of knowledge, and explanatory strength.

In addition to these criteria, others – often called pragmatic criteria – are used in assessing theories. Notable among them are: clarity; internal consistency, i.e. the absence of contradictions in the theory; external consistency, i.e. the absence of contradictions between the theory and other established theories or judgments that are preanalytic, i.e. which are considered but naive, or a matter of reflective common sense; simplicity; predictive power; explanatory power; and completeness.

The question has been raised whether and, if so, how theories can be true or false. Significant in this regard was the work of the English philosopher Frank Plumpton Ramsey (CE 1903–30), who formulated the concept of a *Ramsey sentence*, a sentence that results from conjoining all the sentences in a theory (e.g. all sentences in common-sense psychology – which include a variety of theoretical terms, from "soul" to "instinct"), replacing each theoretical term with a predicate variable (e.g. "soul" with S and "instinct" with I), and quantifying existentially over the said variables, which yields the formalized sentence $(\exists x)Sx\&(\exists x)Ix\&\ldots\&\exists xNx$. This sentence is often claimed to exhaust the cognitive content of the theory. Some try to interpret it in nominalist terms, while others argue that, in referring to theoretical properties, realism is implied. In response, sympathizers of nominalism have proposed merely representational interpretations of Ramsey sentences.

A related result is *Craig's theorem*, a theorem other than Craig's interpolation theorem (see LOGIC). The theorem relevant here says that any recursively enumerable set of sentences can be axiomatized. On the basis of this theorem, philosophers have argued that one can eliminate theoretical terms from empirical theories. For if an empirical theory can be axiomatized in first-order logic, then the set of the empirical consequences of the axioms is recursively enumerable. If so, by Craig's theorem, for this latter set, there is a set of axioms that contain only empirical or observational terms: the *Craig-reduct* or, simply, *reduct*.

Some philosophers would argue that, when contrasting *preanalytic* judgments with theories, it is more appropriate to call them *pretheoretical* judgments. Also, the concepts involved in such judgments are often called *primitive* concepts, a use which is analogous to that of primitive in the expression primitive symbols used to denote the vocabulary of logical or logistic systems.

See also: metaphysics; philosophy; philosophy of science

Further reading

Bartlett, Robert C. and Collins, Susan D. (1999) *Action and Contemplation: Studies in the Moral and Political Thought of Aristotle*, Albany, NY: State University of New York Press.

Leplin, Jarrett (1995) *The Creation of Ideas in Physics: Studies for a Methodology of Theory Construction*, Dordrecht and Boston: Kluwer Academic Publishers.

theory-laden *see* philosophy of science

theory of appearing *see* perception

theory of descriptions *see* description

theory of effluxes *see* perception

theory of knowledge *see* epistemology

theory of relativity *see* philosophy of science

theory of signs *see* philosophy of language

theory of the Forms *see* Platonism

theory of types Also called *type theory*, this is any of a variety of theories according to which every existing item falls into specifiable, perhaps mutually exclusive, categories, called types, where the term type is derived from the Latin *typus* and the Greek *typos*, meaning "impression," "image," or "model."

The term type has various meanings more or less associated with its etymology. The German sociologist Max Weber (CE 1864–1920), for example, held that *ideal types* were useful guiding constructs. On his view, an ideal type of person is a type of person resulting from the influences of social organization and historical conditioning.

In ordinary language, the term type also appears in such combined terms as *archetype*, i.e. an original form, model, or pattern after which an item is made; *prototype*, i.e. the first or initial example of a series of items; and *stereotype*, i.e. a simplified and standardized conception that is charged with social meaning and generally shared by members of a group.

In modern philosophical discussions, the term type appears in the expression *type theory* or its synonym, the *theory of logical types*, both of them denoting a theory first outlined by the English philosopher Bertrand Arthur William Russell (CE 1872–1970) in his *The Principles of Mathematics*. The theory of logical types was partly prompted by *non-predicative* or *impredicative* definitions, i.e. any definition of a concept or property (called an impredicative or non-predicative concept or property) in terms of the totality to which it belongs, e.g. the set of all sets that are not members of themselves. When predicating terms of a given type of terms of the same type, these definitions can lead to paradoxes called *paradoxes of self-reference*. Russell suggested that these paradoxes arise as a result of presupposing that classes and their members form a single, homogenous type, which leads to self-referential incoherence. By contrast, he held, the universe of logic is stratified into a hierarchy of types, where individuals – i.e. such things as chairs, persons, and trees – are members of type 0 or type of level 0; classes of individuals are members of type 1 or type of level 1; classes of classes of individuals are members of type 2 or type of level 2; and so on.

The said paradoxes do not arise in this context, because no class cuts across types. However, other paradoxes are not resolved by Russell's initial suggestion. An example is that of *semantic paradoxes* such as that involved in the liar paradox – "I am lying right now" – which, for perspicuity purposes, can also be formulated as follows: "This proposition itself is false." If the proposition is true, then it is

false and, conversely, if false, then it is true. Other semantic paradoxes include *Berry's paradox* and *Richard's paradox*, which rely on the definability of numbers, and Grelling's paradox or the *paradox of heterologicality*. To address the difficulty raised by these latter paradoxes, Russell suggested *ramified type theory*, where a hierarchy of properties replaces that of classes in his initial suggestion. The level of an individual is the basic level and its type is 0. At the next level or type 1, there are only properties of individuals (as in "*x* is a cat" and "*x* is as fast as any other cat"); at the next, there are only properties of properties of individuals, and so on. Properties whose level or type exceed that of their arguments – i.e. of the items over which they range by one – are said to be predicative. Russell attributed the said paradoxes to some form of illicit self-reference and, accordingly, introduced the draconian *vicious-circle principle*, according to which all such self-reference in properties and propositions is illicit.

In this way, ramified type theory is freed from the said paradoxes; but is also made inadequate as a basis for classical mathematics. For many theorems of classical mathematics violate the vicious-circle principle. For example, a theorem of real analysis says that every bounded set N of real numbers (which are identified with some predicated properties of rational numbers) has a least upper bound. Given the said identification, the first step in the strategy typically used to prove the theorem is to define the least upper bound of a bounded set N of real numbers as the property P that some real number in the set has, and then prove that this property, P, is itself a real number. However, since P quantifies over real numbers, the vicious-circle principle prevents it from being a real number itself, which undermines the proof. To address this difficulty, Russell proposed the *axiom of reducibility* or *reducibility axiom*, according to which, for any property P, there is a predicative property Q that is true of exactly the same things as P.

Russell's solution was too *ad hoc*, which led the German mathematician Ernst Zermello (CE 1871–1953) to propose an axiomatic alternative, *Axiomatic Set Theory*, which included the *axiom of separation* (for any set A and property P, there is a set $\{x|x\varepsilon A$ and x has $P\}$. This axiom requires a previous set, A, from which members are separated by the property P, so that sets leading to paradoxes by collecting all items with P cannot be formed.

A concern with semantic paradoxes, especially that of the liar, led to some significant contributions by the Polish-American mathematician and logician Alfred Tarski (CE 1901–83), who formulated *Tarskian semantics*. He regarded semantics or the theory of meaning as the study of a language's expressions and the objects to which they refer. This theory deals with the problem of truth through an analysis of the predicate "true" that is used to characterize sentences. The resulting type of theory – truth-conditional theory of meaning or truth-conditional semantics – holds (on one of the various versions of these theories) that specifying the meaning of a term or sentence must involve the specification of truth conditions, e.g. in specifying the meaning of the sentence "some birds fly," one must specify truth conditions by means of a Tarskian biconditional, e.g. the one following: "some birds fly" is true if and only if some birds indeed fly.

Tarski's semantics is a *truth value semantics*: it starts with a formal language L in which no semantic notions can be expressed, hence in which the liar paradox cannot arise. Then, using another language – the metalanguage – the predicate "true-in-L" is defined. It applies to the true sentences in L and only to them. This process of defining higher levels of language can continue indefinitely. Tarski used the liar paradox to prove what has come to be called *Tarski's theorem*: the truth predicate for the first-order language of arithmetic cannot be defined in arithmetic (see MEANING; USE–MENTION DISTINCTION). In this and related discussions, theories about theories are called *metatheories*.

See also: logic; meaning; philosophy of language; philosophy of mathematics; truth

Further reading
Copi, Irving M. (1971) *The Theory of Logical Types*, London: Routledge & K. Paul.
Hindley, J. Roger (1997) *Basic Simple Type Theory*, Cambridge, UK and New York, NY, USA: Cambridge University Press.
Jacobs, Bart (1999) *Categorical Logic and*

Type Theory, New York and Oxford: Elsevier Science.

theory of virtue *see* virtue; ethics

theory, relative frequency *see* probability

theory, scientific *see* philosophy of science

theory, virtue *see* virtue; ethics

theosophy *see* mysticism

Theravāda Buddhism *see* Buddhism

thermodynamics, laws of *see* philosophy of science

thesis *see* dialectic

theurgy From the Latin *theurgia* and this from the Greek *theurgeia*, i.e. "magic," this term, like the term magic, denotes the belief that divinities, demons, or analogous powers can influence natural events or states, and the practices aimed at controlling such influences for some human purpose.

In the Greco-Roman world, the first individual to be described as a theurgist (in Greek, *theurgos*) was an author named Julian, about whom little is known, who was a contemporary of the Stoic philosopher and Roman emperor Marcus Aurelius – Marcus Annius Verus, also called Marcus Aurelius Antoninus (CE 121–80). Julian's claim to fame is his commentary on the *Chaldean Oracles*, a second-century CE poem that described how the soul descended into the realm of matter and, possibly, after its purification, ascended through the concentric circles of the universe towards its eternal home.

Theurgy became influential among some Neoplatonic authors, who saw it as a way to wisdom and virtue, even though the founder of Neoplatonism, the Egypto-Roman philosopher Plotinus (CE 204–70), distrusted theurgy as evidenced in his *Against the Gnostics*. The Tyre-born Neoplatonic philosopher Porphyry (CE 234–*c*. 305), for example, contributed to spreading the use of the term *theurgos* in his *Philosophy of the Oracles*. However, his adherence to theurgy ceased after meeting Plotinus. By contrast, Porphyry's disciple, the Syrian philosopher Iamblichus (*c*. CE 245–325), who started the Syrian School, wrote a commentary to the *Chaldean Oracles*, where he emphasized theurgy as a complement to philosophical reasoning in the search for enlightenment. Also, the Constantinople-born philosopher Proclus (CE 410–85), in his *Plato's Theology*, described theurgy as a power higher than all human wisdom.

The influence of theurgy in the Greco-Roman world reached its peak during the rule of the Roman Emperor Flavius Claudius Julianus or Julian the Apostate (CE 331–63), but tended to be rejected by a majority of later Neoplatonic authors. Those who still defended theurgy tried to distinguish between it and magic, but Christian authors – e.g. the philosopher Augustine (CE 354–430; born in the African city of Thagaste) – rejected the distinction and theurgy with it, which he considered to be associated with a criminal sort of curiosity. The interest in theurgy was briefly revived during the Renaissance.

Among the many items used in theurgy, the mandala has been influential in Hinduism, Buddhism, and, though Islam does not condone magic, in Islam. The term *mandala* is originally a Sanskrit term meaning "circle" or "round." In Hindu and Buddhist rituals and meditation practices, mandalas are diagrams, typically divided into four parts and inscribed inside a circle, which represent the various divinities or their symbols. On occasion inscribing them in sand, paper, or other media, incantations – i.e. specific combinations of language and sounds – are performed and spirits are believed to enter the mandalas. So used, mandalas are believed to provide control over divine powers. In this regard, a mandala is analogous to a *mantra* – from the Sanskrit *man*, i.e. "think" – which are sacred utterances. Indeed, mantras are sometimes inscribed in mandalas.

The term mantra initially denoted the *Rgveda*, then all of the *Vedas*. Mantras were used to invoke the gods associated with the Vedas. Eventually, only their first syllables were used, e.g. *om*, the first syllable of the Gayatri mantra, a Rgveda verse addressing the sun. Eventually, om came to denote being and to be used to begin and end every mantra. *Tantrism*, from the Sanskrit *tantra*, i.e. "warp" or "loom," is a nineteenth-century term coined by Western scholars from texts called *Tantras*,

to denote unorthodox doctrines and practices found in Hinduism, Buddhism, and Jainism.

In Islam, the term for mandala is *mandalah*, which denotes a magical operation similar to that of the Hindu mandala. It consists in drawing an inkspot surrounded by verses from the Quran on the palm of a young boy's hand, and making incantations supposed to cause the boy to see visions inside the inkspot drawing when asked specific questions.

See also: myth; philosophy of religion

Further reading
Berchman, Robert M. (1998) *Mediators of the Divine: Horizons of Prophecy, Divination, Dreams, and Theurgy in Mediterranean Antiquity*, Atlanta, GA: Scholars Press.
Shaw, Gregory (1995) *Theurgy and the Soul: The Neoplatonism of Iamblichus*, University Park, PA: Pennsylvania State University Press.

Thing *see* ens

thing in itself *see* Kantian philosophy

third-man argument *see* Platonism

third-order policy problems *see* philosophy, sociopolitical

thirdness *see* pragmatism

Thomism The theology and philosophy of the philosopher Thomas Aquinas (CE 1225–74), born near Naples (in what is now Italy), and the development of his philosophical approach by his followers in later centuries. There are three main eras of Thomistic influence: thirteenth- and fourteenth-century Thomism; sixteenth-and seventeenth-century Thomism or second Thomism; and nineteenth-and twentieth-century Thomism, the period of its greatest influence.

There are various doctrines Thomism shares with Aristotelianism, though not always with the thought of Aristotelianism's founder, the Greek philosopher Aristotle (384–322 BCE). One is that of *hylomorphism* (from *hyle*, "matter," and *morphe*, "form"). It says that all ordinary things are composed of matter – the principle of potentiality and passivity – and form – the principle of actuality and activity. A criticism of this view is that hylomorphism treats changes that are not substantial – e.g.

that of solid into liquid water – as if they were substantial. Some Aristotelians and Thomists have replied that this is not a problem with hylomorphism, but with how to apply the doctrine. Others have proposed a modification of hylomorphism, namely *hylosystemism*, according to which natural objects are made up of parts that are themselves substantial. Further, the natural objects have generic features that are constant – e.g. that of being water – and specific features that change – e.g. that of being solid. That is, when water liquefies, though there are substantial changes, there are no generic changes and, strictly speaking, the substantial changes are not of homogeneous substances, but of energy systems.

Another notion Thomism shares with Aristotelianism is that of *form* in the various senses of this term: *substantial* – the essence of a kind; *accidental* – an item's feature other than those belonging to its essence; *sensible* – that of external objects separated from matter through sense-perception; *formal* – an item's essence as constituent of its being; *natural* – not man-made; *artificial* – man-made; *physical* – of a particular thing; *metaphysical* – of the thing's genus; *subsistent* – capable of existing without matter; *non-subsistent* or *material* – existing only in matter.

Thomism, however, has a somewhat more complex notion of the relation between form and matter. For traditional Aristotelians, matter was a substrate or substratum that constituted the individuation principle, form placed an item into its species, and formed matter yielded an individual substance. While for Thomism, formed matter only yields the essence of an individual substance and, for it to exist, in addition, existence and essence must be combined. The Thomistic term used for the matter of perceivable substances is *signate matter*.

Also, though traditionally substance is opposed to accident and what is substantial is opposed to what is accidental, in Thomism, in addition, what is substantial is also opposed to what is supersubstantial, i.e. God. For a feature of the divine essence is to be *supersubstantial*, i.e. to exceed all substantiality.

A significant controversy here concerns the problem of the *unity* of form versus the *plurality* of forms. The controversy became virulent around CE 1270, apparently because the issue was not merely that of substantial unity of soul and body, but also that of the nature of the body of Christ between the time of his death and of his resurrection. Many non-Thomist authors adopted the plurality of forms doctrine. Thomism adopted the unity of form doctrine, though different Thomist authors understood it differently. Aquinas held the moderate view that, though matter is passive, when infused with form, it participated in it becoming a living thing.

Another controversy concerned universals. Aquinas held a moderate version of realism. It implied *ante rem*, *in re*, and *post rem* realism in that it suggested *ante rem* universals or *universale ante rem*, i.e. universals before the thing, which existed in God's mind; *in re* universals or *universale in re*, i.e. universals in the thing, which were numerically distinct but alike in all members of a species; and *post rem* universals or *universale post rem*, i.e. universals after the thing, which were abstract universal concepts in the mind.

Various concepts formulated by Aristotelians have been adopted by other thinkers. Notable among these are *natura naturans* and *natura naturata*. These are best known in association with the work of the Jewish philosopher of Spanish and Portuguese descent Baruch Spinoza (CE 1632–77), who characterized *natura naturans* as that which is in itself and is conceived by itself; in other words, God as a free cause, and *natura naturata* as everything that follows from God's necessary nature or its attributes, or their modes in so far as they are considered as things that are in God and cannot be conceived without God. The Arabic philosopher Ibn Rushd (CE 1126–98) introduced the term *natura naturata* when commenting on Aristotle's *De coelo* I, 1, and further developed the notion of *natura naturans* and that of *natura naturata* in his *Tahafut al tahafut* (*Contradiction of the Contradiction*), disp. 5, dub. 5. This distinction was widely used by later medieval and Renaissance authors.

Despite its indebtedness to Aristotelianism, Thomism is very much of an independent philosophical position. For, first, it involves a conception of the law that the Ancient Greeks and at least early Aristotelianism had not developed as thoroughly as the Roman and Arabic worlds did and passed on to Western Europeans in the Middle Ages. Second, it involves a Christian conception of the universe and the individual person. In this regard, for example, though reminiscent of Aristotelian arguments, Aquinas's arguments concerning God's existence stand very much on their own. There are five of them, i.e. the *quinque viae* or five ways: from motion, from the nature of efficient cause, from possibility and necessity (or from contingent beings), from gradation, and from the governance of the world (see PHILOSOPHY OF RELIGION). Also, though Aquinas thought reason could attain knowledge that God exists and a meaningful understanding of God's attributes, he thought most humans could not succeed in such endeavor. This is where the *theological virtues* are crucial. They are *faith*, i.e. a virtue whereby one accepts God's revelation; *hope*, i.e. a virtue whereby one trusts in God's assistance in attaining the infinite good; and, first and foremost, *charity*, i.e. the virtue or habitual form that inclines us to love God for His own sake.

The latter discussion indicates the manner in which Thomist ethics is different from Aristotelian ethics. For one, the good we seek is not Aristotelian worldly happiness; but Christian ultimate happiness. Second, some crucial Thomist notions were either absent or undeveloped in much of Aristotelian thought. They were partly the result of Stoicism's influences on Roman lawyers and later conceptions of the law; partly the result of the development of highly complex societies and organizations in the Roman and Arabic worlds and in the late Middle Ages Europe; and quite significantly the result of Christian thought and practice. These notions include, first, the *eternal law* – i.e. the eternal and universal moral principles; second, the *natural law* – i.e. the eternal law as it is embodied in and understood by humans; third, the *human law* – i.e. the laws humans do and need to create to deal with their particular circumstances; and fourth, the *divine* law which, among other things, takes care in the

afterlife of redressing wrongs that were not redressed on earth.

In the nineteenth century, Pope Leo XII's encyclical *Aeterni Patris* stimulated the development of *neo-Thomism*, a movement that revived interest in Aquinas's work far into the twentieth century. It was part of *neo-scholasticism*, which displayed an interest in other medieval authors, though Aquinas was thought to formulate their common doctrines best. Notable among neo-Thomist authors have been the French-born Jacques Maritain (CE 1882–1973) and Étienne Gilson (CE 1884–1978), and the still living German philosopher Karl Rahner.

See also: Aristotelianism; Christianity; Scholasticism

Further reading
Hassel, David J. (1968) *Christian Philosophy and Thomism: An Introduction to Their Problematics*, Chicago: Loyola University Press.
McCool, Gerald A. (1992) *From Unity to Pluralism: The Internal Evolution of Thomism*, New York: Fordham University Press.

thought *see* philosophy of mind

thought experiment *see* philosophy

thought, language of *see* philosophy of mind

three laws of thought *see* logic

three stages, law of the *see* positivism

three-valued logic *see* logic

Three Ways *see* mysticism

threshold *see* philosophy of mind

t'i, yung *see* Chinese philosophy

Tiamat *see* myth

Tibetan Buddhism *see* Buddhism

t'ien *see* Chinese philosophy

t'ien-jen ho-i *see* Chinese philosophy

t'ien li, jen-yü *see* Chinese philosophy

t'ien ming *see* Chinese philosophy

T'ien-T'ai School *see* Chinese philosophy; Japanese philosophy

tika *see* Māori philosophy

Tikkun *see* cabala

time *see* metaphysics; philosophy of science

time, absolute *see* philosophy of science

time, becoming of *see* philosophy of science

time, mathematical *see* philosophy of mathematics

time, relative *see* philosophy of science

time-slice *see* philosophy of mathematics

time, space– *see* philosophy of science

timocracy *see* philosophy, sociopolitical

token *see* action; philosophy of mind

token physicalism *see* philosophy of mind

token-reflexive *see* egocentric

token–token identity *see* philosophy of mind

Toledo Translators School *see* Arabic philosophy

tolerance *see* encyclopedism; ethics

tolerance, principle of *see* reductionism

toleration *see* ethics

tonk *see* logic

top-down *see* explanation

topic-neutral *see* philosophy of mind

Torah *see* Jewish philosophy; Judaism

total evidence *see* probability

total ordering *see* ordering

totemism *see* myth

totum simul *see* metaphysics

trace *see* Continental philosophy

tracking *see* skepticism

Tractarian *see* analysis

traditionalism *see* philosophy, sociopolitical

traducianism *see* myth

tragedy *see* philosophy of literature

transcendence *see* transcendent

transcendent From the Latin *transcendens* (pl. *transcendentes*), the term transcendent was used in the Middle Ages to denote properties that transcend an *ens* or entity, or the passions of an *ens* or entity. However, after the fourteenth century, this meaning was reserved for the terms *transcendental* (in Latin, *transcendentale*) and *transcendentals* (in Latin, *transcendentalia*) (see CATEGORY). Instead, transcendent and to transcend have been used in a somewhat spatial sense, so that to be transcendent or to transcend is to have gone from one place to another or to be beyond a certain limit or point, e.g. in the sense that pi, a transcendental number, is non-algebraic, i.e. is beyond algebra. In philosophy, a more frequent use is to apply transcendent to *transeunt causation* (see CAUSAL LAW), i.e. to agent causation whose effects are outside the agent, as in someone's hanging up the phone. In this sense, transcendent is the opposite of *immanent*, which applies to agent causation whose effect is not outside the agent, as in someone's thinking.

These distinctions have prompted valuational differences where some people think what is immanent is superior, while others using the term transcendent to indicate that something is highly valuable or important. Indeed, in this sense, the term transcendent has been applied to God indicating both, that God is beyond and that God is at a higher – indeed, the highest – level of significance and value in relation to this world.

This sense of transcendent and the feature of being transcendent, i.e. *transcendence*, is metaphysical or theological and, sometimes, involves such a sharp separation between what is transcendent and this world of ours, that it is correlated with the epistemological conception of God or the Absolute as *transintelligible*, i.e. beyond all comprehension.

In the philosophy of history, however, there has been discussion of a specific form of being transcendent, that of being *transhistorical*, i.e. both to exist in history and try to go beyond history, which some philosophers have contraposed to being *metahistorical*, i.e. being entirely outside of or beyond history. In this sense, God is often conceived as metahistorical, but not transhistorical. Human beings are characteristically transhistorical in that they develop in history while trying to attain a permanence that withstands history as in, for example, the classics.

From an epistemological standpoint, the notion of transcendence has played a significant role concerning the subject–object dichotomy (see OBJECT); for example in Augustinian thought, where the soul is said to transcend itself. Also, in coming to know an object, the subject is sometimes said to transcend towards the object. And, in Kantian philosophy and phenomenology (see the respective entries), a kind of transcendental thinking, i.e. transcendental idealism, is said to transcend both subject and object at least at some level, though not in the sense in which transcendent means to go beyond reality.

There is also *New England Transcendentalism*, which used the Kantian notion of transcendence and fostered the transcendental standpoint as suitable for describing reality. This is the sense in which the term transcendental was used when instituting the *Transcendental Club of Boston* in CE 1836. Notable among this movement was the United States philosopher and essayist Ralph Waldo Emerson (CE 1803–82). He was especially interested in individual development through self-reliance, i.e. reliance on oneself, one's own ideas, one's own powers, and, for Emerson, one's social, cultural, and natural environment, as an antidote to mediocrity and sheer commercialism. Accordingly, his studies focused on the great individuals of history, on the assumption that their self-development through the self-reliant development of their ideas can be of use to others.

As previously indicated, his process involved one's reliance on immediately available resources: oneself, one's social and natural environment, one's cultural environment. Emerson called these resources the *over-soul*, which he considered a source of insight and strength.

Worthy of note here is the (*philosophical*) *Zürich School*, *not* to be confused with the (*psychoanalytic*) *Zürich School* inspired by the Swiss psychoanalyst Carl G. Jung CE 1875–1961). The tenets of the (philosophical) Zürich School were formulated in the journal *Dialectica*, which began publication in the Swiss city of Neuchâtel in 1947. The school's most notable member was the French philosopher

of science and literary analyst Gaston Bachelard (CE 1884–1962). His approach, like that of his associates, was a philosophy of *dépassement* (French for transcendence) aimed at moving beyond pure empiricism and pure rationalism; acknowledging that knowledge is crucially unfinished and bodies of belief – however established – are always open to revision; and evaluating dialectic in an effort to apply it to the process where, at each time, opposite beliefs and theories claim finality and closure.

See also: Kantian philosophy; phenomenology

Further reading
Gray, Henry David (1917) *Emerson: A Statement of New England Transcendentalism as Expressed in the Philosophy of its Chief Exponent*, Stanford, CA: Stanford University.
Marsh, James L. (1999) *Process, Praxis, and Transcendence*, Albany: State University of New York Press.
Olson, Alan M. and Rouner, Leroy S. (1981) *Transcendence and the Sacred*, Notre Dame, IN: University of Notre Dame Press.

transcendental *see* transcendent

transcendental aesthetic *see* Kantian philosophy

transcendental analytic *see* Kantian philosophy

transcendental argument *see* Kantian philosophy; phenomenology

transcendental deduction *see* Kantian philosophy

transcendental dialectic *see* Kantian philosophy

transcendental ego *see* phenomenology

transcendental idealism *see* Kantian philosophy

transcendental logic *see* phenomenology

transcendental numbers *see* philosophy of mathematics

transcendental paralogisms *see* Kantian philosophy

transcendental-phenomenological idealism *see* phenomenology

transcendental phenomenology *see* phenomenology

transcendental subjectivity *see* phenomenology

transcendental term *see* category

transcendentalia *see* category

transcendentalism *see* transcendent

transcendentals *see* category

transeunt causation *see* causal law

transferable utility *see* decision

transfinite number *see* philosophy of mathematics

transformation rule *see* philosophy of language

transformational grammar *see* philosophy of language

transformism *see* biology

transhistorical *see* transcendent

transintelligible *see* transcendent

transitive *see* relation

transitivity *see* relation

translation, problems of *see* philosophy of language

translation, radical *see* philosophy of language

transmigration of souls *see* Platonism

transparent context *see* opacity

transvaluation of values *see* ethics

trap, collective *see* decision

trap, conflict *see* decision

trap, externality *see* decision

trap, linguistic *see* analytic

trap, non-co-operation *see* decision

trap, parameter *see* decision

trap, sliding-reinforcer *see* decision

trap, time delay *see* decision

trap, total ignorance *see* decision

Tree of Porphyry *see* Neoplatonism

triadism *see* metaphysics

trichotomy, law of *see* relation

trikāya *see* Buddhism

triloka *see* Hinduism

trimurti *see* Hinduism

Trinitarianism *see* Arianism

Trinity *see* Arianism; Christianity

tritheism *see* Arianism

trivium *see* philosophy of education

trope *see* skepticism

tropos *see* skepticism

trust *see* faith

trustee *see* ethics

truth From the Anglo-Saxon *treowth*, i.e. "fidelity" (the Latin term being *veritas* and the Greek *aletheia*), the term truth ordinarily denotes the presumed object of knowledge and aim of inquiry. In this context, the term truth and its associated adjective, true, are used in at least two senses. In one sense, they are used to describe propositions, in which case their opposites respectively are *falsity* and *false*. In another sense, they are used to describe reality or fact, in which case, their opposites respectively are, for example, appearance and apparent; or illusion and illusory; or mere belief and merely believed; or fiction and fictional.

The question eventually arose: "What is truth?" By this it was meant: what features characterize truth? In India, the question led to the formulation of *theories of intrinsic truth*, according to which truth is self-evident, and found to be so in a non-reflective way. These theories have no exact parallels in Western thought. There is a Western distinction of truths of fact versus truths of reason, and truths of reason are said to be self-evident. However, this is because they are formulated either as tautologies (i.e. declarative sentences that are true just in virtue of their form), e.g. the proposition "either Fido is a cat or Fido is not a cat," or as analytic statements (i.e. declarative sentences that are true just in virtue of the meaning of their terms), e.g. "bachelors are unmarried" (see ANALYTIC–SYNTHETIC DISTINCTION) However, these sentences, if self-evident, are reflectively found to be so; while intrinsic truths are found to be self-evident more in the manner we may, in thinking, immediately realize or intuit that there is thought.

There is more than one variety of theories of intrinsic truth. Those advocated by the are Mīmāmsā and Advaita-Vedānta Schools (see HINDUISM), consider only truth, not falsity to be intrinsic. While the SĀMKHYA-YOGA School (see HINDUISM), considers falsity to be intrinsic as well. According to all these schools, whatever is not an intrinsic truth (or, for the Sāmkhya-Yoga, an intrinsic truth or an intrinsic falsity), is an *extrinsic* truth or falsity, i.e. its being a truth or a falsity depends on conditions external to it. In fact, on this account, all Western theories of truth are of extrinsic truth. There are also Indian theories of truth, e.g. the Nyāya-Vaiśeṣika (see HINDUISM), which make room for extrinsic truth and criticize intrinsic truth theories on the grounds that they cannot account for falsity, or doubt, and can provide no way of telling whether a truth is indeed self-evident or whether we are merely certain that it is, even if it turns out not to be so.

Most conspicuous among theories of external truth is the *correspondence* theory of truth, according to which, roughly, something – a declarative sentence, a belief, a judgment – is true if it corresponds to some conditions external to it such as a fact, a state of affairs, or an event. There are more or less strict ways of interpreting this theory. In the stricter interpretation, the correspondence theory is a *picture* theory or a *pictorial* theory of truth. That is, what is true – say, a declarative sentence – has a structure that pictures what makes it true: namely, a structure in the world.

The problem is that it is often difficult, and sometimes impossible, to find a part of reality that corresponds to each part of a declarative sentence, i.e. to such things as nouns, verbs, and adverbs. For example, consider the sentence "This cake is for you." Even if the noun "cake" corresponds to a particular cake and the pronoun "you" to a particular person, it is doubtful that the demonstrative "this" or the copula "is" correspond to anything out there, let alone that there is some part of reality to which the preposition "for" corresponds!

This problem has led philosophers to propose weaker versions of the correspondence theory of truth. In one weaker interpretation, something is true if it can be correlated with a fact; and it is false if it cannot, or if its negation can be correlated with a fact. However, this version has at least two shortcomings. First, it multiplies the world's entities infinitely, because it creates an intermediary world of facts (or meanings of declarative sentences) between what is true (the sentences) and reality. Second, it raises and fails to answer the question: "When are facts related to reality, i.e. to such things as states of affairs or events?" In effect, it only has rephrased the problem that got people started, while complicating the universe infinitely.

A still weaker version holds that something is true if it says what is the case. For example, to say that the declarative sentence "Some birds fly" is true is to say that it says what is the case: some birds fly. This interpretation of the theory is closer to the common-sense notion of truth and to the common conception that truths are about something – that is, that they have referents in the world. At this point, however, the question arises: "Is truth redundant when calling something true is merely shorthand for repeating what it says?"

Some philosophers accept this or analogous implications. For example, the *deflationary* theory of truth is the theory that acknowledges the basic, uncontroversial point that a proposition is true if and only if what it says is the case – e.g. "triangles have three sides" is true if and only if, indeed, triangles have three sides; however, by contrast with other theories, it asserts that this is all that is needed to characterize truth. Indeed, on this theory, to say that the proposition "What Mary said is true" is only shorthand for the infinite conjunction of conditional propositions "If Mary said that it rained in Cheshire, CT, on May 2, 1998, then it rained in Cheshire, CT, on May

2, 1998; and if Mary said the high school was packed on the next day, then it was packed on the next day; etc." Along these lines, the *redundancy* theory of truth holds that corresponding instances of "it is true that *p*" and "*p*" have exactly the same meaning; while the *minimalist* theory of truth denies that they have the same meaning and, instead, holds that they are equivalent.

Still other advocates of the deflationary theory of truth doubt the existence of propositions and consider sentences to be carriers of truth. Hence, they adopt the *disquotation* theory of truth, characterized by the disquotation principle or Tarski's (T) schema: "*p* is true if and only if *p*." Tarski himself did not consider this principle to be an adequate theory of truth. Instead, he thought it formulated what any adequate definition of truth must imply. His own account is the *semantic* theory of truth (see MEANING; THEORY OF TYPES).

The difficulties inherent in the correspondence version have led some thinkers to adopt a different theory of extrinsic truth, namely the *coherence* theory of truth. At one time, the *consensus gentium* (Latin for "people's agreement") was a central criterion of truth; but it has lost favor. Coherentism somehow embodies the old intent of the *consensus gentium* criterion. It associates truth with the structure of knowledge or justified beliefs and holds that truth is a property of those beliefs that are justified in virtue of their relations to other beliefs, specifically in virtue of their belonging to a coherent – i.e. free from contradictions – system of beliefs that, overall, is better than alternative systems with regard to such criteria as clarity, comprehensiveness, and explanatory power.

This theory is attractive when immediate verification is impossible and hypothetical reasoning is imperative. Yet, as an all-encompassing theory of truth, it has serious drawbacks. One is that it offends common-sense notions of truth, for on its basis, such common-sensically true sentences as "Some birds fly" and "The Soviet Union ceased to exist in late 1990" are true only if they belong to an entire system of sentences whose consistency is greater than that of competing systems. However, there is no conclusive proof that there is such a system, let alone a method for discovering it. Even if such a system could be demonstrated, those common-sensically true sentences – however obvious their truth – would be, at best, true to a degree lesser than probabilistic certainty, because dependent on the system that would at best have such a degree of confirmation.

The third theory of extrinsic truth may escape some of these implications. It is the *pragmatic* theory of truth. There are various versions of this theory. Perhaps the best known version was formulated by the United States philosopher Charles Sanders Peirce (CE 1839–1914). According to it, roughly, those things that are true – declarative sentences, beliefs, or judgments – are so if they were to withstand the indefinite scrutiny of inquiry were the inquiry to be continued indefinitely, whether or not it does continue. By contrast with the coherence theory of truth, this theory makes it possible for the sentence "Some birds fly" to be fully, not just partially, true. Further, such sentences as "Some birds fly" and "The desk on which I am writing is solid" are substantiated enough by previous inquiry to be known to be true *right now*. Yet, this theory appears to presuppose a convergence toward a final set of opinions – the truth – that would survive the indefinite test of inquiry. However, on its own terms, the theory cannot establish this presupposition.

As indicated, Peirce's conception emphasizes the notion of a *community of inquiry*, i.e. the unlimited community constituted by the unlimited or indefinite generations of inquirers who would engage in the (in principle) unending critical scrutiny of views formulated for testing in science. Even though individual humans and groups are fallible, humans need not give up hope of finding truth. For inquiry, especially scientific inquiry, is self-corrective and, in the long run, falsities will be recognized and discarded in favor of believing truth (where *the real* or *the fact* or *the truth* is what is then believed). Peirce thought that the law of large numbers was in favor of this epistemico-evolutionary result.

A different pragmatic conception of truth was formulated by the United States philosopher John Dewey (CE 1859–1952). He held that the purpose of knowledge was to bring about some change in our experience, and that, for this purpose, some hypotheses are more effective than others. We may be inclined to call these hypotheses true or the truth. Dewey, however, thought these terms suggested too much of a static correspondence between the world of discourse and the world out there. Hence, instead of using the term truth, he used the expression *warranted assertability*, which denoted successful cognition in the previously mentioned sense of being a hypothesis effective in changing our experience.

Doubts about coherentism and pragmatism, however, have led some philosophers, weary of ominous relativistic implications, to argue that the correspondence theory, however minimal, is not that bad after all, and that on the versions discussed, truth need not be redundant. For the redundancy claim is based on the claim that the declarative sentence "It is true that some birds fly" adds no descriptive content to "Some birds fly," and that, at most, it adds emphatic content. It is like saying "Yeah! Some birds fly." If this objection is sound, however, it establishes not that truth itself is redundant, but only that truth claims are redundant. Moreover, it is doubtful that all or even most truth claims are thus redundant. For "It is true that some birds fly" is only one among various truth claims that one can make about the declarative sentence "Some birds fly." Another is "The declarative sentence 'Some birds fly' is true." By contrast with "Some birds fly," this truth claim is not about birds and flying. It is about *the sentence* "Some birds fly." Hence, it is not redundant.

See also: epistemology; knowledge; logic; philosophy of language; philosophy of mathematics; philosophy of science

Further reading

Chatterjee, Satischendra (1950) *The Nyāya Theory of Knowledge*, Calcutta: University of Calcutta Press.
Horwich, Paul (1994) *Theories of Truth*, Aldershot and Brookfield, USA: Dartmouth.
Kirkham, Richard L. (1995 [1992]) *Theories of Truth: A Critical Introduction*, Cambridge, MA: MIT Press.

truth, coherence theory of *see* truth

truth condition *see* epistemology

truth-conditional semantics *see* meaning

truth-conditional theory of meaning *see* meaning

truth, correspondence theory of *see* truth

truth, deflationary theory of *see* truth

truth, disquotation theory of *see* truth

truth-functional connectives *see* logic

truth functions *see* logic

truth, minimalist theory of *see* truth

truth, picture theory of *see* truth

truth, pictorial theory of *see* truth

truth, pragmatic theory of *see* truth

truth predicate *see* meaning; theory of types

truth, redundancy theory of *see* truth

truth, semantic theory of *see* meaning

truth table *see* logic

truth value *see* logic

truth value gaps *see* philosophy of mathematics

truth value semantics *see* meaning

truthlikeness *see* probability

truths of fact *see* truth

truths of reason *see* truth

T-sentence *see* meaning

Ts'its'tsi'nako *see* myth

tu quoque *see* fallacy

Tübingen School *see* idealism

Turing degree *see* degree

Turing machine *see* computer theory

Turing machine functionalism *see* philosophy of mind

Turing test *see* computer theory

twice-born *see* caste

twice divided line *see* Platonism

Twin-Earth *see* meaning

two swords, doctrine of the *see* philosophy, sociopolitical

twofold-truth theory *see* Arabic philosophy

tychism *see* determinism

type *see* theory of types

type physicalism *see* philosophy of mind

type, ramified *see* theory of types

type, simple *see* theory of types

type–token distinction *see* theory of types

type–type identity *see* philosophy of mind

types, theory of *see* theory of types

typology *see* category

tyranny *see* philosophy, sociopolitical

tzu jan *see* Chinese philosophy

U

U *see* logic

Übermensch *see* ethics

ubi *see* metaphysics

ubiquity *see* metaphysics

ubiquous *see* metaphysics

uchronie *see* Kantian philosophy

ultimate situations *see* existentialism

Ultimate, the Great *see* Chinese philosophy; Confucianism

ultramontanism *see* philosophy, sociopolitical

umuzima *see* abazimu

umuzimu *see* abazimu

Umwelt *see* phenomenology

uncertainty principle *see* philosophy of science

unconditioned, the *see* philosophy of religion

unconscious, the *see* psychoanalysis

uncountable *see* set

undecidable *see* philosophy of mathematics

underclass *see* Marxism

underdetermination, perceptual *see* perception

underdetermination, theoretical *see* operationalism

understanding Like *intellect* (from the Latin *intelligere*: "to understand"), this term denotes the faculty, power, or disposition to know, by contrast with other faculties, powers or dispositions such as feeling and will. By contrast with *nous*, the Greek term for the highest type of thinking (sometimes considered to be the faculty of intellectual intuition), understanding is closer to *dianoia*, the Greek term for the faculty we exercise when, for example, we work our way through the steps of an argument. It should be mentioned here that the Greek philosopher Plato (428–348 BCE) respectively uses *nous* and *dianoia* – the corresponding adjective is dianoetic – to denote the highest and second levels of the faculties in the line of truth simile (see PLATONISM).

The notion of understanding or intellect was significantly developed in Aristotelian thought, which divided it into a *passive* part that receives information through the senses, and an *active* part that creates and interrelates ideas. While some Arabic philosophers considered the active intellect or active understanding to be the immortal part of the human soul, nominalist medieval philosophers questioned the existence of a rational basis for accepting the existence of an active intellect. Thomism followed Aristotelian thought on this matter.

In modern times, empiricist philosophers have distinguished between sensations and reflection, roughly following the traditional passive–active intellect distinction. The German philosopher Immanuel Kant (CE 1724–1894), however, took a conceptualist approach to knowledge and reality, giving the concept of understanding a pivotal role in his philosophy. Kant sought to uncover the conceptual forms, or pure concepts of the understanding, or categories of the understanding (which had been previously called *Reflexionsbegriffe*, i.e. concepts of reflection), which, in attaining knowledge, he held were required by our constitution. His position was that while concepts without intuitions – all of which, for humans, are sensible intuitions, i.e. acquired through the senses – were empty, intuitions without concepts were blind, leaving us with a mere manifold or multiplicity of unintelligibly scattered impressions. Here, transcendental reflection made it possible to determine the conceptual or sensory origin of given representations. This was the *transcendental deduction of the categories*, i.e. an argument – called in general a transcendental argument – whereby it is shown which ones they are, given the undoubted assumption that we have representations.

Kant held that everything sensed has quality, quantity, relation, and modality, and, using these headings, outlined his table of judgments (a list of the necessary forms of judgments needed for any finite understanding), from which he derived his table of categories (the concepts involved in such judgments), listing twelve categories, three under each heading. Under quality were reality (or the positive), negation, and limitation. Under quantity, he listed unity, plurality, and totality. Relation covered inherence and subsistence, causality and dependence, and community. Modality included possibility–impossibility, existence–non-existence, and necessity–contingency. Necessity and possibility are now sometimes respectively called apodictic modality and problematic modality. For Kant, they corresponded to apodictic judgments and problematic judgments. In Kantian philosophy, these categories of the understanding are constitutive, while other concepts are regulatory or regulative, i.e. direct our thinking. Examples of the latter are heuristic or methodological principles aimed at providing teleological explanations (see KANTIAN PHILOSOPHY).

The neo-Kantian German philosopher Wilhelm Dilthey (CE 1833–1911) used the notion of understanding, or interpretation, or COMPREHENSION (in German, *das Verstehen*), as involving all of our mental powers. He con-

ceived of understanding as a form of apprehension of mental life – which he understood as distinct from nature – by reference to the meaning of its manifestations.

A related topic is the concept, measurement, and sources of intelligence. In the first place, this term is used to translate the Latin *intelligentia*, a term that has been used with many meanings such as understanding or intellect, reason, that which is intelligible (*nous*), and the intelligible spheres or angels of cabalistic thought. In contemporary psychology, intelligence denotes a faculty or family of faculties, or a function or family of functions, aimed at resolving theoretical or practical problems individual organisms – e.g., but not exclusively, human beings – face. Besides controversies concerning the concept of intelligence, there are controversies concerning its measurement and sources, most notably the controversy concerning the extent to which intelligence is inherited and whether there are group differences in intelligence that are caused by genetic factors.

See also: Arabic philosophy; Aristotelianism; empiricism; Kantian philosophy; philosophy of mind

Further reading
Broadie, Alexander (1989) *Notion and Object: Aspects of Late Medieval Epistemology*, Oxford and New York: Clarendon Press and Oxford University Press.
Hume, David (1999) *An Enquiry Concerning Human Understanding*, Oxford and New York: Oxford University Press.
Smith, Norman Kemp (1953) *Immanuel Kant's Critique of Pure Reason*, London: Macmillan.

understanding, categories of the *see* Kantian philosophy

undistributed middle term *see* syllogism

unexpected-examination paradox *see* paradox

Ungrund *see* mysticism

unified-field theory *see* philosophy of science

unified science *see* positivism

uniformity of nature, principle of the *see* induction

unio mystica *see* mysticism

union *see* set

union of egoists *see* ethics

unit class *see* set

unitarianism *see* Arianism

unities, the three *see* aesthetics

unity *see* category

unity in diversity *see* aesthetics; philosophy of education

unity of form *see* Thomism

unity of science *see* positivism

unity, organic *see* holism

universal *see* abstract

universal characteristic *see* calculus

universal class *see* set

universal, concrete *see* idealism

universal constructor *see* computer theory

universal disposition *see* disposition

universal generalization *see* logic

universal grammar *see* philosophy of language

universal instantiation *see* logic

universal quantifier *see* logic

universal relation *see* relation

universal simulator *see* computer theory

universale ante rem *see* Thomism

universale in re *see* Thomism

universale post rem *see* Thomism

universalia *see* abstract

universalism *see* Christianity

universality *see* ethics

universalizability *see* ethics

universals *see* abstract

universe *see* metaphysics

universe of discourse *see* logic

university *see* humanism; madrasah; philosophy of education

univocal *see* ambiguity

univocity *see* ambiguity

unknowable, the *see* explanation

unlimited community *see* pragmatism; truth

unmoved mover *see* chain of being

unsaturated *see* reference

unsolvability, degree of *see* degree

Upanishads *see* Hinduism

Uppsala School *see* positivism

Urform *see* Kantian philosophy

Urintuition *see* philosophy of mathematics

use–mention distinction A distinction between two ways in which terms and sentences are part of discourse. They are *used* when they refer to or state something; while they are *mentioned* when they are the subject matter of discourse, i.e. they are exhibited to talk about them or examine their features. In the sentence "the word 'word' is short," the word "word" is used in its first occurrence and mentioned in its second occurrence. *Corner quotes*, or *corners*, or *quasi-quotes* are a notational device useful in this context. They provide a convenient way of talking generally about expressions of unspecified kinds without mixing levels of language as in A & B by putting corners or quotes around the expression instead, as in: "A & B." The sentence or term between quotes is said to be in the *object language*, while whatever is not between quotes is in the *metalanguage*, i.e. the language used to talk about the sentence or term. This is useful to avoid confusion when, for example, one uses English to talk about English. It is also useful to avoid fallacious inferences resulting from ambiguity between what sentences or terms are used and which ones are mentioned. Finally, it is useful in constructing and interpreting a formal language – our object language or the language we mention or talk about – by using, as a metalanguage, a language we already know, say, English or Spanish. Any theorem proven within the metalanguage is sometimes called a *metatheorem* to distinguish it from any theorem proven within the object language.

The use–mention distinction is identical with the distinction made by the medieval English philosopher Walter Burleigh (CE 1275–*c*. 1373) between *suppositio formalis* or formal supposition and *suppositio materialis* or material supposition. Formal supposition is the supposition made in using language to talk about extra-linguistic entities, as in saying "hand is a part of the body." While material supposition is the supposition made in using language to talk about language itself, as in saying "hand is a short word." Using corner quotes in the latter case, we could make clear what we are talking about by writing "hand" is a short word or, since the sentence is also being exhibited, by writing "'hand' is a short word."

See also: meaning; philosophy of language; theory of types; truth

Further reading
Lee, Benjamin (1997) *Talking Heads: Language, Metalanguage, and the Semiotics of Subjectivity*, Durham: Duke University Press.
Quine, W.V. (1961 [1951]) *Mathematical Logic*, fourth printing of the revised edn, Cambridge, MA: Harvard University Press.

uūl *see* Akhbārīs

Uṣūlīs *see* Akhbārīs

utilitarian calculus *see* utilitarianism

utilitarianism A family of ethical theories holding that, in assessing actions, policies, practices, institutions, and character and character traits, only their consequences matter, and the consequences that matter are those affecting the common good, i.e. the general well-being of those affected by them (though this notion is not used so much by utilitarian writers as it is by natural-law theorists).

The principles involved in utilitarianism are principles of beneficence – and the background attitudes and traits are forms of benevolence – in the *positive* versions of these theories that aim at bringing about good. By contrast, they are principles of non-maleficence in the *negative* versions that aim only at avoiding harm or misery. Some further subdivisions are those of *act-utilitarianism*, where the consequences of the act are all that is taken into account in

evaluating an act, by contrast with *rule-utilitarianism*, sometimes also called *indirect utilitarianism* or *indirect consequentialism*, where the consequences of generally following the rule of performing a certain act are taken into account to assess the rule, but only rules thus established are used to assess acts regardless of the acts' consequences. Act-utilitarians sometimes accuse rule-utilitarians of *rule fetishism*, i.e. of treating moral rules as *fetishes*: objects eliciting unquestioning reverence, respect, or devotion. Rule-utilitarians accuse act-utilitarians of immorality in that their views make room, for example, for framing the innocent when this would bring about the greatest happiness of the population at issue.

A notion crucial to all these approaches is that of the *collective consequences*, i.e. the consequences brought about by the joint occurrence of individually performed actions. They are sometimes called *indirect consequences* – or *side-effects* – and contrasted with *direct consequences*, i.e. those consequences of an act that are not the result of any contributions by any other acts.

As it is plain by now, there are many versions of utilitarianism, some applied under other names. One difference concerns the manner in which the value of the consequences is determined. In the earlier version of utilitarianism formulated by the English philosopher Jeremy Bentham (CE 1748–1832), they were assessed by means of the *hedonic calculus*, also called *felicific calculus*, a version of the *utilitarian calculus* – any calculus of consequences – that involved assessing and, to the extent possible, measuring the intensity, duration, certainty or uncertainty, propinquity or remoteness, fecundity, purity, and extent of the pleasures or pains constituting the consequences. Later versions of the utilitarian calculus focused on conceptions of utility as the good or happiness understood in a variety of ways – from the satisfaction of personal preferences, through the satisfaction of needs, to, as in *well-being*, a combination of health, prosperity, and satisfaction of ordinary wants or desires – thus significantly broadening utilitarianism. In any case, such calculations of happiness involve, first, *intrapersonal utility comparison*, i.e., briefly, comparison by a given person of the various degrees in which alternative consequences would tend to make him or her happier or unhappier. Second, since in most ethical problems of significance, more than one person is affected, the said calculations also involve *interpersonal utility comparison*, i.e., briefly, comparison of the various degrees in which alternative consequences would tend to make affected persons happier or unhappier than others.

In addition to the previous types of utilitarianism, there is *ideal utilitarianism*, the view that certain things such as knowledge or being autonomous are good whether or not people value them. In this connection, the English philosopher William Paley (CE 1743–1805) formulated *theological utilitarianism*, according to which the common good is what God wills and, in the long run, egoism and altruism would coincide.

At a worldlier level, there is also a version of utilitarianism often used in business and policy making: *cost–benefit analysis*, whereby the desirable consequences of each course of action are quantified in monetary terms thus becoming *benefits*, the undesirable consequences are quantified thus becoming *costs*, the benefit over cost ratio is calculated for each course of action, and that action (or, if there is more than one, any of these) is chosen which has the highest ratio. This is sometimes also called *cost-effectiveness analysis*. Most often, however, the latter expression denotes a procedure whereby the aims to be pursued are decided independently of benefit-to-cost ratios – e.g. by selecting those that accord with principles of justice – and, only then, cost–benefit analysis is used to select the cheapest way of reaching those aims. So, combined with other principles, cost-effectiveness analysis is not a strictly utilitarian approach.

An economic notion that has played a significant role in ethics – especially in utilitarianism – and the philosophy of economics is that of *expected utility* – a notion understood in such ways as likely, probable, or not unlikely satisfaction of preferences – and, in particular, that of *declining marginal utility*, i.e. that equal marginal increments of money (or other goods) tend to bring about less satisfaction – less utility, less happiness – to people, the more money these people have. Often, this notion is used to argue for equality of income distribution.

Finally, there have been attempts at formulating versions of utilitarianism that do not rely on the hedonic calculus. Instead, they rely on comparative census information to determine whether alternative courses of action being assessed would satisfy a minimum standard of provisions characterized by the needs of those affected.

See also: ethics; philosophy, sociopolitical

Further reading
Albee, Ernest (1990 [1902]) *A History of English Utilitarianism*, Bristol: Thoemmes.
Bayles, Michael D. (1968) *Contemporary Utilitarianism*, Garden City, NY: Doubleday.
Quinton, Anthony (1973) *Utilitarian Ethics*, New York: St Martin's.

utility *see* utilitarianism

utility, cardinal *see* decision

utility, transferable *see* decision

Utopia *see* philosophy, sociopolitical

Utopian socialism *see* philosophy, sociopolitical

Uttara-Mīmāmsā *see* Hinduism

utterer's meaning *see* meaning

utu *see* Māori philosophy

V

v *see* logic

vagueness *see* ambiguity

Vaiśeṣika *see* Nyāya-Vaiśeṣika School

Valentinianism *see* Christianity

valid *see* logic

validation *see* abduction; justification

validity *see* logic

value From the Latin *valere*, i.e. "to be strong" or "to be worth," the term value denotes the worth of something. When this worth is understood in economic terms, then value denotes *economic* value, i.e. the market value of something or, roughly, its price. There are uses of the term value, however, in which it denotes *non-economic* value, i.e. the non-economic worth of something. Values are studied in the branch of philosophy called axiology or value-theory.

Values are involved in *evaluations* or judgments of value, i.e. judgment to the effect that an item has such features as that of being beautiful or ugly, humorous or humorless, and, in ethics, good or bad, right or wrong, justified or unjustified. Evaluation, however, like assessment, may refer to the process of considering the pros and cons of alternative courses of action (e.g. in risk assessment, the risks and benefits involved with alternative courses of actions), or to the product resulting form such process: the actual judgment that a given course of action is preferable to the alternative ones. Despite using the term JUDGMENT in these contexts, not all philosophers agree that it

denotes any item capable of being true or false. In this regard, they contrast values with facts.

In addition, some argue that facts are recognized, while values are selected or preferred, and from this conclude that values are subjective. Others argue that being selected or preferred does not make values worthy of being selected or preferred and, given the way we talk about and conceive of at least some values, we are committed to the view that at least some values are objective. Examples of these are *ethical* or *moral* values, i.e. values involved in the subject matter of ethics; *cognitive* values, i.e. values involved in the subject matter of such branches of inquiry as science, epistemology, and the philosophy of science; and some *aesthetic* values or values involved in the subject matter of aesthetics.

Philosophers have classified values in a variety of ways and for a variety of purposes. For example, a crucial distinction is made between *extrinsic* or *instrumental* value, i.e. the worth something has for the sake of something else, and *intrinsic* value, i.e. the worth something has for its own sake. An additional notion often used in this regard is that of *intermediate* value, i.e. the worth something has both for its own sake and for the sake of something else. For example, engaging in pleasant and moderate exercise has value for its own sake and because it contributes to good health. In Deweyan pragmatism, given its central conception of the means–ends continuum, all values are intermediate.

Philosophers have formulated conceptions of desire or want – i.e. of the felt disposition to have, do, or experience something – which are parallel to some of the notions of value just discussed. For example, an extrinsic or instrumental desire is the desire one has for something because it is conducive to something else one desires. When, and only when, this is the only reason, the desire is *strictly extrinsic*. Intrinsic desire is the desire of something for its own sake. When, and only when, this is the only reason, the desire is *strictly intrinsic*.

As for other conceptions of value, there is that of *inherent* value: to say that an item is inherently valuable is to say that its experience, awareness, or contemplation is intrinsically valuable. In addition, there is contributory value: to say that an item has *contributory* value is to say that it contributes to the value of some whole of which it is a part.

The notion of intrinsic value has raised the question: "What is it for something to have worth for its own sake?" Two types of answers have been offered. The first is that for something to have intrinsic value is for it to have value in virtue of its intrinsic nature. That is, to say enjoying a walk in the park has intrinsic value is to say that it has value just in virtue of the nature of enjoying a walk in the park. By contrast, the second answer is that for something to have intrinsic value is for it to be appropriate or fitting to desire it, prefer it, or favor it regardless of anything else.

There is also the question of whether values exist and, if so, how they relate to facts. Some deny the existence of values and say that there exist only facts (or objects, or events, or states of affairs), and that having attitudes (which are facts of our mental life) about facts are all there is to evaluation and values. Others, as indicated, deny that attitudes about facts such as desiring or preferring can account for the facts being worth desiring or preferring, and point to an item or set of items that is a final value – e.g. happiness in Aristotelian thought – and the standard for all other values. Still others reject the notion of a final value in this goal-oriented sense, but – as in Kantian philosophy – assign supreme value to rules or principles for passing judgments of value. In addition, some who reject all the preceding views see values as embedded in or based on nature, e.g. as relations between objects and living individuals. There are also those who agree that selecting or preferring something does not make it valuable; but reject all objectivist accounts just discussed, and argue that what is selected or preferred are goods, not values. Hence, they conclude, values are not identical with facts, or reducible to facts, and, at most, emerge from or supervene on facts (see SUPERVENIENCE).

See also: aesthetics; ethics; judgment; supervenience

Further reading
Frondizi, Risieri (1963) *What is Value?*, La Salle, IL, Open Court.
Perry, Ralph Barton (1967 [1954]) *General Theory of Value: Its Meaning and Basic Principles Construed in Terms of Interest*, Cambridge, MA: Harvard University Press.
Shapiro, Michael J. (1993) *Reading "Adam Smith": Desire, History, and Value*, Newbury Park, CA: Sage Publications.

value, cognitive *see* value

value, contributive *see* value

value, contributory *see* value

value, extrinsic *see* value

value, final *see* value

value, inherent *see* value

value, instrumental *see* value

value, intermediate *see* value

value, intrinsic *see* value

value of a variable *see* logic

value, surplus *see* Marxism; philosophy of economics

value theory *see* value

value, truth- *see* logic

variable *see* logic

variable, bound *see* logic

variable, free *see* logic

variable, regressor *see* induction

variable response *see* induction

variable state *see* philosophy of science

variable-sum game *see* decision

variable, value of a *see* logic

variation, concomitant *see* induction

varna *see* caste

vasana *see* Buddhism

Vedānta *see* Hinduism

Vedas *see* Hinduism

veil of ignorance, the *see* justice

velleity *see* intention

Venn diagram *see* syllogism

vera causa *see* causal law

verifiability criterion *see* positivism

verifiability, principle of *see* positivism

verifiability theory of meaning *see* positivism

verification, doctrine of *see* positivism

verisimilitude *see* probability

Vermutungsevidenz *see* justification

Verstehen *see* explanation

verum ipsum factum *see* philosophy of history

vestigia dei *see* Christianity

via antiqua *see* philosophy of religion

via eminentiae *see* philosophy of religion

via moderna *see* philosophy of religion

via negationis *see* philosophy of religion

viae *see* philosophy of education; philosophy of religion

vibratiuncle *see* associationism; philosophy of mind

vice *see* ethics; virtue

vicious circle *see* reasoning

vicious regress *see* reasoning

Victorines *see* Platonism

Vienna Circle *see* positivism

Vijñânavâda *see* Hinduism

vijnapti *see* Hinduism

vinculum substantiale *see* Scholasticism

vindication *see* abduction; justification

violence *see* philosophy, sociopolitical

virtù *see* philosophy, sociopolitical

virtue From the Latin *virtus*, i.e. "manliness," the term virtue is used in a manner parallel to that of the Greek *arete*, i.e. "excellence" (which, initially, had no ethical connotation), to denote an excellent character, which is contrasted with a flawed character or *vice*. Often, virtue is understood as consisting in an excellent combination of characteristics or traits – usually understood as dispositions – of persons, the virtues, which are contrasted with flawed traits or *vices*.

Two main categories of virtue and the virtues have been distinguished: One is that of *intellectual* virtue and intellectual virtues (from the Latin *intelligere* – "to understand" – and *virtus*), also called *dianoetic* virtues (from the Greek *dianoia*: "intellect" or "mind"). They are also called *epistemic* virtue and epistemic virtues, and are thought to be significant in the discovery of truth, the avoidance of error, and other cognitive activities.

The other main category is that of *moral* virtue and moral virtues, which are thought to be significant in leading a good life. In medieval philosophy, some of the moral virtues were called the *cardinal* virtues (from the Latin *cardo*, i.e. "hinge"), because of their prominence. Though the name had not been previously used, this notion followed the practice in Ancient Greek philosophy – say, in the Platonic dialogues – where one of the crucial virtues was courage – an English term derived from the Latin *cor* (heart) – while the others were wisdom, temperance, and justice.

Virtue and the virtues, as well as vice and the vices, are studied in the type of philosophical theory called *virtue theory*. When applied to ethics (instead, say, of being applied to epistemology), virtue theory is nowadays called *character ethics* or *agent-based ethics*, or *virtue ethics*. This is the ethical side of virtue theory. Yet, it should be noted that the practical (and not merely ethical) scope of virtue theory also covers the study of epistemic or intellectual virtue.

Virtue ethics focuses primarily on the kind of persons we should be and character traits, attitudes, and motives for action we should have, and assesses actions and even policies from the standpoint of what those persons would judge or do. The ethics formulated by the Greek philosopher Aristotle (BCE 384–322) is an example of character ethics. It crucially distinguishes between extrinsic or instrumental desires (desires of items for the sake of something else), and intrinsic desires (desires of items for their own sake), holds that the desire for happiness is intrinsic and happiness the goal of life, and characterizes happiness dynamically, as an activity of the soul whereby humans flourish by acting in accordance with the mean. This is a form of balance or harmony (from the Greek *harmos*: a "fitting" or "joining"), lying somewhere between excess and defect in the display of such traits as benevolence, generosity, fairness, honesty, and courage. It accordingly is an ethics of self-realization that, in the Greek context, concerned individuals-in-society, not individuals regardless of their society.

What helps or hinders their acting this way is a *hexis* (from the Greek *hexo*, "to have," or "to be disposed"), i.e. a disposition or state which is not a mere passion (*pathe*) one cannot control, nor a faculty (*dunamis*) of the soul, but a state of character whereby one makes a decision. The development of *phronesis*, i.e. practical wisdom, helps in determining the mean. The corresponding practice is the exercise of the virtues that, for Aristotle, since it is done for its own sake, cannot be theoretical knowledge or even the knowledge involved in *poiēsis*, i.e. "production," an activity characteristic of crafts.

An analogous doctrine of the mean can also be found in Chinese philosophy. It was formulated in arguably the most philosophical of ancient Chinese documents, the *Chung Yung* (*Doctrine of the Mean*), which already existed in the early Han dynasty (206 BCE–CE 220) and was brought into prominence by the Chinese Confucian philosopher Chu Hsi (CE 1130–1200). According to the Chinese Doctrine of the Mean, the ultimate principle is rather metaphysical in that it is said to be *ch'eng* (or sincerity) because totally beyond illusion and delusion, and one's conduct should strike harmony: the appropriate mean between deficiency and excess.

Kantian philosophy views virtue in a deontological perspective (the perspective of its principle, the categorical imperative), which focuses on features of the actions it serves to evaluate themselves, not on the value of their consequences. The categorical imperative is the moral law when applied to imperfect beings like humans, who are often driven at least partly by their inclinations, not by what Kantian ethics considers the only source of moral worth: the good will, i.e. the settled determination to do one's duty. Indeed, in order to act from this motivation, human beings often need to exercise *fortitude*, or strength of will, which is the central Kantian moral virtue.

See also: disposition; epistemology; ethics; Kantian philosophy; philosophy of mind; rationality

Further reading
Baur, Michael (1998) *Virtues and Virtue Theories*, Washington, DC: National Office of the American Catholic Philosophical Association, The Catholic University of America.
Montmarquet, James A. (1993) *Epistemic Virtue and Doxastic Responsibility*, Lanham, MD: Rowman & Littlefield Publishers.
Pincoffs, Edmund (1971) "Quandary ethics," *Mind*, LXXX(320), October, pp. 552–71.
Putman, Daniel A. (1998) *Human Excellence: Dialogues on Virtue Theory*, Lanham, MD: University Press of America.

virtue theory *see* virtue; ethics

virtues, cardinal *see* virtue

virtues, intellectual *see* epistemology; virtue

virtues, moral *see* ethics; virtue

virtues, theological *see* Thomism

vis insita *see* philosophy of science

Vishistādvaita-Vedānta *see* Hinduism

Vishnu *see* Hinduism

vital force *see* biology; vitalism

vital lies *see* faith; existentialism

vitalism From "vital" plus "-ism," where "vital" is derived from the Latin *vita*: "life," plus the adjectival particle *-alis*, the term vitalism denotes the view that each *organism* – a term that, in Antiquity, used to mean "instrument" but, in the Middle Ages, came to mean a "body equipped with instruments" and, since the eighteenth century, means "biological body" – includes some controlling vital force that cannot be reduced to chemical or physical terms. Many intermediate positions have been formulated between the previous two positions, e.g. methodological reductionism, or the view that the analysis, explanation, and prediction of biological phenomena in chemical or physical terms is merely a way of studying them, not a doctrine in metaphysics.

All the views just discussed conflict with *organismic biology*, which rejects reductionism, vitalism, and their variants on the grounds that the whole organism cannot be reduced to the sum of its parts, whether these are interpreted as merely chemical or physical, or as including a vital force as well.

Sometimes, vitalism is also used to denote the view according to which the universe itself can be understood by analogy with living things. This latter type of vitalism is a form of ANIMISM and was frequently held during the Renaissance. In modern times, some biologists and philosophers of biology have held a view called *neo-vitalism*, namely that an irreducible mental-like principle is embedded in all organisms and suffices to determine their structure and behavior. Another version of neo-vitalism holds that the said principle suffices only to direct, cause, or suspend organic movements. Among those who upheld neo-vitalism have been the German philosopher Johannes Reinke (CE 1849–1931), the Estonian-German philosopher Jacob von Uexküll (CE 1864–1944) and, most notably, the German philosopher and biologist Hans Driesch (CE 1867–1941), who held that mechanical causality, though existent in organic processes, is involved in an entelechial and non-mechanical causality.

See also: animism; biology; mechanism

Further reading
Driesch, Hans (1914) *The History and Theory of Vitalism*, rev. and in part rewritten for the English edn by the author, London: Macmillan.
Schubert-Soldern, Rainer (1962) *Mechanism and Vitalism: Philosophical Aspects of Biology*, London: Burns & Oates.

vivencia *see* phenomenology

vocation *see* existentialism

void *see* atomism

volition *see* intention

voluntarism Any philosophical position that makes our understanding of phenomena dependent on our or God's ability to control them. For example, *ethical* voluntarism is the doctrine that moral concepts or principles are somehow chosen by us. *Doxastic* voluntarism is the doctrine that we largely can control what we believe. Among doxastic voluntarists, the French philosopher and mathematician Blaise Pascal (CE 1623–62), the Danish philosopher Søren Kierkegaard (CE 1813–55), and the United States philosopher William James (CE 1842–1910) held forms of *theological* voluntarism: the doctrine that religious belief significantly involves choice on the part of believers. A related form is *optimistic* voluntarism, i.e. the doctrine that the world is good because God chose to make it that way. In addition, *historical* voluntarism is the doctrine that the choices of individual human beings are major determinants of historical developments. This view sharply contrasts with *historical determinism*, which, for example, is held by Marxists, who believe that economic conditions determine historical developments, and individuals and their choices are merely incidental. *Metaphysical* voluntarism is the doctrine associated with the German philosopher Arthur Schopenhauer (CE 1788–1860) that the will, understood as a meaningless striving for survival, is the organizing principle of the world.

Voluntarism is traditionally opposed to *intellectualism*, a family of doctrines that attribute a superior status to intelligence, the intellect, the understanding, or reason. They do so either (1) by considering these faculties to be the only adequate instruments of knowledge; (2) by considering them superior to the will, or (3) by considering reality or parts thereof to be intelligible by their means, (4) by considering humans to be destined for knowledge, (5) by considering all the relations between individual subjects and their world to be cognitive, or (6) by combining some or all of these views.

Not all voluntarism is *anti-intellectualism*, though, in some regard, it is non-intellectualism. For example, those contemporary views that deny that all the relations between individual subjects and their world are cognitive are, in this regard, non-intellectualist, though they need not be anti-intellectualist. For they are compatible with other intellectualist positions, even that which says that humans are destined for knowledge.

Various nineteenth- and twentieth-century philosophers focused on the power of thinking. For example, the French philosopher Alfred Fouillée (CE 1838–1912) argued for the reality of human freedom by appeal to the voluntaristic notion of *idea-force* or *thought-force*; that is, the effectiveness of the mind evidenced by the tendency of ideas to become actualized. Along similarly voluntaristic lines, pragmatist philosophers thought of ideas as the sum of their practical consequences, or this sum plus the consequences of holding the ideas, or as instruments and plans of action.

See also: decision; philosophy, sociopolitical

Further reading

Bonansea, Bernardino M. (1965) *Duns Scotus' Voluntarism*, Washington, DC: Catholic University of America Press.
Stebbing, Lizzie Susan (1914) *Pragmatism and French Voluntarism, with Especial Reference to the Notion of Truth in the Development of French Philosophy from Maine de Biran to Professor Bergson*, Cambridge, UK: The University Press.

voluntary euthanasia *see* euthanasia

Vorstellung *see* perception

vortex theory *see* Cartesianism

voting as a decision procedure *see* philosophy, sociopolitical

voting paradox *see* paradox

w *see* logic

wairua *see* Māori philosophy

wājib *see* philosophy of religion

wang, pa *see* Chinese philosophy

want *see* intention

war From the Old High German *werra*, i.e. "strife," the term war denotes a sustained military conflict between two or more countries or – as in a civil war – organized parties within a country. A related notion is that of a *cold war*, i.e. an intense political, economic, military, and ideological rivalry between states short of military conflict, and its associated notion, the *balance of terror*, i.e. the balance thought to prevent actual war by the terror involved in mutually assured destruction, as in the twentieth-century cold war between the NATO allies and the Soviet Union.

The concept and reality of war have prompted the question: "Can a war be justified?" Some believe it cannot and accordingly advocate pacifism. Others believe it sometimes can and, accordingly, have developed theories aimed at stating when a war is justified. One such theory is the theory of *bellum justum* or just-war theory, of which there are various versions, which began to be formulated in Ancient Rome and found their more developed formulations during the Middle Ages. On all versions, however, the war must be fought for a just cause, but interpretations differ on what a just cause is. In Ancient Rome, a just cause was typically revenge or defense concerning the honor or safety of Rome. On a more recent interpretation, a just cause is that of bringing about a state of affairs required by principles of justice.

The United Nations' relevant documents identify aggression as a necessary condition for a war to be just on the part of those defending against aggression. Other conditions have included that the war be declared by proper authority; that the antagonist be notified of the declaration of war; and that the antagonist be given the opportunity to reach a peaceful settlement before the initiation of hostilities.

A condition elaborated after the onset of Christianity involves the *principle of proportionality*: that the response must be proportionate to harm caused by the aggression. This raises the question: "Can it ever be just to cause any collateral harm, specifically civilian casualties, resulting from military action?" The *principle of double effect* is often advanced as the only justification of such harm. Traditionally, this principle says that one may act in ways that foreseeably lead to deadly results, so long as, first, one's action has a good result; second, one did not intend the deadly result to occur as an end or as a means; third, one did not bring about the good result by means of the deadly one; and fourth, the good result was sufficiently significant to outweigh the deadly one. The twentieth-century development of nuclear and other weapons of mass destruction has raised questions concerning the justifiability of any war using such weapons. Some have argued that no such war is justified. Others have argued that some are, but that the just-war theory is totally inadequate for addressing the problem of whether they are justified (see balance of terror, below).

The above discussion concerns *jus ad bellum*, i.e. the conditions that make war justified. They are contrasted with *jus in bellum*, i.e. the manner in which war should be conducted. Already in Ancient Rome, there were *jus in bellum* rules, e.g. the rule that those who surrendered should be given protection. In the twentieth century, *jus in bellum* concerns have been rekindled by civil wars and independence wars involving *terrorism*, i.e. the use of terror – from hostage-taking through the threat of various injustices up to and including killings – for political aims. There are various forms of terrorism. One is *state terrorism*, i.e. the official use of terrorism by the state against its citizens or subjects, as in the Serbian ethnic cleansing policies in Kosovo. Another is *paramilitary terrorism*, i.e. the use of terrorism by individuals or groups organized along military lines – indeed, sometimes including members of the military who may be acting under orders but not under military command – as in the Kosovo case and the late 1970s dirty war in Argentina. Still another is *international terrorism*, which has partly international political aims and, if backed by a state against some foreign power or its nationals, is done secretly (for, otherwise, it would be an act of war).

These acts are sometimes defended on the grounds that they are prompted by aggression and have a just cause. The reply has often been based on at least one of the conditions involving the principle of double effect. For those harmed by terrorist acts are intentionally harmed. Hence, it is not the case, as the principle requires, that those engaging in terrorist acts did not intend the harmful results – say, loss of freedom, maiming, or death – to occur as an end or as a means. They did.

A similar argument is made concerning the justifiability of the balance of terror in the high-tech weapons arms race. It is argued that civilian populations are targeted and, hence, the balance of terror is unjustified. The reply has been to say that the balance of terror is supposed to produce terror, in order to prevent any more terrible harm such as actual maiming and death. However, the objectors reply, first,

that the terror has already produced actual harm, e.g. we are all hostages to the threat; and second, that it is not justified to threaten to do what would be unjustified to do.

As for the place of war among human institutions, some thinkers have seen war as an extension of diplomacy. Fearing that this view might open the door to the excesses of gunboat diplomacy, its critics have tended to perceive war as a breakdown of diplomacy. Yet, this latter position has been criticized on the grounds that it is unrealistic and, indeed, in failing to deal with the fluidity of confrontational situations, it closes the door to opportunities for peace.

See also: ethics; philosophy, sociopolitical

Further reading

Christopher, Paul (1994) *The Ethics of War and Peace*, Englewood Cliffs, NJ: Prentice Hall.

Clausewitz, Carl von (1994) *On War*, Princeton, NJ: Princeton University Press, 1976; German edition: *Vom Kriege. Hinterlassenes Werk*, Berlin, F. Dümmler, 1832, 1834.

Wasserstrom, Richard A. (1970) *War and Morality*, Belmont, CA: Wadsworth.

warranted assertability *see* truth

Warsaw School *see* positivism

wave mechanics *see* philosophy of science

wayward causal chain *see* causal law

(weak) law of large numbers *see ars conjectandi*, under ars

weak semantic completeness *see* completeness

weak soundness *see* logic

weak supervenience *see* supervenience

weakness of will *see* akrasia

wealth *see* capitalism

Weber–Fechner Law *see* philosophy of mind

wedge argument *see* fallacy

welfare economics *see* philosophy of economics

welfare liberalism *see* philosophy, sociopolitical

well-being *see* ethics; utilitarianism

well-formed formula *see* logic

well-ordered set *see* ordering

well-ordering *see* ordering

Weltanschaung *see* philosophy; philosophy of language

Wertrationalität *see* rationality

Western Marxism *see* Marxism

wff *see* logic

whanaungatanga *see* Māori philosophy

wheel of rebirth *see* Buddhism

white-horse paradox *see* Chinese philosophy

whole *see* holism

wide content *see* philosophy of mind

wide reflective equilibrium *see* ethics

will *see* intention

will, free *see* determinism

will, general *see* philosophy, sociopolitical

will to believe *see* faith; justification

will to power *see* ethics

will, weakness of *see* akrasia

Wille *see* Kantian philosophy

wisdom From the Middle and Old English *wīs* plus the particle "-dom," where *wīs* is akin to "wit" or "sagacity," and, of course, to "wise," the term wisdom is used in the dispositional sense of sagacity, discernment, or insight, and in the resulting sense of knowledge or right judgment(s) attained in the exercise of the said disposition. An analogous dichotomy can be found in the Greek word *sophia*, i.e. "wisdom," which used to denote an ability to engage in a given activity. So it was used by the Greek epic poet Homer (eighth century BCE) in the *Iliad* (xv, 412), to denote a carpenter's skill to build a boat. Soon, however, it designated the skill involved in any art whatsoever, and the Greek historian Herodotus (484?–425? BCE) used it to denote practical intelligence or prudence.

In some cultures other than that of Ancient Greece, the equivalent terms for wisdom involve analogous differences in emphasis if not meaning. One example is arguably the Arabic word for wisdom, *hīkma* (which also means PHILOSOPHY, though this may be a result of the word's having been selected to translate Greek philosophical works). In Africa, the Akan word for wisdom is *nyansa* (or its possible equivalent, *adwen*, which means "thinking"), and denotes the capacity for philosophical thinking understood as an inborn mental faculty. In fact, *nyansa* has some of the same additional connotations as the Greek term for wisdom, *sophia*: skill, learning, practical knowledge.

The Greek philosopher and religious sect leader Pythagoras (570–500 BCE) is credited with having used *sophia* in coining the term *philosophia*, Greek for philosophy (from the Greek *philos*: "lover" or "friend of," and *sophia*). Here again, the question was left open concerning whether this wisdom should be primarily a disposition or primarily a body of knowledge and, down the centuries, some philosophers emphasized the former, others the latter. In Socratic philosophy, *sophia* was a crucial disposition that yielded the modest knowledge of one's own intellectual limitations, thus helping each particular individual become a good person. In Platonic thought, *sophia* had, besides its more traditional meanings, the theoretical meaning of a superior virtue that, as a result, yielded knowledge of right and wrong, e.g. for the members of the superior class in charge of governing the ideal republic. In Aristotelian thought, *sophia* became even more theoretical, but kept the disposition-result dichotomy by denoting theoretical reason and the resulting rather contemplative science of first principles. Indeed, it was contrasted with *phronesis* or practical reason.

This theoretical emphasis receded during the Hellenistic period, which returned to more Socratic personal concerns focusing on the features of a good human being. These could take the form of skeptical wisdom's withholding judgment or, as in Stoic wisdom, of civic concerns that, though intellectual, were aimed at practical activities such as those involved in being a good citizen. In addition, the influence of Christianity contributed to the development of a religious wisdom that focused on acting prudently, in accordance with God's commands and motivated by faith, not, as in the Gnostic tradition, by knowledge (even if Gnostic knowledge could be mystical). This led to the Neoplatonic conception of a superior wisdom that is a kind of illumination from above. This conception was predominant during the Middle Ages, so that *sophia* was sometimes translated as *intelligentia*, i.e. UNDERSTANDING; other times as *prudentia*, i.e. prudence, but most frequently as *sapientia*, i.e. superior knowledge, which medieval philosophers understood as a knowledge made possible by divine grace.

Modern and contemporary philosophical conceptions of wisdom and philosophy have oscillated among all the conceptions of wisdom just described. Some philosophers, for example, have emphasized philosophy as a kind of scientific knowledge and relegated wisdom in its dispositional senses to being the subject of study of psychology or education. Others have done the opposite, conceiving of philosophy as a process of inquiry about questions of fundamental and lasting significance where wisdom as a disposition to face up to such questions is crucial, and any resulting knowledge, if possible, is secondary. Still others have attempted to strike some balance along the range of positions between the extremes just described.

See also: Greek philosophy; philosophy

Further reading
Curnow, Trevor (1999) *Wisdom, Intuition and Ethics*, Aldershot: Ashgate.
Painter, Mark A. (1999) *The Depravity of Wisdom: The Protestant Reformation and the Disengagement of Knowledge from Virtue in Modern Philosophy*, Aldershot, Hants, UK and Brookfield, VT: Ashgate.
Shankman, Steven (2000) *The Siren and the Sage: Knowledge and Wisdom in Ancient Greece and China*, London and New York: Cassell.

withdrawal and return *see* philosophy of history

women's movement *see* feminist philosophy

wonder *see* philosophy

woof *see* logic

word *see* existentialism

work *see* Marxism; philosophy of economics

works, justification by *see* justification

world *see* metaphysics

world-game *see* existentialism

world soul *see* Stoicism

world year *see* age of the world

worldlines *see* philosophy of science

worldview *see* philosophy; philosophy of language

worth, moral *see* Kantian philosophy

worth of one's life *see* existentialism

wu *see* Chinese philosophy; Taoism

wu-hsing *see* Chinese philosophy

wu wei *see* Chinese philosophy; Taoism

Würzburg School *see* philosophy of mind

X *see* logic

Y

Y *see* logic

Yahweh Originally, as a sign of reverence, written YHWH, this term denotes the God of Israel. It is also written Yahwe, Yahveh, Yahve, Jahveh, Jahve, Jahweh, and Jahwe. This name is supposed to have been revealed to Moses as the previously mentioned four Hebrew consonants, YHWH, called the *tetragrammaton*. After the Exile (sixth century BCE), and especially from the third century BCE on, Jews no longer use the name Yahweh. One reason for this change was that, as Judaism proselytized in the Greco-Roman world, the more common noun Elohim (that could be understood in the plural as meaning gods, but is translated as God or Lord in the Christian Bible) was used to make plain the universal sovereignty of Israel's God over all others. A second reason is that the name YHWH was increasingly thought to be too sacred to be uttered. Instead, in the synagogue ritual, the Hebrew word Adonai ("My Lord") was used. This term was translated as Kyrios ("Lord") in the *Septuagint*, the Greek version of the Old Testament.

Between the sixth and the tenth centuries CE, the term Jehovah was created by the Masoretes (the writers or compilers of the *Masorah*: the critical and explanatory notes on the Hebrew text of the Old Testament), who were trying to reproduce the original text of the Hebrew Bible. In the process, they replaced the vowels of the name YHWH with the vowel signs of the Hebrew words Adonai or Elohim, thus producing the artificial name Jehovah (YeHo-WaH). Christian scholars after the Renaissance and Reformation used the term Jehovah for YHWH; however, in the nineteenth and twentieth centuries biblical scholars again began to use the term Yahweh.

See also: Jewish philosophy; Judaism

Further reading
Davies, William David (1984) *Cambridge History of Judaism*, London: Cambridge University Press.
Eisen, Arnold (1998) *Rethinking Modern Judaism: Ritual, Commandment, Community*, Chicago, IL and London: University of Chicago Press.

Yajurveda *see* Hinduism

yang *see* Chinese philosophy

yi *see* Chinese philosophy

yin-yang *see* Chinese philosophy

Yin-yang-chia *see* Chinese philosophy

yoga *see* Sāmkhya-Yoga

Yogācāra Buddhism *see* Buddhism

Young Hegelians *see* idealism; Marxism

yu *see* Chinese philosophy; Taoism

yü *see* Chinese philosophy

yugas *see* age of the world

yung *see* Chinese philosophy

Z

Z *see* logic

Zarathustra *see* Zoroastrianism

zazen *see* Zen

Zen The terms *Zen*, i.e. "meditation" in Japanese, and *Ch'an*, i.e. "meditation" in Chinese, are both used to designate a branch of Buddhism, often called *Zen Buddhism*, which is a subdivision of Mahāyāna Buddhism influenced by Theravāda Buddhism.

Though it originated in India, Ch'an achieved prominence in China in the sixth and seventh centuries CE and was brought to Japan in the twelfth century CE, where it has prospered to the present day.

The Japanese term *Goke-shichishū* ("five houses–seven schools") – also called the *Southern School* – denotes the seven schools of Ch'an (Zen) that stemmed from five lineages (houses) during the T'ang period. The term Southern School is used to contrast it with the *Northern School*. For the latter was strongly influenced by Indian Meditation Buddhism, while the Southern School showed influences of Chinese Taoism and, generally, Chinese literary culture.

The five houses–seven schools of Goke-shichishū were *Rinzai, Igyō, Sōtō, Ummon*, and *Hōgen*, plus two additional schools: *Yōgi-ha*, the Yōgi School, and *Oryō-ha*, the Oryō School. Besides these, there is a secondary lineage of Ch'an (Zen) in Japan, the *Gozu* School, which declined during the Song dynasty. At any rate, the three major schools of Zen in Japan are Rinzai, Sōtō, and the least influential of the three and, in fact, a subsidi-ary lineage of Rinzai (*Lin-chi* in Chinese), namely *Obaku*, which combines Zen meditation with Pure Land Buddhism recitation of the *nembutsu* chant (*nien-fo* in Chinese). Obaku came to Japan in the seventeenth century CE.

The earliest main text of Zen Buddhism is *The Platform Sutra* from the eighth century CE. One of the earliest compilations of Zen works is *Keitoku dentoroku* (*Ching-te ch'uan-teng-lu* in Chinese). It was the work of the Chinese monk Tao-hsüan (Japanese: Dōsen) in CE 1004. It reported the deeds and sayings of more than 600 Zen masters in thirty volumes, and it significantly contributed to fix the *kōans* – phrases, teachings, or stories used in Zen training. A notable compilation is the *Hekigan Roku* or *Hekigan Shū* (in Chinese, *Pi-yen Lu* or *Pi-yen Chi*), also called the *Blue Cliff Records* or *Blue Cliff Collection*, which is a collection of 100 stories of previous Masters made by Setchō (in Chinese, Hsueh-tou; CE 980–1052), one of the greatest Chinese Zen Masters, who added his commentaries to each story. Additional commentaries were added by the Chinese Zen Master Engo (in Chinese, Yuan-Wu; CE 1063–1135), whose disciples published the entire set of stories and commentaries under the *Hekigan Roku* title in CE 1125. This work was translated into Japanese in the thirteenth century and has been the most popular of Zen collections ever since.

Dō is the Japanese way of pronouncing the Chinese character for *Tao*. Like the latter, the word means "way." In Japanese Buddhism, *dō* (also *Buddha-dharma, butsudō*, and, with less of a practical emphasis, *buppō*) generally means following the Buddha on the way of ENLIGHTENMENT or *gedatsu*, the release or liberation through which enlightenment is attained. In this latter meaning, *gedatsu* is also used in Zen Buddhism. As a result, in Japan, the various spiritual-practical ways of training permeated with Zen mind are known as Zen. They distinguish between individuals who show *goseki*, a "trace of enlightenment" – i.e. have experienced it but, in practice, the enlightenment has not become natural – and those in which an individual has achieved profound enlightenment, which in Zen is supposed to leave no trace.

Also, in Zen, the term *jakumetsu* ("stillness-extinction") is the Japanese pronunciation of the character by means of which the Sanskrit term nirvana is translated into Chinese. Jakumetsu is said to be undefinable, in that it cannot be grasped by thought (*fukashigi*) or formulated by words (*fukasetsu*). All that can be said about it is negative statements to the effect that it is not this or the other thing. Yet, what can be described are the conditions under which *jakumetsu* is attained, namely in this life and in complete unity with, as well as at peace with, *samsāra*: the world of appearances.

As for ways of trying to attain the previously described states, Zen practitioners describe a number of them. A misguided one is *gufu-shogyō-zen* (fool's Zen), the style of meditation in which one thinks of orthodox doctrines, by contrast with *zazen*, the true Zen practice whereby one frees one's mind from dependence on thinking, including thinking of Zen doctrines, however holy they may be. It is also worth noticing that *zazen* requires *gyō-jū-za-ga*, literally "walking-sitting-lying," meaning uninterrupted attention throughout one's entire daily life. In *zazen*, *jiriki*, or one's own power, is the attempt to attain enlightenment through one's own efforts, a notion sometimes contrasted with *tariki*, or the power of the other, which indicates, as the Pure Land Buddhism School holds, that merely believing in Buddha and calling on his name suffices to attain enlightenment. In this connection, Zen masters also point to *joriki* ("power of mind") as a power or force that arises from the concentrated mind, and leads to responding to unexpected circumstances rightly and with

presence of mind. Those who develop *joriki* are no longer slaves to their passions. Yet, *joriki* does not suffice to overcome the illusory world. *Satori* or sudden awakening is also necessary.

Various Japanese training ways have been influenced by Zen. One of them is *chadō*, the tea way, which in Japan is also called *cha-no yū*, i.e. "hot tea water" or, simply, "tea." Both names imply that it is not a matter of ceremony an individual performs with the tea as object. Instead, *chadō* is supposed to be a non-dualistic, tea-only, state of consciousness in which many arts – from pottery and architecture to *kadō*, the way of flowers – come together to produce a work of art that lasts just for a while. In it, all human senses participate in a manner that curbs dualistic intellectual inclinations.

Besides training ways, there are *jūkūkinkai* or the "ten main precepts," of which there are exoteric and esoteric forms. In their exoteric form, they forbid taking a life, stealing, being unchaste, lying, selling or buying alcohol, talking about others' bad deeds, praising oneself and deprecating others, giving help reluctantly, aggression, and slandering. In their esoteric form, Zen practitioners vow not to desist from the true *dharma*, to keep on seeking enlightenment, to covet nothing and not to be stingy, to be compassionate towards all beings, not to speak ill of any Buddhist teaching, not to be attached to anything, not to hold false views, to encourage others to seek enlightenment, to teach Mahāyāna views to Hīnayāna followers, to be charitable towards *bodhisattvas*.

There is also *mondō* or encounter dialogue. One of the main styles of *koan* training (i.e. Zen training that uses *koans*, the name for such things as phrases from *sutras*, and episodes from ancient masters' lives), *mondō* is a dialogue between Zen masters or between a Zen master and student in which one party asks questions concerning a problem of concern, and the other responds in a symbolic manner supposed to elicit an answer from the person who asked. A famous example is that of a monk who asked Chao-chou "What is the meaning of the patriarch coming from the West?," to which Chao-chou replied "The oak tree over in the garden."

Some expressions formulating central philosophical ideas in Zen serve to reflect the path from ignorance to enlightenment. In order of ascendance toward enlightenment, they are:

1 *dai-gidan*, i.e. "doubt." In Zen, doubt is not an element of SCEPTICISM, but perplexity, probing inquiry, and intense self-questioning.
2 *dai-funshi*, i.e. "resolve," used to mean the inflexible determination to dispel great doubt (*dai-gidan*). *Dai-funshi*, *dai-shinkon*, and *dai-gidain* are the three pillars of the practice of *zazen*.
3 *dai-shinkon*, i.e. "faith," means a faith that is deeply rooted, unshakable, and untainted by belief in anything supernatural or by superstition.
4 *ichiji-fusetsu*, i.e. "silence," means the Buddha and the *soshigata*, the patriarchs, and all their instruction made use of no single word to describe ultimate reality, because it is not sayable. Hence, all the teachings of the Buddha and the Zen masters are pointers towards the truth, not descriptions of the truth itself.
5 *moku-funi*, i.e. "non-duality," which denotes the non-dualistic nature of reality.
6 *dai-anjin*, i.e. "serenity," used to mean complete enlightenment.

Other Zen notions of philosophical significance deal with mental life. Notable among them are:

1 *nen*, the Japanese pronunciation of the Chinese character constituted by two components, one for *present,* and the other for *heart*, *mind*, or *consciousness*. It is used in the sense of *moment of consciousness*, as well as in that of *intensive non-dualistic thought*.
2 *ninkyō-funi*, an expression denoting the Zen realization that subject or person and object or phenomenon are not distinct.
3 *sengio*, literally "fish weir," this expression means the reality sought by Zen practitioners in direct experience can at best be sought by using scriptures and practical techniques as supportive of one's efforts (like the fish weir in trying to catch fish), but it cannot be found in them.
4 *shiki*, literally "consciousness," of which, according to Buddhism, there are eight kinds: sight, sound, smell, taste, touch, intellect, *manas* or the source of awareness, and *ālaya-vijñāna* or storehouse consciousness (a concept developed by Buddhist metaphysicians in India to deal, for example, with the problem of delayed karmic effect, and that of causation at a temporal distance).

In addition, there are Zen notions of philosophical significance that deal with the nature and components of the universe. Among these are:

1 *mu*, i.e. "nothing," "not," "nothingness," "is not," "has not," "not any." Becoming acquainted with the world of *mu* is the first step in Zen training. As for *mu-ichimotsu*, it means not-one thing and was coined to denote the absence of substance, which is taken to mean that all things are but manifestations of emptiness.
2 *shinnyo* is "suchness," or the true nature of all things that is neither thinkable, nor describable, nor graspable unity of what is relative and what is absolute, attributes and their absence.
3 *ri-bi*, literally "truth," "the secret (*bi*) principle (*ri*)," this expression denotes a sort of cosmic principle, where *ri* denotes an absolute emptiness manifested in all things and *bi* denotes the unobstructed nature of this manifestation.

The influence of Zen on Chinese and Japanese cultures has been very pronounced and can be recognized in the simple style of much of their architecture, as well as in their gardens and paintings. A notable example of this influence is also that of *nō*, the dance-drama of Japan, which relies only on essential means of expression.

See also: Buddhism; Japanese philosophy

Further reading
Abe, Masao (1985) *Zen and Western Thought*, London: Macmillan.
Dumoulin, Heinrich (1988–90) *Zen Buddhism: A History, vol. I: India and China, vol. II: Japan*, New York: Macmillan.
Sekida, Katsuki (1989) *Zen Training: Methods and Philosophy*, Tokyo: Weatherhill.

Zend-Avesta *see* Zoroastrianism

Zeno's paradoxes *see* paradox

zero-sum game *see* decision

Zionism *see* Judaism

Zoroastrianism The religion of *Zoroaster* – a corrupt Greek form of the Persian *Zarathustra* – and of all of Persia prior to the Persians' conversion to Islam. Its founder, Zarathustra, probably lived sometime after 1000 BCE and Zoroastrianism flourished during much of the first millennium BCE. It soon became Persia's national religion and expanded throughout the Near East. After Zarathustra's death, a priesthood developed and organized doctrines and ceremonies, performed rites, and codified the scriptures in the *Avesta* (for a time, and apparently because of a mistake in translation, called *Zend-Avesta* in the Western world). This book was destroyed during the Alexandrian army's invasion in the fourth century BCE, and further losses occurred when Zoroastrianism was crushed by the Islamic invasion of CE 636. The remaining scriptures were collected in five parts: the *Yasna*, liturgical works that include the *Gathas*, hymns attributed to Zarathustra; the *Vispered*, a supplementary ritual; the *Vendidad*, an account of creation; and the *Khorda Vesta*, a collection of prayers.

Zoroastrianism represents a purification of the Aryan-Indian folk-religions and provides a clear example of religious dualism through its cosmology: Originally, there were two powerful divinities, the good spirit, Ahura Mazda or Ormazd, and the evil spirit, Ahriman or Angra Mainyu. The history of the world is the struggle between these two divinities; but Ahura Mazda will eventually triumph, bringing about the kingdom of heaven. There will be a judgment, and the wicked, i.e. those who, according to the accounting of their actions, have done more evil than good, will be plunged into hell. The righteous, i.e. those who have done more good than evil, will eternally live in Ahura Mazda's kingdom in fellowship with each other and Ahura Mazda's angels. In offering this cosmology, Zoroastrianism also provides a clear example of *ethical dualism* – the view that there are two moral principles or forces, good and evil, opposed to each other.

Among sects originated in Zoroastrianism are *Manicheism*, which kept the Zoroastrian dualism, and India's *Parseism*, which still recognizes Zarathustra as its prophet and the *Avesta* as its scriptures, but has become monotheistic, rejecting the evil spirit, Ahriman.

See also: Christianity; Judaism; myth; philosophy of religion

Further reading

Boyce, Mary (1996) *A History of Zoroastrianism*, 3rd impression, with corrections, Leiden and New York: E.J. Brill.

Dhalla, Maneckji Nusservanji (1985 [1963]) *History of Zoroastrianism*, Bombay: K.R. Cama Oriental Institute.

Zürich School (philosophical) *see* dialectic; transcendent

Zürich School (psychoanalytic) *see* psychoanalysis

Zweckrationalität *see* rationality